FEMINISM IN LITERATURE

A Gale Critical Companion

FEMINISM IN LITERATURE

A Gale Critical Companion

Volume 3: 19th Century, Authors (C-Z)

Foreword by *Amy Hudock, Ph.D.*
University of South Carolina

Jessica Bomarito, Jeffrey W. Hunter, Project Editors

THOMSON
™
GALE

Detroit • New York • San Francisco • San Diego • New Haven, Conn. • Waterville, Maine • London • Munich

THOMSON

GALE

™

Feminism in Literature, Vol. 3

Project Editors
Jessica Bomarito, Jeffrey W. Hunter

Editorial
Tom Burns, Jenny Cromie, Kathy D. Darrow, Michelle Kazensky, Jelena O. Krstović, Michael L. LaBlanc, Julie Landelius, Michelle Lee, Allison McClintic Marion, Ellen McGeagh, Joseph Palmisano, Linda Pavlovski, James E. Person Jr., Thomas J. Schoenberg, Marie Toft, Lawrence J. Trudeau, Russel Whitaker

Indexing Services
Synapse, the Knowledge Link Corporation

Permissions
Emma Hull, Lori Hines, Shalice Shah-Caldwell

Imaging and Multimedia
Lezlie Light, Daniel Newell, Kelly A. Quin

Product Design
Michael Logusz, Pamela Galbreath

Composition and Electronic Capture
Carolyn Roney

Manufacturing
Rhonda Williams

Product Manager
Janet Witalec

LIBRARY OF CONGRESS CATALOGING-IN-PUBLICATION DATA

Feminism in literature : a Gale critical companion / foreword by Amy Hudock ; Jessica Bomarito, project editor, Jeffrey W. Hunter, project editor.
    p. cm. -- (Gale critical companion collection)
    Includes bibliographical references and index.
    ISBN 0-7876-7573-3 (set hardcover : alk. paper) -- ISBN 0-7876-7574-1 (vol 1) -- ISBN 0-7876-7575-X (vol 2) -- ISBN 0-7876-7576-8 (vol 3) -- ISBN 0-7876-9115-1 (vol 4) -- ISBN 0-7876-9116-X (vol 5) -- ISBN 0-7876-9065-1 (vol 6)
    1. Literature--Women authors--History and criticism. 2. Women authors--Biography. 3. Women--History. I. Bomarito, Jessica, 1975- II. Hunter, Jeffrey W., 1966- III. Series.
    PN471.F43 2005
    809'.89287--dc22
                                                    2004017989

Printed in the United States of America
10 9 8 7 6 5 4 3 2

CONTENTS

v

VOLUME 2

VOLUME 3

VOLUME 4

VOLUME 5

Anna Akhmatova 1889-1966
Russian poet, essayist, and translator

Isabel Allende 1942-
Chilean novelist, essayist, journalist, short
story writer, memoirist, playwright, and
juvenile fiction writer

VOLUME 6

Virginia Woolf 1882-1941
   English novelist, critic, essayist, short story
   writer, diarist, autobiographer, and
   biographer

CONTENTS

When I was a girl, I would go to the library with my class, and all the girls would run to the Nancy Drew books, while the boys would head toward the Hardy Boys books—each group drawn to heroes that resembled themselves. Yet, when I entered formal literary studies in high school and college, I was told that I should not read so much in the girls' section any more, that the boys' section held books that were more literary, more universal, and more valuable. Teachers and professors told me this in such seemingly objective language that I never questioned it. At the time, the literary canon was built on a model of scarcity that claimed that only a few literary works could attain "greatness"—defined according to a supposed objective set of aesthetic criteria that more often than not excluded women authors. New Criticism, a way of reading texts that focuses on a poem, short story, or novel as an autonomous artistic production without connections to the historical and social conditions out of which it came, ruled my classrooms, making the author's gender ostensibly irrelevant. Masculine experience was coded as universal, while women's experience was particular. Overall, I had no reason to question the values I had been taught, until I encountered feminism.

Feminism, sometimes put in the plural *feminisms*, is a loose confederation of social, political, spiritual, and intellectual movements that places women and gender at the center of inquiry with

the goal of social justice. When people in the United States speak of feminism, they are often referring to the mainstream liberal feminism that grew out of the relationship between grassroots civil rights movements of the 1960s and 1970s and these movements' entrance into the academy through the creation of Women's Studies as an interdisciplinary program of study in many colleges and universities. Mainstream liberal feminism helped many women achieve more equity in pay and access to a wider range of careers while it also transformed many academic disciplines to reflect women's achievements. However, liberal feminism quickly came under attack as largely a movement of white, heterosexual, university-educated, middle-class women who were simply trying to gain access to the same privileges that white, middle-class men enjoyed, and who assumed their experiences were the norm for a mythical universal "woman." Liberal feminists have also been critiqued for echoing the patriarchal devaluation of traditional women's nurturing work in their efforts to encourage women to pursue traditional men's work, for creating a false opposition between work and home, and for creating the superwoman stereotype that can cause women to believe they have failed if they do not achieve the perfect balance of work and home lives. Other feminisms developed representing other women and other modes of thought: Marxist, psychoanalytic, social/radical, lesbian, trans- and bi-sexual, black womanist, first nations, chicana, nonwestern, postcolonial, and approaches that even question the use of "woman" as a unifying signifier in the first place. As Women's Studies and these many feminims gained power and credibility in the academy, their presence forced the literary establishment to question its methodology, definitions, structures, philosophies, aesthetics, and visions as well at to alter the curriculum to reflect women's achievements.

Once I learned from Women's Studies that women mattered in the academy, I began exploring women in my own field of literary studies. Since male-authored texts were often the only works taught in my classes, I began to explore the images of women as constructed by male authors. Many other women writers also began their critique of women's place in society studying similar sites of representation. Mary Wollstonecraft's *A Vindication of the Rights of Women* (1792), Margaret Fuller's *Woman in the Nineteenth Century* (1845), Simone de Beauvoir's *The Second Sex* (1949*)*, and Kate Millet's *Sexual Politics* (1969) explored how published images of women can serve as a means of social manipulation and control—a type of gender propaganda.

However, I began to find, as did others, that looking at women largely through male eyes did not do enough to reclaim women's voices and did not recognize women's agency in creating images of themselves. In *Sexual/Textual Politics* (1985), Toril Moi further questioned the limited natures of these early critical readings, even when including both male and female authors. She argued that reading literature for the accuracy of images of women led critics into assuming their own sense of reality as universal: "If the women in the book feel real to me, then the book is good." This kind of criticism never develops or changes, she argued, because it looks for the same elements repetitively, just in new texts. Also, she was disturbed by its focus on content rather than on how the text is written—the form, language, and literary elements. Moi and others argued for the development of new feminist critical methods.

However, examination of images of women over time has been fruitful. It has shown us that representation of women changes as historical forces change, that we must examine the historical influences on the creators of literary texts to understand the images they manufacture, and that we cannot assume that these images of women are universal and somehow separate from political and culture forces. These early explorations of woman as image also led to discussions of

femininity as image, not biologically but culturally defined, thus allowing analysis of the feminine ideal as separate from real women. This separation of biological sex and socially constructed gender laid the foundation for the later work of Judith Butler in *Gender Trouble: Feminism and the Subversion of Identity* (1990) and Marjorie Garber's *Vested Interests: Cross Dressing and Cultural Anxiety* (1992) in questioning what IS this thing we call "woman." These critics argued that gender is a social construct, a performance that can be learned by people who are biologically male, female, or transgendered, and therefore should not be used as the only essential connecting element in feminist studies. The study of woman and gender as image then has contributed much to feminist literary studies.

Tired of reading almost exclusively texts by men and a small emerging canon of women writers, I wanted to expand my understanding of writing by women. As a new Ph. D. student at the University of South Carolina in 1989, I walked up the stairs into the Women's Studies program and asked the first person I saw one question: were there any nineteenth-century American women writers who are worth reading? I had recently been told there were not, but I was no longer satisfied with this answer. And I found I was right to be skeptical. The woman I met at the top of those stairs handed me a thick book and said, "Go home and read this. Then you tell me if there were any nineteenth-century American women writers who are worth reading." So, I did. The book was the *Norton Anthology of Literature by Women* (1985), and once I had read it, I came back to the office at the top of the stairs and asked, "What more do you have?" My search for literary women began here, and this journey into new terrain parallels the development of the relationship between western feminism and literary studies.

In *A Room of Her Own* (1929), Virginia Woolf asks the same questions. She sits, looking at her bookshelves, thinking about the women writers who are there, and the ones who are not, and she calls for a reclaiming and celebrating of lost women artists. Other writers answered her call. Patricia Meyer Spacks's *The Female Imagination: A Literary and Psychological Investigation of Women's Writing* (1972), Ellen Moers's *Literary Women: The Great Writers* (1976), Elaine Showalter's *A Literature of Their Own: British Women Novelists from Brontë to Lessing* (1977), and Sandra Gilbert and Susan Gubar's *The Madwoman in the Attic* (1979) are a few of the early critical studies that explored the possibility of a tradition in women's literature.

While each of these influential and important books has different goals, methods, and theories, they share the attempt to establish a tradition in women's literature, a vital means through which marginalized groups establish a community identity and move from invisibility to visibility. These literary scholars and others worked to republish and reclaim women authors, expanding the number and types of women-authored texts available to readers, students, and scholars.

Yet, I began to notice that tradition formation presented some problems. As Marjorie Stone pointed out in her essay "The Search for a Lost Atlantis" (2003), the search for women's traditions in language and literature has been envisioned as the quest for a lost continent, a mythical motherland, similar to the lost but hopefully recoverable Atlantis. Such a quest tends to search for similarities among writers to attempt to prove the tradition existed, but this can sometimes obscure the differences among women writers. Looking to establish a tradition can also shape what is actually "found": only texts that fit that tradition. Traditions are defined by what is left in and what is left out, and the grand narratives of tradition formation as constructed in the early phases of feminist literary criticism inadvertently mirrored the exclusionary structures of the canon they were revising.

Some critics began discussing a women's tradition, a lost motherland of language, in not only what was written but also how it was written: in a female language or *ecriture feminine*. Feminist thinkers writing in France such as Hélène Cixous, Julia Kristeva, and Luce Irigaray argued that gender shapes language and that language shapes gender. Basing their ideas on those of psychoanalyst Jacques Lacan, they argued that pre-oedipal language—the original mother language—was lost when the law and language of the fathers asserted itself. While each of these writers explored this language differently, they all rewrote and revisioned how we might talk about literature, thus offering us new models for scholarship. However, as Alicia Ostriker argued in her essay, "Notes on 'Listen'" (2003), for the most part, women teach children language at home and at school. So, she questioned, is language really male and the "the language of the father," or is it the formal discourse of the academy that is male? Ostriker and others question the primacy of the father as the main social/language influence in these discussions. Other critics attacked what came to be known as "French Feminism" for its ahistorical, essentializing approach to finding a women's

tradition in language. Despite its problems, it offered much to the general understanding of gender and language and helped us imagine new possible forms for scholarship.

The idea that language might be gendered itself raised questions about how aesthetic judgement, defined in language, might also be gendered. Problems with how to judge what is "good" literature also arose, and feminist literary critics were accused of imposing a limited standard because much of what was being recovered looked the same in form as the traditional male canon, only written by women. Early recovered texts tended to highlight women in opposition to family, holding more modern liberal political views, and living nontraditional lives. If a text was "feminist" enough, it was included. Often times, this approach valued content over form, and the forms that were included did not differ much from the canon they were reacting against. These critics were still using the model of scarcity with a similar set of critical lens through which to judge texts worthy of inclusion. However, because later scholars started creating different critical lenses through which to view texts does not mean we need to perceive difference as inequality. Rather, texts that differ greatly began to be valued equally for different reasons. In order to do this, critics had to forfeit their tendency to place literary forms on a hierarchical model that allows only one at the apex. Instead, they exchanged the structure of value from one pyramid with a few writers at the apex for one with multiple high points, a model which celebrates a diversity of voices, styles, and forms. The model functioning in many past critical dialogues allowed for little diversity, privileging one type of literature—western, male, linear, logical, structured according to an accepted formula—over others—created by women and men who fail to fit the formula, and, thus, are judged not worthy. Creating hierarchies of value which privilege one discourse, predominantly Anglo male, over another, largely female, non-Anglo, and nonwestern undermines the supposed "impartiality" of critical standards. Breaking down the structure of canon formation that looks for the "great men" and "great women" of literature and instead studies what was actually written, then judging it on its own terms, has the potential for less bias. Challenging the existence of the canon itself allows more writers to be read and heard; perhaps we can base our understanding of literature not on a model of scarcity where only a few great ones are allowed at the top of the one peak, but where there are multiple peaks.

Another problem is that the tradition that was being recovered tended to look most like the critics who were establishing it. Barbara Smith's essay "Toward a Black Feminist Criticism" (1977) and bell hooks's *Ain't I a Woman? Black Women and Feminism* (1981) argued that academic feminism focused on the lives, conditions, histories, and texts of white, middle-class, educated women. Such writers revealed how the same methods of canon formation that excluded women were now being used by white feminists to exclude women of color. They also highlighted the silencing of black women by white women through the assumption that white womanhood was the norm. These writers and others changed the quest for one lost Atlantis to a quest for many lost continents as anthologies of African American, Chicana, Native American, Asian, Jewish, lesbian, mothers, and many more women writers grouped together by identity began to emerge. *This Bridge Called My Back: Writings by Radical Women of Color* (1981), edited by Ana Castillo and Cherríe Moraga, is one such collection. Yet, while these and other writers looked for new traditions of women's writing by the identity politics of the 1980s and 1990s, they were still imposing the same structures of tradition formation on new groups of women writers, still looking for the lost Atlantis.

Western feminist critics also began looking for the lost Atlantis on a global scale. Critiques from non-western critics and writers about their exclusion from feminist literary histories that claimed to represent world feminisms is bringing about the same pattern of starting with an exploration of image, moving to recovery of writers and traditions, then a questioning of recovery efforts that we have seen before. Now, however, all these stages are occurring at the once. For example, American feminist critics are still attempting to make global primary texts available in English so they can be studied and included at the same time they are being critiqued for doing so. Chandra Talpade Mohanty in "Under Western Eyes: Feminist Scholarship and Colonial Discourses" (1991) argues that systems of oppression do not affect us all equally, and to isolate gender as the primary source of oppression ignores the differing and complex webs of oppressions non-western women face. Western tendencies to view non-western women as suffering from a totalizing and undifferentiated oppression similar to their own "universal" female oppression cause feminist literary critics to impose structures of meaning onto non-western texts that fail to reflect the actual cultures and experiences of the writers. Therefore, to simply add the women from non-western literary traditions into existing western timelines, categories, and periodizations may not fully reflect the complexity of non-western writing. In fact, critics such as Gayatri Chakravorty Spivak, Ann DuCille, and Teresa Ebert argue post-colonial and transnational critics have created yet another master narrative that must be challenged. Yet, before the westernness of this new, transnational narrative can be addressed, critics need to be able read, discuss, and share the global texts that are now being translated and published before we can do anything else; therefore, this reclaiming and celebration of a global women's tradition is a necessary step in the process of transforming the very foundations of western feminist literary criticism. But it is only an early step in the continual speak, react, revise pattern of feminist scholarship.

Some critics argue that the ultimate goal of feminist literary history should be to move beyond using gender as the central, essential criteria—to give up looking for only a woman's isolated traditions and to examine gender as one of many elements. In that way, we could better examine female-authored texts in relationship with male-authored texts, and, thus, end the tendency to examine texts by women as either in opposition to the dominant discourse or as co-opted by it. As Kathryn R. King argues in her essay "Cowley Among the Women; or, Poetry in the Contact Zone" (2003), women writers, like male writers, did not write in a vacuum or only in relationship to other women writers. King argues for a more complex method of examining literary influence, and she holds up Mary Louise Pratt's discussion of the contact zone in *Imperial Eyes: Travel Writing and Transculturation* (1992) as a potential model for exploring the web of textual relationships that influence women writers. Pratt argues that the relationship between the colonized and the colonizer, though inflected by unequal power, often creates influence that works both ways (the contact zone). Using Pratt's idea of mutual influence and cultural hybridity allows, King argues, women's literary history to be better grounded in social, historical, philosophical, and religious traditions that influenced the texts of women writers.

So, what has feminism taught me about literary studies? That it is not "artistic value" or "universal themes" that keeps authors' works alive. Professors decide which authors and themes are going to "count" by teaching them, writing scholarly books and articles on them, and by making sure they appear in dictionaries of literary biography, bibliographies, and in the grand narratives of literary history. Reviewers decide who gets attention by reviewing them. Editors and publishers decide who gets read by keeping them in print. And librarians decide what books to buy and to keep on the shelves. Like the ancient storytellers who passed on the tribes' history from generation to generation, these groups keep our cultural memory. Therefore, we gatekeepers, who are biased humans living in and shaped by the intellectual, cultural, and aesthetic paradigms of an actual historical period must constantly reassess our methods, theories, and techniques, continually examining how our own ethnicities, classes, genders, nationalities, and sexualities mold our critical judgements.

What has literary studies taught me about feminism? That being gendered is a text that can be read, interpreted, manipulated, and altered. That feminisms themselves are texts written by real people in actual historical situations, and that feminists, too, must always recognize our own biases, and let others recognize them. That feminism is forever growing and changing and reinventing itself in a continual cycle of statement, reaction, and revision. As the definitions and goals of feminisms change before my eyes, I have learned that feminism is a process, its meaning constantly deferred.

—Amy Hudock, Ph.D.
University of South Carolina

The Gale Critical Companion Collection

In response to a growing demand for relevant criticism and interpretation of perennial topics and important literary movements throughout history, the Gale Critical Companion Collection (GCCC) was designed to meet the research needs of upper high school and undergraduate students. Each edition of GCCC focuses on a different literary movement or topic of broad interest to students of literature, history, multicultural studies, humanities, foreign language studies, and other subject areas. Topics covered are based on feedback from a standing advisory board consisting of reference librarians and subject specialists from public, academic, and school library systems.

The GCCC is designed to complement Gale's existing Literary Criticism Series (LCS) , which includes such award-winning and distinguished titles as *Nineteenth-Century Literature Criticism* (*NCLC*), *Twentieth-Century Literary Criticism* (*TCLC*), and *Contemporary Literary Criticism* (*CLC*). Like the LCS titles, the GCCC editions provide selected reprinted essays that offer an inclusive range of critical and scholarly response to authors and topics widely studied in high school and undergraduate classes; however, the GCCC also includes primary source documents, chronologies, sidebars, supplemental photographs, and other material not included in the LCS products. The graphic and supplemental material is designed to extend the usefulness of the critical essays and provide students with historical and cultural context on a topic or author's work. GCCC titles will benefit larger institutions with ongoing subscriptions to Gale's LCS products as well as smaller libraries and school systems with less extensive reference collections. Each edition of the GCCC is created as a stand-alone set providing a wealth of information on the topic or movement. Importantly, the overlap between the GCCC and LCS titles is 15% or less, ensuring that LCS subscribers will not duplicate resources in their collection.

Editions within the GCCC are either single-volume or multi-volume sets, depending on the nature and scope of the topic being covered. Topic entries and author entries are treated separately, with entries on related topics appearing first, followed by author entries in an A-Z arrangement. Each volume is approximately 500 pages in length and includes approximately 50 images and sidebar graphics. These sidebars include summaries of important historical events, newspaper clippings, brief biographies of important figures, complete poems or passages of fiction written by the author, descriptions of events in the related arts (music, visual arts, and dance), and so on.

The reprinted essays in each GCCC edition explicate the major themes and literary techniques of the authors and literary works. It is important to note that approximately 85% of the essays reprinted in GCCC editions are full-text, meaning that they are reprinted in their entirety, including footnotes and lists of abbreviations. Essays are selected based on their coverage of the seminal works and themes of an author, and based on the importance of those essays to an appreciation of the author's contribution to the movement and to literature in general. Gale's editors select those essays of most value to upper high school and undergraduate students, avoiding narrow and highly pedantic interpretations of individual works or of an author's canon.

Scope of Feminism in Literature

Feminism in Literature, the third set in the Gale Critical Companion Collection, consists of six volumes. Each volume includes a detailed table of contents, a foreword on the subject of feminism in literature written by noted scholar Amy Hudock, and a descriptive chronology of key events throughout the history of women's writing. Volume 1 focuses on feminism in literature from antiquity through the 18th century. It consists of three topic entries, including Women and Women's Writings from Classical Antiquity through the Middle Ages, and seven author entries on such women writers from this time period as Christine de Pizan, Sappho, and Mary Wollstonecraft. Volumes 2 and 3 focus on the 19th century. Volume 2 includes such topic entries as United States Women's Suffrage Movement in the 19th Century, as well as author entries on Jane Austen, Charlotte Brontë, and Elizabeth Barrett Browning. Volume 3 contains additional author entries on figures of the 19th century, including such notables as Kate Chopin, Emily Dickinson, and Harriet Beecher Stowe. Volumes 4, 5, and 6 focus on the 20th century to the present day; volume 4 includes coverage of topics relevant to feminism in literature during the 20th century and early 21st century, including the Feminist Movement, and volumes 5 and 6 include author entries on such figures as Margaret Atwood, Charlotte Perkins Gilman, Sylvia Plath, and Virginia Woolf.

Organization of Feminism in Literature

A *Feminism in Literature* topic entry consists of the following elements:

- The **Introduction** defines the subject of the entry and provides social and historical information important to understanding the criticism.

- The list of **Representative Works** identifies writings and works by authors and figures associated with the subject. The list is divided into alphabetical sections by name; works listed under each name appear in chronologi-

cal order. The genre and publication date of each work is given. Unless otherwise indicated, dramas are dated by first performance, not first publication.

- Entries generally begin with a section of **Primary Sources**, which includes essays, speeches, social history, newspaper accounts and other materials that were produced during the time covered.

- Reprinted **Criticism** in topic entries is arranged thematically. Topic entries commonly begin with general surveys of the subject or essays providing historical or background information, followed by essays that develop particular aspects of the topic. Each section has a separate title heading and is identified with a page number in the table of contents. The critic's name and the date of composition or publication of the critical work are given at the beginning of each piece of criticism. Unsigned criticism is preceded by the title of the source in which it appeared. Footnotes are reprinted at the end of each essay or excerpt. In the case of excerpted criticism, only those footnotes that pertain to the excerpted texts are included.

- A complete **Bibliographical Citation** of the original essay or book precedes each piece of criticism.

- Critical essays are prefaced by brief **Annotations** explicating each piece. Unless the descriptor "excerpt" is used in the annotation, the essay is being reprinted in its entirety.

- An annotated bibliography of **Further Reading** appears at the end of each entry and suggests resources for additional study. In some cases, significant essays for which the editors could not obtain reprint rights are included here.

A *Feminism in Literature* author entry consists of the following elements:

- The **Author Heading** cites the name under which the author most commonly wrote, followed by birth and death dates. Also located here are any name variations under which an author wrote. If the author wrote consistently under a pseudonym, the pseudonym will be listed in the author heading and the author's actual name given in parentheses on the first line of the biographical and critical information. Uncertain birth or death dates are indicated by question marks.

- A **Portrait of the Author** is included when available.

- The **Introduction** contains background information that introduces the reader to the author that is the subject of the entry.

- The list of **Principal Works** is ordered chronologically by date of first publication and lists the most important works by the author. The genre and publication date of each work is given. Unless otherwise indicated, dramas are dated by first performance, not first publication.

- Author entries are arranged into three sections: **Primary Sources**, **General Commentary**, and **Title Commentary**. The Primary Sources section includes letters, poems, short stories, journal entries, novel excerpts, and essays written by the featured author. General Commentary includes overviews of the author's career and general studies; Title Commentary includes in-depth analyses of seminal works by the author. Within the Title Commentary section, the reprinted criticism is further organized by title, then by date of publication. The critic's name and the date of composition or publication of the critical work are given at the beginning of each piece of criticism. Unsigned criticism is preceded by the title of the source in which it appeared. All titles by the author featured in the text are printed in boldface type. However, not all boldfaced titles are included in the author and subject indexes; only substantial discussions of works are indexed. Footnotes are reprinted at the end of each essay or excerpt. In the case of excerpted criticism, only those footnotes that pertain to the excerpted texts are included.

- A complete **Bibliographical Citation** of the original essay or book precedes each piece of criticism.

- Critical essays are prefaced by brief **Annotations** explicating each piece. Unless the descriptor "excerpt" is used in the annotation, the essay is being reprinted in its entirety.

- An annotated bibliography of **Further Reading** appears at the end of each entry and suggests resources for additional study. In some cases, significant essays for which the editors could not obtain reprint rights are included here. A list of **Other Sources from Gale** follows the further reading section and provides references to other biographical and critical sources on the author in series published by Gale.

Indexes

The **Author Index** lists all of the authors featured in the *Feminism in Literature* set, with references to the main author entries in volumes 1, 2, 3, 5, and 6 as well as commentary on the featured author in other author entries and in the topic volumes. Page references to substantial discussions of the authors appear in boldface. The Author Index also includes birth and death dates and cross references between pseudonyms and actual names, and cross references to other Gale series in which the authors have appeared. A complete list of these sources is found facing the first page of the Author Index.

The **Title Index** alphabetically lists the titles of works written by the authors featured in volumes 1 through 6 and provides page numbers or page ranges where commentary on these titles can be found. Page references to substantial discussions of the titles appear in boldface. English translations of foreign titles and variations of titles are cross-referenced to the title under which a work was originally published. Titles of novels, dramas, nonfiction books, films, and poetry, short story, or essay collections are printed in italics, while individual poems, short stories, and essays are printed in roman type within quotation marks.

The **Subject Index** includes the authors and titles that appear in the Author Index and the Title Index as well as the names of other authors and figures that are discussed in the set, including those covered in sidebars. The Subject Index also lists hundreds of literary terms and topics covered in the criticism. The index provides page numbers or page ranges where subjects are discussed and is fully cross referenced.

Citing Feminism in Literature

When writing papers, students who quote directly from the *FL* set may use the following general format to footnote reprinted criticism. The first example pertains to material drawn from periodicals, the second to material reprinted from books.

Bloom, Harold. " Feminism as the Love of Reading," *Raritan* 14, no. 2 (fall 1994): 29-42; reprinted in *Feminism in Literature: A Gale Critical Companion*, vol. 6, eds. Jessica Bomarito and Jeffrey W. Hunter (Farmington Hills, Mich: Thomson Gale, 2004), 29-42.

Coole, Diana H. "The Origin of Western Thought and the Birth of Misogyny," in *Women in Political Theory: From Ancient Misogyny to Contemporary Feminism* (Brighton, Sussex: Wheatsheaf Books, 1988), 10-28; reprinted in *Feminism in Literature: A Gale Critical Companion*, vol. 1, eds. Jessica Bomarito and Jeffrey W. Hunter (Farmington Hills, Mich: Thomson Gale, 2004), 15-25.

Feminism in Literature *Advisory Board*

The members of the *Feminism in Literature* Advisory Board—reference librarians and subject specialists from public, academic, and school library systems—offered a variety of informed perspectives on both the presentation and content of the *Feminism in Literature* set. Advisory board members assessed and defined such quality issues as the relevance, currency, and usefulness of the author coverage, critical content, and topics included in our product; evaluated the layout, presentation, and general quality of our product; provided feedback on the criteria used for selecting authors and topics covered in our product; identified any gaps in our coverage of authors or topics, recommending authors or topics for inclusion; and analyzed the appropriateness of our content and presentation for various user audiences, such as high school students, undergraduates, graduate students, librarians, and educators.

We wish to thank the advisors for their advice during the development of *Feminism in Literature*.

Suggestions are Welcome

Readers who wish to suggest new features, topics, or authors to appear in future volumes of the Gale Critical Companion Collection, or who have other suggestions or comments are cordially invited to call, write, or fax the Product Manager.

Product Manager, Gale Critical Companion
  Collection
Thomson Gale
27500 Drake Road
Farmington Hills, MI 48331-3535
1-800-347-4253 (GALE)
Fax: 248-699-8054

The editors wish to thank the copyright holders of the excerpted criticism included in this volume and the permissions managers of many book and magazine publishing companies for assisting us in securing reproduction rights. We are also grateful to the staffs of the Detroit Public Library, the Library of Congress, the University of Detroit Mercy Library, Wayne State University Purdy/ Kresge Library Complex, and the University of Michigan Libraries for making their resources available to us. Following is a list of the copyright holders who have granted us permission to reproduce material in this edition of *Feminism in Literature*. Every effort has been made to trace copyright, but if omissions have been made, please let us know.

Copyrighted material in Feminism in Literature was reproduced from the following periodicals:

African American Review, v. 35, winter, 2001 for "'The Porch Couldn't Talk for Looking': Voice and Vision in *Their Eyes Were Watching God*" by Deborah Clarke; v. 36, 2002 for "Phillis Wheatley's Construction of Otherness and the Rhetoric of Performed Ideology" by Mary McAleer Balkun. Copyright © 2001, 2002 by the respective authors. Both reproduced by permission of the respective authors.—*Agora: An Online Graduate Journal,* v. 1, fall, 2002 for "Virgin Territory: Murasaki Shikibu's Ôigimi Resists the Male" by Valerie Henitiuk. Copyright © 2001-2002 Maximiliaan van Woudenberg. All rights reserved. Reproduced by permission of the author.—*American Literary History,* v. 1, winter, 1989 for "Bio-Political Resistance in Domestic Ideology and *Uncle Tom's Cabin*" by Lora Romero. Copyright © 1989 by Oxford University Press. Reproduced by permission of the publisher and the author.—*American Literature,* v. 53, January, 1982. Copyright © 1982, by Duke University Press. Reproduced by permission.—*The American Scholar,* v. 44, spring, 1975. Copyright © 1975 by the United Chapters of Phi Beta Kappa. Reproduced by permission of Curtis Brown Ltd.—*The Antioch Review,* v. 32, 1973. Copyright © 1973 by the Antioch Review Inc. Reproduced by permission of the Editors.—*Ariel: A Review of International English Literature,* v. 21, January, 1990 for "Female Sexuality in Willa Cather's *O Pioneers!* and the Era of Scientific Sexology: A Dialogue between Frontiers" by C. Susan Wiesenthal; v. 22, October, 1991 for "Margaret Atwood's *Cat's Eye*: Re-Viewing Women in a Postmodern World" by Earl G. Ingersoll. Copyright © 1990, 1991 The Board of Governors, The University of Calgary. Both reproduced by permission of the publisher and the author.—*Atlantis: A Women's Studies Journal,* v. 9, fall, 1983. Copyright © 1983 by Atlantis. Reproduced by permission.—*Black American Literature Forum,* v. 24, summer, 1990 for "Singing the Black Mother: Maya Angelou and Autobiographical Continuity" by Mary Jane Lupton. Copyright © 1990 by the author. Reproduced by permission of the author.—*The Book Collector,* v. 31, spring, 1982. Reproduced by permission.—*The CEA Critic*, v. 56, spring/summer, 1994 for "Feminism and Children's Literature: Fitting *Little Women* into the American Literary Canon" by Jill P. May. Copyright © 1994 by the College English Association, Inc. Reproduced by permission of the publisher and the author.—*The Centennial Review*, v. xxix, spring, 1985 for "'An Order of Constancy': Notes on Brooks and the Feminine" by Hortense J. Spillers. Michigan State University Press. Copyright © 1985 by *The Centennial Review*. Reproduced by permission of the publisher.—*Chaucer Review*, v. 37, 2003. Copyright © 2003 by The Pennsylvania State University. All rights reserved. Reproduced by permission.—*Christianity and Literature*, v. 51, spring, 2002. Copyright © 2002 by the Conference on Christianity and Literature. Reproduced by permission.—*CLA Journal*, v. XXXIX, March, 1996. Copyright © 1966 by The College Language Association. Used by permission of The College Language Association.—*Classical Quarterly*, v. 31, 1981 for "Spartan Wives: Liberation or Licence?" by Paul Cartledge. Copyright © 1981 The Classical Association. Reproduced by permission of Oxford University Press and the author.—*Colby Library Quarterly*, v. 21, March, 1986. Reproduced by permission.—*Colby Quarterly*, v. XXVI, September 1990; v. XXXIV, June, 1998. Both reproduced by permission.—*College English*, v. 36, March, 1975 for "Who Buried H. D.?: A Poet, Her Critics, and Her Place in 'The Literary Tradition'" by Susan Friedman. Copyright © 1975 by the National Council of Teachers of English. Reproduced by permission of the publisher and the author.—*Connotations*, v. 5, 1995-96. Copyright © Waxmann Verlag GmbH, Munster/New York 1996. Reproduced by permission.—*Contemporary Literature*, v. 34, winter, 1993. Copyright © 1993 by University of Wisconsin Press. Reproduced by permission.—*Critical Quarterly*, v. 14, autumn, 1972; v. 27, spring, 1985. Copyright © 1972, 1985 by Manchester University Press. Both reproduced by permission of Blackwell Publishers.—*Critical Survey*, v. 14, January, 2002. Copyright © 2002 Berghahn Books, Inc. Reproduced by permission.—*Critique: Studies in Modern Fiction*, v. XV, 1973. Copyright © by *Critique*, 1973. Copyright © 1973 by Helen Dwight Reid Educational Foundation. Reproduced with permission of the Helen Dwight Reid Educational Foundation, published by Heldref Publications, 1319 18th Street, NW, Washington, DC 20036-1802.—*Cultural Critique*, v. 32, winter, 1995-96. Copyright © 1996 by *Cultural Critique*. All rights reserved. Reproduced by permission.—*Denver Quarterly*, v. 18, winter, 1984 for "Becoming Anne Sexton" by Diane Middlebrook. Copyright © 1994 by Diane Middlebrook. Reproduced by permission of Georges Bou-

chardt, Inc. for the author.—*Dissent*, summer, 1987. Copyright © 1987, by Dissent Publishing Corporation. Reproduced by permission.—*The Eighteenth Century*, v. 43, spring, 2002. Copyright © 2002 by Texas Tech University Press. Reproduced by permission.—*Eighteenth-Century Fiction*, v. 3, July, 1991. Copyright © McMaster University 1991. Reproduced by permission.—*Emily Dickinson Journal*, v. 10, 2000. Copyright © 2000 by The Johns Hopkins University Press for the Emily Dickinson International Society. All rights reserved. Reproduced by permission.—*The Emporia State Research Studies*, v. 24, winter, 1976. Reproduced by permission.—*Essays and Studies*, 2002. Copyright © 2002 Boydell & Brewer Inc. Reproduced by permission.—*Essays in Literature*, v. 12, fall, 1985. Copyright © 1985 Western Illinois University. Reproduced by permission.—*Feminist Studies*, v. 6, summer, 1980; v. 25, fall, 1999. Copyright © 1980, 1999 by *Feminist Studies*. Both reproduced by permission of Feminist Studies, Inc., Department of Women's Studies, University of Maryland, College Park, MD 20724.—*French Studies*, v. XLVIII, April, 1994; v. LII, April, 1998. Copyright © 1994, 1998 by The Society for French Studies. Reproduced by permission.—*Frontiers*, v. IX, 1987; v. XIV, 1994. Copyright © The University of Nebraska Press 1987, 1994. Both reproduced by permission.—*Glamour*, v. 88, November 1990 for "Only Daughter" by Sandra Cisneros. Copyright © 1996 by Wendy Martin. All rights reserved. Reproduced by permission of Susan Bergholz Literary Services, New York.—*Harper's Magazine*, for "Women's Work" by Louise Erdrich. Copyright © 1995 by *Harper's Magazine*. All rights reserved. Reproduced from the May edition by special permission.—*History Today*, v. 50, October, 2000; v. 51, November, 2001. Copyright © 2000, 2001 by The H. W. Wilson Company. All rights reserved. Reproduced by permission.—*The Hudson Review*, v. XXXVI, summer, 1983. Copyright © 1983 by The Hudson Review, Inc. Reproduced by permission.—*Hypatia*, v. 5, summer, 1990 for "Is There a Feminist Aesthetic?" by Marilyn French. Copyright by Marilyn French. Reproduced by permission.—*International Fiction Review*, v. 29, 2002. Copyright © 2002. International Fiction Association. Reproduced by permission.—*Irish Studies Review*, spring, 1996 from "History, Gender and the Colonial Movement: Castle Rackrent" by Colin Graham. Reproduced by permission of Taylor & Francis and the author.—*Journal of Evolutionary Psychology*, v. 7, August, 1986. Reproduced by permission.—*Journal of the Midwest Modern Language Association*, v. 35, 2002 for "The Gospel According to Jane Eyre: The Suttee and the Seraglio" by Maryanne C. Ward. Copyright © 2002 by The Midwest Modern Language Association. Reproduced by permission of the publisher and the author.—*Journal of the Short Story in English,* autumn, 2002. Copyright © Université d'Angers, 2002. Reproduced by permission.—*Keats-Shelley Journal,* v. XLVI, 1997. Reproduced by permission.—*Legacy,* v. 6, fall, 1989. Copyright © The University of Nebraska Press 1989. Reproduced by permission.—*The Massachusetts Review,* v. 27, summer, 1986. Reproduced from *The Massachusetts Review,* The Massachusetts Review, Inc. by permission.—*Meanjin,* v. 38, 1979 for "The Liberated Heroine: New Varieties of Defeat?" by Amanda Lohrey. Copyright © 1979 by *Meanjin.* Reproduced by permission of the author.—*MELUS,* v. 7, fall, 1980; v. 12, fall, 1985; v.18, fall, 1993. Copyright © MELUS: The Society for the Study of Multi-Ethnic Literature of the United States, 1980, 1985, 1993. Reproduced by permission.—*Modern Drama,* v. 21, September, 1978. Copyright © 1978 by the University of Toronto, Graduate Centre for Study of Drama. Reproduced by permission.—*Modern Language Studies,* v. 24, spring, 1994 for "Jewett's Unspeakable Unspoken: Retracing the Female Body Through *The Country of the Pointed Firs*" by George Smith. Copyright © Northeast Modern Language Association 1990. Reproduced by permission of the publisher and author.—*Mosaic,* v. 23, summer, 1990; v. 35, 2002. Copyright © 1990, 2002 by *Mosaic.* All rights reserved. Acknowledgment of previous publication is herewith made.—*Ms.,* v. II, July, 1973 for "Visionary Anger" by Erica Mann Jong; June 1988 for "Changing My Mind About Andrea Dworkin" by Erica Jong. Copyright © 1973, 1988. Both reproduced by permission of the author.—*New Directions for Women,* September-October, 1987 for "Dworkin Critiques Relations Between the Sexes" by Joanne Glasgow. Copyright © 1987 New Directions for Women, Inc., 25 West Fairview Ave., Dover, NJ 07801-3417. Reproduced by permission of the author.—*The New Yorker,* 1978 for "Girl" by Jamaica Kincaid. Copyright © 1979 by Jamaica Kinkaid. All rights reserved. Reproduced by permission of the Wylie Agency; v. 73, February 17, 1997 for "A Society of One: Zora Neal Hurston, American Contrarian" by Claudia Roth Pierpont. Copyright © 1997 by The New Yorker Magazine, Inc. All rights reserved. Reproduced by permission of the author.—*Nineteenth-Century Feminisms,* v. 2, spring-summer, 2000. Reproduced by permission.—*Nineteenth-Century French Studies,* v. 25, spring-summer, 1997. Copyright © 1977 by *Nineteenth-Century French Studies.* Reproduced by permission.—*Novel,* v. 34, spring, 2001. Copyright © NOVEL Corp. 2001. Reproduced with permission.—*Oxford Literary Review,* v. 13, 1991. Copyright © 1991 the *Oxford Literary Review.* All rights reserved. Reproduced by permission.—*P. N. Review,* v. 18, January/February, 1992. Reproduced by permission of Carcanet Press Ltd.—*Papers on Language & Literature,* v. 5, winter, 1969. Copyright © 1969 by The Board of Trustees, Southern Illinois University at Edwardsville. Reproduced by permission.—*Parnassus,* v. 12, fall-winter, 1985 for "Throwing the Scarecrows from the Garden" by Tess Gallagher; v. 12-13, 1985 for "Adrienne Rich and Lesbian/Feminist Poetry" by Catharine Stimpson. Copyright © 1985, 1986 by Poetry in Review Foundation. Both reproduced by permission of the publisher and the respective authors.—*Philological Papers,* v. 38, 1992. Copyright © 1992 by *Philological Papers.* Reproduced by permission.—*Philological Quarterly,* v. 79, winter, 2000. Copyright © 2001 by the University of Iowa. Reproduced by permission.—*Quadrant,* v. 46, November, 2002 for "The Mirror of Honour and Love: A Woman's View of Chivalry" by Sophie Masson. Copyright © 2002 Quadrant Magazine Company, Inc. Reproduced by permission of the publisher and the author.—*Raritan,* v. 14, fall, 1994. Copyright © 1994 by *Raritan: A Quarterly Review.* Reproduced by permission.—*Resources for American Literary Study,* v. 22, 1996. Copyright © 1996 by The Pennsylvania State University. Reproduced by permission of The Pennsylvania State University Press.—*Revista Hispánica Moderna,* v. 47, June, 1994. Copyright © 1994 by Hispanic Institute, Columbia University. Reproduced by permission.—*Rhetoric Society Quarterly,* v. 32, winter, 2002. Reproduced by permission of the publisher, conveyed through the Copyright Clearance Center.—*Romanic Review,* v. 79, 1988. Copyright © 1988 by The Trustees of Columbia University in the City of New York. Reproduced by permission.—*The Russian Review,* v. 57, April, 1998. Copyright © 1998 *The Russian Review.* Reproduced by permission of Blackwell Publishers.—*San Jose Studies,* v. VIII, spring, 1982 for "Dea, Awakening: A Reading of H. D.'s *Trilogy*" by Joyce Lorraine Beck. Copyright © 1982 by Trustees of the San Jose State University Foundation. Reproduced by permission of the publisher and the author.—*South Atlantic Review,* v. 66, winter, 2001. Copyright © 2001 by the South Atlantic Modern Language Association. Reproduced by permission.—*Southern Humanities Review,* v. xxii, summer, 1988. Copyright © 1988 by Auburn University. Reproduced by permission.—*The Southern Quarterly,* v. 35, spring, 1997; v. 37, spring-summer, 1999. Copyright © 1997, 1999 by the University of Southern Mississippi. Both reproduced by permission.—*Southern Review,* v. 18, for "Hilda in Egypt" by Albert Gelpi. Reproduced by permission of the author.—*Soviet Literature,* v. 6, June, 1989. Reproduced by permission of FTM Agency Ltd.—*Studies in American Fiction*, v. 9, autumn, 1981. Copyright © 1981 Northeastern University. Reproduced by permission.—*Studies in American Humor*, v. 3, 1994. Copyright © 1994 American Humor Studies Association. Reproduced by permission.—*Studies in the Humanities*, v. 19, December, 1992. Copyright © 1992 by Indiana University Press of Pennsylvania. Reproduced by permission.—*Studies in the Novel*, v. 31, fall 1999; v. 35, spring, 2003. Copyright © 1999, 2003 by North Texas State University. Reproduced by permission.—*Textual Practice*, v. 13, 1999 for "Speaking Un-likeness: The Double Text in Christina Rossetti's 'After Death' and 'Remember'" by Margaret Reynolds. Copyright © 1999 Routledge. Reproduced by permission of the publisher and the author.—*The Threepenny Review*, 1990 for "Mother Tongue" by Amy Tan. Reproduced by permission.—*Transactions of the American Philological Association*, v. 128, 1998. Copyright © 1998 American Philological Association. Reproduced by permission of The Johns Hopkins University Press.—*Tulsa Studies in Women's Literature*, v. 6, fall, 1987 for "Revolutionary Women" by Betsy Erkkila. Copyright © 1987, The University of Tulsa. All rights reserved. Reproduced by permission of the publisher and the author.—*The Victorian Newsletter*, v. 82, fall, 1992 for "Revisionist Mythmaking in Christina Rossetti's 'Goblin Market': Eve's Apple and Other Questions" by Sylvia Bailey Shurbutt; v. 92, fall, 1997 for "The Poet and the Bible: Christina Rossetti's Feminist Hermeneutics" by Lynda Palazzo; spring, 1998 for "'No Sorrow I Have Thought More About': The Tragic Failure of George Eliot's St. Theresa" by June Skye Szirotny. All reproduced by permission of The Victorian Newsletter and the author.—*Victorians Institute Journal*, v. 13, 1985. Copyright © Victorians Institute Journal 1985. Reproduced by permission.—*Women: A Cultural Review*, v. 10, winter, 1999 from "Consorting with Angels: Anne Sexton and the Art of Confession" by Deryn Rees-Jones. Copyright © 1999, by Taylor & Francis Ltd. Reproduced by permission of the publisher and the author. (http://www.tandf.co.uk/journals).—*Women and Language*, v. 13, March 31, 1995; v. 19, fall, 1996. Copyright © 1995, 1996 by Communication Department at George Mason University. Reproduced by permission of the publisher.—*Women's Studies: An Interdisciplinary Journal*, v. 3, 1975; v. 4, 1976; v. 17, 1990; v. 18, 1990; v. 23, September, 1994; v. 30, 2001. Copyright © 1975, 1976, 1990, 1994, 2001 Gordon and Breach Science Publishers S.A. Reproduced by permission.—*Women's Studies in Communication*, v. 24, spring, 2001. Reproduced by permission.—*Women's Writing*, v. 3, June, 1996. Reproduced by permission of the publisher; v. 4, 1997 for "(Female) Philosophy in the Bedroom: Mary Wollstonecraft and Female Sexuality" by Gary Kelly. Copyright © Triangle Journals Ltd, 1997. All rights reserved. Reproduced by permission of the publisher and the author.—*World & I*, v. 18, March, 2003. Copyright © 2003 News World Communications, Inc. Reproduced by permission.—*World Literature Today*, v. 73, spring, 1999. Copyright © 1999 by the University of Oklahoma Press. Reprinted by permission of the publisher.—*World Literature Written in English*, v. 15, November, 1976 for "Doris Lessing's Feminist Plays" by Agate Nesaule Krouse. Copyright © 1976 by WLWE. Reproduced by permission of the publisher and the author.

Copyrighted material in Feminism in Literature *was reproduced from the following books:*

Acocella, Joan. From *Willa Cather and the Politics of Criticism*. University of Nebraska Press, 2000. Copyright © 2000, by Joan Acocella. All rights reserved. Reproduced by permission.—Aimone, Joseph. From "Millay's Big Book, or the Feminist Formalist as Modern," in *Unmanning Modernism: Gendered Re-Readings*. Edited by Elizabeth Jane Harrison and Shirley Peterson. University of Tennessee Press, 1997. Copyright © 1997 by The University of Tennessee Press. All rights reserved. Reproduced by permission of The University of Tennessee Press.—Allende, Isabel. From "Writing as an Act of Hope," in *Paths of Resistance: The Art and Craft of the Political Novel*. Edited by William Zinsser. Houghton Mifflin Company, 1989. Copyright © 1989 Isabel Allende. Reproduced by permission of the author.—Angelou, Maya. From *And Still I Rise*. Random House, 1978. Copyright © 1978 by Maya Angelou. Reproduced by permission of Random House, Inc. and Time Warner Books UK.—Arenal, Electa. From "The Convent as Catalyst for Autonomy: Two Hispanic Nuns of the Seventeenth Century," in *Women in Hispanic Literature*. Edited by Beth Kurti Miller. University of California Press, 1983. Copyright © 1983 by The Regents of the University of California. Reproduced by permission of the publisher and the author.—Arndt, Walter. From "Introduction: I The Akhmatova Phenomenon and II Rendering the Whole Poem," in *Anna Akhmatova: Selected Poems*. Edited and translated by Walter Arndt. Ardis, 1976. Reproduced by permission.—Atwood, Margaret. From *Second Words*. Anansi Press Limited, 1982. Copyright © 1982, by O. W. Toad Limited. All rights reserved. Reproduced by permission of the author.—Baker, Deborah Lesko. From "Memory, Love, and Inaccessibility in *Hiroshima mon amour*," in *Marguerite*

Duras Lives On. Edited by Janine Ricouart. University Press of America, 1998. Copyright © 1998 University Press of America, Inc. All rights reserved. Reproduced by permission.—Barlow, Judith E. From "Into the Foxhole: Feminism, Realism, and Lillian Hellman," in *Realism and the American Dramatic Tradition.* Edited by William W. Demastes. University of Alabama Press, 1996. Copyright © 1996, The University of Alabama Press. Reproduced by permission.—Barratt, Alexandra. From *Women's Writing in Middle English.* Edited by Alexandra Barratt. Longman Group UK Limited, 1992. Copyright © Longman Group UK Limited 1992. Reproduced by permission.—Barrett Browning, Elizabeth. From "A Letter to Mary Russell Mitford, September 18, 1846," in *Women of Letters: Selected Letters of Elizabeth Barrett Browning and Mary Russell Mitford.* Edited by Meredith B. Raymond and Mary Rose Sullivan. Twayne Publishers, 1987. Reproduced by permission of The Gale Group.—Barrett Browning, Elizabeth. From "Glimpses into My Own Life and Literary Character," in *The Brownings' Correspondence,* Vol. 1. Edited by Phillip Kelley and Ronald Hudson. Wedgestone Press, 1984. All rights reserved. Reproduced by permission of Eton College.—Bassard, Katherine Clay. From *Spiritual Interrogations: Culture, Gender, and Community in Early African American Women's Writing.* Princeton University Press, 1999. Copyright © 1999 by Katherine Clay Bassard. Reproduced by permission of Princeton University Press.—Beauvoir, Simone de. From "The Independent Woman," in *The Second Sex.* Translated by H. M. Parshley. Alfred A. Knopf, Inc., 1952. Copyright © 1952, renewed 1980 by Alfred A. Knopf, Inc. All rights reserved. Reproduced by permission of Alfred A. Knopf, Inc., a division of Random House, Inc. and The Random House Group.—Behrendt, Stephen. From "Mary Shelley, Frankenstein, and the Woman Writer's Fate," in *Romantic Women Writers: Voices and Countervoices.* Edited by Paula R. Feldman and Theresa M. Kelley. University Press of New England, 1995. Copyright © 1995 by University Press of New England. All rights reserved. Reproduced by permission.—Bell, Barbara Currier and Carol Ohmann. From "Virginia Woolf's Criticism: A Polemical Preface," in *Feminist Literary Criticism: Explorations in Theory.* Edited by Josephine Donovan. The University Press of Kentucky, 1989. Copyright © 1975, 1989 by The University Press of Kentucky. Reproduced by permission of The University Press of Kentucky.—Berry, Mary Frances. From *Why ERA Failed: Politics, Women's Rights, and the Amending Process of the Constitution.* Indiana University Press, 1986. Copyright © 1986 by Mary Frances Berry. All rights reserved. Reproduced by permission.—Birgitta of Sweden. From *Life and Selected Revelations.* Edited with a preface by Marguerite Tjader Harris, translation and notes by Albert Ryle Kezel, introduction by Tore Nyberg from *The Classics of Western Spirituality.* Paulist Press, 1990. Copyright © 1990 by the Order of St. Birgitte, Rome. Translation, notes and Foreword copyright © 1990 by Albert Ryle Kezel, New York/Mahwah, NJ. Reproduced by permission of Paulist Press. www.paulistpress.com.—Blundell, Sue. From *Women in Ancient Greece.* British Museum Press, 1995. Copyright © 1995 Sue Blundell. Reproduced by permission of the author.—Bogan, Louise. From *The Blue Estuaries: Poems 1923-1968.* Farrar, Straus & Giroux, Inc., 1968. Copyright © 1968 by Louise Bogan. Copyright renewed 1996 by Ruth Limmer. All rights reserved. Reproduced by permission of Farrar, Straus and Giroux, LLC.—Booth, Alison. From "Not All Men Are Selfish and Cruel," in *Greatness Engendered: George Eliot and Virginia Woolf.* Cornell University Press, 1992. Copyright © 1992 by Cornell University Press. Reproduced by permission of the publisher, Cornell University Press.—Brammer, Leila R. From *Excluded from Suffrage History: Matilda Joslyn Gage, Nineteenth-Century American Feminist.* Greenwood Press, 2000. Copyright © by Leila R. Brammer. All rights reserved. Reproduced by permission of Greenwood Publishing Group, Inc., Westport, CT.—Britzolakis, Christina. From *Sylvia Plath and the Theatre of Mourning.* Oxford at the Clarendon Press, 1999. Copyright © 1999 by Christina Britzolakis. All rights reserved. Reproduced by permission of Oxford University Press.—Broe, Mary Lynn. From "Bohemia Bumps into Calvin: The Deception of Passivity in Lillian Hellman's Drama," in *Critical Essays on Lillian Hellman.* Edited by Mark W. Estrin. G. K. Hall, 1989. Copyright © 1989 by Mark W. Estrin. All rights reserved. Reproduced by permission of The Gale Group.—Brontë, Charlotte. From "Caroline Vernon," in *Legends of Angria: Compiled from The Early Writings of Charlotte Brontë.* Edited by Fannie E. Ratchford. Yale University Press, 1933. Copyright © 1933 by Yale University Press. Renewed 1961 by Fannit Ratchford. Reproduced by permission.—Brooks, Gwendolyn. From *Blacks.* The David Company, 1987. Copyright © 1945, 1949, 1953, 1960, 1963, 1968, 1969, 1970, 1971, 1975, 1981, 1986 by Gwendolyn Brooks Blakely. All rights reserved. Reproduced by consent of Brooks Permissions.—Brown-Grant, Rosalind. From "Christine de Pizan: Feminist Linguist Avant la Lettre?," in *Christine de Pizan 2000: Studies on Christine de Pizan in Honour of Angus J. Kennedy.* Edited by John Campbell and Nadia Margolis. Rodopi, 2000. Copyright © Editions Rodopi B. Reproduced by permission.—Brownmiller,

ings in *Renaissance Women's Drama: Criticism, History, and Performance 1594-1998.* Edited by S. P. Cerasano and Marion Wynee-Davies. Bucknell University Press 1981. Reproduced by permission of Associated University Presses and the author.—Coultrap-McQuin, Susan. From *Doing Literary Business: American Women Writers in the Nineteenth Century.* The University of North Carolina Press, 1990. Copyright © 1990 Susan Coultrap-McQuin. All rights reserved. Used by permission of the University of North Carolina Press.—Daly, Brenda. From *Lavish Self-Divisions: The Novels of Joyce Carol Oates.* University Press of Mississippi, 1996. Copyright © 1996 by the University Press of Mississippi. All rights reserved. Reproduced by permission.—Davis, Cynthia J. "What 'Speaks in Us': Margaret Fuller, Woman's Rights, and Human Nature," in *Margaret Fuller's Cultural Critique: Her Age and Legacy.* Edited by Fritz Fleischmann. Peter Lang, 2000. Copyright © 2000 Peter Lang Publishing. All rights reserved. Reproduced by permission.—de Gouges, Olympe. From "The Rights of Women," in *Women in Revolutionary Paris 1789-1795: Selected Documents.* Edited and translated by Daline Gay Levy, Harriet Branson Applewhite, and Mary Durham Johnson. University of Illinois, 1979. Reproduced by permission.—Depla, Annette. From "Women in Ancient Egyptian Wisdom Literature," in *Women in Ancient Societies: An Illusion of the Night.* Edited by Léonie J. Archer, Susan Fischler, and Maria Wyke. Macmillan Press Ltd, 1994. Copyright © The Macmillan Press Ltd 1994. Reproduced with permission of Palgrave Macmillan and Routledge/Taylor & Francis Books, Inc.—Deutsch, Sarah Jane. From "From Ballots to Breadlines: 1920-1940," in *No Small Courage: A History of Women in the United States.* Edited by Nancy F. Cott. Oxford University Press, 2000. Copyright © 2000, by Sarah Jane Deutsch. All rights reserved. Used by permission of Oxford University Press.—Dever, Carolyn. From "Obstructive Behavior: Dykes in the Mainstream of Feminist Theory," in *Cross-Purposes: Lesbians, Feminists, and the Limits of Alliance.* Indiana University Press, 1997. Copyright © 1997, by Indiana University Press. All rights reserved. Reproduced by permission.—Donawerth, Jane. From "Women's Poetry and the Tudor-Stuart System of Gift Exchange," in *Women, Writing, and the Reproduction of Culture in Tudor and Stuart Britain.* Edited by Mary E. Burke, Jane Donawerth, Linda L. Dove, and Karen Nelson. Syracuse University Press, 2002. Reproduced by permission.—Doolittle, Hilda. From *HERmione.* New Directions Publishing, 1981. Copyright © 1981 by the Estate of Hilda Doolittle. Reproduced by permission of New Directions Publishing Corp.—Douglas, Ann. From *The Feminization of American Culture.* Anchor Press/Doubleday, 1988. Copyright © 1977 by Ann Douglas. Used by permission of Alfred A. Knopf, a division of Random House, Inc.—Driver, Dorothy. From "Reconstructing the Past, Shaping the Future: Bessie Head and the Question of Feminism in a New South Africa," in *Black Women's Writings.* Edited by Gina Wisker. St. Martin's Press, 1993. Copyright © 1993, by Editorial Board, Lumière (Co-operative) Press Ltd. All rights reserved. Reprinted by permission of Palgrave Macmillan.—DuBois, Ellen Carol. From *Remembering Seneca Falls: Honoring the Women Who Paved the Way: An Essay.* Reproduced by permission of the author.—DuBois, Ellen Carol. From "Taking the Law Into Our Own Hands: Bradwell, Minor and Suffrage Militance in the 1870s," in *One Woman, One Vote: Rediscovering the Woman Suffrage Movement.* Edited by Marjorie Spruill Wheeler. NewSage Press, 1995. Copyright © 1995 by NewSage Press and Educational Film Company. All rights reserved. Reproduced by permission.—DuBois, Ellen Carol. From the introduction to *Feminism and Suffrage: The Emergence of An Independent Women's Movement in America.* Cornell University Press, 1978. Copyright © 1978 by Cornell University. All rights reserved. Used by permission of Cornell University Press.—DuBois, Ellen Carol. From "The Limitations of Sisterhood: Elizabeth Cady Stanton and the Division of the American Suffrage Movement, 1875-1902" in *Women and the Structure of Society.* Duke University Press, 1984. Copyright © 1984 by Duke University Press, Durham, NC. All rights reserved. Used by permission.—DuBois, Ellen Carol. From *Woman Suffrage and Women's Rights.* New York University Press, 1998. Copyright © 1998 by New York University. All rights reserved. Reproduced by permission of the publisher and the author.—DuBois, Ellen Carol. From "Woman Suffrage Around the World: Three Phases of Suffragist Internationalism," in *Suffrage and Beyond: International Feminist Perspectives.* Edited by Caroline Daley and Melanie Nolan. Auckland University Press, 1994. Copyright © by Auckland University Press 1994. All rights reserved. Reproduced by permission of the publisher and the author.—Ducrest, Stéphanie-Félicité. From "The Influence of Women on French Literature," in *Women Critics: 1660-1820: An Anthology.* Indiana University Press, 1995. Copyright © 1995 by Indiana University Press. All rights reserved. Reproduced by permission.—Dworkin, Andrea. From *Letters from a War Zone: Writings 1976-1989.* E. P. Dutton, 1988. Copyright © 1988 by Andrea Dworkin. Reproduced by permission of Elaine Markson Literary Agency.—Echols, Alice.

From *The Sixties: From Memory to History.* Edited by David R. Farber. University of North Carolina Press, 1994. Copyright © 1994 by the University of North Carolina Press. Used by permission of the Publisher.—Ehrenreich, Barbara and Deirdre English. From *For Her Own Good: 150 Years of the Experts' Advice to Women.* Anchor Books/Doubleday, 1978. Copyright © 1978 by Barbara Ehrenreich and Deirdre English. All rights reserved. Used by permission of Doubleday, a division of Random House.—Elbert, Sarah. From *A Hunger for Home: Louisa May Alcott and Little Women.* Temple University Press, 1984. Copyright © 1984 by Temple University. All rights reserved. Reproduced by permission of the author.—Emecheta, Buchi. From "Feminism with a Small 'f'!," in *Criticism and Ideology: Second African Writers' Conference.* Edited by Kirsten Holst Petersen. Scandinavian Institute of African Studies, 1988. Copyright © 1988 by Scandinavian Institute of African Studies. All rights reserved. Reproduced by permission of Nordic Africa Institute.—Ensler, Eve. From *The Vagina Monologues: The V-Day Edition.* Villard, 2001. Copyright © 1998, 2001 by Eve Ensler. All rights reserved. Reproduced by permission of Villard Books, a division of Random House, Inc.—Enstad, Nan. From *Ladies of Labor, Girls of Adventure: Working Women, Popular Culture, and Labor Politics at the Turn of the Twentieth Century.* Columbia University Press, 1999. Copyright © 1999 Columbia University Press, New York. All rights reserved. Republished with permission of the Columbia University Press, 61 W. 62nd St., New York, NY 10023.—Ezell, Margaret J. M. From "Women and Writing," in *A Companion to Early Modern Women's Writing.* Edited by Anita Pacheco. Blackwell Publishing Ltd, 2002. Copyright © 2002 by Blackwell Publishers Ltd. Reproduced by permission of Blackwell Publishers.—Fallaize, Elizabeth. From "Resisting Romance: Simone de Beauvoir, *The Woman Destroyed* and the Romance Script," in *Contemporary French Fiction by Women: Feminist Perspectives.* Edited by Margaret Atack and Phil Powrie. Manchester University Press, 1990. Reproduced by permission of the author.—Feng, Pin-chia. From *The Female Bildungsroman* by Toni Morrison and Maxine Hong Kingston: A Postmodern Reading. Peter Lang, 1998. Copyright © 1988 Peter Lang Publishing, Inc. All rights reserved. Reproduced by permission.—Ferree, Myra Marx and Beth B. Hess. From *Controversy and Coalition: The New Feminist Movement across Three Decades of Change.* Twayne Publishers, 1994. Copyright © 1994 by Twayne Publishers. All rights reserved. Reproduced by permission of The Gale Group.—Fishkin, Shelley Fisher. From an interview with Maxine Hong Kingston, in *Conversations with Maxine Hong Kingston.* Edited by Paul Skenazy and Tera Martin. University Press of Mississippi, 1998. Copyright © 1998 by University Press of Mississippi. All rights reserved. Reproduced by permission of the author.—Fishkin, Shelley Fisher. From "Reading Gilman in the Twenty-First Century," in *The Mixed Legacy of Charlotte Perkins Gilman.* Edited by Catherine J. Golden and Joanna Schneider Zangrando. University of Delaware Press, 2000. Copyright © 2000 by Associated University Press. Reproduced by permission.—Fleischmann, Fritz. From "Margaret Fuller, the Eternal Feminine, and the 'Liberties of the Republic'," in *Women's Studies and Literature.* Edited by Fritz Fleischmann and Deborah Lucas Schneider. Palm & Enke, 1987. Reproduced by permission.—Foster, M. Marie Booth. From "Voice, Mind, Self: Mother-Daughter Relationships in Amy Tan's *The Joy Luck Club* and *The Kitchen God's Wife,*" in *Women of Color: Mother-Daughter Relationships in 20th-Century Literature.* Edited by Elizabeth Brown-Guillory. University of Texas Press, 1996. Copyright © 1996 by the University of Texas Press. All rights reserved. Reproduced by permission.—Fowler, Robert Booth. From *Carrie Catt: Feminist Politician.* Northeastern University Press, 1986. Copyright © 1986 by R. B. Fowler. All rights reserved. Reproduced by permission.—Fraiman, Susan. From "The Humiliation of Elizabeth Bennett," in *Refiguring the Father: New Feminist Readings of Patriarchy.* Edited by Patricia Yaeger and Beth Kowaleski-Wallace. Southern Illinois University Press, 1989. Copyright © 1989 by the Board of Trustees, Southern Illinois University. All rights reserved. Reproduced by permission.—Francis, Emma. From "Is Emily Brontë a Woman?: Femininity, Feminism, and the Paranoid Critical Subject," in *Subjectivity and Literature from the Romantics to the Present Day.* Edited by Philip Shaw and Peter Stockwell. Pinter, 1991. Copyright © Emma Francis. All rights reserved. Reproduced by permission of the author.—Freedman, Estelle B. and Erna Olafson Hellerstein. From an introduction to *Victorian Women: A Documentary Account of Women's Lives in Nineteenth-Century England, France, and the United States.* Edited by Erna Olafson Hellerstein, Leslie Parker Hume, and Karen M. Offen. Stanford University Press, 1981. Copyright © 1981 by the Board of Trustees of Leland Stanford Junior University. Reproduced with permission of Stanford University Press, www.sup.org.—Frenk, Susan. From "The Wandering Text: Situating the Narratives of Isabel Allende," in *Latin American Women's Writing: Feminist Readings in Theory and Crisis.* Edited by Anny Brooksbank Jones and Catherine Davies. Oxford at the Clarendon Press, 1996. Copyright © 1996

ACKNOWLEDGMENTS

All rights reserved. Reproduced by permission of Routledge/Taylor & Francis and the author.—Gubar, Susan. From "Sapphistries," in *Re-reading Sappho: Reception and Transmission.* Edited by Ellen Greene. University of California Press, 1996. Copyright © 1996 by The Regents of The University of California. Reproduced by permission of the publisher and the author.—Gunther-Canada, Wendy. From *Rebel Writer: Mary Wollstonecraft and Enlightenment Politics.* Northern Illinois University Press, 2001. Copyright © 2001 by Northern Illinois University Press. All rights reserved. Reproduced by permission.—Hagen, Lyman B. From *Heart of a Woman, Mind of a Writer, and Soul of a Poet: A Critical Analysis of the Writings of Maya Angelou.* University Press of America, 1997. Copyright © 1997 by University Press of America. All rights reserved. Reproduced by permission.—Hallett, Judith From "The Role of Women in Roman Elegy: Counter-Cultural Feminism," in *Women in the Ancient World: The Arethusa Papers.* Edited by John Peradotto and J. Sullivan. State University of New York Press, 1984. Reproduced by permission of the State University of New York Press.—Hansberry, Lorraine. From *A Raisin in the Sun.* Modern Library, 1995. Copyright © 1958, 1986 by Robert Nemiroff, as an unpublished work. Copyright © 1959, 1966, 1984, 1987, 1988 by Robert Nemiroff. All rights reserved. Reproduced by permission of Random House, Inc., Jewell Gresham-Nemiroff and Methuen Publishing Ltd.—Harris, Susan K. From "'But is it any good?' Evaluating Nineteenth-Century American Women's Fiction," in *The (Other) American Traditions: Nineteenth-Century Women Writers.* Edited by Joyce W. Warren. Rutgers University Press, 1993. Copyright © 1993 by Rutgers University Press. All rights reserved. Reproduced by permission of the author.—Head, Bessie. From "Despite Broken Bondage, Botswana Women Are Still Unloved," in *A Woman Alone: Autobiographical Writings.* Selected and edited by Craig MacKenzie. Heinemann, 1990. Copyright © 1990, by The Estate of Bessie Head. Reproduced by permission of Johnson & Alcock.—Head, Bessie. From "The Woman from America," in *A Woman Alone: Autobiographical Writings.* Selected and edited by Craig MacKenzie. Heinemann, 1990. Copyright © 1990, by The Estate of Bessie Head. Reproduced by permission of Johnson & Alcock.—Hellerstein, Erna, Leslie Parker Hume and Karen M. Offen from an introduction to *Victorian Women: A Documentary Account of Women's Lives in Nineteenth-Century England, France, and the United States.* Edited by Erna Olafson Hellerstein, Leslie Parker Hume, and Karen M. Offen. Stanford University Press, 1981. Copyright © 1981 by the Board of Trustees of the Leland Stanford Junior University. Reproduced with permission of Stanford University Press, www.sup.org.—Henderson, Bruce. From *Images of the Self as Female: The Achievement of Women Artists in Re-envisioning Feminine Identity.* Edited by Kathryn N. Benzel and Lauren Pringle De La Vars. The Edwin Mellen Press, 1992. Copyright © 1992 by Kathryn N. Benzel and Lauren Pringle De La Vars. All rights reserved. Reproduced by permission.—Hill, Mary A. From "Charlotte Perkins Gilman: A Feminist's Struggle with Womanhood," in *Charlotte Perkins Gilman: The Woman and Her Work.* Edited by Sheryl L. Meyering. UMI Research Press, 1989. Copyright © 1989 by Sheryl L. Meyering. All rights reserved. Reproduced by permission of Boydell & Brewer, Inc.—Hobby, Elaine. From *Virtue of Necessity: English Women's Writing 1649-88.* The University of Michigan Press, 1989. Copyright © 1988 by Elaine Hobby. All rights reserved. Reproduced by permission of the author.—Hoffert, Sylvia D. From an introduction to *When Hens Crow: The Woman's Rights Movement in Antebellum America.* Indiana University Press, 1995. Copyright © 1995 by Sylvia D. Hoffert. All rights reserved. Reproduced by permission.—Hurston, Zora Neale. From *Their Eyes Were Watching God.* Perennial Library, 1990. Copyright © 1937 by Harper & Row, Publishers, Inc. Renewed 1965 by John C. Hurston and Joel Hurston. Reproduced by permission of Time Warner Books UK. In North America by HarperCollins Publishers Inc.—James, Adeola. From "Bessie Head's Perspectives on Women," in *Black Women Writers across Cultures.* Edited by Valentine Udoh James, James S. Etim, Melanie Marshall James, and Ambe J. Njoh. International Scholars Publications, 2000. Copyright © 2000, by International Scholars Publications. All rights reserved. Reproduced by permission.—Jardine, Alice A. From an interview with Marguerite Duras, translated by Katherine Ann Jensen, in *Shifting Scenes: Interviews on Women, Writing, and Politics in Post-68 France.* Edited by Alice A. Jardine and Anne M. Menke. Columbia University Press, 1991. Copyright © 1991 Columbia University Press, New York. All rights reserved. Reprinted with the permission of the publisher.—Jelinek, Estelle C. From "The Paradox and Success of Elizabeth Cady Stanton," in *Women's Autobiography: Essays in Criticism.* Edited by Estelle C. Jelinek. Indiana University Press, 1980. Copyright © Estelle C. Jelinek. Reproduced by permission of the author.—Juhasz, Suzanne. From "Maxine Hong Kingston: Narrative Technique & Female Identity," in *Contemporary American Women Writers: Narrative Strategies.* Edited by Catherine Rainwater and William J. Scheik. The University Press of Kentucky, 1985. Copyright © 1985 by The University Press of

Kentucky. Reproduced by permission.—Kaminer, Wendy. From "Feminism's Identity Crisis," in *Public Women, Public Words: A Documentary History of American Feminism.* Edited by Dawn Keetley and John Pettegrew. First published in *The Atlantic.* Reproduced by permission of the author.—Kaplan, Cora. From "Pandora's Box: Subjectivity, Class and Sexuality in Socialist Feminist Criticism," in *Making a Difference: Feminist Literary Criticism.* Edited by Gayle Greene and Coppélia Kahn. Methuen & Co., 1985. Copyright © 1985 Gayle Greene and Coppélia Kahn. All rights reserved. Reproduced by permission of Routledge and the author.—Keetley, Dawn and John Pettegrew. From "Identities through Adversity," in *Public Women, Public Words: A Documentary History of American Feminism.* Edited by Dawn Keetley and John Pettegrew. Madison House Publishers, Inc., 1997. Copyright © 1997 by Madison House Publisher, Inc. All rights reserved. Reproduced by permission.—Kelly, Gary. From *Revolutionary Feminism: The Mind and Career of Mary Wollstonecraft.* St. Martin's Press, 1996. Copyright © 1996 by Gary Kelly. All rights reserved. Reproduced by permission of Palgrave Macmillan.—Kempe, Margery. From "Margery Kempe's Visit to Julian of Norwich," in *The Shewings of Julian Norwich.* Edited by Georgia Ronan Crampton. Medieval Publishing Institute, 1994. Reproduced by permission.—Kempe, Margery. From *The Book of Margery Kempe.* Translated by B. A. Windeatt. Penguin, 1985. Copyright © B. A. Windeatt, 1985. All rights reserved. Reproduced by permission.—Kirkham, Margaret. From *Jane Austen, Feminism, and Fiction.* Harvester Press Limited, 1983. Copyright © Margaret Kirkham, 1983. All rights reserved. Reproduced by permission.—Klemans, Patricia A. From "'Being Born a Woman': A New Look at Edna St. Vincent Millay," in *Critical Essays on Edna St. Vincent Millay.* Edited by William B. Thesing. G. K. Hall, 1993. Copyright © by 1993 by William B. Thesing. All rights reserved. Reproduced by permission of The Gale Group.—Knapp, Bettina L. From *Gertrude Stein.* Continuum, 1990. Copyright © 1990 by Bettina L. Knapp. All rights reserved. Reproduced by permission.—Kolodny, Annette. From "Dancing Through the Minefield: Some Observations on the Theory, Practice, and Politics of a Feminist Literary Criticism," originally published in *Feminist Studies,* 1980. Copyright © 1980 by Annette Kolodny. All rights reserved. Reproduced by permission of the author.—Kumin, Maxine. From "How It Was," in *The Complete Poems: Anne Sexton.* Houghton Mifflin Company, 1981. Copyright © 1981, by Maxine Kumin. All rights reserved. Reproduced by permission of Houghton Mifflin and The Anderson Literary Agency.—Lam-

onica, Drew. From *We Are Three Sisters: Self and Family in the Writing of the Brontës.* University of Missouri Press, 2003. Copyright © 2003 by The Curators of the University of Missouri. All rights reserved. Reproduced by permission.—Larsen, Jeanne. From "Lowell, Teasdale, Wylie, Millay, and Bogan," in *The Columbia History of American Poetry.* Edited by Jay Parini. Columbia University Press, 1993. Copyright © 1993 Columbia University Press, New York. All rights reserved. Reprinted with permission of the publisher.—Lascelles, Mary. From *Jane Austen and Her Art.* Oxford University Press, 1939. Reproduced by permission of Oxford University Press.—Lavezzo, Kathy. From "Sobs and Sighs Between Women: The Homoerotics of Compassion in *The Book of Margery Kempe,*" in *Premodern Sexualities.* Edited by Louise Fradenburg and Carla Freccero. Routledge, 1996. Copyright © 1996 by Routledge. All rights reserved. Reproduced by permission of Routledge/Taylor & Francis and the author.—Lessing, Doris. From a preface to *The Golden Notebook* in *A Small Personal Voice.* Edited by Paul Schleuter. Alfred A. Knopf, Inc., 1974. Copyright © 1974 by Doris Lessing. All rights reserved. Reproduced by permission of Jonathan Clowes, Ltd.—Levertov, Denise. From *Poems, 1960-67.* New Directions, 1966. Copyright © 1967, by Denise Levertov. All rights reserved. Reproduced by permission of New Directions Publishing Corporation and in the UK by Pollinger Limited and the proprietor.—Logan, Shirley Wilson. From *"We are Coming": The Persuasive Discourse of Nineteenth-Century Black Women.* Southern Illinois University Press, 1999. Copyright © 1999 by the Board of Trustees, Southern Illinois University. All rights reserved. Reproduced by permission of Southern Illinois University Press and the University of South Carolina Press.—Lorde, Audre. From *The Black Unicorn.* Norton, 1978. Copyright © 1978, by Audre Lorde. All rights reserved. Reproduced by permission of W. W. Norton & Company and Charlotte Sheedy Literary Agency.—Lumsden, Linda J. From *Rampant Women: Suffragists and the Right of Assembly.* The University of Tennessee Press, 1997. Copyright © 1997 by The University of Tennessee Press. Reproduced by permission of The University of Tennessee Press.—Lunardini, Christine A. *From Equal Suffrage to Equal Rights: Alice Paul and the National Women's Party, 1910-1928.* New York University Press, 1986. Copyright © 1986 by New York University. All rights reserved. Reproduced by permission of the author.—Madsen, Deborah L. From "Sandra Cisneros," in *Understanding Contemporary Chicana Literature.* Edited by Matthew J. Bruccoli. University of South Carolina Press, 2000. Copyright © 2000 by University of South Carolina. Reproduced by permission.—Marder, Herbert. From *Feminism & Art: A Study of Virginia Woolf.* University of Chicago Press, 1968. Copyright © 1968 by the University of Chicago. All rights reserved. Reproduced by permission of the publisher and the author.—Marilley, Suzanne M. From *Woman Suffrage and the Origins of Liberal Feminism in the United States.* Harvard University Press, 1996. Copyright © 1996 by the President and Fellows of Harvard College. All rights reserved. Reproduced by permission Harvard University Press.—Marsh-Lockett, Carol P. From "What Ever Happened to Jochebed? Motherhood as Marginality in Zora Neale Hurston's *Seraph on the Suwanee*," in *Southern Mothers: Facts and Fictions in Southern Women's Writing.* Edited by Nagueyalti Warren and Sally Wolff. Louisiana State University, 1999. Reproduced by permission.—Mason, Nicholas. From "Class, Gender, and Domesticity in Maria Edgeworth's *Belinda*," in *The Eighteenth-Century Novel*, Vol. 1. Edited by Susan Spencer. AMS Press, 2001. Reproduced by permission.—Massardier-Kenney, Françoise. From *Gender in the Fiction of George Sand.* Rodopi, 1985. Copyright © Editions Rodopi B. V. Reproduced by permission.—McCracken, Ellen. From "Sandra Cisneros' *The House on Mango Street*: Community-Oriented Introspection and the Demystification of Patriarchal Violence," in *Breaking Boundaries: Latina Writing and Critical Readings.* Edited by Asunción Horno-Delgado, Eliana Ortega, Nina M. Scott, and Nancy Saporta Sternbach. University of Massachusetts Press, 1989. Copyright © 1989 by The University of Massachusetts Press. All rights reserved. Reproduced by permission.—McNamara, Jo Ann. From "Women and Power through the Family Revisited," in *Gendering the Master Narrative: Women and Power in the Middle Ages.* Edited by Mary C. Erler and Maryanne Kowaleski. Cornell University Press, 2003. Copyright © 2003 by Cornell University Press. Used by permission of Cornell University Press.—Meisenhelder, Susan. From "Ethnic and Gender Identity in Zora Neale Hurston's *Their Eyes Were Watching God*," in *Teaching American Ethnic Literatures: Nineteen Essays.* Edited by John R. Maitino and David R. Peck. University of New Mexico Press, 1996. Copyright © 1996, by the University of New Mexico Press. All rights reserved. Reproduced by permission.—Mellor, Anne K. From "Possessing Nature: The Female in Frankenstein," in *Romanticism and Feminism.* Edited by Anne K. Mellor. Indiana University Press, 1988. Copyright © 1988 by Indiana University Press. All rights reserved. Reproduced by permission.—Mermin, Dorothy. From *Godiva's Ride: Women of Letters in England, 1830-1880.* Indiana University Press, 1993. Copyright © 1993 by Dorothy Mermin. All rights reserved. Repro-

duced by permission.—Millay, Edna St. Vincent. From "Sonnet III of Fatal Interview," in *Collected Sonnets of Edna St. Vincent Millay.* HarperCollins, 1952. Copyright © 1931, 1958 by Edna St. Vincent Millay and Norma Millay Ellis. All rights reserved. Reproduced by permission of Elizabeth Barnett, Literary Executor.—Millay, Edna St. Vincent. From "First Fig," in *Collected Poems of Edna St. Vincent Millay.* HarperCollins, 1952. Copyright © 1922, 1950 by Edna St. Vincent Millay. Reproduced by permission of Elizabeth Barnett, Literary Executor.—Millay, Edna St. Vincent. From "I, Being Born a Woman and Distressed," in *Collected Poems of Edna St. Vincent Millay.* HarperCollins, 1952. Copyright © 1923, 1951 by Edna St.Vincent Millay and Norma Millay Ellis. All rights reserved. Reproduced by permission of Elizabeth Barnett, Literary Executor.—Millett, Kate. From "How Many Lives Are Here...," in *The Feminist Memoir Project.* Edited by Rachel DuPlessis and Ann Snitow. Three Rivers Press, 1998. Copyright © 1998 by Rachel DuPlessis and Ann Snitow. All rights reserved. Used by permission of Crown Publishers, a division of Random House, Inc. and Sanford J. Greenburger Associates.—Moi, Toril. From "Who's Afraid of Virginia Woolf? Feminist Readings of Woolf," in *New Casebooks: 'Mrs. Dalloway' and 'To the Lighthouse.'* Edited by Su Reid. St. Martin's Press, 1993. Copyright © Su Reid 1993. All rights reserved. Reproduced by permission of Palgrave Macmillan.—Moore, Marianne. From *The Selected Letters of Marianne Moore.* Edited by Bonnie Costello. Alfred A. Knopf, 1997. Copyright © 1997 by the Estate of Marianne Moore. Introduction, annotations and additional editorial material copyright 1997 by Bonnie Costello. All rights reserved. Reproduced by permission of Alfred A. Knopf, Inc., a division of Random House, Inc.—Morgan, Winifred. From "Alice Walker: *The Color Purple* as Allegory," in *Southern Writers at Century's End.* Edited by Jeffrey J. Folks and James A. Perkins. The University Press of Kentucky, 1997. Copyright © 1997 by The University Press of Kentucky. All rights reserved. Reproduced by permission.—Morrison, Toni. From *Race-ing Justice, En-Gendering Power.* Pantheon Books, 1992. Copyright © 1992 by Toni Morrison. All rights reserved. Used by permission International Creative Management, Inc.—Morrison, Toni. From "What the Black Woman Thinks About Women's Lib," in *Public Women, Public Words: A Documentary History of American Feminism.* Edited by Dawn Keetley and John Pettegrew. Madison House, 1997. Copyright © 1997 by Toni Morrison. Reproduced by permission of International Creative Management, Inc.—Mortimer, Armine Kotin. From "Male and Female Plots in Staël's *Corinne*," in *Correspondences:*

Studies in Literature, History, and the Arts in Nineteenth-Century France: Selected Proceedings of the Sixteenth Colloquium in Nineteenth-Century French Studies, The University of Oklahoma-Norman, October 11th-13th, 1990. Edited by Keith Busby. Rodopi, 1992. Copyright © Editions Rodopi B. V. Reproduced by permission.—Motard-Noar, Martine. From "From Persephone to Demeter: A Feminist Experience in Cixous's Fiction," in *Images of Persephone: Feminist Readings in Western Literature.* Edited by Elizabeth T. Hayes. University Press of Florida, 1994. Copyright © 1994 by Board of Regents of the State of Florida. All rights reserved. Reproduced with the permission of the University Press of Florida.—Mukherjee, Bharati. From *The Middleman and Other Stories.* Viking, 1988. Copyright © 1988, by Bharati Mukherjee. All rights reserved. Reprinted by permission of Penguin Group Canada and the author.—Mumford, Marilyn R. From "A Feminist Prolegomenon for the Study of Hildegard of Bingen," in *Gender, Culture, and the Arts: Women, the Arts, and Society.* Edited by Ronald Dotterer and Susan Bowers. Associated University Presses, 1993. Copyright © 1993 by Associated University Presses.—Oates, Joyce Carol. From *Where I've Been, and Where I'm Going.* Plume, 1999. Copyright © The Ontario Review, 1999. All rights reserved. Reproduced by permission of Plume, an imprint of Penguin Putnam Inc. In the United Kingdom by John Hawkins & Associates, Inc.—Okely, Judith. From "Re-reading The Second Sex," in *Simone de Beauvoir: A Re-Reading.* Virago, 1986. Reproduced by permission of the author.—Ovid. From "Sappho to Phaon," in *The Sappho Companion.* Edited by Margaret Reynolds. Chatto and Windus, 2000. Copyright © Margaret Reynolds 2000. Reproduced by permission of the editor.—Pan Chao. From *Pan Chao: Foremost Woman Scholar of China.* Edited by Nancy Lee Swann. University of Michigan Center for Chinese Studies, 1932. Copyright © The East Asian Library and the Gest Collection, Princeton University. Reproduced by permission.—Parks, Sheri. From "In My Mother's House: Black Feminist Aesthetics, Television, and *A Raisin in the Sun*," in *Theatre and Feminist Aesthetics.* Edited by Karen Laughlin and Catherine Schuler. Farleigh Dickinson University Press, 1995. Copyright © 1995 by Associated University Presses. All rights reserved. Reproduced by permission.—Paul, Alice. From *Party Papers: 1913-1974.* Microfilming Corporation of America, 1978. Reproduced by permission of Sewall-Belmont House and Museum.—Paz, Octavio. From "The Response," in *Sor Juana or, The Traps of Faith.* Translated by Margaret Sayers Peden. Cambridge, Mass.: The Belknap Press of Harvard University Press, 1988. Copyright © 1988 by the President and Fellows of Harvard College. All rights reserved. Reproduced by permission.—Perkins, Annie. From "The Poetry of Gwendolyn Brooks (1970s-1980s)," in *Women Making Art: Women in the Visual, Literary, and Performing Arts Since 1960.* Edited by Deborah Johnson and Wendy Oliver. Peter Lang, 2001. Copyright © 2001 Peter Lang Publishing, Inc., New York. Reproduced by permission.—Pierpont, Claudia Roth. From *Passionate Minds: Women Rewriting the World.* Alfred A. Knopf, 2000. Copyright © 2000 by Claudia Roth Piepont. All rights reserved. Reproduced by permission of Alfred A. Knopf, Inc., a division of Random House, Inc.—Plath, Sylvia. From *The Bell Jar.* Faber & Faber, 1966; Harper & Row, 1971. Copyright © 1971 by Harper & Row, Publishers, Inc. Reproduced by permission Faber & Faber Ltd. In the United States by HarperCollins Publishers Inc.—Pryse, Marjorie. From "Origins of American Literary Regionalism: Gender in Irving, Stowe, and Longstreet," in *Breaking Boundaries: New Perspectives on Women's Regional Writing.* Edited by Sherrie A. Inness and Diana Royer. University of Iowa Press, 1997. Copyright © 1997 by the University of Iowa Press. All rights reserved. Reproduced by permission.—Radice, Betty. From an introduction to *The Letters of Abelard and Heloise.* Translated by Betty Radice. Penguin Books, 1974. Copyright © Betty Radice, 1974. Reproduced by permission of Penguin Books, a division of Penguin Putnam Inc.—Rendall, Jane. From an introduction to *The Origins of Modern Feminism: Women in Britain, France and the United States 1780-1860.* Macmillan, 1985. Copyright © Jane Rendall 1985. All rights reserved. Reproduced by permission of Palgrave Macmillan.—Rich, Adrienne. From "Vesuvius at Home: The Power of Emily Dickinson," in *On Lies, Secrets, and Silence: Selected Prose 1966-1978.* W. W. Norton & Company, Inc., 1979. Copyright © 1979 by W. W. Norton & Company, Inc. Reproduced by permission of the author and W. W. Norton & Company, Inc.—Rich, Adrienne. From "When We Dead Awaken: Writing as Re-Vision," in *Arts of the Possible: Essays and Conversations.* W. W. Norton & Company, Inc., 2001. Copyright © 2001 by Adrienne Rich. Reproduced by permission of the publisher and the author.—Richmond, M. A. From *Bid the Vassal Soar: Essays on the Life and Poetry of Phillis Wheatley and George Moses Horton.* Howard University Press, 1974. All rights reserved. Copyright © 1974 by Merle A. Richmond. Reproduced by permission.—Risjord, Norman K. From *Representative Americans: The Colonists.* Second Edition. Rowman & Littlefield Publishers, Inc., 2001. Copyright © 2001 by Rowman & Littlefield Publishers, Inc. All rights reserved. Reproduced by permission.—Robbins,

ACKNOWLEDGMENTS

Ruth. From *Transitions: Literary Feminisms.* St. Martin's Press, 2000. Reproduced with permission of Palgrave Macmillan.—Rohrbach, Erika. From H. D. and Sappho: 'A Precious Inch of Palimpsest'," in *Re-Reading Sappho: Reception and Transmission.* Edited by Ellen Greene. University of California Press, 1996. Copyright © 1996 by The Regents of the University of California. Reproduced by permission.—Rosenman, Ellen Bayuk. From *"A Room of One's Own": Women Writers and the Politics of Creativity.* Twayne, 1995. Copyright © 1995 by Twayne Publishers. All rights reserved. Reproduced by permission of The Gale Group.—Rosslyn, Wendy. From "Don Juan Feminised," in *Symbolism and After: Essays on Russian Poetry in Honour of Georgette Donchin.* Edited by Arnold McMillin. Bristol Classical Press, 1992. Copyright © 1992 by Gerald Duckworth & Co. Ltd. All rights reserved. Reproduced by permission of The School of Slavonic Studies in the University of London.—Sanders, Valerie. From "Women, Fiction and the Marketplace," in *Women and Literature in Britain: 1800-1900.* Edited by Joanne Shattock. Cambridge University Press, 2001. Copyright © Cambridge University Press 2001. Reproduced by permission of Cambridge University Press.—Sandler, Martin W. From *Against the Odds: Women Pioneers in the First Hundred Years of Photography.* Rizzoli International Publications, Inc., 2002. Copyright © 2002, by Martin W. Sandler. All rights reserved. Reproduced by permission of the author.—Saunders, Corinne. From *Rape and Ravishment in the Literature of Medieval England.* D. S. Brewer, 2001. Copyright © Corinne J. Saunders 2001. All rights reserved. Reproduced by permission.—Scheick, William J. From *Authority and Female Authorship in Colonial America.* The University Press of Kentucky, 1998. Copyright © 1998 by The University Press of Kentucky. Reproduced by permission of The University Press of Kentucky.—Schroeder, Patricia R. From "Remembering the Disremembered: Feminist Realists of the Harlem Renaissance," in *Realism and the American Dramatic Tradition.* Edited by William W. Demastes. University of Alabama Press, 1996. Copyright © 1996, by the University of Alabama Press. All rights reserved. Reproduced by permission.—Selous, Trista. From *The Other Woman: Feminism and Femininity in the Work of Marguerite Duras.* Yale University Press, 1988. Copyright © 1988 by Yale University. All rights reserved. Reproduced by permission.—Sexton, Anne. From "All God's Children Need Radios," in *No Evil Star: Selected Essays, Interviews, and Prose of Anne Sexton.* Edited by Steven E. Colburn. The University of Michigan Press, 1985. Copyright © Anne Sexton. Reproduced by permission of SLL/Sterling Lord Literistic.—Shaw,

Harry B. From *"Maud Martha*: The War with Beauty," in *A Life Distilled: Gwendolyn Brooks, Her Poetry and Fiction.* Edited by Maria K. Mootry and Gary Smith. University of Illinois Press, 1987. Copyright © 1987 by the Board of Trustees of the University of Illinois. Reproduced by permission.—Shiach, Morag. From an introduction to *Hélène Cixous: A Politics of Writing.* Routledge, 1991. Copyright © 1991 by Morag Shiach. All rights reserved. Reproduced by permission of the publisher and the author.—Showalter, Elaine. From *A Literature of Their Own: British Women Novelists from Brontë to Lessing.* Princeton University Press, 1977. Copyright © 1977 by Princeton University Press. Renewed 2005 Princeton University Press, 1999 exp. Paperback edition. Reproduced by permission of Princeton University Press.—Showalter, Elaine. From *Sister's Choice: Tradition and Change in American Women's Writing.* Oxford at the Clarendon Press, 1991. Copyright © 1991, by Elaine Showalter. All rights reserved. Reproduced by permission of Oxford University Press.—Sigerman, Harriet. From "Laborers for Liberty," in *No Small Courage: A History of Women in the United States.* Edited by Nancy F. Cott. Oxford University Press, 2000. Copyright © 2000 by Oxford University Press, Inc. Copyright © 1994, 2000 by Harriet Sigerman. All rights reserved. Used by permission of Oxford University Press.—Signori, Lisa F. From *The Feminization of Surrealism: The Road to Surreal Silence in Selected Works of Marguerite Duras.* Peter Lang, 2001. Copyright © 2001 Peter Lang Publishing, Inc., New York. All rights reserved. Reproduced by permission.—Silko, Leslie Marmon. From *Storyteller.* Seaver Books, 1981. Copyright © 1981, by Leslie Marmon Silko. All rights reserved. Reproduced by permission.—Simson, Rennie. From "Afro-American Poets of the Nineteenth Century," in *Nineteenth-Century Women Writers of the English-Speaking World.* Edited by Rhoda B. Nathan. Greenwood Press, 1986. Copyright © 1986 by Hofstra University. All rights reserved. Reproduced by permission of Greenwood Publishing Group, Inc., Westport, CT.—Sizer, Lyde Cullen. From *The Political Work of Northern Women Writers and the Civil War, 1850-1872.* The University of North Carolina Press, 2000. Copyright © 2000 The University of North Carolina Press. All rights reserved. Reproduced by permission.—Smith, Hilda L. From "Introduction: Women, Intellect, and Politics: Their Intersection in Seventeenth-Century England," in *Women Writers and the Early Modern British Political Tradition.* Edited by Hilda L. Smith. Cambridge University Press, 1998. Copyright © Cambridge University Press 1998. Reproduced with the permission of Cambridge University Press.—Smith,

Johanna M. From "'Cooped Up': Feminine Domesticity in *Frankenstein*," in *Case Studies in Contemporary Criticism: Mary Shelley's* **Frankenstein.** Edited by Johanna M. Smith. St. Martin's Press, 1992. Copyright © 1992 by Bedford Books of St. Martin's Press. All rights reserved. Reproduced by permission.—Smith, Sidonie. From "Resisting the Gaze of Embodiment: Women's Autobiography in the Nineteenth Century," in *American Women's Autobiography: Fea(s)ts of Memory.* Edited by Margo Culley. University of Wisconsin University Press, 1992. Copyright © 1992 The Board of Regents of the University of Wisconsin System. All rights reserved. Reproduced by permission.—Smith, Sidonie. From *Where I'm Bound: Patterns of Slavery and Freedom in Black American Autobiography.* Greenwood Press, 1974. Copyright © 1974 by Sidonie Smith. All rights reserved. Reproduced by permission of Greenwood Publishing Group, Inc., Westport, CT.—Snyder, Jane McIntosh. From *The Woman and the Lyre: Women Writers in Classical Greece and Rome.* Southern Illinois University Press, 1989. Copyright © 1989 by the Board of Trustees, Southern Illinois University. All rights reserved. Reproduced by permission.—Sor Juana Ines de la Cruz. From *The Answer = La respuesta.* Edited by Electa Arenal and Amanda Powell. The Feminist Press, 1994. Copyright © 1994 by Electa Arenal and Amanda Powell. All rights reserved. Reproduced by permission of The Feminist Press at the City University of New York. www.feministpress.org.—Spender, Dale. From "Introduction: A Vindication of the Writing Woman," in *Living by the Pen: Early British Women Writers.* Edited by Dale Spender. Teachers College Press, 1992. Copyright © 1992 by Teachers College. All rights reserved. Reproduced by permission.—Staley, Lynn. From *Margery Kempe's Dissenting Fictions.* Pennsylvania State University Press, 1994. Copyright © 1994 The Pennsylvania State University. All rights reserved. Reproduced by permission.—Stehle, Eva. From *Performance and Gender in Ancient Greece: Nondramatic Poetry in Its Setting.* Princeton University Press, 1997. Copyright © 1997 by Princeton University Press. All rights reserved. Reproduced by permission of Princeton University Press.—Stein, Gertrude. From "Degeneration in American Women," in *Sister Brother: Gertrude and Leo Stein.* Edited by Brenda Wineapple. G. Putnam's Sons, 1996. Copyright © 1996 by Brenda Wineapple. All rights reserved. Used by permission of G. Putnam's Sons, a division of Penguin Group (USA) Inc. and Bloomsbury Publishing Plc.—Stott, Rebecca. From *Elizabeth Barrett Browning.* Pearson Education Limited, 2003. Copyright © Pearson Educated Limited 2003. All rights reserved. Reproduced by permission.—Straub, Kristina. From *Divided Fictions: Fanny Burney and Feminine Strategy.* University Press of Kentucky, 1987. Copyright © 1987 by the University Press of Kentucky. Reproduced by permission.—Swann, Nancy Lee. From *Pan Chao: Foremost Woman Scholar of China.* Russell & Russell, 1968. Copyright © The East Asian Library and the Gest Collection, Princeton University. Reproduced by permission.—Tanner, Laura E. From *Intimate Violence: Reading Rape and Torture in Twentieth-Century Fiction.* Indiana University Press, 1994. Copyright © 1994, by Laura E. Tanner. All rights reserved. Reproduced by permission.—Terborg-Penn, Rosalyn. From *African American Women in the Struggle for the Vote, 1850-1920.* Indiana University Press, 1998. Reproduced by permission.—Tharp, Julie. From "Women's Community and Survival in the Novels of Louise Erdrich," in *Communication and Women's Friendships: Parallels and Intersections in Literature and Life.* Edited by Janet Doubler Ward and JoAnna Stephens Mink. Bowling Green State University Popular Press, 1993. Copyright © 1993 by Bowling Green State University Popular Press. Reproduced by permission of the University of Wisconsin Press.—Trilling, Lionel. From "Emma and the Legend of Jane Austen," in *Beyond Culture: Essays on Literature and Learning.* Harcourt Brace Jovanovich, 1965. Copyright © 1965 by Lionel Trilling. All rights reserved. Reproduced by permission of the Wylie Agency, Inc.—Turner, Katherine S. H. From "From Classical to Imperial: Changing Visions of Turkey in the Eighteenth Century," in *Travel Writing and Empire: Postcolonial Theory in Transit.* Edited by Steve Clark. Zed Books, 1999. Copyright © Katherine S. H. Turner. Reproduced by permission.—Van Dyke, Annette. From "Of Vision Quests and Spirit Guardians: Female Power in the Novels of Louise Erdrich," in *The Chippewa Landscape of Louise Erdrich.* Edited by Allan Chavkin. The University of Alabama Press, 1999. Copyright © 1999, by The University of Alabama Press. Copyright © 1999. All rights reserved. Reproduced by permission.—Waelti-Waters, Jennifer and Steven C. Hause. From an introduction to *Feminisms of the Belle Époque: A Historical and Literary Anthology.* Edited by Jennifer Waelti-Waters and Steven C. Hause. University of Nebraska Press, 1994. Copyright © The University of Nebraska Press, 1994. All rights reserved. Reproduced by permission.—Wagner-Martin, Linda. From "Panoramic, Unpredictable, and Human: Joyce Carol Oates' Recent Novels," in *Traditions, Voices, and Dreams: The American Novel since the 1960s.* Edited by Melvin J. Friedman and Ben Siegel. University of Delaware Press, 1995. Copyright © 1995 by Associated University Presses, Inc. Reproduced by permission.—Wagner-Martin, Linda. From *Sylvia Plath: A Literary Life.*

St. Martin's Press, 1999. Copyright © 1999 by Linda Wagner-Martin. All rights reserved. Reproduced by permission of Palgrave Macmillan.—Walker, Alice. From *Revolutionary Petunias & Other Poems.* Harcourt Brace Jovanovich, 1971. Copyright © 1970, 1971, 1972, 1973, renewed 1998 by Alice Walker. All right reserved. Reproduced by permission of Harcourt Inc. In the British Commonwealth by David Higham Associates.—Watts, Linda S. From *Rapture Untold: Gender, Mysticism, and the 'Moment of Recognition' in Works by Gertrude Stein.* Peter Lang, 1996. Copyright © 1996 Peter Lang Publishing, Inc., New York. All rights reserved. Reproduced by permission.—Weatherford, Doris. From *A History of the American Suffragist Movement.* ABC-CLIO, 1998. Copyright © 1998 by The Moschovitis Group, Inc. Reproduced by permission of Moschovitis Group, Inc.—Weeton, Nellie. From "The Trials of an English Governess: Nelly Weeton Stock," originally published in *Miss Weeton: Journal of a Governess.* Edited by Edward Hall. Oxford University Press (London), H. Milford, 1936-39. Reproduced by permission of Oxford University Press.—Weston, Ruth D. From "Who Touches This Touches a Woman," in *Critical Essays on Alice Walker.* Edited by Ikenna Dieke. Greenwood Press 1999. Reproduced by permission of Greenwood Publishing Group, Inc., Westport, CT.—Wheeler, Marjorie Spruill. From an introduction to *One Woman, One Vote: Rediscovering the Woman Suffrage Movement.* Edited by Marjorie Spruill Wheeler. NewSage Press, 1995. Copyright © 1995 by NewSage Press and Educational Film Company. All rights reserved. Reproduced by permission.—Willard, Charity Cannon. From *Christine de Pizan: Her Life and Works.* Persea Books, 1984. Copyright © 1984 by Charity Cannon Willard. Reproduced by permission.—Willis, Sharon A. From "Staging Sexual Difference: Reading, Recitation, and Repetition in Duras' *Malady of Death,*" in *Feminine Focus: The New Women Playwrights.* Edited by Enoch Brater. Oxford University Press, 1989. Copyright © 1989 by Oxford University Press, Inc. Reproduced by permission of Oxford University Press.—Winter, Kate H. From *Marietta Holley: Life with "Josiah Allen's Wife."* Syracuse University Press, 1984. Copyright © 1984 by Syracuse University Press. All rights reserved. Reproduced by permission.—Woolf, Virginia. From "George Eliot," in *The Common Reader,* Harcourt, Brace & Company, 1925, L. & V. Woolf, 1925. Copyright 1925 by Harcourt Brace & Company. Renewed 1953 by Leonard Woolf. Reprinted by permission of Harcourt, Brace & Company and The Society of Authors.—Wynne-Davies, Marion. From an introduction to *Women Poets of the Renaissance.* Edited by Marion Wynne-Davies.

Routledge, 1999. Reprint. Copyright © 1998 by J. M. Dent. All rights reserved. Reproduced by permission of Routledge/Taylor & Francis and the author—Yalom, Marilyn. From "Toward a History of Female Adolescence: The Contribution of George Sand," in *George Sand: Collected Essays.* Edited by Janis Glasgow. The Whitson Publishing Company, 1985. Reproduced by permission of the author.—Yu Xuanji. From "Joining Somebody's Mourning and Three Beautiful Sisters, Orphaned Young," in *The Clouds Float North: The Complete Poems of Yu Xuanji.* Translated by David Young and Jiann I. Lin. Wesleyan University Press, 1998. Copyright © 1998 by David Young and Jiann I. Lin. All rights reserved. Reproduced by permission.

Photographs and Illustrations in Feminism in Literature were received from the following sources:

16th century men and women wearing fashionable clothing, ca. 1565 engraving. Hulton/Archive.—A lay sister preparing medicine as shown on the cover of *The Book of Margery Kempe,* photograph. MS. Royal 15 D 1, British Library, London.—Akhmatova, Anna, photograph. Archive Photos, Inc./Express Newspaper.—Alcott, Louisa May, drawing. The Granger Collection, New York.—Alcott, Louisa May, photograph. Archive Photos, Inc.—Allen, Joan, Joanne Camp, Anne Lange, and Cynthia Nixon, in a scene from the play "The Heidi Chronicles," photograph. Time Life Pictures/Getty Images.—Allende, Isabelle, photograph. Getty Images.—An estimated 5,000 people march outside the Minnesota Capitol Building in protest to the January 22, 1973 Supreme Court ruling on abortion as a result of the "Roe vs. Wade" case, photograph. AP/Wide World Photos.—Angelou, Maya, photograph. AP/Wide World Photos.—Anthony, Susan B., Frances Willard, and other members of the International Council of Women, photograph. Copyright © Corbis.—Atwood, Margaret, photograph by Jerry Bauer. Copyright © Jerry Bauer.—Autographed manuscript of Phillis Weatley's poem "To the University of Cambridge." The Granger Collection, New York.—Beller, Kathleen as Kate in the 1980 film version of Margaret Atwood's novel, *Surfacing,* photograph. Kobal Collection/Surfacing Film.—Blackshear, Thomas, illustrator. From a cover of *The Bluest Eye,* written by Toni Morrison. Plume, 1994. Reproduced by permission of Plume, a division of Penguin USA.—Broadside published by the National American Woman Suffrage Association, featuring "Why Women Want to Vote." The Library of Congress.—Brontë, Anne, Emily and Charlotte, painting by Patrick Branwell Brontë, located at the National Portrait Gallery,

1939, photograph. Copyright © Corbis-Bettmann.—Brontë, Charlotte, painting. Archive Photos.—Brooks, Gwendolyn, holding a copy of *The World of Gwendolyn Brooks,* photograph. AP/Wide World Photos.—Brown, John Mason (right) talking to National Book Award winners Marianne Moore, James Jones, and Rachel Carson, in New York City, NY, 1952, photograph. AP/Wide World Photos.—Brown, Rita Mae, photograph. AP/Wide World Photos.—Browning, Elizabeth Barret, 1848, illustration. Copyright © Corbis-Bettmann.—Burney, Fanny, engraving. Archive Photos, Inc.—Carter, Angela, photograph by Jerry Bauer. Copyright © Jerry Bauer.—Cather, Willa, photograph. AP/Wide World Photos.—Catherine the Great, illustration. Copyright © Archivo Iconografico, S.A./Corbis.—Catt, Carrie Chapman, photograph. The Library of Congress.—Cavendish, Margaret Lucas, engraving. Mary Evans Picture Library.—Child, Lydia Maria, photograph. The Library of Congress.—Childress, Alice, photograph by Jerry Bauer. Copyright © Jerry Bauer.—Chin, Tsai and Tamlyn Tomita in the 1993 film production of Amy Tan's *The Joy Luck Club.* Buena Vista/Hollywood/The Kobal Collection.—Chopin, Kate, photograph. The Library of Congress.—Cisneros, Sandra, 1991, photograph by Dana Tynan. AP/Wide World Photos.—Cixous, Hélène, photograph. Copyright © Bassouls Sophie/Corbis Sygma.—Class on a field trip to Library of Congress, photograph by Frances Benjamin Johnston. Copyright © Corbis.—Cleopatra VII, illustration. The Library of Congress.—Cyanotype by Frances Benjamin Johnson, ca. 1899, of girls and a teacher in a high school cooking class, photograph. Copyright © Corbis.—de la Cruz, Juana Inez, painting. Copyright © Philadelphia Museum of Art/Corbis-Bettmann.—de Pizan, Christine, writing in her study, photograph. MS. Harley 4431, f.4R. British Library, London.—Dickinson, Emily, photograph of a painting. The Library of Congress.—Doolittle, Hilda, 1949, photograph. AP/Wide World Photos.—Duras, Marguerite, photograph. AP/Wide World Photos.—Dworkin, Andrea, 1986, photograph. AP/Wide World Photos.—Edgeworth, Maria, engraving. The Library of Congress.—Eliot, George, photograph. Copyright © The Bettman Archive.—Emecheta, Buchi, photograph by Jerry Bauer. Copyright © Jerry Bauer.—Emily Dickinson Homestead in Amherst, Massachusetts, photograph. Copyright © James Marshall/Corbis.—Erdrich, Louise, photograph by Eric Miller. AP/Wide World Photos.—French, Marilyn, photograph by Jerry Bauer. Copyright © Jerry Bauer.—Friedan, Betty, president of the National Organization for Women, and other feminists march in New York City, photograph. Copyright © JP Laffont/Sygma/Corbis.—Friedan, Betty, with

Yoko Ono, photograph. Copyright © Bettmann/Corbis.—Frontpiece and title page from *Poems on Various Subjects, Religious and Moral,* written by Phillis Wheatley. Copyright © The Pierpont Morgan Library/Art Resource, NY.—Fuller, Margaret, painting by John Plumbe. The Library of Congress.—Gandhi, Indira, photograph. Copyright © Corbis-Bettmann.—Garrison, William Lloyd, (bottom right), with the Pennsylvania Abolition Society, photograph. National Portrait Gallery.—Gilman, Charlotte Perkins, cover photograph. Copyright © Corbis.—Gilman, Charlotte P., photograph. Copyright © Corbis-Bettmann.—Godwin, Mary Wollstonecraft, illustration. Copyright © Corbis-Bettmann.—Hansberry, Lorraine, photograph by David Attie. AP/Wide World Photos.—Head, Bessie, photograph. Reproduced by the kind permission of the Estate of Bessie Head.—"Head of Medusa," marble sculpture by Gianlorenzo Bernini. Copyright © Araldo de Luca/Corbis.—Hellman, Lillian, photograph. AP/Wide World Photos.—Hurston, Zora Neale looking at "American Stuff," at the *New York Times* book fair, photograph. The Library of Congress.—Hurston, Zora Neale, photograph by Carl Van Vechten. The Carl Van Vechten Trust.—Hypatia, conte crayon drawing. Copyright © Corbis-Bettmann.—Illustration depicting a woman's body being the subject of political and social conflict, photograph. Barbara Kruger/Mary Boone Gallery.—Jolie, Angelina (right), and unidentified person, in the film *Foxfire,* photograph by Jane O'Neal. The Kobal Collection/O'Neal, Jane.—Karloff, Boris, in movie *Frankenstein;* 1935, photograph. The Kobal Collection.—Kingston, Maxine Hong, photograph by Jerry Bauer. Copyright © Jerry Bauer.—"La Temptation," depicting Adam and Eve in the Garden of Paradise. The Library of Congress.—Lessing, Doris, photograph by Jerry Bauer. Copyright © Jerry Bauer.—Luce, Clare Booth, portrait. Copyright © UPI/Bettmann Archive.—Manuscript page from *The Book of Ladies,* by Christine de Pizan. Bibliotheque Nationale de France.—Manuscript page of *Vieyra Impugnado,* written by Sor Margarita Ignacia and translated to Spanish by Inigo Rosende. Madrid: Antonio Sanz, 1731. The Special Collections Library, University of Michigan.—Martineau, Harriet, engraving. The Library of Congress.—Migrant mother with child huddled on either shoulder, Nipomo, California, 1936, photograph by Dorothea Lange. The Library of Congress.—Millay, Edna St. Vincent, photograph. AP/Wide World Photos.—Montagu, Lady Mary Wortley, engraving. Archive Photos, Inc.—Moore, Marianne, photograph by Jerry Bauer. Copyright © Jerry Bauer.—Morrison, Toni, 1993, photograph. AP/Wide World Photos.—Murasaki, Lady, looking out from the veranda of a monastery, illustration

ACKNOWLEDGMENTS

from *Tale of Genji*. Copyright © Asian Art Archae-ology, Inc./Corbis.—National League of Women Voters' Headquarters, photograph. Copyright © Corbis-Bettmann.—National Women's Suffrage Association (NWSA), during a political convention in Chicago, Illinois, photograph. Copyright © Bettmann/Corbis.—Naylor, Gloria, photograph. Marion Ettlinger/AP/Wide World Photos.—Oates, Joyce Carol, 1991, photograph. AP/Wide World Photos.—October 15, 1913 publication of the early feminist periodical, *The New Freewoman*, photograph. McFarlin Library, Department of Special Collections, The University of Tulsa.—Paul, Alice (second from right), standing with five other suffragettes, photograph. AP/Wide World Pho-tos.—Pfeiffer, Michelle, and Daniel Day-Lewis, in the film *The Age of Innocence*, 1993, photograph by Phillip Caruso. The Kobal Collection.—Plath, Sylvia, photograph. AP/Wide World Photos.—Poster advertising *Uncle Tom's Cabin*, by Harriet Beecher Stowe, "The Greatest Book of the Age," photograph. Copyright © Bettmann/Corbis.—Rich, Adrienne, holding certificate of poetry award, Chicago, Illinois, 1986, photograph. AP/Wide World Photos.—Rossetti, Christina, 1863, photograph by Lewis Carroll. Copyright © UPI/Bettmann.—Russell, Rosalind and Joan Crawford in the 1939 movie *The Women*, written by Clare Boothe Luce, photograph. MGM/The Kobal Col-lection.—Salem Witch Trial, lithograph by George H. Walker. Copyright © Bettmann/Corbis.—Sand, George, illustration. Copyright © Leonard de Selva/Corbis.—Sand, George, photograph. The Library of Congress.—Sanger, Margaret, Miss Clara Louise Rowe, and Mrs. Anne Kennedy, arranging the first American Birth Control Conference, photograph. Copyright © Underwood and Under-wood/Corbis.—Sappho, bronze sculpture. The Library of Congress.—Sappho, illustration. The Library of Congress.—Sappho performing out-doors, illustration. The Library of Congress.—"Sara in a Green Bonnet," painting by Mary Cassatt, c. 1901. National Museum of American Art, Smith-sonian Institution, Washington, DC, U.S.A.—Scene from the film *Mill on the Floss*, by George Eliot, engraving. Hulton Archive/Getty Images.—Segwick, Catherine Maria, slide. Archive Photos, Inc.—Sexton, Anne, photograph. Copyright © Bettmann/Corbis.—Sexton, Anne, with her daugh-ters Joy and Linda, photograph. Time Life Pictures/Getty Images.—Shelley, Mary Wollstonecraft, painting by Samuel John Stump. Copyright © Cor-bis-Bettmann.—Stael, Madame de, color litho-graph. Archive Photos, Inc.—Stanton, Elizabeth Cady, illustration. Copyright © Bettmann/Cor-bis.—Stanton, Elizabeth Cady, photograph. AP/Wide World Photos.—Stein, Gertrude (left), arriv-ing in New York aboard the S. S. Champlain with her secretary and companion Alice B. Toklas, photograph. AP/Wide World Photos.—Stein, Ger-trude, photograph by Carl Van Vechten. The Estate of Carl Van Vechten.—Steinem, Gloria, photograph. AP/Wide World Photos.—Stowe, Har-riet Beecher, photograph. Copyright © Bettmann/Corbis.—Suffrage parade in New York, New York, October 15, 1915, photograph. The Library of Congress.—Supporters of the Equal Rights Amend-ment carry a banner down Pennsylvania Avenue, Washington, DC, photograph. AP/Wide World Photos.—Sur la Falaise aux Petites Dalles, 1873. Painting by Berthe Morisot. Copyright © Francis G. Mayer/Corbis.—Tan, Amy, 1993, photograph. AP/Wide World Photos.—*Time*, cover of Kate Mil-lett, from August 31, 1970. Time Life Pictures/Stringer/Getty Images.—Title page of *A Vindication of the Rights of Woman: With Strictures on Political and Moral Subjects*, written by Mary Wollstonecraft. William L. Clements Library, University of Michi-gan.—Title page of *Adam Bede*, written by George Eliot. Edinburgh & London: Blackwood, 1859, Volume 1, New York: Harper, 1859. The Graduate Library, University of Michigan.—Title page from *De L'influence des Passions sur le Bonheur des Indivi-dus et des Nations*, (A Treatise on the Influence of the Passions upon the Happiness of Individuals and of Nations), written by Stael de Holstein, photograph. The Special Collections Library, University of Michigan.—Title page from *Evelina*, written by Fanny Burney, photograph. The Special Collections Library, University of Michigan.—Title page from *Mansfield Park*, written by Jane Austen. The Special Collections Library, University of Michigan.—Title page of *Mary, A Fiction*, written by Mary Wollstonecraft.—Title page from *Youth and the Bright Medusa*, written by Willa Cather. New York, Alfred A Knopf. The Special Collections Library, University of Michigan.—Title page of *A New-England Tale*, written by Catharine Maria Sedgewick. New York: E. Bliss and E. White, 1822. The Special Collections Library, University of Michigan.—Title page of *Aurora Leigh*, written by Elizabeth Barrett Browning. New York, Boston: C. S. Francis and Co., 1857. The Special Collections Library, University of Michigan.—Title page of *Mrs. Dalloway*, written by Virginia Woolf. London: Hogarth Press, 1925. The Special Collections Library, University of Michigan.—Title page of *The Dial: A Magazine for Literature, Philosophy, and Reli-gion*. Boston. Weeks, Jordan and Company (etc.); London, Wiley and Putnam (etc.). Volume 1. The Special Collections Library, University of Michi-gan.—Title page of *The House of Mirth*, written by Edith Wharton. New York: C. Scribner's Sons, 1905. The Special Collections Library, University of Michigan.—Title page of *The Little Review*,

March 1916. The Purdy/Kresge Library, Wayne State University.—Title page of *Woman in the Nineteenth Century,* written by Sarah Margaret Fuller. New York, Greeley and McElrath. 1845. The Special Collections Library, University of Michigan.—Title page of *Wuthering Heights,* written by Emily Brontë. New York: Harper and Brothers. 1848. The Special Collections Library, University of Michigan.—Truth, Sojourner, photograph. Archive Photos, Inc.—Tubman, Harriet, photograph. The Library of Congress.—Victoria, Queen of England, illustration. The Library of Congress.—Walker, Alice, 1989, photograph. AP/Wide World Photos.—Welles, Orson, as Edward Rochester, with Joan Fontaine as Jane Eyre, in the film *Jane Eyre,* photograph. The Kobal Collection.—Wharton, Edith, photograph. AP/Wide World Photos.—Wheatley, Phillis, photograph. Copyright © The Bettman Archive.—Winfrey, Oprah, as Celie and Danny Glover as Albert with baby in scene from the film *The Color Purple,* written by Alice Walker, directed by Steven Spielberg, photograph. The Kobal Collection.—Women in French Revolution, invade assembly, demanding death penalty for members of the aristocracy, Woodcut. Copyright © Bettmann/Corbis.—Women workers in a shoe factory in Lynn, Massachusetts, photograph. Copyright © Corbis.—Woodhull, Victoria, reading statement before House Committee, drawing. The Library of Congress.—Woolf, Virginia, photograph. AP/Wide World Photos.—Woolson, Constance Fenimore, engraving. Archive Photos.

● = historical event

■ = literary event

1570 B.C.

● Queen Ahmose Nefertari, sister and principal wife of King Ahmose, rules as "god's wife," in a new position created by a law enacted by the King.

C. 1490 B.C.

● Queen Hatshepsut rules as pharaoh, several years after the death of her husband, King Thutmose II.

C. 1360 B.C.

● Queen Nefertiti rules Egypt alongside her husband, pharaoh Akhenaten.

C. 620 B.C.

● Sappho is born on the Isle of Lesbos, Greece.

C. 600 B.C.

■ Sappho organizes and operates a *thiasos,* an academy for young, unmarried Greek women.

● Spartan women are the most independent women in the world, and are able to own property, pursue an education, and participate in athletics.

C. 550 B.C.

● Sappho dies on the Isle of Lesbos.

C. 100 B.C.

● Roman laws allow a husband: to kill his wife if she is found in the act of adultery, to determine the amount of money his wife is owed in the event of divorce, and to claim his children as property.

69 B.C.

● Cleopatra VII Philopator is born in Egypt.

36 B.C.

● Marriage of Antony and Cleopatra.

C. 30 B.C.

● Cleopatra VII Philopator commits suicide in Egypt.

18

● Emperor Augustus decrees the *Lex Julia,* which penalizes childless Roman citizens, adulterers, and those who marry outside of their social rank or status.

C. 370

- Hypatia is born in Alexandria, Egypt.

415

- Hypatia is murdered in Alexandria, Egypt.

C. 500

- Salians (Germanic Franks living in Gaul) issue a code of laws which prohibit women from inheriting land; the law is used for centuries to prevent women from ruling in France.

592

- Empress Suiko (554-628) becomes the first woman sovereign of Japan.

C. 690

- Wu Zetian (624-705) becomes the only female emperor of Imperial China.

C. 700

- Japanese legal code specifies that in law, ceremony, and practice, Japanese men can be polygamous—having first wives and an unlimited number of "second wives" or concubines—, but women cannot.

877

- Lady Ise, Japanese court lady, is born. She is considered one of the most accomplished poets of her time and her poems are widely anthologized.

935

- Hrotsvitha (also Hrotsvit or Roswitha), considered the first German woman poet, is born.

940

- Lady Ise dies.

950

- Publication of the *Kagero Nikki* (*The Gossamer Years*), a diary written by an anonymous Japanese courtesan. The realism and confessional quality of the work influence the works of later court diarists.

C. 960

- Japanese poet Izumi Shikibu, known for her expression of erotic and Buddhist themes, is born. Her body of work includes more than 1,500 *waka* (31-syllable poems).

C. 1002

- Sei Shonagon, Japanese court lady, writes *Makura no Soshi* (*The Pillow Book*), considered a classic of Japanese literature and the originator of the genre known as *zuihitsu* ("to follow the brush") that employs a stream-of-consciousness literary style.

C. 1008

- Murasaki Shikibu writes *Genji Monogatari* (*The Tale of Genji*), considered a masterpiece of classical prose literature in Japan.

C. 1030

- Izumi Shikibu dies.

1098

- Hildegard von Bingen is born in Bermersheim, Germany.

C. 1100

- Twenty women troubadours—aristocratic poet-composers who write songs dealing with love—write popular love songs in France. About twenty-four of their songs survive, including four written by the famous female troubadour known as the Countess of Dia, or Beatrix.

1122

- Eleanor of Aquitaine is born in Aquitaine, France. Her unconventional life is chronicled for centuries in books and dramatic works.

C. 1150

- Sometime in the twelfth century (some sources say 1122), Marie de France, the earliest known female French writer and author of *lais*, a collection of twelve verse tales written in octosyllabic rhyming couplets, flourished. She is thought to be the originator of the *lay* as a poetic form.

C. 1170

- Marie of Champagne (1145-1198), daughter of King Louis VII of France and Eleanor of Aquitaine, cosponsors "courts of love" to debate points on the proper conduct of knights toward their ladies. Marie encourages Chrétien de Troyes to write *Lancelot,* and Andreas Capellanus to write *The Art of Courtly Love.*

1179

- Hildegard von Bingen dies in Disibodenberg, Germany.

C. 1200

- Women shirabyoshi performances are a part of Japanese court and Buddhist temple festivities. In their songs and dances, women performers dress in white, male attire which includes fans, court caps, and swords. This form of traditional dance plays an important role in the development of classical Japanese noh drama.

1204

- Eleanor of Aquitaine dies on 1 April.

C. 1275

- Japanese poet and court lady Abutsu Ni (1222?-1283) writes her poetic travel diary, *Izayoi Nikki (Diary of the Waning Moon)* on the occasion of her travel to Kyoto to seek inheritance rights for herself and her children.

C. 1328

- The French cite the Salic Law, which was promulgated in the early medieval period and prohibits women from inheriting land, as the authority for denying the crown of France to anyone—man or woman—whose descent from a French king can be traced only through the female line.

1346

- Famous mystic St. Birgitta of Sweden (c.1303-1373) founds the Roman Catholic Order of St. Saviour, whose members are called the Brigittines. She authors *Revelations,* an account of her supernatural visions.

1347

- Caterina Benincasa (later St. Catherine of Siena) is born on 25 March in Siena, Italy.

C. 1365

- Christine de Pizan is born in Venice, Italy.

C. 1373

- Margery Kempe is born in King's Lynn (now known as Lynn), in Norfolk, England.

1380

- St. Catherine of Siena dies on 29 April in Rome, Italy.

C. 1393

- Julian of Norwich (1342?-1416?), the most famous of all the medieval recluses in England, writes *Revelations of Divine Love,* expounding on the idea of Christ as mother.

1399

- Christine de Pizan writes the long poem "Letter to the God of Love," which marks the beginning of the *querelle des femmes* (debate on women). This attack on misogyny in medieval literature triggers a lively exchange of letters among the foremost French scholars of the day, and the *querelle* is continued by various European literary scholars for centuries.

1429

- Joan of Arc (1412-1431)—in support of Charles I, who is prevented by the English from assuming his rightful place as King of France— leads liberation forces to victory in Orléans.

1431

- Joan of Arc is burned at the stake as a heretic by the English on 30 May. She is acquitted of heresy by another church court in 1456 and proclaimed a saint in 1920.

C. 1431

- Christine de Pizan dies in France.

C. 1440

- Margery Kempe dies in England.

1451

- Isabella of Castile, future Queen of Spain, is born. She succeeds her brother in 1474 and rules jointly with her husband, Ferdinand of Aragon, from 1479.

1465

- Cassandra Fedele, who becomes the most famous woman scholar in Italy, is born in Venice.

1469

- Laura Cereta, outspoken feminist and humanist scholar, is born in Brescia, Italy.

1485

- Veronica Gambara is born in Italy. Her court becomes an important center of the Italian Renaissance, and Gambara earns distinction as an author of Petrarchan sonnets as well as for her patronage of the artist Corregio.

1486

- *Malleus Maleficarum* (*The Hammer of Witches*), an encyclopedia of contemporary knowledge about witches and methods of investigating the crime of witchcraft, is published in Europe. The volume details numerous justifications for women's greater susceptibility to evil, and contributes to the almost universal European persecution of women as witches that reaches its height between 1580 and 1660 and makes its way to Salem, Massachusetts in 1692.

1492

- Marguerite de Navarre is born on 11 April in France.

1499

- Laura Cereta dies in Brescia, Italy.

C. 1512

- Catherine Parr is born in England.

1515

- Teresa de Alhumadawas (later St. Teresa de Ávila) is born on 28 March in Gotarrendura, Spain.

1524

- Courtesan Gaspara Stampa, widely regarded as the greatest woman poet of the Renaissance, is born in Padua, Italy.

1533

- Queen Elizabeth I is born on 7 September in Greenwich, England, the daughter of King Henry VIII and his second wife, Anne Boleyn.

1536

- King Henry VIII of England beheads his second wife, Anne Boleyn, on 19 May. Boleyn is convicted of infidelity and treason after she fails to produce the desired male heir.

1538

- Vittoria Colonna (1492-1547), an influential woman in Renaissance Italy, achieves distinction as a poet with the publication of her first book of poetry.

1548

- Catherine Parr dies in England.

1549

- Marguerite de Navarre dies in France.

1550

- Veronica Gambara dies in Italy.

1554

- Gaspara Stampa dies on 23 April in Venice, Italy.

1555

- Moderata Fonte (pseudonym of Modesta Pozzo) is born in Venice, Italy.

1558

- Elizabeth I assumes the throne of England and presides over a period of peace and prosperity known as the Elizabethan Age.

- Cassadra Fedele dies in Venice. She is honored with a state funeral.

1559

- Marguerite de Navarre completes her *L'Heptaméron des Nouvelles* (the *Heptameron*), a series of stories primarily concerned with the themes of love and spirituality.

1561

- Mary Sidney, noted English literary patron, is born in England. She is the sister of poet Sir Philip Sidney, whose poems she edits and publishes after his death in 1586, and whose English translation of the Psalms she completes.

1565

- French scholar Marie de Gournay is born on 6 October in Paris. Known as the French "Minerva" (a woman of great wisdom or learning), she is a financial success as a writer of treatises on various subjects, including *Equality of Men and Women* (1622) and *Complaint of Ladies* (1626), which demand better education for women.

1582

- St. Teresa de Avila dies on 4 October in Alba.

1592

- Moderata Fonte (pseudonym of Modesta Pozzo) dies in Venice, Italy.

C. 1600

- Catherine de Vivonne (c. 1588-1665), Madame de Rambouillet, inaugurates and then presides over salon society in Paris, in which hostesses hold receptions in their salons or drawing rooms for the purpose of intellectual conversation. Salon society flourishes in the seventeenth and eighteenth centuries, and stimulates scholarly and literary development in France and England.

- Geisha (female artists and entertainers) and prostitutes are licensed by the Japanese government to work in the pleasure quarters of major cities in Japan.

1603

- Queen Elizabeth I dies on 24 March in Surrey, England.

- Izumo no Okuni is believed to originate kabuki, the combination of dance, drama, and music which dominates Japanese theater throughout the Tokugawa period (1600-1868).

1607

- Madeleine de Scudéry, one of the best-known and most influential writers of romance tales in seventeeth-century Europe, is born on 15 November in Le Havre, France.

C. 1612

- American poet Anne Bradstreet is born in Northampton, England.

1614

- Margaret Askew Fell, who helps establish the Society of Friends, or Quakers, and becomes known as the "mother of Quakerism," is born in Lancashire, England. Quakers give women unusual freedom in religious life. An impassioned advocate of the right of women to preach, Fell publishes the tract *Women's Speaking Justified, Proved and Allowed of by the Scriptures* in 1666.

1621

- Mary Sidney dies in England.

C. 1623

- Margaret Lucas Cavendish, later Duchess of Newcastle, is born in England. She authors fourteen volumes of works, including scientific treatises, poems, and plays, and her autobiography *The True Relation of My Birth, Breeding and Life* (1656).

1631

- Katherine Phillips (1631-1664), who writes poetry under the pseudonym "Orinda," is born. She is the founder of a London literary salon called the Society of Friendship that includes such luminaries as Jeremy Taylor and Henry Vaughn.

C. 1640

● Aphra Behn is born.

C. 1645

● Deborah Moody (c. 1580-c. 1659) becomes the first woman to receive a land grant in colonial America when she is given the title to land in Kings County (now Brooklyn), New York. She is also the first colonial woman to vote.

C. 1646

● Glückel of Hameln, who records her life as a Jewish merchant in Germany in her memoirs, is born in Hamburg.

1651

● Juana Ramírez de Asbaje (later known as Sor Juana Inés de la Cruz) is born on 12 November on a small farm called San Miguel de Nepantla in New Spain (now Mexico).

1670

■ Aphra Behn becomes the first professional woman writer in England when her first play *The Forced Marriage; or, The Jealous Bridegroom,* is performed in London.

1672

● Anne Bradstreet dies on 16 September in Andover, Massachusetts.

C. 1673

■ Francois Poulain de la Barre publishes *The Equality of the Sexes,* in which he supports the idea that women have intellectual powers equal to those of men. His work stimulates the betterment of women's education in succeeding centuries.

1673

● Margaret Lucas Cavendish, Duchess of Newcastle, dies in England.

1676

■ After being captured and then released by Wampanaoag Indians, Puritan settler Mary White Rowlandson (1636-1678) writes what becomes a famous account of her captivity.

1689

● Mary Pierrpont (later Lady Mary Wortley Montagu) is born on 26 May in London, England.

● Aphra Behn dies on 16 April and is buried in the cloisters at Westminster Abbey.

1692

● The Salem, Massachusetts, witch hysteria begins in February, and eventually leads to the execution of eighteen women convicted of witchcraft in the infamous Salem Witchcraft Trials (1692-1693).

C. 1694

■ Mary Astell (1666-1731) publishes the treatise *A Serious Proposal to the Ladies* in two volumes (1694-1697). In the work, Astell calls for the establishment of private institutions where single women live together for a time and receive quality education.

1695

● Sor Juana Inés de la Cruz dies on 17 April at the Convent of St. Jerome in Mexico.

1701

● Madeleine de Scudéry dies on 2 June in Paris, France.

C. 1704

■ Sarah Kemble Knight (1666-1727), a Puritan author, records her arduous journey from Boston to New York to settle the estate of her cousin.

C. 1713

■ Anne Kingsmill Finch (1661-1720) writes many poems dealing with the injustices suffered by women of the aristocratic class to which she belonged. As Countess of Winchilsea, she becomes the center of a literary circle at her husband's estate in Eastwell, England.

1728

● Mercy Otis Warren is born on 14 September in Barnstable, Massachusetts.

1729

- Catherine the Great is born on 2 May in Germany as Sophia Friederica Augusta.

1744

- Abigail Adams is born Abigail Smith on 11 November in Weymouth, Massachusetts.

1748

- Olympe de Gouges, French Revolutionary feminist, is born Olympe Gouze in Montauban, France. She plays an active role in the French Revolution, demanding equal rights for women in the new French Republic.

1752

- Frances "Fanny" Burney is born on 13 June in England.

C. 1753

- Phillis Wheatley is born in Africa.

1759

- Mary Wollstonecraft is born on 27 April in England.

1762

- Lady Mary Wortley Montagu dies on 21 August in London, England.
- Catherine the Great becomes Empress of Russia.

1766

- Germaine Necker (later Madame de Staël) is born on 22 April in Paris, France.

1768

- Maria Edgeworth is born on 1 January at Black Bourton in Oxfordshire, England.

1774

- Clementina Rind (1740-1774) is appointed publisher of the *Virginia Gazette* by the House of Burgesses in Virginia.

1775

- Jane Austen is born on 16 December at Steventon Rectory, Hampshire, England.

1776

- Men and women who hold property worth over 50 pounds are granted suffrage in New Jersey.

C. 1780

- Madame Roland (1754-1793), formerly Marie Philppon, hosts an important salon where revolutionary politicians and thinkers debate during the French Revolution. An outspoken feminist, she presses for women's political and social rights.

1784

- Hannah Adams (1758-1831) becomes the first American woman author to support herself with money earned from writing, with the publication of her first book, *View of Religions* (later *Dictionary of Religions*).
- Phillis Wheatley dies on 5 December in Boston, Massachusetts.

1787

- Catherine Sawbridge Macaulay publishes *Letters on Education*, an appeal for better education of women.
- Mary Wollstonecraft's *Thoughts on the Education of Daughters: With Reflections on Female Conduct, in the More Important Duties of Life* is published by J. Johnson.

1789

- Catharine Maria Sedgwick is born on 28 December in Stockbridge, Massachusetts.
- Olympe de Gouges writes *The Declaration of the Rights of Women and Citizen,* a 17-point document demanding the recognition of women as political, civil, and legal equals of men, and including a sample marriage contract that emphasizes free will and equality in marriage.

1792

- Sarah Moore Grimké is born on 26 November in Charleston, South Carolina.

Mary Wollstonecraft's *A Vindication of the Rights of Woman, with Strictures on Political and Moral Subjects* is published by J. Johnson.

1793

- Lucretia Coffin Mott is born on 3 January in Nantucket, Massachusetts.
- Olympe de Gouges is executed by guillotine for treason on 3 November.
- Madame Roland is executed in November, ostensibly for treason, but actually because the Jacobins want to suppress feminist elements in the French Revolution.

1796

- Catherine the Great dies following a stroke on 6 November in Russia.

1797

- Mary Wollstonecraft Shelley is born on 30 August, in London, England.
- Mary Wollstonecraft dies on 10 September in London, England, from complications following childbirth.
- Sojourner Truth is born Isabella Bomefree in Ulster County, New York.

1799

- Mary Wollstonecraft's *Maria; or, The Wrongs of Woman: A Posthumous Fragment* is published by James Carey.

1801

- Caroline M. (Stansbury) Kirkland is born on 11 January in New York City.

1802

- Lydia Maria Child is born on 11 February in Medford, Massachusetts.

1804

- George Sand (pseudonym of Armandine Aurore Lucille Dupin) is born on 1 July in Paris, France.
- The Napoleonic Code is established in France under Napoleon I, and makes women legally subordinate to men. The code requires women to be obedient to their husbands, bars women from voting, sitting on juries, serving as legal witnesses, or sitting on chambers of commerce or boards of trade.

1805

- Angelina Emily Grimké is born on 20 February in Charleston, South Carolina.

1806

- Elizabeth Barrett Browning is born on 6 March in Coxhoe Hall, Durham, England.

1807

- Germaine de Staël's *Corinne, ou l'Italie* (*Corinne, or Italy*) is published by Nicolle.
- Suffrage in New Jersey is limited to "white male citizens."

1808

- Caroline Sheridan Norton is born on 22 March in England.

1810

- (Sarah) Margaret Fuller is born on 23 May in Cambridgeport, Massachusetts.
- Elizabeth Cleghorn Gaskell is born on 29 September in London, England.

1811

- Harriet Beecher Stowe is born on 14 June in Litchfield, Connecticut.
- Jane Austen's *Sense and Sensibility* is published by T. Egerton.

1813

- Harriet A. Jacobs is born in North Carolina.
- Jane Austen's *Pride and Prejudice* is published by T. Egerton.

1814

- Mercy Otis Warren dies on 19 October in Plymouth, Massachusetts.

1815

● Elizabeth Cady Stanton is born on 12 November in Johnstown, New York.

● King Louis XVIII of France outlaws divorce.

1816

● Charlotte Brontë is born on 21 April in Thornton, Yorkshire, England.

▇ Jane Austen's *Emma* is published by M. Carey.

1817

● Madame Germaine de Staël dies on 14 July in Paris, France.

● Jane Austen dies on 18 July in Winchester, Hampshire, England.

1818

● Emily Brontë is born on 30 July in Thornton, Yorkshire, England.

● Lucy Stone is born on 13 August near West Brookfield, Massachusetts.

● Abigail Adams dies on 28 October in Quincy, Massachusetts.

▇ Jane Austen's *Northanger Abbey and Persuasion* is published by John Murray.

▇ Educator Emma Hart Willard's *A Plan for Improving Female Education* is published by Middlebury College.

▇ Mary Wollstonecraft Shelley's *Frankenstein; or, The Modern Prometheus* is published by Lackington, Hughes, Harding, Mavor & Jones.

1819

● Julia Ward Howe is born on 27 May in New York City.

● George Eliot (pseudonym of Mary Ann Evans) is born on 22 November in Arbury, Warwickshire, England.

1820

● Susan B. Anthony is born on 15 February in Adams, Massachusetts.

1821

● Emma Hart Willard establishes the Troy Female Seminary in Troy, New York.

1822

● Frances Power Cobbe is born on 4 December in Dublin, Ireland.

1823

● Charlotte Yonge is born 11 August in Otterbourne, Hampshire, England.

1825

● Frances Ellen Watkins Harper is born on 24 September in Baltimore, Maryland.

1826

● Matilda Joslyn Gage is born on 24 March in Cicero, New York.

1830

● Christina Rossetti is born on 5 December in London, England.

● Emily Dickinson is born on 10 December in Amherst, Massachusetts.

▇ *Godey's Lady's Book*—the first American women's magazine—is founded by Louis Antoine Godey and edited by Sarah Josepha Hale (1788-1879).

1832

● Louisa May Alcott is born on 29 November in Germantown, Pennsylvania.

▇ George Sand's *Indiana* is published by Roret et Dupuy.

1833

● Oberlin Collegiate Institute—the first coeducational institution of higher learning— is established in Oberlin, Ohio.

1836

● Marietta Holley is born on 16 July near Adams, New York.

1837

● Mt. Holyoke College—the first college for women—is founded by Mary Lyon in South Hadley, Massachusetts.

- Alexandria Victoria (1819-1901) becomes Queen Victoria at the age of eighteen. Her reign lasts for 63 years, the longest reign of any British monarch.

1838

- Victoria Woodhull is born on 23 September in Homer, Ohio.

- Sarah Moore Grimké's *Letters on the Equality of the Sexes, and the Condition of Woman* is published by I. Knapp.

1840

- Frances "Fanny" Burney dies on 6 January in London, England.

- Ernestine Rose (1810-1892) writes the petition for what will become the Married Woman's Property Law (1848).

C. 1844

- Sarah Winnemucca is born on Paiute land near Humboldt Lake in what is now Nevada.

1845

- Margaret Fuller's *Woman in the Nineteenth Century* is published by Greeley & McElrath.

1847

- Charlotte Brontë's *Jane Eyre* is published by Smith, Elder.

- Emily Brontë's *Wuthering Heights* is published by T. C. Newby.

1848

- The first women's rights convention is called by Lucretia Coffin Mott and Elizabeth Cady Stanton on 19 July and is held in Seneca Falls, New York on 20 July.

- Emily Brontë dies on 19 December in Haworth, Yorkshire, England.

- New York State Legislature passes the Married Woman's Property Law, granting women the right to retain possession of property they owned prior to marriage.

1849

- Maria Edgeworth dies on 22 May in Edgeworthstown, her family's estate in Ireland.

- Sarah Orne Jewett is born on 3 September in South Berwick, Maine.

- Amelia Bloomer publishes the first issue of her Seneca Falls newspaper *The Lily,* which provides a forum for both temperance and women's rights reformers.

- The first state constitution of California extends property rights to women in their own name.

1850

- Margaret Fuller drowns—along with her husband and son—on 19 July in a shipwreck off of Fire Island, New York.

- The first National Woman's Rights Convention, planned by Lucy Stone and Lucretia Mott, is attended by over one thousand women on 23 and 24 October in Worcester, Massachusetts.

- Elizabeth Barrett Browning's *Poems,* containing her *Sonnets from the Portuguese,* is published by Chapman & Hall.

- *The Narrative of Sojourner Truth,* transcribed by Olive Gilbert, is published in the Boston periodical, the *Liberator.*

1851

- Mary Wollstonecraft Shelley dies on 1 February in Bournemouth, England.

- Kate Chopin is born on 8 February in St. Louis, Missouri.

- Sojourner Truth delivers her "A'n't I a Woman?" speech at the Women's Rights Convention on 29 May in Akron, Ohio.

1852

- Harriet Beecher Stowe's *Uncle Tom's Cabin; or, Life among the Lowly* is published by Jewett, Proctor & Worthington.

- Susan B. Anthony founds The Women's Temperance Society, the first temperance organization in the United States.

1853

- Charlotte Brontë's *Villette* is published by Smith, Elder.

- Paulina Kellogg Wright Davis (1813-1876) edits and publishes *Una,* the first newspaper of the women's rights movement.

1854

- Margaret Oliphant's *A Brief Summary in Plain Language of the Most Important Laws Concerning Women,* a pamphlet explaining the unfair laws concerning women and exposing the need for reform, is published in London.

1855

- Charlotte Brontë dies on 31 March in Haworth, Yorkshire, England.

- Elizabeth Cady Stanton, speaking in favor of expanding the Married Woman's Property Law, becomes the first woman to appear before the New York State Legislature.

1856

- Harriot Eaton Stanton Blatch is born on 20 January in Seneca Falls, New York.

1857

- Elizabeth Barrett Browning's *Aurora Leigh* is published by Chapman & Hall.

1858

- Emmeline Pankhurst is born on 4 July in Manchester, England.

- Anna Julia Haywood Cooper is born on 10 August in Raleigh, North Carolina.

1859

- Carrie Chapman Catt is born on 9 January in Ripon, Wisconsin.

1860

- Charlotte Perkins Gilman is born on 3 July in Hartford, Connecticut.

- Jane Addams is born on 6 September in Cedarville, Illinois.

1861

- Victoria Earle Matthews is born on 27 May in Fort Valley, Georgia.

- Elizabeth Barrett Browning dies on 29 June in Florence, Italy.

- Harriet Jacobs's *Incidents in the Life of a Slave Girl, Written by Herself,* edited by Lydia Maria Child, is published in Boston.

1862

- Edith Wharton is born on 24 January in New York City.

- Ida B. Wells-Barnett is born on 16 July in Holly Springs, Mississippi.

- Julia Ward Howe's "The Battle Hymn of the Republic" is published in the *Atlantic Monthly.*

1864

- Caroline M. (Stansbury) Kirkland dies of a stroke on 6 April in New York City.

1865

- Elizabeth Cleghorn Gaskell dies on 12 November in Holybourne, Hampshire, England.

1866

- The American Equal Rights Association—dedicated to winning suffrage for African American men and for women of all colors—is founded by Susan B. Anthony and Elizabeth Cady Stanton on 1 May. Lucretia Coffin Mott is elected as the group's president.

- Elizabeth Cady Stanton runs for Congress as an independent; she receives 24 of 12,000 votes cast.

1867

- Catharine Maria Sedgwick dies on 31 July in Boston, Massachusetts.

1868

- Susan B. Anthony and Elizabeth Cady Stanton found the New York-based weekly newspaper, *The Revolution,* with the motto: "The true republic—men, their rights and nothing more; women, their rights and nothing less," in January.

- Julia Ward Howe founds the New England Woman Suffrage Association and the New England Women's Club.

- Louisa May Alcott's *Little Women; or, Meg, Jo, Beth, and Amy* (2 vols., 1868-69) is published by Roberts Brothers.

1869

- John Stuart Mill's treatise in support of women's suffrage, *The Subjection of Women,* is published in London.

● Emma Goldman is born on 27 June in Kovno, Lithuania.

■ Louisa May Alcott's *Hospital Sketches and Camp and Fireside Stories* is published by Roberts Brothers.

● Women are granted full and equal suffrage and are permitted to hold office within the territory of Wyoming.

● The National Woman Suffrage Association is founded by Elizabeth Cady Stanton and Susan B. Anthony in May in New York City.

● The American Woman Suffrage Association is founded by Lucy Stone, Julia Ward Howe, and others in November in Boston, Massachusetts.

1870

■ *The Woman's Journal*, edited by Lucy Stone, Henry Blackwell, and Mary Livermore, begins publication on 8 January.

■ Victoria Woodhull and Tennessee Claflin publish the first issue of their controversial New York weekly newspaper, *Woodhull and Claflin's Weekly*.

1871

● Women are granted full and equal suffrage in the territory of Utah. Their rights are revoked in 1887 and restored in 1896.

● Victoria Woodhull presents her views on women's rights in a passionate speech to the House Judiciary Committee, marking the first personal appearance before such a high congressional committee by a woman.

● Wives of many prominent U. S. politicians, military officers, and businessmen found the Anti-Suffrage party to fight against women's suffrage.

1872

● Victoria Woodhull, as a member of the Equal Rights Party (or National Radical Reform Party), becomes the first woman candidate for the office of U.S. President. Her running mate is Frederick Douglass.

● Susan B. Anthony and 15 other women attempt to cast their votes in Rochester, New York, in the presidential election. Anthony is arrested and fined $100, which she refuses to pay.

● Sojourner Truth attempts to cast her vote in Grand Rapids, Michigan in the presidential election but is denied a ballot.

1873

● Colette is born on 28 January in Burgundy, France.

● Maria Mitchell (1818-1889), astronomer and faculty member at Vassar College, establishes the Association of the Advancement of Women.

● Willa Cather is born on 7 December in Back Creek Valley, Virginia.

● Sarah Moore Grimké dies on 23 December in Hyde Park, Massachusetts.

■ Louisa May Alcott's *Work: A Story of Experience* is published by Roberts Brothers.

1874

● Gertrude Stein is born on 3 February in Allegheny, Pennsylvania.

● Amy Lowell is born on 9 February in Brookline, Massachusetts.

1876

● George Sand dies on 9 June in Nohant, France.

● Susan Glaspell is born on 1 July (some sources say 1882) in Davenport, Iowa.

1877

● Caroline Sheridan Norton dies on 15 June in England.

1878

● Passage of the Matrimonial Causes Act in England enables abused wives to obtain separation orders to keep their husbands away from them.

● The "Susan B. Anthony Amendment," which will extend suffrage to women in the United States, is first proposed in Congress by Senator A. A. Sargent.

1879

● Margaret Sanger is born on 14 September in Corning, New York.

● Angelina Emily Grimké dies on 26 October in Hyde Park, Massachusetts.

1880

- Christabel Pankhurst is born on 22 September in Manchester, England.

- Lydia Maria Child dies on 20 October in Wayland, Massachusetts.

- Lucretia Coffin Mott dies on 11 November in Philadelphia, Pennsylvania.

- George Eliot (pseudonym of Mary Ann Evans) dies on 22 December in London, England.

1881

- Hubertine Auclert founds *La Citoyenne* (*The Citizen*), a newspaper dedicated to female suffrage.

- The first volume of *A History of Woman Suffrage* (Vols. 1-3, 1881-1888; Vol. 4, 1903), edited and compiled by Susan B. Anthony, Elizabeth Cady Stanton, Ida Harper Husted, and Matilda Joslyn Gage, is published by Fowler & Welles.

1882

- Virginia Woolf is born on 25 January in London, England.

- Sylvia Pankhurst is born on 5 May in Manchester, England.

- Aletta Jacobs (1854-1929), the first woman doctor in Holland, opens the first birth control clinic in Europe.

1883

- Sojourner Truth dies on 26 November in Battle Creek, Michigan.

- Olive Schreiner's *The Story of an African Farm* is published by Chapman & Hall.

1884

- Eleanor Roosevelt is born on 11 October in New York City.

1885

- Alice Paul is born on 11 January in Moorestown, New Jersey.

- Isak Dinesen is born Karen Christentze Dinesen on 17 April in Rungsted, Denmark.

1886

- Emily Dickinson dies on 15 May in Amherst, Massachusetts.

- H. D. (Hilda Doolittle) is born on 10 September in Bethlehem, Pennsylvania.

1887

- Marianne Moore is born on 15 November in Kirkwood, Missouri.

- Article five of the Peace Preservation Law in Japan prohibits women and minors from joining political organizations and attending meetings where political speeches are given, and from engaging in academic studies of political subjects.

1888

- Louisa May Alcott dies on 6 March in Boston, Massachusetts, and is buried in Sleepy Hollow Cemetery in Concord, Massachusetts.

- Susan B. Anthony organizes the International Council of Women with representatives from 48 countries.

- Louisa Lawson (1848-1920) founds Australia's first feminist newspaper, *The Dawn*.

- The National Council of Women in the United States is formed to promote the advancement of women in society. The group also serves as a clearinghouse for various women's organizations.

1889

- Anna Akhmatova is born Anna Adreyevna Gorenko on 23 June in Bolshoy Fontan, Russia.

1890

- The National American Woman Suffrage Association (NAWSA) is formed by the merging of the American Woman Suffrage Assocation and the National Woman Suffrage Association. Elizabeth Cady Stanton is the NAWSA's first president; she is succeeded by Susan B. Anthony in 1892.

1891

- Zora Neale Hurston is born on 15 (some sources say 7) January in Nostasulga, Alabama. (Some sources cite birth year as c. 1901 or 1903, and birth place as Eatonville, Florida).

● Sarah Winnemucca dies on 16 October in Monida, Montana.

1892

● Edna St. Vincent Millay is born on 22 February in Rockland, Maine.

● Djuna Barnes is born on 12 June in Cornwall on Hudson, New York.

● Rebecca West (pseudonym of Cicily Isabel Fairfield) is born on 21 December in County Kerry, Ireland.

■ Charlotte Perkins Gilman's *The Yellow Wallpaper* is published in *New England Magazine*.

■ Frances E. W. Harper's *Iola Leroy; or, Shadows Uplifted* is published by Garrigues Bros.

● Olympia Brown (1835-1926), first woman ordained minister in the United States, founds the Federal Suffrage Association to campaign for women's suffrage.

■ Ida Wells-Barnett's *Southern Horrors. Lynch Law in All its Phases* is published by Donohue and Henneberry.

1893

● Lucy Stone dies on 18 October in Dorchester, Massachusetts.

● The National Council of Women of Canada is founded by Lady Aberdeen.

● Suffrage is granted to women in Colorado.

● New Zealand becomes the first nation to grant women the vote.

1894

● Christina Rossetti dies on 29 December in London, England.

1895

■ The first volume of Elizabeth Cady Stanton's *The Woman's Bible* (3 vols., 1895-1898) is published by European Publishing Company.

1896

● Harriet Beecher Stowe dies on 1 July in Hartford, Connecticut.

● Idaho grants women the right to vote.

● The National Assocation of Colored Women's Clubs is founded in Washington, D.C.

1897

● Harriet A. Jacobs dies on 7 March in Cambridge, Massachusetts.

1898

● Matilda Joslyn Gage dies on 18 March in Chicago, Illinois.

■ Charlotte Perkins Gilman's *Women and Economics* is published by Small Maynard.

● The Meiji Civil Law Code, the law of the Japanese nation state, makes the patriarchal family, rather than the individual, the legally recognized entity.

1899

● Elizabeth Bowen is born on 7 June in Dublin, Ireland.

■ Kate Chopin's *The Awakening* is published by Herbert S. Stone.

1900

■ Colette's *Claudine a l'ecole* (*Claudine at School*, 1930) is published by Ollendorf.

● Carrie Chapman Catt succeeds Susan B. Anthony as president of the NAWSA.

1901

● Charlotte Yonge dies of bronchitis and pneumonia on 24 March in Elderfield, England.

1902

● Elizabeth Cady Stanton dies on 26 October in New York City.

● Women of European descent gain suffrage in Australia.

1903

● The Women's Social and Political Union, led by suffragists Emmeline and Christabel Pankhurst, stage demonstrations in Hyde Park in London, England.

1904

● Frances Power Cobbe dies on 5 April.

● Kate Chopin dies following a cerebral hemorrhage on 22 August in St. Louis, Missouri.

- Susan B. Anthony establishes the International Woman Suffrage Alliance in Berlin, Germany.

C. 1905

- Lillian Hellman is born on 20 June in New Orleans, Louisiana.

1905

- Austrian activist and novelist Bertha von Suttner (1843-1914) receives the Nobel Peace Prize.

1906

- Susan B. Anthony dies on 13 March in Rochester, New York.

- Finnish women gain suffrage and the right to be elected to public office.

1907

- Victoria Earle Matthews dies of tuberculosis on 10 March in New York City.

- Mary Edwards Walker, M.D.'s pamphlet on women's suffrage, "Crowning Constitutional Argument," is published.

- Harriot Stanton Blatch founds the Equality League of Self-Supporting Women, later called the Women's Political Union.

1908

- Simone de Beauvoir is born on 9 January in Paris, France.

- Julia Ward Howe becomes the first woman to be elected to the American Academy of Arts and Letters.

1909

- Sarah Orne Jewett dies on 24 June in South Berwick, Maine.

- Swedish author Selma Lagerlöf (1858-1940) becomes the first woman to receive the Nobel Prize for Literature.

- "The Uprising of the 20,000" grows from one local to a general strike against several shirtwaist factories in New York City. Over 700 women and girls are arrested, and 19 receive workhouse sentences. The strike is called off on 15 February 1910. Over 300 shops settle with the union, and workers achieve the terms demanded.

- Jeanne-Elisabeth Archer Schmahl (1846-1915) founds the French Union for Woman Suffrage.

1910

- Julia Ward Howe dies of pneumonia on 17 October in Newport, Rhode Island.

- The Women' Political Union holds the first large suffrage parade in New York City.

- Suffrage is granted to women in Washington State.

- Jane Addams's *Twenty Years at Hull House* is published by Macmillan.

1911

- Frances Ellen Watkins Harper dies on 22 February in Philadelphia, Pennsylvania.

- A fire at the Triangle Shirtwaist Factory in New York City on 25 March claims the lives of 146 factory workers, 133 of them women. Public outrage over the fire leads to reforms in labor laws and improvement in working conditions.

- Suffrage is granted to women in California.

- Edith Wharton's *Ethan Frome* is published by Scribner.

1912

- Suffrage is granted to women in Arizona, Kansas, and Oregon.

- A parade in support of women's suffrage is held in New York City and draws 20,000 participants and half a million onlookers.

1913

- Muriel Rukeyser is born on 15 December in New York City.

- Willa Cather's *O Pioneers!* is published by Houghton.

- Ida Wells-Barnett founds the Alpha Suffrage Club in Chicago.

- Suffrage is granted to women in Alaska.

- The Congressional Union is founded by Alice Paul and Lucy Burns.

1914

- Marguerite Duras is born on 4 April in Gia Dinh, Indochina (now Vietnam).

- The National Federation of Women's Clubs, which includes over two million white women and women of color, formally endorses the campaign for women's suffrage.

- Suffrage is granted to women in Montana and Nevada.

- Margaret Sanger begins publication of her controversial monthly newsletter *The Woman Rebel,* which is banned as obscene literature.

1915

- Charlotte Perkins Gilman's *Herland* is published in the journal *Forerunner.*

- *Woman's Work in Municipalities,* by American suffragist and historian Mary Ritter Beard (1876-1958), is published by Appleton.

- Icelandic women who are age 40 or older gain suffrage.

- Members of the NAWSA from across the United States hold a large parade in New York city.

- Most Danish women over age 25 gain suffrage.

1916

- Ardent suffragist and pacifist Jeannette Pickering Rankin (1880-1973) of Montana becomes the first woman elected to the U. S. House of Representatives. She later votes against U. S. involvement in both World Wars.

- The Congressional Union becomes the National Women's Party, led by Alice Paul and Lucy Burns.

- NAWSA president Carrie Chapman Catt unveils her "Winning Plan" for American women's suffrage at a convention held in Atlantic City, New Jersey.

- Suffrage is granted to women in Alberta, Manitoba, and Saskatchewan, Canada.

- Margaret Sanger opens the first U. S. birth-control clinic in Brooklyn, New York. The clinic is shut down 10 days after it opens and Sanger is arrested.

- Margaret Sanger's *What Every Mother Should Know; or, How Six Little Children were Taught the Truth* is published by M. N. Maisel.

1917

- Gwendolyn Brooks is born on 7 June in Topeka, Kansas.

- The National Women's Party becomes the first group in U.S. history to picket in front of the White House. Picketers are arrested and incarcerated; during their incarceration, Alice Paul leads them in a hunger strike. Many of the imprisoned suffragists are brutally force-fed, including Paul. The suffragettes' mistreatment is published in newspapers, the White House bows to public pressure, and they are released.

- White women in Arkansas are granted partial suffrage; they are able to vote in primary, but not general, elections.

- Suffrage is granted to women in New York.

- Suffrage is granted to women in Estonia, Latvia, and Lithuania.

- Women in Ontario and British Columbia, Canada, gain suffrage.

- Suffragists and members of the NAWSA, led by president Carrie Chapman Catt, march in a parade in New York City.

- Margaret Sanger founds and edits *The Birth Control Review,* the first scientific journal devoted to the subject of birth control.

1918

- Willa Cather's *My Antonia* is published by Houghton.

- Suffrage is granted to women in Michigan, Oklahoma, and South Dakota; women in Texas gain suffrage for primary elections only.

- President Woodrow Wilson issues a statement in support of a federal constitutional amendment granting full suffrage to American women.

- A resolution to amend the U.S. constitution to ensure that the voting rights of U.S. citizens cannot "be denied or abridged by the United States or any state on account of sex" passes in the House of Representatives.

- President Wilson urges the Senate to support the 19th amendment, but fails to win the two-thirds majority necessary for passage.

- Women in the United Kingdom who are married, own property, or are college graduates over the age of 30, are granted suffrage.

- Women in Austria, Czechoslovakia, Germany, Luxembourg, and Poland gain suffrage.

- Women in New Brunswick and Nova Scotia, Canada, gain suffrage. Canadian women of British or French heritage gain voting rights in Federal elections.

- Marie Stopes's *Married Love* and *Wise Parenthood* are published by A. C. Fifield.

- Harriot Stanton Blatch's *Mobilizing Woman-Power,* with a foreword by Theodore Roosevelt, is published by The Womans Press.

1919

- Women in the Netherlands, Rhodesia, and Sweden gain suffrage.

- Doris Lessing is born on 22 October in Kermanshah, Persia (now Iran).

- The "Susan B. Anthony Amendment," also known as the 19th Amendment to the U. S. Constitution, after it is defeated twice in the Senate, passes in both houses of Congress. The amendment is sent to states for ratification.

1920

- The 19th Amendment to the U.S. Constitution is ratified by the necessary two-thirds of states and American women are guaranteed suffrage on 26 August when Secretary of State Bainbridge Colby signs the amendment into law.

- The NAWSA is reorganized as the National League of Women Voters and elects Maud Wood Park as its first president.

- Bella Abzug is born on 24 July in New York City.

- Icelandic women gain full suffrage.

- Edith Wharton's *The Age of Innocence* is published by Meredith.

- Colette's *Cheri* is published by Fayard.

1921

- Betty Friedan is born on 4 February in Peoria, Illinois.

- Edith Wharton receives the Pulitzer Prize for fiction for *The Age of Innocence.*

- Margaret Sanger organizes the first American Conference on Birth Control in New York City.

1922

- Irish women gain full suffrage.

- Grace Paley is born on 11 December in New York City.

- Edna St. Vincent Millay's *The Ballad of the Harp-Weaver* is published by F. Shay.

1923

- Edna St. Vincent Millay receives the Pulitzer Prize for Poetry for *The Ballad of the Harp-Weaver.*

- Margaret Sanger opens the Birth Control Clinical Research Bureau in New York to dispense contraceptives to women under the supervision of a licensed physician and to study the effect of contraception upon women's health.

- Margaret Sanger founds the American Birth Control League.

- The Equal Rights Amendment (ERA), written by Alice Paul, is introduced in Congress for the first time in December.

1924

- Phyllis Schlafly is born on 15 August in St. Louis, Missouri.

- Shirley Chisolm is born on 30 November in Brooklyn, New York.

1925

- Amy Lowell dies on 12 May in Brookline, Massachusetts.

- *Collected Poems of H.D.* is published by Boni & Liveright.

- Virginia Woolf's *Mrs. Dalloway* is published by Harcourt.

1926

- Marietta Holley dies on 1 March near Adams, New York.

- Marianne Moore becomes the first woman editor of *The Dial* in New York City, a post she holds until 1929.

- Carrie Chapman Catt and Nettie Rogers Schuler's *Woman Suffrage and Politics; the Inner Story of the Suffrage Movement* is published by Charles Scribner's Sons.

- Grazia Deledda receives the Nobel Prize in Literature.

1927

- Victoria Woodhull dies on 10 June in Norton Park, England.

- Virginia Woolf's *To the Lighthouse* is published by Harcourt.

1928

- Maya Angelou is born Marguerite Johnson on 4 April in St. Louis, Missouri.

- Emmeline Pankhurst dies on 14 June in London, England.

- Anne Sexton is born on 9 November in Newton, Massachusetts.

- Virginia Woolf's *Orlando* is published by Crosby Gaige.

- Women are granted full suffrage in Great Britain.

- Gertrude Stein's *Useful Knowledge* is published by Payson & Clarke.

- Sigrid Undset receives the Nobel Prize in Literature.

1929

- Adrienne Rich is born on 16 May in Baltimore, Maryland.

- Marilyn French is born on 21 November in New York City.

- While Arthur M. Schlesinger Sr. reads her speech for her, Margaret Sanger appears in a gag on a stage in Boston where she has been prevented from speaking.

- Virginia Woolf's *A Room of One's Own* is published by Harcourt.

1930

- Lorraine Hansberry is born on 19 May in Chicago, Illinois.

- Cairine Wilson is appointed the first woman senator in Canada.

1931

- Jane Addams receives the Nobel Peace Prize.

- Toni Morrison is born Chloe Anthony Wofford on 18 February in Lorain, Ohio.

- Ida B. Wells-Barnett dies on 25 March in Chicago, Illinois.

1932

- Sylvia Plath is born on 27 October in Boston, Massachusetts.

1933

- Gertrude Stein's *The Autobiography of Alice B. Toklas* is published by Harcourt.

- Frances Perkins (1882-1965) is appointed Secretary of Labor by President Franklin D. Roosevelt, and becomes the first female cabinet member in the United States.

1934

- Gloria Steinem is born on 25 March in Toledo, Ohio.

- Kate Millett is born on 14 September in St. Paul, Minnesota.

- Lillian Hellman's *The Children's Hour* debuts on 20 November at Maxine Elliot's Theatre in New York City.

1935

- Jane Addams dies of cancer on 21 May in Chicago, Illinois.

- Charlotte Perkins Gilman commits suicide on 17 August in Pasadena, California.

- The National Council of Negro Women is founded by Mary McLeod Bethune (1875-1955).

1936

- First lady Eleanor Roosevelt begins writing a daily syndicated newspaper column, "My Day."

- Margaret Mitchell's *Gone with the Wind* is published by Macmillan.

1937

- Hélène Cixous is born on 5 June in Oran, Algeria.

- Bessie Head is born on 6 July in Pietermaritzburg, South Africa.

- Edith Wharton dies on 11 August in St. Brice-sous-Foret, France.

- Zora Neale Hurston's *Their Eyes Were Watching God* is published by Lippincott.

- Margaret Mitchell (1900-1949) receives the Pulitzer Prize in Letters & Drama for novel for *Gone with the Wind*.

- Anne O'Hare McCormick becomes the first woman to receive the Pulitzer Prize in Journalism, which she is given for distinguished correspondence for her international reporting on the rise of Italian Fascism in the *New York Times*.

1938

- Joyce Carol Oates is born on 16 June in Lockport, New York.

- Pearl Buck receives the Nobel Prize in Literature.

1939

- Germaine Greer is born on 29 January near Melbourne, Australia.

- Lillian Hellman's *The Little Foxes* debuts on 15 February at National Theatre in New York City.

- Margaret Atwood is born on 18 November in Ottawa, Ontario, Canada.

- Paula Gunn Allen is born in Cubero, New Mexico.

- French physician Madeleine Pelletier (1874-1939) is arrested for performing abortions in Paris, France; she dies later the same year. Throughout her medical career, Pelletier advocated women's rights to birth control and abortion, and founded her own journal, *La Suffragist*.

1940

- Emma Goldman dies on 14 May in Toronto, Ontario, Canada.

- Maxine Hong Kingston is born on 27 October in Stockton, California.

- Harriot Eaton Stanton Blatch dies on 20 November in Greenwich, Connecticut.

1941

- Virginia Woolf commits suicide on 28 March in Lewes, Sussex, England.

1942

- Erica Jong is born on 26 March in New York City.

- Isabel Allende is born on 2 August in Lima, Peru.

- Ellen Glasgow (1873-1945) receives the Pulitzer Prize for her novel *In This Our Life*.

- Margaret Walker (1915-1998) becomes the first African American to receive the Yale Series of Young Poets Award for her collection *For My People*.

1944

- Alice Walker is born on 9 February in Eatonton, Georgia.

- Martha Gellhorn (1908-1998) is the only woman journalist to go ashore with Allied troops during the D-Day invasion of Normandy, France in June.

- Buchi Emecheta is born on 21 July in Yaba, Lagos, Nigeria.

- Rita Mae Brown is born on 28 November in Hanover, Pennsylvania.

- Women are granted suffrage in France and Jamaica.

1945

- Eleanor Roosevelt becomes the first person to represent the U. S. at the United Nations. She serves until 1951, is reappointed in 1961, and serves until her death in 1962.

- Gabriela Mistral receives the Nobel Prize in Literature.

- Louise Bogan is named U. S. Poet Laureate.

1946

- Gertrude Stein dies of cancer on 27 July in Neuilly-sur-Seine, France.

- Andrea Dworkin is born on 26 September in Camden, New Jersey.

- Mary Ritter Beard's *Woman as a Force in History: A Study in Traditions and Realities* is published by Macmillan.

- Eleanor Roosevelt becomes chair of the United Nations Human Rights Commission. She remains chair until 1951.

1947

- Carrie Chapman Catt dies on 9 March in New Rochelle, New York.

- Willa Cather dies on 24 April in New York City.

- Dorothy Fuldheim, a newscaster in Cleveland, Ohio, becomes the first female television news anchor at WEWS-TV.

1948

- Susan Glaspell dies on 27 July in Provincetown, Massachusetts.

- Ntozake Shange is born Paulette Linda Williams on 18 October in Trenton, New Jersey.

- Leonie Adams is named U. S. Poet Laureate.

1949

- Simone de Beauvoir's *Le deuxième sexe* (*The Second Sex*, H. M. Parshley, translator: Knopf, 1953) is published by Gallimard.

- Elizabeth Bishop is named U. S. Poet Laureate.

- Gwendolyn Brooks's *Annie Allen* is published by Harper.

1950

- Gloria Naylor is born on 25 January in New York City.

- Edna St. Vincent Millay dies of a heart attack on 19 October at Steepletop, Austerlitz, New York.

- Gwendolyn Brooks receives the Pulitzer Prize for poetry for *Annie Allen*.

1951

- Marianne Moore's *Collected Poems* is published by Macmillan.

- Marguerite Higgins (1920-1960) receives the Pulitzer Prize for Journalism in overseas reporting for her account of the battle at Inchon, Korea in September, 1950.

1952

- Amy Tan is born on 19 February in Oakland, California.

- Rita Dove is born on 28 August in Akron, Ohio.

- bell hooks is born Gloria Jean Watkins on 25 September in Hopkinsville, Kentucky.

- Marianne Moore receives the National Book Critics Circle award for poetry and the Pulitzer Prize for poetry for *Collected Poems*.

1953

- *A Writer's Diary: Being Extracts from the Diary of Virigina Woolf*, edited by Leonard Woolf, is published by Hogarth.

- The International Planned Parenthood Federation is founded by Margaret Sanger, who serves as the organization's first president.

- Women are granted suffrage in Mexico.

1954

- Louise Erdrich is born on 7 June in Little Falls, Minnesota.

- Colette dies on 3 August in Paris, France.

- Sandra Cisneros is born on 20 December in Chicago, Illinois.

1955

- On 1 December American civil rights activist Rosa Parks (1913-) refuses to move from her seat for a white passenger on a Montgomery, Alabama bus and is arrested.

1956

- The Anti-Prostitution Act, written and campaigned for by Kamichika Ichiko, makes prostitution illegal in Japan.

1958

- Christabel Pankhurst dies on 13 February in Los Angeles, California.

1959

- Susan Faludi is born on 18 April in New York City.

- Lorraine Hansberry's *A Raisin in the Sun* debuts in March at the Ethel Barrymore Theatre in New York City.

- Lorraine Hansberry becomes the youngest woman and first black artist to receive a New York Drama Critics Circle Award for best American play for *A Raisin in the Sun*.

1960

- Zora Neale Hurston dies on 28 January in Fort Pierce, Florida.

- Sylvia Pankhurst dies on 27 September in Addis Ababa, Ethiopia.

- The U.S. Food and Drug Administration approves the first oral contraceptive for distribution to consumers in May.

- Harper Lee's *To Kill a Mockingbird* is published by Lippincott.

1961

- H. D. (Hilda Doolittle) dies on 27 September in Zurich, Switzerland.

- Harper Lee receives the Pulitzer Prize for the novel for *To Kill a Mockingbird.*

- President John F. Kennedy establishes the President's Commission on the Status of Women on 14 December and appoints Eleanor Roosevelt as head of the commission.

1962

- Isak Dinesen dies on 7 September in Rungsted Kyst, Denmark.

- Eleanor Roosevelt dies on 7 November in New York City.

- Naomi Wolf is born on 12 November in San Francisco, California.

- Doris Lessing's *The Golden Notebook* is published by Simon & Schuster.

1963

- Betty Friedan's *The Feminine Mystique* is published by Norton and becomes a bestseller.

- Sylvia Plath's *The Bell Jar* is published under the pseudonym Victoria Lucas by Heinemann.

- Sylvia Plath commits suicide on 11 February in London, England.

- Barbara Wertheim Tuchman (1912-1989) becomes the first woman to receive the Pulitzer Prize for general nonfiction for *The Guns of August.*

- The Equal Pay Act is passed by the U.S. Congress on 28 May. It is the first federal law requiring equal compensation for men and women in federal jobs.

- Entitled *American Women,* the report issued by the President's Commission on the Status of Women documents sex discrimination in nearly all corners of American society, and urges the U.S. Supreme Court to clarify legal status of women under the U.S. Constitution.

1964

- Anna Julia Haywood Cooper dies on 27 February in Washington, DC.

1965

- Lorraine Hansberry dies of cancer on 12 January in New York City.

- Women are granted suffrage in Afghanistan.

1966

- Anna Akhmatova dies on 6 March in Russia.

- Margaret Sanger dies on 6 September in Tucson, Arizona.

- National Organization for Women (NOW) is founded on 29 June by Betty Friedan and 27 other founding members. NOW is dedicated to promoting full participation in society for women and advocates for adequate child care for working mothers, reproductive rights, and the Equal Rights Amendment to the U.S. Constitution.

- Anne Sexton's *Live or Die* is published by Houghton.

- Nelly Sachs (1891-1970) receives the Nobel Prize in Literature, which she shares with Shmuel Yosef Agnon.

1967

- Anne Sexton receives the Pulitzer Prize for poetry for *Live or Die.*

- Senator Eugene McCarthy, with 37 cosponsors, introduces the Equal Rights Amendment in the U.S. Senate.

1968

- Audre Lorde's *The First Cities* is published by Poets Press.

1969

- Joyce Carol Oates's *them* is published by Vanguard Press.

- Shirley Chisolm becomes the first African American woman elected to Congress when she takes her seat in the U.S. House of Representatives on 3 January.

- Golda Meir (1898-1978) becomes the fourth Prime Minister of Israel on 17 March.

- California adopts the nation's first "no fault" divorce law, allowing divorce by mutual consent.

1970

- Toni Morrison's *The Bluest Eye* is published by Holt.

- Germaine Greer's *The Female Eunuch* is published by MacGibbon & Kee.

- Maya Angelou's *I Know Why the Caged Bird Sings* is published by Random House.

- Kate Millett's *Sexual Politics* is published by Doubleday and becomes a bestseller.

- Joyce Carol Oates receives the National Book Award for fiction for *them.*

- The Equal Rights Amendment passes in the U.S. House of Representatives by a vote of 350 to 15 on 10 August.

- Bella Abzug is elected to the U.S. House of Representatives on 3 November.

- The Feminist Press is founded at the City University of New York.

- *Off Our Backs: A Women's News Journal* is founded in Washington, D.C.

- *The Women's Rights Law Reporter* is founded in Newark, New Jersey.

1971

- Josephine Jacobsen is named U. S. Poet Laureate.

1972

- Marianne Moore dies on 5 February in New York City.

- *Ms.* magazine is founded; Gloria Steinem serves as editor of *Ms.* until 1987. The 300,000 copy print run of the first issue of *Ms.* magazine sells out within a week of its release in January.

- Shirley Chisolm becomes the first African American woman to seek the presidential nomination of a major political party, although her bid for the Democratic Party nomination is unsuccessful.

- The Equal Rights Amendment is passed by both houses of the U.S. Congress and is signed by President Richard M. Nixon. The amend-

ment expires in 1982, without being ratified by the required two-thirds of the states; it is three states short of full ratification.

- President Nixon signs into law Title IX of the Higher Education Act banning sex bias in athletics and other activities at all educational institutions receiving federal assistance.

- Women's Press is established in Canada.

1973

- The U.S. Supreme Court, in their decision handed down on 21 January in *Roe v. Wade,* decides that in the first trimester of pregnancy women have the right to choose an abortion.

- Elizabeth Bowen dies of lung cancer on 22 February in London, England.

- Rita Mae Brown's *Rubyfruit Jungle* is published by Daughters, Inc.

- Erica Jong's *Fear of Flying* is published by Holt and becomes a bestseller.

- Alice Walker's *In Love and Trouble: Stories of Black Women* is published by Harcourt.

- The Boston Women's Health Book Collective's *Our Bodies, Ourselves: A Book By and For Women* is published by Simon and Schuster.

1974

- Andrea Dworkin's *Women Hating* is published by Dutton.

- Adrienne Rich receives the National Book Award for *Diving into the Wreck: Poems, 1971-1972.*

- Anne Sexton commits suicide on 4 October in Weston, Massachusetts.

- Katharine Graham (1917-2001), publisher of the *Washington Post,* becomes the first woman member of the board of the Associated Press.

1975

- Paula Gunn Allen' essay "The Sacred Hoop: A Contemporary Indian Perspective on American Indian Literature" appears in *Literature of the American Indian: Views and Interpretations,* edited by Abraham Chapman and published by New American Library.

- Hélène Cixous and Catherine Clement's *La Jeune nee (The Newly Born Woman,* University of Minnesota Press, 1986) is published by Union Generale.

Margaret Thatcher is elected leader of the Conservative Party and becomes the first woman to head a major party in Great Britain.

Susan Brownmiller's *Against our Will: Men, Women, and Rape* is published by Simon and Schuster.

1976

Andrea Dworkin's *Our Blood: Prophecies and Discourses on Sexual Politics* is published by Harper.

Maxine Hong Kingston's *The Woman Warrior: Memoirs of a Girlhood among Ghosts* is published by Knopf.

Maxine Hong Kingston's receives the National Book Critics Circle award for general nonfiction for *The Woman Warrior.*

Barbara Walters (1931-) becomes the first female network television news anchorwoman when she joins Harry Reasoner as coanchor of the *ABC Evening News.*

Shere Hite's *The Hite Report: A Nationwide Study of Female Sexuality* is published by Macmillan.

1977

Alice Paul dies on 9 July in Moorestown, New Jersey.

Marilyn French's *The Women's Room* is published by Summit.

Toni Morrison's *Song of Solomon* is published by Knopf.

Toni Morrison receives the National Book Critics Circle Award for fiction for *Song of Solomon.*

Labor organizer Barbara Mayer Wertheimer's *We Were There: The Story of Working Women in America* is published by Pantheon.

Women's Press is established in Great Britain.

1978

The Pregnancy Discrimination Act bans employment discrimination against pregnant women.

Tillie Olsen's *Silences* is published by Delcorte Press/Seymour Lawrence.

1979

Margaret Thatcher becomes the first woman prime minister of Great Britain. She serves until her resignation in 1990, marking the longest term of any twentieth-century prime minister.

Barbara Wertheim Tuchman becomes the first woman elected president of the American Academy and Institute of Arts and Letters.

Mother Teresa (1910-1997) receives the Nobel Peace Prize.

Sandra M. Gilbert and Susan Gubar's *The Madwoman in the Attic: The Woman Writer and the Nineteenth-Century Imagination* is published by Yale University Press.

1980

Muriel Rukeyser dies on 12 February in New York City.

Adrienne Rich's essay "Compulsory Heterosexuality and Lesbian Experience" is published in *Signs: Journal of Women in Culture and Society.*

1981

bell hooks's *Ain't I a Woman: Black Women and Feminism* is published by South End Press.

Sylvia Plath's *Collected Poems,* edited by Ted Hughes, is published by Harper.

Sandra Day O'Connor (1930-) becomes the first woman Justice of the U.S. Supreme Court, after being nominated by President Ronald Reagan and sworn in on 25 September.

Women of Color Press is founded in Albany, New York by Barbara Smith.

Cleis Press is established in Pittsburgh, Pennsylvania, and San Francisco, California.

This Bridge Called My Back: Writings by Radical Women of Color, edited by Cherríe Moraga and Gloria Anzaldúa, is published by Persephone Press.

Maxine Kumin is named U. S. Poet Laureate.

1982

Djuna Barnes dies on 19 June in New York City.

Sylvia Plath is posthumously awarded the Pulitzer Prize in poetry for *Collected Poems.*

Alice Walker's *The Color Purple* is published by Harcourt.

Carol Gilligan's *In a Different Voice: Psychological Theory and Women's Development* is published by Harvard University Press.

1983

- Rebecca West dies on 15 March in London, England.

- Gloria Steinem's *Outrageous Acts and Everyday Rebellions* is published by Holt.

1984

- Sandra Cisneros's *The House on Mango Street* is published by Arte Publico.

- Lillian Hellman dies on 30 June in Martha's Vineyard, Massachusetts.

- Geraldine Ferraro (1935-) becomes the first woman to win the Vice-Presidential nomination and runs unsuccessfully for office with Democratic Presidential candidate Walter Mondale.

- Firebrand Books, publisher of feminist and lesbian literature, is established in Ann Arbor, Michigan.

- bell hooks's *Feminist Theory: From Margin to Center* is published by South End Press.

1985

- Margaret Atwood's *The Handmaid's Tale* is published by McClelland & Stewart.

- Wilma P. Mankiller is sworn in as the first woman tribal chief of the Cherokee nation. She serves until 1994.

- Gwendolyn Brooks is named U. S. Poet Laureate.

1986

- Simone de Beauvoir dies on 14 April in Paris, France.

- Bessie Head dies on 17 April in Botswana.

- Rita Dove's *Thomas and Beulah* is published by Carnegie-Mellon University Press.

- Sylvia Ann Hewlett's *A Lesser Life: The Myth of Women's Liberation in America* is published by Morrow.

1987

- Toni Morrison's *Beloved* is published by Knopf.

- Rita Dove receives the Pulitzer Prize for poetry for *Thomas and Beulah*.

1988

- Toni Morrison receives the Pulitzer Prize for fiction for *Beloved*.

- *The War of the Words,* Volume 1 of Sandra M. Gilbert and Susan Gubar's *No Man's Land: The Place of the Woman Writer in the Twentieth Century,* is published by Yale University Press.

1989

- Amy Tan's *The Joy Luck Club* is published by Putnam.

1990

- Naomi Wolf's *The Beauty Myth: How Images of Beauty Are Used against Women* is published by Chatto & Windus.

- The Norplant contraceptive is approved by the FDA on 10 December.

- Camille Paglia's *Sexual Personae: Art and Decadence from Nefertiti to Emily Dickinson* is published by Yale University Press.

- Wendy Kaminer's *A Fearful Freedom: Women's Flight from Equality* is published by Addison-Wesley.

- Laurel Thatcher Ulrich's *A Midwife's Tale: The Life of Martha Ballard, Based on Her Diary, 1785-1812* is published by Knopf.

- Judith Butler's *Gender Trouble: Feminism and the Subversion of Identity* is published by Routledge.

1991

- Susan Faludi's *Backlash: The Undeclared War Against American Women* is published by Crown.

- Antonia Novello (1944-) is appointed by President George H.W. Bush and becomes the first woman and first person of Hispanic descent to serve as U. S. Surgeon General.

- Bernadine Healy, M.D. (1944-) is appointed by President George H.W. Bush and becomes the first woman to head the National Institutes of Health.

- Suzanne Gordon's *Prisoners of Men's Dreams: Striking Out for a New Feminine Future* is published by Little, Brown.

- Laurel Thatcher Ulrich receives the Pulitzer Prize for history for *A Midwife's Tale: The Life of Martha Ballard, Based on Her Diary, 1785-1812.*

1992

- Carol Elizabeth Moseley Braun (1947-) becomes the first African American woman elected to the U. S. Senate on 3 November.

- Carolyne Larrington's *The Feminist Companion to Mythology* is published by Pandora.

- Marilyn French's *The War against Women* is published by Summit.

- Clarissa Pinkola Estes's *Women Who Run with the Wolves: Myths and Stories of the Wild Woman Archetype* is published by Ballantine.

- Naomi Wolf's *Fire with Fire: The New Female Power and How It Will Change the Twenty-first Century* is published by Random House.

- Mona Van Duyn is named U. S. Poet Laureate.

1993

- Appointed by President Bill Clinton, Janet Reno (1938-) becomes the first woman U.S. Attorney General when she is sworn in on 12 March.

- Toni Morrison receives the Nobel Prize in Literature.

- Toni Morrison receives the Elizabeth Cady Stanton Award from the National Organization for Women.

- Canada's Progressive Conservative party votes on 13 June to make Defense Minister Kim Campbell the nation's first woman prime minister. Canadian voters oust the Conservative party in elections on 25 October as recession continues; Liberal leader Jean Chrétien becomes prime minister.

- On 1 October Rita Dove becomes the youngest person and the first African American to be named U. S. Poet Laureate.

- Faye Myenne Ng's *Bone* is published by Hyperion.

1994

- The Violence Against Women Act tightens federal penalties for sex offenders, funds services for victims of rape and domestic violence, and provides funds for special training for police officers in domestic violence and rape cases.

- Mary Pipher's *Reviving Ophelia: Saving the Selves of Adolescent Girls* is published by Putnam.

1995

- Ireland's electorate votes by a narrow margin in November to end the nation's ban on divorce (no other European country has such a ban), but only after 4 years' legal separation.

1996

- Marguerite Duras dies on 3 March in Paris, France.

- Hillary Rodham Clinton's *It Takes a Village, and Other Lessons Children Teach Us* is published by Simon and Schuster.

1998

- Bella Abzug dies on 31 March in New York City.

- Drucilla Cornell's *At the Heart of Freedom: Feminism, Sex, and Equality* is published by Princeton University Press.

1999

- Susan Brownmiller's *In Our Time: Memoir of a Revolution* is published by Dial Press.

- Gwendolyn Mink's *Welfare's End* is published by Cornell University Press.

- Martha C. Nussbaum's *Sex and Social Justice* is published by Oxford University Press.

2000

- Gwendolyn Brooks dies on 3 December in Chicago, Illinois.

- Patricia Hill Collins's *Black Feminist Thought: Knowledge, Consciousness, and the Politics of Empowerment* is published by Routledge.

- Jennifer Baumgardner and Amy Richards's *Manifesta: Young Women, Feminism, and the Future* is published by Farrar, Straus, and Giroux.

2002

- Estelle B. Freedman's *No Turning Back: The History of Feminism and the Future of Women* is published by Ballantine.

- *Colonize This! Young Women of Color on Today's Feminism*, edited by Daisy Hernandez and Bushra Rehman, is published by Seal Press.

2003

- Iranian feminist and human rights activist Shirin Ebadi (1947-) receives the Nobel Peace Prize.

- Louise Glück is named U. S. Poet Laureate.

- *Catching a Wave: Reclaiming Feminism for the 21st Century,* edited by Rory Cooke Dicker and Alison Piepmeier, is published by Northeastern University Press.

2004

- The FDA approves the contraceptive mifepristone, following a 16-year struggle by reproductive rights activists to have the abortion drug approved. Opponents made repeated efforts to prevent approval and distribution of mifepristone.

- *The Fire This Time: Young Activists and the New Feminism,* edited by Vivien Labaton and Dawn Lundy Martin, is published by Anchor Books.

- *The Future of Women's Rights: Global Visions and Strategies,* edited by Joanna Kerr, Ellen Sprenger, and Alison Symington, is published by ZED Books and Palgrave Macmillan.

KATE CHOPIN

(1851 - 1904)

(Full name Katherine O'Flaherty Chopin) American novelist and short story writer.

A popular local colorist during her lifetime, Chopin is now recognized as an important figure in nineteenth-century American fiction and as a major figure in feminist literature. Her best-known work, *The Awakening* (1899), depicts a woman's search for sexual freedom in the repressive society of the American South during the Victorian era. The novel's frank treatment of guilt-less adultery inspired critical backlash and public condemnation when it was published, and this negative reception caused Chopin to abandon her literary career. Chopin was largely ignored until the 1950s, when critical interest in her works began to enjoy a significant revival. Modern scholars now view *The Awakening* as a masterpiece of its time. Feminist critics are particularly interested in Chopin's novel for its insights into the condition of women at the turn of the century, and for its comment on the institution of marriage as well as female independence and sexuality.

BIOGRAPHICAL INFORMATION

Born on February 8, 1851, in St. Louis, Missouri, Chopin was the daughter of Thomas O'Flaherty, a prominent businessman, and Eliza Faris. Chopin's father died when she was four years old, and her childhood was profoundly influenced by her mother, grandmother, and great-grandmother, who were descendants of French Creole pioneers. Chopin also spent time with her family's Creole and mulatto slaves, whose dialects she mastered. Chopin read the works of Walter Scott, Edmund Spencer, and other writers who were not represented among the encyclopedias and religious books in the family library, but despite her bookish nature Chopin was an undistinguished student at the convent school she attended. She graduated at the age of seventeen and spent two years as a belle of fashionable St. Louis society. In 1870, she married a wealthy Creole cotton magnate, Oscar Chopin, and moved with him to New Orleans. For the next decade, Chopin pursued the demanding social and domestic schedule of a wealthy New Orleans wife, the recollection of which would serve as material for *The Awakening*. By 1880, however, financial difficulties made it necessary for Chopin's steadily growing family to move to Cloutierville in Natchitoches Parish, located in Louisiana's Red River bayou region. There, Chopin's husband managed the family plantations until his death in 1883. Afterward, Chopin insisted on assuming her husband's managerial responsibilities, which brought her into contact with almost every aspect of the family business and every segment of the community. She was particularly intrigued by the French Acadian, Creole, and mulatto sharecroppers who worked the plantations. The impressions she gathered of these people and of Natchitoches Parish life were later reflected in her fiction.

In the mid-1880s, Chopin sold most of her property and left Louisiana to live with her mother in St. Louis. Family friends, who had found her letters entertaining, encouraged Chopin to write professionally, and she soon began writing short stories. These early works show the influence of her favorite authors, especially the French writers Guy de Maupassant, Alphonse Daudet, and Molière. At this time, Chopin also read the works of Charles Darwin, Thomas Huxley, and Herbert Spencer in order to keep abreast of trends in scientific thinking, and she began questioning the benefits of certain mores and ethical constraints imposed by society on human nature. After an apprenticeship marked by routine rejections, she published the novel *At Fault* in 1890. This work displayed many of the shortcomings of a first novel and failed to interest readers, but Chopin soon began to publish her short stories in the most popular American periodicals. With the publication of the collections *Bayou Folk* (1894) and *A Night in Acadie* (1897), her growing reputation as a skillful local colorist was established. In 1899, Chopin completed her ambitious novel *The Awakening*, which was received with hostility by critics despite general acknowledgement of Chopin's mature writing skills. Chopin's reputation as a writer was severely damaged by the negative reception of *The Awakening*; she had difficulties finding publishers for her later works and was ostracized from local literary groups. Demoralized, she wrote little during the rest of her life. She died of a cerebral hemorrhage on August 22, 1904.

MAJOR WORKS

The short stories collected in *Bayou Folk* and *A Night in Acadie* established Chopin as an important writer of local-color fiction. Set primarily near Natchitoches Parish, these tales of Creole and Cajun life are noted for meticulous descriptions of setting, precise dialect, and an objective point of view. The stories in *Bayou Folk* and *A Night in Acadie* attempt honest examinations of sexuality, repression, freedom, and responsibility—themes Chopin was to explore more fully in *The Awakening*. "Her Letters," for example, a story published in the magazine *Vogue* in 1895, tells with great realistic detail the story of a man driven to suicide

by the suspicion of his late wife's infidelity, commenting subtly on patriarchal control as well as frankly displaying some of the key challenges of the institution of marriage. Scholars consider *The Awakening* Chopin's best-known work, remarkable in that it was written during the morally uncompromising climate of 1890s America. Psychologically realistic, *The Awakening* is the story of Edna Pontellier, a conventional wife and mother who experiences a spiritual epiphany and an awakened sense of independence that change her life. The theme of sexual freedom, and the consequences women must face to attain it, is supported by sensual imagery that acquires symbolic meaning as the story progresses. This symbolism emphasizes the conflict within Pontellier, who realizes that she can neither exercise her newfound sense of independence nor return to life as it was before her "awakening." For example, the sexual candor of the Creole community on Grand Isle, the novel's setting, is contrasted with the conventional moral strictures of New Orleans; birds in gilded cages and free-flying birds are juxtaposed; and the protagonist selects for her confidantes both the domesticated, devoted Adele Ratignolle and the passionate Madame Reisz, an antisocial and unattractive pianist. Critics consider Chopin's careful presentation of the constraints on married and unmarried women in *The Awakening* to be her most sophisticated and radical commentary on feminist themes.

CRITICAL RECEPTION

The Awakening was very much ahead of its time; critics were outraged at its moral statements, and Chopin was shunned by southern literary society. After the furor over the novel had passed, it was largely ignored until the 1930s, when Daniel S. Rankin published a study of Chopin's works that included a highly favorable assessment of the book. During the succeeding decades, critical debate surrounding *The Awakening* has focused on Chopin's view of women's role in society, the significance of the main character's awakening and her subsequent suicide, and the possibility of parallels between the lives of Chopin and her protagonist. Per Seyersted has noted her secretive, individualistic nature and her evident enjoyment of living alone as an independent writer. Priscilla Allen has posited that male critics allow their preconceptions about "good" and "bad" women to influence their interpretations of Chopin's novel, arguing that they too often assume Edna Pontellier's first priority should have been her family and not herself. Like Allen, Seyersted brings a feminist interpretation to *The Awakening* and points out that the depiction of passionate, independent women in Chopin's other fiction supports the theory that she was in fact concerned about the incompatibility of motherhood and career for women living during the late nineteenth century.

PRINCIPAL WORKS

At Fault (novel) 1890

Bayou Folk (short stories) 1894

A Night in Acadie (short stories) 1897

The Awakening (novel) 1899

The Complete Works of Kate Chopin. 2 vols. [edited by Per Syersted] (novels, short stories, and prose) 1969

A Kate Chopin Miscellany [edited by Syersted and Emily Toth] (letters and journals) 1979

Kate Chopin's Private Papers (journals and prose) 1998

PRIMARY SOURCES

KATE CHOPIN (NOVEL DATE 1899)

Chopin, Kate. "Chapter 10." In *The Awakening*, pp. 68-77. Chicago: Herbert S. Stone & Co., 1899.

In the following novel excerpt, Chopin's heroine, Edna Pontellier, experiences a feeling of liberation during her inaugural "solo" swim.

At all events Robert proposed it, and there was not a dissenting voice. There was not one but was ready to follow when he led the way. He did not lead the way, however, he directed the way; and he himself loitered behind with the lovers, who had betrayed a disposition to linger and hold themselves apart. He walked between them, whether with malicious or mischievous intent was not wholly clear, even to himself.

The Pontelliers and Ratignolles walked ahead; the women leaning upon the arms of their husbands. Edna could hear Robert's voice behind them, and could sometimes hear what he said. She wondered why he did not join them. It was unlike him not to. Of late he had sometimes held away from her for an entire day, redoubling his devotion upon the next and the next, as though

to make up for hours that had been lost. She missed him the days when some pretext served to take him away from her, just as one misses the sun on a cloudy day without having thought much about the sun when it was shining.

The people walked in little groups toward the beach. They talked and laughed; some of them sang. There was a band playing down at Klein's hotel, and the strains reached them faintly, tempered by the distance. There were strange, rare odors abroad—a tangle of the sea smell and of weeds and damp, new-plowed earth, mingled with the heavy perfume of a field of white blossoms somewhere near. But the night sat lightly upon the sea and the land. There was no weight of darkness; there were no shadows. The white light of the moon had fallen upon the world like the mystery and the softness of sleep.

Most of them walked into the water as though into a native element. The sea was quiet now, and swelled lazily in broad billows that melted into one another and did not break except upon the beach in little foamy crests that coiled back like slow, white serpents.

Edna had attempted all summer to learn to swim. She had received instructions from both the men and women; in some instances from the children. Robert had pursued a system of lessons almost daily; and he was nearly at the point of discouragement in realizing the futility of his efforts. A certain ungovernable dread hung about her when in the water, unless there was a hand near by that might reach out and reassure her.

But that night she was like the little tottering, stumbling, clutching child, who of a sudden realizes its powers, and walks for the first time alone, boldly and with over-confidence. She could have shouted for joy. She did shout for joy, as with a sweeping stroke or two she lifted her body to the surface of the water.

A feeling of exultation overtook her, as if some power of significant import had been given her to control the working of her body and soul. She grew daring and reckless, overestimating her strength. She wanted to swim far out, where no woman had swum before.

Her unlooked-for achievement was the subject of wonder, applause, and admiration. Each one congratulated himself that his special teachings had accomplished this desired end.

"How easy it is!" she thought. "It is nothing," she said aloud; "why did I not discover before that it was nothing. Think of the time I have lost splashing about like a baby!" She would not join the groups in their sports and bouts, but intoxicated with her newly conquered power, she swam alone.

She turned face seaward to gather in an impression of space and solitude, which the vast expanse of water, meeting and melting with the moonlit sky, conveyed to her excited fancy. As she swam she seemed to be reaching out for the unlimited in which to lose herself.

Once she turned and looked toward the shore, toward the people she had left there. She had not gone any great distance—that is, what would have been a great distance for an experienced swimmer. But to her unaccustomed vision the stretch of water behind her assumed the aspect of a barrier which her unaided strength would never be able to overcome.

A quick vision of death smote her soul, and for a second of time appalled and enfeebled her senses. But by an effort she rallied her staggering faculties and managed to regain the land.

She made no mention of her encounter with death and her flash of terror, except to say to her husband, "I thought I should have perished out there alone."

"You were not so very far, my dear; I was watching you," he told her.

Edna went at once to the bath-house, and she had put on her dry clothes and was ready to return home before the others had left the water. She started to walk away alone. They all called to her and shouted to her. She waved a dissenting hand, and went on, paying no further heed to their renewed cries which sought to detain her.

"Sometimes I am tempted to think that Mrs. Pontellier is capricious," said Madame Lebrun, who was amusing herself immensely and feared that Edna's abrupt departure might put an end to the pleasure.

"I know she is," assented Mr. Pontellier, "sometimes, not often."

Edna had not traversed a quarter of the distance on her way home before she was overtaken by Robert.

"Did you think I was afraid?" she asked him, without a shade of annoyance.

"No; I knew you weren't afraid."

"Then why did you come? Why didn't you stay out there with the others?"

"I never thought of it."

"Thought of what?"

"Of anything. What difference does it make?"

"I'm very tired," she uttered, complainingly.

"I know you are.

"You don't know anything about it. Why should you know? I never was so exhausted in my life. But it isn't unpleasant. A thousand emotions have swept through me to-night. I don't comprehend half of them. Don't mind what I'm saying; I am just thinking aloud. I wonder if I shall ever be stirred again as Mademoiselle Reisz's playing moved me to-night. I wonder if any night on earth will ever again be like this one. It is like a dream. The People about me are like some uncanny, half-human beings. There must be spirits abroad to-night."

"There are," whispered Robert. "Didn't you know this was the twenty-eighth of August?"

"The twenty-eighth of August?"

"Yes. On the twenty-eighth of August, at the hour of midnight, and if the moon is shining—the moon must be shining—a spirit that has haunted these shores for ages rises up from the Gulf. With its own penetrating vision the spirit seeks some one mortal worthy to hold his company, worthy of being exalted for a few hours into realms of the semi-celestials. His search has always hitherto been fruitless, and he has sunk back, disheartened, into the sea. But to-night he found Mrs. Pontellier. Perhaps he will never wholly release her from the spell. Perhaps she will never again suffer a poor, unworthy earthling to walk in the shadow of her divine presence."

"Don't banter me," she said wounded at what appeared to be his flippancy. He did not mind the entreaty, but the tone with its delicate note of pathos was like a reproach. He could not explain; he could not tell her that he had penetrated her mood and understood. He said nothing except to offer her his arm, for, by her own admission, she was exhausted. She had been walking alone with her arms hanging limp, letting her white skirts trail along the dewy path. She took his arm, but she did not lean upon it. She let her hand lie listlessly as though her thoughts were elsewhere—somewhere in advance of her body, and she was striving to overtake them.

Robert assisted her into the hammock which swung from the post before her door out to the trunk of a tree.

"Will you stay out here and wait for Mr. Pontellier?" he asked.

"I'll stay out here. Good-night."

"Shall I get you a pillow?"

"There's one here," she said feeling about, for they were in the shadow.

"It must be soiled; the children have been tumbling about."

"No matter." And having discovered the pillow, she adjusted it beneath her head. She extended herself in the hammock with a deep breath of relief. She was not a supercilious or an overdainty woman. She was not much given to reclining in the hammock, and when she did so it was with no catlike suggestion of voluptuous ease, but with a beneficent repose which seemed to invade her whole body.

"Shall I stay with you till Mr. Pontellier comes?" asked Robert, seating himself on the outer edge of one of the steps and taking hold of the hammock rope which was fastened to the post.

"If you wish. Don't swing the hammock. Will you get my white shawl which I left on the windowsill over at the house?"

"Are you chilly?"

"No; but I shall be presently."

"Presently?" he laughed. "Do you know what time it is? How long are you going to stay out here?"

"I don't know. Will you get the shawl?"

"Of course I will," he said, rising. He went over to the house, walking along the grass. She watched his figure pass in and out of the strips of moonlight. It was past midnight. It was very quiet.

When he returned with the shawl she took it and kept it in her hand. She did not put it around her.

"Did you say I should stay till Mr. Pontellier came back?"

"I said you might if you wished to."

He seated himself again and rolled a cigarette, which he smoked in silence. Neither did Mrs. Pontellier speak. No multitude of words could have been more significant than those moments of silence, or more pregnant with the first-felt throbbing of desire.

When the voices of the bathers were heard approaching, Robert said good-night. She did not answer him. He thought she was asleep. Again she watched his figure pass in and out of the strips of moonlight as he walked away.

THE NATION (REVIEW DATE 3 AUGUST 1899)

SOURCE: "Recent Novels: *The Awakening*." *The Nation* 69, no. 1779 (3 August 1899): 96.

In the following review of The Awakening, *the critic condemns Chopin for having written an immoral novel.*

[Mrs. Chopin's] *The Awakening* is the sad story of a Southern lady who wanted to do what she wanted to. From wanting to, she did, with disastrous consequences; but as she swims out to sea in the end, it is to be hoped that her example may lie for ever undredged. It is with high expectation that we open the volume, remembering the author's agreeable short stories, and with real disappointment that we close it. The recording reviewer drops a tear over one more clever author gone wrong. Mrs. Chopin's accustomed fine workmanship is here, the hinted effects, the well-expended epithet, the pellucid style; and, so far as construction goes, the writer shows herself as competent to write a novel as a sketch. The tint and air of Creole New Orleans and the Louisiana seacoast are conveyed to the reader with subtle skill, and among the secondary characters are several that are lifelike. But we cannot see that literature or the criticism of life is helped by the detailed history of the manifold and contemporary love affairs of a wife and mother. Had she lived by Prof. William James's advice to do one thing a day one does not want to do (in Creole society, two would perhaps be better), flirted less and looked after her children more, or even assisted at more *accouchements*—her *chef d'œuvre* in self-denial—we need not have been put to the unpleasantness of reading about her and the temptations she trumped up for herself.

GENERAL COMMENTARY

SANDRA M. GILBERT AND SUSAN GUBAR (ESSAY DATE 1989)

SOURCE: Gilbert, Sandra M., and Susan Gubar. "The Second Coming of Aphrodite: Kate Chopin's Fantasy of Desire." In *No Man's Land: The Place of the Woman Writer in the Twentieth Century*, pp. 83-119. New Haven: Yale University Press, 1989.

In the following essay, Gilbert and Gubar offer an overview of Chopin's place in the intellectual climate of her time and examine the feminist vision of The Awakening.

The radiant Venus of antiquity, the foam-born Aphrodite, has not passed unscathed through the dreadful shades of the Middle Ages. Her dwelling is no longer Olympus, nor the shores of a per-

ABOUT THE AUTHOR

WILLA CATHER ON *THE AWAKENING*: JULY 8, 1899

A Creole *Bovary* is this little novel [*The Awakening*] of Miss Chopin's. Not that the heroine is a Creole exactly, or that Miss Chopin is a Flaubert—save the mark!—but the theme is similar to that which occupied Flaubert. There was, indeed, no need that a second *Madame Bovary* should be written, but an author's choice of themes is frequently as inexplicable as his choice of a wife. It is governed by some innate temperamental bias that cannot be diagrammed. This is particularly so in women who write, and I shall not attempt to say why Miss Chopin has devoted so exquisite and sensitive, well-governed a style to so trite and sordid a theme. She writes much better than it is ever given to most people to write, and hers is a genuinely literary style; of no great elegance or solidity; but light, flexible, subtle, and capable of producing telling effects directly and simply.

Cather, Willa. Excerpt from "Four Women Writers: Atherton, Ouida, Chopin, Morris." In *The World and the Parish, Vol. II: Willa Cather's Articles and Reviews, 1893-1902*, edited by William M. Curtin, p. 694. Lincoln: University of Nebraska Press, 1970. Originally published under a different title in the *Leader*, July 8, 1899.

fumed archipelago. She has retired into the depths of a cavern, magnificent, it is true, but illumined by fires very different from those of benign Apollo.
—Charles Baudelaire, 1861

Then to me so lying awake a vision
Came without sleep over the seas and touched me,
Softly touched mine eyelids and lips; and I too,
Full of the vision,

Saw the white implacable Aphrodite,
Saw the hair unbound and the feet unsandalled
Shine as fire of sunset on western waters.
—A. C. Swinburne, 1865

I was born under the star of Aphrodite, Aphrodite who was also born on the sea, and when her star is in the ascendant, events are always propitious to me.

—Isadora Duncan, 1927

Swiftly re-light the flame,
Aphrodite, holy name . . .

return, O holiest one,
Venus whose name is kin

to venerate,
venerator.

—H. D., 1945

Although the New Women imagined by Olive Schreiner and Charlotte Perkins Gilman either suffer from or repudiate the erotic, the relationship between late nineteenth-century feminism and female desire was by no means clear cut. To be sure, many suffragists recoiled from the free-love advocate Victoria Woodhull because of her unsavory reputation, but both Elizabeth Cady Stanton and Susan B. Anthony emphatically endorsed her work for the vote in the early 1870s. Exclaimed Stanton, using the occasion to attack the prevailing double standard, "When the men who make laws for us in Washington can . . . declare themselves . . . unspotted from all the sins mentioned in the Decalogue, then we will demand that every woman who makes a constitutional argument on our platform shall be as chaste as Diana," while Anthony wrote to Woodhull enthusiastically urging her to "Go ahead doing, bright, glorious, young and strong spirit, and believe in the best love and hope and faith of S. B. Anthony."[1] Even more radically than Stanton and Anthony, however, some women in this period began not only to excuse or justify but to celebrate the transgressive sexuality of the "fallen woman." For Kate Chopin, in fact, such a woman paradoxically became a resonant symbol of the same need for drastic social change that impelled Schreiner and Gilman in various ways to renounce erotic desire. Ultimately, Aphrodite, the goddess of love—not Mary, the mother of God—became Chopin's ideal.

In February 1899, while *The Awakening* was still in press, Kate Chopin wrote a poem called **"The Haunted Chamber,"** in which a male speaker tells the tale "Of a fair, frail, passionate woman who fell." Narrated in neat couplets, the story seems at first merely an item for masculine delectation, an after-dinner diversion:

It may have been false, it may have been true.
That was nothing to me—it was less to you.
But with bottle between us, and clouds of smoke
From your last cigar, 'twas more of a joke
Than a matter of sin or a matter of shame
That a woman had fallen, and nothing to blame,
So far as you or I could discover,
But her beauty, her blood and an ardent lover.

But surprisingly, as the night wears on, the speaker, left alone with his thoughts, finds himself haunted by this fallen woman's fate. When "the lights were low," he confesses,

> And the breeze came in with the moon's pale
>   glow
> The fair, faint voice of a woman, I heard.
> 'Twas but a wail, and it spoke no word.
> It rose from the depths of some infinite gloom
> And its tremulous anguish filled the room.[2]

Unspoken and unspeakable, the destiny of one lost lady symbolizes the wordless wail of every woman whose passion for self-fulfillment had been forbidden or forgotten.

That such forbidden passion was a major theme for Kate Chopin became clear to American readers two months later, when *The Awakening*—a novel that might be seen as a book-length vindication of the rights of women like the "fair, frail" heroine of "**The Haunted Chamber**"—was published. But the irony and urbanity of Chopin's poem suggest that she was hardly prepared for the outrage that greeted her novel on the same subject. The novel "leaves one sick of human nature," complained one critic; "the purport of the story can hardly be described in language fit for publication," asserted another. Even Willa Cather, who admired Chopin's art and was eventually to produce her own tales of lost ladies, deplored the fact that the author had "devoted so exquisite and sensitive . . . a style to so trite and sordid a theme."[3] Within a few months, the libraries of St. Louis, Missouri, Chopin's native city, had banned the book; Chopin was shunned by a number of acquaintances; and, according to her biographer, Per Seyersted, she was refused membership in the St. Louis Fine Arts Club.[4]

At first the novelist attempted an insouciant self-defense:

> Having a group of people at my disposal, I thought it might be entertaining (to myself) to throw them together and see what would happen. I never dreamed of Mrs. Pontellier making such a mess of things and working out her own damnation as she did. If I had had the slightest intimation of such a thing I would have excluded her from the company. But when I found out what she was up to, the play was half over and it was then too late.[5]

But as time passed, the wound to Chopin's aesthetic morale became ever more painful. Her royalties from the book were minimal, and her third collection of short stories was rejected by *The Awakening*'s publisher. The "moving procession of human energy," the writer confided in a sorrowful essay entitled "**A Reflection**," "has left me by the roadside!"[6]

Ironically, this daughter of a distinguished and pious Catholic family found herself in a position where her own authorial "torment" reflected the pain experienced by the heroine of "**The Haunted Chamber.**" At first a "conscientious mother" of six—indeed, according to her daughter, a model "Lady Bountiful" of the Louisiana neighborhood where she had settled for a while after her marriage—and later an "inconsolable" widow, Chopin had ventured into chambers haunted by the erotic, the illicit, the "sordid".[7] Yet though censorious reviewers and confused readers were shocked by what seemed to be her unprecedented boldness, this artist had been, from early in her career, a very different person from the decorous "Lady Bountiful" that the world believed her to be. Indeed, even as a feminist she had swerved significantly from the essentially puritanical creed that was espoused by many New Women and that would eventually become a central tenet of Gilman's Herland.[8]

On her honeymoon, Chopin had quite fortuitously encountered one "Miss Clafflin" *(sic)*. A sister of Victoria Woodhull, this "fussy, pretty, talkative little woman," wrote Chopin in her diary, "entreated me not to fall into the useless degrading life of most married ladies—but to elevate my mind [and] I assured her I would do so."[9] Living in New Orleans, she had followed "Miss Clafflin's" advice in her own way, adventurously exploring the city and taking notes on scenes that impressed her, attending the theater and the opera, and continuing her compendious reading during long summers at Grand Isle, the resort where *The Awakening* is set. By the time that, as a young widow, Chopin seriously embarked on literary projects, she had abandoned the Catholicism of her girlhood and become an acolyte of the "direct and simple" stories of Maupassant, whom she defined as "a man who had escaped from tradition and authority, who had entered into himself and looked out upon life through his own being and with his own eyes."[10]

Though such "escapes" also fascinated Olive Schreiner and Charlotte Perkins Gilman, the ones envisioned by Chopin were in some ways more controversial. Despite its radical polemics, after all, Schreiner's *African Farm* was morally acceptable enough to become a best-seller, and, though they were notably revolutionary, Gilman's critical and creative works were not greeted with significant opprobrium. But *The Awakening* was almost universally excoriated or deprecated for more than three decades. Perhaps, however, that was because, unlike many of her female contemporaries,

Chopin was aligned with a particularly sensational, largely male-dominated fin-de-siècle rhetoric, a rhetoric which explored, and often defended, what society defined as "damnation."

* * *

Kate Chopin was born in St. Louis in 1851, three years after the publication of *Jane Eyre* and *Wuthering Heights,* two years before the appearance of *Uncle Tom's Cabin,* and six years before the publication of *Aurora Leigh.* In that year, Emily Dickinson was twenty-one, just returned from Mary Lyon's Ladies Seminary at Mount Holyoke, where, already a rebel, she had refused to "accept Christ" during an evangelical revival, while Marian Evans, not yet George Eliot, had produced her translation of Strauss's theologically revisionary *Lebens Jesu* (1846). As for male artists, just four years after Chopin's birth, Walt Whitman was to bring out the first version of *Leaves of Grass,* a work whose sensual frankness and stylistic freedom made it at least as daring in 1855 as **The Awakening** was in 1899. By 1851, moreover, Richard Wagner's epochal *Tannhäuser,* with its shocking depiction of a fiery Venusberg, had already had its premiere in Germany, and within little more than a decade it was to be performed in Paris, where it would be defended by Charles Baudelaire, whose own controversial masterwork, *Les Fleurs du mal,* had appeared in 1857.

It is relevant to review this history because Kate Chopin has often, especially in recent years, been detached from the rich intellectual fabric of the age that nurtured her. Originally seen by her most sympathetic critics as a "local colorist," a purely American phenomenon like George Washington Cable or Mary E. Wilkins Freeman, she has lately been upgraded by even keener enthusiasts to a sort of feminist sociologist but still defined as an artist whose principal sources of energy were empirical observation and political theorizing. Paradoxically, however, in their dislike of the novel's erotic boldness and their willful refusal to sympathize with Edna's "unfocused yearning," some of **The Awakening**'s earliest reviewers came closer to understanding its content and origins.

The novel "is like one of Aubrey Beardsley's hideous but haunting pictures with their disfiguring leer of sensuality," declared a reviewer for the *Los Angeles Sunday Times,* for instance.[11] Three decades later, the writer of the first full-length study of Kate Chopin elaborated upon this position. "**The Awakening** follows the current of erotic morbidity that flowed strongly through the literature of the last two decades of the nineteenth

century," observed Daniel Rankin, adding that Kate Chopin, in an attack "of the prevailing artistic vertigo," had absorbed such diverse influences as Schopenhauer, Wagner, "the Russian novel," and Maeterlinck, while sharing in "the mania for the exotic" that turned so many fin-de-siècle imaginations toward femmes fatales like Haggard's Ayesha, Wilde's Salome, and Flaubert's Salammbô.[12] Rankin was thinking in terms that were just being explored in Mario Praz's *The Romantic Agony,* though his descriptive phrases, like those of the *Los Angeles Times* reviewer, had an emphatically negative moral cast. Beneath the judgmental surface, however, we can discern an accurate definition of who and what Kate Chopin was: a woman of the nineties, a writer of the fin de siècle.

What did it mean, though, to be a *woman* of letters during the fin de siècle, that era whose French label gives it a faintly sinister, voluptuously apocalyptic air?[13] Superficially, at least, the phrase *fin de siècle* meant, for some literary women as for many literary men, a kind of drawing-room sophistication—smoking Turkish cigarettes, subscribing to *The Yellow Book,* reading (and translating) French fiction, all of which Chopin did, especially during the St. Louis years of her widowhood, which were also the years of her major literary activity. More integrally, the fin de siècle was associated with the artistic and intellectual rebels mentioned by Rankin and by Chopin's early reviewers, with, that is, such figures as Beardsley and Wilde, and with their most significant precursors: Swinburne, Pater, Whitman, Wagner, Baudelaire. To such women as Chopin (along with Victoria Woodhull, Emma Goldman, and others), however, the second half of the nineteenth century had also offered the revolutionary concept of "free love," an idea which in some ways qualified, and was sometimes at odds with, the even newer persona of the New Woman. In addition, as we have seen, to be a woman of the nineties meant to have come of age in a new kind of literary age, an era whose spirit was shared and shaped by significant female imaginations.

Like many of her contemporaries, Kate Chopin began quite early to read the works of such ancestresses as Austen, the Brontës, and Eliot. Early and late, moreover, she admired the writings of the iconoclastic George Sand, in honor of whom she evidently named her only daughter "Lélia." In addition, she knew the works of American writers from Stowe to Jewett as well as those of British women from Barrett Browning to

Schreiner, for she belonged to a circle in St. Louis where the writings of such figures were actively discussed.[14] Like the fictions of so many women, however, her earliest full-length narrative—the 1890 novel *At Fault*—dramatizes its author's ambivalent affiliation with the female literary tradition through a complex engagement with that most inescapable of women's novels, *Jane Eyre*. Indeed, like Barrett Browning's *Aurora Leigh*, Eliot's "The Lifted Veil," and other female fictions, *At Fault* depends on crucial elements of the *Jane Eyre* plot: specifically, a husband helplessly shackled to a mentally "incompetent" wife (in this case an alcoholic rather than a madwoman), a "pure" woman who insists on the holiness of wedlock, a fire that destroys much of the husband's property, and a providential death that happily resolves the unhappy triangle.[15]

Unfortunately, though, what had worked so well in 1847 for Charlotte Brontë, almost as well in 1856 for Barrett Browning, and comparatively well in 1859 for Eliot, helped the apprentice Chopin not at all. The splitting of her female protagonist into a sober and noble heroine, on the one hand, and a drunken ignoble double, on the other, seemed for Chopin actually to block the sort of feminist speculation such a strategy had energized in Brontë's novel. Equally hampering were the Gothic elements of fire, murder, and providential death, which had given metaphorical intensity to *Aurora Leigh* and "The Lifted Veil" as well as to *Jane Eyre*. In the forties, Brontë had pioneeringly used such properties of mystery and melodrama to vitalize the theater of desire in which her heroine was a central actor. By the nineties, however, with femmes fatales and New Women making both social and literary history, it seemed specious to fracture the female protagonist.

Whether the heroine was Haggard's Ayesha or Schreiner's Lyndall, events that seemed as "sad and mad and bad" as one of Chopin's reviewers called Edna Pontellier's fate occurred precisely because the mad rebellious woman and the sane submissive woman were now really inhabitants of the same body, and their life-and-death struggle took place not in an attic or a parlor but in the troubled female consciousness.[16] Yet that struggle, often an essential subject of literature by women, must be not only analyzed but rendered, as Chopin had learned from Brontë and other literary foremothers. After the failure of *At Fault*, therefore, she evidently realized that her most pressing task was to learn how to narrate a modern female psychomachia without actually dividing the female personality into two warring selves.

In their different ways, of course, writers like Haggard and Schreiner confronted the same problem, as they set out to record the adventures of the femme fatale or of the New Woman. On the one hand, despite her Medusan powers, the sweetly beautiful but fatal Ayesha has been angelically loyal to her Kallikrates for a millennium, and though she is shown from the first to be belligerent in her relations with other women, she is only gradually revealed to be mad, monstrous, murderous in her relations with all of male culture, and only at the very end of the novel, when she "devolves" into a creature "no larger than a monkey," is her ontological identity revealed. On the other hand, though Schreiner's New Womanly Lyndall is a more complex figure than many late nineteenth-century femmes fatales, she is characterized through a reversal of the dramatic denouement that reveals Ayesha's "true" self. At first, she is seen as strange and rebellious, but later, especially in her angelic death scenes, she becomes a noble victim. Moreover, whether or not New Women consistently used this dramatic pattern to explore their heroines' psychic development, they tended to resort to discursive debates among their characters, a major strategy of Schreiner's; they tended, that is, to tell rather than show the meaning of the conflicts their heroines experienced.[17]

To Chopin, however, such solutions were plainly unacceptable. Inheriting Charlotte Brontë's feminist passion, she also inherited a sense of dramatic coherence comparable to Brontë's, an equally intense poetic energy, and a similar commitment to narrative urgency. At the same time, Chopin preferred a disinterested Flaubertian voice to an impassioned Brontë-esque or Dickensian one. Her version of the feminist psychomachia, therefore, would have to have both the fierce vitality of *Jane Eyre* and the scrupulous restraint of *Madame Bovary*. But how could she negotiate the passage from the clumsily derivative *At Fault* to such a paradoxical romance? To put the question another way, how could she move, as a woman writer, from the often melodramatic or sentimental conventions that shaped even the most "realistic" nineteenth-century novels to the more elliptical structures of twentieth-century fiction?

At first, for Chopin, "local color" writing offered both a mode and a manner that could mediate between the literary forms she had inherited and those she had begun to envision. Like such American contemporaries as Grace King and Constance Woolson, Sarah Orne Jewett and Mary E. Wilkins Freeman—the last two of whom she particularly admired—she could work in what seemed to be a minor, understated (and therefore "ladylike") mode which nevertheless allowed her to explore a number of subversive themes.[18] Because the "local color" writer is in a sense a sort of ethnologist or cultural anthropologist, the recounting of tales based on idiosyncratic customs, folk character, and regional behavior could help her to narrate fictions with the almost scientific detachment of Chekhov, Maupassant, and Flaubert. More important, by reporting odd practices that were part of a region's "local color," she could even tell what would ordinarily be shocking stories without fear of the moral outrage that a more "mainstream" work like *The Awakening* would evoke. Finally, by detaching herself from a specific set of customs she could learn to detach herself from all customs. Like so many other regionalists—among male authors, for instance, Twain, Yeats, and Joyce, and, among women, especially Freeman and, as we shall later show, Edith Wharton and Willa Cather—she could move from theorizing about a particular subcultural group to theorizing about culture itself.

Modest as they may seem, some of Chopin's stories suggest the ways in which large issues had always been implicit in what conservative critics approvingly called her "delightful sketches."[19] With its triangle of upper-class heroine, lower-class heroine, and upper-class lover, for instance, **"At the 'Cadian Ball"** (1892) dramatizes the hierarchies that structure even so apparently simple a society as that of *"La Côte Joyeuse,"* for the local farm girl—Calixta—has ultimately to watch her well-born sweetheart—Alcée—pledge his allegiance to Clarisse, his aristocratic fiancée (*CW* [*The Complete Works of Kate Chopin*] 1:219-27). Recounting a man's repudiation of a young wife whom he believes to have black origins, **"Desirée's Baby"** (1893) goes further and interrogates the arbitrary race distinctions that could divide man from wife, child from parent, in such a culture (*CW* 1:240-45). **"At Chênière Caminada"** (1894), set at the summer resort that was to play so crucial a part in *The Awakening,* and **"Nég Creol"** (1897), set in a very different New Orleans from the *quartier* inhabited by either Edna Pontellier or Kate Chopin herself, offer poignant portraits of southern ladies from the sympathetically delineated point of view of working-class men—one white, one black—into whose consciousness a decorous lady like Chopin

herself might not have been expected to enter (*CW* 1:309-18 and 505-10).

Perhaps even more radically, **"The Story of an Hour"** (1894), **"Athenaïse"** (1896), and **"The Storm"** (comp. 1899) question the very institution of marriage. **"The Story of an Hour"** records a wife's sense of liberation and ecstasy on hearing a false report of her husband's death (*CW* 1:352-54); **"Athenaïse"** explores the rebellious feelings of a runaway bride (*CW* 1:426-54); and **"The Storm"** dramatizes a brief but volcanic—indeed, proto-Lawrentian—sexual encounter between Calixta and Alcée, the lovers who were separated by class lines in **"At the 'Cadian Ball"** (*CW* 2:596-96). Similarly, **"Lilacs"** (1896) movingly delineates the love between two strikingly dissimilar women—a nun and a kind of courtesan—and protests the social rules which would condemn such a relationship (*CW* 1:355-65). In all these pieces, although Chopin appears to begin by setting herself a comparatively limited narrative task, she ultimately confronts large, even (as in **"Desireée's Baby," "The Storm,"** and **"Lilacs"**) deeply "improper" social questions to which many fin-de-siècle artists were coming from other directions.

In an important essay on "The Decadent and the New Woman," Linda Dowling has suggested that both these turn-of-the-century intellectual "types" shared the "fundamental desire of the *fin de siècle avant garde*: the dream of living beyond culture, the dream of pastoral."[20] To say this, however, is to say that artists like Beardsley and Wilde, with literary goals quite distinct from Chopin's, had also begun to speculate on the nature of culture as well as on the nature of nature itself—on the nature, that is, of what is beyond or beneath culture. As Holbrook Jackson put it in 1913, "the intellectual, imaginative and spiritual activities of the Eighteen Nineties [were] concerned mainly with the idea of social life or, if you will, of culture . . . it was a time when people went about frankly and cheerfully endeavoring to solve the question 'How to Live.'"[21] Confronting such questions through her quasi-anthropological work as a local colorist, Chopin must also have been influenced by the kinds of related speculations she would have encountered in French literature and in *The Yellow Book* as well as in the New Woman fictions of Schreiner or, indeed, of such other contemporaries as George Egerton and Sarah Grand.

Of course, however, as they fantasized "living beyond culture," two such different beings as the decadent and the New Woman yearned toward drastically different versions of the revitalized natural world that Dowling calls "pastoral." The New Woman, for instance, frequently dreamed of a transfigured society where both "sex distinction" and the "sex-passion" had dissolved away.[22] As Schreiner put it in one of her "allegories," in the highest heaven sex "does not exist," and as Gilman sought to demonstrate in *Herland,* the most intense sexual pleasure derives, at least for women, from an erotics of the maternal.[23] In the words of one British suffragist, "How can we [women] possibly be Freewomen if, like the majority of men, we become the slaves of our lower appetites?"[24] Such male artists as Beardsley and Wilde, however, envisioned a society transfigured not beyond but through homosexual or heterosexual eroticism. What Lord Henry Wotton in Wilde's *The Picture of Dorian Gray* (1891) called "the new Hedonism," wrote the critic and author Grant Allen in 1894, would repudiate "the asceticism that deadens the senses," and do so specifically through a revitalizing of the erotic which would return men and women to the Eden of polymorphous perversity from which Protestant morality, with its threats of "damnation," had cast them out.[25]

Because Chopin had come to cultural theory through a figurative as well as a literal subscription to *The Yellow Book,* and through both the antipuritanical traditions of French literature and the scrupulously empirical observations of literary anthropology, she was disinclined even to try to imagine a de-eroticized pastoral Eden. Rather, she dreamed of a specifically sexual culture beyond culture, a sensual Eden whose heroine's motto might be defined by a passage from one of Victoria Woodhull's most famous speeches of the mid-century: "I will love whom I may . . . I will love as long or as short a period as I can. . . . I will change this love when [conditions] indicate that it ought to be changed; and . . . neither you nor any law you can make shall deter me."[26]

At the same time, Chopin must have seen that the erotic pastoralism which both she and Woodhull were inclined to espouse usually involved either a misogynistic exploitation of the female, as in the brilliant pornographic text which Aubrey Beardsley first published with the title *Under the Hill* and which later appeared as *Venus and Tannhäuser,* or in a misogynistic revulsion against the female, as in Haggard's *She* or Wilde's *Salome.*[27] From the sardonic extreme unction Flaubert as narrator intones over the corpse of Emma Bovary

to the pornographic Black Masses of Aleister Crowley and his prurient celebrations of Venus as "Daughter of Lust" and "Sister of shame," the French and decadent writers alike used the erotic image of woman to annihilate culture through blasphemy and to picture a world whose sexual energy arose specifically from its sacrilegious concentration on the female, its self-nauseating worship of Venus's hellish and adorable flesh.[28] Without denying or deriding the erotic, as so many New Women tended to do, Chopin strove to purify it of such decadent misogyny.

But in formulating her feminist dream of a sexual culture beyond culture, Chopin—like Woodhull before her and Gilman after her—was aligning herself with a strain of nineteenth-century thinking about eroticism that, although historians have tended to ignore or repress its existence, was real and vivid in its time. As Peter Gay has recently argued, the now notorious views of the British doctor William Acton have been mistakenly taken to represent a monolithic Victorian notion of female sexuality. "The majority of women (happily for them) are not much troubled with sexual feelings of any kind," wrote Acton in 1857, adding that the "married woman has no wish to be treated on the footing of a mistress."[29] But in fact, as Gay demonstrates throughout *The Education of the Senses,* a female capacity for sexual desire and pleasure—a capacity assumed by both the theories of Woodhull and the fiction of Chopin—was, if not taken for granted, at least affirmed by many of these women's contemporaries.

"I have come to the conclusion," wrote Elizabeth Cady Stanton in 1881, "that the first great work to be accomplished for women is to revolutionize the dogma that sex is a crime, marriage a defilement and maternity a bane," and in 1883 she complained that "Walt Whitman seems to understand everything in nature but woman . . . he speaks as if the female must be forced to the creative act, apparently ignorant of the great natural fact that a healthy woman has as much passion as a man."[30] In the same vein, the medical pioneer Elizabeth Blackwell declared in 1884 that the "physical pleasure which attends the caresses of love is a rich endowment of humanity, granted by a beneficent Creative power."[31] More empirically, in 1892 one Dr. Clelia Mosher undertook to survey some four dozen American women about their sexual reactions, and, as Gay reports her results, "More than a third of [her] respondents claimed that they reached orgasm 'always' or 'usually.'"[32]

But, as we have seen, even in the seventies Victoria Woodhull had become both mystical and explicit about erotic pleasure. "In a perfected sexuality shall continuous life be found," she exclaimed at a Spiritualists' Camp Meeting in Vineland, New Jersey, adding that "I never had sexual intercourse with any man of whom I am ashamed to stand side by side before the world with the act . . . if I want sexual intercourse with one hundred men I shall have it. . . . And this sexual intercourse business may as well be discussed now, and discussed until you are so familiar with your sexual organs that a reference to them will no longer make the blush mount to your face any more than a reference to any other part of your body."[33]

As if elaborating on Woodhull's assertions, the British sexologist Edward Carpenter insisted in the first edition of his widely read *Love's Coming of Age* that "Sex is the allegory of love in the physical world." In fact, he remarked, "the state of enforced celibacy in which vast numbers of women live to-day [should] be looked upon as a national wrong, almost as grievous as that of prostitution." And, anticipating—perhaps, indeed, influencing—Kate Chopin's celebration of Edna Pontellier's "splendid body," he fulminated that the Victorian prudery which kept nakedness "religiously covered, smothered away from the rush of the great purifying life of Nature" was itself a cause of prurience, for "Sexual embraces [should] receive the benison of Dame Nature, in whose presence alone, under the burning sun or the high canopy of the stars . . . their meaning can be fully understood."[34] Following Carpenter's lead, moreover, his friend and disciple Havelock Ellis was soon to develop a theory of female sexuality which defined woman's eroticism (in terms that strikingly prefigure the recent arguments of such French feminists as Hélène Cixous and Luce Irigaray) as "more massive and more diffuse than male sexuality."[35]

Sharing the views of all these thinkers, Chopin dreamed of yet a third version of pastoral, a sacramental rather than sacrilegious garden of earthly delights, a culture beyond culture whose energy would arise from the liberation and celebration of female desire. And she insisted that this Eden should be ruled by a Venus who would be as free and regal as Beardsley's (or Crowley's) was degraded and whimsical. But her vision of such a goddess surely gained its strength from the same movement toward theological revision that not only fostered the theories of J. J. Bachofen and Jane Ellen Harrison but also inspired *The Woman's*

Bible produced by Elizabeth Cady Stanton and others, along with Florence Nightingale's hope for a "female Christ" and Mary Baker Eddy's argument that because "the ideal woman corresponds to Life and to Love . . . we have not as much authority for considering God masculine as we have for considering Him feminine."[36] Even more specifically, Chopin's visionary eroticism was energized by the same impulse that led Victoria Woodhull to speculate "that the long-lost Garden of Eden is the human body" and Woodhull's acolyte Laura Cuppy Smith to characterize the free love advocate, during her appearance at Vineland, as "The Redeemer," and "virtue and respectability as the two thieves on the cross."[37] Finally, Chopin's sense of the goddess's sacramental sensuality may have been fortified not just by the fervent radicalism of Woodhull and her disciples but also by the radical eroticism of Walt Whitman, an eroticism that Chopin and others clearly saw as transcending the tendency toward misogyny to which Stanton objected.[38]

Equally important, however, was the revisionary female aesthetic that Chopin constructed as, in striving to imagine the healthy eroticism of a culture beyond culture, she searched through the myths she had inherited from patriarchal civilization itself. For in reexamining such myths she began, if only half-consciously and tentatively, to create a narrative structure in which she might coherently dramatize the female psychomachia that was her central subject, a structure that would prove more viable than the unwieldy literary frameworks upon which so many other New Women depended. As her son sketched it in 1899, not long after the publication of *The Awakening,* the room in which Chopin worked was emblematic of her philosophical as well as literary goals. "There were hardly any ornamentations in it," her biographer tells us, "apart from a few paintings on the wall and a candle and a naked Venus on the bookshelf."[39] Abandoning both the religion in which she had been raised and the nineteenth-century literary conventions she had learned, Chopin evidently understood her own desire to revitalize and vindicate the pagan presence of the goddess of love.

* * *

Toward the end of *The Awakening* there is a dinner party scene which has been ignored by many critics though it has fascinated and puzzled a few. On the verge of leaving her husband's house for a nearby cottage that she hopes will become both a spiritual and material room of her own, Edna Pontellier has invited a "select" group of

FROM THE AUTHOR

EXCERPT FROM A NEWSPAPER ARTICLE IN WHICH CHOPIN ANSWERS THE QUESTION "IS LOVE DIVINE?"

It is as difficult to distinguish between divine love and the natural, animal life, as it is to explain just why we love at all. In a discussion of this character between two women in my new novel I have made my heroine say: "Why is it I love this man? Is it because his hair is brown, growing high on his temples; because his eyes droop a bit at the corners, or because his nose is just so much out of drawing?"

One really never knows the exact, definite thing which excites love for any one person, and one can never truly know whether this love is the result of circumstances or whether it is predestination. I am inclined to think that love springs from animal instinct, and therefore is, in a measure, divine. One can never resolve to love this man, this woman or child, and then carry out the resolution unless one feels irresistibly drawn by an indefinable current of magnetism. This subject allows an immense field for discussion and profound thought, and one could scarcely voice a definite opinion in a ten minutes talk. But I am sure we all feel that love—true, pure love, is an uncontrollable emotion that allows of no analyzation and no vivisection.

Chopin, Kate. Excerpt from "'Is Love Divine?' The Question Answered by Three Ladies Well Known in St. Louis Society." In *Kate Chopin's Private Papers*, edited by Emily Toth and Per Syersted, pp. 219-20. Bloomington, Ind.: Indiana University Press, 1998.

friends to join her at a birthday dinner which will also be a celebration of her departure from one household and her entrance into another. Splendid in gold satin and lace "the color of her skin," she presides over an equally splendid table, which is similarly decked in "pale yellow satin," lit by "wax candles in massive brass candelabra," and heaped with "full, fragrant roses."[40] More strikingly still, "the ordinary stiff dining chairs" have been "discarded for the occasion and replaced by the most commodious and luxurious which could be collected throughout the house" while "before each guest [stands] a tiny glass that [sparkles] like a garnet gem," containing a magical-looking cocktail.

Enthroned at the head of the table, Edna herself appears equally magical, for there is "something in her attitude, in her whole appearance, which [suggests] the regal woman, the one who rules, who looks on, who stands alone." At the same time, however—even in the midst of triumphant merrymaking which climaxes in one of the women guests weaving a pagan garland of roses to crown the dark curls of the handsome young man beside her—we are told that Edna feels an "old ennui overtaking her . . . a chill breath that seemed to issue from some vast cavern wherein discords wailed" (chap. 30). Ranging as it does from sumptuous feasting to secret sadness, from gorgeousness to gloom, the dinner party chapter is, as Cynthia Griffin Wolff observes, "one of the longest sustained episodes in the novel."[41]

Perhaps it is because so many contemporary critics would agree with Lawrence Thornton's description of *The Awakening* as a "political romance"[42] that so few have paid close attention to this scene. Though in the past few decades *The Awakening* has become one of the most frequently analyzed American novels, writers about the book commonly describe Edna's party as just one more occasion on which Chopin's half-mad housewife experiences "unfocused yearning" for romantic transfiguration or social liberation.[43] Yet, besides occupying an exceptionally long and elaborate chapter in a novel of economical, obliquely rendered episodes, Edna's dinner party constitutes an extraordinarily complex literary structure. What does it mean, after all, when the narrator of this apparently "realistic" work suddenly calls her heroine "the regal woman, the one who rules, who looks on, who stands alone"? The vocabulary of such a description seems more appropriate to a fantasy or a fairy tale, and yet this mysterious definition seems also to evoke the narrator's next perception of the "chill breath" her queenly heroine feels, together with Edna's equally mysterious sense of "acute longing which always summoned into her spiritual vision the presence of the beloved one." Who or what, indeed, is the oddly vague "beloved one"? And why, finally, does the enigmatically wise Mademoiselle Reisz take her leave of Edna with a French sentence—*"Bonne nuit, ma reine, soyez sage"*—that seems to confirm our feeling that this magical hostess is clothed in a paradoxical veil of power and vulnerability?

As a speculative explanation of these puzzles, we will argue that *The Awakening* is a female fiction which both draws upon and revises fin-de-siècle hedonism to propose a feminist myth of Aphrodite/Venus as an alternative to the patriarchal western myth of Jesus. In the novel's unfolding of this implicit myth, the dinner party scene is of crucial importance, for here, as she presides over a Swinburnian Last Supper, Edna Pontellier (if only for a moment) "becomes" the powerful goddess of love and art into whose shape she was first "born" in the gulf near Grand Isle and in whose image she will be suicidally borne back into the sea at the novel's end. Thus when Victor, the darkhaired young man who was ritually garlanded at the climax of the feast, tells his friend Mariequita that "Venus rising from the foam could have presented no more entrancing a spectacle than Mrs. Pontellier, blazing with beauty and diamonds at the head of the board," he is speaking what is in some sense the truth about Kate Chopin's heroine.

To see *The Awakening* in these terms is not, of course, to deny that it is also the work most critics have thought it is: a "Creole Bovary," a feminist "critique of the identity of 'mother-women,'" "a New Orleans version of the familiar transcendentalist fable of the soul's emergence, or 'lapse' into life," "a eulogy on sex and a muted elegy on the female condition," a turn-of-the-century "existentialist" epiphany, and "a tough-minded critique of the Victorian myths of love."[44] Taken together, all these definitions of the novel suggest the range of political, moral, and philosophical concerns on which Chopin meditates throughout this brief but sophisticated work. What unifies these often divergent matters, however, is the way in which, for all its surface realism, *The Awakening* is allusively organized by Kate Chopin's half-secret fantasy of the second coming of Aphrodite.

To be sure, Chopin's "Creole Bovary" has always been understood to be, like its French precursor, a novel that both uses fantasy and comments upon that genre in order to establish the character of its heroine and the nature of her character. But many critics see such fantasies as, like Emma Bovary's, symptoms of inadequacy, of an "over-idealization of love" and a "susceptibility to romantic codes." People like Edna Pontellier and Emma Bovary, wrote Willa Cather in 1899, "are the spoil of the poets, the Iphigenias of senti-

ment." Edna's commitment to fantasy, concludes Cynthia Griffin Wolff in a somewhat extreme summary of this position, is the ultimate mark of the "schizoid" personality which causes her "disintegration."[45] We will show, however, that the details of desire which the text of *The Awakening* records ultimately shape themselves into a tale of romantic transfiguration that not only uses and comments upon fantasy but actually becomes a fantasy, albeit a shadowy one. Both seriously and ironically, this work of Kate Chopin's demonstrates, from a female point of view, just what would "really" happen to a mortal, turn-of-the-century woman who tried to claim for herself the erotic freedom owned by the classical queen of love.

We will argue, moreover, that to see this novel as such a shadowy fantasy or fantasy *manqué* is to begin to explain a number of qualities that have puzzled its detractors as well as its admirers: its odd short chapters, its ambiguous lyricism (what Cather called its "flexible iridescent style"), its editorial restraint, its use of recurrent images and refrains, its implicit or explicit allusions to writers like Whitman, Swinburne, and Flaubert, and its air of moral indeterminacy. In addition, we will suggest that to see *The Awakening* as such a fantasy is to begin to grasp the purpose of some of the scenes in the book that have always appeared problematic. Finally, we will show that, in creating this generically equivocal fantasy, Kate Chopin was working in a mode of mingled naturalism and symbolism analogous to the one explored by her near contemporary George Moore and his younger countryman James Joyce. Learned from such varied continental precursors as Turgenev and Maupassant, this artful combination of surface and symbol evolved through Moore's *The Untilled Field* (1903) and Joyce's *Dubliners* (1914) to a culmination in *Ulysses* (1922). But Kate Chopin in America, inheriting the same tradition and similar techniques, also began to explore the mythic radiance which might at any moment flash through ordinary reality. As a woman writer, however, she saw such epiphanies from a feminine point of view and in what we would call feminist terms. Indeed, the next literary women to employ comparable modes would be such modernists as May Sinclair, Virginia Woolf, Katherine Mansfield, and even at times Willa Cather herself—and they too, in particular Woolf, would often use these techniques to articulate new visions of the feminine.

* * *

Appropriately enough, Kate Chopin's portrait of Aphrodite as a "Creole Bovary" begins and ends at a seaside resort, on the margin between nature and culture, where a leisured or, anyway, a lucky few may be given the chance to witness the birth of erotic power in the foam. But to start with, despite the nearness of the sea and the incessant sound of its "seductive" voice, Chopin offers scenes that are determinedly realistic, low-key, landbound. In addition, as if briefly acknowledging Flaubert's influence, she opens her novel about a woman's fateful transformation by examining her heroine from a stolid male perspective. *Madame Bovary,* of course, begins with a brief summary of Charles Bovary's history, including a description of the way Emma Roualt appears to the bovine but passionate young physician whom she will soon marry. Similarly, the author-omniscient of the first chapter of **The Awakening** emphasizes the point of view of Edna Pontellier's conventional husband, Léonce.

Like Madame Bovary's husband-to-be, who at one point gazes at Emma as she stands beneath a parasol which colors "the white skin of her face with shifting reflections" (13), Mr. Pontellier watches from a porch of the main building of Madame Lebrun's Grand Isle summer colony as "a white sunshade [advances] at a snail's pace from the beach" with his wife Edna and her friend Robert Lebrun strolling "beneath its pink-lined shelter" (chap. 1). In both cases, the woman appears first as an object, and Edna, whether she "is" herself or the walking sunshade that contains her, is presented as she seems to Léonce: valuable, even treasured, but nevertheless, a *thing* to be guarded rather than a person to be heard or heeded. Even this early in her novel, however, and even while acknowledging her debt to Flaubert, Chopin swerves from him by emphasizing this last point. For where the French novelist creates sympathy for Charles with his devastating portrait of the first Madame Bovary, a skinny, pimpled Jocasta who is not only old enough to be the young doctor's mother but had been chosen for him by his mother, Chopin immediately characterizes Léonce as an impatient businessman who scrutinizes his wife for sunburn "as one looks at a valuable piece of personal property which has suffered some damage" (chap. 1).

Most of **The Awakening** is told from Edna's perspective, with occasional editorial interpolations from the narrator, but despite its unrepresentative point of view and its air of almost impressionistic improvisation, this opening chapter constitutes a surprisingly complete introduction to the problems and personae of the novel. As an overture, in fact, it includes many of the major le-

itmotifs of the work to follow: symbolic objects (houses, clothing, jewelry, food); symbolic activities (piano playing, swimming, housecleaning, gambling); symbolic figures, both human and inhuman (the birds, the lady in black, the twins, Edna and Robert, Mr. Pontellier, Madame Lebrun); symbolic places (the Gulf, the beach, the city, the summer colony on Grand Isle), and crucial relationships (husbands and wives, mothers and children).

First encountered here, most of these ultimately extraordinary elements appear as vividly physical as objects in a painting by Renoir or Seurat. It is only as one scene dissolves into another, as the narrative point of view gradually enters Edna's strengthening consciousness, and as objects and activities insistently recur, like parts of a protracted dream, that they gain what eventually becomes an almost uncanny significance. Porches and pianos, mothers and children, skirts and sunshades—these are the props of domesticity, the key properties of what in the nineteenth century was called "woman's sphere," and it is in this sphere, on the edge of a blue gulf, that Edna Pontellier is securely caged when she first appears in the novel that will tell her story. In a larger sense, however, she is confined in what is not only literally a "woman's sphere" but also, symbolically speaking, a Woman's House, a place to which, in civilized as in primitive cultures, women are ritually consigned at crucial times in their lives.[46] Here, therefore, every object and figure has both a practical domestic function and a female symbolic significance.

The self-abnegating "mother-women" who seem "to prevail that summer at Grand Isle" (chap. 4), the mutually absorbed young lovers who always appear in the neighborhood of the sepulchrally religious lady in black, Edna's own children trailed by their omnipresent quadroon nurse with her "faraway meditative air," imperious Mademoiselle Reisz in her "rusty black lace" (chap. 9), the Farival twins "always clad in the virgin's colors" (chap. 9), the skirt-dancing little girl in black tulle, even Edna herself sharing out her husband's gift of *friandises*—all seem like faintly grotesque variations on the figures from *La Vie d'une femme* who appear in Charlotte Brontë's *Villette* (1853): the young girl, the bride, the mother, the widow. That the *pension* in which all these women have gathered is ruled by the pretty widow Madame Lebrun, who sews and oversees in a light airy room with a view at the top of the house, seems quite appropriate. At the same time, however, it seems equally appropriate that the novel opens with the comical curse of the caged parrot—*"Allez vous-en! Allez vous-en! Sapristi!"*—and with the information that this bird also speaks "a language which nobody understood, unless it was the mocking bird that hung on the other side of the door" (chap. 1). For these birds together prefigure both Edna's restlessness and her irony, her awakening desire for freedom and her sardonic sense that freedom may ultimately be meaningless, as well as what the world sees as the incomprehensibility of the language in which she struggles to tell the tale of her desire.

Before these problems are fully stated, however, Chopin begins to explore her heroine's summer of discontent through a series of "realistic" interactions between Edna and her husband. Indeed, though the technique of these exchanges may be derived in part from French writers like Flaubert and Maupassant, the scenes themselves are most thematically indebted to the female literary tradition in English of which Kate Chopin was also an ambivalent heiress. Thus, depicting Léonce's casual self-absorption and Edna's mild rebelliousness, the narrator of *The Awakening* at first seems primarily concerned to represent with Austenian delicacy a marriage on the edge of (George) Eliotian fissures. Pontellier is not, of course, either a Casaubon or a Grandcourt, but that seems to be Chopin's revisionary point. As she depicts his imperiousness in swift understated domestic episodes—the scene in chapter three when he wakes Edna and the children, for instance, or his offhand gifts of money and *friandises*—Chopin shows that he, too, is possessed by the possessive male will which speaks differently but equally in the tyrannical husbands of *Middlemarch* (1871-72) and *Daniel Deronda* (1876).

At the novel's start, therefore, Edna's "awakening" is both domestic and prosaic. Like Dorothea Brooke and Gwendolyn Harleth, she awakens from the romantic dreams of girlhood first to find herself a married woman and then to find that the meaning of marriage is quite different from what she had supposed. Like another nineteenth-century heroine, Emily Brontë's Catherine Earnshaw Linton, she experiences what Chopin calls "an indescribable oppression" which seems to come at least in part from her sense of herself as, in Brontë's words, "the wife of a stranger; an exile, and outcast . . . from what had been [her] world." For when, like the subject of one of Emily Dickinson's poems, she rose to "His Requirements" and took on "the honorable work of Woman and of Wife," she seems to have accepted a confinement that excludes all visions of "Amplitude and Awe."[47]

For George Eliot's comparatively docile Dorothea and her chastened Gwendolyn, even for Emily Brontë's more satanically ambitious Catherine, such a recognition of domestic entrapment, along with its corollary spiritual diminution, is the product of a long process of social reconciliation that must ultimately end in these heroines accepting their own comparative powerlessness. For Edna, however, whose author is struggling both to reinscribe and to revise the insights of her precursors, this maritally induced recognition of "her position in the universe as a human being, and . . . her relations as an individual to the world within and about her" (chap. 6) presages a more complicated, more metaphysical awakening to the visionary intimations both of her own selfhood and her own sexuality.

To be sure, once she has left her husband's bed to sit on the porch and listen to "the everlasting voice of the sea," Edna has already, like Eliot's and Brontë's heroines, acquired what her author ironically calls "more wisdom than the Holy Ghost is usually pleased to vouchsafe to any woman" (chap. 6). But, like Emily Dickinson, Chopin seeks to record not only the body's rebellion at confinement but the soul's "moments of Escape" (J.512), along with the visions of power that empower such escapes. In addition, because she is a fiction writer, she wants to create a narrative that will enact those visions. After Edna's first prosaic discoveries of spiritual uneasiness, therefore, her "awakenings" become increasingly fantastic and poetic, stirrings of the imagination's desire for "Amplitude" and "Awe" rather than protests of the reason against unreasonable constraint.

Paradoxically, it is just Edna's realistic awakenings to domestic confinement and her domestic confinement itself which make possible these later, more visionary awakenings. Specifically, Edna awakens to the possibilities as well as the problems of "her position in the universe" because she has come to spend the summer in what is both literally and figuratively a female colony, a sort of Herland. For Madame Lebrun's *pension* on Grand Isle is very much a woman's place, not only because it is owned by a woman and dominated by "mother-women" but also because, as in many summer colonies, its principal inhabitants are actually women and children whose husbands and fathers visit only on weekends. It is no doubt for this reason that, as Chopin observes, "that summer at Grand Isle [Edna] had begun to loosen a little the mantle of reserve that had always enveloped her" (chap. 7) and had begun to do so under "the influence," first, of the sensual Adèle Ratignolle and, later, of the more severe Mademoiselle Reisz.

From the eighteenth century on, middle-class women's culture has often been fragmented by the relegation of each wife to a separate household, by the scattering of such households to genteel suburbs, and by the rituals of politeness that codified interchanges between the ladies of these separate households.[48] While husbands joined together in a public community of men, women were isolated in private parlors or used, as Thorstein Veblen observed, in stylized public appearances, as conspicuous consumers to signify their husbands' wealth.[49] Only a few situations, most notably the girls' school and the summer hotel, offered the isolated lady any real chance to participate in a community of women. And, as *The Awakening* shows, for married women of Edna Pontellier's age and class, the communal household of the vacation hotel provided a unique opportunity to live closely with other women and to learn from them.[50] Our use of the word "colony" is, therefore, deliberately ambiguous. For if a summer colony like Madame Lebrun's *pension* is a place where women have been colonized—that is, confined by the men who possess them—it is also a place where women have established an encampment of their own, an outpost of the dream queendom that Charlotte Perkins Gilman was eventually to imagine in *Herland*.

Finally, then, Nancy Cott's punning use of the phrase "the Bonds of Womanhood" is also useful here.[51] For in the close-knit summer colony locks become links: bonds in the negative sense of "fetters" gradually give way to bonds in the positive sense of "ties." This transformation of bondage into bonding makes it possible for both Adèle Ratignolle, the "mother-woman," and her antithesis, Mademoiselle Reisz, the spinster-artist, to facilitate Edna's passage into the metaphorically divine sexuality that is *her* fated and unique identity. Responding to Adèle's questions and caresses in chapter seven, for instance, Edna begins to comprehend the quest for significant desire that has shaped her life. Similarly, responding in chapter nine to the implicit challenge posed by Mademoiselle Reisz's music, Edna becomes conscious that "the very passions themselves were aroused within her soul, swaying it, lashing it, as the waves daily beat upon her . . . body."

The oceanic imagery embedded in Chopin's description of Edna's response to Mademoiselle Reisz's music is neither casual nor coincidental; rather, it suggests yet another agency through which Madame Lebrun's predominately female summer colony on Grand Isle awakens this Creole Bovary. For Chopin's Aphrodite, like Hesiod's, is born from the sea, and born because the colony where she comes to consciousness is situated, like so many places that are significant for women, outside culture, beyond the limits and limitations of the cities where men make history, on one of those magical shores that mark the margin where nature and culture intersect. Here power can flow from outside, from the timelessness or from, in Mircea Eliade's phrase, the "Great Time" that is free of historical constraints,[52] and here, therefore, the sea can speak in a seductive voice, "never ceasing, whispering, clamoring, murmuring, inviting the soul to wander for a spell in abysses of solitude; to lose itself in mazes of inward contemplation" (chap. 6).

It is important, then, that not only Edna's silent dialogues with Mademoiselle Reisz but also her confessional conversations with Adèle Ratignolle incorporate sea imagery. Reconstructing her first childhood sense of selfhood for Adèle, Edna remembers "a meadow that seemed as big as the ocean" in which as a little girl she "threw out her arms as if swimming when she walked, beating the tall grass as one strikes out in the water" (chap. 7). Just as significantly, she speculates that, as she journeyed through this seemingly endless, uncontained and uncontainable grass, she was most likely "running away from prayers, from the Presbyterian service, read in a spirit of gloom by my father that chills me yet to think of." She was fleeing, that is, the interdictions of patriarchal culture, especially of patriarchal theology, and running into the wild openness of nature. Even so early, the story implies, her search for an alternative theology, or at least for an alternative mythology, had begun. In the summer of her awakening on Grand Isle that quest is extended into the more formalized process of learning to swim.

Edna's education in swimming is, of course, symbolic, representing both a positive political lesson in staying afloat and an ambiguously valuable sentimental education in the consequences of getting in over your head. More important, however, is the fact that swimming immerses Edna in an *other* element—an element, indeed, of otherness—in whose baptismal embrace she is renewed, reborn. That Chopin wants to emphasize this aspect of Edna's learning process is made clear by the magical occasion on which her heroine's first independent swim takes place. Following Mademoiselle Reisz's evocative concert, "someone, perhaps it was Robert [Edna's lover-to-be], thought of a bath at that mystic hour and under that mystic moon." Appropriately, then, on this night which sits "lightly upon the sea and land," this night when "the white light of the moon [has] fallen upon the world like the mystery and softness of sleep" (chap. 10), the previously timid Edna begins for the first time to swim, feeling "as if some power of significant import had been given her" and aspiring "to swim far out, where no woman had swum before." Her new strength and her new ambition are fostered by the traditionally female mythic associations of moonlight and water, as well as by the romantic attendance of Robert Lebrun and the erotically "heavy perfume of a field of white blossoms somewhere near."

At the same time, Chopin's description of the waves breaking on the beach "in little foamy crests . . . like slow white serpents" suggests that Edna is swimming not only with new powers but into a kind of alternative paradise, one that depends upon deliberate inversions of conventional theological images, while the author's frequent reminders that this sea is a *Gulf* reinforce our sense that its waters are at least as metaphysical as those of, say, the Golfo Placido in Conrad's *Nostromo* (1904). Thus, even more important than Edna's swim are both its narrative and its aesthetic consequences, twin textual transformations that energize the rest of Chopin's novel. In swimming away from the beach where her prosaic husband watches and waits, Edna drifts away from the shore of her old life, where she had lingered for twenty-eight years, powerless and reticent. As she swims, she struggles not only toward a female paradise but out of one kind of novel—the work of nineteenth-century "realism" she had previously inhabited—and into a new kind of work, a mythic/metaphysical romance that elaborates her female fantasy of paradisal fulfillment.

In a sense these textual transformations can be seen as merely playful fantasies expressed by Robert and Edna as part of a "realistically" rendered flirtation. When closely analyzed, though, they must be understood to have a metaphorical intensity far keener than what would appear to be their mimetic function, and through such intensity they create a ghostly subtextual narrative which persists with imagistic insistence from Edna's baptismal swimming scene in chapter ten through her last, suicidal swim in chapter thirty-nine. For when Edna says "I wonder if any night on earth will ever again be like this one," she is beginning to place herself in a tale that comes poetically "true." Her dialogue with Robert, as the two return from the moonlit Gulf, outlines the first premises of this story. "It is like a night in a dream," she says. "The people about me are like some uncanny, half-human beings. There must be spirits abroad tonight" (chap. 10). Robert's reply elaborates upon this idea. "It is the twenty-eighth of August," he observes, and then explains:

> On the twenty-eighth of August, at the hour of midnight, and if the moon is shining—the moon must be shining—a spirit that has haunted these shores for ages rises up from the Gulf. With its own penetrating vision the spirit seeks some one mortal worthy to hold him company, worthy of being exalted for a few hours into realms of the semicelestials. His search has always hitherto been fruitless, and he has sunk back, disheartened, into the sea. But tonight he found Mrs. Pontellier. Perhaps he will never wholly release her from the spell. Perhaps she will never again suffer a poor, unworthy earthling to walk in the shadow of her divine presence.
>
> [chap. 10]

Fanciful as it seems, this mutual fantasy of Edna's and Robert's is associated both with a change in their relationship and with a change in Edna. Sitting on the porch in the moonlight, the two fall into an erotic silence that seems to be a consequence of the fiction they have jointly created: "No multitude of words could have been more significant than those moments of silence, or more pregnant with the first-felt throbbings of desire" (chap. 10). And the next day, when Edna awakens from her night of transformative dreaming, she finds herself "blindly following whatever impulse moved her, as if she had placed herself in alien hands for direction, and freed her soul of responsibility" (chap. 12).

The scenes that follow—Edna's awakening of Robert (chap. 12), their voyage (again, chap. 12) to the Chênìere Caminada, their attendance at church (chap. 13), Edna's nap at Madame Antoine's cottage (again, chap. 13), and their return to Grand Isle (chap. 14)—constitute a miniature fable of further transformation, a sort of wistful adult fairy tale that lies at the heart of this desirous but ultimately sardonic fantasy for adult women. Journeying across the gulf to Mass on the nearby island called Chênìere Caminada—the island of live oaks—Edna and Robert find themselves in the surreal company of the lovers, the lady in black, and a barefooted Spanish girl, Robert's sometime girlfriend, with the allegorically theological name of *Mariequita*.[53]

Yet, despite this society, Edna feels as if she were being borne away from some anchorage which had held her fast, whose chains had been "loosening" (chap. 12), and together with Robert she meditates on "pirate gold" and on yet another voyage, this one to the legendary island of "Grande Terre," where they will "climb up the hill to the old fort and look at the little wriggling gold snakes and watch the lizards sun themselves." When she finally arrives at the "quaint little Gothic church of Our Lady of Lourdes," therefore, she is overcome by "a feeling of oppression and drowsiness." Like Mariequita, the Church of Our Lady of Lourdes is named for the wrong goddess; and Edna struggles, as she did when "running away from prayers" through the Kentucky meadow, to escape its "stifling atmosphere . . . and reach the open air."

Everything that happens after Edna leaves the church further implies that she has abandoned the suffocation of traditional Christian (that is, patriarchal) theology for the rituals of an alternative (female and feminist) religion. Attended by Robert, she strolls across the "low, drowsy island," stopping once, almost ceremonially, to drink water that a "mild-faced Acadian" is drawing from a well. At "Madame Antoine's cot," again almost ceremonially, she undresses, bathes, and lies down "in the very center of [a] high, white bed," where, like a revisionary Sleeping Beauty, she sleeps for almost a whole day. When she awakens, for perhaps the most crucial time in this novel of perpetual "awakening," she wonders, as if she were a female Rip Van Winkle. "How many years have I slept? . . . The whole island seems changed. A new race of beings must have sprung up . . . and when did our people from Grand Isle disappear from the earth?" (chap. 13).

Again, almost ritually, Edna bathes, and then she eats what appear to be two sacramental meals. First, she enters a room where she finds that though "no one was there . . . there was a cloth spread upon the table that stood against the wall, and a cover was laid for one, with a crusty brown loaf and a bottle of wine beside the plate." She bites "a piece from the brown loaf, tearing it with strong, white teeth," and drinks some of the wine. Then, after this solitary communion, she dines *à deux* with Robert, who serves her "no mean repast." Finally, as the sun sets, she and Robert sit reverently at the feet of fat matriarchal Madame Antoine, who tells them "legends of the Baratarians and the sea," so that, as the moon rises, Edna imagines she can hear "the whispering voices of dead men and the click of muffled gold" (chap. 13).

Having bathed, slept, feasted, communed, and received quasi-religious instruction, Edna seems to have entered a fictive world, a realm of gold where extraordinary myths are real and ordinary reality is merely mythical. Yet of course the pagan paradise into which she has been initiated is quite incompatible with the postulates of gentility and Christianity by which her "real" world lives. Metaphorically speaking, Edna has become Aphrodite, or at least an ephebe of that goddess. But what can be—must be—her fate? Shadowing her earlier "realism" with the subtextual romance she has developed in these chapters of swimming and boating, sleeping and eating, Chopin devotes the rest of her novel to examining with alternate sadness and sardonic verve the sequence of oppressions and exaltations that she imagines would have befallen any late-nineteenth-century woman who experienced such a fantastic transformation. If Aphrodite, or at least Phaedra, were reborn as a fin-de-siècle New Orleans housewife, says Chopin, Edna Pontellier's fate would be her fate.[54]

* * *

The rest of *The Awakening* is primarily a logical elaboration of the consequences of Edna's mythic metamorphosis. Having awakened to her "true" self—that is, to an apparently more authentic way of formulating her identity—Edna begins "daily casting aside that fictitious self which we assume like a garment with which to appear before the world" (chap. 19). Yet as the episodes on the Chênière Caminada reveal, neither she nor her author are eschewing fictions and fantasies altogether. Rather, Chopin has allowed the moon, the sea, the female summer colony, and Madame Antoine to recreate Edna Pontellier as a quasi-mythic character in search of a story that can accommodate her and her power. That such a tale will be both hard to find and hard to tell, however, is revealed almost at once by Robert Lebrun's abrupt departure from Grand Isle. Though he is the would-be lover of a newly incarnated goddess, he experiences himself as Hippolytus to Edna's Phaedra, Tristan to her Isolde, even Léon to her Emma, and thus he conscientiously strives to do what is both morally and fictionally "right," assuming that because he is a "good" man and not a seducer, the traditional plot in which he imagines himself enmeshed now calls for renunciation.

By the end of the novel, Edna will have created a different story, one in which she would have Robert play Adonis to her Aphrodite: "no longer one of Mr. Pontellier's possessions to dispose of or not," she will declare that, like the Queen of Love, "I give myself where I choose" (chap. 36), as if dramatizing Victoria Woodhull's assertion that "I will love whom I may [and] neither you nor any law you can make shall deter me." But in chapter fifteen, as Chopin's heroine struggles toward such a new project, she finds herself incapable of proposing any serious plot alternatives. She does notice, though, that Robert has announced his plans "in a high voice and with a lofty air [like] some gentlemen on the stage." Perhaps for this reason, she retires to her cottage to tell her children a story which she does not—evidently cannot—end, so that "instead of soothing, it excited them . . . [and] she left them in heated argument, speculating about the conclusion of the tale" (chap. 15).

The tale of Edna's own life moves just as haltingly to its strange conclusion. As she gradually becomes aware that she is "seeking herself and finding herself," she attempts with increasing intensity to discard, deny, and even destroy the social conventions by which she has lived: her wedding ring, her "reception day," even her "charming home" that has been so well-stocked with Mr. Pontellier's "household gods." Yet though she stamps on her ring, "striving to crush it, . . . her small boot heel [does] not make an indenture, not a mark upon the little glittering circlet" (chap. 14). And though she plots to move out of her big house on Esplanade Street into a smaller cottage nearby, a home of her own which she fictionalizes as the "Pigeon House," her husband counters with a fiction of his own "concerning the remodeling of his home, changes which he had long contemplated, and which he desired carried forward during his temporary absence" (chap. 32).

Edna's painting, her gambling, and her visits to the races, as well as her relationships with Mademoiselle Reisz and Adèle Ratignolle, with the Flaubertian Alcée Arobin (clearly a sort of Rodolphe) and his friends Mr. and Mrs. Highcamp, constitute similar efforts at revisionary self-definition. Painting, for instance, lets her try to recreate both her present and her past in more satisfactory forms. Mademoiselle Reisz brings her closer to Robert, and to the oceanic passions and poetic ideas that had inspired her feelings for him from the first. Adèle Ratignolle reinforces her sense of the "blind contentment" implicit in the sequestered domesticity she has rejected (chap. 18). Her trips to the racetrack remind her of the freedom of her Kentucky childhood, when the "race-horse

was a friend and intimate associate" (chap. 25), a spirit like herself, let loose in illimitable fields. And her rapidly developing sexual relationship with Arobin acts "like a narcotic upon her," offering her a "cup of life" (chap. 28) that drugs and drains her awakening egotism even while her choice to drink it manifests the new freedom she is trying to taste.

Yet none of these activities or relationships succeeds in yielding an open space in the plot where Edna finds herself. In fact, precisely because her entanglements have a social reality that gives them plausibility as therapeutic possibilities, none is equal to the intensity of what is by now quite clearly Edna's metaphysical desire, the desire that has transformed her and torn her away from her ordinary life into an extraordinary state where she has become, as Chopin's original title for the novel put it, "a solitary soul." Stranded in this state, having been visited by the Holy Ghost of the allegorically resonant "Gulf," who rarely vouchsafes so much "ponderous" wisdom "to any woman," she can only struggle to make her own persuasive fictions, like the story she tells at a party about "a woman who paddled away with her lover one night in a pirogue and never came back. They were lost amid the Baratarian Islands, and no one ever heard of them or found trace of them from that day to this" (chap. 23).

As Edna eventually realizes, even such a fiction betrays desire into the banalities of conventional romance, so that ultimately her dinner party in chapter thirty is the best, the most authentically self-defining, "story" she can tell. Here she actually enacts the part of the person she has metaphorically become: "the regal woman, the one who rules, who looks on, who stands alone." Yet, as the sadness which shadows this scene implies, in the context of the alternative theology through which Chopin mythologizes this "solitary" heroine's life, the story of Edna's dinner party is the tale of a Last Supper, a final transformation of will and desire into bread and wine, flesh and blood, before the "regal woman's" inevitable crucifixion by a culture in which a regenerated Aphrodite has no viable role. More specifically, it is a Last Supper that precedes Edna's betrayal by a plot that sets both Adèle Ratignolle, the "mother-woman," and Robert Lebrun, the stereotypical lover, against her. In one way or another, each of these characters will remind her of her instrumentality—Adèle, exhausted by childbirth, whispering that she must "think of the children," and Robert passionately envisioning a transaction in which Mr. Pontellier might "set" Edna "free" to belong to *him* (chap. 36).

Finally, therefore, Chopin's heroine can think of only one way "to elude them," to become absolutely herself, and that is through her much-debated last swim. Once again, however, our interpretation of this denouement depends on our understanding of the mythic subtextual narrative that enriches it. Certainly if we see Edna's decision to swim into the sea's "abysses of solitude" as simply a "realistic" action, we are likely to disapprove of it, to consider it, as a number of critics have, "a defeat and a regression, rooted in a self-annihilating instinct, in a romantic incapacity to accommodate . . . to the limitations of reality."[55] But, if we attend to the metaphoric patterns of Chopin's novel, Edna's last swim may not seem to be a suicide—that is, a death—at all, or, if it is a death, it is a death associated with a resurrection, a sort of pagan female Good Friday that promises an Aphroditean Easter. In fact, because of the way it is presented, Edna's supposed suicide enacts not a refusal to accept the limitations of reality but a subversive questioning of the limitations of both reality and "realism." For, swimming away from the white beach of Grand Isle, from the empty summer colony and the oppressive imperatives of marriage and maternity, Edna swims, as the novel's last sentences tell us, not into death but back into her own life, back into the imaginative openness of her childhood.

It is notable, in this regard, that in depicting Edna's last swim Chopin swerved from precursors like Flaubert and Pierre Louÿs and also charted a very different path from the ones chosen by such contemporaries as Haggard and Schreiner or such a descendant as Edith Wharton. All these writers not only show the desirous Aphroditean woman dead but actually linger over the details of her mortification. Flaubert, for instance, follows his censorious extreme unction with horrifying visions of Emma's dead mouth "like a black hole at the bottom of her face," pouring forth "black liquid . . . as if she were vomiting" (241-42). In *Aphrodite,* Louÿs undercuts his Chrysis's triumphant epiphany as Aphrodite with a ghastly picture of her corpse, a "thread of blood" flowing from one "diaphanous nostril" and "some emerald-colored spots . . . softly [tinting] the relaxed belly."[56] And as we have seen, Haggard emphasizes the bestial horror into which his Venus/Persephone "devolves" as she dies.

Similarly, even though Schreiner and Wharton are far gentler with their heroines, both linger with a certain necrophiliac interest over their protagonists' lovely remains. After Lyndall expires—narcissistically studying herself in a mirror—Schreiner comments that the "dead face that the glass reflected was a thing of marvellous beauty and tranquillity," while in *The House of Mirth,* brooding on the dead "semblance of Lily Bart" (who is in any case, as we shall later show, a less Aphroditean woman than any of these other heroines), Wharton imagines Lily's "estranged and tranquil face" definitively motionless and thereby, through that motionlessness, offering her watching lover "the word which made all clear."[57] By contrast, Chopin never allows Edna Pontellier to become fixed, immobilized. Neither perfected nor corrupted, she is swimming when we last see her; nor does she ever, in Dickinson's words, "Stop for Death." To be sure, we are told that "her arms and legs were growing tired," that "exhaustion was pressing upon and overpowering her" (chap. 39). It is clear enough that both reality and "realism" will contain her by fatiguing and drowning her. Yet Chopin seems determined to redeem Edna through a regeneration of myth.

Thus, as she enters the water for her last swim, this transformed heroine finally divests herself of "the unpleasant, pricking garments" of her old life as a "real" woman—a wife, mother, and mistress—and stands "naked under the sky . . . like some new-born creature, opening its eyes in a familiar world that it had never known." Together, her ceremonial nakedness, the paradoxically unknown familiarity of the world she is entering, and the "foamy wavelets [that curl and coil] like serpents about her ankles" (chap. 39) tell us that she is journeying not just toward rebirth but toward a genre that intends to propose new realities for women by providing new mythic paradigms through which women's lives can be understood. Even in the last sentences of Chopin's novel, Edna Pontellier is still moving. *And how, after all, do we know that she ever dies?* What critics have called her "suicide" is simply our interpretation of her motion, our "realistic" idea about the direction in which she is swimming. Yet as Chopin's last words—incorporating a memory from Edna's childhood—tell us, that direction is toward the mythic, the pagan, the aphrodisiac. "There was the hum of bees, and the musky odor of pinks filled the air." Defeated, even crucified by the "reality" of nineteenth-century New Orleans, Chopin's resurrected Venus may be returning to Cyprus or Cythera.[58]

* * *

This reading of *The Awakening* is, of course, hyperbolic, so that it is certainly not intended to displace those interpretations which honor the text's more obvious aims. Rather, it is meant to suggest the tension between realistic and mythic aesthetic strategies that complicates Chopin's brilliant novel. More, it is meant to underscore the literary history as well as the poetical significance of the goddess Aphrodite in the nineteenth and twentieth centuries. Finally, it is intended to clarify the dialectical relationship into which Chopin, as an innovative feminist mythmaker, entered not only with ancestresses like the Brontës, Dickinson, and Eliot but also with such crucial male precursors as Flaubert, Whitman, and Swinburne.

If we once again compare Chopin's novel to Flaubert's *Madame Bovary,* we can see that where the French writer censures what he considers the destructive, even nihilistic power of the female imagination, Chopin honors what is positive in that power, never copying Flaubert (the way Cather and others thought she did) but always responding to him. For Flaubert, water is, as D. L. Demorest noted in 1931, the "symbol of Venus the delectable" (as it is for Chopin), but this means in Flaubert's case that throughout *Madame Bovary* "images of fluidity" dissolve and resolve to "evoke all that is disastrous in love." Emma's girlish sentimentality, for example, is represented in what the writer himself called "milky oceans of books about castles and troubadours" while the final horror of her imagination pours as black liquid, a sort of morbid ink, from her dead mouth, as if she were vomiting the essential fluid which had inscribed the romantic fictions that killed her and would eventually destroy her uxorious husband.[59]

Such Flaubertian images slowly filter the idea of the fluid female imagination—the idea, that is, of female fluency—through what Jean-Paul Sartre called "a realism more spiteful than detached," and it is possible to speculate that they are general defensive strategies against the developing cultural power of women as well as specific defenses by which Flaubert armored himself against Louise Colet, a woman of letters on whom he felt helplessly dependent, strategies, to quote Sartre again, "in the diplomacy of Flaubert with regard to this pertinacious poetess."[60] Whatever the source of Flaubert's anxieties, however, Chopin defends herself and other literary women vigorously against such Flaubertian defenses, for she consistently revises his negative images of female "fluency" to present not a spitefully "realistic" but a metaphysically lyric version of the seductive mazes of the sea from which her Aphrodite is

born, substituting the valorizations of myth and fantasy for the devaluations of "realism."

In this revisionary struggle, Chopin was aided by aesthetic strategies learned from other male precursors. From Whitman and Swinburne, for instance, she learned to imagine the sea the way she did—as, implicitly, "a great sweet mother" uttering "the low and delicious word 'death'" even while rocking her heroine in life-giving "billowy drowse."[61] In a sense, in fact, her Edna Pontellier is as much a cousin of the twenty-eight-year-old "twenty-ninth bather" in Whitman's "Song of Myself" as she is a niece of Flaubert's Emma Bovary. "Handsome and richly dressed," like Whitman's woman, Edna has had "twenty-eight years of womanly life, and all so lonesome," hiding "aft the blinds of the window," and now, "dancing and laughing," she comes along the beach to bathe in the waters of life. Yet again, much as she had learned from Whitman, Chopin departs from him to create a woman who does not enter the sea to "seize fast" to twenty-eight young men but rather to seize and hold fast to herself. Similarly, she revises Swinburne to create an ocean that is not simply an other—a "fair, green-girdled mother"—but also a version of self, intricately veined with "mazes of inward contemplation" and sacramental precisely because emblematic of such subjectivity.[62]

Because of this last gesture, the sea of Chopin's *Awakening* has much in common with the mystically voluptuous ocean Emily Dickinson imagines in the love poem "Wild Nights—Wild Nights!" (J.249). For when Dickinson exclaims "Rowing in Eden, / Ah! the Sea! / Might I but moor / Tonight in thee!" she is imagining an ocean of erotic energy that will transform and transport *her,* an ocean that exists *for* her and in some sense *is* her. More, in identifying this sea with Eden, she is revising the vocabulary of traditional Christian theology so as to force it to accommodate the urgency of female desire. Such a revision is exactly the one that Chopin performed throughout *The Awakening.* Thus where the extreme unction that Flaubert intones over the corpse of Emma Bovary functions as a final exorcism of the ferocity of the imagining and desirous woman, Chopin's redefined sacraments of bread and wine or crimson cocktails function, like Dickinson's, to vindicate female desire in yet another way. For in creating a heroine as free as Aphrodite, a "regal woman" who "stands alone" and gives herself where she "pleases," Chopin was taking an important step in the historical female struggle both to imagine an independently desirous female self and to envision a deity who would rule and represent a strong female community, a woman's colony transformed into a woman's country.

To be sure, as we suggested in the discussion of *She,* men from Wagner (in *Tannhäuser*) to Baudelaire (writing on Wagner), Swinburne (in "Laus Veneris," "Sapphics," and by implication his version of "Phaedra"), William Morris (in "The Hill of Venus"), Beardsley (in *Venus and Tannhäuser*), and Pierre Louÿs (in *Aphrodite* and *Songs of Bilitis*) had begun, almost obsessively, to dramatize encounters with the goddess of love, who in the past, as Paul Friedrich notes in his study of *The Meaning of Aphrodite,* had often been "avoided" by poets and scholars because they found her female erotic autonomy both "alarming" and "alluring."[63] But for the most part these aesthetically revolutionary nineteenth-century artists used Aphrodite in the same way Haggard used Ayesha and Flaubert used Emma Bovary—to objectify new fears about female power.

Wagner's Tannhäuser, for instance, only escapes damnation—after he has sung of his "unquenchable" longing for the "honeyed fascination" of Venus—when the saintly Elizabeth sacrifices herself to save his soul; Swinburne's Tannhäuser, imprisoned in the Venusberg, feels himself to be confined in "the sea's panting mouth of dry desire" and knows that "sudden serpents hiss across [his Venus's] hair"; Morris's hero sees his Venus as "a curse unto the sons of men" and falls from her embrace into "a night whereof no tongue can tell"; Beardsley's Tannhäuser is first attired, at the Venusberg, in a "dear little coat of pigeon rose silk that hung loosely about his hips, and showed off the jut of his behind to perfection" and then "as a woman," in a costume in which, with humiliating irony, he "looked like a Goddess."[64] For Chopin, however, as for such feminist descendants as Isadora Duncan and H. D., Aphrodite/Venus became a radiant symbol of the liberation of desire that turn-of-the-century women had begun to allow themselves to desire.

The source of Aphrodite's significance for this revisionary company of women is not hard to discern. Neither primarily wife (like Hera), mother (like Demeter), nor daughter (like Athena), Aphrodite is, and has her erotic energy, for herself. As Friedrich observes, moreover, all her essential characteristics—her connections with birds and water, her affinity for young mortal men, her nakedness, her goldenness, and even her liminality, as well as her erotic sophistication—empower her in one way or another.[65] Her dove- or swan-

drawn chariot enables her to travel between earth and sky, while her sea-birth places her between earth and sea. Naked yet immortal, she moves with ease between natural and supernatural, human and inhuman, nature and culture. Golden and decked in gold, she is associated with sunset and sunrise, the liminal hours of awakening or drowsing that mediate between night and day, dream and reality.

Appropriately, then, Aphrodite is the patron goddess of Sappho, whom Virginia Woolf called "the supreme head of song" and whose lyric imagination was fostered by unique erotic freedom.[66] And because this goddess became a crucial image of female divinity during the fin de siècle, Kate Chopin made her a model for a "regal," sea-born, gold-clad, bird-haunted woman whose desire for freedom, and for a younger man, edged her (first) out of a large patriarchal mansion into a small female cottage and (then) across the shadowline that separates the clothing of culture from the nakedness of nature. Violent though it was, after all, the origin of the queen of love might have seemed compelling to a protofeminist like Chopin. According to Hesiod, Aphrodite was born when the father god Ouranos was castrated by his son Kronos at the behest of the mother goddess Gaia: after his torn-off genitals were cast into the sea, "shining white *aphros,* / 'foam' arose from the flesh of the god, and in this a girl / came into being . . . a revered and beautiful goddess."[67]

* * *

It is no coincidence that Kate Chopin imagined her Venus rising from the foam of a ceremonial dinner party in 1899, the same year that another American artist, Isadora Duncan, was beginning to dance the dances of Aphrodite in London salons while the classicist Jane Ellen Harrison, who would soon recover the matriarchal origins of ancient Greek religion, chanted Greek lyrics in the background. The daughter of a "bold-minded St. Louis Irish girl about the same age as . . . Kate Chopin," Duncan had always been affected by her own birth "under the star of Aphrodite," and later she was to sit "for days before the *Primavera,* the famous painting of Botticelli," and create a dance

> in which I endeavored to realise the soft and marvelous movements emanating from it; the soft undulation of the flower-covered earth, the circle of nymphs and the flight of the Zephyrs, all assembling about the central figure, half Aphrodite, half madonna, who indicates the procreation of spring in one significant gesture.

Musing on the "sweet, half-seen pagan life, where Aphrodite gleamed through the form of the gracious but more tender Mother of Christ," this prophetess of the beauty of female nakedness was struggling, as Chopin had, to see the power of the pagan through the constraints of the Christian and the triumph of the female through the power of the pagan.[68] She was striving, as H. D. later would, to "relight the flame" of "Aphrodite, holy name," and of "Venus, whose name is kin / / to venerate, / venerator."[69] And she was laboring, as Chopin had, to define the indefinable mythic essence of "a familiar world that [she] had never known."

Like Chopin's and H. D.'s, too, Duncan's revisionary program marked an apex of feminist confidence in the erotic authority of Aphrodite. But even as these artists sought to reimagine the ancient powers of the queen of love, some women who were their contemporaries or descendants had begun to reiterate the old feminine (and feminist) mistrust of female sensuality. By the nineties, for instance, that once "terrible syren" Victoria Woodhull was righteously denying that she had ever advocated free love, and by 1920 a dark and bitter vision of Venus appeared at the center of Willa Cather's "Coming Aphrodite!"[70] In part a retelling of Louÿs's *Aphrodite,* this brilliantly ironic tale also so intensively subverts the allusive terms of **The Awakening** that it might almost be considered an extension of Cather's earlier censorious review of Chopin's novel.[71] Specifically, Cather's story portrays an ambitious Illinois farm girl named *Edna* Bowers who, along with studying "Sapho" [sic] and "Mademoiselle de Maupin" (30), has resolved to become a great actress-singer called "Eden Bower"—a name drawn from Christina Rossetti's equally censorious Victorian poem about Eve's sinfulness and from Dante Gabriel Rossetti's frightening vision of Lilith and the serpent dominating "Eden Bower" in a poem of that title.[72]

Willful and wily, Edna/Eden has casually stepped outside ordinary social confinement and made herself erotically independent. When Cather's story begins, she is being kept (entirely for her own convenience and in the furtherance of her career) by a handily absent Chicago millionaire in a New York apartment next door to a studio occupied by Don Hedger, a struggling painter. Tracing the stages of their romance, Cather splits Chopin's erotic and artistic Edna into two characters: the metaphysically awakened painter, who falls in love with Eden by peering at her through a hole in the wall of his closet, and the physically awakened Eden, whom he watches

while, like a latterday Isadora, she exercises naked before a mirror until, like both Edna and Isadora, she takes on a mythic radiance. Thus, at the tale's intensest, Hedger thinks of her body "as never having been clad, or as having worn the stuffs and dyes of all the centuries but his own." And "for him [Eden has] no geographical associations unless with Crete, or Alexandria, or Veronese's Venice. She [is] the immortal conception, the perennial theme" (22).

Throughout the tale, however, Cather hints that when this unclothed Aphrodite ceases to be paradigmatic and becomes personal, or, to put it differently, when she refuses to be merely an artwork—a "conception" or a "theme"—and asserts herself as an autonomous being, she becomes not an embodiment of Eden but a troublesome and anti-Edenic Eve. Early on, for instance, she threatens Hedger's masculinity by scorning his allegorically phallic bulldog "Caesar" (who does, in fact, "seize her" and is in return seized and silenced by his master, who is himself seized by desire). Later, when Hedger tells an extravagant story about a sexually voracious Aztec princess who gelds a captive prince and destroys a series of lovers, we understand the fable to be a monitory one: the power of female desire may be castrating, even murderous. Finally, therefore, Cather separates Hedger and Eden with the suggestion that Eden's desirousness also implies a greed that would ruin the career of Hedger, the "true" artist. And indeed, by the end of the tale this anti-Edenic Eve's ambition has led to a death of the soul even more terrible than the dissolution Cather associated with Edna Pontellier's erotic dreams.

Now a major international star, scheduled to sing in an operatic version of Louÿ's *Aphrodite,* Eden has learned that Hedger, whom she hasn't seen in twenty years, has become an originatory figure, "decidedly an influence in art," and it is plain that he has become this by freeing himself from her influence. As she drives off in her luxurious car, her face turns

> hard and settled, like a plaster cast; so a sail, that has been filled by a strong breeze, behaves when the wind suddenly dies. Tomorrow night the wind would blow again, and this mask would be the golden face of Aphrodite. But a "big" career takes its toll, even with the best of luck.
>
> [63]

Cather's point seems clear enough: as in Louÿs's novel and as in Hedger's fable of "The Forty Lovers of the Queen," female erotic autonomy, symbolized by the golden nakedness of Aphrodite, is doomed to rigidify, not only repelling any lover unlucky enough to remain captive but also reifying the shining queen of love herself. As D. G. Rossetti said of Lilith in his "Eden Bower," it might be said of *this* Eden Bower that "Not a drop of her blood was human, / But she was made like a soft sweet woman."[73]

There is no doubt that Willa Cather had a number of personal motives for imagining a story like "Coming, Aphrodite!" which reinterprets Aphrodite so bitterly, motives that probably included both a deep distrust of heterosexual desire and a covert identification with the closeted (male) artist who admires and desires the naked girl next door.[74] If we look at the tale as a revisionary critique of *The Awakening,* however, we can see that the creator of Edna/Eden Bower(s) is withdrawing unsympathetically from Chopin's Edna at least in part because that earlier Aphrodite had to swim away from the solid ground of patriarchal reality and die into what was no more than a myth of erotic power. As Mademoiselle Reisz tells Edna, the artist "must possess the courageous soul. . . . The brave soul. The soul that dares and defies" (chap. 21), but Edna, naked and defeated on the beach, is haunted by a bird with a broken wing, "reeling, fluttering, circling disabled down, down to the water" (chap. 38).

Given her own anxieties, Cather must have needed to clarify this problem for herself; and, after all, her ambivalence toward female eroticism was representatively female even while it had personal origins. More, hers were worries that accurately, if paradoxically, summarized Chopin's own wounded reaction to the hostile reviews *The Awakening* received. Thus Cather implicitly decides in "Coming, Aphrodite!" that Edna Pontellier cannot be an artist *because* she is desirous. Art, which requires courage and demands survival, must be left to the (male) Hedgers of this world, who hedge their bets by renouncing desire and protecting themselves against women with a snarling canine Caesar. Yet, as Chopin understood, it is precisely because she is desirous that Edna becomes an artist in the first place, and her art, as at her dinner party, is as much an art of eroticism as it is a "pure" aesthetic activity.

Despite Woodhull's recantation and Cather's skepticism, however, Chopin was not the last feminist to revise patriarchal visions of Aphrodite/Venus. Just two decades after the publication of *The Awakening,* Amy Lowell produced in "Venus Transiens" a love poem to her companion, Ada Russell, which reinvented the image of the goddess of love as an homage to her beloved:

Tell me,
Was Venus more beautiful
Than you are,
When she topped
The crinkled waves,
Drifting shoreward
On her plaited shell?[75]

And more than a half century after Chopin's controversial novel appeared, Muriel Rukeyser clarified at least one strand of the feminist rebelliousness that impelled the fin-de-siècle writer's vision of the second coming of Aphrodite, drawing explicitly upon Hesiod's account of the inception of the goddess to write in "The Birth of Venus" that the queen of love was "born in a / tidal wave of the father's overthrow, / the old rule killed and its mutilated sex."[76]

Yet these feminist visions of Aphroditean empowerment were by no means universal. So recent a writer as Anne Sexton, for instance, could see no way to free herself from the problems that Cather had outlined. In a posthumous volume, *Words for Dr. Y.,* her daughter Linda Gray Sexton printed a piece called "To Like, To Love" in which the poet addresses "Aphrodite, / my Cape Town lady / my mother, my daughter" and admits that, though "I dream you Nordic and six foot tall, / I dream you masked and blood-mouthed," and in the end "you start to cry, / you fall down into a huddle, / you are sick . . . // because you are no one."[77] For women, striving to liberate desire, there was evidently a key moment of Aphroditean rebirth—the neo-Swinburnian moment when Edna enthroned herself in gold satin at the head of a fictive dinner table and Isadora Duncan theatrically brooded before Botticelli's *Primavera*—and then, as Virginia Woolf wrote of the erotic in a slightly different context, "the close withdrew; the hard softened. It was over—the moment."[78] "Realism," implies Cather, may be more than a fictional mode; it may in fact reflect a social reality in which the golden Aphrodite is no more than a metal mask.

A number of male writers, too, became increasingly contemptuous of the ancient goddess of love in these years. Most notably—where such precursors as Wagner, Swinburne, Baudelaire, and even the satiric Beardsley had at least expressed a kind of anxious respect for what they saw as Venus's horrific powers—D. H. Lawrence had his hero, Rupert Birkin, scornfully declare in *Women in Love* (1920) that "Aphrodite is born in the first spasm of universal dissolution" (chap. 14); and Lawrence's persistent portrayals of the "seething electric female ecstasy" of desire that intermittently afflicts characters from Ursula (in *The Rain-*

bow [1915]) and Gudrun (in *Women in Love*) to Kate (in *The Plumed Serpent* [1926]) embody references to the "shining white *aphros*," or "foam" out of which the erotic goddess arose.[79] By the end of his life, moreover, Lawrence had transformed the classical deity into a figure of fun. Railing in *Pansies* (1929) against "The modern Circedom," he asked

> What does she want, volcanic Venus? as she goes
> fuming round?
> What does she want?
> She says she wants a lover, but don't you believe
> her. . . .

and he added sardonically

> How are we going to appease her, maiden and
> mother now a volcano of rage?
> I tell you, the penis won't do it.[80]

At the same time, however, it is significant that among recent poets it was a male artist, Wallace Stevens, who produced one of the most celebratory lyrics about the desire implicit in *The Awakening*'s allusive structure. Stevens's vision may have been facilitated by his freedom from the anxieties that serious identification with a mythic female entails for a woman (as both Chopin and Cather, in their different ways, discovered), and it may also have been fostered by his espousal of a philosophy of existential hedonism which neither Wagner nor Swinburne nor Lawrence would ever have shared. In any case, whatever the reason, when, in "The Paltry Nude Starts on a Spring Voyage" (1919), Stevens's "discontent" goddess, "Tired of the salty harbors," embarks, like Edna Pontellier, on her first voyage out, the twentieth-century poet imagines the kind of second coming of Aphrodite for which Chopin's novel had earlier implicitly yearned. The paltry nude's journey, Stevens insists,

> . . . is meagre play
> In the scurry and water-shine
> As her heels foam—
> Not as when the goldener nude
> Of a later day
>
> Will go, like the centre of sea-green pomp,
> In an intenser calm,
> Scullion of fate,
> Across the spick torrent, ceaselessly,
> Upon her irretrievable way.[81]

Still, because Chopin was a woman writer, her fantasized Aphrodite was at least as different from Stevens's "goldener nude" as Stevens's goddess was from, say, Lawrence's "Volcanic Venus." Chopin, after all, painfully dreamed a surrogate self into the ancient divinity's sacred nakedness. Imagining (even if failing to achieve) transforma-tion, the erotically awakened author of *The Awakening* was haunted in the chamber of the realism she had inherited by her longing for a redemptive Aphrodite, who would go "like the centre of sea-green pomp" into a future of different myths and mythic difference.

Notes

EPIGRAPHS: Baudelaire, "Richard Wagner and Tannhäuser in Paris," in *The Painter of Modern Life and Other Essays,* trans. and ed. Jonathan Mayne (London: Phaidon Press, 1964), pp. 122-23; Swinburne, "Sapphics," in *The Works of Algernon Charles Swinburne* (Philadelphia: David McKay, n.d.), pp. 82-83; Duncan, *My Life* (New York: Liveright, 1927), p. 10; H. D., "Tribute to the Angels," *Collected Poems, 1912-1944,* ed. Louis L. Martz (New York: New Directions, 1983), p. 554.

1. Both quoted in Sachs, *"The Terrible Siren,"* pp. 78-80, 80-81.

2. *The Complete Works of Kate Chopin,* ed. Per Seyersted, with a foreword by Edmund Wilson (Baton Rouge: Louisiana State University Press, 1969), p. 733. Further references to works by Chopin (except *The Awakening*) will be to this edition, and page numbers will be included in the text, preceded by the citation *CW*.

3. Reviews of *The Awakening* in *The Mirror* 9 (May 4, 1899), *The Providence Sunday Journal* (June 4, 1899), and (by Cather) in *The Pittsburgh Leader* (July 8, 1899) are all included in Margaret Culley, ed., *The Awakening: A Norton Critical Edition* (New York: W. W. Norton, 1976), pp. 146, 149, 153.

4. See Per Seyersted, *Kate Chopin* (Oslo: Universitetsforlaget, and Baton Rouge: Louisiana State. University Press, 1969), p. 175.

5. Quoted in Seyersted, p. 176.

6. Quoted in Seyersted, p. 181.

7. See Cather, as quoted in Culley, p. 153.

8. For useful analyses of the distinctions between nineteenth- and twentieth-century feminist attitudes toward female sexuality, see Cott, pp. 41-49, 150-52. Although Cott argues that "Schreiner was also a prophetess of women's sexual release" (p. 41), she adduces statements by a number of early twentieth-century feminists whose radical advocacy of women's "sex rights" aligned their views more nearly with those of Woodhull or Chopin.

9. See Seyersted, p. 33. Seyersted declares that "It was apparently Victoria [Woodhull] that Kate Chopin met," but by the early seventies Woodhull had long been defining herself as "Mrs. Woodhull," whereas her sister, Tennessee Claflin (also known as "Tennie C. Claflin"), went by the name "Miss Claflin." In addition, Tennessee Claflin was always described as "fussy, pretty, talkative," while Woodhull appears to have had a more majestic and commanding presence. For further details about the differences (and similarities) between the notorious sisters, see Sachs, passim.

10. Quoted in Seyersted, p. 51.

11. Review in *The Los Angeles Sunday Times* (June 25, 1899), quoted in Culley, p. 152.

12. Daniel S. Rankin, *Kate Chopin and Her Creole Stories* (Philadelphia: University of Pennsylvania Press, 1932), p. 175.

13. The equation of *fin de siècle* with *fin du globe* is wittily made in Oscar Wilde's *The Picture of Dorian Gray*: "'Fin de siècle,' murmured Sir Henry. 'Fin du globe,' answered his hostess. 'I wish it were *fin du globe*,' said Dorian with a sigh. 'Life is a great disappointment.'" (*The Writings of Oscar Wilde*, 3:326.)

14. On Chopin's reading, see Seyersted, passim, but especially pp. 25 (for her reading of Austen and Charlotte Brontë, among others), 63 (for her familiarity with "Whitman, Flaubert, Zola, Swinburne, and Wilde"), 52 and 101 (for her admiration of Jewett and Freeman), and 206 (for her familiarity with *The Yellow Book*).

15. *At Fault* is included in *The Complete Works of Kate Chopin*, 2:741-880.

16. For "sad and mad and bad," see the review from the *St. Louis Post-Dispatch* (May 20, 1899), quoted in Culley, p. 149.

17. On the New Woman novel, see chap. 2 of this volume as well as Showalter, *A Literature of Their Own*, pp. 182-239; and Lloyd Fernando, *New Women in the Late Victorian Novel*, passim.

18. For a discussion of Chopin's involvement in "local color" writing, see Seyersted, pp. 80-83; although, as we have noted, Chopin did admire Jewett and Freeman, Seyersted cites an interview with Daniel Rankin in observing that "she refused to be considered a local colorist and resented being compared as such to [George Washington] Cable and Grace King" (p. 83).

19. On Chopin's "delightful sketches," see the review from the *Chicago Times-Herald* (June 1, 1899), quoted in Culley, p. 149. For an incisive analysis of one aspect of the social criticism formulated in Chopin's sketches, see Anna Shannon Elfenbein, *Women on the Color Line: Evolving Stereotypes and the Writings of George Washington Cable, Grace King, Kate Chopin* (Charlottesville: University Press of Virginia, 1988), pp. 117-57.

20. Linda Dowling, "The Decadent and the New Woman in the 1890's," *Nineteenth-Century Fiction*, 33:4 (March 1979): 450.

21. Holbrook Jackson, *The Eighteen Nineties: A Review of Art and Ideas at the Close of the Nineteenth Century*, with an intro. by Karl Beckson (1913; New York: Capricorn, 1966), pp. 29-30.

22. For "sex-distinction," see Schreiner, *Stories, Dreams, and Allegories* [London: 1924], pp. 156-59; Carpenter discusses "the sex-passion" (with approval) in chap. 1 of *Love's Coming of Age*.

23. Schreiner, *Stories*, pp. 156-59; but on Schreiner's attitude toward sexuality, see also Weeks, *Sex, Politics and Society*, p. 167: "Influenced both by [Havelock] Ellis and Edward Carpenter, with both of whom she was on close personal relations, Schreiner's work was clearly within the feminist radical tradition which, while recognising 'inherent differences' dictated by reproductive divisions and hence the rationale of separate functions, stressed the importance of female eroticism in its own (not male) terms."

24. Kathryn Oliver, writing in *The Freewoman* (Feb. 25, 1912, p. 252), quoted in Weeks, p. 164.

25. Grant Allen, "The New Hedonism," *Fortnightly Review* (March 1894), quoted in Jackson, p. 28. The "new Hedonism," declares Allen, "was to recreate life, and to save it from [a] harsh, uncomely Puritanism."

26. See Schneir, *Feminism*, p. 154.

27. *Venus and Tannhäuser* is included in Beckson, ed. *Aesthetes*, pp. 9-46.

28. In his portrayal of the extreme unction administered to Emma Bovary, Flaubert describes the priest stroking oil "upon the eyes that had so coveted all worldly goods . . . upon the nostrils that had been so greedy of the warm breeze . . . Upon the mouth that had spoken lies . . . upon the hands that had taken delight in the texture of sensuality . . . upon the soles of the feet, so swift when she had hastened to satisfy her desires." See Gustave Flaubert, *Madame Bovary*, ed. and with a substantially new translation by Paul de Man (New York: Norton Critical Edition, 1965), p. 237. Further references will be to this edition, and page numbers will be included in the text. For Aleister Crowley, see "Ode to Venus Callipyge" and other poems, in Crowley, *White Stains*, ed. John Symonds (London: Duckworth, 1973; first published in 1898 "in an edition of 100 copies, most of which were destroyed in 1924 by H. M. Customs"), p. 50 and passim.

29. Acton (1857, 1865), quoted in Gay, *Education of the Senses*, p. 153.

30. Stanton, in *Elizabeth Cady Stanton, As Revealed in Her Letters, Diary and Reminiscences*, ed. Theodore Stanton and Harriot Stanton Blatch, 2 vols. (1922) 2:183, 210; quoted in Gay, *Education of the Senses*, p. 119.

31. Blackwell, in *The Human Element in Sex: Being a Medical Inquiry into the Relation of Sexual Physiology to Sexual Morality* (1884, 1894), p. 14; quoted in Gay, *Education of the Senses*, p. 159.

32. Mosher's survey is discussed in Gay, *Education of the Senses*, p. 136. Gay also cites a range of other European and American authorities who affirmed the reality of female eroticism: he quotes, for instance, the "eminent Scottish gynecologist, J. Matthews Duncan" as believing that "in women desire and pleasure are in every case present, or are in every case called forth by the proper stimulants" (*Education of the Senses*, p. 135); he notes that the French doctor Auguste Debay thought "women's 'sexual system' is more 'extensive' than the man's; her imagination is livelier, her sensitivity greater. Hence she 'trembles, shudders under the amorous embrace and savors pleasure during the whole time that sexual excitement lasts'" (Gay, *Education of the Senses*, p. 151); and he cites the assertion of the American sociologist Lester Ward that "All desires are alike before nature—, equally pure, equally respectable. . . . Nature knows no shame. She affects no modesty" (Gay, *Education of the Senses*, p. 131).

33. Woodhull is quoted in Sachs, pp. 219, 222-23. For further discussion of the "free love" movement in the nineteenth-century United States, see Hal D. Sears, *The Sex Radicals: Free Love in Victorian America* (Lawrence: The Regents Press of Kansas, 1977), and Taylor Stoehr, *Free Love in America: A Documentary History* (New York: AMS Press, 1979).

34. Carpenter, *Love's Coming of Age*, pp. 26, 9, 22.

35. "More massive and diffuse"; this characterization of Ellis's belief is from Paul Robinson's excellent chapter on the sexologist in Robinson, *The Modernization of Sex: Havelock Ellis, Alfred Kinsey, William Masters and Virginia Johnson* (New York: Harper & Row, 1976), p. 18; significantly (though Robinson does not note this) the concept echoes Auguste Debay's beliefs, as they are reported by Gay (see note 28, above). For the theories of Cixous and Irigaray, see, for example, Cixous in Cixous and Clement, *The Newly Born Woman,* p. 94: "Women have almost everything to write . . . about the infinite and mobile complexity of their becoming erotic . . . [about] woman's body with a thousand and one fiery hearths"; and Irigaray, *This Sex Which is Not One,* trans. Catherine Porter (French ed., 1977; Ithaca: Cornell University Press, 1985), p. 28: *"woman has sex organs more or less everywhere. She finds pleasure almost anywhere"* (emphasis Irigaray's).

36. Eddy, *Science and Health,* p. 517.

37. Both quoted in Sachs, pp. 273 and 219.

38. Dowling observes that though "Whitman and 'Whitmania' . . . are scarcely mentioned in New Woman fiction, [they] were . . . persistently invoked . . . to explain the New Woman phenomenon" for "not only had the poet of 'barbaric yawp' hymned the new primitivism sought by the decadent spirit, he had promised simultaneously that sex . . . would be the means by which conventional culture would be transcended" (Dowling, pp. 451-52).

39. Seyersted, p. 62.

40. *The Awakening,* chap. 30; since there are so many different editions of this novel, all references will be to chapter numbers and will be given in the text.

41. Wolff, "Thanatos and Eros: Kate Chopin's *Awakening,*" *American Quarterly* 25 (Oct. 1973): 463.

42. Thornton, *"The Awakening*: A Political Romance," *American Literature* 52 (March 1980): 51.

43. Ibid., p. 64. Even those writers who analyze the feast more sympathetically tend to be perfunctory, bewildered, or both in their treatment of the event. Bernard J. Koloski, for instance, the first critic to identify the lines from Swinburne quoted by one of the dinner guests, reads the scene entirely in terms of those lines as Edna's Swinburnian "Song Before Death" (see Koloski, "The Swinburne Lines in *The Awakening,*" *American Literature* 45 [1974]: 608-10). Only Seyersted, still Chopin's most perceptive critic, defines the party as "a sensuous feast with subtle overtones of a ritual for Eros" (Seyersted, p. 157).

44. Cather, review of *The Awakening,* in Culley, pp. 153-55; Helen Taylor, Introduction to *The Awakening* (London: The Women's Press, 1978), p. xviii; Warner Berthoff, *The Ferment of Realism: American Literature, 1884-1919* (New York: Free Press, 1965), p. 89; Seyersted, p. 161; Stanley Kauffman, "The Really Lost Generation," *The New Republic* 155 (Dec. 3, 1966): 22, 37-38; Otis B. Wheeler, "The Five Awakenings of Edna Pontellier," *The Southern Review* 11 (1975): 118-28.

45. Thornton, p. 51; Cather (in Culley), p. 154; Wolff, pp. 453-54.

46. See, for instance, "Feminine Secret Societies," in Eliade, *Myths, Dreams, and Mysteries: The Encounter between Contemporary Faiths and Archaic Realities,* trans. Philip Mairet (New York: Harper Torchbooks, 1967), pp. 214-18.

47. Brontë, *Wuthering Heights,* ed. William M. Sale, Jr. (New York: Norton Critical Edition, 1972), p. 107; J.732, in *The Poems of Emily Dickinson,* ed. Thomas Johnson, 3 vols. (Cambridge: Harvard University Press, Belknap Press, 1955). Further references will be to this edition, and poem numbers will be included in the text, preceded by *J.*

48. For an essay which explores the paradoxically positive aspects of the privatized world of nineteenth-century women, see Carroll Smith-Rosenberg, "The Female World of Love and Ritual: Relations Between Women in Nineteenth-Century America," *Signs* 1 (Autumn 1975): 1-29.

49. See Veblen, *The Theory of the Leisure Class* (1899; New York: Modern Library, 1931), passim, but especially chap. 3 ("Conspicuous Leisure"), 4 ("Conspicuous Consumption"), 6 ("Pecuniary Canons of Taste"), and 7 ("Dress as an Expression of the Pecuniary Culture").

50. For a more ambivalent depiction of the American vacation hotel, see the first five chapters of Edith Wharton, *The Buccaneers* (New York: Appleton, 1938), and our discussion of Wharton's own attitude, chap. 5 of this volume, p. 129.

51. Cott, *The Bonds of Womanhood: "Woman's Sphere" in New England, 1780-1835* (New Haven: Yale University Press, 1977).

52. On "Great Time," see Eliade, *The Myth of the Eternal Return, or Cosmos and History,* trans. Willard R. Trask, Bollingen Series 46 (Princeton: Princeton University Press, 1954).

53. Although we are suggesting that "Mariequita" or "little Mary" evokes just the theological orthodoxy from which Edna will seek to flee, in a discussion of Balzac's "The Girl with the Golden Eyes," Shoshana Felman claims that "Mariquita" *[sic]* is a Spanish slang term for an effeminate man, a point which (if it has relevance here) would certainly complicate Chopin's erotic plot; see Shoshana Felman, "Rereading Femininity," *Yale French Studies* 62 (1981): 30-31.

54. Besides Chopin's overt and covert allusions to the power of Aphrodite, there are, of course, several other echoes of the Phaedra story in *The Awakening,* notably the seaside setting of much of the novel, the passion of an older married woman for a single younger man, and the suicide of the heroine.

55. Suzanne Wolkenfeld, "Edna's Suicide: The Problem of the One and the Many," in Culley, p. 220.

56. *Collected Works of Pierre Louÿs* (1896; New York: Shakespeare House, 1951), p. 178.

57. Schreiner, *The Story of an African Farm,* p. 271; Wharton, *The House of Mirth* (1905; New York: New American Library, 1964), pp. 338, 342.

58. The crucifixion imagery at the end of *The Awakening* may be subtly reinforced by the fact that, when Edna encounters Victor at the beginning of chapter 39, the young man is hammering nails into the porch: "I walked up from the wharf . . . and heard the hammering," she says.

59. D. L. Demorest, ["Structures of Imagery in *Madame Bovary*"], in the Norton Critical *Madame Bovary,* p. 280; Flaubert, letter to Louise Colet (March 3, 1852), ibid., p. 311.

60. Sartre, ["Flaubert and *Madame Bovary*: Outline of a New Method"], in Norton Critical *Madame Bovary*, p. 303; ibid., note 3.

61. See Swinburne, "The Triumph of Time," l. 257; Whitman, "Out of the Cradle Endlessly Rocking," l. 168, and "Song of Myself," ll. 452, 199-224; and Swinburne, "The Triumph of Time," l. 265. Portions of this last poem do, however, foreshadow the denouement of *The Awakening*: disappointed in love, the speaker dreams of a suicide by drowning, and imagines himself first casting off his clothes and then being reborn in the sea:

> This woven raiment of nights and days,
>   Were it once cast off and unwound from
>   me,
> Naked and glad would I walk in thy ways,
>   Alive and aware of thy ways and thee;
> Clear of the whole world, hidden at home,
> Clothed with the green and crowned with
>   the foam,
> A pulse of the life of thy straits and bays,
>   A vein in the heart of the streams of the
>   sea.
>
>   [281-88]

62. For a more extensive (and slightly different) discussion of Chopin's use of Whitmanesque imagery, see Elizabeth Balkman House, "*The Awakening*; Kate Chopin's 'Endlessly Rocking' Cycle," *Ball State University Forum* 20:2 (1979): 53-58.

63. Friedrich, *The Meaning of Aphrodite* (Chicago: University of Chicago Press, 1978), p. 1.

64. Wagner, *Tannhäuser*, Paris version (1861), trans. Peggie Cochrane (London: The Decca Record Co., 1971), Act 2; Swinburne, "Laus Veneris," in *The Poetry of Swinburne*, with an intro. by Ernest Rhys (New York: Modern Library, n.d.), pp. 13, 16; Morris, "The Hill of Venus," in *The Collected Works of William Morris*, with an intro. by his daughter May Morris, vol. 6, *The Earthly Paradise: A Poem IV* (London and New York: Longmans Green, 1911), pp. 295, 303; Beardsley, *Venus and Tannhäuser in Aesthetes*, pp. 37, 46.

65. Friedrich, passim, but esp. pp. 33-35, 132-48.

66. Woolf, *A Room of One's Own* (New York: Harcourt Brace, 1929), p. 69. For further discussion of Sappho's freedom, see also Woolf, "A Society," in *Monday or Tuesday* (New York: Harcourt Brace, 1921), and pp. 224-25 in this volume.

67. *Theogony*, in *The Poems of Hesiod*, trans. with intro. and comments by R. M. Frazer (Norman: University of Oklahoma Press, 1983), p. 36.

68. On Harrison and Duncan, see Jill Silverman, "Introduction to 'Andre Levinson on Isadora Duncan,'" *Ballet Review* 6:4 (1977-78): 4. Silverman notes that Harrison also "guided the young dancer through the Greek collections at the British Museum," and adds that "Harrison's . . . glorification of matriarchal structures in archaic Greece . . . undoubtedly influenced the early development of Duncan's art." On Duncan's mother and Chopin, see Elizabeth Kendall, "Before the World Began," *Ballet Review* 6:4 (1977-78): 24. For Duncan on Aphrodite, see *My Life*, pp. 113-14.

69. The passage from H. D. that we have cited here is, of course, a late one, but its celebratory tone is prefigured by the tone of a number of earlier references to the goddess; see, for instance, "Fragment Forty-one" (from *Heliodora*, 1924), with its invocation of "Aphrodite, shameless and radiant" (*Collected Poems*, p. 182), and "Songs from Cyprus" (in *Red Roses for Bronze*, 1931), with its characterization of Aphrodite as "her who nurtures, / who imperils all" (*Collected Poems*, p. 281).

70. On Woodhull's recantation, see Sachs, p. 294, quoting Woodhull's claim in 1880 that she "has been most unrighteously associated with what is known by the name of Free Love. No viler aspersion was ever uttered. No greater outrage could be inflicted on a woman."

71. "Coming, Aphrodite!" in Cather, *Youth and the Bright Medusa* (1920; New York: Vintage, 1975). Further references will be to this edition, and page numbers will be included in the text. This story also exists in a somewhat bowdlerized version which was published as "Coming, Eden Bower!" in the *Smart Set* (August 1920). For a detailed study of variants between these two texts, see the appendix to *Uncle Valentine and Other Short Stories: Willa Cather's Uncollected Short Fiction, 1915-1929*, ed. Bernice Slote (Lincoln: University of Nebraska Press, 1973). Perhaps the two most significant changes are the title change and the change in the opera that Eden Bower stars in: in the *Smart Set* version, she sings Clytemnestra in Straus's *Elektra*, while in the book version she sings Aphrodite in Erlanger's *Aphrodite*, based on Louÿs's novel. Both changes suggest Cather's consciousness of the erotic centrality of Aphrodite in the story she really wanted to write. For further background information, see Slote's introduction to *Uncle Valentine*, pp. xxi-xxii.

72. C. Rossetti, "Eve," in *The Complete Poems of Christina Rossetti*, ed. and intro. by R. W. Crump (Baton Rouge: Louisiana State University Press, 1979), 1:156-59; D. G. Rossetti, "Eden Bower," in *The Collected Works of Dante Gabriel Rossetti* (London: Ellis and Scrutton, 1886), 1:308-14.

73. D. G. Rossetti, p. 308.

74. On Cather's sexual ambivalence, see James Woodress, *Willa Cather* (New York: Pegasus, 1970), pp. 86-87, 91-94, and Sharon O'Brien, *Willa Cather: Emerging Voice* (New York: Oxford University Press, 1987), chap. 6, "Divine Femininity and Unnatural Love," pp. 117-46.

75. Lowell, "Venus Transiens," in *The Complete Poetical Works of Amy Lowell*, with an intro. by Louis Untermeyer (Cambridge: Houghton Mifflin, The Riverside Press, 1955), p. 210.

76. Rukeyser, "The Birth of Venus," in Rukeyser, *Body of Waking* (New York: Harper & Row, 1958), p. 44.

77. Sexton, *Words for Dr. Y.*, ed. Linda Gray Sexton (Boston: Houghton Mifflin, 1978), pp. 38-39.

78. Woolf, *Mrs. Dalloway* (1925; New York: Harcourt Brace, 1953), p. 47.

79. For a characterization of female desire that Lawrence also very likely uses to represent what he regards as the inappropriate clitoral orgasm, see, for instance, *The Rainbow*, chap. 11; *Women in Love*, chap. 24; and especially *The Plumed Serpent*, chap. 26. Note, for example, "The throes of Aphrodite of the foam . . . The beak-like friction of Aphrodite of the foam, the friction which flares out in circles of phosphorescent ecstasy" that Lawrence censures in chap. 26 of *PS*.

80. See "Female Coercion," "Volcanic Venus," and "What Does She Want?", in *The Complete Poems of D. H.*

Lawrence, ed. Vivian de Sola Pinto and F. Warren Roberts (New York: Penguin, 1977), pp. 538-39.

81. Stevens, "The Paltry Nude Starts on a Spring Voyage," in *The Collected Poems of Wallace Stevens* (New York: Alfred A. Knopf, 1955), pp. 5-6.

REBECCA DICKSON (ESSAY DATE SPRING-SUMMER 1999)

SOURCE: Dickson, Rebecca. "Kate Chopin, Mrs. Pontellier, and Narrative Control." *The Southern Quarterly* 37, nos. 3-4 (spring-summer 1999): 38-43.

In the following essay, Dickson outlines Chopin's place in the context of her female predecessors such as Jane Austen and Charlotte Brontë, and contends that in The Awakening *"Chopin envisioned and portrayed a woman more firmly in control of her own story and her own body than any of her predecessors had imagined."*

Until the twentieth century, the vast majority of plots created by, for, and about women were focused on an ingenue and were controlled by men, either quietly or overtly. Even when a young woman is the center of the story, and even if male characters seldom appear in a given novel, a man with his financial power inevitably holds the key to a heroine's happiness while patriarchal economic, political, and moral structures determine her identity and behavior. So, in the end a man controls a woman's story. By the end of the nineteenth century, however, that domination was being challenged on many fronts. Kate Chopin was one writer whose work significantly disrupts this male control of plot and narrative, often by manipulating another male-controlled institution: marriage. Although she employs this strategy in many earlier works, it is in ***The Awakening***, with its surprising protagonist Edna Pontellier, that Chopin most forcefully challenges male-determined stories. With Mrs. Pontellier, Chopin rejects assessing women according to their sexual status. In so doing, she continues a project that a handful of nineteenth-century women writers had devoted themselves to: gaining a measure of narrative control for women.

Nineteenth-century women writers were highly constrained by the traditional heroine that eighteenth-century authors had created: she was invariably an ingenue, a young naive virgin who had to find a husband while maintaining her chastity. That virginity, vital and frequently referred to, seriously limited the heroine's options. As Susan Morgan tells us, when virginity is considered an unmarried woman's most valuable asset, as it certainly was in the eighteenth and nineteenth centuries, men will control both women and culture because male actions determine a woman's sexual status and social identity. Consider, as Morgan does, the novels of the eighteenth century: when a single young heroine encounters a man, she can only hope he is kind while she defends her all-important virginity from his demanding sexuality. The man, on the other hand, has several choices: he may ignore the woman (in which case she may become a spinster, generally construed a sorry fate), he may act nobly (the virgin thus becomes a wife), he may act ignobly (he may seduce her, and she becomes a fallen woman), or he may act viciously (he may rape her, likewise defining her as fallen). Often a heroine's highest accomplishment in an eighteenth- or nineteenth-century novel is that she maintains her virtue when it is threatened by temptation or male aggression. But this achievement is based on non-action, by what a woman does not do. As Morgan puts it, if a woman can "make *nothing* happen . . . that would constitute a happy ending" (348). Meanwhile, men act; they control the labels that are conferred on heroines (spinster, wife, whore)—in short, they control the plot.

Two bestselling American novels from the eighteenth century illustrate this male dominance of narrative: both Susanna Rowson's *Charlotte Temple* (1791) and Hannah Foster's *The Coquette* (1797) focus on a good-hearted but naive young woman who is seduced and abandoned by a man. In both novels, the patriarchally constructed seduction plot ineluctably unfolds. Both women must regret being seduced, and do; both women must sink emotionally, socially, economically, and do; both women must die, and do. Well-loved by American readers and considered highly instructive, these novels were still in print in Chopin's lifetime, and she likely read one or both of them. She certainly was familiar with the seduction tale, in which men have choices while women effectively do not, in which male actions determine the predictable plot, and where young women are valued according to the condition of their vaginas.

Not all novels written about ingenues end unhappily, of course. In Susan Warner's bestselling *The Wide Wide World* (1850), a novel Chopin did read (Toth 51), the heroine, young Ellen Montgomery, whose innocence is repeatedly stressed, faces one taxing experience after another. By learning to suppress her emotional impulses, however, she survives with hymen intact and is rewarded with a virile minister as her husband. Maria Susanna Cummins's *The Lamplighter* (1854), another bestseller when Chopin was a girl, similarly focuses on a young virgin whose happiness is entirely defined by men or their institutions; like Ellen, young Gerty Flint's innocence is her key trait, and she too must learn to be passive. While Ellen and Gerty are presented first and foremost as ingenues who must overcome their stubborn, emotional natures, their male counterparts, Natty Bumppo and Huck Finn, are presented as adventurous souls who express their frustrations by escaping "sivilization." That Huck, who is the same age as Gerty and Ellen, is also a virgin, is irrelevant to his story. From such works, readers learn to ask of women, is she chaste? whom will she marry? But of men we ask, what is he like? what has he done? The cultural effects of these wildly differing questions are obviously enormous. Perhaps this disparity explains why Chopin read so many European writers, for several European women novelists were asking different questions about women.

Jane Austen, a writer on the other side of the nineteenth century whom Chopin read,[1] was largely uninterested in the classic ingenue. In defending Austen's sexless tales, Morgan maintains that in not focusing on sexual intrigues and virgins, Austen allows her protagonists to concern themselves with something other than their virtue by making that virtue simply a given. Consequently, a woman's sexual status ceases to be the engine of plot, if not wholly irrelevant. Catherine Morland, Elizabeth Bennet, Emma Woodhouse, and Marianne Dashwood never cower with bosoms heaving for fear of some man's aggression. Each of them meets new people, reconsider themselves and their assumptions, decide they were wrong in some key matter, and change for the better. As Morgan makes clear, given the literary history of heroines, Austen's innovation is vital, for her protagonists have a chance to engage in self-reflection and self-correction, which are imperative in becoming mature adults. After Austen, heroines had a precedent for growing up, and sometimes had the emotional freedom to do so.

Chopin also read Charlotte Brontë, whose protagonists are much like Austen's: their virtue is presumed, which allows them to concern themselves with other matters. Brontë is determined to keep narrative control in her heroine's hands, so determined that in *Jane Eyre* (1847) she maims and blinds the puissant Rochester in order to give Jane a more dominant role in their relationship. In *Villette* (1853) she drowns the male protagonist, enabling Lucy Snowe to maintain her independence as a teacher and thinker. Brontë also wrote *Jane Eyre* and *Villette* in a bold first person, which is unusual in novels by women in the nineteenth

century and another strategy for allowing women some control over their own stories.

But Chopin read French writers as often as she did English ones, and since she was intrigued with women who broke conventions, she read George Sand.[2] Sand, like Austen, shuns the ingenue. Consider her most famous novels: in *Indiana* (1832) the exploits of a married woman who has an affair are followed, and in *Lélia* (1833) a nun who feels that her life and work have been meaningless is encountered. Sand also developed a new form of narrative that Isabelle Naginski calls androgynous, a "double-voiced discourse" through which she could express her own complex identity while simultaneously reflecting the changing role of women in France and Western culture (2-4). There was no place in Sand's complex narrations for the conventional young heroine whose virtue was paramount.

Chopin was also familiar with American writers such as Sarah Orne Jewett and Mary Wilkins Freeman, who were shifting their focus from the ingenue to other characters: widows, old women, poor women, married women. Seldom do Jewett and Freeman write of the young virgin who will marry at the end of the story, and we know that Chopin frankly admired their works (**Miscellany** 90). Certainly their narrative choices influenced her own.

To wrest control of narrative from male authors and characters as these writers did, the virgin must be removed and the male-determined plot rejected. But while each of the above writers took these critical steps, their fiction betrays their limitations. Austen's heroines develop character and mature, and they enter marriages that promise to be unusually egalitarian and fulfilling, but Austen never offers a glimpse of female desire. Though in many of her works Sand portrays physical love as healthy, she too hesitates to depict female sexuality. Brontë still feels compelled to lock the sensual woman firmly in the attic, and Jewett and Freeman ignore or restrain female desire. In contrast, Chopin places a sexual woman center stage in the form of a Protestant-bred Kentuckian who has married a pillar of New Orleans's creole community. Significantly, however, we never see *The Awakening*'s Edna Pontellier express herself sexually with her husband. In that notable omission, Chopin takes the battle for narrative control to an entirely new level.

What Chopin is playing with in ***The Awakening*** (1899) are the reader's expectations of heroines and married women. A nineteenth-century reader would have expected the heroine to be young and unmarried, for both in fiction and in everyday life, then as now, a married woman's life is generally dismissed as uninteresting and plotless. Once married, Western culture assumes that a woman's future—sexually, economically, and socially—has been settled.[3] But Chopin recognized that the married woman could be a more promising heroine than the ingenue. With a married woman, the titillating question about a heroine's sexual status becomes moot, giving the writer room to develop her character, instead of the fate of her virginity. A married woman also has greater freedom than a single woman, something that was certainly true for the married women on the Grand Isle of Chopin's novel. While the lady in black serves as an apparently self-appointed chaperone for the unmarried lovers who are forever trying to elude curious eyes, Edna may involve herself in a heated relationship with Robert and no one thinks it unusual. Fully accustomed to unflagging sexual loyalty in women, even her husband Léonce considers Edna's actions innocuous. "[T]he Creole husband is never jealous," Chopin explains, "with him the gangrene passion is one which has become dwarfed by disuse" (*CW* [*The Complete Works*] 5: 891).

Given this assumption, Chopin may place her married heroine where a single woman of the 1890s simply could not otherwise go. A married woman might attend the horseraces with a man whom she barely knows; a single woman of "good" family could not. A father would hardly let his single daughter move into her own "pigeon-house," but Edna's husband does not object. Kate Chopin herself took full advantage of the freedoms allowed a married woman. While in Germany on their honeymoon, she and her husband Oscar wanted to visit the university in Bonn, but they were told that it would be unseemly for a woman to be observed by the all-male students. The new Mrs. Chopin tried to persuade the curator that "being married might in a manner abate the[ir] interest" (*Miscellany* 73). Her strategy failed, but it reveals Chopin's awareness of the license allowed married women. A few weeks later, the nineteen-year-old Mrs. Chopin strolled through Zurich unescorted, a pleasure which she herself finds remarkable (*Miscellany* 81).

Chopin's interest in married women as protagonists is evident in many of her short stories as well as in her two surviving novels (Thérèse Lafirme of *At Fault* is a widow).[4] In *The Awakening,* Chopin eschews the ingenue almost entirely; she devotes little ink to the few virgins present

and portrays them generically. The female half of the two lovers on Grand Isle, presumably a virgin, has no name, no face, and no identity other than being part of a couple. Chopin gently makes fun of the Farival twins, who are fourteen and always clad in virginal white and blue; she allows Mademoiselle Reisz to despise them openly (*CW* 16: 931). Mademoiselle herself is cantankerous, old, and wise, and her alleged virginity is irrelevant.[5] And Mariequita, young and unmarried, is savvy and sensual rather than demure and passive. Given the language surrounding Mariequita and the stories she tells (12: 914-16; 39: 997-98), the reader can assume that she knows as much about sex as does Edna, a matron of twenty-nine.

Freed by marriage from the ingenue's pursuit of a spouse and from the wife's dreary labor by her husband's wealth, Edna has time for self-reflection. Since her husband can afford a nanny, she has time to pensively reconsider her own childhood, when she ran away from Presbyterian prayers to explore green meadows "idly, aimlessly, unthinking and unguided" (*CW* 7: 897). With Adèle's encouragement, Edna tries to articulate her own story, to trace how she shifted from a girl running from church to a woman learning how to swim, both symbolically and physically. She no longer concerns herself with silly infatuations for a cavalry officer or tragedian and instead tentatively attempts to understand the underlying rebellious impulses that prompted her to create those fantasies.

Because there is no pressing need to find a man, Edna can also immerse herself in others' stories. The visitors on Grand Isle share gossip and read racy novels, and Edna joins in (albeit shyly at first). Robert tells her of himself and his adventures (*CW* 2: 884) and of what could be found on the islands around Grand Isle (12: 915-16). When Edna and Robert visit Chênière Caminada, Madame Antoine entertains them with accounts of ships, Baratarian pirates, and other exploits (13: 920). Edna's impressionable mind embraces such tales, as she gradually learns to construct her own. When Dr. Mandelet dines with the Pontelliers, Léonce tells stories of his childhood, Edna's father tells a somber and self-involved yarn, and the doctor recounts a didactic tale about a woman who returns to her "legitimate" love. And then Edna tells her own story, one she makes up about "a woman who paddled away with her lover one night in a pirogue and never came back" (23: 953). Novice though she is, she proves a compelling storyteller:

[E]very glowing word seemed real to those who listened [to Mrs. Pontellier]. They could feel the hot breath of the Southern night; they could hear the long sweep of the pirogue through the glistening moonlit water . . . ; they could see the faces of the lovers, pale, close together, rapt in oblivious forgetfulness, drifting into the unknown.

(23: 953)

Chopin here emphasizes that Edna is doing what the men are doing—telling stories—but she is also trumping them: she rejects Dr. Mandelet's conclusion as to what should happen when a woman wanders sexually. She tells a fib as well, which, of course, a good Protestant girl is taught not to do: she insists that hers is a true tale, an account she heard from Madame Antoine. But Edna's story is her own, an oral landmark in her personal history that she is shaping as never before.

The last months of Edna's life do make for a remarkable story, one that she alone has constructed. Consider Edna's plot: she falls in love with a man while on vacation one summer; loses that lover; learns that she can make her own money (through gambling, through painting); rejects her father's autocratic influence; finds a new lover; removes herself from her husband's house and his economic and social protection; and announces she will not be owned by a man. Several key figures among Edna's acquaintance recognize the unexpected shape her story is taking and try to impose their more conventional plots upon it. But Edna consistently repels every attempt to appropriate her story, especially those offered by men.

While on Grand Isle, Léonce is oblivious to Edna's emerging independence, but once back in New Orleans, where she has social obligations, he tries to rein her in. He expresses outrage over a wife who is not comporting herself properly, but Edna is unimpressed—she is perfectly content to eat her dinners alone while he dines at his club. She battles with Léonce, at times fiercely, at times fondly, and consistently wins. Alcée Arobin, a practiced womanizer, also needs to control women, but through illicit liaisons rather than the marital proprieties. While Edna explores her own character and potential, Alcée tries to reduce their relationship to a mere adulterous affair that he manipulates through shallow compliments, practiced sensuality, and oily devotion. But he fails and is often frustrated when Edna's attention wanders. Edna so firmly maintains control of their affair that Alcée becomes passive and effeminate: while she is moving out of Léonce's house, he

dons a dustcap for her and becomes her servant, following her directives (*CW* 29: 968).

Robert frequently tries to impose his story upon Edna's, especially when he senses that she has experienced something meaningful. After her swim, he tries to make her achievement fit his fanciful myth of a Gulf spirit that occasionally seeks out a worthy human recipient. Edna quickly cuts him off: "Don't banter me" (*CW* 10: 909-10). She knows she has accomplished something personally momentous, and Robert's mythicizing annoys her. After Edna abandons the heavy atmosphere of the little church on Chênière Caminada and awakes to explore her own body in Madame Antoine's cottage, Robert, who realizes that Edna's flight from church is significant, tries to commandeer her story once again. When Edna invents a tale of a new race of beings having sprung up, Robert interjects his own fancies about her merely having slept for a hundred years. Edna ignores his interjection (13: 919) and maintains firm control of their relationship. It is her idea to go to Chênière Caminada, and it is she who sends for Robert. When they meet in New Orleans at Catiche's "small, leafy corner," Edna decrees that he share her dinner, and then abruptly asks him why he has avoided her. They argue, but he goes back to the "pigeon-house" with her, where she leans over and kisses him for the first time. In response, he attempts to redirect their relationship to a more traditional course by telling her he wants her to be his wife. She simply mocks him:

"You have been a very, very foolish boy, wasting your time dreaming of impossible things when you speak of Mr. Pontellier setting me free! I am no longer one of Mr. Pontellier's possessions to dispose of or not. I give myself where I choose. If he were to say, 'Here, Robert, take her and be happy; she is yours,' I should laugh at you both."

His face grew a little white. "What do you mean?" he asked.

(36: 992)

Certainly Robert should go pale, for this woman wants to control not only her story, but his as well, which is contrary to everything he has learned about the known universe. It is hardly surprising that he disappears after Edna's announcement that she is no longer a possession.

Seeing Edna after her summer on Grand Isle, kindly Dr. Mandelet also recognizes that she is transforming, sexually and otherwise. Despite the fact that he is impressed with Edna's shift from a "listless woman . . . into a being who . . . seemed palpitant with the forces of life" and even though "[s]he reminded him of some beautiful, sleek animal waking up in the sun," Dr. Mandelet cannot approve of Edna's story (*CW* 23: 952). He tries to intervene, first with his didactic dinner tale. After Adèle's baby is born, he tries again to interrupt Edna's narrative, gently cajoling her to confide in him. But Edna will not cooperate. She is wary of the doctor's efforts and will not allow Dr. Mandelet to advise her on how to handle her marriage or her children, however well-intentioned he may be.

Edna does, however, allow women to help shape her story. The devoted mother Adèle is the first to see that Edna's attempt to understand and express herself could have serious consequences. Immediately after their conversation in which Edna speaks candidly of her experiences, Adèle warns Robert to leave Edna alone (*CW* 8: 899-901). A woman who rethinks her own story destabilizes patriarchal structures, and as one who has cheerfully resigned herself to home and husband, Adèle is alarmed by Edna's behavior. Hours after Edna announces to Robert that men no longer control her, Adèle imparts a haunting message that finally ends Edna's exploratory tale: "Think of the children, Edna. Oh think of the children! Remember them!" (37: 995).

In a narrative created by a woman, for women, about a woman trying to elude male control, it is fitting then that a woman's words send Edna to her final swim. Even in its unsettling conclusion, *The Awakening* remains a woman's narrative. The reality of suicide aside, and the ramifications of Adèle's patriarchal acquiescence notwithstanding, Chopin's fictive resolution of Edna's story bids a metaphoric adieu to male control of female narrative—a woman serves as the catalyst for Edna's final act, not a man. Women—Adèle, Mademoiselle Reisz, who encourages Edna's rejection of the conventional, and Mariequita, whose open sensuality Edna admires—have more influence on Edna's story than the men in her life. The women shape her narrative from beginning to end. Thus it is ironic and deliciously subversive that Chopin undermines male control of the human story with a married woman as her primary tool.

Among the handful of nineteenth-century women writers who were determined to give women some control not only of their lives, but of stories themselves are Austen, Sand, Brontë, Jewett, and Freeman. But with the publication of *The Awakening* at the end of the century, Chopin envisioned and portrayed a woman more firmly in control of her own story and her own body than any of her predecessors had imagined. In so doing, Kate Chopin joins them in their effort to de-center the cult of the virgin—she posits the inadequacy of a woman's sexual label in defining her identity by creating a narrative that focuses on personal exploration and transformation rather than on a woman's sexual status. And, predating Virginia Woolf by nearly thirty years, Chopin suggests that what a woman most needs is a pigeon-house of her own, where she may construct her own story. On this the hundredth anniversary of *The Awakening,* it is fitting that we place Chopin in the international pantheon of writers to which she belongs, among those writers who knew that women had to envision themselves in control—in their novels, in their social narratives—before they could learn to navigate their own lives.

Notes

1. See Seyersted's discussion of Chopin's reading (25-26) or her reading list in the *Miscellany* (87-88).

2. Seyersted points out that though we have no record that Chopin read Sand, her daughter Lelia believed that she was named after Sand's famous heroine (101).

3. This attitude is most obvious in pre-twentieth-century novels, but it is also evident in today's mainstream movies and romance fiction.

4. An incomplete list of Chopin's stories about married women includes: "The Going Away of Liza," "A Visit to Avoyelles," "In Sabine," "A Respectable Woman," "The Story of an Hour," "Her Letters," "Athénaïse," and "The Storm."

5. Given Mlle. Reisz's open and effusive love for Edna, Mademoiselle may have been sexually active with women, which further disrupts male control of narrative.

Works Cited

Chopin, Kate. *The Complete Works.* Ed. Per Seyersted. Baton Rouge: Louisiana State UP, 1969.

———. *A Kate Chopin Miscellany.* Ed. Per Seyersted and Emily Toth. Natchitoches, LA: Nortgwestern State UP, 1979.

TITLE COMMENTARY

The Awakening

CAROLYN L. MATHEWS (ESSAY DATE 3 SEPTEMBER 2002)

SOURCE: Mathews, Carolyn L. "Fashioning the Hybrid Women in Kate Chopin's *The Awakening.*" *Mosaic* 35, no. 3 (3 September 2002): 127-49.

In the following excerpt, Mathews examines the meaning of the clothing imagery in The Awakening *and contends that Chopin "uses dress as a means of representing female subjectivity."*

During the years surrounding the turn into the twentieth century, discourse on dress proliferated, resulting in what fashion historian Joan Severa calls "a universal understanding of style" (454). Americans of the period purchased more clothing per capita than ever before, and manuals like Dorothy Quigley's *What Dress Makes of Us* or Mary Haweis's *The Art of Dress* appeared alongside books on dress reform like J. H. Kellogg's *The Evils of Fashionable Dress.* Early feminists such as Charlotte Perkins Gilman addressed the topic . . . as did highly respected American psychologists such as William James and G. Stanley Hall. While Hall's 1898 study on motivation in dress interpreted clothing as a means of social conformity (Ewen 79), James singled out garments as instrumental in establishing self; he writes that "we [. . .] identify ourselves with them" (280). The fervency with which dress became a serious subject within scientific and economic discourse is perhaps best illustrated by Thorstein Veblen's now classic book entitled *The Theory of the Leisure Class: An Economic Study of Institutions,* wherein he describes women's dress as the most "apt illustration" of the principles underlying the whole of his economic theory. Treating it as an emblem of conspicuous consumption, Veblen interprets female attire within the context of women's historical role as commodities of exchange. Because the wife functions as property, he argues, her costly attire is meant to pronounce her "uselessness" and lack of "productive labour" (170), thereby announcing "to all observers" (179) her husband's social and economic status.

The positions etched out by thinkers like Veblen, Gilman, Hall, and James establish cultural precedents for Kate Chopin's use of clothing in **The Awakening,** her controversial 1899 novel about marriage and female sexuality. Critics over the course of the past four decades have explicitly acknowledged Chopin's reliance on clothing and images of undressing to suggest her character Edna's sense of oppression and eventual liberation. Per Seyersted, for example, refers to acts of disrobing throughout the novel, arguing that this action at the novel's end "symbolizes a victory of self-knowledge" (194). Other critics have read Edna's disrobing conversely, attributing Edna's demise not to societal forces, as Seyersted suggests, but to the character's lack of an integrated self or to personal limitations that make change impossible. Suzanne Wolkenfeld, for example, calls the disrobing a "regression to the animality of infancy" (223). Robert Collins, tracing in its entirety the pattern of garment imagery, argues that disrobing

"symbolizes Edna's dissatisfaction with fiction-making" but that the way in which the imagery is used "suggests that Chopin viewed Edna's suicide [. . .] as a failure of imagination" (177). The attention to dress in Chopin criticism verifies the importance of garment imagery in the novel, but to date no critic has placed this pattern within the context of nineteenth-century discourse on dress.

My examination of the novel's clothing imagery maps out the specific socially grounded meanings encoded in Chopin's extensive and specific inclusion of details of dress; it is an analysis revealing that the writer uses dress as a means of representing female subjectivity. I begin by establishing the discursive background for use of dress in the novel and then focus on its depiction of working-class and non-white women, particularly in terms of their clothing, to show how Chopin depended upon social class and racial stereotypes to revise nineteenth-century feminist discourse on self-ownership. By exploring the novel's use of clothing as signals for particular constructions of nineteenth-century womanhood, I argue that the novel insinuates upon readers a model for female subjectivity that substantially amends the era's dominant form, which assumed middle-class propriety, moral superiority, and motherhood. Chopin's version of the female self in effect merges elements from presumably opposed social contexts—from lower-class as well as upper-class settings, for example—thus positing a hybrid formation that works culturally to unsettle categories of nineteenth-century thought.

Although writers of the late nineteenth and early twentieth centuries often disagreed in their judgements regarding societal emphasis on dress, they consistently posited dress as a semiotic system of signs wherein sartorial details work together to articulate the wearer's social identity. In 1892, for example, Helen Ecob wrote, "Character of dress is the external *sign* of the social, intellectual, and moral status of the wearer" (230, emph. mine). Because women's social identities were inexorably tied to marriage, many writers were quick to point out how women's clothing signalled immobility and their lack of self-ownership. Material evidence of the period supports these rulings, for the lady's gown, sewn from over twenty yards of fabric and worn over multiple "skirts," hand-embroidered drawers, a corset, and undervests, weighed nearly twenty pounds. When she added outdoor wraps, she carried twenty-five to thirty pounds of fabric (Ewen and Ewen 106). The appearance of inactivity was no mere illusion. Heavily boned bodices and tightly fitted sleeves prevented wearers from reaching tiny hook-and-eye fasteners sewn down the back (Bradfield 28), and a maid often assisted. Dress reformers of the late nineteenth century were especially quick to note the connection between women's dress and their lack of productivity. Like Veblen, they viewed women's clothing in relation to issues of ownership. "A Symposium on Women's Dress," published in October 1892 by *The Arena,* for example, chronicles opinions of artists, physicians, and women "crippled" by fashion as arguments for making "improved" dress the sign of "good breeding" (621). . . . Divine providence, Darwin, art, health, and motherhood were all recruited to carry forth the symposium's call for a more rational dress, and throughout, the plea for women's rights surfaces. Observing the link between dress and middle-class women's roles, E. M. King pessimistically predicts the defeat of dress reform: "Dress reformers may well despair, for I perceive that their hopes can never be fulfilled until they go, both in theory and practice, to the very root of the matter. Women must take their rightful place in the sphere of humanity. They must respect and reverence their own bodies and have their rightful sovereignty over them" (King 629). King's writing clearly demonstrates the cultural weight of thought linking female clothing and lack of self-ownership. Kate Chopin mined this vein of thought when she used dress to signal meanings related to female sovereignty, but she used social-class coding to insure that Edna's position not just as wife but as middle-class wife comes under scrutiny.

Propriety and the whole cult of respectability that directed the lives of middle-class Americans of this era lie at the heart of Edna Pontellier's quest for self-ownership. As John Kasson's study of manners in America shows, upper-middle- and leisure-class women recognized correct form in dress as integral to setting themselves apart from the lower classes. "Correct form" specified particular styles, fabrics, and colours for different hours of the day and different activities. As historical work by both Philippe Perrot and Penelope Byrde illustrate, women like Edna Pontellier purchased expansive wardrobes so that they might appropriately attire themselves for morning, afternoon, or evening as they religiously observed differences between country and city dress and between street wear and calling attire. Like other middle-class women of the period, Edna performs time-consuming rituals of dress, preparing her toilette several times a day. She begins her day, for example, in a "white morning gown" (73), a laced and flounced gar-

ment worn by middle-class women as they directed their household staffs. Later she changes into a tailor-made street gown to make informal morning calls (73). If she were to make the more formal afternoon calls, she would don a visiting dress or formal day gown, or if she were to receive callers, she would wear a reception gown, intricately constructed with layers of flouncing, scalloped frills, piping, tucks, and insets of brocade. Edna's failure to be thus attired first brings into the open the Pontellier's marital conflicts. Angered that his wife has not kept her formal reception day, Mr. Pontellier says, "It's just such seeming trifles that we've got to take seriously; such things count" (71). Standing as fictional counterpart to Veblen's insistence that women's dress functioned as an expression of the husband's social position, the conflict serves as one of many reminders of Edna's initial lack of autonomy and self-ownership.

Margit Stange has noted that *The Awakening* builds toward a "turning point [. . .] at which Edna, deciding to leave Léonce's house, resolves 'never again to belong to another than herself'" (203). Arguing that the novel dramatizes nineteenth-century rhetoric of self-ownership, Stange explains Edna's rejection of her role as middle-class wife within the context of domestic feminists' campaigns for voluntary motherhood. This reform movement, which began in 1840 with Lucinda Chandler's plea that each woman take "control over her own person independent of the desires of her husband" (qtd. in Stange 107), used the term *self-ownership* to denote a woman's right to refuse marital sex and thus to limit family size. Stange argues that when Edna turns Mr. Pontellier out of her bed with talk of the "eternal rights of women" (Chopin 85), she uses discourse typical of domestic feminists of the period. Stange maintains, though, that the character profoundly alters these feminists' version of self-ownership, which held that women's sexuality was integrally tied to motherhood. They vehemently opposed birth-control devices, fearing that contraception would create a threatening sexual freedom that would ultimately dissolve the family. While Stange notes that Edna declares herself "free to have sex with whomever she chooses," she does not discuss Chopin's method for revising domestic feminism and asserting female sexuality. It is this gap in Stange's discussion that attention to clothing addresses. Because *The Awakening* associates proper dress with middle-class identity and its opposite—impropriety and states of undress—with working-class and non-white women, it strips self-ownership of its straight-laced passionlessness. Female sexuality emerges as an integral aspect of self-ownership, but at the expense of working-class and non-white women.

My analysis of Chopin's representation of social class borrows from the methodology of Peter Stallybrass and Allon White, who, in *The Politics and Poetics of Transgression,* theorize a system for mapping out interconnected meanings within given cultures. Arguing that European cultures "think themselves" by way of the oppositions "high"/"low" or "top"/"bottom," they show how hierarchical classifications can be cross-referenced to reveal meaning (2). Within a given culture's system of symbolization, social classes, the human body, psychic forms, and geographic space are all laid out through the high/low opposition that correlates each domain to the other three. A disruption of the hierarchy within one domain affects all other domains (3). The validity of such a cultural matrix is evidenced in everyday speech when undesirable locations are called the "armpit" of the world or when verbal insults function by way of a synecdoche that sums up the whole person with some choice, lower-anatomy substitute like "ass-hole." While Stallybrass and White do not address fashion as a domain that can be cross-referenced with other significant domains, their use of Bakhtin's conceptions of the classical body and the grotesque certainly apply to women's fashion of the period. Arguing that the body and meaning are related discursively, they show that the classical body consistently denotes the *"form* of the high official culture" (21, emph. Stallybrass and White's). This body, closed, perfect, and pure, is without orifice. Pedestalled and symmetrical, monumental and distant, the classical body expresses the same values articulated in "tasteful," "refined" female dress of the late nineteenth century. The cross-referencing between the human body and social class that Stallybrass and White observe occurs with remarkable frequency in fashion commentary of this period. One etiquette-manual writer insisted, for example, that "nothing so quickly points out the low-bred as loudness of conduct or flashiness of dress" (qtd. in Kasson 98). Another advisor articulated the link between conspicuous display and women's sexual bodies when he suggested that loudness in dress invited sexual advances (Kasson 163).

Discussions of tasteful dress that engaged Chopin's contemporaries enable readers today to interpret with closer historical accuracy the implied cultural "high" or "low" of certain details of dress in *The Awakening.* For instance, Edna Pontellier looks "handsome and distinguished" in her street gown, a description that Carol Mac-Curdy reads as commentary on Edna's lack of femininity (55). Yet even a cursory glance at fashion magazines of the period reveals the frequency with which "handsome" was applied to women's public attire ("Two"; "Long"). Chopin's Edna, never appearing in public in costumes overly rich in fabric or too eye-catching in colour, epitomizes the tasteful dresser. . . . Linked in prescriptive fashion commentary with those of "high-breeding," understated, tasteful attire like Edna's identified wearers as respectably middle class, an assumption that explains why a writer for *The Jewish Daily News* so emphatically urged her mostly immigrant readers to "seek refinement" ("Just") in their dress. Working-class women, and especially non-white or newly Americanized ones, occupied by virtue of class and ethnicity a culturally "low" social and economic position. By dressing tastefully (like those "high"-bred), they might unsettle cultural categories that enabled unequal power relations among the social classes and among races. Fed by fears of miscegenation, a general stereotyping of non-white and working-class women as sexually promiscuous occurred with blatant candour at the turn of the century (McNall 25-26), and it is no surprise that Chopin depended upon such assumptions in her depiction of Mariequita, the Spanish servant girl who serves within the novel as cultural "low" to the demure and tasteful "high" of Edna Pontellier.

In *The Reversible World: Symbolic Inversion in Art and Society,* Barbara Babcock examines how given cultures use language, art, and religion to symbolically invert commonly held cultural codes, values, and norms. While a belief turned on its head can work culturally toward different ends, sometimes reinforcing the dominant view and sometimes challenging it, an inversion nonetheless presents an alternative. Such symbolic inversion occurs in Chopin's use of Mariequita not simply as a foil for Edna but as a character whose race and class enable Edna to break with the conventions of middle-class marriage. And, as theories regarding cultural matrixes would predict, the "high"/"low" opposition between Edna and the servant girl works across different domains. "Low" in terms of social class, Mariequita is also associated with the lower body—most often genitalia and feet. Glaringly underdeveloped as a character, she appears in only two scenes of *The Awakening,* an inclusion underscoring her symbolic function since these particular scenes occur at structurally pivotal points in the narrative. First appearing in the *Chênière Camanada* episode, which is most often identified as the scene of Edna's sexual awakening, Mariequita appears once more at the novel's end just before Edna's suicide. The incomplete portrayal works to focus readers' attention on two aspects of characterization that the novel presents clearly: her social class and her body. Not simply lower class, but of the lowest, the servant class, Mariequita in each scene flaunts a lack of propriety with her body—the slimy feet she bares, the "eyes" she "makes" at Robert, the "mouths" she "makes" sassing old Beaudelet (52). An example of what Bakhtin calls the "grotesque," which stands in opposition to "the bourgeois individualist conception of the body" (Stallybrass and White 22), Mariequita's body becomes integral in Edna's conception of subjectivity. Like another of the novel's dark women—the "generous" Verta Cruz girl who gives Robert an embroidered pouch (122) or the "stunning girls" who kept Arobin occupied in Mexico (123)— Mariequita calls forth sexual associations inseparable from her race and class, and these cultural assumptions enable what Michele Birnbaum has called "Edna's racial surrogacy" (314), her identification with "the marginalized[,] which both affirms her class position and allows her to critique the sexual constraints associated with it" (304). Kasson's study of nineteenth-century manners validates Birnbaum's conclusions, for he shows that, to middle-class Americans of Chopin's period, cleanliness, manners, and taboos regarding body functions and sexuality were paramount in etching out an identity counter to that of the supposedly "low bred." Functioning as "low-others" against whom middle-class Americans measured their own superiority, people low on the socioeconomic ladder—workers and non-whites—were *essential* to middle-class constructions of self, Kasson maintains. As he demonstrates, these low-others served as a sort of symbolic repository for all that the middle class excluded when setting themselves apart— impropriety, poor taste, filth, and unacceptable sexual desires. It was these cultural codes that allowed Chopin to use Mariequita to revise domestic feminists' concept of self-ownership, and the move entailed a highlighting of the contrast between the tastefully clad and properly middle-class wife, Edna Pontellier, and the barefoot and sexually promiscuous Mariequita.

When Mariequita appears on the boat in the *Chênière Camanada* segment with bare, dirty feet, she inverts the middle-class toilette through undress—a term I use to denote matters of dress set in opposition to bourgeois propriety, decorum, and cleanliness. Rejoinders to Edna's prim, stocking-protected and shoe-enclosed lower extremities (55), such feet marked the person as racially and intellectually inferior, according to physiognomic treatises like Alexander Walker's *Intermarriage; or How and Why Beauty, Health and Intellect Result from Certain Marriages and Deformity, Disease and Insanity from Others*. Further, their very sliminess, along with the basket of shrimps, implies work and appropriateness determined by function rather than fashion. Bakhtin's notion of the carnival as a cultural ritual of inversion clarifies the significance of Chopin's focus on feet in the *Chênière Camanada* segment. The carnival, in privileging the grotesque body with its teeming lower parts (feet, buttocks, genitals), allowed members of the upper class voyeuristic gazes at all that they excluded from their own definitions of self (Stallybrass and White 48, 128). With just this sort of voyeurism, Edna looks at Mariequita's bare feet, "noticing the sand and slime between her brown toes." She observes the girl's sexually alluring eye-play, and she "like[s] it all" (52). Later, when Edna removes "the greater part of [her clothes]" (55) in Madame Antoine's cottage to experience her body for the first time, the shoes and stockings are the only articles of clothing specified. The removal of her clothing and her bathing precede the removal of her shoes and stockings, the illogical sequence thus highlighting the feet. This baring of feet recalls the earlier image of the sexually free and barefooted Mariequita, and it works on a symbolic level to invert middle-class gender codes of propriety, sexual taboos, immobility, and lack of self-ownership. The feet and *undress* function as symbols of the culturally "low" and become for Edna Pontellier symbols of the sexual freedom she desires.

By mid-novel, Edna has taken control of her body and bed as domestic feminists since 1840 had been advocating, but she has not accepted as warrant for her action their insistence on female passionlessness. By merging what in the nineteenth century was a male prerogative—possessive individualism—with elements of lower-class or non-white female subjectivity, Chopin posits a "hybrid" construction of womanhood that pulls from both the conventions of the middle class and the repository of "low," rejected qualities that the middle class associated with those beneath them in the social hierarchy. The symbolic relation between dress and female selfhood is underscored in the analogy used as Mr. Pontellier muses over Edna's behaviour: "He could see plainly that she was not herself. That is, he could not see that she was becoming herself and daily casting aside that fictitious self which we assume *like a garment* with which to appear before the world" (77, emph. mine). While this oft-quoted passage has been used to celebrate Edna's emerging selfhood, readers should not overlook Chopin's method, which works at the expense of the low-others of nineteenth-century culture—those of low economic status, particularly non-white women.

While Chopin's use of hybridization could seem little more than a stitching together of dress associations from different social classes, her reliance on these associations underscores just how profoundly particular symbolic representations align with actual social forms. Barefootedness is not simply an arbitrary choice within Chopin's novel; rather, it has a very concrete correlative in the material and social world of turn-of-the-century America. Only servant girls like Mariquita, who could not afford to ruin shoes by shrimping in them, would appear barefooted; middle-class women did not even bare their feet to swim. And, as Stallybrass and White argue, when opposite poles of categories like propriety/impropriety mix in actual social practice, a hybrid cultural formation results. Fusing contradictory elements, these hybrid formations interrogate "the rules of inclusion, exclusion and domination" that structure a society (43). Hybridization, Stallybrass and White write, "produces new combinations and strange instabilities in a given semiotic system[;] it therefore generates the possibility of shifting *the very terms of the system itself*" (58, emph. Stallybrass and White's). In social practice, hybridization might, for example, produce constructions of womanhood that could ultimately shift definitions of male and female. Chopin includes two characters who function as such cultural hybrids. Adele Ratignolle and Mademoiselle Reisz each successfully blends elements of the "high" and "low," and, as hybrid constructions of womanhood, each pulls from a closet of possibilities the seemingly incompatible to assemble a costume that signifies the disruption of established hierarchies.

Most often read as the embodiment of traditional womanhood, Adele Ratignolle is the mother-woman bedecked in fluttering garments that suit "her rich, luxuriant beauty" (33). Appearing at the novel's onset in stark contrast to Edna, who wears the "symmetrical" lines associated in the 1890s with the New Woman, Adele dresses in "pure white, with a fluffiness of ruffles" and "draperies" (33). Fashion commentary of 1898

noted that such a dress should give the illusion that the wearers, or "aery habitations," are composed "of stuff less solid than flesh and blood" (Cunnington 402). The language here echoes discourse on motherhood prevalent during the nineteenth century—writings in which mothers appear as angels or soft spirits "hovering in soothing caresses" (Melendy 45). Imaging Adele and the other mother-women first as domestic chickens, caged by their maternal instinct, which in turn transforms them into ministering angels, Chopin blends motherhood, spirituality, and femininity, portraying Adele as the epitome of ideal womanhood. Adele, however, cannot be pigeon-holed, for her maternal qualities are often overshadowed by an erotic appeal associated elsewhere in the novel with low-others. Receiving Edna in a "negligé which left her arms almost wholly bare and exposed the rich, melting curves of her white throat" (75), Adele displays an improper level of undress, thoroughly at odds with middle-class "correct form." The emphasis on her whiteness, however, permeates the image, whitewashing the eroticism borrowed from the lower classes and non-white models of womanhood with an assertion of what Birnbaum calls "colonizing whiteness" (316). Readers inclined to read the novel's unmistakable emphasis on whiteness as a purely aesthetic choice must reckon with the racial implications present in Chopin's representation of white female subjects. Whether we read this emphasis as another example of colonization or as Chopin's effort—albeit compromised—to unsettle cultural hierarchies, the fact remains that Adele resists easy categorization and thus cannot be dismissed as an uncomplicated emblem of nineteenth-century womanhood. Both physical and spiritual, sensual and chaste, she merges the "high" and "low" of the culture, and as hybrid "sensual Madonna" (30), she serves as model for Edna's growing comfort with her own body (see: Shaw 66; Wershover 29; Stone 25).

While Adele demonstrates the possibility of women's constructing hybrid selves, her choice to pursue motherhood as vocation limits her capacity for challenging dominant gender roles. A more fully alternative self emerges in Mademoiselle Reisz, the reclusive artist whose music evokes in Edna intense passions. Undoubtedly playing a significant role in Edna's decision to pursue her art and move out of her husband's house, Mademoiselle Reisz puts forth an appearance befitting her eccentric temperament. Summed up as having "absolutely no taste in dress," she wears one ornament, "a batch of rusty black lace with a bunch of artificial violets," which sits to the side of her false hair (44). With these adornments, however, she makes a uniquely anti-fashion statement. Anti-fashion, a mode of dress that often functions as a sign of protest, included during the nineteenth century the bohemian garb worn by French artists, the bloomer costume propounded by dress reformers, and the outmoded styles worn by eccentric individualists like Mademoiselle (see: Davis 5-27; Barwick 48-70; Hollander 363-65). False hair—clumps of curls with comb—had fallen out of fashion by 1879, and, while millinery like Mademoiselle's violets and black lace embellished ladies' evening wear in stop-and-go cycles throughout the nineteenth century, only in the 1870s did such pieces enjoy general daytime use (Cunnington 302-05). Mademoiselle Reisz's clinging to these outmoded styles of her youth makes a potentially political statement, for, in America's burgeoning consumer society, women who resisted the sway of fashion fulfilled an oppositional role, contesting consumerism by rejecting what Veblen observed to be women's primary function under capitalism: consumption. The prunella gaiter that Mademoiselle mends during one of Edna's visits further underscores her opposition to normative female roles. Utilitarian and practical rather than ornamental, gaiters, which were button shoes with a cloth upper section, are pictured in the 1894 *The Woman's Book* as a part of a reform business ensemble (213). Clearly in contrast with the ruffled tea gowns and velvet-trimmed walking dresses shown elsewhere in *The Woman's Book,* the suit and gaiters adopt the idiom of men's dress, insistently expressing seriousness, activity, and purposeful work. . . . Fashion historians and theorists like Joanne Finkelstein (107-29) or Fred Davis (33-54) have discussed the importance of more "masculine" dress for nineteenth-century unmarried women who entered the professions (see also Ewen and Ewen 88-97). Mademoiselle's gaiter suggests in its very functionality her mobility, her leaving her home to teach music and perform. Of course, Mademoiselle Reisz's "old prunella gaiter," shabby and in need of mending, is no careful addendum to a three-piece suit. Indeed, like the other of the material details of her life—the three-room apartment in a racially mixed neighbourhood or the "dingy and battered" buffet (81)—the gaiter implies not only women's changing life options but also the economic hardship that often accompanied a choice to shun marriage in favour of independence.

Chopin includes only three specific details about Mademoiselle's attire, one of them the outdated but ultra-feminine false hair and violets, the second the masculine-coded gaiters, and a third the red flannel rag that she wears around her neck when she is sick. This final detail works to punctuate a point of friction where body, gender identity, and subjectivity interconnect, for elsewhere in the novel red functions as a symbol for female sexuality, a point that Christina Giorcelli makes in her essay on *The Awakening* (112). While Giorcelli makes no mention of Mademoiselle's red rag, her argument about the symbolic use of red lends support for Kathryn Seidel's reading of Mademoiselle, which examines the character within the context of late-nineteenth-century representations of lesbians. Showing that Mademoiselle, like the lesbian characters in works of George Sand, Zola, de Maupassant, and O. Henry, displays physical deformity, flaunts her hostility of domestic occupation, and pursues art as a vocation, Seidel argues that Chopin's treatment here draws on nineteenth-century stereotypes of lesbians, a position that becomes all the more pointed within Chopin's colour-coding of female sexuality. Notwithstanding the implication of a "twistedness," Mademoiselle's sexuality significantly resists classification within the binary categories male/female. In an odd mix that makes Mademoiselle the antithesis of ideal female beauty and the antithesis of ideal male beauty, Chopin blurs categories of male and female. Dependent on men neither economically nor romantically, Mademoiselle nonetheless lacks the economic power she might enjoy were she an independent male, a social reality of unmarried professional women's lives that further works to blur traditional gender codes. Although Mademoiselle appears to involve herself only vicariously in romance, her lesbianism nevertheless opens a powerfully transgressive space. In its refusal to fit into strictly binary gender configurations, it acknowledges a female subjectivity that defines itself not simply by opposing normative categories but by tossing the markers of those categories willy-nilly into a hybrid mix. Hybrid from the top of her head (where ultra-feminine, evening millinery sits askew at all hours of the day) to the tips of her toes (where gaiters accented with the idiom of masculine dress leak), Mademoiselle Reisz lives out the artistic life amid the common and racially mixed. The artist who "dares and defies," Chopin suggests, chooses *anti-* as her mode of life, art, and dress, and she mixes categories, particularly gender categories, at will.

The sort of hybrid anti-fashion favoured by Mademoiselle Reisz marks Edna's dress at only one point in *The Awakening.* As she prepares to declare her economic independence and take up her life as an artist in her pigeon house, she works in an "old blue gown, with a red silk handkerchief knotted at random around her head" (105). In putting on a dress discarded because it has gone out of fashion, Edna foregoes special work clothing, the morning gowns and wrappers that were "a luxury" enjoyed only by the upper and middle classes (Hall 52-53). Instead, she employs a mode of dress customary for members of the lower classes, who adapted their worn dress-up clothing to meet the daily needs of work. Edna's anti-fashion outfit fabricates an identity that takes its inception from the working class, but it clearly alters the materials. Edna's gown, though old, was never working-class dress-up wear. And her red handkerchief, though knotted peasant style, is—unlike Mariequita's red servant's kerchief—made of silk. Turning the peasant's rag into an odd mix that simultaneously signifies wealth *and* its lack, Edna dons for the first time a sort of hybrid anti-fashion, and she has "never looked handsomer" (105). Once again, Chopin builds Edna's subjectivity by calling upon imagery of low-others; in effect, Edna plays at transgressing class boundaries, a game that Birnbaum rightly sees as reinforcement of class and race difference. Yet, by choosing clothing not typically favoured by middle-class women, Edna comes the closest at this point to truly outfitting herself to venture forth with self-possession. Outfitted for work, foregoing attire bought through bourgeois marriage, she puts on her own version of Mademoiselle's outmoded, anti-fashion ensemble, planning to take up the independent life. Edna's plans, of course, never materialize. Sartorially speaking, she cannot make a habit of anti-fashion. Abandoning the pieced-together costume that most becomes her, Edna celebrates her exit as wife wearing an opulent gown of gold satin.

The description of Edna in her gold gown at her gala birthday dinner puts into place the opposition most significant to her subjectivity—solitary artist/mother-woman. Amid the "soft fall of lace encircling her shoulders," Chopin writes, there is something in Edna's appearance that suggests "the regal woman, the one who rules, who looks on, who stands alone" (109). Regal imagery appears in only one other scene—when Adele walks toward her children with the majesty "which queens are sometimes supposed to possess" (31). This repetition suggests that power for women emanates from two possible positions: motherhood and solitude. While historians have thoroughly documented the discourse on mother-

hood, showing that it clearly enhanced women's power during this period (see: Gordon 111-15; Leach 85-90), the implications of solitariness are much harder to sort through but critically vital in discussing a novel originally entitled *A Solitary Soul*. Because solitariness exists as both a category of Edna's thought and as a concept scrutinized by Chopin, only by teasing apart character zone and authorial voice can readers unravel its implications. Chopin's position emerges in her description of Edna's shimmering gown, for, when read against the background created by other uses of dress in the novel, the rich folds and excess of the gown's folds perfectly exemplifies the sort of opulence that Veblen linked with the show of the *husband's* power—not the wife's. Because the novel has brought into question both consumerism and a husband's ownership of his wife, there is little reason to read Chopin's description of Edna's appearance at the dinner as a statement of female power. Edna in effect fabricates the solitary artist with materials taken directly from the garb she aims to put aside, and she crowns herself with a diamond tiara, a gift from the husband she desires to escape.

Edna's inability to sustain the sort of boundary crossing needed to construct a new sort of female selfhood that can pull her present role—motherhood—into an innovative one that would merge motherhood and artistic pursuit surfaces in the character's visit to Iberville. Immediately following her move into the pigeon house, this visit pulls her toward merger with her children; arms "clasp" and cheeks "press" as Edna gives her children "all of herself." Yet, Chopin defines motherhood as a reciprocal relationship, for, although Edna gives all of herself, she also "gather[s] and fill[s] herself with [her children's] young existence" (115). Edna continues to span this threshold while in transit between Iberville and New Orleans when the presence of the children lingers "like the memory of a delicious song" (116). The synaesthesia merging sound and taste suggests other fusions as well—thresholds where autonomy meets love, where middle-class convention meets non-conventional social practice, where self-possession need not negate ties to others. Unable to remain within this liminal space where motherhood meets solitude, though, Edna reaches the city "alone" (116), and she is left to imagine a utopian world where ties to the social world disappear.

Just as Edna's clothing throughout the novel has marked her social class and gender identity, so her rejection of clothing symbolically closes off these sites of subjectivity. Chopin prepares the reader for her character's final rejection of the social world during the island awakening scene when she divests herself of her constraining garments to nap in Madame Antoine's cottage. Conventions of nineteenth-century utopian fiction undergird this episode (Rose 1-5), as when Edna wakes to pretend with Robert to have slept "precisely one hundred years" (57). She perceives the island as "changed" and imagines that a "new race of beings [. . .] have sprung up," leaving only herself and Robert as "past relics" (57). With this imaginary leap into an Edenic future rich with sensual pleasures and devoid of former social ties, Chopin suggests the sort of premature utopianism that Terry Eagleton has attributed to many nineteenth-century Marxists. Such utopias then and now, he argues, simply risk "making us ill" (229) with desire, for they suggest no starting point from which "a feasible future might germinate" (230). Edna's need to rupture all ties with the existing world in order to construct a new self surfaces in the quick question she asks: "And when did our people from Grand Isle disappear from the earth?" (57). With her own people gone, she might enter a utopian paradise where no demands from the past impinge. The utopian vision ends abruptly and significantly with the word *really*: "But *really*, what has become of Monsieur Farival and the others?" (57, emph. mine). In reality, Chopin suggests, a future severed from our present selves simply cannot be. The future must incorporate the present if it is to be feasible. Only a dialectical relationship between present and future can ultimately fuse into one hybrid self the oppositions that, if kept isolated, threaten destruction.

Not knowing how to incorporate her own past—motherhood—into her construction of a new sort of female self, Edna fabricates through her death the solitary woman. Having told Adele "I would give my life for my children; but I wouldn't give myself," she goes to Grande Isle at the novel's end to undress and stand "naked under the sky" (136). The utopian dress-reform movement provides a context for reading Edna's final divesting. While some utopian reformers advocated wearing flesh-coloured tights and Greek-style draperies . . . , others simply advocated a free and non-conventional nudity (see: Banner 147-53; Rigel 397). These latter dress reformers, espousing an abrupt shift from constricting corsets to liberating nudity, brandished a violent break between present and future. Edna Pontellier embodies with her death this same sort

of divide. All she can do is throw off the worn, pricking garments of the world, for she can find no vestments to clothe solitariness in a world indisputably social. Her new woman, clothed only in the undress of simple cultural negation, gives up the struggle for liberation. No clothes become her.

Edna's rejection, at the novel's end, of all dress and thus all possible female social identities illustrates her inability to reconcile the contradictions elemental to a hybrid construction of womanhood. Edna's limitations, however, are secondary to my point. Kate Chopin clearly recognized the necessity of women's looking beyond dominant, middle-class figurations of womanhood for models of liberated practice. By creating characters that merged the dress and supposed behaviour from a variety of sites, she was able to forward alternative female identities. Her use of stereotyped social class, racial, and lesbian models of female sexuality most certainly encumbers readers' unconditional praise of Chopin's use of hybridization as a means of representing an alternative female subject, and any interpretation must come to grips with the way nineteenth-century "low-others" are integral to the options that Chopin offers in **The Awakening**. Yet the writer's awareness that social change for women must entail innovative forms that pull from a variety of social contexts is noteworthy. Rather than simply restating commonly accepted forms, Chopin combined in new ways social forms already present within the culture.

In 1896, a writer for *Godey's Magazine* predicted a revolution in dress, prophesizing a future when women would "wear the garments once considered as the prerogative of our husbands and brothers." She asked with disdain if the woman of the future would be "a hybrid sort of creature" who with her raiment would suggest "both sexes" (Montaigu 435). For Montaigu and for the public at large, dress at the turn into the twentieth century revealed more than mere fashion statements. These contemporaries of Kate Chopin could read with ease subtle cues intoned with gender connotations, and they were adept at scrutinizing each others' dress for signs of taste, character, and respectability. Not surprisingly, modern readers lack specific knowledge about sartorial choices of the period and are thus left to read clothing imagery as simple detail or as satisfying bits of local colour. Yet, when seemingly transparent details of dress are placed solidly within the discursive field of late-nineteenth-and early-twentieth-century America, the socially significant meanings that contemporaneous readers took for granted emerge. As this reading of Chopin's novel demonstrates, an interdisciplinary approach that melds literary study, fashion history and theory, and social history can open late-nineteenth and early-twentieth-century texts by recovering meanings lost as fashions faded. Without a doubt, Kate Chopin represented the changing silhouette of American womanhood.

Works Cited

Babcock, Barbara. *The Reversible World: Symbolic Inversion in Art and Society.* Ithaca, NY: Cornell UP, 1978.

Banner, Lois W. *American Beauty.* New York: Knopf, 1983.

Barwick, Sandra. *A Century of Style.* Boston: George Allen and Unwin, 1984.

Birnbaum, Michele A. "'Alien Hands': Kate Chopin and the Colonization of Race." *American Literature* 66 (1994): 301-23.

Bradfield, Nancy. *Costume in Detail: Women's Dress, 1730-1930.* Boston: Plays, 1968.

Byrde, Penelope. *Nineteenth Century Fashion.* London: B.T. Batsford, 1992.

Chopin, Kate. *The Awakening: A Complete Authoritative Text with Biographical and Historical Contexts, Critical History, and Essays from Five Contemporary Critical Perspectives.* Ed. Nancy Walker. Boston: Bedford, 1993.

Collins, Robert. "The Dismantling of Edna Pontellier: Garment Imagery in Kate Chopin's *The Awakening.*" *Southern Studies* 23 (1984): 176-90.

Cunnington, C. Willett. *English Women's Clothing in the Nineteenth Century.* London: Faber and Faber, 1937.

Davis, Fred. *Fashion, Culture, and Identity.* Chicago: U of Chicago P, 1992.

Eagleton, Terry. *The Ideology of the Aesthetic.* Cambridge, MA: Basil Blackwell, 1990.

Ecob, Helen Gilbert. *The Well-Dressed Woman: A Study in the Practical Application To Dress of the Laws of Health, Art and Morals.* New York: Fowler and Wells, 1892.

Ewen, Stuart. *All Consuming Images: The Politics of Style in Contemporary Culture.* New York: Basic, 1988.

Ewen, Stuart, and Elizabeth Ewen. *Channels of Desire: Mass Images and the Shaping of American Consciousness.* Minneapolis: U of Minnesota P, 1992.

Finkelstein, Joanne. *The Fashioned Self.* Philadelphia: Temple UP, 1991.

Gilman, Charlotte Perkins. *Women and Economics: A Study of the Economic Relation between Men and Women as a Factor in Social Evolution.* 1898. New York: Harper and Row, 1966.

Giorcelli, Christina. "Edna's Wisdom: A Transitional and Numinous Merging." *New Essays on* The Awakening. Ed. Wendy Martin. Cambridge, UK: Cambridge UP, 1988. 109-40.

Gordon, Linda. *Woman's Body, Woman's Right: A Social History of Birth Control in America.* New York: Grossman, 1976.

Hall, Lee. *Common Threads: A Parade of American Clothing.* Boston: Little, Brown, 1992.

Haweis, Mary Eliza Joy. *The Art of Dress.* London: Chatto and Windus, 1979.

Hollander, Anne. *Seeing through Clothes.* New York: Avon, 1980.

James, William. *The Principles of Psychology.* Vol. I. Cambridge, MA: Harvard UP, 1981.

"Just between Ourselves, Girls." *The Jewish Daily News.* 14 December 1902: English page.

Kasson, John F. *Rudeness and Civility: Manners in Nineteenth-Century Urban America.* New York: Hill and Wang, 1990.

Kellogg, J. H. *The Evils of Fashionable Dress.* Battle Creek, MI: The Office of the Health Reformer, 1876.

King, E. M. Untitled essay. *Symposium on Women's Dress.* Part 2. *The Arena* 35 (October 1892): 629-30.

Leach, William. *True Love and Perfect Union: The Feminist Reform of Sex and Society.* New York: Basic, 1880.

"Long Cloaks for Early Autumn." *Harper's Bazar* 7 July 1900: 616-17.

MacCurdy, Carol A. "*The Awakening*: Chopin's Metaphorical Use of Clothes." *Publications of the Mississippi Philological Association* (1985): 58-66.

McNall, Sally Allen. "Immigrant Backgrounds to *My Antonia*: A Curious Social Situation in Black Hawk." *Approaches to Teaching Cather's My Antonia.* Ed. Susan J. Rosowski. New York: MLA, 1989. 22-30.

Melendy, Mary Ries. *Perfect Womanhood for Maidens-Wives-Mothers.* N.p.: Boland, 1903.

Montaigu, Countess Annie de. "Fashion, Fact, and Fancy." *Godey's Magazine* (April 1896): 435-50.

Perrot, Philippe. *Fashioning the Bourgeoisie: A History of Clothing in the Nineteenth Century.* Trans. Richard Bienvenu. Princeton: Princeton UP, 1994.

Quigley, Dorothy. *What Dress Makes of Us.* New York: E.P. Dutton, 1897.

Rigel, Robert E. "Women's Clothes and Women's Rights." *American Quarterly* 15 (1963): 396-97.

Rose, Anita. "Reconfiguring the 'Other' in Late Nineteenth-Century British Utopian Literature." Diss. U of North Carolina at Greensboro, 1996.

Seidel, Kathryn Lee. "Art is an Unnatural Act: Mademoiselle Reisz in *The Awakening.*" *Mississippi Quarterly* 46 (1993): 199-214.

Severa, Joan L. *Dressed for the Photographer: Ordinary Americans and Fashion, 1840-1900.* Kent, OH: Kent State UP, 1995.

Seyersted, Per. *Kate Chopin: A Critical Biography.* Baton Rouge: Louisiana State UP, 1969.

Shaw, Pat. "Putting Audience in Its Place: Psychosexuality and Perspective in *The Awakening.*" *American Literary Realism* 23.1 (fall 1990): 61-69.

Stallybrass, Peter, and Allon White. *The Politics and Poetics of Transgression.* Ithaca, NY: Cornell UP, 1986.

Stange, Margit. "Personal Property: Exchange Value and the Female Self in *The Awakening.*" *The Awakening: A Complete Authoritative Text with Biographical and Histori-*

cal Contexts, Critical History, and Essays from Five Contemporary Critical Perspectives. Ed. Nancy Walker. Boston: Bedford, 1993. 201-17.

Stone, Carole. "The Female Artist in Kate Chopin's *The Awakening*: Birth and Creativity." *Women's Studies* 13 (1986): 23-32.

"A Symposium on Women's Dress." Part 1. *The Arena* 34 (September 1892): 488-507.

———. Part 2. *The Arena* 35 (October 1892): 621-34.

"Two New Yachting Gowns." *Harper's Bazar* 28 July 1900: 814-15.

Veblen, Thorstein. *The Theory of the Leisure Class: An Economic Study of Institutions.* 1899. New York: B. W. Huebsch, 1912.

Walker, Alexander. *Intermarriage; or How and Why Beauty, Health and Intellect Result from Certain Marriages and Deformity, Disease and Insanity from Others.* Birmingham: Edward Baker, 1897.

Wershoven, C. J. "*The Awakening* and *The House of Mirth*: Studies in Arrested Development." *American Literary Realism* 19.3 (1986/87): 27-41.

Wolkenfeld, Suzanne. "Edna's Suicide: The Problem of the One and the Many." *The Awakening: An Authoritative Text, Contexts, Criticism.* Ed. Margaret Culley. New York: Norton, 1976. 218-24.

The Woman's Book: Dealing Practically with the Modern Conditions of Home-Life, Self-Support, Education, Opportunities, and Every-Day Problems. New York: C. Scribner's Sons, 1894.

FURTHER READING

Bibliographies

Green, Suzanne Disheroon, and David J. Caudle. *Kate Chopin: An Annotated Bibliography of Critical Works.* Westport, Conn.: Greenwood Press, 1999, 274 p.

Provides a comprehensive survey of criticism on Chopin published between 1976 and 1998, including annotated entries for books, essays, dissertations, biographical studies, and bibliographical works.

Seyersted, Per and Emily Toth. "Bibliography of Kate Chopin's Writings" and "Writings on Kate Chopin." In *A Kate Chopin Miscellany*, pp. 203-11; 212-61. Natchitoches, La.: Northwestern State University Press, 1979.

Contains a detailed bibliography of Chopin's writings and of critical study of Chopin's works.

Biography

Toth, Emily. *Kate Chopin.* New York: William Morrow and Company, 1990, 528 p.

Questions long-held views on Chopin's life and writing; includes appendices, photographs, and a select bibliography.

Criticism

Allen, Priscilla. "Old Critics and New: The Treatment of Chopin's *The Awakening*." In *The Authority of Experience: Essays in Feminist Criticism*, edited by Arlyn Diamond and Lee R. Edwards, pp. 224-38. Amherst: University of Massachusetts Press, 1977.

Examines the critical reception over time given to The Awakening.

Beer, Janet. "*Sister Carrie* and *The Awakening*: The Clothed, the Unclothed, and the Woman Undone." In *Soft Canons: American Women Writers and the Masculine Tradition,* edited by Karen L. Kilcup, pp. 167-83. Iowa City: University of Iowa Press, 1999.

Compares the heroines of Chopin's The Awakening and Theodore Dreiser's Sister Carrie.

Burns, Karin Garlepp. "The Paradox of Objectivity in the Realist Fiction of Edith Wharton and Kate Chopin." *Journal of Narrative Theory* 29, no. 1 (winter 1999): 27-61.

Analyzes the use of objectivity and its feminist implications in Edith Wharton's The Custom of the Country and Chopin's The Awakening.

Crosland, Andrew. "Kate Chopin's 'Lilacs' and the Myth of Persephone." *ANQ: A Quarterly Journal of Short Articles, Notes, and Reviews* 14, no. 1 (winter 2001): 31-4.

Provides a concise analysis of Chopin's short story "Lilacs," paying particular attention to its mythological allusions.

Ewell, Barbara C. "Unlinking Race and Gender: *The Awakening* as a Southern Novel." *The Southern Quarterly* 37, nos. 3-4 (spring-summer 1999): 30-7.

Examines how The Awakening was shaped by the culture and history of the late-nineteenth-century South and compares Chopin's commentary on gender to her understanding of racial inequalities.

Koloski, Bernard. *Kate Chopin: A Study of the Short Fiction.* New York: Twayne Publishers, 1996, 165 p.

Surveys Chopin's short stories and reprints reviews and essays on Chopin's life and work as a short story writer.

Petry, Alice Hall, ed. *Critical Essays on Kate Chopin.* New York: G. K. Hall, 1996, 257 p.

Reprints both early and modern reviews and essays devoted to Chopin's works.

Rich, Charlotte. "Reconsidering *The Awakening*: The Literary Sisterhood of Kate Chopin and George Egerton." *The Southern Quarterly* 41, no. 3 (spring 2003): 121-36.

Discusses the influence of George Egerton's writings on The Awakening, *stressing the similarities between Chopin's novel and Egerton's* Keynotes.

Rankin, Daniel S. *Kate Chopin and Her Creole Stories.* Philadelphia: University of Pennsylvania Press, 1932, 339 p.

Provides critical discussion of Chopin's short stories and details about her life in relation to her work.

Schweitzer, Ivy. "Maternal Discourse and the Romance of Self-Possession in Kate Chopin's *The Awakening*." In *Gendered Agents: Women and Institutional Knowledge,* edited by Silvestra Mariniello and Paul Bové, pp. 161-91. Durham, N.C.: Duke University Press, 1998.

Contrasts the protagonists of Nathaniel Hawthorne's The Scarlet Letter and Chopin's The Awakening, particularly noting that Edna Pontellier experiences motherhood while Hester Prynne does not.

Simons, Karen. "Kate Chopin on the Nature of Things." *The Mississippi Quarterly* 51, no. 2 (spring 1998): 243-52.

Highlights the influence of the Roman poet and philosopher Lucretius on The Awakening.

Wade, Carl. "Conformity, Resistance, and the Search for Selfhood in Kate Chopin's *The Awakening.*" *The Southern Quarterly* 37, no. 2 (winter 1999): 92-104.

Departs from the typical regionalist and feminist readings of The Awakening *to explore the novel's place in the tradition of realist fiction.*

OTHER SOURCES FROM GALE:

Additional coverage of Chopin's life and career is contained in the following sources published by the Gale Group: *American Writers Retrospective Supplement,* Vol. 2; *American Writers Supplement,* Vol. 1; *Authors and Artists for Young Adults,* Vol. 33; *Beacham's Guide to Literature for Young Adults,* Vols. 11, 15; *Concise Dictionary of American Literary Biography 1865-1917; Dictionary of Literary Biography,* Vols. 12, 78; *DISCovering Authors; DISCovering Authors: British Edition; Exploring Novels; Exploring Short Stories; Feminist Writers; Literature and Its Times,* Vol. 3; *Literature Resource Center; Modern American Women Writers; Novels for Students,* Vol. 3; *Reference Guide to American Literature,* Ed. 4; *Reference Guide to Short Fiction,* Ed. 2; *Short Stories for Students,* Vol. 17; *Short Story Criticism,* Vols. 8, 68; *Twayne's United States Authors; Twentieth-Century Literary Criticism,* Vol. 127; and *World Literature Criticism Supplement.*

EMILY DICKINSON

(1830 - 1886)

American poet.

Dickinson has been hailed by critics as one of the most important and original poets to emerge from the American literary tradition. However, the poet received none of this critical acclaim during her lifetime. The few editors who actually appraised Dickinson's verse faulted her language as too unsentimental and plain to suit contemporary tastes. Further, the structure of her poems was not as polished as the conventional romantic verse that was published in the leading periodicals of the day. Modern critics have come to recognize that Dickinson's poetic style was in fact decades ahead of its time and that she anticipated the modern poetry movement of the twentieth century by using simple words and images to meditate on such profound universal concepts as nature, death, and immortality. Feminist scholars have examined Dickinson's poems and letters in an effort to gain some insight into how the poet responded to the gender-restrictive values of the mid-nineteenth-century patriarchal society. These critics have concluded that while as a person Dickinson succumbed to a life of social marginality and seclusion, as a poet she opened a new frontier of feminine power and assertiveness through her transcendent and imaginative verse.

BIOGRAPHICAL INFORMATION

Dickinson was born on December 10, 1830, in Amherst, Massachusetts. She was the eldest child of Edward Dickinson, a prominent lawyer, politician, and treasurer of Amherst College, and Emily Norcross Dickinson. The Dickinsons were a close-knit family governed by her father, a demanding, family-oriented patriarch. Indeed, Emily and her younger sister Lavinia never married, devoting their lives to the domestic obligations and care of the other members of the Dickinson family. Emily's brother, Austin, followed in his father's footsteps by becoming a partner in the family law practice and by succeeding his father as treasurer of Amherst College. Austin also built a house next to the Dickinson family homestead. As a youth, Emily received a formal education befitting a member of a prosperous New England family. She attended primary school for four years beginning in 1835; she then matriculated at Amherst Academy from 1840 to 1847. Upon graduating from the Amherst Academy, Dickinson enrolled in Mount Holyoke Female Seminary for one year from 1847 to 1848. Electing not to continue her studies at Mount Holyoke after her first year, Dickinson settled down in Amherst and resumed her domestic and familial obligations. During this time, she became acquainted with a number of prominent religious, political, and literary figures who paid visits to her father at Amherst. Among these visitors was Samuel Bowles, the owner and editor of the *Springfield Republican,* from whom Dickinson would seek advice and send poems in the hope of being recognized as a serious poet. Failing to recognize her talent, Bowles refused to publish Dickinson's poems in his periodical and even discouraged her from writing more verses.

In 1854 Dickinson traveled with her mother to Washington, D.C., to visit Edward, who was at the time serving a term as a representative to the United States Congress. On their return trip to Amherst, the Dickinsons visited a family friend in Philadelphia. Several biographers have speculated that while in Philadelphia, Dickinson met and fell in love with a married minister who begged her to elope with him. These scholars have further contended that this love affair and Dickinson's decision to end it precipitated her withdrawal into seclusion and her increasingly eccentric behavior. It is important to note that apart from one family account of this affair there is no evidence to substantiate the claim that it ever occurred. Nevertheless, not long after this trip Dickinson did become more reclusive and eccentric. She withdrew to the family homestead in Amherst, refusing even to venture to her brother's house next door. Whereas she had previously received and entertained numerous guests at the homestead, Dickinson now refused all visitors. She began to dress in only white attire, an act which some scholars have argued was a symbolic attempt to present herself as a nun, a virgin, a poet, or some combination of the three. Her few companions during this time included Lavinia and Austin. Dickinson's attachment to Austin's children and his wife, Susan, was especially close.

Biographers have generally agreed that Dickinson experienced a grave emotional crisis in the early 1860s. Although no evidence has been discovered to shed light onto the nature of this crisis, some scholars have pointed out that this time frame coincides with Bowles's public rejection of Dickinson's unsentimental brand of poetry in the *Springfield Republican,* although he did not specifically identify her as the offender. At about the same time, Dickinson's poetry output surged; in 1862 alone she is thought to have composed more than three hundred poems. After her rift with Bowles, Dickinson sought out a new patron who would recognize the value of her poetry. She initiated a correspondence with Thomas Wentworth Higginson, the literary editor of the *Atlantic Monthly,* sending him some of her poems and soliciting his advice on their merit. Like Bowles, Higginson never published any of Dickinson's

verse in his periodical, but he did serve as a sympathetic advisor to her literary endeavors. Throughout this period, Dickinson remained in seclusion at Amherst, except for brief trips to Boston in 1864 and 1865 to receive medical care for an eye condition. Whatever familial security Dickinson felt ended abruptly in 1874 when her father died unexpectedly. Not long after Edward's death, Dickinson's mother became an invalid, relying on her children for complete care until her own death in 1882. Dickinson herself died two years later on May 15, 1886, after a prolonged battle with a kidney disorder known as Bright's disease.

MAJOR WORKS

Literary scholars have discovered nearly eighteen hundred poems written by Dickinson. Some academics have posited that even more verses might be in existence as appendixes to Dickinson's voluminous correspondence with family, friends, and literary acquaintances, but that they have not yet been recognized by the letter recipients' inheritors. Those poems authoritatively attributed to Dickinson have been collected by scholars and each one assigned an identifying number since Dickinson did not give a title to most of her verses. Given the sheer number of Dickinson's poems, the poet afforded herself the opportunity to explore a wide variety of subjects, including the austerity and beauty of nature; experiences of love and loss; a skeptical attitude toward religion and immortality; and a morbid fascination with death. This last preoccupation is especially apparent in Poem 712 (also known as "Because I could not stop for Death—"), in which eternal rest is imagined as a carriage ride. Regardless of the subject, Dickinson's poetry represents an innovative formal technique that heralded the preeminent stylistic developments of the twentieth century: she developed a highly personal system of symbol and allusion, assigning complex meanings to colors, places, times, and seasons; she experimented with compression, enjambment, and unusual rhyme schemes; and she employed an idiosyncratic use of capitalization and punctuation, including the liberal use of dashes. The result is a distinctive and revolutionary poetic style quite unlike that of her nineteenth-century contemporaries.

Feminist scholars have identified a number of Dickinson's poems which directly comment upon the role and experiences of women within a repressive patriarchal order. In addition, some of these critics have suggested that many more poems can be interpreted as the poet's opinion of gender issues if one were to assume that the speaker in each verse is a female. For example, Poem 271 ("A solemn thing—it was—I said—") presents the image of "a woman—white," which may be a reference to a bride, a novice nun, or a female poet. At the conclusion, the speaker of the poem finds satisfaction in her "'small' life," which some commentators have suggested is a rejection of conventional female roles in favor of pursuing those that she finds more fulfilling. A similar theme of empowerment has been detected in Poem 657 ("I dwell in Possibility—"), which many critics have maintained is a commentary on the ability of the female artist to subvert the oppressive limitations of the patriarchal order through the transcendental power of poetry. Though her poems were not grouped into published collections during her lifetime, Dickinson did sew certain poems into "fascicles," or small booklets, indicating that she viewed them as related meditations on a central theme. Her fascicle 22, which includes Poem 271, is one example. Scholars have focused on the poems in this fascicle—which reflect on such subjects as domestic life, liberty, human relationships, and spiritual redemption—as verses indicative of Dickinson's desire to defy the social and gender conventions of her day.

CRITICAL RECEPTION

Just as literary editors failed to recognize Dickinson's literary talent during her lifetime, late-nineteenth-century critics dismissed her first posthumous collection of verses entitled *Poems* (1890). While these reviewers asserted that Dickinson's unconventional use of meter, rhyme, and imagery was technically defective and dispassionate, the poems found an eager and receptive public audience. In order to meet the popular demand for Dickinson's verses, her estate published a second series of *Poems* in 1891 and a third series in 1896. In the early twentieth century, Dickinson's oeuvre influenced the poets who belonged to the Imagist movement, particularly Amy Lowell. Members of this movement, which advocated the employment of free verse and the expression of concepts and feelings through simple, precise images, found in Dickinson's pioneering tropes and images the framework in which to express their own revolutionary ideas about poetry. Along with the popular and literary acceptance of Dickinson's poems in the twentieth century, scholars and critics began to recognize

the profound achievement of creating such sophisticated and technically innovative verse without the of assistance of any literary antecedents. Commentators have since analyzed nearly every aspect of Dickinson's poems from a myriad of critical perspectives, including linguistic, stylistic, psychoanalytical, philosophical, and historical. In the late twentieth century, feminist critics began to study Dickinson's poems in an effort to understand how they were shaped by the poet's experiences within the socially and morally codified patriarchal climate of mid-nineteenth-century America. These scholars have examined, among other issues, the difficulties Dickinson faced in reconciling her gender with the vocation of poet, the significance of her decision to retire from society, her use of language as a means of rebellion, and her importance to later writers. In addition, some critics have focused on Dickinson's relationships with the women in her life and her creation of a female-centered poetry, while others have concentrated on her interactions with men and her struggle to publish poetry in a male-dominated literary environment. Once deemed as eccentric, both Dickinson's poems and her way of life are now more commonly recognized as an uncompromising commitment to artistic expression and, in the opinion of some critics, as an attempt to undermine the restrictive masculine culture of her time.

PRINCIPAL WORKS

Poems (poetry) 1890

Poems second series (poetry) 1891

Letters of Emily Dickinson. 2 vols. (letters) 1894

Poems third series (poetry) 1896

The Single Hound: Poems of a Lifetime (poetry) 1914

The Complete Poems of Emily Dickinson (poetry) 1924

Further Poems of Emily Dickinson (poetry) 1929

Emily Dickinson Face to Face: Unpublished Letters with Notes and Reminiscences (letters) 1932

Unpublished Poems of Emily Dickinson (poetry) 1935

Bolts of Melody: New Poems of Emily Dickinson (poetry) 1945

Poems. 3 vols. (poetry) 1955

Letters. 3 vols. (letters) 1958

Complete Poems (poetry) 1960

The Poems of Emily Dickinson. 3 vols. (poetry) 1998

PRIMARY SOURCES

EMILY DICKINSON (POEM DATE 1861?)

SOURCE: Dickinson, Emily. "271." In *The Complete Poems of Emily Dickinson,* edited by Thomas H. Johnson, pp. 123-24. Boston: Little, Brown and Company, 1960.

Literary scholars have speculated that the following poem by Dickinson was written circa 1861.

271

A solemn thing—it was—I said—
A woman—white—to be—
And wear—if God should count me fit—
Her blameless mystery—

A hallowed thing—to drop a life
Into the purple well—
Too plummetless—that it return—
Eternity—until—

I pondered how the bliss would look—
And would it feel as big—
When I could take it in my hand—
As hovering—seen—through fog—

And then—the size of this "small" life—
The Sages—call it small—
Swelled—like Horizons—in my vest—
And I sneered—softly—"small"!

EMILY DICKINSON (POEM DATE 1862?)

SOURCE: Dickinson, Emily. "652." In *The Complete Poems of Emily Dickinson,* edited by Thomas H. Johnson, pp. 324-25. Boston: Little, Brown and Company, 1960.

Literary scholars have speculated that the following poem by Dickinson was written circa 1862.

652

A Prison gets to be a friend—
Between its Ponderous face
And Ours—a Kinsmanship express—
And in its narrow Eyes—

We come to look with gratitude
For the appointed Beam
It deal us—stated as our food—
And hungered for—the same—

We learn to know the Planks—
That answer to Our feet—
So miserable a sound—at first—
Nor ever now—so sweet—

As plashing in the Pools—
When Memory was a Boy—
But a Demurer Circuit—
A Geometric Joy—

The Posture of the Key
That interrupt the Day

To Our Endeavor—Not so real
The Cheek of Liberty—

As this Phantasm Steel—
Whose features—Day and Night—
Are present to us—as Our Own—
And as escapeless—quite—

The narrow Round—the Stint—
The slow exchange of Hope—
For something passiver—Content
Too steep for looking up—

The Liberty we knew
Avoided—like a Dream—
Too wide for any Night but Heaven—
If That—indeed—redeem—

EMILY DICKINSON (POEM DATE 1862?)

SOURCE: Dickinson, Emily. "657." In *The Complete Poems of Emily Dickinson,* edited by Thomas H. Johnson, p. 327. Boston: Little, Brown and Company, 1960.

Literary scholars have speculated that the following poem by Dickinson was written circa 1862.

657

I dwell in Possibility—
A fairer House than Prose—
More numerous of Windows—
Superior—for Doors—

Of Chambers as the Cedars—
Impregnable of Eye—
And for an Everlasting Roof
The Gambrels of the Sky—

Of Visitors—the fairest—
For Occupation—This—
The spreading wide my narrow Hands
To gather Paradise—

EMILY DICKINSON (POEM DATE 1863?)

SOURCE: Dickinson, Emily. "712." In *The Complete Poems of Emily Dickinson,* edited by Thomas H. Johnson, p. 350. Boston: Little, Brown and Company, 1960.

Literary scholars have speculated that the following poem by Dickinson was written circa 1863.

712

Because I could not stop for Death—
He kindly stopped for me—
The Carriage held but just Ourselves—
And Immortality.

We slowly drove—He knew no haste
And I had put away
My labor and my leisure too,
For His Civility—

We passed the School, where Children strove
At Recess—in the Ring—
We passed the Fields of Gazing Grain—
We passed the Setting Sun—

Or rather—He passed Us—
The Dews drew quivering and chill—
For only Gossamer, my Gown—
My Tippet—only Tulle—

We paused before a House that seemed
A Swelling of the Ground—
The Roof was scarcely visible—
The Cornice—in the Ground—

Since then—'tis Centuries—and yet
Feels shorter than the Day
I first surmised the Horses' Heads
Were toward Eternity—

GENERAL COMMENTARY

ADRIENNE RICH (ESSAY DATE 1976)

SOURCE: Rich, Adrienne. "Vesuvius at Home: The Power of Emily Dickinson." *On Lies, Secrets, and Silence: Selected Prose 1966-1978*, pp. 157-84. New York: W. W. Norton, 1979.

In the following essay, originally published in 1976, Rich celebrates Dickinson's poetry as a work of genius that was partly a response to the patriarchal culture of the nineteenth century but also informed by the poet's relationships with women. Rich also asserts that poetry was the primary goal of Dickinson's life, not the by-product of other events, as has been claimed by some critics.

I am travelling at the speed of time, along the Massachusetts Turnpike. For months, for years, for most of my life, I have been hovering like an insect against the screens of an existence which inhabited Amherst, Massachusetts, between 1831 and 1884. The methods, the exclusions, of Emily Dickinson's existence could not have been my own; yet more and more, as a woman poet finding my own methods, I have come to understand her necessities, could have been witness in her defense.

"Home is not where the heart is," she wrote in a letter, "but the house and the adjacent buildings." A statement of New England realism, a directive to be followed. Probably no poet ever lived so much and so purposefully in one house; even, in one room. Her niece Martha told of visiting her in her corner bedroom on the second floor at 280 Main Street, Amherst, and of how Emily Dickinson made as if to lock the door with an imaginary key, turned and said: "Matty: here's freedom."

I am travelling at the speed of time, in the direction of the house and buildings.

Western Massachusetts: the Connecticut Valley: a countryside still full of reverberations: scene of Indian uprisings, religious revivals, spiritual confrontations, the blazing-up of the lunatic fringe of the Puritan coal. How peaceful and how threatened it looks from Route 91, hills gently curled above the plain, the tobacco-barns standing in fields sheltered with white gauze from the sun, and the sudden urban sprawl: ARCO, Mac-Donald's, shopping plazas. The country that broke the heart of Jonathan Edwards, that enclosed the genius of Emily Dickinson. It lies calmly in the light of May, cloudy skies breaking into warm sunshine, light-green spring softening the hills, dogwood and wild fruit-trees blossoming in the hollows.

From Northampton bypass there's a 4-mile stretch of road to Amherst—Route 9—between fruit farms, steakhouses, supermarkets. The new University of Massachusetts rears its skyscrapers up from the plain against the Pelham Hills. There is new money here, real estate, motels. Amherst succeeds on Hadley almost without notice. Amherst is green, rich-looking, secure; we're suddenly in the center of town, the crossroads of the campus, old New England college buildings spread around two village greens, a scene I remember as almost exactly the same in the dim past of my undergraduate years when I used to come there for college weekends.

Left on Seelye Street, right on Main; driveway at the end of a yellow picket fence. I recognize the high hedge of cedars screening the house, because twenty-five years ago I walked there, even then drawn toward the spot, trying to peer over. I pull into the driveway behind a generous 19th-century brick mansion with wings and porches, old trees and green lawns. I ring at the back door—the door through which Dickinson's coffin was carried to the cemetery a block away.

For years I have been not so much envisioning Emily Dickinson as trying to visit, to enter her mind, through her poems and letters, and through my own intimations of what it could have meant to be one of the two mid-19th-century American geniuses, and a woman, living in Amherst, Massachusetts. Of the other genius, Walt Whitman, Dickinson wrote that she had heard his poems were "disgraceful." She knew her own were unacceptable by her world's standards of poetic convention, and of what was appropriate, in particular, for a woman poet. Seven were published in her lifetime, all edited by other hands; more than a thousand were laid away in her bedroom chest, to be discovered after her death. When her sister discovered them, there were decades of struggle over the manuscripts, the manner of their presentation to the world, their suitability for publication, the poet's own final intentions. Narrowed-down by her early editors and anthologists, reduced to quaintness or spinsterish oddity by many of her commentators, sentimentalized, fallen-in-love with like some gnomic Garbo, still unread in the breadth and depth of her full range of work, she was, and is, a wonder to me when I try to imagine myself into that mind.

I have a notion that genius knows itself; that Dickinson chose her seclusion, knowing she was exceptional and knowing what she needed. It was, moreover, no hermetic retreat, but a seclusion which included a wide range of people, of reading and correspondence. Her sister Vinnie said, "Emily is always looking for the rewarding person." And she found, at various periods, both women and men: her sister-in-law Susan Gilbert, Amherst visitors and family friends such as Benjamin Newton, Charles Wadsworth, Samuel Bowles, editor of the Springfield *Republican* and his wife; her friends Kate Anthon and Helen Hunt Jackson, the distant but significant figures of Elizabeth Barrett, the Brontës, George Eliot. But she carefully selected her society and controlled the disposal of her time. Not only the "gentlewoman in plush" of Amherst were excluded; Emerson visited next door but she did not go to meet him; she did not travel or receive routine visits; she avoided strangers. Given her vocation, she was neither eccentric nor quaint; she was determined to survive, to use her powers, to practice necessary economies.

Suppose Jonathan Edwards had been born a woman; suppose William James, for that matter, had been born a woman? (The invalid seclusion of his sister Alice is suggestive.) Even from men, New England took its psychic toll; many of its geniuses seemed peculiar in one way or another, particularly along the lines of social intercourse. Hawthorne, until he married, took his meals in his bedroom, apart from the family. Thoreau insisted on the values both of solitude and of geographical restriction, boasting that "I have travelled much in Concord." Emily Dickinson— viewed by her bemused contemporary Thomas Higginson as "partially cracked," by the 20th century as fey or pathological—has increasingly struck me as a practical woman, exercising her gift as she had to, making choices. I have come to imagine her as somehow too strong for her envi-

ronment, a figure of powerful will, not at all frail or breathless, someone whose personal dimensions would be felt in a household. She was her father's favorite daughter though she professed being afraid of him. Her sister dedicated herself to the everyday domestic labors which would free Dickinson to write. (Dickinson herself baked the bread, made jellies and gingerbread, nursed her mother through a long illness, was a skilled horticulturist who grew pomegranates, calla-lillies, and other exotica in her New England greenhouse.)

Upstairs at last: I stand in the room which for Emily Dickinson was "freedom." The best bedroom in the house, a corner room, sunny, overlooking the main street of Amherst in front, the way to her brother Austin's house on the side. Here, at a small table with one drawer, she wrote most of her poems. Here she read Elizabeth Barrett's "Aurora Leigh," a woman poet's narrative poem of a woman poet's life; also George Eliot; Emerson; Carlyle; Shakespeare; Charlotte and Emily Brontë. Here I become, again, an insect, vibrating at the frames of windows, clinging to panes of glass, trying to connect. The scent here is very powerful. Here in this white-curtained, high-ceilinged room, a redhaired woman with hazel eyes and a contralto voice wrote poems about volcanoes, deserts, eternity, suicide, physical passion, wild beasts, rape, power, madness, separation, the daemon, the grave. Here, with a darning-needle, she bound these poems—heavily emended and often in variant versions—into booklets, secured with darning-thread, to be found and read after her death. Here she knew "freedom," listening from above-stairs to a visitor's piano-playing, escaping from the pantry where she was mistress of the household bread and puddings, watching, you feel, watching ceaselessly, the life of sober Main Street below. From this room she glided downstairs, her hand on the polished bannister, to meet the complacent magazine editor, Thomas Higginson, unnerve him while claiming she herself was unnerved. "Your scholar," she signed herself in letters to him. But she was an independent scholar, used his criticism selectively, saw him rarely and always on *her* premises. It was a life deliberately organized on her terms. The terms she had been handed by society—Calvinist Protestantism, Romanticism, the 19th-century corseting of women's bodies, choices, and sexuality—could spell insanity to a woman genius. What this one had to do was retranslate her own unorthodox, subversive, sometimes volcanic propensities into a dialect called metaphor: her native language. "Tell all the Truth—but tell it Slant—." It is always what is under pressure in us, especially under pressure of concealment—that explodes in poetry.

The women and men in her life she equally converted into metaphor. The masculine pronoun in her poems can refer simultaneously to many aspects of the "masculine" in the patriarchal world—the god she engages in dialogue, again on *her* terms; her own creative powers, unsexing for a woman, the male power-figures in her immediate environment—the lawyer Edward Dickinson, her brother Austin, the preacher Wadsworth, the editor Bowles—it is far too limiting to trace that "He" to some specific lover, although that was the chief obsession of the legend-mongers for more than half a century. Obviously, Dickinson was attracted by and interested in men whose minds had something to offer her; she was, it is by now clear, equally attracted by and interested in women whose minds had something to offer her. There are many poems to and about women, and some which exist in two versions with alternate sets of pronouns. Her latest biographer, Richard Sewall, while rejecting an earlier Freudian biographer's theory that Dickinson was essentially a psychopathological case, the by-product of which happened to be poetry, does create a context in which the importance, and validity, of Dickinson's attachments to women may now, at last, be seen in full. She was always stirred by the existences of women like George Eliot or Elizabeth Barrett, who possessed strength of mind, articulateness, and energy. (She once characterized Elizabeth Fry and Florence Nightingale as "holy"—one suspects she merely meant, "great.")

But of course Dickinson's relationships with women were more than intellectual. They were deeply charged, and the sources both of passionate joy and pain. We are only beginning to be able to consider them in a social and historical context. The historian Carroll Smith-Rosenberg has shown that there was far less taboo on intense, even passionate and sensual, relationships between women in the American 19th-century "female world of love and ritual," as she terms it, than there was later in the 20th century. Women expressed their attachments to other women both physically and verbally; a marriage did not dilute the strength of a female friendship, in which two women often shared the same bed during long visits, and wrote letters articulate with both physical and emotional longing. The 19th-century close woman friend, according to the many diaries and letters Smith-Rosenberg has studied, might be a far more important figure in a woman's life than the 19th-

century husband. None of this was condemned as "lesbianism." We will understand Emily Dickinson better, read her poetry more perceptively, when the Freudian imputation of scandal and aberrance in women's love for women has been supplanted by a more informed, less misogynistic attitude toward women's experiences with each other.

But who, if you read through the seventeen hundred and seventy-five poems—who—woman or man—could have passed through that imagination and not come out transmuted? Given the space created by her in that corner room, with its window-light, its potted plants and work-table, given that personality, capable of imposing its terms on a household, on a whole community, what single theory could hope to contain her, when she'd put it all together in that space?

"Matty: here's freedom," I hear her saying as I speed back to Boston along Route 91, as I slip the turnpike ticket into the toll-collector's hand. I am thinking of a confined space in which the genius of the 19th-century female mind in America moved, inventing a language more varied, more compressed, more dense with implications, more complex of syntax, than any American poetic language to date; in the trail of that genius my mind has been moving, and with its language and images my mind still has to reckon, as the mind of a woman poet in America today.

In 1971, a postage stamp was issued in honor of Dickinson; the portrait derives from the one existing daguerreotype of her, with straight, center-parted hair, eyes staring somewhere beyond the camera, hands poised around a nosegay of flowers, in correct 19th-century style. On the first-day-of-issue envelope sent me by a friend there is, besides the postage stamp, an engraving of the poet as popular fancy has preferred her, in a white lace ruff and with hair as bouffant as if she had just stepped from a Boston beauty-parlor. The poem chosen to represent her work to the American public is engraved, alongside a dew-gemmed rose, below the portrait:

> If I can stop one heart from breaking
> I shall not live in vain
> If I can ease one life the aching
> Or cool one pain
> Or help one fainting robin
> Unto his nest again
> I shall not live in vain.

Now, this is extremely strange. It is a fact, that in 1864, Emily Dickinson wrote this verse; and it is a verse which a hundred or more 19th-century versifiers could have written. In its undistin-

ABOUT THE AUTHOR

MARTHA DICKINSON BIANCHI REMEMBERS HER AUNT EMILY

She was "eternally preoccupied with death" as any of Pater's giant Florentines, but though the supernatural had the supreme hold on her imagination and conjecture, every lesser mystery was a panic and an ecstasy. If she could contrive to outwit domestic vigilance and smuggle a box of fresh-laid eggs to my Mother, on the sly, it savored to her of piracy and brigandage. She was averse to surveillance of every description and took pains to elude it in these little traffics of her heart as in the enigmas of her Being. "Give me liberty or give me death—but if you can, give me liberty!" was her frequent cry. . . .

Physically timid at the least approach to a crisis in the day's event, her *mind* dared earth and heaven. That apocrypha and apocalypse met in her, explains her tendency so often mistaken for blasphemy by the superficial analyst.

The advance and retreat of her thought, her transition from arch to demure, from elfin to angelic, from soaring to drowning, her inescapable sense of tragedy, her inimitable perception of comedy, her breathless reverence and unabashed invasion upon the intimate affairs of Deity and hearsay of the Bible, made her a comrade to mettle inspiration and dazzle rivalry. Unlike the dullard, brilliancy was no effort for her. She revelled in the wings of her mind,—I had almost said the fins too,—so universal was her identification with every form of life and element of being. She usually liked men better than women because they were more stimulating. I can see her yet, standing in the spacious upper hall a Summer afternoon, finger on lip, and hear her say, as the feminine callers took their departure—"Listen! Hear them kiss, the traitors!" To most women she was a provoking puzzle. To her, in turn, most women were a form of triviality to be escaped when feasible.

Bianchi, Martha Dickinson. Excerpt from "The Editor's Preface." In *The Single Hound: Poems of a Lifetime*, by Emily Dickinson, pp. xiii-xv. Boston: Little, Brown, and Company, 1914.

guished language, as in its conventional sentiment, it is remarkably untypical of the poet. Had she chosen to write many poems like this one we would have no "problem" of non-publication, of editing, of estimating the poet at her true worth. Certainly the sentiment—a contented and unambiguous altruism—is one which even today might in some quarters be accepted as fitting from a female versifier—a kind of Girl Scout prayer. But we are talking about the woman who wrote:

> He fumbles at your Soul
> As Players at the Keys
> Before they drop full Music on—
> He stuns you by degrees—
> Prepares your brittle Nature
> For the Ethereal Blow
> By fainter Hammers—further heard—
> Then nearer—Then so slow
> Your breath has time to straighten—
> Your brain—to bubble Cool—
> Deals—One—Imperial—Thunderbolt—
> Then scalps your naked Soul—
>
> When winds take Forests in their Paws—
> The Universe—is still—
>
> (#"315")

Much energy has been invested in trying to identify a concrete, flesh-and-blood male lover whom Dickinson is supposed to have renounced, and to the loss of whom can be traced the secret of her seclusion and the vein of much of her poetry. But the real question, given that the art of poetry is an art of transformation, is how this woman's mind and imagination may have used the masculine element in the world at large, or those elements personified as masculine—including the men she knew; how her relationship to this reveals itself in her images and language. In a patriarchal culture, specifically the Judeo-Christian, quasi-Puritan culture of 19th-century New England in which Dickinson grew up, still inflamed with religious revivals, and where the sermon was still an active, if perishing, literary form, the equation of divinity with maleness was so fundamental that it is hardly surprising to find Dickinson, like many an early mystic, blurring erotic with religious experience and imagery. The poem I just read has intimations both of seduction and rape merged with the intense force of a religious experience. But are these metaphors for each other, or for something more intrinsic to Dickinson? Here is another:

> He put the Belt around my life—
> I heard the buckle snap—
> And turned away, imperial,
> My Lifetime folding up—
> Deliberate, as a Duke would do
> A Kingdom's Title Deed

Henceforth, a Dedicated sort—
Member of the Cloud.

Yet not too far to come at call—
And do the little Toils
That make the Circuit of the Rest—
And deal occasional smiles
To lives that stoop to notice mine—
And kindly ask it in—
Whose invitation, know you not
For Whom I must decline?

(#"273")

These two poems are about possession, and they seem to me a poet's poems—that is, they are about the poet's relationship to her own power, which is exteriorized in masculine form, much as masculine poets have invoked the female Muse. In writing at all—particularly an unorthodox and original poetry like Dickinson's—women have often felt in danger of losing their status as women. And this status has always been defined in terms of relationship to men—as daughter, sister, bride, wife, mother, mistress, Muse. Since the most powerful figures in patriarchal culture have been men, it seems natural that Dickinson would assign a masculine gender to that in herself which did not fit in with the conventional ideology of womanliness. To recognize and acknowledge our own interior power has always been a path mined with risks for women; to acknowledge that power and commit oneself to it as Emily Dickinson did was an immense decision.

Most of us, unfortunately, have been exposed in the schoolroom to Dickinson's "little-girl" poems, her kittenish tones, as in **"I'm Nobody! Who Are You?"** (a poem whose underlying anger translates itself into archness) or

I hope the Father in the skies
Will lift his little girl—
Old fashioned—naughty—everything—
Over the stile of "Pearl."

(#"70")

or the poems about bees and robins. One critic—Richard Chase—has noted that in the 19th century "one of the careers open to women was perpetual childhood." A strain in Dickinson's letters and some—though by far a minority—of her poems was a self-diminutization, almost as if to offset and deny—or even disguise—her actual dimensions as she must have experienced them. And this emphasis on her own "littleness," along with the deliberate strangeness of her tactics of seclusion, have been, until recently, accepted as the prevailing character of the poet: the fragile poetess in white, sending flowers and poems by messenger to unseen friends, letting down baskets of gingerbread to the neighborhood children from her bedroom window; writing, but somehow naively. John Crowe Ransom, arguing for the editing and standardization of Dickinson's punctuation and typography, calls her "a little home-keeping person" who, "while she had a proper notion of the final destiny of her poems . . . was not one of those poets who had advanced to that later stage of operations where manuscripts are prepared for the printer, and the poet's diction has to make concessions to the publisher's style-book." (In short, Emily Dickinson did not wholly know her trade, and Ransom believes a "publisher's style-book" to have the last word on poetic diction.) He goes on to print several of her poems, altered by him "with all possible forbearance." What might, in a male writer—a Thoreau, let us say, or a Christopher Smart or William Blake—seem a legitimate strangeness, a unique intention, has been in one of our two major poets devalued into a kind of naïveté, girlish ignorance feminine lack of professionalism, just as the poet herself has been made into a sentimental object. ("Most of us are half in love with this dead girl," confesses Archibald MacLeish. Dickinson was fifty-five when she died.)

It is true that more recent critics, including her most recent biographer, have gradually begun to approach the poet in terms of her greatness rather than her littleness, the decisiveness of her choices instead of the surface oddities of her life or the romantic crises of her legend. But unfortunately anthologists continue to plagiarize other anthologies, to reprint her in edited, even bowdlerized versions; the popular image of her and of her work lags behind the changing consciousness of scholars and specialists. There still does not exist a selection from her poems which depicts her in her fullest range. Dickinson's greatness cannot be measured in terms of twenty-five or fifty or even 500 "perfect" lyrics, it has to be seen as the accumulation it is. Poets, even, are not always acquainted with the full dimensions of her work, or the sense one gets, reading in the one-volume complete edition (let alone the three-volume variorum edition) of a mind engaged in a lifetime's musing on essential problems of language, identity, separation, relationship, the integrity of the self; a mind capable of describing psychological states more accurately than any poet except Shakespeare. I have been surprised at how narrowly her work, still, is known by women who are writing poetry, how much her legend has gotten in the way of her being re-possessed, as a source and a foremother.

I know that for me, reading her poems as a child and then as a young girl already seriously writing poetry, she was a problematic figure. I first read her in the selection heavily edited by her niece which appeared in 1937; a later and fuller edition appeared in 1945 when I was sixteen, and the complete, unbowdlerized edition by Johnson did not appear until fifteen years later. The publication of each of these editions was crucial to me in successive decades of my life. More than any other poet, Emily Dickinson seemed to tell me that the intense inner event, the personal and psychological, was inseparable from the universal; that there was a range for psychological poetry beyond mere self-expression. Yet the legend of the life was troubling, because it seemed to whisper that a woman who undertook such explorations must pay with renunciation, isolation, and incorporeality. With the publication of the **Complete Poems,** the legend seemed to recede into unimportance beside the unquestionable power and importance of the mind revealed there. But taking possession of Emily Dickinson is still no simple matter.

The 1945 edition, entitled **Bolts of Melody,** took its title from a poem which struck me at the age of sixteen and which still, thirty years later, arrests my imagination:

> I would not paint—a picture—
> I'd rather be the One
> Its bright impossibility
> To dwell—delicious—on—
> And wonder how the fingers feel
> Whose rare—celestial—stir
> Evokes so sweet a Torment—
> Such sumptuous—Despair—
>
> I would not talk, like Cornets—
> I'd rather be the One
> Raised softly to the Ceilings—
> And out, and easy on—
> Through Villages of Ether
> Myself endured Balloon
> By but a lip of Metal
> The pier to my Pontoon—
>
> Nor would I be a Poet—
> It's finer—own the Ear—
> Enamored—impotent—content—
> The License to revere,
> A privilege so awful
> What would the Dower be,
> Had I the Art to stun myself
> With Bolts of Melody!
>
> (#"505")

This poem is about choosing an orthodox "feminine" role: the receptive rather than the creative; viewer rather than painter, listener rather than musician; acted-upon rather than active. Yet even while ostensibly choosing this role she wonders "how the fingers feel / whose rare-celestial—stir— / Evokes so sweet a Torment—" and the "feminine" role is praised in a curious sequence of adjectives: "Enamored—*impotent*—content—." The strange paradox of this poem—its exquisite irony—is that it is about choosing not to be a poet, a poem which is gainsaid by no fewer than one thousand seven hundred and seventy-five poems made during the writer's life, including itself. Moreover, the images of the poem rise to a climax (like the Balloon she evokes) but the climax happens as she describes, not what it is to be the receiver, but the maker and receiver at once: "A Privilege so awful / What would the Dower be / Had I the Art to stun myself / With Bolts of Melody!"—a climax which recalls the poem: "He fumbles at your soul / As Players at the Keys / Before they drop full Music on—" And of course, in writing those lines she possesses herself of that privilege and that "dower." I have said that this is a poem of exquisite ironies. It is, indeed, though in a very different mode, related to Dickinson's "little-girl" strategy. The woman who feels herself to be Vesuvius at home has need of a mask, at least, of innocuousness and of containment.

> On my volcano grows the Grass
> A meditative spot—
> An acre for a Bird to choose
> Would be the General thought—
>
> How red the Fire rocks below—
> How insecure the sod
> Did I disclose
> Would populate with awe my solitude.
>
> (#"1677")

Power, even masked, can still be perceived as destructive.

> A still—Volcano—Life—
> That flickered in the night—
> When it was dark enough to do
> Without erasing sight—
>
> A quiet—Earthquake style—
> Too subtle to suspect
> By natures this side Naples—
> The North cannot detect
>
> The Solemn—Torrid—Symbol—
> The lips that never lie—
> Whose hissing Corals part—and shut—
> And Cities—ooze away—
>
> (#"601")

Dickinson's biographer and editor Thomas Johnson has said that she often felt herself possessed by a demonic force, particularly in the years 1861 and 1862 when she was writing at the height of her drive. There are many poems besides "**He**

put the Belt around my Life" which could be read as poems of possession by the daemon—poems which can also be, and have been, read, as poems of possession by the deity, or by a human lover. I suggest that a woman's poetry about her relationship to her daemon—her own active, creative power—has in patriarchal culture used the language of heterosexual love or patriarchal theology. Ted Hughes tells us that

> the eruption of (Dickinson's) imagination and poetry followed when she shifted her passion, with the energy of desperation, from (the) lost man onto his only possible substitute,—the Universe in its Divine aspect . . . Thereafter, the marriage that had been denied in the real world, went forward in the spiritual . . . just as the Universe in its Divine aspect became the mirror-image of her "husband," so the whole religious dilemma of New England, at that most critical moment in its history, became the mirror-image of her relationship to him, of her "marriage" in fact.[1]

This seems to me to miss the point on a grand scale. There are facts we need to look at. First, Emily Dickinson did not marry. And her non-marrying was neither a pathological retreat as John Cody sees it, nor probably even a conscious decision; it was a fact in her life as in her contemporary Christina Rossetti's; both women had more primary needs. Second: unlike Rossetti, Dickinson did not become a religiously dedicated woman; she was heretical, heterodox, in her religious opinions, and stayed away from church and dogma. What, in fact, *did* she allow to "put the Belt around her Life"—what *did* wholly occupy her mature years and possess her? For "Whom" did she decline the invitations of other lives? The writing of poetry. Nearly two thousand poems. Three hundred and sixty-six poems in the year of her fullest power. What was it like to be writing poetry you knew (and I am sure she did know) was of a class by itself—to be fuelled by the energy it took first to confront, then to condense that range of psychic experience into that language; then to copy out the poems and lay them in a trunk, or send a few here and there to friends or relatives as occasional verse or as gestures of confidence? I am sure she knew who she was, as she indicates in this poem:

> Myself was formed—a carpenter—
> An unpretending time
> My Plane—and I, together wrought
> Before a Builder came—
>
> To measure our attainments
> Had we the Art of Boards
> Sufficiently developed—He'd hire us
> At Halves—

> My Tools took Human—Faces—
> The Bench, where we had toiled—
> Against the Man—persuaded—
> We—Temples Build—I said—
>
> (#"488")

This is a poem of the great year 1862, the year in which she first sent a few poems to Thomas Higginson for criticism. Whether it antedates or postdates that occasion is unimportant; it is a poem of knowing one's measure, regardless of the judgments of others.

There are many poems which carry the weight of this knowledge. Here is another one:

> I'm ceded—I've stopped being Theirs—
> The name They dropped upon my face
> With water, in the country church
> Is finished using, now,
> And They can put it with my dolls,
> My childhood, and the string of spools,
> I've finished threading—too—
>
> Baptized before, without the choice,
> But this time, consciously, of Grace—
> Unto supremest name—
> Called to my Fill—the Crescent dropped—
> Existence's whole Arc, filled up
> With one small Diadem.
>
> My second Rank—too small the first—
> Crowned—Crowing—on my Father's breast—
> A half unconscious Queen—
> But this time—Adequate—Erect—
> With Will to choose—or to reject—
> And I choose—just a Crown—
>
> (#"508")

Now, this poem partakes of the imagery of being "twice-born" or, in Christian liturgy, "confirmed"—and if this poem had been written by Christina Rossetti I would be inclined to give more weight to a theological reading. But it was written by Emily Dickinson, who used the Christian metaphor far more than she let it use her. This is a poem of great pride—not pridefulness, but *self-confirmation*—and it is curious how little Dickinson's critics, perhaps misled by her diminutives, have recognized the will and pride in her poetry. It is a poem of movement from childhood to womanhood, of transcending the patriarchal condition of bearing her father's name and "crowing—on my Father's breast—." She is now a conscious Queen, "Adequate—Erect / With Will to choose, or to reject—."

There is one poem which is the real "onlie begetter" of my thoughts here about Dickinson; a poem I have mused over, repeated to myself, taken into myself over many years. I think it is a poem about possession by the daemon, about the dangers and risks of such possession if you are a woman, about the knowledge that power in a woman can seem destructive, and that you cannot live without the daemon once it has possessed you. The archetype of the daemon as masculine is beginning to change, but it has been real for women up until now. But this woman poet also perceives herself as a lethal weapon:

> My life had stood—a Loaded Gun—
> In Corners—till a Day
> The Owner passed—identified—
> And carried me away—
>
> And now We roam in Sovereign Woods—
> And now We hunt the Doe—
> And every time I speak for Him—
> The Mountains straight reply—
>
> And do I smile, such cordial light
> Upon the Valley glow—
> It is as a Vesuvian face
> Had let its pleasure through—
>
> And when at Night—our good Day done—
> I guard My Master's Head—
> 'Tis better than the Eider-Duck's
> Deep Pillow—to have shared—
>
> To foe of His—I'm deadly foe—
> None stir the second time—
> On whom I lay a Yellow Eye—
> Or an emphatic Thumb—
>
> Though I than he—may longer live
> He longer must—than I—
> For I have but the power to kill,
> Without—the power to die—
>
> (#"754")

Here the poet sees herself as split, not between anything so simple as "masculine" and "feminine" identity but between the hunter, admittedly masculine, but also a human person, an active, willing being, and the gun—an object, condemned to remain inactive until the hunter—the *owner*—takes possession of it. The gun contains an energy capable of rousing echoes in the mountains and lighting up the valleys; it is also deadly, "Vesuvian;" it is also its owner's defender against the "foe." It is the gun, furthermore, who *speaks for him.* If there is a female consciousness in this poem it is buried deeper than the images: it exists in the ambivalence toward power, which is extreme. Active willing and creation in women are forms of aggression, and aggression is both "the power to kill" and punishable by death. The union of gun with hunter embodies the danger of identifying and taking hold of her forces, not least that in so doing she risks defining herself—and being defined—as aggressive, as unwomanly,

("and now we hunt the Doe") and as potentially lethal. That which she experiences in herself as energy and potency can also be experienced as pure destruction. The final stanza, with its precarious balance of phrasing, seems a desperate attempt to resolve the ambivalence; but, I think, it is no resolution, only a further extension of ambivalence.

> Though I than he—may longer live
> He longer must—than I—
> For I have but the power to kill,
> Without—the power to die—

The poet experiences herself as loaded gun, imperious energy; yet without the Owner, the possessor, she is merely lethal. Should that possession abandon her—but the thought is unthinkable: "He longer *must* than I." The pronoun is masculine; the antecedent is what Keats called "The Genius of Poetry."

I do not pretend to have—I don't even wish to have—explained this poem, accounted for its every image; it will reverberate with new tones long after my words about it have ceased to matter. But I think that for us, at this time, it is a central poem in understanding Emily Dickinson, and ourselves, and the condition of the woman artist, particularly in the 19th century. It seems likely that the 19th-century woman poet, especially, felt the medium of poetry as dangerous, in ways that the woman novelist did not feel the medium of fiction to be. In writing even such a novel of elemental sexuality and anger as *Wuthering Heights,* Emily Brontë could at least theoretically separate herself from her characters; they were, after all, fictitious beings. Moreover, the novel is or can be a construct, planned and organized to deal with human experiences on one level at a time. Poetry is too much rooted in the unconscious; it presses too close against the barriers of repression; and the 19th-century woman had much to repress. It is interesting that Elizabeth Barrett tried to fuse poetry and fiction in writing "Aurora Leigh"—perhaps apprehending the need for fictional characters to carry the charge of her experience as a woman artist. But with the exception of "Aurora Leigh" and Christina Rossetti's "Goblin Market"—that extraordinary and little-known poem drenched in oral eroticism—Emily Dickinson's is the only poetry in English by a woman of that century which pierces so far beyond the ideology of the "feminine" and the conventions of womanly feeling. To write it at all, she had to be willing to enter chambers of the self in which

Ourself behind ourself, concealed—
Should startle most—

and to relinquish control there, to take those risks, she had to create a relationship to the outer world where she could feel in control.

It is an extremely painful and dangerous way to live—split between a publicly acceptable persona, and a part of yourself that you perceive as the essential, the creative and powerful self, yet also as possibly unacceptable, perhaps even monstrous.

Much Madness is divinest sense—
To a discerning Eye—
Much sense—the starkest Madness.
'Tis the Majority
In this, as All, prevail—
Assent—and you are sane—
Demur—you're straightway dangerous—
And handled with a chain—

(#"435")

For many women the stresses of this splitting have led, in a world so ready to assert our innate passivity and to deny our independence and creativity, to extreme consequences: the mental asylum, self-imposed silence, recurrent depression, suicide, and often severe loneliness.

Dickinson is *the* American poet whose work consisted in exploring states of psychic extremity. For a long time, as we have seen, this fact was obscured by the kinds of selections made from her work by timid if well-meaning editors. In fact, Dickinson was a great psychologist; and like every great psychologist, she began with the material she had at hand: herself. She had to possess the courage to enter, through language, states which most people deny or veil with silence.

The first Day's Night had come—
And grateful that a thing
So terrible—had been endured—
I told my soul to sing—

She said her Strings were snapt—
Her Bow—to Atoms blown—
And so to mend her—gave me work
Until another Morn—

And then—a Day as huge
As Yesterdays in pairs,
Unrolled its horror in my face—
Until it blocked my eyes—

My Brain—begun to laugh—
I mumbled—like a fool—
And tho' 'tis years ago—that Day—
My brain keeps giggling—still.

And Something's odd—within—
That person that I was—

And this One—do not feel the same—
Could it be Madness—this?

(#"410")

Dickinson's letters acknowledge a period of peculiarly intense personal crisis; her biographers have variously ascribed it to the pangs of renunciation of an impossible love, or to psychic damage deriving from her mother's presumed depression and withdrawal after her birth. What concerns us here is the fact that she chose to probe the nature of this experience in language:

The Soul has Bandaged moments—
When too appalled to stir—
She feels some ghastly Fright come up
And stop to look at her—

Salute her—with long fingers—
Caress her freezing hair—
Sip, Goblin, from the very lips
The Lover—hovered—o'er—
Unworthy, that a thought so mean
Accost a Theme—so—fair—

The soul has moments of Escape—
When bursting all the doors—
She dances like a Bomb, abroad,
And swings upon the hours . . .

The Soul's retaken moments—
When, Felon led along,
With shackles on the plumed feet,
And staples, in the Song,

The Horror welcomes her, again,
These, are not brayed of Tongue—

(#"512")

In this poem, the word "Bomb" is dropped, almost carelessly, as a correlative for the soul's active, liberated states—it occurs in a context of apparent euphoria, but its implications are more than euphoric—they are explosive, destructive. The Horror from which in such moments the soul escapes has a masculine, "goblin" form, and suggests the perverse and terrifying rape of a "bandaged" and powerless self. In at least one poem, Dickinson depicts the actual process of suicide:

He scanned it—staggered—
Dropped the Loop
To Past or Period—
Caught helpless at a sense as if
His mind were going blind—
Groped up—to see if God was there—
Groped backward at Himself—
Caressed a Trigger absently
And wandered out of Life.

(#"1062")

The precision of knowledge in this brief poem is such that we must assume that Dickinson had, at least in fantasy, drifted close to that state in which the "Loop" that binds us to "Past or Period" is "dropped" and we grope randomly at what remains of abstract notions of sense, God, or self, before—almost absent-mindedly—reaching for a solution. But it's worth noting that this is a poem in which the suicidal experience has been distanced, refined, transformed through a devastating accuracy of language. It is not suicide that is studied here, but the dissociation of self and mind and world which precedes.

Dickinson was convinced that a life worth living could be found within the mind and against the grain of external circumstance: "Reverse cannot befall / That fine prosperity / Whose Sources are interior—." (#"395") The horror, for her, was that which set "Staples in the Song"—the numbing and freezing of the interior, a state she describes over and over:

> There is a Languor of the Life
> More imminent than Pain—
> 'Tis Pain's Successor—When the Soul
> Has suffered all it can—
>
> A Drowsiness—diffuses—
> A Dimness like a Fog
> Envelopes Consciousness—
> As Mists—obliterate a Crag.
>
> The Surgeon—does not blanch—at pain
> His Habit—is severe—
> But tell him that it ceased to feel—
> That creature lying there—
>
> And he will tell you—skill is late—
> A Mightier than He—
> Has ministered before Him—
> There's no Vitality.
>
> (#"396")

I think the equation surgeon-artist is a fair one here; the artist can work with the materials of pain; she cuts to probe and heal; but she is powerless at the point where

> After great pain, a formal feeling comes—
> The nerves sit ceremonious, like Tombs—
> The stiff Heart questions was it He, that bore,
> And Yesterday, or Centuries before?
>
> The Feet, mechanical, go round—
> Of Ground, or Air, or Ought—
> A Wooden way
> Regardless grown,
> A Quartz contentment, like a stone—
>
> This is the Hour of Lead
> Remembered, if outlived
> As Freezing persons, recollect the Snow—
> First—Chill—then Stupor—then the letting go—
>
> (#"341")

For the poet, the terror is precisely in those periods of psychic death, when even the possibility of work is negated; her "occupation's gone." Yet she also describes the unavailing effort to numb emotion:

> Me from Myself—to banish—
> Had I Art—
> Impregnable my Fortress
> Unto All Heart—
>
> But since Myself—assault Me—
> How have I peace
> Except by subjugating
> Consciousness?
>
> And since We're mutual Monarch
> How this be
> Except by Abdication—
> Me—of Me?
>
> (#"642")

The possibility of abdicating oneself—of ceasing to be—remains.

> Severe Service of myself
> I—hastened to demand
> To fill the awful longitude
> Your life had left behind—
>
> I worried Nature with my Wheels
> When Hers had ceased to run—
> When she had put away her Work
> My own had just begun.
>
> I strove to weary Brain and Bone—
> To harass to fatigue
> The glittering Retinue of nerves—
> Vitality to clog
>
> To some dull comfort Those obtain
> Who put a Head away
> They knew the Hair to—
> And forget the color of the Day—
>
> Affliction would not be appeased—
> The Darkness braced as firm
> As all my strategem had been
> The Midnight to confirm—
>
> No drug for Consciousness—can be—
> Alternative to die
> Is Nature's only Pharmacy
> For Being's Malady—
>
> (#"786")

Yet consciousness—not simply the capacity to suffer, but the capacity to experience intensely at every instant—creates of death not a blotting-out but a final illumination:

> This Consciousness that is aware
> Of Neighbors and the Sun
> Will be the one aware of Death
> And that itself alone

Is traversing the interval
Experience between
And most profound experiment
Appointed unto Men—

How adequate unto itself
Its properties shall be
Itself unto itself and none
Shall make discovery.

Adventure most unto itself
The Soul condemned to be—
Attended by a single Hound
Its own identity.

(#"822")

The poet's relationship to her poetry has, it seems to me—and I am not speaking only of Emily Dickinson—a twofold nature. Poetic language—the poem on paper—is a concretization of the poetry of the world at large, the self, and the forces within the self; and those forces are rescued from formlessness, lucidified, and integrated in the act of writing poems. But there is a more ancient concept of the poet, which is that she is endowed to speak for those who do not have the gift of language, or to see for those who—for whatever reasons—are less conscious of what they are living through. It is as though the risks of the poet's existence can be put to some use beyond her own survival.

The Province of the Saved
Should be the Art—To save—
Through Skill obtained in themselves—
The Science of the Grave

No Man can understand
But He that hath endured
The Dissolution—in Himself—
That man—be qualified

To qualify Despair
To Those who failing new—
Mistake Defeat for Death—Each time—
Till acclimated—to—

(#"539")

The poetry of extreme states, the poetry of danger, can allow its readers to go further in our own awareness, take risks we might not have dared; it says, at least: "Someone has been here before."

The Soul's distinct Connection
With immortality
Is best disclosed by Danger
Or quick Calamity—

As Lightning on a Landscape
Exhibits Sheets of Place—

Not yet suspected—but for Flash—
And Click—and Suddenness.

(#"974")

Crumbling is not an instant's Act
A fundamental pause
Dilapidation's processes
Are organized Decays.

'Tis first a cobweb on the Soul
A Cuticle of Dust
A Borer in the Axis
An Elemental Rust—

Ruin is formal—Devil's work
Consecutive and slow—
Fail in an instant—no man did
Slipping—is Crash's law.

(#"997")

I felt a Cleaving in my Mind
As if my Brain had split—
I tried to match it—Seam by Seam—
But could not make them fit.

The thought behind, I strove to join
Unto the thought before—
But Sequence ravelled out of Sound
Like Balls—upon a Floor

(#"937")

There are many more Emily Dickinsons than I have tried to call up here. Wherever you take hold of her, she proliferates. I wish I had time here to explore her complex sense of Truth; to follow the thread we unravel when we look at the numerous and passionate poems she wrote to or about women; to probe her ambivalent feelings about fame, a subject pursued by many male poets before her; simply to examine the poems in which she is directly apprehending the natural world. No one since the 17th century had reflected more variously or more probingly upon death and dying. What I have tried to do here is follow through some of the origins and consequences of her choice to be, not only a poet but a woman who explored her own mind, without any of the guidelines of orthodoxy. To say "yes" to her powers was not simply a major act of nonconformity in the 19th century; even in our own time it has been assumed that Emily Dickinson, not patriarchal society, was "the problem." The more we come to recognize the unwritten and written laws and taboos underpinning patriarchy, the less problematical, surely, will seem the methods she chose.

Note

1. *A Choice of Emily Dickinson's Verse*, p. 11.

TITLE COMMENTARY

"A solemn thing—it was—I said" (Poem 271)

MARCIA FALK (ESSAY DATE 1989)

SOURCE: Falk, Marcia. "Poem 271." *Women's Studies* 16, nos. 1-2 (1989): 23-7.

In the following essay, Falk interprets poem "271" as a chronicle of self-discovery in which the narrator rejects the role of bride or nun.

In the first publication of Emily Dickinson's poem #**"271"** (in 1896, ten years after Dickinson's death), the poem was entitled **"Wedded"** by the editors. The editorial assumption that this passionate lyric was intended as a paean to marriage is typical of the way Dickinson's work and life have been treated by the critics until recently. It is much to the credit of feminist scholars in the recent past that readers have begun to see the poet and the poetry on their own terms, rather than filtered through the lens of heterosexist assumptions and values. The revisioning of poem #**"271"** as an expression of the poet's consecration to her art—an interpretation that sees the "woman—white" as Dickinson's private symbol for the role of the poet—falls within this new line of criticism. Insofar as it rejects the idea that the poem is a celebration of traditional marriage, this interpretation offers an important corrective to the earlier view. However, I believe that it does not yet fully take into account the logical development of the poem's argument—its unexpected *turns* of thought—and the literary and social conventions that the poem rests upon and ultimately transforms. I would like, therefore, to propose another alternative, a different dialogue with this poem.

I am going to begin by asserting the view—surprising though it may at first seem in the context of this feminist forum—that the "woman—white" is a double symbol for the traditional female roles of bride and nun, both of which, of course, are marriage roles—that is, roles of dependent relationship to a male other (or Other). Indeed, I think it is impossible to ignore these conventional readings of the "woman—white," no matter what information we have about Dickinson's biography. That Dickinson never married, that she chose to dress in white, that she dedicated herself fiercely to her poetry at about the time this poem was written—these are all facts of interest and importance, but they cannot obliterate, for us as readers any more than for Dickinson as writer, the common symbolic as-

sociations of the image of "a woman—white." In our culture, such an image cannot but call to mind the bridal gown and, perhaps secondarily, the novice's habit. Moreover, as we shall see as we read through the poem, Dickinson develops the bridal image thematically as the poem progresses, making it the foundation of a sophisticated poetic structure.

Having said this, however, I want to follow with the claim that the poem is finally *not* about choosing to be a bride or a nun, but about the process by which the speaker comes to reject such a choice. Indeed, the poem is not about the choice of any vocation or the adoption of any role. Rather, it is about the overthrowing of roles and idealizations in favor of embracing an autonomous, self-created life. Such a life is one of real and particular experiences—as contrasted with idealized, gender-determined roles—and no matter how this life is viewed by the world, no matter how "small" and inconsequential it may seem to external authorities and "Sages," it swells proud and large in the speaker's own "vest."

But the poem does not begin with this realization; it ends there. The following is an outline of the sequence of thoughts and events that leads to this defiant conclusion.

The poem recounts a mini-narrative, describing first what the speaker *once thought* ("A solemn thing—it *was*—I said—" [emphases mine]), followed by how she came to consider this idea ("I pondered how the bliss would look—"), and finally stating what she now believes and feels ("And then— / . . . I sneered—"). The sequence of actions completed by the first person narrator—I said, I pondered, and then I sneered—summarizes the poem's story, which is, in effect, the tale of a change of heart and mind.

Once, the speaker tells us, she proclaimed it "a solemn thing" to be a "woman—white" (a bride to man or God). She believed this role to be sanctioned by God and cloaked in blamelessness (purity) and mystery (sexuality, passion). While the almost-oxymoronic phrase "blameless mystery" calls to mind the miraculous Virgin Birth (and, hence, associations of the convent), it also suggests the paradoxes of our culture's idealized image of the secular bride, especially the adolescent one: virtuous and virginal, yet seductive and sexual. Consider, for a moment, the classic style of wedding gowns: white, of course, and floor-length, covering the body from top—often beginning at the neck, with lace—to the very bottom, and even trailing beyond; yet form-fitting at the torso and often quite low-cut at the bust beneath the conveniently transparent lace; thus projecting the deliberately confusing message of chastity that seduces, modesty that reveals. To be both virgin and femme fatale was once an ideal shared by many American young women, living as they did in a culture deeply conflicted about sexuality in general and female sexuality in particular. In the first stanza of the poem, the speaker describes the aspirations she once embraced and the convictions she espoused when she declared it "solemn" to be a bride.

In the second stanza, the speaker continues to refer back to this earlier stage of life when she imagined her own future as a woman. "The purple well," another richly associative symbol, seems to emerge out of the symbol of the "woman— white," and to extend its meanings in both secular and religious domains. Thus, as a vaginal image, the well suggests female sexuality, while as a sacred image drawn from the body of nature—an image which is also associated with women, especially in biblical and other religious sources—it can represent a spiritual passageway, a site of revelation, a source of life. Although purple may appear to be the opposite of white—the one the symbolic color of lifeblood and passion, the other of innocence and purity—such a joining of opposites only completes in imagery the paradox implied in the "blameless mystery" of the first stanza. White becomes purple, as bridal innocence yields to marital passion, or religious self-renunciation leads to union with the Divine. To the adolescent imagination, the virgin ideal leads naturally into an idealized life of passion, be that passion sexual or religious. For the youthful persona of the speaker's past, the possibilities of "the purple well" seem infinite, "plummetless"; indeed, this well is a fount of eternal life, promising to "return—Eternity" to her.

The last two lines of the stanza are syntactically difficult, and it is tempting to read "Eternity—until—" as a reversal for the sake of the rhyme. But there seems to be more than rhyme at stake here. Placing "until" after "eternity," Dickinson cuts eternity short, and the word "until" becomes the turning point between the two halves of the poem: I said all of this *until* . . . I pondered.

In the second half of the poem, the vision changes, as thought supersedes the adolescent imaginings recounted in the first two stanzas. The speaker now *ponders* the "bliss" about which she had earlier only fantasized, wondering whether the life she had envisioned will seem as "big" once she possesses it as it had seemed when she had only imagined it. At a distance, she notes, this bliss was necessarily blurred by "fog," the fog of unreality. The logic of the laws of perspective is reversed here. Normally, things seem larger the closer they are brought into view. But here, the speaker questions whether her fantasies will seem—will "feel," to be precise—as big when they are owned, held in the hand, as they did when they were only glimpsed from far away. The answer, unspoken but already implied in the doubting, implied in the question itself, is a frank and resounding "no."

No, the life of the bride or the nun will not seem so large to her once she owns it. Having seen that her fantasies were misguided, overblown, the speaker now has the insight that her life is *already large*. It is already full and whole as "Horizons"— that is, a world in itself—swelling in her "vest" (a metonymy for her body, hence her Self, to replace the image of the gown or habit implied by the "woman—white"). This is the revelation of the fourth stanza. The so-called "Sages"—male authorities, society's standard-bearers—may have deemed her life "small," incomplete, unworthy. In *their* eyes, she may need to dedicate herself to a groom or to a God in order to be made whole, to be saved. But to this false vision she now replies with defiant and self-confident restraint—"softly," with only a sneer. With a sarcasm strongly implied by the use of quotation marks, Dickinson inverts the meaning of the Sages' word: "small" becomes, by implication, infinitely large. The speaker's choice to be her own Self—not to give her Self over to a male other, or to any other-defined role—seems fully valid now, not needing further argument or explanation. Indeed, her choices do not concern the outside world at all, for they are hers alone to make.

Having achieved this self-sufficiency, the speaker has completed her journey, arriving from adolescence to adulthood. She has gone from would-be bride ("woman—white—to be") to true mother of her Self. Her journey has taken her through an idealized anticipation of sexual, or mystical, union (the life dropped into the bottomless "purple well"), and then through a conceptualizing period (when she ponders). It is in this period of conceptualization/conception that she comes to reject the false "bliss," and in its stead to conceive—virginally, as it were, without union with a male other—a new identity, one which she will eventually hold in her own hands. This embryonic ("'small'") new identity then swells large in the womb of her "vest," until finally she is ready to defy the paternal authorities, become her own parent, and give birth to a new Self.

In poem #"508," Dickinson will subsequently write:

> I'm ceded—I've stopped being Theirs—
> . . . . .
> A half unconscious Queen—
> But this time—Adequate—Erect,
> With Will to choose, or to reject,
> And I choose, just a Crown—

The speaker of #"508" makes clear just how crucial was the choice of her own identity, an identity contrasted with the one imposed on her by others. The speaker of poem #"271" describes a similar choice and provides a similar contrast; however, she reveals not just the end of the process but also the internal stages along the way—and this revelation is what makes the poem so poignant. Thus poem #"271" depicts the temptations that are at first succumbed to, the robes that are eventually cast off, and the idols that must finally be overthrown before the Crown of the Self can be donned.

The genius of poem #"271" lies in the subtle interrelationship between its imagery and its structure, and in its bold appropriation and transformation of elemental cultural conventions. By an exquisitely crafted use of her art, Dickinson has taken the theme of bride-become-wife-and-mother (or, virgin-become-nun-or-Madonna) and converted it into the story of a woman's creation of her Self. She has done far more than reject tradition here; she has passed through it, transcended it, and made from it something wholly new.

"I dwell in Possibility—" (Poem 657)

A. JAMES WOHLPART (ESSAY DATE WINTER 2001)

SOURCE: Wohlpart, A. James. "A New Redemption: Emily Dickinson's Poetic in Fascicle 22 and 'I dwell in Possibility.'" *South Atlantic Review* 66, no. 1 (winter 2001): 50-83.

In the following essay, Wohlpart argues that the poems that make up fascicle 22, particularly "I dwell in Possibility—," illustrate the gender constraints implicit in a patriarchal culture and Dickinson's attempt to undermine the foundations of that culture.

It was a life deliberately organized on her terms. The terms she had been handed by society—Calvinist Protestantism, Romanticism, the nineteenth-century corseting of women's bodies,

choices, and sexuality—could spell insanity to a woman genius. What this one had to do was retranslate her own unorthodox, subversive, sometimes volcanic propensities into a dialect called metaphor: her native language.
—Adrienne Rich, "Vesuvius at Home: The Power of Emily Dickinson"

In 1983, in her introduction to *Feminist Critics Read Emily Dickinson,* Suzanne Juhasz outlined a revisionary stance that she felt was necessary to appreciate fully Dickinson's poetry.[1] In reaction to traditional criticism, which suggested that Emily Dickinson turned to poetry—a masculine activity—because of her failure as a woman or which read the poetry in light of a specific cultural context altogether ignoring concerns of gender, Juhasz posited the need for critical inquiry that was founded on the fact that Emily Dickinson was simultaneously a woman and a poet. Included in this collection of essays, Sandra M. Gilbert offered a reading that detailed the way in which Emily Dickinson structured her "life/text"—an emblematic conjoining of herself as woman with her poetry—"around a series of 'mysteries' that were distinctly female, deliberately exploring and exploiting the characteristics, even the constraints, of nineteenth-century womanhood so as to transform and transcend them" (23).

In the 1980s, critics offered revealing analyses of Emily Dickinson's poetry in connection to the concerns of domesticity that were central to her life and her work. The primary focus of these readings was the way in which Emily Dickinson transformed the limitations of nineteenth-century gender roles into a powerful force that allowed her to refigure the world around her. Suzanne Juhasz, in *The Undiscovered Continent,* describes Emily Dickinson's concern with the domestic economy, witnessed in her retreat from the external world into an internal, created space, as a "strategy," explaining that

> Dickinson chose to keep to her house, to her room, to live in her mind rather than the external world, in order to achieve certain goals and to circumvent or overcome certain forces in her environment and experience that were in opposition to these goals—particularly, the expectations and norms that a patriarchal society creates for women, especially problematic when a woman wants to be a poet.
>
> (4-5)

Juhasz and others demonstrated that Dickinson used the home and domestic concerns, which represent an integral component of the cultural constraints of the nineteenth century, as a force for subverting the patriarchal society that surrounded her.[2]

The readings of the 1980s, which opened a new avenue for Dickinson criticism, culminated in the 1990s with such works as Paula Bennett's *Emily Dickinson: Woman Poet* and Betsy Erkkila's *The Wicked Sisters: Woman Poets, Literary History, and Discord.* Bennett grappled with the paradoxical implications of the role of domesticity in Emily Dickinson's poetry, admitting that, even while "Dickinson herself appears to have had little sympathy with the values of spirituality, purity and service underlying the role she chose to play,"

> there is no way we can separate Dickinson from the domestic life she led or from the role of 'poetess' she chose to play. . . . [F]or whatever reservations Dickinson had concerning domesticity, all the evidence suggests that she nevertheless identified strongly with women and with many aspects of domestic life. . . . Her submergence into the women's sphere and her presentation of herself as 'poetess' (a *woman* poet) was, therefore, a good deal more than simply a role she played in order to keep from playing others.
>
> (13)

Erkkila explains that "What made Dickinson's female world unique was that it became, for her at least, not an initiation into but a form of *resistance to* the structures of male power as they were embodied in home and school, church and state, workplace and marketplace" (19). As Erkkila, Juhasz, and others have noted, the home, for Emily Dickinson, was a creative space that allowed for a reaction against the domestic economy of the nineteenth century. Rather than a place for woman as server of others, the home became a place for woman as creator.

Dickinson's manipulation of domestic imagery, at once accepting and subverting the values of her culture, suggests the possibility of a heightened awareness of the critical significance of her poetry, a kind of self-consciousness not only about the poems created but also about the creative process itself. Indeed, Dickinson very often used her poetry to explore her own poetic—that is, the meaning of her poetry and her role as poet.[3] Because she had committed herself to a project that countered cultural expectations, and because she launched that project from the very seat of those expectations, Emily Dickinson often became self-reflective as she explored the ramifications of being a woman poet against the expectations of nineteenth-century womanhood. Such a concern for defining her poetic, then, was necessarily tied to explorations of domesticity; indeed, in her poems about creativity we can perhaps most clearly see the way in which Dickinson trans-

formed the home and the activities of the home into a poetic force that undermined nineteenth-century culture.

One such obvious example of domestic concerns explicitly intersecting with poetic concerns is in the private publication of her poetry in the form of the fascicle. R. W. Franklin, who has produced the most extensive scholarship on Emily Dickinson's manuscripts, suggests that the gathering of poems into fascicles, "a personal enactment of the public act" of publication, may have been motivated by the desire "to reduce disorder in her manuscripts" (Introduction ix). Yet he goes on to note that as the binding of poems progressed, the fascicles became less a record of completed poems and more of "a continuing workshop where, in producing a new copy for friends or in reading among the poems, she would enter the specific poetic process again" (Introduction x). Such a view of the fascicles—as an organic workshop—is very much linked to domestic concerns in that it embodies the view of Dickinson's poetry as living things used to nurture her relationships. Wendy Martin notes that "The word fascicle, which her sister Lavinia used to describe the packets of sewn poems, is . . . a botanical term referring to a flower pattern in which the petals spring irregularly from the top of a main stem like a peony. In binding her poems into fascicular packets, Emily Dickinson chose an appropriate form for the blossoming of her poems; each poem was a petal, each packet a flower" (144). The organic metaphors used to describe the publication process—whether through considering the writing process or the botanical reference—suggests that the fascicles were living things, part of Emily Dickinson's garden.[4] Moreover, both the physical nature and the content of the fascicles link them to a domestic economy. The physical method of binding the poems—sewing them together into a unit—"converted traditional female thread-and-needle work into a different kind of housework and her own form of productive industry" (Erkkila 38).

With the 1981 publication of Emily Dickinson's poems in manuscript form, critics have begun to explore the significance of the arrangement of poems in the fascicle form. The most extensive consideration of this issue, Sharon Cameron's *Choosing Not Choosing,* engages the manuscripts in all their complexity—considering the importance of variants in the poems, of clusters or groupings of poems within fascicles, of the relationships of poems within these clusters, and of the relationships of clusters to each other. Cameron is ultimately concerned with the way in which these variants and multiple relationships complicate each other in order to produce an "excess of meaning" (43).[5] M. L. Rosenthal and Sally M. Gall, on the other hand, engage Fascicles 15 and 16 in order to demonstrate that Emily Dickinson used the form of the fascicle to provide order, albeit conditional, to her chaotic emotions: "The poems penetrate a life of secret turmoil, each striking a certain held pitch of awareness; and the fascicles mobilize these little systems of subjective energy into larger ones, permitting a more complex equilibrium among effects" (48). Others, such as Ruth Miller and William Shurr, have argued that a repeated drama occurs throughout the fascicles; for instance, Miller identified two primary dramas: of a woman, striving for acceptance or knowledge, failing, and then placing hope in an afterlife; or of a poet, seeking truth about the world, and then celebrating the relation between the mortal and the immortal, the natural and the spiritual (*Poetry of Emily Dickinson* 249).

While there is a great deal of disagreement about the way in which Emily Dickinson's fascicles are to be considered, Cameron, Rosenthal and Gall, and Miller all suggest that the fascicles present poems in ways that allow for interesting interactions among poems or groupings of poems that amplifies the meanings and possibilities of the poems.[6] Indeed, at the 1997 MLA convention, Eleanor Heginbotham argued that certain poems might play specific roles within a fascicle, acting as a central poem for the movement of the fascicle, or that two poems might intentionally face one another within a fascicle, creating a tension that is resolved elsewhere. With these contexts in mind, I would like to turn to an analysis of **"fascicle 22"** (arranged in 1862), with a special focus on what I consider a central poem in this cluster, **"I dwell in Possibility,"** one of Emily Dickinson's preeminent poems about poetry and the poet. Central to my analysis will be an awareness of the way in which Emily Dickinson wrote from the perspective of a woman poet who concerned herself with undermining the foundations of the cultural beliefs that surrounded her through the private publication of her works.

As a woman, Dickinson experienced the dichotomization of her culture—a polarization of male and female, culture and nature, spiritual and physical, this life and afterlife, sin and salvation—as constraint; rather than working to reconcile the binary oppositions of her culture, however, Emily Dickinson offered a poetic that undermines the ground of these oppositions in order to

subvert the cultural norms that imprisoned her and thus to expand into limitlessness and freedom.[7] Ultimately, the liberation that lies at the heart of Emily Dickinson's poetic in **"fascicle 22"** and **"I dwell"** subverts orthodox, religious views on redemption and can most clearly be defined as the establishment of interrelationships with the natural world and with other humans that enable her to transform the quotidian into the sacred.[8] Dickinson subverts her culture's views on redemption in two primary ways: first, through offering a re-valuation of culturally opposed dichotomies, such as this life versus the afterlife and the physical versus the spiritual, in order to question the foundation of these oppositions, and, second, through reclaiming and revisioning the Garden of Eden, the originary space of these dichotomies. In **"fascicle 22"** with **"I dwell"** as a central poem, using images of the house and the garden, Emily Dickinson demonstrates that the dichotomies that originate from such institutions as religion, which create a prison especially for women and which pervade and dominate our lives, might be overcome through grasping the physical and temporal interconnectedness of all things—of the natural landscape as well as of humans.[9]

The first grouping of poems, including **"A Prison gets to be a friend—"** (J"652," F"456"), **"Nature—sometimes sears a Sapling—"** (J314, F457), and **"She dealt her pretty words like Blades—"** (J479, F458), describes the way in which humans not only accept and become accustomed to cultural constraints but also how we refuse to engage the truth about these experiences because it is too painful.[10] As a result of our cultural constraints and disregard for truth, we become separated from nature, which is also here linked to the female poet. Significantly, Dickinson's description of the binary opposition between culture and nature—set up most clearly in a juxtaposition of the first two poems—posits the way in which we become comfortable and even happy in our cultural beliefs even though they imprison us. Set against this state of comfort, the poet, linked to nature and the feminine, offers a critique that creates pain and discomfort but ultimately is tied to freedom. The opposition between the poet and our cultural beliefs, which is set up in this first grouping, is central to the movement of the fascicle as a whole. While the central poem of the fascicle, **"I dwell,"** offers a renewed vision of redemption, a kind of escape from our cultural system, the last grouping of poems in the fascicle returns to the concept of constraint explored here.

"A Prison gets to be a friend—" describes the process and the effects of acculturation, especially the way in which, as we grow older, we willingly replace our "freedom" with a "prison."[11] The opening of the poem explains that, between our prison and ourselves,

> . . . a Kinsmanship express—
> And in it's narrow Eyes—
>
> We come to look with gratitude
> For the appointed Beam
> It deal us—stated as our food—
> And hungered for—the same—
>
> (ll. 3-8)

According to Dickinson, humans not only come to accept their prisons as kin, but also come to be grateful for the attention we receive from our imprisoning systems; more importantly, we come to hunger for this attention as if it were our sustenance. Because of our acculturating experience, we lose sight of the freedom we experienced as children—"As plashing in the Pools— / When Memory was a Boy—" (ll. 13-14)—and perceive the prison as more real than liberation:

> . . . Not so real
> The Cheek of Liberty—
>
> As this Phantasm Steel—
> Whose features—Day and Night—
> Are present to us—as Our Own—
>
> (ll. 19-23)

Dickinson suggests that the culturally created beliefs that guide our daily activities and define our selves—the beliefs that imprison us—are not real, are "Phantasm." Yet, significantly, we do not perceive the illusory nature of these systems; rather, because our beliefs provide a framework for navigating daily life, even though they simultaneously constrain us, they become more real than the liberty that we have abandoned.

The poem concludes, linking the imprisonment described in the poem to religion and reiterating the way in which we accept cultural beliefs—and, here, specifically, a belief in redemption in the afterlife—as the norm:

> The Liberty we knew
> Avoided—like a Dream—
> Too wide for any Night but Heaven—
> If That—indeed—redeem—
>
> (ll. 29-32)

As humans grow older, accepting cultural beliefs, we consider the freedom of our childhood, a freedom that we experienced naturally, as fantasy and can not even imagine liberation except insofar as it is connected to the afterlife. The acculturation process replaces our freedom with imprisonment, and relegates freedom ("redemption") to the spiritual world. Moreover, we have not only lost our ability to perceive true liberty, but also our ability to imagine—in the "Night"—this liberty. Consequently, we place our hopes for redemption elsewhere, in the afterlife, a hope that Dickinson questions in the final line.

This first poem begins to set up some of the binary oppositions that Dickinson will seek to undermine later in the fascicle—especially the dichotomies of this life and the afterlife, and sin and salvation—and to connect this project to poetry. While she does not dispel the polarities here, she does question them in the final line of the poem—"If That [Heaven]—indeed—redeem—" (l. 32), suggesting that the hope for redemption and freedom placed on the spiritual afterlife may be misplaced. But she is also concerned with the relation between the prison of culture and poetry:

> We learn to know the Planks—
> That answer to Our feet—
> So miserable a sound—at first—
> Nor even now—so sweet—
>
> (ll. 9-12)

On one level, these lines describe the sound of pacing on the floor of a prison cell that we have become accustomed to. On another level, however, they describe the way in which her poetry (the metrical feet of her poetic lines) adjust to, though they never completely harmonize with, the prison. Such a negative depiction will be significant to my reading of the fascicle as a whole, which ends rather despairingly in the limitations of religion described in the first poem of the fascicle.

The second poem in the first grouping, "Nature—sometimes sears a Sapling—", counterbalances the first poem through a description of the way in which Nature impacts both the natural world and humans. The first part of the poem depicts the harmful effects of Nature on the landscape:

> Nature—sometimes sears a Sapling—
> Sometimes—scalps a Tree—
> Her Green People recollect it
> When they do not die—
>
> Fainter Leaves—to Further Seasons—
> Dumbly testify—
>
> (ll. 1-6)

Not only do these first lines demonstrate that pain is a natural part of life—the searing of the sapling and the scalping of the tree—they also demonstrate that this pain is part of the cycle of life—the fainter leaves that grow in later seasons.

In this way, Dickinson insinuates a cyclical view of time, one that will be built on later in the fascicle, and asserts that pain is a part of growth.[12] But she also demonstrates that humans respond differently to the pain: "We—who have the Souls— / Die oftener—Not so vitally—" (ll. 7-8). Humans, who are more delicate and fragile than the natural landscape—we die more often—die in a different way than the natural world, for we die "Not so vitally—" suggesting that our death is not that of our mortal bodies but of our "Souls." The pain of Nature, then, does not kill humans; rather, humans become separated from Nature, the cause of discomfort, because our fragile natures, unlike that of the sapling and the tree, cannot withstand the pain. Such a depiction of the human reaction to pain explains the reason for our acceptance of cultural constraints elaborated in the opening poem.

While the first two poems work together to delineate a nice contrast between culture—a familiar prison—and nature—a discomforting force, the third poem, **"She dealt her pretty words like Blades—"**, ties the two together and links them directly to the role of the poet. Like **"Nature—sometimes sears a Sapling—"**, **"She dealt her pretty words,"** which describes how "She" creates a "vulgar grimace in the Flesh," also focuses on how poorly humans react to pain and the way in which we create customs to gloss over the "pretty words" that are "like Blades":

> To Ache is human—not polite—
> The Film upon the eye
> Mortality's old Custom—
> Just locking up—to Die.

(ll. 9-12)

Culture, which determined that it is not appropriate to reveal our discomfort, is described here as a film that skews our sight, imprisoning us in a kind of death in life. Because this poem follows **"Nature—sometimes sears a Sapling—"** and because it deals with similar issues, the "She" of the poem might refer to Nature; yet, because "She" deals with words, the pronoun simultaneously refers to the poet who offers a truth that cannot be borne by her audience, thus connecting the female poet with Nature.[13] The first three poems of the fascicle, then, set up a clear distinction between culture—which is defined as a limitation or constraint, a custom or habit, such as placing our hope for redemption in the afterlife, that separates us from our freedom—and nature or the poet—which is connected to freedom, but also to a pain that humans cannot tolerate and thus that they disassociate themselves from.

The next grouping of poems, including **"'Why do I love' You, Sir?"** (J480, F459), **"The Himmaleh was known to stoop"** (J481, F460), and **"We Cover Thee—Sweet Face—"** (J482, F461), deals with the importance and power of human relationships. These poems, which depict a fragile relation between a dominant male lover and a passive female devotee, have been read metaphorically as delineations of the various aspects of the poet's self; Gelpi notes that Dickinson's love poems describe a "subjective drama, and both figures in the drama are first and last psychological factors . . . the 'other' [in the poems] is a projected personification of the poet's emotional and religious needs much more than any person she has known and loved. 'He' is real but not actual, and his reality is self-referential. 'He' is a protagonist/antagonist in the drama of identity" (*Tenth Muse* 247-48). Others have more recently read these poems in relation to Dickinson's creative powers, suggesting that the male lover might refer to the creative dimension of her personality, "her own inner agency, which she feared would desert or destroy her" (Martin 103).[14] While I certainly think that such readings add depth to our understanding of Emily Dickinson and her views of creativity, I want to consider these poems not as statements about Dickinson's multifaceted self, or about Emily Dickinson as a poet, but rather as statements that attempt to describe in some fashion the power of human relationships.

The first poem in this grouping, **"'Why do I love' You, Sir?"** replies to the question of the opening line through several parallels in the natural world—between the wind and the grass, the lightning and the eye—that demonstrate that love is beyond explanation and beyond language: "And reasons not contained— / —Of Talk— / There be—" (ll. 14-16). The dash at the start of line 15, a truncated line, mirrors the fact that there is a great deal about love that cannot be contained in words.[15] While the poem demonstrates that love is inexplicable, it concludes with evidence of love's power:

> The Sunrise—Sir—compelleth Me—
> Because He's Sunrise—and I see—
> Therefore—Then—
> I love Thee—

(ll. 17-20)

The poem, which opens with the question "'Why do I love'" (note that the rest of the first line, "You, Sir?" is not in quotations and thus that the question is more about why humans love than it is about why she loves him), concludes without providing an answer beyond the fact that she is compelled to love. The power and force of love, a power that cannot be captured in language, becomes the only explanation for the love.

The next two poems, "**The Himmaleh was known to stoop**" and "**We Cover Thee—Sweet Face—**", describe the effect of relationships—the way in which relationships allow the meanest thing to become great, to expand beyond its normal proportions. The low daisy of the first poem, which puts forth her petals in a field full of daisies for the Himmaleh, is amplified: "Her Universe / Hung out it's Flags of Snow—" (ll. 5-6). The lowly flower suddenly recognizes herself as a "Universe" at the same time that her white flowers—the "Flags of Snow"—are spread out for others to see. Likewise, in the second poem, the narrator, who must continually con her lover in order to receive attention, concludes that she would be "Augmented . . . a Hundred fold— / If Thou would'st take it—now—" (ll. 11-12). Taken together, this series of poems describes the way in which relationships enrich us beyond our normal state, offering a nice contrast to the first grouping of poems, which define the role of culture in delimiting us. In addition, this grouping begins the process of subverting cultural norms, a process emphasized in the second half of the fascicle, through offering a re-valuation of the devalued, passive, female position, a position which expands as the "Universe" and is "Augmented . . . a Hundred fold."[16] Moreover, these three poems lead to the next series of poems, which explicitly describes the liberation and expansion of the self into the universe, and to the central poem, "**I dwell in Possibility**" which is also concerned with relationships, and especially the relation of the poet to her "Visiters—the fairest—".

The third grouping of poems, including "**Of Being is a Bird**" (J"653," F"462"), "**A long—long Sleep—A famous—Sleep—**" (J"654," F"463"), "**Without this—there is nought—**" (J"655," F"464"), and "**The name—of it—is 'Autumn'—**" (J"656," F"465"), centers on describing the experience of liberation and expansion and suggests an interconnection of nature and humans. The first poem compares our "Being" to the free flight of a bird that floats upon the heavens and "measures with the Clouds / In easy—even—dazzling pace—" (ll. 6-7). The ease with which the bird associates with the clouds in the heavens belies the magnificence of her feat, linking the poem to the second grouping. The poem concludes noting that the only difference between our being and the bird is that "a Wake of Music / Accompany their feet—"

(ll. 9-10), suggesting that birds can not only experience this sense of freedom but that they can also sing about it.[17] The second poem draws on the freedom experienced in the first poem of this series while beginning to undermine the binary oppositions (here, night versus day) that pervade our culture, thus building on the first two groupings of poems. The "long Sleep" not only "makes no show for Morn," but it also does not "look up—for Noon" (ll. 2, 8), suggesting that this famous sleep is independent of the boundaries of night and day that guide our temporal lives. The third poem in this series returns to the concept of expansion and ties into the second grouping of poems that revealed the importance of relationships. The poem opens, referring to love, "Without this—there is nought—" (l. 1) and concludes:

> I wished a way might be
> My Heart to subdivide—
> Twould magnify—the Gratitude—
> And not reduce—the Gold—
>
> (ll. 9-12)

Here, the narrator expresses her desire to offer her love to as many humans as possible; with this magnification of relationships, however, her love is not thinly spread and thus weakened but is rather increased without reducing its intensity or power. Again, the concept of magnification is introduced, as in the second grouping, and is tied to an exploration of relationships.

The concluding poem in this series, "**The name—of it—is 'Autumn'—**", links the natural landscape and humans while also describing time as cyclical rather than being demarcated by boundaries (day and night). In the poem, autumn is described through human characteristics: "An Artery—upon the Hill— / A Vein—along the Road—" (ll. 3-4), thus linking humans and the natural landscape as well as humans and the seasons. When the wind upsets the autumnal clouds, the "Scarlet Rain" "sprinkles Bonnets—far below—" (ll. 8-9), offering a physical communion of nature and humans, before it "eddies like a rose—away— / Upon Vermillion Wheels—" (ll. 11-12). Although a poem about autumn might conjure images of death and decay, here the references to the beauty and the "Wheels" of the season suggest a concern not with time ending but with time as a cycle, as a part of a natural process—very much like "**Nature—sometimes sears a Sapling—**" and "**She dealt her pretty words like Blades—**" in the first grouping of poems. In addition, the cycles of time include both the natural landscape and humans which are linked in the poem.[18] Such a link, which exists in many Dickinson poems, can also be seen in her letters. In February 1855, in a letter to Susan Gilbert, Dickinson metaphorically connects her observation of nature (and the seasonal cycles of nature) with her feelings for her friend, her relationships: "Sweet and soft as summer, Darlings, maple trees in bloom and grass green in sunny places—hardly seems it possible this is winter still; and it makes the grass spring in this heart of mine and each linnet sing, to think that you have come" (L 178).

The central poem in **"fascicle 22," "I dwell in Possibility—"** (J657, F466), draws on the themes and motifs registered in the first three groupings of poems. Centrally concerned with defining poetry and the role of the poet, **"I dwell"** works to undermine the religious dichotomies of Dickinson's culture—sin versus salvation, physical versus spiritual, this life versus afterlife—not through reconciliation but rather through subverting the foundation of these dichotomies.[19] The opening lines of the poem begin to assert this stance: "I dwell in Possibility— / A fairer House than Prose—" (ll. 1-2). Dickinson, describing her vocation through the domestic image of the house, sets up a distinction between the house of poetry and the house of prose, the former founded on openness and multiplicity—like the cycles of nature—the latter by contrast founded on clear cut distinctions—such as night and day, sin and salvation. The house of poetry is "More numerous of Windows— / Superior—for Doors—" (ll. 4-5), linking poetry to relationships and thus interconnectedness. Significantly, the house of poetry is also tied to nature:

> Of Chambers as the Cedars—
> Impregnable of Eye—
> And for an Everlasting Roof
> The Gambrels of the Sky—
>
> (ll. 5-8)

and thus completes the depiction: prose arises from culture and creates constraint and limitation because it is founded on polarities; poetry arises from nature and creates freedom and liberation because it sees past polarities and is based on interconnectedness.

Dickinson concludes the poem further defining her conception of the expansion at the heart of her poetic. She notes:

> For Occupation—This—
> The spreading wide my narrow Hands
> To gather Paradise—
>
> (ll. 9-12)

Here, Dickinson suggests that poetry, as a vocation, creates a change in her being. She moves from narrowness, a symbolic reference to human depravity and sin borrowed from orthodox, Puritan religion, to expansion. The capitalization of the word "Hands" suggests a parallel between the poet as creator and God as creator. Thus, poetry as a vocation allows her to overcome and move beyond limitations as set by a traditional view of humans and become infinite, ultimately "gather[ing] Paradise." Because Dickinson has moved beyond conventional religious beliefs, the paradise referred to here is not the paradise of traditional religion but a revised and renewed paradise—one founded on a unique interrelation of the natural world (the house is compared to cedars and connected to the sky) and humans (the house includes multiple entrances).[20]

A similar revisioning of Heaven, one based on human relationships and often connected to nature, can be seen in Dickinson's letters.[21] In a letter to Susan Gilbert, Dickinson notes "Dear Children—Mattie—Sue—for one look at you, for your gentle voices, I'd exchange it all. The pomp—the court—the etiquette—they are of the earth—will not enter Heaven" (L 178). Here Dickinson redefines the state of salvation; rather than existing in something as royal as the afterlife, heaven and thus redemption exist through relationships. Similarly, in a letter to Mrs. J. G. Holland in January 1856, Dickinson notes "While I sit in the snows, the summer day on which you came and the bees and the south wind, seem fabulous as *Heaven* seems to a sinful world—and I keep remembering it till it assumes a *spectral* air, and nods and winks at me, and then all of you turn to phantoms and vanish slowly away" (L 182). Dickinson's relation to her friend, as "Heaven," is troped as a summer day, connecting her redefinition of paradise to a relationship with and interconnection between humans and nature.[22]

As the central poem in the fascicle, then, **"I dwell"** works to undermine rather than merely reconcile the polarities of her culture in two specific ways. First, in this poem the home becomes the site of her occupation, thus subverting the separation of the public sphere and the private sphere that occurred in the nineteenth century and that devalued the domestic and the female. In Jeanne Holland's analysis of Dickinson's various forms of publication, from the fascicle to the household scrap, she asserts that "As a nineteenth-century woman writer . . . Dickinson retires to the domestic to confront, and thwart as best she can, its ideological stranglehold" (154). Yet Dickinson's objective was not merely to oppose the constraints of nineteenth-century womanhood or

ON THE SUBJECT OF...

AN EARLY REVIEW OF *LETTERS OF EMILY DICKINSON*

Transcendentalism should claim Emily Dickinson for its own as her prose and verse alike fulfill the intention with absolute simplicity, and complete independence of the fetters of rhyme. The "Letters" show the same irregularity of expression, and also a singular quality of "hidden music," which become impressive on further acquaintance. The "Letters" are surcharged with original thought, and they are not subject to the slight disadvantage under which the poems labor. Mrs. Mabel Loomis Todd edits the "Letters" for publication. It has been well said by her that if in Emily Dickinson's work there is frequently no rhyme where rhyme should be, a subtle something, welcome and satisfying, takes its place.

The epigrammatic quality of Miss Dickinson's writing is strongly marked. The thought is often vigorous and expressed with terseness, sometimes even in a brusque manner. So it happens that her poetic fancies are wild flowers—no conventional blooms, but at best "garden escapes." For many years Miss Dickinson lived the life of a recluse, and her disinclination for general society was carried to an unusual degree. Her biographer says that in later years Emily Dickinson rarely addressed the envelopes of her letters; it seemed as if her sensitive spirit shrank from the publicity which even her handwriting would undergo in the observation of indifferent eyes. Various expedients were resorted to. Obliging friends sometimes performed this office, and sometimes a printed newspaper label was pasted upon the envelope, but the actual strokes of her own pencil were, so far as possible, reserved for friendly eyes. If it is not good for man to be alone, the same objection applies to feminine desire to retire from the world. The incident shows that the wish to retreat far from the madding crowd can easily be rendered ridiculous when indulged to excess.

"New Publications." *Philadelphia Public Ledger* (7 December 1894): 15-6. Reprinted in *Emily Dickinson's Reception in the 1890s*, edited by Willis J. Buckingham, p. 377. Pittsburgh, Pa.: University of Pittsburgh Press, 1989.

domesticity; rather she offers a re-valuation of the domestic sphere that provides a basis for the re-valuation of other cultural paradigms that exist as constraints. Second, returning to paradise as the Garden of Eden, Dickinson returns to the originary space of polarities (before sin, the fall, separation from God and nature, before the creation of culture) and reclaims that space as one where she entertains "Visiters—the fairest—" (l. 9). Such a re-visioning of paradise as a renewed Garden of Eden to be gathered through extended, welcoming arms offers a new form of redemption, one based not on the afterlife but rather on this life—and specifically on the interconnectedness of and relationships in this life.

The first grouping of poems in the second half of the fascicle, including "**A Solemn thing within the Soul**" (J483, F467), "**Whole Gulfs—of Red, and Fleets—of Red—**" (J658, F468), "**My Garden—like the Beach—**" (J484, F469), and "**The First Day, when you praised Me, Sweet**" (J659, F470), alternates between poems focusing on garden imagery and poems focusing on time. Both "**A Solemn thing**" and "**My Garden**," with references to gardens, describe the movement from seeming insignificance to significance; yet this apparently clear cut distinction is erupted with the assertion that the smallest and meanest thing is really no different from the greatest, thus subverting the foundations of these distinctions and building on the second grouping of poems in the first half of the fascicle. "**A Solemn thing within the Soul**" occurs within the Garden of Eden—and thus before the fall—and depicts the slow process of becoming "ripe": "Your chance in Harvest moves / A little nearer—Every Sun" (ll. 14-15). While Judith Farr notes that the focus of the poem is on "the reunion of God with his creation" (63), in this garden the end of the process is not the most significant, for it is "Wonderful—to feel the Sun / Still toiling at the Cheek" (ll. 7-8) while you "golden hang" (l. 3). The experience of ripening within the garden is one that offers its own form of communion, not only with God but also with nature (the "Sun" as God and as nature).[23] Similarly, "**My Garden—like the Beach—**" suggests that the garden, which ultimately creates her poetry, like the grains of sand on the beach which create the pearl, are equally significant, for it is the garden and the beach which offer the foundation for the existence of the sea and poetry (l. 2). These two garden poems within this series build on "**I dwell**" in that they undermine distinctions and polarities (in the first, sinner vs. redeemed; in the second, garden vs. poetry or sand vs. pearl) and depict the interconnectedness of all things. The glorification of the insignificant—the sand, the garden, the ripening Soul—creates a re-valuation that interrupts traditional distinctions and thus allows for a perception of the interconnectedness of all things.

The other two poems in this series, interpolated with the garden poems, also deal with seeming polarities through references to time and also undermine these polarities through careful delineation of the value associated to units of time. **"The First Day, when you praised Me, Sweet"** seems to offer a distinction between two time periods, before the day she was praised—"The Minor One—that gleamed behind—" (l.7)—and after that day—"And Vaster—of the World's" (l. 8). Yet these two sets of days are both described as "Gold"; the only distinction (beyond the fact that one is past and one looks to the future) is that they are separated by "That Day" that she received praise, the day that "Glows Central—like a Jewel" (ll. 4-5). While this kind of demarcation between two periods generally leads humans to a different valuation of those periods, Dickinson suggests that such a dichotomization not happen—that we see the separating moment as unique, but that time flow around it. Building on the awareness of time as cyclical, such a perception allows for a sense of constant renewal. Similarly, while **"Whole Gulfs—of Red, and Fleets—of Red—"** dramatizes a sunset, it does not, recalling **"A long—long Sleep,"** offer the sunset as a marker for creating distinctions or differences between night and day, one time period and another. The moment, which appears to divide, really only makes us recognize the value of what lies on either side and, ultimately, the equal value of these units of time. Gelpi notes that Dickinson's struggle to live in the moment created a unique dilemma, for to live in the moment meant that she must dwell on that moment, allowing other moments of time to slip away; the result was a kind of melding of time around the moment: "one found one's self living not just in the present but in the past and even the future; a life dedicated to apprehending the immediate intensity became alarmingly caught up in retrospection and anticipation" (*The Mind of the Poet* 103). Such a perception alters our relationship to time through uniting disparate moments within the flow of time.

The second grouping of poems in the last half of **"fascicle 22,"** including **"To make One's Toilette—after Death"** (J485, F471), **"'Tis good—the looking back on Grief—"** (J660, F472), **"I was the slightest in the House—"** (J486, F473), and

"You love the Lord—you cannot see—" (J487, F474), reiterates the project of the fascicle and **"I dwell"**—that the polarities and distinctions offered through orthodox religion create limitations and constraints and that her house—the house of poetry—offers freedom from these constraints. Three of the poems in this series focus specifically on the oppression of religious dogma. **"To make One's Toilette—after Death"** suggests that it is easier to prepare for the day when a friend has died than it is when the friend has been "wrenched / By Decalogues—away—" (ll. 7-8), possibly referring to the many friends of Dickinson who were swayed by the religious awakenings of the nineteenth century and joined the church. The loss of friends in this life to orthodox religion becomes worse than the loss of friends to death because of the continued presence of the friends, a presence which acts as a constant reminder of the loss.[24] **"I was the slightest in the House—"** concludes that

> I never spoke—unless addressed—
> And then, 'twas brief and low—
> I could not bear to live—aloud—
> The Racket shamed me so—
>
> (ll. 10-13)

The organized religion that pervades Dickinson's culture causes a racket that creates shame (the guilt of sin) but also that silences and devalues women—"I was the slightest in the House— / I took the smallest Room—" (ll. 1-2). Significantly, the overwhelming presence of religion abnegates her own thoughts and exploration of a wider world: "Let me think—I'm sure— / That this was all—" (ll. 8-9). The next poem, **"You love the Lord—you cannot see—"**, builds on this idea, suggesting that most humans spend their time consumed with traditional rituals that are empty:

> You love the Lord—you cannot see—
> You write Him—every day—
> A little note—when you awake—
> And further in the Day.
>
> (ll. 1-4)

Yet the poem also offers a solution to the racket of religion through the house of poetry: "But then His House—is but a Step— / And Mine's—in Heaven—You see" (ll. 7-8). Access to God's house, to heaven, occurs through one step, death; yet her house, the house of poetry as identified in **"I dwell,"** is already heaven because it recaptures the paradise of the Garden of Eden.

The value that has been placed within the distinction between sin and salvation, this life and the afterlife is reversed in these poems—it is easier to lose a friend to the afterlife than to lose her in this life—and thus the differentiation is interrupted. The other poem in this series, significantly placed as the second poem in this series of four poems, reiterates the process so crucial to "**fascicle 22**" of breaking down or undermining the dichotomies and polarities, and the consequent values, that are part of our culture. "**'Tis good—the looking back on Grief—**" again suggests that though we often value certain experiences differently, no differentiation should be made between these experiences:

> And though the Wo you have Today
> Be larger—As the Sea
> Exceeds it's Unremembered Drop—
> They're Water—equally—
>
> (ll. 9-12)

Grief, like all experiences, when fully and truly experienced, does not have any distinctions; a small grief and a large grief are both overpowering and overwhelming—are "Water—equally." If we differentiate between the two, we devalue the "small" grief which is equally profound. By extension, Dickinson suggests in this series of poems that this life is as valuable as the afterlife, that redemption should not be relegated to a spiritual existence after we die but rather that it can and should be experienced in our temporal lives.

While the movement of the entire fascicle up to, and immediately after, "**I dwell in Possibility**" is concerned with offering a poetic of liberation and freedom that undermines the cultural and religious dichotomies of sin and salvation, and thus redefining redemption, the final grouping of poems in the fascicle reasserts the religious dichotomies and thus suggests that maintaining the poetic of redemption is difficult if not impossible. "**Myself was formed—a Carpenter—**" (J"488," F"475"), "**We pray—to Heaven—**" (J"489," F"476"), "**He fumbles at your Soul**" (J"315," F"477"), and "**Just Once! Oh least Request!**" (J"1076," F"478") increasingly assert the dominance of a traditional God who judges and condemns. "**Myself was formed—a Carpenter—**" is tied to the theme of the fascicle in that it suggests that her work as a poet, linked to Christ's work through the image of the carpenter, should not be measured according to traditional cultural values:

> a Builder came—
>
> To measure our attainments—
> Had we the Art of Boards
> Sufficiently developed—He'd hire us
> At Halves—
>
> (ll. 4-8)

The narrator, with her tools, "Against the Man—persuaded— / We—Temples build—I

said—" (ll. 11-12). While the poet offers something grander than the builder desires or understands, her art is diminished through the valuation offered by her culture.[25] Indeed, the next two poems in the cluster, "**We pray—to Heaven—**" and "**He fumbles at your Soul**," indicate that the traditional values of her society, on the afterlife and the God of the afterlife, dominate; the heaven of the first poem, while it can not be located—"There's no Geography" (l. 9)—is the central concern of humans: "We pray—to Heaven— / We prate—of Heaven—" (ll. 1-2), just as the God of the second poem, who "fumbles at your Soul" (l. 1), "Deals—One—imperial—Thunderbolt— / That scalps your naked Soul—" (ll. 11-12), suggesting the imperious and dominating nature of God in mid-nineteenth-century American culture.[26]

The concluding poem of "**fascicle 22**," "**Just Once! Oh least Request!**" with its unanswered questions to the God described as "Adamant," "a God of Flint," and "remote" (ll. 2, 6, 8), depicts the poet herself returning to traditional religious beliefs. Unable to maintain her poetic of redemption in the face of a society that cannot hear the painful truth or experience the liberation of her poetic, the poet has no choice but to put her request "Just Once" to God who offers the only salvation that humans perceive even though she knows that this request will not be acknowledged. Such a recognition is reflected, occasionally, in Dickinson's letters; in a letter to Louise and Frances Norcross in 1861, Dickinson describes a little boy who is

> restricted to Martin Luther's works at home. It is a criminal thing to be a boy in a godly village, but maybe he will be forgiven. . . . If angels have the heart beneath their silver jackets, I think such things could make them weep, but Heaven is so cold! It will never look kind to me that god, who causes all, denies such little wishes. It could not hurt His glory, unless it were a lonesome kind. I 'most conclude it is.
>
> (L 234)

Dickinson's desire for angels to show their hearts or for God to allow the boy something else to read than Luther's works is countered with her recognition that Heaven is remote, cold, uncaring—and in control of all.

Significantly, this last poem delimits the expansion and liberation at the heart of Dickinson's poetic as outlined in "**fascicle 22**" and "**I dwell.**" While the first half of the fascicle leading up to the central poem describes the power of interconnectedness and human relationships (especially in the second grouping) as the foundation for liberation (in the third grouping), "**Just**

Once! Oh least Request!" with its emphasis on our relationship to a remote God, returns to the prison of culture delineated in the opening poem of the fascicle and thus brings the movement of the fascicle full circle. Indeed, the domestic imagery central to the fascicle (especially the house and garden), is appropriate for this movement of despair that opens and closes the fascicle, with the hope at the center of the fascicle, for the house that Emily Dickinson lived in, while it constituted the space that allowed her to write, create, and thus re-valuate her culture, was also the house of her father who formally joined the church in 1850 and increasingly pressured his daughter, the last hold out, to convert as well. As Cynthia Griffin Wolff notes, "The notion of 'House' brings together a number of Dickinson's concerns: her autonomy, her authority, her right to inherit the earth, her right to possess herself of god's heroic grandeur as well, and her right to create poetry through which these ambitions could be realized" (431).[27]

The house of poetry in "fascicle 22," which offers a re-valuation of domesticity and a new redemption through interconnectedness, meanwhile must contest with the dominant house of prose, with its confinement and oppression. Jeanne Holland's analysis of the scraps that represent Dickinson's later form of private publication suggests that moving away from the fascicle, a form that closely mirrored public forms of publication, to the scrap, a more refined domestic technology of publication, was an attempt to "materially locat[e] her poems in the private home. It is significant that her writing on household refuse coincides with her agoraphobic withdrawal from public life" and more fully "reflects and shapes her explorations in the domain of selfhood and writing" (141). This movement did not erase the conflict between patriarchy and poetry, as Holland demonstrates in her analysis of the manuscript of "Poem 1167," "Alone and in Circumstance—" (dated 1870), which includes a stamp with a locomotive on it, a representation of her father. Rather, it allowed Dickinson the opportunity in her later poetry to more fully question "the oppositions between locomotive/poetry, father/daughter, male/female" (147). Yet in the early part of her career, the late 1850s and early 1860s, Dickinson felt very keenly the constraining power of the patriarchal culture that surrounded her. She notes, in the conclusion of a letter to John L. Graves dated April 1856, what "a conceited thing indeed, this promised Resurrection!" (L 184),

suggesting her frustration at the overbearing power of patriarchal systems.

I want to conclude this paper with reference to another poem, "They shut me up in Prose—" (J613, F445), that was composed around 1862 and situated in "fascicle 21." In this poem, Dickinson also develops her conception of the paradoxical relationship between constraint and liberation using house imagery, here the house of prose. In this poem, she suggests that those in power—ministers or parents—use "prose" as a method of confinement: "They shut me up in Prose— / As when a little Girl / They put me in the Closet—".[28] While the poem opens with a description of her constraint, the conclusion of "They shut me up" suggests that residing (or being confined) in the house of prose does not, ultimately, limit or constrain the narrator:

> . . . Could themself have peeped—
> And seen my Brain—go round—
> They might as wise have lodged a Bird
> For Treason—in the Pound—
>
> Himself was but to will
> And easy as a Star
> Abolish his Captivity—
> And laugh—No more have I—

Significantly, the epistemological freedom that the narrator experiences derives from her confinement in the house of prose; without the captivity, the narrator would never have been able to enact the abolishment of her captivity—would never have been able to access her freedom. Dickinson here suggests that a dialectical relation exists between constraint and liberation, between prose and poetry, and that, ultimately, it is the confinement of prose that provides Dickinson the opportunity to create the transcendence of poetry. Such a tension, significantly, is traced in the movement of "fascicle 22" as a whole, which, while it opens and closes with conceptions of constraint, has as its central conception that of liberation, a liberation that is offered through subverting the foundations of Dickinson's culture.

Notes

1. I would like to thank the College of Arts and Sciences at Florida Gulf Coast University for support with professional development in writing this paper. I would especially like to acknowledge the assistance of Lisa Crocker, who provided me with research on many of the poems in this paper and who aided in editing the text.

2. Other critics who explored Emily Dickinson's poetry within the context of domesticity in the 1980s include Cheryl Walker, *The Nightingale's Burden*; Wendy

Martin, *An American Triptych*; and Suzanne Juhasz, "Writing Doubly: Emily Dickinson and Female Experience."

Gertrude Hughes, in "Subverting the Cult of Domesticity: Emily Dickinson's Critique of Woman's Work," argues that Dickinson re-valued the gendered experiences of the nineteenth century, an argument akin to my own:

> Like her daily life, her poems are filled with the flower-tending, letter-writing, music-playing, and sickroom nursing that were canonically assigned to her, but the poems do not use these in prescribed ways. Whereas the convention prescribed that such homely occupations existed to provide background and support for male activities, Dickinson decided for herself what constituted trivia and what 'firmament,' and she also decide whether male activities deserved support or scorn.
>
> (18)

I will extend this argument to fascicle 22 and especially "I dwell" where Dickinson uses the locus of the home to redefine and re-valuate such culturally determined beliefs as what constitutes redemption.

3. For a detailed analysis of Dickinson's metapoetics—that is, of her reflection on poetry and the role of the poet—see Raab.

4. In her third letter to T. W. Higginson, dated July 1862, Dickinson describes her poems as "Blossom[s] from my Garden" (L 268). That Dickinson's poetry originates from her garden will be significant to my reading of "I dwell in Possibility" which centers on the way in which she reclaims and revisions the Garden of Eden.

5. Cameron states, early on, that "In Dickinson's fascicles—where 'variants' are more than the editorial term for discrete delimited choices—variants indicate both the desire for limit and the difficulty in enforcing it. The difficulty in enforcing a limit to the poems turns into a kind of limitlessness, for . . . it is impossible to say where the text ends because the variants extend the text's identity in ways that make it seem potentially limitless" (6). While Cameron would certainly argue against such a thing, I would suggest that one reading of fascicle 22 is in fact an exploration of the thematic significance of the concept of limitlessness, a reading that I will pursue here. Significantly, as Cameron notes, the variants to poems within fascicles increased in 1861, about the same time that Dickinson arranged the poems in fascicle 22.

6. Cameron makes the most comprehensive argument concerning the compounding of a multiplicity of meanings, suggesting that a thematic approach to the fascicles that does not engage the variants and inter-relationships is not, indeed, reading Dickinson. I would suggest, rather, that a thematic approach such as the one that I pursue here might act as one reading of a fascicle which could easily, even comfortably though possibly contradictorily, be joined by other readings which privilege other poems and discern different groupings within the fascicles. My reading, then, would only be the beginning of a series of readings that would allow for a compounding of meanings, all of which might be expected to interact, to lead to questionings, to lead to problematization.

7. Many critics have noted the conflict in Emily Dickinson's poetry between constraint and transcendence, especially in relation to her conception of her vocation as poet. Many of these readings posit the conflict as one between Puritanism and Transcendentalism without considering the importance of gender.

For those critics who consider the conflict to be an unresolved tension that offers complexity to Dickinson's work, see Albert Gelpi, *The Tenth Muse: The Psyche of the American Poet,* and Hyatt Waggoner, *American Poets,* who provide perhaps the strongest background for this discussion. See also Carter, who suggests that Dickinson experienced "a continuing and never-resolved conflict between the secularism represented by Emerson's Transcendentalism and the Christianity represented by her family and her New England heritage" (85), and New, who locates Dickinson not in Romanticism nor in nihilism but in a third position, "that of a theologically answered doubt," that New defines through Kierkegaard (4). As I will note later, New proceeds to read "I dwell" as a thoroughly Transcendental poem (6-7).

On the other hand, Weisbuch argues ultimately that the second world, that of Puritan limitation, overwhelms the first: "The veto power of Dickinson's second pain-filled world stands ready to negate or qualify the self-legislated grandeur of the first. . . . Dickinson would insist on testing her fictions, and they would often fail. The resultant despair is not simply a worldly pessimism; it is directed not against 'so fair a place' as nature but against her own visions which have neglected a limit. Her second world is 'second' because it is logically subsequent to her hopes. . . . In this second world, the Transcendental possibilities of the first tantalize only to torture" (*Emily Dickinson's Poetry* 2). For similar readings, see Wilner, Yin, and Eberwein, "'Graphicer for Grace.'"

My reading of Dickinson's poetic, following the lines of many of the feminist critics of the 1980s and 1990s, is founded on a concern for gender as a tool for subverting traditional cultural values. As Jeanne Holland notes in her analysis of Dickinson's private publishing efforts, "The ideological split between 'male' literary creativity and 'female' domestic labor collapses in Dickinson's experience. Because she combines ideological positions that her culture struggles to separate—indeed her late works meld literary creativity and domesticity—Dickinson's multiply [sic for multiple?] gendered perspective enables her to resist . . . possessive individualism" (152).

8. Dickinson's rebellion against orthodox religion can be seen in many letters and poems, especially in her descriptions of refusing to go to service with her family and remaining home, instead, to write letters to her friends. This rebellion can also be seen in "Some keep the Sabbath going to Church—" (J324; F236), which concludes: "So instead of getting to Heaven, at last— / I'm going, all along" (ll. 11-12). The distinction between the heaven of orthodox religion—based on faith in the afterlife—and the heaven of this life is at the heart of Dickinson's redefinition of redemption.

Several other critics have also noticed this rebellion. Margaret Homans, in "Emily Dickinson and Poetic Identity," suggests that Dickinson reacted against both orthodox religion and Emersonian Transcendentalism, and especially their gendered foundations, in developing her poetic. In relation to Transcendentalism, she notes that, while Emerson works from polarities to a state of reconciliation, Emily Dickinson "works toward undermining the whole concept of oppositeness" (140), an argument that I will build on.

In addition, in "Writing Doubly," Suzanne Juhasz notes that in many of Dickinson's poems, rather than staging a conflict between two polarities (either/or), she offers simultaneity (both/and); while patriarchal culture devalues female experience as domestic and trivial, Dickinson's poetry reacts against this devaluation and asserts the grandness of the female experience not in order to cancel out the former but only to offer a simultaneous and contradictory view. Again, my reading will build on this argument, relating it specifically to the poems in fascicle 22.

9. I am following the organization of the fascicle suggested in the Variorum edition of Dickinson's works, edited by Franklin (Dickinson, *The Poems of Emily Dickinson: A Variorum Edition* 476-92). Fascicle 22 includes the following poems, grouped according to my own strategy:

FIRST PART

Grouping One

> J652/F456 A Prison gets to be a friend—
>
> J314/F457 Nature—sometimes sears a Sapling—
>
> J479/F458 She dealt her pretty words like Blades—

Grouping Two

> J480/F459 'Why do I love' You, Sir?
>
> J481/F460 The Himmaleh was known to stoop
>
> J482/F461 We Cover Thee—Sweet Face—

Grouping Three

> J653/F462 Of Being is a Bird
>
> J654/F463 A long—long Sleep—A famous—Sleep—
>
> J655/F464 Without this—there is nought—
>
> J656/F465 The name—of it—is 'Autumn'—

Central Poem

> J657/F466 I dwell in Possibility—

SECOND PART

Grouping One

> J483/F467 A Solemn thing within the Soul
>
> J658/F468 Whole Gulfs—of Red, and Fleets—of Red—
>
> J484/F469 My Garden—like the Beach—
>
> J659/F470 The First Day, when you praised Me, Sweet

Grouping Two

> J485/F471 To make One's Toilette—after Death
>
> J660/F472 'Tis good—the looking back on Grief—

> J486/F473 I was the slightest in the House—
>
> J487/F474 You love the Lord—you cannot see—

Grouping Three

> J488/F475 Myself was formed—a Carpenter—
>
> J489/F476 We pray—to Heaven—
>
> J315/F477 He fumbles at your Soul
>
> J1076/F478 Just Once! Oh least Request!

My analysis will follow what I perceive to be an organizational pattern in the fascicle. I will analyze three groupings of poems in the first half of the fascicle, with a special emphasis on the first grouping, that set up the primary themes and motifs, including especially the concept of constraint or limitation, the importance of relationships, and the experience of liberation or freedom. These first three groupings will lead up to a reading of the central poem of the fascicle, "I dwell in Possibility," a poem which delineates the role of poetry and the poet in relation to the themes and motifs introduced in the first half of the fascicle. In this poem, Dickinson most clearly undermines the binary oppositions of her culture—especially relating to religion—through returning to, and redefining, the Garden of Eden—symbolically the foundation for the dichotomies that pervade nineteenth-century culture. I will then analyze three groupings of poems in the last half of the fascicle that fall away from "I dwell" through repeating the theme of "I dwell" but also through suggesting that maintaining the undifferentiated state is difficult or perhaps even impossible.

10. While I will consistently note both Johnson's and Franklin's numbers for the poems when I first introduce them, when citing Dickinson's poems, I will use Johnson; if Franklin offers a significant alternative, I will note the Franklin version in a footnote.

11. Several critics have offered differing readings of this poem. Roger Lundin interprets the poem within intellectual contexts of the nineteenth century that suggest that Dickinson's concern with the disorientation that occurred as a result of the advance of human knowledge led to a growing awareness that the universe does not display an ordered design (135-37). James Guthrie reads the poem within the context of Dickinson's problems with her sight and her experiences as a patient (69-71). Finally, Eleanor Heginbotham glosses the poem in relation to references to Milton ("'Paradise fictitious,'" 59).

12. Wolff provides a nice gloss of this poem, reading it within a biblical context—Jacob's struggle with God. While this struggle wounds Jacob, it also offers him a new identity—"a new 'self' empowered to exercise the authority he had won" (149-50). While I certainly agree that the pain in the poem is connected to the possibility for growth, I suggest that Dickinson is concerned with differentiating nature's response to this pain from human's response.

13. While Weisbuch suggests that this poem describes the "misuse of the word's power" ("Prisming Dickinson" 210), Gelpi offers a reading similar to mine, noting the connection between poetry, which depicts life, and pain (*The Mind of the Poet* 137).

14. Betsy Erkkila notes that in the Master Letters and love poems, the narrator offering herself up to the male lover "might be read as an attempt to invest . . .

[herself] with masculine subjectivity and power. But because masculine presence would threaten to overpower the woman, her romantic passion is often most intense when the male figure is either absent or unavailable" (66). See also Adrienne Rich (104-05, 109).

15. Franklin does not truncate these lines:

> And reasons not contained—Of Talk—
> There be—preferred by Daintier Folk—
>
> (ll. 14-15)

Significantly, the four other stanzas of the poem, even in Franklin, include truncated lines, which, like the Johnson version of these lines, builds on the theme of the inexplicability of human love.

16. In reference to Poem 481 and others like it, Robert Smith offers a nice reading of the way in which Dickinson created a "*masochistic aesthetic*" that used the "thematics of domination and submission" in order to subvert "power hierarchies." Such a thematics, according to Smith, creates a "representative space . . . from within which poet and readers alike are able to explore and demystify the brutal conjunction of power and pleasure in intersubjective relations" (2).

17. In a letter to Dr. and Mrs. J. G. Holland, written in the summer of 1862, Dickinson makes a similar parallel: "My business is to love. I found a bird, this morning, down—down—on a little bush at the foot of the garden, and wherefore sing, I said, since nobody hears? One sob in the throat, one flutter of bosom— 'My business is to sing'—and away she rose! How do I know but cherubim, once, themselves, as patient, listened, and applauded her unnoticed hymn?" (L 269).

18. In "Terrains of Difference," Joanne Feit Diehl notes that "poem 656 ['The name—of it—is 'Autumn'—'] disrupts conventional literary distinctions between the internal and the external, between nature and culture, between the body and all that lies beyond it. In addition to its brilliantly descriptive view of autumn, Dickinson's text constitutes a re-examination of the relationship between nature and the human, presenting a vision of the world as body and of seasonal (therefore cyclical) occurrence as a willed or volitional event" (87).

19. Many readings of "I dwell in Possibility" suggest that this poem reflects Emersonian Transcendentalism. See Judith Farr, who notes that "I dwell" "makes the association frequent in Emerson between sky and paradise while her allusion to fairest visitors is to those transcendental emissaries, the muses, or sources of artistic inspiration to whom she alludes in a number of poems about the poetic process. Poem 657 describes the creative responsiveness Emerson praised in *Nature*: 'Every spirit builds itself a house, and beyond its house a world, and beyond its world a heaven'" (51). See also Douglas Robinson, who notes: "Certainly her attachment to Emersonianism was strong. In her very Emersonian poem 'I Dwell in Possibility' (657) . . . 'Possibility' tropes nature while enacting *NATURE*: 'Build, therefore, your own world.' The poem *is* Dickinson's world, her dwelling place or house of poetry" (25). Likewise, Frederick L. Morey reads the poem in the light of Emersonian Transcendentalism and Kantian metaphysics (33). Finally, while the context of Doriani's study is "the Christian prophetic tradition,"

and especially that tradition as it existed in Puritan New England, the emphasis on prophecy links the study to considerations of Emersonian Transcendentalism (1); Doriani's reading of "I dwell" focuses on the religious terms of Dickinson's vocation (142). See also Diehl, "Emerson, Dickinson, and the Abyss," and McElderry for discussions of Dickinson and Transcendentalism.

Significantly, most other readings focus on the concepts of liberation and limitlessness; see Juhasz, "'I dwell in Possibility': Emily Dickinson in the Subjunctive Mood"; Miller, "Poetry as Transitional Object" (449-50); and Julia Walker (21). Only Benfey reads this poem as emphasizing limitation and negation: "The doors and windows of the first stanza seem, in retrospect (on rereading, that is), to be there less in the service of openness than for the possibility of closing them when necessary: they serve as much to exclude as to include" (34).

20. Elisa New interprets the final lines of the poem in terms of Emersonian Transcendentalism: "in these lines Dickinson lays out not only the promise of poetic innovation that her work will fulfill, a wrenching of the poem away from the prose dictions that afford available paraphrase, but also promise of an alternative, more commodious theology than that to which American poetry is used. 'Possibility' implies both a poetic and a theological movement. By 'spreading wide [her] narrow Hands' the poet will gather in a redemption neither guaranteed nor made particularly available by her forebears' faith, a redemption whose paradoxes will deepen and compound" (7).

New's analysis of the connection between Dickinson's poetic and theology parallels my own, yet I don't read Dickinson's beliefs as grounded in Emersonian transcendentalism, which very often works towards reconciling binary oppositions (see Homans 140). Dickinson, rather, works through oppositions in order to envelope and encompass; specifically here she works through constraints and limitations in order to reach freedom, a strategy common in her works that suggests the importance of constraints as a part of the process for attaining liberation. Amy Cherry notes that "the limitations of the prison are what keep her writing. She needs the boundaries so she can attempt to overcome them" (21). I will return to this idea in my conclusion.

21. For two interesting discussions of Dickinson's views on and symbolic uses of Heaven in her poetry, see Guthrie (Chapter 4) and Wolff (321-42).

22. Significantly, even when Emily Dickinson maintains a traditional view of Paradise, as existing only in the afterlife, she still defines it through relationships; in a letter to Mrs. J. G. Holland in 1856, Dickinson notes that she wishes that she were in the afterlife, "which makes such promises. . . . And I'm half tempted to take my seat in that Paradise of which the good man writes, and begin forever and ever *now*, so wondrous does it seem. My only sketch, profile, of Heaven is a large, blue sky, bluer and larger than the *biggest* I have seen in June, and in it are my friends—all of them— every one of them—those who are with me now, and those who were 'parted' as we walked, and 'snatched up to Heaven'" (L 185). Yet even after this, she suggests that she envisions two distinct paradises: "If roses had not faded, and frosts had never come, and one had not fallen here and there whom I could not

waken, there were no need of other Heaven than the one below—and if god had been there this summer, and seen the things that I have seen—I guess that he would think His Paradise superfluous" (L 185). Significantly, Dickinson admits that maintaining the vision of this life as paradise is difficult, primarily because of the presence of death which interrupts the cycles of life, the flow of time, key concepts in her poetic and revisioned redemption.

Many other letters maintain the real presence of the paradise of this life; see, for instance, letters 193 and 305.

23. Both Wolff and Lundin suggest that the narrator in the poem is suspended between two worlds—the "heaven above and the abyss below" (Lundin 159)—suggesting that her "glimpse into Heaven, then, is not glorious but terrifying" (Wolff 306). Such a reading ignores the significance of the garden imagery in the poem which suggests that becoming ripe allows the soul to fall into the garden, a garden of redemption before the fall; in this reading, only one world exists, that of possibility and hope.

24. For a strong discussion of Emily Dickinson's reaction to the revivals that occurred in and around Amherst throughout her life, and their impact on her family and friends, see Chapter 3 in Gelpi, *The Mind of the Poet.*

25. Judith Farr also discusses this poem, in connection with "I was the slightest in the house" and "A Solemn Thing it was I said," noting that in these poems, "Dickinson's speaker offers herself in solitude to nature's influence and predicates the sacramental connection between landscape and humanity, between landscape and the divine, which was the hypothesis of the romantics and a chief principle of Ruskin" (51). While I agree that such a connection is established in fascicle 22, I have suggested in my reading of "I dwell" especially that it differs somewhat from that of the romantics; more importantly, in looking at the movement within the fascicle, by the time Dickinson gets to "Myself was formed a Carpenter," which is in the final grouping, she is moving away from the ability to maintain this sacred connection. While Guthrie rightly notes that this poem offers a high valuation of poetry (132), this claim comes in response to the devaluation of her work by "the Man," a symbolic representative of the dominant, patriarchal culture.

26. Wolff describes this domination in sexual terms: "God rapes us one by one; however, He has violated us collectively, too, for His violence has vitiated the very culture in which we have been reared" (280). For other discussions of this poem, see Fast, who suggests that the poem is concerned with poetic inspiration; Juhasz, who reads the poem in relation to "the nature and uses of power itself" ("Poem 315" 66); and Ringler-Henderson, who reads the poem as depicting "a devastating psychic and emotional storm" (70).

27. For a nice discussion of the role of place, and especially the home, in Emily Dickinson's thinking, see Eberwein, "Dickinson's Local, Global, and Cosmic Perspectives."

28. Robert Weisbuch has rightly linked the reference to prose in this second poem to the "rigidities of puritanism" that existed in the Dickinson family (*Emily Dickinson's Poetry* 4). Weisbuch concludes: "The House of Prose, of conventional and prosaic conformity, here [in "They shut me up"] becomes a punitive closet; but the House of Possibility, of imaginative epistemological freedom, exists wherever the mind is" (*Emily Dickinson's Poetry* 5).

Works Cited

Benfey, Christopher E. G. *Emily Dickinson and the Problem of Others.* Amherst: U of Massachusetts P, 1984.

Bennett, Paula. *Emily Dickinson: Woman Poet.* Iowa City: U of Iowa P, 1990.

Cameron, Sharon. *Choosing Not Choosing: Dickinson's Fascicles.* Chicago: U of Chicago P, 1992.

Carter, Steve. "Emily Dickinson and Mysticism." *ESQ* 24 (1978): 83-95.

Cherry, Amy L. "'A Prison gets to be a friend': Sexuality and Tension in the Poems of ED." *Dickinson Studies* 49 (June 1984): 9-21.

Dickinson, Emily. *The Letters of Emily Dickinson.* Vol. 2. Ed. Thomas H. Johnson. Cambridge: Harvard UP, 1958.

———. *The Poems of Emily Dickinson.* Vols. 1 and 2. Ed. Thomas H. Johnson. Cambridge: Harvard UP, 1955.

———. *The Poems of Emily Dickinson: A Variorum Edition.* Vol. 1. Ed. R. W. Franklin. Cambridge: Harvard UP, 1998.

Diehl, Joanne Feit. "Emerson, Dickinson, and the Abyss." *Modern Critical Views: Emily Dickinson.* Ed. Harold Bloom. New York: Chelsea House, 1985. 145-160.

———. "Terrains of Difference: Reading Shelley and Dickinson on Autumn." *Women's Studies* 16 (1989): 87-90.

Doriani, Beth Maclay. *Emily Dickinson: Daughter of Prophecy.* Amherst: U of Massachusetts P, 1996.

Eberwein, Jane Donahue. "Dickinson's Local, Global, and Cosmic Perspectives." *The Emily Dickinson Handbook.* Ed. Gudrun Grabher, Roland Hagenbuchle, and Cristanne Miller. Amherst: U of Massachusetts P, 1998. 27-43.

———. "'Graphicer for Grace': Emily Dickinson's Calvinist Language." *Studies in Puritan American Spirituality* 1 (Dec. 1990): 170-201.

Erkkila, Betsy. *The Wicked Sisters: Women Poets, Literary History, and Discord.* New York: Oxford UP, 1992.

Farr, Judith. *The Passion of Emily Dickinson.* Cambridge: Harvard UP, 1992.

Fast, Robin Riley. "Poem 315." *Women's Studies* 16 (1989): 55-59.

Franklin, R. W. *The Editing of Emily Dickinson: A Reconsideration.* Madison: U of Wisconsin P, 1967.

———. Introduction. *The Manuscript Books of Emily Dickinson.* Ed. R. W. Franklin. Cambridge: Harvard UP, 1981. ix-xxii.

Gelpi, Albert J. "Emily Dickinson and the Deerslayer: The Dilemma of the Woman Poet in America." *Shakespeare's Sisters: Feminist Essays on Women Poets.* Ed. Sandra M. Gilbert and Susan Gubar. Bloomington: Indiana UP, 1979. 122-34.

———. *Emily Dickinson: The Mind of the Poet.* Cambridge: Harvard UP, 1966.

————. *The Tenth Muse: The Psyche of the American Poet.* Cambridge, Mass.: Harvard UP, 1975.

Gilbert, Sandra M. "The Wayward Nun beneath the Hill: Emily Dickinson and the Mysteries of Womanhood." *Feminist Critics Read Emily Dickinson.* Ed. Suzanne Juhasz. Bloomington: Indiana UP, 1983. 22-44.

Guthrie, James R. *Emily Dickinson's Vision: Illness and Identity in Her Poetry.* Gainesville: UP of Florida, 1998.

Heginbotham, Eleanor. "Dickinson's Aesthetics and Fascicle 21." *Unfastening the Fascicles: An EDIS Roundtable at the 1997 MLA. http://jefferson.village.virginia.edu/dickinson/fascicle/hegin.html.* 18 June 1998.

————. "'Paradise fictitious': Dickinson's Milton." *Emily Dickinson Journal* 7.1 (1998): 55-74.

Holland, Jeanne. "Scraps, Stamps, and Cutouts: Emily Dickinson's Domestic Technologies of Publication." *Cultural Artifacts and the Production of Meaning: The Page, the Image, and the Body.* Ed. Margaret J. M. Ezell and Katherine O'Brien O'Keeffe. Ann Arbor: U of Michigan P, 1994. 139-181.

Homans, Margaret. "Emily Dickinson and Poetic Identity." *Emily Dickinson.* Ed. Harold Bloom. New York: Chelsea House, 1985. 129-44.

Hughes, Gertrude Reif. "Subverting the Cult of Domesticity: Emily Dickinson's Critique of Women's Work." *Legacy* 3 (Spring 1986): 17-28.

Juhasz, Suzanne. "'I dwell in Possibility': Emily Dickinson in the Subjunctive Mood." *Emily Dickinson Bulletin* 32 (1977): 105-109.

————. "Introduction: Feminist Critics Read Emily Dickinson." *Feminist Critics Read Emily Dickinson.* Ed. Suzanne Juhasz. Bloomington: Indiana UP, 1983. 1-21.

————. "Poem 315." *Women's Studies* 16 (1998): 61-66.

————. *The Undiscovered Continent: Emily Dickinson and the Space of the Mind.* Bloomington: Indiana UP, 1983.

————. "Writing Doubly: Emily Dickinson and Female Experience." *Legacy* 3 (Spring 1986): 5-15.

Keller, Karl. *The Only Kangaroo Among the Beauty: Emily Dickinson and America.* Baltimore: Johns Hopkins UP, 1979.

Lundin, Roger. *Emily Dickinson and the Art of Belief.* Grand Rapids: William B. Eerdmans, 1998.

Martin, Wendy. *An American Triptych: Anne Bradstreet, Emily Dickinson, Adrienne Rich.* Chapel Hill: U of North Carolina P, 1984.

McElderry, B. R., Jr. "Emily Dickinson: Viable Transcendentalist." *ESQ* 44 (1966): 17-21.

Miller, Ruth. "Poetry as a Transitional Object." *Between Reality and Fantasy: Transitional Objects and Phenomena.* Ed. Simon A. Grolnick and Leonard Barkin, in collaboration with Werner Muensterberger. New York: Jason Aronson, 1978. 449-68.

————. *The Poetry of Emily Dickinson.* Middletown: Wesleyan UP, 1968.

Morey, Frederick L. "Dickinson-Kant, Part III: The Beautiful and the Sublime." *Dickinson Studies* 67 (1988): 3-60.

New, Elisa. "Difficult Writing, Difficult God: Emily Dickinson's Poems Beyond Circumference." *Religion and Literature* 18.3 (Fall 1986): 1-27.

Oberhaus, Dorothy Huff. *Emily Dickinson's Fascicles: Method and Meaning.* University Park: Pennsylvania SUP, 1995.

————. "Emily Dickinson's Fascicles: Method and Meaning of a Christian Poet." *Literature and Belief* 15 (1995): 1-21.

Raab, Josef. "The Metapoetic Element in Dickinson." *The Emily Dickinson Handbook.* Ed. Gudrun Grabher, Roland Hagenbuchle, and Cristanne Miller. Amherst: U of Massachusetts P, 1998. 273-95.

Rich, Adrienne. "Vesuvius at Home: The Power of Emily Dickinson." *Shakespeare's Sisters: Feminist Essays on Women Poets.* Ed. Sandra M. Gilbert and Susan Gubar. Bloomington: Indiana UP, 1979. 99-121.

Ringler-Henderson, Ellin. "Poem 315." *Women's Studies* 16 (1989): 67-71.

Robinson, Douglas. "Two Dickinson Readings." *Dickinson Studies* 70 (1989): 25-35.

Rosenthal, M. L., and Sally M. Gall. *The Modern Poetic Sequence: The Genius of Modern Poetry.* New York: Oxford UP, 1983.

Shurr, William H. *The Marriage of Emily Dickinson: A Study of the Fascicles.* Lexington: UP of Kentucky, 1983.

Smith, Robert McClure. "Dickinson and the Masochistic Aesthetic." *Emily Dickinson Journal* 7.2 (1998): 1-21.

Waggoner, Hyatt H. *American Poets: From the Puritans to the Present.* 1968. Baton Rouge: Louisiana SUP, 1984.

Walker, Cheryl. *The Nightingale's Burden: Women Poets and American Culture before 1900.* Bloomington: Indiana UP, 1982.

Walker, Julia M. "ED's Poetic of Private Liberation." *Dickinson Studies* 45 (June 1983): 17-22.

Weisbuch, Robert. *Emily Dickinson's Poetry.* Chicago: U of Chicago P, 1972.

————. "Prisming Dickinson; or, Gathering Paradise by Letting Go." *The Emily Dickinson Handbook.* Ed. Gudrun Grabher, Roland Hagenbuchle, and Cristanne Miller. Amherst: U of Massachusetts P, 1998. 197-223.

Wilner, Eleanor. "The Poetics of Emily Dickinson." *ELH* 38 (1971): 126-54.

Wolff, Cynthia Griffin. *Emily Dickinson.* New York: Knopf, 1987.

Yin, Joanna. "'Arguments of Pearl': Dickinson's Response to Puritan Semiology." *Emily Dickinson Journal* 2.1 (1993): 65-83.

"*Because I could not stop for Death—*" (Poem 712)

KEN HILTNER (ESSAY DATE 2000)

SOURCE: Hiltner, Ken. "Because I, Persephone, Could Not Stop for Death: Emily Dickinson and the Goddess." *Emily Dickinson Journal* 10, no. 2 (2000): 22-42.

In the following essay, Hiltner interprets Dickinson's poem "Because I could not stop for Death—" as a retelling of the Greek myth of Persephone and as a critique of patriarchal exogamy (the practice of a father choosing his daughter's husband from an outside group). Hiltner also suggests that Dickinson's choice not to publish her poetry can be viewed as her preference to remain separate from male-dominated society.

Though it is doubtful Emily Dickinson will ever be described as a "Classicist," we know that the poet not only studied Latin at Amherst Academy, but had at her disposal in the libraries of the Academy, Mount Holyoke Female Seminary, and the family's Homestead a wide variety of classical textbooks as well as original and translated works by Homer, Sophocles, Horace, Cicero, Virgil, and others.[1] Latin words and phrases appear throughout the poet's body of work, from the early "Sic transit glories mundi" (Fr2/J3), to late references to "ignis fatuus" and "illume" in **"Those dying then"** (Fr1581/J1551). We also know that the Amherst poet made inspired use of such classically influenced writers as Shakespeare, Milton, and the Romantic poets.[2] Furthermore, a provocative case has been made that Dickinson's familiarity with Latin quantitative metrics and caesurae strongly influenced the poet's meter, capitalization, and internal punctuation.[3] Yet, in spite of this classical background, perhaps because critics still reluctantly find the reclusive poet provincial or simply turned inward (and hence away from, among other things, the ancient traditions), Dickinson's use of classical material has virtually escaped the attention of critics.[4] Indeed, what Jack Capps somewhat pejoratively noted decades ago is still widely accepted today: Dickinson "found no place in her own writing for the involved apparatus of classical . . . mythology" (72).[5]

Or did she? In the present essay I propose to use one of Dickinson's most anthologized poems, **"Because I could not stop for Death"** (Fr **"479"**/ J**"712"**), to demonstrate that the poet not only used classical sources (in this case the Homeric "Hymn to Demeter"), but, in producing a new and startling version of the myth of Persephone, framed a devastating critique of patriarchal exogamy as that which would not only take her away from mother, sister, and friends, but the mother's realm of the imaginary as well. As we shall see, more than just a speculative critique, this approach to patriarchal exogamy may underscore a number of the poet's life decisions, not the least of which being her reluctance to publish

Since the discovery in 1777 of a single surviving medieval manuscript of the Homeric "Hymn to Demeter," writers have flocked to retell the story of the mother who was willing to sacrifice so much in order to save her daughter. Both Percy

Bysshe and Mary Wollstonecraft Shelley offered early versions of the myth: his in verse in the "Song of Proserpine," and hers as the unpublished drama "Proserpine." But it was not until mid-century that a virtual avalanche of works let loose which either directly referenced the myth or featured characters reenacting the story. A partial list includes Nathaniel Hawthorne (*Tanglewood Tales*), Elizabeth Barrett Browning ("Aurora Leigh"—a favorite of Dickinson's), Helen Hunt Jackson ("Demeter"—Jackson was, of course, one of Dickinson's correspondents), Alfred Tennyson ("Demeter and Persephone"), H. D. ("Demeter"), Edgar Lee Masters ("Persephone"), Gertrude Atherton ("The Foghorn"), Amy Clarke ("Persephone"), Margaret Atwood (*Procedures for Underground* and *Double Persephone*), Sylvia Plath ("Two Sisters of Persephone"), Edith Wharton, Willa Cather, Ellen Glasgow, Virginia Wolfe, Colette, and many more.[6] The myth has also attracted the attention of literary critics such as Adrienne Rich (*Of Woman Born*), Susan Gubar ("Mother, Maiden, and the Marriage of Death"), and Luce Irigaray (*Marine Lover of Friedrich Nietzsche*). Indeed, Susan Gubar sees Persephone as nothing less than "the central mythic figure for women" (302).

It will be easiest to understand why this myth captured the imagination of so many by moving to Dickinson's poem, but not before addressing the crucial question of where the poet encountered the Homeric "Hymn to Demeter": at first glance a copy of the "Hymn" does not appear to be included in the libraries of Amherst Academy, Mount Holyoke, or the family Homestead. But, after sifting through the classical reference books available to the poet, we find a number of different versions of Persephone's tale. Both Thomas Bulfinch's *The Age of Fable or Beauties of Mythology* (Houghton #2133) and John Lempriere's *A Classical Dictionary*, which were available in the Dickinson's home library, contain extended retellings of the myth. However, though these rather freely recounted versions appear to have been somewhat influenced by the "Hymn," it is clear that they owe a greater debt to Ovid's "The Rape of Persephone" appearing in his *Metamorphosis*. Both Bulfinch and Lempriere follow Ovid's version of the tale in omitting the role that Helios (the sun) played. Additionally, these versions end with Persephone's time spent half with Hades and half with her mother. In the Homeric "Hymn"—and, as I shall argue, in Dickinson's poem—the sun does play a role, while the tale crucially divides the year into three parts, with Persephone spending only one third of her time with Hades. This

The Emily Dickinson homestead in Amherst, Massachusetts.

still leaves unanswered the question of where Dickinson encountered the "Hymn."

Buried in Charles Anton's *Classical Dictionary*—which was a required reference book at Amherst Academy—under "Ceres" (Demeter's Latin name) is a version of the "Hymn" which, while omitting certain lines, is an otherwise faithful, and indeed beautiful, translation. This is hardly surprising as Anton's (which should not be confused with Lempriere's work of the same name) was no ordinary classical dictionary. It has been persuasively argued that Hawthorne used Anton's dictionary, which was widely respected and available at mid-century, as the basis for all the classical myths recounted in his *Tanglewood Tales*, including his version of the Demeter story.[7] What made Anton's work so unusual was that, though he added introductions and commented on classical myths, he preferred to use slightly abridged translations of the earliest available versions of the myths. In contrast, Lempriere's work strayed far from the classical sources in order to give the "work the charm of a story-book" (4). In that Anton's translation of the "Hymn" is so faithful to the original, as well as Dickinson's likely source of

the myth, all references to the "Hymn" (unless otherwise noted) will be to this edition as we move to the Amherst's poet's own version of the myth.

> Because I could not stop for Death—
> He kindly stopped for me—
> The Carriage held but just Ourselves—
> And Immortality.
>
> We slowly drove—He knew no haste
> And I had put away
> My labor and my leisure too,
> For His Civility—
>
> We passed the School, where Children strove
> At Recess—in the Ring—
> We passed the Fields of Gazing Grain—
> We passed the Setting Sun—
>
> Or rather—He passed us—
> The Dews drew quivering and chill—
> For only Gossamer, my Gown—
> My Tippet—only Tulle—
>
> We paused before a House that seemed
> A Swelling of the Ground—
> The Roof was scarcely visible—
> The Cornice—in the Ground—

Since then—'tis Centuries—and yet
Feels shorter than the Day
I first surmised the Horses' Heads
Were toward Eternity

(Fr479)

That the poem depicts Death as a bridegroom has hardly been lost on critics, but whether Death is a "chivalrous gentleman" (Capps 88), or a "gentleman suitor" who is revealed to be a "kind of rapist" (Wardrop 88), has certainly been contested—as it has been regarding the Homeric "Hymn" where the suitor Hades arrives in his "golden Chariot" (330). Hawthorne, for example, held that Persephone was surprisingly content with having been abducted by Hades and taken to his palace: Persephone "being of a cheerful and active disposition . . . was not quite so unhappy as you may have supposed. The immense palace had a thousand rooms, and was full of beautiful and wonderful objects" (322). However, recent critics have been especially wary of efforts on the part of writers like Hawthorne to "reframe positively" the "violent . . . behavior" of Hades, instead of naming it "directly as kidnapping and rape" as did the "ancients" (Carlson 15). Before moving to the question of rape in relation to Dickinson's poem, it might be helpful to quickly cite some obvious lines which indicate that the poem's speaker is, in fact, Persephone and the "gentleman suitor," Hades.

As the "Hymn" opens, Persephone is found to be gathering "the rose, the violet, the crocus, [and] the hyacinth" (330), which for the goddess of young plants and fertility was "My labor and my leisure too"—as was such an activity for gardener Emily Dickinson. Because the abduction in the "Hymn" was nearly "unheard and unseen by gods" (330), it passed even the field of vision of "Gazing Grain"—Persephone's mother Demeter (goddess of grain), who, failing to see the abduction, went feverously looking for her missing daughter. "Fields of Gazing Grain," of course, also wonderfully paints Persephone, flying in the "golden Chariot" of Hades (330), looking down to clearly seeing her mother's fields, yet sadly unseen by Demeter. However, there were two witnesses to the abduction, the most important for now being "King Helios (the sun), whose eye nothing on Earth escapes" (330) as he too streaked across the sky in a chariot, causing the poem's speaker to first believe that "We passed the Setting Sun" in his chariot, though she quickly realizes that "He passed us."

But, why is it that Helios did the passing? To approach this question we need realize that the poem's third quatrain, in three lines each begin-ning with "We passed," wonderfully depicts three spans of time (a day, a season, and a lifetime) being broken into appropriately three phases. As mentioned earlier, the Homeric "Hymn" (unlike the retellings of Persephone's story by Ovid, Bulfinch, and Lempriere) depicts the year separated into three parts with Persephone spending one third of her time with Hades and two thirds with Demeter. Anthon's extended commentary, which is an attempt to explain the "scientific" basis of the "Hymn," offers that "the time which the corn [Persephone, who like Demeter is also a goddess of corn] is away . . . [is] . . . about four months" (330), as this is the time needed for the sown corn to reach maturity. This time before reaching maturity forms the first third of the day of the abduction (line one of quatrain three where "We passed the School"), the first third of life (childhood, "where Children strove / At Recess—in the Ring"), and of course, the first third of the year: spring. The second third of the day is witness to the "Fields of Gazing Grain," the adult period of life where the mature grain has grown tall, which is also the second third of the year as summer yields to autumn. The final third of the day of the abduction, the time of the "Setting Sun," is old age and winter. The fact that it is Helios who "passed" the speaker adds double meaning as the sun not only sets on the day, but also moves lower in the sky as autumn turns to winter. As Judith Farr succinctly summarizes the third quatrain, in it "Dickinson describes childhood (when ring games are played), maturity (fields of grain), and old age (setting sun)" (330).

Using a three-part structure for days, seasons, and life is a notable departure for Dickinson, who consistently prefers a fourfold division. As Rebecca Patterson has noted, Dickinson "associates each quarter of the compass with its traditional time of day and season of the year . . . she has also two symbolic movements of the sun corresponding to her North-South and East-West divisions. On this double axis she has literally suspended hundreds of poems" (181). Barton Levi St. Armand has taken this notion of Dickinson's "fourfold universe" (277) further to not only include days, seasons, and life, but color-based, religious, geographical, and other fourfold cycles.[8] The influence of the "Hymn" on the poet seems clear here, for in no other poem does Dickinson so thoroughly use a tripartite structure. As we delve further into the Amherst poet's retelling of the myth, the significance of the Threefold will become far more apparent.

However, as distinct as these three phases may be, the third quatrain also joins them by virtue of repeated circular images: "the Ring," the circle shaped "Sun," and the overarching image of Helios making his journey across the sky. Though days, seasons, and lifetimes seem to come to an end, they merely turn back on themselves to circularly repeat. Night and winter are not endings, but rather preludes to morning and spring. Similarly, when maturity leads to a new birth, life continues past death. (This last circular notion, of life living past death through birth, is an important one to which we need return.) As Bettina Knapp has further noted, in the third quatrain "The parataxis ("We passed . . . We Passed . . . We Passed") and the alliterations ("Fields of Gazing Grain" and "the setting Sun") depict a continuity of scenes, thereby emphasizing the notion of never-endingness" (92).

As the fourth quatrain opens it is clear that we have been led to the third arc of the circle as the day ends when "He [Helios] passed us" as the sun sets. It is in this third part of the year, with Helios low in the sky, that "The Dews drew quivering and chill" with the onslaught of winter. This is also the effect of Demeter's passive resistance to the abduction of Persephone: using the only leverage at her disposal, to bring "quivering and chill" to the Earth, in the fourth quatrain Demeter is attempting to effect the return of Persephone.

In the fifth quatrain the sun has set on life as the palace ("House") of Hades—which is also a fresh grave, "A Swelling of the Ground" comes into view. Yet the sixth quatrain, which begins by assuring us that the speaker is a contemporary Persephone, speaking centuries after the abduction occurred, ends with the notion that life too has turned back on itself to achieve immortality.

Though it seems clear Dickinson's poem is a retelling of the myth of Persephone as it appears in the "Hymn," the greater question of why the poet chose to retell the tale also compels us to ask why so many writers—especially women—have offered up their own versions of the myth. While it might seem the myth is principally concerned with the agricultural change of seasons (a subject to which Dickinson frequently returned), this is increasingly becoming acknowledged as a something of a "cover story." As classical philologist Adriana Cavarero notes, "The agricultural symbology is superimposed on . . . [the myth] . . . as an external artifice. It does not contribute to mediating and resolving the conflict" (58). That "conflict" centers on certain marital practices as patriarchal institutions.

Before the events of the myth are put into motion, unbeknownst to both Persephone and Demeter, a deal had been brokered between Hades and Persephone's father, Zeus, whereby Persephone had been given to Hades. As Irigaray has noted, "As a piece of property, Persephone belongs to the men" (112), and as property herself, Demeter need not have been consulted. However when Demeter finds that "the ravisher is Pluto [Hades], who, by the permission of her sire [Zeus], had carried away" her daughter, she becomes "Incensed at the conduct of Jupiter [Zeus]" (330). This of course leads to Demeter, as goddess of fertility, going on "strike" until Persephone is returned.

As psychologist Kathie Carlson has noted, traditionally this behavior on Demeter's part has been "presented as pathological: neurotic, depressive, overpossessive, narcissistic, a midlife 'folly,'" and so forth. Persephone, on the other hand, "is seen as naïve, innocent and teasing, lacking depth, and needing to break away from her mother." With Persephone unable "to separate from a 'binding' mother," traditionally her "rape is recast" as a much needed "initiation" (14-15). Hawthorne's retelling of the myth generally takes this position—as do, unfortunately, many of the versions penned by men. On the other hand, certain men, most notably Jung, realized that the Demeter/Persephone myth hardly depicts pathological behavior, but rather "exists on the plane of the mother-daughter experience, which is alien to man, and shuts him out. In fact, the psychology of the Demeter cult bears all the features of a matriarchal order of society" (177).

Or, more accurately, we might say "a matriarchal order of society" under siege. As Helene Foley has noted "In the 'Hymn' Zeus attempts to impose on Persephone a form of marriage new to Olympus . . . in modern terms we would characterize it as a patriarchal and virilocal exogamy (a marriage between members of two different social groups arranged by the father of the bride in which the bride resides with her husband)" (105). Generally when the Greek gods married, it involved a goddess from Olympus marrying a god from Olympus with the couple continuing to reside in the same location, but as most Olympian gods and goddesses were barred from Hades' realm, this meant that Persephone and Demeter were forever separated by her marriage. Of course, the myth speaks to human patriarchal marriage practices, common in ancient Greece, whereby daughters, unlike sons, were forced not only to leave home, but often compelled to live at a distance sufficient to effectively separate them from mother and family. As such, Foley adds, "The Hymn thus takes apart the benign cultural institution we see functioning without tension . . . and shows the price paid by mother and daughter for accepting for the first time a marriage that requires a degree of separation and subordination to the male" (109). When this patriarchal institution is functioning invisibly, attention is turned away from the institution itself as resistance to the mother/daughter separation is seen as "pathological" and "unnatural" on the part of the women.

It is furthermore clear that such patriarchal exogamy, when carried to the myth's extreme, in which the prospective wife not only has no role in the choice of her husband, but also has no knowledge of her marriage until her husband comes to "take" her, results in nothing less than rape. Dickinson's retelling of the myth, in which the speaker has no choice or prior knowledge of her husband or marriage, also, as Daneen Wardrop has noted, "recounts the events of rape" (88). In addition to having meaning for any woman living under patriarchal exogamy—regardless of where of when—it has been suggested that the myth of Persephone "mirrors mythically the usurpation and gradual assimilation of an older southern European religion of the Mother Goddess by the earliest forces of patriarchy . . . Mythically, this assimilation was repeatedly pictured as the Goddess being raped, dismembered, slain by a hero, or married (and subordinated) to the invading god" (Carlson 3). In short, this myth, which still speaks to existing patriarchal marital practices, may have first originated when those practices where forced on a culture that, if not matriarchal, at least had greater gender equality.

While Jung believed the myth of Demeter/Persephone was an archetype shared by all women, it should be clear that it is a myth shared only by women of certain patriarchal cultures; however, given the ubiquity of these cultures, the impression is that the archetype is truly universal. Adrienne Rich has similarly noted that the myth seems universal: every "daughter . . . must have longed for a mother whose love for her and whose power were so great as to undo rape and bring her back from death. And every mother must have longed for the power of Demeter, the efficacy of her anger" (240). As a near-universal archetype, it is hardly surprising that so many women writers used the "Hymn to Demeter" to express their own experiences of patriarchy. Such a woman was Emily Dickinson.

Though Dickinson (who, to borrow Carlson's words, like Demeter has been "presented as patho-

logical: neurotic, depressive," and so forth (14), has often been depicted as unwilling to leave her father's home, so it may be her mother's home the poet chose not to leave. Aside from the vicious separation of mother and daughter, the most devastating effect of patriarchal exogamy is that it generally undermines communities of women. With women constantly being traded about by patriarchal power, it is not only the relationship between mother and daughter that is severed, but that between sisters, as well as bonds with friends who live nearby. In Dickinson's case the relationships at risk would have been with her sister [Emily described her bond with Lavinia as "early, earnest, indissoluble," (L827)], close friends and relatives (Dickinson called her sister-in-law Susan an "Avalanche of Sun" in her life, L755), and her mother (after losing her mother Dickinson lamented, "When we were children and she journeyed, she always brought us something. Now would she bring us but herself, what an only Gift," L792).

In the version of the "Hymn" Dickinson had in her possession, Anton notes that Hades either took Persephone from the company of "Venus, Minerva, and Diana," who were "the companions of their sister for the occasion," or "the sirens" who were her "attendants" (330). In either case, and in the unabridged Hymn, Persephone is taken away from a community of women described as "sisters." Moreover, after Demeter realizes that Hades is the kidnaper/rapist, she leaves Olympus—and the male god who betrayed her in allowing the abduction to take place—to settle in Eleusis. There she resides in a community populated largely by woman, Queen Metanira and her daughters. A salient feature of the myth is not only that Persephone is snatched from a community of woman, but also that having lost the company of her daughter, Demeter seeks solace by joining a similar community.

One of the most unusual features of Dickinson's retelling of the myth is that it is told in the first person by Persephone. None of the ancient variants of the myth are told by Persephone, and many of the nineteenth and twentieth-century versions told by women, like Shelley's unpublished drama (written shortly after she lost a child), are either told by or emphasize the role of Demeter. Unlike these versions, Dickinson's poem tells the story of a woman willingly taken away from her community of loved ones. Dickinson's life, on the other hand, tells the story of a woman unwilling to be taken away from the company of those she loved.

It is on this point that so much of the poem pivots: unlike Persephone in the Homeric "Hymn," the speaker in Dickinson's poem is surprisingly content to be taken off by Death. In the "Hymn," Hades literally "carried her off [kicking and] shrieking for aid" (330). The mood of Dickinson's poem, by contrast, is thoroughly calm, with Hades acting "kindly" towards Persephone, driving "slowly" with "no haste." Hades in general is found to possess marked "Civility." Now, of course, whether we have linked the poem with Persephone's story or not, it is clear that these words are dripping with irony. How indeed does a woman calmly accept a suitor when he intends to forever take her away from family and friends? I would argue that this is one of the central questions Dickinson asks in the poem.

Though so many ancient and nineteenth-century retellings of the myth focused on how the mother Demeter was unwilling to allow her daughter to be taken, Dickinson asks how Persephone could let herself be taken, calmly and willingly, as the poem makes so clear. In accordance with patriarchal exogamy as it existed in the nineteen century, girls and young woman were, with remarkably calm resignation, allowing themselves to be taken away from everything and everyone they loved. In the "Hymn," Demeter not only protests patriarchal exogamy, but also successfully overcomes it for two thirds of the year. Yet Persephone, whose name before the abduction, Kore, literally means in Greek "the girl," is presented as a helpless waif who has no role in her own recovery. As Dickinson looked about her, she found a world populated by Kores, willingly and calmly accepting a fate dictated to them by patriarchal power.

And yet, the Amherst poet is surprisingly sympathetic to the speaker of her poem. But, why be sympathetic to a speaker—and to women— who were making a choice the poet clearly rejected in her own life? The answer involves that third passenger in the carriage: for "The Carriage held" not "just Ourselves," but also "Immortality." To understand the role of immortality, not just in Dickinson's poem but in the "Hymn" as well, we can again turn to Jung, who held that regarding the myth of Demeter and Kore:

> We could . . . say that every mother contains her daughter in herself and every daughter her mother, and that every woman extends backward into her mother and forward into her daughter. This participation and intermingling gives rise to that particular uncertainly as regards time: a woman lives earlier as a mother, later as a daughter. The conscious experiencing of these ties produces the feeling that her life is spread out over generations—the first step towards the immediate experience and conviction of being outside time, which brings with it a feeling of immortality.
>
> (162)

The relationship between mother and daughter is unlike that between sisters or friends. As Jung suggests, in many respects they share a life, lived before as mother, then as daughter becoming mother, and later as daughter, and so forth. The speaker of the poem, unlike Dickinson, is not cut off from this life. I have argued that one of the central questions asked by the poem is how a woman accepts a suitor when he intends to take her away forever from mother, sister, and friends; yet, how does she not? Though she might remain within her community of women, in failing to accept a marriage co-opted by patriarchal exogamy, a woman nonetheless cuts herself off from her (to borrow Jung's words) "life . . . spread out over generations," and with it, her "feeling of immortality."

We hear two voices in the poem, one unspoken (Dickinson's), and the other, the voice of a woman in a carriage traveling down a road not taken. The other voice is, in fact, also Emily Dickinson's, but as three women telling their single story. To unfold this notion, we need return again to the "Hymn."

In accordance with Jung's argument that mother and daughter begin to merge into one, when Demeter and Persephone are shown in Greek painting and sculpture, they are frequently indistinguishable.[9] This is because, though Hades abducts the Kore (the "girl"), a woman, Persephone, emerges from the experience. (It is for this reason that the myth has traditionally been seen as an "initiation" rite, though rape as a rite of passage certainly needs to be questioned.) The Kore changes into the woman Persephone, who assumes all the significance, power, and appearance of Demeter. In Anton's version of the myth this is especially clear as he interchangeably refers to both Demeter and Persephone as goddess of corn and grain (330). In order to speak of these two indistinguishable goddesses who were both the goddess of grain, the Greeks typically adopted the dual mode (to Theo) to speak of the two who are one. Still, both are inescapably related to the Kore, who is the future of one (as Demeter's daughter), and the past of the other (as the Kore from whom the woman Persephone has grown).

Yet, we cannot stop at the two who are one goddess, for there is also a third: her name was Hecate, whom I mentioned earlier (but failed to name) as the second witness to Persephone's abduction. As the "Hymn" notes in Anton's translation, while Demeter was searching for Persephone, "Hecate met her . . . [and] . . . together they proceeded to Helios" for news of the abduction (330). From this point on, Hecate becomes the constant companion of Demeter until the Kore emerges as Persephone, at which point "Hecate arrives to congratulate Persephone, and henceforth becomes her attendant" (330, emphasis added). Janet Wolf explains the significance of Hecate to the myth as she notes that while Demeter and Persephone

> were a sacred duo . . . each related to the other as past and future . . . There is, however, a third woman with an important role in the myth, that is the ambiguous goddess Hecate . . . the triad of Persephone, Demeter, and Hecate does indeed represent the three phases of the moon, the seasonal cycle, and woman at the three stages of their life cycles, i.e., woman as maiden, nymph [mother], and crone.
>
> (33)

Carlson adds:

> all may appear together, dynamic and intertwined . . . in the Goddess: Maiden, Mother, Crone, the feminine three-in-one . . . a dynamic, ever-repeating cycle . . . the Triple Goddess.
>
> (141-41)

Together Persephone, Demeter, and Hecate form a trinity known simply as the "Goddess"—an ancient mythic figure who likely preceded the Greek pantheon of gods historically.

With the threefold Goddess in mind, we can return to Dickinson's poem which, as noted earlier, in quatrain three creates a threefold cycle of days, seasons, and life. However, if we look at the six-quatrain poem as a whole, it is clear that it is also divided into three sections (each made of two quatrains) with one each given to Persephone, Demeter, and Hecate.

The first section, voiced by the Kore, is the quiet, relaxed account of a girl willingly giving up "My labor and my leisure too" as she is being taken off. Hades is described here as "kindly," and as having "Civility," because the girl, who does not possess the knowledge of a woman, cannot fully understand what is in store for her.[10] Both introductory quatrains proceed at a leisurely pace as "We slowly drove—He knew no haste."

But in the second section, voiced by the Kore becoming Persephone, everything speeds up as "We passed . . . / We Passed . . . / We passed." Persephone's double, the protesting Demeter, is also present in this section as she brings "quiver-

ing and chill" to the Earth.[11] Kore, dressed in a something resembling a wedding "gown" that is "only Gossamer," is, in Knapp's words, experiencing an "elopement of sorts" (93)—in quatrains three and four, Kore, being raped, is becoming Persephone. But with the rape comes knowledge. As noted earlier, the third quatrain is itself a single day (the day of the rape) that is also a season and a lifetime. A lifetime divided into three parts: childhood, "where Children strove" (Kore); maturity, "Fields of Gazing Grain" (Demeter); and old age, "the Setting Sun" (Hecate). On that day in which Kore became Persephone, she gained knowledge of life as past (Kore), present (Persephone/Demeter), and future (Hecate) spread out before her. In the poem's closing lines she remembers it as "the Day / I first surmised the Horses' Heads / Were toward Eternity."

But Persephone does not voice those closing lines: the poem's third section (quatrains five and six) belongs to Hecate. As noted earlier, the "Hymn" tells us that after Persephone's return, Hecate "becomes her attendant" who will accompany her back to Hades' realm (330). Kore, who became Persephone, who in turn became Demeter, now becomes Hecate, who will enter that "House that seemed / A Swelling of the Ground" as the cycle of the Goddess completes itself. But as the Goddess, who "first surmised" on that day of her rape, "Centuries" ago, "the Horses' Heads / Were toward Eternity"—she will return from rape and death once again as Persephone.

Dickinson's likely wrote the poem when she was thirty-two years old.[12] No longer a Kore, and with the specter of Hecate before her, she assumed the voice of the Goddess—the Maiden Kore, the Mother Demeter, and the Crone Hecate—in order to explore marriage as that which would in many ways take her away from everything she loved in life, yet, in the uneasy bargain, enter her into a life of immortality. As she speaks for the Goddess, she reveals patient sympathy for women ripped away from family and home, yet cannot help but see this as a horrific fate they capitulated to with calm willingness of a child.

To further understand the significance of Dickinson's rejection of separation from mother and home, it will be helpful to consider the psychology of the Persephone myth. As the myth depicts the separation of daughter from mother, it has been argued that

> the Freudian theory of psychosexual development . . . [appears] . . . to embody and illustrate a cultural logic analogous to that found in the Homeric "Hymn to Demeter." In both, the strategies

of resistance to patriarchal domination have an internal logic and coherence, and both culminate in a validation of the patriarchal order.

(Katz 212)

Simply put, the "Hymn" depicts the Kore (the "girl") making the transition from the preoedipal to the oedipal stage of development. Though mother and daughter both object, the daughter is nonetheless separated from the mother by the intrusion of the father.

However, much the same way that Jung's "universal" archetype of Persephone's myth is now understood to be dependent on whether a culture is patriarchal, Freud's notion of the universal transition from the preoedipal to oedipal stage has certainly been questioned. In bringing together object-relation psychology, sociology, and cross-cultural anthropology, Nancy Chodorow finds girls, though always moving from preoedipal to oedipal phases; nonetheless, doing so in widely differing ways. In certain groups, such as largely matriarchal Atjehnese families in Indonesia, Chodorow finds girls and women often having flexible and nearly nonexistent ego boundaries separating them from their mothers and other female relatives. In practice in Atjehnese culture, "the mother-daughter tie and other female kin relations remain important from a woman's childhood through her old age. Daughters stay closer to home in both childhood and adulthood and remain involved in particularistic role relations. Sons and men are more likely to feel uncomfortable at home and spend work and play time away from the house" (260).

In directly applying Chodorow's approach to the Homeric "Hymn of Demeter," Helene Foley finds that "Ego boundaries between Demeter and Persephone are barely developed" throughout the "Hymn" (127). In that father Zeus's attempt to assert patriarchal order is only marginally successful (separating Demeter and Persephone for just one third of the year), Demeter largely succeeds in keeping a strong postoedipal bond between mother and daughter intact. This is not to say that Persephone fails to make the transition to the oedipal stage when she becomes an individual separated from others by ego boundaries, but that these boundaries need not separate her from her mother's realm. What the "Hymn" then depicts is a challenge to Freud's claim that, for the oedipal stage to be successfully negotiated, firm ego boundaries need be thrown up between mother and daughter. Indeed, viewed from the eye-opening perspective of the "Hymn," the very notion that daughters need be separated from moth-

ers—what Freud argued was an essential stage of development—can itself be seen as patriarchy at work.

Though Foley's application of Chodorow to the "Hymn" is revealing in itself, Jacques Lacan's take on the oedipal exchange, especially as interpreted by French feminist thinkers, adds a whole new dimension to the subject. Lacan held that the preoedipal or "imaginary" stage is a preliterate time before the father and his law is insinuated, thereby inaugurating the oedipal, or "symbolic" stage. Writers such as Irigaray and Julia Kristeva have noted that the imaginary stage is decidedly feminine, being associated with the body, feelings, the non-rational, the unconscious, and speech. On the other hand, these thinkers have taken the symbolic to be principally male, involving the mind, rationality, the conscious, and written language. Given that, in classic Freudian (and Lacanian) terms, we should all fully enter the oedipal (symbolic) phase, this clearly involves a break with much that is feminine.

It is this break that Hélène Cixous sees both as a horrid shattering of a wonderful state of oneness (a prelinguistic unity) of mother and child, and as the imposition of the law of the father: "we are born into [his] language and [his] language speaks [to] us, dictates its law" (14). As noted earlier, what Demeter is fighting against in the "Hymn" is a world controlled by patriarchal power, but these French feminist thinkers reveal the remarkable extent of that power, especially regarding written language. In the West, written language—its grammar, its metaphors, and its meaning—has always been controlled by the male realm of the symbolic. As French feminist Xavière Gauthier has noted, this presents a profound difficulty for the woman who desires to write: How can she find her "place within the linear, grammatical, linguistic system that orders the symbolic . . . the law," when much that is feminine lies outside that very symbolic order?

Historically this difficulty became especially apparent when, in the second half of the nineteenth century, "believing themselves to be emancipated, women had access to universities where they were fed by force a language in which everything, verbs and subjects, was masculine" (Gauthier 162). Not surprisingly, as Gauthier notes, to "speak 'the language of Man'" was a maddening situation for women: "If there is a madman, then its definitely the Woman" (162, Gauthier's emphasis). In considering this "madwoman," though without reference to Gauthier, Gilbert and Gubar found that "by the end of the nineteenth century," even though often representing a part of themselves as monstrous and mad, "women were not only writing, they were conceiving fictional worlds in which patriarchal images and conventions were severely, radically revised" (44). As empowering as this may seem, there still remains Gauthier's overarching concern that if women do "begin to write and write as men do, they will enter history subdued and alienated," yet it is "history that, logically speaking, their speech should disrupt" (162-63, Gauthier's emphasis).

This situation essentially presents women with an oedipal dilemma: either enter the male symbolic order so that they may write, or remain silent in the feminine imaginary realm. Josephine Donovan adds that

> At no point in women's history was this dilemma more acute than at the turn of the [twentieth] century, because it was then that . . . women genuinely had the option of entering patriarchal civilization, the realm of the Symbolic. Before that they had remained segregated in woman-centered communities that sustained separate non-oedipal cultural traditions.
>
> (15)

Though Donovan's focus is on works written at the close of the century by Wharton, Cather, and Glasgow, I believe applying her thesis to Dickinson's 1862 work reveals the poem to be something of a harbinger of what was to come—especially as Donovan notes how this oedipal dilemma was indeed a reenactment of the myth of Persephone:

> The Persephone-Demeter myth allegorizes the historical mother-daughter transition that occurred towards the end of the nineteenth century in the Western world. Partly as a result of the nineteenth-century women's movement, young middle- to upper-class women were leaving their mothers' bowers in increasing numbers and entering such institutions of the male-dominated sphere as universi ties and the professions. In the process these women were leaving behind the women's sphere of "love and ritual," which had its own traditions and values . . . Like Demeter, late nineteenth-century mothers were struggling to keep their daughters "home," thereby sustaining women's culture, otherwise doomed by the daughter's abduction/betrayal. The daughters, on the other hand, were eager to expand their horizons, to engage in new systems of discourse, like Persephone, unaware that such involvement entailed patriarchal captivity.
>
> (44)

Certainly for thousands of years daughters had been taken from their mother's homes by suitors, but in the second half of the nineteenth century daughters were leaving home—and the preoedipal feminine world of the imaginary—to eagerly and willingly enter the patriarchal realm of the symbolic.

This reveals a great irony of the nineteenth century "women's movement," for, in order to defy patriarchy, there was a great "movement of women," especially women writers, away from their mother's homes—which startlingly reenacted the myth of Persephone as these women surprisingly found themselves in a new captivity dictated by patriarchy, especially the patriarchal nature of written language. The new and improved nineteenth-century Hades, no longer content with abducting a single woman (and for centuries having perfected a system of training women to calmly and willingly be taken by him) envisioned a brave new world where women by the tens of thousands could be lured away from family and home to become captives in his palace. As enticing as this new carriage ride may have seemed to many, Emily Dickinson declined its offer.

The last two decades of Dickinson studies have witnessed a number of ground-breaking works which have found the Amherst poet working outside the limits of the male language of the symbolic. In Margaret Homans's now classic deconstructive reading of Dickinson's poems, she argues that, though the maternal presence is lost in infancy, Dickinson's writing nonetheless gives voice to what is seemingly absent. Shortly after Homans's work appeared, Joanne Feit Diehl argued that Dickinson challenged the tradition of the male Romantic poets. Building on these and other writers, Mary Loeffelholz, in introducing Lacan into her own deconstructive approach, found the male literary tradition which Dickinson subverted as itself expressive of the symbolic. Works by Cristanne Miller, Helen McNeil, and others have also built upon the general notion that Dickinson, in rejecting the traditional male realm of the symbolic, was attempting to work out a distinctly feminine mode of expression.

Whereas Donovan argues that Wharton, Cather, and Glasgow were seduced by the prospect of expressing themselves through the symbolic, it is clear from the works of the aforementioned critics that Dickinson was not so easily ensnared. I earlier remarked that the lines from the Persephone poem, "I had put away / My labor and my leisure too," suggest the tending of young flowers, a leisurely labor both for Persephone and Dickinson. But for Dickinson, her labor and leisure, was, first and foremost, poetry. The poet plainly understood that it was not only from mother and home that she was to be taken, but from the tending of her poetry as well. Hades arrives in the poem as more than just a man who has come to claim his woman; his arrival announces what patriarchy demands (along with Freud and Lacan) as an essential stage in the "maturity" of all women: their delivery from the mother's realm (with its culture, traditions, values, and unique communication) to the father's domain of the symbolic. Dickinson, though sympathetic with women who sought immortality through writing as they left the realm of their mothers, also clearly sees this as a road away from a distinctly feminine mode of expression.

It is not only (critics have noted) Dickinson's mode of expression which reveals the poet's rejection of the "patriarchal suitor," but her recalcitrance about letting the poems themselves leave the realm she shared with her mother, sister, and friends. This becomes especially clear when we consider the early publication history of the Persephone poem. Todd and Higginson likely cut the work's fourth quatrain from the 1890 edition of Dickinson's *Poems* because it dared an image of the speaker "quivering" in a "Gossamer . . . Gown." But, as noted earlier, Dickinson's entire retelling of Persephone's tale pivots on the third and fourth quatrains, which renders the image of a woman exposed and quivering at the moment of rape. The image is disquieting precisely because Dickinson, in not subscribing to the patriarchal notion of Kore undergoing a much-needed "initiation," is reclaiming the ancient conviction that this indeed was rape. As a result, the edited poem's tone, now more influenced by the first two quatrains (Kore's section), is that of a child calmly and willingly accepting the unknown as a suitor. In so editing the work, Todd and Higginson converted Dickinson's poem, which protested patriarchal exogamy, into something akin to Hawthorne's retelling of the myth: an endorsement of those very patriarchal practices. Furthermore, the editorial decision to give the poem the title **"The Chariot,"** which, though perceptively hinting at the poem's classical pedigree; nonetheless, does little to introduce the essential patriarchal conflict explored by the work. Though these revisions were made after the poet's death, Dickinson unquestionably understood that consigning her poems to the realm of the symbolic would risk their being brutally ravished.

Withal, the event chronicled in the "Hymn" and Dickinson's poem is not a painful but necessary growth out of childhood but rather a death. The Goddess, the poem's three-in-one speaker, is describing the death of that which linked her with home, mother, sister, friends, feelings and expression. What she is relating is nothing less than the death of much that gave her life. Though well aware of the regenerative power of the Goddess, knowing that she too could live through rape and death, Dickinson choose not to achieve immortality at the cost of killing the relations that bound her to her world. Even if Emily Dickinson had never encountered the Homeric "Hymn to Demeter," it is likely she would have produced her Persephone poem—not to give new life to an ancient myth, but, in boldly writing the story of a woman traveling a road not taken, to silently give expression to the poet's own life and its decisions.

Notes

1. Regarding the poet's exposure to Latin at Amherst Academy, Dickinson mentions in a letter to Jane Humphrey, "I am in the class that you used to be in Latin—besides Latin I study History and Botany I like the school very much indeed" (L3). Furthermore, Dickinson wrote to Abiah Root that she was attending classes in "Mental Philosophy, Geology, Latin, and Botany" (L6). Capps and Lowenberg have been used to determine the availability of classical books and authors to Dickinson.

2. See Jack Capps's *Emily Dickinson's Reading: 1836-1886* for the availability and influence of these writers on Dickinson.

3. For the influence of Latin grammar on Dickinson, see both Cuddy's "The Influence of Latin Poetics on Emily Dickinson's Style," as well as her "The Latin Imprint of Emily Dickinson's Poetry: Theory and Practice."

4. I say "virtually" escaped critical attention for in 1976 Nancy McClaran made a brief (two page) case that Dickinson's "Of Death I try to think like this" makes a reference to Virgil.

5. More recently, Jane Donahue Eberwein has echoed a similar sentiment: "Dickinson, despite her modestly classical education, paid little attention to Greek deities or classical ideals" (233).

6. For a broad survey of works referencing the Demeter myth, see Helene Foley's *The Homeric "Hymn to Demeter"* (151-69). Josephine Donovan also offers a book-length analysis of the myth in Wharton, Cather, Glasgow, Wolfe, and Colette.

7. Hugo McPherson's *Hawthorne as Myth-Maker* is a book-length treatment of Hawthorne's use of Anthon's *Classical Dictionary* in the writing of *Tanglewood Tales*. McPherson argues that in retelling the myth of Persephone, Hawthorne "relied on the simple but exhaustive account given in Anton under 'Ceres'" (99)—the same passage I am arguing Dickinson used in writing her own version of the Persephone myth.

8. For Dickinson's creation of a "fourfold universe," see Barton Levi St. Armand's *Emily Dickinson and Her Culture*, especially his chart of "Dickinson's Mystic [Fourfold] Day" on 317.

9. For the similarities of Demeter and Persephone in Greek painting and sculpture, see Frazer, 462.

10. A treatment of the Greek use of the dual mode in reference to Demeter and Persephone can be found in Pakkanen, 106-07.

11. For the likely date of the poem's creation see both Johnson's variorum edition of the poems (volume 1, page 492) and Franklin's *The Manuscript Books of Emily Dickinson* (volume 1, page 508).

12. On the notion of Dickinson rejecting male language, see Homans's *Woman Writers and Poetic Identity: Dorothy Wordsworth, Emily Brontë, and Emily Dickinson,* Diehl's *Dickinson and the Romantic Imagination,* Loeffelholz's *Dickinson and the Boundaries of Feminist Theory,* Miller's *Emily Dickinson: A Poet's Grammar,* and McNeil's *Emily Dickinson.*

Works Cited

Unless otherwise indicated the following abbreviations are used for reference to the writings of Emily Dickinson

Fr: *The Poems of Emily Dickinson.* ed. R. W. Franklin. 3 vols. Cambridge, MA: Harvard UP, 1998. Citation by poem number.

J: *The Poems of Emily Dickinson.* ed. Thomas H. Johnson. 3 vols. Cambridge, MA: Harvard UP, 1955. Citation by poem number.

L: *The Letters of Emily Dickinson.* ed. Thomas H. Johnson and Theodora Ward. 3 vols. Cambridge, MA: Harvard UP, 1958. Citation by letter number.

Anton, Charles. *A Classical Dictionary: Containing an Account of the Principal Proper Names Mentioned in Ancient Authors.* New York: Harper and Brothers, 1841.

Bulfinch, Thomas. *The Age of Fable or Beauties of Mythology.* Boston: Sanborn, Carter and Bazin, 1855.

Capps, Jack L. *Emily Dickinson's Reading: 1836-1886.* Cambridge, MA: Harvard UP, 1966.

Carlson, Kathie. *Life's Daughter/Death's Bride: Inner Transformations Through the Goddess Demeter/Persephone.* Boston: Shambhala Press, 1997.

Cavarero, Adriana. *In Spite of Plato: A Feminist Rewriting of Ancient Philosophy.* Trans. Serena Anderlini-D'Onofrio and Aine O'Healy. New York: Routledge, 1995.

Chodorow, Nancy. "Family Structure and Feminine Personality." In Helene Foley, *The Homeric "Hymn to Demeter."* Princeton: Princeton UP, 1994. 243-65.

Cixous, Hélène. "Castration or Decapitation?" *Signs* 7 (1981): 41-49.

Cuddy, Lois A. "The Influence of Latin Poetics on Emily Dickinson's Style." *Comparative Literature Studies* 13 (1976): 214-29.

———. "The Latin Imprint of Emily Dickinson's Poetry: Theory and Practice." *American Literature* 50 (1978): 74-84.

Diehl, Joanne Feit. *Dickinson and the Romantic Imagination.* Princeton: Princeton UP, 1981.

Donovan, Josephine. *After the Fall: The Demeter-Persephone Myth in Wharton, Cather, and Glasgow.* University Park: Pennsylvania State UP, 1989.

Eberwein, Jane Donahue. *Dickinson, Strategies of Limitation.* Amherst, MA: U of Massachusetts, P, 1985.

Farr, Judith. *The Passion of Emily Dickinson.* Cambridge, MA: Harvard UP, 1992.

Foley, Helene. *The Homeric "Hymn to Demeter."* Princeton: Princeton UP, 1994.

Franklin, R. W., ed., *The Manuscript Books of Emily Dickinson.* Cambridge, MA: Harvard UP, 1981.

Frazer, J. C. *The Golden Bough.* New York: Macmillan, 1992.

Gauthier, Xavière. "Is There Such a Thing as Women's Writing?" in *New French Feminisms: An Anthology.* Ed. Elaine Marks and Isabelle de Courtivron. New York: Schocken, 1980. 162-65.

Gilbert, Sandra M., and Susan Gubar. *The Madwoman in the Attic.* New Haven: Yale UP, 1979.

Hawthorne, Nathaniel. *The Centenary Edition of the Works of Nathaniel Hawthorne.* ed. William Charvat et al. Volume VII. Columbus, OH: Ohio State UP, 1972.

Homans, Margaret. *Woman Writers and Poetic Identity: Dorothy Wordsworth, Emily Brontë, and Emily Dickinson.* Princeton: Princeton UP, 1980.

Jung, C. G. "The Psychological Factors of the Kore." *Essays on a Science of Mythology: The Myth of the Divine Child.* Princeton: Princeton UP, 1967.

Katz, Marilyn Arthur. "Politics and Pomegranates Revisited." In Helene Foley, *The Homeric "Hymn to Demeter."* Princeton: Princeton UP, 1994. 243-65.

Knapp, Bettina. *Emily Dickinson.* New York: Continuum, 1989.

Irigaray, Luce. *Marine Lover of Friedrich Nietzsche.* Trans. Gillian C. Gill. New York: Columbia UP, 1991.

Lempriere, John. *A Classical Dictionary; Containing a Copious Account of all the Proper Names Mentioned in Ancient Authors.* New York: A. T. Goodrich, 1816.

Loeffelholz, Mary. *Dickinson and the Boundaries of Feminist Theory.* Urbana: U of Illinois P, 1991.

Lowenberg, Carlton. *Emily Dickinson's Textbooks.* Lafayette, CA: private printing, 1986.

McClaran, Nancy. "Dickinson's 'Of Death I Try to Think Like This.'" *Explicator* 35 (1976): 18-19.

McNeil, Helen. *Emily Dickinson.* London and New York: Virago, 1986.

McPherson, Hugo. *Hawthorne as Myth-Maker.* Toronto: U of Toronto P, 1969.

Miller, Cristanne. *Emily Dickinson: A Poet's Grammar.* Cambridge MA: Harvard UP, 1987.

Pakkanen, Petra. *Interpreting Early Hellenistic Religion; A Study Based on the Mystery Cult of Demeter and the Cult of Isis.* Helsinki, 1996.

Patterson, Rebecca. *Emily Dickinson's Imagery.* Amherst: U of Massachusetts P, 115.

Rich, Adrienne. *Of Woman Born: Motherhood as Experience and Institution.* New York: W. W. Norton, 1976.

St. Armand, Barton Levi. *Emily Dickinson and Her Culture: The Soul's Society.* Cambridge, MA: Harvard UP, 1984.

Wardrop, Daneen. *Emily Dickinson's Gothic: Goblin with a Gauge.* Iowa City: U of Iowa P, 1996.

Wolf, Janet S. "'Like an Old Tale Still': Paulina, 'Triple Hecate,' and the Persephone Myth in The Winter's Tale." *Images of Persephone: Feminist Readings in Western Literature*. Ed. Elizabeth T. Hayes. Gainesville: UP of Florida, 1994.

FURTHER READING

Bibliographies

Duchac, Joseph. *The Poems of Emily Dickinson: An Annotated Guide to Commentary Published in English, 1890-1977*. Boston, G. K. Hall, 1979, 658 p.

A comprehensive survey of criticism on Dickinson published between 1890 and 1977.

———. *The Poems of Emily Dickinson: An Annotated Guide to Commentary Published in English, 1978-1989*. Boston, G. K. Hall, 1993, 525 p.

A comprehensive survey of criticism on Dickinson published between 1978 and 1989.

Biographies

Habegger, Alfred. *My Wars are Laid Away in Books: The Life of Emily Dickinson*. New York: Random House, 2001, 764 p.

Comprehensive account of Dickinson's life.

Wolff, Cynthia Griffin. *Emily Dickinson*. Reading, Mass.: Addison-Wesley, 1988, 635 p.

Provides an in-depth bio-critical survey of Dickinson's life and career.

Criticism

Eberwein, Jane Donahue. "Ministerial Interviews and Fathers in Faith." *Emily Dickinson Journal* 9, no. 2 (2000): 6-15.

Discusses the two ministers who served the Amherst, Massachusetts church that Dickinson's family attended, speculating on the influence that they may have had on her work.

Grabher, Gudrun Roland Hagenbüchle, and Cristanne Miller, eds. *The Emily Dickinson Handbook*. Amherst: University of Massachusetts Press, 1998, 480 p.

Comprehensive reference source containing essays on the poet's life and work; also contains commentary on the state of modern Dickinson scholarship.

Landry, H. Jordan. "Animal/Insectual/Lesbian Sex: Dickinson's Queer Version of the Birds and the Bees." *Emily Dickinson Journal* 9, no. 2 (2000): 42-54.

Interprets Dickinson's use of insect and bird imagery as the poet's means of reimagining gender and sexual roles.

Martin, Wendy, ed. *The Cambridge Companion to Emily Dickinson*. Cambridge: Cambridge University Press, 2002, 248 p.

Collection of scholarly essays focusing on Dickinson's biography and the publication history of her works, her poetic strategies and themes, and the cultural contexts inferred from her poetry.

Messmer, Marietta. *A Vice for Voices: Reading Emily Dickinson's Correspondence*. Amherst: University of Massachusetts Press, 2001, 280 p.

Surveys Dickinson's letters in an effort to elucidate the poet's inspiration and literary genius.

Ramirez, Anne West. "Harriet Beecher Stowe's Christian Feminism in *The Minister's Wooing*: A Precedent for Emily Dickinson." *Christianity and Literature* 51, no. 3 (spring 2002): 407-24.

Examines the similarities between Dickinson's verse and Stowe's novel, outlining the women's shared cultural history.

Raymond, Claire. "Emily Dickinson as the Un-named, Buried Child." *Emily Dickinson Journal* 12, no. 1 (2003): 107-22.

Analyzes Dickinson's narrative technique of assuming the voice of a dead child and considers the device as a comment on gender roles and identity.

Shoobridge, Helen. "'Reverence for each Other Being the Sweet Aim': Emily Dickinson Face to Face with the Masculine." *Emily Dickinson Journal* 9, no. 1 (spring 2000): 87-111.

Employs the theories of Luce Irigaray to examine Dickinson's letters, suggesting that the poet's intention was to communicate with and educate men.

Vendler, Helen. "Emily Dickinson Thinking." *Parnassus: Poetry in Review* 26, no. 1 (2001): 34-56.

Detailed analysis of Dickinson's treatment of time in her poetry.

OTHER SOURCES FROM GALE:

Additional coverage of Dickinson's life and career is contained in the following sources published by the Gale Group: *American Writers; American Writers Retrospective Supplement*, Vol. 1; *Authors and Artists for Young Adults*, Vol. 22; *Concise Dictionary of American Literary Biography, 1865-1917; Dictionary of Literary Biography*, Vols. 1, 243; *DISCovering Authors; DISCovering Authors: British Edition* and *Canadian Edition; DISCovering Authors Modules: Most-studied Authors and Poets; DISCovering Authors 3.0; Exploring Poetry; Literature Resource Center; Modern American Women Writers; Nineteenth-Century Literature Criticism*, Vols. 21, 77; *Poetry Criticism*, Vol. 1; *Poetry for Students*, Vols. 1, 2, 3, 4, 5, 6, 8, 10, 11, 13, 16; *Poets: American and British; Reference Guide to American Literature*, Ed. 4; *Something about the Author*, Vol. 29; *Twayne's United States Authors; World Literature Criticism; World Poets*; and *Writers for Young Adults*.

MARIA EDGEWORTH

(1768 - 1849)

English novelist, short story writer, essayist, and playwright.

Although Edgeworth wrote in a variety of genres, she is primarily associated with the early English novel of manners and the Irish regional novel. She also produced a number of didactic children's tales that were popular in her own time, but are largely forgotten today. Her most highly-regarded works are *Castle Rackrent: An Hibernian Tale* (1800), a novel based on a family memoir written by Edgeworth's grandfather, and *Belinda* (1801), a three-volume novel of manners.

BIOGRAPHICAL INFORMATION

Born January 1, 1768, at Black Bourton in Oxfordshire, Edgeworth was the eldest daughter of Anna Maria Elers and the educator and inventor Richard Lovell Edgeworth, the most significant figure in her life and in her writing career. In 1773, Edgeworth's mother died and her father remarried almost immediately. He would eventually father a total of twenty-two children by four different wives, and the demands of caring for her many siblings caused Edgeworth to leave school at the age of fifteen. In 1782, her father moved the family to Edgeworthstown, his ancestral estate in

Ireland, and became active in Irish politics and economic reform. During this time, in addition to overseeing the education of the younger children, Edgeworth assisted her father as his secretary. She began writing children's stories to amuse her brothers and sisters, and together with her father produced a volume of essays on childrearing, *Practical Education* (1798). She then turned to novel writing, publishing her first novel in 1800 and her second a year later.

Edgeworth's work was widely read, but she was uncomfortable with public attention, preferring the quiet domestic life she advocated for women. Despite numerous invitations to visit England, she made her first trip—in the company of her father, stepmother, and sister—in 1813. She was introduced to many of the leading intellectuals and literary figures of her time, and while Edgeworth herself was warmly received, her father was not, which disturbed her greatly and contributed to her withdrawal from literary society. She returned to Ireland where she continued writing, administering the education of her younger siblings, the last of whom was born in 1812, and helping to manage the family estate. Her father died in 1817 after a long illness and Edgeworth was charged with completing his autobiography. His *Memoirs* were finally published in 1820, and again her father's unpopularity led to widespread attacks in the press. Flaws in her writing were invariably attributed to the contaminating influence of her father's social and political ideas. Although she was stung by such criticism of her father, his death enabled her to venture again into the literary societies of both England and Scotland. At the same time, she gained control of the family estate—which had been mismanaged by her brother—and capably handled all facets of its operation until 1839. She continued writing, publishing her last novel, *Helen,* in 1834, and a children's story, *Orlandino,* in 1848. She died on May 22, 1849, at the age of eighty-one at the family estate in Edgeworthstown.

MAJOR WORKS

In 1795 Edgeworth published *Letters for Literary Ladies,* a three-part work consisting of an exchange of correspondence between two men on the education of women, followed by an epistolary novella featuring two young female characters, and "An Essay on the Noble Science of Self-Justification." With this work, Edgeworth joined the contemporary literary debate on women's rights, but unlike such revolutionary feminists as Mary Wollstonecraft, she advocated a more conventional role for women—one that restricted their intellectual activities to the domestic sphere, where they might exercise their influence through mediation rather than direct participation in public discourse. Her next work, *The Parent's Assistant* (1796), was a collection of didactic short stories intended for children. Edgeworth's most critically acclaimed work was her first novel, *Castle Rackrent,* an account of four generations of the Rackrent family narrated by Thady Quirk, the family's loyal retainer. The work drew on the family history of the Edgeworths and incorporated social criticism of both the Anglo-Irish gentry and the middle class. It is considered one of the first English novels to represent working-class life, and is also regarded as the first Irish regional novel. Edgeworth's next effort, *Belinda,* employed the conventions of the novel of manners to attack the excesses and moral bankruptcy of the fashionable elite, while at the same time warning against the vulgarity the author associated with the middle class. The work's eponymous heroine was charged with finding a middle ground between female independence and domesticity.

CRITICAL RECEPTION

By many accounts, Edgeworth was the most commercially successful as well as the most critically acclaimed female writer of her time. Today, however, her novels and essays are not widely read, although her work has attracted considerable attention from feminist theorists and literary historians. While she is considered an early feminist or proto-feminist by some scholars, largely because of her advocacy of education for women, others believe her writings reinforce the power of the patriarchy by encouraging women to confine themselves to domestic life. Marilyn Butler suggests that *Castle Rackrent* can be read as a progressive, even radical, work that anticipates the nineteenth-century realist novel. She contends that in the novel "old aristocratic stories of male dominance and legitimacy are being challenged by democratized women-centered plots of family life in which servants, including female servants, wield power, and almost anything is negotiable." Similarly, Edgeworth's 1809 story "Ennui," from *Tales of Fashionable Life* (1809-12), features three main characters who are powerful women and authority figures according to Butler. Nicholas Mason takes issue with those critics who insist that Edgeworth's work exhibits complicity with the patriarchy because of its emphasis on domesticity. Mason maintains that her version of domesticity extends beyond gender issues and encompasses issues of class as well: "more than a system for proper female behavior, the domesticity Edgeworth advocates is a summons for all members of polite society, whether female or male, to live up to their gender- and class-based responsibilities." Gender issues aside, most critics acknowledge Edgeworth's innovations in literary form, including her contribution to the development of the novel of manners and the regional novel, and her innovations in subject matter, particularly her representations of working-class characters.

PRINCIPAL WORKS

Letters for Literary Ladies (essays) 1795

The Parent's Assistant (short stories) 1796-1800

Practical Education [with Richard Lovell Edgeworth] (essays) 1798; also published as *Essays on Practical Education* 1815

Castle Rackrent: An Hibernian Tale (novel) 1800

Belinda (novel) 1801

Moral Tales for Young People (short stories) 1801

Essay on Irish Bulls [with Richard Lovell Edgeworth] (essay) 1802

Popular Tales (short stories) 1804

Leonora (novel) 1806

Tales of Fashionable Life (short stories) 1809-12

Patronage (novel) 1814

Comic Dramas (plays) 1817

Harrington, a Tale, and Ormand, a Tale (novels) 1817

**Memoirs of Richard Lovell Edgeworth, Esq.; Begun by Himself and Concluded by His Daughter, Maria Edgeworth.* 2 vols. [with Richard Lovell Edgeworth] (biography) 1820

Helen (novel) 1834

Orlandino (juvenilia) 1848

---

*   Edgeworth completed her father's autobiography after his death in 1817.

PRIMARY SOURCES

MARIA EDGEWORTH (ESSAY DATE 1799)

SOURCE: Edgeworth, Maria. "Answer to the Letter from a Gentleman to His Friend, Upon the Birth of a Daughter." In *Letters for Literary Ladies, Second Edition, Revised*, 58-83. London: J. Johnson, 1799.

In the following excerpt, Edgeworth's male letter writer discusses the proper education for women.

No woman can foresee what may be the taste of the man with whom she may be united; much of her happiness, however, will depend upon her being able to conform her taste to his: for this reason I should therefore, in female education, cultivate the general powers of the mind, rather than any particular faculty. I do not desire to make my daughter merely a musician, a painter, or a poet; I do not desire to make her merely a botanist, a mathematician, or a chemist; but I wish to give her early the habit of industry and attention, the love of knowledge, and the power of reasoning: these will enable her to attend to excellence in any pursuit to which she may direct her talents. You will observe, that many things which formerly were thought above the comprehension of women, or unfit for their sex, are now acknowledged to be perfectly within the compass of their abilities, and suited to their situation.—Formerly the fair sex was kept in Turkish ignorance; every means of acquiring knowledge was discountenanced by fashion, and impracticable even to those who despised fashion;—our books of science were full of unintelligible jargon, and mystery veiled pompous ignorance from public con-

tempt: but now writers must offer their discoveries to the public in distinct terms, which every body may understand; technical language no longer supplies the place of knowledge, and the art of teaching has been carried to such perfection, that a degree of knowledge may now with ease be acquired in the course of a few years, which formerly it was the business of a life to attain. All this is much in favour of female literature. Ladies have become ambitious to superintend the education of their children, and hence they have been induced to instruct themselves, that they may be able to direct and inform their pupils. The mother, who now aspires to be the esteemed and beloved instructress of her children, must have a considerable portion of knowledge. Science has of late *"been enlisted under the banners of imagination"*, by the irresistible charms of genius; by the same power, her votaries will be led *"from the looser analogies which dress out the imagery of poetry to the stricter ones which form the ratiocination of philosophy.*—Botany has become fashionable; in time it may become useful, if it be not so already. Chemistry will follow botany. Chemistry is a science well suited to the talents and situation of women; it is not a science of parade; it affords occupation and infinite variety; it demands no bodily strength; it can be pursued in retirement; it applies immediately to useful and domestic purposes: and whilst the ingenuity of the most inventive mind may in this science be exercised, there is no danger of inflaming the imagination, because the mind is intent upon realities, the knowledge that is acquired is exact, and the pleasure of the pursuit is a sufficient reward for the labour.

A clear and ready knowledge of arithmetic is surely no useless acquirement for those who are to regulate the expenses of a family. Economy is not the mean "penny wise and pound foolish" policy which some suppose it to be; it is the art of calculation joined to the habit of order, and the power of proportioning our wishes to the means of gratifying them. The little pilfering temper of a wife is despicable and odious to every man of sense; but there is a judicious, graceful species of economy, which has no connexion with an avaricious temper, and which, as it depends upon the understanding, can be expected only from cultivated minds. Women who have been well educated, far from despising domestic duties, will hold them in high respect; because they will see that the whole happiness of life is made up of the happiness of each particular day and hour, and that much of the enjoyment of these must depend upon the punctual practice of those virtues which are more valuable than splendid.

It is not, I hope, your opinion, that ignorance is the best security for female virtue. If this connexion between virtue and ignorance could once be clearly proved, we ought to drown our books deeper than ever plummet sounded:—I say *we*—for the danger extends equally to both sexes, unless you assert that the duties of men rest upon a more certain foundation than the duties of the other sex: if our virtues can be demonstrated to be advantageous, why should theirs suffer for being exposed to the light of reason?—All social virtue conduces to our own happiness or that of our fellow-creatures; can it weaken the sense of duty to illustrate this truth?—Having once pointed out to the understanding of a sensible woman the necessary connexion between her virtues and her happiness, must not those virtues, and the means of preserving them, become in her eyes objects of the most interesting importance? But you fear, that even if their conduct continued to be irreproachable, the manners of women might be rendered less delicate by the increase of their knowledge; you dislike in the female sex that daring spirit which despises the common forms of society, and which breaks through the reserve and delicacy of female manners:—so do I:—and the best method to make my pupil respect these things is to show her how they are indispensably connected with the largest interests of society: surely this perception of the utility of forms apparently trifling, must be a strong security to the prudential reserve of the sex, and far superior to the automatic habits of those who submit to the conventions of the world without consideration or conviction. Habit, confirmed by reason, assumes the rank of virtue. The motives that restrain from vice must be increased by the clear conviction, that vice and wretchedness are inseparably united.

Do not, however, imagine, my dear sir, that I shall attempt to lay moral demonstration before *a child*, who could not possibly comprehend my meaning; do not imagine that because I intend to cultivate my daughter's understanding, I shall neglect to give her those early habits of reserve and modesty which constitute the female character.—Believing, as I do, that woman, as well as man, may be called a bundle of habits, I shall be peculiarly careful, during my child's early education, to give her as many good habits as possible; by degrees as her understanding, that is to say as her knowledge and power of reasoning shall increase, I can explain the advantages of these

habits, and confirm their power by the voice of reason. I lose no time, I expose myself to no danger, by this system. On the contrary, those who depend entirely upon the force of custom and prejudice expose them themselves to infinite danger. If once their pupils begin to reflect upon their own hoodwinked education, they will probably suspect that they have been deceived in all that they have been taught, and they will burst their bonds with indignation.—Credulity is always rash in the moment she detects the impositions that have been practised upon her easy temper. In this inquiring age, few have any chance of passing through life without being excited to examine the motives and principles from which they act: is it not therefore prudent to cultivate the reasoning faculty, by which alone this examination can be made with safety? A false argument, a repartee, the charms of wit or eloquence, the voice of fashion, of folly, of numbers, might, if she had no substantial reasons to support her cause, put virtue not only out of countenance, but out of humour.

You speak of moral instinct. As far as I understand the term, it implies certain habits early acquired from education; to these I would add the power of reasoning, and then, and not till then, I should think myself safe:—for I have observed that the pupils of habit are utterly confounded when they are placed in circumstances different from those to which they have been accustomed.—It has been remarked by travellers and naturalists, that animals, notwithstanding their boasted instinctive knowledge, sometimes make strange and fatal mistakes in their conduct, when they are placed in new situations:—destitute of the reasoning faculty, and deceived by resemblances, they mistake poison for food. Thus the bull-frog will swallow burning charcoal, mistaking it for fire-flies; and the European hogs and poultry which travelled to Surinam poisoned themselves by eating plants that were unknown to them.

You seem, my dear sir, to be afraid that truth should not keep so firm a hold upon the mind as prejudice; and you produce an allusion to justify your fears. You tell us that civil society is like a building, and you warn me not to tear down the ivy which clings to the walls, and braces the loose stones together.—I believe that ivy, in some situations, tends to pull down the walls to which it clings.—You think it is not worth while to cultivate the understandings of women, because you say that you have no security that the conviction of their reason will have any permanent good effect upon their conduct; and to persuade me of this, you bid me observe that men who are superior to women in strength of mind and judgment, are frequently misled by their passions. By this mode of argument, you may conclude that reason is totally useless to the whole human race; but you cannot, with any show of justice, infer that it ought to be monopolized by one-half of mankind. But why should you quarrel with reason, because passion sometimes conquers her?—You should endeavour to strengthen the connexion between theory and practice, if it be not sufficiently strong already; but you can gain nothing by destroying theory.—Happiness is your aim; but your unpractised or unsteady hand does not obey your will: you do not at the first trial hit the mark precisely.—Would you, because you are awkward, insist upon being blind?

The strength of mind which enables people to govern themselves by their reason, is not always connected with abilities even in their most cultivated state: I deplore the instances which I have seen of this truth, but I do not despair; on the contrary, I am excited to inquire into the causes of this phenomenon; nor, because I see some evil, would I sacrifice the good upon a bare motive of suspicion. It is a contradiction to say, that giving the power to discern what is good is giving a disposition to prefer what is bad. I acknowledge with regret, that women who have been but half instructed, who have seen only superficially the relations of moral and political ideas, and who have obtained but an imperfect knowledge of the human heart, have conducted themselves so as to disgrace their talents and their sex; these are conspicuous and melancholy examples, which are cited oftener with malice than with pity. But I appeal to examples amongst our contemporaries, to which every man of literature will immediately advert, to prove, that where the female understanding has been properly cultivated, women have not only obtained admiration by their useful abilities, but respect by their exemplary conduct.

I apprehend that many of the errors into which women of literature have fallen, may have arisen from an improper choice of books. Those who read chiefly works of imagination, receive from them false ideas of life and of the human heart. Many of these productions I should keep as I would deadly poison from my child; I should rather endeavour to turn her attention to science than to romance, and to give her early that taste for truth and utility, which, when once implanted, can scarcely be eradicated. There is a wide difference between innocence and ignorance: ignorant women may have minds the most debased and perverted, whilst the most cultivated understanding may be united with the most perfect innocence and simplicity.

Even if literature were of no other use to the fair sex than to supply them with employment, I should think the time dedicated to the cultivation of their minds well bestowed: they are surely better occupied when they are reading or writing than when coqueting or gaming, losing their fortunes or their characters. You despise the writings of women:—you think that they might have made a better use of the pen, than to write plays, and poetry, and romances. Considering that the pen was to women a new instrument, I think they have made at least as good a use of it as learned men did of the needle some centuries ago, when they set themselves to determine how many spirits could stand upon its point, and were ready to tear one another to pieces in the discussion of this sublime question. Let the sexes mutually forgive each other their follies; or, what is much better, let them combine their talents for their general advantage.—You say, that the experiments we have made do not encourage us to proceed—that the increased care and pains which have been of late years bestowed upon female education have produced no adequate returns; but you in the same breath allow that amongst your contemporaries, whom you prudently forbear to mention, there are some instances of great talents applied to useful purposes. Did you expect that the fruits of good cultivation should appear before the seed was sown? You triumphantly enumerate the disadvantages to which women, from the laws and customs of society, are liable:—they cannot converse freely with men of wit, science, and learning, nor even with the artist, or artificers; they are excluded from academies, public libraries, &c. Even our politeness prevents us, you say, from ever speaking plain truth and sense to the fair sex:—every assistance that foreign or domestic ingenuity can invent to encourage literary studies, is, as you boast, almost exclusively ours: and after pointing out all these causes for the inferiority of women in knowledge, you ask for a list of the inventions and discoveries of those who, by your own statement of the question, have not been allowed opportunities for observation. With the insulting injustice of an Egyptian task-master, you demand the work, and deny the necessary materials.

I admit, that with respect to the opportunities of acquiring knowledge, institutions and manners are, as you have stated, much in favour of our sex; but your argument concerning time appears to me to be unfounded.—Women who do not love dissipation must have more time for the cultivation of their understandings than men can have, if you compute the whole of life:—whilst the knowledge of the learned languages continues to form an indispensable part of a gentleman's education, many years of childhood and youth must be devoted to their attainment.—During these studies, the general cultivation of the understanding is in some degree retarded. All the intellectual powers are cramped, except the memory, which is sufficiently exercised, but which is overloaded with words, and with words that are not always understood.—The genius of living and of dead languages differs so much, that the pains which are taken to write elegant Latin frequently spoil the English style.—Girls usually write much better than boys; they think and express their thoughts clearly at an age when young men can scarcely write an easy letter upon any common occasion. Women do not read the good authors of antiquity as school-books, but they can have excellent translations of most of them when they are capable of tasting the beauties of composition.—I know that it is supposed we cannot judge of the classics by translations, and I am sensible that much of the merit of the originals may be lost; but I think the difference in pleasure is more than overbalanced to women by the time that is saved, and by the labour and misapplication of abilities which are spared. If they do not acquire a classical taste, neither do they imbibe classic prejudices; nor are they early disgusted with literature by pedagogues, lexicons, grammars, and all the melancholy apparatus of learning.— Women begin to taste the pleasures of reading, and the best authors in the English language are their amusement, just at the age when young men, disgusted by their studies, begin to be ashamed of alluding to literature amongst their companions. Travelling, lounging, field sports, gaming, and what is called pleasure in various shapes, usually fill the interval between quitting the university and settling for life.—When this period is past, business, the necessity of pursuing a profession, the ambition to shine in parliament, or to rise in public life, occupy a large portion of their lives.—In many professions the understanding is but partially cultivated; and general literature must be neglected by those who are occupied in earning bread or amassing riches for their family:—men of genius are often heard to complain, that in the pursuit of a profession, they are obliged to contract their inquiries and concentrate their powers; statesmen lament that they must often

pursue the *expedient* even when they discern that it is not *the right*; and men of letters, who earn their bread by their writings, inveigh bitterly against the tyranny of booksellers, who degrade them to the state of "literary artisans".—"Literary artisans," is the comprehensive term under which a celebrated philosopher classes all those who cultivate only particular talents or powers of the mind, and who suffer their other faculties to lose all strength and vigour for want of exercise. The other sex have no such constraint upon their understandings; neither the necessity of earning their bread, nor the ambition to shine in public affairs, hurry or prejudice their minds: in domestic life they have leisure to be wise.

Far from being ashamed that so little has been done by female abilities in science and useful literature, I am surprised that so much has been effected. On natural history, on criticism, on moral philosophy, on education, they have written with elegance, eloquence, precision, and ingenuity. Your complaint that women do not turn their attention to useful literature is surely ill-timed. If they merely increased the number of books in circulation, you might declaim against them with success; but when they add to the general fund of useful and entertaining knowledge, you cannot with any show of justice prohibit their labours: there can be no danger that the market should ever be overstocked with produce of intrinsic worth.

GENERAL COMMENTARY

MARILYN BUTLER (ESSAY DATE SPRING 2001)

SOURCE: Butler, Marilyn. "Edgeworth's Ireland: History, Popular Culture, and Secret Codes." *Novel* 34, no. 2 (spring 2001): 267-92.

In the following essay, Butler discusses Edgeworth's Irish fiction and its relationship to historical events.

During the 1990s more critical work has appeared on the Anglo-Irish "national novel" than in any decade since 1800-1810 when, by common consent, the sub-genre first appeared. The new edition of Edgeworth in twelve volumes is a contribution to this collective effort, but the edition is appearing after what is effectively a "school" of Anglo-Irish postcolonial criticism. In the course of the 1990s Tom Dunne, Seamus Deane, Terry Eagleton, and most recently Kevin Whelan have between them established an essentialist line, not closely concerned with the text, on what they see more broadly as a body of writing initially by Anglicized and Protestant Irish writers that made the "writing of Ireland" a topic dominated by the colonial relationship with England and addressed to the English.[1] Some of the postcolonial group argue that the relationship has from the first been hierarchical: they instance the debate Edmund Spenser borrowed from a dialogue by the Greek, Lucian, that of Civility versus Incivility, which survived into the nineteenth century with the Irish permanently cast in the role of barbarians. Critics vary somewhat in the closeness with which they make such general propositions fit individual writers. Whelan is most dogmatic in fitting the colonizer-stereotype to Edgeworth and in the process giving her a specific political role:

> By properly playing their civilising leadership role, the [Protestant] Irish gentry could also wean the native Hibernians from clan to state loyalties; their assent thus ensuring the hegemony of that landed class.
>
> (Whelan, Foreword xiii-xiv)

The proposition I shall put in my reexamination of Edgeworth's Irish writing is that when read closely all five of the works concerned indeed exhibit political objectives, but they are not these. Edgeworth has other objectives, including but not limited to nationalism, that prove her much more expressively committed than has hitherto appeared to the history, language, culture, and future of Irish people.

The best critical writing on Edgeworth in this decade has been more nuanced and more responsive to the texts themselves, as are the articles of Mitzi Myers, W. J. McCormack, Ina Ferris, and Katie Trumpener's excellent overview of the Irish "national novel," *Bardic Nationalism* (1998). Ferris and Trumpener however have defined this new genre narrowly, by only one of the formats in which it appeared, the fictionalized travelogue as allegorical romance, as used by Sydney Owenson in *The Wild Irish Girl,* which I regard as too concentrated on antiquarianism and too bluntly propagandist to offer an adequate basis for a discussion of how novelists collectively learned to represent nationhood as a social and cultural concept. Instead, I offer an account of Edgeworth's characteristic themes and methods when representing the Irish and how she developed them as a rich, ambitious blueprint for the national novel.

Edgeworth as a fiction-writer distinguishes her characters, with a new subtlety in relation to their gender, class and nationality, by what they have been reading. In her best, most bookish fiction of upper-class life she introduces a novel kind of sub-

ABOUT THE AUTHOR

MYERS DESCRIBES EDGEWORTH'S IDEAL READER

For all Edgeworth's reputation as mimetic mirror, the ideal reader her stories expect knows a lot about literature, knows the eighteenth-century traditions of romance and philosophical tale, and can appreciate her blurring of genres as hybrid forms that address the lived issues of women's lives. Her romantic impossibilities and unnatural incidents achieve their effects not because they seamlessly resolve contradictions and bestow the illusion of closure, but because their sophisticated variations on stylized genres befriend her readers as well as her protagonists. They playfully make us laugh; they purposively make us—as Edgeworth's characters are always enjoined to do—think for ourselves.

Myers, Mitzi. Excerpt from "'We Must Grant a Romance Writer a Few Impossibilities': 'Unnatural Incident' and Narrative Motherhood in Maria Edgeworth's *Emilie de Coulanges*." *The Wordsworth Circle* 27 (Summer 1996): 151-57.

text that makes reading and conversations on reading an indicator of rationality and moral worth.[2] An indicator of the opposite, as well, as in her satirical treatment of great men in her two most trenchant anti-Whiggish political novels, *Vivian* (1812) and *Patronage* (1814).[3] In general terms, Edgeworth's characteristic use of allusive conversations conveys a sense of knowledge shared. The name of an author or the title of a book not only opens up other imagined worlds, but also gives us access to the world of books, the reading community, and (by the early 1800s) a specific community, local or national, which may never before have been described as an entity.

In the Irish tales after *Castle Rackrent*, classic scenes of conversation in high life occur, especially in the opening chapters. These were particularly noticed by reviewers, since the Irish *Ennui* (1809) and *The Absentee* (1812) were each in turn hailed as Edgeworth's best work so far. In the body of the tale, however, where the setting is Ireland, she innovatively alludes to and incorporates popular culture: from recent or current Dublin and Belfast writing in English, satire, lampoon, and United Irish broadsheet propaganda; from the rural Gaelic-Irish tradition, folksong, story, legend, nationalist history, and occasionally magic. Edgeworth's level of encryption in the Irish tales is then a distinctive phenomenon, not recurring elsewhere in her own work or in the work of Irish predecessors or contemporaries. It is an intellectually self-conscious attempt at a group portrait of a hybrid, often disunited people who may have their own languages, some of them secret. It plainly addresses different readerships, either within the one nation or outside it. There is an implicit assumption behind this mode of writing that the English Protestant reader and the Gaelic Catholic reader will have a different reading experience. This is to set down in outline the case for a re-reading of Edgeworth's Irish tales for their intellectuality, their technical virtuosity, their role in literary history, and their move to open up the novel and literature itself to popular language.

A book that uses literary language and other literary devices demands the attention of its readers. A novel stands or falls by its use of language, narration, and plot—not by who the writer is. "Identity," in the simple sense of national or racial or religious identity, cannot itself explain the allegiances and motivations of even a single writer, especially when the writer consciously addressed a diverse public. Edgeworth from the outset wrote fiction for different audiences—between 1792 and 1801, lively short stories for children of various ages and "lessons" cast as dialogues for parents teaching at home; after 1801, novels and novellas set in English high-life; a sub-genre of these introducing French or Frenchified main characters; and her Irish tales, which also have sub-plots or substantial episodes introducing English or French characters.

The language Edgeworth uses in these different genres and sub-genres is tailor-made for its imagined audiences. In the children's tales the main child character, who is either decidedly rich and spoilt or decidedly poor and spunky, may be eight, ten, or twelve to fourteen—in the last case, he or she is struggling with an often dark adult world, and vocabulary and sentence-lengths adjust accordingly. Edgeworth's adaptability fosters her experimental plotting. She uses non-realistic devices from (say) fairy tale and a playful allusiveness to other texts in both dialogue and third-person narration. Her High Society is sometimes scientifically informed or chic and Parisian, that is, well-read in literary classics in English or

French, reaching back to 1600 or before. Or, it can be intermittently raffish, as in *Belinda* (1801), from the introduction of other voices quoting more or less exactly from current newspaper items, fashionable scandals, popular caricature, advertisements, reviews, and the subculture of a big house, the servants' quarters belowstairs.

By characters' easy cross-references to their reading, the Edgeworth text supplies its real-life context. Books by 1800 had a cosmopolitan readership: novels were popular, bookish novels more popular than most. Edgeworth was speedily translated into French from this time, and responded by creating for her readership three socially tiered societies: metropolitan France, metropolitan England, and rural Ireland. Intellectuals of the late Enlightenment were fully aware of the social and political impact of the Europe-wide and Atlantic print network, of belonging to a reading public that knew itself by reading *Reviews,* memoirs, travels, and novels. Dugald Stewart, philosopher and mentor of the early *Edinburgh Review,* considered the circulating print network a guarantee of nineteenth-century progress.

Edgeworth, then, is not narrowly concerned with inventing either the national novel or the naturalistic novel, though she contributes to both; she participates in a historical process by developing a more stylized, consciously intellectual cosmopolitan novel, an intrinsically comparative and interactive exercise. Her high-life scenes in London Society portray a wartime English plutocracy driven by greed as illustrated by the London marriage market in *Belinda.* It is an idle, discontented class, further enfeebled by its own love-affair with French old-régime cynicism and amorality—as Edgeworth shows in her epistolary novel of espionage and adultery, *Leonora* (1806, pub. 1805), and *Patronage* (1814). Not exactly satire as Pope's generation understood it (though Pope is a leading presence in these novels), Edgeworth's high-life fiction is critical in a form understood by (for example) Jeffrey, Croker, and Jeremy Bentham.[4]

Edgeworth's Irish tales and the *Essay on Irish Bulls* are among her best, most characteristic writings. All five works are consistently and deliberately historical, but in an idiosyncratic mode that relies on quotation, the naming of authors and books, and allusions to familiar thoughts and ideas. These techniques make characters knowable, but in a new way, by having them reveal their own cultural milieu, deepened for the reader by the use of real-life people and the words they used. Radcliffe's gothic *Mysteries of Udolpho* and

Scott's *Waverley* or *Ivanhoe* are obviously historical in that the author dates the action in a past age, but their authors' interests cannot be said to be more historical than those of Edgeworth, whose method is theoretically more organic and intrinsic. Her three later Irish tales all seem to situate the action in 1798 or later; yet the flow of names in narrative and dialogue is topographical, historical, literary, and cultural, embedding the characters richly in their own pasts and giving the reader access to the past. Her invented Ireland is fed by a broad stream of references to the history, personalities, and families of the island, its local place names and topography, its extant documents and archives, especially those bearing on the ownership of land.

Edgeworth's first solo book and for some her masterpiece, **Castle Rackrent** brings together in a narrational *tour de force* the archive of her own extended family, focusing on (yet also masking) its internal quarrels over money, land, and religion in North Longford between 1688 and 1709. Given that this is what Thady's narration actually is, Edgeworth misleads her readers in providing **Castle Rackrent** with the subtitle: "An Hibernian Tale/Taken from Facts, and from the Manners of the Irish Squires before the year 1782." The subtitle makes a point of being historical; yet, since the book was published in the beginning of the year 1800, only eighteen years on, it hardly reaches back into history. Critics beginning with Thomas Flanagan have unsuspiciously connived with her by interpreting **Rackrent** as a study of big historical events, such as the loss of the notionally independent Protestant-Ascendancy parliament, and the incorporation in 1800 of the Irish constituencies and some Irish peers into the parliament at Westminster. It is better to assume Edgeworth was out to puzzle her reader, or even play a joke, as she was doing in the contemporaneous **Essay on Irish Bulls** (1802). This could explain why we have yet to see a satisfactory explanation of how **Castle Rackrent** is supposed to be rendering such public events; or why the manners of squires a generation earlier might be relevant to such a theme; or whether, indeed, **Rackrent** qualifies as either a national tale or historical tale at all.

The story, told by the aged steward Thady M'Quirk, serves as the fictionalized memoir of his service of four successive squires on a remote Irish estate over a period of eighty years. The Rackrent family chronicles, it is now generally conceded, really do derive from a similar family memoir not fictional at all. It was written in the late 1760s by

Maria Edgeworth's grandfather Richard Edgeworth (1701-70) from family papers; complete with legal documents, it is available in the National Library of Ireland. Richard Edgeworth stops at the point when both his parents died within a few weeks of each other, that is, in the year 1709, when he was only eight. The orphan boy was left alone as the couple's only surviving child. Half a century later he recalls his father, Frank, dying heartbroken after losing the lands and title deeds to the new house he had built at Edgeworthstown. That dark scene closes the memoir, known in the family as the "Black Book of Edgeworthstown," and it also closes Maria Edgeworth's tale of Sir Condy, last of the Rackrents.

The first Edgeworth to settle near Mastrim, afterwards known as Edgeworthstown, was the emigré English lawyer Francis Edgeworth. The Dublin-based husband of Jane Tuite, a firmly Catholic woman from nearby County Westmeath, Francis bought a medium-sized estate at Cranalagh, north of Mastrim, when it came on the market as part of an official reapportionment in 1619. The original owners of the property were O'Farrells, still in 1619 the dominant family in a territory known as Annaly until its modernization in 1570 as County Longford. Francis Edgeworth and others like him benefited from this second wave of anti-baronial modernization: big Old Irish or Old English estates were reduced in size as new gentlemen-farmers from further east or from England were introduced as improvers. Francis Edgeworth was the first of a line of four squires who lived at Cranalagh, two miles north of Mastrim, until Frank, the fourth, built his new house at what became Edgeworthstown.

But Maria Edgeworth changes the real-life story by making the first of the Rackrents an Irishman by descent. This was a purposeful decision: the central family in all four of her Irish tales is of Gaelic origin. Sir Patrick O'Shaughlin, a spendthrift and jolly hospitable host, takes over the house and small estate from a relative on condition he changes to the English name. As a type Sir Patrick strongly resembles Captain John Edgeworth, who inherited the property from his father Francis in 1627, a landlord nicknamed by his tenants "Shaen Mor," Irish for "Big John." The fictional landlords between Sir Patrick and Sir Condy, who are called Sir Murtaugh and Sir Kit, are not specific portraits, but contrasting types pieced together, without regard for chronology, from one striking figure in the real memoirs, and one equally notorious neighbor—of whom more will be said. The original for the mean half-crazy lawyer Murtaugh was not an Edgeworth eldest son, and thus a legitimate heir, but the unfortunate Frank's younger brother Robert, a Catholic; a still younger brother and another Catholic, Ambrose, tricked Frank out of his house with the help of a perjured witness, as one of the glossary notes describes.[5]

Thady's fictional narrative allegedly covers eighty years, with considerable fidelity to small detail and notable omissions. His life-story matches landlord régimes spanning eighty-two years in the Edgeworth family chronicle. Instead of representing the era immediately prior to 1782, as the subtitle claims, the annals recount the eighty years prior to that, ending in 1709. Consequently, they cover Irish history through two periods of religious and dynastic war, followed in the 1690s by William of Orange's penal legislation against the Catholic gentry—the most determined scheme yet devised to break up big Catholic estates and disrupt a basic precept of English law, the rule of inheritance by the eldest son, and thus of ongoing family wealth and power. It is those two civil wars, of 1641 and 1688, that stand as the largest omission from Thady's narrative.

The Irish local historian Raymond Gillespie, editor of a collection of new essays on County Longford (1991), in his own contribution to the volume narrates the real-life slow decline of the county's leading Catholic family, the O'Farrells. He brings out elements in their story—a major schism between two branches of the family; then, incompetence, bad luck, backwardness, absenteeism, and in the senior branch, sterility—factors that regularly appear in Edgeworth's history of the Rackrents. There was, however, a point of difference: whereas the O'Farrells ran out of male heirs in mid-century, the Edgeworths by the 1690s had all too many quarrelsome siblings. Edgeworth holdings in County Longford had once belonged to the northern branch of the O'Farrells, which farmed the more boggy and mountainous terrain between Granard, near the Westmeath border, westward toward Roscommon and northward toward Leitrim. The Edgeworths were sharply reminded of the old owners by a dramatic incident in the house at Cranalagh during the rebellion of 1641. Big John was away from home, as the "Black Book" tells it. Tenants and local men broke into the house, stripped John's wife Mary, English Protestant daughter of Sir Hugh Cullum of Derbyshire, and drove her out naked into the countryside. A family servant, Brian Farrell, seized the couple's child, the future Sir John, then aged three, and fiercely declared he would kill him. He

stoutly prevented the mob from proceeding with their main aim after plundering the house, which was to burn it down: the Farrells, he said, the real owners of the estate, might want to live in it. That done, he left with the child and hid him in the bog until he could be spirited away. Brian Farrell's descendents continued to live on the estate into the next century. He was, in his way, a double agent and prototype of Thady, though in a different political cause.

Since Gillespie, another Irish local historian, W. A. Maguire, in a 1996 article on County Longford, decisively re-sources the best-known episode in *Castle Rackrent,* indeed the best-known episode in Edgeworth, that of the "Madwoman in the Attic." In the process he uncovers an original for the one Rackrent who was not an Edgeworth. In the novel, the third of the dynasty, Sir Kit, incarcerates his Jewish wife for years because she would not give up her jewels. The real story referred to was public knowledge in the late eighteenth century, thanks to an obituary in the *Gentleman's Magazine* for Lady Cathcart, once wife of an Irish gentleman, Colonel Hugh Maguire. But the obituary wrongly located their household in County Fermanagh and for two centuries that location, relatively remote from Edgeworthstown, was assumed to be correct.

Maguire shows that the episode occurred in the 1760s in a Catholic household four miles north of Edgeworthstown called Castle Nugent. The owner was indeed Colonel Hugh Maguire, who was the nephew on his mother's side of the celebrated Grace Nugent—the subject of an Irish song by the poet and harpist Carolan and the name of the heroine of *The Absentee* (1812), after *Rackrent* the best-known of Edgeworth's Irish tales. The curious intricacy of plotting and the localism uncovered by this discovery has consequences for Edgeworth's readers. She can incorporate the history of neighboring families; in doing so she merges the real-life experience of Catholic and Protestant Longford gentry. A very high proportion of Thady's narration and many of the yarns that flesh out the glossary notes select archival material from the *Black Book*—not realism, so much as "the real."

Quite separately from these local and family contributions, through the device of allegory the story of *Castle Rackrent* refers to *national* history of the same era. Edgeworth left in a family copy of *Castle Rackrent* a pencilled note of a footnote she intended to add, but never did add, that applies to a line in Thady's narrative, "as I have lived so will I die, true and loyal to the family" (10).

Edgeworth's jotting merely says "Loyal High Constable." That ironic allusion to a real title (Lord High Constable) would have brought in James Butler, second Duke of Ormond. By virtue of his office, he carried the crown at the coronation of the Protestant William and Mary, and afterwards at the coronation of Queen Anne. The second Duke inherited the office, though an altered title, from his grandfather, the first Duke, also James Butler (1610-88), who was elevated both to the Dukedom and to the title of Lord High *Steward* by Charles II at the Restoration—to reward him, gratefully but almost costlessly, for his stalwart support of the Stuart monarchs as their greatest servant in Ireland. As Steward, the first Duke carried the crown at Charles's coronation in 1661 and at the Catholic James II's coronation in 1685, thus beginning the family's tradition of truth and loyalty to four monarchs of the family.

Even before the accession of the Protestant Elector of Hanover as George I, however, the second Duke was no longer in favor and may have been planning a secret coup to bring James Edward, the Old Pretender, back to London before the arrival of the Elector of Hanover. Early in 1715, anticipating his impeachment and the sequestration of his vast Munster estates, he fled to the Continent to join James Edward's court in exile and to lead a Spanish fleet that in 1719 attempted to assist the Jacobite rising of 1715 against George I. It was indeed loyalty from the Jacobite perspective: equivocation, followed by treason, for Hanoverians.

Thady's resonant allusion to the second Duke in the novel's first paragraph need not make Thady a Jacobite; Edgeworth's codes tend to be more equivocal than that. Though it can be characterization, it reads better as allegory: Thady's service of the four Rackrents, who are so close to four Edgeworths, is analogous with the two Dukes' service of the last four Stuarts. *Castle Rackrent* reads as the requiem for an unlamented century, that of Europe-wide civil wars driven by religion and devious statecraft. A failed line of English-Irish landlords, disinherited by 1709, replicates the feckless, reckless, amorous Stuart dynasty, whose reign over the Three Kingdoms (England, Scotland and Ireland) ended in 1714.

It is sour and failing family history and national history that graphically merges in *Castle Rackrent*. But even more is perhaps at stake: what the Great House generally signified in feudal times. As it plainly tilts at the irresponsible Stuarts, *Castle Rackrent* also challenges the system—traditional landownership or the aristocratic system of proprietorship, sustained by male primogeniture on the one hand, profitable marriages and the strategic extension of kinship on the other. Great-House stateliness is debunked when Castle Rackrent's annals are handed over to an illiterate Irish chronicler to relate. The entire social system, based on kinship and alliances, is shown crumbling away as, in each generation, wealth-bearing brides make off with what they can salvage in money and durables. Even Thady's granddaughter Judy manages to rescue something from the wreck of Condy's affairs, and to frustrate the schemes of the men of her family, Thady and Jason. Perhaps the social changes posited here would need a timespan longer than 82 years, which may be why Edgeworth in her subtitle gives herself to 1782. Read this way, the glossary note on "the raking pot of tea," served after midnight in the bedrooms where women rule, is a key to *Rackrent*'s radicalism and a useful signpost to the nineteenth-century realist novel that is on its way (33, 65n). Old aristocratic stories of male dominance and legitimacy are being challenged by democratized women-centered plots of family life in which servants, including female servants, wield power, and almost anything is negotiable.

Castle Rackrent began in 1793-94 as an impromptu act of mimicry, delivered to a family audience that knew the family past, and made vivacious by being retold in the Hibernian vernacular of an ancient steward. The annals of the last landlord were added after a break of two years, and were in place by 1798. At this time, a plan for an *Essay on Irish Bulls,* to be jointly authored by Maria Edgeworth and her father Richard Lovell Edgeworth (hereafter RLE), had been in place since the summer of 1797, but little or no writing on the book-length *Essay* could have been done.[6] In short, there is a clear break between *Castle Rackrent* and Edgeworth's other Irish writing, beginning with the *Essay.* True to its title, the latter serves as a trial run for Edgeworth's later fictional constructions of Ireland.

Rackrent is already a carefully considered work, as is apparent from the last-minute framing paratext, consisting of preface, glossary, and probably the first footnote to the text. Despite the spoken idiom in which it is delivered, Thady's narrative has real claims to be taken seriously as history, both for its detail based on fact and for its coolly detached commentary on seventeenth-century Longford and its landlordism. But *Castle Rackrent* avoids contemporary political allusions, except for a sly joke in the closing paragraph at the expense of the Warwickshire Militia, for (presumably) being drunk and disorderly and reported as such in the press. In that respect it differs from the overtly and boldly political *Essay on Irish Bulls* (May 1802), and from the semi-hidden politics of Edgeworth's elegant later Irish tales.

As a family the Edgeworths lived in Clifton, Bristol, for most of 1792-93, and resumed life in a fast-politicizing Ireland in 1794. By this time the United Irishmen were fully operative in both Belfast and Dublin. Their press had become an excellent tool for disseminating reformist, indeed revolutionary ideas by a combination of satire of the rulers and generalized consensual objectives, attractive to liberals whether Catholic or Protestant. More to the point from the perspective of Edgeworthstown, two of the United Irish leaders, Archibald Hamilton Rowan and William Drennan, were in the dock for their part in these seditious publications. RLE was acquainted with both men since his days as a reformist Volunteer in 1782-83; he had corresponded subsequently with Drennan and took Belfast newspapers at Edgeworthstown. As he followed the trial of Hamilton Rowan, RLE would have noted the line adopted by John Philpot Curran, the impressive counsel for the defense, that freedom of speech was the issue. The Irish people were being denied what the English boasted of having, and by extension the Irish liberal press might also be subjected to official censorship or closed down. As Curran put it when summing up in Rowan's case:

> *England is marked by a natural avarice of freedom, which she is studious to engross and accumulate, but most unwilling to impart . . . the policy of England has ever been, to govern her connexions more as colonies than as allies.*
>
> (213)

Hamilton Rowan was found guilty but escaped to France; Drennan was acquitted; and so, too, in 1795, was the editor of a United-Irish newspaper, the *Northern Star*.

Also in 1795, RLE intervened in national affairs by offering the Dublin government a device of obvious strategic importance, a telegraph (which he spelt *tellograph*) of his own invention. Maria Edgeworth wrote the paper RLE gave to the Royal Irish Academy on 27 June 1795, "**A Secret and Swift Messenger.**"[7] It gave advance notice of the feat he achieved on 24 August, a message successfully conveyed by telegraph from Scotland to Ireland. RLE explained to his fellow academicians that he was less concerned with the simple mechanics of his invention than with the utility and symbolic significance of a universal sign-language, a project worked on by seventeenth-century

predecessors such as the English mathematician and inventor John Wilkins and, on the Continent, Fontenelle and Leibnitz ("**Secret**" 122-23). Their aim was to improve worldwide communications by inventing a device for instantaneous translation. Once the codebook was established and disseminated, a telegraph could serve as such a device. But the military interest in a telegraph was likely to be different: to ensure that the transmission of military information was *not* readable by an enemy. Neither RLE's codebook nor his tellograph was adopted by Dublin. This may have been because in both County Longford and Dublin RLE himself was considered a security risk.

RLE was aware of the military need for a secure form of coding and decoding. It may already have occurred to him that books and a freely circulating press, such as that achieved by the United Irishmen, provided opportunities for passing secret messages as well as information. In an ambiguous aside to the academicians he hinted at this: "The press is an engine which every person can make use of to convey his ideas to the public" ("**Secret**" 124). From then on he revived cryptography as a favorite pursuit. And, in the form of riddles, obscure hints, and allusions to underground networking, hidden and double messages became a feature of his daughter's Irish writing.

Security and the removal of an inflammatory circulating press meanwhile continued to preoccupy the most powerful figure in Ireland, the chief law officer John Fitzgibbon, Earl of Clare. By April 1797 he succeeded in shutting down the last of the United Irish newspapers, *The Press*. His comment in the previous month on the United Irish movement succinctly identifies its constituent parts: "a deluded peasantry aided by more intelligent treason" (Whelan, *Tree of Liberty* 73). The *Essay on Irish Bulls* was adopted as a project that summer. The press, and Fitzgibbon, were salient elements in the eventual work. From the outset, the author's own security (against a minister looking for treason) was a real issue, so that the *Essay* was probably conceived as a kind of maze, a puzzling family game. It opens by giving readers a variety of clues about where it is coming from. In the first chapter of the 1802 edition we learn that the basic idea was a joke Jonathan Swift sent to a friend in London, Lord Bathurst, in 1730—he proposed to write a book on the so-called "Irish bull," as a verbal blunder, supposedly characteristic of the Irish, that proved their stupidity. Swift's book, he promised, would put this calumny against his nation into reverse: the English had themselves invented the bull; if it conveyed anyone's stupidity, it was theirs.

This theme is indeed faithfully followed, rather too much so, by the Edgeworths. There is, however, another hint on the title page, in a Latin epigraph from Juvenal which refers to Democritus, the ancient Greek scientist, philosopher, and doctor. It is not Democritus himself who becomes a direct source for **Irish Bulls,** but the seventeenth-century philosopher, doctor, and utopian Robert Burton, who signs himself "Democritus Junior" in the 100-page Introductory Address to his massive medical work *The Anatomy of Melancholy* (1621).

With Swift as the work's inspiration, the book's considerable resources open up the books of others, most comprehensively from the ancient world and Ireland's, Britain's, and Europe's seventeenth century. Though the anthology consists of prose rather than poetry, it is eclectic in its forms, for these are often oral and informal: bulls, other jokes, testimony in court, vernacular wit, vernacular oratory, libels, travesty, misinformation, and coded meanings. In a more formal philosophical dialogue, however, the "Bath Coach Conversation" between representatives of the Three Kingdoms, an Englishman, a Scotsman, and an Irishman, and in contributions from Scottish-Enlightenment cultural critics, literary critics, linguists, and rhetoricians, discussion ranges across the many genres encompassed by Comedy, the topic of "the low" as a legitimate literary concern, and the status of dialect speech as opposed to written and literary language. In the history of genre-study or formalism, the **Essay** deserves a mention, particularly for its inclusiveness: prose, dialect, vulgarisms, and the low are all in.

If on the other hand Burton is taken for the presiding genius of **Irish Bulls,** the **Essay** reads as an engagingly unorthodox cultural history of early modern Europe, especially the turbulent dystopic history of seventeenth-century religious war, as coolly surveyed by Democritus Junior, or Voltaire, or Charles II's best propagandist, Roger L'Estrange. Burton writes eloquently of a Europe preoccupied with war, want, poverty, and crime, and more compactly of the "dream of a better world," or utopianism, the literary genre that is a blueprint for an ideal commonwealth. The representation of England is conveyed in the **Essay** disproportionately by figures who could come from Burton's dystopic panorama and by quotations from English lawyers and administrators, newspapermen and pamphleteers, partisans and libelers of the mid-to-late seventeenth century. Even more

bitterly a war of words breaks out in the **Essay** each time Edgeworth touches on the Anglo-Irish government's part in the 1798 Rebellion and its aftermath. This indeed is a covert strand in the **Essay,** visible as a strand only by those who experienced the events described or sympathized with its main victims, the ordinary people.[8]

The **Essay** provides the first and the most elaborate of Edgeworth's imagined Irelands. Where **Castle Rackrent** was the chronicle of a family or at most a locality, what she achieves in **Irish Bulls** is clearly a much richer, more complex national community, by using differentiated voices and accents, groups of people, styles of discourse to evoke the Irish lower orders in their topographical milieus, urban and rural, and their past, as print culture or overheard voices record them. Each of the subsequent **Tales** picks up the multi-stranded format, each makes use of some aspect of ephemeral popular culture, each contests a metropolitan or Anglicized view by way of an undercover subtext, either invisible or unintelligible to non-Irish eyes. The **Tales** borrow the technique developed in the **Essay** for presenting an energized group portrait. Yet even the **Essay** has limits. It is not quite a cultural portrait of the Irish as a whole, still less of the three Kingdoms. Instead it gives an uncritical and likeable impression of the Catholic masses, offset on one side by a liberal, inclusive anthology of scholars of the Scottish Enlightenment on culture, literature, language, and society, and on another side by a less favorable impression of the English (and Anglo-Irish) as not altogether creditable lawyers, judges, and administrators.

The **Essay** sees to it that the Irish come off best, the English worst. Hibernian speakers in their workplaces or when appearing before a magistrate are as eloquent, we are being urged, as the great writers and thinkers of the ancient world or of civilized early-modern Britain and Europe, from More's *Utopia* on. The **Essay** is politically highly partisan. It is cast as in part an answer to a polemical Protestant Unionist, Richard Musgrave, author of *Memoirs of the Different Rebellions in Ireland, 1641, 1688, 1798* (1801), a work that insists that all three Irish Rebellions were incited and led by Catholic priests, fought by their flocks. Hence Edgeworth's deliberately humorous, diverse, and well-documented portrayal of an apparently peaceable Irish population. And equally, her trail of references throughout the **Essay** to an unpopular, demonized Unionist politician, John Fitzgibbon, Earl of Clare, whose repressive policies had first closed down the liberal press, then unleashed the troops and Yeomanry to bully, torture, and hang suspects in the rebel counties who came their way.

The uneven representation of the people of the Three Kingdoms has the effect of equalizing their status and losing the idea of English hegemony, since the metropolitan center remains an empty space; the State itself in London is notable as an absentee. What is not omitted is the recent debacle of the 1798 Rebellion, and its harsh suppression from Dublin by a powerful cabal of three—an intervention headed by Fitzgibbon in his capacity as chief law officer. Clare offended liberals and constitutionalists as well as radicals and activists by the orders he gave in 1797 and 1798 to arrest men of military age on suspicion and use torture in order to get them to talk. Village blacksmiths were suspect in the eyes of the authorities from the outset, as potential makers of pikes. Catholic priests were seen as the ringleaders once violence broke out: after the defeats inflicted on the rebel forces, the priests were the first to be hanged in Wexford and Wicklow without benefit of trial. At the end of chapter III, Maria Edgeworth quotes accounts in the Dublin press of Clare's provocative demeanor, his boast of carrying a pistol as he walked through the streets of Dublin, along with the cruelty of General Lake, an Englishman, who scoured the Wexford countryside in search of men to hang under Clare's orders. She keeps the scenes in readers' minds and manipulates their responses by contrasting the Lord Chancellor's behavior with the gallant war record overseas since the Rebellion of two Scottish officers, General Abercromby and his next-in-command, Colonel John Moore, in Holland and Egypt. These two soldiers were particular heroes for those opposed to the Irish Government in Ireland because they publicly criticized Lord Clare's orders and the consequent behavior of many military units, as in Sir Ralph Abercromby's remarkable statement recorded in the press on 26 February 1798 that the militia were more dangerous to their friends than their enemies.[9]

In an entirely different vein, the Edgeworths create an encyclopedic jestbook going back to Greece and Asia Minor, ancient Carthage and Phoenicia—the last two, possible Celtic homelands, though the historically-skeptical Edgeworths do not claim this. Herodotus's history of the ancient Greeks recurs, as an analogue for Irish experience in ancient times rather than as itself Irish. The talented but outnumbered Greeks, fighting their big bully and near neighbor, the Persian Empire, snatched some famous victories by brains and cheek, made the great emperor Xerxes look very silly, and managed to survive, even to flower—as the resilient Irish, confronting the English, generally do. Other Greek writers, Aristophanes, Democritus, Plato, and above all the Scythian Greek-speaking Lucian—outsider, fantasist and skeptic—all figure as founding fathers of critical High Comedy, the true intellectual ancestors of the modern Irish. An Irish bibliography on the last page names Swift, Sterne, the Sheridan family, and an impressive proportion of the best eighteenth-century comic dramatists on the London as well as the Dublin stage. Implicitly there is a fusion here, or several fusions, between High Comedy and liberalism, and between Dublin-based intellectuals and writers and the Irish people. But the method Edgeworth has adopted seems more neutral than this: partisan inferences must be made by individual readers.

As a composite picture of the Irish, the *Essay* anticipates the *Tales*, making tales in miniature, in the form of three inset stories, succinct epitomes of the strained relations of the Irish with their British neighbors. In **"Little Dominick,"** a school story for children, a pedantic Welsh schoolmaster bullies his small Irish pupil and ridicules the boy's English. **"The Hibernian Mendicant,"** a tragic ballad, has an Irishman and an English soldier quarreling over the Irishman's girl, so that between them they kill her. The longest of the three, **"The Irish Incognito,"** retells Lucian's charming fantasy, **"A True Story,"** ingeniously substituting a boxing match between the English and the Irish champions for Lucian's war in space between the Moonites and the Sunites. But Phelim O'Mooney of Cork, traveling as Sir John Bull, goes from Ireland to England, rather than in the other direction. His quest for a wealthy wife lands him in jail, and then with relief brings him home, in a manner more characteristic of modern stage comedy.

Small touches in each of these short stories illustrate Edgeworth's use of codes and riddling. Dominick in the schoolroom is being mocked for his Hibernian reversal of the normal English usage of "shall" and "will." A bigger Scottish boy in the same class hums a tune to support Dominick—"Will ye no come back again?"—a Jacobite song, as the unpleasant teacher suspiciously observes. Again, **"The Hibernian Mendicant"** could be an "aisling," a form of Irish ballad, but it is also a story of the type used by Swift in the posthumously published **"The Unfortunate Lady"** (1748). It is an allegory in which the Lady in question is Ireland, wronged and oppressed by one or both of her big neighbors.[10] Phelim's quest-romance consistently interweaves genres in the comic range with popular pursuits (the boxing match) and State politics (the sale by the French revolutionary government of Philippe Egalité's china). Philippe, Duke of Orleans, the French King's cousin but also a supporter of Revolution, is one of Edgeworth's intermittent devices for bringing to mind the United Irishman Lord Edward Fitzgerald, through his wife Pamela, who was rumored to be Philippe Egalité's illegitimate daughter.[11] Edgeworth in the *Essay on Irish Bulls* has taught herself to keep up to a dozen themes or strands separate and in play. Providing glimpses of sympathetic thinkers, writers, even heroes of 1798 by means of a name or association is one method. But the nagging theme of English injustice always somehow seems more visible than the rest, rather as Burke, evoking the crowd-scenes of the French Revolution, saw a gallows at the end of every vista.

Ennui has a prefatory section, understandably close to Robert Burton, since Edgeworth began to plan her next Irish tale late in 1803. The first five chapters explore the fashionable malaise "ennui," alternatively known in the eighteenth century as hypochondria, in the seventeenth century as melancholy, and nowadays idiomatically as depression. The title and theme is the fullest acknowledgment Edgeworth gives of her continuing interest in Burton. She hints at this by providing what looks like a preface—the first five chapters in England, which function as a full-dress historical review of the unhealthy lives of the European upper orders from the late Roman empire on. In the middle of the five chapters Edgeworth introduces the Irish nurse Ellinor O'Donoghoe, a character second only in importance in the novel to the Anglicized peer and "hero," Lord Glenthorn. Ellinor is established in a bravura passage in which Glenthorn, the tale's official narrator, inexactly recollects the tales Ellinor told him of Irish history and myth as he lay concussed on his sickbed. After this, in chapter IV Glenthorn experiences one of the trials of high life, discovery of his neglected young wife's adultery and their subsequent divorce.

For this episode, Edgeworth uses a real-life scandal still identifiable at the time of *Ennui*'s publication (1809). Glenthorn's cuckolding, his offer to forgive his wife, and later the court proceedings, are all based on the actual divorce case (1789-92) of Henry Cecil, briefly Lord Burghley, later Marquess of Exeter, who died in 1804. Edgeworth knew the story well, even very well,

since the adulterer in the case was the Reverend Edward Sneyd, her father's brother-in-law, and at the height of the proceedings in 1789 Sneyd took refuge at Edgeworthstown. The aspect of the story Edgeworth used was the aristocratic husband's apathy and enervation: the Judge, Lord Kenyon, the jury, and the press thought Cecil's inertia so odd that they suspected him of colluding with the runaways. The introduction of this recent scandal has a subtle bearing on the standing in the novel of Anglo-Irish ruling families. Henry Cecil was a direct descendant of the English statesman, William Cecil, Lord Burghley. As Elizabeth's chief counsellor, William Cecil was patron to ambitious men who came to Ireland from the 1580s as soldiers, administrators, and planters—and often passed the name of Cecil on to their descendants, some of the leading figures of the Protestant Ascendancy.

It is an important feature of *Ennui* that it works on two levels, as both a story with strong characters and scenes, and a foray into magic realism and the hidden Ireland. It is in certain ways the most closely observed of Edgeworth's Irish tales: three very different examples of naturalistic episodes on a rising scale are Glenthorn's set-piece comic encounter on the road with an irrepressible coach-driver; his surreal account, echoing real-life press coverage and local Longford stories, of the heroic deeds and horrors of 1798; and his domestic and village encounters with his loving but now alienated mother, Ellinor O'Donoghoe. If *Castle Rackrent* is a linear masculinist family chronicle, endlessly subverted by the women with whom the Rackrents ally themselves, *Ennui* virtually reverses this pattern. Its estate and neighborhood are more multi-stranded and complex, the people dangerously divided into hostile camps. Glenthorn feels oppressed by their numbers, as they wait in crowds to speak to him, and is soon further pressured by the hawkish Protestant gentry, who both command the local Yeomanry and engross the magistracy. The people have independent energies, and together they are conspiring. Nevertheless, the estate's affairs and the novel's plot turn out to be in the hands of three powerful women, all authority-figures and, under different rules of legitimacy, together standing for a hybrid Ireland.

Glenthorn is, naturally, set up as the regular metropolitan male authority-figure and aristocrat, who could be expected to have significant encounters with wild Irish Womanhood. Neither of the other women is as violent as Ellinor, when she suddenly springs at the head of Glenthorn's horse so that the animal throws him against the stone pillars of his gate. Taken up for dead, he awakes to find her in the room beside him. In a blurred state, he listens to her stories. In retrospect, he pieces together, for himself and the reader, her manipulative campaign to "Irish" him. From his sickbed he first sees her simply, uncritically, even sentimentally as his nurse and even a mother-figure. After this he becomes more exact about the stories she told during his convalescence:

> I listened or not, just as I liked; any way *she was con-tint. She was inexhaustible in her anecdotes of my ancestors all tending to the honour and glory of the family; she had also an excellent memory for all the insults, or traditions of insults, which the Glenthorns had received for many ages back, even to the times of the old kings of Ireland; long and long before they stooped to be* lorded; *when their "names, which it was a pity and a murder, and moreover a burning shame, to change, was O'Shaughnessy."*

Her own voice, her attitudes, her favorite hero, have entered their conversations:

> *She was well stored with histories of Irish and Scottish chiefs. The story of O'Neill, the Irish black-beard, I am sure I ought to remember, for Ellinor told it to me at least six times.*

(175)

Despite her care, Ellinor has had only partial success in telling Glenthorn about Shane O'Neill, in English eyes Blackbeard, the fearsome rebel and barbarian of the early years of Elizabeth's reign. Forgetting the first name, Glenthorn's narration would permit a careless reader, that is a Glenthorn, to think instead of Hugh O'Neill, Earl of Tyrone, Elizabeth's much more courtly and less barbaric opponent. He makes even less of her still more Gaelic reminiscences:

> *Then she had a large assortment of fairies and* shad-owless *witches, and* banshees; *and besides, she had legions of spirits and ghosts, and haunted castles without end, my own castle of Glenthorn not ex-cepted. . . . For many a long year, she said, it had been her nightly prayer, that she might live to see me in my own castle; and often and often she was coming over to England to tell me so, only her husband, as long as he lived, would not let her set out on what he called a fool's errand: but it pleased God to take him to himself last fair day, and then she resolved that nothing should hinder her to be with her own child against his birthday: and now, could she see me in my own Castle Glenthorn, she would die* contint—*and what a pity but I should be in it! I was only a lord, as she said, in England; but I could be all as one as a king in Ireland.*

(175)

It is a piece of writing that resists abridgement: the inner free speech of an imperceptive narrator

and sick man, a collage that dangerously assumes no harm in Ellinor's ramblings on Irish legend, Shane O'Neill, and sinister apparitions. "We resist efforts by those who . . . employ artifice to change our determinations," Glenthorn compla-cently comments in retrospect, still underestimat-ing Ellinor (175). Coming back to the passage on a second reading, one finds that Ellinor's political commitments stand out, as does (perhaps) her knowingness as a secret agent in the cause of Ireland. While the last remains a possibility, in mythological terms Ellinor has an uncanny resem-blance to the banshee (in Gaelic, *bean si*) who foretells and delivers the fall of a great house.

Edgeworth's Irish country-house life is more populated and, within the conventions of satire, more plausible than Owenson's version in *The Wild Irish Girl*. In a style appropriate to stage comedy, simplified types, rather than characters, indicate that the main occupations of the Irish provincial gentry are husband-hunting and keep-ing boredom at bay. Young Irish women compet-ing for scarce eligible men direct their jokes at Gl-enthorn and at an Englishman, Lord Craigle-thorpe, who is collecting materials for a book of travels. This figure was taken by reviewers and probably most readers for the modern traveller, John Carr, whose *Stranger in Ireland* (1805) became a subject for burlesque in England. Craiglethorpe is represented as supercilious and lazy, and it is plain that the company sees an amusing resem-blance between him and Glenthorn. Since Gl-enthorn already has one discreditable English double in Henry Cecil, matters for our hero, can, it seems, only get worse, as indeed they do. He tries to propose to Lady Geraldine, a sprightly but dowerless Irish noblewoman, and she turns him down, despite title and wealth, for not being good enough.

Craiglethorpe meanwhile is being misled by the mischievous ladies, a confrontation that older Irish readers must have recognized. In 1776 an English traveler, Richard Twiss, toured Ireland notoriously borrowing "facts" and stories from (for example) the discredited and superseded Fynes Morrison and, with the help of Morrison and others, finding Irish ladies ugly, vulgar, and drunken (355).[12] Dublin manufacturers retaliated by marketing a chamberpot that bore on the inside a caricature of Twiss's face. Edgeworth had several times reintroduced Twiss and his cleverest tormentor, a Dublin poet and satirist called Wil-liam Preston, as one of her nice pairings of ill-informed English and ingenious Irish in the *Essay on Irish Bulls.* Presumably in order to reduce Glenthorn's standing still further, Edgeworth takes him to Killarney and has him do there what the hapless Twiss seems to have done in real life: he quotes his description of the scenery from another author's guidebook (*Ennui* 250-51, n226).

Ennui's Anglo-Irish world is full of names that are historically suggestive. They provide an impressionistic chart of the layering of the Irish population by successive waves of British immigrants, from the twelfth-century barons on. Geraldine represents those barons as a member of the Norman Fitzgerald family, Earls of Kildare and Dukes of Leinster. Equally, the man she prefers to Glenthorn, Cecil Devereux, represents the next large wave of English immigrants, the Elizabethans. His first name, Cecil, evokes the Elizabethan statesman William Cecil; his surname, that of Robert Devereux, Earl of Essex, Elizabeth's Irish Commander-in-Chief; the heiress-at-law to the Glenthorn estate, Cecilia Delamere, is yet another Elizabethan arriviste. Giving us three more Cecils can be no oversight; though Cecil and Cecilia are presented as virtuous, they are heavily outnumbered in the novel's pack of Englishmen, beginning with the aristocrats Henry Cecil and Glenthorn, if indeed we can think of them as two people rather than one. It looks as if the introduction of the scandalous Henry were designed to discredit the English aristocracy/Anglo-Irish gentry as a caste, in much the same way as digging up the Twiss story throws ridicule on English travelers as arbiters of Ireland. Such a reading of the satirical strand in *Ennui* conflicts, of course, with recent critical claims that Edgeworth's Irish tales are "Whiggish," or for Whelan "effete Whiggism," and that her underlying goal is to ensure "the hegemony of that landed class" (Whelan, Foreword ix, xiv).

Once the story moves to Ireland, Glenthorn's contact with the people is made more interesting than the upper-class scenes. It turns on his ongoing, flawed relationship with Ellinor, a mother and son irremediably divided by their upbringing and cultural experiences, whose half-understandings and frustrated feelings are depicted in a series of natural domestic meetings. It is also through Ellinor and her sons that Glenthorn builds up without knowing it a bystander's picture of the 1798 Rebellion, the familiar myths and legends of the Rebellion common to Wexford, Wicklow, and Longford, where in September the rising was finally crushed by the defeat of Humbert's French and Irish army at the Battle of Ballinamuck a few miles northwest of Edgeworthstown. The stories included the hiding of arms and use of ancient secret passageways, police and Yeoman brutality, the torturing of blacksmiths to find weapons, summary justice on suspects, and the "cute" servant planning to betray his master to the terrorists outside the walls.

Looking back, we find magic has been implied throughout *Ennui*. The hero's encounters in Ireland with three powerful women, each representing a different strand of the Irish people in history, capture him and transform him. Three times he changes, and three times he changes his name. The last change of name, part of it imposed by the modern Anglicized wife, Cecilia Delamere, who owns the title-deeds of the estate and now ruined castle, is the most striking because of its ancient suggestiveness. "The O'Donoghoe" is a name from the Gaelic-Irish history of County Kerry in the remote southwest—a folk hero who was an Irish counterpart of Arthur, the "once and future King." In old age, after a happy reign, the O'Donoghoe walked out on the surface of Lake Killarney, then under the water. He had told his people that when they needed him he would return, and legend says he was occasionally seen. It can't be more clumsy plotting, it has to be after authorial deliberation that at the very end of *Ennui* a man who now thinks of himself as by descent a Gaelic Irishman, named O'Donoghoe De-la-mere, comes back to his own land and people near the southwest coast of Ireland, and takes up the task of bettering their conditions. Cecilia's surname De-la-mere puns ingeniously: over the *sea*, but also over the *mere* or lake. For the English reader, her (or her mother's) snobbish requirement that he adopt her name is yet another sign of Glenthorn's enslavement to a female principle. For the Irish reader, the symbolic return of the Gaelic hero is much the stronger reading. The Irish plotlines knot in a finale that prophesizes the future restoration of the land—to an Irish population not solely Gaelic, for it is represented here by Ellinor's hybrid sons.

Is *Ennui* the most accomplished of the Romantic-era Irish national tales? Reasons for such a view include its weaving together of contested history and story, as well as its energized use of stereotyped figures of the native Irish. The best of these are bred out of colonial paranoia—best of all, as Edgeworth herself thought, Ellinor the nurse, but also Joe Kelly, the treacherous servant and, more topically and popularly, the blacksmith, seen as a figure of folkloric significance and heroism at this time. Myth is used here with special boldness in the finale. All three later *Tales* however exhibit an element of virtually postmodern skepticism about the possibility of a stable individual identity (a stability denied by the shape-shifting, namechanging characters), and by the democratizing, universalizing recruitment of old story that distinguishes the Edgeworth tale from clumsier rivals.

The plot of *The Absentee,* non-magical and less historical, has a coded subtext turning on Edgeworth's use of the song "Gracey Nugent," written in Irish by the harper Carolan, who died in 1739. Again, it is a woman, this time the heroine, who represents Ireland, and whose story the sympathetic reader must attend to. The heroine shares her name with an Irish popular song: it is the song-title that is the key, for it brings in many other songs, in fact whole traditions of popular and patriotic Irish song. First it represents, rather loosely, the tradition of the "aisling."[13] The historical Grace Nugent must have been considered a lady, for her uncle was the Duke of Tyrconnell, James II's Lord Lieutenant in Ireland, who himself features (as a dog) in the satirical Protestant song, *Lilliburlero.* Grace's own song is not an interesting example, for it reads like any conventional lyric paying tribute to a beauty. Early in the eighteenth century these poems, routinely featuring a woman, could show her forlorn, perhaps homeless and wandering, perhaps abandoned by her lover. She appears to figure Ireland; her absent husband or lover alludes to the Stuart King or Pretender over the water or perhaps to his sympathizers and followers, the exiled Catholic gentlemen known as the "Wild Geese." Later in the eighteenth century the Jacobite associations of these songs began to fade, and the heroines acquired common village names, such as (in English) Maureen, Sheila, or Eileen (Ellinor). Such women now represented the rural Catholic masses; Grace's village god-daughter and namesake in the novel may be Edgeworth's acknowledgement of the more popular nature of Irish song.

In still earlier songs of the aisling type, the woman's virtue is called in question, much as Catholic and Stuart legitimacy was denied in seventeenth- and eighteenth-century Ireland. This story-line also enters the novel, and the virtue of Grace's Catholic mother, a Miss St. Omer, and thereby Grace's own legitimacy, are both suspected. Edgeworth had encountered Carolan's poem to Grace Nugent in Charlotte Brooke's edition, with accompanying English translation, of *Reliques of Irish Poetry* (1789). The real Grace Nugent had been a near neighbor, living at Castle Nugent four miles north of Edgeworthstown, a member of a family less or more friendly with the Edgeworths for generations (Maguire 146-59). Brooke, who became a celebrated author after her book was published, also lived before her death in 1793 near the town of Longford and corresponded with Edgeworth. Edgeworth apparently worked a special, Gaelic set of variations that lightly evokes the changing nature of the ballad heroine over time, and uses the history traced by the genre to tell a story about the trials of Grace's forlorn mother. A group of real-life literary women, and of fictitious village women, this time stand in for an Ireland where the Gaelic strand still seems powerful, even dominant.

The edition of *The Absentee* (1989) by W. J. McCormack and Kim Walker lays out the political significance of the name Nugent as referring to real-life leading Catholics, Jacobites, and "Wild Geese." Our edition suggests that the text refers to other real-life Nugents who played a political role in Irish and pro-Catholic campaigns. The first of these was an Irish-born MP in the Westminster Parliament, Earl Nugent, who proposed both religious and financial reforms on Ireland's behalf in 1778. The second, still more significant for the novel's denouement, was a minor political song-writer of the 1790s.

Towards the end, Grace does turn out to be legitimate, but, puzzlingly, she also acquires an English-sounding grandfather called Reynolds, so that her name, awkwardly, becomes Grace Nugent Reynolds or just "Miss Reynolds." Her identity has strangely begun to merge, but for three letters, with that of a real-life Irishman, George Nugent Reynolds, author of songs such as "The Catholic's Lamentation," also known as "Green were the fields where my forefathers dwellt-O," and "Kathleen O'More." These songs appeared in Dublin journals regarded as politically suspect by the government because of their links with the United Irishmen. The journals were the *Sentimental and Masonic Magazine,* Carey's *Evening Star,* and Watty Cox's *Irish Magazine,* which typically signed the songs with the poet's initials, "G-e R-s" and "G-e R-n-lds." George Nugent Reynolds, a Protestant gentleman from South Leitrim, was then a well-known contributor to general magazines supportive of the United Irishmen in the very years, 1794 to 1797, when the government was shutting other parts of this press down.

In 1799, during the tense round-up following the Rebellion, George became a notable public figure. His celebrity was enhanced thanks to the severity shown him by the unpopular John Fitzgibbon, Earl of Clare, who deprived him of his office as a Justice of the Peace on the grounds that his loyalty was in doubt. George retaliated by addressing Fitzgibbon with a defiant open letter, immediately published in Watty Cox's suspect magazine. Referring to Fitzgibbon's Catholic antecedents, Nugent Reynolds said he would have behaved more like a gentleman if he had been educated, as his father intended, in the Jesuit college at St. Omer. In times of crisis and press censorship, resistance movements relied on songs or fiction with double meanings or cryptic press items to circulate rebel messages. The use of such songs and such messages by a writer would have constituted an expression of sympathy with the Catholic side. In this particular quarrel, the author's tactic of distancing herself from the harsh policies of the Dublin Government seems unmistakable.

The finale of *The Absentee* celebrates in the novel's closing rituals the homecoming of Grace as the legitimate heiress of a remote divided Irish estate, in some sense that Lord and Lady Clonbrony and their son Lord Colambre are not. For local Irish readers, the real-life estate referred to would have been identifiable as Colambre, three miles south of Granard near the Westmeath border. But Colambre in real life was not yoked to Clonbrony, as it is in the novel. It is linked to Castle Nugent, the home of a Longford branch of the Catholic Nugent family. The real-life Clonbrony, some two miles west, was close to Kilshruly, at the end of the seventeenth century the family seat of the Catholic younger branch of the Edgeworth family, whose owner, the intriguing Robert Edgeworth, tried and for a while succeeded in unseating the Protestant senior branch of the family at Edgeworthstown.[14] In short, the historical placenames have Catholic associations, as does Grace's own name. Where a novel adopts the traditions of stage comedy, it arrives at closure in a marriage, but often at something deeper, a restitution. This is the case in *The Absentee* as in *Ennui.* Grace's homecoming has an equivalent or greater historical depth than that of Ellinor O'Donoghoe's son, for it is celebrated in a mighty bonfire that, according to the villager who describes it, could be "seen . . . from all parts of the three counties" (*Absentee* 200), a fiery echo of ancient-world sunworship.

In *Ormond* (1817), Edgeworth returns to the manner of her most theoretical construction of Ireland and most ambitiously composite book, the *Essay on Irish Bulls. Ormond*'s plot is a maze of classic quest-plots ancient and modern: Harry Ormond relives the experiences of Telemachus, wandering son of the wandering Ulysses; Tom Jones, who is also in quest of a father; Shakespeare's Prince Hal; Spenser's Red Cross Knight; and Sidney's prince Musidorus in *Arcadia.*[15] More elaborately than anywhere else, Edgeworth weaves together quests, poetic fantasies, and idealistic projects from the later Elizabethan period of about 1580 to about 1700 and locates them in the southwest and middle of Ireland, in County Longford and Munster. The novel is her most sustained and artful literary collage, a composite portrait of Irish (meaning Irish-resident) men and women over the two centuries that began with the arrival of the first Elizabethan planters. One remarkable character, the eccentric self-styled "King" Corny, incorporates the scientific and technological projects, the old and new learning, above all the social idealism, egalitarianism, and republicanism that (in addition to land-hunger and greed) sustained the century's fervor to re-make paradise on either side of the Atlantic. Edgeworth often uses fairy-tale and classical and early-modern fantasy, all long-established literary languages, but in *Ormond* she comes closer to attempting a utopia, a more philosophical and complex mode. The world the politician Sir Ulick makes for himself in provincial Ireland is a dystopia full of the quarrels and hatreds familiar enough in seventeenth-century religious wars, and revived in the post-Union Irish countryside, Edgeworth suggests, in the sectarian squabbles fought by educationalists setting up an Irish school system. The utopia to be built on the remote Black Islands that Edgeworth comes near to imagining in *Ormond* is a changing and imperfect one—a mixture of Corny's superseded paternalism with the idealism of a group of friends.

Corny is an important figure in *Ormond,* and his place in the historical allegory needs consideration. His home is an island in Lough Ree, largest of the Shannon lakes, the natural boundary between Annaly and Connaught in the west; its southern tip, where Munster begins. The Shannon system is the dominant geographical feature of central Ireland, which is Edgeworth's Ireland. The islands that dot its many lakes are often associated with the long history of Ireland as a dark-age "land of saints," and the medieval era of abbeys, churches, hermitages, and defensive towers, buildings in stone that survived only as ruins. Their name, "the Black Islands," comes however from the *Arabian Nights*: this is also a kind of Arcadia. Traditionally, utopias too are found on islands, sometimes on magical islands that appear and disappear so that they cannot be found again. The key is that Corny's home is an ideal place, where we see many ideas tried out and dreams of the future conceived. Corny, whose closest confidant is the local priest, embodies Catholic Ireland. His lifestyle and attitudes are old-fashioned and seem to belong to the early-to-mid seventeenth century, when Ireland and especially Munster was also the homeland of projectors, inventors, plantation-makers—at their most eminent for the English, Robert Boyle, later of the Royal Society, and Sir William Petty—but also many other scholars, including Ireland's early-modern Gaelic-language historians, such as Geoffrey Keating and the Anglican scholar Archbishop Ussher, who had friendly relations with Celtic scholars.

In *Ormond,* however, one Elizabethan Munster planter William Herbert (died 1593) stands for the rest; and this real-life story, sketched into the plot, is the Protestant and English modernizing counterpart of Corny's benign traditional patriarchy. William Herbert of Castleisland, near Tralee in west Munster, was in real life a man of literature and learning. He wrote a poem to Sir Philip Sidney, a treatise in Latin on Ireland, and he subscribed to the mystical Platonism of the sixteenth-century Florentine school. On the Welsh borders other gentlemen shared the same enthusiasms: William Herbert married Florence, the daughter of William Morgan of Llantarnan, Monmouthshire, a Neo-Platonist, if his daughter's first name is any indication. William Herbert has given his name to the novel's idealized landlord, Herbert Annaly; his wife Florence Herbert gives her name to Herbert Annaly's sister, whom Ormond eventually marries. In real life William Herbert quarreled with a neighbor, Sir Edward Denny of Tralee, whom Herbert accused of encouraging pirates on the coast. That episode figures in the novel, when Herbert Annaly becomes involved in a fracas with smugglers on the seashore that causes his death. In one respect, however, William Herbert is an insufficient model for Herbert Annaly. It was his son-in-law, Edward Herbert of Cherbury, Lord Castleisland in the Irish peerage, who was the ecumenical thinker, a conscientious objector to England's sectarian Civil War of the 1640s, and a man who wrote his own autobiography as a chivalric, dream-like Arcadian romance: a book that had a cult following among RLE's friends of the Lunar Society of Birmingham after its publication by Horace Walpole in 1764. In style, Herbert's *Life* is a model for RLE's own first volume of his *Memoirs,* which in 1817, as Maria wrote *Ormond,* he made her promise to complete.[16]

Corny in his youth had been the contemporary of the father of "White" and "Black" Connal; this fact confirms his place among the Gaelic Old Irish landowners of Annaly, or County Longford. It suggests he lived between the sixteenth and seventeenth centuries, when the dominant O'Farrells divided themselves into two factions, White and Yellow, one group to lead largely provincial lives, based on farming, in backward, boggy North Longford, before the line of male heirs failed them. Meanwhile the more sophisticated Yellow O'Farrells communicated with the English and French Court at both Westminster and Versailles. After her father has pressed Dora to marry White Connal, he suddenly dies. Dora throws in her lot with the soldier Black Connal, whom she accompanies to Versailles, as a Catholic gentleman's daughter in the late seventeenth century might well have done. Dora's separate adventure, a subtly unhappy story, complements the book's many male quest-romances, while its glamour puts London's attractions in the shade. It stands as a reminder that the Irish Catholic gentry had stood for civility in history in ways beyond the reach of English squires. Because Dora in Sidney's *Arcadia* was actually Pamela, the tale also offers a wry suggestion of the many historical occasions when Irish and French united against the English.

To return to the question with which I began this investigation of Edgeworth's diverse cultural materials: in what sense does Edgeworth write "national novels"? All Edgeworth's writing on Ireland, even the relatively local *Castle Rackrent, is* concerned with its nationhood. Work on the densely literary *Essay on Irish Bulls* sophisticated Edgeworth's approach, by requiring her to reflect on what a nation is when it is less than an autonomous state. To judge from the materials she includes in the *Essay* as in some way Irish (such as the High Comedy of the ancient Greeks), Edgeworth considers that a nation's group identity rests on its shared experiences, as these have been passed down in history and story over time: in sharing land, particularly a land with well-defined borders such as an island, and in sharing a language, with all that that implies of popular literature in its many genres, written and oral. Language is problematic, however, for the Irish have two languages, one of which, the Gaelic Irish tongue, is used almost entirely by the Old Irish part of the population, while the other, Hibernian English, is treated by the English as an inferior dialect. Religion, for other nations a cohesive factor, has been and is divisive in Ireland's case. Edgeworth restricts her references to religion, before *Ormond* at least, to what is for her the straightforward issue of Catholic Emancipation. Together, these Irish elements—historical, topographical, linguistic, and literary—determine the language used in Edgeworth's Irish fiction, both in narration and dialogue, and introduce an unusual variety of alternative plots, often based on fairy and folk tale, myth, and still more informal forms, such as scandal and practical jokes. Finally, the linguistic elements include secret codes and are problematic because they are exclusive and divisive. But since Edgeworth's apprenticeship as an Irish writer took place in the 1790s, swift and secret communication was essential to her inclusive uncensorious non-doctrinaire account of the Irish in time, as a complex, hybrid people.

This self-conscious, intellectual, and very detailed method of indeed constructing a people out of a large body of written materials, past and present, as well as the spoken words of contemporaries, is highly unusual, and to conventional novel-readers often strange, obscure, and politically hard to interpret. With hindsight, Edgeworth emerges as both a theorist of cultural history and natural identity, a true if unsung pioneer of the historical novel and a novelist with a powerful vision of what the nineteenth-century novel is there to do.

Notes

1. See Dunne, "A Gentleman's Estate" 96-101 and "Haunted by History" 68-91; Deane 30-40; Eagleton 161-77; and Whelan, Foreword ix-xxiv.

2. See *Leonora* (1806), Edgeworth's epistolary novel of international espionage and seduction, which features the letters of Mme de P—, a former Countess and (in a plot located in Britain and Paris during the Peace of Amiens, 1802-03) an active politician. Most of P—'s literary allusions are to old-régime and seventeenth-century writings, e.g., by Rochefoucault, Voltaire, and Sévigné. *Emilie de Coulanges*, in *Tales of Fashionable Life*, is a dialogic novella about a triangle of three French and English upper-class women: the external cultural reference-points include the Renaissance paintings the English hostess Mrs. Somers collects.

3. See also the wide intellectual range but imperfect comprehension betrayed by the Whig peer Lord Glistonbury in *Vivian* (146-47) and the dialogues between Lord Oldborough and Commissioner Falconer in *Patronage* (VI.21-26, VII.66-67).

4. Some of Edgeworth's early reviewers and readers complained that she was a critic of the aristocratic system, e.g., of nepotism and patronage in the professions (*Patronage*) and bought votes in Parliament (*Vivian*). But Bentham published a two-part anonymous letter in consecutive issues of Leigh Hunt's *Examiner* (February 1814) extolling her criticisms. In private he urged her not to retract the least point. The identity of Bentham as the author of the *Examiner* letter was established by Dinwiddy.

5. "We gained the day by this piece of honesty" (*Castle Rackrent* 34). See glossary note to text (66n).

6. Letter from Frances Beaufort [from 1798, the fourth Mrs. RLE] to her brother William Beaufort, 2 July 1797. Her predecessor, Mrs. Elizabeth (Sneyd) Edgeworth was already at work designing the vignettes (of two bulls) which eventually preceded and followed the text.

7. The full title used on publication was "An Essay on the Art of Conveying Secret and Swift Intelligence."

8. See the discussion below of the 1798 Rebellion and, for Maria's use of utopianism from the *Essay on Irish Bulls* on, much of it via Robert Burton and Sir John Davies, see Butler "Edgeworth, the United Irishmen and 'More Intelligent Treason.'"

9. See Butler and Desmarais, ed., *Essay on Irish Bulls* (85, 99, and notes 53, 54, 108, 210).

10. There are suggestive parallels to "The Hibernian Mendicant" in two anonymous stories, "Ierne" [Ireland] and "A True Story," which both appeared in a short-lived Irish satirical newspaper, *The Anti-Union* (1798-99).

11. See *Essay on Irish Bulls*, "Little Dominick" (*The Novels* I.89-95); "The Hibernian Mendicant" (*The Novels* I.112-16); "The Irish Incognito" (*The Novels* I.134-51).

12. See Leerssen 355.

13. My discussion of the aisling is indebted to Eoin.

14. For the use made of Robert Edgeworth in *Castle Rackrent*, see *The Black Book of Edgeworthstown*.

15. See also, Fénelon, Archbishop of Cambrai, *Télémaque* (1699), classic work of a moralist and educator widely admired for his enlightened spiritual Catholicism; Fielding, *Tom Jones* (1748-49); *Henry IV*, Pts I and II; *The Faerie Queene*, Bk I. In *Arcadia* (1598) prince Musidorus glimpses the king's daughter Pamela, falls in love with her, and dresses as a shepherd, Dorus, in order to woo her—a model for Ormond's private courtship of "King" Corny's daughter Dora, whose name confirms the allusion to Sidney. Pamela was the name of Lord Edward Fitzgerald's wife.

16. Edward Herbert's *Autobiography* (in later editions, *Life*) was discovered in ms by one of his descendants, and first published by Horace Walpole (Strawberry Hill, 1764) with a frontispiece of Isaac Oliver's portrait (1616) of Herbert, dressed in black, covered by a shield, and lying by a woodland stream. The shield bears the inscription "Magia Naturalis"; behind Herbert is a caparisoned knight's horse, evidence of a battle. The scene depicts one of many quarrels or duels (allegorized as knightly encounters) in Herbert's then unpublished *Autobiography*. Herbert's most contentious works, those relating to religion, were not available in English, though on the Continent the Latin *De Veritate* (1624) was soon translated into French. Charles Blount's *Religione Laici* (1683) is substantially taken from Herbert. Herbert's version (1663), *The Religion of the Gentiles,* was translated into English by W. Lewis (1705). The Lunar Society's interests in alchemy and the scientific thought of the Renaissance are captured by the painter, Joseph Wright of Derby, who uses Oliver's portrait of Herbert, without attribution or explanation, as the model for his painting (1780) of the friend of Darwin and Wedgwood and English admirer and patron of Rousseau, Sir Brooke Boothby.

Works Cited

Beaufort, Frances. Letter to William Beaufort. 2 July 1797. Ms. 13176. Edgeworth Letters, to 1817. National Library of Ireland, Dublin.

Bentham, Jeremy. "A Pupil of Miss Edgeworth's." *Examiner* 20 February 1814: 124-26; 27 February 1814: 140-41.

Burton, Robert. *The Anatomy of Melancholy.* Oxford: John Lichfield and James Short, for Henry Cripps, 1621.

Butler, Harriet Jessie [Edgeworth] and Harold Edgeworth Butler, ed. *The Black Book of Edgeworthstown and other Edgeworth Memories,* 1585-1817. London: Faber & Gwyer, 1927. 46-52.

Butler, Marilyn. "Edgeworth, the United Irishmen and 'More Intelligent Treason.'" Ed. Chris Fauske and Heidi Kaufman. *An Uncomfortable Authority: Maria Edgeworth and Her Contexts.* Newark: U of Delaware P, 2003.

Carr, John. *Stranger in Ireland: or, A tour in the southern and western parts of that country in 1805.* Shannon: Irish UP, 1806.

Curran, John Philpot. *Collected Speeches, with a new Memoir of his Life.* Dublin. 1815.

Deane, Seamus. *Strange Country: Modernity and Nationhood in Irish Writing Since 1790.* Oxford: Clarendon, 1997. 30-40.

Dinwiddy, J. R. "Jeremy Bentham as a Pupil of Miss Edgeworth's." *Notes and Queries* 29 (June 1982): 208-10.

Dunne, Tom. "'A Gentleman's Estate should be a moral school': Edgeworthstown in Fact and Fiction, 1760-1840." Ed. Gillespie and Moran. 95-121.

———. "Haunted by History: Irish Romantic Writing, 1800-1850." Ed. Roy Porter and Mikulás Teich. *Romanticism in a National Context.* Cambridge: Cambridge UP, 1988. 68-91.

Eagleton, Terry. *Heathcliff and the Great Hunger: Studies in Irish Culture.* London: Verso, 1997. 161-77.

Edgeworth, Maria. *The Novels and Selected Works of Maria Edgeworth.* 12 vols. General Ed. Marilyn Butler, with Mitzi Myers. London: Pickering & Chatto, 1999.

———. *The Absentee.* Vol. V. Ed. Heidi Van de Veire and Kim Walker.

———. *Castle Rackrent.* Vol. I. Ed. Tim McLoughlin and Marilyn Butler.

———. *Emilie de Coulanges.* Vol. V. Ed. Heidi Van de Veire and Kim Walker.

———. *Ennui.* Vol. I. Ed. Tim McLoughlin and Marilyn Butler.

———. *Irish Bulls.* Vol. I. Ed. Marilyn Butler and Jane Desmarais.

———. *Leonora.* Vol. III. Ed. Marilyn Butler and Susan Manly.

———. *Ormond.* Vol. VIII. Ed. Claire Connolly.

———. *Patronage.* Vols. VI-VII. Ed. Connor Carville.

———. *Vivian.* Vol. IV. Ed. Claire Connolly.

Edgeworth, Richard. *The Black Book of Edgeworthstown.* Ms. National Library of Ireland, Dublin.

Edgeworth, Richard Lovell. "An Essay on the Art of Conveying Secret and Swift Intelligence." *Transactions of the Royal Irish Academy* VI (1797): 95-139. Rpt. in *Nicholson's Journal* II (1798-99).

Eoin, Máirín nic. "Secrets and Disguises? Caitlín Ní Uallacháin and other female personages in eighteenth-century Irish political poetry." *Eighteenth-Century Ireland* XI (1996): 7-45.

Ferris, Ina. "Narrating Cultural Encounter: Lady Morgan and the Irish National Tale." *Nineteenth-Century Literature* 51 (1996): 287-303.

Flanagan, Thomas. *The Irish Novelists, 1800-1850.* New York: Columbia UP, 1959. 69-79.

Gillespie, Raymond. "A Question of Survival: The O'Farrells and Longford in the Seventeenth Century." Ed. Gillespie and Moran. 13-29.

Gillespie, Raymond and Gerard Moran, ed. *Longford: Essays in County History.* Dublin: Lilliput, 1991.

"Ierne." *The Anti-Union* 1 Jan. 1799: 9-12.

Leerssen, Joep. *Mere Irish and Fíor-Ghael: Studies in the Idea of Irish Nationality, its Development, and Literary Expression Prior to the Nineteenth Century.* 2nd ed. Cork: Cork UP, 1996.

Maguire, W. A. "Castle Nugent and *Castle Rackrent*; fact and fiction in Maria Edgeworth." *Eighteenth-Century Ireland* XI (1996): 146-59.

McCormack, W. J. "The Tedium of History: an approach to Maria Edgeworth's *Patronage* (1814)." *Ideology and the Historians.* Ed. Ciaran Brady. Dublin: Lilliput P, 1991. 77-98.

Musgrave, Robert. *Memoirs of the Different Rebellions in Ireland, From the Arrival of the English: Also, a particular Detail of that Which Broke Out the 23d of May, 1798; with the History of the Conspiracy which Preceded It.* 1801.

Myers, Mitzi. "Goring John Bull: Maria Edgeworth's Hibernian High Jinks versus the Imperialist Imaginary." *Cutting Edges: Postmodern Critical Essays on Eighteenth-Century Satire.* Ed. James E. Gill. Knoxville: U of Tennessee P, 1995. 367-94.

Obituary for Lady Cathcart. *Gentleman's Magazine* August 1789: 766-67.

Swift, Jonathan. Letter to Lord Bathurst. Oct. 1730. Vol 3. *The Correspondence of Jonathan Swift.* Ed. Harold Williams. Oxford: Clarendon, 1963. 409-412.

"A True Story." *The Anti-Union* 17 Jan. 1799: 37-40.

Trumpener, Katie. *Bardic Nationalism: The Romantic Novel and the British Empire.* Princeton: Princeton UP, 1997.

Twiss, Richard. *A Tour in Ireland in 1775.* London: n.p., 1776.

Whelan, Kevin. Foreword. "Writing Ireland, Reading England." *The Wild Irish Girl: A National Tale* by Sydney Owenson, Lady Morgan. Ed. Claire Connolly and Stephen Copley. London: Pickering & Chatto, 2000. ix-xxiv.

———. *The Tree of Liberty: Radicalism, Catholicism, and the Construction of Irish Identity 1760-1830.* Cork: Cork UP, 1996.

Castle Rackrent

COLIN GRAHAM (ESSAY DATE SPRING 1996)

SOURCE: Graham, Colin. "History, Gender and the Colonial Moment: *Castle Rackrent.*" *Irish Studies Review,* no. 14 (spring 1996): 21-24.

In the following essay, Graham examines Edgeworth's treatment of the concept of union—between male and female and between England and Ireland—in Castle Rackrent.

For Irish literary and cultural criticism, *Castle Rackrent* (1800) is placed almost irresistibly at the moment of the Act of Union; it sets a narrative which faces back to a pre-Union 'chaos' against an authorising 'Preface' which looks with anticipation to the new post-Union century. I want to examine how the squeezed historical moment of Union, balanced precariously on the thinnest definition of *fins de siècle* and the gender issues inherent in the text, can be made vital to uncovering a critique of the legislative merging of Britain and Ireland. Edgeworth's text, I will suggest, expresses its scepticism about the phenomenon of Union through an analogous train of thought which uses a gendered notion of union. And Union in *Castle Rackrent* is a concept pressurised by its existence *between* male and female, Irish and English, eighteenth and nineteenth centuries. Union thus becomes both a marital and political act in *Castle Rackrent,* and each union is viewed as a relationship of power in which dominance and counter-dominance co-exist, so that *Castle Rackrent* can eventually be read as a text which supports the notion that dominant discursive formations can be undercut without their knowledge.

Using post-colonial criticism may be contentious in a Irish cultural setting (as Gerry Smyth has recently commented, its status is 'uncertain and its relationship with indigenous initiatives troubled'),[1] and certainly it needs to be adapted and exploited in the specific context of Ireland. This, and the theoretical relationship between gender and post-colonialism, constitute an infinitely wider issue than can be dealt with here, and I want to assume a degree of applicability in looking at how the ideas of Homi Bhabha can be used to untangle some of the possibilities inherent in Edgeworth's text.

In his 'Introduction' to *The Location of Culture* Bhabha says:

Beginnings and endings may be the sustaining myths of the middle years; but in the *fins de siècle,* we find ourselves in the moment of transit where space and time cross to produce complex figures of difference and identity, past and present, inside and outside, inclusion and exclusion.[2]

Castle Rackrent can be usefully set in the context of these comments on the *fins de siècle,* not because it can be made a paradigmatic text in Bhabha's critique but because it reveals a conflict in terms which echo Bhabha's polarities of beginnings, endings and myths against difference and identity. *Castle Rackrent* can be read as a text which defines its historical moment in terms of cultural politics and gender through an examination of the competing versions of a time that is both an ending and a beginning.

In order to uncover the complexities of gender and history at play in *Castle Rackrent* I want to use Bhabha's essay 'Sly Civility' as a means to understanding his notions of the doubleness of colonial/official discourses and how alternative, ironising forms can be inserted into the official;[3] my aim is to turn these onto how *Castle Rackrent* addresses gender and history at the same moment.

Bhabha's essay has two functions. First, he attempts to establish what he calls the 'ambivalence at the very origins of colonial authority'.[4] In the broadest terms this could be seen as the gap between dominance and liberality in Western thought; the dichotomies between notions of the civilising mission of empire (and all the ideologies and narratives of domination which this carries) and the trappings of freedom, individuality and humanism which are basic to Western thought and exist in tandem with dominance in an Imperial context. Bhabha explores this 'space' in the predominant discourse in many ways, but perhaps his best example comes in his use of that arch utterer of imperial truths, Thomas Babington Macaulay. Bhabha quotes Macaulay's essay on Warren Hastings in which he says that Hastings' 'instructions, being interpreted, mean simply, "Be the father and the oppressor of the people'; be just and unjust, moderate and rapacious".'[5] Of this piece of colonial advice, Bhabha says:

What is articulated in the doubleness of colonial discourse is not simply the violence of one powerful nation writing out the history of another. 'Be the father and the oppressor . . . just and unjust' is a mode of contradictory utterance that ambivalently reinscribes, across differential power relations, both coloniser and colonised. For it reveals an agnostic uncertainty contained in the incompatibility of empire and nation; it puts on trial the very discourse of civility within which representative government claims its liberty and empire its ethics.[6]

The 'agnostic uncertainty' Bhabha describes in colonial discourse, where its self-contradictions cannot close on each other, constitutes the space into which a counter-discourse can press its resistance; it is notable how Bhabha's configuration of this resistant space parallels the terms he uses to describe the *fins de siècle*; the complex against the simple, the uncertain against the solid. Having established this space, Bhabha moves on to his second major purpose, to identify the means by which 'interpretation and misappropriation' can enter the space. He envisages this counter-discourse in the terms described by the title of his essay—'Sly Civility'; a phrase taken from Archdeacon Potts's writing in 1818 about Indian natives. Potts says:

> If you urge them [Indian natives] with their gross and unworthy misconceptions of the nature and the will of God, or the monstrous follies of their theology, they will turn it off with a sly civility perhaps, or with a popular and careless proverb. You may be told that 'heaven is wide place, and has a thousand gates'; and that their religion is one by which they hope to enter.[7]

Bhabha suggests that sly civility, a resistance which can never quite be construed entirely as resistance or acquiescence, deepens a crisis of paranoia in colonial discourse and widens the space in its doubleness. The importance of Bhabha's description of this psycho-political split is that it breaks the configuration of colonial interaction originally set up by Edward Said's notion of Orientalism in which the dominant West is entirely dominant as a discourse. Textuality in the colonial context changes from the monolithic and complacent to being complex and unsettled (while still reflecting dominance). For my purposes the idea of sly civility can usefully build a notion of textuality in which texts can be inscribed with both dominant *and* counter-discourses; in which colonial textuality can be self-parodying of its own dominance through the unwitting inclusion of sly civilities. Perhaps the liminal position of Ireland in the colonial encounter (on the threshold of what might be called entire colonisation, but complicated by geography and blurred race issues) is central to producing texts which are not fixed in their cultural and discursive positions. Added to this wider cultural context in the case of *Castle Rackrent* is the historically liminal position it occupies on the verge of the century and of a newly legislated polity.

Sly civility describes with some degree of accuracy the textual tactics at play in *Castle Rackrent,* and these tactics insist in this case on a paralleled linkage between a coloniser-colonised relationship and the gender relationships of marriage. The crucial factor in aligning colonial and gender relations in Edgeworth is the very notion of Union—as political event and as social marriage; as proffered beginnings placed (inappropriately) in a time of disorientation. Marriages are central to the narratives of *Castle Rackrent,* and they are the points of which Edgeworth most obviously aligns cultural and sexual politics. But for the beginnings of Edgeworth's contemplation of sly civility in union/Union we can look back to her '**Essay on Self-Justificiation**' (1785). In this deeply ironic and shifting text she describes the means by which women can subvert, counter, even control dominant male discourses without the man's knowledge:

> Nothing provokes an irascible man, interested in debate, and possessed of an opinion of his own eloquence, so much as to see the attention of his hearers go from him: you will then, when he flatters himself that he has just fixed your eye with his very best argument, suddenly grow absent.[8]

The tactics described here are those of the provoking frustration which Bhabha sees colonists worrying over in India. The authority of a discourse is undermined by the deliberate exploitation of the apparent incapacities of those subjected to it: the 'feminine' inability to concentrate; the native's inability to discourse 'rationally' on religion. Yet these are the very incapacities which justify the initial dominance. On either side of this paradox is the doubleness Bhabha describes. Edgeworth's '**Essay**' instils a gendered, subaltern consciousness which exists in the same social context as its dominant, and which may even exist beside but without the knowledge of that which it undermines. It is a textual quality derived from this sly civility of self-justification which is embedded in *Castle Rackrent,* and which makes it such a complex text in historical, cultural and gender terms.

The possibilities of this type of reading of *Castle Rackrent* are immense, but I want to suggest two examples of how the text can benefit from a Bhabha-derived critique of its particular positioning of history and gender at the moment of Union. Both examples illustrate the possibilities for reading which Bhabha's ideas offer, yet neither allows his theory to fit exactly or complacently as an epistemological framework for the text. This, in turn, reiterates the notion implicit in Bhabha's essays that colonial discourse and its countering discourses co-exist in unpredictable and continually ironic ways; a cultural condition he sees replicated to some degree by the historical moment of the *fins de siècle*.

Figuring the Act of Union as a marriage aligns gender questionably but temptingly alongside politico-cultural relations and allows the component discourses of the text to clash in variant ways. The two examples I am going to use suggest that gender can exist on either the 'official' or 'unofficial' side of colonial discourse; taken together they constitute a sceptical and radical examination of the potential of the political and gender Unions which circulate in **Castle Rackrent.** Marilyn Butler reminds us that the 'Preface' to **Castle Rackrent** is, most likely, a work of collaboration between Maria Edgeworth and Richard Lovell Edgeworth.⁹ Given this knowledge, it might be tempting to view the work as the kind of dialogue of gendered sly civility which Bhabha transcribes in colonial terms. This need not necessarily involve dissecting the language or authorship of the text in gender terms. As the 'Preface' says, 'there is much uncertainty even in the best authenticated ancient and modern histories' (p. 61), and the 'Preface' itself replicates this textual ambiguity about authenticity, authority and written history. It ends with the hope and projected potential of the Act of Union: 'When Ireland loses her identity by an union with Great Britain, she will look back with a smile of good-humoured complacency on the Sir Kits and Sir Condys of her former existence' (p. 63). The teleology of assimilation and loss of identity here are already undermined by the **'Essay on Self-Justification'**, which has contorted the notion of the possibility of a post-union 'good-humoured smile'. At the very least the **'Essay'** implies that the husband can never be certain of the intention of what appears as complacency and compliance. The loss of identity is thus, according the Essay, available only to the most superficial understandings of union/Union; and against the certainty of beginnings are set the complex figures of misunderstood interactions.

From here we can see how the Preface configures any manner of unofficial discourse it might include—and this leads us inevitably to its discussion of Thady's voice. In a text which assumes an *ignorant* English reader (p. 63) it seems vital to know if the 'Irishness' of the text is understood as a counterpart or a counter to 'Englishness'. The 'editor' of the Preface says that she/he:

> had it once in contemplation to translate the language of Thady into plain English; but Thady's idiom is incapable of translation, and besides, the authenticity of his story would have been more exposed to doubt if it were not told in his own characteristic manner.
>
> (p. 63)

The grammatical construction suggests an elision of the knowledge of sly civility: by not translating Thady's idiom its existence as something which may cast doubt on the 'complacent' loss of 'Irish' identity after Union is never, as the Preface says, 'exposed to doubt'. Indeed, it may be this which makes Thady untranslatable; not because he is insurgent (as an ideological or representative character he is certainly not), but because his otherness to 'plain English' is a reminder of the difficulty of union, and because this notion of misunderstood idiom in Union is tied, in gender and political terms, to the polite insurgency described by Edgeworth's **'Essay on Self-Justification'**.

The Preface, at least partly as a double-authored text, may then already signal the role of gender in simultaneously covering and exploiting the spaces opened by sly civility. The Union is understood in its ideal terms, but this is undercut by the notion of Thady's language as untranslatable. How the process of loss of identity is constituted (and it is significantly 'her identity' that needs to be lost) is unexplained.

Given these enclosing presumptions about the text, through Bhabha's writings, Edgeworth's **'Essay'** and the Edgeworths' 'Preface', the text can effectively be opened and examined in many ways. One of the most obvious is through the metaphor and narrative device of marriage which closes the Preface as a projected mode of hope. Yet the text itself delineates a succession of failing marriages and unions. This is not to insist on a continual parallel between Ireland and femininity in Union; rather, the work uses a gender perspective on the difficulties, perhaps impossibilities of union. Sir Condy and Mrs Jane, for example, come to represent a marriage which the woman would never have entered into with a fuller knowledge:

> my lady couldn't abide the smell of the whiskey punch. 'My dear', says [Condy], 'you liked it well enough before we were married, and why not now?' 'My dear', said she, 'I never smelt it, or I assure you I should never have prevailed upon myself to marry you.' 'My dear, I am sorry you did

not smell it, but we can't help that now', returned my master, without putting himself in a passion, or going out of his way, but just fair and easy helped himself to another glass, and drank it off to her health.

(pp. 91-2)

If it can be argued that this is merely narrativity, a 'novelistic' marriage without resonances through gender into politics, the footnote which accompanies the incarceration of Sir Kit's Jewish wife goes further in pushing the political into gender spheres. The 'editor' tells the story of a Colonel McGuire's wife who was imprisoned by her husband for over twenty years. The footnote ends:

> These circumstances may appear strange to the English reader; but there is no danger in the present times, that any individual should exercise such tyranny as Colonel McGuire's with impunity, the power now being all in the hands of government, and there being no possibility of obtaining from parliament an act of indemnity for any cruelties.

(p. 79)

Such a reassurance (which, like much of the text, is addressed with some irony to the English reader) rests, of course, on the authority of an Act of Parliament. Apart from a potentially deliberate and joking ambiguity about which Parliament is referred to, the authority which the editorial voice invests in this legislation echoes that hopeful note in the Preface about the effects of the Act of Union. The same undermining process, an ironic interjection into the discourse of safety in legislation, begs the obvious question of whether Sir Kit's behaviour would have been different after political Union and parliamentary legislation. Indeed, it would be possible to argue that Sir Kit's treatment of his wife is not a pre-Union but a post-union/Union phenomenon, which comes about as much through the frictions of cultural as through gender fusions. Kit's wife's Jewishness is continually emphasised by Thady's account, functioning mainly as a definition of her non-Irishness. When she calls a turf stack 'a pile of black bricks', describes a bog as 'a very ugly prospect', and laughs 'like one out of their right mind', and hears the place name Allyballycarricko'shaughlin, Sir Kit '[stands] by whistling all the while'. As Thady says: 'I verily believe she laid the corner stone of all her future misfortunes at that very instant; but I said no more, only looked at Sir Kit' (pp. 77-8).

Gender, cultural nationality and the doubly squeezed history represented by the Act meet at this moment in the text, pressuring the notion of Union as benign change, implying dissent beyond the beginning of assimilation, allowing a space for the insertion of what remains outside the teleology and remit of the dominant. In *Castle Rackrent* the cultural politics of metaphoric marriages becomes laden with this possibility of sly civility. The text pushes towards the notion of marriage as the appropriate construction for understanding the union/Union, yet ironises its own expressed belief in the ability of union to facilitate a loss of identity tantamount to a discursive monologism. Its notion of the untranslatable idiom (necessary for the treasured notion of 'authenticity') can be used to place its delineation of the cracks in colonial, dominant discourses in the context of Bhabha's idea of the double articulation of colonialism and sly civility. And Edgeworth's text expresses something implied but unexplored in Bhabha's essay—that the double-facedness of the coloniser may be seen from outside the coloniser's discourse, but, if seen, it cannot be articulated; it can only be mimicked, parodied in sly civility. A knowledge of the space between the double-face of colonialism can only be voiced where the coloniser is deaf to it. However small this space may be, any insertion into it begins the process of undermining and exploding the authority of colonialism. To borrow the metaphor Edgeworth uses in advising a woman on how to gain the sympathy of bystanders when confronted by her irascible husband, 'the simple scratching of a pick-axe, properly applied to certain veins in a mine, will cause the most dreadful explosions'.[10] Both the Act of Union, and its place at the turn of the century, restate the need for this space to be understood and utilised. The available interpretative terrain may be under pressure when caught between genders, centuries and cultures, but through its *fins de siècle* positioning it becomes all the more capable of rendering the complexities of cultural interaction. *Castle Rackrent* pressures the notion and the moment of Union through a gendered understanding of cultural interaction; against the colonial discourse which implies a loss of identity it pits an awareness of dissent which is dangerous for its untranslatable, slyly civil qualities. *Castle Rackrent* mobilises 'a disturbance of direction'[11] against sustaining myths, making the most of the spaces in the fusions of history undertaken by the Act of Union and the very notion of the *fins de siècle*.

Notes

1. G. Smith, 'The Past, the Post and the Utterly changed: Intellectual Responsibility and Irish Cultural Criticism', *Irish Studies Review* no. 10 (1995), p. 27.

2. H. K. Bhabha, 'Introduction: The Location of Culture', *The Location of Culture* (Routledge, 1994), p. 1.

3. H. K. Bhabha, 'Sly Civility', *The Location of Culture*, pp. 93-101.

4. Bhabha, 'Sly Civility', p. 95.

5. Bhabha, 'Sly Civility', p. 95.

6. Bhabha, 'Sly Civility', pp. 95-6.

7. Quoted in Bhabha, 'Sly Civility', p. 99.

8. M. Edgeworth, 'An Essay on the Noble Science of Self-Justification', *Letters for Literary Ladies*, ed. Claire Connolly (Everyman, 1994), p. 70.

9. M Edgeworth, *'Castle Rackrent' and 'Ennui'* (Penguin, 1992), p. 347. All further references to this text are cited in parentheses.

10. Edgeworth, 'Essay on Self-Justification', p. 70.

11. Bhabha, 'Introduction: The Location of Culture', p. 1.

Belinda

NICHOLAS MASON (ESSAY DATE 2001)

SOURCE: Mason, Nicholas. "Class, Gender, and Domesticity in Maria Edgeworth's *Belinda*." In *The Eighteenth-Century Novel*, Vol. 1, edited by Susan Spencer, pp. 271-85. New York: AMS Press, 2001.

In the following excerpt, Mason examines Edgeworth's second novel as a work that encourages both males and females of the aristocracy and the middle class to accept the responsibilities associated with their social standing.

In 1847 the publishers Simpkin and Marshall contacted Maria Edgeworth, requesting that she prepare an autobiographical preface for a new edition they were planning of her novels. At the time, Edgeworth was seventy-nine years old and still widely considered one of England's greatest novelists. Comfortable in her status among readers, Edgeworth saw no need for further self-promotion through such a preface and decided to decline the publishers' request. In her *Memoirs,* she explained, "As a woman, my life, wholly domestic, cannot afford anything interesting to the public. . . . I have no story to tell."[1]

For those familiar with Edgeworth's fiction, this equation of domesticity with dullness should be somewhat surprising, since on several occasions her form of choice was the *domestic* novel. In fact, one of the most commonly discussed aspects of Edgeworth's work in recent criticism has been its domestic focus. This is particularly true of her second novel, *Belinda* (1801), a text which, after well over a century of neglect, has once again begun to attract the attention of readers and critics. Much of the commentary on *Belinda* from the past two decades has focused on the novel's advocacy of a domestic lifestyle for women. Beth Kowaleski-Wallace, for instance, has claimed that this novel is complicit in a "new-style patriarchy" that attempts to make domestic life seem the natural choice for women. Anne Mellor has called *Belinda* a "textbook case of the new feminine Romantic ideology" insofar as it suggests that the ideal domestic woman combines the positive traits of both genders. And Colin B. Atkinson and Jo Atkinson have discussed how the character Harriet Freke exemplifies Edgeworth's beliefs that women should worry more about properly fulfilling their duties at home and less about gaining new rights.[2]

As I hope to make clear in the pages to follow, I appreciate much of what these scholars have done to illuminate the central role domesticity plays in *Belinda.* Nevertheless, my goal in this essay is to move beyond the somewhat narrow definition of domesticity brought to *Belinda* in previous essays and to examine the domestic issues in the novel in terms of a broader definition that includes not only gender, but social class as well. In essence, my argument holds that more than a system for proper female behavior, the domesticity Edgeworth advocates is a summons for all members of polite society, whether female or male, to live up to their gender- and class-based responsibilities.

I

It is only fitting that in the midst of Edgeworth's collaborations with her father to reform educational practices in Britain she should write a novel setting out to reform the domestic conduct of her readers. That Edgeworth has didactic aims in *Belinda* is made clear in the novel's prefatory pages, where she casts what is to follow as a "Moral Tale" rather than a novel, with all of that genre's lurid connotations. This "moral tale" is the story of Belinda Portman and the various characters she encounters upon going up to London to be the protégée of the famed wit Lady Delacour. At the outset of the novel, Belinda supposes that having Lady Delacour as a guide to polite culture will help her acquire the manners and connections needed to make a desirable match. Soon into the story, however, Belinda becomes disillusioned after discovering the profligacy and social irresponsibility that characterize the lives of Lady Delacour and her circle. Belinda's dissatisfaction with high society only deepens when Lady Delacour recounts to her the life of sin and degradation she has led, a lifestyle that is now taking its toll through a serious wound to her breast she received during her escapades. While Belinda laments the Lady's past behavior, she takes hope that Lady Delacour has reached such depths that she may be ripe for a reformation. After a long struggle to help restore Lady Delacour's physical and moral well-being, Belinda at last leads her guardian to accept her responsibilities as a wife, a mother, and an aristocrat. In the end, Lady Delacour demonstrates her new selflessness by orchestrating Belinda's union with Clarence Hervey, another aristocratic character who has come to understand his social obligations during the course of the novel.

From this brief synopsis, readers familiar with Nancy Armstrong's landmark study of the novel, *Desire and Domestic Fiction,* might recognize how Edgeworth's plot in many ways conforms to the norms for domestic novels of the late eighteenth and early nineteenth centuries. According to Armstrong, the form of fiction which "rose" in the mid-eighteenth century traces its roots to the popular conduct book tradition. So effective was the novel at assimilating the social function of the conduct book, in fact, that from *Pamela* forward the novel became firmly established as the genre with the greatest power to influence society's perceptions of how women should act. In Armstrong's estimation, "The rise of the novel hinged upon a struggle to say what made a woman desirable."[3] Rather than inscribing different codes of behavior for different ranks, as had been done in conduct books of previous centuries, the eighteenth-century novel set out to win all levels of society over to middle-class ideals of domesticity. One of the chief ways this was carried out was through a direct attack on aristocratic manners. The nobleman came to be seen as a spendthrift who, like Richardson's Mr. B, considered women, particularly those of the lower classes, to be his sexual chattel. Even worse in the eyes of writers of conduct books and novels, however, was the aristocratic woman, who had abandoned her motherly duties for a life of self-display at card tables and dancing halls. So powerful was this novelistic juxtaposition of the corrupt aristocratic woman and the loving middle-class mother that by the early nineteenth century the domestic woman had become the prototype for women of all classes. Armstrong concludes that, in very real ways, eighteenth-century novelists paved the way for the cult of domesticity, which, in turn, paved the way for the ascendancy of the middle class.

Although much of what Armstrong states concerning the domestic novel proves useful in studying **Belinda,** it is her notion of the novel both enacting and facilitating domesticity's conquest over aristocratic corruption that I would like to take up here. As might be expected in an early nineteenth-century novel of manners, most of the characters in **Belinda** belong to the privileged orders of society. Lady Delacour, for instance, has both wealth and station, having inherited over 100,000 pounds from her father and acquired the rank of viscountess through marriage. Her friend and confidante, Clarence Hervey, comes from a very affluent and highly respected family that has provided him with an Oxford education, a large fortune, a seat in Parliament, and connections in the governments of both the church and the state. Other characters coming from the privileged ranks include the estate-holding Percival family, the baronet Sir Philip Baddely, and the libertine Harriet Freke. Of the novel's major characters, in fact, only Belinda and Dr. X lack rank and wealth, although both come from respectable enough backgrounds to grant them admission to polite society.

One need not read far to see how poorly these upper-class characters are doing in living up to their pedigrees. Most of the minor aristocratic characters are fairly harsh caricatures of England's decadent elite. Sir Philip Baddely, for instance, goes through life depending wholly upon his rank and fortune to gain him access to any polite society, as he otherwise lacks every grace and talent of the proper English gentleman. He drinks heavily, peppers his sentences with "damme's," and, when pressed, can contribute nothing more to polite conversation than questions such as "Don't you think the candles want snuffing famously?" (139).[4] Among the female characters of the privileged classes, Harriet Freke is set up to be the most contemptible, as with her zeal for hunting, cross-dressing, and Wollstonecraftian feminism, she violates all guidelines for proper feminine behavior.[5] Several other minor characters, ranging from the swindling Mrs. Luttridge to the rakish Colonel Lawless to the gambling Mr. Vincent, further extend Edgeworth's catalog of upper-class vices.

While the novel's two major aristocratic characters, Lady Delacour and Clarence Hervey, eventually come around to a sense of their domestic responsibilities, in the early stages of the narrative they, too, represent all that is wrong with England's nobility. Of the pair, Lady Delacour is cast as the more degenerate, as her longer life has provided her greater exposure to the corrupting influences of high society. In relating her history to Belinda, she discloses such misdeeds as squandering her entire fortune, bringing about the death of an admirer in a duel, using her wealth to sway an election, and ruining an innocent gardener in an attempt to show up her rival, Mrs. Luttridge.[6] Even more damning than these public sins of commission, however, are her domestic sins of omission. As a wife, she has alienated her in-laws and driven her husband to gaming and drink; as a mother, her neglect has led to her first child being stillborn, her second child dying as an infant from inadequate nursing, and her third child being sent away to be raised by a wet-nurse and the staff of a boarding school. So overwhelming is the cumulative effect of Lady Delacour's offenses that when she has finished confessing her sordid history, Belinda cannot help but "tremble at the idea of being under the guidance of one, who was so little able to conduct herself" (61).

Lady Delacour, in essence, is the type of decadent aristocratic woman so regularly warned against in the conduct books and domestic fiction of this era. If, as Armstrong suggests, one of the primary social functions of the late eighteenth- and early nineteenth-century novel was to clear the way for middle-class domesticity by undermining the prestige of the aristocracy, the character of Lady Delacour would seem to be functioning very much as a weapon in this campaign. Several critics, most notably Kowaleski-Wallace, Mellor, and Greenfield, have written insightfully about the ideological function of the Lady Delacour character, with the critical consensus being that, in Kowaleski-Wallace's words, "Lady Delacour's narrative records the process of internalizing a specific image of womanhood."[7] While I certainly agree that Lady Delacour's story is grounded in gendered discourse, I believe we need to be careful to read this character's narrative in terms of her position not only as a woman, but as an *aristocratic* woman. In other words, the tale of Lady Delacour's fall and redemption serves as an excellent example of the extent to which class and gender expectations were linked together in the domestic ideal of the late eighteenth and early nineteenth centuries.

That Lady Delacour's depravity in the first half of the novel is marked by a simultaneous transgression of gender- and class-based expectations is best evidenced in one of the novel's more intriguing episodes, the "dueling-and-ducking" scene of chapter IV. After years of heated competition for supremacy in the cut-throat circles of London's high society, Lady Delacour and Mrs. Luttridge are provoked by a fashionable pamphlet "upon the Propriety and Necessity of Female Duelling" to clothe themselves in men's attire and engage in the traditionally masculine act of dueling. When all the necessary preparations have been made, however, both ladies lose their nerve and agree to fire their pistols into the air and depart in peace. According to Lady Delacour's account,

> I had scarcely discharged my pistol, when we heard a loud shout on the other side of the barn, and a crowd of town's people, country people, and hay makers, came pouring down the lane towards us with rakes and pitch forks in their hands. [T]he untutored sense of propriety amongst these rusticks was so shocked at the idea of a duel fought by women in *men's clothes,* that I verily believed they would have thrown us into the river with all their hearts. Stupid blockheads! I am convinced that they would not have been half so much scandalised if we had boxed in petticoats.
>
> (51-52)

That the mob would react in this way to women dressing in men's clothing and engaging in a duel would certainly have been satisfying to many of Edgeworth's original readers, since a concerted effort was being made in the conduct literature of this period to warn against masculinity in working-class women and effeminacy in working-class men.[8] At least from Lady Delacour's perspective, the riot was wholly in response to the violation of gender codes that had taken place.

In reexamining the story, however, one has to believe that more than gender violations were involved in this mob action. Simply put, this group of laborers most likely would not have reacted in the same way had these been working-class women, as inherent in almost any form of mob action is an element of class conflict. This was particularly true during the age in which *Belinda* is set, when mobs increasingly functioned as a medium by which workers could forcefully communicate their grievances to the privileged classes. In the case of Lady Delacour's duel, the protest appears to have been the laborers' way of reminding the indecorous noblewomen of what was socially acceptable, both in terms of gender *and* class. In this respect, this scene serves as the most fitting image of the degenerate condition Lady Delacour—and, by extension, her entire class—is in at the beginning of the novel. The traditional office of the privileged classes to dictate propriety to their social inferiors has been completely forfeited and assumed by, of all groups, the working poor.

Although the novel's other major upper-class character, Clarence Hervey, certainly has less to repent of than Lady Delacour, he too shows a proclivity toward the aristocratic degeneracy so clearly warned against in conduct literature. Chronologically speaking, Hervey first enters the narrative in the afore-mentioned dueling-and-ducking scene, where his involvement comes by virtue of the fact that it is he who has written the pamphlet on the necessity of female dueling which incites the ladies to take up their pistols. From the two brief discussions of this pamphlet in the novel, it is difficult to tell whether Hervey intends the treatise to be ironic or not. But, even if he does have satiric intentions, he leaves enough room for misinterpretation to convince several educated women, including the quick-witted Lady Delacour, that there is no shame in putting one's life on the line in the defense of honor.

To his credit, after the ladies have actually taken up arms, Hervey tries to make amends for his pamphlet by rescuing the duelists from the ignominy of being "ducked," or dunked, by the mob of laborers. His choice of methods for distracting the crowd, however, only raises further questions about his readiness to uphold his lofty station in society. Just as the mob is about to plunge the ladies into the water, Hervey appears, dressed in formal regimental attire, driving a herd of pigs, and declaring that he has entered into a hundred-guinea wager that his pigs can outrun a Frenchman's turkeys. Lady Delacour reports that "at the news of this wager, and at the sight of the gentleman turned pig-driver, the mob were in raptures" (52). Although Hervey eventually loses the wager, he saves the ladies from further disgrace. The lingering question, however, is whether Hervey might not have chosen a more genteel manner of diverting the mob's attention.

When Hervey next appears in the novel, he once again raises doubts about his sense of propriety. In a scene that contains the novel's second occurrence of cross-dressing and Hervey's second wager, he bets Lady Delacour fifty guineas that he can dress in a hoop and, his beard aside, conduct himself in so feminine a manner that he might deceive the purblind Lady Boucher into taking him for a woman. Hervey is about to complete a successfully feminine performance when he stumbles in an "unladylike" manner while picking up a comb Lady Delacour has purposely dropped. That he could come so close to pulling the caper off would most likely have not endeared Hervey to the majority of Edgeworth's readers, since, as noted above, much of the domestic literature of the age was devoted to training women and men to act in a manner befitting their gender.

If the cross-dressing is not worrisome enough, the haste with which Hervey enters into his second sizable wager of the novel suggests that he lacks the self-control and maturity to manage his wealth. This suspicion is confirmed in the following chapters, where Hervey wagers with Sir Philip Baddely "for ten guineas—for any money you please" that he can beat him in a walking race. When he loses this bet after being forced to dodge an approaching child, he accepts a double-or-nothing challenge to out-swim Baddely in the Serpentine River, even though he has never learned how to swim. As we discover later in the novel when Belinda lists Mr. Vincent's gambling addiction as one of her primary reasons for rejecting him, excessive wagering—with its implications of financial irresponsibility, fast company, and long nights spent outside the home—was for the aristocratic man as much a sign of a lack of domesticity as sending off children to boarding schools and being a regular on the social circuit was for the aristocratic woman. Despite his occasional displays of impressive talents and good manners, then, the Hervey of the first third of the novel appears to be on a course toward full-fledged rakishness.

II

Although the first half of **Belinda** may suggest otherwise, the novel is ultimately not so much a coronach on the demise of the English aristocracy as a prospectus for its reformation and revival. Admittedly, at the story's end, many of the minor characters, including Sir Phillip Baddely, Harriet Freke, and Mrs. Luttridge, continue to function as reminders of the hollowness of a privileged life misspent. Nevertheless, the characters we are led to care about—Lady Delacour and Clarence Hervey—have had their eyes opened to the gratification to be found in a distinctively aristocratic form of domesticity that includes not only attention to one's spousal and filial obligations within the home, but, on an extended level, one's paternal (or maternal) duties to the community over which one presides. In order for Lady Delacour and Hervey to appreciate their responsibilities both "Abroad and at Home,"[9] however, they need the guidance of characters who already have an understanding of the joy that can be found in basing one's life on correct principles.

The most central of these exemplary characters is Belinda, who must herself undergo a conversion of sorts before she can begin to bring about the betterment of others. Preconditioned by her aunt, Mrs. Stanhope, to believe that fortune and rank are the only paths to happiness, Belinda learns through observing Lady Delacour how miserable someone in so seemingly comfortable an existence can be. Belinda muses, "If Lady Delacour, with all the advantages of wealth, rank, wit and beauty, has not been able to make herself happy in this life of fashionable dissipation, why should I follow the same course, and expect to be more fortunate?" (62). After rejecting Lady Delacour's example, Belinda turns to the Percival family as her model. Patterned after Edgeworth's own family, the Percivals represent all that the privileged classes should be. The parents enjoy a relationship based on love and mutual respect, the children are eagerly immersed in learning, and the family opens its doors to all who wish to share in their happiness. In his relations with others, Mr. Percival acts with dignity and fairness, treating even his tenants respectfully. In one scene that reveals Mr. Percival's understanding of the expanded requirements of domesticity for aristocrats, he visits a couple who for years labored industriously on his estate before being reduced to poverty when old age restricted their ability to work. Rather than turning this couple over to the mercy of the parish, Mr. Percival adheres to the codes of paternalism and provides them with a new home and all the necessities for a comfortable retirement. Mr. Percival's wife, Lady Anne, is even more impressive to Belinda, as she possesses such a degree of inward and outward beauty that others are instantly drawn to her. Belinda observes how Lady Anne combines natural feminine sensibility with a large supply of reason and knowledge, and, as a result, she is "the chosen companion of her husband's understanding" (204).[10] After spending a season with the Percivals, Belinda is converted. She resolves that from here on she will use this family's example to "establish in her own understanding, the exact boundaries between right and wrong" (219).

With the zeal of a convert, Belinda sets out to win Lady Delacour over to the Percivals' mode of living and to induce her to use her rank and wealth to benefit those around her. Key to Belinda's success as a reformer is her loyal friendship and her example as one who refuses to live life according to the dictates of fashionable society. These qualities make Lady Delacour so trusting of her that the viscountess is willing to use her protégée as a confessor of sorts. Being able to share the great secret of her breast "cancer" with Belinda

has an immediate, liberating effect on Lady Delacour, as it allows her to once again regain her authority as the lady of the house from Marriott, the servant who has hitherto used her knowledge of the secret to maintain power over her employer. One of the first signs that Belinda's project with Lady Delacour is taking effect comes in the Lady's spirited proclamation, "I will not live a slave" (146). The real epiphany in Lady Delacour's life, however, takes place several months later, when Belinda goes to live with the Percivals to quell suspicions that she seeks to be the next Lady Delacour. In a moment of jealousy mixed with fear of losing her only real friend, Lady Delacour renounces all she has built her former life upon, symbolically smashing her coronet upon a marble hearth and exclaiming, "Vile bauble! Must I lose my only friend for such a thing as you? Oh, Belinda! do not you see that a coronet cannot confer happiness?" (195). Soon after this, Lady Delacour's physical and mental ailments take her to the brink of death, and only when Belinda charitably returns and forgives her does her recovery begin.

In their analyses of the domestic ideology in *Belinda,* several critics have discussed in detail the changes Lady Delacour undergoes from this point forward. What is missing in most readings of this transformation, however, is an acknowledgment of the social dimension of Lady Delacour's domestic reformation. In addition to accepting her obligations as a wife and a mother, she must also learn to fulfill her duties as an aristocratic woman, which in Edgeworth's system entails not only a return from the whist table to the home, but proper religion, charitable treatment of the worthy poor, and a genuine desire to improve the lives of those with whom one comes in contact. Therefore, equally significant in her reformation as her revitalized relationships with Lord Delacour and her daughter, Helena, is her return from Methodism to orthodox religion, her reparations to the gardener whom she has previously cheated, and her diligent efforts to unite Belinda and Hervey. Only when she has completed all of these tasks can she claim to have fulfilled her commission as an aristocratic woman. That she has accomplished this by the novel's end is made manifest in the closing pages, where she once again has assumed her rightful position as the director of the narrative, pointing the other characters in the paths their lives will take when the novel concludes.

The other major reformation project in the second half of *Belinda* is that which the sage-like Dr. X undertakes with Hervey. These two characters first meet at the low point of Hervey's immature early years, when Dr. X saves the young man from drowning during his swimming contest with Baddely. Being a man of great accomplishments himself, Dr. X can better appreciate Hervey's prodigious talents than anyone else, which makes him all the more cognizant of the way his friend is wasting his life going from lark to lark. Several weeks after he saved Hervey from drowning, Dr. X feels familiar enough with his young friend to confront him about the way he is using his gifts. Dr. X's rebuke on this occasion serves as the novel's most direct edict on the social dimension of domesticity for the aristocratic male:

> What a pity, Mr. Hervey, that a young man of your talents and acquirements, a man who might be any thing, should—pardon the expression—choose to be—nothing—should waste upon petty objects powers suited to the greatest—should lend his soul to every contest for frivolous superiority, when the same energy concentrated might ensure honourable preeminence among the first men in his country.—Shall he, who might not only distinguish himself in any science or situation, who might not only acquire personal fame, but, O, far more noble motive!—who might be permanently useful to his fellow creatures, content himself with being the evanescent amusement of a drawing-room?
>
> (105-06)

Dr. X's blunt reproach produces almost instantaneous effects in Hervey. From this point forward, he forsakes the follies of his youth and begins to assume the until-then vacant role of the hero of the tale. As his first noble act, he decides to assist Belinda in "wean[ing] Lady Delacour, by degrees, from dissipation, by attaching her to her daughter, and to Lady Anne Percival" (113). Beyond this, he proceeds to rescue Mrs. Ormond from penury, to tutor and support the orphaned Virginia St. Pierre, and, in his most selfless act, to prevent his rival, Mr. Vincent, from squandering a fortune and committing suicide. Although in the latter half of the novel Hervey is still far from perfect—as is evidenced in the blunders he commits while attempting to cultivate a Rousseauvian relationship with Virginia—he has taken Dr. X's counsel to heart and devoted his talents to the service of others. In this respect, he has become worthy of both his station in life and the love of Belinda.

III

It should be noted that, as was the case earlier in the novel when the mob acted as enforcers of virtue, once again here the reformation of aristocratic characters has been overseen by individuals of lower social standing. Although her connection to Lady Delacour suggests that Belinda comes from a somewhat respectable family, it is evident at several points in the text that she possesses neither the status nor the fortune to be ranked among the aristocracy. One of the most revealing glimpses into her social position comes when Baddely, who, as a baronet, is himself near the bottom of the upper-class pecking order,[11] assumes that "a niece of Mrs. Stanhope's [is his] lawful prize" (132). Consequently, when Belinda eventually rejects his marriage proposal, he is mortified, having never expected to be turned down by one so far below him in rank and fortune. Even further down the social ladder than Belinda is Dr. X, a member of the professional class who lacks the fortune to retire from his practice. Other than the servants, Dr. X is the only significant character who is actually seen at work during the novel. However wise and well-educated the doctor may be, he can never transcend his middle-class roots in the eyes of many aristocrats, including Baddely, who expresses absolute disbelief that Belinda and Hervey would prefer the doctor's company to his own. At one point, Baddely taunts Hervey that he is bound to become a "doctor of physic, or a methodist parson" if he continues to associate with such a decidedly middle-class individual (108).

At first glimpse, then, by positioning the two great reformers of the novel somewhere between the nobility and the working class, Edgeworth might be said to be reflecting—and encouraging—a society much like the one Armstrong describes, in which the middle-class domestic ideals of conduct literature were gaining ascendancy over decaying aristocratic traditions. This is certainly the pattern with Belinda's regeneration of Lady Delacour and Dr. X's tutelage of Hervey. But upon further reflection, it should be sufficiently clear that the middle class does not monopolize the role of exemplar within the narrative. As I noted earlier, the novel's original enforcer of domestic ideals is not a member of the middle ranks, but a "crowd of town's people, country people, and hay makers . . . with rakes and pitch forks in their hands." Beyond this, the prototype of domesticity within the novel is not the family of a merchant or a banker, but the Percivals, an aristocratic family, complete with their titles, their leisure, and their tenantry. Only after living with the Percivals does Belinda come to a lasting appreciation of domestic roles and the happiness that comes when the mother stays at home with her husband and children. In a reversal of what early nineteenth-century readers would have come to expect, it is the aristocratic Lady Anne who serves as the ultimate model for the middle-class Belinda, not vice versa.

Why Edgeworth should complicate the traditional pattern by refusing to allow domesticity to be solely the domain of the middle or any other class warrants examination. From a biographical angle, unlike many women novelists of the late eighteenth and early nineteenth centuries, Edgeworth did not come from the middle ranks of society. In fact, her family was very much in the tradition of the old British aristocracy, tracing their position as wealthy landowners to the reign of James I, when Frances Edgeworth was awarded six hundred acres in the Irish midlands as part of a movement to establish a Protestant gentry in Ireland.[12] While their Edgeworthstown estate was by no means among the largest in Ireland, it provided the Edgeworths with a sizable enough income from rents that the extremely large family could live comfortably without working—the true litmus test of aristocracy—and could afford such luxuries as regular trips to England and boarding school expenses.[13] From this position near the top of the social hierarchy, Edgeworth tended to see nothing remiss in society's being divided into classes. On one occasion she remarked that she would leave debates over the class system to the politician and the legislator and go forward with her designs for separate educational curricula for the different classes.[14]

Edgeworth was not devoid of opinion, however, on such issues as the distribution of wealth—she did, in fact, write "An enquiry into the causes of poverty in Ireland" while still in her teens—and the ascendancy of the middle class. In fact, if anything, Edgeworth's corpus shows her to be extremely concerned with issues of class. While at various points in her writing Edgeworth levies sharp criticisms at the behavior of every rank of society, including her own, she reserves much of her harshest censure for the middle class, particularly those among it who aspire to possess more power than they are entitled to by birth. During the Defender uprisings of 1798, Edgeworth's father, Richard Lovell Edgeworth, had objected to attempts by middle-class tradesmen to lead the community's defense efforts, stating that the people would be foolish to follow leaders who lacked "fortune, knowledge, birth, or education."[15] That the daughter shared many similar beliefs is evident in her writing. In her first and most famous novel, *Castle Rackrent* (1800), the villain is Old Thady's son, Jason, who quickly, shrewdly, and ruthlessly climbs the social ladder,

rising from his original position as the Rackrent family's domestic servant, to a position as their agent, before at last being their dispossessor when he accumulates the means to force the ancient family from their estate. In a scene from this novel that anticipates the riotous ducking-and-dueling episode in *Belinda*, the tenants on the Rackrent estate, upon learning that a member of the aspiring middle class has taken over the castle, "one and all gathered in great anger against . . . Jason, and terror at the notion of his coming to be landlord over them, and they cried, No Jason! No Jason!—Sir Condy! Sir Condy! Sir Condy Rackrent for ever!" (79).[16]

In a later novel, *The Absentee* (1812), Edgeworth suggests that the entire social order comes under threat when the middle class rises to power. Not only does the tenantry suffer under the hands of a middle-class agent lacking the education or paternalistic instincts needed to preside over society, but the treasured traditions of polite culture become bastardized when the middle class takes on aristocratic airs. One of the more ridiculous scenes in a novel filled with caricatures of social pretentiousness is of a middle-class woman—in this case, the sister of a corrupt Irish agent—attempting to host an aristocratic-style dinner party. Upon first observing the spectacle created by the woman's efforts, one of the visiting lords "was much amused by the mixture, which was now exhibited to him, of taste and incongruity, ingenuity and absurdity, genius and blunder; by the contrast between the finery and vulgarity, the affectation and ignorance of the lady of the villa" (87).[17]

Although no scenes such as these, in which the middle class is skewered for their pretensions, are to be found in *Belinda*, these episodes from other novels suggest that Edgeworth's biases against the middle class might very well have led to her refusal to position domesticity as an exclusively middle-class virtue. Any suggestion that Edgeworth refused to ascribe domesticity to the middle class because of her prejudices against this group, however, raises another, more vexing question: why would a writer so wary of middle-class ascendancy write a novel championing the central virtue of the middle class's emergent ideology? It would seem that Edgeworth would want to do anything *but* advocate an ideology that threatened to transfer power from her own class to one made up of merchants and tradesmen. If, however, by the end of the eighteenth century domesticity had been so naturalized that it could no longer be identified as a distinctively middle-class ideal,

Edgeworth's advocacy of it would not have seemed a conflict of interest. Instead, domesticity might have appeared to her as a universal truth which transcended class and national boundaries.

The idea that domesticity had achieved such prominence by the early nineteenth century is born out in Armstrong's study. Of the progression of this domestic revolution she writes, "Richardson successfully introduced into fiction the highly fictional proposition that a prosperous man desired nothing so much as the woman who embodied domestic virtue. By Austen's time, this proposition had acquired the status of truth."[18] Further evidence for the naturalization of domesticity occurring during this period comes in the now-common recognition among social historians that the late eighteenth and early nineteenth centuries saw a tremendous growth in the social and political influence of the middle class. If one accepts the notion that middle-class culture became dominant in Britain in the late eighteenth and early nineteenth centuries, it is not difficult to see how the originally middle-class virtue of domesticity could have been well on its way to being naturalized by the time Edgeworth began writing her novel in 1800.

Viewed as a historical document, **Belinda** supports the argument that domesticity was beginning to be taken as a universal, timeless truth during this era. While it is true that at the end of the novel segments of the aristocracy remain caught up in the dissolute life of fashion, the examples of the Percivals, Lady Delacour, and Hervey suggest that domesticity was just as expedient for those possessing rank and fortune as it was for those lacking such advantages. In fact, for the aristocracy of Edgeworth's era, domesticity was all the more requisite, since in addition to implying stewardship over the home, it also carried with it an obligation to fulfill centuries-old paternalistic duties towards one's tenants or subjects. That Lady Delacour and Hervey came to understand this is evidenced in the increased attention they paid to the needs of their families and those of lesser rank following their respective reformations. In the end, the prevailing virtue in the world of Edgeworth's novel is a domesticity that requires behavior befitting both one's gender and one's social class.

Notes

1. This excerpt from Edgeworth's privately printed *Memoirs* is quoted in Marilyn Butler, *Maria Edgeworth: A Literary Life,* (Oxford: Clarendon, 1972), 9.

2. Beth Kowaleski-Wallace, "Home Economics: Domestic Ideology in Maria Edgeworth's *Belinda*," *The Eighteenth Century* 29 (1988), 242-62; Anne Mellor, *Romanticism and Gender,* (New York: Routledge, 1993), 42-45; Colin B. Atkinson and Jo Atkinson, "Maria Edgeworth, *Belinda,* and Women's Rights," *Eire-Ireland: A Journal of Irish Studies* 19 (1984): 94-118. See also Susan Greenfield, "'Abroad and at Home': Sexual Ambiguity, Miscegenation, and Colonial Boundaries in Edgeworth's *Belinda*," *PMLA* 112 (1997): 214-28.

3. Armstrong, *Desire and Domestic Fiction: A Political History of the Novel,* (Oxford: Oxford UP, 1987), 4-5.

4. Maria Edgeworth, *Belinda,* ed. Eiléan Ni Chuilleanain, (Rutland, VT: Everyman, 1993). All page references are to this edition.

5. Freke's transgressive masculinity and corrupting influence upon her companions make her a favorite subject of much of the recent criticism on *Belinda.* See particularly Atkinson and Atkinson, Mellor, and Greenfield.

6. During this period, moralists in Britain became increasingly outraged over the excessive lifestyles of aristocrats like Lady Delacour. Apropos to *Belinda,* Leonore Davidoff and Catherine Hall recount how "Aristocratic claims for leadership had long been based on lavish display and consumption while the middle class stressed domestic moderation. In particular, aristocratic disdain for sordid money matters, their casual attitude to debt and addiction to gambling which had amounted to a mania in some late eighteenth-century circles, were anathema to the middling ranks whose very existence depended on the establishment of creditworthiness and avoidance of financial embarrassment" (*Family Fortunes: Men and Women of the English Middle Class, 1780-1850,* [Chicago: U of Chicago P, 1987], 21).

7. Kowaleski-Wallace, "Home Economics," 243.

8. See Armstrong, 20; Atkinson and Atkinson, 104.

9. As most analyses of domesticity in *Belinda* have pointed out, Edgeworth originally gave her novel the title *Abroad and at Home* to contrast the life spent in high society with the more rewarding life centered around the home.

10. In her delineation of masculine and feminine Romantic ideologies, Mellor shows how the Percivals' marriage is the type of union aspired to by many women writers of the late eighteenth and early nineteenth centuries. See Mellor, 43-44.

11. The title of baronet, contrived and sold as part of a fund-raising ploy by James I, was not part of the traditional English peerage, which was comprised of dukes, marquesses, earls, viscounts, and barons. Baronets did not hold seats in the House of Lords, were addressed as "Sir" rather than "Lord," and generally enjoyed far less prestige than peers. Part of their relative lack of power, no doubt, was due to the simple fact that in England a baronet was much more common than a peer. In 1800, for example, there were only 267 peers in England as opposed to 699 baronets (see John Cannon, *Aristocratic Century: The Peerage of Eighteenth-Century England,* [Cambridge: Cambridge UP, 1991], 32). Lest we think that Baddely and his fellow baronets were completely devoid of distinction, however, it should be pointed out that in all eras of English history prior to the twentieth century, the aristocracy—including peers, baronets, and knights—accounted for less than one percent of the total

population. Cannon, in fact, calculates that in 1801 the aristocracy accounted for a minuscule 0.0000857 percent of the total population (33n.).

12. See Elizabeth Kowaleski-Wallace, *Their Fathers' Daughters: Hannah More, Maria Edgeworth, and Patriarchal Complicity,* (New York: Oxford UP, 1991), 141.

13. For a detailed description of the Edgeworth family's income and lifestyle during their years at Edgeworthstown House, see Butler, 78-145.

14. My thanks to George Watson for providing this quote from Edgeworth's *The Parent's Assistant* (1796) in his introduction to *Castle Rackrent,* Oxford World's Classics edition, ed. George Watson (Oxford: Oxford UP, 1980), xxii.

15. This quotation comes from a letter of 30 April 1795 from Richard Lovell Edgeworth to Lord Charlemont. See Butler, 117.

16. Maria Edgeworth, *Castle Rackrent,* Oxford World's Classics edition, ed. George Watson (Oxford: Oxford UP, 1980).

17. Maria Edgeworth, *The Absentee,* Oxford World's Classics edition, eds. W. J. McCormack and Kim Walker (Oxford: Oxford UP, 1988).

18. Armstrong, 135.

FURTHER READING

Biography

Lawless, Emily. *Maria Edgeworth,* New York: Macmillan. 1904, 220 p.

Offers a biography of Edgeworth from the English Men of Letters series.

Criticism

Gallagher, Catherine. "The Changeling's Debt: Maria Edgeworth's Productive Fictions." In *Nobody's Story: The Vanishing Acts of Women Writers in the Marketplace, 1670-1820,* pp. 257-327. Berkeley: University of California Press, 1994.

Discusses Edgeworth's privileged position within the early nineteenth-century literary marketplace.

Gamer, Michael. "Maria Edgeworth and the Romance of Real Life." *Novel* 34, no. 2 (spring 2001): 232-66.

Analyzes Edgeworth's unique approach to literary realism.

Greenfield, Susan C. "'Abroad and at Home': Sexual Ambiguity, Miscegenation, and Colonial Boundaries in Edgeworth's *Belinda*." *PMLA* 112, no. 2 (March 1997): 214-28.

Examines the oppositions between public and private spheres and between England and the British West Indies in Belinda.

Hoad, Neville. "Maria Edgeworth's *Harrington*: The Price of Sympathetic Representation." In *British Romanticism and the Jews: History, Culture, Literature,* edited by Sheila A. Spector, pp. 121-37. New York: Palgrave, 2002.

Studies Edgeworth's attempt to represent Jews in a sympathetic manner, which is complicated by issues of gender as well as social and economic class.

Kirkpatrick, Kathryn. "The Limits of Liberal Feminism in Maria Edgeworth's *Belinda*." In *Jane Austen and Mary Shelley and Their Sisters,* edited by Laura Dabundo, pp. 73-82. Lanham, Md.: University Press of America, 2000.

Discusses Edgeworth's Lady Anne Percival as a model for female domestic virtue.

Kowaleski-Wallace, Beth. "Reading the Father Metaphorically." In *Refiguring the Father: New Feminist Readings of Patriarchy,* edited by Patricia Yaeger and Beth Kowaleski-Wallace, pp. 296-316. Carbondale, Ill.: Southern Illinois University Press, 1989.

Considers Edgeworth's relationship to her father and its influence on her life and writing career.

McCann, Andrew. "Conjugal Love and the Enlightenment Subject: The Colonial Context of Non-identity in Maria Edgeworth's *Belinda*." *Novel* 30, no. 1 (fall 1996): 56-77.

Examines Edgeworth's attempt in Belinda *to encourage the abolition of slavery in the colonies and replace it with the culture of wage-labor.*

Narain, Mona. "A Prescription of Letters: Maria Edgeworth's *Letters for Literary Ladies* and the Ideologies of the Public Sphere." *The Journal of Narrative Technique* 28, no. 3 (fall 1998): 266-86.

Discusses issues of feminine identity and the woman writer through an examination of Edgeworth's Letters for Literary Ladies.

Page, Judith. "Maria Edgeworth's *Harrington*: From Shylock to Shadowy Peddlers." *The Wordsworth Circle* 32, no. 1 (winter 2001): 9-13.

Examines Edgeworth's use of Gothic conventions to situate the figure of the Jew as an outcast in Harrington.

Schaffer, Julie. "Not Subordinate: Empowering Women in the Marriage-Plot—The Novels of Frances Burney, Maria Edgeworth, and Jane Austen." *Criticism* 34, no. 1 (winter 1992): 51-73.

Comparative study of three marriage-plot novels: Burney's Evelina, *Edgeworth's* Belinda, *and Austen's* Pride and Prejudice.

OTHER SOURCES FROM GALE:

Additional coverage of Edgeworth's life and career is contained in the following sources published by the Gale Group: *British Writers Supplement,* Vol. 3; *Dictionary of Literary Biography,* Vols. 116, 159, 163; *Feminist Writers; Literature Resource Center; Nineteenth-Century Literature Criticism,* Vols. 1, 51; *Something about the Author,* Vol. 21; *Twayne's English Authors;* and *World Literature and Its Times,* Ed. 3.

GEORGE ELIOT

(1819 - 1880)

(Pseudonym of Mary Ann—or Marian—Evans) English novelist, essayist, poet, editor, short story writer, and translator.

Eliot is a respected novelist of the late nineteenth century, and her work has been praised for its penetrating psychological analysis and profound insight into human character. Generally played against the backdrop of English rural life, Eliot's novels explore moral and philosophical issues with a realistic approach to character and plot development. *Middlemarch* (1871) is frequently studied by feminist critics for its careful consideration of a woman's place in a male-dominated world, although critics disagree over whether this novel, and Eliot's other works, display proto-feminist ideas or reinforce patriarchal systems.

BIOGRAPHICAL INFORMATION

Eliot was born November 22, 1819 to a strict Methodist family whose views she accepted until her friendship with the skeptical philosophers Charles Bray and Charles Hennell brought her to challenge the rigid religious principles of her upbringing. This questioning of values also inspired her first published work, a translation of *Das Leben Jesu* (*The Life of Jesus*; 1846) by the German religious philosopher D. F. Strauss. The incident caused a rift with her father, but Eliot later reconciled with him and lived with him until his death in 1849.

After her father's death, Eliot moved to London and became acquainted with John Chapman, who hired her as an assistant editor on the *Westminster Review* and introduced her to his literary circle. This group included the philosopher Herbert Spencer, who introduced Eliot to writer and intellectual George Henry Lewes. Although Lewes was married (he was legally prohibited from divorcing his estranged wife), the two openly lived together until Lewes's death in 1878, defying the strict moral code of the Victorian era. Lewes's influence on Eliot's writing was great: it was he who first encouraged her to write fiction, and he acted as an intermediary between the pseudonymous "George Eliot" and her first publisher, *Blackwood's Magazine*. Eliot's literary success eventually brought the couple social acceptance, but just over a year after Lewes's death she married John Walter Cross, a banker twenty years her junior, and again met with public outrage. Seven months after her marriage the novelist suddenly died and was buried in Highgate Cemetery, North London.

MAJOR WORKS

Although she was a prolific writer in many genres, Eliot is chiefly known for her sequence of novels that begin by drawing heavily from her rural English background and grow gradually wider in scope. *Scenes of Clerical Life* (1858) includes three sketches with a provincial setting and is noted for its well-drawn characters and keen rendering of Midland dialect. *Adam Bede* (1859) presents realistic images of daily life in a quiet rural community undercut with unfulfilled love and selfishness resulting in tragedy and hard-won self-awareness. *The Mill on the Floss* (1860) tells the story of Maggie Tulliver's inability to conform to the rigidly traditional society in which she lives, and *Silas Marner* (1861) deals with an alienated miser whose life is transformed by his adoption of an abandoned child.

Eliot broadened her thematic goals with the historical novel *Romola* (1863) as well as *Felix Holt* (1866), which is often characterized as a political novel but features a conventional courtship narrative more typically associated with domestic fiction. *Middlemarch*, widely considered Eliot's finest achievement, presents a comprehensive picture of English provincial life while developing moral and philosophical issues such as the relationship of the individual to society. Eliot's last novel, *Daniel Deronda* (1876), examines a broad spectrum of nineteenth-century European society and is regarded as her most ambitious yet perhaps her least successful work.

CRITICAL RECEPTION

Eliot's critical acclaim came early, with the publication of *Adam Bede*. During her lifetime, the writer's work generally met with popular and critical success, although novels such as *Felix Holt* and *Daniel Deronda* have consistently been considered less accomplished than *Adam Bede* and *Middlemarch*. Eliot's reputation endured a significant decline, however, from her death through the early twentieth century, when her novels were often dismissed as heavy, didactic, and overly scholarly. However, Virginia Woolf was influential in reviving interest in Eliot's works as early as 1925, addressing Eliot's unique treatment of the nature of femininity, and F. R. Leavis's essays in the 1940s effectively reaffirmed the significance of Eliot's achievement.

The onset of the feminist movement sparked another reevaluation of Eliot's work, although critics have remained sharply divided about the novelist's treatment of women's issues. As Zelda Austen notes in her 1976 essay, feminists have often claimed that Eliot tends to engage in an anti-feminist reinforcement of the systems under which her heroines often suffer. For example, some feminist scholars of *Felix Holt* have criticized Holt's character, claiming his objections to Esther's refinement and aesthetic sensibilities make him no more desirable a suitor than Transome, who believes that women are meant to be decorative rather than functional. Other critics, however, claim Eliot as a proto-feminist figure whose complex thinking about the place of a woman in an oppressive society was instrumental in setting the stage for the women's literary liberation that would eventually follow.

PRINCIPAL WORKS

The Life of Jesus [translator; as Marian Evans] (essay) 1846

The Essence of Christianity [translator; as Marian Evans] (essay) 1854

*Scenes of Clerical Life (novel) 1858

Adam Bede (novel) 1859

The Mill on the Floss (novel) 1860

Silas Marner, the Weaver of Raveloe (novel) 1861

Romola (novel) 1863

Felix Holt, the Radical (novel) 1866

The Spanish Gypsy: A Poem (poetry) 1868

Middlemarch: A Study of Provincial Life (novel) 1871-72

The Legend of Jubal, and Other Poems (poetry) 1874

Daniel Deronda (novel) 1876

Impressions of Theophrastus Such (essays) 1879

The George Eliot Letters 9 vols. (letters) 1954-78

* All of Eliot's novels were originally published serially in magazines.

PRIMARY SOURCES

(REVIEW DATE 14 APRIL 1860)

SOURCE: "The Mill on the Floss." *Saturday Review* 9, no. 233 (14 April 1860): 470-71.

In the following review, the anonymous critic's qualified praise of The Mill on the Floss *offers a provocative example of the contemporary response to a female novelist.*

To speak the simple truth, without affectation of politeness, [*Adam Bede*] was thought to be too good for a woman's story. It turns out that a woman was not only able to write it, but that she did not write it by any lucky accident. The *Mill on the Floss* may not, perhaps, be so popular as *Adam Bede,* but it shows no falling off nor any exhaustion of power. We may think ourselves very fortunate to have a third female novelist not inferior to Miss Austen and Miss Brontë; and it so happens that there is much in the works of this new writer that reminds us of these two well-known novelists without anything like copying. George Eliot has a minuteness of painting and a certain archness of style that are quite after the manner of Miss Austen, while the wide scope of her remarks, and her delight in depicting strong and wayward feelings, show that she belongs to the generation of Currer Bell, and not to that of the quiet authoress of *Emma*. Where all excel, it is of no use to draw up a sort of literary class-list, and pronounce an opinion as to the comparative merits of these three writers; but no one can now doubt that the lady who, with the usual pretty affectation of her sex, likes to look on paper as much like a man as possible, and so calls herself George Eliot, has established her place in the first rank of our female novelists.

She has done us all one great kindness, for she has opened up a field that is perfectly new. She has, for the first time in fiction, invented or disclosed the family life of the English farmer, and the class to which he belongs. . . . There is nothing in which George Eliot succeeds more conspicuously than in [the] very nice art of making her characters like real people, and yet shading them off into the large group which she is describing. Some notion of what it requires to make a good novelist may be obtained by reflecting on all that is implied in the delineation of three farmer's daughters and their husbands with separate and probable characters, and in allotting them suitable conversation, and following the turns and shifts of their minds within the narrow limits of the matters that may be supposed to interest them. It is this profusion of delineative power that marks the *Mill on the Floss,* and the delineations are given both by minute touches of description and by dialogues. To write dialogue is much harder than merely to describe, and George Eliot trusts greatly to the talk of her farmers' wives in order to make her conception of these sisters come vividly before us. Both in the description and in the dialogue there are exhibited a neatness of finish, a comprehensiveness of detail, and a relish for subdued comedy that constantly bring back to our recollection the best productions of Miss Austen's genius. Like Miss Austen, too, George Eliot possesses the art of taking the reader into her confidence. We seem to share with the authoress the fun of the play she is showing us. She joins us in laughing at her characters, and yet this is done so lightly and with such tact that the continuity of the story is not broken. Every one must remember the consummate skill with which Miss Austen manages this, and if we do not quite like to acknowledge that our old favourite has been equalled, we must allow that George Eliot performs the same neat stroke of art with a success that is little inferior.

Portraiture, however, and the description of farmers and their wives, only occupies one portion of George Eliot's thoughts. There is a side of her mind which is entirely unlike that of Miss Austen, and which brings her much closer to Charlotte Brontë. She is full of meditation on some of the most difficult problems of life. She occupies herself with the destinies, the possibilities, and the religious position of all the people of whom she cares to think. Especially she seems haunted with the thought of the amazing discrepancy between what she calls "the emmet-life" of these British farmers, and the ideal of Christianity. She dwells on the pettiness, the narrowness, the paganism of their character. She even takes a pleasure in making the contrast as strong as she can. In her stern determination to paint what she conceives to be the truth, to soften nothing and not to exalt and elevate where she profoundly believes all to be poor and low, she shocks us with traits of character that are exceptional, however possible. (p. 470)

As it seems to us, the defect of the *Mill on the Floss* is that there is too much that is painful in it. And the authoress is so far led away by her reflections on moral problems and her interest in the phases of triumphant passion, that she sacrifices her story. We have such entire changes of circumstances, and the characters are exhibited under such totally different conditions of age and mental development, that we get to care nothing for them. . . . We hope that some time George Eliot will give us a tale less painful and less discursive. There is something in the world and in the quiet walks of English lower life besides fierce mental struggles and wild love. We do not see why we should not be treated to a story that would do

ABOUT THE AUTHOR

**NINETEENTH-CENTURY REVIEWER ON
ELIOT'S "WOMANLINESS OF THOUGHT"**

[The womanliness of thought about human relations] is in a more impassioned way the attitude of George Eliot: and there is something worth thinking of in this coincidence. The feelings and thoughts of women about the larger relations and more abstract motives of human life have been singularly inarticulate. While feeling much, they have accepted men's interpretations of their feelings, as they have taken their creeds from men, though themselves the religious sex. If George Eliot and Olive Schreiner are true interpreters of the way women would feel about society could they get at their own feelings clearly, the womanly standard for human society is first, that sort of minute and transcendental justice that we call altruism, second, love of truth, and third, private love, as the ruling forces. The most penetrating passages are those in which the appeal is made to men to understand what they are doing to each other by injustices.

Anonymous. An excerpt from "Dreams." *The Overland Monthly* 19, no. 110 (February 1892): 223-24.

justice to George Eliot's powers, and yet form a pleasing and consistent whole. (p. 471)

GENERAL COMMENTARY

VIRGINIA WOOLF (ESSAY DATE 1925)

SOURCE: Woolf, Virginia. "George Eliot." In *Collected Essays*, Vol. 1, pp. 196-204. London, England: Hogarth, 1966.

In the following essay, originally published in her 1925 The Common Reader, Woolf highlights the complexity of Eliot's thinking about womanhood and "feminine aspirations."

The beauty of [George Eliot's] first books, *Scenes of Clerical Life, Adam Bede, The Mill on the Floss,* is very great. It is impossible to estimate the merit of the Poysers, the Dodsons, the Gilfils, the Bartons, and the rest with all their surroundings and dependencies, because they have put on flesh and blood and we move among them, now bored, now sympathetic, but always with that unquestioning acceptance of all that they say and do, which we accord to the great originals only. The flood of memory and humour which she pours so spontaneously into one figure, one scene after another, until the whole fabric of ancient rural England is revived, has so much in common with a natural process that it leaves us with little consciousness that there is anything to criticise. We accept; we feel the delicious warmth and release of spirit which the great creative writers alone procure for us. As one comes back to the books after years of absence they pour out, even against our expectation, the same store of energy and heat, so that we want more than anything to idle in the warmth as in the sun beating down from the red orchard wall. If there is an element of unthinking abandonment in thus submitting to the humours of Midland farmers and their wives, that, too, is right in the circumstances. We scarcely wish to analyse what we feel to be so large and deeply human. And when we consider how distant in time the world of Shepperton and Hayslope is, and how remote the minds of farmer and agricultural labourers from those of most of George Eliot's readers, we can only attribute the ease and pleasure with which we ramble from house to smithy, from cottage parlour to rectory garden, to the fact that George Eliot makes us share their lives, not in a spirit of condescension or of curiosity, but in a spirit of sympathy. She is no satirist. The movement of her mind was too slow and cumbersome to lend itself to comedy. But she gathers in her large grasp a great bunch of the main elements of human nature and groups them loosely together with a tolerant and wholesome understanding which, as one finds upon rereading, has not only kept her figures fresh and free, but has given them an unexpected hold upon our laughter and tears. (p. 200)

But in the midst of all this tolerance and sympathy there are, even in the early books, moments of greater stress. Her humour has shown itself broad enough to cover a wide range of fools and failures, mothers and children, dogs and flourishing midland fields, farmers, sagacious or fuddled over their ale, horse-dealers, inn-keepers, curates, and carpenters. Over them all broods a certain romance, the only romance that George Eliot allowed herself—the romance of the past.

The books are astonishingly readable and have no trace of pomposity or pretence. But to the reader who holds a large stretch of her early work in view it will become obvious that the mist of recollection gradually withdraws. It is not that her power diminishes, for, to our thinking, it is at its highest in the mature **Middlemarch,** the magnificent book which with all its imperfections is one of the few English novels written for grown-up people. . . . Those who fall foul of George Eliot do so, we incline to think, on account of her heroines; and with good reason; for there is no doubt that they bring out the worst of her, lead her into difficult places, make her self-conscious, didactic, and occasionally vulgar. Yet if you could delete the whole sisterhood you would leave a much smaller and a much inferior world, albeit a world of greater artistic perfection and far superior jollity and comfort. (pp. 201-02)

The more one examines the great emotional scenes [in **The Mill on the Floss**] the more nervously one anticipates the brewing and gathering and thickening of the cloud which will burst upon our heads at the moment of crisis in a shower of disillusionment and verbosity. It is partly that her hold upon dialogue, when it is not dialect, is slack; and partly that she seems to shrink with an elderly dread of fatigue from the effort of emotional concentration. She allows her heroines to talk too much. She has little verbal felicity. She lacks the unerring taste which chooses one sentence and compresses the heart of the scene within that. (p. 203)

Yet, dismiss the heroines without sympathy, confine George Eliot to the agricultural world of her 'remotest past', and you not only diminish her greatness but lose her true flavour. That greatness is here we can have no doubt. The width of the prospect, the large strong outlines of the principal features, the ruddy light of the early books, the searching power and reflective richness of the later tempt us to linger and expatiate beyond our limits. But it is upon the heroines that we would cast a final glance. . . . [The problem with all Eliot's heroines is that they cannot live] without religion, and they start out on the search for one when they are little girls. Each has the deep feminine passion for goodness, which makes the place where she stands in aspiration and agony the heart of the book—still and cloistered like a place of worship, but that she no longer knows to whom to pray. In learning they seek their goal; in the ordinary tasks of womanhood; in the wider service of their kind. They do not find what they seek, and we cannot wonder. The

Tom and Maggie are overwhelmed by a flood in this illustration from *The Mill on the Floss.*

ancient consciousness of woman, charged with suffering and sensibility, and for so many ages dumb, seems in them to have brimmed and overflowed and uttered a demand for something—they scarcely know what—for something that is perhaps incompatible with the facts of human existence. George Eliot had far too strong an intelligence to tamper with those facts, and too broad a humour to mitigate the truth because it was a stern one. Save for the supreme courage of their endeavour, the struggle ends, for her heroines, in tragedy, or in a compromise that is even more melancholy. But their story is the incomplete version of the story of George Eliot herself. For her, too, the burden and the complexity of womanhood were not enough; she must reach beyond the sanctuary and pluck for herself the strange bright fruits of art and knowledge. Clasping them as few women have ever clasped them, she would not renounce her own inheritance—the difference of view, the difference of standard—nor accept an inappropriate reward. Thus we behold her, a

FROM THE AUTHOR

ELIOT ON ELIZABETH BARRETT BROWNING'S *AURORA LEIGH*

Mrs. Browning is, perhaps, the first woman who has produced a work which exhibits all the peculiar powers without the negations of her sex; which superadds to masculine vigour, breadth, and culture, feminine subtlety of perception, feminine quickness of sensibility, and feminine tenderness. It is difficult to point to a woman of genius who is not either too little feminine, or too exclusively so. But in this, her longest and greatest poem, Mrs. Browning has shown herself all the greater poet because she is intensely a poetess.

Eliot, George. An excerpt from "Belles Lettres." In *Westminster Review.* O.S. 67, 1867, pp. 306-26.

memorable figure, inordinately praised and shrinking from her fame, despondent, reserved, shuddering back into the arms of love as if there alone were satisfaction and, it might be, justification, at the same time reaching out with 'a fastidious yet hungry ambition' for all that life could offer the free and inquiring mind and confronting her feminine aspirations with the real world of men. Triumphant was the issue for her, whatever it may have been for her creations, and as we recollect all that she dared and achieved, how with every obstacle against her—sex and health and convention—she sought more knowledge and more freedom till the body, weighted with its double burden, sank worn out, we must lay upon her grave whatever we have it in our power to bestow of laurel and rose. (pp. 203-04)

SHERRI CATHERINE SMITH (ESSAY DATE JUNE 1996)

SOURCE: Smith, Sherri Catherine. "George Eliot, Straight Drag and the Masculine Investments of Feminism." *Women's Writing* 3, no. 2 (June 1996): 97-111.

In the following essay, Smith discusses Eliot's "nuanced understanding of the binary that underwrites gender hierarchy" and reveals the function of misogyny in her feminist tendencies.

I

"There was clearly no suspicion that I was a woman"[1], George Eliot marvelled in 1858, no telltale sign that the mysterious and applauded author of **"The Sad Fortunes of the Reverend Amos Barton"** was in fact Marian Evans, erstwhile translator, journalist, and editor of the *Westminster Review*. There might have been pleasure enough in knowing that one had hoodwinked a readership inclined to believe women the intellectual and aesthetic inferiors of men. But for Eliot, the pleasure of the deception was almost perverse. Not only had her first story met with the approval of the very society that had shunned her for eloping with a married man, but Eliot herself received the misreading as a kind of compliment, a testimony both to the respect that she believed manhood warranted and to her ingenuity in harnessing that respect by acting like a man.

Eliot did much to support such an impression of herself. Even her earlier translations and critical essays were shaped in large part by the anonymous male persona she assumed long before she emerged on the literary scene as the novelist "George Eliot." Her theatricals also extended beyond her authorial persona to encompass her everyday conduct with her closest friends and literary acquaintants. While the novelist Eliza Lynn Linton remembered her to be "uncouth," "unkempt," "unwashed and unbrushed," this reputation for gracelessness suited Eliot quite well in the social contexts in which she often found herself. A great number of intellectual men regularly invited her to gatherings made up chiefly of other intellectual men, and where the parties and soirées were of mixed company, Eliot could routinely be found fraternizing with the men.[2]

When Jacques Derrida remarked 120 years later that "[f]eminism is nothing but the operation of a woman who aspires to be like a man"[3], Eliot, no doubt, would have made a choice candidate for admission into the feminist fold. But it was a sisterhood to which she never wanted to belong, on either a personal or a political level. Convinced that "women were interested only in ephemeral subjects and not likely to use their vote wisely," Eliot did not support John Stuart Mill's proposal to alter the language of the Second Reform Bill to include women in the franchise.[4] Moreover, Eliot shied away from projects associated with women, including projects of a practical rather than a strictly political nature, which might otherwise have engaged her interest and energies. When approached by Bessie Rayner Parkes about contributing to the fledgling *English Woman's Jour-*

nal, for example, Eliot refused on the grounds that "a public display of inferior work by women would do more harm than good."[5] Her infamous essay, "Silly Novels by Lady Novelists," written just before she took up the novel-writing craft herself, is also unabashedly critical of the "foolish facility" that most women mistake for "mastery."[6] More baffling still, especially to feminist literary critics, is the conservatism of Eliot's novels.[7] Most of her fictional heroines seem almost ritually unable to achieve the level of autonomy and possibility that Eliot herself enjoyed.

While Eliot's gender politics may be difficult for today's feminists to classify, Eliot was not ambivalent about the practicalities of self-fulfillment. Attracted to erudite circles, she went where she could find them. And her animosity toward most women's activism was, above all, self-interested. Still, Eliot's discordant relations with women appear so germane to the pleasure she took in the company and discourse of men that she is left vulnerable to the charge of misogyny. Are her respective sentiments toward men and women fundamentally unrelated, or does her desire to act like a man in fact *facilitate* her disaffection toward women? Christina Crosby, among others, has speculated in this vein: "As the Prophetess of Humanity, Eliot had to rule women out. . . . One might ask her what [Daniel] Deronda's mother asks her son: 'You speak as men do—as if you felt yourself wise. What does it all mean?'"[8]

If we are talking about where to place an unruly Eliot in a history of feminism, then Crosby's question invites us to complicate that history, to take account of the misogyny not only in Eliot but also in feminism.[9] To that end, Eliot's reluctance to identify with women as a class—despite her commitment *as a woman* to overcome the ascription of social and intellectual deficiencies—opens up an important perspective on the paradox inherent in Derrida's definition of feminism as well as in that branch of academic feminism which champions the quest for "equality" as the central creed of women's movements over the past two centuries. The suggestion that feminist objectives merely duplicate male desire (for control, knowledge, self-possession, and the like) would seem to recommend a feminism set against itself, or at least one willing to risk its collective goals in the interest of the unsystematic attempts of individual women to make it in a man's world.[10] Many theorists have looked at the apparent conflict of interests in egalitarian feminism and have concluded that this tack is best abandoned, not only because it slowly erodes the coalitional politics that often justify feminism as a critical method but also because it advances like a snake eating its own tail, using what is most appealing about humanist incorporation to destroy the specificity of women's bodies and women's experience. As Nancy Cott has noted, however, paradox is part of the very nature of feminism:

> [Feminism] aims for individual freedoms by mobilizing sex solidarity. It posits that women recognize their unity while it stands for diversity among women. It requires gender consciousness for its basis yet calls for the elimination of prescribed gender roles.[11]

The paradoxes of feminism demand a variety of methods, most of which are in conflict with one another. It is with this understanding that I propose a re-examination of one strategy that is quickly and unfortunately losing currency among feminist theorists today. Specifically, my purpose here is to consider the political and aesthetic advantages of masculinism in Eliot's critical writing and to show how Eliot's identification with men should be regarded as an outgrowth of feminism at the same time it appears to be—and perhaps *is*—a rejection of it. While part of my assessment will involve taking sober account of the misogyny that made Eliot's feminism such an oxymoron to the nineteenth-century women's movement[12], I also intend to describe the excesses of her feminism as sites of ingenuity and resourcefulness. If "feminism continues to require its own forms of serious play," to use Judith Butler's formulation[13], then Eliot's investments in the masculine become politically significant for us today as studies in impersonation, "in-vestment," drag. A closer look at Eliot's life and work not only brings to light the risks of this type of feminist play but also clarifies the returns we can expect on such questionable investments.

II

The satisfactions of drag have already been claimed for feminism by Judith Butler in her landmark text on gender performativity.[14] Much like Eliot, Butler does not shrink from a strategic appreciation of so-called masculine modes of behavior. She contends, in fact, that feminism *must* work "within the terms of power itself" or, more precisely, engage in deliberate play with the male/female binary which structures identity politics.[15] But as to method and purpose, Eliot and Butler part ways altogether. Butler views *gay* drag as a more conspicuous, and hence politically necessary, version of the gender performances already undertaken by straight men and women.

Revealing gender as performative would consequently undermine its status as a natural and apparently fixed determinant of power. Eliot, on the other hand, invests herself in masculinity *as a straight woman,* not in order to displace gender distinction but, as I will show, in order to exploit its significance.

Above all, gender is illusory for Butler, and because such "illusions of [gendered] substance" underwrite the subjugation of women, Butler believes that the logic and political efficacy of gender must be challenged. This is best accomplished by multiplying gender distinction *ad nauseam,* "to the point where it no longer makes sense."[16] Where gender codes overflow, "masculine" and "feminine" attributes will inevitably turn up on bodies that are not correlatively sexed. Both the lesbian parody of heterosexual exchange (e.g., "butch" and "femme") and gay drag, for example, effectively dislocate gender from a physiological and psychological essence, according to Butler, and thus double back to publish the performative and unprotected nature of normative heterosexuality.

What is most striking about Butler's central trope, gay drag, is that she uses it as though it were feminism's last, best hope, even though it is meant only to help her speak more shrewdly about heterosexual paradigms. If, "[i]n imitating gender, drag implicitly reveals the imitative structure of gender itself—as well as its contingency"[17], then further attention to "the imitative structure of gender itself" might be in order. Is gay drag the only thing that is going to reveal this structure to us?[18] Or is there any room for such play—such "gender trouble"—in the everyday practices of heterosexual populations? Despite George Eliot's ambiguous sociosexual posturing, she repeatedly rebuffed the lesbian advances of Elma Stuart and Edith Simcox, telling Simcox that "she had never all her life cared very much for women."[19] Eliot, then, would be unwilling to associate her "masculine" *social* predilections with some sort of *libidinal* interest in women. But if gay drag makes the gender binary available to feminism for subversive ends, as Butler argues, then perhaps something like straight drag would do the trick as well.[20]

By the age of 26, Eliot had become quite used to participating in a rigorous, intellectual, and masculine world, well aware, also, of the very conventions that had linked reason with masculinity in the first place. She had already completed translations of Alexandre Rudolf Vinet's *Mémoire sur les libertés des cultes* and David Friedrich Strauss's *Das Leben Jesu,* and when her unorthodox friend and confidant Charles Bray purchased the Coventry *Herald,* he found in Eliot a clever columnist and book reviewer. Eliot, in fact, had been moving quite comfortably within the Coventry intelligentsia for nearly 5 years. Yet, remarkably, she refused to reconceptualize her strength of intellect as an unsexed human attribute. She chose, instead, to account for her intellectual authority by reinventing her social identity. In other words, rather than feminize her intellect, Eliot set out to resolve the apparent social incongruities of her life by masculinizing her public and private persona.

The complex nature of Eliot's investment in the masculine becomes more intelligible if we examine a tongue-in-cheek letter that she sent to Bray in October of 1846. In the letter, Eliot spins a tale about a German professor who appears on her doorstep asking for her hand in marriage. The suitor, a Professor Bücherwurm ("Bookworm"), has come to London to "secure a translator in the person of a wife" and, at the recommendation of others, has determined that Eliot presents "the required combination of attributes": the ability to translate German, "a very decided ugliness of person," and a fortune sufficient to the publishing and smoking needs of the prolific scholar. Although she pleases him in most respects, he is compelled to confess that "I am rather disappointed to see that you have no beard, an attribute which I have ever regarded as the most unfailing indication of a strong-minded woman." Thrilled to be saved "from the horrific disgrace of spinsterhood," Eliot accepts the proposal and allays the professor's sole misgiving with the following response:

> As to my want of beard I trust that defect may be remedied, since I doubt not there must be creams and essences which gentlemen . . . employ to cherish the too reluctant down, and it is an interesting physiological experiment yet to be tried, whether the feminine lip and chin may not be rendered fertile by this top-dressing.
>
> [21]

Eliot's sense of her own large and manly physical features clearly amuses her, for she recognizes that the earnest self-deprecation of homely femininity turns out to be of a piece with the daily masculine affectations of any unfortunately effeminate young gentleman. She has no particular interest here in detaching her genius from the norm of masculinity, for in suggesting that a gentleman's *toilette* could produce the desired effects on either a man or a woman, she implies that the norm of masculinity is itself detached and available.

That this anecdote is conceived in the context of a traditional marriage proposal ensures that the "femaleness" of Eliot's body is not forgotten, however. The professor has come to London to take a *wife,* after all, not simply a translator. Here we see the dynamics of what Butler calls the "compulsory system" or "situation of duress under which gender performance always and variously occurs."[22] By narrating a domestic scene, Eliot presents first the orthodoxy of the "original," the expectation that biological sex retains its essence beneath her investment in masculinity. But the link between masculinity and reason—scrupulously maintained as it is in the image of a bearded, strongminded woman—actually begins to call the female body into question. Eliot notes that "the Professor prefers as a female garb a man's coat, thrown over what are justly called the *petticoats,* so that the dress of a woman of genius may present the same sort of symbolical compromise between the masculine and feminine attire of which we have an example in the breastplate and petticoat of the immortal Joan."[23] Once the professor accepts Eliot as a "woman of genius," Eliot's femaleness inevitably turns into femininity, a garb rather than an essence, as much an effect as the cultivation of facial hair. Accordingly, as the professor's translator-wife, Eliot enters a new sphere of action and influence that both depends upon and undermines the "compulsory system" that gives it social intelligibility. Unwilling to displace gender distinction altogether, Eliot never discards her petticoats; they give shape to the difference which distinguishes masculinity as politically serviceable to her. By putting a man's coat over her petticoats, therefore, she claims her social, intellectual, and professional freedoms out of the very sexual differences that she appears to contest.

So it is with pointed irony that 8 years after such raillery, in the course of praising the intellect of French women, Eliot turns to rebuke her British sisters for deigning to imitate men. In her 1854 review essay, **"Woman in France,"** Eliot writes:

> With a few remarkable exceptions, our own feminine literature is made up of books which could have been better written by men; . . . when not a feeble imitation, they are usually an absurd exaggeration of the masculine style, like the swaggering gait of a bad actress in male attire.
>
> [24]

Eliot's brusqueness and lack of sympathy with women in general makes some sense so long as her identification with men takes on the character of a personal project of self-determination and success. But why admonish other women for choosing the same course for themselves? Why celebrate French women who "wrote what they saw, thought, and felt . . . without any intention to prove that women could write as well as men, without affecting manly views or suppressing womanly ones"?[25]

Eliot's discrimination between the mimicry of other women and her own intellectual cross-dressing derives from her assessment of the quality of the performance and the measure of dissonance that the impersonation generates. As I have suggested above, Butler valorizes drag as parody, pastiche, a "failed copy," as it were—the protraction of observable distance between sex, gender, and the gender performance.[26] Because the drag queen is subversive only in her failure to "pass" as a straight woman, bad acting, for Butler, turns out to be feminism's chief stratagem. Eliot, on the other hand, would find such parodic impersonations unconvincing, absurd, unproductive. Instead, the careful, contrived style of social intercourse in the seventeenth-century French salon captures Eliot's attention as the gender performance *par excellence,* valued not only for its self-consciousness but also for its precision.

The evolution of social interaction between French men and women was founded first of all on what Eliot believed to be an earnest appreciation of sexual difference. Because the reigning "womanly characteristics" of the day included "affection," "imagination," and a "dread of what overtaxes [the] intellectual energies," these "*réunions* of both sexes" forced French women, on the one hand, to invent a "new standard of taste" and French men, on the other, to conform to it. Exalted sentiment and "simplicity of language" were all the rage in the salon; "everything was admissible, if only it were treated with refinement and intelligence." Hence, the great thinkers of the day (Balzac, Richelieu, La Rochefoucauld, to name a few) were expected to "present their best ideas in the guise most acceptable to intelligent and accomplished women." And the by-product? An increase in dramatic facility with every attempt at self-presentation, and a decrease in the margin between acting the part of the genius and acting the part of the man.[27]

In sum, Eliot's regard for this highly stylized form of social interaction ("*genre précieux,*" as she calls it) is grounded not only in its performative character but also in its inherent attachment to the original ideas of the French men who frequented the salons. No mere pretense, the "guise" here is a form or genre, a kind of *ad hoc* self-fashioning, yes, but with roots embedded in a larger history of genius, intellectual communion, and liberty of thought and practice. Eliot goes on to critique some of the later imitative salons, where "simplicity degenerated into affectation, and nobility of sentiment was replaced by an inflated effort to outstrip nature."[28] But what Eliot wants to duplicate in her own life is this so-called *original "genre précieux,"* where to cross-dress, even metaphorically, is to do more than simply put on the trappings of masculinity; it is, rather, to be implicated in those myriad histories which underwrite the political significance of masculinity. Eliot, therefore, finds masculine traits and accoutrements to be insufficient as feminist ends in themselves. Women who imitate men badly are merely foolish rather than subversive, and remain unqualified to abandon the feminine sphere of thought and duty for larger social responsibilities and privileges.[29] Given this attention to the meaning as well as the shape of masculinity, Eliot's defence of *genre précieux* is particularly provocative today in the face of renewed feminist interest in essentialism and the body.[30] Although Eliot does not overlook the fact that gender is a mobile construct, she does appreciate an originality in gender that Butler misses, an essential promise of intellectual and social privilege that makes mimicking the observable silhouette of gender alone an inadequate strategy for her.

These subtle distinctions between the mobility and the originality of gender become somewhat clearer, at least theoretically, in a brief essay called **"Notes on Form in Art"** (1868). Eliot essentially re-evaluates prevailing aesthetic philosophies, offering in their stead an expressly organic reading of the constitutive elements of art, including, most importantly, form.

> *Even in the plastic arts Form obviously, in its general application, means something else than mere imitation of outline, more or less correctness of drawing or modelling—just as, with reference to descriptive poetry, it means something more than the bare delineation of landscape or figures. . . . Artistic form, as distinguished from mere imitation, begins in sculpture and painting with composition or the selection of attitudes and the formation of groups, let the objects be of what order they may. . . . [T]he choice and sequence of images and ideas—that is, of relations and groups of relations—are more or less not only determined by emotion but intended to express it.*[31]

Form is no mere frontage that can be imitated by the student without recourse to the idea that unifies a particular work of art. To capture and reproduce form, then, one must have some sense, or aesthetic sensibility, for the "design" or purpose that governs it.

Not surprisingly, Eliot applies her analysis of art to the human organism, the "highest Form." This analogy has its own significance in the context of her aesthetic inquiry, but it also helps us to reread Eliot's skepticism about the democratization of English society in general and the women's movement specifically. Eliot suggests that it is pointless to regard affectation or "airs of superiority" as the effects of "true culture." Such pretenses are nothing more than "mere acquisitions carried about, and not knowledge thoroughly assimilated so as to enter into the growth of the character."[32] Where form (or gender) is reduced to "mere acquisitions," the return on one's investment is negligible. Masculinity is politically useful for Eliot only in so far as it is socially and intrinsically linked with genius. Silly lady novelists, on the other hand, have atomized gender and culture, copying the "mere outline" of what they deem to be socially empowering. Although it is important to remember that Eliot does not consider the "masculine" to be available exclusively to men, she is never tempted to feminize the power, privilege and society that she seeks. "Women become superior in France," she notes, "by being admitted to a common fund of ideas, to common objects of interest with men."[33] Eliot recognizes that, at least for Victorian society, the value attached to these "ideas" and "objects of interest" proceeds from the judgement of men and governs the aspirations of men—even if some of those "men" are only playing at it.

III

In suggesting that we consider the resource of non-libidinal appropriations of masculinity by women, I have concentrated on a figure from the nineteenth century whose life and work were fashioned out of the expectation that equality between men and women would be worth pursuing personally and locally but that such equality must be manufactured from the very differences that threaten to suppress its further possibilities. Therefore we should take care not to construe Eliot's play at being a man as disregard for an "original" difference between herself and her model. The originality of gender—and hence its value—comes, for Eliot, out of history itself, out of the narratives that precede and follow traditions, institutions and nations, giving meaning to social and political order as well as to "the growth of the character." These histories are intrinsic to the experiences and identities of both individuals and groups, and while they may not be "essential," they are inevitable, at least within the contexts in which they are told.

Still, there are problems with using Eliot as a case-study for feminism today, problems that may be obscured by the antiseptic character of academic writing as well as by the historical and critical distance that scholarly work presupposes. David Lehman has wisely reminded us of Orwell's dictum that "[t]he problem of jargon . . . is that it can all too easily confer a bogus veneer of respectability on barbarous behavior."[34] What I want to consider now are the liabilities of a theoretical analysis of a role model for feminism. What dilemmas ensue when we celebrate, or perhaps construct, behaviors in Eliot that we would condemn in our own academic departments and political life?[35]

In her retrospective on feminism and the academy over the last 30 years, Mary Ellen S. Capek admits that what has been judged by many as feminist progress may have become, in fact, a new form of "barbarous behavior":

> With few exceptions . . . , writers cited in the current debates about feminist literary theory are white scholars writing from bases in prestigious institutions, often writing in traditional male academic writing styles. This is not to knock success. In the process of staking our claims in the academy, however, we need not abstract ourselves from our sources. . . . As we struggle for tenure and recognition in the academy, tools that have helped us deconstruct embedded sexism and heterosexism in texts too often fail to help us find the embedded racism and classism, those status needs that shape our own language and styles of discourse.
>
> 36

In reconsidering the intersection of race, class, gender, and sexual preference, Capek believes that contemporary feminist appropriations of "male academic writing styles" are no longer about a feminist assault on the Old Boys Club.[37] According to Capek, the "status needs" that have driven the individual feminist to mimic masculine virility have left intact other forms of discrimination (racism and classism) and thus support a picture of feminism that is corrosive at best, spurious at worst. Should we be surprised, then, when stories of Eliot's repeated affronts against her female contemporaries and friends as well as her frequent

opposition to the women's movement begin to lose their theoretical appeal upon closer inspection?

Furthermore, were we to follow Eliot in her insistence that mimicking mannerism isn't enough—that we must reach further into the heart of masculinity to find genius, to find a solid basis on which to build notions of responsibility and freedom for women—then we would come into direct conflict with feminist theorists and philosophers such as Elizabeth Grosz, Carole Pateman, Sandra Harding, Teresa de Lauretis and Dale Spender, who have been instrumental in piloting a systematic critique of knowledges in the interest of maintaining "an essential difference between a feminist and a non-feminist understanding" of "woman, women, and the world."[38] These theorists read the quest for equality as both delusive and distracting, and propose instead a feminist program for theorizing women's specificity *en route* to securing women's autonomy from rather than equality with men. This strategy, it is argued, works toward not only disabling men as a dominant class but also undermining their position as a standard for comparison. Eliot's reliance on a masculinist definition of genius would ultimately defeat the purpose of that investment for feminism, according to these critics, and contribute "to the very forms of male dominance feminism should be trying to combat."[39]

Without further elaboration, these two brief examples illustrate the likelihood of theoretical slippage when feminists try to write a coherent and continuous history of feminism.[40] Why, for example, don't feminists of earlier generations ever appear adequate to the collective cause of later generations, and what are we to do with this inadequacy, this inappropriateness, this annoying naïveté, if not to disavow it? Have we given up too much when we theorize the possibilities that inhere in a nineteenth-century feminist strategy of straight drag? And what fundamental contradictions are produced by calling this strategy "feminist" in the first place?

We would not go wrong in remembering the slogan with which Fredric Jameson christened the preface of his book, *The Political Unconscious.* "Always historicize!" he exhorts, and with that in mind, Eliot's investment in masculinity takes on a radically contingent character.[41] We begin to see that the narrative which links masculinity with both genius and its consequent philosophical and political liberties is a narrative that is subtly transformed every time women tap into its logic. Over time, as this narrative shifts under the inclinations of feminist play, the terms of that play will shift as well, in response to the specificities of what is original to masculinity at given moments in history. Hence the so-called inadequacy of Eliot's investments, from a late twentieth-century feminist perspective, reflects not Eliot's lack of relevance as a feminist but masculinity's lack of fixity and unity as a cultural and historical product. For if it is true that "the pervasive threat of misogyny brought into being feminist discourse," to quote Susan Gubar, then where that threat migrates, feminist discourse will tend to follow.[42]

The nature of these misogynist and feminist migrations, however, goes beyond a simple game of follow the leader. Even Susan Gubar's dialogic theory—where feminism and misogyny are said to "bob and weave" or "feint and jab" their way through history[43]—does not account for feminism's own investments in masculinity *in feminist terms*. Although Eliot's intellectual cross-dressing emerged first and foremost from personal ambition, defined by a set of goals achievable in her lifetime (respect, intellectual and vocational fulfillment, public mobility), her value as a role model for feminism turns on a different axis altogether, one that draws our attention to the marked historicity not only of straight drag but of feminism itself.

In the first instance, we learn from Eliot to read straight drag as a means (of critique), not an end (to inequality). In forcing us to recognize that straight drag is neither ahistorical nor revolutionary, this lesson heightens our awareness of the broad spectrum of women's oppressions and fosters, more generally, a healthy realism to counter the utopian strains of some feminist theory and activism. Thus, we see that even as straight drag mimics potency, it is ultimately impotent (at least in a revolutionary sense) and must repeat itself in order to put any critical strain on misogyny. When the feminist woman "aspires to be like a man," both the narrative and physical features said to constitute masculinity lose their political importance as a mark of difference, and misogyny is forced to revise its justifications and move on. Acting like a man, then, does not have to be about women suppressing the historical specificity of their own gendered subjectivity, nor must it mean that women think themselves historically, if not essentially, inferior to men and hence rely on legislation to answer this inequality. Rather, straight drag—a non-utopian feminist *strategy*—simply publishes the fault lines concealed by the story that unifies masculinity and power. What it does not do is produce any sort of equality that should ever satisfy us.

This tack, of course, repeatedly compels misogyny to reconsolidate masculinity, to invent new marks of difference even as it loses the efficacy of its old ones. Hence the crisis of feminism in an age of backlash: if feminist play invokes new and reactionary forms of misogyny, feminism could be said to circulate the very thing it seeks to disrupt. Furthermore, straight drag, by definition, is unable to bring about any end to masculinity as an organic product of history and culture and is limited, at best, to motivating the perpetual mutation of the political functions of masculinity. While it is true, then, that feminism is to some extent implicated in misogyny, it is not the repetition or mimicry of masculinity itself that puts the integrity of the feminist project at risk, but the way in which straight drag obliges misogyny to reinvent itself in order to survive. More specifically, if Eliot is to be labelled a misogynist, it is not her manliness that should give us pause but the fact that her play will, over time, render the identification of masculinity with intellectual authority politically moot and force the narratives which underwrite sexual hierarchy to reinvest in another site of sexual difference—say, for instance, citizenship.

It could be argued that the reactions and consequences which feminism invites by virtue of its critical methods stand beyond the scope of feminist responsibility. I would assert, to the contrary, that this is perhaps the only real risk feminism ever takes—and it is, indeed, *feminism's* distinctive wager. There is still room for women to agitate "as duplicate men" precisely because the benefits of such agitation have been repeatedly embraced, however grudgingly, by almost anyone willing to call herself a feminist today. Recognizing and then taking responsibility for the limitations of egalitarian feminism has, for example, enabled someone like Elizabeth Grosz to build a theory of sexual difference atop, as well as in spite of, a foundation of legislative progress for women over the past 150 years. This is not to say that Grosz is uninterested in critiquing equality politics. Such a critique is clearly one of her chief aims in re-evaluating knowledges that have been produced by men and uncritically mimicked by women. But where feminism begins to accept its byproducts for what they are likely to bring with them, critics such as Grosz are compelled to presuppose, even as they investigate, the hallmarks of egalitarian feminism. Along with the prohibitive perspective of phallocentric institutions comes the irresistible materiality of women's greater access to education; the pernicious "double load" and equitable child custody laws are available only as a package deal. Whatever beginnings, means, or ends feminism is ready to avow—without going so far as to sanction wholesale—constitutes the measure of feminism's responsibility to itself.

Today, a feminist's contributions as a woman will always also include her satisfactions in emulating men (whether she argues for equality or not) because the material resources and institutional supports on which her work depends are rooted in feminisms of equality. This wider frame of reference also gives the feminist access to a larger battery of techniques and perspectives that compel greater nuance in comprehending and describing the nature of women's oppressions. The risks of this expansiveness may mean that the future of feminism is uncertain, but its past will be less so, since the paradox of what feminism wants will always require the divisions, gaps, misunderstandings and multiple origins that define feminism historically, no matter what is in or out of vogue at the time.

Notes

1. George Eliot (6 December 1857) "Journal Entry," The George Eliot Letters (Ed. Gordon S. Haight; New Haven: Yale University Press, 1954-55), vol. 2, p. 409.

2. Ina Taylor (1989) A Woman of Contradictions: The Life of George Eliot (New York: William Morrow and Company, Inc.), pp. 67, 103-105.

3. Jacques Derrida (1978) Spurs: Nietzsche's Styles/Éperons: Les Styles de Nietzsche (tr. Barbara Harlow; Intro. Stefano Agosti; Chicago: University of Chicago Press, 1979), p. 65.

4. Taylor, A Woman of Contradictions, p. 188.

5. Ibid., p. 171.

6. George Eliot (October 1856) "Silly Novels by Lady Novelists," Westminster Review, 56, p. 254.

7. For a good summary of feminist reaction to George Eliot's fiction, see Ellen Ringler (1983) "Middlemarch: A Feminist Perspective," Studies in the Novel, 15.1, pp. 55-61. For a more recent picture of Eliot's reception history among feminists, see Jeanie Thomas (1988) Reading Middlemarch: Reclaiming the Middle Distance (Ann Arbor: UMI Research Press), pp. 47-65; Laurie Langbauer (1990) Women and Romance: The Consolations of Gender in the English Novel (Ithaca: Cornell University Press), pp. 188-232.

8. Christina Crosby (1991) The Ends of History: Victorians and "The Woman Question" (New York: Routledge), pp. 42-43.

9. See Susan Gubar's recent work on "feminist misogyny." As Gubar puts it, "although feminism historically has not been the condition for misogyny's emergence, the pervasive threat of misogyny brought into being feminist discourse." The two are lifelong "slam dance" partners in dialogic relation to one another, co-implicated in one another's projects to such a degree that traces of both feminism and misogyny can be teased out of virtually every major author and work of the literary canon (Susan Gubar [1995] "Feminist Misogyny: Mary Wollstonecraft and the Paradox of 'It Takes One to Know One,'" Feminism Beside Itself [Eds Diane Elam & Robyn Wiegman; New York: Routledge], pp. 142, 144).

10. Some critics have begun to challenge openly the notion that collectivity is politically necessary or desirable at all for feminism, although I am not sure to what extent this shift can ever be achieved self-consciously. I am thinking, in particular, of the anthology Feminism Beside Itself, co-edited by Diane Elam & Robyn Wiegman, as well as its companion conference held at Indiana University in April of 1995. In both cases, the governing logic of the editors/organizers betrays an orchestration behind the discord—perhaps a remnant of anxieties about giving up the political leverage of unity too soon?

11. Nancy Cott (1987) The Grounding of Modern Feminism (New Haven: Yale University Press), p. 5.

12. Karin Cope might argue that my refusal to absolve or "exonerate" Eliot is a presumption of greater authority on the part of my feminism because of its apparently more enlightened (read: later) position in feminist history, and is likewise an attempt to reify the shifting moral values that label someone a role model in one age and a misanthrope in another. Cope's point is well taken, although my desire to preserve Eliot's misogyny in all its offensiveness does not stem from my disappointment in her as a feminist "foremother." Rather, I simply want to take seriously this example of feminism's masculine investments in order to understand more clearly how feminism might be served by them. Karin Cope (1995) "'Moral Deviancy' and Contemporary Feminism: The Judgment of Gertrude Stein," in Feminism Beside Itself, pp. 155-178.

13. Judith Butler (1990) Gender Trouble: Feminism and the Subversion of Identity (New York: Routledge), p. viii.

14. Butler, Gender Trouble.

15. Ibid., p. 30.

16. Ibid., pp. 146, 127.

17. Ibid., p. 137 (Butler's emphasis).

18. As Diana Fuss assesses the problem, "[m]uch lesbian-feminist theory sets up the lesbian subject as a natural agent of subversion, an inherent revolutionary subject." While Butler makes several attempts to distance herself from this sort of valorization (particularly in her discussion of Monique Wittig in chapter 3, part 3), her theory of gender performativity is too dependent on gay drag to avoid this problem altogether (Diana Fuss [1989] Essentially Speaking: Feminism, Nature and Difference [New York: Routledge], p. 46).

19. Gordon S. Haight (1968) *George Eliot: A Biography* (Oxford: Oxford University Press), p. 535; see also Taylor, *A Woman of Contradictions*, pp. 207-209.

20. The lack of theoretical attention given to straight drag becomes even more remarkable when Butler quotes Parker Tyler's "The Garbo Image" in an epigraph: "Garbo 'got in drag' whenever she took some heavy glamour part, whenever she melted in or out of a man's arms, whenever she simply let that heavenly-flexed neck . . . bear the weight of her thrown-back head. . . . How resplendent seems the art of acting! It is all *impersonation,* whether the sex underneath is true or not" (Butler, *Gender Trouble*, p. 128). Although I am interested primarily in Butler's oversight with regard to straight forms of cross-sexual drag, one wonders why she does not use this epigraph to launch an extended analysis of what might turn out to be the most subversive form of drag - an excess of femininity on the female body.

21. George Eliot (21 October 1846) "George Eliot to Charles Bray," in *The George Eliot Letters*, 9 vols (Ed. Gordon S. Haight; New Haven: Yale University Press, 1954-55, 1978), vol. 8, pp. 13, 14.

22. Butler, *Gender Trouble*, p. 139.

23. Eliot, "George Eliot to Charles Bray," p. 15.

24. George Eliot (October 1854) "Woman in France: Madame de Sablé," *Westminster Review*, 62, p. 448.

25. Ibid., p. 449. Elsewhere, Eliot praises Margaret Fuller's *Woman in the Nineteenth Century* because "[t]here is no exaggeration of woman's moral excellence or intellectual capabilities, no injudicious insistence on her fitness for this or that function hitherto engrossed by men" (George Eliot [13 October 1855] "Margaret Fuller and Mary Wollstonecraft," *The Leader*, 6, p. 988).

26. Butler, *Gender Trouble*, pp. 146, 137.

27. Eliot, "Woman in France," pp. 452-453.

28. Ibid., p. 453.

29. It is worth noting that ethical responsibility and aesthetic genius were always linked in Eliot's mind. Both were the chief measure of a masculinity to which she aspired; both were void of the femininity which she often disparaged: "For it must be plain to every one who looks impartially and extensively into feminine literature, that its greatest deficiencies are due hardly more to the want of intellectual power than to the want of those moral qualities that contribute to literary excellence—patient diligence, a sense of the responsibility involved in publication, and an appreciation of the sacredness of the writer's art" (Eliot, "Silly Novels," p. 319).

30. See, for example, Elizabeth Grosz (1994) *Volatile Bodies: Toward a Corporeal Feminism* (Bloomington: Indiana University Press); Rosi Braidotti (1991) *Patterns of Dissonance* (Cambridge: Polity Press); Naomi Schor & Elizabeth Weed (Eds) (1994) *the essential difference* (Bloomington: Indiana University Press); Diana Fuss, *Essentially Speaking*.

31. George Eliot (1868) "Notes on Form in Art," in Rosemary Ashton (Ed.) (1992) *George Eliot: Selected Critical Writings* (Oxford: Oxford University Press), pp. 356-357.

32. Eliot, "Margaret Fuller," p. 989.

33. Eliot, "Woman in France," p. 472.

34. David Lehman (1992) *Signs of the Times: Deconstruction and the Fall of Paul de Man* (New York: Poseidon Press), p. 89.

35. Here again Karin Cope's insightful essay is relevant as I consider the extent to which feminists of an earlier generation can be ethically appropriate or politically expedient role models for later generations, given the contingency of moral value and politics (Karin Cope, "'Moral Deviancy' and Contemporary Feminism").

36. Mary Ellen S. Capek (1992) "Post-Tweeds, Pipes, and Textosterone: Perspectives on Feminism, Literary Studies, and the Academy," in *The Knowledge Explosion: Generations of Feminist Scholarship* (Eds Cheris Kramarae & Dale Spender; New York: Teachers College Press), pp. 74-75.

37. For further reflection on the question of academic writing and feminism, see Ruth-Ellen Boetcher Joeres (1992) "Editorial: On Writing Feminist Academic Prose," *Signs*, 17, pp. 701-704.

38. Teresa de Lauretis (1994) "The Essence of the Triangle or, Taking the Risk of Essentialism Seriously: Feminist Theory in Italy, the US, and Britain," *the essential difference*, p.1. See also Elizabeth Gross & Carole Pateman (Eds) (1986) *Feminist Challenges: Social and Political Theory* (Boston: Northeastern University Press); Sandra Harding & Merrill B. Hintikka (Eds) (1983) *Discovering Reality: Feminist Perspectives on Epistemology, Metaphysics, Methodology and the Philosophy of Science* (Dordrecht: Reidel); Dale Spender (Ed.) (1981) *Men's Studies Modified: The Impact of Feminism on Academic Knowledge* (London: Pergamon).

39. Elizabeth Grosz (1994) "Sexual Difference and the Problem of Essentialism," in *the essential difference*, pp. 90-91, 82. Judith Allen provides an excellent bibliographic history of the emergence of the feminist critique of knowledges in the late 1970s and its commitments up to the present day (Judith A. Allen [1992] "Feminist Critiques of Western Knowledges: Spatial Anxieties in a Provisional Phase?" in *Beyond the Disciplines: The New Humanities* [Ed. K. K. Ruthven; Canberra: Australian Academy of the Humanities], pp. 57-77).

40. For a discussion of some of the assumptions of periodization and classification that have kept historians of feminism locked into unproductive methods of historiography, see Judith Allen (1990) "Contextualising Late-Nineteenth-Century Feminism: Problems and Comparisons," *Journal of the CHA/Revue de la S.H.C.*, pp. 17-36.

41. Fredric Jameson (1981) *The political Unconscious: Narrative as a Socially Symbolic Act* (Ithaca: Cornell University Press), p. 9.

42. Gubar, "Feminist Misogyny," p. 142. This is not to say that men and masculinity are logically prior to women and femininity, or that women are or should be defined relative to men. But it would be a mistake to think that feminism as a political and theoretical *strategy* is not guided in important ways by the character of the misogyny and patriarchalism it aims to undermine.

43. Ibid.

TITLE COMMENTARY

Felix Holt, the Radical

ALISON BOOTH (ESSAY DATE 1992)

SOURCE: Booth, Alison. "Not All Men Are Selfish and Cruel: *Felix Holt* As a Feminist Novel." In *Gender and Discourse in Victorian Literature and Art,* edited by Antony H. Harrison and Beverly Taylor, pp. 143-60. DeKalb: Northern Illinois University Press, 1992.

In the following essay, Booth explores the gender conflict in Felix Holt, *asserting that the novel is an "unassimilated feminist argument."*

Once George Eliot had established herself as a great woman of letters in such works as the unpopular but authoritative *Romola,* she found herself in a difficult position. The stakes were higher perhaps even than they had been when she vindicated the fallen, strong-minded woman, Marian Evans "Lewes," in the wise reminiscences of the clerical George Eliot. That gentleman had now been promoted to the position of Victorian sage, which could easily take the fun out of the novelist's job. Yet while she was expected to teach, she was still expected to dazzle; overt preaching was taboo in the Victorian almost as much as in the modern aesthetic code. Further, her now public womanhood burdened her; the suspicion cast on any woman not minding her domestic business could poison a political novel by a woman, not to mention a novel recklessly broaching the "woman question." In *Felix Holt, the Radical,* Eliot veers close to feminist special pleading, yet the novel has always appeared to be political only in the traditional sense (and her traditional politics have irritated many); she can "pass" as a male historical novelist of a superior order, experimenting in artful form and allusion, avoiding Scott's anachronism, elevating her readers' understanding and taste. Yet it is important to see, behind the mask of the great novelist, a writer politically situated, one who recognized the interdependence of the public and private spheres and who, perhaps more than she realized, indicted the injustices of patriarchy in a drama of class and gender in a small Midlands town in the Reform Era.

In *Felix Holt* (1866) Eliot disguised her arguments about gender and class in an apparently impartial history of everyday life; she in effect responded to an immediate political threat, the second Reform Bill, by advocating gradual amelioration of private life and, above all, of women's lot. Like her friends and associates who campaigned in the 1850s and 1860s for such things as women's higher education and the right for married women to own property, she adhered to an ideology of influence, a belief in women's vocation for sympathy as a basis for social reform.[1] She hoped to foster feminine influence but entertained no political ambitions of remaking woman in man's image—and still less of eliminating class along with sexual differences.[2] Eliot mistrusted partisan politics as a kind of institutionalization of unfeminine egocentrism and competition, and while she, like so many of her contemporaries, perceived an affinity between women and oppressed classes and peoples, the bonds of the common life as she portrays them are uneasy at best. In particular, she suggests an ingrained antagonism between imperious men and all "others," redefining "radical" to mean, one who repudiates *his* ties to the past, to family life, and to the feminine.

Eliot's evident constraints in dealing with the electoral conflicts compressed in the subtitle "the Radical" become more intelligible and even excusable when seen in light of her feminist politics, which affirm what the self-promoting votemongers would like to leave behind. In the epigraph to chapter 21, an unidentified opportunist (perhaps lawyer Jermyn or his informer Christian) complains, "'Tis grievous, that with all amplification of travel both by sea and land, a man can never separate himself from his past history."[3] Eliot might simply be echoing the platitude that there are no shortcuts in moral life and illustrating it with alarming scenes of social upheaval, but she is applying these conservative brakes because men who desire mobility have generally stored their women at home as too heavy to carry along. Thus Mrs. Transome's lover, Jermyn, has left her behind in his own career of reputable villainy, like Jason believing that he is "not at all obliged to" his Medea, only to face the vengeance of consequences (512-13). Eliot's consequential world, in which there can be no revolutions or magical escapes from the past, also gives voice to Medea's rage, a disturbance of the peace more truly radical, in the usual sense, than any riot on election day.

The feminism of *Felix Holt* for the most part is sealed off from the public political action of committees or votes, while its ladies are perceived as under siege not only by patriarchs but also by the masses. Eliot begs her social questions: Which misogynist "radical" is Esther Lyon to marry? Which fate is better for the workers in the short run, brute subjection or brute rebellion? But she seeks to appease the classes and the sexes within the tradition of the novel of manners, through a slightly eccentric marriage in which the heiress marries the poor man (forfeiting her wealth) and seems prepared to help him run a kind of workers' institute.[4] Uneasy about pressing too political a message in her novel, she preferred to publish a more explicit statement about class and electoral politics (but *not* the "woman question") as a nonfictional appendix: "Address to Working Men, by Felix Holt" (1867). *Felix Holt* may be seen as an attempt to subsume the agitation for women's suffrage in the 1860s under scenes of "masculine" political life from the 1830s, in the locale and period of Eliot's youth, working within literary and social traditions.[5] Perhaps it is no wonder, given the complexity of its aims, that this is one of the least read of Eliot's novels.

In outline these aims are very much those of *Middlemarch,* another study of the English Midlands in the 1830s with interwoven masculine and feminine histories. Although the two novels differ enormously in power and design, many of the elements of the acknowledged masterpiece appear in the preceding work, with an almost inverted emphasis. Such inversion makes *Felix Holt* the more revealing articulation of a hushed politics. Eliot's earlier novel leaves the political issues of class and gender surprisingly exposed and unresolved, whereas the "greater" novel marginalizes scenes of political life and feminist protest as minor episodes or as hints in the prelude and finale. Is it partly the dictum that great art is not political that has devalued *Felix Holt* and that hampered Eliot as she wrote it?[6] *Felix Holt,* almost in spite of Eliot, seems an *overtly* radical text, even as it repudiates masculine "radicalism." The bitter protests of Mrs. Transome in particular arrest our attention (and readers from the beginning have found her the most compelling feature of the novel). That ailing woman, before being put to bed and "soothe[d] . . . with a daughter's tendance" by Esther, says, "Men are selfish . . . and cruel. What they care for is their own pleasure and their own pride." "Not all," is Esther's rather inadequate response to these "painful" words (597).

In *Felix Holt,* Eliot appears to reconcile interdependent spheres, the private and the public, much as though she would justify patriarchal society as the natural order modeled on the family, yet she alters the scale of values: the private, associated with women, the powerless, and personal relations, becomes the predominant factor in human history. Thus the novel implies that social progress relies on some form of fellow-feeling and on the sympathy that women are conditioned to extend rather than on practical measures or on the active pursuit of change usually reserved for young men. Eliot's narrator declares, "[T]his history is chiefly concerned with the private lot of a few men and women; but there is no private life which has not been determined by a wider public life" (129). By implication, one cannot understand public life without reading the history of private lots.

Most critics of the novel address a perceived strain between these political and "personal" strands, some accounting for it in terms of conflicting generic intentions. During composition, Eliot does seem to have been doubly concerned with the accuracy of a historical-political novel on the Reform Era and with the effectiveness of a tragedy in novel form.[7] According to Fred C. Thomson, Eliot's notebooks indicate that *Felix Holt* originated in Eliot's study of classical tragedy as she worked on *The Spanish Gypsy* and that the interest in electioneering politics was worked up later.[8] Like the tendency to suppress "the Radical," the subtitle on the original title page, this view that the story of the Transomes takes precedence over the depiction of changing social conditions is suspect (part of a bias toward timeless, apolitical art?), but it is hard to deny that the circumstances of the election, the legal machinery that conveys Esther to Transome Court, and the reconciliation and marriage of Esther and Felix lack Mrs. Transome's fire.[9] Arnold Kettle, reversing Thomson's ordering, claims that the original study of two kinds of radical was deflected by Eliot's interest in "the position of woman" and "moral responsibility" (106).[10] Whatever Eliot's process of creation, it seems that critics resist the idea that the plots centering on Mrs. Transome, Esther, Felix, and Harold might be more than incidentally related; in other words, they presume that the plots centering on men's politics and on women's relationships are disparate if not rivalrous, that private and public spheres remain alien to each other. In spite of the manifest analogies in the novel between the politics of the drawing room and of the hustings, the accounts of Eliot's having been distracted from one sphere into the other persist. Even in light of these analogies, it is impossible to make a fully coherent novel out of *Felix Holt.* There is, especially, a surplus of feminist protest—surplus because narrator, characters, and plot largely ignore it.

The tragedy of Mrs. Transome is that of a woman who is unable to renounce her personal desires and who finds no wider calling; she is a pettier prototype of the Alcharisi, the dark double of the great woman of letters. Female ambition without voluntary self-sacrifice is always a disturbing force in Eliot's work. As though to contain this force, the novel shows a more dispassionate interest in things as they were: the history of the Reform Era as it opened and quickly closed the possibility of extending political rights to workers and women.[11] In addition to tragic form and historical accuracy, Eliot juggled the conventions of plot and plausibility, consulting the Comtean lawyer Frederic Harrison on the legal details of her plot.[12] Harrison's and John Blackwood's praise of the "politics" of the first two volumes dispelled Eliot's "depression as to [the novel's] practical effectiveness," though she remained "in that state of utter distrust and anxiety about my work which is usually the painful accompaniment of authorship with me."[13] She was not, of course, discouraged from attempting a similar synthesis of diverse elements again: Eliot assured Harrison that she would "keep the great possibility (or impossibility)" of creating an effective microcosm of social relations "perpetually in my mind," and we may speculate that *Middlemarch* developed as a result. Eliot acknowledged the risk she had taken in attempting political art. After the publication of *Felix Holt*, she noted "the severe effort of trying to make certain ideas thoroughly incarnate"; "aesthetic teaching," she now maintained, would necessarily become offensive when "it lapses . . . from the picture to the diagram."[14] The artful world of *Felix Holt* at times seems reduced to a two-dimensional tract, but it does not disintegrate into unrelated private and public narratives.[15]

The conservative tenor of this novel may be primarily attributed to a *resistance* to such disintegration of the gendered spheres. *Felix Holt* offers radical insight into the correspondence between the lots of English ladies and the fate of all citizens of the Empire, between historical events and moments in the domestic interior; and the insight is occluded by the enfranchised actors in the drama. Mrs. Transome's battle with her son is more than coincidentally linked with the battle between ancient right and the rioting rabble on election day. In addition, while the novel dramatizes the possibility of gradual progress in obscure lives—in a realistic historical framework—it also invokes a spiritual counterhistory, cyclical rather than teleological, perpetuating hidden conflicts in gender relations. Mrs. Transome's and Esther's complementary stories have a mythical quality, as though like Demeter and Persephone they enact the recurring seasons, while Mrs. Transome recognizes that home is a Dantesque hell. The complex structure of the novel—shifting between plots, households, times, points of view—draws analogies between the private choices of women and men and the transitional epochs in which they live, implying, for instance, that there is more promise in Esther's growing awareness than in any extension of the franchise or triumph of a politically enlightened faction.

The power of *Felix Holt* derives from irreconcilable differences between men and women and their respective fields of power and influence in English society. What cannot be put asunder, according to the outlook of this novel, also cannot be joined without masking the rough margins. Familiar forms have been twisted out of shape; emphasis falls unexpectedly. There are dark family secrets, musty wills, lovers' lockets, but nothing more sensational arises than an anticlimactic riot. To most readers, Mrs. Transome and Matthew Jermyn broadcast their secret affair long before their son Harold knows of it, while the dispute between the Transomes, Durfeys, and Bycliffes—all the legal matter of base fees and remainder-men that Frederic Harrison supplied—remains hardly more than it appears to Esther, a muddle of prerogatives magically invoked to change lives.[16] Even the title raises doubts, not only as to the sense in which "Radical" applies to a man who opposes what would become the Chartist program (395-403) but also as to the centrality of the fortunate and faith-upholding Felix Holt to the moral drama of the novel. Happy is he who holds on by the roots, the title seems to say, yet Felix must undo his father's errors and resist his mother, while Esther must escape her inheritance.[17] The patriarch is rather shabbily represented on the one hand by imbecile Mr. Transome and dotty Mr. Lyon, who fail in biological fathering, and on the other by devious Lawyer Jermyn and his illegitimate son, Harold, who marries a slave.

If the male line of succession is doubtful, the novel seems reluctant to let matriarchy stand in its stead. E. S. Dallas observed in 1866 that a male author would have named the book after Esther.[18] Indeed, most of the novel centers on the metamorphoses of the heroine, whose namesakes, Dickens's Esther Summerson and Queen Esther, are likewise poor foster daughters who find favor with powerful men. Eliot's Esther earns her moral crown by refusing a luxurious place as chief concubine, but she uses her influence to help her lover and her father, just as Queen Esther saves her cousin and adoptive father, Mordecai. The tragic Vashti, a famous actress in *Villette* (1853), in this novel has become the defeated Mrs. Transome, almost as though Eliot, like another King Ahasuerus, wished to make an example of the rebellious woman.[19] Precedent and tradition are subtly modified, but without overt challenge to patriarchal order.

For all her strong didactic aim, the woman of letters seems more than usually reluctant to commit herself to any particular doctrine; the monologues of the eccentric Rufus Lyon suggest that the preacher must be a kind of outsider. Political activity is shown to be corrupt, idealistic, ineffectual, or irrelevant. Only Felix, manly and dignified, is allowed to seize the author's podium for a time, but he is jailed for his part in civil disorder, while his misguided enthusiasm seems subordinate to the question of his education in the femininity he initially despised. The treatment of class conflict is even more unsatisfactory; the human animals of the Sproxton mines are noted but are offered no real help: only a future relief through the evolutionary enlightenment of the race. Given these evasions, in what sense does Eliot integrate the private with the public life?

To answer this question, we must concentrate on the "woman question" in nineteenth-century England. It seems to have been impossible to cover up the gap between the historic lot of Englishwomen and their potential. Eliot shows how women are denied their due influence, but any protest is rigidly controlled, primarily as the bitter censured outcry of a sinning woman. In the process of writing this novel, I would suggest, Eliot tempered her feminist argument, deflecting attention from female characters onto male and deploying impersonal descriptive passages and a title that subordinated the perspective of the women. Mrs. Transome and Transome Court are only part of the story of 1832, and a less timely part; Esther, similarly, remains outside public life, more like Maggie Tulliver than Romola. The struggles of Harold, Jermyn, Rufus, and Felix, in contrast, appear almost identical with the historical crisis of the novel. It is as though the implied author concurs with at least the first part of Harold's sweeping exclusion of women from historical mobility: "women keep to the notions in which they have been brought up. It doesn't signify what they think—they are not called upon to judge or act" (117). In Eliot's world of course it *does* signify what ladies think and how they judge and act, but they scarcely show signs of the times. In

response to the grand political turmoil of the Reform Era, Eliot offers two private pacifications: Harold, a Byronic colonialist, misogynist, and cynic, is finally swayed by Esther and reconciled with his mother, while Esther adapts herself to (and begins to influence) her romantic hero of the working classes.

These pacifications obey the central principle of **Felix Holt**: that "we" are each one among many, parts of a general pattern of interdependent private and public lives that foil our egotistical plans; hence the impersonal overview of the narrator, particularly in the "Author's Introduction" and in the epigraphs to each chapter, added late to the manuscript. A close look at the way we are conducted into the novel and at the subtle politics of certain unobtrusive scenes will help us uncover the unacknowledged propaganda in the work. A tendency to universalize a Victorian, masculine norm is tempered by a critique of particular manly egotists and radicals of all walks of life.

Eliot's narrator is kin to DeQuincey ("The English Mail-Coach"), Thackeray's showman (chapter 7 in *Vanity Fair*) and the future Theophrastus Such: "Five-and-thirty years ago the glory had not yet departed from the old coach roads," he begins in a comradely tone, savoring a lost era of conservative immobility (75-76). The departed glory must be seen through ever-receding frames of nostalgic retrospect, since elderly gentlemen of 1831 resent the coach itself as an innovation going beyond "packhorses" (20). Then, on a narrated coach ride through the Midlands that is also a chronological history, the traveler "passed rapidly from one phase of English life to another," from pastoral harmony to market towns to manufacturing districts where miners and weavers turn day to night (76-79). Our narrator, like the coachman another "Virgil," will lead us into the Dantesque inferno of untold "human histories," such as the hereditary tragedies lurking on estates like Transome Court that try to resist social change (81-84). Thus we pass through changing social conditions to enter Mrs. Transome's hell in chapter 1—from the public and diachronic to the private and perpetual. At once we focus on a particular yet typical scene, a woman restlessly waiting in her drawing room for a man to return from his affairs in the world outside and to fulfill *her* ambitions. Mrs. Transome will bitterly learn that her son means to rule at home as he did abroad. The novel, then, opens with a wide-circling bird's-eye view, only to perch in a gilded cage with sexual and social politics coming home to roost. Two chapters later the novel reverses this move and examines surrounding conditions, so-called men's affairs of business and politics, in light of such domestic tragedy.

The action of *Felix Holt* is compressed into a brief period of gestation, the nine months from Harold's arrival to Esther's wedding, as though mimicking dramatic unities.[20] This compression, while it implausibly hastens Esther's metamorphosis from a creature of Byronic sensibility to one of Wordsworthian duty, calls attention to the formal design of the work. Each of the main characters undergoes a crisis essential to Eliot's view of tragedy and of society: an "irreparable collision between the individual and the general," that is, between "our individual needs" and "the dire necessities of our lot."[21] Such tragic unity as Eliot might have found in the Transome story alone is subordinate to an inclusive study of society; all the varied lots meet their necessity and discover their interdependence. When we turn in chapter 3 to the humorous history of Treby Magna as though on a layover on another introductory coach ride, or when we abandon Mrs. Transome or Felix for long passages until Esther comes to them in their prisons, we should perceive the pattern in a larger web than the fate of one hero or heroine. Just before Felix, Mrs. Holt, and Rufus Lyon are introduced as analogues to Harold, Mrs. Transome, and Matthew Jermyn, we are asked to attend to the process of the common life:

> And the lives we are about to look back upon . . . are rooted in the common earth, having to endure all the ordinary chances of past and present weather. As to the weather of 1832, the Zadkiel of that time had predicted . . . unusual perturbations in organic existence . . . that mutual influence of dissimilar destinies which we shall see unfolding itself.
>
> (129)

Social history evolves naturally and, as a rule, unpredictably, this suggests, regardless of individual will or perspective. Such a vision may make the "universal custom" of the "subjection of women to men" appear "natural" rather than merely customary, as John Stuart Mill observed in *The Subjection of Women* (1869), a work that like *Felix Holt* elaborated a response to the 1867 Reform Bill.[22] But Eliot's emphasis on organically interdependent social development is aimed not at mystifying class and gender hierarchies—these are exposed as awkward customs in *Felix Holt*— but rather at chastening the egotism of the individual who does not acknowledge "mutual influence" and who denies his subjection to a collective historical plan. Women, the novel shows, may be

egotists, "selfish and cruel," but they perforce acknowledge mutual influence.

As the novel unfolds, however, the law of consequences that the novel enforces against the male radicals, upstarts and opportunists like Harold or Jermyn and their various hired guns, seems to lose its power. Social life may be metaphorically an organism "rooted in the common earth," or it may be as random as stormy weather; disparate elements of the social microcosm and of the narrative that creates it are uprooted and blown out of place. Many of the episodes seem to lack clear relevance; the pretext of a revelatory plot, with its punitive consequences, is often inadequate to account for the amplitude of Eliot's history. At times it seems that Eliot's historical curiosity about the detail of English common life undermines her respect for the public priorities of traditional political history. Perhaps the novel is designed to "denature" the customary and to displace the scene of political progress from the market square to the home.

In the domestic interior it is perhaps easier— and less regressive—to dramatize the ethical imperative of memory, of fidelity to the past, because historically the women's sphere has been forgotten. In Eliot's own conscientious, public-spirited act of memory, she precisely records the detail of past domestic life in order to retrieve evidence of women's experience. She perpetuates the tradition of the apparently apolitical novel that offers a realistic social history, including indisputably political events. Simply to note the trivial matters of lives of the obscure can be, of course, a form of protest. If women have been consigned to lives of repetitive domestic detail, it is time the history of such detail were related. No details of women's lives should be dismissed as "small airs and small notions," as Felix calls them. On the contrary, the key to the history of nineteenth-century parliamentary reform was kept in the work-baskets of mothers, daughters, wives. Yet the novelist saw no solution in women's rivaling men: Mrs. Transome's cold lust for power seems a sign of the self-wounding that comes of angry confrontation with men, as well as a fore-runner of hostile images of suffragettes and women's-libbers. Eliot's narrator remains more sympathetic than hostile, of course, in keeping with her unbiased humanist persona. The novel suggests that the sexes will be reconciled only if men and women are able to change, but they must not fruitlessly resist inevitable sexual differences. These differences, for Eliot, have some positive value in the exclusion of women from power and ownership, which are sources of violence and exploitation. The influence of Esther is presented as the feminine alternative to the corruption of masculine power. Indicting the treatment of women, the novel then, in the forgiving form of Esther, softens the judgment when the case comes to trial. Men are brought to acknowledge women's claims on them. As Harold must accept his dependence on others, Felix must accommodate his idealism to the fact of a wife.

To highlight the false division between the domestic circle and the outside world, women are depicted indoors, looking out; home becomes sanctuary or prison, while life outside beckons as well as threatens. At Transome Court, Esther opens the blinds to see the river and the trees: "She wanted the largeness of the world to help her thought." To Mrs. Transome, the same vista only reflects "boundary" and "line," "the loneliness and monotony of her life" (590, 596). (Compare Dorothea's view from the boudoir at Lowick in **Middlemarch**.) In the end, Esther rejects "a silken bondage" as a lady at the manor in favor of "the dim life of the back street, the contact with sordid vulgarity" (591-92). It appears that the social order itself is founded on the clear demarcation of domestic interior and public exterior, and on the liminal status of women who must pay if they cross the boundary.

In 1832, ladies depend on gentlemen's protection; during the riot, Felix reassures Esther in her home before he tries to lead the mob, only to find himself swept along in its rampage toward Treby Manor. There, as earlier in an inn, his knightly impulse is to rescue the women, but ironically he is forced to pose as the aggressor, brandishing his "sabre" in a lighted window before "a group of women clinging together in terror," frightened as much by him as by the pillagers he is preoccupied in turning away. The soldiers shoot him as though he were the leader of the rabble, wounding "the shoulder of the arm that held the naked weapon which shone in the light of the window." The phallic image of the man who has entered the women's interior remains indelible evidence against him at the trial, in spite of his chivalrous intentions (432). He appears to be another literary martyr to the cause of humbling and reforming men, like Rochester in *Jane Eyre* and Romney in *Aurora Leigh*.

Eliot's political analysis of separate spheres takes the form not only of showing what happens when the threshold is violated but also of examining the significance of domestic details; female characters are represented in relation to household

trappings. Esther is first introduced as the minister's daughter who objects to the smell of ale and tallow candles. Her fastidiousness sets her apart from the vulgar, "weak sisters" who pester their minister Rufus (133), yet she herself threatens her father's and Felix's vocations. Felix sneers at Esther's indulgence in wax candles: "I thank Heaven I am not a mouse to have a nose that takes note of wax or tallow" (140). Catherine Gallagher points out here the conflict of Felix's contempt for such material "signs" and the narrator's realistic method;[23] misogyny and contempt for detail coincide in Felix with an egotistical denial of humanity's common interdependence. Female sensibility is animal-like to Felix: "A fine lady is a squirrel-headed thing, with small airs and small notions, about as applicable to the business of life as a pair of tweezers to the clearing of a forest" (153). He will have to refine his sense of scale in order to learn how the sexes might collaborate in domestic and public life, while Esther will learn that wax candles may come at the price of a woman's freedom.

As though her self-indulgent wish for refinement were granted, Esther is invited to choose a new home that has all the amenities lacking in Malthouse Yard. Transome Court seems like "Paradise" until she recognizes the role of the woman in it; it is "haunted by an Eve gone grey with bitter memories of an Adam who had complained, 'The woman . . . she gave me of the tree, and I did eat'" (585). In contrast with Felix, Harold prefers the decoration to the life, asking Esther to pose in finery like one of the Transome portraits. She refuses, however, to adopt a fixed, false image (498). The portrait of Mrs. Transome in young and hopeful days seems to admonish her to "put out the wax lights that she might get rid of the oppressive urgency of walls and upholstery," and thus to reject her first vanity for a higher vision (47, 586). She is not to be the "doll-Madonna in her shrine" that Eliot criticized in "Margaret Fuller and Mary Wolltonecraft," an essay in which the heroic feminists, certainly not doll-like, are praised for retaining domestic loyalties as well as for not overvaluing women who have been degraded by decorous captivity.[24]

Although like so many heroines Esther faces a choice personified by two lovers, she more clearly dreads two kinds of disempowerment. Both the man who sneers at domestic detail and the man who wants to pile it up around his women are dangerous suitors for a woman who likes self-definition, just as they are distressing sons to their willful mothers.[25] Harold, like Felix, eagerly repudiates female claims on him. Harold's "busy thoughts were imperiously determined by habits which had no reference to any woman's feeling," and he is incapable either of imagining "what his mother's feeling was" or of swaying from his own imperious purpose (93). The radical who repudiates the past, the man who cannot be domesticated, is the man trying to his mother's will; thus Mrs. Holt and Mrs. Transome, "women who appear . . . to have a masculine decisiveness . . . and force of mind," have "come into severe collision with sons arrived at the masterful stage" (535). Whereas Felix is a kind of hippie (his mother grieves that he wears no stock), Harold is no genuine radical but a composite of all the prejudices of the privileged European male: he is imperialist, racist, classist, and sexist. As Esther senses, "to Harold Transome, Felix Holt was one of the common people who could come into question in no other than a public light. She had a native capability for discerning that the sense of ranks and degrees has its repulsions corresponding to the repulsions dependent on difference of race and colour" (522-23). Thus, accepting the power of prejudice, Esther shrinks from telling Harold that she has been intimate with Felix. Yet her repulsion when she hears that Harold's first wife "had been a slave—was bought, in fact" (541) is more than dread of vicarious contact with the alien; it is also dread of the sexually abusive master. Esther's "native" discernment has everything to do with her having been socialized as a woman; she may play along with ranks and degrees, but she begins to find them repulsive in themselves, since race and gender remain, like class, the registers on which the patriarch marks his supremacy.

Somewhat like Gwendolen in *Daniel Deronda,* Esther resists the surrender implied in accepting a man: "The homage of a man may be delightful until he asks straight for love, by which a woman renders homage." Harold's love "seemed to threaten her with a stifling oppression," almost as though she intuits the opinion he declared when he first returned from Smyrna as a widower: "I hate English wives; they want to give their opinion about everything" (94). Perhaps less ominously, after having kissed Felix, "she felt as if she had vowed herself away, as if memory lay on her lips like a seal of possession" (592); he at least has taken the trouble to argue with her opinions. Crudely, she must choose between the radical who sees women as useless delights and the radical who sees women as temptations unless useful. With more conscience and foresight than Mrs.

Transome, Esther chooses duty rather than pleasure (524), the man who scolds rather than the man who flatters her.

In outline, Eliot's novel promises little for women. While Esther seemingly must submit to Felix in the end, for her adultery Mrs. Transome must endure a living hell, dependent on Harold's belated understanding. Yet, as to the necessity for such sacrifices, the narrator offers contradictory commentary, generated especially by the figure of Mrs. Transome. Having married an imbecile, chosen a lover, and with him managed her failing estate, Mrs. Transome is now told she must become "grandmama on satin cushions" (95). Her power has not gained her love, and her illicit affair has rendered her powerless. The narrator can only advise resigned silence: "half the sorrows of women would be averted if they could repress the speech they know to be useless; nay, the speech they have resolved not to utter" (117). It is advice that Eliot herself, in the powerful voice of the narrator, does not follow. Observing Harold's bulldozing egotism, the narrator offers this rebuke:

> It is a fact kept a little too much in the background, that mothers have a self larger than their maternity, and that when their sons have become taller than themselves, and are gone from them to college or into the world, there are wide spaces of their time which are not filled with praying for their boys, reading old letters, and envying yet blessing those who are attending to their shirt-buttons. Mrs. Transome was certainly not one of those bland, adoring, and gently tearful women.
>
> (198)

It may make us uneasy to be told that there are such bland women, but they seem to be relegated to the world of unrealistic fiction. Esther, too, is certainly not one of the quiescent type, but lacking power she can only hope for the less demeaning love that recognizes her as a "woman whose mind was as noble as her face was beautiful." She complains of the injustice to Felix: "It is difficult for a woman ever to try to be anything good . . . when it is always supposed that she must be contemptible." Men may choose "hard" and "great" lots, but women, apart from the rare "Saint Theresas," "must take meaner things, because only meaner things are within [their] reach" (364-67). Esther's growing humility and desire for a truly great lot in life excuse this complaint. She will grow to embody some of a saint's grand calling, but she is a woman, not a saint—that is, she is not destined, as George Eliot was, to join in the vanguard of public historical movements.

For some time it seems likely that Esther will take Harold, a meaner thing within her reach. Mrs. Transome predicts Esther's sacrifice to Harold with the bitterness of one of the damned:

> "This girl has a fine spirit—plenty of fire and pride and wit. Men like such captives, as they like horses that champ the bit. . . . What is the use of a woman's will?—if she tries she doesn't get it, and she ceases to be loved. God was cruel when he made women."
>
> (488)

The narrator understands such bitterness without forgiving it or offering women any recourse. In complaints or reproaches, "poor women, whose power lies solely in their influence, make themselves like music out of tune, and only move men to run away" (437). Pointing out the selfish, cowardly response of men, however, is not the surest way to recommend women's submission. Though the sexes mirror each other unflatteringly, ultimately women appear less base than men. Mrs. Transome's servant Denner comically declares: "I shouldn't like to be a man—to cough so loud, and stand straddling about on a wet day, and be so wasteful with meat and drink. They're a coarse lot, I think" (488). Mrs. Transome tells Jermyn, "I would not lose the misery of being a woman, now I see what can be the baseness of a man" (519).

To all appearances, Harold is the opposite of coarse, but the narrator, like Mrs. Transome and eventually Esther, detects the flaws of egotism beneath his veneer:

> "A woman ought never to have any trouble. There should always be a man to guard her from it." (Harold Transome was masculine and fallible; he had incautiously sat down this morning to pay his addresses by talk about nothing in particular; and, clever experienced man that he was, he fell into nonsense.)
>
> (500)

The corollary of Harold's gallantry is that women should protect men from wounded vanity, much as the narrator does by this backhanded parenthetical excuse. In practice, Victorian gender ideology depends on mutual blindness; thus Harold is uneasy when he suspects that Esther has a mind as well as a beautiful face:

> She was clearly a woman that could be governed. . . . Yet there was a lightning that shot out of her now and then, which seemed the sign of a dangerous judgment; as if she inwardly saw something more admirable than Harold Transome. Now, to be perfectly charming, a woman should not see this.
>
> (525)

The final caustic comment belongs to the wise and, in spite of the counsel of resignation, feminist narrator (the voice seems that of the unguarded Jane Austen in *Northanger Abbey*).

There are signs that the narrator realizes the unsatisfactory compromise in the romantic ending supposedly so devoutly to be wished. Really, Esther cannot do better than to marry, the narrator, in Shakespearean guise, maintains: "she was intensely of the feminine type, verging neither towards the saint nor the angel. She was 'a fair divided excellence, whose fulness of perfection' must be in marriage" (551).[26] Characteristically, Eliot presents feminine independence as the exception to the common order, a possibility for rare spirits like St. Theresa or Romola. Yet an inert and ignorant Angel in the House will spread a curse as much as any demonic Mrs. Transome. Esther must retain her will and aspiration. At her great moment, she assumes the role of a heroine of history:

> When a woman feels purely and nobly, that ardour which breaks through formulas too rigorously urged on men by daily practical needs, makes one of her most precious influences. . . . Her inspired ignorance gives a sublimity to actions . . . that otherwise . . . would make men smile. Some of that ardour which has . . . illuminated all poetry and history was burning today in the bosom of sweet Esther Lyon. In this, at least, her woman's lot was perfect: that the man she loved was her hero; that her woman's passion and her reverence for rarest goodness rushed together in an undivided current.
>
> (571)

The "divided excellence" finds a rare undivided opportunity to act. There could hardly be a more explicit image of the compensations of influence, yet Esther does not consume her life in obeisance to her manly hero. Like another Elizabeth Bennet, she could only be happy with a man "greater and nobler than I am," but she reserves a little of her wealth and, playfully, of her power: "You don't know how clever I am. I mean to go on teaching a great many things"—including Felix—"and you will not attribute stupid thoughts to me before I've uttered them." She will enjoy the "retribution" of demanding that he be worthy of her sacrifice (602-3).[27]

Eliot has captured perfectly the strange balance of power in the ideology of influence; she would later present a more convincing portrait of such a relationship in that of Mary Garth and Fred Vincy, where the man learns virtue by living up to the woman's standard for him. Felix must play the part of Esther's mentor, but it is a role she creates and makes him worthy of. Significantly, the union is cleansed of any hint of sexual mastery. Felix and Esther unite rather as though Maggie and Tom Tulliver were able to prolong their last moment outside of gender difference, like children or angels:

> He smiled, and took her two hands between his, pressed together as children hold them up in prayer. Both of them felt too solemnly to be bashful. They looked straight into each other's eyes, as angels do when they tell some truth.
>
> (556)

Male and female lots have been shown to be separate though tensely intertwined; the fusion at the end belies the instructive disunity of the novel. Felix and Esther leap out of history and out of gendered sexuality in order to unite as novelistic closure demands.

The comments on women's lot in *Felix Holt* are remarkably outspoken, more so than in *Middlemarch* or *Daniel Deronda.* Here lovers and mothers and sons openly negotiate power and ownership, and, in spite of the plot of reconciliation, the sexes seem to glare at each other unappeased. Eliot's drama of 1832 remains a puzzle in which the pieces of private and public life seem to fit and yet do not. Social divisions are exposed along the fault lines of class as well as gender. As in *Romola,* Eliot represents the common people as both the medium of continuity and as a volatile force for change; common people and upper-class women are implicitly linked in their shared exclusion from corrupt modes of power. As before, the novel exalts less the crowd or the suffering masses than individual, uncommon, but obscure beings such as Felix Holt and Rufus Lyon who are willing instruments of progress; the radicalism of their visions is tempered by fellow-feeling, love of tradition, and domestic sentiments. Their influence may be narrow and unsteady, but it is the ingredient heretofore missing from public life, where all men do appear selfish and cruel. Ladies at times are able to collaborate with such decent meliorists as Felix and Rufus, as when Esther rises in court in defense of Felix, "break[ing] through" the rigid systems of men (571). Felix holds an article of faith that "there's some dignity and happiness for a man other than changing his station" (557), but the spirit of the age is against him (as well as his own rejection of vulgar parents). The challenge to inherited station during the Reform Era jarred the Treby Magnas of England out of an apparent slumber of centuries. Eliot appears to dramatize

the crisis of her times primarily in terms of class politics, but public events are upstaged by the skirmishes between men and women, which the novel suggests more profoundly determine the course of human history.

In a commentary on the disjunction between those interlocked spheres, private and public life, Eliot's narrator analyzes a society ostensibly governed by men whose public personae deceive everyone, including themselves—though perhaps not the women who know them in private life. "Under the stimulus of small many-mixed motives . . . a great deal of business has been done in the world by well-clad, and, in 1833, clean-shaven men, whose names are on charity-lists, and who do not know that they are base" (471-72). Certainly, young men who learn to integrate public forms and private relations offer some hope for change. Felix refuses to join the fashionable parade of self-deceiving educated men, but he must also learn to value the trivia of domestic life and to respect as a fellow human being what he mistook for "a squirrel-headed thing." Influential young women such as Esther were beginning in the 1830s to step out of the house and not only to put their own names on the charity lists but also to organize widespread reforms aimed at reconciling public and private morality. The novelist herself was such a reformer, urging that the business of the world be conducted in a less deceptive, impersonal manner, so that signs of authority—upper-class English manhood—could not be mistaken for signs of virtue or merit. The feminist political message is certainly muted, especially by Mrs. Transome's heartlessness and the forced concluding marriage. But such muting, like the moderation of Victorian feminism in general, enabled the very real advances that women like Eliot were able to make. The disjunctions of *Felix Holt* can be attributed largely to the strains on a writer sustaining the position of a great woman of letters, wishing to affirm a continuous tradition yet to integrate the different voices that had been silenced, wishing to narrate a political history of pre-Victorian society that incorporated the private experience of middle-class women, and finally wishing to expose bias and false consciousness while herself appearing impartially human and omniscient. These diverse wishes are impossible to fulfill entirely, of course. Whatever the "many-mixed motives" of the author herself, however, her text makes the most of these contradictions by not resolving them, exposing an unassimilated feminist argument.

Notes

Adapted from Alison Booth, *Greatness Engendered: George Eliot and Virginia Woolf.* Copyright 1992 by Cornell University. Used by permission of the publisher, Cornell University Press.

1. Suzanne Graver, *George Eliot and Community* (Berkeley: University of California Press, 1984), 176-78. Eliot offers a good example of what Naomi Black calls "social feminism." See *Social Feminism* (Ithaca: Cornell University Press, 1989), 1-3.

2. See, for example, *The George Eliot Letters,* ed. Gordon Haight, 9 vols. (New Haven: Yale University Press, 1954-1978), 4:364-65, 467-68.

3. George Eliot, *Felix Holt: The Radical,* ed. Peter Coveney (Harmondsworth: Penguin, 1972), 310. Hereafter cited parenthetically in the text by page number. We are reminded of the warning in the "Author's Introduction" that progress has its price as well as its benefits: "Posterity may be shot, like a bullet through a tube, by atmospheric pressure from Winchester to Newcastle: that is a fine result to have among our hopes; but the slow old-fashioned way of getting from one end of our country to the other is the better thing to have in the memory" (75).

4. Esther Lyon, like Emma Woodhouse, is the spoiled darling of a widower, but she learns to reject the lord of the manor for the yeoman, the Robert Martin figure, Felix Holt. Ellen Moers has pointed out Eliot's alteration of Austen's class scale. See *Literary Women: The Great Writers* (1976; repr. New York: Oxford University Press, 1985), 50.

5. Bonnie Zimmerman, "*Felix Holt* and the True Power of Womanhood," *English Literary History* 46 (1979): 432-37.

6. Obviously, many "great" novels have political themes, and many even stage battle or election scenes (*War and Peace, The Red and the Black, Waverley, Vanity Fair,* and *Middlemarch* come to mind). But it seems that the arbiters of the canon prefer not to be reminded that the implied author is also politically situated and that the novel, much like the tract, takes sides.

7. Early critics of *Felix Holt,* while generally admiring, laid out two lines of attack: against the political novel of the Reform era and against the moral drama of the Transomes, Lyons, and Holts. See David Carroll, *George Eliot: The Critical Heritage* (London: Routledge and Kegan Paul, 1971), 251-70; and Florence Sandler, "The Unity of *Felix Holt,*" in *George Eliot: A Centenary Tribute,* ed. Gordon S. Haight and Rosemary T. VanArsdel (London: Macmillan, 1982), 137. *Felix Holt* was more a critical than popular success (Gordon Haight, *George Eliot: A Biography* [New York: Oxford University Press, 1968], 387). Though it appears to belong in the company of political novels such as Disraeli's *Sybil* or of multiplot social-problem novels such as *Bleak House,* it defies generic expectation. See Raymond Williams, *Culture and Society, 1780-1950* (New York: Columbia University Press, 1958), 103.

8. Fred C. Thomson, "*Felix Holt* as Classic Tragedy," *Nineteenth-Century Fiction* 16 (1961): 47; "The Genesis of *Felix Holt,*" *PMLA* 74 (1959): 576.

9. Norman Vance, "Law, Religion, and the Unity of *Felix Holt,*" in *George Eliot: Centenary Essays and an Unpublished Fragment,* ed. Anne Smith (London: Vision, 1980), 103-20.

10. "'Felix Holt the Radical,'" *Critical Essays on George Eliot,* ed. Barbara Hardy (New York: Barnes & Noble, 1970), 106. David Carroll diagrams the novel's "spheres of politics, religion, and love" as deliberately interrelated, yet he claims that Esther has "usurped Felix's central position" ("*Felix Holt*: Society as Protagonist," in *George Eliot: A Collection of Critical Essays,* ed. George R. Creeger [Englewood Cliffs, N. J.: Prentice-Hall, 1970], 134, 140). See also Michael Edwards, "George Eliot and Negative Form," *Critical Quarterly* 17 (1975): 171; and Joseph Wiesenfarth, "Felix qui non potuit," in *George Eliot's Mythmaking* (Heidelberg: Carl Winter, 1977), 170-85.

11. Eliot's journal and notebooks record extensive research on the economic and political contexts of 1832 in the *Times,* the *Annual Register,* the House of Commons's *Report from the Select Committee on Bribery at Elections* (1835), Mill's *Principles of Political Economy,* Samuel Bamford's *Passages From the Life of a Radical,* and Daniel Neals's *History of the Puritans,* among other sources. See Haight, *George Eliot,* 381; and Thomson, "The Genesis of *Felix Holt,*" 577-83, and the introduction to his edition of *Felix Holt* (Oxford: Clarendon, 1980), xiii-xlii.

12. His suggestion for the statement by the attorney-general was inserted in chapter 35. See Appendix B, 629-37, in Coveney's edition of *Felix Holt,* and the introduction, xxii-xxv, to Thomson's edition. The collaboration was unusual for her (*George Eliot Letters* 4:214-302).

13. *George Eliot Letters,* 4:258.

14. *George Eliot Letters,* 4:300-301.

15. Catherine Gallagher sees *Felix Holt* as a crisis in Eliot's "inductive" method of "metonymic realism," when the social tension of the 1860s made "the discontinuity between facts and values" impossible to ignore (*The Industrial Reformation of English Fiction* [Chicago: University of Chicago Press, 1985], 237-43). The righteous eponymous hero, generally seen as "too good to be true," tries to deny his affiliation with domestic life (see Laurence Lerner, *The Truthtellers* [New York: Schocken, 1967], 49). He has been condemned as a spokesman for Eliot's dread of public upheaval, in line with Arnold's response to the Hyde Park Riots in *Culture and Anarchy* (1869), but he is also the common man "feminized" and elevated by fellow-feeling. Williams, *Culture and Society,* 109, reproaches Eliot for excluding the common people from her vision of the interdependence of public and private life. See W. F. T. Myers, "Politics and Personality in *Felix Holt,*" *Renaissance and Modern Studies* 10 (1966): 27; David Craig, "Fiction and the Rising Industrial Classes," *Essays in Criticism* 17 (1967): 64-74; and Linda Bamber, "Self-Defeating Politics in George Eliot's *Felix Holt,*" *Victorian Studies* 18 (1975): 419-35.

16. The Lyons receive the news of Esther's inheritance as "magic"; Felix says her fitness for ladyship gives "chance sanction to that musty law . . . the appropriate conditions are come at last" (557).

17. Wiesenfarth, "Felix qui non potuit," 177-78.

18. Carroll, *Critical Heritage,* 267. Compare *Little Dorrit,* in which Arthur Clennam undergoes a more dramatic development than the eponymous guiding light; a woman might have named it *Arthur Clennam.*

19. The Book of Esther sets the context of *Felix Holt,* but the heroine's role as political savior of her people has

been privatized. Lawyer Jermyn is Haman the villain-ous minister; Felix, like Mordecai, is an unruly outsider yet a guide for Esther inside the palace. See Zimmerman, "*Felix Holt*," 411n.11. Charlotte Brontë's "Vashti" is judged as a woman rather than as an artist, suggesting a precedent for Eliot's defiant Alcharisi in *Daniel Deronda*.

20. Thomson, "*Felix Holt* as Classic Tragedy," 54.

21. Eliot, "Notes on 'The Spanish Gypsy,'" *George Eliot's Life as Related in Her Letters and Journals,* ed. John W. Cross, 3 vols. (New York: Harper & Brothers, n.d.), 31-32.

22. John Stuart Mill, *The Subjection of Women* (New York: D. Appleton, 1870), 22-23.

23. Gallagher, *Industrial Reformation,* 237-43.

24. "Margaret Fuller and Mary Wollstonecraft," *Essays of George Eliot,* ed. Thomas Pinney (London: Routledge & Kegan Paul, 1963), 201-5.

25. Felix rejects the dishonest occupation of his dead, mountebank father, thus distressing his mother; Harold repudiates his Tory lineage, neglects his imbecile "father," and almost kills Jermyn, his real father, all in a contest of wills with his mother.

26. The quotation is from *King John* 2:1.

27. Coveney points out that Esther's "laugh as sweet as the morning thrush" in this concluding scene echoes the scene in prison when Esther, "like a thrush . . . a messenger of darkness," warns Felix of failure (chapter 45, n. 1; chapter 51, n. 2).

Middlemarch

JUNE SKYE SZIROTNY (ESSAY DATE SPRING 1998)

SOURCE: Szirotny, June Skye. "'No Sorrow I Have Thought More About': The Tragic Failure of George Eliot's St. Theresa." *Victorian Newsletter,* 93 (spring 1998): 17-27.

In the following essay, Szirotny opposes the critical tendency to deny Eliot the status of a proto-feminist, arguing that Middlemarch *is a feminist novel and a damnation of a society that is oppressive to women.*

Whether George Eliot was in some sense a feminist has remained a moot question from her day to this. Though she knew "the supremacy of the intellectual life" (*M* lxxiii, IV:188)[1] and obtained for herself a "masculine" vocation that was life itself to her,[2] though she argued that women have a right to education and that those deprived of love have a special need for independent work (*L* V: 107; see also *DD* xxxvi, III: 96), she speaks guardedly of women's right to self-fulfillment, and ultimately allows none of her idealistic heroines meaningful occupation outside the home. Dinah Morris, Maggie Tulliver, and Dorothea Brooke each makes a "sad . . . sacrifice"

of her yearning for an "epic life" (*M,* Finale, IV: 370; Prelude, I: v, vi); Janet Dempster, Romola de'Bardi, and Fedalma, deprived of love, do not find the work that women need to give them "joy in things for their own sake" (*L* V:107). While George Eliot laments their lack of fulfillment, she insists, especially in her early works, on its necessity.

Prior to the revival of interest in George Eliot in the fifties, most readers had seen her as conservative, if not retrograde, in advocating women's rights—"shar[ing] the conventional Victorian views of a woman's proper role" (Spacks 58).[3] At the same time, readers have always seen *Middlemarch* as posing the Woman Question. And many, like Virginia Woolf, affected by George Eliot's seeming identification with her aspiring heroines,[4] and by her criticism of the oppression women suffer, have sensed that she rebels against women's conventional roles.

Since the seventies, feminists interested in George Eliot have been preoccupied with trying to ascertain her precise position on the Woman Question. At first, feminists, looking for support in one who had successfully rebelled against society's strictures on a woman's pursuing a vocation outside marriage, but, persuaded, as Kate Millet says, that George Eliot's advocacy of women's right to vocations is little more than "an eloquent plea" (139), often denounced one by whom they felt betrayed.[5] then, when her critics had exhausted the vein they worked, others began to reclaim George Eliot as one of them. Some argued that she infuses the conventionally feminine with dignity, rejecting the notion that women's different nature makes them inferior to men.[6] Others suggested that she views women as intellectually equal to men and deserving of the same autonomy, though tempering her enthusiasm for women's pursuit of the vocations men enjoy.[7]

But no one has seen in George Eliot that "healthy anger" that Ellin Ringler regards as appropriate in an author who depicts the imbalance between male and female strength (59). No one disputes Françoise Basch's contention that George Eliot's awareness of woman's tragedy "never leads to militant feminism" (94), or Jeanie G. Thomas's that George Eliot's sensibility is not "a reforming one" (393; cf. 412).[8] Without disputing that George Eliot is ambivalent, I want to suggest that she presents her most authentic view of the Woman Question in *Middlemarch,* and that that novel is a systematic indictment of a society that proscribes achievement for women—an indictment that tears at the very fabric of the social order. I shall show that, in **Middlemarch,** George Eliot denies that women do good by sacrificing, rather than fulfilling, themselves; and, demonstrating that men do appreciable good only when allowed to develop their own potentialities in a sympathetic environment, I will argue that she damns a society that deliberately deprives women of such an environment, only to satisfy its own selfish interests.

I

Though Dorothea yearns to find a channel for doing great good, she fails both in her chosen vocation as helpmate to her first husband and in her attempts to secure independent work. Readers have often explained her failure to do good to Casaubon, her first husband, by saying that she was selfishly concerned to do what she, rather than he, sees as helpful (see Harvey, "Intro." 14-16). But while George Eliot admires Dorothea's ultimate attainment of selflessness, she does not (always allowing for her ambivalence) confound this virtue with doing good, as in her early novels (where a superhuman ideal of selflessness only makes George Eliot irrelevant for the modern reader). On the contrary, she seems to make Dorothea conform to the nineteenth-century ideal of women as self-sacrificing in order to explode the common view and show that a woman does good by fulfilling herself—by following her bliss, to use Joseph Campbell's phrase (see, e.g., *Hero's Journey* 33, 63-66, 210-214).

Intending to do good by trying to make herself into the person Casaubon wants her to be, Dorothea, "shut[ting] her best soul in prison" (xlii, II: 374), becomes a veritable Griselda. But no sooner does she attain this character than she understands that her self-sacrifice will be useless. Prepared to pledge that she will carry on Casaubon's work after his death, she knows she is consigning herself "to work as in a treadmill fruitlessly" (xlviii, III: 94). Only after his death, when "Dorothea's native strength of will was no longer all converted into resolute submission" (liv, III: 198)—when, possibly superstitious, she writes him that she will not go on with his work: *"I could not submit my soul to yours, by working hopelessly at what I have no belief in"* (liv, III: 202)—does she do good.

All her major acts after Casaubon's death show her doing good by following her inner warrant in opposition to society, though readers often cite two of these acts as evidence that Dorothea has finally become self-sacrificing and submissive enough to do good. Learning that Lydgate's reputation is besmirched, she sets about clearing his name. In disregarding others' "cautious weighing of consequences" (lxxii, IV: 180), she is seemingly moved by the same self-sacrificing passion to do good as Fedalma envisions in disciples spending their all, even if vainly, to save Christ from the cross (*SG* I: 154). But doing good being what she likes, she is by no means disregarding her own will. "The idea of some active good within her reach 'haunted her like a passion,' and another's need having once come to her as a distinct image, preoccupied her desire with the yearning to give relief" (lxxvi, IV: 230). Moreover, Dorothea succeeds in helping Lydgate because, in following her own inner warrant, she ignores the world's opposition. George Eliot creates an entire chapter to show that Farebrother, James, Brooke, and Celia all object to Dorothea's involving herself in Lydgate's problems. Likewise, in order to carry out her crowning work of charity—the ministrations that save Rosamond's marriage—Dorothea, believing that Rosamond has robbed her forever of all joy, must clutch her own pain. Yet because "[s]he yearned towards the perfect Right" (lxxx, IV: 282), her apparent self-denial is self-fulfillment—"self-forgetful ardour" (lxxxi, IV: 293). Furthermore, George Eliot seems bent on suggesting that Dorothea acts in opposition to public opinion. Even though no third person presumably knows what Dorothea says to Rosamond, George Eliot says that if Dorothea had not undertaken to save Rosamond, "why, she perhaps would have been a woman who gained a higher character for discretion, but it would certainly not have been as well for [Rosamond, Lydgate, and Ladislaw]" (lxxxii, IV: 309). Finally, defying both Casaubon's and society's proscription, she marries Ladislaw. And because she could have liked nothing better than that she should give Ladislaw "wifely help," she becomes the helpmate Casaubon had rejected, living a life of "beneficent activity" (Finale, IV: 366, 365) by fulfilling herself.

When Dorothea follows her own passionate impulses, she does the good that her renunciations do not accomplish. But despite her ardor, she never succeeds in building cottages, becoming learned, or founding a village. At the end of the novel, she tells her sister that she could never do anything she liked (lxxxiv, IV: 340). What good she accomplishes is "not widely visible" (Finale, IV: 371). And since George Eliot sees doing good as the *summum bonum,* she laments Dorothea's failure—laments it especially because it is not in "the supreme unalterable nature of things" (**"Address to Working Men"** 10).

II

Asking herself in this novel what in the nature of things enables one to do good, George Eliot argues that success requires commitment to follow one's "inward vocation" (*L* VI: 438; *FH* xxvii, II: 181), which in turn requires sympathetic support, especially of a spouse. Ranging over the whole of her society in this "Study of Provincial Life," she depicts each of her main male characters as encountering difficulties at the outset of his career that tempt him to succumb to the pressures of the world—either to ignore "the voices within" (xv, I: 254) in choosing a vocation, or to get entangled in money cares that cause him to abandon his calling. Only by marrying "a good unworldly woman" (xvii, I: 314) whom he cherishes as a partner—an intellectual equal—can he weather the battle with the Adam within and without (see xvii, I: 311-12), and succeed. He who marries one unsympathetic to his concerns or one his equal whom he refuses to regard as a partner—because supported in his vanity by tradition and *a priori* assumptions that women are ornaments, toys, or nurses—fails. Whereas, in **Felix Holt,** Esther says the lot of a woman depends on the love she accepts (xliii, III: 149-50; cf. *M* xxv, II: 58), in **Middlemarch,** George Eliot says the lot of a man depends on the love he accepts (see xv, I: 257).

Different as they are, Lydgate, Casaubon, Bulstrode, and Farebrother, for want of sharing their concerns with a sympathetic wife, all abandon their true vocations and so fail.

Classmates surely would have voted for Lydgate as the man most likely to succeed. "He was one of the rarer lads who early get a decided bent and make up their minds that there is something particular in life which they would like to do for its own sake, and not because their fathers did it" (xv, I: 253). Despite opposition from his guardian, Lydgate in pursuing medicine, which he considers "the grandest profession in the world" (xlv, III: 53; cf. xv, I: 258), is, as Farebrother says, "in the right profession, the work you feel yourself most fit for" (xvii, I: 314). But Lydgate never becomes another Vesalius. For when he tries to enlist his wife's aid, she, not identifying her interests with his, sabotages every one of his expedients for paying their creditors, with the result that he capitulates to the way of the world, renouncing his aspirations in order to amass money. Giving adornment "the first place among wifely functions" (xi, I: 163) and supposing it characteristic "of the feminine mind

to adore a man's pre-eminence without too precise a knowledge of what it consisted in" (xxvii, II: 77), Lydgate supposed he had found the ideal wife in a conventional, small-souled woman. Too late he learns that to have married help, not care, he must have been able to accord equality to a wife who, like Dorothea, would share his concerns.[9]

Casaubon, regarding his scholarship as "an outward requirement," by which he is to acquit himself in the eyes of others (xxix, II: 102), is driven by none of Lydgate's enthusiasm for his work. But, having married a good unworldly woman, he, unlike Lydgate, has help at hand. "[A]nxious to follow [the] spontaneous direction of his thought" (xx, I: 357), Dorothea might have enabled him to refocus his energies; "in spite of her small instruction, her judgment in this matter [of his opus] was truer than his" (xlviii, III: 92). But the same male ego that kept Lydgate from choosing a proper wife keeps Casaubon from seeing in his wife the "heaven-sent angel" (xlii, II: 372) he needs. Like Lydgate, having married "to adorn his life with the graces of female companionship, to irradiate the gloom which fatigue was apt to hang over the intervals of studious labour with the play of female fancy, and to secure . . . the solace of female tendance for his declining years" (vii, I: 104); and expecting his wife to observe "his abundant pen-scratches and amplitude of paper with the uncritical awe of an elegant-minded canary-bird" (xx, I: 363), he regards one who exhibits a mind as something he had to contend against (see xxix, II: 105), and thus he "achieve[s] nothing" (xlii, II: 357).

Bulstrode likewise fails because, like Casaubon, he seeks mastery in marriage and rejects the wifely help at hand. Like Lydgate, he early felt called to his work, but, seduced by the opportunity to make easy money that ultimately leads him to disgrace, he abandoned his dream of becoming a missionary. Candor with his first wife, "a simple pious woman" (lxi, III: 348), would have saved him by forcing him to give up a dishonest trade.

Like Lydgate, Farebrother is a clever man who does not fulfill the promise of his nature (see motto to xvii, I: 301). Possibly influenced by a dominating mother, whose father was a clergyman, he took "the fatal step of choosing the wrong profession" (xl, II: 333). Without interest in the Church, he is no more than "a decent makeshift" of a clergyman (xvii, I: 316). In love with Mary Garth and conscious that a woman may play so important a part in a man's life that "to renounce her may be a very good imitation of heroism" (lxvi, IV: 75), he might well have turned out differently if he had had Fred's luck in winning her. But he did *not* win her, and he cannot do anything remarkable.[10]

Those who succeed are no more ambitious or able, no less liable to difficulties, than those who fail. But Caleb Garth, Fred Vincy, and Will Ladislaw succeed because, truly loving one who identifies her interests with his, each is able to stay focused on his true vocation.

Garth, motivated by his love of "business" (xxiv, II: 45; xl, II: 329; see also lvi, III: 238-39; lxxxvi, IV: 354), has pursued the work that had early been to him as poetry, philosophy, and religion (xxiv, II: 44-45)—the work that he regards as "the most honourable work that is" (xl, II: 329; see also xl, II: 321). But unable to manage finances, he once failed in his business (xxiii, II: 8). Only because he leaned on his exemplary wife, who "[a]doring her husband's virtues" (xxiv, II: 29), devoted herself to supporting his aims, did he ultimately succeed. Only because he so much respected his wife's opinion that he took no important step without consulting her—in fact, allowed her to rule in ninety-nine cases out of a hundred (lvi, III:247)—did he survive his money difficulties to become another Cincinnatus. As Farebrother says, without the partnership with his wife, Garth would hardly have pulled through (xvii, I: 314). With the partnership, Caleb, like his Biblical namesake, sees the promised land.

Fred, at the beginning of the novel, is as unpromising as Lydgate is promising. Desirous of feeding "a good appetite for the best of everything" (xii, I: 210), and pressured by parents to follow a genteel profession, he threatens to follow Bulstrode in letting the desire for money determine his vocation. But "thoroughly in love" (xiv, I: 248) with one who makes the condition of marriage with him renunciation of both his extravagant habits and a vocation in the Church for which he has neither taste nor aptitude, he takes up farming for which he has a penchant. Because he cherishes the love of a good, enlightened woman, he succeeds in becoming a distinguished farmer.

Ladislaw, not having early discovered his vocation, resists pressure that would make him "submissive to ordinary rule" (ix, I: 138)—in settling in a solid profession. Understanding that "[o]ur sense of duty must often wait for some work which shall take the place of dilettanteism [*sic*]" (xlvi, III: 59), he awaits "those messages from the universe which summon [genius] to its peculiar work" (x, I: 141; see also 142). But, abundant only

"in uncertain promises" (xlvii, III: 78), though brilliant (xxxvii, II: 246; lxii, III: 369), he might have remained a dilettante but for his dread of doing what the woman he worships would disapprove (xxxvii, II: 263, 265; lxxvii, IV: 251). Without hope of winning Dorothea, he not only thinks to work at "the first thing that offers" (lxii, III: 377), but, dallying with a married woman, sees himself sliding "into that pleasureless yielding to the small solicitations of circumstance" (lxxix, IV: 272) that destroys Lydgate. With hope of winning Dorothea, he disentangles himself from Rosamond's snares and refuses to compromise himself by accepting Bulstrode's ill-gotten money (lxi, III: 362; lxxxiii, IV: 318). Married to Dorothea, he fulfills his dream of becoming an important reformer (see li, III: 146). For, humble enough to take "the pressure of [everyone's] thought instead of [like Casaubon] urging his own with iron resistance" (l, III: 126), and so respecting Dorothea's opinion (see xxii, I: 385; xxxvii, II: 251) that his feeling for her was "like the inheritance of a fortune" (xlvii, III: 74), he makes a partner of his wife. Readers who judge Ladislaw unworthy of Dorothea because of his dilettantism and dependence on a beloved woman are approving the conformist values George Eliot contemns.

None of her usual ambivalence infects the answer George Eliot gives in these stories to the question what enables one to do good. At the height of her career in 1871, she is writing out of experience that made her believe "devoutly in a natural difference of vocation" (xxii, I: 405) and in the worker's need for a sympathetic spouse. Unattached and lonely for years, during which she lost hope of ever fulfilling her dream of writing a novel (*L* II: 406), during which she could scarcely envision any future for herself except as the lamp-holder Dorothea aspires to,[11] Mary Ann Evans became George Eliot only because, faithful to her "inward vocation,"[12] she linked her life to one who, caring more for her work than for his own (see *L* II: 260; III: 179; IV: 59; V: 175, 215, 261, 322; VI: 380), anxiously watched over her career. Having refused a marriage that would have "involve[d] too great a sacrifice of her mind and pursuits" (*L* I: 184)—having understood the difficulty for "a woman [to] keep her steadfastness / Beneath a frost within her husband's eyes / Where coldness scorches" ("Armgart" ii, *Legend*, 1st ed., 110)—George Eliot succeeded because she formed a liaison with one whose "perfect love and sympathy" stimulated her to "healthful activity" (*L* II: 343).

III

The stories of George Eliot's male characters suggest that Dorothea Casaubon fails to effect great good because she can neither follow her bliss, except in befriending the Lydgates, nor secure her husband's approval. But why is Dorothea, married to Ladislaw—a sympathetic spouse, modelled on George Eliot's helpmate—"absorbed into the life of another" and "only known in a certain circle as a wife and mother" (Finale, IV: 366)? The answer is that the "epic life" she hungers after requires not only nurturing by a spouse but by society. Society's support is not lacking for the males in the novel, for an androcentric world approves of a man's pursuing a vocation, whereas it condemns a woman's ardor for meaningful work outside marriage as "extravagance" (Prelude, I: vii). And in a world where "the social air in which mortals begin to breathe" (Finale, IV: 370) lends no encouragement to the aspiring woman, where Dorothea's ardor finds no answering response in anyone but Ladislaw (xxii, I: 401; xxxvii, II: 252; see also xxviii, II: 89-90), she feels stymied. Never able to rally support for her projects (Celia regards Dorothea's interest in drawing plans for cottages as only a "favourite *fad*" [iv, I: 56]), she gives up. She says she might have done something better if she had been better, but no one in her environs "stated exactly what else that was in her power she ought rather to have done" (lxxxiv, IV: 342; Finale, IV: 366). In passages that enclose Dorothea's story—and George Eliot specifically directed a friend to the Prelude for an explanation of the story (*L* V: 330)—George Eliot plainly tells us that Dorothea fails because she cannot carve a life for herself outside "the framework of things" (xiii, I: 225).[13] Forewarning us in the Prelude that Dorothea is a St. Theresa who is "helped by no coherent social faith and order" (I: vi), George Eliot explains in the Finale that Dorothea's "tragic failure" (Prelude, I: vi) is due to "the conditions of an imperfect social state" (Cabinet ed. III: 464), "[f]or there is no creature whose inward being is so strong that it is not greatly determined by what lies outside it" (IV: 370; cf. *SM* iii, 40; *FH* iii, I: 88; see also *MF* VI, vi, III: 76; *R* xxi, VI: 577; *M*, motto to iv, I: 52).

Some strong souls will say that an unsympathetic environment is too simple-minded an explanation for Dorothea's failure. Assuming that genius will out regardless of circumstances, or perhaps unwilling to assume responsibility for having sent their infecting breath toward Dorothea (see xv, I: 257; see also Finale, IV: 370), some have insisted that Dorothea would have succeeded had she had the ability (as Maggie, had she had the initiative).[14] But George Eliot stresses the worker's need for a sympathetic environment. In "Amos Barton," she had written, "That is a deep and wide saying, that no miracle can be wrought without faith—without the worker's faith in himself, as well as the recipient's faith in him. And the greatest part of the worker's faith in himself is made up of the faith that others believe in him" (ii, 7). In 1863, she commiserated with her friend Barbara Bodichon, who, living abroad, felt cut off from any artistic society that would help her and feed her faith:

> It is hard to believe long together that anything is "worth while" unless there is some eye to kindle in common with our own, some brief word uttered now and then to imply that what is infinitely precious to us is precious alike to another mind. I fancy that, to do without that guarantee, one must be rather insane—one must be a bad poet, or a spinner of impossible theories or an inventor of impossible machinery.
>
> (*L* IV: 119)[15]

In **Middlemarch,** George Eliot concerns herself with the influence of domestic conditions on success. But in other works, she shows that ardent men succeed or fail according as society smiles or frowns on them.[16] The Rev. Mr. Tryan, supported by his congregation, does great good, but his pastoral work is cut short by his early death, due partially to his enemies' persecution of him; dependent on sympathy, suffering acutely from hatred and ridicule ("JR" viii, 203), and seeing death as the only escape (see xviii, 467), he "seemed bent on wearing himself out" (xi, 333). In **"The Lifted Veil,"** written when George Eliot was suffering keenly over idle talk about her authorship, Latimer, endowed with the poet's sensibility but deprived of "the listening ear and answering soul"—suffering from "a fatal solitude of soul"—never becomes a poet: his nature "grew up in an uncongenial medium, which could never foster it into happy, healthy development" (i, 26). Savonarola is a formidable power as long as his party is dominant; when an antagonistic government imprisons him, he loses the faith in himself that no one, lacking external support, can sustain without "a stupid inflexibility of self-confidence" (*R* lxxi, VIII: 146), and withal his influence. Felix Holt, foiled by circumstances in which he is a lone voice crying in the wilderness, argues that he does not fear failure (*FH* xlv, III: 201), but, like Dorothea and George Eliot, he eventually moves away from his old home, presumably in search of a more sympathetic community. Zarca is, except for an assassin's blow, destined to save his people

ADAM BEDE

GEORGE ELIOT

LONDON: J. M. DENT & SONS LTD.
NEW YORK: E. P. DUTTON & CO. INC.

Title page of *Adam Bede*, published in 1859.

because he inspires their "savage loyalty" (*SG* V: 338). Daniel Deronda has good hopes of uniting his people because he feels supported by his ancestors and friends.

Except for Janet, who does not aspire to independent work, all George Eliot's ardent, idealistic heroines, who "care supremely for great and general benefits to mankind" (*DD* xlvi, III: 308), fail to find permanent, fulfilling work outside marriage because the world no more favors their aspirations than Dorothea's. Dinah gives up preaching when it is no longer sanctioned by the Wesleyan Conference. As "the only way of escaping opprobrium, and being entirely in harmony with circumstances" (*MF* I, xi, I: 193), Maggie renounces her aspirations for love and learning. Romola, commanded by Savonarola, abandons her hope to live as "an instructed woman" and devotes herself to charitable labors, for which "[s]he had no innate taste" (*R* xxxvi, VII: 25; xliv, VII: 294). Fedalma, obeying her father's commands, renounces love and undertakes the futile, and hence dreary, task of governing her people.

Behind George Eliot's insistence on the worker's need for sympathy lies her own insatiable need for it, which proceeds from insecurity so deep that she could write in 1859, "[I]t is so dif-

ficult to believe what the world does *not* believe, so easy to believe what the world keeps repeating" (*L* III: 44). Necessary as Lewes's constant support was to her, it was not sufficient. She craved universal praise. Her "extraordinary diffidence" (*L* V: 228) having kept her from writing for years, she was so depressed by adverse criticism that she could continue to write only by ignoring criticism. Lewes wrote in 1862, "A thousand eulogies would not give her the slightest confidence, but one objection would increase her doubts" (*L* IV: 58; see also III: 157, 164, 397; IV: 481; VI: 218, 224, 318). But even general popularity did not satisfy her after the early years of her authorship; she must have understanding and influence (see *L* III: 198; V: 213, 228, 229, 244, 245, 250, 367, 374; VI: 258, 379; *Selections* 370). Repeatedly she wrote her worshippers that their approval, after her husband's, was encouragement she desperately needed. Imagine, she wrote an admirer in 1866,

> the experience of a mind morbidly desponding, of a consciousness tending more and more to consist in memories of error and imperfection rather than in a strengthening sense of achievement—and then consider how such a mind must need the support of sympathy and approval from those who are capable of understanding its aims.
>
> (*L* IV: 300; see also II: 399-400; III: 6, 88, 170, 246, 393; IV: 248, 405, 434; V: 29, 185, 201, 229, 325, 358, 373; VI: 116, 226, 244, 394-95; *Selections* 370, 524)

The adulation did help to dissolve her "paralyzing despondency" (*L* V: 29). Lewes wrote Blackwood in response to the publisher's praise of *Daniel Deronda,* "Your note has been as good as a dose of quinine. As the drooping flower revives under the beneficent rain, so did her drooping spirits under your enthusiastic words" (*L* VI: 228). Though helplessly dependent on others' judgments—"I never think what I write is good for anything till other people tell me so" (*L* II: 260)—she came to have a sort of precarious belief in her power that enabled her to function. As Lewes wrote in 1871, when she was basking in the acclaim that followed publication of Book I of *Middlemarch,* "[S]he begins to feel that her life has indeed not been unavailing" (*L* V: 228). For while "[a]ll the ringing chorus of praise . . . does not stifle her doubt," "by repetition the curing influences *tell,* for they become *massed,* and . . . enable her to *apperceive* the fact that her books are something more than mere amusements" (*L* VI: 226; V: 228; see also II: 406; VI: 219).

Four of her characters, three in poems she wrote while working on *Middlemarch* or shortly after, and the other in the novel succeeding *Mid-*

dlemarch, suggest that the "excessive diffidence" (*L* IV: 58) that paralyzed her in the absence of sympathy is rooted in her neurotic character. Like George Eliot and Zarca (see *SG* I: 153; III: 251), all four fulfill their "Caesar's ambition" for a "[s]upreme vocation" ("**Armgart**" i, *Legend,* 1st ed., 77, 104) by determination to wrest success from a hostile world. But, deprived of their vocations and thus of the world's applause, they are assailed by guilt for the greatness they have secured by refusing to submit to the way of the world and "to be shapen after the average" (xv, I: 257). Recognizing the truth of the angel's words "'Twas but in giving that thou couldst atone / For too much wealth amid [others'] poverty," Jubal renounces his "little pulse of self" and accepts an ignominious death ("**The Legend of Jubal**," *Legend* 1st ed., 45, 38). Accepting the condemnation in her friend's asking, "Where is the rebel's right for you alone?" when there is "the mighty sum / Of claims unpaid to needy myriads" ("**Armgart**" v, *Legend,* Cabinet ed. 130), Armgart, reborn from "that monstrous Self" nurtured by her success, does penance by resigning herself to a life in which she feels herself "Beating upon the world without response" ("**Armgart**" v, *Legend* 1st ed., 140, 133). Arion expiates the "born kingship" ("**Arion**," *Legend* 1st ed., 237) that song confers on him, by consenting to his death. Though Leonora Alcharisi only temporarily loses her voice, she does not resume her glorious career. Behind her mysterious explanation—"I could not go back. All things hindered me—all things"—is loss of will begotten by guilt that she has pursued a career in defiance of her father and society. "I have been forced to obey my dead father," she says. "[E]vents come upon us like evil enchantments" (*DD* li, IV: 45, 29). With thunderous applause in her ears, George Eliot could forget that in writing she, like Leonora, was transgressing her family's and society's proscription against pursuing a vocation. But when the applause died away, then, aware that she had bought success by alienating the love that the child within her could not survive without, she ached for sympathy.

IV

George Eliot's enormous need for sympathetic support, which she shared with many of her female contemporaries, was partly due to the world's belittling of women. She had early understood the *a priori* notions upon which her androcentric society was founded: a woman is intellectually inferior to a man—"[a] man's mind . . . has always the advantage of being masculine,—as the smallest birch-tree is of a higher kind than the most soaring palm,—and even his ignorance is of a sounder quality" (ii, I: 27),[17]—or if undeniably superior, then a "mistake of nature" (*MF* I, ii, I: 14; cf. *M* x, I: 161)—"a woman's no business wi' being so clever" (*MF* I, iii, I: 22)—who would master her husband. In *Middlemarch,* explaining the important role women play in making their husbands successful, George Eliot tries to show that in fact some women are the intellectual and moral equals of men, and that, as she had said in her essay on Fuller and Wollstonecraft, these women are not the threat to men that unenlightened women are. But in her late works, perceiving the oppression and exploitation of women—seeing that society's notions of women's inferiority are only rationalizations of ruthless egoism—understanding at last that society projected its own selfishness on women who pursued vocations, she savagely turned on a world that she more and more saw as stupid and sinister. In *Middlemarch,* she not only indicts society for depriving Dorothea of the support she needs to succeed in the projects she undertakes after marriage, but she bitterly accuses society of consciously and insidiously sacrificing Dorothea on the altar of sexism when she chooses her first husband. In the Finale of the first edition of the novel, George Eliot enumerates the conditions responsible for Dorothea's disastrous choice. She could not have married Casaubon if society "had not smiled on propositions of marriage from a sickly man to a girl less than half his own age—on modes of education which make a woman's knowledge another name for motley ignorance—on rules of conduct which are in flat contradiction with its own loudly-asserted beliefs" (IV: 370). Whatever reason George Eliot had for later deleting these words that have generated much controversy, she did not thereby delete from the novel the argument here.[18]

Society says nothing to disabuse Dorothea of the notion that in making a January-May marriage she is entering on what she thinks is a nurturing father-child relation. For indeed society approves what is in reality the master-slave relation that Casaubon seeks in deliberately choosing as wife "a blooming young lady—the younger the better, because more educable and submissive" (xxix, II: 98). When the "winter-worn husband" (xxxvii, II: 250) tells her, "The great charm of your sex is its capability of an ardent self-sacrificing affection, and herein we see its fitness to round and complete the existence of our own" (v, I: 80), he is clearly expressing a commonplace idea. Dorothea's friends would only substitute one such relation for another in preferring to Casaubon, James, who thought he would have been willing to put up with some predominance in Dorothea, since he could put it down when he liked (ii, I: 27).

In order to judge Casaubon rightly, Dorothea, who, as a woman, had been denied all but a toy-box education (see x, I: 147; iii, I: 39), should have been privy to masculine learning. For what she needed to know was that Casaubon's clergyman's gown concealed no holiness, and his voluminous notes, nothing but dryasdust pedantry—information that her world, regarding Casaubon as "a man of profound learning" (i, I: 9; see also xxx, II: 114) could hardly have supplied. Furthermore, the objections of her circle—"Mrs Cadwallader's contempt for a neighboring clergyman's alleged greatness of soul," "Sir James Chettam's poor opinion of his rival's legs," "Mr Brooke's failure to elicit a companion's ideas," and "Celia's criticism of a middle-aged scholar's personal appearance" (x, I: 143)—could not rightly carry any weight with one "whose notions about marriage took their colour entirely from an exalted enthusiasm about the ends of life" (iii, I: 39; see also v, I: 79).

Readers who argue that "Dodo" is culpable for her mistake in marrying Casaubon point out that none of her friends would have made her mistake (see ix, I: 124). But friends who would have had her marry one (James) who not only would have made her miserable but would not have been so obliging as to leave her a young widow, are hardly wise counselors. If Dorothea's friends happen to be right in opposing her marriage, they are so only because, as George Eliot says in another context, "wrong reasoning sometimes lands poor mortals in right conclusions" (iii, I: 34). Readers who dispute the world's responsibility for Dorothea's marriage often impute to George Eliot an ironical view of her heroine's mistaken notions ("Dorothea . . . retained very child-like ideas about marriage"; "Celia, whose mind had never been thought too powerful, saw the emptiness of other people's pretensions much more readily" [i, I: 7; ii, I: 107]), forgetting that when Dorothea's marriage has failed, George Eliot no more blames Dorothea for her choice of husband than she blames Romola for hers. "Was it [Dorothea's] fault that she had believed in [Casaubon]—had believed in his worthiness?" (xlii, II: 374). Attributing Dorothea's naïveté both to ignorance for which she is not responsible, and to ardor that is more admirable than calculation and prudence,[19] George Eliot

merely smiles at Dorothea's naïveté as she smiles "with some gentleness" (Prelude, I: v) at the innocent child St. Theresa seeking martyrdom. Dorothea's idealizing of Casaubon (see iii, I: 31; v, I: 81; ix, I: 125), which is due to "that simplicity of hers, holding up an ideal for others in her believing conception of them, was one of the great powers of her womanhood" (lxxvii, IV: 252).

Not only Dorothea's ignorance but society's hypocrisy, which Milton says "neither man nor angel can discern" (*Paradise Lost* Bk. III, ll. 682-83), blinds Dorothea. Vociferous as are Dorothea's friends in objecting to her marriage, they do not fundamentally oppose the match. For it satisfies their most deeply rooted concerns that she marry money and social position. Dorothea's uncle and guardian reveals the priorities society dare not flaunt. He tells her he could not "have consented to a bad match. But Casaubon stands well: his position is good" (v, I: 72). Even faced with the disappointment of Mrs. Cadwallader, who consoles herself that Casaubon has money enough (vi, I: 92), shilly-shally Brooke holds firm. "I should have been travelling out of my brief to have hindered [the match]. . . . He is pretty certain to be a bishop, is Casaubon" (vii, I: 110).

Professing to object to Dorothea's sacrifice of herself to Casaubon, her companions, regarding their own interest, actually manipulate her into making a sacrifice of the sort George Eliot had deplored in the forties. According to her pupil, Mary Sibree, Mary Ann

> thought that though in England marriages were not professedly "arrangés," they were so too often practically: young people being brought together, and receiving intimations that mutual interest was desired and expected, were apt to drift into connections on grounds not strong enough for the wear and tear of life; and this, too, among the middle as well as in the higher classes.
>
> (Cross ii, 58)

In fact, George Eliot emphasizes that society covertly approves of the match by implicitly comparing its reactions to Dorothea's two marriages. When Dorothea announces her intention to marry Casaubon, her friends do nothing but grumble behind her back. Brooke refuses to forbid the marriage until she is of age—considering marriage a cure for Dorothea's vagaries, he is disposed to hurry it on when he sees her opposed to marrying James (vii, I: 110)—and her clergyman, who says he knows no harm of Casaubon (viii, I: 114, 118), will not intervene. But when Dorothea marries a second time—marries one neither well born nor possessed of any fortune but his brains (xxx, II: 121)—society does not stand by helpless. Brooke threatens to disinherit her, and all her family excommunicate her. When one critic asks what more society could have done to prevent her marriage to Casaubon, short of putting strychnine in his tea (review of *M* 550; see also Harvey, "Criticism of the Novel" 133-34), the answer is plenty.

If society, while smiling on Dorothea's first marriage, is at the same time dismayed by it, that is so because, as George Eliot says elsewhere, "mortals have a great power of being astonished at the presence of an effect towards which they have done everything, and at the absence of an effect towards which they have done nothing but desire it" (*DD* xxii, II: 64-65). Not to see the malevolent character of a society that regards women as pawns in the marriage game is to identify with the world that George Eliot makes the object of her most trenchant irony—a world that she will excoriate in *Daniel Deronda.*

V

The angry feminist critics of the seventies have largely been silenced by feminist apologists who have rallied around George Eliot since the late seventies. Yet the battle is not over. Christina Crosby, focusing on *Daniel Deronda,* has recently written that George Eliot relegates women to "the realm of reproduction," making them "but instruments to further man's transcendence" (23, 27; see also 161 n. 20). One must still say that George Eliot "occupies a profoundly uneasy position among feminist literary critics," as Ringler wrote in 1983 (55).

And for many this is not likely to change, given certain ineluctable facts. Most important is George Eliot's emphasis on sacrifice and submission ("[a]ll self-sacrifice is good" [*L* I: 268]). But as I have tried to show, George Eliot questions the value of sacrifice in *Middlemarch,* even endorsing Ladislaw's dictum that "[t]he best piety is to enjoy" (xxii, I: 398). Her attitudes toward self-sacrifice and self-fulfillment are not the same throughout her works; at the end of her career, when she wrote *Middlemarch,* she was more given to "innovation" (*TS* ii, 40) than at the beginning.

Certainly, disposed to lead a contemplative, rather than an active, life (see *L* II: 383; IV: 473; V: 324-25, 344); plagued by a "doubting mind" (*L* IV: 472)—by "the labour of choice" (*MF,* II, i, I: 283);[20] and hating to sit in the judgment seat (see

L VI: 418; see also II: 306, 383; IV: 207; V: 76, 344, 367, 471; VII: 44; GE's **"German Wit"** 7), she embarrasses apologists by her hesitancy to take a stand on the Woman Question (see *L* II: 383, 396; IV: 364, 366; V: 58; VII: 44), except in the matter of women's right to a "masculine" education (see *L* IV: 364, 366, 399, 401, 468; **"Woman in France"** 472; **"Art and Belles Lettres"** 642-43). Cherishing "the relation of the sexes and the primary ties of kinship" as "the deepest roots of human wellbeing" (*TS* xvi, 286), she would not hold up a life of achievement as every woman's goal. Moreover, while she did not want any to suffer unjustly (*L* IV: 366; see also 364), she was, like her Armgart, an elitist, especially concerned that exceptional talent not be frustrated.[21] Writing even as a radical youth[22] that "woman does not yet deserve a much better lot than man gives her" (*L* II: 86; see also 157), she had no interest in spurring women on to imitate her in pursuing a career. Believing, as Klesmer insists in *Daniel Deronda,* that good work requires sacrifice[23] and that bad work is an offense,[24] she would not encourage dilettantes. Passionately concerned to disprove the conventional notion that women are inferior—convinced that they have "a precious specialty" (**"Silly Novels"** 461)—she was chiefly concerned with promoting the talented woman (see *L* V: 406).

Furthermore, if she would not encourage women to take up careers, neither would she tell women who needed no prodding to pursue a vocation that they, like her, could succeed if they, like her, were willing to suffer from prejudice. Many feminists are indignant that she did not present models of successful women. Lee R. Edwards says George Eliot could not imagine a world in which Dorothea could have succeeded by force of will ("Women, Energy, and *Middlemarch*" 234, 235-36, 237-38). Clearly she could, since she herself had succeeded by "willing to will strongly" (*L* VI: 166). But she wanted to expose the reasons of her suffering,[25] not celebrate her expensive victory.[26] Having dared to write only in middle age, though early preoccupied with fame (see *L* I: 7, 12, 47, 227, 237, 252; Cross ii, 53), and miserable that her life was of no consequence (*L* II: 93), then, able to write only by battling depression and despair that came partly from "suffer[ing] the slavery of being a girl" (*DD* li, IV: 30), she bitterly resented that, even though blessed with some conditions the most favorable for her development, she paid a terrible price, such as men do not pay, for her "far-resonant action" (*M* Prelude, I: vi). What she wanted to do, in her last three novels, *Middlemarch* especially, was to protest the sexism that made life intolerably hard for women like herself, able and ambitious—George Eliots who never find the living stream in fellowship with their own oary-footed kind (see *M* Prelude, I: vii).

And this brings me to another point. In an effort to ameliorate the conditions under which she labored, George Eliot, always aware of the arguments against granting women equality, wrote not so much for women as for men, especially young men, as still impressionable. At the end of 1867, when she was already contemplating *Middlemarch,* she wrote that "young men . . . are just the class I care most to influence" (*L* IV: 397; see also V: 212-13, 367; VI: 405). Having early understood that woman's lot in an androcentric society is dependent on the lot men give her (see *FH* xxvii, II: 182; xliii, III: 149-50), she strives in *Middlemarch* to enfranchise women not so much by inspiriting women, but by persuading men to see their own self-interest in according women the respect that would free them. Thus, while George Eliot, by showing Dorothea's support of Ladislaw's work, may not seem to have advanced an argument for women's right to an independent occupation, she was, by stressing Ladislaw's acceptance of Dorothea as his equal (if not his superior [see *L* VI: 394]), responding to those, like her Mr. Tulliver, who fail to see that their own interest lies in dispossessing themselves of the notion that women are too stupid to be partners with men.

Add to her ambivalence and elitism, her consciousness that radical views on the position of women did not come well from one damned for her irregular life (see *L* IV: 364, 425), as well as her lack of sympathy for some feminists (*L* V: 58),[27] and one can understand her detachment, except as an "*æsthetic*" (*L* VII: 44), from the battle over the Woman Question.

Yet, despite the certainty that she would not have wanted to be called a feminist (had the word meaning an advocate of equal rights for women existed in her lifetime), I contend that her most authentic self was fiercely, if sometimes covertly, rebellious against the restrictions talented women suffered in pursuing a vocation, and that this self was passionately devoted to abolishing the prejudices of a society that would deny women public vocations. Having tried, unsuccessfully, in her earlier works to reconcile herself to women's sacrifice of their aspirations, as doing good; and having, in her latter years, won the "glorious

achievement" (*R* lxxi, VIII: 147) that emboldened her to release her repressed anger at the establishment, she could express her true self in *Middlemarch.*

Feminists when they sensed in *Middlemarch* "a sacred text" saw more truly than when such of them as Edwards came to regard their original intuition as "an adolescent fantasy" ("Women, Energy, and *Middlemarch*" 238). Ellen Moers says that readers have always been surprised to discover that George Eliot was no feminist (194); and indeed one must disbelieve one's senses to think that George Eliot's experience would have made her other than passionately concerned with the right of women to pursue vocations. With Dorothea, commiserating with Lydgate over the failure of his life's work, George Eliot would have said, "There is no sorrow I have thought more about than that—to love what is great, and try to reach it, and yet to fail" (lxxvi, IV: 237; see also xlii, II: 367; lxxvi, IV: 243). And because in this novel she brilliantly and powerfully makes the case for reform—showing that women are deprived of their right to a public life because egoism and stupidity motivate the sexism of a society that exploits women to its own hurt—she has, I think, produced in *Middlemarch* the greatest feminist novel ever written[28]—a novel that the successes of the feminist movement have not rendered irrelevant in our time.

Notes

1. Abbreviations of George Eliot's works are: Cross—*George Eliot's Life as Related in Her Letters and Journals,* ed. J. W. Cross; DD—*Daniel Deronda;* FH—*Felix Holt;* "JR"—"Janet's Repentance"; L—*The George Eliot Letters;* M—*Middlemarch;* MF—*The Mill on the Floss;* R—*Romola;* SG—*The Spanish Gypsy;* SM—*Silas Marner;* TS—*Impressions of Theophrastus Such.* Unless otherwise noted, references to *M* are to the first edition. In GE's works, part numbers (book, chapter, or scene, or some combination of these) precede page, or volume and page, numbers. GE refers to George Eliot.

2. Saying she lives for her art (see *L* III: 184, 187), GE repeatedly identified her work with her worth: *L* V: 133, 212, 244, 437; VI: 52; IX: 192; see also II: 221; VI: 23, 163; VII: 230; *Selections* 524.

3. Ellen Moers, in her brilliant study *Literary Women,* argues that GE was "no feminist" (194). John Halperin (161) uses the same words. Barbara Hardy says the novelist's "books make their feminist protest in a very muted way": she does not write "as a proselytizing feminist" (52, 51). In her classic study of literary women, Elaine Showalter (24) approvingly quotes Donald Stone as saying that nineteenth-century heroines "are hardly concerned with self-fulfillment in the modern sense of the term."

4. Virginia Woolf says the story of GE's idealistic heroines "is the incomplete version of the story of George Eliot herself" ("George Eliot" 658b; see also 658a). Cf. Woolson 9. Lewes likened GE to Dorothea (*L* V: 163, 308, 332, 338, 352, 360).

5. Lee R. Edwards, in "Women, Energy, and *Middlemarch*," regarding *Middlemarch* as cherishing the values of Dorothea's world (see especially 224, 231, 237), declared that what had been "a sacred text" "can no longer be one of the books of my life" (224, 238). See also her *Psyche as Hero* 91-103. Jenni Calder says GE "diagnoses . . . 'the common yearning of womanhood' [i.e., women's aspirations—a misreading of GE, who, in *M* Prelude I: vi-vii, uses the phrase to mean women's desire for love], and then cures it, sometimes drastically, as if it were indeed a disease" (158). See Zelda Austen 549-61.

6. Several writers see GE's feminism in her very refusal to grant her heroines fulfillment. Patricia Spacks (36-47, 316) and Nancy K. Miller, the latter writing on Maggie (see especially 44), say GE views her heroine's selflessness as fulfilling. Kathleen Blake, in "*Middlemarch* and the Woman Question," claims that *Middlemarch* is "a great feminist work" because in it GE protests that depriving women of their work as helpmates— "[w]omen's work is men" (285, 300)—is depriving them of identity. (Her argument is further supported by GE's repeatedly identifying herself with her work [see n. 2 above], and by her denial that the good of happiness is possible without the exercise of faculty [*L* VIII: 209; see also IV: 155-56, 168; V: 173].) Jeanie G. Thomas sees GE as "profoundly feminist" (393) in acknowledging women's disposition for nurture as a special strength. Susan Fraiman sees the author of *The Mill on the Floss* questioning whether women do not more effectively build character through social interaction than men through self-culture.

7. Sandra M. Gilbert and Susan Gubar attribute to GE covert rage against the patriarchal society that oppresses women, but argue that, in her later works, considering that "the injustice of masculine society bequeathes to women special strengths and virtues" (498), she balances her vengefulness against the countenancing of women's renunciation (499; see also 530). George Levine finds an ideal of vocations open to women "fully present in George Eliot's world," but colliding with "a strain of misogyny" that makes self-sacrifice "quintessentially the women's vocation" (13, 4). Blake, in a revision of her earlier article, more explicitly sees GE as arguing for women's right to a public life, but not as protesting the "self-postponement" women suffer in making men their work (*Love* 41). Carol A. Martin says GE protests against the obstacles that prevent women from realizing their aspirations, but seasons her protest with moderation. Gillian Beer says that GE, though "persistently work[ing] at the central dilemmas of feminism in her time," "was not . . . either a feminist theorist or activist" (1). Similarly, Deirdre David sees GE as sympathetic with intelligent women's desire for cultural and social power, but says her views of women's "womanly" character and love for the past make her complicit with male authority; she was not "actively feminist" (251 n. 3). Suzanne Graver, in "'Incarnate History,'" no longer seeing GE as ambivalent toward feminism (64), argues that, in *M*, GE tries to fuse women's ethics of care and of rights—but says

she legitimizes, as well as challenges, the *status quo* (73-74). (Earlier, in "Mill, *Middlemarch*, and Marriage" and *George Eliot and Community*, Graver argues that GE's responses to the Woman Question are contradictory. Like Spacks, Graver finds that "George Eliot's belief in the redemptive power of suffering caused her to see the very liabilities women suffered in marriage as contributing to their moral evolution" ["Mill," 62].)

8. GE's contemporary Abba Gould Woolson is a possible exception. She says GE holds that "society is bound to promote [her heroines' ideals] by every means in its power. If, instead of this, it employs its institutions, customs, and prejudices towards crushing them out. GE would assign the whole structure of civilized society, as tending to the waste of its noblest energies, and to the cramping and debasement of the individual soul" (78; see also 46-47)

9. Lydgate's story powerfully illustrates GE's argument, in her article on Fuller and Wollestonecraft, that men, by denying women partnership in marriage jeopardize their vocations.

10. Mary suggests that one reason she married Fred rather than Farebrother was that she could save the former, not the latter. When Fred tells her that Farebrother was far worthier of her than he, she retorts, "To be sure he was, . . . and for that reason he could do better without me" (Finale, IV: 362-63; see also lvii, III: 277).

11. In 1849, she wrote, "[T]he only ardent hope I have for my future life is to have given to me some woman's duty, some possibility of devoting myself where I may see a daily result of pure calm blessedness in the life of another" (*L* I: 322).

12. See *L* II: 419; III: 24, 63, 202, 226-27, 405, 417; IV: 28, 123, 347; VI: 335-36, 379; VII: 215. She protested that she could not write to please others (see *L* II: 400, III: 393).

13. GE uses the same phrase in *SM* xi, 209.

14. Some suggest that Dorothea is stupid; see Leslie Stephen 180, Felicia Bonaparte 128, pp. below. Most argue she is handicapped by not having GE's genius; see Laurence Lemer 119; Patricia Beer 181; Zelda Austen 553-54; Marlene Springer 140, 142; George Levine 8; Carol A. Martin 22. But we do not know that she is not extremely intelligent. Brilliant Ladislaw respects her opinion (see p. above); dying Casaubon trusts her to complete his work (l, III: 119-20); Lovegood says she has "a real *genus*" (*sic*) for planning cottages (iii, I: 45); even Brooke admits that Dorothea is "clever enough for anything" (xxx, II: 114); and GE compares her to St. Theresa (Prelude, I: vi; x, I: 148; Finale, IV: 370), probably the most learned female saint, and to St. Catherine of Alexandria (liv, III: 195-96), patron of students.

15. See also *L* IV: 494; VI: 96; *MF* I, viii, I: 139; *M* lxviii, IV: 96; *DD* xlv, III: 300; liv, IV: 106-07. Virginia Woolf wrote, "Literature is strewn with the wreckage of men who have minded beyond reason the opinions of others" (*Room* iii, 85). Csikszentmihalyi writes: "Most of us deep down believe that a person who is creative will prevail regardless of the environment." But "even the greatest genius will not accomplish anything without the support of society and culture" (330).

Closely related to GE's notion that sympathy is necessary to one's successful pursuit of an occupation is her notion that sympathy may be essential for one's stability. Janet Dempster, Hetty Sorrel, Silas Marner, Esther Lyon, Rosamond Vincy, Gwendolen Harleth, and Mirah Lapidoth are saved from despair by another's sympathy, while Catherina Sarti, Latimer, and Don Silva are destroyed by rejection. Cut off from others' sympathy, Latimer, like GE, who in 1840 attributed a fit of sensitiveness to her need for sympathy (*L* I: 75), develops diseased psychic powers.

16. Silas Marner, who continues his weaving though "cut off from faith and love" (ii, 35), might seem to be an exception. But the world does not reject his work. Moreover, his work does not involve his ego; he weaves "like the spider, from pure impulse, without reflection" (*SM* ii, 26). See *L* VI: 48.

17. Cf. the impressions of GE's friend and biographer, Oscar Browning, after looking over examination papers, that, "irrespective of the marks he might give, the best woman was intellectually the inferior of the worst man" (qtd. in Woolf, *Room* iii, 81).

18. Readers have seen GE's excising of the offending words as admission of her mistake. But it is more likely that she deleted the words on grounds that she had already made the meaning of her story clear (she expressed a doubt that there should have been an Epilogue [*L* V: 405]). Furthermore, she may have had second thoughts about inflicting on her readers so savage an excoriation of society; elsewhere in her writings she deleted passages to tone down her original.

19. GE comments ironically on the superior insight Celia has about Casaubon by virtue of feeling less than Dorothea: "To have in general but little feeling, seems to be the only security against feeling too much on any particular occasion" (vii, I: 107).

20. GE uses similar phrases in "JR" xxiv, 525; / *R* lxi, VII: 705 (2 references); lxviii, VIII: 133.

21. In 1857, she wrote a friend, "'La carrière ouverte aux talen[t]s,' whether the talents be feminine or masculine, I am quite confident is a right maxim. Whether 'La carrière ouverte à la sottise,' be equally just, when made equally universal, it would be too much like 'taking sides' for me to say" (*L* II: 396). Feminists have criticized GE for isolating herself from her sister artists (see Showalter 107), but one can scarcely blame a woman naturally reserved, who was spit at by "the world's wife" (*MF* VII: ii, III: 249, 253). Incidentally, indifference to one's sisters is not now thought reason for questioning a woman's feminism.

22. GE became more conservative after her liaison with Lewes, and, then, after working through personal issues in her fiction, returning in later years to something approximating the radicalism she adopted after her apostasy.

23. In 1864, GE said that study, hard work, and heroism "must always go to the doing of anything difficult" (*L* IV: 159). See also I: 277; III: 177, 467; "Silly Novels" 460; *DD*, xxiii, II: 97. Lewes thought GE was performing a service in setting forth in *DD* "the arduousness and difficulties of a career so facile in imagination" (*L* VI: 193).

24. See *L* II: 210, 396 n.7; III: 226, 241; IV: 367, 376, 425, 467; V: 33, 185, 212; VI: 113, 409; VII: 3; VIII: 384;

"Silly Novels" 460-61. In 1879, GE refused to encourage a young writer whom she thought unpromising (*L* VII: 177-78).

25. In 1874, GE wrote, "[W]hat evil can be got rid of on a sudden? Only it makes a difference when the evil is recognized as an evil, because then action is adjusted to gradual disappearance instead of contemplated permanence" (*L* VI: 47).

26. Woolf, "George Eliot" (658b), saw GE's work as wearing her life away, as indeed GE herself did (*L* VI: 415).

27. GE insisted that women should remain feminine (*L* IV: 468; V: 406).

28. Was Lewes alluding to the feminist message of the novel when he wrote in December 1871 that he has "all along felt that women would owe [GE] peculiar gratitude for that book" (*L* V: 225)?

Works Cited

Austen, Zelda. "Why Feminist Critics Are Angry with George Eliot." *College English* 37 (Feb. 1976): 549-61.

Basch, Françoise. *Relative Creatures: Victorian Women in Society and the Novel, 1837-67.* Trans. Anthony Rudolph. London: Allen Lane, 1974.

Beer, Gillian. *George Eliot.* Bloomington: Indiana UP, 1986.

Beer, Patricia. *Reader, I Married Him: A Study of the Women Characters of Jane Austen, Charlotte Brontë, Elizabeth Gaskell and George Eliot.* London: Macmillan, 1974.

Blake, Kathleen. "*Middlemarch* and the Woman Question." *Nineteenth-Century Fiction* 31 (Dec. 1976): 285-312.

———. *Love and the Woman Question in Victorian Literature: The Art of Self-Postponement.* Brighton, Sussex: Harvester, 1983.

Bonaparte, Felicia. *Will and Destiny: Morality and Tragedy in George Eliot's Novels.* New York: New York UP, 1975.

Calder, Jenni. *Women and Marriage in Victorian Fiction.* New York: Oxford UP, 1976.

Crosby, Christiana. *The Ends of History: Victorians and "the Woman Question."* New York: Routledge, Chapman & Hall, 1991.

Csikszentmihalyi, Mihaly. *Creativity: Flow and the Psychology of Discovery and Invention.* New York: Harper Collins, 1996.

David, Deirdre. *Intellectual Women and Victorian Patriarchy: Harriet Martineau, Elizabeth Barrett Browning, George Eliot.* Ithaca: Cornell UP, 1987.

Edwards, Lee R. *Psyche as Hero: Female Heroism and Fictional Form.* Middletown, CT: Wesleyan UP, 1984.

———. "Women, Energy, and *Middlemarch*." *Massachusetts Review* 13 (winter-spring 1972): 223-38.

Eliot, George. "Address to Working Men, by Felix Holt." *Blackwood's Edinburgh Magazine* 103 (Jan. 1868): 1-11.

———. "Amos Barton." *Blackwood's Edinburgh Magazine* 81 (Jan.-Feb. 1857): 1-22, 153-72.

———. "Art and Belles Lettres." *Westminster Review* 65 (April 1856): 625-50.

———. *Daniel Deronda.* 1st ed. 4 vols. Edinburgh: Blackwood, 1876.

———. *Felix Holt, the Radical.* 1st ed. 3 vols. Edinburgh: Blackwood, 1866.

———. *The George Eliot Letters.* Ed. Gordon S. Haight. 9 vols. New Haven: Yale UP, 1954-78.

———. *George Eliot's Life as Related in Her Letters and Journals.* Ed. J[ohn] W[alter] Cross. New ed. Edinburgh: Blackwood, [1887].

———. "German Wit: Heinrich Heine." *Westminster Review* 65 (Jan. 1856): 1-33.

———. *Impressions of Theophrastus Such.* 1st ed. Edinburgh: Blackwood, 1879.

———. "Janet's Repentance." *Blackwood's Edinburgh Magazine* 82 (July-Nov. 1857): 55-76, 189-206, 329-44, 457-73, 519-41.

———. *The Legend of Jubal and Other Poems.* 1st ed. Edinburgh: Blackwood, 1874.

———. *The Legend of Jubal and Other Poems, Old and New.* Cabinet ed. Edinburgh: Blackwood, 1879.

———. "The Lifted Veil." *Blackwood's Edinburgh Magazine* 86 (July 1859): 24-48.

———. "Margaret Fuller and Mary Wollstonecraft." *Leader* 6 (Oct. 13, 1855): 988-89.

———. *Middlemarch.* 1st ed. 4 vols. Edinburgh: Blackwood, 1871-72.

———. *Middlemarch.* Cabinet ed. 3 vols. Edinburgh: Blackwood, 1878.

———. *The Mill on the Floss.* 1st ed. 3 vols. Edinburgh: Blackwood, 1860.

———. *Romola. Cornhill Magazine* 6 (July-Dec. 1862): 1-43, 145-86, 289-318, 433-70, 577-604, 721-57; 7 (Jan. June 1863): 1-30, 145-71, 281-309, 417-40, 553-76, 681-705; 8 (July-Aug. 1863): 1-34, 129-53.

———. *Selections from George Eliot's Letters.* Ed. Gordon S. Haight. New Haven: Yale UP, 1985.

———. *Silas Marner.* 1st ed. Edinburgh: Blackwood, 1861.

———. "Silly Novels by Lady Novelists." *Westminster Review* 66 (Oct. 1856): 442-61.

———. *The Spanish Gypsy.* 1st ed. Edinburgh: Blackwood, 1868.

———. "Woman in France: Madame de Sablé." *Westminster Review* 62 (Oct. 1854): 448-73.

Fraiman, Susan. "*The Mill on the Floss,* the Critics, and the Bildungsroman." *PMLA* 108 (Jan. 1993): 136-50.

Gilbert, Sandra M., and Susan Gubar. *The Madwoman in the Attic: The Woman Writer and the Nineteenth-Century Literary Imagination.* New Haven: Yale UP, 1979.

Graver, Suzanne. *George Eliot and Community: A Study in Social Theory and Fictional Form.* Berkeley: U of California P, 1984.

———. "'Incarnate History': The Feminisms of *Middlemarch.*" *Approaches to Teaching Eliot's "Middlemarch."* Ed. Kathleen Blake. New York: MLA, 1990. 64-74.

———. "Mill, *Middlemarch,* and Marriage." *Portraits of Marriage in Literature.* Ed. Anne C. Hargrove and Maurine Magliocco. Macomb: Western Illinois UP, 1984. 55-65.

Halperin, John. *Egoism and Self-Discovery in the Victorian Novel: Studies in the Ordeal of Knowledge in the Nineteenth Century.* New York: Burt Franklin, 1974.

Hardy, Barbara. *The Novels of George Eliot: A Study in Form.* London: Athlone P, 1959.

Harvey, W. J. "Criticism of the Novel: Contemporary Reception." *Middlemarch: Critical Approaches to the Novel.* Ed. Barbara Hardy. London: Athlone P, 1967.

———. "Introduction." *Middlemarch.* Harmondsworth: Penguin, 1965.

The Hero's Journey: The World of Joseph Campbell. Ed. Phil Cousineau. San Francisco: Harper & Row, 1990.

Lerner, Laurence. *George Eliot and Her Readers: A Selection of Contemporary Reviews.* Ed. John Holmstrom and Lerner. London: Bodley Head, 1966.

Levine, George. "Repression and Vocation in George Eliot: A Review Essay." *Women and Literature* 7 (Spring 1979): 3-13.

Martin, Carol A. "George Eliot: Feminist Critic." *Victorian Newsletter* 65 (Spring 1984): 22-25.

Miller, Nancy K. "Emphasis Added: Plots and Plausibilities in Women's Fiction." *PMLA* 96 (Jan. 1981): 36-48.

Millett, Kate. *Sexual Politics.* Garden City, NY: Doubleday, 1970.

Moers, Ellen. *Literary Women.* Garden City, NY: Doubleday, 1963.

Review of *Middlemarch. Canadian Monthly and National Review.* 3 (June 1873): 549-52.

Ringler, Ellin. "*Middlemarch*: A Feminist Perspective." *Studies in the Novel* 15 (spring 1983): 55-61.

Showalter, Elaine. *A Literature of Their Own: British Women Novelists from Brontë to Lessing.* Princeton: Princeton UP, 1977.

Spacks, Patricia Meyer. *The Female Imagination.* New York: Alfred A. Knopf, 1975.

Springer, Marlene. "Angels and Other Women in Victorian Literature." *What Manner of Woman: Essays on English and American Life and Literature.* Ed. Springer. New York: New York UP, 1977.

Stephen, Leslie. *George Eliot.* New York: Macmillan, 1902.

Thomas, Jeanie G. "An Inconvenient Indefiniteness: George Eliot, *Middlemarch,* and Feminism." *University of Toronto Quarterly* 56 (spring 1987): 392-415.

Woolf, Virginia. "George Eliot." *Times Literary Supplement* 20 Nov. 1919: 657-58.

———. *A Room of One's Own.* London: Hogarth P, 1929.

Woolson, Abba Gould. *George Eliot and Her Heroines: A Study.* New York: Harper, 1886.

FURTHER READING

Bibliography

Baker, William and John C. Ross. *George Eliot: A Bibliographical History.* London, England: British Library Publications, 2002, 676 p.

Provides a detailed and thorough bibliography of published critical commentary on Eliot's life and works through 2001.

Biography

Haight, Gordon S. *George Eliot: A Biography.* New York: Oxford University Press, 1968, 616 p.

> *Offers a definitive biography.*

Criticism

Austen, Zelda. "Why Feminist Critics Are Angry with George Eliot." *College English* 37, no. 6 (February 1976): 549-61.

> *Explains why feminists often criticize Eliot's novels, particularly* Middlemarch, *for reinforcing patriarchal systems; however, Austen argues that feminists have "something to learn" from Eliot's subtle thinking about a woman's place in a male-dominated society.*

Critical Essays on George Eliot, edited by Barbara Hardy. New York: Oxford University Press, 1970, 192 p.

> *Contains essays on Eliot's individual novels, with commentary on Eliot's oeuvre by W. J. Harvey and John Bayley.*

Dee, Phyllis Susan. "Female Sexuality and Triangular Desire in *Vanity Fair* and *The Mill on the Floss.*" *Papers on Language & Literature* 35, no. 4 (fall 1999): 391-416.

> *Compares female sexuality in William Makepeace Thackeray's and Eliot's novels, addressing the ways in which female characters "struggle to escape the male-initiated bonds of sexual desire."*

Dillon, Steven. "George Eliot and the Feminine Gift." *Studies in English Literature* 32, no. 4 (autumn 1992): 707-21.

> *Explores the "gift," which refers to the protestant religious gift associated with John Milton, in terms of femininity in Eliot's works.*

Heller, Deborah. "George Eliot's Jewish Feminist." *Atlantis* 8, no. 2 (spring 1983): 37-43.

> *Explores the complexity of Eliot's attitude towards Judaism and feminism in* Daniel Deronda.

Hudd, Louise. "The Politics of a Feminist Poetics: 'Armgart' and George Eliot's Critical Response to *Aurora Leigh.*" In *Poetry and Politics (Essays and Studies 49),* edited by Kate Flint, pp. 62-83. Cambridge, England: D. S. Brewer, 1996.

> *Discusses Eliot's critical response to Elizabeth Barrett Browning's epic poem* Aurora Leigh, *using examples from Eliot's writings in the* Westminster Review *to show that Eliot is engaging in a feminist debate.*

Gilbert, Sandra M. and Susan Gubar. "George Eliot as the Angel of Destruction." In *The Madwoman in the Attic: The Woman Writer in the Nineteenth-Century Literary Imagination,* pp. 478-535. New Haven: Yale University Press, 1979.

> *In a seminal feminist interpretation of* Middlemarch *Gilbert and Gubar suggest that the novel should be read*

as an attempt on Eliot's part to resolve the conflict between two opposing sides of her personality, her "man's mind" and "woman's heart."

Graver, Suzanne. "'Incarnate History': The Feminisms of *Middlemarch.*" In *Approaches to Teaching Eliot's Middlemarch,* edited by Kathleen Blake, pp. 64-74. New York: Modern Language Association, 1990.

> *Addresses Eliot's ambivalence towards feminism in* Middlemarch *and suggests approaches to the novel in the classroom.*

Lovesey, Oliver. "The Other Woman in *Daniel Deronda.*" *Studies in the Novel* 30, no. 4 (winter 1998): 505-20.

> *Comments on the marginalization and restriction of female characters in* Daniel Deronda.

Ringler, Ellin. "*Middlemarch*: A Feminist Perspective." *Studies in the Novel* 25, no. 1 (spring 1983): 55-60.

> *Argues that "feminists' uneasiness" about Eliot's novels in general and* Middlemarch *in particular is justified because Eliot ultimately reinforces "disjunctures between male and female social power."*

Sypher, Eileen. "Resisting Gwendolen's 'Subjection': *Daniel Deronda*'s Proto-Feminism." *Studies in the Novel* 28, no. 4 (winter 1996): 506-24.

> *Contends that Gwendolen Harleth, one of the heroines in Eliot's* Daniel Deronda, *displays many characteristics of early feminist thought because of her resistance to the limitations imposed by men.*

West-Burnham, Joss. "Travelling towards Selfhood: Victorian Religion and the Process of Female Identity." In *Women's Lives into Print: The Theory, Practice and Writing of Feminist Auto/Biography,* edited by Pauline Polkey, pp. 80-95. Basingstoke, England: Macmillan, 1999.

> *Discusses Eliot's transition from faith to unbelief, including a suggestion of the implications of religion on the feminist tendencies in Eliot's writing.*

OTHER SOURCES FROM GALE:

Additional coverage of Eliot's life and career is contained in the following sources published by the Gale Group: *British Writers,* Vol. 5; *British Writers: The Classics,* Vol. 1; *British Writers Retrospective Supplement,* Vol. 2; *Concise Dictionary of British Literary Biography,* 1832-1890; *Contemporary Novelists,* Ed. 7; *Contemporary Popular Writers; Dictionary of Literary Biography,* Vols. 21, 35, 55; *DISCovering Authors; DISCovering Authors: British Edition; DISCovering Authors: Canadian Edition; DISCovering Authors Modules: Most-studied Authors and Novelists; DISCovering Authors 3.0; Literary Movements for Students,* Vol. 1; *Literature and Its Times Supplement,* Vol. 1; *Literature Resource Center; Nineteenth-Century Literature Criticism,* Vols. 4, 13, 23, 41, 49, 89, 118; *Novels for Students,* Vol. 17; *Poetry Criticism,* Vol. 20; *Reference Guide to English Literature,* Ed. 2; *Reference Guide to Short Fiction,* Ed. 2; *Short Stories for Students,* Vol. 8; *Twayne's English Authors; World Literature and Its Times,* Vol. 3; and *World Literature Criticism.*

MARGARET FULLER

(1810 - 1850)

American essayist, critic, travel writer, translator, and poet.

A pioneer of nineteenth-century feminism, Margaret Fuller was a well-respected social and literary critic. She is best known as the founding editor of the Transcendentalist journal *The Dial,* and as the author of the feminist treatise *Woman in the Nineteenth Century* (1845).

BIOGRAPHICAL INFORMATION

Sarah Margaret Fuller was born May 23, 1810, in Cambridgeport, Massachusetts. She was the eldest of seven surviving children of Margaret Crane and Timothy Fuller, a Harvard graduate and attorney who served in the Massachusetts State Senate, the Massachusetts House of Representatives, and the United States House of Representatives. Fuller displayed superior intellectual skills at an early age and her father decided to personally oversee her education, which included rigorous study of classical languages and literature. She began studying Latin grammar at the age of five and progressed to Greek, French, Italian, and German. However, the demands of her father's strict educational program took its toll on her health as a child, causing Fuller to later regret having "no natural childhood." In 1821, recognizing that she

had little social interaction with other children outside the family, the Fullers sent their daughter to Dr. John Park's school in Boston, which she attended for little more than a year. Her only other formal schooling was at Susan Prescott's school in Groton, which she attended from 1824 to 1826.

Fuller was exposed at a young age to the intellectual life of Boston and Cambridge; she impressed many of the Harvard students and faculty with her wit and learning, although she earned the disapproval of an equal number by her failure to adhere to contemporary standards of demure femininity. In 1833, Timothy Fuller moved the family to Groton where Fuller, cut off from her friends in Boston, assumed much of the care and education of her siblings. Two years later, her father's sudden death from cholera forced Fuller into the teaching profession as a way to help support her mother and her younger sisters and brothers. Back in Boston, she taught at Bronson Alcott's Temple School in 1836, supplementing her income with night classes in German and Italian poetry for adults. A year later she left Boston to teach in Albert Gorton Greene's school in Providence. By 1839, her family's financial situation had improved and Fuller joined her mother in Boston, where she resumed her friendships with the leading figures of the Transcendentalist movement, among them Ralph Waldo Emerson, Nathaniel Hawthorne, Henry Wadsworth Longfellow, Amos Bronson Alcott, and Horace Greeley.

That same year, she started the first of her annual "Conversations," a lecture and discussion series for adult women—some of them her former students—and began editing the Transcendentalist journal, *The Dial,* serving without pay for the first two years. She resigned from the position in 1842 and the magazine ended publication two years later under Emerson's editorship. In 1844, Fuller moved to New York and took over as literary editor of Greeley's *New York Daily Tribune.* She became one of America's first foreign correspondents when she traveled to Europe in 1846 and sent dispatches back to the *Tribune.* In 1847 Fuller traveled to Italy where she met Giovanni Ossoli with whom she had a son the following year; it is unclear whether or not the couple married. They were returning to America in 1850 when their ship ran aground and sank off Fire Island on July 19. Fuller's body was never recovered, nor was the manuscript of her final book.

MAJOR WORKS

Fuller's professional writing career began with her work on *The Dial,* the first issue of which appeared in July, 1840. Since she had some difficulty convincing other writers to contribute to the magazine, Fuller wrote a great deal of the material featured in the first several issues herself. In 1844, she published *Summer on the Lakes,* a collection of travel essays written after her 1843 tour of the Great Lakes with her friend Sarah Clarke. Two years later, *Papers on Literature and Art,* consisting of essays previously published in periodicals, was published. The work covered a wide variety of subjects, from reviews of current books and exhibitions to an essay on her own critical perspective called "A Short Essay on Critics."

Fuller's best-known work is *Woman in the Nineteenth Century,* an extended treatise on the status of women. A shorter version had appeared two years earlier in *The Dial* under the title "The Great Lawsuit." Fuller called for complete equality between males and females, and compared the struggle for women's rights with the abolition movement. She insisted that all professions be opened to women and contended that women should not be forced to submit to the men in their lives: husbands, fathers, or brothers. The book was highly controversial in its time; critics believed Fuller's notions would destroy the stability and sanctity of the home. Some objections were lodged on religious grounds as her ideas were considered contrary to the divine order.

CRITICAL RECEPTION

Aside from the controversial nature of Fuller's theories, early criticism of her writings focused on her literary style, which was modeled on that of the classics, but was considered far too ornate and lengthy. Contemporary assessments of her work were also colored by resistance to Fuller's strong personality. In addition, the heavy-handed editing of her papers and diaries after her death—by such famous contemporaries as William Henry Channing, James Freeman Clark, and Ralph Waldo Emerson—suppressed some of the more controversial aspects of her life and work. As a result, succeeding generations of critics, given such a distorted view of the woman and her writings, have underestimated her contributions to the nineteenth-century struggle for women's equality. While *Woman in the Nineteenth Century* was considered the inspiration for the 1848 women's rights convention in Seneca Falls, the work virtually disappeared after the publication of a second edition in 1855. Since the 1970s, Fuller's work has been reexamined and her critical reputation restored primarily through the efforts of feminist scholars.

Suggesting that Fuller's unusual writing method has been misunderstood by critics, Fritz Fleischmann explains that, for her, writing was a process of discovery: "Fuller writes to find out 'what she means,' rather than to expound on what she means; and her method of writing is in full consonance with her purpose and her message." Annette Kolodny (see Further Reading) also contends that Fuller's style, so thoroughly dismissed by her contemporaries, was actually ahead of its time; Kolodny praises the revolutionary nature of Fuller's theories and the "even greater daring of her rhetorical strategies." Cynthia J. Davis acknowledged that Fuller was searching for a "degendered rhetorical form," but more importantly, according to Davis, was the fact that "Fuller not only degendered rhetoric, she degendered bodies, and this was a radical thing to do, even within a feminist tradition." But the radical nature of her work and her failure to conform to conventional standards of femininity made Fuller a self-proclaimed outsider in nineteenth-century culture, according to Michaela Bruckner Cooper. "While Fuller stressed her difference from others," Cooper reports, "she does not always do so confidently. Frequently, anxiety about her status as a woman and writer surfaces." Nonetheless, many critics today praise Fuller as a pioneer feminist whose writings, in some cases, anticipate the work of scholars today.

PRINCIPAL WORKS

Summer on the Lakes, in 1843 (travel essays) 1844

Woman in the Nineteenth Century (essays) 1845

Papers on Literature and Art (criticism) 1846

Memoirs of Margaret Fuller Ossoli 2 vols. (memoirs) 1852

Woman in the Nineteenth Century and Kindred Papers Relating to the Sphere, Conditions, and Duties of Woman (essays) 1855

At Home and Abroad; or; Things and Thoughts in America and Europe (essays and letters) 1856

Life Without and Life Within (essays, criticism, and poetry) 1860

The Writings of Margaret Fuller (essays, criticism, letters, poetry, and memoirs) 1941

The Letters of Margaret Fuller 6 vols. (letters) 1983-94

PRIMARY SOURCES

MARGARET FULLER (ESSAY DATE 1843)

SOURCE: Fuller, Margaret. "The Great Lawsuit." In *Public Women, Public Words: A Documentary History of American Feminism,* edited by Dawn Keetley and John Pettegrew, pp. 187-90. Madison, Wisc.: Madison House, 1997.

In the following excerpt, from an essay which first appeared in The Dial *in July, 1843, Fuller compares the status of women with the status of slaves and urges women to avoid letting love and marriage constitute their entire existence.*

. . . Of all its banners, none has been more steadily upheld, and under none has more valor and willingness for real sacrifices been shown, than that of the champions of the enslaved African. And this band it is, which, partly in consequence of a natural following out of principles, partly because many women have been prominent in that cause, makes, just now, the warmest appeal in behalf of woman.

Though there has been a growing liberality on this point, yet society at large is not so prepared for the demands of this party, but that they are, and will be for some time, coldly regarded as the Jacobins of their day.

"Is it not enough," cries the sorrowful trader, "that you have done all you could to break up the national Union, and thus destroy the prosperity of our country, but now you must be trying to break up family union, to take my wife away from the cradle, and the kitchen hearth, to vote at polls, and preach from a pulpit? Of course, if she does such things, she cannot attend to those of her own sphere. She is happy enough as she is. She has more leisure than I have, every means of improvement, every indulgence."

"Have you asked her whether she was satisfied with these indulgences?"

"No, but I know she is. She is too amiable to wish what would make me unhappy, and too judicious to wish to step beyond the sphere of her sex. I will never consent to have our peace disturbed by any such discussions."

"'Consent'—you? it is not consent from you that is in question, it is assent from your wife."

"Am I not the head of my house?"

"You are not the head of your wife. God has given her a mind of her own."

"I am the head and she the heart."

"God grant you play true to one another then. If the head represses no natural pulse of the heart, there can be no question as to your giving your consent. Both will be of one accord, and there needs but to present any question to get a full and true answer. There is no need of precaution, of indulgence, or consent. But our doubt is whether the heart consents with the head, or only acquiesces in its decree; and it is to ascertain the truth on this point, that we propose some liberating measures."

Thus vaguely are these questions proposed and discussed at present. But their being proposed at all implies much thought, and suggests more. Many women are considering within themselves what they need that they have not, and what they can have, if they find they need it. Many men are considering whether women are capable of being and having more than they are and have, and whether, if they are, it will be best to consent to improvement of their condition.

The numerous party, whose opinions are already labelled and adjusted too much to their mind to admit of any new light, strive, by lectures on some model-woman of bridal-like beauty and gentleness, by writing or lending little treatises, to mark out with due precision the limits of woman's sphere, and woman's mission, and to prevent other than the rightful shepherd from climbing the wall, or the flock from using any chance gap to run astray.

Without enrolling ourselves at once on either side, let us look upon the subject from that point of view which to-day offers. No better, it is to be feared, than a high house-top. A high hill-top, or at least a cathedral spire, would be desirable.

It is not surprising that it should be the Anti-Slavery party that pleads for woman, when we consider merely that she does not hold property on equal terms with men; so that, if a husband dies without a will, the wife, instead of stepping at once into his place as head of the family, inherits only a part of his fortune, as if she were a child, or ward only, not an equal partner.

We will not speak of the innumerable instances, in which profligate or idle men live upon the earnings of industrious wives; or if the wives leave them and take with them the children, to perform the double duty of mother and father, follow from place to place, and threaten to rob them of the children, if deprived of the rights of a husband, as they call them, planting themselves in their poor lodgings, frightening them into paying tribute by taking from them the children, running into debt at the expense of these otherwise so overtasked helots. Though such instances abound, the public opinion of his own sex is against the man, and when cases of extreme tyranny are made known, there is private action in the wife's favor. But if woman be, indeed, the weaker party, she ought to have legal protection, which would make such oppression impossible.

And knowing that there exists, in the world of men, a tone of feeling towards women as towards slaves, such as is expressed in the common phrase, "Tell that to women and children;" that the infinite soul can only work through them in already ascertained limits; that the prerogative of reason, man's highest portion, is allotted to them in a much lower degree; that it is better for them to be engaged in active labor, which is to be furnished and directed by those better able to think, & c. & c.; we need not go further, for who can review the experience of last week, without recalling words which imply, whether in jest or earnest, these views, and views like these? Knowing this, can we wonder that many reformers think that measures are not likely to be taken in behalf of women, unless their wishes could be publicly represented by women?

That can never be necessary, cry the other side. All men are privately influenced by women; each has his wife, sister, or female friends, and is too much biassed by these relations to fail of representing their interests. And if this is not enough, let them propose and enforce their wishes with the pen. The beauty of home would be destroyed, the delicacy of the sex be violated, the dignity of halls of legislation destroyed, by an attempt to introduce them there. Such duties are inconsistent with those of a mother; and then we have ludicrous pictures of ladies in hysterics at the polls, and senate chambers filled with cradles.

But if, in reply, we admit as truth that woman seems destined by nature rather to the inner circle, we must add that the arrangements of civilized life have not been as yet such as to secure it to her. Her circle, if the duller, is not the quieter. If kept from excitement, she is not from drudgery. Not only the Indian carries the burdens of the camp, but the favorites of Louis the Fourteenth accompany him in his journeys, and the washer-woman stands at her tub and carries home her work at all seasons, and in all states of health. . . .

Under these circumstances, without attaching importance in themselves to the changes demanded by the champions of woman, we hail them as signs of the times. We would have every arbitrary barrier thrown down. We would have every path laid open to woman as freely as to man. Were this done, and a slight temporary fermentation allowed to subside, we believe that the Divine would ascend into nature to a height unknown in the history of past ages, and nature, thus instructed, would regulate the spheres not only so as to avoid collision, but to bring forth ravishing harmony. . . .

A writer in a late number of the New York Pathfinder, in two articles headed "Femality," has uttered a still more pregnant word than any we have named. He views woman truly from the soul, and not from society, and the depth and leading of his thoughts is proportionably remarkable. He views the feminine nature as a harmonizer of the vehement elements, and this has often been hinted elsewhere; but what he expresses most forcibly is the lyrical, the inspiring and inspired apprehensiveness of her being.

Had I room to dwell upon this topic, I could not say anything so precise, so near the heart of the matter, as may be found in that article; but, as it is, I can only indicate, not declare, my view.

There are two aspects of woman's nature, expressed by the ancients as Muse and Minerva. It is the former to which the writer in the Pathfinder looks. It is the latter which Wordsworth has in mind, when he says,

"With a placid brow,
Which woman ne'er should forfeit, keep
   thy vow."

The especial genius of woman I believe to be electrical in movement, intuitive in function, spiritual in tendency. She is great not so easily in classification, or re-creation, as in an instinctive seizure of causes, and a simple breathing out of what she receives that has the singleness of life, rather than the selecting or energizing of art.

More native to her is it to be the living model of the artist, than to set apart from herself any one form in objective reality; more native to inspire and receive the poem than to create it. In so far as soul is in her completely developed, all soul is the same; but as far as it is modified in her as woman, it flows, it breathes, it sings, rather than deposits soil, or finishes work, and that which is especially feminine flushes in blossom the face of earth, and pervades like air and water all this seeming solid globe, daily renewing and purifying its life. Such may be the especially feminine element, spoken of as Femality. But it is no more the order of nature that it should be incarnated pure in any form, than that the masculine energy should exist unmingled with it in any form.

Male and female represent the two sides of the great radical dualism. But, in fact, they are perpetually passing into one another. Fluid hardens to solid, solid rushes to fluid. There is no wholly masculine man, no purely feminine woman.

History jeers at the attempts of physiologists to bind great original laws by the forms which flow from them. They make a rule; they say from observation what can and cannot be. In vain! Nature provides exceptions to every rule. She sends women to battle, and sets Hercules spinning; she enables women to bear immense burdens, cold, and frost; she enables the man, who feels maternal love, to nourish his infant like a mother. Of late she plays still gayer pranks. Not only she deprives organizations, but organs, of a necessary end. She enables people to read with the top of the head, and see with the pit of the stomach. Presently she will make a female Newton, and a male Syren.

Man partakes of the feminine in the Apollo, woman of the Masculine as Minerva.

Let us be wise and not impede the soul. Let her work as she will. Let us have one creative energy, one incessant revelation. Let it take what form it will, and let us not bind it by the past to

man or woman, black or white. Jove sprang from Rhea, Pallas from Jove. So let it be.

If it has been the tendency of the past remarks to call woman rather to the Minerva side,—if I, unlike the more generous writer, have spoken from society no less than the soul,—let it be pardoned. It is love that has caused this, love for many incarcerated souls, that might be freed could the idea of religious self-dependence be established in them, could the weakening habit of dependence on others be broken up.

Every relation, every gradation of nature, is incalculably precious, but only to the soul which is poised upon itself, and to whom no loss, no change, can bring dull discord, for it is in harmony with the central soul.

If any individual live too much in relations, so that he becomes a stranger to the resources of his own nature, he falls after a while into a distraction, or imbecility, from which he can only be cured by a time of isolation, which gives the renovating fountains time to rise up. With a society it is the same. Many minds, deprived of the traditionary or instinctive means of passing a cheerful existence, must find help in self-impulse or perish. It is therefore that while any elevation, in the view of union, is to be hailed with joy, we shall not decline celibacy as the great fact of the time. It is one from which no vow, no arrangement, can at present save a thinking mind. For now the rowers are pausing on their oars, they wait a change before they can pull together. All tends to illustrate the thought of a wise contemporary. Union is only possible to those who are units. To be fit for relations in time, souls, whether of man or woman, must be able to do without them in the spirit.

It is therefore that I would have woman lay aside all thought, such as she habitually cherishes, of being taught and led by men. I would have her, like the Indian girl, dedicate herself to the Sun, the Sun of Truth, and go no where if his beams did not make clear the path. I would have her free from compromise, from complaisance, from helplessness, because I would have her good enough and strong enough to love one and all beings, from the fullness, not the poverty of being. . . .

But men do *not* look at both sides, and women must leave off asking them and being influenced by them, but retire within themselves, and explore the groundwork of being till they find their peculiar secret. Then when they come forth again, renovated and baptized, they will know how to turn all dross to gold, and will be rich and free though they live in a hut, tranquil, if in a crowd. Then their sweet singing shall not be from passionate impulse, but the lyrical overflow of a divine rapture, and a new music shall be elucidated from this many-chorded world.

Grant her then for a while the armor and the javelin. Let her put from her the press of other minds and meditate in virgin loneliness. . . .

A profound thinker has said "no married woman can represent the female world, for she belongs to her husband. The idea of woman must be represented by a virgin."

But that is the very fault of marriage, and of the present relation between the sexes, that the woman does belong to the man, instead of forming a whole with him. Were it otherwise there would be no such limitation to the thought.

Woman, self-centered, would never be absorbed by any relation; it would be only an experience to her as to man. It is a vulgar error that love, _a_ love to woman is her whole existence; she also is born for Truth and Love in their universal energy. Would she but assume her inheritance, Mary would not be the only Virgin Mother. Not Manzoni alone would celebrate in his wife the virgin mind with the maternal wisdom and conjugal affections. The soul is ever young, ever virgin.

And will not she soon appear? The woman who shall vindicate their birthright for all women; who shall teach them what to claim, and how to use what they obtain? Shall not her name be for her era Victoria, for her country and her life Virginia? Yet predictions are rash; she herself must teach us to give her the fitting name.

MARGARET FULLER (ESSAY DATE 1845)

SOURCE: Fuller, Margaret. "Woman in the Nineteenth Century." In _Margaret Fuller: A Brief Biography with Documents,_ Eve Kornfeld, pp. 175-76. Boston: Bedford Books, 1997.

In the following excerpt, from a text originally published in 1845, Fuller denounces the notion that women should be better educated, not for their own sakes, but so that they might serve as better companions for their husbands and better mothers to their children.

Another sign of the times is furnished by the triumphs of female authorship. These have been great and constantly increasing. Women have taken possession of so many provinces for which men had pronounced them unfit, that though these still declare there are some inaccessible to them, it is difficult to say just _where_ they must stop.

The shining names of famous women have cast light upon the path of the sex, and many obstructions have been removed. When a Montagu could learn better than her brother, and use her lore afterward to such purpose, as an observer, it seemed amiss to hinder women from preparing themselves to see, or from seeing all they could, when prepared. Since Somerville has achieved so much, will any young girl be prevented from seeking a knowledge of the physical sciences, if she wishes it?[1] . . .

Whether much or little has been done or will be done, whether women will add to the talent of narration, the power of systematizing, whether they will carve marble, as well as draw and paint, is not important. But that it should be acknowledged that they have intellect which needs developing, that they should not be considered complete, if beings of affection and habit alone, is important.

Yet even this acknowledgment, rather conquered by woman than proffered by man, has been sullied by the usual selfishness. So much is said of women being better educated, that they may become better companions and mothers _for men._ They should be fit for such companionship, and we have mentioned, with satisfaction, instances where it has been established. Earth knows no fairer, holier relation than that of a mother. It is one which, rightly understood, must both promote and require the highest attainments. But a being of infinite scope must not be treated with an exclusive view to any one relation. Give the soul free course, let the organization, both of body and mind, be freely developed, and the being will be fit for any and every relation to which it may be called. The intellect, no more than the sense of hearing, is to be cultivated merely that she may be a more valuable companion to man, but because the Power who gave a power, by its mere existence, signifies that it must be brought out towards perfection.

In this regard of self-dependence, and a greater simplicity and fulness of being, we must hail as a preliminary the increase of the class contemptuously designated as old maids. . . .

Note

1. Lady Mary Wortley Montagu (1689-1762) was an English author; Mary Somerville (1780-1872) was a Scottish mathematician and scientist.

GENERAL COMMENTARY

FRITZ FLEISCHMANN (ESSAY DATE 1987)

SOURCE: Fleischmann, Fritz. "Margaret Fuller, the Eternal Feminine, and the 'Liberties of the Republic'." In *Women's Studies and Literature,* edited by Fritz Fleischmann and Deborah Lucas Schneider, pp. 39-57. Erlangen, Germany: Palm & Enke, 1987.[1]

In the following excerpt, Fleischmann discusses some of the problems with Fuller's work that have frustrated literary scholars from Fuller's time to the present.

I.

Woman in the Nineteenth Century (1845) is one of the most fascinating, but also one of the most frustrating texts in the literature of feminist thought, as generation after generation of critics has demonstrated. The reasons for this frustration are not clear. Is it the lack of feminist bravado, or moral uplift? (Fuller's friend Caroline Sturgis thought that it was "not a book to take to heart, and that is what a book upon woman should be" (Houghton MS, quoted from Chevigny 233). Is it Fuller's intellectuality, her erudition, that readers have found forbidding? Lydia Maria Child wrote in response to another Fuller book, *Summer on the Lakes,* "your house is too full; there is too much furniture for your rooms" (Houghton MS, quoted ibid.). Is it that the book misses the political point by not demanding the vote for women vociferously enough, as John Neal argued: "You might as well educate slaves—and still keep them in bondage"? (Houghton MS, quoted in Chevigny 235) Is it that, as Emerson remarked, Fuller's "pen was a non-conductor" and that, as V. L. Parrington and others in the 20th century have found, she was "in no sense an artist, scarcely a craftsman" (quoted in Robinson 84)?

While most of these charges can be refuted or explained, they represent a body of reaction to Fuller's book that points at a deeper irritation. A prominent school of Fuller criticism holds that Fuller's real vocation lay in abandoning "literature" for "history," self-centered pedantry for political action. Perhaps the best-known recent source is *The Feminization of American Culture,* in which Ann Douglas speaks of "the crippling narcissism of [Fuller's] transcendental years" (Douglas 340), albeit a narcissism that was "born of utter necessity and . . . that was somewhere intended to self-destruct, if only through its own excesses" (328). Douglas argues that Fuller's achievement lay precisely in shedding that narcissism for her "essential vision" that "was not literary, not metaphorical, but historical" (337).

A century before Douglas, in a text published posthumously in 1877, Harriet Martineau[2] had put the matter even more drastically. Here is her well-know dictum about the "Conversations":

> While Margaret Fuller and her adult pupils sat "gorgeously dressed," talking about Mars and Venus, Plato and Goethe, and fancying themselves the elect of the earth in intellect and refinement, the liberties of the republic were running out as fast as they could go, at a breach which another sort of elect persons were devoting themselves to repair: and my complaint against the "gorgeous" pedants was that they regarded their preservers as hewers of wood and drawers of water, and their work as a less vital one than the pedantic orations which were spoiling a set of well-meaning women in a pitiable way.
>
> (*Harriet Martineau's Autobiography,* ed. Maria Weston Chapman [Boston: James R. Osgood & Co., 1877] 2: 381-82. Quoted from Chevigny 229.)

Unfortunately, the alleged opposition between a "literary" and a "historical" side or phase distorts both the complexity and the consistency of Fuller's development. What, for instance, are we to make of her remark to her students at the Greene Street School in Providence, Rhode Island, recorded in her student Evelina Metcalf's journal for December 18, 1838, that history "was a study peculiarly adapted to females"—that while "it was not to be expected that women would be good Astronomers or Geologists or Metaphysicians . . . they could and are expected to be good historians"? (Shuffelton 42) The fact is that while Fuller's involvement with social and political issues became increasingly overt, even dominant, towards the end of her life, her interest in history and politics was already fed by her childhood readings in Greek and Roman history, continued during her collaboration with her father on a history of the early American Republic, and infused her major works. Just as Fuller often frustrated contemporary reformers like Martineau for lack of fervor to adopt their cause, she has often frustrated modern feminists who feared that, as Christina Zwarg has phrased it, "her feminism was far too 'textual' in origin" and who therefore tended to focus "on her 'late' revolutionary career in Italy, because there at last she began to write 'history' and this made it possible to reclaim her as our proper 'feminist' foremother" (Zwarg 7).

In this paper, I intend to look at how Fuller approaches the notions of gender and history in a way that may account for the trouble she has always given certain readers, but that also shows her to be deeply concerned about the social and political issues that dominated the public dis-

ABOUT THE AUTHOR

**PARRINGTON ATTEMPTS TO EXPLAIN
FULLER'S REPUTATION IN THE EARLY
TWENTIETH CENTURY: 1927**

The written record that Margaret Fuller left is
quite inadequate to explain her contemporary reputation. In no sense an artist, scarcely
a competent craftsman, she wrote nothing
that bears the mark of high distinction either
in thought or style. Impatient of organization
and inadequately disciplined, she threw off
her work impulsively, not pausing to shape it
to enduring form. Yet she was vastly talked
about, and common report makes her out to
have been an extraordinary woman who
creatively influenced those with whom she
came in contact. Like Alcott, her power lay in
brilliant talk. Her quick mind seems to have
been an electric current that stimulated other
minds to activity, and created a vortex of
speculation wherever she passed. Hungry for
ideas, intellectually and emotionally vibrant,
she caught her inspirations from obscure
impulses of a nature thwarted and inhibited
from normal unfolding; and in her sensitive
oscillations she was often drawn away from
polar principles to which she would later
swing back. There was quite evidently a
fundamental unrest within her, a conflict of
impulses, that issued in dissatisfaction; and
this contradiction was aggravated by intense
emotions, which both quickened her mind
and distorted it.

Parrington, Vernon Louis. Excerpt from "Margaret
Fuller, Rebel." Reprinted in *Critical Essays on
Margaret Fuller,* edited by Joel Myerson. Boston:
G. K. Hall, 1980.

course of her time. Choosing as my central text
Woman in the Nineteenth Century (1845), the
genesis of which spans the "transcendental"
period in Fuller's life,[3] I will endeavor to demonstrate how Fuller spins her mythological and
romantic notion of the "eternal feminine" into a
transcendental and political yarn which ties her
securely to the "liberties of the republic."

The collective irritation of so many readers
has to do with the *method* and the *challenge* of
Woman. Fuller irritates because she challenges her
friends and her American audience to think
certain cherished premises through to their conclusions and to *act* on these conclusions. This
double challenge has been splendidly laid out by
David M. Robinson in a 1982 *PMLA* article.
Woman, Robinson argues,

> uses the central intellectual commitment of the
> transcendental movement, the belief in the pos-
> sibility of "self-culture," or the continual spiritual
> growth of the soul, to diagnose, and prescribe a
> remedy for, the condition of women. The work
> thus stands as a translation of transcendental
> idealism into the social and political realm and as
> an exemplary bridge between romantic philoso-
> phy and social reform.
>
> (Robinson 84)

If "the development of a divine will or self,"
the end of self-culture, is denied to women, the
"social sources of the denial" have to be addressed,
and "transcendental moral idealism" finds itself
challenged to engage in a "political commitment
to feminism" to uphold its ideals. At the same
time, however, the whole nation is challenged to
live up to its "democratic heritage reinforced by
the transcendental revolution" (Robinson 85, 86,
94, 96), a heritage endangered by slavery, imperialism, and other forms of self-betrayal. In the part
of ***Woman*** added to "**The Great Lawsuit**" during
its revision, Fuller writes:

> last week brought news which threatens that a
> cause identical with the enfranchisement of Jews,
> Irish, women, ay, and of Americans in general,
> too, is in danger, for the choice of the people
> threatens to rivet the chains of slavery and the
> leprosy of sin permanently on this country,
> through the annexation of Texas!
>
> Ah! if this should take place, who will dare again
> to feel the throb of heavenly hope, as to the
> destiny of this country?
>
> (***Woman*** 198)

While Robinson does an excellent job outlining the development of Fuller's "historical consciousness, growing out of her need to put self-
culture into practice" (90), even he has problems
with Fuller's *method*. By "method" I mean her approach to writing as *discovery,* as a way to isolate
her ideas, place and test them in different contexts—historical, mythological, religious, pragmatic—, to resist closure as long as possible, to
take back and qualify as soon as introduced, to
emphasize the *process* of thinking rather than the
completed thought, the process of growth rather
than the finished product. Some critics have tried
to describe this method as arising out of an oral
tradition, or an example of the "potential angelic

artistry implicit in Fuller's idea of Woman." "Put most positively," William J. Scheick writes, "**Woman** shares with other Transcendental works an acknowledgement of its oral heritage when it celebrates spontaneity, continuous inspiration, perpetual discovery, and improvisation" (Scheick 293). Most recently, Christina Zwarg has characterized Fuller's work "as a kind of object lesson in reading," marked by a "relentless effort to disrupt what might be called the tidy binary and hence hierarchizing structures of meaning with a disorderly third term" (Zwarg 12, 13).

All of this makes it hard to come to grips with this text, to pin it down; this is why paradoxes, contradictions, vague descriptions seem to remain and irritate. For instance, when Fuller defines the most successful form of marriage as a "pilgrimage towards a common shrine," even the patient Robinson wonders "[w]hether or not Fuller herself was entirely sure of what she meant here" (Robinson 92). But that isn't the point. Fuller writes to find out "what she means," rather than to expound what she means; and her method of writing is in full consonance with her purpose and her message. The message is transcendental: it is the destiny of Man" (by which she means "both man and woman") "to ascertain and fulfil the law of his being" (**Woman** 83); the purpose of **Woman** is then to deconstruct the metaphor of gender in this transcendental framework.

In the discussion to follow, I use the term "eternal feminine" not so much because of Fuller's Goethe scholarship (which figures prominently in her book), but because she uses that notion to launch a radical inquiry into the constitution of gender and gendered discourse, to ask in what degree the "feminine" or "masculine" is indeed eternal, constant, and how much of it is contingent, historical, changing, and changeable.

II.

That Fuller's original interest in the question was autobiographical is well-documented. For much of her life, she thought of her gender as a problem. Just one famous journal entry from the **Memoirs** will have to suffice as an exemplary statement: "I love best to be a woman; but womanhood is at present too straitly-bounded to give me scope" (**Memoirs** 1: 297). More revealing for our present purpose are the semantic struggles with gender regularly undergone when her friends, or Fuller herself, attempt to describe her. Here is Frederic Henry Hedge's reminiscence of Fuller at the age of thirteen: her mind

was what in woman is generally called a masculine mind; that is, its action was determined by ideas rather than sentiments. And yet, with this masculine trait, she combined a woman's appreciation of the beautiful in sentiment and the beautiful in action. Her intellect was rather solid than graceful, yet no one was more alive to grace.

(**Memoirs** 1: 95)

Emerson writes, "She had a feeling that she ought to have been a man, and said of herself, 'A man's ambition with a woman's heart, is an evil lot.'" He quotes from a poem of hers, "**To the Moon**":

"But if I steadfast gaze upon thy face,
A human secret, like my own, I trace;
For, through the woman's smile looks the male
   eye."

(**Memoirs** 1: 229)

In response to George Sand's writing, Fuller confided to her journal in 1835, "I have always thought . . . that I would not write, like a *woman,* of love and hope and disappointment, but like a *man,* of the world of intellect and action. But now I am tempted . . ." (Higginson 188). In an undated statement on Sand, she writes, "I am astonished at her insight into the life of thought. She must know it through some man" (**Memoirs** 1: 247). In 1839, she remarks about the same writer, "She has genius, and a manly grasp of mind, but not a manly heart! Will there never be a being to combine a man's mind and woman's heart, and who yet finds life too rich to weep over?" (Houghton MS, quoted from Chevigny 58)

But half a decade later, in **Woman**, the personal has become the general, the political and the semantic question. Opening up a dialogue with Miranda, her thinly disguised self, Fuller introduces her as raised by a father "who cherished no sentimental reverence for woman, but a firm belief in the equality of the sexes" (101). Her inheritance was self-reliance. "A dignified sense of self-dependence was given as all her portion, and she found it a secure anchor. Herself securely anchored, her relations with others were established with equal security. . . . The world was free to her, and she lived freely in it" (102). Is it praise or condemnation, Miranda is asked, to call an exceptional woman "manly"? Miranda objects to the term: heroic qualities, she says, are always described as "manly," but "persistence and courage are the most womanly no less than the most manly qualities. . . . Let it not be said, wherever there is energy or creative genius, "She has a masculine mind"" (104).

Then what kind of mind *does* she have? Who makes up these categories?

The present definition of womanhood, says Fuller, comes from the male authors of "little treatises, intended to mark out with precision the limits of woman's sphere, and woman's mission, to prevent other than the rightful shepherd from climbing the wall, or the flock from using any chance to go astray" (96). If women are not sheep, what are they? Clearly, their relations to men cannot define them. In a series of passages dealing with the arguments for a traditional "woman's sphere," Fuller examines the allegation that men are "representing women fairly at present" (100). That argument is familiar: although women have no public voice, they are protected by the "virtual representation" of their menfolk, who will not treat them unfairly. As Fuller's contemporary John Neal had already pointed out, "virtual representation" of the American colonies in Parliament had been alleged by the English government to justify taxation without representation (Fleischmann 156); the absurdity of that claim was now acknowledged. Fuller, however, plays on the double meaning of "representation": Can men *represent* women fairly in their own minds, can they take a just view? No, she says, because their view is in turn limited by their relations with women: "the sentiment will vary according to the relations in which [they are] placed. The lover, the poet, the artist are likely to view her nobly. The father and the philosopher have some chance of liberality; the man of the world, the legislator for expediency, none" (100).

Men's perceptions are affected by the "relations" in which they stand. Women's whole identity, however, has been grounded in their "relations," and this notion Fuller sets out to dismantle in her book: "a being of infinite scope," she writes, "must not be treated with an exclusive view to any one relation" (146). Women must be allowed to develop fully; "they should not be considered complete, if beings of affection and habit alone" (146). In one of her excursions into Greek and Roman mythology, Fuller remarks that Diana, Minerva, and Vesta were "alike in this,—that each was self-sufficing" (111). She praises Goethe because he "aims at a pure self-subsistence" for women. All of his women characters, "though we see them in relations, we can think of as unrelated" (171). In her summary at the end of the book, Fuller divides "self-subsistence" into two subcategories: "self-reliance" and "self-impulse"; she predicts that "Woman, self-centred, would never be absorbed by any one relation; it would be only an experience to her as to man" (206). All of these terms—"self-centered," "self-reliant"—

posit an identity for women that is marked by internal growth rather than external rule, an identity that is located in a self that only relies on God and may therefore approximate what Emerson in his essay "Self-Reliance" (1841) called "the aboriginal Self, on which a universal reliance may be grounded" (Emerson 268). This identity, of course, is never complete, never closed, never static, but always growing, dynamic, in flux. In "**The Great Lawsuit. Man versus Men. Woman versus Women,**" the title of the original *Dial* essay which later became **Woman,** Fuller had located the conflict not between men and women, but between men, women, and their potential selves. In lamenting the loss of the original title due to certain "objections," she restated her intentions in her "Preface" to **Woman:**

> I meant, by that title, to intimate the fact that, while it is the destiny of Man, in the course of the Ages, to ascertain and fulfil the law of his being, so that his life shall be seen, as a whole, to be that of an angel or messenger, the action of prejudices and passions, which attend, in the day, the growth of the individual, is continually obstructing the holy work that is to make the earth a part of heaven. By Man I mean both man and women: these are the two halves of one thought. I lay no especial stress on the welfare of either. I believe that the development of the one cannot be effected without that of the other. My highest wish is that this truth should be distinctly and rationally apprehended, and the conditions of life and freedom recognized as the same for the daughters and the sons of time; twin exponents of a divine thought.
>
> . . . I solicit of women that they will lay it to heart to ascertain what is for them the liberty of law. It is for this, and not for any, the largest, extension of partial privileges that I seek.
>
> (83)

For women to "ascertain what is for them the liberty of the law" requires certain consequences:

(1) a new regard for "the class contemptuously designated as old maids" (146). Fuller throws in old bachelors for good measure and remarks of the whole category of Aunts and Uncles that they, more than others, "are thrown upon themselves," where they must "find peace and incessant life" (147) or despair. But their task remains the same as everyone else's: "as the breaking of no bond ought to destroy a man, so ought the missing of none to hinder him from growing" (148). (In this phrase, "bond" plays a role analogous to "wealth" in Thoreau's famous sentence in the "Conclusion" to *Walden*: "We

are often reminded that if there were bestowed on us the wealth of Croesus, our aims must still be the same, and our means essentially the same" [Thoreau 218].)

(2) A second consequence is that women, not men, must discover what is good for them; hence, they must lead themselves:

. . . I would have woman lay aside all thought . . . of being taught and led by men. . . . I would have her free from compromise, from complaisance, from helplessness, because I would have her good enough and strong enough to love one and all beings, from the fulness, not the poverty of being. Men, as at present instructed, will not help this work, because they are also under the slavery of habit. (164)

(3) A third consequence follows from the previous two, and it applies equally to women and men: "We must have units before we can have union," an Emersonian phrase (150) which Fuller paraphrases as follows: "Give the soul free course, let the organization, both of body and mind, be freely developed, and the being will be fit for any and every relation to which it may be called" (146).

"Units before union"—how can this self-centered unity, this wholeness, be achieved without reducing female identity to biological gender, or to the "functions"—mother, wife, cook, nurse, etc.—commonly associated with women? And how can one describe such an identity without constantly borrowing from a gendered vocabulary that has marked off the "non-feminine" as "masculine," and vice versa, in which the "masculine" functions as the norm and the "feminine" as the other? How can woman expand a restricted notion of femininity without constantly borrowing from masculine attributes, without encroaching on male territory, without using a masculine vocabulary?

III.

In a paper published last year in *Amerikastudien/American Studies*, Jane Flax told us that "[t]he single most important advance in feminist theory is that the existence of gender has been problematized. Gender can no longer be treated as a simple 'natural fact'" (Flax 198). Defining gender as "relational" (both "a social relation and a relational category of analysis" [202], Flax describes the workings of gender in these terms:

Through gender relations two types of persons are created: males and females. Male and female are posited as exclusionary categories. One can be

only one gender, never the other or both. The actual content of being a male or female and the rigidity of the categories themselves are highly variable across cultures and times. Nevertheless, gender relations as far as we have been able to understand them have been (more or less) relations of domination. That is, the totality of gender has been (more) defined and (imperfectly) controlled by one of its interrelated aspects—the male.

(202)

In a survey of contemporary feminist theory, Flax finds that when

feminist discourse defines its problematic as "woman," it too ironically privileges the man as unproblematic or exempted from determination by gender relations. From the perspective of social relations, men and women are both prisoners of gender, although in highly differentiated but interrelated ways.

(202)

Feminist theory that intends to study gender as "a practical social relation" must undertake "a close examination of the meanings of male and female and the consequences of being assigned to one or the other gender within concrete social practices" (203).

This program, then, is twofold: (1) to examine "the meanings of male and female," and (2), to find out what being assigned a "male" or "female" label entails in actual practice.

Let us look at how Fuller handles this assignment in **Women**. We have already seen her critique of social practice: women are assigned a male-defined "sphere" that limits their growth. Early in the book, Fuller defines "male" and "female" as metaphorical principles that are somehow interdependent. In the already-quoted passage from the "Preface," she refers to "man and woman" as "the two halves of one thought" (83). A few pages later, the same metaphor occurs when we are told "that the idea of Man, however imperfectly brought out, has been far more so than that of Woman, that she, the other half of the same thought, the other chamber of the heart of life, needs now to take her turn in the full pulsation, and that improvement in the daughters will best aid in the reformation of the sons of this age" (90). It is worth noting that "improvement in the daughters" is to have a redemptive function. But what improvement is being sought, and what is the idea of Woman that must be more clearly "brought out?" Civil liberties for women, while important, cannot be the primary goal: "Here, as elsewhere, the gain of creation consists always in the growth of individual minds" (91). Women's minds, then, but not only they, should be "improved": "we welcome everything that tends to strengthen the fibre and develop the nature on more sides" (153). But what women want and need is not power, money, fame; their need "is for that which is the birthright of every being capable to receive it,—the freedom . . . of the universe, to use its means" (120). The only reason women ever aspire to what men have is because men "prevent them from finding out what is fit for themselves. Were they free, were they wise fully to develop the strength and beauty of woman; they would never wish to be men, or man-like" (120).

To discover what the idea of woman/Woman is, Fuller embarks on that extended series of excursions into history, literature, mythology, and religion that has made **Woman** famous and notorious, a "house full of furniture." She rejects the idea that woman is the victim of history, although she acknowledges the victimization of women as individuals. She discusses women as artists, rulers, divinities, or characters in literature not so much to create a female track record, a history of role models, as to look at them as manifestations of the idea of Woman in its many varieties. The idea transcends and survives actual social practices ("Whatever may have been the domestic manners of the ancients, the idea of woman was nobly manifested in their mythologies and poems" [111]), and it transcends national and individual differences (119). But this idea must necessarily have many different manifestations. Nature's variety is the model: "we must admit the same varieties that she admits" (135).

It is necessary to "bring out" the idea of Woman more fully because of the transcendental creed that "the highest ideal man can form of his own powers, is that which he is destined to attain. Whatever the soul knows how to seek, it cannot fail to obtain" (87). Therefore, if women are to approximate Universal Womanhood, they must listen to the poets and prophets of all ages who have obtained glimpses of that ideal. A second reason is the posited redemptive function. Taking her cue from the prominent role of women in the abolition movement, Fuller writes that

> woman, if, by a sympathy as to outward condition she is led to aid the enfranchisement of the slave, must be no less so, by inward tendency, to favor measures which promise to bring the world more thoroughly and deeply into harmony with her nature.
>
> (160)

This brings us back to our starting point: what is the "idea," the "nature," the "genius" of woman? Fuller's conventional language belies the intensity of her struggle to break up the boundaries of restrictive gender definition, a struggle which eventually leads her to separate what I have called the Eternal Feminine from actual women.

> The growth of man is two-fold, masculine and feminine.
> As far as these two methods can be distinguished they are so as
> Energy and Harmony,
> Intellect and Love.
> Or by some such rude classification, for we have not language primitive and pure enough to express such ideas with precision.
>
> (201)

Fuller's language, in fact, sounds often enough like stereotyping:

> The especial genius of woman I believe to be electrical in movement, intuitive in function, spiritual in tendency. She excels not so easily in classification, or re-creation, as in an instinctive seizure of causes, and a simple breathing out of what she receives that has the singleness of life, rather than the selecting and energizing of art.
>
> (161)

By contrast, "the intellect, cold, is ever more masculine than feminine" and needs to be "warmed by emotion" (151-52). In a transcendental value system which privileges the "magnetic and intuitive" as the more fully human than the purely intellectual (Robinson 93), this seemingly restrictive and conventional categorization is reversed: "The electrical, the magnetic element in woman has not been fully brought out at any period. Every thing might be expected from it; she has far more of it than man" (**Woman** 152). Robinson puts Fuller's shift of emphasis in context:

> While Emerson and his followers glorified reason over understanding and poetic intuition over calculating intellect, Fuller simply extended this argument by identifying exactly those more valued qualities as predominant in woman. . . . The culture of woman, therefore, fulfills perfectly the transcendental hopes for the progressive glorification of the race.
>
> (94)

At this point, however, I part ways with Robinson, who argues that Fuller reverses her line of reasoning to stress the need for women's increased intellectual development. What I see instead is a consistent attempt to identify a program, a category (Keitel's terms) conventionally labelled as "feminine" but immediately removed to a level of abstraction that prevents its attribution to real women:[4]

. . . it is no more the order of nature that it should be incarnated pure in any form, than that the masculine energy should exist unmingled with it in any form.

Male and female represent the two sides of the great radical dualism. But, in fact, they are perpetually passing into one another. Fluid hardens to solid, solid rushes to fluid. There is no wholly masculine man, no purely feminine woman.

(161)

Between the category of the Eternal Feminine, at the highest remove, and the real women of the book's audience lies the level of mythology which allows Fuller to differentiate without being unduly restrictive. Robert D. Richardson has shown that Margaret Fuller's use of myth creates a point of leverage, a distant perspective from which she can approach the American scene with a nobler idea of woman (Richardson 178). In the Greek Pantheon, held up as a counter model to Jewish or Christian mythology, Fuller finds that, in Richardson's words, "the female principle had equal dignity with the male; it was not a secondary, male-derived, or fallen nature" (179). Sarah Sherman, who has studied the "resuscitation" of Greek goddesses in New England, finds a "highly self-conscious literary, even religious tradition" (63) that gave woman writers like Sarah Orne Jewett a vocabulary to talk about women. Sherman speculates that some of this interest may have been "kindled by Margaret Fuller's 1841 'Conversations on Mythology'" (64). Other connections with Fuller surface here, such as an 1869 *Atlantic Monthly* article on "The Greek Goddesses" by Thomas Wentworth Higginson, who also happens to be the best 19th century biographer of Fuller. Higginson writes, "'In [Greek] temples the sexes stood equal, goddess was as sublime as god, priestess the peer of priest. . . . In Protestant Christian Churches, on the other hand, nothing feminine is left but the worshippers, and they indeed are feminine, three to one'" (quoted in Sherman 65).

In **Woman,** as I have said, myth gives Fuller a non-restrictive way to differentiate: "There are two aspects of woman's nature, represented by the ancients as Muse and Minerva" (160). By the Muse she means "the unimpeded clearness of the intuitive powers which a perfectly truthful adherence to every admonition of the higher instincts would bring to a finely organized human being" (162). In "the present crisis" of American women, the preference must be given "to the Minerva side" (defined as a more intellectual form of womanhood in which woman "partakes" of the masculine [162]).

On the third, most specific ("lowest," if you like) level of discourse, Fuller talks about real women and men. Having identified an "eternal" idea of woman and having compared various manifestations in literature and mythology, Fuller creates a vision of social harmony in which gender as a rigid dividing line, as a ground for self-definition, has disappeared. "Relations" between men and women have lost their limiting function; the prison of gender is open. As for the social "functions," each is useful and good as long as it is not the sole ground for the self: "Penelope is no more meant for a baker or weaver solely, than Ulysses for a cattle-herd" (105).

If Fuller reconceptualizes gender as a relation, to use Jane Flax's terminology, it is a relation not of mutual blindness and imprisonment, but of recognition and emancipation. This enables her to disconnect gender from power or domination. For, as Flax reminds us, "In order to sustain domination, the interrelation and interdependence of one group upon another must be denied" (211).

Fuller puts these two "quotations" at the head of **Woman** (82).

"Frailty, they name is WOMAN."
"The Earth waits for her Queen."—then changes
    them to
Frailty, they name is MAN.
The Earth waits for its King.

She saw clearly that woman, kept in a position of weakness, could never become a queen, only a servant, her mate no king, only a master: "he could never reach his true proportions, while she remained in any wise shorn of hers" (202).

IV.

For Americans, the liberation of the Eternal Feminine from the prison of gender has far-reaching political implications. In the United States, that "spot, where humanity was, at last, to have a fair chance to know itself" (198), a time is approaching "[when] man and woman may regard one another as brother and sister" (203). David M. Robinson has characterized Fuller's perspective in **Woman** as "millenial," in line with some of the evangelical tendencies of her age. But, as he points out, "the thrust of [her] rhetoric is motivation for political change" (Robinson 95).

That Fuller cared very much about the "liberties of the republic" is amply evident in her book. One example is her growing sympathy with the anti-slavery struggle, which reflects not only the abolitionists' "appeal in behalf of woman," but also "a natural following out of principles" on Fuller's part (**Woman** 94). Another is her careful and poignant discussion of how political reforms are to be brought about. She contrasts Fourier's emphasis on institutional changes with Goethe's call for individual self-culture:

> Fourier says, As the institutions, so the men! All follies are excusable and natural under bad institutions.
>
> Goethe thinks, As the man, so the institutions! There is no excuse for ignorance and folly. A man can grow in any place, if he will.
>
> Ay! but Goethe, bad institutions are prison walls and impure air that make him stupid, so that he does not will.
>
> And thou, Fourier, do not expect to change mankind at once, or even in three generations. . . . If these attempts are made by unready men, they will fail.
>
> Yet we prize the theory of Fourier no less than the profound suggestion of Goethe. Both are educating the age to a clearer consciousness of what man needs, what man can be, and better life must ensue.
>
> (168)

The "better life" to "ensue," Fuller maintains, has now its best chance on the shores of the New World. Her faith in her country's destiny "to elucidate a great moral law, as Europe was to promote the mental culture of man" (92) pulls her disparate impulses together, affirming her conviction that both self-culture and political involvement are needed to promote the growth of the individual and the nation. The promise of that "better life" carries an obligation; it will only be fulfilled "if this land carry out the principles from which sprang our national life" (203).

Notes

1. An earlier version of this paper was presented at the 34th Annual Convention of the German Association for American Studies, University of Bremen, June 10, 1987.

2. On the Martineau-Fuller relationship and on Fuller's views on abolitionism, see Chevigny 210-223 and 228-230, and Kearns. Fuller's letter criticizing Society in America, which caused Martineau's lifelong displeasure, is now reprinted in Hudspeth 1: 307-310.

3. Woman has three main sources: Fuller's earlier work on Goethe and German literature, her "Conversations" about mythology and art, and her involvement with Emerson and the Dial. Tracing those sources back enables us to see that the book's genesis stretches over a period of thirteen years. In 1832, Fuller began an intensive study of German with her friend James Freeman Clarke. Mastering the language in three months, she read Goethe, Schiller, Novalis, Tieck, Koerner, Richter, and other writers of the German romantic movement. Over the next decade, she became an acknowledged authority on German literature; her work from that period includes translations of Goethe's Tasso and numerous shorter pieces, Eckermann's Conversations with Goethe (publ. 1839), the Correspondence of Fraeulein Guenderode with Bettina von Arnim (publ. 1842), three major essays on Goethe, numerous articles on other German writers, and a projected (but never finished) biography of Goethe. Her "Conversations" in Boston and Cambridge began in the winter of 1839 and continued until 1844. Her friendship with Emerson started in 1836; her editorship of the Dial lasted from July, 1840 to July, 1842. It was there that her first version of Woman in the Nineteenth Century appeared in July, 1843 under the title "The Great Lawsuit. Man versus Men. Woman versus Women." The revision of this text into Woman adds material but retains most of the original version. The Margaret Fuller of Woman in the Nineteenth Century, therefore, is still essentially the transcendental Fuller of 1843, Douglas's desperate narcissist and Martineau's "gorgeous pedant."

4. I am paraphrasing the following passage from Evelyne Keitel's 1983 essay, "Frauen, Texte, Theorie": "If one posits a specifically feminine not as an empty category or as a program but attributes it to real women, it appears objectified, attainable, and deprived of its revolutionary character. If, in the discussion about a female aesthetic, the feminine were made into an absolute, these discussions could no longer fulfill their function as the instrument of a comprehensive cultural criticism" (Keitel 840; translation mine).

Works Cited

Chevigny, Bell Gale. *The Woman and the Myth: Margaret Fuller's Life and Writings*. Old Westbury, NY: Feminist Press, 1976.

Douglas, Ann. *The Feminization of American Culture*. New York: Avon, 1978.

Emerson, Ralph Waldo. *Essays and Lectures*. New York: Library of America, 1983.

Flax, Jane. "Gender as a Problem: In and For Feminist Theory." *Amerikastudien/American Studies* 31 (Fall 1986): 193-213.

Fleischmann, Fritz. *A Right View of the Subject: Feminism in the Works of Charles Brockden Brown and John Neal*. Erlanger Studien 47. Erlangen: Palm & Enke, 1983.

Fuller, Margaret. *Memoirs of Margaret Fuller Ossoli*. [Ed. R. W. Emerson, W. H. Channing, and J. F. Clarke.] 2 vols. Boston: Phillips, Sampson and Co., 1852.

——. *Margaret Fuller: Essays on Life and Letters*. Ed. Joel Myerson. New Haven, Ct.: College and University Press, 1978. [All citations from *Woman in the Nineteenth Century* refer to this edition.]

——. *The Letters of Margaret Fuller*. Ed. Robert Hudspeth. Vol. I: 1839-41. Ithaca: Cornell University Press, 1983.

Higginson, Thomas Wentworth. *Margaret Fuller Ossoli*. American Men and Women of Letters Series. New York: Chelsea House, 1981.

Kearns, Francis E. "Margaret Fuller and the Abolition Movement." *Journal of the History of Ideas* 25 (1964): 120-127.

Keitel, Evelyne. "Frauen, Texte, Theorie. Aspekte eines problematischen Verhaeltnisses." *Das Argument* 142 (1983): 830-841.

Richardson, Robert D., Jr. "Margaret Fuller and Myth." *Prospects* 4 (1979): 168-84.

Robinson, David M. "Margaret Fuller and the Transcendental Ethos: *Woman in the Nineteenth Century*." *PMLA* 97 (1982): 83-98.

Scheick, William J. "The Angelic Ministry of Margaret Fuller's *Woman in the Nineteenth Century*." *Essays in Literature* 11.2 (Fall 1984): 293-98.

Sherman, Sarah W. "Victorians and the Matriarchal Mythology: A Source for Mrs. Todd." *Colby Library Quarterly* 22.1 (March 1986): 63-74.

Shuffelton, Frank. "Margaret Fuller at the Greene Street School: The Journal of Evelina Metcalf." *Studies in the American Renaissance* 1985: 29-46.

Thoreau, Henry David. *Walden and Civil Disobedience*. Ed. Owen Thomas. New York: Norton, 1966.

Zwarg, Christina L. "The Impact of Post-Modernist Criticism on American Literature." 20 pp. Presented at the 1987 NEMLA Spring Conference. I wish to thank Professor Zwarg for sending me a copy of her paper and for permission to quote from it.

CYNTHIA J. DAVIS (ESSAY DATE 2000)

SOURCE: Davis, Cynthia J. "What 'Speaks in Us': Margaret Fuller, Woman's Rights, and Human Nature." In *Margaret Fuller's Cultural Critique: Her Age and Legacy*, edited by Fritz Fleischmann, pp. 43-54. New York: Peter Lang, 2000.

In the following excerpt, Davis explores Fuller's relationship to the organized women's suffrage movement.

Speaking at a Woman's Rights Conference held in Worcester, Massachusetts, only weeks after Margaret Fuller Ossoli drowned off Fire Island, suffragist Paulina Wright Davis invoked this tragedy as more than mere personal loss. As Davis shared with the women there gathered, "To [Fuller] I, at least, had hoped to confide the leadership of this movement. It can never be known if she would have accepted it; the desire had been expressed to her by letter" (qtd. in Flexner 346). Yet another letter, this one dated some seventeen years later, provides additional evidence of Fuller's importance to the first wave of feminist movement: in 1867, a young suffragist named Mary Livermore confided to Susan B. Anthony that "I have always believed in the ballot for woman at some future time—always, since reading Margaret Fuller's **'Woman in the Nineteenth Century,'** which set me to thinking a quarter of a century ago" (Stanton et al. 2: 921). Livermore's debt to Fuller was so great that she would base her suffrage lecture, "What shall we do with our Daughters?" on ideas culled from **Woman in the Nineteenth Century.** And in perhaps the most indelible tribute, Elizabeth Cady Stanton, Susan B. Anthony,

ABOUT THE AUTHOR

KOLODNY DESCRIBES FULLER'S CRITICAL NEGLECT.

To read Fuller today is to be impressed anew with the sheer revolutionary daring of her attempt both to question existing gender hierarchies and to disrupt accepted sexual practices. Unfortunately, the potential impact of her arguments was long ago obscured amid the reluctance of critics seriously to analyze the even greater daring of her rhetorical strategies. As a result, when the second wave of feminist theorists in the United States began to call for a pluralistic discourse that was both collaborative and noncoercive, they showed no awareness that Fuller had earlier responded to that same challenge.

Kolodny, Annette. Excerpt from "Inventing a Feminist Discourse: Rhetoric and Resistance in Margaret Fuller's *Woman in the Nineteenth Century*." *New Literary History* 25, no. 2 (spring 1994): 355-82. Copyright 1994 by Annette Kolodny. All rights reserved.

and Matilda Joslyn Cage dedicated their monumental *History of Woman Suffrage* to nineteen women, among them Margaret Fuller, "Whose Earnest Lives and Fearless Words, in Demanding Political Rights for Women, have been, in the Preparation of these Pages, a Constant Inspiration to The Editors."

The genealogical connection between Fuller and the woman's rights movement is both extensive and underexplored. Bell Gale Chevigny maintains,

> In a sense, it is remarkable that Fuller became a feminist at all. Certainly identification with other women did not come easily to her. In the absence of a movement, criticism of other women was the natural recourse of a woman seeking to break out of the limited world her sisters seemed to accept, and this was accentuated in Fuller's case by her goals of unlimited self-development. To defend herself from discouragement, Fuller cultivated in private her sense of exceptionality and presented herself publicly as a woman of singular destiny. Her feminism never eradicated these habits.
>
> (210)

But as Chevigny also acknowledges, Fuller would gradually hearken the call to uplift not only herself but women as a group, perhaps nowhere more evidenced than in the "Conversations" she held for women beginning in November 1839 and continuing for roughly five winters. While these loosely structured discussions, mostly centered around the nature of women's inherent destiny and how best to fulfill it, bolstered Fuller's own confidence in her powers of expression and intellect, their benefit to the women attendees seems to have been the more profound (cf. Chevigny 210-15). For instance, among the some forty or so women who eventually attended these "Conversations" was the young Elizabeth Cady Stanton, who would go on to future prominence as one of the leaders of the woman suffrage movement. Stanton's one winter with Fuller was enough to compel her to deem these Cambridge Conversations in retrospect "A Vindication of Woman's Right to think" (Stanton et al. 1: 801).

Our dating of the nineteenth-century suffrage movement from the now-famous conference in Seneca Falls in 1848 often obscures the fact that Margaret Fuller (whose major works were all published by 1845) was clearly considered by many nineteenth-century women as the *sine qua non* of the woman's rights movement. Had she lived beyond 1850, might Fuller have directed women's struggle for equality in directions other than those it traveled without her guidance? And for all the early suffragists' acknowledged indebtedness to Fuller, is this a debt that was ever honorably paid? Did the suffrage movement of the nineteenth century, not to mention its resurgence as a second wave of feminist movement in the latter half of the twentieth, define its terms and strategies in ways that truly honor Fuller's legacy? These two questions provide the impetus behind the ensuing assessment of Fuller's vision of "woman in the nineteenth century" and her contributions to the feminist movement.

In our own day, divergent critical views have tended either to strengthen or unravel the ties that bind Fuller and the organized suffrage campaign inaugurated while Fuller was in Italy. On the one hand, Ann Douglas, in *The Feminization of American Culture,* divorces Fuller from the women around her and their Declaration of Sentiments, whether these be fictional or nonfictional manifestoes. On the other, Sandra M. Gustafson, in an article in *American Quarterly,* argues for a continuity between these sentiments and Fuller's own rhetoric. Fuller's concern with sincerity and lack of artifice in both spoken and written word—a concern that is central to a sentimental tradition—

impelled her, in Gustafson's words, to use "sentimental ideals to justify antisentimental forms" (50).

Gustafson focuses on Fuller's search for an appropriate *degendered rhetorical* form. It is beyond the scope of her project to consider what I believe to be Fuller's more radical aim: her attempt in **Woman in the Nineteenth Century** (1845) to displace a more traditional emphasis on *deeply gendered corporeal* forms. In other words, in **Woman** Fuller not only degendered rhetoric, she degendered bodies, and this was a radical thing to do, even within a feminist tradition. Thus when Gustafson claims that Fuller is dedicated "to an integral female self and its adequate expression" (39), I believe she wrongly and retroactively genders Fuller's famously neuter "sovereign self." But neither would I agree with Ann Douglas when she argues that "Fuller's life can be viewed as an effort to find what she called her 'sovereign self' by disavowing . . . the realm of 'feminine' fantasy for the realm of 'masculine' reality" (262). Instead I would suggest, *contra* both Douglas and Gustafson, that in the final analysis Fuller disavowed *both* femininity and masculinity for an identity that transcended or at least incorporated both. Thus when Gustafson claims that for Fuller, "women and men, writing and speech are all invested with material forms" (54), she assigns Fuller's understandings of masculinity and femininity a materiality that I believe is nowhere evidenced in **Woman.**

It is, precisely, this resistance to materiality—the *abstract nature* of Fuller's representations of masculinity and particularly femininity—that intrigues me here. Up against a culture that was increasingly medicalizing and essentializing woman's nature and even against an emergent woman's rights movement that would ultimately ground woman's rights in natural rights and in woman's special nature, Fuller's failure precisely to locate gender identity within the body renders unstable and unnatural a gendered dichotomy that would, alas, become increasingly stable and natural after her death. In fact, in Fuller's **Woman,** an abstract generic "soul" displaces concrete gendered essences as that which is contained within bodies, whether male or female. The net effect of this is that in **Woman,** Fuller unites far more than she divides men and women. While Fuller's emphasis on soul may be directly attributed to Transcendentalism rather than to some radical feminism, the fact that it is after all a woman arguing for the disembodied, transparent I(ball?)

pushes Transcendentalism's potential radicalism into territories where no beard nor bard had gone before.

Indeed, it is possible that, since woman more closely approximates what Fuller deems the "singleness of life" (115), woman more closely approximates the "I." Herein may lie the explanation for why Fuller, herself a woman, resists splitting that I into its gendered pronouns—into he/she, or even into those other objectifying dichotomies me/you, or us/them. Illustrating this is the essay upon which **Woman** is based, "**The Great Lawsuit**" (1843), wherein the opposing sides are not Man v. Woman, but Man v. Men, Woman v. Women—with Fuller arguing on behalf of the former "abstraction" (that is, on behalf of "Man" and "Woman"). She thus disavows not only the specific and flawed bodies implicit in terms like "men" and "women," but also the ideology that assigns such divisions weight and substance. Fuller's understanding of the category "Man" as an abstraction is made clearer in her preface to **Woman,** where she writes, "By Man I mean both man and woman, the two halves of one thought" (xiii). Some fifty years after Fuller wrote **Woman,** Kate Chopin's Edna Pontellier—an avid reader of Emerson's "Self-Reliance" as was Fuller—would graphically demonstrate the limits of Transcendentalism when its proponent found herself constrained by a desired and desiring female body. Writing at midcentury, Fuller did not see that body as necessarily constraining in part because she refused to see it as necessarily female. Ideally, this unwillingness to specify a distinctly "female" body should have paved the way for other women in the nineteenth century to posit transcendence as a collective goal. That is, if Fuller's arguments had meant as much to them as the suffragists whom I quoted at the beginning of this paper suggest, these women would have sought a transcendence that comes *not* from seeking, à la the Transcendentalists, a unity of the soul with Nature, but rather, à la Fuller, a liberating of the soul from *nature*—in the sense of biology, corporeality, the too, too sullied female flesh.

Fuller, in fact, explicitly distinguishes a woman's gender from her nature at a time when the two were fast becoming synonymous: hence in **Woman** she contends that "what woman needs is not as a *woman* to act or rule, but as a *nature* to grow, as an intellect to discern, as a soul to live freely and unimpeded . . ." (38, emphasis added). Here, the freedom and lack of impediments she believes to be guaranteed any soul are conferred upon woman precisely by identifying her as soul

versus the traditional identification of woman with (or as) body. Fuller's treatise provides women with a loophole of retreat from the increasingly essentialized and pathologized woman's nature (even, rightly or wrongly, from their sexual nature—hence Fuller's emphasis on celibacy *contra* Edna Pontellier). It thus provides them with a means of escape from their confinement in woman's sphere, in a "woman's place" where and when that confinement is based on the penalty of biology.

This is not to say that Fuller didn't often subscribe to rather conservative notions of masculine and feminine traits and capabilities: many of her arguments for ending women's oppression are grounded in traditional views of women as the gentler, purer, more spiritual sex. Not infrequently, she laments her own "femality"—especially to the extent it proved a hindrance to her writing—and endows men with more daring, genius, and resolve. For instance, in the reading notes she took about George Sand, Fuller exclaimed:

> I am astonished at her insight into the life of thought. She must know it through some man. Women, under any circumstances, can scarce do more than dip the foot in this broad and deep river; they have not strength to contend with the current . . . when it comes to interrogating God, the universe, the soul, and, above all, trying to live above their own hearts, they dart down to their own nests like so many larks.
> (**M Memoirs of Margaret Fuller Ossoli**1: 295)

When Fuller did confront the limitations of the female body, it was typically to acknowledge their status as encumbrance, as delineating the very difference that she strove to eradicate or at least transcend. In her less hopeful moments, she seems inclined to reinscribe the male-mind/female-body split: "the very outline [sic, CJD] of the feminine form were yielding," she laments, "and we could not associate them with a prominent self-conscious state of the faculties" (qtd. in Russell 43). There were even times when she grew despondent about the consequences of extant gender differences. As she remarked bitterly in **Life Without and Life Within,** "Woman is the flower, man the bee. She sighs out melodious fragrance, and invites the winged laborer. He drains her cup, and carries off the honey. She dies on the stalk; he returns to the hive, well fed, and praised as an active member of the community" (Chevigny 279).

But intriguingly, this debased and debasing femininity—as her remarks about Sand illustrate—is not for Fuller associated with the "body" per se so much as it is specifically associated with the "heart." While she still identifies masculinity with the "mind," this replacement of "body" with "heart" in the traditional male/female, mind/body dichotomies is significant. For the fact that both organs—mind and heart—can be contained within one body (*any* body) parallels Fuller's belief—a not uncommon one in the circles in which she traveled—that there were masculine and feminine currents in each woman or man. As Fuller herself put it in a journal entry: "The Woman in me kneels and weeps in tender rapture; the Man in me rushes forth, but only to be baffled. . . . Yet the time will come, when, from the union of this tragic king and queen, shall be born a radiant sovereign self" (***M*** 2: 136). Or, perhaps more pertinently, as she contends in ***Woman***: "Male and female represent the two sides of the great radical dualism. But in fact, they are perpetually, passing into one another. . . . There is no wholly masculine man, no purely feminine woman" (115-16); "It is no more the order of nature that [femininity] should be incarnated pure in any form, than that the masculine energy should exist unmingled with it in any form" (115).

Divorcing gendered traits from gendered forms, what Fuller works toward here is not so much androgyny—the blending of masculine and feminine into a sort of third amorphous gender—as simultaneity, not one melded sex but both at once, and more. That this is so is evidenced by the emblem that she chooses to represent her utopian view of a post-dichotomous world: in lieu of gendered binaries, Fuller offers up a "zodiac of the busts of gods and goddesses, arranged in pairs . . . [where] male and female heads are distinct in expression, but equal in beauty, strength, and calmness. . . . Could the thought thus expressed be lived out, there would be nothing more to be desired. There would be unison in variety, congeniality in difference" (55). Fuller here turns the boundary line that ideologically divides the genders on its side, transforming it into a continuum on which every body ranges between the masculine and feminine poles. But even this is not entirely correct. For throughout most of ***Woman***, Fuller displaces the conventional gendered poles of male and female, and in their place positions (generic) Man at one end and the Divinity that is the perfect soul in all of us at the other. She thus unites all Men (that is, all people) in their striving toward one common desire and destiny—to shed the body and become soul: "all soul is the same" (115), she claims; "there is but one law for souls" (37).

While according to Fuller all of us can and will eventually become souls, because we are still (abstract) Men and not yet souls, we are still male and female. However, as I have suggested, Fuller believes that we can be both these things at once. Or, at the very least, *she* believes she can be both male and female at once. She writes: "I have been always wishing to call myself into the arms of some other nature. . . . This was womanish, I own. I am not yet a man" (qtd. in Russell 29-30). "Not yet a man" implies that she is and can move toward manliness despite her self-proclaimed womanishness—and thus that this possibility may indeed be open to every body, regardless of sex.

Fuller's emphasis on synchronicity, variety, and continuation—on "not yet"—highlights a concept central to Fuller's notion of gender identity: temporality. As Fuller puts it herself in a journal entry: "I love best to be a woman; but womanhood is at present too straitly-bounded to give me scope. At hours, I live truly as a woman; at others, I should stifle" (***M*** 1: 297). Being a woman—what many would presume to be an ontological fact—may be a state she "loves best," but for Fuller in the present moment it is too confining. With her qualifying clause Fuller suggests that she (and perhaps others) can somehow choose to "be" *other* than a woman—to transcend ontology—at certain moments. This is borne out by her claim in her next sentence that "at hours" she lives as a woman—which would suggest, however implausibly, that at other hours she does not.

In thus emphasizing the constitutive temporality of gender identity—living "as a woman" suggests subversively that womanhood is a metaphorical rather than an ontological state—Fuller anticipates theories of gender popularized in our own day by feminist theorists, most notably by Denise Riley. Riley's *"Am I That Name?": Feminism and the Category of "Women" in History*, written some 140 years after ***Woman***, echoes Fuller in contending that no human subject is ever interpellated by a single dominant ideology (such as gender) all the time. There are moments, Riley stipulates in accordance with Fuller, when females are not "women," when "women" do not think of themselves nor are hailed as such. As Riley puts it: "anyone's body is—the classifications of anatomy apart—only periodically either lived or treated as sexed, therefore the gendered division of human life into bodily life cannot be adequate or absolute. Only at times will the body impose itself or be arranged as that of a woman or a man" (103). While this may seem a potentially liberating view of gender identity, especially when juxtaposed with those who would fix gender within the body as a timeless essence, it is not without its dangers. For is it not possible that in so stressing temporality both Fuller and Riley underemphasize, even ignore the extent to which "anatomical difference" still figures (it makes a difference) in constructing and even predetermining the subject and social positioning of many women? In other words, while we may want to celebrate this temporality, we must not lose sight of the unfortunately still myriad ways in which particular social configurations and power structures work to narrow the range of our choices of identities at any given moment. The celebration of gender as a temporal construct, as an identity that we do not identify with at all moments, may be premature; it fails to acknowledge that the choice of how we live our lives and bodies is not, in the final analysis, solely up to us, but also depends upon the transformation of the dominant social discourses that still, as often as not, narrate us.

That this is so is, ironically, documented in the narrative distortions and revisions Margaret Fuller herself was subjected to over time. Take, for example, Hawthorne's satiric profile of Fuller as Zenobia in the *Blithedale Romance* (this from the author who had hoped that Fuller would prove "a very woman after all," no better than "the weakest of her sisters" [qtd. in Douglas 266-67]). Other famous examples include Emerson's, James Freeman Clarke's and W. H. Channing's blacking out and excising of Fuller's papers for their **Memoirs of Margaret Fuller Ossoli,** Fuller's brother Arthur's attempts to paint a more "womanly" portrait of his sister in the 1855 edition of **Woman**—paying in his preface "tribute to her domestic virtues and fidelity to all home duties" (v)—, and Horace Greeley's assessment that "great and noble as [Fuller] was, a good husband and two or three bouncing babies would have emancipated her from a great deal of cant and nonsense" (qtd. in Douglas 280).

Finally, there are Henry James's anxious and often condescending musings about the "Margaret-ghost" who haunts him and other writers in his biography of *William Whetmore Story and His Friends* (1903; cf. Rowe). Intriguingly, in James's formulation, it is not Fuller's actual and imposing presence—"Margaret's mountainous me," as Emerson immortalized her—that looms over these male writers, but a ghost-like apparition. If James is correct, then the most disturbing or haunting thing about Fuller (for these men) is her representing, after death, the disembodied

femininity she argued for in life. Although Poe never meant it as such, perhaps we should then read his infamous quip that there are three types of people—"men, women and Margaret Fuller" (Chevigny 19)—as a (backhanded) compliment, pointing not to her "freakishness" (as I am sure Poe intended), but to Fuller's remarkable ability to transcend convincingly—to posit an alternative to—gendered categories.

In **Woman,** Fuller famously concludes that "It is not woman, but the law of right, the law of growth, that speaks in us, and demands the perfection of each being in its kind" (177). But Fuller's distorted reputation—filtered as it has been through these male writers' manipulations—demonstrates that such questions as "what speaks in us" and "when" may be less important, ultimately, than such questions as "who's listening?" and "how is that which is spoken being heard?"

All of which returns us, in conclusion, to the vexed problem of Fuller's reception, her lasting legacy. At the beginning of this essay, I suggested that early woman's rights figures did indeed listen to Fuller speaking, that they did read and respond to her words. But questions remain: did these women also distort them, filtering Fuller's aspirations through pre-existing ideologies, and taming them of their political punch? In particular, did they defuse Fuller's potentially radical notion that gender identity is not and should not be grounded in two distinct and different anatomies?

Certainly not intentionally, and perhaps not beyond recognition. But even as early as the Declaration of Sentiments (written primarily by Fuller protégée Elizabeth Cady Stanton just three years after **Woman** was published), we see the first slide down the slippery slope toward gender essentialism that the early woman's rights movement ultimately assumed and that Fuller so assiduously avoided. We might start with the rhetorical discontinuities. While (as I have pointed out) in **Woman** Fuller works to minimize the differences between men and women, the rhetoric of the Declaration of Sentiments ranges men against women: nearly every sentence begins as follows: "He has never permitted her . . . ," "he has taken from her . . . ," "he has compelled her . . . ," "he has denied her" (*Proceedings* 6-7). While Fuller strove throughout her career to find a common "I," the suffragists were clearly already willing to see the world as divided into shes and hes, pronouns that they grounded in essential differences. Moreover, it is clearly a "she" declaring her sentiments throughout the 1848 manifesto, while Fuller's 1845 treatise is famously ambiguous about who is speaking. In *Woman,* Fuller reflects not only in the content but the style and grammar of her prose her willingness to play with gendered categories that remained fixed and oppositional in the Declaration of Sentiments.

Elsewhere, it is true, the Declaration's rhetoric owes a great debt to Fuller, a debt it acknowledges with such Fulleresque proclamations as ". . . it is time [woman] should move in the enlarged sphere which her great Creator has assigned her" (*Proceedings* 4). But at other moments, the Declaration's attempts to speak for women translates as an essentialized woman "speaking in us" that Fuller largely avoids. In part, this translation is the result of the Declaration's grounding of woman's rights in "natural rights"—a concept borrowed from the liberal humanist and rationalist tradition as handed down from Locke and Jefferson. While the framers of the Declaration of Sentiments emphasize "natural rights" as a means of affording women the rights granted to (then only male) citizens, by grounding those rights in nature they risk encouraging the view of women as having fixed and timeless natures, a view of women Fuller strove throughout her career to obstruct and make abstract.

"Natural rights" are based on that ultimate abstraction "human nature." This is an abstraction, however, that quickly becomes concrete, as the political experiment that is the United States amply demonstrates. Just as the "created-equal" "Man" of the Declaration of Independence quickly materialized as the white propertied man of the Constitution, so too did the "woman" endowed by nature with inalienable rights of the Declaration of Sentiments quickly materialize as the white bourgeois woman of "bleeding Kansas." That Sojourner Truth had later to ask "Ain't I a Woman?" (Stanton et al. 1: 115-17) only confirms the extent to which the framers of the Declaration of Sentiments had a specific body in mind when invoking the apparently inclusive category "Woman" throughout their Declaration.

Paulina Wright Davis was right, then, to rue Fuller's untimely demise, for even as early as *Woman* Fuller was quick to point out what the suffragists acknowledged too little, too late. As Fuller contends, "Those who think the physical circumstances of Woman would make a part in the affairs of national government unsuitable, are by no means those who think it impossible for negresses to endure field-work, even during pregnancy, or for the sempstresses to go through their killing labors" (35). This sort of recognition would

WOMAN

IN THE

NINETEENTH CENTURY.

BY S. MARGARET FULLER.

" Frei durch Vernunft, stark durch Gesetze,
Durch Sanftmuth gross, und reich durch Schätze,
Die lange Zeit dein Busen dir verschwieg."

"I meant the day-star should not brighter rise,
Nor lead like influence from its lucent seat;
I meant she should be courteous, facile, sweet,
Free from that solemn vice of greatness, pride;
I meant each softest virtue there should meet,
Fit in that softer bosom to reside;
Only a (heavenward and instructed) soul
I purposed her, that should, with even powers,
The rock, the spindle, and the shears control
Of destiny, and spin her own free hours."

NEW-YORK:
GREELEY & McELRATH, 160 NASSAU-STREET.
W. Osborn, Printer, 88 William-street.
1845.

Title page of *Woman in the Nineteenth Century.*

have saved the suffrage movement, and women in the nineteenth century in general, a great deal of divisiveness.

History tends to repeat itself when it is not thoroughly critiqued and revised. It is one of the central ironies for those of us indebted to feminist principles that some one hundred years have made us virtually no wiser than our early foremothers. The second wave, after all, has itself been impeded by the snares of essentialism and racism that also slowed the impetus of the earlier wave and which Fuller explicitly warned against. Both of these "isms" have threatened to rupture the modern feminist movement, leading to acrimonious debate about, as well as the formation of splinter groups organized around, differences *between* women. The feminist movement, like the sex, is decidedly not "one," and this fact yields both positive and negative consequences. On the one hand, unlike our antecedents, modern feminists have learned and learned relatively quickly that these differences are real, important, and informative of not just gender identity but gendered struggle. Experience has taught us that gender, race, class, sexuality, religious affiliation and other modes of classification are not pop-beads on a necklace that can be separated out from one another so that we may speak as a woman in one context, a Caucasian in another, a member of the middle class in a third, and so on. Rarely does a savvy critic use the singular "woman" as an all-inclusive, unqualified noun anymore, and this avoidance should not be taken as reflecting merely superficial motivations or good training. What it indicates, I hope, is a paradigmatic shift in feminist consciousness concerning the multiple and contingent ways in which gender has and might come to matter (quite literally) in the world. On the other hand, who among us is not dismayed that the American media have gotten away with labeling this a "post-feminist age," and who among us is not concerned that our own internal grievances have not in some small or large way facilitated this labeling process?

I should make clear in closing that my lament is not some nostalgic longing for what might have been had Fuller lived. I am not suggesting that Fuller's disembodied, degendered approach to subjectivity (in her published if not her private musings) is ultimately preferable. Fuller's abstractions are at once too general and too individualized, with all the well-documented problems that attend either flaw. Still, Fuller did offer an alternative, a road not taken. Her application of liberal humanistic philosophy to women's rights issues resists or sidesteps the traps of restrictive essentialism and disingenuous universalism that later and even today risk bogging down the feminist movement.

I also recognize that Fuller alone could not have altered this course. Ultimately, what stretched the suffrage struggle out over seven-plus long and hard-fought decades in this country, what continues to make the struggles for gender equity and justice so vital today, was not so much Fuller's or any one inspirational leader's individual death. Instead, responsibility lies with a widespread social, political, and economic opposition to women's advancement. What Emerson concluded about Fuller when he deemed her an "athletic soul, which *craved an atmosphere larger than it found*" (Chevigny 1, emphasis added) applies as well to other women in both the nineteenth and twentieth centuries who likewise discovered their atmosphere to be both stultifying and claustrophobic. After all, while Emerson grants Fuller the status of soul, what he could not grant was the transcendence Fuller and other women craved once they found themselves inhibited by the very real pressures of being, not just for a moment, not just at times, but in the last instance, in others' eyes, a woman.[1]

Note

1. Portions of this text have appeared in an essay entitled "Margaret Fuller, Body and Soul" in the March 1999 issue of *American Literature*.

Abbreviations

CC: Lydia Maria Child. *The Collected Correspondence of Lydia Maria Child, 1817-1880.* Ed. Patricia G. Holland, Milton Meltzer, and Francine Krasno. Millwood, NY: Kraus Microform, 1980.

EMF: Margaret Fuller. *The Essential Margaret Fuller.* Ed. Jeffrey Steele. New Brunswick, NJ: Rutgers UP, 1992.

FMW: Fuller Manuscripts and Works, Houghton Library, Harvard University.

FP: Margaret Fuller Papers, Massachusetts Historical Society.

HCW: *The History of the Condition of Women, in Various Ages and Nations.* Vols. 4 and 5 of *Ladies' Family Library.* Boston: John Allen, 1835.

LMF: Margaret Fuller. *The Letters of Margaret Fuller.* Ed. Robert N. Hudspeth. 6 vols. Ithaca, NY: Cornell UP, 1983-94.

LNY: Lydia Maria Child. *Letters from New York.* 1843. Freeport, NY: Books for Libraries P, 1970.

"LNY": "Letters from New-York" (column).

PMF: Margaret Fuller. *The Portable Margaret Fuller.* Ed. Mary Kelley. New York: Viking Penguin, 1994.

SL: Lydia Maria Child. *Lydia Maria Child: Selected Letters, 1817-1880.* Ed. Milton Meltzer, Patricia G. Holland, and Francine Krasno. Amherst: U of Massachusetts P, 1982.

Works Cited

Chevigny, Bell Gale. *The Woman and the Myth: Margaret Fuller's Life and Writings.* New York: Feminist P, 1976.

Chopin, Kate. *The Awakening.* 1899. New York: Bantam, 1981.

Douglas, Ann. *The Feminization of American Culture.* New York: Knopf, 1978.

Emerson, Ralph Waldo. "Self Reliance." *Selections from Ralph Waldo Emerson.* Ed. Stephen E. Whicher. Boston: Houghton Mifflin, 1960.

Flexner, Eleanor. *Century of Struggle: The Women's Rights Movement in the United States.* Rev. ed. Cambridge, MA: Harvard UP, 1975.

Fuller, S. Margaret. *Woman in the Nineteenth Century.* New York: Greeley & McElrath, 1845.

——. *Woman in the Nineteenth Century and Kindred Papers Relating to the Sphere, Condition, and Duties of Woman.* Ed. Arthur B. Fuller. 1874. New York: Greenwood, 1968.

Gustafson, Sandra. "Choosing a Medium: Margaret Fuller and the Forms of Sentiment." *American Quarterly* 47 (1995): 34-65.

Hawthorne, Nathaniel. *The Blithedale Romance.* 1852. Ed. Seymour Gross and Rosalie Murphy. New York: Norton, 1978.

Myerson, Joel. *Margaret Fuller: An Annotated Secondary Bibliography.* New York: Burt Franklin, 1977.

———. *Margaret Fuller: A Descriptive Bibliography.* Pittsburgh: U of Pittsburgh P, 1978.

Proceedings of the Woman's Rights Convention, Held at Seneca Falls, N.Y. July 19th & 20th, 1848. John Dick: Rochester, 1848.

Riley, Denise. *"Am I That Name?": Feminism and the Category of "Women" in History.* Minneapolis: U of Minnesota P, 1988.

Rowe, John Carlos. "Swept Away: Henry James, Margaret Fuller, and 'The Last of the Valerii.'" *Readers in History: Nineteenth-Century American Literature and the Contexts of Response.* Ed. James L. Machor. Baltimore: Johns Hopkins UP, 1993. 32-53.

Russell, Roberta Joy. "Margaret Fuller: The Growth of a Woman Writer." Ph.D. diss. U of Connecticut, 1983. Ann Arbor: UMI, 1985. 8317725.

Stanton, Elizabeth Cady, Susan B. Anthony, and Matilda Joslyn Gage. *History of Woman Suffrage.* 2 vols. 1881-1882. Salem, NH: Ayer, 1985.

TITLE COMMENTARY

Summer on the Lakes

MICHAELA BRUCKNER COOPER (ESSAY DATE 2000)

SOURCE: Cooper, Michaela Bruckner. "Textual Wandering and Anxiety in Margaret Fuller's *Summer on the Lakes.*" In *Margaret Fuller's Cultural Critique: Her Age and Legacy,* edited by Fritz Fleischmann, pp. 171-87. New York: Peter Lang, 2000.

In the following excerpt, Cooper contends that Fuller's writing in Summer on the Lakes *demonstrates anxiety and a lack of confidence in herself as a writer.*

The history of female reading and writing is a continuous effort to overcome the anxiety attendant upon the limitations of gender roles and narrative forms; but female readers and writers are working to alter history, first by articulating the sources of ambivalence.

(Singley 8)

In "Female Language, Body, and Self," a chapter in the anthology *Anxious Power: Reading, Writing, and Ambivalence in Narrative by Women,* Carol Singley examines women's ambiguous relationship with language, one that is often fraught with anxiety. If language gives expression to a distinct self, Singley argues, women have developed an ambivalent relationship with it because of their predominantly complementary or contingent positions as wives, mothers, or daughters (7). When I first read Margaret Fuller's *Summer on the Lakes,* I was struck not only by the self-consciousness in her writing, but especially by the ways in which Fuller subverts the stance of the controlling and self-confident reader and writer by giving voice repeatedly to the kind of anxiety Singley alludes to.

In the summer of 1843, Margaret Fuller and her friend Sarah Clarke took off together on a tour to the Midwest. During the trip, Fuller kept an extensive journal, which she later began to organize into what was to become her "first original book (her previous books having been translations from the works of German authors)" (Kolodny 113). In the record of her trip to Niagara Falls, the Great Lakes, and finally the Wisconsin Territory, Fuller skillfully interweaves her observations and impressions of the landscape and its inhabitants with associations that such impressions evoke.

Within the context of her journey and her later work on the journal she kept during the trip, Fuller works out ideas about America's past and future, the plight of Native Americans, and the role of women settlers. She creates a text that integrates various narratives, poetry, and dialogues into the flow of her observations about the West. The resulting text, *Summer on the Lakes,* however, is much more than an accumulation of recollections and interpretations of what Fuller saw and heard during her trip. In it, she practices a kind of cultural critique that is driven by a need to examine culture contextually and investigate self-consciously the locations from which the cultural critic speaks, a strategy that is aided by Fuller's ambivalent stance toward her own role as a woman writer. Such an approach implicitly invites the reader, as cultural critic, to follow Fuller's example.

The revision process of *Summer on the Lakes* was time-consuming since Fuller was occupied with teaching and her Conversations, and she had also decided to do some more research about the Great Lakes region before finishing her book (Blanchard 196). Locating adequate sources was a tricky enterprise. Fuller convinced the authorities to allow her access to the Harvard University library, which served also "as a kind of private club to which a gentleman could retreat after dinner" (Blanchard 197). Paula Blanchard reveals to some degree the ambiguous status (both outsider and socially connected) that Fuller had to cope with both as a woman and as a writer within the predominantly male Transcendentalist establishment. It was, however, this status that provided her with unique insights into the lives and conditions of the settler women and Native Americans she encounters during her trip.

Throughout her life, Fuller was aware that the unique circumstances of her education had endowed her with qualities that set her apart from most of the women of her time. In a passage included in *Memoirs of Margaret Fuller Ossoli*, Fuller writes,

> from a very early age I have felt that I was not born to the common womanly lot. I knew I should never find a being who could keep the key to my character; that there would be none on whom I could always lean, from whom I could always learn; that I should be a pilgrim and sojourner on earth, and that the birds and foxes would be surer of a place to lay the head than I.
>
> (*M* 98-99)

Fuller relates her outsider status to that of the traveler who is nowhere at home, the woman who has escaped the confinements of her assigned role as wife and mother and thus ends up, metaphorically and literally, without a home. Because she does not fit into a preexisting model of womanhood, it will be hard, if not impossible, for her female friends and her fellow Transcendentalists, to understand or "keep the key to [her] character."

While Fuller stresses her difference from others, she does not always do so confidently. Frequently, anxiety about her status as a woman and writer surfaces. A possible source is the conflicted nature of her early education brought about by the radical shift it underwent when Fuller was ten years old: "The first phase of her education was over, and from now on the emphasis would increasingly shift from the intellectual sphere to the social . . . As she approached her teens, the intellectual momentum of her early years was not only slowed but deliberately deflected" (Blanchard 35). While up to that point Timothy Fuller had instructed his daughter in English and Latin, subjects usually only taught to boys, he decided to enroll her in Dr. Park's school for girls where "she would . . . be told to make herself less conspicuous, not to compete, not to speak her mind boldly, and to pay more attention to the practical details of everyday life" (35).

The lessons learned at Dr. Park's school would shape Fuller's life and work. Blanchard points out that because of Fuller's extensive domestic responsibilities, particularly after her father's death, "her own work would have to give way to the higher priority accorded to household duties" (77). Although Fuller was aware of the limitations her training for traditional womanhood and incessant domestic duties imposed on her intellectual work, she also, Margaret Vanderhaar Allen argues, "partially accepted the conventions of women's and men's distinct roles. To the extent that she did so, her friends and family praised her as a 'true' woman" (137). Fuller wasn't immune to the dictates of female good looks and proper attire. In *Margaret Fuller: A Psychological Biography,* Katherine Susan Anthony speculates that Fuller envied and sought to imitate the beautiful Anna Barker, who later married Samuel Gray Ward, the man whom many thought Fuller was in love with, by "struggl[ing] with curl-papers night after night when French and metaphysics had had their due" (35).

Fuller's awareness about her double role as writer and woman often surfaces in her writing as self-questioning. Various critics, such as Jeffrey Steele,[1] Christina Zwarg,[2] Nicole Tonkovich,[3] Stephen Adams,[4] and Julie Ellison[5] have paid attention to Fuller's self-conscious stance as an author, and in some of these critical discussions the emergence of a resistant subjectivity in Fuller's text is treated as strong and confident. I would argue, however, that the particular strength of Fuller's text lies in its author's willingness to draw anxious speculations about her own tenuous position into the realm of legitimate representation. In *Summer on the Lakes,* this position is embodied in the person of the writer as traveler. Thus traveling becomes a trope for both physical and textual wandering. While Fuller moves her body across the Midwest, seeing new places, encountering settler families and Native Americans, she also embarks on a textual journey among various and often mutually contesting or overlapping discourses that shape her response to the landscape and the people she encounters on her trip. Through her shifting position, she can speak both from within the patriarchal culture and from outside it. Teresa De Lauretis calls such a fluid position the "space-off" (26), a helpful term for an examination of *Summer on the Lakes.* The space-off, in classical cinema, is "the space not visible in the frame, but inferable from what the frame makes visible," and in avant-garde cinema, the space-off exists "alongside the represented space" (26). By occupying the space-off, women can look at the world from a point that is always elsewhere, that simultaneously affirms the existence of the dominant culture, and comments upon it and resists it from an outside position. In *Summer on* the Lakes, Fuller can thus, for example, employ and subvert familiar styles of writing, as she does in the case of landscape writing about the sublime, which inscribes experience within a rigid vocabulary. Furthermore, by focusing on the space-off as the field of legitimate representation in her description of the western landscape, and white as well as Native American women, Fuller expands the margins of her discourse, while at the same time foregrounding the limitations of traditional male narratives of westward expansion and progress.

De Lauretis' theory of the space-off is particularly helpful in an examination of Fuller's narrator and observer because of its consideration of the shifting positionality of the spectator. This theory includes "the spectator (the point where the image is received, reconstructed and reproduced in/as subjectivity)" (26). Thus, the image does not exist autonomously but is always dependent on its connection to a spectator who brings an interpretive frame of reference to it that will shape her reading. By showing that the spectator, as interpreter, participates in the representation, De Lauretis points to the kind of self-conscious examination of the observer's position that Fuller engages in.

In the beginning of Summer, Fuller describes her life as a text to be read: "Since you are to share with me such foot-notes as may be made on the pages of my life during this summer's wandering, I should not be quite silent as to this magnificent prologue to the, as yet, unknown, drama" (71). Fuller's subsequent efforts at opening up the borders of the patriarchal text are already contained and foreshadowed here. Her choice of metaphor is interesting insofar as footnotes are the marginal sites for explanations seen as distracting from the main text. By making those footnotes central to her text, Fuller breaks down the barriers between the "main text" and that which is seen as subordinate or marginal.

Fuller voices some unease about the potential reception of Summer on the Lakes: "And now you have the little all I have to write. Can it interest you? To one who has enjoyed the full life of any scene, of any hour, what thoughts can be recorded about it, seem like the commas and semicolons in the paragraphs, mere stops. Yet I suppose it is not so to the absent" (75). She questions the significance of her contribution—"Can it interest you?"—and then proceeds to divide her audience into two categories. She seems to refer here to the male privilege of mobility and access to wider realms of experience, which she also represents,

the person "who has enjoyed the full life of any scene." For such a person, Fuller's text will be inadequate as representation. Instead, by directing her text to those who did not have the freedom or privilege to share her travels, Fuller already sets her readers up for one of the major issues of her text, her narrative of the lives and hardships of women, who occupy the place of the absent other because they were not traditionally included in representations of the American West.

In the tale of the Seeress of Prevorst, an account Fuller inserted in her chapter on Wisconsin, she works out the kind of displacement that is a precondition to the self-conscious cultural critique she envisions. Drawing from the account of the German physician Justinus Kerner, *Die Seherin von Prevorst* (1829), she describes events in the life of Friederike Hauffe, a somnambulist and clairvoyant "immersed in the inward state" and "free from bodily bonds, and the hindrances of space and time" (Fuller 157). Although Fuller emphasizes the contrast that this story provides between the "vision of an exalted and sensitive existence, which seemed to invade the next sphere" and "the spontaneous, instinctive life" among the rough settlers of the Midwest she observes during her trip, there are also significant connections between the narrative of the seeress and her accounts of life on the frontier (144-45). These are already signified in the seeress's volatile position at the border between the material and the spiritual world and in turn reflect Fuller's own anxiety about her volatile position as the author of a text that constantly questions itself. The mystic Hauffe, who "saw herself often out of the body; saw herself double," thus signifies women's displacement and the kind of outlook that is made possible by such a displacement (158). For the seeress, it is a displacement from the physical world to a realm beyond. For Fuller, it seems to designate a position that is on the boundary looking either way and that exemplifies the anxiety about being taken over by either one; but, more importantly, anxiety in the text seems to arise from her efforts at writing the space-off into her discourse. Thus, the narration of the tale and the enunciation of a relationship between different histories present a strategy of textual wandering that shapes Fuller's text.

Fuller justifies the inclusion of the tale of Friederike Hauffe by placing it into the context of her watching the many new immigrants getting off the boat in Wisconsin. "[S]oon [the immigrants'] tales . . . will be so mingled with those of the Indian, that the very oak trees will not know them apart" (170). The history that these immigrants bring with them will become part of their newly gained cultural knowledge and of the history of their new home. Their reading of new experiences and environments, and her reading of them in turn, will be partially shaped by their past. At the same time, an unsettling sense of loss is inherent in the concept of acculturation, as Fuller envisions it, that reflects her ambivalent treatment of the plight of Native Americans in **Summer on the Lakes.** However, while here she seems to suggest that acculturation is an almost organic process that occurs naturally and harmoniously, at other places in her text she also undercuts this point by lamenting and resisting the extinction of Native Americans and the loss of their rich cultural heritage.

Observing the immigrants who get off the boat, Fuller laments the limitations imposed on her own search for new stories and new experiences: "Could I but have flown at night through such mental experiences, instead of being shut up in my little bedroom at the Milwaukee boarding house, this chapter would have been worth reading" (170). It is notable that Fuller connects her limited access to those experiences and tales that she thinks would interest her reader to the need for economic independence and thus ties her situation indirectly to gender. "Had I been rich in money, I might have built a house, or set up in business," Fuller speculates during her stay in Milwaukee (170). Instead, she is "obliged to walk the streets and pick up what I could in casual intercourse" in order to find out more about the city (170). Fuller's physical journey across the Great Lakes and the prairie is thus significantly defined by the traveler's, and particularly the female traveler's, loss of control. Traveling as a woman, Fuller has to depend on others, usually men, to accompany her on her journey, and even to make such a journey financially possible. Her trip to the Midwest became affordable only after Fuller "reluctantly accepted a gift of fifty dollars from her friend, the liberal Universalist minister, James Freeman Clarke" (Kolodny 113). Fuller was accompanied by Clarke and his sister Sarah, and, upon Clarke's return to the East, by his brother William Hull Clarke, who took the two women on a trip through the prairie in a horse-drawn covered wagon (113). Near the end of **Summer,** disappointed because she might not see the Pictured Rocks, Fuller laments her lack of control over her situation and the ways in which her access to new experiences depends on others: "It did not depend on me; it never has, whether such things shall be done or not" (216).

Fuller's anxiety is caused both by physical confinement related to gender and by discursive confinements; thus she is concerned that her limited access to experience will prevent her from writing those stories that are sanctioned and deemed interesting. Through the practice of textual wandering, Fuller tries self-consciously to allay, if not escape, the anxieties arising both from her literal place in time and space and from her position within the discourses about the West. Through textual wandering, the inclusion of multiple, seemingly irrelevant narratives, Fuller inscribes the displacement brought about by the out-of-body experience she describes in the narrative about the Seeress. Textual wandering in this sense signifies an out-of-body experience of sorts, not, as in the case of Friederike Hauffe, into the beyond of death, but into the unrepresented margins of representations of life on the western frontier.

In her description of Niagara Falls, Fuller sets the tone for her subsequent efforts at anxiously employing and questioning traditional modes of representation. While staying at the Falls, she frequently expresses frustration at not being able to look upon Niagara with "feelings . . . entirely [her] own" (77). Her impression of the Falls is always tied to previous texts known to her which are hard to escape. She thus apologizes to her readers for the insignificance of her own description and then proceeds to insert "a brief narrative of the experience of another, as being much better than anything I could write" (75). The unnamed author, from whose description of Niagara Falls Fuller quotes, is also concerned about the predictability of one's response: "'I expected to be overwhelmed . . . but, somehow or other, I thought only of comparing the effect on my mind with what I had read and heard . . . And, provoked with my stupidity in feeling most moved in the wrong place, I turned away'" (76). Upon returning at night, however, this visitor is finally moved when seeing the Falls a second time in moonlight. The included description seems to attest on the one hand to Fuller's own anxiety about this experience. Feeling most moved in the wrong place herself, she is aware that her text parts with traditional ways of seeing, in this case a master narrative that predicts and shapes the viewer's response to the Falls.[6] Unlike Fuller, the author of the inserted text occasionally comes around to the conventional way of seeing. Thus, Fuller's inclusion of this particular excerpt might be explained through its simultaneous addressing and masking of Fuller's own anxieties—addressing because it serves to question the legitimacy of her own reading, and masking because it replaces an unconventional or resistant reading with a conventional one.

Anxiety about reading and writing also plays a significant role in Fuller's discussion of the lives of women and Native Americans. In such descriptions, Fuller simultaneously writes the position of the space-off into her text and foregrounds the precariousness of a position that is always in danger of being taken over by dominant discourses. Taking a closer look at such a description, I have found it helpful to draw on some conventions of nineteenth-century landscape painting since there are similarities between the visual and textual representation or lack of representation of white settler women and Native American women.

Fuller both reinvokes and transcends the idea of the West as adventurous and free by describing men's existence there as relatively unburdened by excessive hardship: "The men can find assistance in field labor, and recreation with the gun and fishing-rod" (106). For the women, however, the new life is much more difficult and, literally and metaphorically, unsettling. Having unwillingly followed their husbands into the wilderness, these women are often unfit for their lot (106). By describing the lives of women and Native Americans in the West, Fuller textually represents a space that was usually not "visible in the frame" of visual art for in spite of women's participation "in all stages of western development," their appearance in western art is infrequent and contradictory to historical fact (Schoelwer 135).

In her essay "The Absent Other: Women in the Land and Art of Mountain Men," Susan Prendergast Schoelwer focuses primarily on women's role on the fur trade frontier. However, her discussion of women and Native Americans provides some helpful insights into the context that Fuller was responding to in **Summer on the Lakes.** Schoelwer argues that "the legendary absence of women" from paintings of the fur trade frontier "really means the absence of white women" (143). Written texts depict trapper life as "one of manly self-indulgence, of continual hunting and fishing, of absolute freedom from the demands and constraints of civilization—taxes, mortgages, wives, the law" (143). In order to fulfill their sexual desires, however, trappers often "took Indian wives or, at least, companions" (143). In her description of pioneer women, Fuller entered into

territory that had been excluded in the representations of male artists. The presence of women in these representations, although not explicit, was often inferable. Thus, for example, in George Caleb Bingham's *Fur Traders Descending the Missouri,* the role of the absent woman is suggested. In this painting, a fur trader and his son "paddle downriver to deliver their catch to Saint Louis" (160). Although no woman is depicted in this scene, she is nevertheless inscribed into the composition by providing "the biological link" between father and son, as Schoelwer succinctly argues (161). Also "[h]er economic production, manifest in the buffalo skin-covered pack that rests between . . . [father and son]" suggests a significant role for the mother which "[the painting's] content explicitly denies" (161). The trapper's son, "not yet fully independent, leans heavily on this tangible reminder of the mother" (161). It is in her exploration of women's sphere as the locus of hard labor and "economic production" on the western frontier that Fuller transcends the frames of traditional representation.

At the same time, however, as Fuller confidently writes into her text the lives of women who had been mostly absent from earlier representations, she gives voice to an anxiety about her own shortcomings and the dangers involved when competing texts call for her attention: "I have fixed my attention almost exclusively on the picturesque beauty of this region; it was so new, so inspiring. But I ought to have been more interested in the housekeeping of this magnificent state, in the education she is giving her children, in their prospects" (132). In passages such as this one, Fuller evokes the split between two texts that are at odds with each other. On the one hand, there is the world of the picturesque which represents dominant ways of seeing, such as those she explores in her description of Niagara Falls, and on the other hand, there is the world of suffering and hardship, a world in the space-off of traditional representations of the West. She reprimands herself for having been swayed too much in one direction. Her focus on the picturesque has sidetracked her examination of some of the harsher aspects in the lives of women settlers, lives that revolve around domestic tasks such as housekeeping and education of the young. While Fuller is interested in describing the sublimity of the landscape, she also voices the fear that dominant representations, such as those generated by conventions of the picturesque, crowd out stories about the lives of women and Native Americans.

The rupture between these competing texts is reiterated over and over again in **Summer on the Lakes,** and in her description of the antagonism that the settlers feel toward Native Americans, Fuller foregrounds it again vividly. She focuses her attention on a man who "though in other respects of most kindly and liberal heart, showed the aversion that the white man soon learns to feel for the Indian on whom he encroaches, the aversion of the injurer for him he has degraded" (138-39). She juxtaposes this description with the settler's own account of the killing of a deer, "the most graceful I ever beheld [as he says]—there was something so soft and beseeching in his look, I chose him at once; took aim and shot him dead" (139). Fuller shows here the split between a typical sublime narrative on the one hand and a buried or suppressed narrative of suffering on the other. The description of the deer becomes emblematic of both the settlers' treatment of Native Americans and Fuller's anxiety about the narratives that compete for her attention. It is significant that her exploration of this ambiguity occurs in the same chapter in which she includes the narrative of the Seeress of Prevorst with its emphasis on the dangers of the threshold experience. The graceful deer, like the Native Americans, is doomed to death. At the same time, however, in the settler's description of the hunt, the reality of this dooming is sidetracked, suppressed through an exclusive emphasis on the deer's graceful beauty as measured in terms of its value to the hunter. Fuller seems to retell through this account a different version of the dangers of a sublime narrative that obscures suffering while it asserts at the same time the hunter's control and agency—"'I chose him at once.'" In the context of Fuller's anxiety about reading and writing, the patriarchal text seems to be always a text about death, and a text that, through its exclusionary practices and the setting of textual boundaries, writes death and thus inscribes and reaffirms its control. Suffering occurs outside the boundaries of that patriarchal text and, like footnotes, does not have a place in it.

More generally, Fuller replicates the kind of displacement reflected in the story of the seeress and her description of the hunter in an ongoing exploration of her own discursive positionality. Throughout **Summer on the Lakes,** she foregrounds her often precarious negotiation between some of the discourses that shape her responses to the landscape and to the people she encounters. In these negotiations, Fuller is anxious about the dangers of having her experiences usurped by a discourse that will prevent her from writing about the suffering she sees. When writing about the Native Americans who have gathered at Mackinaw to receive their annual payment from the American government, Fuller shows her struggle with other discourses. She is intrigued by the romanticism of the scene she witnesses, its "gipsy charm," even to the point of invoking one of its well-known representatives: "Continually I wanted Sir Walter Scott to have been there. If such romantic sketches were suggested to him, by the sight of a few gipsies, not a group near one of these fires but would have furnished him material for a separate canvass" (175). Fuller, however, quickly checks herself and shifts the focus of her attention: "I was so taken up with the spirit of the scene, that I could not follow out the stories suggested by these weatherbeaten, sullen, but eloquent figures" (175). Again, as during her trip to Niagara Falls, a narrative that privileges traditional ways of seeing (in this case conventions of the picturesque) threatens to crowd out a narrative of suffering and poverty, and traces of such a struggle persistently remain, as for example in Fuller's evocation of the "sullen, but eloquent figures" who still display their noble qualities even in the face of adversity. Such traces show the complexity and ambivalence of Fuller's stance by placing her both within the dominant culture and at its margins.

While acknowledging the suffering of various of her subjects, Fuller also frequently tries to keep at bay a narrative of pain by invoking romantic or classical connotations. At one point during her travels, she describes the site of an ancient Native American village in terms of "a Greek splendor, a Greek sweetness" (100). In praise of the site's natural splendor, Fuller expresses the belief that "Rome and Florence are suburbs compared to this capital of nature's art" (101). However, her depiction of the Edenic character of Native Americans does not describe their present situation, but refers to an invented past. She has little hope that their situation will change for the better.

> I have no hope of liberalizing the missionary, of humanizing the sharks of the trade, of infusing the conscientious drop into the flinty bosom of policy, of saving the Indian from immediate degradation, and speedy death. The whole sermon may be preached from the text, "Needs be that offenses must come, yet wo them by whom they come." Yet, ere they depart, I wish there might be some masterly attempt to reproduce, in art or literature, what is proper to them, a kind of beauty and grandeur, which few of the every-day crowd have hearts to feel, yet which ought to leave in

the world its monuments, to inspire the thought of genius through all ages.

(189)

Fuller describes the artist as a helpless on-looker, who can at best employ her creative efforts in order to preserve visually or textually a larger sense of vanishing cultures. Stressing the special obligation of the artist who might have a strong perception of the iniquities perpetrated against Native Americans, Fuller renounces all earthly responsibility for their gradual removal. Retributions, if they come, will be the acts of God rather than interventions by human beings. She seems to draw here on the idea of the artist developed by Emerson in "The Poet," which was written at about the same time Fuller was working on *Summer.*

In "The Poet," Emerson describes poets as "liberating gods" who "are free and . . . make free" (319). Through their imagination, they help a reader "to escape the custody of that body in which he is pent up, and of that jail-yard of individual relations in which he is enclosed" (317). The dissolution of such bonds, however, comes at a price and raises questions about the ethics of the artist's detached stance. The artist, rather than becoming an agent of change, becomes a silent if unwilling accomplice in the maintenance of the status quo. In journal entries he made during the fall and winter of 1843, Emerson writes that his audience misunderstands him when it expects him to turn into action what he writes about in his essays: "They mistook me. I am and always was a painter" (Whicher 216). In another entry during the same year he writes, "[m]y genius loudly calls me to stay where I am, even with the degradation of owning bank-stock and seeing poor men suffer, whilst the Universal Genius apprises me of this disgrace and beckons me to the martyr's and redeemer's office" (217). Even though he is aware of inequities among people, Emerson remains detached from them. In her description of the artist and her disbelief in the possibility of any change coming from within the ranks of "the sharks of the trade," Fuller follows Emerson's sympathetic but detached artist. Hers is not an agent of political change in the name of greater justice for all, but an observer and preserver of historical facts, a painter of portraits or collector of skulls (Fuller 211).

For Fuller, the artist thus always stays at a remove from her subject, freed from "the jail-yard of individual relations." At the same time, and unlike Emerson, she reassigns the artist the role of

historiographer, for, unable to affect the course of historical events, the artist records them after the fact in order to secure them a lasting place in history. In such a role, however, the artist also becomes a silent if unwilling accomplice in the systematic extinction of Native Americans because representations reflect and revalidate oppressive colonial discourses through their textual usurpation and objectification of native peoples.[7]

Fuller's discussion at times also bears out the threat of such usurpation since, despite her efforts at self-consciousness, she frequently employs elements that resemble those used in nineteenth-century colonial writing. In *The Rhetoric of Empire,* David Spurr describes colonial discourse as that discourse which "designate[s] a space within language that exists both as a series of historical instances and as a series of rhetorical functions" (7). Colonial discourse, Spurr argues, always originates within a colonial situation. Quoting from George Balandier's 1963 definition, Spurr writes, "the colonial situation is characterized by the domination imposed by a foreign minority, 'racially' and culturally different, over a weaker indigenous majority in the name of racial (or ethnic) superiority" (5-6). The two cultures are separated by technological advancement and economic power on the one hand, and the lack thereof on the other (6). Spurr discusses how the spectator's position is determined by colonial discourses. In her description of Native Americans in *Summer on the Lakes,* Fuller frequently occupies the position of the colonial observer.

When she writes about the camp at Mackinaw, Fuller draws comparisons between Native American ways of life and ancient traditions. While affirming the close relationship between the Native Americans and nature, she simultaneously distances each individual from such a primal relationship by inserting a model of Roman nobility between him or her and nature. While in Milwaukee, Fuller sees a Native American chief who reminds her of "a real Roman, more than six feet in height, erect, and of a sullen, but grand gait and gesture. He wore a deep red blanket, which fell in large folds from his shoulders to his feet, did not join in the dance, but slowly strode about through the streets, a fine sight" (142). By ascribing to Native Americans the attributes of ancient nobility, Fuller tries to evoke in her audience sympathy for their plight, and shows, as Lucy Maddox convincingly argues, that they are the "more appropriate claimants to the American Wilderness" (143). However, by representing them as aesthetic objects, Fuller simultaneously denies the subjectivity of these same Native Americans for her audience.

Exploring Native American ways of life on the one hand as representations of a sublime aesthetics, Fuller also resorts to the other extreme in her description of Native American women by employing the stereotype of woman as inferior beast. While earlier she lamented the fact that "the Red man" is either "exalt[ed] . . . into a Demigod or degrad[ed] . . . into a beast," she now falls into this same two-dimensional pattern (175). Furthermore, through her focus on the physical bodies of Native American women, Fuller participates in a discourse of colonialism that objectifies the native other as inferior. In colonial writing, Spurr argues, "the body is that which is most proper to the primitive, the sign by which the primitive is represented" (22). In her depiction of Native American women's burdened lives, Fuller makes use of a stereotype current among Western artists, that of Native American women as "beasts of burden" (Schoelwer 165). For European Americans, Native American women "must have appeared antithetical to the presumed natural condition of women" because they carried out what was considered male labor (165). Schoelwer questions whether "the widespread denigration of Indian Women as 'beasts of burden' may have represented not so much a description of their condition as an indicator of cultural anxieties evoked by unfamiliar conceptions of gender" (165). Fuller's description could thus be viewed as a gauge of her absorption within a patriarchal discourse that casts women as delicate objects who live a life of leisure alien to hard physical labor. Although Fuller describes the Native American women at Mackinaw as exhibiting "decorum and delicacy," she also states that "they *do* occupy a lower place than women among the nations of European civilization" (178). Thus, she casts Native American women as doubly other, twice removed from European civilization through their inferiority both to European American and Native American men and to European American women. By arguing that these women not only "inherit submission," but also "[p]erhaps suffer less than their white sisters, who have more aspiration and refinement," Fuller suppresses a narrative about suffering that she had previously affirmed (178). In doing this, she both affirms traditional ideas of the superiority of Western civilization, and the superiority of European American women in particular, and at the same time usurps the

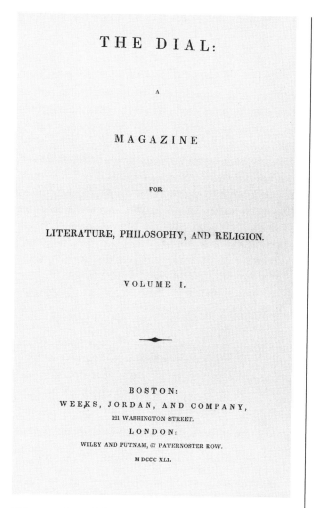

THE DIAL:

A

MAGAZINE

FOR

LITERATURE, PHILOSOPHY, AND RELIGION.

VOLUME I.

BOSTON:
WEEKS, JORDAN, AND COMPANY,
121 WASHINGTON STREET.
LONDON:
WILEY AND PUTNAM, 67 PATERNOSTER ROW.
M DCCC XLI.

Title page from Volume 1 of *The Dial: A Magazine for Literature, Philosophy, and Religion.*

identity of Native American women by objectifying them as brute and senseless victims of oppression. By representing Native Americans through the lens of Western history and denying them a voice in her text, Fuller thus obscures their positions as complex subjects.

Fuller's complex and often conflicted example of cultural critique and the stance of the cultural critic invites in turn a self-conscious exploration of my own position as a reader and critic of women's texts. For me, the significance of her critique lies in its anxious treatment of the writer's involvement in dominant discourses. Another, even more important aspect is its explicit iteration of the precariousness of its own situation, part of what I have previously called the anxiety of writing. For me, as a feminist critic and reader of women's texts, anxiety arises not only from the awareness of my complicity in dominant discourses, but also from my efforts at including within textual speculations the tensions and fears that arise from my attempts at expanding, as Fuller does, the boundaries of my critical text.

It is an anxiety about my involvement, as a cultural critic, in academic discourses that privilege the critic's control over her own text and the texts she reads. But there is also a more deeply seated anxiety about the possibilities and dangers of cultural critique, an anxiety that is intricately connected to issues of nationality. As a German woman living in the U. S. studying American literature, and as a woman within academia practicing cultural criticism, I am forced to think about my own role and responsibilities as an interpreter of languages, discourses, and cultures. This makes me more sensitive to the temptation, as a reader and writer of texts, to usurp and objectify the texts I study, and to the need to interrogate the claims to critical authority inscribed in the discourses I use. In the context of these issues, Fuller's *Summer on the Lakes* generates questions about the ethics of a cultural critique, about the privileged, detached position of the observer, her position as the subject of the gaze.

I have often had to contend with the critical assumption that interpretive authority is irretrievably tied to one's nationality. My being on the borderline between two languages and two cultures has loosened up such real or imagined connections, and thus has been a constant reminder of the precariousness of the very idea of cultural authority. And my constant wandering between languages and cultural contexts has also been an inevitable reminder of the interpretive possibilities of such a double-stance. Thus, I have come to see the strengths and benefits of a cultural critique not in its closeness to arbitrary standards of authenticity, but in the cultural critic's ongoing efforts at questioning her role and motivations as a participant in and reader of cultural texts. Such questioning becomes possible only when one is willing to temporarily wander between interpretive contexts and the beliefs and assumptions that define them.[8]

A shift in frames of reference—in my case a physical shift between countries—makes negotiation possible, even necessary. Such shifts are not exclusively contingent on physical wandering; however, it is necessary for the kind of cultural critique Fuller tentatively envisions for the critic to *wander* among and probe the limits of the discourses that shape her reality. In doing so, Fuller also builds a bridge between the past and the responsibilities of those who live in the present. By including autobiographical experience in my scholarship, I hope to show the relevance of such probings in my reading of texts. And yet I feel an anxiety about voicing these ideas, about including what should be footnotes to my critical enterprise, or suppressed entirely, in the main text, and, like Margaret Fuller, I feel tempted to ask my readers not to "blame me that I have written so much about Germany" (170). But Fuller's own attempts at forging a link between multiple, often contesting voices and her anxieties about reading and writing in ways that stray from convention point out possible routes in my own search for a self-conscious cultural critique. In *Summer on the Lakes,* we can see that within such a critique an interrogation of the interpreter's contingent, always limited, point of view is indispensable.[9]

Notes

1. Jeffrey Steele points out that it was a "sense of personal disjunction [which] helped Fuller interpret the ways in which the victims of racial and sexual oppression had been compartmentalized into categories that isolated them from effective political sympathy" (xiii).

2. Christina Zwarg argues that "[t]he double frame of the translator . . . [was] lending her [Fuller] something of an anthropologist's sensibility to the dynamic of culture contact" (98). By questioning the treatment of Native Americans, Fuller positions herself at the margins of the dominant culture. At the same time, however, she also speaks from within that culture. Zwarg thus discusses the complex and contradictory involvement of Fuller's feminist discourse in traditional patriarchal discourses. She sees Fuller's successful negotiation among the discourses that constitute her writing as symptomatic of an emergence of "critical agency" (124).

3. Like Zwarg, Nicole Tonkovich argues that Fuller consciously employs textual strategies that enable her to resist the dominant discourses that inscribe her as a white, educated woman from the East. Tonkovich focuses on Fuller's resistance to the "fictively unified subjectivity upon which traditional nineteenth-century masculine notions of authorship depended" (95). By combining multiple narratives and various fictive selves with "techniques of parody," Fuller subverts such attempts at unity (95).

4. Stephen Adams makes a case for the strong role of subjective perception in Fuller's writing. He argues that *Summer on the Lakes* presents Fuller's successful attempt at creating a new heterogeneous form by skillfully weaving together multiple narratives (247-49). However, "beneath the surface disjointedness, digressiveness, and fragmentation" of the text, romantic works such as Fuller's "strive for a deep unity" (251).

5. Ellison's discussion, although it does not focus primarily on *Summer on the Lakes,* is nevertheless helpful for an analysis of this text. Like Adams, Ellison emphasizes Fuller's heterogeneous style of writing (283). Rather than focusing, however, as Adams does,

on the hidden Romantic unifying tendencies in Fuller's work, Ellison stresses the dynamics that construct a subject's historicity. Heterogeneity, Ellison argues, "refers not to a random mixture of styles, but to a structured movement among certain discourses and the cultural positions associated with them" (283). The self in Fuller's writing is the site at which "the many languages of the mind . . . and of society" intersect (223). As for Steele, for Ellison the subject does not exist beyond ideology, but is able to move along the various discourses that constitute it.

6. Elisabeth McKinsey points out that several stock conventions provided guidelines for written representations of the Falls. There was in fact a "vocabulary of the sublime." Writers often were "concerned much more with emotions and psychic responses to the cataract than with its physical description [and thus] they emphasize adjectives more than nouns, and the nouns they do use are particularly value laden and affective." Besides the word "dreadful," which is also a part of Fuller's description, such words as "dazzling stupendous . . . profound, overwhelming, eternal, wonder, prodigy, abyss, and chasm" are elements of stock descriptions of the Falls (43).

7. In a study of the works of women travel writers, Sara Mills asks, "[a]re we [feminist critics] going to be critical of some of the positions exemplified in the texts, for example, colonialist or racial statements, and will we be judging these works against some feminist standard? Or are we writing about them as part of a larger project concerned with the construction of an alternative women's history?" (28). In my reading of Fuller's text, these two questions often threaten to cancel each other out. An exclusive focus on Fuller's text in relation to an alternative tradition of women's writing—one that would foreground her resistance to dominant discourses and her affirmation of the hardships in the lives of both white and Native American women—could be in danger of obfuscating her text's simultaneous complicity in those discourses. On the other hand, focusing solely on Fuller's participation in discourses that reinscribe stereotypes about Native Americans, I might diminish the feminist message embedded in her critique. However, in the course of this project I have come to realize that such fears are based on the assumption that a feminist message has to be consistent and in control of its various meanings in order to be meaningful. Thus, I argue that rather than representing mutually exclusive positions, both of the questions Mills raises are intricately tied into the emergence of an anxiety about reading and writing in Fuller's text.

8. For me the kind of distancing that is necessary for such negotiations was facilitated through my displacement as a foreigner in this country. Ongoing probings and shiftings between different cultural texts and the discourses, as well as national languages, through which they are constructed and which in turn they construct, have forced me to take up various, often conflicting positions that put me at shifting distances both from the cultural texts of my native Germany and from those of North America. In a longer version of this paper, I explore this conflict within the particular context of my reading and rereading of the German Holocaust.

9. This paper is part of a chapter on Margaret Fuller from my dissertation, which experiments with and explores the uses of personal voice and autobiographical experience in literary criticism. Thus, my reading of *Summer on the Lakes* and Fuller's role as cultural critic is also a reading of myself, albeit an abbreviated one in this excerpt, caught between cultures as a German woman reading, writing, and teaching in the United States.

FURTHER READING

Bibliography

Myerson, Joel. *Margaret Fuller: An Annotated Bibliography of Criticism, 1983-1995*. Westport, Conn.: Greenwood, 1998, 160 p.

Annotates studies of Fuller from 1983-1995, and includes an extensive index.

Biographies

Capper, Charles. *Margaret Fuller: An American Romantic Life, The Public Years*. London: Oxford University Press, 2004, 423 p.

Focuses on Fuller's emergence from private into public life. Volume one of a two-volume set.

Howe, Julia Ward. *Margaret Fuller (Marchesa Ossoli)*. Boston: Roberts Brothers, 1883, 298 p.

Offers a biography of Fuller from the Famous Women Series.

Criticism

Adams, Kimberly VanEsveld. "'Would [Woman] But Assume Her Inheritance, Mary Would Not Be the Only Virgin Mother'." In *Our Lady of Victorian Feminism: The Madonna in the Work of Anna Jameson, Margaret Fuller, and George Eliot*, pp. 118-47. Athens, Ohio: Ohio University Press, 2001.

Analyzes Fuller's use of the Madonna as a symbol of empowerment for women.

Kolodny, Annette. "Margaret Fuller's First Depiction of Indians and the Limits of Social Protest: An Exercise in Women's Studies Pedagogy." *Legacy* 18, no. 1 (2001): 1-20.

Asserts that Fuller's review essay "Romaic and Rhine Ballads," sheds light not only on Fuller's skill as a Germanist, but also reveals her first published thoughts on the condition of the American Indian.

Poe, Edgar Allan. "Sarah Margaret Fuller." In *Critical Essays on Margaret Fuller*, edited by Joel Myerson, pp. 35-39. Boston: G. K. Hall & Co., 1980.

Praises Fuller's literary reviews and Woman in the Nineteenth Century, *while finding fault with many elements of her writing style.*

Rosowski, Susan J. "Margaret Fuller, an Engendered West, and Summer on the Lakes." *Western American Literature* (August 1990): 125-44.

Discusses Fuller's autobiographical writing and her connections to the American West—two areas of Fuller scholarship Rosowski contends are largely neglected by critics.

Steele, Jeffrey. "Lunar Flowers: Exploring the Divine Feminine." In *Transfiguring America: Myth, Ideology, and*

Mourning in Margaret Fuller's Writing, pp. 65-82. Columbia, Mont.: University of Missouri Press, 2001.

Studies Fuller's mystical essays for the Dial *within their historical context.*

Zwarg, Christina. "The Work of Trauma: Fuller, Douglass, and Emerson on the Border of Ridicule." *Studies in Romanticism* 41, no. 1 (spring 2002): 65-88.

Discusses the rhetorical strategies employed in the writings on emancipation by Fuller, Douglass, and Emerson.

OTHER SOURCES FROM GALE:

Additional coverage of Fuller's life and career is contained in the following sources published by the Gale Group: *American Writers Supplement,* Vol. 2; *Dictionary of Literary Biography,* Vols. 183, 223, 239; *Concise Dictionary of Literary Biography, 1640-1865; Feminist Writers; Literary Movements for Students,* Vol. 1; *Literature Resource Center; Nineteenth-Century Literature Criticism,* Vols. 5, 50; and *Something about the Author,* Vol. 25.

MARIETTA HOLLEY

(1836 - 1926)

(Also wrote under the pseudonym Jemymah) American novelist, short story writer, poet, playwright, and autobiographer.

Holley was a well-known regional novelist of late-nineteenth-century America. Her folksy, opinionated, and comic characters garnered much commercial success in her day, and she was often compared to Mark Twain. Her work explores topical issues such as women's suffrage, racial relations, class divisions, temperance, war, and the treatment of women in society.

BIOGRAPHICAL INFORMATION

Holley was born in Jefferson County, New York on July 16, 1836. The youngest of seven children, she grew up on a farm and had a special interest in music. As a young woman, she helped support her family by selling handicrafts and giving music lessons to young women from prosperous families. Holley also wrote verse, and in 1857 she began to publish her work in the local newspaper, *The Jefferson County Journal,* under the pseudonym Jemymah. In 1872, Elisha Bliss, Mark Twain's publisher, commissioned her to write a humorous novel; *My Opinions and Betsey Bobbet's* was published in 1873. With the success of this book, she became a well-known public figure,

despite the fact that she rarely left her home in Jefferson County. A strong supporter of the suffrage movement, Holley explored many controversial social and political issues in her fiction. She died at home in Jefferson County on March 1, 1926.

MAJOR WORKS

Several of Holley's novels feature a comic protagonist named Samantha Smith Allen, a sensible, middle-aged woman who acts as a counterbalance to her husband, Josiah Allen, a diminutive and weak man with a penchant for crazy schemes. Another major character in these works is Samantha's friend Betsey Bobbet, a stereotypically skinny, ugly old maid who believes—unlike Samantha—that women are inferior to men and should be treated accordingly. Holley uses these characters as well as the traditional tools of the humorist—exaggeration, satire, vernacular language, malapropisms, and misspelling—to explore and expound on the salient issues of the day. For example, in *My Opinions and Betsey Bobbet's* she presents the case for women's suffrage and the need for economic independence for women. In *Samantha Among the Brethren* (1890) she questions the subservient role of women in the church. *Samantha at Saratoga* (1887), *Samantha at the St. Louis Exposition,* (1904), and *Around the World with Josiah Allen's Wife* (1905) explore such controversial issues as the obsession with fashion, the problem of racial discrimination, and the relationship between capital and labor in the early twentieth century.

CRITICAL RECEPTION

Critics maintain that Holley's novels and short fiction draw from several American literary traditions: the insights and details of the regional writer, the vernacular humor used by earlier humorists, and the sentimental style of late-nineteenth-century literature. In fact, Holley's work is often compared to that of American humorists such as Frances Whitcher and Mark Twain. Commentators have mixed opinions of her satirical depiction of the realities of country life. Some perceive it as an insightful and amusing caricature of rural existence in late-nineteenth-century America, while others view her humor as weak and tiresome. Popular in her day, Holley's work fell into obscurity by the mid-twentieth century. With the increased attention to feminist issues and literature in the late twentieth century, critics reassessed Holley's fiction. Her treatment of controversial subjects—such as the suffrage movement, racial exploitation, and the exploitation of the American worker—is considered by some scholars as engaging social and political commentary. Feminist critics have also examined Holley's use of humor to advance the cause of women, to attack the sentimental tradition, and to challenge women's ideas about themselves.

PRINCIPAL WORKS

My Opinions and Betsey Bobbet's (novel) 1873

Josiah Allen's Wife as a P. A. and P. I., Samantha at the Centennial (novel) 1877

Betsey Bobbet: A Drama (play) 1880

The Lament of the Mormon Wife (prose poem) 1880

My Wayward Pardner; or, My Trials with Josiah, America, The Widow Bump, and Etcetery (novel) 1880

Miss Richards' Boy, and Other Stories (short stories) 1883

Sweet Cicely; or, Josiah Allen as Politician (novel) 1885

Miss Jones' Quilting (novel) 1887

Poems (poetry) 1887

Samantha at Saratoga (novel) 1887

Samantha Among the Brethren (novel) 1890

The Widder Doodle's Courtship, and Other Sketches (short stories) 1890

Samantha on the Race Problem (novel) 1892

Tirzah Ann's Summer Trip, and Other Sketches (short stories) 1892

Samantha at the World's Fair (novel) 1893

Josiah's Alarm, and Abel Perry's Funeral (novel) 1895

Samantha in Europe (novel) 1896

Samantha at the St. Louis Exposition (novel) 1904

Around the World with Josiah Allen's Wife (novel) 1905

Samantha vs. Josiah, Being the Story of a Borrowed Automobile and What Came of It (novel) 1906

Samantha on Children's Rights (novel) 1909

Josiah's Secret: A Play (play) 1910

Samantha at Coney Island and a Thousand Other Islands (novel) 1911

Josiah Allen on the Woman Question (novel) 1914

Samantha on the Woman Question (novel) 1914

The Story of My Life (autobiography) 1931

PRIMARY SOURCES

MARIETTA HOLLEY (ESSAY DATE 1906)

SOURCE: Holley, Marietta. "'A Male Magdalene,' from *Samantha vs. Josiah*." In *The Oxford Book of Women's Writing*, edited by Linda Wagner-Martin and Cathy N. Davidson, pp. 56-62. London: Oxford University Press, 1995.

In the following excerpt, originally published in 1906 in her Samantha vs. Josiah, Being the Story of a Borrowed Automobile and What Came of It, *Holley addresses the issue of the double sexual standard.*

I attended a beautiful party yesterday; it wuz a anniversary, and carried on regardless of style and expense. Over seven wuz invited, besides the happy folks who gin the party. And the cookin' wuz, I do almost believe, as good as my own. That's dretful high praise, but Miss Chawgo deserves it. It wuz to celebrate their weddin' day, which occurred the year before at half past two, and dinner wuz on the table at exactly that hour.

There wuz Josiah and me, Miss Bizer Kipp and Lophemia, she that wuz Submit Tewksbury, and her husband, and Widder Bassett and her baby.

That made a little over seven; the baby hadn't ort to count so high as a adult. The party wuz all in high sperits, and all dressed well and looked well, though Miss Bassett whispered to me that Miss Kipp had flammed out a little too much.

She wuz very dressy in a pink flowered shally with lots of ribbins kinder floatin', but she felt and said that she wuz celebratin' a very auspicious occasion with very dear friends, which made us lenitent to her. Weddin' anniversaries are now and agin happy and agreeable, and the male party here, Nelt Chawgo, how much! how much that young man had to be thankful for! yes indeed!

And Id'no but I might jest as well tell about it now as any time while in history's pages the gay party is settin' 'round the bountifully spread table.

I'll make the story short as possible. Most three years ago we had a new arrival in Jonesville, a young grocery man by the name of Nelson Chawgo; the young folks all called him Nelt. He bought out old uncle Simon Pettigrew, his good will and bizness, though so fur as the good will went I wouldn't paid a cent fur it, or not more than a cent, anyway. Uncle Sime abused his wife, wuz clost as the bark to a tree, and some mentioned the word "sand" in connection with his sugar, and "peas" with his coffee, and etcetery, etcetery. But his bizness wuz what might be called first rate; he had laid up money and retired triumphant at seventy-one.

But to resoom. Uncle Sime Pettigrew's place of bizness wuz a handsome one, a new brick block with stun granite trimmin's, some stained glass over the doors and winders, and everything else it needed for comfort and respectability. He had a big stock of goods and whoever bought 'em and set up bizness in that handsome new block would have been looked up to even if he had been an old man with a bald head, rumatiz and a wooden leg.

But when it wuz a young, handsome, unmarried man, you may imagin he made a sensation to once, and he wuz as handsome a chap as you would often see, light completed with sort o' melancholy blue eyes and curly brown hair and mustash.

The Jonesvillians and Loontowners went into ecstacies over him the first day he appeared in meetin', he wuz so beautiful. They acted fairly foolish; they praised him up so and wuz so enthusiastick. But it is my way to keep calmer and more demute. I will try to restrain my emotions if I have to tie a string to 'em and haul 'em back if I find 'em liable to go too fur. I never could bear anybody

or anything that slopped over, from a oriter to a kettle of maple syrup, and I kep' holt of my faculties and common sense in this case, and several of the sisters in the meetin'-house got mad as hens at me, and importuned me sharp as to why I didn't go into spazzums of admiration over him.

And I sez, "He is sweet-lookin', I can't deny that, but there is a kinder weak and waverin' expression to his face that would cause me anxiety if I wuz his Ma."

But when I promulgated these ideas to the other sistern, sister Bizer Kipp especially, she most took my head off. She said his face wuz "Bea-u-tiful, just perfection."

But I still repeated what I had said in a megum tone, and with my most megumest mean, but I agreed with her in a handsome way that Nelt wuz what would be called very, very sweet and winsome, and would be apt to attract female attention and be sought after. And so he wuz. As days rolled on he grew to be the rage in Jonesville, a he-belle, as you may say. Groceries lay in piles on wimmen's buttery shelves and sickness wuz rampant, caused by a too free use of raisins and cinnamon and all-spice. They are too dryin'.

And still the wimmen flocked to his counters as if they couldn't buy enough stuff, and they priced peanuts, and got samples of cast-steel soap, and acted. No place of amusement wuz considered agreeable or endurable without Nelt Chawgo; no party wuz gin without his name stood first on the list, and when he got there he wuz surrounded by a host of the fair sect showerin' attention on him, anxious to win a smile from him.

He wuz doin' dretful well in bizness, and doin' well in morals so fur as I knew. He wuz payin' attention in a sort of a languid, half-hearted way, to Lophemia Kipp. She wuz a pretty girl, sister Kipp's only child. It wuz very pleasin' to her Ma. Folks thought she wuz the one that had brought it about; she acted so triumphant and big feelin' about it, and told everybody how active Nelt wuz in the meetin'-house, and how well he wuz doin' in bizness, and how strong and stimulatin' his tea and coffee wuz.

Folks thought, as I say, that she had more to do about his payin' attention to Lophemia than she did, fur it wuz thought that she had gin her heart to young Jim Carter, old lawyer Carter's youngest boy. He had gone west on a ranch, and it wuz spozed he carried her heart with him. It wuz known he carried her picture, took standin', with a smile on the pretty lips and a happy glow in the eyes, rousted up it wuz spozed by young

Jim himself. He went with her to the photographer's; that wuz known, too. Miss Kipp had boasted a sight about him, his good looks and his good bizness and his attentions to Lophemia till Nelt come.

Sister Kipp hain't megum, she is one of the too enthusiastick ones whose motto is not "Love me little love me long," but "Love me a immense quantity in a short time." It stands to reason that if the stream is over rapid the pond will run out sooner; if the stream meanders slow and stiddy, it will last longer.

Well, 'tennyrate she wuz all took up with Nelt Chawgo, and praisin' him us as she had to the very skies you may imagin my feelin's when one day she fairly bust into my settin'-room, out of breath and red in the face, and sez: "I've discovered the dretfulest thing! the awfulest, the most harrowin'! Nelt Chawgo, that young he-hussy, shall never enter my doors agin!"

"Whyee!" sez I, "what's the matter?"

Sez she, "He's a lost young man, a ruined feller!"

"Whyee!" sez I agin, and I sunk right down in my tracts in a rockin'-chair, she havin' sunken down in one opposite; and sez I, "I hain't mistrusted it. He has acted modest and moral; I can't believe it!"

"But it is so," sez she. "He has been ruined. Angerose Wilds, a dashin' young woman up in the town of Lyme, is responsible."

"I have hearn of her," sez I. "She had quite a lot of money left her, and is cuttin' a great swath."

"Well," sez sister Kipp, "she has deceived and ruined Nelt Chawgo, and then deserted him; it has all been proved out, and he shall never speak to Lophemia agin, the miserable outcaster!"

Well, I wuz dumbfoundered and horrowstruck like all the rest of Jonesville, but I, as my way is, made inquiries and investigations into the matter. And the next time I see Miss Kipp, and she begun to me awful about Nelt, runnin' him down all to nort, I sez to her, "I have found out some things that makes me feel more lenitent towards Nelson Chawgo."

Oh, how she glared at me. "Lenitent!" sez she, "I'd talk about lenity to that villian, that low ruined creeter!"

"Well," sez I, "I have inquired and found out that Angerose Wilds jest follered Nelt up with attentions and flatteries, and it is spozed up in Lyme that he wuz tempted and fell under a promise of marriage." And I spoke with considerable indignation about this woman who wuz beautiful and rich and holdin' her head high.

But Miss Kipp treated it light and sez: "Oh, young wimmen must sow their wild oats, and then they most always settle down and make the best of wives."

But agin I mentioned extenuatin' circumstances. Sez I, "Miss Wilds wuz noble and galliant in her bearin'; she wuz rich and handsome, and she turned his thoughtless head with her flatteries, and won his pure and unsophistocated heart, so it wuz like wax or putty in her designin' hands, and then at the last she turned her back on him and wouldn't have nothin' to say to him." But these mitigatin', extenuatin' circumstances didn't mitigate or extenuate a mite with Miss Kipp.

Sez she bitterly, "Couldn't he have repulsed her attentions? Couldn't he have kep' his manly modesty if he had been a mind to? Wuz there any need of his fallin' to the depths of infamy he sunk to? No, he is lost, he is ruined!" sez she.

Sez I, "Sister Kipp, don't talk so scornfully; don't say ruined," sez I. "Fall is a good word to use in such a case; folks can fall and git up agin— mebby he will. But ruined is a big word and a hard one; it don't carry any hope with it; it breathes of despair, agony and eternal loss."

"Well," sez she, "it ort to in his case. I shall draw my skirts away from him and go by on the other side. Before his ruin he wuz a sweet, lovely young man but now he is lost. I shall have nothin' to do with him, nor Lophemia shan't."

But I still tried to draw her attention to the facts I had promulgated that Miss Wilds, too, wuz not guiltless. But she wuz sot and wouldn't yield.

She said his sect wuz considered stronger-minded than our sect, with heftier brains and mightier wills, and so it stood to reason that if he wuz tempted by one of the weaker and more feather-brained, he could have saved himself and her, too, from ruin.

There wuz some sense in her talk, I had to admit that there wuz. But I kep' on wavin' my mantilly of charity as high as I could, hopin' that some of the folds, even if it wuzn't nothin' but the end of the tabs, might sort o' shadder Nelt a little, for he wuz indeed a object of pity.

And we couldn't none of us look ahead and see the thrillin' eppisode that wuz in front on him. No, a thick veil of despair seemed to hang down in front on him. And I didn't mistrust that it wuz my hands that wuz goin' to push that veil aside and let some rays lighten up the darkness. But more of that anon and bimeby.

When the news got out about Nelt Chawgo, Jonesville society wuz rent to its very twain. The two factions led on by Miss Kipp and Nelt's friends waged a fearful warfare, some jinin' one side and some the other.

Some on 'em, the old conservative ones, wuz for overlookin' the hull matter so fur as Nelt wuz concerned and throwin' the hull blame onto the female woman up to Lyme on the safe old ground, trod so long by the world at large, that he wuz a man and so such sin in him wuzn't a sin. It wuz sin in a woman, a deep and hopeless sin that forever barred the guilty one from the pail of respectable society.

But I held to the firm belief that if she carried the pail he ort to, and visey versey. My idee wuz that they ort to carry the pail between 'em. They said it wuz sin in the woman, a turrible and hopeless sin, but in him it wuzn't. It come under the head of wild oats, which when planted thick in youth and springin' up rank, prepared the ground for a rich after crop of moral graces.

This wuz old well-established doctrine that had been follered for years and years, so they felt it wuz safe.

But one night to a church sociable when Miss Kipp had brung the subject up and one of our foremost deacons, Deacon Henzy, wuz advancin' these idees, she that wuz Nancy Butterick, who had come to Jonesville to deliver a lecture in the interests of the W. C. T. U., she sassed Deacon Henzy right back and sez she:

"The idee of thinkin' that the same sin when committed by a man and a woman ort to be laid entirely onto the party that is in the law classed with lunaticks and idiots." Sez she, "That hain't good logic. If a woman is a fool she hadn't ort to be expected to have her brain tapped and run wisdom and morality, and if she is a lunatick she might be expected to cut up and act."

She wuz educated high, Nancy wuz, and knew a sight in the first place, as folks have to, to amount to much, for all education can do anyway is to sharpen the tools that folks use to hew their way through the wilderness of life.

Sez she, "The male sect is in the eyes of the Law the gardeens of females, and ort to act like gardeens to 'em and try to curb their folly and wickedness and restrain it instead of takin' advantage of it, and fallin' victims to their weakness."

Sez she, "When a oak tree falls it falls heavier than a creepin' vine, a creepin' up and hangin' to it, and it would be jest as sensible to lay the hull of the blame on the creeper for the fall of the oak, as to put the hull of the blame on the Lyme woman."

Why, she brung up lots of simelys that fairly bristled with eloquence, and Deacon Henzy sassed her back in his way of thinkin'; it wuz a sight to hear 'em talkin' pro and con. . . .

. . . I thought Jane Ann looked queer, but I went on and sez: "Oh, if that woman could look and see the wreck she has made of that once happy and good young man, it must be she would be struck with remorse. They say she is handsome and well off, and holds her head high, while her victim is dyin' under the contempt and scorn of the world. Nobody will associate with him. Why, my Josiah draws his pantaloons away from him for fear of the contamination of his touch. He's weighed down under the scorn of the world and his own remorse. He is ruined in his bizness, and he's goin' into the gallopin' consumption as fast as he can gallop."

Jane Ann gin me such a queer look here that I involuntary follered her gaze and looked at the handsome stranger. Her work had fell into her lap, her face wuz red as blood, and she busted into tears, sayin:

"I am Angerose Wilds! I am the guilty wretch that wuz the means of that sweet and innocent young creature's fall; I am the one to blame. But," sez she with her streamin' eyes lifted to mine, "I never realized until you brung it before me the extent of my crime, but I will atone for the evil as fur as I can. I will marry him and so do all I can to lift him up and make an honest man of him, and set him right in the eyes of the community. And," sez she, while the tears chased each other down her cheeks, "Poor Nelt! poor boy! how you have suffered; and I alone am the guilty cause!"

But here I interfered agin, held up by Justice and Duty. "Don't say, mom, that you alone are to blame; divide it into two bundles of guilt, take one on your own back and pack the other onto hisen. It hain't fair for one to bear it alone, male or female."

Josiah come that very minute and I had to bid them a hasty adoo. But the last words that galliant appearin' handsome woman whispered to me wuz: "I will make an honest man of him; I will marry him."

And if you'll believe it, she did. It all ended first rate, almost like a real novel story. It seems that woman wuz so smut with remorse when it wuz brought before her in a eloquent and forcible manner; and she realized the almost irreparable wrong she had committed aginst that lovely and innocent young man, she offered him the only reparation in her power; she offered him honorable marriage, which he accepted gladly, and they got married the next week, and he brought her to Jonesville the follerin' Monday, and they sot up housekeepin' in a handsome two-story-and-a-half house, and are doin' well and bid fair to make a respectable couple.

We buy the most of our groceries there; not all, for I am megum in groceries as well as in everything else. I buy some of the other grocer, not bein' willin' to hurt his fellin's, his wife bein' a member of the same meetin'-house. But Miss Kipp can't be megum any more than my own dear pardner can. She come 'round immegiate and unanimous, and said their marriage made 'em both all that could be desired. She buys all her groceries of him; she sez his tea is cheaper and takes a spunful less in a drawin'. But I don't believe it; I believe she steeps it longer. 'Tennyrate she bought of him all her fruit and candy and stuff for Lophemia Carter's weddin', which took place some time ago.

Well, this party I sot out to tell you about wuz to celebrate the first anniversary of the Chawgo and Wilds weddin', and wuz a joyful event.

After we got home Josiah wuz so nerved up (part on't wuz the strong coffee), that I had to read three truthful articles out of the scrap-book; he a settin' leanin back in his chair a listenin' and a makin' comments on each one on 'em as I finished readin' 'em.

His talk bein' some like the little pieces they play between songs, interludes, I believe they call 'em, only his talk wuzn't all the time melogious; no, indeed; fur from it. There wuz minor cords in it, and discords, and flats and sharps, yes indeed!

GENERAL COMMENTARY

KATE H. WINTER (ESSAY DATE 1984)

SOURCE: Winter, Kate H. "Prologue." In *Marietta Holley: Life with "Josiah Allen's Wife,"* pp. 1-10. Syracuse, N.Y.: Syracuse University Press, 1984.

In the following excerpt, Winter offers an overview of Holley's writing, touching on the author's use of humor for feminist causes, her works' historical and geographical context, and the literary traditions from which they emerged.

She was called the Female Mark Twain in the popular press, and it was claimed that she had as large an audience as Twain's. From 1873 to 1914 Marietta Holley was one of America's most popular writers, creating one of its most endearing characters—Samantha—and making "Josiah Allen's Wife" a household phrase. In twenty-one books and uncounted short stories, Samantha regaled the country with her "episodin' and allegorin'" in works dealing with the issues personal and political that occupied the thinkers of the age. In fact, during the early years of her literary career, there were many who simply did not believe that Josiah Allen's Wife was a woman at all because the humor, satire, and political arguments were so vigorous and shrewd.

Her works are squarely in the tradition of the male literary comedians—Mark Twain, Josh Billings, Bill Arp, Artemus Ward, and Petroleum V. Nasby. Stylistically Holley depended for much of her humor on the upcountry dialect and the proverbs and maxims mixed with extravagant images that were the stuff of the "crackerbox philosophers." In using cacography and peculiar orthography, she was actually attempting a phonetic transcription of New York State's North Country speech, and in this she was fairly consistent and systematic, unlike Artemus Ward and Josh Billings. Furthermore, Samantha has certain characteristic phrases that she repeats frequently, habits of speech that make her a rounded character, things like "anon or oftener," "to resoom," "episodin' and allegorin'," and "foremothers."

Holley's character used humor for a new end—propaganda for the feminist movement, which had previously been the butt of much comedy. Using the same character types—the wise sage, the foolish foil, the love-starved spinster—she reverses the reader's sympathies to undermine the conventions of the culture regarding the respective roles of men and women. Whereas other comedians had made the woman, particularly the woman's rights advocate, a laughing-stock, Holley created a cast of lesser characters who exemplified the absurdities of intemperance and antisuffrage while she maintained the stalwart central character of Samantha as a right-minded, simple country woman whose habits of speech might have been laughable but whose habits of thought were sound and serious. In a further twist, Samantha satirizes women as well as men, thereby winning her male readers with her fair-mindedness as well as her patience and sympathy for her husband, the foolish Josiah.

The earlier women humorists Ann Stephens and Frances Whitcher had primarily concerned themselves with the impact of genteel values on American women, calling attention to the injustices, abuses, and indignities that the tradition of gentility imposes on women. Ann Stephens, the first American woman humorist to write in the vernacular, chose a male naive narrator, Jonathan Slick, for her 1843 work *High Life in New York,* and employed the same epistolary mode that Seba Smith had used. Whitcher, using the dramatic monologue, created a female comic figure in Widow Bedott. It remained for Holley to create a sympathetic comic woman, and she did so even as the peak of interest in dialect humor was being passed.

Holley was one of the first published fiction writers to emerge out of the North Country region of New York State. Her precursor, Frances Whitcher, was from the upstate village of Whitesboro, near Utica. Two years younger than Holley, Whitcher had enjoyed the advantages of town life over farm life and had thus begun publishing earlier. *The Widow Bedott Papers,* published in book form in 1855, created the first feminine comic figure to be portrayed at length, the widow who satirized an eastern small town's genteel society.

But Widow Bedott is not a sympathetic character at all, and she follows in the tradition of Shillaber's Mrs. Partington. However, Whitcher did create a character who presaged Holley's feminist spokeswoman, a writer of woman's rights essays named Samantha Hocum. This character, although still a satirical figure in Whitcher's scheme, may have been the inspiration for Holley's eloquent feminist Samantha Smith Allen. Whitcher's work, which first appeared anonymously in *Neal's Saturday Gazette* in 1846, emerged just on the surge of demand for dialect humor, a wave of popularity on which Holley was carried for more than thirty years.

Two other women writers of the "feminine fifties" also lived and wrote upstate: Emily Chubbock Judson of Eaton, who used the pseudonym Fanny Forester, published *Alderbrook* in 1847; Sarah J. Clarke, born in Pompey and known to her readers as Grace Greenwood, had produced *Greenwood Leaves* in 1850. Both short fiction writers, they produced collections that were best-sellers.

Holley's vernacular humor connected the tradition of the women's sentimental novels and stories, which these women practiced within, with the later "B'gosh school" of fiction that Irving

Bacheller, another North Country writer, explored and expanded. In his novels Bacheller drew as heavily as Holley on the dialect, manners, and values of the region, although he tended toward a more realistic mode of narrative than she did. At the other extreme are the stories of Philander Deming, Holley's contemporary. Born and reared in Schoharie County outside the southern boundary of the North Country, Deming drew heavily for his narratives on the habits and ethics of the people he knew from the summers he spent running a sawmill in the Adirondacks. As much in touch with the realities of upstate survival as Holley, he chose to etch in chiseled prose the harsh life of the upcountry. It was a fictional chronicle that Walter Edmonds in the 1930s continued in his upstate novels, blending the realism of Deming with his own strong narrative gifts.

Like all the North Country writers of the nineteenth century, Holley shared the sense that politicians were just neighbors and politics an activity as much connected with all their lives as farm chores and church meetings. Segregated from the rest of the nation by terrain as well as by choice, North Country people maintained a strong moral solicitude for the country as a whole and a willingness to pronounce opinion on political matters. The region had been a "germinating ground for politicians" from Cleveland to Roosevelt. The presence of real political figures and the assumption that they would listen to the thoughtful women and men of the country informed much of the thinking and writing that came out of the upstate region.

In any encounter with a politician, Samantha takes it upon herself to admonish, congratulate, or advise him regarding his stand on the issues most important to her. When she goes into New York City in the first novel, it is especially to see Horace Greeley, who was to run for president. Although she admires him, she disagrees with him on "biled vittles, Wimmen's Rights, and cream biscuits," and she is determined to set him straight on the central matter at least. In the same way, she accosts President Grant at the centennial. He had earned Samantha's wrath by pressing the prosecution of Susan B. Anthony after she and sixteen other women had voted in the 1872 presidential election in Rochester, New York. She preaches to him for several pages before she concludes:

> And then I advised the Nation (through Ulysses) what to do in the great cause of Wimmen's Rights. I talked eloquent on that subject, and in closin' I drawed his mind back a few years to the time

when a great war was goin' on between justice and injustice, and how God wrought out of it the freedom of a race, before He gave the victory. I reminded him that another great battle was goin' on between temperance and intemperance, and how, in that warfare, I believed God was helpin another race of human female beins to liberty; by showin' to man how He enabled *them* to win greater victories than had ever crowned *man's* efforts, and provin' what *they* would do for God and humanity if the power was given them.

In this same manner, Samantha talks with many of the movers and shakers of the 1870s, trying to persuade them through her sturdy common sense to adopt her views on woman's rights and temperance much as her campaigning sisters actually buttonholed politicians during the century of petitioning for the vote.

The primary concern for Holley was to gain the ballot for women. Holley, like Philander Deming, had witnessed the toll on women of the desolate, painful, and fearful life in the rural districts of New York State. This made both writers sensitive to the plight of women, who held no political power. Irving Bacheller would likewise recognize the drudgery and hardship of farm and woodland life for women, but with his bent for nostalgia and pastoral idyll, he more often masked the reality with an aura of rustic sainthood, portraying the women as angelic, patient, virtuous mother-women. Elevated to such a pedestal, women were as powerless as ever to gain their fair measure of dignity and independence. Sainthood was not what Samantha or Holley sought. Against Josiah's argument that a woman's place is on a pedestal—to keep her from the polls—Samantha argues:

> I just as lives be on a pedestal as not, I'd kinder love to if I could set, I always did enjoy bein' riz up, if I had nothin' to do only to stay up there sometime, but wimmin have to git round so much it wouldn't work. . . . But that hain't the main reason I'm agin it, it is too tuckerin' a job for wimmin.

> Tuckerin' to be enthroned on a pedestal with the male sect lookin' up to you and worshippin' you. . . . How under the sun can I or any other woman be up on a pedestal and do our own housework, cookin', washin' dishes, sweepin', moppin', cleanin' lamps, blackin' stoves, washin', ironin', makin' beds, quiltin' bed quilts, gittin' three meals a day, biled dinners and bag puddin's and mince pies and things, to say nothin' of custard and pumpkin pies that will slop over on the level, do the best one can! How could you keep 'em inside the crust histin's yourself up and down?

To all of this Josiah angrily answers, "They could manage it if their minds wuz strong enough." It is against that sort of logic and literalness that Samantha struggles in both the private and public domain. Samantha frequently insisted:

> I never contended that wimmen was perfect, far from it. You have heerd me say in the past, that I thought wimmen was meaner than pusly about some things. I say so still. My mind haint changed about wimmen, nor about pusly. But justice is what I have been a contendin' for; justice, and equal rights, and a fair dividin' of the burdens of life is my theme.

Central New York State women already had developed a tradition of political activism and feminist unrest. Elizabeth Cady Stanton and Susan B. Anthony took up the cause of woman's rights, especially the right to the ballot, in Geneva in 1848. Frances Willard, head and heart of the Women's Christian Temperance Union, was born in Churchville, New York; Dr. Mary Walker, advocate of women's rights and a surgeon in the Civil War, was born in Oswego, New York. While these women carried on the work of campaigning for the vote by lecturing, petitioning, and convening, Holley used Samantha's voice to reach other audiences with the truth about the injustices and indignities of a woman's place in society. At the same time, Samantha chronicled the homely events and hard work that set the rhythm of life for country women: the domestic trials of planting and harvesting, cooking and canning, washing and sewing, often for a large household of children and hired hands. From her stories we know the ceaseless toil of farm life as well as the spirit and turmoil of life in a small New York State town not quite of the New England character but very like it. Holley's works clearly depict the realities and rigors of such a life and thereby give us a glimpse of a time and place that otherwise went largely unrecorded. Such attention to domestic detail recounted with both humor and irritation made her works enormously popular with women readers.

Although her humor appealed most obviously to the masses of women who supported popular fiction, it also reached the reformers who were struggling with their own advocacy of woman's rights and temperance, and stage adaptations brought the arguments of Betsey, Josiah, and Samantha to audiences in colleges, churches, rural districts, and the theaters of Boston and New York City. Holley's impact across the nation is difficult to assess because we have no methods, few reliable criteria, and no way of judging influence from popularity. Obviously one publisher thought that it was worth it when he advanced her $14,000 for her world's fair book in 1893. All the early works were quickly successful; their first printings soon sold out and several were translated into French. In 1887 her *Samantha at Saratoga* was the year's best-seller.

Soon Holley was sought out by leading feminists and temperance leaders, including Anthony and Willard. The woman suffrage movement, having been diverted by the Civil War and then divided by factionalism, sought her support. The temperance movement, having begun in the 1840s as a response to the position of women at the mercy of drinking men, informally merged with the woman suffrage movement under Willard's direction when she saw the vote as both a means and an end. Under the evangelical banner of Home Protection, women petitioned for local option. Suddenly more women were conscious of their political strength, and soon the Women's Christian Temperance Union represented more than two hundred thousand women in every state in the Union. Holley was enjoined to appear with them, write for them, and finally even to tailor the Samantha novels to suit their own goals by killing off Josiah. Clearly they believed in the breadth of Samantha's influence, as did clergy who petitioned Holley to write novels concerning their own reform strategies, most notably for the consequences of manumission in the South and the position of women in the Protestant church. So powerful was her influence felt to be that she was invited to address the United States Congress on woman's rights. Men who would not listen to a feminist speaker's arguments would read Holley's books with delight, accepting through her humor the subversive notions of suffragist thought.

The popular literature of the period from the 1820s to the 1870s was predominantly that of women writing for women, a body of fiction through which "American women became authors and readers." This popular domestic fiction was written by the likes of E.D.E.N. Southworth, Caroline Lee Hentz, Susan Warner, and Marion Harland as well as a horde of lesser-known writers, producing the works that outsold the literary output of Hawthorne, Melville, Thoreau, and Whitman.

Novel and short story alike relied on an overplot that affirmed for women a life-script they could pray and hope for, one in which a girl, beset by adversities, becomes a strong, happy woman. Typically, a young girl, abandoned or left without a guardian in the world, confronts that world, marshals all her talents and determination, and carves out a life for herself by asserting her right to make her own way, although most often the fiction ends in an appropriate marriage for her. The message seemed to be that through independence and self-reliance a woman could find ample use for her wits and her gifts, struggling to achieve a sense of selfhood along the way and participating in a new feminine heroism. With that attained, there was no reason to marry, although, in fact, marriage to a man who appreciated her strength of character was a kind of reward for her virtue. Holley adapted the conventional narrative line and the didactic intention of these earlier writers to her own feminist and prohibitionist motives. In Holley's novels we see the young woman after the wedding, fourteen years after, when other tests of her character, stamina, and adaptability arise. To get the message of her more pragmatic feminism to as many women and men as possible, she wrapped it in the vernacular humor that the public had come to appreciate from Jack Downing and Frances Whitcher. Taking the notion of home-centeredness that the sentimental or domestic novelist had used, Holley turned it to her own purposes by taking up the life of one of these heroines after the marriage vows are said. Holley's Samantha books pick up the narrative well after the honeymoon, when cast-iron affection rather than passion has taken hold.

Taking the pragmatic, moderate feminism of the writers of women's novels, Holley sketched the overplot, particularly in the characters of Tirzah Ann and Betsey Bobbett, showing the failure of the pink-and-white tyranny. After the Civil War, the "matrilineal piety" of Catharine Beecher, Harriet Beecher Stowe, Sarah Orne Jewett, and Charlotte Perkins Gilman was an attempt to provide new heroines, role models for the late nineteenth-century readers. Holley sent forward the bustling, substantial, thoroughly indomitable farm wife, Samantha Allen. At the center of the stories Samantha presides, the antithesis of the genteel maiden, the maiden-turned-matron.

So Holley's Samantha stories draw on three literary traditions—the rustic humorists and literary comedians, the domestic fiction of the feminine fifties, and the emerging local-color movement—melding them in a unique way that no writer has since done. Like the vernacular humorists, Holley fixed her works in the voices of dialect speakers. But like the other North Country writers, Holley's work is also rooted in a sense of place. There is always an awareness of seasons and landscape even when Samantha is traveling through new territory. Holley is, in this way, a regionalist interested in portraying Americans who differ slightly in detail from other Americans rather than what is unique and picturesque. Hers is a democratic and panoramic vision of the nation, yet her work anticipates the women local colorists like Harriet Beecher Stowe, Sarah Orne Jewett, and Mary Wilkins Freeman in her depiction of the details of life in a circumscribed area, a single district of New York.

The manners and customs as well as the quirky speech of the New Englanders who settled the North Country are plainly recorded in the novels. The cycle of socials and church services that sustained the upcountry folk, the domestic scenes, the rustic voices all record a life in the near-wilderness of the upper regions of New York. Deming was sketching the harsh, cramped life of the North Country in stories less like Holley's than Jewett's and Freeman's—taut, lapidary prose pieces with little of the dialect and none of the humor of Holley's work. It was not until Irving Bacheller recreated the Yankee settlers and their habits of speech and being that the Yorker dialect humor was again heard in fiction. By the time Irving Bacheller's *Eben Holden* was published in 1900, Holley was nearly worn out with the crusading spirit that had fortified Samantha. Bacheller, espousing lesser reforms, picked up the thread of vernacular humor and local color that Holley had spun.

Like most of the women local colorists, Holley treated both the grim difficulty of country life and the hardship of domestic care, but hers was a vision tempered with laughter. Like the others, she also created a fictional community of characters: Jewett sketched Deephaven, Rose Terry Cooke depicted Bassett, and Holley described Jonesville.

Like them she also worked best in the short forms. Her novels are typically sketches hung together on a thin narrative strand that often keep the same characters. Unlike the sentimental writers who viewed hearth and home as an attitude as much as a place, the local colorists and Holley have in mind a very fixed place and a sense of rootedness. Holley's works remain centered at the Allen hearth even when, in the later works, Samantha is launched on her travels and everything is compared to home but suffers in the comparison. Holley and these writers take the sentimental heroine forward, retaining her sense of independence and self-reliance, often to eccentricity, but showing her alone and childless, often telling her story herself.

Holley begins to seem like this heroine come to life. As others have noted, there appears to be a pattern in the lives of popular women writers of the nineteenth century. Many were widows with children or single women with families to support. Disclaiming any literary aspirations, these women had the better excuse for their literary ambitions—writing out of economic necessity. Holley's situation is consistent with the pattern. She came from a modest background and never truly wanted a public life. Her father had belonged to the farming class that was rapidly losing status. Her life was one of retreat as she remained single and celibate, choosing to live in rural New York State most of the time, using her childhood home as a base. She was perhaps uncommonly devoted to her mother. As with many of the other local colorists, she did her best work early in her career and outlived her reputation. Like Whitcher, Holley was a retiring sort whose avoidance of public life incurred the charge of haughtiness. Like Jewett, Holley was accused of being critical of the culture that had nurtured her, a charge that was a misunderstanding of her sympathy as well as her devotion to accuracy of detail. Holley's was a life of ambivalence and conflicting images: public acclaim and private loneliness, urban gentility and upstate rusticity, maidenhood and marriage, poetry and prose, art and life, snow and roses. Her creative reconciliation of these disparities makes hers a life worth scrutiny.

GWENDOLYN B. GWATHMEY (ESSAY DATE 1994)

SOURCE: Gwathmey, Gwendolyn B. "'Who Will Read the Book, Samantha?': Marietta Holley and the Nineteenth-Century Reading Public." *Studies in American Humor* 3, no. 1 (1994): 28-50.

In the following essay, Gwathmey investigates the popularity of Holley's writing on contemporary audiences.

One reviewer writing for *The Critic* in February, 1886, wrote patronizingly of Marietta Holley's humor that "a little of it is really amusing" but that "it is, after all, the kind of humor which is 'popular,' though not destined to be immortal." That reviewer, however, did not bargain on the feminist critics of the late 20th century who, in their quest to recover "lost" women writers, have unearthed Marietta Holley and given her a second chance at immortality.

Marietta Holley was born in 1836 in Jefferson County, New York, where she lived all her life.[1] Although she began by publishing sentimental verses in local newspapers, she became famous for her humorous dialect sketches which featured an overweight, middle-aged, rustic housewife named

Samantha Allen. Samantha, American humor's first "funny female," was an outspoken advocate for women's rights, and it is upon her remarkable combination of politics and humor that Holley's modern reputation is based.[2] Yet feminist critics who have appropriated Holley and her writings have not offered a complete picture of what Samantha meant to her 19th century reading public. Without setting myself in opposition to these critics, I want to raise a series of historical questions designed to complicate the Marietta Holley that they have reconstructed. What was it that made her so popular? How did her readers respond to her use of dialect? How can we understand her appeal to a vast public despite reviews which were repeatedly and increasingly condescending? How does she speak to the larger issue of sentimentality in 19th century women's fiction? In short, what can we learn about 19th century readers and reading practices from Marietta Holley's work?

Holley's popularity was phenomenal. An oft-quoted review in *The Critic* suggests that "As 'Josiah Allen's Wife,' she has entertained as large an audience, I should say, as has been entertained by the humor of Mark Twain."[3] The first printings of her early books sold out rapidly; some were even translated into French. *Samantha at Saratoga* was the year's best-seller in 1887 (Winter, 6). Funk and Wagnall's had so much confidence in Samantha's popularity that they offered Holley an advance of $14,000 in 1893 for *Samantha at the World's Fair* (Winter, 3). In New York and Chicago, Betsey Bobbet clubs sprang up where friends would read aloud chapters from the Samantha books, sometimes acting out the parts dramatically (Winter, 68). In short, Samantha's name was a household word in 19th century America (Williams, 16).

It is no wonder that feminists of Holley's own time such as Susan B. Anthony and Frances Willard recognized Samantha's propaganda value: not only did she write about women's rights, temperance, and the sexual double standard, she also had a ready-made, adoring public. Anthony and Willard wooed Holley assiduously. Willard asked her to be a delegate at the 1877 Woman's Christian Temperance Union convention; Anthony invited her to the 1878 National Woman Suffrage Association convention. Holley, however, despite her admiration for these women and her sympathy for their causes, consistently declined their invitations to appear in public, even when Anthony suggested that she go incognito.[4]

For many of the same reasons that Samantha appealed to early feminists, she was an exciting

"find" for critics as feminist energies swept the academy in the 1980s. But like Anthony and Willard, who pushed Holley to do political work she was unwilling or unable to do, modern critics have had a tendency to push her too hard, to try to make her do more political work than is convincing. The argument has been made, for instance, that 19th century women humorists such as Holley were deliberately debunking the sentimental strain that dominated women's literature of the period.[5] According to this argument, women humorists were in conscious and deliberate rebellion against the sentimentality that dominated writing by and for women at the time—and they used wit as "an antidote to the pious religiosity of the sentimental novel and poem" (Walker, 7).

The difficulty with this argument is that a number of 19th century women humorists wrote not only humor, but a great deal of sentimental prose as well. Holley herself regularly combined both styles within a single book. Although modern feminist critics have privileged the humorous Holley over the sentimental one, preferring to think of the latter as deliberately satirical and flagrantly insincere, this reading of Holley's work is incomplete. It is impossible to ignore the fact that much of her sentimental prose, overblown though it may seem to our sensibilities, elaborates upon the evils of alcohol—a subject that was as dear to Holley's heart as that of women's suffrage.

In *Sweet Cicely*, the young heroine's husband degenerates steadily as a result of his drinking habit. Eventually he gets into a barroom brawl and murders a man; he dies in the State prison where he awaits his trial. Holley describes the way in which Cicely, left with a four year old son, responds to these events:

> She rousted up out of her deathly weakness and heart-broken, stunted calm,—for such it seemed to be for the first two or three years after her husband's death. She seemed to make an effort almost like that of a dead man throwin' off the icy stupor of death, and risin' up with numbed limbs, and shakin' off the death-robes, and livin' agin. She rousted up with jest such a effort, so it seemed, for the boy's sake. . . .

> It wus jest like death for her to face the curius gaze of the world again; for, like a wounded animal, she had wanted to crawl away, and hide her cruel woe and disgrace in some sheltered spot, away from the sharp-sot eyes of the babblin' world.

> But she endured it. She came out of her quiet home, where her heart had bled in secret; she came out into society again; and she did every thing she could, in her gentle, quiet way. She joined temperance societies,—helped push 'em

forward with her money and her influence. With other white-souled wimmen, gentle and refined as she was, she went into rough bar-rooms, and knelt on their floors, and prayed what her sad heart wus full of,—for pity and mercy for her boy, and other mothers' boys,—prayed with that fellowship of suffering that made her sweet voice as pathetic as tears, and patheticker, so I have been told.

(*Cicely*, 24-5)[6]

This is undeniably "sentimental" prose of the kind that modern taste deplores—pious and overblown. Yet there is no hint of insincerity here; there is no indication of sarcasm, condescension, or parody. There is no rhetorical fillip that would send the reader the signal to read this passage as a veiled attack on sentimental prose. It doesn't make sense to suppose that Holley intends mockery when she is expounding one of her most pressing themes.

Critics who have read Holley and other 19th century women writers as attacking the sentimental tradition are making the implicit claim that sentimentalism (as we conceive of it now) and feminism are incompatible, that a feminist writer of the late 19th century could not, by definition, also be a sentimental writer.[7] In fact, however, Holley resists this reading; she cries out to be read as both a sentimental writer *and* a feminist.

It is easy for modern readers to overlook the sentimental side of Holley because of the way in which Holley has been reconstituted by critics. She exists for us today simply as a woman humorist who wrote on "the woman question."[8] The handful of critical articles that have been written about Holley tend to focus on her as a humorist.[9] Jane Curry, a leading Holley scholar, published a 1983 collection entitled **Samantha Rastles the Woman Question** which serves as a sort of Holley's Greatest Hits. It consists of excerpts from fewer than half of the twenty-five books Holley published; these excerpts are all, of course, related to "the woman question," and they are all humorous.[10]

Yet if this picture is the only one we have of Holley's work, how are we to understand some of the 19th century reviews which respond to Holley not on the basis of her humor, but rather on the basis of her sentimentality? In reviewing **Miss Richard's Boy, and Other Stories** in 1883, for instance, (one of the books from which Curry did not select excerpts), the *Independent*'s reviewer writes: "The tone of the stories is high and pure. There is, perhaps, too much of sentiment and sensation in them for the best taste, and they do not display original imaginative power" (Jan. 1883). In a long review of **Samantha in Europe**

(another volume ignored by Curry), editor B. O. Flower of *The Arena* writes with high praise of the "common-sense philosophy and the high religious and ethical teachings" which Holley "clothes in such simple, quaint, and humorous garb." Flower considers the book "peculiarly interesting" by virtue of the "high ethical teachings which are woven as threads of gold throughout the web and woof of the narrative" (Mar. 1896). Obviously this is a completely different Holley from the one Curry's collection represents.

My point is obvious: modern critics have reconstructed Marietta Holley to suit their own political agendas. The Holley that we have today is not the same Holley that 19th century audiences loved so much. While some critics insist that writers such as Holley used humor to bash the stereotype of the sentimental woman writer, the evidence suggests that it isn't quite that simple. For instance, in a biographical note on Holley in one anthology of American women's humor, there is a throwaway sentence that tells us: "In her youth, Holley wrote pious, sentimental poetry, as does Samantha's fictional adversary Betsey Bobbet, and throughout her life considered her poetry to be more important than the 'Samantha' books for which she became widely known" (Walker & Dresner, 99). Holley was not unequivocally bashing the sentimental writings that characterize her era; in fact, she produced many of those pieces herself—and was *proud* of them.

It is important to keep in mind that late 20th century readers consider sentimentality a bad thing; we are uncomfortable with sentiment itself—which we define as emotional, spiritual, or pious expressions offered with an unacceptable degree of sincerity. Although this sort of "sentimentality" is something we wish to avoid at all costs, the readers and writers of the 19th century viewed it differently. They were quite comfortable with religious, moralistic language; they valued "Truth" and sound teaching. Didacticism was an acceptable part of their fictional tradition.

The words "sentiment" and "sentimentality" have oscillated historically between positive and negative connotations. The OED defines "sentiment" as "Refined and tender emotion; exercise or manifestation of 'sensibility'; emotional reflection or meditation; appeal to the tender emotions in literature or art. Now chiefly in derisive use, conveying imputation of either insincerity or mawkishness." In other words, there was a point in time when "sentiment" was a good thing, but a shift occurred during the 19th century and the words "sentiment" and "sentimentality" began to carry negative overtones. Such a shift would have been gradual, of course, which means that there must have been a significant period of time during which the word "sentiment" held a double currency in the culture; there would have been "good" and "bad" types of sentiment.[11] It is precisely during this period that Holley was writing; this is also the period denominated by historians as the heyday of women's "sentimental" fiction.

The confusion surrounding the use and meanings of these terms leads critics into trouble when they argue that Holley and other 19th century women humorists were attacking "sentimentality." Rather, Holley practiced what she considered to be "good" sentimentality and attacked what she considered to be "bad." It was not the presence of emotion and feeling, per se, that bothered Holley in the literature being produced by her contemporaries. On the contrary, sincere emotion was something she approved and incorporated freely into her own work. Addiction to "superficial emotion," however, Holley did not approve. She completely rejects the standard romantic plot of 19th century "sentimental" fiction. This plot typically features a young girl, often orphaned, who weathers the vicissitudes of fortune only to win the heart and hand of the romantic hero at the end of the novel. Holley would have none of that. She created a character who is middle-aged and fat, and who has been married so many years that she is long past the stage of harboring any romantic illusions about what marriage means.

It is from her platform of clear-sightedness with respect to the institution of marriage that Samantha critiques the notorious Betsey Bobbet, queen of "insincerity and mawkishness." Betsey Bobbet is "awful sentimental, I have seen a good many that had it bad, but of all the sentimental creeters I ever did see Betsey Bobbet is the sentimentalist, you couldn't squeeze a laugh out of her with a cheeze press" (Curry, 69). The phrase "had it bad" indicates that Betsey's sentimentalism is a disease, that she is, indeed, "addicted to indulgence in superficial emotion." She is also a great one for hypocrisy and insincerity, as the following description makes clear:

> She thinks she talks dreadful polite and proper, she says "I was cameing" instead of "I was coming," and "I have saw" instead of "I have seen," and "papah" for paper, and "deah" for dear. I don't know much about grammer, but common sense goes a good ways. She writes the poetry for the Jonesville Augur, or "Augah," as she calls it. She used to write for the opposition paper, the

Jonesville Gimlet, but the editer of the Augur, a long haired chap, who moved into Jonesville a few months ago, lost his wife soon after he come there, and sense that she has turned Dimocrat, and writes for his paper stiddy.

(Curry, 70)

Betsey, ever in search of a husband, has changed her party allegiance simply in order to gain access to the new widower. Samantha despises Betsey for her airs, for her disingenuous behavior, and, it is true, for her very bad poetry, which is always aimed at a male target—the latest widower in town. What disgusts Samantha here is sentimentality at its worst: manipulativeness and indirection—the absence of straightforwardness and "common sense."[12]

Her instinct for the straightforwardness and no-nonsense made Samantha Allen appealing; her anti-sentimental persona played into a popular tradition in American humor—that of the "crackerbox philosopher"—in which a sage but homely figure delivers wisdom on a variety of subjects but always with the salt of "common sense."[13] Just as Holley deliberately placed herself in the tradition of the "crackerbox philosopher," so she placed herself squarely into the tradition established by the Literary Comedians. She was almost certainly familiar not only with Frances Whitcher's *Widow Bedott Papers*, but also with the writings of the Literary Comedians Artemus Ward, Josh Billings, and Petroleum V. Nasby, all of whose writings appeared in excerpted form in the local newspapers. Holley used many of the stylistic tools standardized by the Literary Comedians and Funny Fellows: she misquotes the Bible and the classics; she uses dialect, puns, ridiculous catalogues, bad grammar, mixed metaphors, anticlimax, and cacography (Winter, 43-44).

Strategically, Holley made the right move when she cast Samantha as a rustic philosopher and country bumpkin; the popular persona softened the impact of the fact that Samantha was not only a woman, but an outspoken feminist. Because Samantha was an unthreatening figure, even the resistant reader would have been more inclined to give ear to her message. More subtly still, Holley appropriated the appeal of the anti-intellectual tradition in American humor in a new way; the 19th century reader identified with Samantha's anti-intellectualism, only to find that this identification entailed a simultaneous alignment with Samantha's feminism. But such speculation about Holley's strategy in creating Samantha must give way to some biographical information.

FROM THE AUTHOR

A CONVERSATION BETWEEN JOSIAH ALLEN AND SAMANTHA ALLEN ON A WOMAN'S PLACE

He looked almost mortified, but still he murmured as if mechanically. "It's the wimmen's place to marry and not to vote."

"Josiah Allen," says I, "Anybody would think to hear you talk that a woman couldn't do but just one of the two things any way—marry or vote, and had got to take her choice of the two at the pint of the bayouet. And anybody would think to hear you go on, that if women could live in any other way, she wouldn't be married, and you couldn't get her to." Says I looking at him shrewdly, "if marryin' is such a dreadful nice thing for wimmen I don't see what you are afraid of. You men act kinder guilty about it, and I don't wonder at it, for take a bad husband and there ain't no kind of slavery to be compared to wife slavery."

Holley, Marietta. Excerpt from "A Allegory on Wimmen's Rights." In her *My Opinions and Betsey Bobbet's*. Toronto: Robertson's Cheap Series, 1877.

According to Kate Winter, her biographer, Holley believed herself to be most talented as a writer of poetry. When she first sought publication in book form, she sent a variety of materials—poetry, a sentimental story, and a sketch in dialect by "Josiah Allen's Wife"—to Elisha Bliss, head of the American Publishing Company (Bliss was already publishing Mark Twain, Josh Billings, and Bret Harte). Bliss responded immediately. He wanted more of Samantha. This was a disappointment to Holley, who expostulated that she had much rather write in her serious, more "literary" style. Bliss overrode her objections, and her first novel, *My Opinions and Betsey Bobbet's*, was underway (Winter, 40-41). Elisha Bliss knew what the American public wanted to read.

Holley's preference for her poetry and for her more serious style of writing remained with her, and after her reputation was established as a humorist, she would occasionally exploit it for the sake of publishing work more to her own taste. Hence such efforts as *Miss Richard's Boy and Other Stories* (1883)—a book of short stories written in the sentimental vein popular in ladies' magazines of the period—and *Poems* (1887), the contents of which would be considered, by today's standards, insipid.[14]

If Holley was not entirely willing to be a dialect humorist, she certainly made the best of her situation. She seems to have used the genre to her advantage in every way, allowing the dialect itself to do some of her political work for her. The dialect made Samantha unthreatening; she was not "superior"—in social or educational status—to any of her readers. If anything, the readers felt themselves to be "above" Samantha. Holley was exploiting a dynamic reminiscent of Shakespeare's fools—out of the mouth of the rustic comes wisdom. Dialect was critical to the creation of this unpretentious, uneducated, but truth-seeing philosopher.

Richard Brodhead argues that reading in late 19th century America was a practice "strongly conjoined with experiential acquisitiveness, a disposition with two parts: a habit of assuming that others are more fully alive than oneself and a presumption that there is no reason not to appropriate that life for oneself" (205). Entertainment, therefore, is understood as an almost parasitic relationship whereby the reader gains pleasure by appropriating the experience of someone in the text. Regionalism, with its rustic characters and dialect, plays into this economy perfectly. Brodhead defines regionalism as

> the literature that posits that someone else's way of living and talking is more "colorful" than one's own (culturally superior) way, in other words, that a primary vitality absent from the refined is present in the backward, *and* that this other life can be annexed for the cultivated class's leisured recreation, made pleasurably inhabitable in print.
> (205-6)

The fact that the character's life "can be annexed" by the reader and "made pleasurably inhabitable in print" suggests the psychological process of identification that goes along with reading, and the way in which readers are empowered by their identification with various characters.

Whether or not her use of "colorful" dialect was an actual selling point for Holley, it is unlikely that it deterred readers in the way that such prose might do today. According to Blair and McDavid, dialect humor had been considered "deliciously funny" by readers for much of the 19th century. They give several reasons for this:

During a period when many of the orators and highly admired literati used styles that were particularly elegant and highfalutin, less structured, less ornate, and more earthy writings seemed both refreshingly lifelike and incongruous. It was an age, too, when schoolmarms and dictionary makers were stuffy and stern about spelling, elegant diction, and grammar; therefore, assaults on all three seemed both naughty and funny. Sectional and class differences were more marked, important, and interesting then than they now are. Readers evidently were familiar with unlearned speech and more tolerant and comfortable with it than many of us are today. And people felt no need, it seems, to hurry their fireside reading.

(Blair & McDavid, xxiii)

Holley's use of dialect placed her into a well-known (and beloved) tradition. And given her evident distaste for things "elegant and highfalutin" in general, it is no surprise that she found herself using dialect; clearly she and her readers still enjoyed bursting the balloons of stuffiness.[15]

The fact that Holley was a dialect humorist does not fully account for the tremendous popularity of her well-loved Samantha. Kate Winter suggests that part of her appeal lay in her middle-of-the-road position in all things, even the feminist cause in which she so firmly believed: "her conservatism and pragmatism based on a sense of justice and expediency won audiences that would otherwise be antagonistic to her feminist ideals" (51). Jane Curry agrees that "Samantha's constant stance is that of 'megumness' ['mediumness']," that she always makes a point of seeing all sides of a question. She criticizes both the ladies of fashion, with their unhealthy corsets, and also the immodest women who have taken to wearing trousers in public (Curry, 6).

Winter gives a number of other suggestions about Samantha's popularity. For a postwar audience, her "ardent nativism" seemed a healing influence after the sectionalism and divisiveness of the Civil War. Winter also cites Samantha's implacable logic, her eagerness to note the accomplishments of women in all arenas, and her "hardy self-confidence, independence, and intellectual vigor" which "belied the prevailing notion that women were weak, passive, mindless, and powerless" (51). Holley also took advantage of the popularity of the travel writing genre; Samantha went to the St. Louis Exposition, to Europe, to the World's Fair, and to Coney Island, among other places.[16] Most important, though, is the intangible fact that Samantha was an extremely appealing point of identification for many women readers. She is the voice in the text that always has the last word. She wins the arguments. It is always Josiah who, subdued by Samantha's logic, leaves the room.

II.

All of this leads to the question of Holley's popularity. Trying to establish what makes a given writer popular is a difficult task, even more difficult when that writer lived and wrote a hundred years ago. We are really asking "Who read this writer, and *how* was she read?" The answer is hard to find. The most obvious source of information on how a 19th century writer was read lies in contemporary reviews, but this source is problematic, particularly in the case of a "popular" writer like Holley. The first problem is simply that reviews of her work are hard to find. She was triply marginalized: a woman writer, a humorist, and a writer whose books were sold by subscription (which was considered to be a second-class form of publication).[17] Reviews of her work, when they do appear, tend to be extremely short—notices, rather than real reviews.

But the bigger problem for the 20th century critic exploring how Holley was received by her contemporaries is that there is a tremendous discrepancy between Holley's critical reception and her public one. Despite the fact that her books sold phenomenally well for such a long period of time, her reviewers, on the whole, tended to be either openly critical, or condescendingly tolerant of Holley: "Miss Holley's humor is homely but none the less attractive to thousands of readers" (*Critic* Jan. 1905); "Three hundred and eighty-one pages (pictures included) are comprised within the covers of this handsomely made book. At least a hundred pages too many, for, however amusing the efforts and adventures of the renowned Samantha may be, she becomes wearisome long enough before the last chapter is reached" (*Lit. World* Mar. 1886). Former readers may expect of the new book at hand "only a large amount of somewhat heterogeneous social and political satire, sometimes droll and sometimes dull, sometimes very shrewd and to the point, and sometimes dogmatic and shallow, sometimes moderate and true, and sometimes burlesqued beyond all judgment: linked together by the faintest possible thread of narrative" (*Overland* Mar. 1886). One reviewer refers to Holley's Samantha sketches as "pious little stories" (*Critic* Sep. 1906). Another speaks of Holley's "satire and weakly witty garrulity, which has flowed on so unchangingly out of the pages of *Peterson's Magazine* down to the present" (*Independent* Jan. 1905). These samples show the general tone taken toward Holley's work by professional critics.[18] Despite their disdain, however, Holley's popularity persisted.

Perhaps the last review cited offers us another place to turn in trying to understand how Holley was read and understood in her own day. As that reviewer reminds us, her fiction was published first (and often thereafter) in *Peterson's Magazine*. She also published in *Harper's, Godey's Lady's Book, Lippincott's, Ladies Home Journal,* and other magazines catering primarily to female audiences.[19]

Peterson's Magazine was the most popular women's magazine in America for over two decades after the Civil War (Mott, 309). It had billed itself from its beginning as a magazine "edited and written both by and for women" (although in reality its owner, Charles J. Peterson, was the editor) and announced proudly that "We shall rely chiefly, if not altogether, on female pens."[20] According to Mott's *History of American Magazines, Peterson's* contained a combination of fashions and "light literature." The stories and illustrations were all very similar, and, to the 20th century mind, very "sentimental." Here is Mott's summary paragraph in his chapter on *Peterson's*:

> Though not of any considerable literary importance, *Peterson's Magazine* was for some two decades the most popular women's magazine in America. Its hand-colored fashion plates were equal to those of *Godey's*. When the pages of its earlier volumes are opened today to its tender sentimentalism of picture, story, and poem, it brings us, in spite of dust and broken bindings, the authentic atmosphere of a phase of early Victorianism which is not without charm.
>
> (Mott, 311)[21]

Mott considers Holley's Samantha stories to have offered "some relief from treacle," but he neglects to mention that Holley also published sentimental poetry and stories in *Peterson's*.[22]

If we accept *Peterson's* as fairly typical of the type of magazine in which Holley published, what conclusions can we draw about her readers? Mott refers to its reflecting a "phase of early Victorianism"; perhaps this idea accounts for what seems to be a very conservative strain in such magazines. In them, the "cult of true womanhood" is continually reinforced. True femininity is defined in terms of domesticity. Woman's sphere is the home; her expressive realm is that of emotion.[23]

Surprisingly, the outspoken Samantha, with her explicit feminist sympathies, fits rather well into the world of sentimental ladies' magazine fiction. In fact, Samantha affirms the values espoused by these magazines. One way Holley achieves this

compatability is by using a strategic pseudonym. Though Samantha is the protagonist and the narrator of the sketches, the pseudonym Holley chooses is "Josiah Allen's Wife." By presenting herself as a wife, first and foremost, Samantha distances herself somewhat from her own feminist agenda. Holley eventually admitted that she chose the pseudonym very deliberately: "probably I thought it would soften somewhat the edge of unwelcome argument to have the writer meekly claim to be the wife of Josiah Allen and so stand in the shadow of a man's personality."[24]

Samantha depicts herself as very much immersed in the daily details of a domestic existence. She never indicates that she wishes to be anything other than "Josiah's wife."[25] She constantly affirms her love for Josiah (though she frequently accompanies this with the comment that she doesn't know *why* she loves him). She is extremely active in her church and community. In short, she represents Holley's suggestion that the entire domestic superstructure of America would not collapse if women should be given the right to vote. Undoubtedly this reassurance would have contributed to her popularity among a fairly conservative female audience.

At precisely the same moments that Samantha locates herself most distinctly in the domestic sphere, however, we see hints of a subversive agenda. She outspokenly criticizes, for instance, the ideology that denominates woman the "angel in the house." When Josiah insists that women should be on a pedestal, Samantha refuses. Being up on a pedestal sounds nice, she says, but it is too "tuckerin" for women:

> How under the sun can I or any other woman be up on a pedestal and do our own housework, cookin', washin' dishes, sweepin', moppin', cleanin' lamps, blackin' stoves, washin', ironin', makin' beds, quiltin' bed quilts, gittin' three meals a day, day after day, biled dinners and bag puddin's and mince pies and things, to say nothin' of custard and pumpkin pies that will slop over on the level, do the best you can; how could you keep 'em inside the crust histin' yourself up and down?
>
> (Curry, 45)

This relentless catalogue of her chores continues for two more full paragraphs as Samantha highlights the incongruity inherent in Josiah's expectation that a woman should both grace her pedestal *and* get her housework done.

These catalogues (which occur elsewhere in her writing) presented an interesting and complex reading opportunity for Holley's 19th century readers. In such paragraphs, readers who were happy with the notion that woman's sphere was the home could find no explicit resentment or dissatisfaction in Samantha with regard to her domestic duties. Yet readers who were inclined to resent the narrowness of woman's sphere might pick up on the weight of three such paragraphs; they might read this passage as a covert critique of the status quo.

Ann Douglas, in her book *The Feminization of American Culture,* writes of a 19th century female educator and editor named Harriet Farley who offers an explicit rationale for such conservatism as we see in Holley:

> "To convince people," Farley explained, "we must gain access to them": to do this, we cannot assault them with opinions contrary to their own. We cannot alarm them by revealing the deprivation which could suggest our rage, and their danger. We must sugarcoat the proverbial pill. In an immensely telling, if trite phrase, Farley summed up her doctrine: we must "do good by stealth." . . . Farley was advocating the decorous deviousness which was the presiding policy in Sarah Hale's *Godey's Lady's Book,* from which ladies learned to cajole as well as obey their superiors, or in Catharine Beecher's Hartford Female Seminary, where girls were instructed always to "move in curves."
>
> (Douglas, 71)

Although Farley was writing in connection with labor reform, it seems to me that the strategy she outlines is precisely that which Holley applies. Kate Winter disagrees, arguing that Holley refused the strategy of Beecher and Farley by making her satirical attacks "open and direct" (55). But while it is true that Holley was outspoken, she carefully created a non-threatening protagonist to "gain access" to her audience without alienating them; she was carefully cushioning her attack. Her great popularity reflects the palatability of Holley's "sugarcoated" pills.

III.

In her 1887 novel ***Sweet Cicely,*** Holley designs an interesting episode. Josiah receives an unexpected letter which is addressed in such poor handwriting that, according to Josiah, "the postmaster had a awful time a tryin' to make out who it was to. I should think, by his tell, it wus the dumbest writin' that ever wus seen. I should think, by his tell, it went ahead of yourn" (*Cicely,* 92).[26] When Josiah opens the letter, he finds that the writing inside matches that on the envelope. He stares at it for a bit, then Samantha asks him who sent it.

He determines that the letter comes from the headquarters of the Railroad Company. He tells Samantha:

> "As near as I can make out, it is a free pass for me to ride on the railroad."
>
> Says I, "Why, that can't be, Josiah Allen. Why should they give you a free pass?"
>
> "I don't know," says he. "But I know it is one. The more I look at it," says he, growin' excited over it,—"the more I look at it, the plainer I can see it. It is a free pass."

Samantha doesn't believe it for a minute, and Josiah throws the letter into her lap so that she can see for herself:

> I looked at it close and sever, but not one word could I make out, only I thought I could partly make out the word "remove," and along down the sheet the word "place," and there was one word that did look like "free." And Josiah jumped at them words; and says he,—
>
> "It means, you know, the pass reads like this, for me to remove myself from place to place, free. Don't you see through it?" says he.

Josiah decides to put his pass to the test, and he spends the next year riding the rails for free, visiting family in various places, and thoroughly enjoying his sense of importance. As Josiah reads the pass, it is due to expire on April 4, so he decides to write and get it renewed. An answer comes by return mail, and it is written in a hand easily read:

> It seemed there wus a mistake. It wuzn't a free pass, it wus a order for Josiah Allen to remove a pig-pen from his place on the railroad-track within three days.
>
> There it wuz, a order to remove a nuisence; and Josiah Allen had been a ridin' on it for a year, with pride in his mean, and haughtiness in his demeanor.

This incident has a lot to say about the perils and pitfalls of reading and interpreting texts. The illegible handwriting suggests the many possibilities for obfuscation and ambiguity that are inherent in any written text. Interpretation is a much more complicated process even than deciphering bad handwriting. Josiah finds three "key words" in the text. He fastens onto them; they suit his needs. He then creates a context for these three key words—he virtually rewrites the text. This rewriting process is essential to the reading/interpretation process itself.[27] Readers fasten onto bits and pieces of a text that are appealing and useful to them. They then recreate the text for themselves. Hence, each reader reads a "different" text. In fact, Holley has provided a useful paradigm for the reading process in general. As readers, we are all like Josiah. Our interpretations tend to reflect our desires; we are prone to read into a text exactly what we wish to find there; we construct meanings that suit our purposes and make us happy. This process is what makes reading satisfying to us.

Holley's recognition of the slipperiness of reading and interpretation reflects the characteristic of her own books that makes them most remarkable—they were (and are) open to widely varied interpretations depending upon the agenda of the particular reader. Holley's books offered multiple points of identification for a wide range of 19th century readers, and by gathering for herself such a varied audience, she assured herself of success. Winter describes *Sweet Cicely* as "one of her strongest works, showing Holley at the peak of her ability to handle the rustic humor, the temperance genre, and the sentimental domestic novel all at once in an almost seamless narrative" (Winter 91). In other words, Holley could do it all—travel narrative, sentimental prose, poetry, rustic humor—even within the covers of a single book. I suspect that it is precisely this protean quality of her books that made them so popular. Here was the proverbial "something for everyone."

In the "Prefais" to her first book **My Opinions and Betsey Bobbet's,** Holley sketches a conversation between Samantha and Josiah in which Samantha announces her intention to "rite a book" and Josiah repeatedly asks the annoying (and unsettling) question, "Who will read the book Samantha?" Samantha admits that this question fills her with "agonizin' aprefension," but she refuses to be talked out of the project. Josiah repeats the insidious question even in his sleep: "Who will read the book?" When Samantha pokes him to wake him up, he mutters "I wont pay out 1 cent of my money to hire any body to read it." Recognizing the petty nature of Josiah's fear (he doesn't *care* if no one reads the book; he just wants to avoid financial involvement), Samantha says:

> I pitied him, for I was afraid it would end in the Nite Mair, and I waked him up, and promised him then and there, that I never would ask him to pay out 1 cent to hire any body 2 read it. He has perfect konfidence in me and he brightened up and haint never said a word sense against the idee, and that is the way this book came to be rote.
>
> (**My Opinions**, vii)

The incredible anxiety that fills this "Prefais" is not simply the fear that no one will *like* her book. Samantha's (read Holley's) fear is that no

one will even *read* it. Perhaps her bravest act as a woman writer was to write the book despite her doubt. Unable to imagine a community of readers for her book, she wrote it anyway. And once the book was "rote" of course, she didn't have to hire any readers. They paid her.

Notes

1. For basic biographical details on Holley see Jane Curry's entry in the *Dictionary of Literary Biography.* Kate Winter has written a full biography, *Marietta Holley: Life with "Josiah Allen's Wife".*

2. The postwar humorists had been denominated Funny Fellows by the press, a label sometimes rendered "Phunny Phellows" to reflect their stylistic trait of abominable spelling. See Blair and McDavid, eds., *The Mirth of a Nation: America's Great Dialect Humor* (Minneapolis: U of Minnesota P, 1983), pp. xviii-xix. Blair modifies the label to apply to female humorists; see his *Horse Sense in American Humor* (Chicago: U of Chicago P, 1942), p. 231.

3. *Critic* 46.1 (Jan. 1905):6. Blair judges this to be an overstatement, but he agrees that Holley's popularity was tremendous; see *Horse Sense,* p. 231.

4. Winter and Curry have explained Holley's refusal to attend such conventions as a function of her painful shyness, even reclusiveness.

5. See for instance Nancy Walker, "Wit, Sentimentality, and the Image of Women in the Nineteenth Century," *American Studies* XXII.2: 5-22.

6. Here it is worth quoting a review from *The Athenaeum* 97:50 (10 Jan. 1891): "Afflicting as [Holley] is in her humorous moments, her strivings after pathos—and they are numerous and prolonged—are even more productive of acute mental dyspepsia. . . . The style adopted is a mixture of unbridled dialect and high-falutin' melodrama. Here is one sample: 'She rousted up out of her deathly weakness and heart-broken stunted calm.'"

7. Here we are confronted with a debate which has loomed large in contemporary criticism. The idea that sentimental prose works to undermine the feminist cause has been set forth by Ann Douglas in *The Feminization of American Culture.* The opposite position, that sentimentalism is a strong and valid expression of feminism, has been argued by Jane Tompkins in *Sensational Designs.*

8. She merits a single brief entry in *The Heath Anthology of American Literature,* a representative conversation between her and Josiah about whether or not "wimmen" have any business participating in the 1888 Methodist Conference (Josiah, of course, reminds Samantha that "the word laymen *always* means woman when she can help men in any way, but *not* when he can help her, or in any other sense"). Lauter, Paul, et al., eds., *The Heath Anthology of American Literature* (Lexington: D. C., 1990), p. 758. From Holley's *Samantha Among the Brethren.*

9. See for instance: Melody Graulich, "'Wimmen is my theme, and also Josiah': The Forgotten Humor of Marietta Holley" (*American Transcendental Quarterly* (Summer/Fall 1980); Cheri L. Ross, "Nineteenth-Century American Feminist Humor: Marietta Holley's

Samantha Novels" (*Journal of the Midwest MLA* 22.2 (Fall 1989)); and Patricia Williams, "The Crackerbox Philosopher as Feminist: The Novels of Marietta Holley" (*American Humor: An Interdisciplinary Newsletter* 7.1 (Spring 1980)).

10. Curry also performs a one-woman show of Samantha sketches. The tape of this performance is available, and very funny. The sketches have all been put together around two principles: they must be humorous, and they must relate specifically to "the woman question."

11. I place the terms "good" and "bad" in quotation marks to acknowledge my awareness that they are themselves problematic, contingent terms. I use them simply to schematize the evolution of the terms "sentiment" and "sentimentality." They reflect the distinction suggested by the OED where the phrase "in favourable sense" is opposed to "in derisive use."

12. In the introduction to *Redressing the Balance,* Walker and Dresner recognize Samantha's role clearly: "Like Jonathan Slick, the 'wise fool' figure of Ann Stephens's work, and the popular personae of early nineteenth-century "Down East" humor, Samantha exposes pretentiousness and hypocrisy through her ability to see and call a spade a spade" (Walker and Dresner, xxix).

13. See Williams, "The Crackerbox Philosopher as Feminist" and Walter Blair, *Horse Sense.* Blair writes: "To our general way of thinking, horse sense is the same thing as common sense, homespun philosophy, pawkiness, crackerbox philosophy, gumption, or mother-wit, and it is, therefore, permissible to use these terms interchangeably" (vi). The tradition of horse sense in American humor, according to Blair, starts with Ben Franklin and includes the Literary Comedians of the 19th century (Josh Billings, Artemus Ward, Jack Downing, etc.), Mark Twain, and figures like Will Rogers and James Thurber in the 20th century. Blair, by including Holley in his 1942 anthology, gave her a respectable place in the canon of American humor. After this time, she received little critical notice until her "rediscovery" by feminist critics in the 80s.

14. Winter suggests that Holley hoped finally "to find recognition for the work that she considered to be the most worthy" but that the volume "was mainly a curiosity to her reading public." See pp. 40-41.

15. There are some reviewers who register their annoyance with Holley's use of cacography. One reviewer of *Sweet Cicely* (who finds the book "wearisome" on the whole), remarks that "the 'fonetic' spelling lost its novelty long ago" (*Literary World* 17:102-103, 20 Mar. 1886). Another critic calls Holley's spelling "bewilderingly phonetic" (*Dial* 47: 464. Dec 1, 1909).

16. In fact, Samantha went to a lot of places that Holley had never been. A great deal of her travel writing was based strictly on thorough research. See Curry, *DLB* [*Dictionary of Literary Biography*], p. 207 and Winter, p. 62.

17. I am indebted to Professor Louis Budd for this insight, and for his assistance in thinking through the problems that arise in turning to book reviews as a source of information about 19th-century reading practices. For details on the process of selling by subscription, see James D. Hart, *The Popular Book,* pp. 150-153, and Mott, *Golden Multitudes,* pp. 155-158. Blair and Mc-

David contrast the "issuers of subscription books" to "reputable publishers" (p. xx).

18. Professor Budd points to the fact that critics during this period were developing a sense of professionalism which may have encouraged this patronizing, cynical tone. It is also important to remember that critics read with very different agendas than the average reader. The professional critic was reading very fast (and not for pleasure) and was looking for something to *say* about a book.

19. The fact that many of her books were serialized in these magazines may account for their episodic nature. See Winter, p. 48.

20. Mott p. 307. Mott cites *Ladies National Magazine,* III, 128 (April, 1843). The publication was not called *Peterson's Magazine* until 1848.

21. Note the trivialization of women's writing for women that is implicit in Mott's opening clause here.

22. Kate Winter notes that Holley's first publication in *Peterson's* was a poem entitled "The Haunted Castle" (Winter, p. 38). It is true that because the public liked Samantha so much, Holley found herself selling more and more "Samantha" stories; her market forced her to set aside her beloved poetry.

23. It would be interesting to consider the question of whether the contents of these women's magazines dictated, or were dictated by, women's tastes.

24. Quoted in Winter, pp. 38-39. From Holley, "How I Wrote My First Books," *Harper's Bazaar* (September 1911), p. 404.

25. It wasn't until her fourth book (*My Wayward Pardner, or, My Trials with Josiah, America, the Widow Bump, and Etcetery*) came out in 1880 that Holley's own name appeared on the title page. Here, under the byline "Josiah Allen's Wife," was a parenthesis in which the name "Marietta Holley" appeared in small type. See Winter, p. 69.

26. According to Winter, Holley herself had handwriting that was virtually illegible. See Winter, p. 117.

27. This is, of course, one of the insights of the reader-response theorists.

Works Cited

Blair, Walter. *Horse Sense in American Humor.* Chicago: U of Chicago P, 1942.

Blair, Walter, and Raven I. McDavid, Jr., eds. *The Mirth of a Nation: America's Great Dialect Humor.* Minneapolis: U of Minnesota P, 1983.

Brodhead, Richard. *Cultures of Letters: Scenes of Reading and Writing in Nineteenth-Century America.* Chicago: U of Chicago P, 1993.

Curry, Jane, ed. *Samantha Rastles the Woman Question.* Urbana: U of Illinois P, 1983.

——. "Marietta Holley." *Dictionary of Literary Biography.* Ed. Stanley Trachtenberg. Vol. 11. Detroit: Book Tower, 1982.

Douglas, Ann. *The Feminization of American Culture.* New York: Knopf, 1977.

Flower, B. O. Rev. of *Samantha in Europe,* by Marietta Holley. *Arena* March 1896: 688-89.

Graulich, Melody. "'Wimmen is my theme, and also Josiah': The Forgotten Humor of Marietta Holley." *American Transcendental Quarterly: A Journal of New England Writers* (Summer/Fall 1980): 187-98.

Hart, James D. *The Popular Book: A History of America's Literary Taste.* New York: Oxford UP, 1950.

Holley, Marietta. *My Opinion and Betsey Bobbet's.* Hartford: American Publishing, 1873.

———. *Sweet Cicely.* New York: Funk and Wagnalls, 1887.

Lauter, Paul, et al., eds. *The Heath Anthology of American Literature.* 2 vols. Lexington: D. C. Heath, 1990.

Morris, Linda A. *Women's Humor in the Age of Gentility: The Life and Works of Frances Miriam Whitcher.* Syracuse: Syracuse UP, 1992.

Mott, Frank L. *Golden Multitudes: The Story of Best Sellers in the United States.* New York: Bowker, 1947.

———. *A History of American Magazines.* 4 vols. Cambridge: Harvard UP, 1957.

Oxford English Dictionary. 2nd ed. Oxford: Clarendon P, 1989.

Rollins, Alice W. "Woman's Sense of Humor." *The Critic* 1.13 (29 Mar. 1884): 145-46.

Ross, Cheri L. "Nineteenth-Century American Feminist Humor: Marietta Holley's 'Samantha Novels'." *Journal of the Midwest MLA* 22.2 (Fall 1989): 12-25.

Sanborn, Kate. *The Wit of Women.* New York: Funk and Wagnalls, 1885.

Sewell, David R. *Mark Twain's Languages: Discourse, Dialogue, and Linguistic Variety.* Berkeley: U of California P, 1987.

Rev. of *Around the World with Josiah Allen's Wife,* by Marietta Holley. *Critic* Dec. 1905: 580.

Rev. of *Around the World with Josiah Allen's Wife,* by Marietta Holley. *New York Times Saturday Review* 18 Nov. 1905: 774.

Rev. of *Miss Richards' Boy, and other Stories,* by Marietta Holley. *Independent* 18 Jan. 1883: 12.

Rev. of *Poems,* by Marietta Holley. *New York Tribune* 5 Sept. 1888: 8.

Rev. of *Samantha at the St. Louis Exposition,* by Marietta Holley. *Critic* Jan. 1905: 6.

Rev. of *Samantha at the St. Louis Exposition,* by Marietta Holley. *Independent* 26 Jan. 1905: 212.

Rev. of *Samantha in Europe,* by Marietta Holley. *Chautauquan* 7 March 1896: 767.

Rev. of *Samantha on Children's Rights,* by Marietta Holley. *Dial* 1 Dec. 1909: 464.

Rev. of *Samantha vs. Josiah,* by Marietta Holley. *Critic* Sept. 1906: 286.

Rev. of *Sweet Cicely,* by Marietta Holley. *Athenaeum.* 10 Jan. 1891: 50.

Rev. of *Sweet Cicely,* by Marietta Holley. *Critic* 20 Feb. 1886: 93.

Rev. of *Sweet Cicely,* by Marietta Holley. *Overland Monthly* March 1886: 336.

Rev. of *Sweet Cicely,* by Marietta Holley. *Literary World* 20 March 1886: 102-103.

Walker, Nancy, and Zita Dresner, eds. *Redressing the Balance: American Women's Literary Humor from Colonial Times to the 1980s.* Jackson: UP of Mississippi, 1988.

Walker, Nancy. "Wit, Sentimentality, and the Image of Women in the Nineteenth Century." *American Studies* XXII.2: 5-22.

Williams, Patricia. "The Crackerbox Philosopher as Feminist: The Novels of Marietta Holley." *American Humor: An Interdisciplinary Newsletter* 7:1 (Spring 1980): 16-21.

Winter, Kate. *Marietta Holley: Life with "Josiah Allen's Wife".* Syracuse: Syracuse Univ. P, 1984.

FURTHER READING

Biography

Winter, Kate H. *Marietta Holley: Life with "Josiah Allen's Wife."* Syracuse, N.Y.: Syracuse University Press, 1984, 182 p.

Offers a critical biography that attempts to understand the forces that shaped Holley and her work.

Criticism

Armitage, Shelley. "Marietta Holley: The Humorist as Propagandist." *Rocky Mountain Review of Language and Literature* 34, no. 4 (fall 1980): 193-201.

Analyzes Holley's use of humor, asserting that it exposes and challenges women's ideas about themselves.

Curry, Jane. *Marietta Holley.* New York: Twayne Publishers, 1996, 114 p.

Offers a full-length critical study; includes a detailed biography and chapters on Holley's most important writings.

Ericson, E. E. "The Dialect of Up-State New York: A Study of the Fold-Speech in Two Works of Marietta Holley." *Studies in Philology* 42, no. 3 (July 1945): 690-707.

Provides a linguistic study of Samantha at Saratoga *and* Samantha at the St. Louis Exposition.

Graulich, Melody. "'Wimmen is my theme, and also Josiah': The Forgotten Humor of Marietta Holley." *American Transcendental Quarterly* (summer-fall 1980): 187-97.

Urges renewed critical and popular attention to Holley's fiction.

Morris, Linda A. "Marietta Holley: Feminist Innovator." In *Women Vernacular Humorists in Nineteenth-Century America: Ann Stephens, Francis Whitcher, and Marietta Holley,* pp. 186-225. New York: Garland Publishing, 1988.

Examines Holley's influence on American vernacular humorists and shows how those impacted were informed by her feminist perspective.

Ross, Cheri L. "Nineteenth-Century American Feminist Humor: Marietta Holley's Samantha Novels." *Journal of the Midwest Language Association* 22, no. 2 (fall 1989): 12-25.

Places Holley's fiction within the context of nineteenth-century American humor and examines her work in relation to current feminist humor theory.

Templin, Charlotte. "Marietta Holley and Mark Twain: Cultural-Gender Politics and Literary Reputation." *American Studies* 39, no. 1 (spring 1998): 75-91.

Traces the similarities between the work of Holley and that of Mark Twain, outlining the reasons for their disparate literary reputations.

Walker, Nancy. "Wit-Sentimentality, and the Image of Women in the Nineteenth Century." *American Studies* 22, no. 2 (1981): 5-22.

Includes a discussion of Holley as a feminist writer who used humor to attack the sentimental tradition.

Winter, Kate. "Marietta Holley, 'Josiah Allen's Wife.'" *Legacy* 2, no. 1 (spring 1985): 3-5.

Provides a stylistic overview of Holley's work.

Winter, Kate H. "Marietta Holley (Josiah Allen's Wife) (1836-1926)." In *Nineteenth-Century American Women Writers: A Bio-Critical Sourcebook,* edited by Denise D. Knight, pp. 224-30. Westport, Conn.: Greenwood Press, 1997.

Overview of Holley's life, her major works and themes, and the critical reception of her writing.

OTHER SOURCES FROM GALE:

Additional coverage of Holley's life and career is contained in the following sources published by the Gale Group: *Contemporary Authors,* Vol. 118; *Dictionary of Literary Biography,* Vol. 11; *Literature Resource Center;* and *Twentieth-Century Literary Criticism,* Vol. 99.

HARRIET JACOBS

(1813 - 1897)

(Also wrote under the pseudonym Linda Brent)
American autobiographer.

Jacobs's *Incidents in the Life of a Slave Girl, Written By Herself* (1861), stands out from the male-dominated slave narrative genre in its unique point of view and especially in its focus on the sexual exploitation of the female slave. Soon after the publication of *Incidents*, which Jacobs penned under the pseudonym of Linda Brent, questions arose regarding the text's authenticity. Many believed the book to have been written by its white abolitionist editor, Lydia Maria Child. Doubts about the narrative's veracity and its true author persisted into the twentieth century, and *Incidents* was consequently neglected by historians and critics alike. In 1981, however, Jean Fagan Yellin discovered Jacobs's correspondence with Child, and with another abolitionist friend, Amy Post. The letters, along with the rest of Yellin's research, assured the authenticity of Jacobs's narrative; and since then *Incidents* has received critical attention. A great deal of modern criticism has focused on Jacobs's exploitation of the sentimental domestic genre and on the differences between Jacobs's work and slave narratives such as Frederick Douglass's *Narrative of Frederick Douglass, an American Slave*. Feminist scholars have also explored Jacobs's notions of selfhood and womanhood, her treatment of the female body, and the impact of her work on the genre of the slave narrative.

BIOGRAPHICAL INFORMATION

Jacobs was born a slave in North Carolina around 1813. Her parents were both slaves, but her grandmother had been emancipated and owned her own home, earning a living as a baker. When Jacobs was six years old, her mother died, and she was sent to the home of her mother's mistress, Margaret Horniblow. Horniblow taught Jacobs to read, spell, and sew; she died when Jacobs was eleven or twelve, and willed the young girl to Mary Mathilda Norcom, Horniblow's three-year-old niece. While living in the Norcom household, Jacobs suffered the sexual harassment of Dr. James Norcom, Mary's father and a prominent physician. Dr. Norcom threatened Jacobs with concubinage when she was sixteen years old. Rather than submit to the doctor, Jacobs became the mistress of a white slaveholding neighbor of the Norcoms and soon announced that she was pregnant. She bore two children, both fathered by this white neighbor. At the age of twenty-one, Jacobs ran away, believing that Norcom would see to the children in her absence. In her narrative, Jacobs wrote that at this time she hid for seven years in the attic crawlspace of her grandmother's home, where her children lived unaware of their mother's presence. The children were purchased by their father shortly after Jacobs went into hiding; they were allowed to continue living with their grandmother. Jacobs finally succeeded in fleeing north in 1842. There, she reunited with her children and tried to establish a home for her family. In 1850, the passage of the Fugitive Slave Law, which stated that anyone caught aiding a fugitive slave was subject to punishment, threatened her safety, and Jacobs once again went into hiding. In 1852, her employer, Mrs. Nathaniel Parker Willis, purchased Jacobs for $300 to free her. Soon after, Jacobs was urged by Amy Post to write her life's story, and she spent five years doing so. After trying for three years to get her narrative published, Jacobs finally succeeded in 1861. Throughout the Civil War and Reconstruction, Jacobs and her daughter continued to fight for the rights of African Americans. Jacobs died in 1897.

MAJOR WORKS

Incidents in the Life of a Slave Girl details the horrific experiences endured by Jacobs. In the preface to her book, Jacobs states that her "adventures may seem incredible," but assures readers that her "descriptions fall short of the facts." She describes her life as a slave from her early years, when she did not even know she was a slave, to the violence and exploitation she endured as a teenager at the hands of her master, and finally to her repugnance at the thought of her well-meaning employer purchasing her in order to free her. Although Jacobs wrote *Incidents* in the style of the sentimental novel, she seems to argue against the conception of womanhood that the sentimental novel conventionally upholds. While appealing to a northern, white, female audience at a time when "true womanhood" meant chastity and virtue, Jacobs argues that slavery makes it impossible for a black woman to live a virtuous, chaste life. As she champions some of the conventions of the sentimental genre by emphasizing the primacy and significance of motherhood and domesticity, Jacobs also demonstrates how the institution of slavery threatens and destroys white and black women alike. In this respect, *Incidents* differs markedly from typical, male slave narratives, which emphasize the ways in which slavery destroys masculinity. Nevertheless, a common quality shared by male slave narratives and Jacobs's *Incidents* is the feeling of triumph the writer describes as he or she reclaims a sense of self.

CRITICAL RECEPTION

Incidents received little critical attention until Yellin's research revealed the authenticity of the narrative. This research established Jacobs as the sole author of *Incidents* and clarified Child's limited role as editor. Since then, many critical studies have focused on the way in which *Incidents* exploits the conventions of the domestic literature genre or the slave narrative. Feminist scholars have also been interested in comparing Jacob's female perspective to that of male writers and have also analyzed the treatment and politicization of the female body in her narrative. Other issues that feminist commentators have explored include Jacobs's notion of the self, her exploration of the idea of "true womanhood," her assertion of the black female slave voice, her subversive critique of the domestic genre, and her writing as an act of defiance and liberation.

PRINCIPAL WORKS

Incidents in the Life of a Slave Girl, Written by Herself [as Linda Brent] (autobiography) 1861

PRIMARY SOURCES

HARRIET A. JACOBS (ESSAY DATE 21 JUNE 1853)

SOURCE: Jacobs, Harriet A. "Letter from a Fugitive Slave. Slaves Sold Under Peculiar Circumstances." *The New York Tribune* (21 June 1853): 6.

In the following essay, Jacobs's first publication, the pseudonymous writer presents an account of the violation of her "sister," presenting materials she would use in Incidents in the Life of a Slave Girl.

SIR: Having carefully read your paper for some months I became very much interested in some of the articles and comments written on Mrs. Tyler's Reply to the Ladies of England. Being a slave myself, I could not have felt otherwise. Would that I could write an article worthy of notice in your columns. As I never enjoyed the advantages of an education, therefore I could not study the arts of reading and writing, yet poor as it may be, I had rather give it from my own hand, than have it said that I employed others to do it for me. The truth can never be told so well through the second and third person as from yourself. But I am straying from the question. As Mrs. Tyler and her friend Bhains were so far used up, that he could not explain what those peculiar circumstances were, let one whose peculiar sufferings justifies her in explaining it for Mrs. Tyler.

I was born a slave, reared in the Southern hot-bed until I was the mother of two children, sold at the early age of two and four years old. I have been hunted through all of the Northern States, but no, I will not tell you of my own suffering—no, it would harrow up my soul, and defeat the object that I wish to pursue. Enough—the dregs of that bitter cup have been my bounty for many years.

And as this is the first time that I ever took my pen in hand to make such an attempt, you will not say that it is fiction, for had I the inclination I have neither the brain or talent to write it. But to this very peculiar circumstance under which slaves are sold.

My mother was held as property by a maiden lady; when she marries, my younger sister was in her fourteenth year, whom they took into the family. She was as gentle as she was beautiful. Innocent and guileless child, the light of our desolate hearth! But oh, my heart bleeds to tell you of the misery and degradation she was forced to suffer in slavery. The monster who owned her had no humanity in his soul. The most sincere affection that his heart was capable of, could not make him faithful to his beautiful and wealthy bride the short time of three months, but every stratagem was used to seduce my sister. Mortified and tormented beyond endurance, this child came and threw herself on her mother's bosom, the only place where she could seek refuge from her persecutor; and yet she could not protect her child that she bore into the world. On that bosom with bitter tears she told her troubles, and entreated her mother to save her. And oh, Christian mothers! you that have daughters of your own, can you think of your sable sisters without offering a prayer to that God who created all in their behalf! My poor mother, naturally high-spirited, smarting under what she considered as the wrongs and outrages which her child had to bear, sought her master, entreating him to spare her child. Nothing could exceed his rage at this what he called

impertinence. My mother was dragged to jail, there remained twenty-five days, with Negro traders to come in as they liked to examine her, as she was offered for sale. My sister was told that she must yield, or never expect to see her mother again. There were three younger children; on no other condition could she be restored to them, without the sacrifice of one. That child gave herself up to her master's bidding, to save one that was dearer to her than life itself. And can you, Christian, find it in your heart to despise her? Ah, no! not even Mrs. Tyler; for though we believe that the vanity of a name would lead her to bestow her hand where her heart could never go with it, yet, with all her faults and follies, she is nothing more than a woman. For if her domestic hearth is surrounded with slaves, ere long before this she has opened her eyes to the evils of slavery, and that the mistress as well as the slave must submit to the indignities and vices imposed on them by their lords of body and soul. But to one of those peculiar circumstances.

At fifteen, my sister held to her bosom an innocent offspring of her guilt and misery. In this way she dragged a miserable existence of two years, between the fires of her mistress's jealousy and her master's brutal passion. At seventeen, she gave birth to another helpless infant, heir to all the evils of slavery. Thus life and its sufferings was meted out to her until her twenty-first year. Sorrow and suffering has made its ravages upon her—she was less the object to be desired by the fiend who had crushed her to the earth; and as her children grew, they bore too strong a resemblance to him who desired to give them no other inheritance save Chains and Handcuffs, and in the dead hour of the night, when this young, deserted mother lay with her little ones clinging around her, little dreaming of the dark and inhuman plot that would be carried out into execution before another dawn, and when the sun rose on God's beautiful earth, that broken-hearted mother was far on her way to the capitol of Virginia. That day should have refused her light to so disgraceful and inhuman an act in your boasted country of Liberty. Yet, reader, it is true, those two helpless children were the sons of one of your sainted Members in Congress; that agonized mother, his victim and slave. And where she now is God only knows, who has kept a record on high of all that she has suffered on earth.

And, you would exclaim, Could not the master have been more merciful to his children? God is merciful to all of his children, but it is seldom that a slaveholder has any mercy for hs [sic] slave child. And you will believe it when I tell you that mother and her children were sold to make room for another sister, who was now the age of that mother when she entered the family. And this selling appeased the mistress's wrath, and satisfied her desire for revenge, and made the path more smooth for her young rival at first. For there is a strong rivalry between a handsome mulatto girl and a jealous and faded mistress, and her liege lord sadly neglects his wife or doubles his attentions, to save him being suspected by his wife. Would you not think that Southern Women had cause to despise that Slavery which forces them to bear so much deception practiced by their husbands? Yet all this is true, for a slaveholder seldom takes a white mistress, for she is an expensive commodity, not as submissive as he would like to have her, but more apt to be tyrannical; and when his passion seeks another object, he must leave her in quiet possession of all the gewgaws that she has sold herself for. But not so with his poor slave victim, that he has robbed of everything that can make life desirable; she must be torn from the little that is left to bind her to life, and sold by her seducer and master, caring not where, so that it puts him in possession of enough to purchase another victim. And such are the peculiar circumstances of American Slavery—of all the evils in God's sight to most to be abhorred.

Perhaps while I am writing this you too, dear Emily, may be on your way to the Mississippi River, for those peculiar circumstances occur every day in the midst of my poor oppressed fellow-creatures in bondage. And oh ye Christians, while your arms are extended to receive the oppressed of all nations, while you exert every power of your soul to assist them to raise funds, put weapons in their hands, tell them to return to their own country to slay every foe until they break the accursed yoke from off their necks, not buying and selling this they never do under any circumstances.

And because one friend of a slave has dared to tell of their wrongs you would annihilate her. But in Uncle Tom's Cabin she has not told the half. Would that I had one spark from her store house of genius and talent I would tell you of my own sufferings—I would tell you of wrongs that Hungary has never inflicted, nor England ever dreamed of in this free country where all nations fly for liberty, equal rights and protection under your

stripes and stars. It should be stripes and scars, for they go along with Mrs. Tyler's peculiar circumstances, of which I have told you only one.

A FUGITIVE SLAVE.

TITLE COMMENTARY

Incidents in the Life of a Slave Girl

JOANNE M. BRAXTON (ESSAY DATE SUMMER 1986)

SOURCE: Braxton, Joanne M. "Harriet Jacobs' *Incidents in the Life of a Slave Girl*: The Re-Definition of the Slave Narrative Genre." *The Massachusetts Review* 27, no. 2 (summer 1986): 379-87.

In the following essay, Braxton explores the impact of Jacobs's slave narrative on the male-dominated genre.

"Rise up, ye women that are at ease! Hear my voice, ye careless daughters! Give ear unto my speech."

Isaiah, XXX, original epigram from ***Incidents in the Life of a Slave Girl***

"READER, be assured this narrative is no fiction."
Preface by the Author,
Incidents in the Life of a Slave Girl

I believe, with James Olney, that students of autobiography are themselves vicarious autobiographers, and I know that I read every text through my own experience, as well as that of my mother and my grandmothers.[1] As black American women, we are born into a mystic sisterhood, and we live our lives within a magic circle, a realm of shared language, reference, and allusion within the veil of our blackness and our femaleness.[2] We have been as invisible to the dominant culture as rain; we have been knowers, but we have not been known. This paradox is central to what I suggest we call the Afra-American experience.

It was in the world of Afra-American autobiography that I first met her on the conscious plane, but then I realized that I had known the outraged mother all my life. With her hands on her hips and her head covered with a bandanna, she is the sassiest woman on the face of the earth, and with good reason. She is the mother of Frederick Douglass travelling twelve miles through the darkness to share a morsel of food with her mulatto son and to reassure him that he is somebody's child. She travels twelve miles back again before the dawn. She sacrifices and improvises for the survival of flesh and spirit, and as mother of the race, she is muse to black poets, male and female alike. She is known by many names, the most exalted being "Momma." Implied in all of her actions and fueling her heroic ones is outrage at the abuse of her people and her person.

She must be the core of our black and female experience, this American Amazon of African descent, dwelling in the moral and psychic wilderness of North America. Yet when I surveyed the literature of the critical wilderness proliferated from that moral and psychic one, I found her absent. I imagined our ancestor mothers lost forever in that fearsome place in search of a tradition to claim them.

The treatment of the slave narrative genre has been one of the most skewed in Afro-American literary criticism. It has been almost always the treatment of the narratives of heroic male slaves, not their wives or sisters. By focusing almost exclusively on the narratives of male slaves, critics have left out half the picture.

In general, the purpose of the slave narrative genre is to decry the cruelty and brutality of slavery and to bring about its abolition. In addition, the genre has been defined as possessing certain other characteristics, including a narrator who speaks in a coherent, first person voice, with a range and scope of knowledge like that of an unlettered slave and a narrative movement which progresses from South to North, and culminates in an escape from slavery to a freedom which is both an inner and outer liberation. The prevalent themes of the genre include the deprivation of food, clothing, and shelter, the desire for instruction (frequently for religious instruction, which is thwarted), physical brutality, the corruption of families (usually white), the separation of families (usually black), the exploitation of slave workers and, in some narratives, especially those written by women, abuse of the sexuality and reproductive powers of the slave woman.

The resistance to a gynocritical or gynocentric approach to the slave narrative genre has been dominated by male bias, by linear logic, and by either/or thinking. We have been paralyzed by issues of primacy, and authorship, and by criteria of unity, coherence, completion, and length. Academic systems, which do not value scholarship on black women or reward it, have told us that we are not first, not central, not major, not au-

thentic. The suggestion has been that neither the lives of black women nor the study of our narratives and autobiographies have been legitimate.

I want to supplement the either/or thinking that has limited the consideration of evidence surrounding the narratives of women, and the inclusion of such works in the slave narrative genre. Instead of asking "Is it first? Is it major? Is it central? Does it conform to established criteria?" this study asks, "How would the inclusion of works by women change the shape of the genre?"

To begin with, the inclusion of works by women would push the origin of the slave narrative genre back by two years, and root it more firmly in American soil, for the genre begins, not with *The Interesting Narrative of Olaudah Equiano, or Gustavus Vassa, the African,* published in London in 1789, but with the narrative of a slave woman entitled "Belinda, or the Cruelty of Men Whose Faces Were Like the Moon," published in the United States in 1787, a narrative of a few pages which would be considered too short by conventional standards.[3]

Traditionally, the 1845 *Narrative of the Life of Frederick Douglass, An American Slave, Written by Himself,* has been viewed as the central text in the genre, and based on this narrative, critic Robert Stepto has defined the primary Afro-American archetype as that of the articulate hero who discovers the "bonds among freedom, literacy, and struggle."[4] Once again, the narrative experience of the articulate and rationally enlightened female slave has not been part of the definition. Stepto, in his otherwise brilliant work on the *Narrative of Frederick Douglass, An American Slave, Written by Himself* (1845), makes no attempt to define a corresponding female archetype; I propose that we consider as a counterpart to the articulate hero the archetype of the outraged mother. She appears repeatedly in Afro-American history and literary tradition, and she is fully represented in Harriet "Linda Brent" Jacobs' *Incidents in the Life of a Slave Girl: Written by Herself* (1861).

Although Thayer and Eldridge published *Incidents in the Life of a Slave Girl* in Boston in 1861, not until 1981 did Jean F. Yellin publish evidence establishing Jacobs' historical identity and the authorship of her narrative. Marion Starling, a black woman, had argued for the authenticity of the Jacobs narrative as early as 1947, but male critics like Sterling Brown and Arna Bontemps contested that authorship.[5] The issue was complicated by the fact that Lydia Maria Child had edited the Jacobs narrative, which was published under the pseudonym, Linda Brent.

In general, the kinds of questions asked about the text prohibited scholars from seeing *Incidents* as part of the slave narrative genre and prevented them from looking for historical evidence to establish Jacobs' authorship. Yellin found such evidence readily available in the form of letters from Jacobs to Lydia Maria Child, from Jacobs to her confidante, Rochester Quaker Amy Post, and also in letters from Lydia Maria Child to John Greenleaf Whittier and William Lloyd Garrison, as well as the apprentice pieces Jacobs published in the New York *Tribune*.[6]

Another piece of external evidence overlooked by many scholars is a May 1, 1861 review of *Incidents* which appeared in the London *Anti-Slavery Advocate* written by a reviewer who had knowledge of the manuscript in both the original and published versions and who also had talked with the author. This *Anti-Slavery Advocate* review contains a wonderful description of Jacobs and her text:

> We have read this book with no ordinary interest, for we are acquainted with the writer; and have heard many of the incidents from her own lips, and have great confidence in her truthfulness and integrity. Between two and three years ago, a coloured woman, about as dark as a southern Spaniard or a Portuguese, aged about five-and-forty, with a kind and pleasing expression of countenance, called on us, bearing an introductory letter from one of the most honoured friends of the anti-slavery cause in the United States. This letter requested our friendly offices on behalf of Linda, who was desirous of publishing her narrative in England. It happened that the friends at whose house we were then staying were so much interested by this dusky stranger's conversation and demeanour, that they induced her to become their guest for some weeks. Thus we had an excellent opportunity of becoming acquainted with one of the greatest heroines we have ever met with. Her manners were marked by refinement and sensibility, and by an utter absence of pretense or affectation; and we were deeply touched by the circumstances of her early life which she then communicated, and which exactly coincide with those of the volume now before us.[7]

This kind of evidence establishes both the authenticity and primacy many critics have denied *Incidents in the Life of a Slave Girl.* Had these scholars asked the same questions of *Incidents* they asked of male narratives, had they looked for external evidence and examined it carefully, they would have come to the conclusion that Linda Brent wrote this narrative herself.

But as I have suggested, questions about unity, length, primacy and authorship are not the most important ones we can ask of such a narrative. We can more profitably ask how reading the work modifies an understanding of the slave narrative genre. However, the fact remains that the established criteria used to define the slave narrative genre have systematically excluded women; this paper calls those criteria into question.

When viewed from a gynocritical or gynocentric perspective, *Incidents* arrives at the very heart and root of Afra-American autobiographical writing. Although other works appear earlier, this full-length work by an Afra-American writing about her experiences as a slave woman is indeed rare. Yet despite its rarity, *Incidents* speaks for many lives; it is in many respects a representative document.

Incidents is descended both from the autobiographical tradition of the heroic male slaves and a line of American women's writings that attacks racial oppression and sexual exploitation. It combines the narrative pattern of the slave narrative genre with the conventional literary forms and stylistic devices of the 19th century domestic novel in an attempt to transform the so-called "cult of true womanhood' and to persuade the women of the north to take a public stand against slavery, the most political issue of the day. The twin themes of abolition and feminism are interwoven in Jacobs' text.

Like Harriet Beecher Stowe's hybrid, *Uncle Tom's Cabin, Incidents* focuses on the power relationships of masters and slaves and the ways in which (slave) women learn to manage the invasive sexuality of (white) men. Unlike Stowe, who demonstrates her anxiety about the authorship of *Uncle Tom's Cabin* by saying that God wrote it, the author of *Incidents* claims responsibility for every word, and yet she publishes under the pseudonym "Linda Brent."

Although I had read the critical literature on women's autobiography, it was *Incidents* that taught me that the silences and gaps in the narrative of women's lives are sometimes more significant than the filled spaces.[8] "Linda Brent" obscures the names of persons and places mentioned in the text, and although she denies any need for secrecy on her own part, she writes that she deemed it "kind and considerate toward others to pursue this course."[9] Thus she speaks as a disguised woman, whose identity remains partly obscured. A virtual "madwoman in the attic," Linda leads a veiled and unconventional life. Her dilemma is that of life under slavery as a beautiful, desirable female slave, object of desire as well as profit.

Linda adheres to a system of black and female cultural values that motivate her actions and inform the structure of this text. First of all, the author's stated purpose is to "arouse the woman of the North to a realizing sense of the condition of two millions of women at the South" (Jacobs, p. 1). If the white women of the North know the true conditions of the slave women of the South, then they cannot fail to answer Jacobs' call to moral action.

In order to balance our understanding of the slave narrative genre, we need first to read those narratives written by women (and to read them closely), and secondly to expand the range of terms used in writing about those narratives. An analysis of the imagery, thematic content, uses of language, and patterns of narrative movement in *Incidents in the Life of A Slave Girl* moves us closer to a characterization of the behavior of the outraged mother and to a more balanced understanding of the slave narrative genre.

As one who is small and relatively powerless in the face of her oppression, the outraged mother makes use of wit and intelligence to overwhelm and defeat a more powerful foe. In her aspect as trickster, "Linda" employs defensive verbal postures as well as various forms of disguise and concealment to outwit and escape Dr. Flint, the archetypal patriarchal rapist slavemaster:

1. She must conceal her quest for literacy and her ability to read in order to prevent the master from slipping her foul notes in an attempt to seduce her.

2. She must conceal her love for a free black man she eventually sends away for his own good, as well as the identity of the white man who becomes the father of her children and who eventually betrays her.

3. She conceals her pregnancy from everyone.

4. She must conceal her plans to run away, working hard and attempting to appear contented during the time she formulates these plans.

5. When Linda "runs away," she is disguised as a man and taken to the Snaky Swamp, a location she finds more hospitable than landed slave culture.

6. She is then concealed in the home of a neighboring white woman (a slaveholder sympathetic to her plight), and, finally, in a crawl space in her grandmother's house for seven years.

7. While concealed in her grandmother's house, Linda deceives the master by writing letters a friend mails from New York. When Flint takes off to New York to look for the fugitive, she is practically in his own back yard.

8. Linda is taken to the North in disguise, and even after she arrives there, she must conceal her identity with a veil, which she only removes when her freedom is purchased by a group of Northern white women. Through quick-thinking, the use of sass and invective, and a series of deceptions, Linda finally realizes freedom for herself and her children.

"Sass" is a word of West African derivation associated with the female aspect of the trickster figure. The OED attributes the origin of "sass" to the "sassy tree," the powerfully poisonous Erythophloeum quineense (Cynometra Manni). A decoction of the bark of this tree was used in West Africa as an ordeal poison in the trial of accused witches, women spoken of as being wives of Exu, the trickster god. According to the 1893 *Autobiography* of Mrs. Amanda Smith,

> I don't know as any one has ever found what the composition of this sassy wood really is; but I am told it is a mixture of certain barks. There is a tree there which grows very tall, called the sassy wood tree, but there is something mixed with this which is very difficult to find out, and the natives do not tell what it is. They say that it is one of their medicines that they use to carry out their law for punishing witches; so you cannot find out what it is.

"The accused had *two gallons* to drink. If she throws it up, she has gained her case," Mrs. Smith wrote.[10] So "sass" can kill.

Webster's Third International Dictionary defines "sass" as talking impudently or disrespectfully to an elder or a superior, or as talking back. Throughout the text, Linda uses "sass" as a weapon of self-defense whenever she is under sexual attack by the master; she returns a portion of the poison he has offered her. In one instance Dr. Flint demands: "Do you know that I have a right to do as I like with you,—that I can kill you, if I please?" Negotiating for respect, Linda replies: "You have tried to kill me, and I wish you had; but you have no right to do as you like with me" (Jacobs, p. 62). "Sass" is an effective tool that allows "Linda" to preserve her self-esteem and to increase the psychological distance between herself and the master. She uses "sass" the way Frederick Douglass uses his fists and his feet, as a means of expressing her resistance.

It is a distinctive feature of the outraged mother that she sacrifices opportunities to escape without her children; Linda is motivated by an overwhelming concern for them, a concern not apparent in the narratives of the questing male slaves. This concern is shown in chapter titles like "A New Tie to Life," "Another Link to Life," "The Children Sold," "New Destination for the Children," and "The Meeting of Mother and Daughter."

The outraged mother resists her situation not so much on behalf of herself as on behalf of her children. She is part of a continuum; she links the dead, the living, and the unborn. "I knew the doom that awaited my fair baby in slavery, and I determined to save her from it, or perish in the attempt. I went to make this vow at the graves of my poor parents, in the burying ground of the slaves" (Jacobs, pp. 137-38). In the case of Jacobs' narrative, the sense of the continuum of *women's* oppression is also clear.

It is the prospect of her daughter's life under slavery that finally nerves Jacobs to run away. "When they told me my new-born babe was a girl, my heart was heavier than it had ever been before. Slavery is a terrible thing for men; but it is far more terrible for women," Jacobs wrote. "Superadded to the burden common to all, *they* have wrongs, and sufferings and mortifications peculiarly their own" (Jacobs, p. 119).

Another important difference between this narrative and those of the heroic male slaves is that Linda celebrates the cooperation and collaboration of all the people, black and white, slave and free, who make her freedom possible. She celebrates her liberation and her children's as the fruit of a collective, not individual effort.

The inclusion of **Incidents in the Life of a Slave Girl, Written by Herself** in the slave narrative genre and the autobiographical tradition of black Americans, permits a more balanced view of that genre and that tradition, presenting fresh themes, images, and uses of language. **Incidents** occupies a position as central to that tradition as the 1845 *Narrative of Frederick Douglass*. Only in this perspective does the outraged mother emerge as the archetypal counterpart of the articulate hero.

Further study of all such texts and testimonies by women will allow us to fill out an understanding of that experience and culture which I have designated as Afra-American, and help us correct and expand existing analyses based too exclusively on male models of experience and writing. The study of black women's writing helps us to transform definitions of genre, of archetype, of narrative traditions, and of the African-American experience itself.

Notes

1. See James Olney, "Autobiography and the Cultural Moment" in *Autobiography: Essays Theoretical and Critical* (Princeton: Princeton UP, 1980), p. 26.

2. See Robert Stepto's "Teaching Afro-American Literature: Survey or Tradition," in *Afro-American Literature: The Reconstruction of Instruction,* ed. Dexter Fisher and Robert B. Stepto (New York: Modern Language Association, 1979), pp. 8-25. Within the "continuum of [black] artistic endeavor" described by Stepto as a *temenos* or "magic circle" exists yet another realm of artistic expression and meaning, that of the black woman, the Afra-American.

3. A woman called "Belinda" wrote "The Cruelty of Men Whose Faces Were Like the Moon: the Petition of an African Slave to the Legislature of Massachusetts." The title of the text suggests an awareness of racial and sexual oppression that is both race and sex specific. Belinda speaks to the cruelty of men, white men, whose moon-like faces symbolize strangeness, spiritual barrenness and death. See "Belinda: or the Cruelty of Men Whose Faces Were Like the Moon" in *American Museum and Repository of Ancient and Modern Fugitive Pieces, Prose and Poetical Volume I* (June, 1787).

4. See Robert B. Stepto, "Narration, Authentication, and Authorial Control in Frederick Douglass' *Narrative* of 1845," in *Afro-American Literature: The Reconstruction of Instruction,* pp. 178-91. See also Robert B. Stepto, *Beyond the Veil* (Urbana: U of Illinois P, 1979), chapters 1-3.

5. See Arna Bontemps, "The Slave Narrative: An American Genre," Introduction to *Great Slave Narratives* (Boston: Beacon, 1969), vol. XV; John W. Blassingame, "Critical Essay on Sources," in *The Slave Community* (New York: Oxford UP, 1972), pp. 233-34; and Jean F. Yellin, "Written by Herself: Harriet Brent Jacobs' Slave Narrative,"in *American Literature* 53 (November, 1981), 480-85.

6. Jean Yellin first disclosed the existence of Jacobs' autobiographical apprentice piece, "Letter From a Fugitive Slave," in "Written by Herself: Harriet Brent Jacobs' Slave Narrative." "Letter From a Fugitive Slave," published in the New York *Tribune,* 21 June 1853, treats the subject matter which later becomes *Incidents* in Mrs. Jacobs' distinctive style. Mrs. Jacobs' correspondence with Rochester Quaker Mrs. Amy Post verifies her claim to authorship of these letters to the *Tribune.*

7. Rev. of *Incidents, Anti-Slavery Advocate,* London, England, May 1, 1861.

8. In "Women's Autobiographies and the Male Tradition," her introduction to *Women's Autobiography* (Bloomington: U of Indiana P. 1980), Estelle Jelinek discusses some of the differences between the autobiographies of men and women.

9. Harriet "Linda Brent" Jacobs, "Preface by the Author," *Incidents in the Life of a Slave Girl: Written by Herself* (Boston: Thayer and Eldridge, 1861), p. 1. Subsequently referred to in the text as "Jacobs."

10. See Amanda Smith's *Autobiography* (Chicago: Meyer and Brother, 1893), pp. 386-89.

SIDONIE SMITH (ESSAY DATE 1992)

SOURCE: Smith, Sidonie. "Resisting the Gaze of Embodiment: Women's Autobiography in the Nineteenth Century." In *American Women's Autobiography: Fea(s)ts of Memory,* edited by Margo Culley, pp. 75-110. Madison: University of Wisconsin Press, 1992.

In the following excerpt, Smith explores how Jacobs asserts her selfhood in her narrative, staking her claim to humanness despite her status as a slave, an African, and a woman.

Making herself into a "talking book" entitled **Incidents in the Life of a Slave Girl, Written by Herself,** Jacobs engaged the mythology of "race" in order to give "voice" to herself and "face" to her people through alternative myths of empowerment (Gates 11-12). In the process she struggled to break the chains of slavery by breaking the chain of being which would relegate her as an "African" to the lowest rung of the ladder and by intervening in the constraints of generic expectations which would reappropriate her "life" in narrative. Engaging the conventions of self-mastery and authority, she staked her claim in the territory of the "human." The black woman, however, had a far more complex struggle for "selfhood" on her hands than either the white woman or the black man. Doubly the site of Western culture's totalizing representations, doubly "embodied" as "African" and "woman," doubly colonized in the territory of rape and enforced concubinage, the slave woman confronted conflated destinies, discourses, and identifications. Marginalized vis-à-vis both "metaphysical" and "embodied [white]" selfhoods, Jacobs travels arduously toward both territories as she narrates a paradigmatic tale of spiritual and rhetorical as well as physical journeys from bondage to "freedom."

Unwilling to accept the conditions of slavery, "Linda Brent" (the name of Jacobs' protagonist) determines to escape her circumstances, eluding her master by hiding in her grandmother's attic for seven years and then fleeing north to New York where she finds work, regains her children, and achieves freedom, not through self-agency but through the agency of her employer. At the center of Jacobs' escape story is "Brent's" will, her determination to figure life on her own terms. Agency functions as the sign of her resistance to her status as slave, subjected always to another's will. Describing her struggle with her master, Doctor Flint, "Brent" foregrounds this agency, figuring the struggle in metaphors of warfare, that quintessential masculine domain: "The war of my life had begun; and though one of God's most powerless creatures, I resolved never to be conquered"

(Jacobs 19).[1] Through this "hand-to-hand" combat, "Brent" literally and figuratively wrests agency from the master as her prerogative, beating the master at his own game, outwitting "the man." The narrative presents "Brent" as an avatar of the "self-made man," bent on achieving freedom by means of iron will, intelligence, courage, self-sacrifice, and perseverance as well as moral purposefulness. Both story and text affirm her "individuality" and "metaphysical selfhood" despite her qualified achievement in the North and her continuing struggle "to affirm the self in a hostile, or indifferent, environment" (Genovese 172).

As a narrative of self-determining agency, Jacobs' text participates in the tradition of the male slave narrative. But other positionings toward "selfhood" in the text cause Jacobs' narrative to deviate from that androcentric paradigm. For unlike the male slave narrator Jacobs has to attend as she writes to another story of "selfhood." Not only does she confront "Brent's" estrangement from "metaphysical selfhood"; she confronts synchronously her estrangement from "true [white] womanhood" and its sentimental narrative frames. The ideology of "true womanhood" elaborated by feminist historians looking at the nineteenth century, assigned to the "true woman" what Barbara Welter has described as "four cardinal virtues—piety, purity, submissiveness and domesticity" (Welter 21).[2] But that assignment implied another assignment—one directed at unprivileged women, women of color and working-class women. Hazel V. Carby argues that while the establishment of "what constituted a woman and womanhood" may have brought "coherence and order to the contradictory material circumstances of the lives of women," it did so by "balancing opposing definitions of womanhood and motherhood [for white and black women], each dependent on the other for its existence" (Carby, *Reconstructing Black Womanhood* 24, 25). For instance, the fragile physique characteristic of the "true woman" contrasted markedly to the bodily strength desirable in the black female slave.[3] Moreover, the fierce purposefulness of a slave woman's efforts to escape her bondage violated the code of submissiveness so central to "true womanhood." Any effort by a black woman to establish her consonance with "true womanhood" involved a crossing over from one definitional territory to another's definitional territory, a crossing over to a place whose boundaries depended on keeping black woman in their place.[4]

Inevitably, black and white women experienced differing relationships to their bodies. A white woman exercized some control over her body. Despite the discourse labeling her naturally lustful, despite the implicit fear of her sexuality evidenced in the most elaborate defenses of her goodness and purity, she could achieve some modicum of power by resisting the temptations of the flesh and keeping her body clean, chaste. By maintaining her virginity and her "reputation," she could secure marriage and with it social legitimacy. After marriage she could fulfill her duty by bearing legitimate children for the patrilineage. Or she could maintain her virginity and serve her family as dutiful daughter or her cause as selfless evangelist. Enshrined in her "separate sphere," she could secure a certain cultural status and currency (literally and figuratively).

While neither male nor female slaves had control over their own bodies, the female slave suffered physical violation of her body beyond what the male slave suffered, a reality to which Jacobs painfully alludes: "When they told me my new-born babe was a girl, my heart was heavier than it had ever been before. Slavery is terrible for men; but it is far more terrible for women. Super-added to the burden common to all, they have wrongs, and sufferings, and mortifications peculiarly their own" (77). Within that "peculiar institution" the fate of woman was itself "peculiar." If in the discursive regimes of "embodied selfhood" the white woman always carried in her the potential for illicit and disruptive sexuality, the black woman lived in that crawlspace of sexual lasciviousness by virtue of the mark that was her skin color. Her black body condemned her to an inescapable essentialism since in the mythology of "race," it served as her defining characteristic, the very sign of her unrepressed and unrepressible sexuality, her licentiousness and insatiability. From the less authoritative discourse of the chain of being to the more scientifically respectable discourse of medical pathology, black female sexuality became synonymous with abnormal sexual appetite.[5] Effectively, her body stood as an invitation to white male desire. And so the white master satisfied his "purient" sexual desire and his desire for human capital on the female slave's body in one act. In this way her body functioned as the vessel for reproducing "chattel" for the system (since children followed the mother) and for shielding the white woman from "uninhibited" sexual practices; both uses maintained colonial relationships of power.

Despite these apparently intractable cultural obstacles, Jacobs seeks to establish in her narrative some relationship (albeit partially contestatory as I will argue later) to "true womanhood" by situating "Brent" inside shared boundaries with white women. Perhaps the recognition of a shared community with white northern women was abetted by the feminist politics of the two women with whom she worked and corresponded during the writing of her narrative, Lydia Maria Child and Amy Post. "The publication of Jacobs's autobiography," suggests Andrews, "constituted a double opportunity, for as woman and slave, Jacobs dramatized the feminist analysis of the parallel slavery of race and sex. . . . From the feminist point of view, which labeled true womanhood white slavery and submissive wifehood prostitution, Jacob's multiply marginal identity qualified her amply as one of the most truly representative women of her time" (247-48). And yet her "representative" status was undermined by other positionings. She was after all, as Andrews reminds us, a domestic servant, a woman on the margins of the domestic domain of woman. And the narrative inevitably revealed certain postures antithetical to the postures of the "true woman": her wilfullness noted above, her not always suppressed anger, her independent critique of both southern and northern society, and her revelation of sexual concubinage.

In response to the great irony of her situation—"the more enormous the crimes committed against her, the less receptive people are to hearing about them, especially from the victim herself"—Jacobs, according to Andrews, seeks to "forestall the wrong kind of reading of her book" by constituting in her text a "woman-identified reader" and "remodeling" through the text the kind of enlightened community that would "offer a truly familial kind of fellowship" (Andrews 249, 253). To this end "Brent" speaks directly to white middle-class northern women, comfortable in their status as "true women." Speaking as a woman to other women whose sympathy, understanding, and action she would enlist in the antislavery crusade, she asks that they identify with her sufferings as a woman who shares their concerns for home and children. This desire to gain common ground with her reader determines the emphases in the narrative on the struggle to achieve control over her body and the related struggle to establish a home for the children of that body.

In tracing the former struggle, however, Jacobs reveals not only her determination to escape sexual exploitation but also her surrender to concubinage, confessing that in resisting her master's will she entered deliberately into liaison with another white man by whom she bore two children. Thus the narrator must position herself as the "fallen" woman whose very utterances, because unspeakable, threaten the sanctity of that protected space of "true womanhood." The reality of this threat is acknowledged by Lydia Maria Child in her introduction:

> I am well aware that many will accuse me of indecorum for presenting these pages to the public; for the experiences of this intelligent and much injured woman belong to a class which some call delicate subjects, and others indelicate. This peculiar phase of Slavery has generally been kept veiled; but the public ought to be made acquainted with its monstrous features, and I willingly take the responsibility of presenting them with the veil withdrawn. I do this for the sake of my sisters in bondage, who are suffering wrongs so foul, that our ears are too delicate to listen to them.
>
> (4)

There is no room for Jacobs' experience as a black woman inside the borders of "true womanhood." Since "silence" surrounds the "indecorous" subject matter and marginalized speaking position of the narrator—"It would have been more pleasant to me to have been silent about my own history" (2)—Jacobs/"Brent" risks rejection by her reader in order to tell the story of her fall from virginity into concubinage, in order to insist on the legitimacy of her experience.

The narrative strategies Jacobs/"Brent" uses to stake her claim as a black woman to a place within the community of "true women" are fascinating and provocative. In tracing her struggle for physical self-determination she appeals rhetorically to her audience by appropriating the very language and narrative conventions of popular fiction, most particularly invoking (and rewriting) the tale of seduction.[6] Presenting herself as a resisting victim of Doctor Flint's sexual aggression, "Brent" figures a story about the forced loss of innocence and the long, anguished struggle to achieve bodily integrity in the face of unremitting emotional and physical abuse. Chronicling her experiences in slavery and out, she foregrounds especially the emotional and physical consequences of her decision to resist sexual victimization, the superhuman self-sacrifice necessary. She suffers separation from her children. Harassed, exhausted, feverish, infected, contorted by the seven-year enclosure inside her grandmother's attic, her body bears the marks of the master's brutality, bares the price of "virtue." At the same time that she testifes to the horrors of that "peculiar institution," therefore, she positions herself as victimized heroine inside the narrative space of "white" fiction.

Jacobs also appeals to white women as mothers by creating "Brent" as the heroic mother whose steel purpose is to achieve freedom and a home for her children and by figuring her story in the rhetoric of domestic fiction with its celebration of the domestic virtues. Presenting herself in what Jean Fagan Yellin reminds us was "the most valued 'feminine' role" of the century" (xxvi), Jacobs emphasizes how hard fought the achievement must be for the female slave, precisely because "motherhood" posed significant problems for the black woman caught in a system that intervened ruthlessly and purposefully in family relationships.[7] Amassing detailed accounts of the difficulties of motherhood in slavery, Jacobs insists on "Brent's" total commitment to her children, to the point of self-sacrifice: "My friends feared I should become a cripple for life; and I was so weary of my long imprisonment that, had it not been for the hope of serving my children, I should have been thankful to die; but, for their sakes, I was willing to bear on" (127). Moreover, Jacobs surrounds "Brent's" struggle as a mother with the struggle of her larger family, a family whose members—grandmother, father, mother, aunts, uncles—she figures as powerful, physically resilient, spiritually hearty, loving, courageous, loyal. She thereby places herself in a noble family lineage, a lineage embodying the highest values of a civilized society, a lineage characterized by spiritual, moral, and social heroism despite the degrading circumstances of slavery. And even as she concludes with an acknowledgment that she can never achieve that "separate sphere" available to white women, she maintains the legitimacy of her desire for equal access: "I still long for a hearthstone of my own, however humble," she concludes, "I wish it for my children's sake far more than for my own" (201).

Finally, "Brent" assumes the narrative posture of the "true woman" who sacrifices herself and her privacy by telling her tale to others for the benefit of her people and their cause, as she earlier sacrifices herself and her comfort for her children and their freedom. Moreover, as Andrews argues, she sacrifices her privacy to benefit her readers: "Jacobs approaches her woman-identified reader with a personal history of secrets whose revelation, she hopes, will initiate that reader into the community of confidence and support that nineteenth-century women needed in order to speak out above a whisper against their oppression" (254).[8]

The closing reference to her failed effort to gain her own "home" underscores the grim reality of Jacobs'/"Brent's" status as exile in her own country and in the country of "ideal [white] womanhood." Ex-slaves, however much they celebrated their freedom, remained second-class citizens, remained strangers in their own land, variously homeless. Pointedly, "Brent" is not even "free" to claim the legitimacy of her experience for herself. Rather she is dependent upon the testimony of Lydia Maria Child, the white abolitionist whose necessary authorization of Jacobs' text points to the ex-slave's reinscription within certain appropriative structures.[9] Moreover, she is dependent upon Child for the editing and marketing of her narrative. As Alice A. Deck suggests, Child's imprint upon the narrative is multiple (33-40). Child herself wrote to Jacobs that she "transpos[ed] sentences and pages, so as to bring the story into continuous order, and the remarks into *appropriate* places"; she requested that Jacobs send her more materials about "the outrages committed on the colored people, in Nat Turner's time," thus emphasizing dramatic details even when they were not a part of Jacobs' personal story: she deleted a last chapter on John Brown because "it does not naturally come into your story and the M.S. is already too long" (quoted in Meltzer and Holland 357). Like other ex-slave narrators, Jacobs finds her narrative and her self-representation subject to and subject of a certain amount of white "paternalistic" control.[10] Yet despite this editorial colonization, the narrative maintains the fierce integrity of an oppositional vision.

Literally as well as figuratively homeless, Jacobs/"Brent" speaks from a position very different from the one Elizabeth Cady Stanton achieves at the conclusion of her narrative. Indeed, she stands in the speaking position of the "deterritorialized," to use the current phrase of Gilles Deleuze and Felix Guattari (17).[11] From her position on the margins, however, Jacobs can "see" both inside and outside white culture, inside and outside "true womanhood" and its supporting ideology. She can "see" the reality of both margin and center more vividly than Stanton who vis-à-vis Jacobs remains in the center of her culture. She has what bell hooks calls a kind of doubled sight.[12]

This doubled sight characterizes Jacobs' stance toward the culturally legitimated discursive regimes she invokes to gain credibility for the "truth" of her tale: those of the seduction novel, domestic fiction, the more common male slave narrative, biblical tropes, picaresque narratives, and the spiritual narrative of the movement of the soul toward salvation and freedom. Since these loci of authority are white and/or male-identified, she engages them from her oppositional position at the margins, often uncomfortably. Negotiating the intersections of multivalent discourses, Jacobs effectively troubles all these centering rhetorics simultaneously. For her deterritorialized vision leads her to probe, unconsciously and consciously, certain gaps in those conventions, certain disturbances in the surfaces of narrative.

From the perspective of the homeless, Jacobs interrogates even as she imitates the ideology of true womanhood, foregrounding its inherent racialized nature. As Carby argues, "*Incidents* demystified a convention that appeared as the obvious, commonsense rules of behavior and revealed the concept of true womanhood to be an ideology, not a lived set of social relations as she exposed its inherent contradictions and inapplicability to her life" (*Reconstructing Black Womanhood* 49). She does so through her figuration of both the northern women whom she addresses and the southern women whom she describes. On the one hand, she suggests that certain white southern women transcend the privileges of their class and status in identifying with her plight and flight, giving her shelter and support. She challenges thereby the totalized vision of white southern women as proslavery. On the other, she condemns the complacency and indifference of northern women, even those associated with the abolitionist cause, revealing her perception of the absence of sisterly concern among them by quoting from the Bible: "Rise up, ye women that are at ease! Hear my voice, ye careless daughters! Give ear unto my speech" (Isaiah 32.9). Or she manifests, albeit mutedly, a certain bitterness toward her northern reader in her comparisons of their life with hers.

But more directly, she unmasks the ideology of "true womanhood" as a fiction in her characterization of southern women who collude in the degradation of other women and deny the primacy of conjugal bonds: "The qualities of delicacy of constitution and heightened sensitivity, attributes of the Southern lady, appear as a corrupt and superficial veneer that covers an underlying strength and power in cruelty and brutality" (Carby, *Reconstructing Black Womanhood* 53-54). In contrast to the ruthless and uncivilized familial relationships of whites, she creates a world of nurturing, supportive black women, a world of strong black relationships. Incorporating episodes that make of white men sexual profligates and moral pigmies, that make of white women uncaring, jealous, petty tyrants, this slave narrator provides a contrast of cultures that reverses ideological notions of "civilized" and "uncivilized," hierarchized as white and black.

Jacobs/"Brent" also challenges the very notion of American "freedom" and "democracy" and in doing so contests the presence of the agency and autonomy associated with American notions of bourgeois individuality. For instance, in a passage cited for its unveiled, assertive voice (Washington 12), "Brent" comments directly on the fact that her "freedom" has been bought for her by a white woman:

> So I was *sold* at last! A human being *sold* in the free city of New York! The bill of sale is on record, and future generations will learn from it that women were articles of traffic in New York, late in the nineteenth century of the Christian religion. It may hereafter prove a useful document to antiquaries, who are seeking to measure the progress of civilization in the United States. I well know the value of that bit of paper; but much as I love freedom I do not like to look upon it. I am deeply grateful to the generous friend who procured it, but I despise the miscreant who demanded payment for what never rightfully belonged to him or his.
>
> (200)

Assuming the authoritative stance of a biblical prophet, Jacobs ("Brent") defiantly, unsentimentally, scorns the hypocrisy of the nation and its founding documents.[13]

Contrary to the conventional figuration and fate of the antagonist of the seduction tale, Jacobs presents her seducer not as any kind of Byronic figure whose power is attractive and redeemable if lethal but rather as a dehumanized pervert, brutalizing and bestial.[14] Turning the tables on the ideology supporting the slave system, Jacobs renders the white man as less than fully human and assigns him a position low on the chain of being. Moreover, she presents herself not as the passive victim but as the iron-willed antagonist who fights her victimization with bravado. "Jacobs' narrator," suggests Yellin, "asserts that—even when young and a slave—she was an effective moral agent" who "takes full responsibility for her actions" (xxx). And she further differentiates between a "selfhood" synonymous simply with bodily chastity and a "selfhood" emanating from self-esteem and integrity as she "abandon[s] her attempt to avoid sexual involvements in an effort to assert her autonomy as a human being" (Yellin xxx; Carby, *Reconstructing Black Womanhood* 60). For instance, she makes a careful distinction between being forcibly raped by her master and choosing her lover: "It seems less degrading to give one's self, than to submit to compulsion"

(55). Ironically, she inverts the tale of seduction; the passive victim chooses her lover, chooses her fall. Moreover, and obviously, her tale of seduction does not end conventionally in death. It ends in a rise to moral integrity and freedom as she transforms her fall into the story of real integrity, persistence, and a moral vision that challenges the simplistic notions of morality associated with "true womanhood." "Still, in looking back, calmly, on the events of my life," she reflects, "I feel that the slave woman ought not to be judged by the same standard as others" (56). Later, when she describes how "Brent" reveals the truth of her past to her daughter Ellen and wins Ellen's acceptance, Jacobs reveals her own narrative priorities: she cares more for a daughter's forgiveness than for the reader's (and larger culture's) forgiveness. As Carby suggests, Jacobs places slavery on trial rather than "Brent's" social deviancy (*Reconstructing Black Womanhood* 61). For these reasons, argues Yellin, Jacobs might be calling for "a new definition of female morality grounded in her own sexual experience in a brutal and corrupt patriarchal racist society" (xxxi). Such a notion of morality would be dependent not solely upon woman's sexual purity but on more complicated, contextual grounds. Such morality would be morality historicized rather than essentialized.

Jacobs/"Brent" rewrites every narrative convention that shadows her text. She rewrites the fiction of domesticity by calling for direct political action and intervention rather than the more limited "influence" of domesticated feminism being promoted by certain white feminists of the period. As a "homeless" woman she sees the self-satisfied complacencies of a feminism that would limit its area of concern to reform and celebration of that separate sphere when political, economic, and social forces limited the access to that sphere to white middle-class women.[15] She rewrites the conventions of sentimental fiction whose heroine's fate is marriage, celebrating instead her achievement of "freedom." She rewrites that other scenario of sentimental fiction, the narrative of death by seduction or captivity, by critiquing the platitudes of a morality that erases the specificities of the slave woman's experience. She also rewrites the conventions of the "male" slave narrative which assumes the representative privilege of the male slave's experience of bondage and escape. Unlike a Frederick Douglass who in his several narratives acknowledges neither the woman who helped him escape (and who later became his wife) nor other networks assisting him as he fled, Jacobs/"Brent" eschews the representation of herself as the isolato, self-contained in her rebellion, figuring herself instead as dependent always on the support of family and friends, particularly her grandmother (see Andrews 253-58; Foster, "'In Respect to Females'" 66-70; McKay 177; Washington 3-15).

Finally, Jacob contests the notion of "selfhood's" fixedness. "I was born a slave; but I never knew it till six years of happy childhood had passed away" (3), writes "Brent" in opening her narrative. Early in the narrative Jacobs introduces the distinction between a "fixed" idea of "selfhood" and a culturally and historically contextual notion of "selfhood" (Genovese 170). By doing so she challenges the mythology of "racial" identity as an essentialized phenomenon. Providing character, nobility, full humanity to her black family, and complex humanity to herself, she deconstructs the stereotypes of black identity spawned in the ideology of "race." Refusing to be figured as the sexually unrepressed primitive black woman whose body constitutes her identity, refusing to be figured as the "mammy" of white children, refusing to be figured as morally and spiritually bankrupt, refusing therefore to be figured as less than fully human, she destabilizes colonial notions of "African-ness."

Moreover, Jacobs foregrounds throughout her text not only the intertextualities of self-representation but also the discursive staging of identity. The discourse of the text resists the finalizing impact of the history in the text. The mutual constitution of "reader" and "narrator" marks the text and its self-representational project as simultaneously fluid and contextual. Novelistic passages introduce the dialogic nature of "self-representation," the indeterminacies of role-playing and multiple voicings (Andrews 280). Life-storytelling becomes the site of "selfhood," now understood as discursive, contextual, communicative, and ultimately "fictive." Thus Jacobs' narrative testifies to the ambiguities of any core of irreducible, essentialist "selfhood."

From her position of "homelessness" at the margins of both slave and white societies, Jacobs interrogates in more complex ways than does Stanton conventional pieties of woman's "embodied selfhood" in the nineteenth century as well as conventional empowerments of "metaphysical selfhood." Out of the friction generated as she engages competing and contradictory discourses that never quite fit the parameters of her historically specific experience in slavery, Jacobs experiments with the elasticities of "self"-representation.

Hers is a particularly provocative narrative, one which adumbrates those disturbances of the territorial boundaries of both "metaphysical" and "embodied" "selfhood" characterizing autobiographies written by women in the twentieth century.

Notes

1. Elizabeth Fox-Genovese (171) explores Jacobs' struggle of wills.

2. For further discussions of "true womanhood," see Spruill; Scott; Clinton; Berg.

3. "Strength and ability to bear fatigue, argued to be so distasteful a presence in a white woman, were positive features to be emphasized in the promotion and selling of a black female field hand at a slave auction" (Carby, *Reconstructing Black Womanhood* 25).

4. What Carby claims for black women after the Civil War applies even more certainly to female slaves before emancipation: "Black women were relegated to a place outside the ideological construction of 'womanhood.' That term included only white women; therefore the rape of black women was of no consequence outside the black community" ("On the Threshold of Woman's Era" 308-9). Carby is elaborating the theories of the black feminist Ida B. Wells who explored the politics of lynching at the end of the nineteenth century. See, for instance, Wells, *On Lynching* (New York, 1969), for a collection of her essays. Carby also explores the politics of the black female body in *Reconstructing Black Womanhood* (26-32).

5. "In the nineteenth century," writes Gilman, "the black female was widely perceived as possessing not only a 'primitive' sexual appetite but also the external signs of this temperament—'primitive' genitalia" (232). Fascination with this phenomenon of physical and physiognomic abnormality reveals itself in the century's preoccupation with the "Hottentot Venus" whose visual characteristics—large buttocks, flat nose, strange labia—function as signs of her phylogenetic place. The critical significance of establishing the difference of black female anatomy lay, according to Gilman, in the following rationalization: "If their sexual parts could be shown to be inherently different, this would be a sufficient sign that the blacks were a separate (and, needless to say, lower) race, as different from the European as the proverbial orangutan" (235). In the catalogue of defining physical characteristics of the female Hottentot, the century read the signs of regression to an earlier state of human evolution. Moreover, in identifying some of those same characteristics as markers of prostitutes (the most sexualized of white women) and in describing the sexual practices of primitive tribes as forms of prostitution, medical anthropologists linked black sexuality and prostitution as two sources of social corruption and disease (syphilis in particular). Sexuality as the dark force in civilized "man" was thus identified with, projected onto, the prostitute and the black female (240-57).

6. Jean Fagan Yellin explores Jacobs' use of the conventions of sentimental fiction in her Introduction (xxix-xxx).

7. Slave marriages were not legally valid. The indiscriminate use of the slave woman's body by white men made fatherhood an absence. Moreover, the subjec-

tion of the female body to the will of the white master, functioning as an effective means of "unmanning" the black male, in one more way destabilized the family and, as Elizabeth Fox-Genovese suggests, left black women with "no satisfactory social definition of themselves as women" (169).

8. See Andrews' extended discussion of the thematics of secrecy in the narrative (254-59).

9. The history of the text's fate at the hands of white abolitionists, critics, and literary historians, however, adds yet another story to her story. The text is legitimized by Lydia Maria Child's attestation that it is the authentic story of the author. Recognizing that "it will naturally excite surprise that a woman reared in Slavery should be able to write so well" (Jacobs 3), Child both explains the author's circumstances and assures the reader that she has acted as editor only. This attestation notwithstanding, the text was labeled fictional by subsequent generations until Jean Fagan Yellin recently verified the authenticity of the places, people, and experiences narrated by "Linda Brent." Ironically, the text as "technology of reason" spoke against itself. See Yellin's Introduction to the text (xiii-xxxv).

10. Deck (34-36) explores the formulaic patterns imposed by white abolitionists on the experiences and narratives of ex-slaves. See also Yellin, *Intricate Knot;* and Stepto.

11. For an elaboration of the deterritorialized nature of women's autobiographical writing, see Kaplan.

12. "Living as we did—on the edge—we developed a particular way of seeing reality. We looked both from the outside in and from the inside out. We focused our attention on the center as well as the margin. We understood both" (hooks preface).

13. See Mary Helen Washington's comments on Jacobs' empowered and assertive voice (11-12).

14. See Andrews (251); and Niemtzow (106). Andrews takes issue with Niemtzow's analysis.

15. Yellin argues that "instead of dramatizing the idea that the private sphere is women's appropriate area of concern . . . *Incidents* embodies a social analysis asserting that the denial of domestic and familial values by chattel slavery is a social issue that its female readers should address in the public arena" (Introduction xxxii). For a discussion of nineteenth-century versions of "domestic feminism" see Baym.

Works Cited

Andrews, William L. *To Tell a Free Story: The First Century of Afro-American Autobiography, 1760-1865.* Urbana: University of Illinois Press, 1986.

Carby, Hazel V. *Reconstructing Black Womanhood: The Emergence of the Afro-American Woman Novelist.* New York: Oxford University Press, 1987.

Clinton, Catherine. *The Plantation Mistress: Woman's World in the Old South.* New York: Pantheon, 1982.

Deleuze, Gilles, and Felix Guattari. "What Is a Minor Literature." In *Kafka: Towards a Minor Literature,* trans. Dana Polan, 16-27. Minneapolis: University of Minnesota Press, 1986.

Foster, Frances Smith. "'In Respect to Females . . .': Difference in the Portrayals of Women by Male and Female Narrators." *Black American Literature Forum,* 15 (Summer 1981), 66-70.

Fox-Genovese, Elizabeth. "To Write My Self: The Autobiographies of Afro-American Women." In *Feminist Issues in Literary Scholarship,* ed. Shari Benstock, 161-80. Bloomington: Indiana University Press, 1987.

Gates, Henry Louis, Jr. "Editor's Introduction: Writing 'Race' and the Difference It Makes." In *"Race," Writing, and Difference,* ed. Gates, 1-20. Chicago: University of Chicago Press, 1986.

Gilman, Sander. "Black Bodies, White Bodies: Toward an Iconography of Female Sexuality in Late Nineteenth-Century Art, Medicine, and Literature." In *"Race," Writing, and Difference,* ed. Henry Louis Gates, Jr., 223-61. Ithaca: Cornell University Press, 1986.

hooks, bell. *Feminist Theory: From Margin to Center.* Boston: South End Press, 1984.

Jacobs, Harriet. *Incidents in the Life of a Slave Girl, Written by Herself.* Ed. Lydia Maria Child. New ed. Jean Fagan Yellin. Cambridge: Harvard University Press, 1987.

Kaplan, Caren. "Deterritorializations: The Rewriting of Home and Exile in Western Feminist Discourse." *Cultural Critique,* 6 (Spring 1987), 187-98.

McKay, Nellie Y. "Race, Gender, and Cultural Context in Zora Neale Hurston's *Dust Tracks on a Road.*" In *Life/Lines: Theorizing Women's Autobiography,* ed. Bella Brodzki and Celeste Schenck, 175-88. Ithaca: Cornell University Press, 1988.

Meltzer, Milton, and Patricia G. Holland, eds. *The Collected Correspondence of Lydia Maria Child, 1817-1880.* Amherst: University of Massachusetts Press, 1982.

Niemtzow, Annette. "The Problematic of Self in Autobiography: The Example of the Slave Narrative." In *The Art of the Slave Narrative,* ed. John Sekora and Darwin T. Turner, 96-109. Macomb: Western Illinois University Press, 1982.

Scott, Ann. *The Southern Lady: From Pedestal to Politics, 1830-1930.* Chicago: University of Chicago Press, 1970.

Spruill, Julia Cherry. *Women's Life and Work in the Southern Colonies.* 1938; rpt. New York: W. W. Norton, 1972.

Stepto, Robert B. *From behind the Veil: A Study of Afro-American Narrative.* Urbana: University of Illinois Press, 1979.

Washington, Mary Helen. "Introduction, Meditations on History: The Slave Woman's Voice." In *Invented Lives: Narratives of Black Women, 1860-1960,* ed. Mary Helen Washington, 3-15. New York: Doubleday Anchor Press, 1987.

Welter, Barbara. *Dimity Convictions: The American Woman in the Nineteenth Century.* Columbus: Ohio State University Press, 1976.

Yellin, Jean Fagan. *The Intricate Knot: Black Figures in American Literature.* New York: New York University Press, 1972.

Yellin, Jean Fagan. Introduction to Jacobs.

ON THE SUBJECT OF...

INCIDENTS IN THE LIFE OF A SLAVE GIRL

It [The narrative] presents features more attractive than many of its predecessors purporting to be histories of slave life in America, because, in contrast with their mingling of fiction with fact, this record of complicated experience in the life of a young woman, a doomed victim to America's peculiar institution—her seven years' concealment in slavery—continued persecutions—hopes, often deferred, but which at length culminated in her freedom—surely need not the charms that any pen of fiction, however gifted and graceful, could lend. They shine by the lustre of their own truthfulness—a rhetoric which always commends itself to the wise head and honest heart. In furtherance of the object of its author, LYDIA MARIA CHILD has furnished a graceful introduction, and AMY POST, a well-written letter; and wherever the names of these two devoted friends of humanity are known, no higher credentials can be required or given. My own acquaintance, too, with the author and her relatives, of whom special mention is made in the book, warrants an expression of the hope that it will find its way into every family, where all, especially mothers and daughters, may learn yet more of the barbarism of American slavery and the character of its victims.

Nell, Wm. C. From "Linda the Slave Girl." *The Liberator*, 24 January, 1861.

JANICE B. DANIEL (ESSAY DATE SPRING 1997)

SOURCE: Daniel, Janice B. "A New Kind of Hero: Harriet Jacobs's *Incidents.*" *The Southern Quarterly* 35, no. 3 (spring 1997): 7-12.

In the following essay, Daniel argues that the new type of hero that Jacobs presents in her autobiographical account is an innovative variation on the traditional male hero of the romance genre.

Harriet Ann Jacobs's autobiographical account of her personal experiences has survived despite its controversial reception. For decades, *Incidents in the Life of a Slave Girl: Written by Herself* was believed to be either a false slave narrative penned by a white abolitionist or the work of Maria Child, her white collaborator. Because of the efforts of Jean Fagan Yellin, however, the literary world has recently acknowledged its authenticity, and its true author has taken her place among other important antebellum writers and Afro-American women authors.

Today Jacobs's work continues to survive amid mixed reactions. Some readers place it in the category of slave narrative, many regard it in the genre of sentimental domestic or seduction novel, and some view it simply in the autobiographical tradition. Also, many scholars place it in historical perspective as another antislavery novel, and others appreciate its more modern radical feminist content. Although the work has no difficulty in fulfilling all of these classifications, attempting to justify any one of them can result in dealing with the tension of ignoring many of the novel's obvious meritorious qualities in order to focus narrowly on a single interpretation. This same type of tension is present when one endeavors to analyze (with intentions to label) the status of its pseudonymous protagonist Linda Brent. She is simultaneously a heroic slave who strives against formidable odds to obtain freedom, a desperate mother who is engulfed in a desperate struggle for the survival of her children, and a woman who openly acknowledges and endures the sexual tribulations of being both a slave and a female. However, there is yet another type of female hero into whom Jacobs successfully combines all of these without the difficulties inherent in ignoring or disqualifying any one category. Jacobs presents in Linda Brent a female version of the hero of the romance mode, a woman who effectively portrays the requirements for this type of hero—requisites that were present in fiction long before the appearance of slave narratives or sentimental novels or feminist tracts. To consider Brent in this role is to be consistent with readers who suggest that Jacobs "projects a new kind of female hero" (Yellin xiv), yet this new kind, upon closer inspection, is actually an innovative rendering of a long-established literary persona.

This "new" kind of hero is a credible version of the "old" male hero identified by scholars of the romance genre. The pattern of Brent's experiences closely parallels that of the traditional hero of the romance as the "incidents" in her quest for freedom lead her down his same mythical path. The parallel is especially striking if we examine Brent's quest in light of special characteristics of the romance mode as explained by Northrop Frye in *The Secular Scripture*. Frye profiles the romance quest with elements such as ascent, descent, double identity, allies, enemies, alienation and trials. Jacobs's labels are different: her destination is "a home found" (168), and her journey is "a perilous passage" (53) filled with "continued persecutions" (80) and "competition in cunning" (128); but her quest is the same search for identity as that of the traditional hero of romance.

Linda Brent's confirmation as a romance hero commences with her earliest remembrances of childhood, in a situation that parallels the romance requirement for the protagonist's questionable origin (Frye 101-03). The first sentence of her narrative affirms her lack of identity as a slave: "I was born a slave; but I never knew it till six years of happy childhood had passed away" (5). Although she knows her parental unit and the origin of her existence, her uncomplicated life in a comfortable home keeps her oblivious of her slave status for the first years of her life. "I was so fondly shielded that I never dreamed I was a piece of merchandise" (5).

In the romance, the hero's status must have a definitive beginning; thus Brent's conscious life as a slave begins with a significant event. "When I was six years old, my mother died; and then, for the first time, I learned, by the talk around me, that I was a slave" (6). Brent soon begins to comprehend the implications of her station in life, and the reader continues to recognize additional parallels to the romance hero. The garment of identity for him has become for her the annual gift of attire from her mistress. "I have a vivid recollection of the linsey-woolsey dress given me every winter by Mrs. Flint. How I hated it! It was one of the badges of slavery" (11).

Her life as a slave, however, is not without the romance hero's pastoral rapport with nature. When her mistress sends her out to play, she runs and jumps and bounds "to gather berries or flowers to decorate her room" (7). Even in her grief for her mother, she finds solace in nature:

> The graveyard was in the woods, and twilight was coming on. Nothing broke the deathlike stillness except the occasional twitter of a bird. My spirit was overawed by the solemnity of the scene. For more than ten years I had frequented this spot, but never had it seemed to me so sacred as now. A black stump, at the head of my mother's grave, was all that remained of a tree my father had planted.
>
> (90)

Any realization of a conscious personal quest, however, does not occur until she has progressed through a period of rebellion.

After the deaths of many loved ones, Brent's "heart rebelled against God, who had taken from me mother, father, mistress, and friend" (10). When the child cannot find comfort in the long-term assurance of an abstract God, she seizes upon the short-term goal of good behavior: "But we, who were slave-children, without father or mother, could not expect to be happy. We must be good; perhaps that would bring us contentment" (18).

Under the ownership of a demanding new master, however, Brent finds that exemplary deportment is impossible, as she encounters the formidable dragon or monster of the romance. Not only does Dr. Flint endeavor to make her life miserable as a servant, but when she begins to grow into young womanhood at the age of fifteen, he suddenly commences sexual harassment:

> My master met me at every turn, reminding me that I belonged to him, and swearing by heaven and earth that he would compel me to submit to him. If I went out for a breath of fresh air, after a day of unwearied toil, his footsteps dogged me. If I knelt by my mother's grave, his dark shadow fell on me even there. The light heart which nature had given me became heavy with sad forebodings.
>
> (28)

She considers herself "struggling alone in the powerful grasp of the demon Slavery" (54). The dragon that guards the treasure hoard in the romance has materialized for her into the form of an institution which grants ownership of her to a man who stands sentry between her and her legal freedom—*and* her sexual freedom. She even extends the metaphor of demon into a menacing animal form: "O, the serpent of Slavery has many and poisonous fangs" (62). Later, when one of her hiding places is in Snaky Swamp, she has to fend off real snakes, but they are only partially as monstrous as the human perpetrators of slavery: "But even those large, venomous snakes were less dreadful to my imagination than the white men in that community called civilized" (113).

Consequently, in Brent's "quest" for identity as a free person, she must conquer the menacing monster however it materializes. Therefore, Dr. Flint's sexual attentions force her into desperate means. After he refuses to allow her free black lover to marry her, and realizing that her childhood is over anyway, she gives herself sexually to another white man whose compassionate nature may lead him to buy her and subsequently to grant her freedom. Reminding her reader that "the condition of a slave confuses all principles of morality, and, in fact, renders the practice of them impossible" (55), she maintains that "the slave woman ought not to be judged by the same standard as others" (56). Thus, she "continues to rebel by rejecting the right of others to apply their standards to her" (Becker 417). Brent also achieves a significant step in her quest for personal freedom by initiating her sexual experience with a man of her own choice: "It seems less degrading to give one's self, than to submit to compulsion" (55). While exhibiting a romance hero's self-reliance, she also "asserts liberty and autonomy as alternative values for slave women" (Nudelman 940).

At this point in the narrative, Brent's quest toward self-actualization is consciously active, but her endeavors do not assume the actual movement of a journey motif until a later time. After the births of her two children, she realizes she must physically relocate herself into free territory where she can take them in order to spare them the experiences of slavery. The news that her son and daughter are to be "broke in" at the plantation motivates her to speak the words that prove to be the pivotal point in her quest: "It nerved me to immediate action" (94). Her decision moves her into a flight that is parallel to the journey of the romance hero, a passage filled with obstacles and trials.

Frye explains that the romance hero's passage must move him into a dangerous descent pattern, into a place where he is isolated, immobile and almost mechanical in behavior (129). In the romance, this place is often a cave, labyrinth, or prison; ironically, Linda Brent's lower region is actually an elevated area—a tiny garret in her grandmother's attic. To get to this hiding place, she must don the traditional romance "disguise," in her case, sailor's clothes and charcoal for her light complexion, and she must survive a terrifying obstacle—concealment in a snake-infested swamp.

Finally, Brent is temporarily safe from her relentless master in a space only nine feet long, seven feet wide, and three feet high—"a dismal hole [that] was to be my home for a long, long time" (113). Enduring these cramped quarters for seven years, she experiences the romance hero's isolation from his social community and demonstrates the stamina required to survive *forza,* violence that threatens the hero's successful quest (Frye 65-66). Whereas Brent has escaped the physical violence typically inflicted on slaves, she must now tolerate the bodily discomfort and pain caused by her restricted environment. A thin roof of shingles exposes her to the intense heat of summer that creates suffocating conditions and to the dreadful chill of winter which numbs and frostbites her extremities. "My limbs were benumbed by inaction, and the cold filled them with cramp. I had a very painful sensation of coldness in my head; even my face and tongue stiffened, and I lost the power of speech" (122). Occasionally, storms soak her clothing and bedding; sometimes hundreds of little red insects "fine as a needle's point" (115) torment her skin with intolerable burning; often, rats and mice running over her bed prohibit rest and sleep; and *always,* stifling air, total darkness, limited movement and tedious monotony are constant trials that compose "long, gloomy days, with no object for my eye to rest upon, and no thoughts to occupy my mind, except the dreary past and the uncertain future!" (117).

Along with *forza* is the corresponding concept of *froda,* or fraud, involving elements of guile and craft that can be used against the hero to hinder progress or that can assist survival and eventual continuation of the quest (Frye 68-70). Fortunately, Brent is well-equipped, in spite of her physical difficulties, to use her own *froda* to her advantage against her shrewd pursuer. First of all, her hiding place is wisely chosen; her own grandmother's house, in the same neighborhood as her master's, is the last place he would consider searching: "there was no place, where slavery existed, that could have afforded me so good a place of concealment" (117). Also, her resourcefulness leads her to create a one-inch hole, her "loophole of retreat" (114), through which to view any activities in the yard below. This opening not only provides her with a psychological balance of reality outside her isolated sphere but also gives her courage and mental stamina to survive by providing visual and aural access to her children who play nearby.

Finally, understanding Dr. Flint's shrewd, persistent nature, Brent "resolves to match my cunning against his cunning" (128). She writes letters to him, dates them ahead and sends them to be mailed from New York and Boston by way of supportive friends and family members. Her garret is a safe haven from which to throw her pursuer off her trail, "from which to spy on her enemy and to wage psychological warfare against him" (Yellin xxviii), and through *froda,* she "challenges the masculine assumption that physical battle is the most effective and heroic" (Sale 708). Also, her letters provide the romance element of twins or double identity. They "project an alter ego in freedom up North" (Andrews 259) while the still-enslaved Brent awaits the appropriate time to continue her journey.

Also operating within her quest is the oracle of the romance, the voice of a god-like figure behind the action who expresses his will and speaks of the ultimate outcome (Frye 107). Brent's oracle is her grandmother who not only has always been her icon of goodness and strength but who also consistently "speaks" to her during her long sojourn in the attic. With a system of different knocks for different meanings, her grandmother comes to her as often as possible to whisper words of counsel, encouragement and assurance that someday Brent will be safe with her children.

The day does finally come when Brent becomes mobile in her quest, and with this forward movement comes the romance "ascent" phase. Even though she is not yet legally free, her relocation in Philadelphia places her at least in the improved condition of being on free soil and temporarily safe from her pursuer. Jacobs's rhetoric indicates an ascent pattern and underscores the momentous rise in Brent's situation; she comes up on the deck of a boat to view the sunrise, to see "the great orb come up slowly out of the water, as it seemed" (158). Here, also, continues the theme of double identity. Not realizing that Brent will be on the same boat, her friend has assumed her first name; and when the two meet on board, Fanny exclaims, "Linda, can this be *you*? or is it your ghost?" (156). When finally among people in the city streets, Brent's real identity is still in question: "My face was so blistered and peeled, by sitting on deck, in wind and sunshine, that I thought they could not easily decide to what nation I belonged" (160).

A trial scene is common near the end of a romance, usually an unjust trial created by society as a whole rather than by an individual (Frye 139). Brent's final trial is a composite of negative experiences brought about by racial prejudice in the northern states. Even though she inhabits free territory, she still must operate as a black person in a white society and as a light-complected female among blacks. Dismayed, she must continue to cope with "the same manifestations of that cruel prejudice, which so discourages the feelings, and represses the energies of the colored people" (176). Then, after sending for her children and living in New York, the passage of the Fugitive Slave Act exacerbates her trepidation:

> All that winter I lived in a state of anxiety. When I took the children out to breathe the air, I closely observed the countenances of all I met. I dreaded the approach of summer, when snakes and slave-holders make their appearance. I was, in fact, a slave in New York, as subject to slave laws as I had been in a Slave State. Strange incongruity in a State called free!
>
> (193)

Brent's trial period clearly parallels that of the romance where "it is much more frequently the individual . . . who has the vision of liberation, and the society they are involved with that wants to remain in a blind and gigantic darkness" (Frye 139).

Her vision of liberation achieves reality, however, when compassionate new friends procure freedom for her and her children. After years of "flying from pillar to post . . . as if the chase was never to end" (198), her journey is over and her quest is complete. Her persecution is ended, and the burden of a flight from slavery has been lifted from her weary shoulders: "I and my children are now free! We are as free from the power of slaveholders as are the white people of the north; and though that, according to my ideas, is not saying a great deal, it is a vast improvement in *my* condition" (201).

Linda Brent has indeed improved her condition by affirming her identity as a free human being, and her quest is parallel to that of the traditional romance hero. Harriet Jacobs portrays an engrossing protagonist who convincingly represents the composite role of heroic slave, heroic mother and heroic female; the persona of romance hero not only adds another dimension to this character but does so without detracting from the exemplary qualities of the others. Furthermore, Brent's capacity in this role convincingly crosses gender lines. Jacobs reverses the idea that heroism is accessible only by traditional male qualities of power and aggressiveness. In his analysis of female heroism, Lee R. Edwards suggests how this might be viable: "The possibility of the woman hero is contingent only on recognizing the aspirations of consciousness as human attributes. . . . Heroism thus read and understood is a human necessity, capable of being represented equally by either sex" (11). The "human necessity" prompting Brent's struggle and survival disregards gender requisites, and Brent emerges as a heroic human being, desiring the consciousness of identity.

Recognition of this "new kind of female hero" as a rendering of an "old" literary male type acquires special significance when we realize that Jacobs's romance hero is effective as a literary transition. Brent's search for identity forms a bridge between the traditional male figure of the past and the unconventional female protagonist of the future. "Jacobs's book may well have influenced Frances Ellen Watkins Harper's pioneering novel *Iola Leroy; Or, Shadows Uplifted* (1892), which in turn helped shape the writings of Zora Neale Hurston and other foremothers of black women writing today" (Yellin xxix). In fact, Hurston's Janie Crawford in *Their Eyes Were Watching God* has recently been considered as a convincing portrayal of the romance heroine (Daniel 66-76). Both Janie and Linda Brent acquire the same important quality of heroic female self-affirmation, the ability to survive on their own.

Critics are generally in consensus that contemporary female protagonists are portrayed with new forms of empowerment:

> By the beginning of the twentieth century, novelists seem readier to abandon the project of entrapping the female heroic character and begin the task of inventing maneuvers whereby she can break out of familial, sexual, and social bondage into an altered and appropriate world.
>
> (Edwards 16)

Undeniably, Brent is entrapped in traditional entanglements of female roles, but Jacobs gives her the "maneuvers" with which to "break out." Equipping her "new kind of hero" with the provisions of the romance hero, Jacobs gives literature a persona who is more appropriate for "an altered and appropriate world." Placing Jacobs's female protagonist in the role of romance hero in no way ignores the fact that Brent's narrative is actually Jacobs's own story. In fact, this persona extends into circumstances of her situation after her quest ends. With the romance hero's cyclical movement back to his place of origin, she eventually revisits the house of her childhood and concealment. Returning under extremely different circumstances, she writes to a friend that "the change is so great I can hardly take it all in" (249).

Because this narrative of "incidents" is not a fictional account does not prevent it from revealing similarities to a fictional genre and to a fictional hero prototype. After all, according to her friend Amy Post, Jacobs was operating in a society that "sanctions laws and customs which make the experiences of the present more strange than any fictions of the past" (204). Certainly, in penning her own story during the popularity of the antislavery novel, Jacobs used the form of narrative that "served as a conduit through which African American women could reach their Anglo sisters" (Foster 101), but her protagonist also

provides writers after her with a "new kind of hero" who transcends race and class and gender and time.

Works Cited

Andrews, William L. *To Tell a Free Story: The First Century of Afro-American Autobiography, 1760-1865*. Urbana: U of Illinois P, 1986.

Becker, Elizabeth C. "Harriet Jacobs's Search for Home." *College Language Association Journal* 35 (1992): 411-21.

Daniel, Janice. "'De understandin' to go 'long wid it': Realism and Romance in *Their Eyes Were Watching God*." *Southern Literary Journal* 24 (Fall 1991): 66-76.

Edwards, Lee R. *Psyche As Hero: Female Heroism and Fictional Form*. Middletown, CT: Wesleyan UP, 1984.

Foster, Frances Smith. *Written by Herself: Literary Production by African American Women, 1746-1892*. Bloomington: Indiana UP, 1993.

Frye, Northrop. *The Secular Scripture: A Study of the Structure of Romance*. Cambridge: Harvard UP, 1976.

Jacobs, Harriet A. *Incidents in the Life of a Slave Girl: Written by Herself*. Ed. Jean Fagan Yellin. Cambridge: Harvard UP, 1987.

Nudelman, Franny. "Harriet Jacobs and the Sentimental Politics of Female Suffering." *English Literary History* 59 (1992): 939-64.

Post, Amy. Appendix. *Incidents in the Life of a Slave Girl: Written by Herself*. By Harriet Ann Jacobs. Cambridge: Harvard UP, 1987. 203-04.

Sale, Maggie. "Critiques from Within: Antebellum Projects of Resistance." *American Literature* 64 (1992): 695-718.

Yellin, Jean Fagan. Introduction. *Incidents in the Life of a Slave Girl: Written by Herself*. By Harriet Ann Jacobs. Cambridge: Harvard UP, 1987. xiii-xxxiv.

FURTHER READING

Biographies

Yellin, Jean Fagan. "'Written by Herself': Harriet Jacobs's Slave Narrative." *American Literature* 53, no. 3 (November 1981): 479-86.

Seminal study that reveals the existence of letters attesting to the authenticity of Jacobs's narrative and illuminating the editorial role of the white abolitionist Lydia Maria Child.

————. "*Legacy* Profile: Harriet Ann Jacobs." *Legacy* 5, no. 2 (fall 1988): 55-61.

Overview of Jacobs's life and her narrative.

————. "Harriet Jacobs's Family History." *American Literature* 66, no. 4 (December 1994): 765-77.

Corrects an error in her 1987 edition of Incidents in the Life of a Slave Girl *regarding the identity of Jacobs's father.*

————. *Harriet Jacobs: A Life*. New York: Perseus Books, 2004, 394 p.

Details Jacobs's life before and after her writing Incidents in the Life of a Slave Girl.

Criticism

Accomando, Christine. "'The laws were laid down to me anew': Harriet Jacobs and the Reframing of Legal Fictions." *African American Review* 32, no. 2 (summer 1998): 229-45.

Contends that Jacobs's narrative includes a sustained legal critique.

Bartholomaus, Craig. "'What Would You Be?': Racial Myths and Cultural Sameness in *Incidents in the Life of a Slave Girl*." *CLA Journal* 39, no. 2 (December 1995): 179-94.

Examines the use of "true womanhood" and other elements in Jacobs's narrative to show how the text refutes negative stereotypes advanced by nineteenth-century scientific theories of race.

Beardslee, Karen E. "Through Slave Culture's Lens Comes the Abundant Source: Harriet A. Jacobs's *Incidents in the Life of a Slave Girl*." *MELUS* 24, no. 1 (spring 1999): 37-61.

Emphasizes the individuality of experience in Jacobs's autobiography even as it offers lessons about the system of slavery, history, culture, and the melding of past and present.

Becker, Elizabeth C. "Harriet Jacobs's Search For Home." *CLA Journal* 35, no. 4 (June 1992): 411-21.

Analyzes the "cult of true womanhood" on Jacobs as a black woman, arguing that her emphasis on the home as the center of female purpose influences every aspect of her narrative.

Boren, Mark Edelman. "Slipping the Shackles of Subjectivity: The Narrator as Runaway in *Incidents in the Life of a Slave Girl*." *Genre* 34, no. 1-2 (spring-summer 2001): 33-62.

Examines the subject position of Jacobs as narrator in her autobiography.

Braxton, Joanne M., and Sharon Zuber. "Silences in Harriet 'Linda Brent' Jacobs's *Incidents in the Life of a Slave Girl*." In *Listening to Silences: New Essays in Feminist Criticism*, edited by Elaine Hedges and Shelley Fisher Fishkin, pp. 146-55. New York: Oxford University Press, 1994.

Discusses the way in which Jacobs uses and transcends the silence imposed upon her by virtue of her being a slave, a woman, and a mother.

Carby, Hazel V. "'Hear My Voice, Ye Careless Daughters': Narratives of Slave and Free Women before Emancipation." In *Reconstructing Womanhood: The Emergence of the Afro-American Woman Novelist*, pp. 40-61. New York: Oxford University Press, 1987.

Explores the influence of the nineteenth-century conception of "true womanhood" on Jacobs's narrative and contends that the author used the events of her life to critique conventional standards of female behavior and to question their relevance for black women's experience.

Cutter, Martha J. "Dismantling 'The Master's House': Critical Literacy in Harriet Jacobs' *Incidents in the Life of a Slave Girl*." *Callaloo* 19, no. 1 (1996): 209-25.

Discusses Jacobs's use of her literacy in a way that liberated her from society's dominant discursive practices.

Dalton, Anne B. "The Devil and the Virgin: Writing Sexual Abuse in *Incidents in the Life of a Slave Girl*." In *Violence, Silence, and Anger: Women's Writing as Transgression*, edited by Deirdre Lashgari, pp. 38-61. Charlottesville: University Press of Virginia, 1995.

Suggests that, through her language and imagery, Jacobs suffered more sexual abuse than she reports in her narrative.

Doherty, Thomas. "Harriet Jacobs's Narrative Strategies: *Incidents in the Life of a Slave Girl*." *Southern Literary Journal* 19, no. 1 (fall 1986): 79-91.

Examines Jacobs's use of the conventions of the sentimental genre and describes the shortcomings of the narrative as a sentimental novel.

Emsley, Sarah. "Harriet Jacobs and the Language of Autobiography." *Canadian Review of American Studies* 28, no. 2 (1998): 145-62.

Discusses the truth of Jacobs's autobiographical account despite its sentimental, unconventional, and fiction-like aspects.

Foreman, P. Gabrielle. "The Spoken and the Silenced in *Incidents in the Life of a Slave Girl* and *Our Nig*." *Callaloo* 13, no. 2 (spring 1990): 313-24.

Explores how Jacobs's autobiography resembles and differs from Harriet E. Wilson's *Our Nig*, focusing on how the two writers negotiate the assertion of their voices.

Fox-Genovese, Elizabeth. *To Write My Self: The Autobiographies of Afro-American Women*, edited by Shari Benstock, pp. 161-80. Bloomington: Indiana University Press, 1987.

Includes a discussion of the differences in tone between Jacobs's autobiography and other works of sentimental domestic literature.

Garfield, Deborah M. "Speech, Listening, and Female Sexuality in *Incidents in the Life of a Slave Girl*." *Arizona Quarterly* 50, no. 2 (summer 1994): 19-49.

Discusses the complexities involved in acts of speaking, writing, and hearing, and in Jacobs's articulation of her experiences in her narrative.

Garfield, Deborah M., and Rafia Zafar. *Harriet Jacobs and* Incidents in the Life of a Slave Girl: *New Critical Essays*, edited by Deborah M. Garfield and Rafia Zafar. New York: Cambridge University Press, 1996, 256 p.

Offers a collection of thirteen critical essays.

Gelder, Ann. "Reforming the Body: 'Experience' and the Architecture of Imagination in Harriet Jacobs's *Incidents in the Life of a Slave Girl*." In *Inventing Maternity: Politics, Science, and Literature, 1650-1865*, edited by Susan C. Greenfield and Carol Barash, pp. 252-66. Lexington: The University Press of Kentucky, 1999.

Discusses the use of and politicization of the female body in Jacobs's narrative.

Gwin, Minrose. "Green-Eyed Monsters of the Slavocracy: Jealous Mistresses in Two Slave Narratives." In *Conjuring: Black Women, Fiction, and Literary Tradition*, edited by Marjorie Pryse and Hortense J. Spillers, pp. 39-52. Bloomington: Indiana University Press, 1985.

Examines the ways in which the stereotypes and relationships of white and black women within the "slavocracy" of the South informs Jacobs's work.

Kaplan, Carla. "Narrative Contracts and Emancipatory Readers: *Incidents in the Life of a Slave Girl*." *Yale Journal of Criticism* 6, no. 1 (spring 1993): 93-119.

Argues that Jacobs attempts to create a new black narrative position that rejects aspects of both the slave narrative genre and romance genre.

Martin, Terry J. "Harriet Jacobs (Linda Brent) (C. 1813-1897)." In *Nineteenth-Century American Women Writers: A Bio-Bibliographical Critical Sourcebook*, edited by Denise D. Knight, pp. 262-69. Westport, Conn.: Greenwood Press, 1997.

Sketch outlining Jacobs's life, major works and themes, and critical response to her writing.

McKay, Nellie Y., and Frances Smith Foster. Introduction to *Incidents in the Life of a Slave Girl*, by Harriet Jacobs, edited by Nellie Y. McKay and Frances Smith Foster, pp. i-xxv. New York: W. W. Norton & Company, 2001.

Reproduces Jacobs's text and presents a selection of contemporary responses, Jacobs's other writings, and critical essays on Incidents in the Life of a Slave Girl.

Mills, Bruce. "Lydia Maria Child and the Ending to Harriet Jacobs's *Incidents in the Life of a Slave Girl*." *American Literature* 64, no. 2 (June 1992): 255-72.

Studies the influence of Lydia Maria Child, the editor of Jacobs's narrative, on the author's writing and on the book's structure and content.

Nayar, Pramod K. "The Dialogic Imperative: The Case of Harriet Jacobs's *Incidents in the Life of a Slave Girl*." *Indian Journal of American Studies* 27, no. 2 (summer 1998): 27-30.

Argues that Jacobs's autobiography can be seen as "dialogic" on several levels: the work is a dialogue to and within herself, a dialogue with white abolitionists, and a dialogue within a dialogue.

Nudelman, Franny. "Harriet Jacobs and the Sentimental Politics of Female Suffering." *ELH* 59, no. 4 (winter 1992): 939-64.

Recounts the ways in which Jacobs's use of the conventions of the sentimental novel and the influence of the "cult of true womanhood" have been analyzed by critics.

Painter, Nell Irvin. Introduction to *Incidents in the Life of a Slave Girl, Written by Herself*, by Harriet Jacobs, edited by Nell Irvin Painter, pp. i-xxxvi. New York: Penguin Books, 2000.

Provides an overview of Jacobs's life, critical assessment of Incidents in the Life of a Slave Girl, *and a review of early notices of the narrative.*

Randle, Gloria T. "Between the Rock and the Hard Place: Mediating Spaces in Harriet Jacobs's *Incidents in the Life of a Slave Girl*." *African American Review* 33, no. 1 (spring 1999): 765-77.

Discusses Jacobs's ability to retain her mental health despite the suffering she endured.

Sanchez-Eppler, Karen. "Righting Slavery and Writing Sex: The Erotics of Narration in Harriet Jacobs *Incidents*." In *Touching Liberty: Abolition, Feminism, and the Politics of the Body*, pp. 83-104. Berkeley: University of California Press, 1993.

Examines the relationship between slavery and the act of writing for Jacobs.

Sherman, Sarah Way. "Moral Experience in Harriet Jacobs's *Incidents in the Life of a Slave Girl*." *NWSA Journal* 2, no. 2 (spring 1990): 167-85.

Argues that the source of moral conflict and ambiguity in Jacobs's work stems from the narrator's struggle with the exploitation and brutality of slavery and idealized conception of "true womanhood."

Skinfill, Mauri. "Nation and Miscegenation: *Incidents in the Life of a Slave Girl*." *Arizona Quarterly* 51, no. 2 (summer 1995): 63-79.

Examines Jacobs's narrative in the context of a capitalist economy and a national discourse of domesticity.

Smith, Valerie. "'Loopholes of Retreat': Architecture and Ideology in Harriet Jacobs's *Incidents in the Life of a Slave Girl*." In *Reading Black, Reading Feminist: A Critical Anthology*, edited by Henry Louis Gates, Jr., pp. 212-26. New York: Meridian, 1990.

Examines the implications of the literal and figurative structures of confinement in Incidents in the Life of a Slave Girl.

Sorisio, Carolyn. "'There is Might in Each': Conceptions of Self in Harriet Jacobs's *Incidents in the Life of a Slave Girl*." *Legacy* 13, no. 1 (1996): 1-18.

Discusses the influence of Romanticism and Transcendentalism on Jacobs's perception of "self."

Walter, Krista. "Surviving in the Garret: Harriet Jacobs and the Critique of Sentiment." *American Transcendental Quarterly* 8, no. 3 (September 1994): 189-210.

Argues that Jacobs's work does not conform to but rather critiques the sentimental tradition.

Warhol, Robyn R. "'Reader, Can You Imagine? No You Cannot': The Narratee as Other in Harriet Jacobs's Text." *Narrative* 3, no. 1 (January 1995): 57-72.

Examines Jacobs's narrative as a reconstruction of the codes that the textual conventions of domestic, sentimental, and Gothic literature promoted in the nineteenth century.

Warner, Anne Bradford. "Santa Claus Ain't a Real Man: *Incidents* and Gender." In *Haunted Bodies: Gender and Southern Texts*, edited by Anne Goodwyn Jones and Susan V. Donaldson, pp. 185-200. Charlottesville: University Press of Virginia, 1997.

Argues that Jacobs reshapes the notion of the narrating person as a trickster and creates a text that is shifting, subversive, spiritual, and satiric.

Washington, Mary Helen. "Meditations on History: The Slave Woman's Voice." In *Invented Lives: Narratives of Black Women 1860-1960*, pp. 3-15. New York: Anchor Press, 1987.

Analyzes Jacobs's use of the sentimental domestic genre in Incidents in the Life of a Slave Girl, *arguing that the work reads more as a slave narrative than a sentimental novel, particularly in the way in which it transcends the boundaries of gender.*

Winifred, Morgan. "Gender-Related Difference in the Slave Narratives of Harriet Jacobs and Frederick Douglass." *American Studies* 35, no. 2 (fall 1994): 73-94.

Compares the different strategies of coping and resistance portrayed in Jacobs's Incidents in the Life of a Slave Girl *and Frederick Doulgass's* Narrative of the Life of Frederick Douglass.

OTHER SOURCES FROM GALE:

Additional coverage of Jacobs's life and career is published in the following sources published by the Gale Group: *African American Writers*, Eds. 1, 2; *Dictionary of Literary Biography*, Vol. 239; *Feminist Writers; Literature and Its Times*, Vol. 2; *Literature Resource Center; Nineteenth-Century Literature Criticism*, Vol. 67; and *Reference Guide to American Literature*, Ed. 4.

SARAH ORNE JEWETT

(1849 - 1909)

(Full name Theodora Sarah Orne Jewett; also wrote under the pseudonyms A. C. Eliot, Alice Eliot, and Sarah O. Sweet) American short story writer, novelist, and poet.

Regarded as a premier writer of American regional, or local color, fiction, Jewett is best known for her short stories about provincial life in New England during the late nineteenth century. Her works are often discussed in conjunction with those of other contemporary local colorists, including Harriet Beecher Stowe, Mary E. Wilkins Freeman, and Rose Terry Cooke, and she is considered an important contributor to the development of the local color movement. Jewett was never an advocate for women's rights, but critics have noted that she presents portraits of strong, self-reliant, and optimistic women, most of whom are unmarried, and shows a concern for women's issues in her works. Feminist scholars have been particularly interested in exploring Jewett's unconventional portraits of women, her subversion of traditional patriarchal literary elements, and her subtle critique of male-dominated society.

BIOGRAPHICAL INFORMATION

Jewett was born September 3, 1849, in the rural port community of South Berwick, Maine, the daughter of Theodore H. Jewett, a wealthy and respected physician, and Caroline F. Perry. As a child she often accompanied her father on his daily rounds to patients' homes, where she met many of the New England characters she later recalled in her fiction. Jewett's youth was for the most part uneventful, secure, and happy. Her fathered tutored her in literature and local history, encouraging her to read from his vast library. Jewett began publishing short stories in 1867 under the pseudonyms A. C. Eliot, Alice Eliot, and Sarah O. Sweet. Her first notable success came just before her twentieth birthday when William Dean Howells accepted the short story "Mr. Bruce" for publication in the *Atlantic Monthly*. Guided by Howells's suggestions as well as her own understanding of life in New England, Jewett subsequently produced a number of successful local color stories for the *Atlantic Monthly*; at Howells's behest, she revised and collected these stories in 1877 in *Deephaven*. The success of *Deephaven* gained Jewett many literary admirers, and her close association with the *Atlantic Monthly* brought her frequently into contact with its editor, James T. Fields, and his wife, Annie, an esteemed philanthropist and literary hostess. Jewett was welcomed into the circle of eminent writers and editors who frequented the Fields's Charles Street salon in Boston. Following the deaths of Jewett's father in 1878 and Charles Fields in 1881, Jewett and Annie Fields cultivated a lifelong friendship. They traveled extensively, making several trips to Europe, during which Jewett met Alfred Tennyson, Matthew Arnold, Henry James, Christina Rossetti, and Rudyard Kipling. Although she thrived on such encounters, Jewett invariably returned to South Berwick every summer to write, believing her travels enabled her to focus more clearly on the unique aspects of her home community. In 1902, Jewett seriously injured her spine in a carriage accident, after which she never returned to writing. She spent her remaining years in leisure, visiting and corresponding with friends. She died from a stroke on June 24, 1909.

MAJOR WORKS

Deephaven, Jewett's first collection of stories, is woven around the observations of a young woman who arrives from the city to spend the summer in the village house of her companion's deceased aunt. In the tales, the narrator reports her impressions of New England country culture and its people to the reader. Jewett used this technique of the outsider-narrator in other works as well. Another important feature of her writing is the description of the natural environment. Her most famous story, "A White Heron," published in 1886 in *A White Heron and Other Stories,* examines the relationship between humanity and the natural world. The young protagonist of the story must choose between love of nature, represented by the heron, and human love, represented by an ornithologist who wants to capture the bird. While "A White Heron" is Jewett's most anthologized work, critics agree that *The Country of the Pointed Firs* (1896) represents her highest achievement. The work has been classified variously as a novel, a series of sketches, and a collection of stories; some critics note that it is in a genre of its own. In the work, which is regarded as the culmination of the author's local color writing, Jewett once again uses the outsider-narrator as the frame. The narrator is a writer from the city who comes to the town of Dunnet Landing in search of a suitable place to work. She stays for the summer as the boarder of Mrs. Almira Todd, an herbalist. As with her other works, Jewett emphasizes setting rather than action, and she offers detailed descriptions of the natural environment and the (mostly female) characters that populate the small town in which the stories take place. In addition to her twelve collections of short stories, Jewett published three novels, juvenile fiction, and a volume of verse. Of these other writings, her novel *A Country Doctor* (1884), about a woman who chooses her career in medicine over marriage, is best known and was clearly influenced by Jewett's experiences growing up as a physician's daughter.

Although Jewett does not explicitly address feminist concerns in her work, much of her writing explores questions about women's roles in society. The 1882 story "Tom's Husband" deals with marriage and female emancipation, and stories such as "Mrs. Bonny" (1876) offer depictions of unconventional women who rely on themselves and are uncontaminated by the male-dominated world. "A White Heron" explores questions about the socialization of girls, gender relations, and the need for women to be true to themselves and to be useful to society. Virtually all of Jewett's fiction contains detailed character studies of unusual women; indeed, some critics have noted that few of her male characters are realistic at all while her descriptions of older females are vivid, sympathetic, and humorous. Jewett also writes extensively about relationships between women, and in *The Country of the Pointed Firs* female friendships form the primary link between the individual and society. Women in Jewett's stories are also depicted as the holders of cultural traditions, those who understand and are identified with the natural environment, and symbols of a receding past in the face of industrialization.

CRITICAL RECEPTION

After the publication of her first collection of short stories, Jewett was considered a writer of national importance. Howells praised her work, and in her preface to *The Country of the Pointed Firs* Willa Cather declared that she would name Jewett's book along with Nathaniel Hawthorne's *The Scarlet Letter* and Mark Twain's *Huckleberry Finn* as three American books that have the possibility of an enduring literary reputation. The popularity of Jewett's work declined after the 1920s, and although some of her stories, most notably "A White Heron," were read in survey courses of American literature, she was considered a minor figure and cited merely as an example of a local colorist. Since the 1970s, however, after feminist critics have reassessed her work, Jewett's reputation has grown and the universality of her writing has been affirmed. Critics have noted that Jewett's fiction rarely addresses questions about women's issues in an overtly political manner, but her work treats women's roles in a patriarchal society. Feminist critics have paid particular attention to the subtle manner in which Jewett critiques the patriarchal establishment with the use of original narrative techniques. They have also examined her depiction of unconventional women, discussed her characters' psychological journeys of self-revelation, and explored her ideas about nature, female heritage and tradition, and the effects of culture on women's psychological development.

PRINCIPAL WORKS

Deephaven (short stories) 1877

Play Days: A Book of Stories for Children (juvenilia and poetry) 1878

Old Friends and New (short stories) 1879

Country By-Ways (short stories) 1881

A Country Doctor (novel) 1884

A Mate of the Daylight, and Friends Ashore (short stories) 1884

A Marsh Island (novel) 1885

A White Heron and Other Stories (short stories) 1886

The Story of the Normans, Told Chiefly in Relation to Their Conquest of England (juvenilia) 1887

The King of Folly Island and Other People (short stories) 1888

Betty Leicester: A Story for Girls (juvenilia) 1890

Strangers and Wayfarers (short stories) 1890

A Native of Winby and Other Tales (short stories) 1893

Betty Leicester's English Xmas: A New Chapter of an Old Story (juvenilia) 1894; republished as *Betty Leicester's Christmas*, 1899

The Life of Nancy (short stories) 1895

The Country of the Pointed Firs (short stories) 1896

The Queen's Twin and Other Stories (short stories) 1899

The Tory Lover (novel) 1901

Stories and Tales. 7 vols. (novel and short stories) 1910

Verses (poetry) 1916

The Best Stories of Sarah Orne Jewett. 2 vols. (short stories) 1925

Sarah Orne Jewett Letters [edited by Richard Cary] (letters) 1967

The Uncollected Short Stories of Sarah Orne Jewett [edited by Richard Cary] (short stories) 1971

PRIMARY SOURCES

SARAH ORNE JEWETT (SHORT STORY DATE 1882)

SOURCE: Jewett, Sarah Orne. "Tom's Husband." *LEGACY* 7 (spring 1990): 30-7.

In the following short story, originally published in the Atlantic Monthly *in 1882, Jewett addresses the question of female liberation in marriage.*

I shall not dwell long upon the circumstances that led to the marriage of my hero and heroine; though their courtship was, to them, the only one that has ever noticeably approached the ideal, it had many aspects in which it was entirely commonplace in other people's eyes. While the world in general smiles at lovers with kindly approval and sympathy, it refuses to be aware of the unprecedented delight which is amazing to the lovers themselves.

But, as has been true in many other cases, when they were at last married, the most ideal of situations was found to have been changed to the most practical. Instead of having shared their original duties, and, as school-boys would say, going halves, they discovered that the cares of life had been doubled. This led to some distressing moments for both our friends; they understood suddenly that instead of dwelling in heaven they were still upon earth, and had made themselves slaves to new laws and limitations. Instead of being freer and happier than ever before, they had assumed new responsibilities; they had established a new household, and must fulfill in some way or another the obligations of it. They looked back with affection to their engagement; they had been longing to have each other to themselves, apart from the world, but it seemed that they never felt so keenly that they were still units in modern society. Since Adam and Eve were in Paradise, before the devil joined them, nobody has had a chance to imitate that unlucky couple. In some respects they told the truth when, twenty times a day, they said that life had never been so pleasant before; but there were mental reservations on either side which might have subjected them to the accusation of lying. Somehow, there was a little feeling of disappointment, and they caught themselves wondering—though they would have died sooner than confess it—whether they were quite so happy as they had expected. The truth was, they were much happier than people usually are, for they had an uncommon capacity for enjoyment. For a little while they were like a sailboat that is beating and has to drift a few minutes before it can catch the wind and start off on the other tack. And they had the same feeling, too, that any one is likely to have who has been long pursuing some object of his ambition or desire. Whether it is a coin, or a picture, or a stray volume of some old edition of Shakespeare, or whether it is an office under government or a lover, when it is fairly in one's grasp there is a loss of the eagerness that was felt in pursuit. Satisfaction, even after one has dined well, is not so interesting and eager a feeling as hunger.

My hero and heroine were reasonably well established to begin with: they each had some money, though Mr. Wilson had most. His father had at one time been a rich man, but with the decline, a few years before, of manufacturing interests, he had become, mostly through the fault of others, somewhat involved; and at the time of his death his affairs were in such a condition that it was still a question whether a very large sum or a moderately large one would represent his estate. Mrs. Wilson, Tom's step-mother, was somewhat of an invalid; she suffered severely at times with asthma, but she was almost entirely relieved by living in another part of the country. While her husband lived, she had accepted her illness as inevitable, and had rarely left home; but during the last few years she had lived in Philadelphia with her own people, making short and wheezing visits only from time to time, and had not undergone a voluntary period of suffering since the occasion of Tom's marriage, which she had entirely approved. She had a sufficient property of her own, and she and Tom were independent of each other in that way. Her only other step-child was a daughter, who had married a navy officer, and had at this time gone out to spend three years (or less) with her husband, who had been ordered to Japan.

It is not unfrequently noticed that in many marriages one of the persons who choose each other as partners for life is said to have thrown himself or herself away, and the relatives and friends look on with dismal forebodings and ill-concealed submission. In this case it was the wife who might have done so much better, according to public opinion. She did not think so herself, luckily, either before marriage or afterward, and I do not think it occurred to her to picture to herself the sort of career which would have been her alternative. She had been an only child, and had usually taken her own way. Some one once said that it was a great pity that she had not been obliged to work for her living, for she had inherited a most uncommon business talent, and, without being disreputably keen at a bargain, her

insight into the practical working of affairs was very clear and far-reaching. Her father, who had also been a manufacturer, like Tom's, had often said it had been a mistake that she was a girl instead of a boy. Such executive ability as hers is often wasted in the more contracted sphere of women, and is apt to be more a disadvantage than a help. She was too independent and self-reliant for a wife; it would seem at first thought that she needed a wife herself more than she did a husband. Most men like best the women whose natures cling and appeal to theirs for protection. But Tom Wilson, while he did not wish to be protected himself, liked these very qualities in his wife which would have displeased some other men; to tell the truth, he was very much in love with his wife just as she was. He was a successful collector of almost everything but money, and during a great part of his life he had been an invalid, and he had grown, as he laughingly confessed, very old-womanish. He had been badly lamed, when a boy, by being caught in some machinery in his father's mill, near which he was idling one afternoon, and though he had almost entirely outgrown the effect of his injury, it had not been until after many years. He had been in college, but his eyes had given out there, and he had been obliged to leave in the middle of his junior year, though he had kept up a pleasant intercourse with the members of his class, with whom he had been a great favorite. He was a good deal of an idler in the world. I do not think his ambition, except in the case of securing Mary Dunn for his wife, had ever been distinct; he seemed to make the most he could of each day as it came, without making all his days' works tend toward some grand result, and go toward the up-building of some grand plan and purpose. He consequently gave no promise of being either distinguished or great. When his eyes would allow, he was an indefatigable reader; and although he would have said that he read only for amusement, yet he amused himself with books that were well worth the time he spent over them.

The house where he lived nominally belonged to his step-mother, but she had taken for granted that Tom would bring his wife home to it, and assured him that it should be to all intents and purposes his. Tom was deeply attached to the old place, which was altogether the pleasantest in town. He had kept bachelor's hall there most of the time since his father's death, and he had taken great pleasure, before his marriage, in refitting it to some extent, though it was already comfortable and furnished in remarkably good taste. People said of him that if it had not been for his illnesses, and if he had been a poor boy, he probably would have made something of himself. As it was, he was not very well known by the towns-people, being somewhat reserved, and not taking much interest in their every-day subjects of conversation. Nobody liked him so well as they liked his wife, yet there was no reason why he should be disliked enough to have much said about it.

After our friends had been married for some time, and had outlived the first strangeness of the new order of things, and had done their duty to their neighbors with so much apparent willingness and generosity that even Tom himself was liked a great deal better than he ever had been before, they were sitting together one stormy evening in the library, before the fire. Mrs. Wilson had been reading Tom the letters which had come to him by the night's mail. There was a long one from his sister in Nagasaki, which had been written with a good deal of ill-disguised reproach. She complained of the smallness of the income of her share in her father's estate, and said that she had been assured by American friends that the smaller mills were starting up everywhere, and beginning to do well again. Since so much of their money was invested in the factory, she had been surprised and sorry to find by Tom's last letters that he had seemed to have no idea of putting in a proper person as superintendent, and going to work again. Four per cent on her other property, instead of eight, which she had been told she must soon expect, would make a great difference to her. A navy captain in a foreign port was obliged to entertain a great deal, and Tom must know that it cost them much more to live than it did him, and ought to think of their interests. She hoped he would talk over what was best to be done with their mother (who had been made executor, with Tom, of his father's will).

Tom laughed a little, but looked disturbed. His wife had said something to the same effect, and his mother had spoken once or twice in her letters of the prospect of starting the mill again. He was not a bit of a business man, and he did not feel certain, with the theories which he had arrived at of the state of the country, that it was safe yet to spend the money which would have to be spent in putting the mill in order. "They think that the minute it is going again we shall be making money hand over hand, just as father did when we were children," he said. "It is going to cost us no end of money before we can make anything. Before father died he meant to put in a good deal of new machinery, I remember. I don't

know anything about the business myself, and I would have sold out long ago if I had had an offer that came anywhere near the value. The larger mills are the only ones that are good for anything now, and we should have to bring a crowd of French Canadians here; the day is past for the people who live in this part of the country to go into the factory again. Even the Irish all go West when they come into the country, and don't come to places like this any more."

"But there are a good many of the old work-people down in the village," said Mrs. Wilson. "Jake Towne asked me the other day if you were n't going to start up in the spring."

Tom moved uneasily in his chair. "I'll put you in for superintendent, if you like," he said, half angrily, whereupon Mary threw the newspaper at him; but by the time he had thrown it back he was in good humor again.

"Do you know, Tom," she said, with amazing seriousness, "that I believe I should like nothing in the world so much as to be the head of a large business? I hate keeping house,—I always did; and I never did so much of it in all my life put together as I have since I have been married. I suppose it is n't womanly to say so, but if I could escape from the whole thing I believe I should be perfectly happy. If you get rich when the mill is going again, I shall beg for a housekeeper, and shirk everything. I give you fair warning. I don't believe I keep this house half so well as you did before I came here."

Tom's eyes twinkled. "I am going to have that glory,—I don't think you do, Polly; but you can't say that I have not been forbearing. I certainly have not told you more than twice how we used to have things cooked. I'm not going to be your kitchen-colonel."

"Of course it seemed the proper thing to do," said his wife, meditatively; "but I think we should have been even happier than we have if I had been spared it. I have had some days of wretchedness that I shudder to think of. I never know what to have for breakfast; and I ought not to say it, but I don't mind the sight of dust. I look upon housekeeping as my life's great discipline;" and at this pathetic confession they both laughed heartily.

"I've a great mind to take it off your hands," said Tom. "I always rather liked it, to tell the truth, and I ought to be a better housekeeper,—I have been at it for five years; though housekeeping for one is different from what it is for two, and one of them a woman. You see you have brought a different element into my family. Luckily, the servants are pretty well drilled. I do think you upset them a good deal at first!"

Mary Wilson smiled as if she only half heard what he was saying. She drummed with her foot on the floor and looked intently at the fire, and presently gave it a vigorous poking. "Well?" said Tom, after he had waited patiently as long as he could.

"Tom! I'm going to propose something to you. I wish you would really do as you said, and take all the home affairs under your care, and let me start the mill. I am certain I could manage it. Of course I should get people who understood the thing to teach me. I believe I was made for it; I should like it above all things. And this is what I will do: I will bear the cost of starting it, myself,—I think I have money enough, or can get it; and if I have not put affairs in the right trim at the end of a year I will stop, and you may make some other arrangement. If I have, you and your mother and sister can pay me back."

"So I am going to be the wife, and you the husband," said Tom, a little indignantly; "at least, that is what people will say. It's a regular Darby and Joan affair, and you think you can do more work in a day than I can do in three. Do you know that you must go to town to buy cotton? And do you know there are a thousand things about it that you don't know?"

"And never will?" said Mary, with perfect good humor. "Why, Tom, I can learn as well as you, and a good deal better, for I like business, and you don't. You forget that I was always father's right-hand man after I was a dozen years old, and that you have let me invest my money and some of your own, and I have n't made a blunder yet."

Tom thought that his wife had never looked so handsome or so happy. "I don't care, I should rather like the fun of knowing what people will say. It is a new departure, at any rate. Women think they can do everything better than men in these days, but I'm the first man, apparently, who has wished he were a woman."

"Of course people will laugh," said Mary, "but they will say that it's just like me, and think I am fortunate to have married a man who will let me do as I choose. I don't see why it is n't sensible: you will be living exactly as you were before you married, as to home affairs; and since it was a good thing for you to know something about housekeeping then, I can't imagine why you should n't go on with it now, since it makes me miserable,

and I am wasting a fine business talent while I do it. What do we care for people's talking about it?"

"It seems to me that it is something like women's smoking: it is n't wicked, but it is n't the custom of the country. And I don't like the idea of your going among business men. Of course I should be above going with you, and having people think I must be an idiot; they would say that you married a manufacturing interest, and I was thrown in. I can foresee that my pride is going to be humbled to the dust in every way," Tom declared in mournful tones, and began to shake with laughter. "It is one of your lovely castles in the air, dear Polly, but an old brick mill needs a better foundation than the clouds. No, I'll look around, and get an honest man with a few select brains for agent. I suppose it's the best thing we can do, for the machinery ought not to lie still any longer; but I mean to sell the factory as soon as I can. I devoutly wish it would take fire, for the insurance would be the best price we are likely to get. That is a famous letter from Alice! I am afraid the captain has been growling over his pay, or they have been giving too many little dinners on board ship. If we were rid of the mill, you and I might go out there this winter. It would be capital fun."

Mary smiled again in an absent-minded way. Tom had an uneasy feeling that he had not heard the end of it yet, but nothing more was said for a day or two. When Mrs. Tom Wilson announced, with no apparent thought of being contradicted, that she had entirely made up her mind, and she meant to see those men who had been overseers of the different departments, who still lived in the village, and have the mill put in order at once, Tom looked disturbed, but made no opposition; and soon after breakfast his wife formally presented him with a handful of keys, and told him there was meat enough in the house for dinner; and presently he heard the wheels of her little phaeton rattling off down the road. I should be untruthful if I tried to persuade any one that he was not provoked; he thought she would at least have waited for his formal permission, and at first he meant to take another horse, and chase her, and bring her back in disgrace, and put a stop to the whole thing. But something assured him that she knew what she was about, and he determined to let her have her own way. If she failed, it might do no harm, and this was the only ungallant thought he gave her. He was sure that she would do nothing unladylike, or be unmindful of his dignity; and he believed it would be looked upon as one of her odd, independent freaks, which always had won respect in the end, however much they had been laughed at in the beginning. "Susan," said he, as that estimable person went by the door with the dust-pan, "you may tell Catherine to come to me for orders about the house, and you may do so yourself. I am going to take charge again, as I did before I was married. It is no trouble to me, and Mrs. Wilson dislikes it. Besides, she is going into business, and will have a great deal else to think of."

"Yes, sir; very well, sir," said Susan, who was suddenly moved to ask so many questions that she was utterly silent. But her master looked very happy; there was evidently no disapproval of his wife; and she went on up the stairs, and began to sweep them down, knocking the dustbrush about excitedly, as if she were trying to kill a descending colony of insects.

Tom went out to the stable and mounted his horse, which had been waiting for him to take his customary after-breakfast ride to the post-office, and he galloped down the road in quest of the phaeton. He saw Mary talking with Jack Towne, who had been an overseer and a valued workman of his father's. He was looking much surprised and pleased.

"I was n't caring so much about getting work, myself," he explained; "I've got what will carry me and my wife through; but it'll be better for the young folks about here to work near home. My nephews are wanting something to do; they were going to Lynn next week. I don't say but I should like to be to work in the old place again. I've sort of missed it, since we shut down."

"I'm sorry I was so long in overtaking you," said Tom, politely, to his wife. "Well, Jack, did Mrs. Wilson tell you she's going to start the mill? You must give her all the help you can."

"'Deed I will," said Mr. Towne, gallantly, without a bit of astonishment.

"I don't know much about the business yet," said Mrs. Wilson, who had been a little overcome at Jack Towne's lingo of the different rooms and machinery, and who felt an overpowering sense of having a great deal before her in the next few weeks. "By the time the mill is ready, I will be ready, too," she said, taking heart a little; and Tom, who was quick to understand her moods, could not help laughing, as he rode alongside. "We want a new barrel of flour, Tom, dear," she said, by way of punishment for his untimely mirth.

If she lost courage in the long delay, or was disheartened at the steady call for funds, she made no sign, and after a while the mill started up, and her cares were lightened, so that she told Tom that before next pay day she would like to go to Boston for a few days, and go to the theatre, and have a frolic and a rest. She really looked pale and thin, and she said she never worked so hard in all her life; but nobody knew how happy she was, and she was so glad she had married Tom, for some men would have laughed at it.

"I laughed at it," said Tom, meekly. "All is, if I don't cry by and by, because I am a beggar, I shall be lucky." But Mary looked fearlessly serene, and said that there was no danger at present.

It would have been ridiculous to expect a dividend the first year, though the Nagasaki people were pacified with difficulty. All the business letters came to Tom's address, and everybody who was not directly concerned thought that he was the motive power of the re-awakened enterprise. Sometimes business people came to the mill, and were amazed at having to confer with Mrs. Wilson, but they soon had to respect her talents and her success. She was helped by the old clerk, who had been promptly recalled and reinstated, and she certainly did capitally well. She was laughed at, as she had expected to be, and people said they should think Tom would be ashamed of himself; but it soon appeared that he was not to blame, and what reproach was offered was on the score of his wife's oddity. There was nothing about the mill that she did not understand before very long, and at the end of the second year she declared a small dividend with great pride and triumph. And she was congratulated on her success, and every one thought of her project in a different way from the way they had thought of it in the beginning. She had singularly good fortune: at the end of the third year she was making money for herself and her friends faster than most people were, and approving letters began to come from Nagasaki. The Ashtons had been ordered to stay in that region, and it was evident that they were continually being obliged to entertain more instead of less. Their children were growing fast too, and constantly becoming more expensive. The captain and his wife had already begun to congratulate themselves secretly that their two sons would in all probability come into possession, one day, of their uncle Tom's handsome property.

For a good while Tom enjoyed life, and went on his quiet way serenely. He was anxious at first, for he thought that Mary was going to make ducks and drakes of his money and her own. And then he did not exactly like the looks of the thing, either; he feared that his wife was growing successful as a business person at the risk of losing her womanliness. But as time went on, and he found there was no fear of that, he accepted the situation philosophically. He gave up his collection of engravings, having become more interested in one of coins and medals, which took up most of his leisure time. He often went to the city in pursuit of such treasures, and gained much renown in certain quarters as a numismatologist of great skill and experience. But at last his house (which had almost kept itself, had given him little to do beside ordering the dinners, while faithful old Catherine and her niece Susan were his aids) suddenly became a great care to him. Catherine, who had been the main-stay of the family for many years, died after a short illness, and Susan must needs choose that time, of all others, for being married to one of the second hands in the mill. There followed a long and dismal season of experimenting, and for a time there was a procession of incapable creatures going in at one kitchen door and out of the other. His wife would not have liked to say so, but it seemed to her that Tom was growing fussy about the house affairs, and took more notice of those minor details than he used. She wished more than once, when she was tired, that he would not talk so much about the house-keeping; he seemed sometimes to have no other thought.

In the first of Mrs. Wilson's connection with manufacturing, she had made it a rule to consult Tom on every subject of importance; but it had speedily proved to be a formality. He tried manfully to show a deep interest which he did not feel, and his wife gave up, little by little, telling him much about her affairs. She said that she liked to drop business when she came home in the evening; and at last she fell into the habit of taking a nap on the library sofa, while Tom, who could not use his eyes much by lamp-light, sat smoking or in utter idleness before the fire. When they were first married his wife had made it a rule that she should always read him the evening papers, and afterward they had always gone on with some book of history or philosophy, in which they were both interested. These evenings of their early married life had been charming to both of them, and from time to time one would say to the other that they ought to take up again the habit of reading together. Mary was so unaffectedly tired in the evening that Tom never liked to propose a walk; for, though he was not a man of peculiarly social nature, he had always been accustomed to pay an occasional evening visit to his neighbors in the village. And though he had little interest in the business world, and still less knowledge of it, after a while he wished that his wife would have more to say about what she was planning and doing, or how things were getting on. He thought that her chief aid, old Mr. Jackson, was far more in her thoughts than he. She was forever quoting Jackson's opinions. He did not like to find that she took it for granted that he was not interested in the welfare of his own property; it made him feel like a sort of pensioner and dependent, though, when they had guests at the house, which was by no means seldom, there was nothing in her manner that would imply that she thought herself in any way the head of the family. It was hard work to find fault with his wife in any way, though, to give him his due, he rarely tried.

But, this being a wholly unnatural state of things, the reader must expect to hear of its change at last, and the first blow from the enemy was dealt by an old woman, who lived near by, and who called to Tom one morning, as he was driving down to the village in a great hurry (to post a letter, which ordered his agent to secure a long-wished-for ancient copper coin, at any price), to ask him if they had made yeast that week, and if she could borrow a cupful, as her own had met with some misfortune. Tom was instantly in a rage, and he mentally condemned her to some undeserved fate, but told her aloud to go and see the cook. This slight delay, besides being killing to his dignity, caused him to lose the mail, and in the end his much-desired copper coin. It was a hard day for him, altogether; it was Wednesday, and the first days of the week having been stormy the washing was very late. And Mary came home to dinner provokingly good-natured. She had met an old school-mate and her husband driving home from the mountains, and had first taken them over her factory, to their great amusement and delight, and then had brought them home to dinner. Tom greeted them cordially, and manifested his usual graceful hospitality; but the minute he saw his wife alone he said in a plaintive tone of rebuke, "I should think you might have remembered that the girls are unusually busy to-day. I do wish you would take a little interest in things at home. The girls have been washing, and I'm sure I don't know what sort of a dinner we can give your friends. I wish you had thought to bring home some steak. I have been busy myself, and couldn't go down to the village. I thought we would only have a lunch."

Mary was hungry, but she said nothing, except that it would be all right,—she did n't mind; and perhaps they could have some canned soup.

She often went to town to buy or look at cotton, or to see some improvement in machinery, and she brought home beautiful bits of furniture and new pictures for the house, and showed a touching thoughtfulness in remembering Tom's fancies; but somehow he had an uneasy suspicion that she could get along pretty well without him when it came to the deeper wishes and hopes of her life, and that her most important concerns were all matters in which he had no share. He seemed to himself to have merged his life in his wife's; he lost his interest in things outside the house and grounds; he felt himself fast growing rusty and behind the times, and to have somehow missed a good deal in life; he felt that he was a failure. One day the thought rushed over him that his had been almost exactly the experience of most women, and he wondered if it really was any more disappointing and ignominious to him that it was to women themselves. "Some of them may be contented with it," he said to himself, soberly. "People think women are designed for such careers by nature, but I don't know why I ever made such a fool of myself."

Having once seen his situation in life from such a stand-point, he felt it day by day to be more degrading, and he wondered what he should do about it; and once, drawn by a new, strange sympathy, he went to the little family burying-ground. It was one of the mild, dim days that come sometimes in early November, when the pale sunlight is like the pathetic smile of a sad face, and he sat for a long time on the limp, frost-bitten grass beside his mother's grave.

But when he went home in the twilight his step-mother, who just then was making them a little visit, mentioned that she had been looking through some boxes of hers that had been packed long before and stowed away in the garret. "Everything looks very nice up there," she said, in her wheezing voice (which, worse than usual that day, always made him nervous); and added, without any intentional slight to his feelings, "I do think you have always been a most excellent house-keeper."

"I'm tired of such nonsense!" he exclaimed, with surprising indignation. "Mary, I wish you to arrange your affairs so that you can leave them for six months at least. I am going to spend this winter in Europe."

"Why, Tom, dear!" said his wife, appealingly. "I could n't leave my business any way in the"—

But she caught sight of a look on his usually placid countenance that was something more than decision, and refrained from saying anything more.

And three weeks from that day they sailed.

GENERAL COMMENTARY

MARILYN E. MOBLEY (ESSAY DATE MARCH 1986)

SOURCE: Mobley, Marilyn E. "Rituals of Flight and Return: The Ironic Journeys of Sarah Orne Jewett's Female Characters." *Colby Library Quarterly* 21, no. 1 (March 1986): 36-42.

In the following essay, Mobley examines Jewett's use of flight imagery to describe her female characters, claiming that this imagery demonstrates her admiration for "self-reliant women."

In light of Sarah Orne Jewett's expressed affection for the rural villages of Maine, it might seem inconsistent that she so often uses flight imagery to describe the real and imaginative journeys of her female characters. Though seemingly contradictory, this characteristic imagery belies an ambivalence toward her native region,[1] and demonstrates an unflinching admiration for its self-reliant women. Challenging the notion that range is masculine and that confinement is feminine,[2] Jewett portrays women who continually contemplate and/or embark on journeys outside the confines of their rural domestic communities. While a different form of flight predominates in each text, certain patterns emerge in her numerous references to birds, holidays and excursions that signify Jewett's attempt to acquaint her readers with the range of experience available to her New England women.[3] The most significant of these patterns—the flight from one's environment to the outside world and the inevitable return home—has the mythic characteristics of ritual and reveals Jewett's complex response to this region, to its women and to her own role as a regional writer. Although inevitable, the return is not a resignation to limitations or failure, but a heroic expression of the desire to remain connected to one's cultural roots; thus, like flight, it is an act of self-affirmation.

With the exception of *The Country of the Pointed Firs*, "A White Heron"[4] presents the most dramatic example of Jewett's flight motifs.

Sylvia's initiatory journey occurs simultaneously on three levels: physically, as an actual adventure, imaginatively, as a "voyage" of discovery, and symbolically, as a passage from ignorance to knowledge. Although the story begins with a description of her as content and secure within her rural setting, Sylvia craves more space than her grandmother's home provides. Consistent with the pastoral resonances in her name is her grandmother's description of her as a "great wand'rer" (164) with whom wild creatures and birds easily identify.[5] Therefore, more significant than the "dream of love" (167) that the ornithologist arouses is the "spirit of adventure" that his inquiries about the white heron inspire.

If the "dream of love" is short-lived, it is because her greater desire is to reach the vantage point where she could "see all the world" (167). Thus, Sylvia does not consider the journey up the tree as a dangerous physical feat, but as a rewarding flight to a greater range of experience, knowledge and freedom. In language customarily attributed to male characters and male quests, we learn of Sylvia's "utmost bravery" in undertaking such a "great enterprise" (168-69). Her journey culminates in two epiphanies: first—the feeling that, like the birds, "she too could go flying" (169), and second—her discovery of the heron's secret nest (169-70). Thus, the portrayal of Sylvia is not only heroic but triumphant.

The nature of her triumph—successfully making the solitary passage from ignorance to knowledge of the world—rehearses the traditional metaphor for the initiatory experience in American literature. If we understand initiation as the first existential ordeal, crisis or encounter with experience in the life of a youth, or more simply as a "viable mode of confronting adult realities,"[6] then we might say Sylvia undergoes an initiation. Yet the traditional pattern of the initiatory journey—that of separation or departure, trial, communication of communal secrets, and return to the community[7]—is not what we have in this story. Although Sylvia returns to her home, her departure has been both real and imaginative, both complete and abortive. In realistic terms, she moves upward but not outward. Only figuratively and psychically does her journey broaden her horizons.

Indeed, if we were to focus solely on the flight or departure itself, it might seem that we have simply another character who attempts to "transcend"[8] the conditions of her rural life. Instead, in Sylvia's return and refusal to reveal communal secrets is a departure from the traditional initia-

tion pattern. Sylvia's refusal to reveal the location of the heron's nest confirms that the journey not only gives her knowledge of the outside world but also courage to reject that world and protect her own. Thus, just as her journey has been a heroic act, so is her decision to deny "the great world . . . for a bird's sake" (170-71). It is a liberating experience that empowers Sylvia to protect the "essential human values"[9] and her harmonious relationship with nature that the hunter threatens. Her ritual of flight and return is not so much a "coming of age" as it is a growing into consciousness.[10]

Despite the realities and the triumphs of Sylvia's ordeal, "A White Heron" remains a highly symbolic, almost metaphysical story. Consequently, Jewett's preoccupation with the need to know the world and the village,[11] and the city and the country appears in oblique terms. In "The Hiltons' Holiday" and "The Flight of Betsey Lane," this same preoccupation is apparent, but it takes on less symbolic, and more explicit, realistic hues. The journeys are therefore horizontal rather than vertical, emphasizing the complimentary needs for self-affirmation and connection to others. For example, the Hilton girls' father suggests their excursion into town as a "treat" or opportunity to "know the world" and "see how other folks do things" (292-93), while their mother advocates the virtues of the country. Her less than enthusiastic response to the proposed trip is emphasized by her stasis in the rocking chair and her questioning "why folks want . . . to go trapesin' off to strange places when such things is happenin' right about 'em" (294). Her words invoke Jewett's own ambivalence toward this region's concomitant self-sufficiency and deprivation.[12]

The characterization of the Hilton girls illustrates how the journey can actually blur the distinctions between town and country. Before the journey, the depiction of the two sisters represents the traditional dichotomy between the female who readily accepts the confines of hearth and home and the one who does not.[13] While Susan Ellen is described as a "complete little housekeeper" (291), Katy is described as one who ventures "out o' doors" to "hark . . . [to] bird[s]" (292). Ironically, the "holiday" trip to town transforms both girls. When they return, their mother perceives that both "children looked different . . . as if they belonged to the town as much as to the country" (304). Their transformation suggests that a woman need not deny one to enjoy the other, but that she could affirm both.

But it is not that the journey itself transforms the girls, but rather that the journey as an excursion into the past changes them. It is in town that the girls learn their family history, listen to the memories of the town's elderly and have their picture taken with their father. Thus, the journey is into the past as a valuable investment in the "riches of association and remembrance" (304) from which they would continually draw on the road to self-discovery.

In short, flight and return are not mutually exclusive experiences, but are the affirmation of desire in Jewett's women. The circularity of the journey does not signify the impoverishment that some have suggested;[14] instead, it signifies the ritualistic pattern of desire, expectation, fulfillment and desire that characterizes the cycle of human experience. In this sense, Jewett is very modern.[15] But as a woman writer, she illustrates that the desire that accompanies a woman's return is not to subdue objects to her own purpose as a man does, but to reconnect and share with the community from which she departed.[16] Accordingly, the Hilton girls, whose lives have been enriched by the day's excursion, share their experiences with their mother, and by so doing, enrich her life as well.

This leads us to "The Flight of Betsey Lane," for the expedition of this elderly spinster is somewhat similar to the excursion of the Hilton girls. But unlike their trip to town, initiated by their father's invitation, Betsey Lane's journey to Philadelphia is inspired by a long hoped for opportunity to "see something of the world before she died" (174). The By-fleet Poor-house, where she resides, has ironic undertones of being both a prison and a haven. Its inhabitants, referred to as "inmates," do not lament their situation, but actually like "the change and excitement" that their winter "residence" provides (172). Yet, as the youngest of the three spinsters, Betsey Lane seeks greater excitement than the poor-house offers. The opportunity to realize her dream comes in the form of one hundred dollars, a sum which furnishes her with a "sense of her own consequence" (179) that is much like the urgent "wish for wings" that Nina Auerbach contends is characteristic of the spinster as hero.[17] Thus, we are prepared for her disappearance to be described as a discovery that she "had flown" (182), and for her departure to be termed a "flitting" (183) and an "escape" (185). In other words, flight has connotations of independent choice, unlimited potential and bird-like freedom from captivity.

While the journey of her friends to search for her is termed a "fruitless expedition" (192), her journey is thoroughly productive. In strictly personal terms, it provides her with much-desired escape from narrow circumstances, with knowledge of the world (almost literally, in that the Centennial she attends is the equivalent of the World's Fair), and with a sense of rejuvenation and fulfillment. Yet her return points to another sense in which her excursion has been productive. When she informs her friends that she has brought each of them a "little somethin'" (192), her words signify more than the material tokens of friendship she gives them. These words also suggest the greater gifts of spiritual renewal she wishes to offer by sharing her journey with them. Again, the female hero's return is characterized by the urgent desire to share and reaffirm communal ties that is almost as urgent as the previous desire to take flight. In sum, Betsey Lane's return also has powers of transformation: it transforms the three friends from mere bean-pickers into a "small elderly company . . . [of] triumphant" women (193). Enriched vicariously through their friend's journey, these women find it easier to endure the realities of their meager existence.

Motifs of flight and return take on their greatest complexity in *The Country of the Pointed Firs*. From the merging of the narrator's story with that of the other characters comes a depiction of Dunnet Landing as both "prison" and "paradise" (37). Men, such as Captain Littlepage, indict this region for its insularity and narrowness (25). But the women see it as "a complete and tiny continent and home" (40). They also provide the flux and vitality that allows the village to survive.[18] Whether it is the daily expeditions of Mrs. Todd, the excursion of Mrs. Blackett to the family reunion, or the flight of Joanna Todd from the community to her self-imposed exile, the ironic journeys of these women sustain the life of this "female landscape."[19] Of all the characters, however, Mrs. Todd and the narrator best illustrate the thematic and structural significances of flight and return.

Mrs. Todd embodies the spirit of the land. While others have been occupationally displaced from the land by industrialization, she survives as a folk herbalist who not only thrives on the soil for her livelihood but moves among her neighbors as one who, like them, "grew out of the soil."[20] Because of her multiple roles as "land-lady, herb gatherer and rustic philosopher" (35), she is more mobile than any of her neighbors. While her trips to gather herbs resemble flight as the freedom of mobility and independence, the journeys to the homes of friends and relatives seem to be flight as escape from solitude or as an excursion from routine. Yet regardless of how often she travels or how much she enjoys administering to the needs of others, she religiously returns to her solitary residence. Thus, while she is depicted as resourceful, heroic and self-reliant, she nevertheless seems tragically alone and imprisoned in "a narrow set of circumstances [which] had caged [her] . . . and held [her] captive" (95). On the other hand, she unselfishly shares with others as if, the narrator observes, she had "been set on this lonely island . . . to keep the balance true, and make up to all her . . . neighbors for other things which they may have lacked" (47). In that she seems to keep some mythic balance between past and present ". . . as if some force of Nature . . . gave her cousinship to . . . ancient deities" (137), Mrs. Todd seems larger than life. When she reminisces about her husband, she retreats into herself and seems tragically human and heroic at the same time. In fact, her grandeur inspires the narrator to compare her to "Antigone" and to view her as a "renewal of some historic soul" (49).

The existential leap from old-fashioned, rustic simplicity to the grandeur and complexity of myth is a crucial one. Myth, an inherently complex narrative that fuses the natural with the supernatural, recalls the value of ritual to give expression to unconscious desires and to affirm our faith in human potential.[21] In the parallel to Antigone is the suggestion that Mrs. Todd heroically affirms this potential at the same time that she must tragically concede to the existence of forces she cannot control. The allusions to classical texts direct us to the universality and complexity of country people and commonplace experience that the narrator grows to comprehend and respect.

The female character who gives unifying perspective and aesthetic complexity to **Pointed Firs** is the narrator. In her mutual roles as visitor/observer and resident/participant, she comes to know the "world" and the "village" in the fullest sense. Her visit is actually a "Return"—as the title of the first chapter informs us—to a rural haven of simplicity or an "unspoiled place"; yet, it is also a flight from an urban prison of complexity and "unsatisfactory normality."[22] In her role as visitor, she journeys from detached ignorance and superiority to involved acceptance and finally to enlightened understanding. Nowhere is this clearer than at the Bowden reunion where she shifts from first

person singular "I" to first person plural "we" (90) to describe that communal celebration. In her role as narrator, she becomes the unifying device that gives thematic and structural continuity to the novel. Her recognition that she cannot remain at Dunnet Landing but must return to Boston, conveys, as does the final chapter title, "A Backward View," that the ultimate reward for the journey out is the opportunity for growth and fulfillment of desire; concurrently, the reward for the journey back is the reservoir of remembrance, self-discovery and renewed desire. Neither journey precludes the significance of the other. The narrator's writing aesthetically affirms both the journey of flight and the journey to return, and thus, preserves what Henry James refers to as "the palpable present."[23] In other words, art can continually shape and recreate the journey.

In the fiction of Sarah Orne Jewett we have just that—art continually recreating the journey. By using the rituals of flight and return in carefully devised circular narrative structures,[24] she exposes the ironies that characterized the lives of many rural women in her time. On her own literary journey, Jewett discovered that she need not be limited by the local color medium; instead she could transform it through her essentially affirmative vision.[25] Indeed, she journeyed beyond the artistic confines of local color into the comprehensive landscape we associate with myth. The achievement of her fiction is that she does not deny the contradictions that emerge, but seeks instead to hold them in balance before us.

Notes

1. Rebecca Wall Nail, "'Where Every Prospect Pleases': Sarah Orne Jewett, South Berwick, and the Importance of Place," in *Critical Essays on Sarah Orne Jewett*, ed. Gwen L. Nagel (Boston: G. K. Hall, 1984), pp. 185-98.

2. Mary Ellmann, *Thinking About Women* (New York: Harcourt Brace and World, 1968), p. 87.

3. Annie Fields, *Letters of Sarah Orne Jewett* (Boston: Houghton Mifflin, 1911), p. 228.

4. Sarah Orne Jewett, *The Country of the Pointed Firs and Other Stories* (Garden City, N.Y.: Doubleday Anchor, 1956). All parenthetical references in the text to "A White Heron," "The Hiltons' Holiday," "The Flight of Betsey Lane" and *Pointed Firs* are to this reprint edition.

5. Carol Pearson and Katherine Pope, *Who Am I This Time? Female Portraits of British and American Literature* (New York: McGraw Hill, 1976), pp. 4-5.

6. Ihab Hassan, *Radical Innocence: Studies in the Contemporary American Novel* (New York: Harper and Row, 1961), p. 41.

7. Virginia Sue Brown Machann, "American Perspectives on Women's Initiations: The Mythic and Realistic Coming to Consciousness," *Dissertation Abstracts International*, XL (Sept. 1979), 1470A.

8. Josephine Donovan, "A Woman's View of Transcendence: A New Interpretation of the Works of Sarah Orne Jewett," *Massachusetts Review*, XXI (1980), 366.

9. A. M. Buchan, *Our Dear Sarah: An Essay on Sarah Orne Jewett* (St. Louis: Committee on Publications at Washington University, 1942), p. 45.

10. Machann, p. 1470A.

11. Willa Cather, *Not Under Forty* (New York: Knopf, 1936), p. 83.

12. Sarah Orne Jewett, "Preface to the 1883 Edition," in *Deephaven and Other Stories,* ed. Richard Cary (New Haven: College and University Press, 1966), p. 31.

13. Donovan, *New England Local Color: A Women's Tradition* (New York: Ungar, 1983), pp. 1-10.

14. Ann Douglas Wood, "The Literature of Impoverishment: The Women Local Colorists in America 1865-1914," *Women's Studies*, I (1972), 3-45.

15. Steven Shaviro, "'That Which Is Always Beginning': Steven's Poetry of Affirmation," *PMLA*, C (March 1985), 220-33.

16. Buchan, p. 45.

17. Nina Auerbach, "Old Maids and the Wish for Wings," in *Woman and the Demon: The Life of a Victorian Myth* (Cambridge: Harvard Univ. Press, 1982), pp. 111-12.

18. Elmer Pry, "Folk-Literary Aesthetics in *The Country of the Pointed Firs*," *Tennessee Folklore Society Bulletin*, XLIV (March 1978), 9.

19. Robin Magowan, "Pastoral and the Art of Landscape in *The Country of the Pointed Firs*," *New England Quarterly*, XXXII (June 1963), 232.

20. Cather, "Preface," *The Country of the Pointed Firs and Other Stories*, p. 4.

21. William Flint Thrall and Addison Hibbard, eds., *A Handbook of Literature* (New York: Odyssey, 1960), pp. 298-99. See also Richard Chase, *The Quest for Myth* (Baton Rouge: Louisiana State Univ. Press, 1949), p. 78.

22. Hyatt H. Waggoner, "The Unity of *The Country of the Pointed Firs*," in *The World of Dunnet Landing: Sarah Orne Jewett Collection*, ed. David Bonnell Green (Lincoln: Univ. of Nebraska Press, 1962), p. 374.

23. Ferman Bishop, "Henry James Criticizes *The Tory Lover*," *American Literature*, XXVII (May 1955), 264, as cited in Richard Cary, *Sarah Orne Jewett* (New York: Twayne, 1962), p. 152.

24. Elizabeth Ammons, "Going in Circles: The Female Geography of Jewett's *Country of the Pointed Firs*," *Studies in the Literary Imagination*, XVI (Fall 1983), 83-92.

25. Louis A. Renza, *"A White Heron" and the Question of Minor Literature* (Madison: Univ. of Wisconsin Press, 1984), p. 196.

KAREN OAKES (ESSAY DATE SEPTEMBER 1990)

SOURCE: Oakes, Karen. "'All that lay deepest in her heart': Reflections on Jewett, Gender, and Genre." *Colby Quarterly* 26, no. 3 (September 1990): 152-60.

In the following essay, Oakes explores some of the major issues in Jewett's works and discusses how The Country of the Pointed Firs *blurs the boundaries of culture, race, and gender.*

In the beginning (or in 1941), God (later known as F. O. Matthiessen) created the American Renaissance.[1] Emerson and Thoreau, Melville and Hawthorne and Whitman he created them. And he saw that it was good.

I give this rather whimsical introduction to my thoughts on Sarah Orne Jewett by way of suggesting how circuitous my route to her has been. Nineteenth-century American literature has, until very recently, focused primarily if not exclusively on the magnetic figures gathered around mid-century. My own education, at an excellent women's college, and later, at a radical university, foregrounded Emerson and company to the obliteration of "lesser" deities. I experienced the pleasure of Jewett—appropriately, it turns out—through the mediation of a friend, who said simply, as if of peach pie, "I think you'll like her."

And I did. The setting of her work conjured the New England of my childhood, her characters and their voices, the members of my extended family. But if my first response to reading **The Country of the Pointed Firs** was pure delight, my second was pure rage. I was staggered that I had never heard her name even once in the course of my elite "formal" education, though I thought I understood why. Jewett's writing has over the years been the source of much critical discord. Is **The Country of the Pointed Firs** a (failed) novel, a set of loosely related sketches, or something else entirely? The flurry of recent interest in her work at times evinces the same jittery quality. Those who love her often prove determined to show how she meets the standards set by American Renaissance writers—or, perhaps more accurately, by Matthiessen and his cohorts—and hence other questions arise such as how to define her main character (which of course assumes that there must be *a main* character) or how to describe her development (which presumes a progressive rather than an accretive model). A recent essay in the feminist journal *Signs* attempts to locate the book within a "new" genre, "narrative of community."[2] But before I focus more specifically on **The Country of the Pointed Firs,** I'd like to rehearse some of the larger issues to which Jewett's work speaks, hoping that you will be patient with my game of hopscotch and will accept my assurance that all the jumps will lead to "home."

Genre, to be sure, is a convenient concept not only for contemporary critics, a peg on which to hang our hats, but also for professors of literature. How else might we lasso the rambunctious variety of texts which we teach? Hence, we imagine courses in "Twentieth-Century American Women's Poetry" and "Nineteenth-Century Women's Fiction," to cite two of the courses I've taught in recent years. Indeed, genre is not only convenient, but, as one contemporary critic argues, "Few concepts of literary criticism are quite as 'literary' as the concept of genre."[3] Genre study is as old as Plato and Aristotle and as new as a course a friend teaches, "The Contemporary Mystery Novel." Of course, the most sophisticated genre criticism explores the overlap of genres within individual works and attempts constantly to recognize or invent new terms.

If genre figures prominently in discussion of Jewett's work, canonical texts have hardly been immune to debate. Is *The Scarlet Letter* a novel or a romance (I think it's a sermon, but that's another paper)? Nor has the debate been only a recent concern, for mid-nineteenth-century reviewers constantly interrogated Whitman's work according to the touchstone of lyric poetry; was *Leaves of Grass,* they asked, poetry, prose, or, as tastemaker Rufus Griswold asserted, trash? Even writers whose work has seemed generically reliable have encountered scrutiny; at a recent conference, one meeting I attended focused on Dickinson's poems as letters and her letters as poems.[4]

Because of the traditional, even self-defining, quality of genre in literary studies, much influential feminist criticism has explored women's relation to genre. Sandra Gilbert and Susan Gubar discuss in *The Madwoman in the Attic* the affinity of narrative to women's lives and the problematics of lyric poetry, just as Virginia Woolf before them had done.[5] Such critics, female and male, have for some time questioned the hegemony of the traditional literary genres of fiction, poetry, and drama, and we can see the concrete consequences of this questioning in revised syllabi and in new anthologies. For example, many in American literature would now consider texts like Charlotte Perkins Gilman's "journal," *The Yellow Wall-Paper,* or Harriet Jacobs' autobiographical *Incidents in the Life of a Slave Girl* to be canonical; and the new *Heath Anthology of American Literature* includes such "non-canonical" works as Afro-

American folk tales. But the larger question these transformations raise is the essentiality of genre as a lens for discussion.

Jewett, I believe, questions radically the notion of genre if we understand that concept to resonate beyond the categories of fiction, poetry, and drama to include the larger matter of boundaries. Her current reputation (or lack thereof) reflects her corseting by critics into forms and attitudes which she refuses to occupy.[6] One of her best readers, Elizabeth Ammons, discusses the image of the circle as a metaphor for the structure of *The Country of the Pointed Firs,* and in so doing she de-emphasizes the norms of development, climax, and denouement which have haunted her critical predecessors, not to mention poor high-school students across the country.[7] We do well to follow Ammons' lead and step outside the boundaries of literary theory into psychological and cultural theory. The work of sociologist Nancy Chodorow is useful here; Chodorow argues that masculine and feminine identity are differently defined, the former by an emphasis on individuation and a need for separateness and the latter by a need for relation and connection with others. Feminine identity, to use her terms, evinces "flexible or permeable ego boundaries." In spite of her focus only on white, middle-class, heterosexual individuals, Chodorow provides a helpful metaphor in connection to the matter of Jewett and genre.[8]

Indeed, the problem of genre is as intimately linked with the matter of gender in Western literature as ham and eggs. Sandra Gilbert suggests this connection in her recent article, "The American Sexual Politics of Walt Whitman and Emily Dickinson," which is grounded in Chodorow's theory. In brief, Gilbert argues that both Whitman and Dickinson wrote something she calls "not-poetry"; but she contrasts the reliance of each on traditional genres. Whitman's poetry ultimately rehearses familiar poetic forms, suggesting a masculine impulse toward individuation, while Dickinson's elides those boundaries, suggesting a feminine impulse toward fluidity and providing a paradigm for the female artist.[9] In a masculine-minded culture, such a model for consciousness, for artistic creation, and even for critical discourse may receive little credence. (I recall here D. H. Lawrence's abhorrence of Whitman: "Always wanting to merge himself into the womb of something or other.")[10]

For Jewett, the impulse to erase boundaries could not have been unambivalent. The popularity and respect accorded to her by her contemporaries was no doubt in some measure due to her apparent acceptance of some traditional boundaries. Literature, for example, should possess a reverence for the past, and *The Country of the Pointed Firs* gestures toward the past in several ways. The city-dwelling narrator's escape to the Maine coastal town of Dunnet Landing echoes the anxiety of an increasingly industrialized country and its desire for a simpler life. The narrator's landlady, Mrs. Todd, is a practitioner of traditional herbal medicine who initiates the former into a tradition of community and family relations. Jewett connects Mrs. Todd not only with the New England past and the American past, however, but also with the Western tradition, as in the central scene where the two characters gather pennyroyal:

> She looked away from me, and presently rose and went on by herself. There was something lonely and solitary about her great determined shape. She might have been Antigone alone on the Theban plain. It is not often given in a noisy world to come to the places of great grief and silence. An absolute, archaic grief possessed this country-woman; she seemed like a renewal of some historic soul, with her sorrows and the remoteness of a daily life busied with rustic simplicities and the scents of primeval herbs.[11]

Jewett's allusions to myth confirm her membership in literary history, yet she simultaneously incorporates herself into a "modern" realistic tradition in her attentiveness to the important issue of humans' alienation from nature. The tone of this passage is unmistakably elegiac, with its emphasis on "places of great grief and silence," on Mrs. Todd's "lonely and solitary figure," and her "absolute, archaic grief."

If paradise is lost, it is also regained and conserved in Jewett's own writing, which she metaphorizes in the narrator's efforts at herb-gathering:

> I was not incompetent at herb-gathering, and after a while, when I had sat long enough waking myself to new thoughts, and reading a page of remembrance with new pleasure, I gathered some bunches, as I was bound to do, and at last we met again higher up the shore, in the plain every-day world we had left behind when we went down to the pennyroyal plot.
>
> (49-50)

A kind of waking dream, writing, like its sister act of reading, accomplishes a conservation of the self and its history. My interest here, however, is not to discuss how Jewett confirms some of the boundaries of her time—among them the idea that women should focus more on the domestic and private than on the public and political realms—but to suggest some of the ways in which she breaks "generic" boundaries, boundaries of kind, of definition, and in so doing commits a radical act for Western culture.[12]

Paula Gunn Allen's work provides an avenue from which we might meet Jewett. In her Introduction to *Spider Woman's Granddaughters*, a collection of short pieces by Native American women, Allen discusses literary convention with a particular emphasis on the convention that specifies the segregation of (for example) "long stories from short, traditional stories from contemporary." Allen's reflections on boundaries is so intense and interesting that I quote it here at length:

> The dogmatism of the Western literary position has consequences that go well beyond the world of literature, which include the Western abhorrence of mixing races, classes, or genders (which is why homosexuality and lesbianism are so distressing to many Western minds). Similarly, the mixing of levels of diction, like the mixing of spiritual beliefs and attitudes, is disdained if not prohibited. This rigid need for impermeable classificatory boundaries is reflected in turn in the existence of numerous institutional, psychological, and social barriers designed to prevent mixtures from occurring. Western literary and social traditionalists are deeply purist, and today, millennia after Aristotle described the features that characterized Greek literature, his descendents proclaim and enforce purism's rules in thousands of ways large and small.

Allen goes on to assert, "Intellectual apartheid of this nature helps create and maintain political apartheid."[13] The impulse for this apartheid, she makes quite clear, is the Western value of purity, a value which circumscribed women of Jewett's era in the dominant culture in precise and well-documented ways, from the sexual to the literary.[14] It seems to me that Jewett's blurring of boundaries, both substantive and structural, in *The Country of the Pointed Firs* represents a dialogue with the notion of purity and a gesture toward the tribal sensibility which Allen describes. Or perhaps, in other terms, we can construct an analogy between the tribal and the psychological feminine.

My route to Jewett has so far been intentionally circuitous since one of my goals is to rehearse the writer's own freedom. Nonlinear, accretive, process-oriented, *The Country of the Pointed Firs* eludes interpretive certainties, refusing to stand still for dissection, yet inviting pleasure. I offer my observations up to this point and those to come less as a map for reading Jewett and more as a meditation on her world.

One important fence which Jewett dismantles is that between culture and nature. Historian Ann Leighton tells us that in early New England, one of women's jobs was to tend the gardens, a source of food and medicine; Jewett's Mrs. Todd occupies this traditional role, growing herbs and dispensing nostrums.[15] But Mrs. Todd's role exceeds its boundaries, for Jewett tells us that "Mrs. Todd was an ardent lover of herbs, both wild and tame." Furthermore, the garden itself supersedes its margins, as wild and tame converge inside the pale. Easily identifiable are the "balm and sage and borage and mint, wormwood and southernwood," in contrast to another corner:

> At one side of this herb plot were other growths of a rustic pharmacopoeia, great treasures and rarities among the commoner herbs. There were some strange and pungent odors that roused a dim sense and remembrance of something in the forgotten past. Some of these might once have belonged to sacred and mystic rites, and have had some occult knowledge handed with them down the centuries; but now they pertained only to humble compounds brewed at intervals with molasses or vinegar or spirits in a small cauldron on Mrs. Todd's kitchen stove.
>
> (3-4)

Jewett indicates the cultural status not only of the garden itself but of its botanical inhabitants, for to the familiar and domesticated herbs she assigns names, while others more mysterious than and antecedent to the tame ones remain unspecified. Mrs. Todd distills "wild" herbs into what were once primordial elixirs but are now only "humble compounds."

Nevertheless, the residue of wildness remains in the description as we discover that Mrs. Todd dispenses her concoctions "to suffering neighbors, who usually came at night as if by stealth, bringing their own ancient-looking vials to be filled." One, however, is more significant than all the rest: "One nostrum was called the Indian remedy, and its price was but fifteen cents; the whispered directions could be heard as customers passed the windows" (4). This "Indian remedy," which elicits Mrs. Todd's connection with untamed nature, is most likely a medium of woman's freedom from her cultural role as mother—namely, an abortifacient; her favorite pennyroyal has been esteemed for the same purpose since at least the mid-seventeenth century. Most of her herbs, in fact, respond to female reproductive needs; a veritable women's health center is Mrs. Todd, whose "garden" is the world.[16]

The mention of the Indian remedy in connection with Mrs. Todd raises an adjacent problem of purity, namely, racial and cultural purity. In an era in which the problems of Native Americans were receiving fresh attention, when Standing Bear had come to Boston to speak on the displacement of the Poncas, when missionary women headed west and the United States government was establishing boarding schools to "help" Native Americans "assimilate," when Jewett's contemporary Mary E. Wilkins (Freeman) had written a novel published in the same year as *The Country of the Pointed Firs*, *Madelon* (1896), whose female protagonist possessed Iroquois blood, and Helen Hunt Jackson had completed *A Century of Dishonor* (1881) and *Ramona* (1885), it would have been impossible for Jewett not to be aware of and, however subliminally, to respond to the notion of ethnic purity.[17] Mrs. Todd, she implies, figures a person whose heritage is (at least metaphorically) mixed-blood, for she possesses the herbal skill not only of her colonial counterparts but of her Indian predecessors. Furthermore, we learn in another story, "The Foreigner," that Mrs. Todd has acquired much of her insight from a woman who parallels the figure of the Indian outsider, a French woman from Jamaica, who significantly cannot speak "Maine" and who horrifies her sober and asexual counterparts by singing and dancing in the meeting-house vestry in a shockingly "natural" manner (170, 167). This "foreigner's" subsequent social exclusion surely speaks to the women's fears of the loss of purity.

If racial or cultural boundaries are an important, if covert, issue in *The Country of the Pointed Firs* and Jewett's work generally, another set of boundaries that the writer rattles is that of gender. Mrs. Todd, while she figures the community's loving mother in her position as herbal doctor, is equally capable of assuming traditional masculine power. When she and the narrator embark to visit Mrs. Todd's mother, Mrs. Todd directs their progress in images which evoke the shape and movement of the book itself: "'You better let her drift; we'll get there 'bout as quick; the tide 'll take her right out from under these old buildin's; there's plenty wind outside'" (32). As paradoxical "lawgiver," Mrs. Todd occupies the seat of power, as we see in the exchange which follows. An onlooker feels compelled to criticize her management, concluding, as some critics have of the book, "'She's lo'ded bad, your bo't is—she's heavy behind's she is now!'" but Mrs. Todd does not relinquish her captaincy: "'That you, Asa? Goodmornin',' she said politely. 'I al'ays liked the starn seat best. When'd you get back from up country?'" (33). Her verbal wit in response to this landlubber indicates her ability to assume masculine power not only in the realm of seamanship but also in the realm which defines all masculine power, language itself (Gilbert and Gubar, 3-92).

This blurring of gender boundaries emerges in any number of characters, from Mrs. Todd's shy brother William to Captain Elijah Tilley, who receives the narrator into his home with his knitting, "a blue yarn stocking," in hand (120). The narrator observes, "There was something delightful in the grasp of his hand, warm and clean, as if it never touched anything but the comfortable woolen yarn, instead of cold sea water and slippery fish" (120). After the death of his wife, Elijah has become domesticated so that his year is shared by feminine and masculine endeavors:

> "No, I take stiddy to my knitting after January sets in," said the old seafarer. . . . "The young fellows braves it out, some on 'em; but, for me, I lay in my winter's yarn an' set here where 'tis warm, an' knit an' take my comfort. Mother learnt me once when I was a lad. . . . They say our Dunnet stockin's is gettin' to be celebrated up to Boston—good quality o' wool an' even knittin' or somethin'. I've always been called a pretty hand to do nettin', but seines is master cheap to what they used to be when they was all hand worked. I change off to nettin' long towards spring. . . ."
>
> (125-26)

What strikes me most about this passage is the convergence of knitting, a traditionally feminine task, with netting, a traditionally masculine one. Even netting possesses feminine overtones in its other meaning of lace-making. Domestic and public realms mesh here in the synthesis of these activities by a single individual and even in the contiguity of the very sounds of the words. Their performer embodies their texture in his doubly-gendered self-creation.

We can meditate at length on Jewett's other deconstructions of boundaries—such as those between humans and nature (Mrs. Todd talks of a tree as if it's a person), between the individual and the community (the narrator and the Bowdens), between life and death (Captain Littlepage's story and Joanna's synchronic presence)—but it seems most important to me to suggest briefly the loosening of the boundaries between the reader and the story itself, between life and art. While all narrative implicitly asks for some measure of our participation or identification, Jewett's hospitality to our presence and our creativity is much more intense than that of other familiar texts.[18] Take, for example, the two books with which Cather grouped *Country* in her estimation of the most enduring works of American literature, *The Adven-*tures of Huckleberry Finn *and* The Scarlet Letter. Both Twain and Hawthorne inscribe their simultaneous narrative presence and absence, Twain with his famous opening injunctions against interpreta-

ABOUT THE AUTHOR

WILLA CATHER ON JEWETT AND *THE COUNTRY OF THE POINTED FIRS*

Born within the scent of the sea but not within sight of it, in a beautiful old house full of strange and lovely things brought home from all over the globe by seafaring ancestors, she spent much of her girlhood driving about the country with her doctor father on his professional rounds among the farms. She early learned to love her country for what it was. What is quite as important, she saw it as it was. She happened to have the right nature, the right temperament, to see it so—and to understand by intuition the deeper meaning of all she saw.

She had not only the eye, she had the ear. From childhood she must have treasured up those pithy bits of local speech, of native idiom, which enrich and enliven her pages. The language her people speak to each other is a native tongue. No writer can invent it. It is made in the hard school of experience, in communities where language has been undisturbed long enough to take on color and character from the nature and experiences of the people. . . .

If I were asked to name three American books which have the possibility of a long, long life, I would say at once, *"The Scarlet Letter," "Huckleberry Finn,"* and *"The Country of the Pointed Firs."* I can think of no others that confront time and change so serenely. . . . It is so tightly yet so lightly built, so little encumbered with heavy materialism that deteriorates and grows old-fashioned. . . . It will be a message to the future, a message in a universal language. . . .

Cather, Willa. An excerpt from "Preface." In *The Country of the Pointed Firs,* 1925.

tion and Hawthorne with his insistence that his narrator/alter ego will "keep the inmost Me behind the veil."[19]

In contrast, Jewett's generosity toward the reader, her feminine fluidity, is quite striking, though our acceptance of it may not be immediate. This generosity emerges in the multiple roles of the narrator and Mrs. Todd, for each is in some sense both writer and reader, artist and interpreter; and Jewett invites the book's reader to participate in these roles as well, suggesting not only their convergence but their interconnection. I haven't space to construct this argument in detail, but let me end my reflections on *The Country of the Pointed Firs* with an incident that is illuminating. On her arrival, the narrator quickly falls into the rhythms of Dunnet Landing and of Mrs. Todd, alternately accompanying her on her gathering forays and "acting as business partner" (6). She says:

> I found the July days fly fast, and it was not until I felt myself confronted with too great pride and pleasure in the display, one night, of two dollars and twenty-seven cents which I had taken in during the day, that I remembered a long piece of writing, sadly belated now, which I was bound to do. To have been patted kindly on the shoulder and called "darlin'," to have been offered a surprise of early mushrooms for supper, to have had all the glory of making two dollars and twenty-seven cents in a single day, and then to renounce it all and withdraw from these pleasant successes, needed much resolution.
>
> (6-7)

In spite of an undertone of irony, pleasure figures largely in the narrator's self-forgetfulness, as it does in my own reading of the book; and the effect of this passage is to render self-consciousness vivid. Yet Mrs. Todd's response is respectful of the other's needs and generous with praise; it is an intimate moment which moves toward publicity, as she affirms, "'I ain't had such a season for years, but I have never had nobody I could so trust. All you lack is a few qualities, but with time you'd gain judgment an' experience, an' be very able in the business.'" She concludes, "'I'd stand right here and say it to anybody'" (7). In spite of the narrator's masculine movement toward "withdrawal," Mrs. Todd's generosity forestalls the possibility of their "separat[ion]" or "estrange[ment]," and the narrator tells us, "on the contrary, a deeper intimacy seemed to begin" (7). It is as if, by affirming her uniqueness, the narrator (and the reader), receiving Mrs. Todd's (Jewett's) reassurance, can relinquish the boundaries of the self:

> I do not know what herb of the night it was that sometimes used to send out a penetrating odor

late in the evening, after the dew had fallen, and the moon was high, and the cool air came up from the sea. Then Mrs. Todd would feel that she must talk to somebody, and I was only too glad to listen. We both fell under the spell, and she either stood outside the window, or made an errand to my sitting-room, and told, it might be very commonplace news of the day, or, as happened one misty summer night, all that lay deepest in her heart.
>
> (7)

This sharing of the "deepest" confidence occurs only seven pages into the story, and it figures the connection that Jewett imagines not only between the narrator and Mrs. Todd, but between the reader and Jewett herself—a connection modeled after Jewett's own "real-life" intimacy with Annie Adams Fields.

Jewett makes me worry about the convenience of genre, like the convenience of all boundaries. Such boundaries—whether those of ethnicity, gender, class, race, age, or sexual orientation—are like convenience food. Not only do they exclude texts, writers, voices, nuances which can't be packaged into a shiny container, they also reify texts, privileging product (interpretation) over process; they enable us to remove literary voices from their social and historical contexts and place them in the stainless steel refrigeration unit of formalist literary criticism, deskinned and deboned. On a still larger scale, these boundaries enable the compartmentalization of the academy into those convenient and competing units, departments. In contrast, Jewett imagines for us the interconnection, multiplicity, and intangibility of knowledge. As one of my students once said after reading *The Country of the Pointed Firs,* "I can't tell you what this book means to me."

Notes

1. F. O. Matthiessen, *American Renaissance: Art and Expression in the Age of Emerson and Whitman* (New York: Oxford Univ. Press, 1941).

2. Sandra A. Zagarell, "Narrative of Community: The Identification of a Genre," *Signs: Journal of Women in Culture and Society* 13 (1988): 498-527. Other recent criticism of Jewett includes: Jennifer Bailey, "Female Nature and the Nature of the Female: a Re-vision of Sarah Orne Jewett's *The Country of the Pointed Firs,*" *Revue Française d'Études Américaines* 8.17 (1983): 283-94; Marcia McClintock Folsom, "'Tact is a Kind of Mind-Reading': Empathic Style in Sarah Orne Jewett's *The Country of the Pointed Firs,*" *Critical Essays on Sarah Orne Jewett,* ed. Gwen L. Nagel (Boston: Hall, 1984), 76-98; Josephine Donovan, "Sarah Orne Jewett's Critical Theory: Notes toward a Feminine Literary Mode" in Nagel, 212-25; Elizabeth Ammons, "Jewett's Witches" in Nagel, 165-84; John C. Hirsh, "The Non-Narrative Structure of *The Country of the Pointed Firs,*" *American Literary Realism* 14 (1981): 286-88; Richard G. Carson, "Nature and the Circles of Initiation in *The*

Country of the Pointed Firs," *Colby Library Quarterly* 21 (1985): 154-60; Sarah W. Sherman, "Victorians and the Matriarchal Mythology: A Source for Mrs. Todd," *Colby Library Quarterly* 22 (1986): 63-74; Marilyn E. Mobley, "Rituals of Flight and Return: The Ironic Journeys of Sarah Orne Jewett's Female Characters," *Colby Library Quarterly* 22 (1986): 36-42; Laurie Crumpacker, "The Art of the Healer: Women in the Fiction of Sarah Orne Jewett," *Colby Library Quarterly* 19 (1983): 155-66; Gwen L. Nagel, "'The prim corner of land where she was queen': Sarah Orne Jewett's New England Gardens," *Colby Library Quarterly* 22 (1986): 43-62; Josephine Donovan, "A Woman's Vision of Transcendence: A New Interpretation of the Works of Sarah Orne Jewett," *Massachusetts Review* 21 (1980): 365-80.

3. Paul Hernadi, *Beyond Genre: New Directions in Literary Classification* (Ithaca: Cornell Univ. Press, 1972), 1.

4. Martha Nell Smith, Chair, "Reading Dickinson's Poems in Letters, Letters in Poems," Div. on Emily Dickinson, NEMLA Convention, 7 Apr. 1990.

5. Sandra M. Gilbert and Susan Gubar, *The Madwoman in the Attic: The Woman Writer and the Nineteenth-Century Literary Imagination* (New Haven: Yale Univ. Press, 1979), 539-80; Virginia Woolf, *A Room of One's Own* (San Diego: Harcourt Brace Jovanovich, 1957), 43-81.

6. Jewett herself may have internalized the standards of the critical community; in a famous letter to Horace Scudder she writes, "But I don't believe I could write a long story. . . . In the first place, I have no dramatic talent. The story would have no plot. I should have to fill it out with descriptions of character and meditations. It seems to me I can furnish the theatre, and show you the actors, and the scenery, and the audience, but there is never any play!" *Sarah Orne Jewett Letters,* ed. Richard Cary (Waterville, Maine: Colby College Press, 1967), 29.

7. Elizabeth Ammons, "Going in Circles: The Female Geography of Jewett's *Country of the Pointed Firs,*" *Studies in the Literary Imagination* 16.2 (1983): 83-92.

8. Nancy Chodorow, *The Reproduction of Mothering: Psychoanalysis and the Sociology of Gender* (Berkeley: Univ. of California Press, 1978), 169. Chodorow's theory is resolutely cultural in its definitions, insisting that "feminine" and "masculine" are not limited by biological sex; hence, the reader should be aware that when I use these terms, I mean psychologically feminine and masculine, unless I specify otherwise.

Adrienne Rich, among others, has pointed out some of the limitations of Chodorow's theory. Rich, "Compulsory Heterosexuality and Lesbian Existence," *Blood, Bread, and Poetry: Selected Prose 1979-1985* (New York: Norton, 1986), 23-75.

9. Sandra M. Gilbert, "The American Sexual Politics of Walt Whitman and Emily Dickinson," *Reconstructing American Literary History,* ed. Sacvan Bercovitch (Cambridge: Harvard Univ. Press, 1986), 123-54.

10. D. H. Lawrence, *Studies in Classic American Literature* (Garden City, N.Y.: Doubleday, 1951), 180.

11. Sarah Orne Jewett, *The Country of the Pointed Firs,* ed. Mary Ellen Chase (New York: Norton, 1981), 49. All subsequent references to Jewett's work cite this edition.

12. Two contemporary feminists who discuss boundary-breaking from distinctive theological perspectives are: Catherine Keller, *From a Broken Web: Separation, Sexism, and Self* (Boston: Beacon, 1986), and Margot Adler, *Drawing Down the Moon: Witches, Druids, Goddess-Worshippers, and Other Pagans in America Today* (Boston: Beacon, 1986).

13. Paula Gunn Allen, *Spider Woman's Granddaughters: Traditional Tales and Contemporary Writing by Native American Women* (Boston: Beacon, 1989), 2, 3.

14. See, for example, Carroll Smith-Rosenberg, "The Female World of Love and Ritual: Relations Between Women in Nineteenth-Century America," *Disorderly Conduct: Visions of Gender in Victorian America* (New York: Knopf, 1985), 53-76; Gilbert and Gubar, 568; Lillian Faderman, *Surpassing the Love of Men: Romantic Friendship and Love between Women from the Renaissance to the Present* (New York: Morrow, 1981), 145-294; John D'Emilio and Estelle B. Freedman, *Intimate Matters: A History of Sexuality in America* (New York: Harper and Row, 1988), 55-221.

15. Ann Leighton, *Early American Gardens: "For Meate or Medicine"* (Amherst: Univ. of Massachusetts Press, 1986).

16. See Ammons, "Jewett's Witches," 175; Crumpacker, 158; Nicholas Culpeper, *Culpeper's Color Herbal,* ed. David Potterton (New York: Sterling, 1983), 142.

17. Jewett's explicit attitude toward racial mixing is less affirmative than we might wish. See Ferman Bishop, "Sarah Orne Jewett's Ideas of Race," *New England Quarterly* 30 (1957): 243-49.

18. Walter J. Ong, "The Writer's Audience Is Always a Fiction," *PMLA* 90 (1975): 9-21.

19. Mark Twain, *The Adventures of Huckleberry Finn* (New York: Washington Square, 1973), n. pag.; Nathaniel Hawthorne, *The Scarlet Letter,* ed. Sculley Bradley et al., 2nd ed. (New York: Norton, 1978), 6-7.

TITLE COMMENTARY

"A White Heron"

LYNN DOLBERG (ESSAY DATE JUNE 1998)

SOURCE: Dolberg, Lynn. "Unanswered Questions, Unquestioned Voices: Silence in 'A White Heron.'" *Colby Quarterly* 34, no. 2 (June 1998): 123-33.

In the following essay, Dolberg suggests that silence is used as an empowering narrative technique in "A White Heron."

Literary history and the present are dark with silences, some the silences for years by our acknowledged great; some silences hidden, some the ceasing to publish after one work appears; some the never coming to book form at all.

Olsen, *Silences*

Since the publication of *Silences* in 1965, "silence" has meant more than absence of speech or text. Tillie Olsen uncovers the various agencies behind things unspoken: how and why has silence come about? Who has silenced whom? Olsen's work makes "silence" a political term; giving voice to the previously muted is now standard practice in Women's Studies. In "Breaking Silence: *The Woman Warrior*," Shirley Nelson Garner outlines the feminist argument clearly:

> It . . . occurs to me that silence or quietness has been just as unquestioned a virtue for women as chastity. . . . For women born into such a cultural tradition, speaking itself becomes an act of assertion. Speaking in public becomes a radical act. . . . To speak with anger relegates one to the realm of whores, witches and madwomen. It is no wonder . . . that feminist artists and writers talk about "breaking silence" as a crucial experience.
>
> (117-18)

Silence is a "feminine" virtue; breaking silence is a feminist act. Olsen's work calls particular attention to the untapped potential of women who, for reasons as various as the women themselves, are unable to record their experiences, ideas, and beliefs. Sometimes, as Garner outlines above, the cultural pressure to remain "feminine" prevails; in other instances, silencing takes a much more concrete form: "Faulkner's 'real life' Dilsey lived and died [within] walking distance from the world-famous writer to whose books, language (and self) she contributed so much—never enabled to read a word he had written, let alone write; tell in her own powerful language, her own imaginings, reality" (Olsen 208). Here is a woman clearly inspirational. Her characteristics are well known to readers of American fiction. Has she any awareness of her fame? What if, as Olsen suggests, she had been able to tell her own story? What might readers learn from this woman's own voice? Literacy commands power and opportunity unavailable to "Dilsey."[1]

Enforced female illiteracy is a partial explanation for the fact that men have for centuries been the primary writers. This primacy leads to the understanding, so hotly contested among today's literary critics, that canonical literature is limited in its scope and, therefore, in its appeal. Jane Austen (one of a few women regularly included in the canon) understands this sentiment: "Yes, yes, if you please, no reference to examples in books. Men have had every advantage of us in telling their own story. Education has been theirs in so much higher a degree; the pen has been in their hands. I will not allow books to prove any thing" (236). Anne Elliot expresses dissatisfaction with books, her words part of Austen's work at transformation of a masculine literary heritage. This pas-

sage forecasts today's canon wars in its assertion that text has little meaning when its perspective is exclusive. What about those writers who prevailed in the face of cultural and societal pressures to remain silent? Do they not deserve some attention for these feats alone? Consistent throughout critical discourses concerning silence is the idea that, spoken or written, absent or present, speech is related to power.

Sarah Orne Jewett is one of many women writers recently reclaimed by feminist critics. Historically, analyses of Jewett held her within specific boundaries; customarily considered a regionalist, Jewett was often understood as limited in theme and focus.[2] In contrast, feminist studies celebrate the woman-centered worlds within her works, finding within these communities a wealth of images, including the pastoral and the divine, and a wealth of dynamic characters, including spiritual and actual mothers, and powerful older women. In contrast to traditional feminist accounts that regard silence as merely oppressive and speech as inherently liberating, I wish to suggest here that an empowering and intimate silence is directly present in Jewett's work, where it represents a theme, a habit, and a narrative technique. Elaine Showalter has suggested that women's fiction speaks a "double-voiced discourse," containing a "dominant" and "muted" story (266). In Showalter's terms I seek to amplify the muted through a reexamination of the dominant, in particular through a close reading of Sarah Orne Jewett's "**A White Heron**." Here silence is present on two levels. The first occurs within the story world— when characters themselves are silent. Silence exists as well within what I will term Jewett's methodological world—within moments when either author or narrator (or both) are silent.

I will begin by simply pointing out some instances of silence in this story. To start within the story world, even Sylvia's cow understands the value of silence. She not only refuses to respond to Sylvia's calls, she also knows that if she remains "still," her bell will remain noiseless and enforce her solitude: "it was her greatest pleasure to hide herself away among the high huckleberry bushes, and though she wore a loud bell she had made the discovery that if one stood perfectly still it would not ring" (1). This scenario (silence in response to intrusive search) is of course parallel to Sylvia's own experience with the inquisitive stranger. When Sylvia encounters the "enemy," her initial responses to him are "almost" inaudible. He demands that she "speak up," and she barely manages a one-word response, answering only after he questions her repeatedly (5-6). Once they arrive at home Sylvia remains silent for the rest of the evening while her grandmother and the young intruder converse. Quiet, Sylvia is nonetheless listening carefully to her companions' conversation and is in fact so distracted by the mention of reward money that she uncharacteristically neglects a hop-toad's comfort. The creature is unable to gain access to his home because of their presence, but Sylvia is far too lost in thought to realize its dilemma: "No amount of thought, that night, could decide how many wished-for treasures the ten dollars, so lightly spoken of, would buy" (12). In fact, beyond her initial three words of direction to the stranger, we have access to only a single word uttered by Sylvia, her own—significant—name.[3]

On a methodological level, Jewett and her narrator are silent on several occasions. We are initially told that Sylvia is afraid of people. We are not, however, told why this is so. Has she had some frightening experience in that "noisy town" where she spent her earlier childhood? Does her fear have to do with the "red-faced boy" she is remembering at the moment she encounters the ornithologist? Or is it simply the result of shyness, not caused by any particular event but rather just part of her nature? The narrator is also silent on the subject of the ornithologist's name. His character is in this way generic—he is initially the "enemy," then "the stranger," the "young man," the "guest," the "ornithologist," the "young sportsman." When Sylvia brings him home, we are told that she "knew by instinct that her grandmother did not understand the gravity of the situation" (6). But we are not told what she believes the cause of this gravity is. Why is Sylvia so threatened?

These are just a few examples—there are many more—to offer evidence of the constancy of silence in this story. But what is this silence about? How is it employed and what is its influence? As I have mentioned, the stranger's initial presence frightens Sylvia, but by the next day she is enjoying his companionship. The language which describes their time together becomes increasingly romanticized:

> As the day waned, Sylvia still watched the young man with loving admiration. She had never seen anybody so charming and delightful; the woman's heart, asleep in the child, was vaguely thrilled by a dream of love. Some premonition of that great power stirred and swayed these young foresters who traversed the solemn woodlands with soft-footed silent care. They stopped to listen to a bird's song; they pressed forward again eagerly, parting the branches,—speaking to each other rarely and in whispers. . . .
>
> (12-13)

Some critics point to the underlying sexual tension in this passage; George Held has stressed the "romantic aura" created by Jewett's alliterative style (64). It is important, certainly, that Jewett herself understood **"A White Heron"** to be a romance. In a letter to Annie Fields, she writes, "Mr. Howells thinks that this age frowns upon the romantic, that it is no use to write romance any more; but dear me, how much of it there is left in every-day life after all. It must be the fault of the writers that such writing is dull, but what shall I do with my 'White Heron' now she is written?" (59). The romance Jewett refers to is in "every-day life"; these lines do not necessitate a romance between Sylvia and her companion. "Every-day life" could describe the romance between child and nature, the romance of possible discovery, the romance that is almost a given within such pastoral surroundings. What is the setting and source of this romance? The couple tread with "soft-footed silent care," they stop to "listen to a bird's song," they speak "rarely" and then only "in whispers." The "premonition" of "that great power" these two experience clearly refers to the "dream of love" in the previous sentence.

But the great power present throughout this story is the power of silence. Perhaps the premonition is that one power (love) will be halted by the other (silence); or, perhaps for Sylvia, the two are somehow intricately connected. This moment is enjoyable to Sylvia only because she is able to exist within the silence she needs. The source of this need is not made explicit, but its urgency is without question. When silence is broken, Sylvia becomes terrified: "she did not lead the guest, she only followed, and there was no such thing as speaking first. The sound of her own unquestioned voice would have terrified her,—it was hard enough to answer yes or no when there was need of that" (13). Societal convention allows Sylvia to follow, not lead, to reject speech unless she is directly addressed. In this way she is able to avoid making a decision about whether or not to share her information about the white heron. On this first day of exploration together, Sylvia embraces silence because it offers her safety. Age and gender have determined her subservient position and Sylvia makes use of this subservience. Silence, described by Olsen and others as the result of oppression, is here turned into an instrument of empowerment. It enables Sylvia to retain her knowledge, save the white heron and, by extension, save herself.

The second portion of this passage also deserves attention: "the sound of her own unquestioned voice would have terrified her." As Held points out, the meaning of this sentence is somewhat obscure (64). On what exactly does Sylvia's fear depend? Is it a fear of speaking unless she is questioned by her companion? Or does she fear speaking without questioning herself about her motives? The clearest interpretation of this line is the former, and yet the second meaning has import here as well. Is this obscurity typical of Jewett's writing? Jewett's critical and technical methods are never clearly laid out in a single essay but must instead be gleaned from her letters and diaries. With respect to her readership, one diary entry written in 1871 seems particularly apt:

> Father said this one day "A story should be managed so that it should *suggest* interesting things to the *reader* instead of the author's doing all the thinking for him, and setting before him in black and white. The best compliment is for the reader to say 'Why didn't he put in "this" or "that."'"
> (cited in Donovan 224, n. 19)

This entry suggests at least a couple of interesting resonances within the present discussion. Certainly in **"A White Heron"** Jewett adds gray to her "black and white" text. What is particularly significant is that at this moment describing Sylvia's "unquestioned voice," Jewett—herself determined to write things "as they are" (**Letters** [Cary] 52)—is not writing with exceptional clarity. Why does she stray from her stated method? The author is silent to her reader's questions about Sylvia's motivations. Although we know that Sylvia, at moments, hopes to spot the white heron, it is clear she is not at all ready to volunteer information. Jewett expands on the questioning process by making determinability about the girl's self-inquiry equally enigmatic. Sylvia fears her unquestioned voice; Jewett poses unanswerable questions. Both withhold information and retain control over their wooded and narrative landscapes.

Sylvia's early morning expedition to determine the heron's exact whereabouts, and to view the ocean for the first time, involves more moments of silence and listening, and a deepening of the parallel between this woodland creature and her natural habitat. As she steals away to begin her search, this parallel is made explicit: "Alas, if the great wave of human interest which flooded for the first time this dull little life should sweep away the satisfactions of an existence heart to heart with nature and the dumb life of the forest!" (15). The harmony of this relationship is contingent upon things unspoken. Further examples support this contingency. Sylvia finds the heron because she knows to hide, motionless and quiet, in a tree; the heron departs "when a company of shouting cat-birds comes . . . vexed by their fluttering and lawlessness" (19). Noise is momentarily equivalent to crime. Upon her return, Sylvia brings her knowledge home but elects to keep her secret unspoken. On this day, however, Sylvia is no longer unquestioned. Jewett gives this moment greater emphasis, for it is one of three instances where the narrative shifts to the present tense; we are told, "the grandmother and the sportsman stand in the door together and question her" (20). On this day, Sylvia is forced into the position of activist. She cannot simply exist in the silence she prefers; she has to refuse the questions and ignore inquiry actively.

The story's final paragraph leaves the reader with more unanswered questions. The paragraph begins with an address: "Dear loyalty, that suffered a sharp pang as the guest went away disappointed later in that day" (21). "Dear loyalty"—is this loyalty to the lost companion, the ornithologist who has left disappointed? Is this loyalty "dear" because it has cost Sylvia companionship? Or does the term of endearment refer to Sylvia's true love, the natural world she has defended? The narrator asks, "Were the birds better friends than their hunter might have been,—who can tell?" The story ends without response to this inquiry, only a directive that the "woodlands and summertime" "remember" and bring treasures and secrets to "this lonely country child" (22).

One reading of this story suggests that Sylvia remains loyal to herself, retains her "nature" and lives independent of male-dominated society like many of Jewett's characters and, indeed, like Jewett herself. That Sylvia is lonely, however, suggests some questioning as to whether or not this isolation is the best choice. Significantly, this loneliness is the result of the intrusion by the stranger. Prior to this visit, Sylvia is content. In the opening section of the story we are told that she whispers, not to any person but to a content, solitary cat, "this [is] a beautiful place to live in, and [I] never should wish to go home" (4). Prior to the hunter's visit Sylvia exists silently in a feminized world, feminized in that it is inhabited only by a woman and a girl (and a female cow) but also in that a conventional feminine role (subservient silent companion) offers protection here. During the stranger's visit there is a moment of romanticized contentment, but it exists conditionally, only within a safe, unquestioned and unquestioning place. After the visit, however, something has changed. Silence (meaning both Sylvia's surroundings and her choice to keep her secret to herself) no longer offers her complete happiness. She is lonely—her rules and her world have been somehow altered by this experience. Jewett's ending to this story lacks conclusion.

Although Sylvia has saved the white heron and retained her nature and her world, she is no longer content. Equivalently, Jewett herself is not content with keeping secrets from her readers by writing enigmatically. She is not merely secretive; she follows her father's advice and offers a series of questions for the reader to contemplate. Perhaps Jewett chooses to remain silent because she does not have the definitive answer, or perhaps she (like her young heroine) elects to keep her knowledge to herself. Perhaps she is not, as yet, fully satisfied with her method; perhaps it is still in process. Jewett does not, however, remain a passive reporter of facts here. Asking questions and not providing responses forces us to respond on some level. Jewett takes a position and incites readerly participation.

Scholars have for years noted Jewett's characters' reluctance to speak and the regularity with which climactic moments hinge on the unspoken, but this notice is usually treated only parenthetically within a larger topic. For example, in "'Tact is a Kind of Mind-Reading': Empathic Style in Sarah Orne Jewett's *The Country of the Pointed Firs*," Marcia McClintock Folsom notes an attention to "hints and unspoken conversation" as part of a larger discussion of Jewett's unsentimental, realistic style (78). Alternatively, in "Archives of Female Friendship and the 'Way' Jewett Wrote," Marjorie Pryse discusses what she describes as the "intertwining of friendship and fiction, of listening and telling": "The process through which the narrator learns how to turn friendship into a 'lifelong affair' becomes the 'plot' of *The Country of the Pointed Firs*. What makes this process possible, and what Jewett equates with the narrator's moral and professional development, is her discovery that listening is as important as telling for the growth of both 'true friendship' and fiction" (64-65). Part of being a good listener, of course, involves a measure of the ability to be silent.

In fact, Jewett's characters often resort to silence and there is no single cause for this practice. Most often, quiet is indicative of deep emotion, as in *A Country Doctor* when Mrs. Thacher is at a loss to express her sadness about the continued absence of her daughter, Adeline: "the good woman could say no more, while her guests understood readily enough the sorrow that had found no words" (6). Jewett also creates moments of contentment when words are disruptions and silence, peace. For example, in *Deephaven*, Kate and Helen often enjoy moments of quiet together: "Sometimes in the evening we waited out at sea for the moonrise, and then we would take the oars again and go slowly in, once in a while singing or talking but oftenest silent" (40). While in these examples within the story world silence typically reflects emotion, we see elsewhere a commitment to silence at the methodological level as well. In *The Country of the Pointed Firs*, for example, Jewett is silent with respect to her narrator. The teller of this tale (a writer) is without a name and in fact, as Sarah Way Sherman has pointed out, initially without the first-person pronoun (203). She is present to us in the observations she makes about her surroundings; in other words, she is present more as the writer of that story, and less as a character in her own right. In fact, this character becomes most alive to us through the lessons that other characters such as William teach her. She learns the value of being a good listener and improves this ability through an appreciation of what silence makes possible. The few details we do gain about the narrator, her relationship to the people of Dunnet Landing, and the place itself become all the more important because they are what sets this narrator apart from the other writer involved here, Jewett herself.

I believe that Jewett's constant attention to this issue of silence is conscious. On one level, certainly, her characters are silent because the writer wishes to depict New England reticence. Of Jewett's mimetic practice, Josephine Donovan observes: "One of the central elements in Jewett's literary credo was that the artist should transmit reality with as little interference and doctoring up as possible." But Jewett is also clearly aware that silence inspires thought, and she wants her readers to think. She wants to teach us something about the nature of silence and does so by using it to shape her content and her purpose. Donovan goes on to discuss Jewett's form: "Implicit in this thesis is the idea that form follows function (that is, content and purpose), rather than the other way around" (212, 213). If we accept Donovan's understanding that Jewett's form follows her function, her form is indebted to silence. The writer is not providing answers but inviting, soliciting and

Cover page of *Deephaven.*

encouraging response. She does not dominate, does not tell her readers how to respond, but she suggests that we participate in a process of discussion (see Oakes).

In this spirit of discussion I turn to one of the more important recent essays on Jewett's work. Richard Brodhead devotes a chapter to Jewett in his *Cultures of Letters: Scenes of Reading and Writing in Nineteenth-Century America.* Brodhead's discussion focuses on cultural structures within nineteenth-century conceptions of regionalism. Engaging *The Country of the Pointed Firs* in particular, Brodhead argues that Jewett's regionalism is "produced . . . in the culture of a quite specific late nineteenth-century upper class" (149) and that Jewett (and her characters) should be situated squarely within the nineteenth-century leisure class: "If . . . we were to focus Jewett on the background not of women's culture but of a nineteenth-century leisure-class culture 'struggling to find expression' we would find for her writing a more concretely specified social home" (144). Brodhead's argument works well with the majority of Jewett's writing; "**A White Heron,**" however, provides an exception. Sylvia and her grandmother do not fit comfortably into the leisure-

class mold; they are not vacationing tourists like Kate and Helen in *Deephaven,* nor are they visiting writers observing a coastal community. In short, Sylvia's concerns (for example, rounding up wayward cows) are not those of the leisure class. "**A White Heron**" also offers an exception to Brodhead's assertions about expression. In much of Jewett's work her characters are indeed struggling to express themselves. Sylvia, however, decides against using her knowledge; the expression she chooses is autonomous silence.

Brodhead also pays attention to Jewett's contributions to nineteenth-century aesthetic understandings of "art" and "artist": "[Jewett] became more dedicated to her art at the price of having that art give up larger functions of social edification and political address embraced by the less 'artistic' domestic-sentimental generation" (173). *The Country of the Pointed Firs* did not and will never have the social and political impact of a work such as *Uncle Tom's Cabin.* But Jewett does not rescind all social and political consideration; commentary—about women's roles in a patriarchal world, about community, about romance—is contained quietly within her form. "Political address" is part of her narrative; "social edification" may indeed be an unstated (silent) goal. As study of "**A White Heron**" suggests, this goal is achieved by her engagement of the reader in creating meaning in response to the troublesome questions, particularly about gender and women's roles, that her silences elicit.

Jewett uses silence as a literary tool. When and how she wields this tool (within the story world and within her method) are indicative of her beliefs. Jewett's independence and love of womankind are everywhere evident in her work, but these beliefs are never more political than in her articulations of silence. She is aware of the gendered relationship between language and power so forcefully articulated by contemporary feminists; indeed, this relationship is often part of her subject matter. The critical discourse which began Jewett studies—by such men as F. O. Matthiessen and Henry James—regularly described her work with diminutive ("feminine") adjectives: "quaint," "little," "innocent," "childlike." These descriptives are all far from threatening and make Jewett's work appear easily kept within its place, easily controlled. But the silence within her work, multilayered, evocative, and as yet unquestioned, is revolutionary.

Notes

1. In a specifically American literary tradition, the slave narrative, literacy is directly connected to freedom. See, for example, the narratives of Frederick Douglass and Harriet Jacobs.

2. For example, Jewett's first biographer, F. O. Matthiessen, feels the need to protect his subject from charges that her subject matter is minor: "Nowhere except in America and at the present time would it be necessary to defend a writer for handling pathos and humour instead of the stronger chords of passion" (150).

3. It is possible, of course, to gain further access to Sylvia by studying Jewett and making connections to the author's own experiences. F. O. Matthiessen calls attention to Jewett's love of the woods surrounding her home and her horror at their gradual destruction: "The increasing destruction of her world gave her a hunted feeling like the last wild thing left in the woods" (23). Sylvia's defense of her home may well stem from Jewett's loyalty to and love of her natural surroundings.

Works Cited

Ammons, Elizabeth. "The Shape of Violence in Jewett's 'A White Heron.'" *Colby Library Quarterly* 22 (1986): 6-15.

Arac, Jonathan, and Harriet Ritvo, eds. *Macropolitics of Nineteenth-Century Literature*. Durham: Duke UP, 1995.

Austen, Jane. *Persuasion*. 1818. Rpt. Baltimore: Penguin, 1972.

Bader, Julia. "The Dissolving Vision: Realism in Jewett, Freeman, and Gilman." In *American Realism: New Essays*. Ed. Eric J. Sundquist. Baltimore: Johns Hopkins UP, 1982. 176-98.

Blanchard, Paula. *Sarah Orne Jewett: Her Life and Her Work*. Reading, MA: Addison-Wesley, 1994.

Brodhead, Richard H. *Cultures of Letters: Scenes of Reading and Writing in Nineteenth-Century America*. Chicago: U of Chicago P, 1993.

Cary, Richard, ed. "Jewett on Writing Short Stories." *Colby Library Quarterly* 6 (1964): 425-40.

——. "The Rise, Decline, and Rise of Sarah Orne Jewett." *Colby Library Quarterly* 9 (1972): 450-63.

——, ed. *Appreciation of Sarah Orne Jewett: 29 Interpretive Essays*. Waterville, ME: Colby College P, 1973.

Donovan, Josephine. "Sarah Orne Jewett's Critical Theory: Notes Toward a Feminine Literary Mode." *Colby Library Quarterly* 18 (1982): 212-25.

Fetterley, Judith, and Marjorie Pryse, eds. *American Women Regionalists, 1850-1910*. New York: Norton, 1992.

Fields, Annie, ed. *Letters of Sarah Orne Jewett*. Cambridge: Riverside P, 1911.

Folsom, Marcia McClintock. "'Tact Is a Kind of Mind-Reading': Empathic Style in Sarah Orne Jewett's *The Country of the Pointed Firs*." *Colby Library Quarterly* 18 (1982): 66-78.

Garner, Shirley Nelson. "Breaking Silence: *The Woman Warrior*." In *The Intimate Critique: Autobiographical Literary Criticism*. Ed. Diane P. Freedman, Olivia Frey, and Frances Murphy Zauhar. Durham: Duke UP, 1993.

Held, George. "Heart to Heart with Nature: Ways of Looking at 'A White Heron.'" In *Critical Essays on Sarah Orne Jewett*. 58-68.

Hovet, Theodore R. "'Once Upon a Time': Sarah Orne Jewett's 'A White Heron' as a Fairy Tale." *Studies in Short Fiction* 15 (1978): 63-68.

Jewett, Sarah Orne. *A Country Doctor*. New York: Meridian, 1986.

——. *The Country of the Pointed Firs and Other Stories*. 1896. Rpt. New York: Anchor, Doubleday, 1989.

——. *Deephaven*. 1877. Rpt. Boston: Houghton, Mifflin, 1889.

——. *Letters*. Revised and enlarged. Ed. Richard Cary. Waterville, ME: Colby College P, 1967.

——. *"A White Heron" and Other Stories*. 1886. Rpt. Cambridge: Riverside P, 1892.

Matthiessen, Francis Otto. *Sarah Orne Jewett*. Boston: Houghton Mifflin, 1929.

Nagel, Gwen L., ed. *Critical Essays on Sarah Orne Jewett*. Boston: G. K. Hall, 1984.

Oakes [Kilcup], Karen. "'All that lay deepest in her heart': Reflections on Jewett, Gender, and Genre." *Colby Quarterly* 26 (1990): 152-60.

Olsen, Tillie. *Silences*. New York: Dell, 1978.

Pryse, Marjorie. "Archives of Female Friendship and the 'Way' Jewett Wrote." *The New England Quarterly* 66 (1993): 47-66.

Renza, Louis A. *"A White Heron" and the Question of Minor Literature*. Madison: U of Wisconsin P, 1984.

Roman, Judith A. *Annie Adams Fields: The Spirit of Charles Street*. Bloomington: Indiana UP, 1990.

Roman, Margaret. *Sarah Orne Jewett: Reconstructing Gender*. Tuscaloosa: U of Alabama P, 1992.

Sherman, Sarah Way. *Sarah Orne Jewett: An American Persephone*. Hanover: UP of New England, 1989.

Showalter, Elaine, ed. *The New Feminist Criticism*. New York: Pantheon, 1985.

Silverstone, Elizabeth. *Sarah Orne Jewett: A Writer's Life*. Woodstock, NY: Overlook P, 1993.

Smith-Rosenberg, Carroll. *Disorderly Conduct: Visions of Gender in Victorian America*. New York: Oxford UP, 1985.

Sutherland, John H., ed. *Papers from the Jewett Conference at Westbrook College*. *Colby Library Quarterly* 22 (March 1986).

The Country of the Pointed Firs

GEORGE SMITH (ESSAY DATE SPRING 1994)

SOURCE: Smith, George. "Jewett's Unspeakable Unspoken: Retracing the Female Body Through *The Country of the Pointed Firs*." *Modern Language Studies* 24, no. 2 (spring 1994): 11-19.

In the following essay, Smith claims that in The Country of the Pointed Firs *Jewett articulates a covert radical feminism as she subverts dominant patriarchal elements of romance and realism in her stories.*

"Misogyny and the idealization of women are constituted in the same impulse: they are two sides to a single sheet of paper."

John Duvall

If we look at the question of regionalism from an intertextual viewpoint, Sarah Orne Jewett comes out as one of the least heard and most radical voices in nineteenth-century American literature. This is to say that while Jewett articulates a covert feminist realism in a quaint Down East voice, her narrative representation of coastal Maine village life speaks also to big name nineteenth-century American novelists through a close dialogical exchange with their phallocentric fictions. Indeed, Jewett carries on several dialogues at once. Picking bones with Poe, Hawthorne, and Melville about the phallic claims of American romance, she argues at the same time with the 'chief exemplars' of the new realism that had replaced romance as the conventional discourse of American patriarchy.[1]

Having said as much we should place Jewett's regional voice within its wider cultural framework. In the mid to late nineteenth century the New Woman arose against the American male hegemony. As the conflict intensified, there ensued a hard fought struggle for control over the female body. Most fiercely contested were issues centered on abortion and lesbianism (Smith-Rosenberg). In the 1850s, '60s, and '70s, abortion rates had reached "disturbing" numbers; in the '80s and '90s, female homosexuality was "discovered" by the sexologists. As with abortion, these "perversions" posed a grave threat to bourgeois patriarchy. Accordingly, the A.M.A. led efforts to rein in the female body, largely through backing anti-abortion legislation and raising the alarm against "Mannish lesbians" and "Genteel, educated women, thoroughly feminine in appearance, thought, and behavior, [who] [. . .] might well be active lesbians" (102). These repressive misogynies went hand in hand with the literary commodification of the female body and the larger realist enterprise that emerged out of and replaced the American romance and its discourse of idealization. In her subversion of romance and realism, Jewett represents, as we shall see, an autonomous female body in terms of abortion and lesbianism.

Jewett's subversive voice speaks these terms from within a regional culture dominated by a patriarchal hegemony that staked its claims to authority on Yankee blue blood. And of course that blood had deep connections with European aristocracy. Thus in *The Country of the Pointed Firs* Jewett links the patriarchal strain of American romance to its origins in the chivalric tradition. In this tradition the romance plays out a variety of themes centering on the fisher king, whose illness—usually involving or suggesting impotence—is reflected in a barren kingdom. As the story goes, the questing hero returns virility to the king and fertility to the land. But the moral lies in the devastating consequence of the king's prior impotence, which semiotically encodes the colossal power and necessity of the life giving patriarchal phallus. To say the least, the affirmed sign here, the *doxa* represented, is none other than the transcendental signifier. In this regard Laurie Finke has recently suggested that the various courtly romances of the Middle Ages "served as a vehicle for the expression and mystification of masculine desire" (109). Using Chretien de Troyes as example, she argues that "In their sophisticated deployment of strategies designed to promote the politics of patrilinear order, Chretien's romances provided a means for articulating and solidifying the hierarchical relationships among men at a time when older feudal ties were being undermined by new social, economic, and political developments" (109-10).

As mid nineteenth-century America shifted from a quasi-feudal Jeffersonian agrarian political economy to that of industrial capitalism, the American romance—particularly as represented in Poe, Hawthorne, and Melville—constructed a cultural discourse similar to the patriarchal strategies Finke has described in Chretien de Troyes. As example of the way Jewett subverts this intertextual alliance, let me mention briefly and schematically the fisher king typology of the old and impotent Bowden alcoholic. In his "patrilineal" role as the habitual impersonator of an officer of the United States Army, he heads the Bowden family reunion procession into the vaulted banquet hall of standing pines. Underscoring these chivalric ironies is the likelihood that the Bowden forebears "sat in the great hall of some old French house in the Middle Ages, when battles and sieges and processions and feasts were familiar things" (105).[2] The parody here hits close to Poe, the alcoholic who so often situates his romance hero (always descended from chivalric lines and usually addicted) within the dark chambers of a feudal manner. There is also, I want to add, much promise in considering the dialogical exchange between Captain Littlepage's tale of "The Waiting Place" and Melville's romance of the sea, such as *Benito Cerino*. In this case the noble phallic power so mysteriously threatened and at the last breath rescued and triumphant in Melville's homo-social romance is replied to and restyled, in Jewett's text, by an impotent old man's hallucinatory nostalgia.

But these are schematic generalizations. Let me draw more specific attention to Elijah Tilley's tale. A sentimentalized patriarchal romance, this episode is dialogically linked with Hawthorne (say, Aylmer's 'absolute' perfection of Georgiana in "The Birthmark") and perhaps more closely with Poe, for whom, as the saying goes, 'the only good woman is a dead woman'. Thus Elijah, "sore stricken and unconsoled at the death of his wife" (118), has for eight years sat alone thinking "it all over," and "some days it feels as if poor dear might step right back into this kitchen" (121). The narrator relates how

> The visible tribute of his careful housekeeping, and the clean bright room which had once enshrined his wife, and now enshrined her memory, was very moving to me; he had no thought for anyone else or for any other place. I began to see her myself in her home,—a delicate-looking faded little woman, who leaned upon his rough strength and affectionate heart, who was always watching for his boat out of this very window, and who always opened the door and welcomed him when he came home.
>
> (122)

In a word, Jewett is constructing in this little vignette a classic patriarchal romance. Thus we should stress the perfect silence and otherness of Elijah's idealized wife. Through Elijah's romance, she undergoes an other world transcendence, and there joins Ligeia, Madeline Usher, and all such heroines, to become what Gilbert and Gubar refer to as the "nineteenth-century angel woman [who] becomes not just a momento of otherness but actually [. . .] an 'Angel of Death'" (24).

But the question remains, was Mrs. Tilley ever alive to begin with? From Elijah's viewpoint, she appears the epitome of the "spiritualized Victorian woman who, having died to her own desires, her own self, her own life, leads a posthumous existence in her own lifetime" (Gilbert and Gubar 25). Within the structure of Elijah's patriarchal romance she has played to perfection the role of one of those "slim, pale, passive beings whose 'charms' eerily recalled the snowy porcelain immobility of the dead" (Gilbert and Gubar 25). Indeed, this "porcelain immobility of the dead" becomes after death the symbol through which Elijah enshrines Mrs. Tilley in his little makeshift tabernacle. To quote: "'[. . .] I'm going to show you her best tea things she thought so much of,'

said the master of the house, opening the door to the shallow cupboard. 'That's real chiny, all of it on those two shelves [. . .] I bought it myself, when we was first married, in the port of Bordeaux'" (124). As Northrop Frye notes, "The precious objects brought back from the quest, or seen or obtained as a result of it, sometimes combine the ritual and the psychological associations." Here he argues that "The Holy Grail [. . .] is connected with Christian Eucharist symbolism; it is related to or descended from a miraculous food provider like the cornucopia, and, like other cups and hollow vessels, it has female sexual affinities [. . .]" (193-94). With Elijah's exaltation of his wife's precious virginity in terms of her china and its symbolic relation to the Christian Eucharist, Jewett tropes courtly love as it often functions within the feudal romance. The significance of this trope is perhaps best explained by Lacan's well-known observation concerning phallic *jouissance* and the courtly love tradition: "For the man, whose lady was entirely, in the servile sense of the term, his female subject, courtly love is the only way of coming off elegantly from the absence of sexual relation" (Lacan 141; qtd. in Finke 109). Added to this is the fact that Elijah's courtly romance belies a crack in its phallic structure:

> There never was one single piece of it broken until—Well, I used to say, long as she lived, there never was a piece broke, but long last I noticed she'd look kind 'o distressed, and I thought 'twas 'count 'o me boastin'. When they asked if they should use it when folks was here to supper, time 'o her funeral, I knew she'd want everything nice, and I said 'certain'. Some o' the women they come runnin' to me an' called me, while they was taken' of the chiny down, an' showed me there was one o' the cups broke an' the pieces wropped in paper and pushed way back here, corner o' the shelf. . . . I guess wa'n't no other secret ever lay between us.
>
> (124-25)

In his disavowal of reality, in his refusal, that is, to read in the broken cup the emblem of his wife's carnal knowledge, Elijah's life adds up to a prolonged imaginary dramatization of the American patriarchal romance. In this Mrs. Tilley plays, before and after death, the perfectly idealized, other worldly, silent "angel woman" whose "contemplative purity" was for Mr. Tilley a "living *memento* of the otherness of the divine." Thusly Elijah enshrines his wife's memory. In her actual life, however, Mrs. Tilley was, as we see, a material being who spoke and did things unspeakable against the strictures of patriarchal law. If nothing else, her unseen and silent sexual reality frames Elijah's lived patriarchal romance within the ideology that Althusser defines as "a 'representation' of the imaginary relationship of individuals to their real conditions of existence" (162). Furthermore, insofar as Elijah's representation of the imaginary parodies Poe, Hawthorne, and Melville, his text exposes their discursive tactics.

As already suggested, Jewett's text also takes on the realism that, largely through Howells, replaces romance as the hegemonic voice of American fiction. Whereas romance idealized the female body as a "mystification of masculine desire," Howells readily appropriates the female body to the discursive construction of middle class marriage. Silas Lapham, for instance, proudly names his top of the line paint "THE PERSIS BRAND," after his wife, and the label on every "pretty" can metonymically represent the female as object of exchange in a patriarchal economy. As commodity object we see the sign of woman in its relation to "business as sacrament," which Weber describes as the aura of holiness that suffused post-Civil War capitalism. And of course, though Howells operates in this subtler mode, later naturalists, such as Norris, Dreiser, and Crane, dramatize a gross and brutal relationship between capital and the female body.

It will be objected though, that not only did Jewett welcome Howells's intervention against the sorry state of sentimentalism into which the once robust tradition of American romance had finally collapsed, but that she admired his critical realism and brought it to bear on her own style (Carter 120). But to say as much and leave it at that silences the claims Jewett brings against the realist commodification of the female body. Along these lines let me argue to begin with that Mrs. Tilley is not the only angel-woman with an *other*, real, unspeakable life. Joanna, the "nun or hermit" of Shell-heap Island, was "Crossed in love." From all indications her crimes of the body, though not of *The Scarlet Letter* variety, drive her into absolute silence and self-imposed ostracism. But of course Joanna's Hawthornesque exile to the other world of Shell-heap Island, like Mrs. Tilley's broken cup 'otherness of the divine', has its realist overtones, and as such it is meant as a minor variation on the major chord that sounds through the silent discourse of "puzzling and queer Mrs. Todd." Dispensing brews, potions, and elixirs to the sick of body and heart, surely Mrs. Todd would seem to represent the archetypal nineteenth-century angel woman.

But in reality Almira Todd contradicts the idealized woman enshrined in the *doxa* out of which Jewett has constructed the patriarchal

side—Elijah Tilley's side—of the dialogical enterprise thus far described. She too keeps hidden the unspeakable secret of the female body, silenced in the hard flat Puritanism of Dunnet Landing. Remembering back to her one real heterosexual love, she confides, "When we was young together his mother . . . done everything she could to part us; and folks thought we both married well, but't wa'n't what either one of us wanted most; an' now we're left alone again, an' might have had each other all the time" (7-8). This lover, with whom she explored the body of her youth, beyond and against the law and covenant of marriage, has now long since disappeared, and no doubt "[. . .] he's forgot our youthful feelin's [. . .] but a woman's heart is different; them feelin's come back when you think you've done with 'em, as sure as spring comes with the year" (8). "The feelin's come back" later on in the novel, in that privileged and mysterious moment on Green Island, when Mrs. Todd reveals to her companion of "deeper intimacy" the secret source of her pennyroyal teas:

> "There, dear, I never showed nobody else but mother where to find this place; 'tis kind of sainted to me. Nathan, my husband, an' I used to love this place when we was courtin', and"—she hesitated, and then spoke softly—"when he was lost, 'twas just off shore tryin' to get in by the short channel there between Squaw Islands, right in sight o' this headland where we'd set an' made our plans all summer long."

As the dialogue continues, we learn something more:

> "T'was but a dream with us," Mrs. Todd said. "I knew it when he was gone. I knew it"—and she whispered as if she were at confession—"I knew afore he started to go to sea. My heart was gone out o' my keepin' before I ever saw Nathan; but he loved me well, and he made me real happy, and he died before he ever knew what he'd had to know if we'd lived together. 'Tis very strange about love. No, Nathan never found out, but my heart was troubled when I knew him at first. There's more women likes to be loved than there is of those that loves. I spent some happy hours right here. I always liked Nathan, and he never knew. But this pennyroyal always reminded me, as I'd sit and gather it and hear him talkin'—it always would remind me of—the other one."
>
> (49)

We needn't overstrain ourselves in the exercise of close reading to get this right: Nathan's ship went down before he and Almira consummated their marriage. Nathan died without knowing that, like Mrs. Tilley, Mrs. Todd had committed her body to an unspeakable knowledge. And like

Elijah, what marriage Nathan knew was lived in the Althusserian imaginary of patriarchal romance.

As for the widow Mrs. Todd: "She might have been Antigone alone on the Theban plain [. . .] An absolute archaic grief possessed this country-woman [. . .]" (49). If the comparison to Antigone standing alone in the desert locates Mrs. Todd in a wasteland, that wasteland is surely Dunnet Landing. Such a claim seems a far cry from the early promise of the novel, sounded in those first sentences giving airy whiteness to the honesty and spiritual health of the old New England coastal village at which we, along with the narrator, had just arrived. One sentence in particular bears repeating: "The tide was high, there was a fine crowd of spectators, and the younger portion of the company followed . . . with subdued excitement up the narrow street of the salt-aired, white clap-boarded little town" (2). Aside from Mrs. Todd's nephew, Johnny Bowden, there *is* no 'younger portion' of Dunnet Landing. While the impotent old-timers repair their nets and fish close in on the bay for a small catch here & there, the aging town, "like its disabled schooners," rots to the water line. And indeed it is the shipping and the fishing that's gone to wrack in these barren times. Critics usually cite the rise of industrialism as the cause of the decline. If we apply the conventions of the grail, however, the decline is clearly for want of youth as well. Why, though, is there no offspring from earlier years, when the wives and husbands of Dunnet Landing were young and presumably fertile? Have they all but Johnny Bowden fled to the cities in pursuit of industrial revolution?

Whatever the reason, Dunnet Landing's infertility and the consequences thereof speak plainly to the phallocentric discourse represented in the fisher king legend as its strands weave through the dialogical tapestry of Jewett's text. Because no questing hero has come to restore patriarchy and fertility to the land, the town rots away, year after year. And yet this scenario doesn't add up. In the first place, instead of a questing knight who would bring potency to the phallus and fertility to the land, we do in fact get an errant woman, whose (phallic) power resides in her pen; and secondly, as we have seen, Jewett's women break the patriarchal law that binds the structure of romance: they break the hymen outside of marriage. Through that rupture they give form to their own realist text.

Which brings us to the very real question of procreation. If, in their 'illegitimate' liaisons, Mrs. Tilley, or Joanna, or Mrs. Todd got pregnant—not to mention all the other presumably childless women of Dunnet Landing—what has become of all the pregnancies? The answer lies hidden in the pungency of Mrs. Todd's favorite herb, pennyroyal. Emitting the fragrance of romance and intertextually engaged as well with the sacramental aura of Lapham's Persis Brand paint, all through *The Country of the Pointed Firs* pennyroyal appears as something of a metonymic representation of Mrs. Todd's character and imbues with ambiguous aromas her "deeper intimacy" with the younger woman who narrates her story: "Among the green grass grew such pennyroyal as the rest of the world could not provide. There was a fine fragrance in the air as we gathered it sprig by sprig and stepped along carefully, and Mrs. Todd pressed her aromatic nosegay between her hands and offered it to me again and again" (48). What Mrs. Todd is offering here is not just a simple bouquet symbolizing complicated love. It is that too, but it is also a gesture of solidarity and political praxis. Mrs. Todd is passing on the secret of pennyroyal, so that her beloved, in her travels beyond Dunnet Landing, might be, like her mentor, a dispenser of pennyroyal potions and teas. In Mrs. Todd's time and place, pennyroyal was a common home-remedy abortifacient.[3]

Now we better understand Mrs. Todd's remark that "pennyr'yal always reminded me, as I'd sit and gather it and hear [Nathan] talkin'—it always reminded me of—the other one." Aborting the progeny of their resistance to patriarchal domination, most forcibly exacted in nineteenth-century America through the institution of marriage, the women in Jewett's feminist text—not the fisher king, not the patriarchal law or the post-Puritan middle-class white male hegemony—give cause to the very real decline of Dunnet Landing. And, it follows, in Jewett's female resides the power to restore the town to health and plenty.[4] According to Sartre, "revolution takes place when a change in institutions is accompanied by a profound modification in the property system" (224). In the representation of abortion, Jewett's multivoiced text articulates not only the liberation of the female body in terms of its sexual autonomy; it also articulates the exercise of that autonomy in the termination of pregnancy, which, obviously, negates all institutional claims of patrilineal ownership. As already suggested, these patrilineal lines are threatened again in the "deeper intimacy" shared between Mrs. Todd and the narrator. While Mrs. Todd's domineering "height and massiveness" of "great determined shape" fits the

A.M.A's description of the "mannish lesbian," the narrator is a "Genteel, educated woman, thoroughly feminine in appearance, thought and behavior, [and] [. . .] might well be [an] active lesbian[ ]." As Jewett's story represents the praxis of abortion and (the proximity of) lesbianism, it stakes out the regional site wherein a dialogical voice contradicts phallic American romance. At the same time, Jewett's materialist realism engenders a narrative discourse that speaks to and against Howells, Norris, Crane, Dreiser, Hemingway, and so many other realists for whom the commodification of the female body 'maintains and reproduces' the ideology of late nineteenth- and early twentieth-century middle-class American patriarchy.

Notes

1. For recent feminist critiques of Jewett's fiction, see especially Singley, Pratt, and Sherman. While Singley argues that Jewett's fiction advances "a rejection of patriarchal norms" (76), Pratt sees Jewett's fiction as a discursive appropriation of the male *Bildungsroman*. Sherman applies Chodorow's theory of matriarchy to the Persephone-Demeter myth as a way of intertextualizing Jewett's feminist strategies. See also Donovan, who argues that Jewett's text constructs "an escape from a masculine time of history into transcending feminine space" (223). Given these analyses it is tempting to approach *The Country of the Pointed Firs* as a feminist utopian novel. Certainly Jewett's text informs and dialogically engages later feminist utopian fiction, particularly Gilman's *Herland*. However, Ann Lane argues that Mary E. Bradley Lane's *Mizora* (1890) "is the only self-consciously feminist utopia published before *Herland*" (Gilman xix), and in my view *The Country of the Pointed Firs* is best understood as a discourse of resistance, whereby phallocentric narrative constructs are undermined through inversion.

2. This and all further quotations from *The Country of the Pointed Firs* are taken from *The Country of the Pointed Firs and Other Stories*, Ed. Mary Ellen Chase. New York: W. W. Norton & Company, 1982.

3. Pennyroyal is defined as an abortifacient in Jacob Bigelow's *American Dictionary of Medicine* (1835), a standard text used widely by American physicians throughout the nineteenth-century and in all likelihood included in Dr. Jewett's medical library. For a discussion of pennyroyal as it was used for abortions in the nineteenth-century American Northeast, see Malcolm Potts. While it is true that pennyroyal was also used along the Maine coast as a mosquito repellent, Jewett leaves no doubt as to whether this is the particular use she has in mind with regard to Mrs. Todd's herbal ministrations. In "William's Wedding" Mrs. Todd recounts how for years she "besmeared" William's face with pennyroyal ointment "under the pretext" of protecting him against mosquitoes on his way to secret rendezvous with Esther (220).

4. Once Jewett's questing hero has fulfilled the ritual of her inverted romance, there is a return to fertility, represented in William's marriage to Esther. No longer will Mrs. Todd smother William's face with pennyroyal ointment, and during the marriage celebration Esther carries a lamb, signifying birth and renewal.

Works Cited

Althusser, Louis. *Lenin and Philosophy*. Trans. Ben Brewster. New York: Monthly Review Press, 1971.

Carter, Everett. *Howells and the Age of Realism*. New York: J. B. Lippincott Company, 1950.

Donovan, Josephine. "Sarah Orne Jewett's Critical Theory: Notes Toward a Feminine Literary Mode." in *Critical Essays on Sarah Orne Jewett*. Ed. Gwen Nagel. Boston: G. K. Hall, 1984.

Duvall, John N. "Murder in the Communities: Ideology In and Around *Light in August*." *Novel: A Forum on Fiction* 20 (Winter 1987):101-22.

Finke, Laurie. "Towards a Cultural Poetics of Romance." *Genre XXII* (Summer 1989): 109-27.

Frye, Northrop. *Anatomy of Criticism*. Princeton: Princeton UP, 1957.

Gilbert, Sandra M. and Susan Gubar. *The Mad Woman in the Attic: The Woman Writer and the Nineteenth-Century Literary Imagination*. New York: Yale UP, 1979.

Gilman, Charlotte Perkins. *Herland*. New York: Pantheon Books, 1979.

Jewett, Sarah Orne. *The Country of the Pointed Firs and Other Stories*. Ed. Mary Ellen Chase. New York: W. W. Norton & Company, 1982.

Lacan, Jacques. *Feminine Sexuality: Jacques Lacan and the ecole freudienne*. Eds. Juliet Mitchell and Jacquiline Rose. New York, London: U of Nebraska P, 1982.

Pratt, Annis. "Women and Nature in Modern Fiction." *Contemporary Literature* 13 (Autumn 1972):476-90.

Sartre, Jean-Paul. *Literary and Philosophical Essays*. Trans. Annette Michelson. New York: Collier Books, 1962.

Sherman, Sarah Way. *Sarah Orne Jewett: American Persephone*. Hanover, London: UP of New England, 1989.

Singley, Carol. "Reaching Lonely Heights: Sarah Orne Jewett, Emily Dickinson, and Female Initiation." *Colby Library Quarterly* 22:1(March 1986):75-82.

Smith-Rosenberg, Carroll. "The Body Politic." *Coming to Terms: Feminism, Theory, Politics*. Ed. Elizabeth Weed. New York, London: Routledge, 1989. 101-21.

FURTHER READING

Bibliographies

Frost, John Eldridge. "Sarah Orne Jewett Bibliography: 1949-1963." *Colby Library Quarterly* 10 (June 1964): 405-17.

Offers a survey of criticism on Jewett published between 1949 and 1963.

Weber, Clara Carter, and Carl J. Weber. *A Bibliography of the Published Writings of Sarah Orne Jewett*. Waterville, Maine: Colby College Press, 1965, 105 p.

Contains a bibliography of Jewett's published writings.

Biographies

Blanchard, Paula. *Sarah Orne Jewett: Her World and Her Work.* New York: Perseus, 2002, 416 p.

Utilizes a feminist framework to review Jewett's life and work.

Cary, Richard. *Sarah Orne Jewett.* New York: Twayne Publishers, 1962, 175 p.

Provides a critical biography by a prominent Jewett scholar.

Matthiessen, Francis Otto. *Sarah Orne Jewett.* New York: Houghton Mifflin Company, 1929, 159 p.

Presents the first critical biography of Jewett.

Criticism

Anderson, Donald. "Jewett's 'Foreigner' in the Estranged Land of Almira Todd." *Colby Quarterly* 38, no. 4 (December 2002): 390-402.

Discusses the character and psychological state of the narrator in "The Foreigner."

Bishop, Ferman. "Sarah Orne Jewett's Ideas of Race." *The New England Quarterly* 30, no. 2 (June 1957): 243-49.

Contends that Jewett believed in the supremacy of the Nordic race.

Brown, Bill. "Regional Artifacts (The Life of Things in the Work of Sarah Orne Jewett)." *American Literary History* 14, no. 2 (summer 2002): 195-226.

Explores how objects are assigned a cultural value in Jewett's fiction.

Cary, Richard, ed. Introduction to *Sarah Orne Jewett Letters,* pp. 3-8. Waterville, Maine: Colby College Press, 1967.

Introduces Jewett's letters and examines what they reveal about her literary tastes.

———, ed. *Sarah Orne Jewett: 29 Interpretive Essays.* Waterville, Maine: Colby College Press, 1973, 305 p.

Collection of critical essays on Jewett's works.

Cather, Willa. "Miss Jewett." In *Not Under Forty,* pp. 76-95. New York: Alfred A. Knopf, 1936.

Offers a character sketch in which Cather praises Jewett's literary style and notes that Jewett's writing conveys an intensely personal experience of life.

Church, Joseph. "Transgressive Daughters in Sarah Orne Jewett's *Deephaven.*" *Essays in Literature* 20, no. 2 (fall 1993): 231-50.

Asserts that the stories in Deephaven are about women's psychological journeys of self-revelation.

———. "A Woman's Psychological Journey in 'The King of Folly Island.'" *Essays in Literature* 23, no. 2 (fall 1996): 234-50.

Contends that "The King of Folly Island" is an example of Jewett working toward greater understanding of the way in which culture and psychology contribute to a women's development.

———. "The Healing Arts of Jewett's *A Country Doctor.*" *Colby Quarterly* 34, no. 2 (June 1998): 99-122.

Provides a psychological analysis of A Country Doctor in which Church argues that the novel mirrors Jewett's development as a writer.

Donovan, Josephine. "A Woman's Vision of Transcendence: A New Interpretation of the Works of Sarah Orne Jewett." *The Massachusetts Review* 21, no. 2 (summer 1980): 365-81.

Presents a new interpretation of several subjects, themes, and characteristics prominent in Jewett's fiction.

———. "Silence or Capitulation: Prepatriarchal 'Mothers' Gardens in Jewett and Freeman." *Studies in Short Fiction* 23, no. 1 (winter 1986): 43-8.

Offers a contemporary feminist reading of Jewett's "A White Heron" and Mary E. Wilkins Freeman's "Evalina's Garden."

———. "Jewett on Race, Class, Ethnicity, and Imperialism." *Colby Quarterly* 38, no. 4 (December 2002): 403-16.

Refutes claims that Jewett's writing is racist, fascist, classicist, and proto-imperialist.

Hohmann, Marti. "Sarah Orne Jewett to Lillian M. Munger: Twenty-Three Letters." *Colby Quarterly* 22, no. 1 (March 1986): 28-35.

Examines Jewett's encouraging letters to a young woman from 1876 to 1882.

Howard, June, ed. *New Essays on* The Country of the Pointed Firs. New York: Cambridge University Press, 1994, 123 p.

Contains a collection of previously unpublished essays on Jewett's best-known work.

Leder, Priscilla. "Living Ghosts and Women's Religion in Sarah Orne Jewett's *The Country of the Pointed Firs.*" In *Haunting the House of Fiction: Feminist Perspectives on Ghost Stories by American Women,* edited by Lynette Carpenter and Wendy K. Kolmar, pp. 26-40. Knoxville: University of Tennessee Press, 1991.

Analyzes how Jewett appropriates the "male" ghost story and adventure narrative and uses them to her own purposes.

Nagel, Gwen L., ed. *Critical Essays on Sarah Orne Jewett.* Boston, Mass.: G. K. Hall & Co., 1984, 254 p.

Collection of critical essays, including an introduction with a detailed bibliographic survey of Jewett's scholarship, early reviews of Jewett's work, and seventeen full-length critical analyses, many dealing with feminist issues.

Pennell, Melissa McFarland. "A New Spiritual Biography: Domesticity and Sorority in the Fiction of Sarah Orne Jewett." *Studies in American Fiction* 18, no. 2 (autumn 1990): 193-206.

Examines Jewett's use of the theme of sisterhood in her stories as a means of stressing female heritage and tradition over patriarchal institutions.

Powell, Betty J. "Speaking to One Another: Narrative Unity in Sarah Orne Jewett's *Old Friends and New.*" *Colby Quarterly* 34, no. 2 (June 1998): 150-71.

Explores the circuitous narrative strategy in Old Friends and New.

Pryse, Marjorie. "Women 'At Sea'; Feminist Realism in Sarah Orne Jewett's 'The Foreigner.'" *American Literary Realism* 15, no. 2 (autumn 1982): 244-52.

Identifies "foreigners" and "foreign" experiences in Jewett's story "The Foreigner."

———. "Archives of Female Friendship and the 'Way' Jewett Wrote." *The New England Quarterly* 66, no. 1 (March 1993): 47-66.

Examines Jewett's diaries and an unpublished holograph to understand how Jewett created fiction out of friendship.

Roman, Margaret. *Sarah Orne Jewett: Reconstructing Gender.* Tuscaloosa: University of Alabama Press, 1992, 245 p.

Argues that nearly all Jewett's work reveals her attempts to break free from patriarchal traditions and its dual norms for men and women.

Sherman, Sarah Way. *Sarah Orne Jewett, An American Persephone.* Hanover, N.H.: University Press of New England, 1989, 333 p.

Traces the literary and religious tradition that Jewett used as a source in her fiction, focusing on the symbol of the Greek goddess Persephone.

Stevenson, Catherine Barnes. "The Double Consciousness of the Narrator in Sarah Orne Jewett's Fiction." *Colby Library Quarterly* 11, no. 1 (March 1975): 1-12.

Analyzes perceptions of Jewett's narrators in Deephaven, "A White Heron," and The Country of the Pointed Firs.

Swartz, Patti Capel. "We Do Not All Go Two by Two; or, Abandoning the Ark." In *Jewett and Her Contemporaries:* *Reshaping the Canon,* edited by Karen L. Kilcup and Thomas S. Edwards, pp. 265-76. Gainesville: University Press of Florida, 1999.

Discusses the ways in which Jewett explored connections between people in her fiction; maintains that her work offers a map for those treasuring solitude despite also needing deep physical and spiritual relationships with others.

Westbrook, Perry D. "Sarah Orne Jewett (1849-1909)." In *Nineteenth-Century American Women Writers: A Bio-Critical Sourcebook,* edited by Denise D. Knight, pp. 270-80. Westport, Conn.: Greenwood Press, 1997.

Provides an overview of Jewett's life, her major works and themes, and the critical response to her writing.

OTHER SOURCES FROM GALE:

Additional coverage of Jewett's life and career is contained in the following sources published by the Gale Group: *American Writers; American Writers: The Classics,* Vol. 2; *American Writers Retrospective Supplement,* Vol. 2; *Contemporary Authors,* Vols. 108, 127; *Contemporary Authors New Revision Series,* Vol. 71; *Dictionary of Literary Biography,* Vols. 12, 74, 221; *Exploring Short Stories; Feminist Writers; Literature Resource Center; Modern American Women Writers; Novels for Students,* Vol. 15; *Reference Guide to American Literature,* Ed. 4; *Reference Guide to Short Fiction,* Ed. 2; *Short Stories for Students,* Vol. 4; *Short Story Criticism,* Vols. 6, 44; *Something about the Author,* Vol. 15; and *Twentieth-Century Literary Criticism,* Vols. 1, 22.

CHRISTINA ROSSETTI

(1830 - 1894)

(Also wrote under the pseudonym Ellen Alleyn) English poet, short story writer, and prose writer.

Rossetti is closely associated with Pre-Raphaelitism—an artistic and literary movement that aspired to recapture the vivid pictorial qualities and sensual aesthetics of Italian religious paintings before 1500—but was equally influenced by the religious conservatism and the asceticism of the Church of England. Scholars have found in her poetry an enduring dialectic between these disparate outlooks as well as an adeptness with a variety of poetic forms. Since the 1970s, feminist scholars have also noted that Rossetti's writings include subtle critiques of nineteenth-century society's treatment of women. It is recognized that Rossetti was no radical feminist—in fact she explicitly rejected the idea of women's suffrage. However, her work does explore relationships between women, the restrictions imposed upon women, the difficulties facing the female writer, and gender ideology. Some critics also argue that her religious verse offers new readings of the Christian scriptures with a uniquely feminist understanding and that her work in general offers a critique of the treatment of women in her age despite the fact that she did not overtly challenge the social order.

BIOGRAPHICAL INFORMATION

Rossetti was born in 1830, four years after her exiled, Italian father settled in London and married Frances Mary Polidori. Demonstrating poetic gifts early in her life, Rossetti wrote sonnets in competition with her brothers William Michael and Dante Gabriel, a practice that is thought to have developed her command of metrical forms. At the age of eighteen, Rossetti began studying the works of the Italian poet Dante Alighieri, who became a major and lasting influence on her poetry, as evidenced in her many allusions to his writing. As a young woman, Rossetti declined two marriage proposals because her suitors failed to conform to the tenets of the Anglican Church. Rather than marry, she chose to remain with her mother, also a devout Anglican. A succession of serious illnesses strongly influenced her temperament and outlook on life; because she often believed herself close to death, religious devotion and mortality became persistent themes in both her poetry and prose. In 1871 she developed Graves's disease and, though she published *A Pageant, and Other Poems* in 1881, she concentrated primarily on works of religious prose, such as *The Face of the Deep: A Devotional Commentary on the Apocalypse,* published in 1892. That same year she was diagnosed with cancer; she died two years later.

MAJOR WORKS

Rossetti's first published poem appeared in the *Athenaeum* when she was eighteen. She became a frequent contributor to the Pre-Raphaelite journal *The Germ,* which her brother Dante Gabriel founded. The title poem of her first collection of poetry, *Goblin Market, and Other Poems* (1862), relates the adventures of two sisters, Laura and Lizzie. The two are taunted by goblin merchants to buy luscious and tantalizing fruits. Though Lizzie is able to resist their coaxing, Laura succumbs. The narrator details Laura's increasing apathy and Lizzie's efforts to save her sister. The poem has been variously interpreted as a moral fable for children, an erotic lesbian fantasy, an experiment in meter and rhyme, and a feminist reinterpretation of Christian mythology. Two other well-known poems in the same volume, "After Death" and "Remember," meditations on death and the afterlife, have also been interpreted by some feminists as subversive texts despite their seemingly complaisant surfaces. The title poem of *The Prince's Progress, and Other Poems* (1866), Rossetti's second major collection, relates a prince's physical, moral, and spiritual journey to meet his bride. In 1874 Rossetti published a collection of prose for children, *Speaking Likenesses*. The title story of the book, which consists of three fantasy stories told to five sisters by their aunt, has been viewed by some critics as an exploration of the suppression of sexuality in girls. Another volume of children's prose, *Sing-Song* (1872), has been seen as a critique of patriarchal and authoritarian family values. Although earlier critics saw Rossetti's devotional verse as exploring humanity's relationship with God and the nature of life in the afterworld, feminist scholars have also noted the way in which the poet revises scripture in feminine terms. The sonnet sequence "Monno Innominanta," included in *A Pageant, and Other Poems,* has traditionally been regarded as a celebration of Rossetti's denial of human love for the sake of religious purity, but feminist thinkers have also seen it as an attempt by the artist to present a portrait that is distinguished from male depictions of herself. Rossetti's later prose works include *Time Flies* (1885), which offers for each day of the year a passage designed to provoke spiritual reflection, and the biblical commentaries *Seek and Find* (1879), *Letter and Spirit* (1883), and *The Face of the Deep*. Rossetti's work of juvenilia *Maude: A Story for Girls* (1897) was written in 1850 but only published after her death. The autobiographical text about the spiritual search of a fifteen-year-old girl offers insights into Rossetti's introspective adolescence.

CRITICAL RECEPTION

Critics generally consider Rossetti's poetry superior to her later nonsecular prose works but observe that much of her most highly regarded verse was also inspired by her deeply held religious beliefs. Faulted by some critics for an alleged indifference to social issues, she is praised by others for her simple diction, timeless vision, and stylistic technique; some critics have claimed further that Rossetti offers in her work a subtle social critique despite its surface conventionality. Early assessments of the poetry and prose focused on the poet's reticence and renunciation of this world in favor of the afterlife, but some late-twentieth-century critics have argued that there are multiple layers and hidden meanings to Rossetti's texts that show a deep and complex concern with women's issues. Much contemporary feminist criticism has focused on "Goblin Market," especially its eroticism and the exploration of the relationship between the two sisters in the story. Critics have noted too that the imagery and language of economics and commerce in the poem comments on the role of women and their literature within the Victorian economy. The poem has also been read as a religious allegory of the Fall and Redemption revised in feminist terms. Rossetti's other poetry and prose has also been reassessed by feminist scholars. These critics acknowledge that Rossetti held conservative views on many issues but claim that a deeper analysis of her work shows her to be uncommonly radical, particularly in her attempt to understand and critique the deeper realities of religion and literature and re-present them in terms that resonate with the female reader.

PRINCIPAL WORKS

Goblin Market, and Other Poems (poetry) 1862

Poems (poetry) 1866

The Prince's Progress, and Other Poems (poetry) 1866

Commonplace, and Other Short Stories (short stories) 1870

Sing-Song: A Nursery Rhyme Book (children's stories) 1872

Speaking Likenesses (juvenilia) 1874

Seek and Find (religious prose) 1879

Called to be Saints: The Minor Festivals Devotionally Studied (religious prose) 1881

A Pageant, and Other Poems (poetry) 1881

Letter and Spirit (religious prose) 1883

Time Flies: A Reading Diary (religious prose) 1885

The Face of the Deep: A Devotional Commentary on the Apocalypse (religious prose) 1892

Verses (poetry) 1893

New Poems (poetry) 1896

Maude: A Story for Girls (juvenilia and verse) 1897

The Poetical Works of Christina Georgina Rossetti (poetry) 1904

The Complete Poems of Christina Georgina Rossetti: A Variorum Edition, 3 vols. 1979-90.

PRIMARY SOURCES

CHRISTINA ROSSETTI (POEM DATE 1862)

SOURCE: Rossetti, Christina. "Dream Land." In *Goblin Market and Other Poems,* p. 17. New York: Dover, 1994.

In the following poem, originally published in 1862, Rossetti meditates on the restfulness and peace of a woman's death and her afterlife, which are familiar themes in much of her verse.

DREAM LAND

Where sunless rivers weep
Their waves into the deep,
She sleeps a charmèd sleep:
  Awake her not.
Led by a single star,
She came from very far
To seek where shadows are
  Her pleasant lot.

She left the rosy morn,
She left the fields of corn,
For twilight cold and lorn
  And water springs.
Through sleep, as through a veil,
She sees the sky look pale,
And hears the nightingale
  That sadly sings.

Rest, rest, a perfect rest
Shed over brow and breast;
Her face is toward the west,
  The purple land.
She cannot see the grain
Ripening on hill and plain;
She cannot feel the rain
  Upon her hand.

Rest, rest, for evermore
Upon a mossy shore;
Rest, rest at the heart's core
  Till time shall cease:
Sleep that no pain shall wake,
Night that no morn shall break
Till joy shall overtake
  Her perfect peace.

GENERAL COMMENTARY

LYNDA PALAZZO (ESSAY DATE FALL 1997)

SOURCE: Palazzo, Lynda. "The Poet and the Bible: Christina Rossetti's Feminist Hermeneutics." *The Victorian Newsletter* 92 (fall 1997): 6-9.

In the following essay, Palazzo argues that in her religious prose Rossetti attempts to recover for the woman reader the hidden realities in the Christian scriptures and thus that her hermeneutics are feminist.

With the anniversary of Christina Rossetti's death in 1994, there has been renewed interest in her work, with an entire volume of *Victorian Poetry* devoted to her poetry and prose, revealing a perceptive and sometimes subversive intelligence at work. However, critical accounts of her theology are still very few, and even fewer those which examine the theology of her devotional prose. One of the more promising articles in the volume, Linda Petersen's "Restoring the Book: The Typological Hermeneutics of the PRB," after an exciting introduction suggesting a reaction in Rossetti's theology against the "subtle yet insistent cultural exclusion of women as active readers of, and writers about, the sacred scriptures" (212) ultimately disappoints by neatly sidestepping the devotional prose and engaging with Rossetti's poetry instead. The reader is left without a confirmation of Rossetti active herself as reader and interpreter of the sacred text. Rossetti is indeed an active participant in the theological developments of the last century, and her approach, imaginative and intuitive rather than "scientific," is closely linked to the religious controversies of her time. She recognizes the potential of controversial developments in nineteenth-century Anglican theology, and although always careful to avoid overstepping the bounds of what she considers legitimate enquiry, develops a method of scriptural interpretation which satisfies both her intellectual need for an imaginative and transformative encounter with a living text, and her personal need as a woman to interpret and understand a "masculine" text.

An earlier article by Joel Westerholm comes nearer to showing Rossetti's active engagement with the scriptural text, especially in his discussion of her response to gender issues. However, he has not placed her satisfactorily within the context of Victorian Anglican theology and consequently is unable to determine the method of her operation. Her "authority" in fact comes from the knowledge that she is working within a rapidly expanding, although at times controversial, field. More credit must be given the SPCK than to assume that they were unaware of any "serious and scholarly biblical interpretation" (14) in her work. There is no evidence either that "in prefaces and editing the church tried to place her back in the contexts it found acceptable" (16). The editing of her work by the SPCK appears to have been minimal (see note 4). The Anglican Church in the nineteenth century was surprisingly open ended and Rossetti's close friendship with such figures as the fiery R. F. Littledale would have kept her up to date with the latest controversies, It is not, as Westerholm suggests, her courage we need to admire, although she certainly had that, but the razor sharp intellect and vision that identified in contemporary theological developments the potential for feminine and feminist theology.

Rossetti's place, in terms of method, is amongst the post-Coleridgeans such as J. H. Newman, Isaac Williams, to whom she acknowledges a debt in the prefatory note of *Seek and Find,* and Benjamin Jowett, in his "On the Interpretation of Scripture." There is evidence in *Seek and Find* and *Letter and Spirit* of a lively interest in controversies such as those that followed the publication of *Essays and Reviews.*[1] Like Jowett, she was fascinated by metaphor and symbol, and the role of the imagination in relation to the scriptures. The methodology of both in fact foreshadows some of the most important developments in modern hermeneutical study, for example Paul Ricoeur in his use of metaphor.

Possibly her earliest attempts at biblical commentary, her unpublished notes on Genesis and Exodus,[2] show her moving away from the popular typological orientation, towards an evaluation of the figurative power of language. As does Coleridge in his "Statesman's Manual," Rossetti notes the potential of metaphor and symbol in the opening up of the text to a multiplicity of interpretations, reader-based interpretations, which make

the Bible live in the contemporary mind, as "living educts of the imagination" (29).

She remarks on a marginal comment for Genesis 2:22:

> *Margin* "builded he a woman: opens the whole subject of the Church born & *built* from our Lord's side. Also consider His parallel with Adam casting in His lot with his lost bride. "Yet without sin." Also the *female* cast out of sin? *Is* it so?

Rossetti is aware of the standard typological association, Eve, type of the Church as bride of Christ, but her focus is on the metaphor "builded," which highlights the tension between God's creation of Eve and the physical building of the church. She is allowing the metaphor to open up imaginative access to a whole series of possibilities, ending with a daring suggestion in her use of "cast out" that Eve's sin had its origin in the sinful flesh of Adam from which she was made.

Her comment on the use of the word bow" found in Genesis 9:13 indicates again that she is exploring the way metaphor gives access to meaning through association with the familiar in the mind of the reader: "13. "My bow"—would this suggest bow and arrows as an antedeluvian mode of hunting, & *thus* familiar and intelligible?" (see note 2). The author's reference to "bow," Rossetti suggests, is chosen specifically because it would facilitate an imaginative connection between the text and the vocabulary of the familiar, thus establishing meaning.

George Landow sees the "deformation" of the popular type into allegory, symbol or correspondence as characteristic of high church exegetes like Keble and Pusey (59), but Rossetti's agenda is different from that of the great Tractarians. She certainly learnt from Keble, and even in later years continued to use her copy of his *Christian Year,* but even her youthful illustrations to his poems in this volume show a very different sensibility from his. Diane D'Amico in a discussion of these illustrations draws our attention to, on the one hand, Rossetti's subjective reading of Keble, "responding to, if not looking for, what in the poetry of *The Christian Year* would serve to mirror her own hopes and fears," and on the other to her use of the feminine figure "when we would expect to see a male figure as the subject of an illustration" (37). More important in terms of her theology, we also see that her choice of emphasis does not correspond to Keble's own. In her illustration of Keble's "Fifth Sunday after Epiphany" she fixes upon a few words only from the epigraph from Isaiah 59: "your iniquities have separated between you and your God." She interprets these in a literal sense, cutting them off momentarily from their immediate referent, and then reproduces them in a figuration of her own: a medusa-like demon, reminiscent of her own "The World," obscures the figure of Christ on the cross. The resulting image, despite its childish characters, is unsettling and provoking. Her brother William Michael noted in his memoir to her **Poetical Works** the "very literal manner" with which she was wont to construe the biblical precepts" (liv), but this was not, as he perhaps thought, the consequence of a closed mind. Rather, it was her fascination with words, and the pictures they conjured up in her imagination. Her method here is as follows: focus on the surface meaning, once the word has been given symbolic or metaphorical status, allows it to be imaginatively transferred from its original context to become active in the individual mind, producing a corresponding metaphor. Benjamin Jowett describes a similar action in his comments on the use of symbol and imagination when he speaks of "the doubling of an object when seen through glasses placed at different angles" (381). In a bolder step than he himself would have dared, the correspondences of Keble's sacramental universe have been transferred to the words of scripture. Language itself has become sacrament. Rossetti follows Jowett (and Coleridge), as she "read[s] scripture like any other book" (338), with "an effort of thought and imagination requiring the sense of a poet was well as a critic . . . demanding much more than learning a degree of original power and intensity of mind" (384). It is an opening up of the mind to the text, an empathy which probes the "is" and "is not"[3] of each metaphor.

Rossetti is aware of a tendency to devalue the text in biblical study and has harsh words to say in **Letter and Spirit** about those who denigrate the face value of scripture: "We protrude mental feelers in all directions above, beneath, around it, grasping, clinging to every imaginable particular except the main point" (85). She is not, as her brother thought, falling into the trap of literalism, nor is she naively adhering to the idea of "common sense" linguistic transparency. We need to grasp the surface of the text, its literal value, in order to have access to meaning. Even so the mind is waylaid by the need to translate into fact, to prove physical truth or falsity: "What was the precise architecture of Noah's Ark?" Rossetti quotes, "Clear up the astronomy of Joshua's miracle.[4] Fix the botany of Jonah's gourd. Must a pedestal be included within the measurement of Nebuchadnezzar's 'golden image'" (86-87).

Rossetti's final volume of devotional prose, **The Face of the Deep,** an exegetical commentary on Revelation, is particularly interesting in that we see Rossetti working directly on the scriptures. The title itself, taken from Genesis 1:2, proclaims its revaluation of the individual word as an access point to personal revelation. Her prefatory note proposes a search of the surface of the sacred text: "If thou canst dive, bring up pearls. If thou canst not dive, collect amber. Though I fail to identify Pardisiacal 'bdellium,' I still may hope to search out beauties of the 'onyx stone'" (7).

The metaphorical nature of the individual word allows her, through grasping its "surface," to glimpse the theological referent, and then as an interpreter, to substitute another "metaphor" taken from her own experience. She begins her commentary by opening her mind and imagination to the language of the text, appropriating words or phrases from it which have called up echoes from her own experience—words which orthodox biblical commentaries may in the past have considered unimportant. Then in her text she restores, not the words themselves, but the figures they have produced in her own mind.

For example in Revelation 1:1 from the phrase "must shortly come to pass" she appropriates the word "shortly," which has a pivotal function, allowing her to include herself in an expanded text: "'Things which must shortly come to pass.'—At the end of 1800 years we are still repeating this 'shortly'" (9). It was this "shortly" for John, "the channel, not the fountain head" of Revelation, and it is still "shortly" for the present generation. But Rossetti doesn't attempt to define the word in her commentary, or explain its meaning; rather she explores the tension between the totally opposite poles it represents. The word has become metaphoric, the figurative sense pointing to a barely glimpsed divine meaning which in turn challenges the literal, forcing the reader to find ways in which such meanings can co-exist, realigning the self as the word becomes productive in the imagination.

Particularly important to Rossetti is the capacity of such a method to satisfy her own need as a woman working in a field almost exclusively dominated by men. **The Face of the Deep** is not addressed exclusively to women, but the frequent use of the address "we women" suggests that, especially in her description of the female figures, she has her female readership in mind. Certainly some of the more prominent figures in Revelation are examined in terms of gender distinction, becoming patterns which Rossetti is able to trace in her own world. Her comment on the "woman clothed with the sun" of Revelation 12:1 is perhaps the best known of these, as it fits well with the "lowest place" theme of her poetry: "she has done all and stands; from the lowest place she has gone up higher . . . triumphantly erect, despite her own frailty" (310). But Rossetti's definition of this frailty gives us more than an echo of her poetry. It is physical weakness, certainly, the lot reserved for women, "unlike the corresponding heritage of man" (310), but is also Eve's punishment for intellectual daring. Rossetti's description of Eve's intellectual sin has the characteristics of her own objections to contemporary Biblical controversy, but the interpreter of the text is female: "Not till she became wise in her own conceit, disregarding the plain obvious meaning of words, and theorising on her own responsibility as to physical and intellectual results, did she bring death into the world" (310).

Protagonists who stand ranged on each side of the gender divide give Rossetti the opportunity to provide guidance in male-female relationships, and there are no doubts as to where her sympathies lie. The outcome on earth of the "war in heaven" of Revelation 12: 7 comes perilously close to a war between the sexes, the newly delivered woman fleeing from the pursuing flood of the (male) dragon. But she avoids the simplistic and uses such generalizations only to highlight important issues for her woman readers.

Rossetti's hermeneutic can be defined as a feminist one in the way she attempts to recover for the woman reader those hidden or suppressed realities of the text. She accepts with humility the feminine implications of even that most loathsome of creatures, the whore of Babylon, whom she admits as "illustrating the particular foulness, degradation, loathsomeness, to which a perverse rebellious woman because feminine not masculine is liable," but her scrutiny picks out the relationship between the whore and the (male) beast upon which she is seated. Since the sacred text is inspired[5] and therefore active "to teach us somewhat we can learn, and in a way by which we are capable of learning" (23), a physical detail of this nature may be considered symbolically and interpreted within the personal circumstance of the reader: "If she removes he is the motor; she is lifted aloft to the extent of his height; her stability depends on his. In semblance he is her slave, in reality her master" (399). In the discussion which follows, on the misuse of physical force, there is an ill disguised bitterness:

> As yet, I suppose, we women claim no more than equality with our brethren in head and heart; whilst as to physical force, we scout it as unworthy to arbitrate between the opposed camps. Men on their side do not scout physical force, but let it be.
> (410)

She thus is able to foreground sections of the text which may have seemed irrelevant to earlier commentators, but which in her own discourse gain meaning. The "kings of the earth" for example, the seducers of Babylon, regret the fall of the whore, but as Rossetti points out, "Adam seems not to have found one word to plead for Eve in the terrible hour of judgement" (418). We are reminded here of her comment from the Genesis notes, "Also the *female* cast out of sin?" and her anguished "*Is* it so?" Cast from the flesh of Adam, Eve's sin is derived from his, but he shows no compassion for her in her suffering. As Rossetti moves her meditation to her own day, the corrupt seducers of Babylon assume contemporary identity:

> *Now* they are the wicked who stand callous amid the fears, torments, miseries of others; not investigating human claims . . . not heeding the burning questions of their day, neighbourhood, nay sometimes their own hearths.
> (418)

But it will not always be so. "Society" Rossetti claims, "may be personified as a human figure whose right hand is man, whose left woman. . . . Rules admit of and are proved by exceptions. There are left-handed people, and there may arise a left-handed society!" (409).

In what she perceives as a world blind in the main to the suffering of women, Rossetti derives comfort from the feminine identity of the Church and its relationship to Christ. In her response to Revelation 19:7 she illustrates the love between Christ and the Church by a revaluation of Christ's own relationship with women; his love, acceptance and consolation, defending her use of this literal interpretation of the feminine identity of the Church, "because it is so lovely a privilege to have stood really and truly in some direct relation to Christ that it may well take precedence of aught figurative" (434). Adding imaginative and emotional detail she fills in the feminine mindset, finally bringing her discourse into the present where womankind "comes forth from the thousand battlefields . . . beds of weariness, haunts of starvation, hospital wards, rescue homes, orphanages . . ." (436).

As Revelation draws to a close and St. John returns to address the Churches, as at the beginning, Rossetti allows the words of St. John to span the centuries and become directly meaningful to her own discourse. His warning in Revelation 22:18-19, "If any man shall take away from the words of the book of this prophecy, God shall take away his part out of the book of life," elicits the response "O Lord, if I myself have fallen into either deadly error against which Thou here testifieth: 'I acknowledge my transgressions'" (548), and for the reader Rossetti adds, "if I have been overbold in attempting such a work as this, I beg pardon" (551).

Rossetti's method has enabled her to bridge the gap between a text increasingly under fire as inaccurate, irrelevant and incomprehensible[6] and the average Victorian sensibility, bewildered in a world fast becoming "modern" at the end of the century. In this she is forward looking to Karl Barth, to Gadamer and to modern hermeneutical trends, but she looks past them also, in her exploration of feminist hermeneutics, which a hundred years later seeks to liberate the Biblical text from participation in the oppression of women, through, as Schneider terms it, an "integral interpretation . . . engaging it in such a way that it can function as locus and mediator of transformative encounter with the living God" (197).

Notes

1. See for example my discussion of the two volumes in "The Prose Works of Christina Rossetti."

2. They were probably written some time before *Seek and Find*. See Packer (330) and Palazzo (62). I am indebted to Mrs. Joan Rossetti for the notes on Genesis, and to Professor Diane D'Amico for help in tracing their whereabouts. See also Palazzo 89, notes 17, 18, 20, and Appendix A, for a reproduction of the notes.

3. Schneider (29). Sandra Schneider uses modern developments in the study of hermeneutics, especially in relation to the use of metaphor, to facilitate a feminist interpretation of the scriptures.

4. Joshua's miracle in particular must have caught her imagination as she attempted to publish a more detailed comment on it in *Seek and Find*. The SPCK [Society for Promoting Christian Knowledge] rejected the passage, but otherwise the editing of the manuscript appears minimal. See Palazzo Appendix B.

5. The nature of the inspiration itself was a controversial topic of the period. Rossetti is closest in her treatment of inspiration to the method of Isaac Williams and his *Apocalypse* and *Genesis*.

6. Attacks on literalism, although useful in correcting the worst excesses of fundamentalism, ultimately tended to devalue the language of the text, for example Matthew Arnold's classification of the words of scripture in his *God and the Bible* as expendable "husks" (156).

Works Cited

Arnold, Matthew. *God and the Bible*. Ed. R. H. Super. Ann Arbor: U of Michigan P, 1970.

Coleridge, S. T. "The Statesman' Manual." *Lay Sermons*. Ed. R. J. White. London: Routledge & Kegan Paul, 1972.

D'Amico, Diane. "Christina Rossetti's *Christian Year*: Comfort for 'the weary heart.'" *Victorian Newsletter* No. 72 (Fall 1987): 37-41.

Jowett, Benjamin. "On the Interpretation of Scripture." *Essays and Reviews*. London Parker & Son, 1860; Greg International, 1970.

Landow, George. *Victorian Types, Victorian Shadows*. Boston: Routledge & Kegan Paul, 1980.

Packer, Lona Mosk. *Christina Rossetti*. Cambridge: Cambridge UP, 1963.

Palazzo, Lynda. "The Prose Works of Christina Rossetti." Unpubl. Diss. U of Durham, 1992.

Petersen, Linda. "Restoring the Book: The Typological Hermeneutics of the PRB." *Victorian Poetry* 32, 3-4 (Autumn-Winter, 1994): 209-27.

Rossetti, Christina. *The Face of the Deep*. London: SPCK, 1892.

——. *Letter and Spirit*. London: SPCK, 1883.

——. *The Poetical Works of Christina Rossetti* with memoir and notes by William Michael Rossetti. London: Macmillan, 1904.

——. *Seek and Find*. London: SPCK, 1897.

Schneider, Sandra M. *The Revelatory Text*. New York: Harper San Francisco, 1991.

Westerholm, Joel. "I Magnify Mine Office: Christina Rossetti's Authoritative Voice in Her Devotional Prose." *Victorian Newsletter* No. 84 (Fall 1993): 11-17.

Williams, Isaac. *Apocalypse with Notes and Reflections*. London: Rivington, 1852.

——. *The Beginning of the Book of Genesis, with Notes and Reflections*. London: Rivington, 1861.

MARGARET REYNOLDS (ESSAY DATE 1999)

SOURCE: Reynolds, Margaret. "Speaking Un-likeness: The Double Text in Christina Rossetti's 'After Death' and 'Remember'." *Textual Practice* 13, no. 1 (1999): 25-41.

In the following essay, Reynolds explores the complexity and subversive nature of Rossetti's poetry, despite its surface simplicity.

Small though not positively short, she might easily be overlooked but would not easily be forgotten.

Christina Rossetti, *Maude: Prose and Verse*
(1850)[1]

Indifferent to language, enigmatic and feminine, this space underlying the written is rhythmic, unfettered, irreducible to its intelligible verbal translation; it is musical, anterior to judgement, but restrained by a single guarantee: syntax.
Julia Kristeva, *Revolution in Poetic Language* (1974)[2]

Once upon a time, Christina Rossetti was simple. Her brother William Michael says that he 'cannot remember ever seeing her in the act of composition'. He admits that this is strange given that he and his younger sister were 'almost constantly in the same house' from the date of her birth up to the year 1876, some forty-six years, woman and girl. Nevertheless, William Michael declares authoritatively that Rossetti's methods of composition were artless and unselfconscious:

> Christina's habits of composing were eminently of the spontaneous kind. I question her having ever once deliberated with herself whether or not she would write something or other, and then, after thinking out a subject, having proceeded to treat it in regular spells of work. Instead of this, something impelled her feelings, or 'came into her head', and her hand obeyed the dictation. I suppose she scribbled lines off rapidly enough, and afterwards took whatever amount of pains she deemed requisite for keeping them in right form and expression.[3]

In spite of never having seen her at it, William Michael knows perfectly well how Christina writes and why. Or rather he knows perfectly well how girls write and why. They get taken over by something to do with feeling and then they take dictation. And they do it secretly. They live in the public eye, always accessible to family scrutiny—'almost constantly in the same house'—and yet, like Jane Austen alerted by the creaking drawing-room door, like Barrett Browning thrusting her manuscript scraps under the cushions, like Christina's own Maude 'slipping out of sight some scrawled paper', the practice of writing is hidden away, kept secret and separate from the performance of social engagement.[4]

Just as when, where and how Rossetti wrote her poems were hidden from her brother, so *what* she wrote was equally obscured. Partly, Rossetti herself made it that way. At an early age Rossetti developed a scrupulous manner which led to her brother teasing that 'she would soon become so polite it would be impossible to live with her'.[5] The hard-bound surface hides the vulnerable self. In a similar way Rossetti's own manuscript notebooks were elaborately tidy; William Michael refers to her 'extremely neat but . . . rather timid and formal script' and to her 'usual excessive neatness of caligraphy [thus]'.[6] Manners maketh the woman and by her hand you shall know her; for if Rossetti herself built up these defensive surfaces, her two brothers, and William Michael in particular in his later role of editor and literary executor, successfully obscured Rossetti further by creating a polished veneer which reflected back his own im-age of the woman poet. His 1904 edition of Rossetti is the main culprit here, neatly controlling the reader's interpretation of the poems by putting them all under individual headings described as 'Some leading themes, or keynotes of feeling, in the poems of Christina Rossetti'. These are: Personal experiences and emotions; Death; The aspiration for rest; Vanity of vanity; Love of animals; Winter; The loveliness of the rose.[7]

William Michael's list betrays his terms. His sister was a woman. Her poems must be feminine, so feminine he will make them. A particular nineteenth-century feminine which makes lyrical utterance into autobiography; death, especially her own death, into the ideal 'most poetical topic'[8] for a woman poet; and all rounded off with devotional themes and subjects drawn from the nursery and the boudoir. The surface, the public image, once again intrudes and the real Rossetti is hidden from view. She is, like her own Maude, 'easily overlooked'.

This is a parable about what has also happened to her poetry. Scrupulously polite, excessively neat, redolently feminine, Rossetti's poetry is none the less 'not easily forgotten'. This is true most obviously in the fact that, in spite of having spent much of the twentieth century labelled as a 'minor lyric voice'[9] Rossetti has yet managed to hold on to her popular appeal. More than that, recently critics have begun to attribute Rossetti's unforgettableness to her 'scandalous' tendencies, to her 'capacity to unsettle', and to the 'instability' of her texts.[10] Dualism, doubleness, repetition, alterity, have long been noted as prime influences and techniques in Rossetti's poetry, but, in fact, that double model is often the very essence of the disturbing quality which marks and which so richly empowers Rossetti's writing. Isobel Armstrong writes of the Victorian double poem, 'The simpler the surface of the poem, the more likely it is that a second and more difficult poem will exist beneath it'.[11] If the surface Rossetti is neat, polite and 'simple', the hidden Rossetti underneath, the one William Michael never saw at work, is perverse, caustic and complex.

The two sonnets '**After Death**' and '**Remember**' were both composed in 1849, '**After Death**' on 28 April and '**Remember**' on 25 July. Both were written out by Rossetti in the same manuscript notebook, now in the Bodleian, and the two poems appeared consecutively, '**Remember**' first, then '**After Death**' in the 1862 edition of *Goblin Market and Other Poems*. Both poems are very well known, much reprinted and, especially in the case of '**Remember**', much loved.

And yet, while they often receive honourable mentions in Rossetti criticism, very little sustained attention has been given to them.[12]

AFTER DEATH

The curtains were half drawn, the floor was
        swept
    And strewn with rushes, rosemary and may
    Lay thick upon the bed on which I lay,
Where thro' the lattice ivy-shadows crept.
5   He leaned above me, thinking that I slept
    And could not hear him; but I heard him
        say:
    'Poor child, poor child:' and as he turned
        away
Came a deep silence, and I knew he wept.
He did not touch the shroud, or raise the fold
10   That hid my face, or take my hand in his,
    Or ruffle the smooth pillows for my head:
    He did not love me living; but once dead
    He pitied me; and very sweet it is
To know he still is warm tho' I am cold.[13]

'**After Death**' already suggests its two-sidedness in its title. There was a life, now there is death (and continuing life), and the one state will be measured against the other. Whether or not this is a 'real' death is open to question. Generally, and because Rossetti so insistently returns to a landscape beyond the grave where a speaking self still feels and knows and haunts the living, it is taken that Rossetti's speaker here is dead and laid out prior to burial. In fact, linguistically speaking, all the phrases the poem uses, 'dead', 'slept', 'shroud', 'cold', could be used, as they conventionally are, as synonyms, euphemisms or exaggerations for some other state dramatically declared to be a death in life.[14]

The shifting context of Rossetti's poem is suggested by the physical scene setting in the first four lines. The curtains are 'half drawn'; the floor is 'strewn', that is, partly covered, with rushes; 'rosemary and may' lie on the bed, and presumably, on her, the poet-speaker. Everything is half covered, both revealed and concealed, not light, nor dark, but both at once. And this is confirmed in the fourth line where 'thro' the lattice ivy-shadows crept'. The lattice, as Catherine Maxwell rightly says, along with the rushes and the detail of the flowers on the bed, situates the poem within a mock medieval tradition of the enclosed lady, the 'high-born maiden' invoked by Tennyson in 'The Lady of Shalott' and by Browning in 'Porphyria's Lover'.[15] But in its simplest descriptive image it also points to the black and white criss-cross, that is, double and contradictory, the half seen, half hidden that is the literary essence of the poem. And, 'thro' the lattice ivy-shadows crept'.

This line is, literally, creepy. While the half seen, half hidden is economically set up in the first lines, there is also a clear sense of barriers crossed, division broken down, laws of place transgressed. The outside world has come into the inside, death has invaded life (or vice versa), and the seen/not seen of the 'lattice' is no protection. 'Ivy-shadows' creep (crept/creep/crypt) from the outside to the inside . . . and on the inside . . . , what happens? 'He leaned above me, thinking that I slept / And could not hear him'. Close juxtaposition of words and phrases in Rossetti is never accidental. The shadows creep through, and 'He', now introduced into the poem's consciousness for the first time, 'he' leans above 'me' in a privacy where he (wrongly) believes himself unobserved and where, consequently, he believes it unnecessary to constrain or curb himself.

We don't know who this 'he' is, but there is a hint. In this secret space, unobserved, 'he' says, 'Poor child, poor child'. Now doubleness and reciprocity, meaning one term by saying another, are trademarks in Rossetti poems. Maxwell has a good stab at this by pointing out that the trick is to turn this apparently conventional term around. If he calls her 'child', then what does she call him? The answer is 'Father'. Maxwell (correctly) positions the poem in the confessional mode, deduces (correctly) that this must be a privileged male given that he is permitted a private interview with a woman alone in her bedroom, puzzles (incorrectly) over who such a man can be 'with no familial or projected familial ties'—and comes up with the ingenious suggestion that this 'he' is a priest.[16]

It's easier than that, of course, and worse than that. The absent term here, the one that cannot be spoken out but only gestured at, is the name of Father. And why is the word unsaid? Because the act of naming would name more than the father, for it would label the argument of the poem too; fix its 'meaning' too overtly. In Lacan's terms the 'nom-du-père' represents the Law of the Father which marks out the border between culture and 'nature abandoned to the law of copulation'.[17] Those borders, those barriers, are all broken down in this poem and the key term which fixes the (new?) knowledge of transgression is left out. In the silences of the poem, through the opposition of one term (child) which obliquely spells another term (father), the semiotic signals its coded message from within the body of the text, while the law of the symbolic remains written on its skin. That the meaning conveyed by Kristeva's semiotic is associated with the child's pre-Oedipal stage contact with the mother's body is significant here. The speaker in this poem may indeed be a 'child' ('Poor child, poor child') and the poem may speak at a moment of transition on to the Oedipal phase. The rhetoric in 'After Death' is 'artless', childlike, uncomplicated, apparently naive, and from within that 'innocence' a message spells itself out. The poem refuses to name the father, and in that absence, that silence, a new knowingness marks the entry into the symbolic. Maud Ellmann says that 'For Lacan . . . incest is bad grammar'. The taboo against it is 'identical with an order in language'.[18] Rossetti's poem, so grammatically precise, so coolly ordered, leaves out the naming to keep her grammar and syntax intact.

But everything else is breached. It is never quite clear in this poem who is the active party. The speaker seems passive ('dead'), but she speaks, and, quite possibly, what she speaks is the secret of her desire. The transgression in this poem may be mutual. Or it may be one-sided, with *either party* constructing a scene of illicit desire. The sestet of the poem, where one would expect to find some change in theme, argument or mood, hots up the sense of anxiety and threat of or the desire for transgression. 'He did not touch the shroud, or raise the fold / That hid my face, or take my hand in his, / Or ruffle the smooth pillows for my head.' It begins with a negative, 'He did not'. But language works in linear progression and functions as explained by de Saussure and endorsed by Lacan only on differences, for there are no positive terms. So we can only go about the process of imagining the negative here by first conceiving the action to be negated. We are invited to *imagine* him doing exactly all these things: touching the shroud, raising the fold to expose her face, taking her hand. . . . If he does not actually carry out these actions—and we are only told so once, so that we are inclined to forget the negative as the list goes on—he still *could* do them, *might* do them, *might long* to do them. As the speaker might long for them to be done. 'He did not . . . ruffle' the pillows so that they are no longer 'smooth' but some implied 'different' term. Rough? Roughed up? Both are suggested by the assonance in spite of the apparent transparency of 'ruffle'. Like Emily Dickinson's poem 'He fumbles at your soul' Rossetti's sonnet places us in a readerly discomfort. We know 'He did not' do these things on this occasion. But has he done them before? Might the speaker wish for him to do them? By prioritizing the negative the poem invites us to imagine some surprise, or regret, in the speaker's

voice, some assumption that the familiar pattern will be, could well be, repeated yet again.

The obscure sense of invasion that governs the opening section of the poem is made very strong here. A should-be-externalized object intrudes disturbingly into a discrete space. In this particular context the room is first invaded, and then the garments, wrapping up, closing off, protecting, identifying ('the fold that hid my face') the very body of the speaker, are all twitched aside by linguistic sleight of hand. In Rossetti's language 'differences' are all, and the pull between the said and the not-said is always making spaces filled with meaning.

Or a space where meaning can be thrown out.

In Kristeva's account of the processes of abjection, she includes a story about 'The improper / unclean', where the subject spits out something which she loathes, but which none the less she has ingested, either under duress or out of some improper desire. This spitting out of the alien matter is painful, terrible, an abjection towards death, but it paradoxically emphasizes and confirms the individuality of the self: 'During that course in which "I" become, I give birth to myself amid the violence of sobs, of vomit.'[19]

Kristeva's language sounds extravagant beside Rossetti's reflecting surfaces, but it suggests something of what is being thrown out, abjected in Rossetti's poetry. In 'After Death' (and in 'Remember') Rossetti's speaker spits out an 'unclean' which weighs into her silences. What she has to say is unpalatable. With a violence which she none the less controls and keeps secret, she throws up a truth about dominance, about power, about sex relations and about transgression. Like the bulimic who exercises control over her body and her self-image by puking up all that she judges redundant, ugly, not herself, Rossetti's verse throws up the weight of her message. And, like the bulimic, she does it in secret, for the story is in code, not on the public surface, hidden away in a privacy of silence.

And yet even in this 'involuntary' spasm there may be a positive process of self-creation. For in the process of throwing up this waste, this secret and unnecessary meaning, the speaker/poet/ Rossetti, otherwise hidden from view, does become 'I', gives birth to a speaking assertive self at the cost of imagining her own 'death'.

In the last three lines of 'After Death' Rossetti's 'I' becomes an 'other' separating herself from the father who 'names' her ('Poor child, poor child') but whom she dare not name. We are told that 'He did not love me living'. How anyone who reads nineteenth-century literature, with its many iconic female corpses, can take this at face value baffles me. He did not love me. Maybe true, but doubtless he used me, controlled me, ignored me, or perhaps he even hated me. And once 'dead'—as opposed to alive, vital, demanding, assertive, self-directed—then certainly he may 'pity' me. Just as Porphyria's lover pitied her, as Lancelot pitied the Lady of Shalott, as the Duke pitied his Last Duchess, as Dickens pitied Little Nell, as Hardy pitied Tess.

So he pities me . . . 'and' . . . Rossetti's speaker here uses '*and*' notice. Not 'but' or 'yet' or 'still'. Her conjunctions, like everything else, are telling. 'And' means that the sentiment which follows, her sentiment, her feeling, expressed for the very first time in the poem, has some direct connection to what went before—that is, his 'not loving' her, but now weeping and 'pitying' her. She does not feel this in spite of what he feels, has felt about her, but *because* of it. And what she feels is pleasure . . . cruel, 'cold', dispassionate pleasure. A pleasure which is 'sweet' with all the erotic and physically realized sensuality (food- and sex-wise) that the word can bear.

In her reading of '**After Death**' Maxwell is troubled by the 'perversity' of 'sweet' here, and rightly so. She points out that its freakish insistent power is connected to the fact that the words 'warm' and 'cold' in the last lines, descriptions of each of the poem's protagonists' respective positions—he is now 'warm' and she is 'cold'—might function as synonyms for 'emotionally susceptible' and 'emotionally detached'.[20] This is the right track, but there is more, much more here. As Isobel Armstrong has shown, 'warm' and 'warmth' in Rossetti's vocabulary very often carry connotations of an intense erotic.[21] In '**After Death**', he—the man who invades, breaks laws, enters in—'still is warm'. If anything, he is even hotter than before, the restraint of 'He did not' pushing at the boundary of suggestion hinting that now, more than ever now, in a moment of intense but rigidly policed desire, would he like to do the things he once did or wished to do. But now she, the speaker, is 'dead' and another taboo, perhaps stronger and yet more deliciously tantalizing than the one she fails to name, denies and bars. And the effects of his thwarted taunted desire are 'sweet' for the speaker. Now, at last, she is 'cold'—calculating, detached, in charge, indifferent, cruel—a dominatrix whose power of denial, or acquiescence, is indeed 'sweet'.

'Perverse' the poem is, not least because the 'père-version' it uncovers and deconstructs is written over with a new text that asserts 'I'. But only if the reader sees. Or rather, only if the reader hears. For Rossetti's readers have to listen to her talking poem and to analyse the hidden traumas described. In the meantime they return as compulsive repetitions.

Listen to what she says in '**Remember**'.

REMEMBER

Remember me when I am gone away,
    Gone far away into the silent land;
    When you can no more hold me by the hand,
Nor I half turn to go yet turning stay.
Remember me when no more day by day
    You tell me of our future that you planned:
    Only remember me; you understand
It will be late to counsel then or pray.
Yet if you should forget me for a while
    And afterwards remember, do not grieve:
    For if the darkness and corruption leave
    A vestige of the thoughts that once I had,
Better by far you should forget and smile
    Than that you should remember and be sad.[22]

The first question to ask is then: remember . . . what?

Of course, the answer looks like 'me'. 'Remember me' is repeated three times in the first eight lines and the title of the sonnet is often mistakenly given as 'Remember Me'. But it's a Rossetti trick. As the poem moves on to the sestet the instruction to 'remember' appears twice, but in neither case is it made clear exactly *what* may, or may not, be remembered there.

'**Remember**' looks like a love poem. But then that might mean that we have already made assumptions about who is speaking to whom which aren't actually in the text. Apart from the fact of a woman's name as author why do we take it that this is a woman speaking? Because, in de Beauvoir's terms, 'He is the Subject, he is the Absolute—she is the Other'.[23] The (supposed) listener/man in this poem is obviously someone out there in the world doing things, he is 'one'; she, the speaker/woman, is clearly 'Other'—she doesn't have an independent existence beyond this relationship. She is anxious that he should remember her (and she goes on about it so much that the implication is that he won't), so that she will exist.

The active/passive opposition set out in this poem further implies a feminine signature. Cixous' 'Sorties' diagram lines up activity, along with sun, culture, day, father, head, logos, with the masculine principle, while the feminine principle lines up with passivity, moon, nature, night, mother, heart, pathos.[24] The ultimate passivity for women, enacted so often in Rossetti's poems, explicit in **'After Death'** and hinted at in **'Remember'**, is death. Not that there's any reason here to explain why this speaker is about to die. The referent is absent, but presumed, because the condition of (assumed) femininity includes the condition of passivity and death. 'The silent land' is pretty vague, and 'the darkness and corruption' not much better, but none the less the idea of this speaker being about to die is quite acceptable in our cultural positioning; women die, men mourn; it's a classic literary trope and one that Rossetti exploits to the full.

So. The nice version of this poem goes: 'Please remember me when I'm dead, but on the other hand, if it's going to make you unhappy to remember me, then I love you so much ("For if the darkness and corruption leave / A vestige of the thoughts that once I had") that I'd rather that you did forget about me so that you can be happy.'

It is true that this reading is in the poem. But it's not the only one. As Angela Leighton has observed, 'Behind Rossetti's "Aesthetic of Renunciation" it is possible to discern an alternative aesthetics of secrecy, self-containment, and caprice'.[25] And the clue to the capricious reading lies in the verbs. The first verb to appear is the odd construction applied to the speaker, '. . . when I am gone away'. That the verb here is 'to be' used in the present tense to convey a future idea, and without any active verb construction—like 'When I have gone away'—applied to the speaker, makes the sentence feel oddly passive. By contrast in the opening octet the listener is given active verbs lining him (it/they/she) up with the masculine principle and making the *listener* the dominant party. 'When you can no more hold me by the hand' . . . so he does the holding; 'I half turn to go yet turning stay' . . . so she makes a move away, but doesn't quite manage that bid for independence; 'when no more day by day / You tell me of our future that you planned' . . . *our* future? that *you* planned? . . . so she didn't have a say in it; 'It will be late to counsel then or pray' . . . OK, is that what he does all the time? Goes on at her giving advice and asking her to do things?

The way these verbs work means that this speaker manages, almost secretly, subtextually, to reveal that the he-listener is the chief actor in their relation. In life she, the speaker, is 'use-value'[26]—he uses her for whatever agenda it is that he has in mind, personal or social, and she has no say in anything. (Except, of course, through the medium of the poem.) He acts and she is acted upon.

Just as he acts and she is acted upon in **'After Death'**. Interestingly, in both poems the same image, the same idea of action, appears. In **'Remember'** the speaker looks towards the day 'When you can no more hold me by the hand'. In **'After Death'** the he-presence in the poem does not 'take my hand in his'. It's a resonant absence—or presence. The father takes the child by the hand; the lover takes the beloved by the hand; patriarchy takes a hand and she is taken, wherever this père-verted discourse is organized.

What about the pretty end then? '. . . if the darkness and corruption leave / A vestige of the thoughts that once I had'. What thoughts are these? Thus far, they all seem to be cross, fed-up thoughts about how he is bullying her and lecturing her. Maybe then *these* are the thoughts which will get left behind, the traces, like fossils left on the face of the earth. And maybe the 'darkness and corruption' here is not death (as in the nice version), but the darkness and corruption of her anger, her distress, at his conventional use of her. No wonder then that he should 'forget and smile' because, maybe, just maybe, what is going on here is not that she wants him to forget so that he can be happy because she loves him so much, but that if he remembers, and *really* remembers the truth, then he will be sad. And the implication is that so he should be, because he's going to realize what a shit he's been all along. 'Better by far' does not sound much like a generous valedictory wish any more; it sounds like a curse, a threat, a bitter promise which is perverse and 'sweet' and cruel in the mouth of the vengeful speaker.

Once upon a time, Christina Rossetti was simple.

But Christina loved games, puns, parodies and secrets, and while William Michael and so many later readers have mooned over the 'broken-hearted'-ness of her poetry, Rossetti has played a joke.[27] Self-effacing, hidden, secret, behind, underneath, are words that are often associated with Rossetti, yet what goes on in that underneath still needs excavation. The curiously throw-away reference to an evolutionary context that appears in **'Remember'** may provide a model. 'Darkness and corruption' may, after all, be the troubled present, the nineteenth century itself, the period of Rossetti's own lived life, fraught with personal and social prohibitions which make indirect speaking necessary. But still in that place a trace may be left of the individual life, of the moment of becoming 'I', a vestige of (self) creation.[28] Others coming after, re-membering Rossetti, will be able to read the trace of the hidden life beneath the cover story.

Not that the one excludes the other. **'After Death'** and **'Remember'** both have (at least) two readings. In each case a subversive text is inscribed within a complaisant poem, but they are simultaneously compatible. The double frame of reference in both poems makes them work like the many paradox pictures of Victorian popular entertainment. One example, published in Germany in the 1880s, is called 'My Wife and My Mother-in-law'. Look at it one way and it's a beautiful young woman, looked at another and it's an ugly old hag. But they are both there and they are both true and there is no rivalry between them.

In 1856 Christina Rossetti wrote a story about a picture called 'The Lost Titian'. It tells the story of Gianni, a colleague and rival of Titian in Renaissance Venice. Gianni is a successful and popular painter, but his life and his methods are suspect, and his position is threatened by Titian's preeminence, soon to be confirmed by the unveiling of his latest masterpiece. One night, in an apparently friendly game of dice, Titian, drunk with wine and success, stakes his newly created work— and Gianni wins. Jealous of the Master's fame, Gianni daubs over the picture with coarse pigments, and then, on the blank surface, he paints 'a dragon flaming, clawed, preposterous'. Falling from favour and beset by debt, Gianni's creditors move in, but even Titian himself does not recognize his own painting. To Gianni's horror, the dragon is none the less claimed by another creditor who takes a fancy to its gaudy show and sets it up as an inn sign. Gianni spends the rest of his life trying to paint a new dragon which will be received in satisfactory exchange, but to no avail. So when Gianni dies, still silent, Titian's masterpiece remains hidden, lost forever. Or perhaps not quite lost.

> Reader, should you chance to discern over wayside inn or metropolitan hotel a dragon pendent, or should you find such an effigy amid the lumber of a broker's shop, whether it be red, green or piebald, demand it importunately, pay for it liberally, and in the privacy of home scrub it. It *may* be that from behind the dragon will emerge a fair one, fairer than Andromeda, and that to you will appertain the honour of yet further exalting Titian's greatness in the eyes of a world.[29]

The double texts of Rossetti's poems are the other way round of course. Underneath the 'fair one' with her smooth surface is a 'preposterous' dragon who none the less is an Andromeda waiting to be unchained. And when that cruel-perverse-Rossetti-dragon is revealed, it will contribute to Rossetti's greatness: 'Reader . . . in the privacy of home scrub it . . .'.

In the privacy of 'home' the 'unheimlich' will be uncovered.[30] 'Uncanny' is a word often associated with Rossetti's poetry and it's a right word. As a good Victorian daughter and sister Rossetti is always at home—'almost constantly in the same house'. And yet her poetry is 'unheimlich' because it speaks, and it says more than it means. Rossetti wrote in secret and she wrote secrets. Not necessarily her own, but everybody's secrets. Her poetry is our talking-cure. Her protagonists speak, confess, tell.[31] In their nightmares and their dreams they compulsively repeat the traumas of desire and loss. Her dead women are the corpses who have fallen (cadaver/cadere) and lost themselves in decay, but they paradoxically project (abject/throw out/ throw up) a hidden self, a vital self, in the process. Squeezed in between, or out between, the spaces in the text is the secret message, written 'in white ink' which seeps and oozes through the page.[32] In Kristeva's terms the semiotic speaks through, or beyond, or out of, the symbolic. The symbolic in Rossetti is always that 'excessively neat' surface held together by the decorum of the 'single guarantee: syntax'. But 'underlying the written', and quite as meaningful, even more powerful, is the silent speaking space, 'enigmatic and feminine . . . rhythmic, unfettered, irreducible to its intelligible verbal translation . . . musical, anterior to judgement'.[33]

But you have to listen hard. At the centre of both **'After Death'** and **'Remember'** there is a silence. In **'After Death'** there 'Came a deep silence' just before the speaker lets out the second bitter text. In **'Remember'** the speaker projects herself into a time when she will be gone away 'into the silent land' and her second bitter text might be remembered. But it has, mostly, been forgotten, or rather, not heard. In the double texts of Rossetti's poems her 'two lips' may speak together but they may also mumble into silence.[34]

Yet I suspect Rossetti herself knew this well enough. Her 'conciseness' could lead to 'obscurity', and that state of obscurity, of being hidden from view, of being overlooked, probably appeared to her an inevitable condition of her status as a Victorian woman who was also a poet.[35] In her prose story **'Speaking Likenesses'** (1874) Rossetti tells a tale about feminine acquiescence and propriety. Flora dreams about a tea-party where a game called 'Self-Help' is invented to be played by a group of grotesque children where 'The boys were players, and the girls were played (if I may be allowed such a phrase)'.[36] The bodies of the boys here are spiky—'One boy bristled with prickly quills like a porcupine'—or they are sharply angled, or covered in fish-hooks. The girls, on the other hand, are gelatinous, oozing, slidey, fluid, and liable to be rubbed away: 'One girl exuded a sticky liquid and came off on the fingers; another, rather smaller, was slimy and slipped through the hands.'[37]

Rossetti's girls, slimy and liable to slide away, prefigure Irigaray's account of the 'mucosity' and flow in a 'feminine syntax'.[38] They also anticipate Kristeva's account of the irony in the critic's slippery task of fixing meaning. 'It is', she writes, speaking of Freud's economy of laughter in *Jokes and Their Relation to the Unconscious,* 'a discharge with two meanings between sense and nonsense'.[39]

Rossetti's work, then, may be distinctively feminine after all. Like the girls in her story, her poetry slips through the fingers. And this is Rossetti's joke. That she will always slip away, dissolve, evaporate, disappear, and the poor critic will be left juggling the remnants of surface and subtext, attempting to 'coagulate an island of meaning upon a sea of negativity'.[40] If the semiotic is 'the nonsense woven indistinguishably into sense'[41] then Rossetti's nonsense story makes sense and the surface-sense of her best-loved poems may be nonsense. For they secrete a secret which 'might easily be overlooked' but which will 'not easily be forgotten'.

Notes

1. Christina Rossetti, *Maude: Prose and Verse,* ed Rebecca Crump (Hamden, CT: Archon Books, 1976), p. 30.

2. Julia Kristeva, 'Revolution in poetic language', trans. Margaret Waller, in *The Kristeva Reader,* ed. Toril Moi (Oxford: Blackwell, 1986), p. 97. Kristeva is paraphrasing Mallarmé's description of the semiotic rhythm in language as she finds it in his 'La Mystérè dans les lettres'.

3. William Michael Rossetti, Preface to *New Poems of Christina Rossetti Hitherto Unpublished or Uncollected,* ed. W. M. Rossetti (London: Macmillan, 1900), pp. xii-xiii.

4. See J. E. Austen-Leigh, 'A Memoir of Jane Austen', in *Persuasion,* ed. D. W. Harding (Harmondsworth, Middlesex: Penguin, 1965), pp. 339-40. For Elizabeth Barrett Browning see Alexandra Sutherland Orr, *Life and Letters of Robert Browning* (London: Macmillan, 1908), p. 202, and Robert Browning to Leigh Hunt, 6 October 1857, *The Correspondence of Leigh Hunt,* ed. Thornton Hunt (London, 1862), Vol. 2, p. 266. For Rossetti's Maude see *Maude: Prose and Verse,* p. 29.

5. William Michael Rossetti, 'Memoir' of Christina Rossetti, in *The Poetical Works* (London: Macmillan, 1904), p. lx.

6. William Michael Rossetti, Preface to *New Poems of Christina Rossetti,* p. ix and his Prefatory Note to Maude (1896) in *Maude: Prose and Verse,* p. 79.

7. *The Poetical Works of Christina Georgina Rossetti,* with Memoir and Notes by William Michael Rossetti (London: Macmillan, 1904), pp. xliii-xliv. The most amusing example of William Michael's wilful rehabilitation here is his listing of 'Goblin Market' under the heading 'Love of Animals'.

8. '. . . death of a beautiful woman is, unquestionably, the most poetical topic in the world'; Edgar Allen Poe, 'The philosophy of composition' in *Essays and Reviews* (New York: Literary Classics of the United States, 1984), p. 19. For a comprehensive study of this theme in the nineteenth century see Elisabeth Bronfen, *Over Her Dead Body: Death Femininity and the Aesthetic* (Manchester: Manchester University Press, 1992). Bronfen includes a chapter on Dante Gabriel Rossetti and his reification of the dead Lizzie Siddall.

9. Stuart Curran, 'The lyric voice of Christina Rossetti', *Victorian Poetry* 9 (1971), pp. 287-99.

10. Isobel Armstrong, 'Christina Rossetti: diary of a feminist reading', in *Women Reading Women's Writing* ed. Sue Roe (Brighton: Harvester, 1987), pp. 117-37; Steven Connor, 'Speaking likenesses': language and repetition in Christina Rossetti's Goblin Market', *Victorian Poetry* 22 (1984), pp. 439-48; Angela Leighton, *Victorian Women Poets: Writing Against the Heart* (Hemel Hempstead: Harvester, 1992), pp. 129-63. See also Isobel Armstrong, *Victorian Poetry: Poetry, Poetics and Politics* (London: Routledge, 1993), pp. 344-67.

11. Isobel Armstrong, *Victorian Poetry: Poetry, Poetics and Politics,* p. 324. Armstrong's analysis of the 'deeply sceptical' form of the Victorian double poem is important to my readings here. I also acknowledge Jerome McGann's influential essay on the techniques in Rossetti's poetry which 'test and trouble the reader by manipulating sets of ambiguous symbols and linguistic structures'. Jerome McGann, 'Christina Rossetti's poems: a new edition and revaluation', *Victorian Studies* 23 (1980), pp. 237-54, and Angela Leighton's chapter on Rossetti in *Victorian Women Poets: Writing Against the Heart* (Hemel Hempstead: Harvester, 1992), pp. 118-63. Other works that deal with the idea of doubleness in Rossetti's work include Winston Weathers, 'Christina Rossetti: the sisterhood of self', *Victorian Poetry* 3 (1965), pp. 81-9; Theo Dombrowski, 'Dualism in the poetry of Christina Rossetti', *Victorian Poetry* 14 (1976), pp. 70-6; Helena Michie, '"There is no friend like a sister": sisterhood as sexual difference', *English Literary History* 52:2 (summer 1989), pp. 401-21; Mary Arseneau, 'Incarnation and repetition: Christina Rossetti, the Oxford Movement and Goblin Market', *Victorian Poetry* 31 (1993), pp. 79-93.

12. The two poems are treated briefly in Dolores Rosenblum's *Christina Rossetti: The Poetry of Endurance* (Carbondale and Edwardsville: Southern Illinois University Press, 1986), pp. 129 and 209-10. More recently Catherine Maxwell has dealt with one in 'The

poetic context of Christina Rossetti's "After Death"', *English Studies* 76:2 (1995), pp. 148-55. While I would agree with and extend some of her propositions, especially in relation to its placing within the context of works by Tennyson and Browning, her reading comes only tentatively at the dark, wilful perversity which is at the centre of the poem and which, in my opinion, explains its peculiar power to attract, and more insidiously, to repel.

13. *The Complete Poems of Christina Rossetti,* ed. Rebecca Crump (Baton Rouge and London: Louisiana State University Press, 1979-1900), Vol. 1, pp. 37-8.

14. The idea of the fallen woman, especially the raped woman as 'dead before death' has its most powerful example in Samuel Richardson's *Clarissa* (1747-49), but it was an image that continued well into the nineteenth century and which is to be found, for instance, in Elizabeth Gaskell's *Ruth* (1853) who actually attempts suicide, and in Elizabeth Barrett Browning's *Aurora Leigh* (1856 (1857)), where Marian Erle repeatedly describes her rape as a 'death' or 'murder' (VI, 769-71, VI, 812-19) and says that she cannot now return to respectable life and marriage because she is unable to 'get up from my grave, / And wear my chin-cloth for a wedding-veil' (IX, 387-97). See Elizabeth Barrett Browning, *Aurora Leigh,* ed. Margaret Reynolds (New York: Norton, 1996), pp. 203, 204 and 297.

15. Catherine Maxwell, 'The poetic context of Christina Rossetti's "After Death"', *English Studies* 76:2 (1995), pp. 145-50.

16. Maxwell, ibid., pp. 145-6.

17. Jacques Lacan, *Ecrits: A Selection,* trans. Alan Sheridan (London: Tavistock, 1977), p. 67.

18. *Psychoanalytic Literary Criticism,* ed. Maud Ellmann (London and New York: Longman, 1994), p. 16, quoting Jacques Lacan, 'The function and field of speech and language in psychoanalysis', in *Ecrits: A Selection,* trans. Alan Sheridan (London: Tavistock, 1977), p. 66. I suppose I must (resignedly) make it clear here that just as Lacan's 'nom-du-père' or the symbolic father is clearly differentiated from any idea of the real father, so the 'father' that I find in this poem is related only to the symbolic function and, perhaps tangentially, to Victorian patriarchy, but it is not necessarily related to any real father including Christina's own. I should also add that as so often in unsanctioned liaisons between family members the bond of silence that grows up might also conceal a compliance or desire on both sides. The speaker's recognition of a desire that is taboo might also place this poem at the moment of entry into the symbolic where such feelings, previously inchoate, are named and categorized for the first time.

19. Julia Kristeva, *Powers of Horror: An Essay on Abjection,* trans. Leon S. Roudiez (New York: Columbia University Press, 1982) pp. 2-3.

20. Maxwell, op. cit. (1995), p. 154.

21. Isobel Armstrong, *Victorian Poetry: Poetry, Poetics and Politics* (London: Routledge, 1993), p. 359.

22. *The Complete Poems of Christina Rossetti,* Vol. I, p. 37.

23. Simone de Beauvoir, Introduction to *The Second Sex* (1949), trans. H. M. Parshley in *New French Feminisms,* ed. Elaine Marks and Isabelle de Courtivron (Brighton: Harvester, 1981), p. 44.

24. Hélène Cixous, 'Sorties' from *The Newly Born Woman* (1975), trans. Ann Liddle in *New French Feminisms,* p. 90.

25. Angela Leighton, '"When I am dead, my dearest": the secret of Christina Rossetti', *Modern Philology* 87 (1990), p. 376. Quoting Sandra Gilbert and Susan Gubar *The Madwoman in the Attic: The Woman Writer and the Nineteenth Century Literary Imagination* (New Haven, CT and London: Yale University Press, 1979), pp. 549-54.

26. Luce Irigaray, *This Sex which is Not One* (1977), trans. Claudia Reeder in *New French Feminisms,* p. 105.

27. 'Touching these same verses, it was the amazement of every one what could make her poetry so broken-hearted as was mostly the case . . .', Christina Rossetti, *Maude: Prose and Verse,* p. 31.

Angela Leighton makes the point that Christina Rossetti's secret was that there was no secret, and that 'At the heart of this unremittingly lovelorn poetry, there is a freakish freedom of purpose and meaning. Over and over again, Rossetti makes a joke of the predictably tragic monotony of love'; Leighton, '"When I am dead my dearest: the secret of Christina Rossetti', *Modern Philology* 87 (1990), p. 379.

28. I suspect that Rossetti's use of 'vestige' in 'Remember' owes something to the title of Robert Chambers' *Vestiges of the Natural History of Creation* which was published in 1844. *Vestiges* included an interesting passage about the loss of the individual life (as opposed to the race) which may be recalled by Rossetti's close juxtaposition of and punning on the word 'once': '. . . if the darkness and corruption leave / A vestige of the thoughts that once I had.' Like Tennyson, Rossetti made contemporary evolutionary theory into a subject for poetry. 'It is clear, moreover, from the whole scope of the natural laws, that the individual, as far as the present sphere of being is concerned, is to the Author of Nature a consideration of inferior moment. Everywhere we see the arrangements for the species perfect; the individual is left as it were, to take his chance amidst the mêlée of the various laws affecting him.' See Chambers, *Vestiges* (1844), p. 377, quoted in *The Poems of Tennyson,* ed. Christopher Ricks (London: Longman, 1969), p. 910.

29. Christina Rossetti, 'The Lost Titian', in *Commonplace and Other Short Stories* (London, 1870), p. 161. Angela Leighton makes a similar point: 'this image of the double painting, the secret masterpiece below and the vivid decoy above, also expresses something of Rossetti's own art; its moral nonsense, whether goblins, crocodiles or dragons, its obliqueness and disguises and, above all, its secret meanings which have been forever concealed, forever lost'; Angela Leighton, *Victorian Women Poets: Writing Against the Heart* (Hemel Hempstead: Harvester, 1992), p. 158.

30. Freud's explanation of how the word 'unheimlich', or uncanny, derives from the word 'heimlich', homely or familiar, is in his 1919 essay on Hoffman's 'The Sandman'; 'The "Uncanny"', The Standard Edition of *The Complete Psychological Works of Sigmund Freud,* trans. James Strachey (London: Hogarth, 1953-74), Vol. XVII, pp. 217-56.

31. From *Studies in Hysteria* (1893-95) on, Freud construes the process of psychoanalysis as one which begins with a therapeutic confession—hence Anna O.'s

designation of his 'talking cure'. That the analysand has to talk, to shape stories about the self, to confess, makes psychoanalytic literary criticism a peculiarly appropriate tool for reading Rossetti's intimate and telling poems. That readers are so willing to act as analyst is partly connected to what Foucault describes as a 'metamorphosis in literature' which takes place in the nineteenth century and where literary texts are no longer seen as fictions, but as a 'confession' extracted 'from the very depths of oneself, in between the words'. See Michel Foucault, *The History of Sexuality, Volume I: An Introduction* (Harmondsworth: Penguin, 1984), p. 59.

32. Hélène Cixous, 'The Laugh of the Medusa', trans. Keith Cohen and Paula Cohen, in *New French Feminisms*, p. 251. Luce Irigaray, *This Sex Which is Not One*, trans. Catherine Porter and Carolyn Burke (Ithaca and London: Cornell University Press, 1985), p. 134.

33. Julia Kristeva, 'Revolution in poetic language', trans. Margaret Waller, in *The Kristeva Reader*, ed. Toril Moi (Oxford: Blackwell, 1986), p. 97.

34. Luce Irigaray, 'Sexual difference', in *The Irigaray Reader*, ed. Margaret Whitford (Oxford: Blackwell, 1991), p. 175.

35. 'Perhaps the nearest approach to a method I can lay claim to was a distinct aim at conciseness; after a while I received a hint from my sister that my love of conciseness tended to make my writing obscure, and I then endeavoured to avoid obscurity as well as diffuseness.' Christina Rossetti to an anonymous admirer, 1888, in the Troxall Collection at Princeton University Library; quoted in Antony H. Harrison, *Christina Rossetti in Context* (Brighton: Harvester, 1988), p. 10.

36. Christina Rossetti, *Speaking Likenesses* (London: Macmillan, 1874), p. 36.

37. Ibid., p. 28. The sexualized character of the boys' and girls' physical characteristics have been noticed by Roderick McGillis: 'these two games . . . reveal a deep fear of sexual violence and a disturbing disrespect for humanity'; in 'Simple surfaces: Christina Rossetti's work for children', in *The Achievement of Christina Rossetti*, ed. David A. Kent (Ithaca and London: Cornell University Press, 1987), p. 227, and by Julia Briggs, 'The symbolism of the boys with their projecting quills or hooks and the sticky, slippery women [thus] is disturbingly sexual', in 'Women writers and writing for children: from Sarah Fielding to E. Nesbit' in *Children and Their Books*, ed. Gillian Avery and Julia Briggs (Oxford: Clarendon Press, 1989), p. 17.

38. Luce Irigaray, *This Sex Which is Not One*, p. 134.

39. Julia Kristeva, 'How does one speak to literature?', in *Desire in Language: A Semiotic Approach to Literature and Art*, ed. Leon S. Roudiez, trans. Thomas Gora, Alice Jardine and Leon S. Roudiez (Oxford: Blackwell, 1981), p. 109.

40. Ibid.

41. Maud Ellmann, *Psychoanalytic Literary Criticism* (London: Longman, 1994), p. 25.

TITLE COMMENTARY

"Goblin Market"

SYLVIA BAILEY SHURBUTT (ESSAY DATE FALL 1992)

SOURCE: Shurbutt, Sylvia Bailey. "Revisionist Mythmaking in Christina Rossetti's 'Goblin Market': Eve's Apple and Other Questions Revised and Reconsidered." *The Victorian Newsletter* 82 (fall 1992): 40-44.

In the following essay, Shurbutt argues that in "Goblin Market" Rossetti revises traditional Christian myths to produce feminist readings of the Fall and the Redemption.

The notion of a woman writer attempting to offer an alternative version to the patriarchal explanation of being is not new: from Amelia Lanier to Virginia Woolf, women writers have attempted to amend traditional Western myth with its misogynist overtones, especially biblical myth so much a part of our Western ethical system. Sometimes blatantly overt (as in Lanier's apology for Eve, Nightingale's declaration of a female Christ or Elizabeth Cady Stanton's dream of a revisionist Woman's Bible), sometimes subtly muted (as in Shelley's retelling of paradise lost in her famous Gothic novel), women writers have sought to revise or reconstruct the patriarchal myths that influence our ethical values and limit the vision of individual possibilities.

Alicia Ostriker evaluates the terrain of myth and the process of revisionist mythmaking in this way: "At first thought," she says, "mythology seems an inhospitable terrain for a woman writer." Juxtaposed to the conquering gods and hardy heroes, "we find the sexually wicked Venus, Circe, Pandora, Helen, Medea, Eve, and virtuously passive Iphigenia, Alcestis, Mary, Cinderella. It is thanks to myth we believe that woman must be either 'angel' or 'monster'" (316). However, emendation of this highly polarized and often negative mythic portrayal of woman has long been an intriguing possibility for women writers. "Whenever a poet employs a figure or story previously accepted and defined by culture, the poet is using myth, and the potential is always present that the use will be revisionist: that is, the figure or tale will be appropriated for altered ends, the old vessel filled with new wine, initially satisfying the thirst of the individual poet but ultimately making cultural change possible" (317). In the case of revisionist mythmaking, Ostriker continues, ". . . old stories are changed, changed utterly, by female experience, so that they can no longer stand as foundations of collective male fantasy. Instead . . . they are corrections; they are representations of what women find divine and demonic in themselves; they are retrieved images of what women have collectively and historically suffered; in some cases they are instructions for survival" (316).

An example of the more subtle revisionist process can be seen in the lines of one of Victorian literature's most discussed and intriguing poetic tales, Christina Rossetti's **"Goblin Market."** While the poem has generated a variety of critical interpretation—from the traditional explanation of the divided self struggling against an over-wrought libido to Rossetti's positing of a "covert (if ambivalently) lesbian world" (Gilbert and Gubar 567) to the poem as paradigm for a nineteenth-century version of anorexia nervosa (Cohen) and finally to the quasi-Freudian interpretation of the story as "conflict between oral sadism and the reality-testing anal stage" (Charles 149)—what Freudians and feminists alike tend to forget, however, are the deeply religious implications of the poem. Indeed, as Dolores Rosenblum writes in a 1982 article in *Victorian Poetry*: "In a sense . . . all Rossetti's poetry is deeply religious, concerned always with the relation of this world to the next" (33). It is this aspect of **"Goblin Market"** that I wish to focus upon, but not in the traditional or orthodox sense, rather as Rossetti's conscious attempt to revise traditional Christian myth in order to produce an alternative, "feminist" reading to the two most fundamental stories in Christian lore—the fall of humankind from grace and our redemption through the blood of Christ. It is pointedly significant that this devoutly religious poet has her *female* Christ figure say in the re-demptive climax of the poem: "Eat me, drink me, love me" (l. 471).

That Rossetti, whom biographers have por-trayed as a model of pious devotion, indeed, whose posthumous poems were altered by brother William Michael "to make them more saintly still" (Auerbach 113), should attempt consciously or unconsciously anything so rebellious in nature as revisionist mythmaking might seem incongruous; however, even her "saintliness" has been estab-lished as slightly unorthodox. As Catherine Musello Cantalupo has stated in her evaluation of Rossetti as a devotional poet, she was "no strict typologist" (275). And Ellen Moers, who calls Ros-setti one of "the greatest religious poets of the nineteenth century," comments specifically on the unique *unorthodoxy* of **"Goblin Market"** (103).

In a work so filled with religious imagery and overtones, something is slightly out of kilter in its pious presentation of one sister's effort to save the other from slipping into concupiscent sin. At the moment when the devout sister Lizzie offers herself as a sacrifice for the other, says Moers, "it is the most eloquent, most erotic moment in the poem" (103). But this combination of eroticism and Christian imagery, itself not extraordinary if viewed in a Pre-Raphaelite context, is not the only puzzling aspect about the poem: there appears within the work a conscious effort to turn biblical and Miltonic myth, with its misogynistic intent, into heroic affirmation of the female, Christ-like principle of loving self-sacrifice and creative self-assertion through rebirth or resurrection.

As early as 1956, in an article entitled "The Feminine Christ," Marian Shalkhauser discussed **"Goblin Market"** as a "Christian fairy tale in which a feminine cast of characters is substituted for the masculine cast of the Biblical sin-redemption sequence" (19). Shalkhauser associ-ated Rossetti's two sisters, Laura and Lizzie, with Adam/Christ figures in a sacrificial drama in which "a feminine Christ redeems a feminine mankind from a masculine Satan" (20). In 1979, Gilbert and Gubar noted Rossetti's use and exploitation of Mil-tonic imagery, but they viewed such exploitation merely in terms of a "lesson in renunciation" (573), an affirmation of the patriarchal ideal of "angel in the house"; they were perhaps short-sighted in failing to see the ultimate power and expression of active autonomy communicated in Rossetti's revisionist myth-making.

One must free oneself from the traditional, patriarchal interpretation of self-sacrifice as ulti-mate expression of feminine submission, in order to understand the implications of the sisters' uniquely *empowering* act of renunciation. Despite Rossetti's seeming acceptance of "woman's place" as defined by a nineteenth-century patriarchy, she appears to have rejected the idea that female self-sacrifice was necessarily indicative of weak-minded submission. Indeed, Diane D'Amico has written of Rossetti's attempt to elevate the female principle and self-sacrifice to deific proportions, with Mary, Eve and Mary Magdalene serving in her writing as "a sort of feminine triptych" (175). D'Amico goes on to explain that Rossetti believed that woman had suffered "difficulty and pain" in her relation-ship with man as defined by the Judeo-Christian mythic scheme: "Even in the case of Adam and Eve, Rossetti did not overlook the verse in Genesis (13:12) in which Adam seems quite willing to let

Eve take all the blame: 'The meanness as well as the heinousness of sin [says Rossetti in **Letter and Spirit** (84)] is illustrated in Adam's apparent effort to shelter himself at the expense of Eve'" (180-81). However, if "Genesis told her of Eve's weakness and shame," continues D'Amico commenting on Rossetti's devotional prose piece **The Face of the Deep,** "Revelation told her of woman's ultimate strength and glory" (191).

The biblical and Miltonic overtones in Rossetti's poem are obvious as the story of the Eve-like Laura's fall is unfolded. Captivated by the seductive call of the satanic goblin men, who appropriately slink, crawl, and slither their way into her consciousness (ll. 70-76), Laura/Eve succumbs to their serpentine enticement and yearns to partake of their luscious and lascivious fruit. Like Milton's serpent before being cursed by god to slither forever legless, the goblin men are "whist-tailed" creatures, full of "airs and graces," whose honeyed words seduce the feckless Laura/Eve. The fruit with which they accomplish their seduction, like Milton's biblical fruit is rife with sexual and creative implication as well as with the power which forbidden knowledge affords. The vivid words Rossetti employs to describe the fruit and, most important, uses in Laura's own description of her voluptuous feast are rich with Pre-Raphaelite color, the details as brilliant as a Burne-Jones painting:

> What melons icy-cold
> Piled on a dish of gold
> Too huge for me to hold,
> What peaches with a velvet nap,
> Pellucid grapes without one seed;
> Odorous indeed must be the meed
> Whereon they grow. . . .
>
> (ll. 175-81)

The goblin men are purveyors not only of sexual liberation and bacchanal pleasures but of creative liberation as well; they hold the keys to the masculine world of creative activity and knowledge. Laura purchases their fruit with her golden lock, an obvious sexual gesture, and in clipping her lock, she trades her chastity for access to the male world of artistic and sexual freedom:

> Stronger than man-rejoicing wine,
> Clearer than water flowed that juice:
> She never tasted such before,
> How should it cloy with length of use?
> She sucked and sucked and sucked the more
> Fruits which that unknown orchard bore,
> She sucked until her lips were sore.
>
> (ll. 130-36)

Rossetti's lines pulsate not only with sexual implication but with the suggestion that Laura's hunger, that her oral craving, goes beyond mere sexual fulfillment; the hunger here is also for knowledge and creative expression, for poetic articulation as well as for carnality. Laura is utterly lost in her sensual abandonment, in the awakening she experiences, and as her words vividly record, she is well able to articulate what she has experienced. Having tasted the forbidden fruit, she becomes God-like in her knowledge and in her ability to create, and, like the artist, she brilliantly portrays for sister Lizzie a portrait of her pleasure feast (ll. 164-83).

However, just as Milton's God feared Adam and Eve's gaining knowledge after tasting the fruit of paradise and cast them out of Eden, the goblin men reject Laura in her new-found knowledge. She too is cast aside and no longer privy to their call to come and feast. She is now a threat—a woman with creative and sexual knowledge, a rival; and like the doomed Jeanie, another willful lass seduced, she is condemned to pine and languish, never again invited to taste of the goblin men's fruit. Unfortunately, having tasted of masculine freedom and knowledge, Laura will forever be dissatisfied with the mundane world of womanly cares and duties; her common-day sphere of kneading dough, churning butter, and whipping cream holds little fascination now; she is as weary-worn and care-ridden as that primal pair banished from paradise and fallen upon a world of tears and pain (ll. 293-98), a world dulled by the postlapsarian shadow.

In her recently published study of Rossetti's poetry, *Christine Rossetti and the Poetry of Discovery,* Katherine Mayberry has recognized the creative self-assertion prominent in Rossetti's portrayal of the fallen sister Laura: "Permeating the verse is a sense of the poet's breathless inebriation with the process of writing. The proliferation of words, rhythms, metaphors, and similes suggests an artist reveling in her creativity, whose love of her craft, like Laura's love of the fruit, is insatiable" (90). Laura's discovery of knowledge and creative self-expression is the narrator's discovery:

> The narrator's apparent enchantment or intoxication with the tools of her art allies her with the wayward Laura, who experiences a comparable inebriation with the goblins' beautiful, abundant fruit. In Laura, Rossetti has produced a natural poet-figure—a character possessing all the impulses and instincts necessary, though not always sufficient, for the creation of art [i. e. her Eve-like curiosity, her instinctive attempt to give literary form to her experiences, and her richly "poetic language"].
>
> (92)

Rossetti's version of "paradise regained," the second half of the poem, is unique in that she presents a female Christ figure who offers much more than merely an aesthetic of renunciation and self-sacrifice, the traditional feminist interpretation of the second half of the poem (Gilbert and Gubar 572). The sacrificial action of Lizzie can more appropriately be viewed as a positive act of defiance and, on Rossetti's part, as revisionist mythmaking.

Taking a silver penny with which to purchase the forbidden fruit for Laura, Lizzie/Christ seeks the goblin men herself. The imagery Rossetti associates with Lizzie at this point is the same traditionally associated with Jesus Christ; it is also imagery which fills the Pre-Raphaelite canvas—the lily (Dante Rossetti's "Ecce Ancilla Domini," Collins's "Convent Thoughts," Hughes's "The Annunciation"), the beacon (Hunt's "The Light of the World), the besieged city (ll. 409-21). Fearlessly, Lizzie faces the taunting goblin men, devilish in their wicked supplication:

Full of airs and graces,
Pulling wry faces,
Demure grimaces,
Cat-like and rat-like,

. . . . .

[They] squeezed and caressed her:
Stretched up their dishes.

(ll. 337-40, 349-50)

The protean forms the goblin men assume are those traditionally associated with Satan: cats, rats, wombats, magpies. As Lizzie confronts this raffish crew, she remains steady, unyielding to their persecution; and in conquering temptation and the flesh, she purchases redemption for her sister, as Christ in his passion bought redemption for fallen humankind. The mythical Christian imagery in the poem at this point is unmistakable:

White and golden Lizzie stood,
Like a lily in a flood,—
Like a rock of blue-veined stone . . .
Like a beacon left alone . . .
Like a royal virgin town
Topped with gilded dome and spire
Close beleaguered by a fleet
Mad to tug her standard down.

(ll. 408-10, 412, 418—21)

Lizzie's is no mean or cowardly act of submission, but one of defiance and action; it is a decisive act of will, and in the face of her strength the goblin men slink and slime their way back into the dark recesses of the earth, back into the primal depths of their origin (ll. 437-46). And Lizzie, having bargained for the "fiery antidote" (l. 559) to

her sister's malaise, returns to Laura and, bruised and dripping with the sticky goblin pulp, charges her sister to embrace her, indeed to "Eat me, drink me, love me" (l. 471). With heroic self-sacrifice, she has purchased salvation for her sister, and the redemption she offers pulsates with eucharistic imagery.

Overcome with the magnitude of her sister's sacrifice—"Lizzie, Lizzie, have you tasted / For my sake the fruit forbidden?" (ll. 477-78)—Laura embraces her sister and accepts the offer of redemption. In so doing, she exorcises her demon spirits, and the act of a woman's tasting the forbidden fruit assumes heroic rather than sinful dimensions:

Swift fire spread through her veins, knocked at
her
   heart,
Met the fire smoldering there
And overbore its lesser flame.

(ll. 506-08)

At length, Laura swoons, and in symbolic death finds rebirth and salvation: "Life out of death . . . Laura awoke as from a dream" (ll. 524, 537).

The sisters go on to become mothers, teachers and story tellers, celebrating the heroic actions of Lizzie and the principle of sisterhood (ll. 543-67). At the end of the poem, the world they inhabit is one curiously absent of men, yet it is a creative world, a world of wisdom and knowledge that the sisters pass on to their children. In her remaking of Miltonic and biblical myth, Rossetti appears to legitimize the creative spirit of the nineteenth-century female, god-like in her ability to create life though seldom sanctioned the freedom to create art.

The sisterhood that Rossetti's poem celebrates is one not only reminiscent of the "Amazon" legends of Greek myth but also similar to those science fiction fantasies of the twentieth century, where female heroes bigger than life create a sisterhood and inhabit a heroic world without men. Perhaps such a sisterhood would seem especially appealing to someone like Rossetti, an individual both disenfranchised and powerless, and allowed little part in "brotherhood." One rather imagines Rossetti, fascinated and deeply interested in the work of her brother and other Pre-Raphaelites, feeling occasionally the intruder, the outcast, perhaps the work of art (as model) but never the artist (see "In an Artist's Studio"). Jerome Bump has written of the irony of Rossetti's exclusion from the "brotherhood": "The first literary victory of the Pre-Raphaelites was the publication of *Gob-*

lin Market and Other Poems, and it was written by the member they excluded" (323). The extent of Rossetti's pain at such exclusion can only be guessed at; certainly, her poetry reveals a longing for fulfillment of heroic potential, though it might not be in precisely the same mode or fashion as that of her male siblings. In **"The Lowest Room"** she questions:

> Why should not you, why should not I
> Attain heroic Strength?
> . . . . .
>
> Who dooms me I shall only be
> The second, not the first?
>
> (ll. 15-16, 19-20)

Rossetti's interest in the concept of sisterhood has been explored by Dorothy Mermin, who notes the poet's work with fallen women, her wish to be an Anglican nun (a goal her sister Maria achieved in 1873), and her interest in joining Nightingale's core of female nurses bound for the Crimea (115). Mermin also speculates that Rossetti's fascination with the concept of a female Christ, not a totally novel idea in the nineteenth century, is due to the influence exerted on her by Nightingale, who writes in *Cassandra,* "The next Christ will perhaps be a female Christ" (112). Certainly, Rossetti's Lizzie follows precisely the mythic/heroic paradigm of a Christ or a Dante or a Buddha—the only variation in this version of the separation, the journey, and the return with redemptive powers is that Rossetti's hero (her Christ) is cast in female guise.

Far from being an affirmation of the angel in the house, typical interpretation of Rossetti's poem, **"Goblin Market"** is revisionist mythmaking in a variety of ways. Here are certainly angels, but they are by no means passive and sacrificial. Rather, both Lizzie and Laura are strong-willed women who defy the nineteenth-century male version of creative and sexual prerogatives, exclusive to a single sex. When Laura/Eve succumbs to the goblin fruit, she is affirming her sexuality, her creativity, and her right to be an intellectual being; in so doing, she intrudes upon the male domain, becoming a threat and thus deemed worthless and no longer privileged to hear their call or share their fruit. Gilbert and Gubar have characterized the goblin fruit and Laura's fall in this way: "Rossetti's 'pleasure-place' is thus quite clearly a paradise of self gratifying art, a paradise in which the lines of **'Goblin Market'**'s masculine fruit-merchants are anticipated by the seductions of the male muse . . ." (571). Yet, in the final analysis, the implication Gilbert and Gubar clearly find for **"Goblin Market"** is both anti-self and

ABOUT THE AUTHOR

ROSSETTI'S CONTRIBUTIONS TO *THE ENGLISH WOMAN'S JOURNAL*

In the late 1870s religious scruples prevented Rossetti from joining the suffragists, and in the late 1880s she even signed a protest against female suffrage. Although *The English Woman's Journal* had a strong feminist tone for its time, it did not directly address the question of parliamentary votes for women. . . .

Of course it is impossible to know whether or not Rossetti would have contributed to the *Journal* had it supported female suffrage. However, the fact that it avoided the issue makes her appearance in the *Journal* all the more understandable. . . .

Rossetti did not include either "Behold, I stand at the door and knock" or "Gone Before" in any of her collected volumes, indicating perhaps that she did not consider them to be among her best work. Nevertheless, their appearance in *The English Woman's Journal* gives them a special place in her canon. They serve as evidence that in the early 1860s Rossetti was willing to have her name associated with a journal that had "an avowedly political purpose" to employ, educate and organize middle-class women . . .

[C]ertainly she was in sympathy with those who wished to expand a woman's sphere of action beyond the home and into the work place. Indeed, in the 1860s, as an unmarried middle-class woman still financially dependent upon her brother, she must have been very sympathetic to such a cause.

D'Amico, Diane. An Excerpt from "Christina Rossetti and *The English Woman's Journal.*" In *The Journal of Pre-Raphaelite Studies* 3, no. 1 (spring 1994).

anti-artist for the female; "like Laura and Jeanie," they say, "Rossetti must learn to suffer and renounce the self-gratifications of art and sensuality" (571). There is, however, little suffering and less renouncing suggested in the final lines of the poem; indeed, the sisters' lives portend not only paradise regained but that Blakean version of "paradise" achieved through experience and testing. As for the sisters'—and Rossetti's—renouncing art and creativity, such is hardly the case. Indeed, what renunciation there is in the poem is uniquely empowering and in itself revisionist, for the sisters do not renounce sexuality or artistic expression on *their own* terms (after all, the conclusion presents full-blossomed women with children, women who carry on a tradition of story-telling and wisdom teaching, modes of artistic expression traditionally associated with the female world and only in recent years legitimized as "real" art); rather, theirs is renunciation of sexuality and artistic expression as defined by the goblin men, by patriarchal tradition.

Katherine Mayberry has written that for Rossetti creating poetry was "a tremendously powerful act, serving as an alembic through which all that was painful or confusing could be rendered beautiful and intelligible. . . . Through the poetic act, Rossetti could recast the unsatisfactory conditions of her temporal existence into beautiful and permanent experience" (109). One might conclude, as well, that in her choice to create, to be a poet, Rossetti went so far as to revise the "myth," the story of her own life: "Even the conditions of being a poet wrought a reinterpretation of the circumstances of Christina Rossetti's own life, changing her singleness from a misfortune into a professional requirement; as with the heroines of her ballads, Rossetti's spinsterhood was a condition that ultimately fostered autonomy, strength, and creativity" (109).

In some respect, what Rossetti was doing in such poems as **"Goblin Market," "Repining," "The Lowest Room," "Moonshine,"** and **"The Heart Knoweth its Own Bitterness"** was what Carolyn Heilbrun calls "writing a woman's life." Heilbrun stresses the importance in women's lives of literature and myth and how, for the most part, women's "stories" have been written by men and the patriarchal myths and traditions which mold us all: "We can only retell and live by the stories we have read or heard. We live our lives through texts. They may be read, or chanted, or experienced electronically, or come to us, like the murmurings of our mothers, telling us what conventions demand. Whatever their form or medium, these stories have formed us all" (37). At the conclusion of **"Goblin Market,"** Rossetti presents women themselves narrating to their children their story, creating their own myth; and their story follows the pattern of Christ in its loving

self-sacrifice and religious intent, though the roles are recast, revised, with the principal players women.

Dorothy Mermin has written that "religious belief," for Rossetti, "both curbed her ambition and offered escape from the restrictions imposed by her sex" (116). Though one might question whether her religious beliefs did indeed curb Rossetti's ambition, there is little doubt that Victorian women like Christina Rossetti provided themselves with a means of empowerment by their devotion to a religion of renunciation and self-sacrifice. Though a Nietzsche might not have seen the possibility of power through self-sacrifice, a host of nineteenth-century women found active and positive possibilities in following the paradigm provided through Christ's passion—certainly, Rossetti sensed the power of the myth and the appeal of revision of that myth to achieve her own sense of heroic self-fulfillment.

Works Cited

Auerbach, Nina. *Woman and the Demon: The Life of a Victorian Myth*. Cambridge: Harvard UP, 1982.

Bump, Jerome. "Christina Rossetti and the Pre-Raphaelite Brotherhood." *The Achievement of Christina Rossetti*. Ed. David A. Kent. Ithaca: Cornell UP, 1987. 322-45.

Cantalupo, Catherine Musello. "Christina Rossetti: The Devotional Poet and the Rejection of Romantic Nature." *The Achievement of Christina Rossetti*. Ed. David A. Kent. Ithaca: Cornell UP, 1987.

Charles, Edna K. *Christina Rossetti: Critical Perspectives 1862-1982*. London: Associated UPs, 1985.

Cohen, Paula. "Christina Rossetti's 'Goblin Market': A Paradigm for Nineteenth-Century Anorexia Nervosa." *University of Hartford Studies in Literature* 17 (1985): 1-18.

D'Amico, Diane. "Eve, Mary, and Mary Magdalene: Christina Rossetti's Feminine Triptych." *The Achievement of Christina Rossetti*. Ed. David A. Kent. Ithaca: Cornell UP, 1987.

Gilbert, Sandra M. and Susan Gubar. *The Madwoman in the Attic: The Woman Writer and the Nineteenth-Century Literary Imagination*. New Haven: Yale UP, 1979.

Heilbrun, Carolyn G. *Writing a Woman's Life*. New York: Ballantine, 1988.

Mayberry, Katherine J. *Christina Rossetti and the Poetry of Discovery*. Baton Rouge: Louisiana State UP, 1989.

Mermin, Dorothy. "Heroic Sisterhood in Goblin Market." *Victorian Poetry* 21 (Summer 1983): 107-118.

Moers, Ellen. *Literary Women*. New York: Oxford UP, 1977.

Ostriker, Alicia. "The Thieves of Language: Women Poets and Revisionist Mythmaking." *Feminist Criticism: Women, Literature and Theory*. Ed. Elaine Showalter. New York: Pantheon, 1985. 314-38.

Rosenblum, Dolores. "Christina Rossetti's Religious Poetry: Watching, Looking, Keeping Vigil." *Victorian Poetry* 20 (Spring 1982): 33-49.

Shalkhauser, Marian. "The Feminine Christ." *Victorian Newsletter* 10 (Autumn 1956): 19-20.

FURTHER READING

Bibliography

Addison, Jane. "Christina Rossetti Studies, 1974-1991: A Checklist and Synthesis." *Bulletin of Bibliography* 52, no. 1 (March 1995): 73-93.

Biographical sketch and extensive bibliography of writings about Rossetti from 1974 to 1991.

Biographies

Battiscombe, Georgina. *Christina Rossetti: A Divided Life.* New York: Holt, Rinehart and Winston, 1981, 233 p.

Focuses on the conflict between the outward calm of Rossetti's life and her internal emotional turmoil.

Marsh, Jan. *Christina Rossetti: A Literary Biography.* New York: Viking Penguin, 1995, 640 p.

Complete, feminist interpretation of Rossetti's life.

Criticism

Adlard, John. "Christina Rossetti: Strategies of Loneliness." *Contemporary Review* 221, no. 1280 (September 1972): 146-50.

Analysis of "Goblin Market" focusing on the adult themes of the poem.

Armstrong, Isobel. "Christina Rossetti: Diary of Feminist Reading." In *Women Reading Women's Writing*, edited by Sue Roe, pp. 115-37. Brighton, England: Harvester Press, 1987.

Discusses Rossetti's place in the literary canon from a feminist perspective.

Bald, Marjory A. "Christina Rossetti." In *Women Writers of the Nineteenth Century*, pp. 233-66. Cambridge, England: Cambridge University Press, 1923.

Discusses the literary sources of Rossetti's poetry and examines her use of symbol, allegory, myth, and dream.

Bloom, Harold. "Dante Gabriel Rossetti (1828), Christina Rossetti (1830-1894)." In *Genius: A Mosaic of One Hundred Exemplary Creative Minds*, pp. 433-39. New York: Warner Books, 2002.

Comparison of aspects of Rossetti's verse with that of her brother, the poet-painter Dante Gabriel Rossetti.

Bristow, Joseph. "'No Friend Like a Sister'?: Christina Rossetti's Female Kin." *Victorian Poetry* 33, no. 2 (summer 1995): 257-82.

Examines the conflicted nature of sisterhood in Rossetti's work.

Charles, Edna Kotin. *Christina Rossetti: Critical Perspectives,* Selinsgrove, Pa.: Susquehanna University Press, 1985, 187 p.

Reviews and explains the scholarship and criticism of Rossetti's works from 1860 to 1982.

D'Amico, Diane. *Christina Rossetti: Faith, Gender and Time.* Louisiana: Louisiana State University Press, 2000, 200 p.

Examines the role that Rossetti's faith and gender had on her writing.

Flowers, Betty S. "'Had Such a Lady Spoken For Herself': Christina Rossetti's 'Monna Innominata'." In *Rossetti to Sexton: Six Women Poets at Texas*, edited by and introduced by Dave Oliphant, pp. 13-29. Austin: University of Texas at Austin, 1992.

Suggests that Rossetti needed to distinguish her "self" from the fictional versions of women created by Dante, Petrarch, and her brother.

Forman, H. Buxton. "Christina Gabriela Rossetti." In *Our Living Poets: An Essay in Criticism*, pp. 231-53. London, England: Tinsley Brothers, 1871.

Early critical assessment of Rossetti as a significant contributor to "real poetry" and the history of female literature.

Garlitz, Barbara. "Christina Rossetti's *Sing-Song* and Nineteenth-Century Children's Poetry." *PMLA* 70, no. 3 (June 1955): 539-43.

Discusses Sing-Song *in relation to other nineteenth-century children's poetry.*

Gilbert, Pamela K. "'A Horrid Game': Woman as Social Entity in Christina Rossetti's Prose." *English* 41, no. 169 (spring 1992): 1-23.

Provides representative examples of Rossetti's neglected longer prose works, including Maude *and* Speaking Likenesses, *and shows how Rossetti critiqued the treatment of women during her era despite the fact that she did not challenge the social order.*

Gilbert, Sandra M. and Susan Gubar. "The Aesthetics of Renunciation." In *The Madwoman in the Attic: The Woman Writer and the Nineteenth-Century Literary Imagination*, pp. 539-80. New Haven: Yale University Press, 1979.

Examines the work of Rossetti and that of other female poets, including Emily Dickinson and Virginia Woolf, in the context of the argument that women writers have experienced difficulty in sustaining an image of themselves as poets.

Harrison, A. H., guest editor. *Victorian Poetry: Centennial of Christina Rossetti, 1830-1894* 32, no. 3-4 (autumn-winter): 1994.

Special edition of the journal devoted to Rossetti.

Holt, Terence. "'Men sell not such in any town': Exchange in *Goblin Market*." *Victorian Poetry* 28, no. 1 (spring 1990): 51-68.

Examines the language and metaphors about economics in "Goblin Market," arguing that the discourse of the marketplace is designed to stress that the market is not the province of women.

Maxwell, Catherine. "The Poetic Context of Christina Rossetti's 'After Death'." *English Studies* 76, no. 2 (March 1995): 143-55.

Offers a close reading of "After Death" that attempts to identify the work's literary merits and not merely understand it in terms of the author's biography or status as a woman.

Melnyk, Julie. "The Lyrical 'We': Self-Representation in Christina Rossetti's 'Later Life'." *Journal of Pre-Raphaelite Studies* 11 (fall 2002): 43-61.

Analysis of the poem "Later Life" that demonstrates one way that Christianity enabled Rossetti to write poetry within and against the Romantic lyric and to find a more satisfying representation of the self.

Palazzo, Lynda. "Christina Rossetti's 'Goblin Market': The Sensual Imagination." *Unisa English Studies* 26, no. 2 (September 1988): 15-20.

Considers "Goblin Market" to be the work of a poet attempting to solve problems caused by the change from Romantic to Victorian values.

———. *Christina Rossetti's Feminist Theology.* London: Palgrave, 2002, 184p.

Depicts Rossetti's prose as foreshadowing later feminist theories.

Parker, Emma. "A Career of One's Own: Christina Rossetti, Literary Success and Love." *Women's Writing* 5, no. 3 (1998): 305-28.

Argues that the themes of loss and longing in Rossetti's work relate less to love than to her ambitions and anxieties as a writer.

Rosenblum, Dolores. "Christina Rossetti: The Inward Pose." In *Shakespeare's Sisters: Feminist Essays on Women Poets,* edited by Sandra M. Gilbert and Susan Gubar, pp. 82-98. Bloomington: Indiana University Press, 1979.

Explores a "doubleness" of opposing themes in Rossetti's poetry, which the Rosenblum contends resulted from the restrictions of being a woman in Victorian England.

Senior, Claire. "Maiden-Songs: The Role of the Female Child in Christina Rossetti's *Speaking Likenesses*." *Journal of Pre-Raphaelite Studies* 11 (fall 2002): 62-94.

Discusses the suppression of sexuality and energy of girls in Rossetti's work.

Sickbert, Virginia. "Christina Rossetti and Victorian Children's Poetry: A Maternal Challenge to the Patriarchal Family." *Victorian Poetry* 31, no. 4 (winter 1993): 385-410.

Examines Rossetti's construction of parenthood and childhood in her children's poetry.

Smulders, Sharon. "Woman's Enfranchisement in Christina Rossetti's Poetry." *Texas Studies in Literature and Language* 34, no. 4 (winter 1992): 568-88.

Argues that much of Rossetti's poetry from the 1850s and 1860s explores the question of women's place in society and literature.

Wiesenthal, Christine. "Regarding Christina Rossetti's 'Reflection'." *Victorian Poetry* 39, no. 3 (fall 2001): 389-406.

Explores the indeterminacy and doubleness of Rossetti's poem "Reflection," which the critic says is a critique of gender ideology.

Woolf, Virginia. "I Am Christina Rossetti." In *Collected Essays,* pp. 54-60. New York: Harcourt, Brace & World, 1967.

An essay originally written in 1930 to commemorate the 100th anniversary of Rossetti's birth that offers a positive assessment of the poet's work.

OTHER SOURCES FROM GALE:

Additional coverage of Rossetti's life and career is contained in the following sources published by the Gale Group: *Authors and Artists for Young Adults,* Vol. 51; *Beacham's Guide to Literature for Young Adults,* Vol. 4; *British Writers,* Vol. 5; *Dictionary of Literary Biography,* Vols. 35, 163, 240; *DISCovering Authors; DISCovering Authors: British Edition; DISCovering Authors: Canadian Edition; DISCovering Authors Modules: Most-studied Authors* and *Poets; DISCovering Authors, 3.0; Exploring Poetry; Literature and its Times Supplement,* Ed. 1; *Literature Resource Center; Nineteenth-Century Literature Criticism,* Vols. 2, 50, 66; *Poetry Criticism,* Vols. 10, 14; *Reference Guide to English Literature,* Ed. 2; *Something About the Author,* Vol. 20; *Twayne's English Authors; World Literature Criticism;* and *Writers for Children.*

GEORGE SAND

(1804 - 1876)

(Pseudonym of Aurore Dupin) French novelist, essayist, and playwright.

A celebrated writer and controversial personality of nineteenth-century France, Sand wrote prolifically in a variety of genres, producing over eighty novels, three collections of short stories, a twenty-volume autobiography, numerous essays, twenty-five dramas, and approximately twenty thousand letters. She remains best known for her novels, which have been praised for their vivid depictions of the peasantry and the countryside, insightful studies of human nature, and natural prose style. Although she was one of the most popular novelists of her time, relatively few of her works are studied today. Instead, she is primarily remembered for her bold behavior while living in Paris as a young woman: wearing men's clothing, espousing equal rights for women, and engaging in love affairs with prominent artistic figures. Feminist scholars who have examined Sand's work have focused on her representations of female characters, her critique of marriage and the relations between the sexes, her deconstruction of gender stereotypes, her exploration of the female body and transvestism, her ideas about masculinity and femininity, and her controversial brand of feminism.

BIOGRAPHICAL INFORMATION

Sand was born Aurore Dupin on July 1, 1804, to parents of dissimilar backgrounds: her mother was a bird seller's daughter, while her father was an officer in Napoleon's army and purportedly an illegitimate descendant of Frederic-Auguste de Saxe, King of Poland. Her parents married just one month before her birth. Following her father's death when she was four, Sand was entrusted to her paternal grandmother's care and was raised at the family estate of Nohant in Berry. There, she was privately tutored until she reached the age of thirteen, at which time she was sent to the Convent of the English Augustinians in Paris for three years. When she was eighteen, Sand married a local army officer, Casimir Dudevant, and eventually became the mother of two children. Dudevant and Sand soon realized that they were incompatible, and after several restless and unhappy years of marriage, Sand left her husband in 1831 to pursue a literary career in Paris. Following the publication of two novels written in collaboration with her lover Jules Sandeau and signed J. Sand, she began her career in earnest with the novel *Indiana* (1832), writing independently under the name George Sand. For the next several decades, Sand remained a prominent member of the artistic and intellectual community in Paris, due to her considerable literary output as well as her friendships with such figures as Honoré de

Balzac and Gustave Flaubert. She also often captured public interest with her romantic involvements, which included relationships with Alfred de Musset and Frederic Chopin. Sand spent her last years in Nohant, where she died in 1876.

MAJOR WORKS

Sand is best known for her bold statements about the rights of women in nineteenth-century society, her exploration of contemporary social and philosophical issues, and her depiction of the lives and language of French provincials. Several of her important early novels, including *Indiana, Valentine* (1832), *Lélia* (1833), and *Jacques* (1834), reflect her rebellion against the bonds of marriage and deal largely with relationships between men and women. Clearly influenced by Lord Byron and Jean Jacques Rousseau, Sand crafted Romantic narratives depicting passionate personal revolt against societal conventions and an ardent feminism, attitudes that outraged her early British and American critics. These novels were extremely popular with the reading public, however, and they established Sand as an important literary voice for her generation. Sand's abiding interest in politics and philosophy is evident in such novels as *Consuelo* (1842-43) and *Le meunier d'Angibault* (1845; *The Miller of Angibault*). These works, dealing specifically with humanitarianism, Christian socialism, and republicanism, have been described by critics as the least plausible of her literary efforts; the tone is often didactic and the plots contrived. Sand is perhaps most renowned for her pastoral novels. Set in her native Berry, *La mare au diable* (1846; *The Haunted Marsh*) *Françoise le champi* (1848; *Francis the Waif*), and *La petite Fadette* (1849; *Little Fadette*) were inspired by her love of the countryside and her sympathy for the peasants. Realistic in background detail and distinguished by their Romantic idealism, they are considered by many scholars to be Sand's finest novels. The most enduring products of her later years are her autobiography, *Histoire de ma vie* (1845-55; *My Life*) and her voluminous correspondence.

CRITICAL RECEPTION

From the beginning of her career, Sand's unconventional lifestyle interfered with serious critical assessment of her works. In spite of moral prejudice, which dominated early critical analyses of her works, she eventually won acceptance as an artist during her lifetime. Throughout the first half of the twentieth century, many critical studies of Sand's oeuvre attempted to establish links between her life and works, particularly focusing on Sand's romantic relationships. Since the early 1970s, critics have concentrated on the works themselves, noting especially her bold exploration of such issues as sexual freedom and independence for women. Many feminist critics have lauded Sand for presenting strong, willful heroines, and for exposing the obstacles faced by women—particularly women artists—in the nineteenth century. Several commentators have argued, however, that Sand's feminism was limited; she consistently advocated equal rights for women in matters of marriage and divorce, yet she subscribed to conventional views on male and female social roles. Some critics have noted that she regarded women to be creatures of emotion and men as thinking beings. However, Sand continues to be viewed as an important feminist, one whose life and work sought to undercut gender stereotypes and rebel against the roles imposed upon women by male-dominated society.

PRINCIPAL WORKS

Indiana (novel) 1832

Valentine (novel) 1832

Lélia (novel) 1833

Jacques (novel) 1834

Lettres d'un voyageur [*Letters of a Traveler*] (travel sketches) 1834-36

André (novel) 1835

Mauprat (novel) 1837

Spiridion (novel) 1839

Les sept cordes de la lyre [*The Seven Strings of the Lyre*] (play) 1840

Le compagnon du tour de France [*The Companion of the Tour of France*] (novel) 1841

Consuelo (novel) 1842-43

Jeanne (novel) 1844

Le meunier d'Angibault [*The Miller of Angibault*] (novel) 1845

La mare au diable [*The Haunted Marsh*] (novel) 1846

Françoise le champi [*Francis the Waif*] (novel) 1848

La petite Fadette [*Little Fadette*] (novel) 1849

Histoire de ma vie [*My Life*] 20 vols. (autobiography) 1854-55

Elle et Lui [She and He] (novel) 1859

Le marquis de villemer [The Marquis of Villemer] (novel) 1861

Flamarande (novel) 1875

Correspondance, 1812-1876 6 vols. (letters) 1883-95

PRIMARY SOURCES

GEORGE SAND (ESSAY DATE 1832)

SOURCE: Sand, George. "Preface to the Edition of 1832." In *Indiana*, translated by G. Burnham Ives, pp. v-xxi. Philadelphia: George Barrie, 1900.

In the following essay, originally included as a preface to the 1832 edition of her novel Indiana, *Sand discusses how the work is a representation of the relationship between women and society.*

If certain pages of this book should incur the serious reproach of tending toward novel beliefs, if unbending judges shall consider their tone imprudent and perilous, I should be obliged to reply to the criticism that it does too much honor to a work of no importance; that, in order to attack the great questions of social order, one must either be conscious of great strength of purpose or pride one's self upon great talent, and that such presumption is altogether foreign to a very simple tale, in which the author has invented almost nothing. If, in the course of his task, he has happened to set forth the lamentations extorted from his characters by the social malady with which they were assailed; if he has not shrunk from recording their aspirations after a happier existence, let the blame be laid upon society for its inequalities, upon destiny for its caprices! The author is merely a mirror which reflects them, a machine which reverses their tracing, and he has no reason for self-reproach if the impression is exact, if the reflection is true.

Consider further that the narrator has not taken for text or devise a few shrieks of suffering and wrath scattered through the drama of human life. He does not claim to conceal serious instruction beneath the exterior form of a tale; it is not his aim to lend a hand in constructing the edifice which a doubtful future is preparing for us and to give a sly kick at that of the past which is crumbling away. He knows too well that we live in an epoch of moral deterioration, wherein the reason of mankind has need of curtains to soften the too bright glare which dazzles it. If he had felt sufficiently learned to write a genuinely useful book, he would have toned down the truth, instead of presenting it in its crude tints and with its startling effects. That book would have performed the functions of blue spectacles for weak eyes.

He does not abandon the idea of performing that honorable and laudable task some day; but, being still a young man, he simply tells you to-day what he has seen, not presuming to draw his conclusions concerning the great controversy between the future and the past, which perhaps no man of the present generation is especially competent to do. Too conscientious to conceal his doubts from you, but too timid to transform them into certainties, he relies upon your reflections and abstains from weaving into the woof of his narrative preconceived opinions, judgments all formed. He plies with exactitude his trade of narrator. He will tell you everything, even painful truths; but, if you should wrap him in the philosopher's robe, you would find that he was exceedingly confused, simple storyteller that he is, whose mission is to amuse and not to instruct.

Even were he more mature and more skilful, he would not dare to lay his hand upon the great sores of dying civilization. One must be so sure of being able to cure them when one ventures to probe them! He would much prefer to arouse your interest in old discarded beliefs, in old-fashioned, vanished forms of devotion, to employing his talent, if he had any, in blasting overturned altars. He knows, however, that, in these charitable times, a timorous conscience is despised by public opinion as hypocritical reserve, just as, in the arts, a timid bearing is sneered at as an absurd mannerism; but he knows also that there is honor, if not profit, in defending lost causes.

To him who should misunderstand the spirit of this book, such a profession of faith would sound like an anachronism. The narrator hopes that few auditors, after listening to his tale to the end, will deny the *moral* to be derived from the facts, a moral which triumphs there as in all human affairs; it seemed to him, when he wrote the last line, that his conscience was clear. He flattered himself, in a word, that he had described social miseries without too much bitterness, human passions without too much passion. He placed the mute under his strings when they echoed too loudly; he tried to stifle certain notes of the soul which should remain mute, certain voices of the heart which cannot be awakened without danger.

Perhaps you will do him justice if you agree that the being who tries to free himself from his lawful curb is represented as very wretched indeed, and the heart that rebels against the decrees of its destiny as in sore distress. If he has not given the best imaginable rôle to that one of his characters who represents *the law,* if that one who represents *opinion* is even less cheerful, you will see a third representing *illusion,* who cruelly thwarts the vain hopes and enterprises of passion. Lately, you will see that, although he has not strewn rose-leaves on the ground where the law pens up our desires like a sheep's appetite, he has scattered thistles along the roads which lead us away from it.

These facts, it seems to me, are sufficient to protect this book from the reproach of immorality; but, if you absolutely insist that a novel should end like one of Marmontel's tales, you will perhaps chide me on account of the last pages; you will think that I have done wrong in not casting into misery and destitution the character who has transgressed the laws of mankind through two volumes. In this regard, the author will reply that before being moral he chose to be true; he will say again, that, feeling that he was too new to the trade to compose a philosophical treatise on the manner of enduring life, he has restricted himself to telling you the story of *Indiana,* a story of the human heart, with its weaknesses, its passions, its rights and its wrongs, its good qualities and its evil qualities.

Indiana, if you insist upon an explanation of every thing in the book, is a type; she is woman, the feeble being whose mission it is to represent *passions* repressed, or, if you prefer, suppressed by *the law*; she is desire at odds with necessity; she is love dashing her head blindly against all the obstacles of civilization. But the serpent wears out his teeth and breaks them in trying to gnaw a file; the powers of the soul become exhausted in trying to struggle against the positive facts of life. That is the conclusion you may draw from this tale, and it was in that light that it was told to him who transmits it to you.

But despite these protestations the narrator anticipates reproaches. Some upright souls, some honest men's consciences will be alarmed perhaps to see virtue so harsh, reason so downcast, opinion so unjust. He is dismayed at the prospect; for the thing that an author should fear more than anything in the world is the alienating from his works the confidence of good men, the awakening of an ominous sympathy in embittered souls, the inflaming of the sores, already too painful, which are made by the social yoke upon impatient and rebellious necks.

The success which is based upon an unworthy appeal to the passions of the age is the easiest to win, the least honorable to strive for. The historian of *Indiana* denies that he has ever dreamed of it; if he thought that he had reached that result, he would destroy his book, even though he felt for it the artless fatherly affection which swaddles the rickety offspring of these days of literary abortions.

But he hopes to justify himself by stating that he thought it better to enforce his principles by real examples than by poetic fancies. He believes that his tale, with the depressing atmosphere of frankness that envelopes it, may make an impression upon young and ardent brains. They will find it difficult to distrust a historian who forces his way brutally through the midst of facts, elbowing right and left, with no more regard for one camp than for the other. To make a cause odious or absurd is to persecute it, not to combat it. It may be that the whole art of the novelist consists in interesting the culprits whom he wishes to redeem, the wretched whom he wishes to cure, in their own story.

It would be giving overmuch importance to a work that is destined doubtless to attract very little notice, to seek to protect it against every sort of accusation. Therefore the author surrenders unconditionally to the critics; a single charge seems to him too serious to accept, and that is the charge that he has written a dangerous book. He would prefer to remain in a humble position forever to building his reputation upon a ruined conscience. He will add a word therefore to repel the blame which he most dreads.

Raymon, you will say, is society; egoism is substituted for morality and reason. Raymon, the author will reply, is the false reason, the false morality by which society is governed; he is the man of honor as the world understands the phrase, because the world does not examine closely enough to see everything. The good man you have beside Raymon; and you will not say that he is the enemy of order; for he sacrifices his happiness, he loses all thought of self before all questions of social order.

Then you will say that virtue is not rewarded with sufficient blowing of trumpets. Alas! the answer is that we no longer witness the triumph of virtue elsewhere than at the boulevard theatres. The author will tell you that he has undertaken to exhibit society to you, not as virtuous, but as necessary, and that honor has become as difficult as heroism in these days of moral degeneration.

Do you think that this truth will cause great souls to loathe honor? I think just the opposite.

GEORGE SAND (ESSAY DATE 1852)

SOURCE: Sand, George. "Introduction." In *Indiana*, translated by G. Burnham Ives, pp. v-xxi. Philadelphia: George Barrie, 1900.

In the following essay, originally written in 1852, Sand discloses her motives for writing her novel Indiana.

I wrote **Indiana** during the autumn of 1831. It was my first novel; I wrote it without any fixed plan, having no theory of art or philosophy in my mind. I was at the age when one writes with one's instincts, and when reflection serves only to confirm our natural tendencies. Some people chose to see in the book a deliberate argument against marriage. I was not so ambitious, and I was surprised to the last degree at all the fine things that the critics found to say concerning my subversive purposes. Criticism is far too acute; that is what will cause its death. It never passes judgment ingenuously. It looks for noon at four o'clock, as the old women say, and must cause much suffering to artists who care more for its decrees than they ought to do.

Under all régimes and in all times there has been a race of critics, who, in contempt of their own talent, have fancied that it was their duty to ply the trade of denouncers, of purveyors to the prosecuting attorney's office; extraordinary functions for men of letters to assume with regard to their confrères! The rigorous measures of government against the press never satisfy these savage critics. They would have them directed not only against works but against persons as well, and, if their advice were followed, some of us would be forbidden to write anything whatsoever.

At the time that I wrote **Indiana,** the cry of Saint Simonism was raised on every pretext. Later they shouted all sorts of other things. Even now certain writers are forbidden to open their mouths, under pain of seeing the police agents of certain newspapers pounce upon their work and hale them before the police of the constituted powers. If a writer puts noble sentiments in the mouth of a mechanic, it is an attack on the bourgeoisie; if a girl who has gone astray is rehabilitated after expiating her sin, it is an attack on virtuous women; if an impostor assumes titles of nobility, it is an attack on the patrician caste; if a bully plays the swashbuckling soldier, it is an insult to the army; if a woman is maltreated by her husband, it is an argument in favor of promiscuous love. And so with everything. Kindly brethren,

devout and generous critics! What a pity that no one thinks of creating a petty court of literary inquisition in which you should be the torturers! Would you be satisfied to tear the books to pieces and burn them at a slow fire, and could you not, by your urgent representations, obtain permission to give a little taste of the rack to those writers who presume to have other gods than yours?

Thank God, I have forgotten the names of those who tried to discourage me at my first appearance, and who, being unable to say that my first attempt had fallen completely flat, tried to distort it into an incendiary proclamation against the repose of society. I did not expect so much honor, and I consider that I owe to those critics the thanks which the hare proffered the frogs, imagining from their alarm that he was entitled to deem himself a very thunderbolt of war.

GENERAL COMMENTARY

MARILYN YALOM (ESSAY DATE 1985)

SOURCE: Yalom, Marilyn. "Towards a History of Female Adolescence: The Contribution of George Sand." In *George Sand: Collected Essays,* edited by Janis Glasgow, pp. 204-15. Troy, N.Y.: Whitson, 1985.

In the following essay, Yalom examines Sand's contribution to a history of female adolescence, concentrating particularly on the author's autobiography and comparing it with works by other women writers.

When the history of female adolescence is written, it will be seen that the writing of George Sand offers a store of portraits and insights unparalleled in her time and place. Both in her autobiographical and fictive works, Sand proved that adolescence was a subject worthy of observation and a "source of poetry."[1] Like her master Rousseau a century earlier, she both excoriated the corrupted state of adolescence among her contemporaries and immortalized the adolescent soul in its physical restlessness, spiritual awakening, and fitful attempts to integrate conflicting social, psychological and biological pressures.

In early nineteenth century France, the idea of adolescence as a period of life distinct from childhood was not yet a familiar concept. As Philippe Ariès has written in *Centuries of Childhood*: "People had no idea of what we call adolescence, and the idea was a long time taking shape. . . . The first typical adolescent of modern times was Wagner's *Siegfried.*"[2] Here, as elsewhere, the concept of adolescence was predicated on a male model. Thus Ariès could write that "... *Siegfried* expressed for the first time that combination of (provisional) purity, physical strength, naturism, spontaneity and *joie de vivre* which was to make the adolescent the hero of our twentieth century, the century of adolescence."[3]

But what about the adolescent heroine? Does she not also have an experiential and a literary tradition? And is hers to be encompassed and adequately represented by the generic masculine?

Another example of this one-sided optic is found in Justin O'Brien's book *The Novel of Adolescence in France*,[4] in which the author deals exclusively with male writers—Jules Renard, Maurice Barrès, Romain Rolland, Raymond Radiguet, Gide, Cocteau, Montherlant—an impressive array to be sure. His reasons for excluding women writers like Sand, whom he hails as "the first person to recognize that there existed a problem of the adolescent and to point out that literature had ignored it," and Colette, whose name is simply listed in an appendix, are questionable: "It appears that the advent of puberty, whose physiological repercussions are so marked in girls, influences them intellectually and spiritually far less than it does boys(!) ..."[5] Had O'Brien been less fettered by received ideas on the nature of women and more open to a genuinely empathic reading of Sand and Colette, to name only the most prominent French women writers with books that fall into the category of the novel of adolescence, he might have been less certain of his criteria for exclusion.

This paper is an initial attempt to explore Sand's contribution to a history of female adolescence. In the interest of space I shall limit myself to **Histoire de ma vie,** though many of Sand's works of fiction offer rich ground for similar investigations. In addition, for the sake of comparison, I shall occasionally draw upon American and English sources contemporary with Sand so as to include certain characteristics of female adolescence which had currency not only in France but elsewhere in the Western world.[6]

In the nineteenth century France the term "enfance" covered anyone who was not an adult. The word "adolescence" had not yet come to be popularly used to designate that period in life between childhood and adulthood, though both Rousseau in his *Confessions* and Sand in **Histoire de ma vie** brought the term into literature. Similarly, in English-speaking countries the term "infancy" had a broad connotation, often designating anyone under eighteen or even twenty-one, and the word "youth" was loosely used to encompass both adolescents and young adults.

In the twentieth century, both French- and English-speaking peoples define adolescence as that period in the life cycle between childhood and adulthood, roughly from twelve to twenty. The first line of demarcation is often clear-cut, a biological fact marking the onset of puberty occurring today, on the average, around age twelve for girls and age fourteen for boys. In the nineteenth century, the average age of puberty took place approximately two years later for both girls and boys. The second line of demarcation is more obscure. When does adolescence end today? When one leaves school? When one begins to earn one's keep? When one marries? Ariès notes that in the twentieth century marriage has ceased to mark the end of adolescence and that the "married adolescent ... (has) become one of the most prominent types of our time."[7]

In the time of George Sand, born in 1804, marriage was clearly viewed not only as the end of "enfance" but as the primary context in which female adolescence had meaning. Though Sand herself made no mention of the onset of menstruation in her autobiography—a subject considered too indelicate for literary reference—French medical literature had long been explicit in its understanding of the interface between the physical and social factors marking the female's transition from girl to woman. For example, the noted doctor Marc Colombat de l'Isère, outlining the hygienic rules concerning puberty and menstruation, wrote that the female adolescent "... needs closest watching. ... Whereas before puberty she existed but for herself alone ... she now belongs to the entire species which she is destined to perpetuate. ... (I)t is of the highest importance to remove young girls from boarding school, when they approach the age of puberty, in order to exercise a constant watch over them."[8]

Sand's grandmother did just the opposite; she placed her ward in a convent school, but the motivation was the same: to place her in a situation of surveillance so that she would be molded to the purposes of society. As a child, Aurore carroused with children of both sexes in the countryside she adored; now she had to be sequestered, literally cloistered with other girls, and the implication is unmistakable. Unchaperoned contact with males is dangerous, overly affectionate contact with other females is also dangerous; girls are enjoined never to be alone or in couples, but always in groups of three or more. "Onanism, that execrable and fatal evil, destroys beauty and health and conducts almost always to a premature grave.'"[9] With puberty, sex had reared its ugly head and was to be repressed in every way for as long or as short a period as was necessary to fashion the adolescent into a marriageable product and marry her off to the best suitor.

This is how George Sand recalls her grand-mother's decision to send her away from the country estate at Nohant, where she had passed most of her childhood, to a convent school in Paris:

> . . . ma grand-mère me dit: «Ma fille, vous n'avez plus le sens commun. Vous aviez de l'esprit, et vous faites tout votre possible pour devenir ou pour paraître bête. Vous pourriez être agréable, et vous vous faites laide à plaisir. Votre teint est noirci, vos mains gercées, vos pieds vont se dé-former dans les sabots. Votre cerveau se déforme et se dégingande comme votre personne. Tantôt vous répondez à peine et vous avez l'air d'un esprit fort qui dédaigne tout. Tantôt vous parlez à tort et à travers comme une pie qui babille pour babiller. Vous avez été une charmante petite fille, il ne faut pas devenir une jeune personne absurde. Vous n'avez point de tenue, point de grâce, point d'à-propos. Vous avez un bon coeur et une tête pitoy-able. Il faut changer tout cela. Vous avez d'ailleurs besoin de *maîtres d'agrément,* et je ne puis vous en procurer ici. J'ai donc résolu de vous mettre au couvent, et nous allons à Paris à cet effect.»[10]

It appears that Aurore's grandmother decided to place her in a boarding school because she could not cope with the tempestuous outbursts and unruly conduct of a young adolescent. Before this decision, Aurore had been allowed to associ-ate with the peasant children who surrounded her grandmother's estate. She spoke their patois, joined in their rustic activities—milking cows and goats, making cheese, dancing country dances, eating wild apples and pears (all of which stood her in good stead later in life when she wrote her pastoral novels). Up to the age of twelve or thirteen she could roam the countryside accord-ing to her fancy and read whatever she liked. Her education had been irregular, consisting of peri-odic excursions to Paris with her grandmother for a smattering of private lessons in handwriting, dancing, music, a bit of geography and history, and back to Nohant with the more regular lessons in Latin and French literature under her father's old tutor, Deschartres.

In the twelve months between her twelfth and thirteenth years, Aurore Dupin grew three inches, attaining a maximum height of five feet two inches. It is at this point that she began to show these signs of adolescence which became the despair of her grandmother—irritability, temper tantrums, outbursts toward her tutor during which she refused to study. Once she threw her books on the floor, exclaiming out loud that she wouldn't study because she didn't want to. At table she began to speak out of turn, laughed at the slightest pretext, was turning by her later ac-counts into a real "enfant terrible."

Home education by one's mother or a tutor was the prevalent pattern for those privileged girls who were educated at all. As outlined by Albertine Necker de Saussure in a widely read treatise on the education of French girls,[11] there was to be es-sentially no difference in the education of girls and boys up to the age of ten. But after the age of ten, according to Necker de Saussure and other authors of educational manuals, girls should be educated differently in view of the role they would later play as wives and mothers. At this point, the mother-educator, if she educates her daughter at home, or the school, if the girl is at boarding school, should educate the sexes separately. Au-rore was sent off to school a little later than girls of her same class, probably because her grand-mother, a widow living in the country, wanted to keep her with her, but when the signs of adoles-cence became too visible, Mme Dupin was forced to think in terms of her grand-daughter's future, and this entailed taming her and transforming her from an unmannered country girl into a mar-riageable young lady.

Thus Aurore was packed off to a convent school at age thirteen. The description of her convent years in *Histoire de ma vie* reveals the picture of an active, energetic, curious thirteen-year-old. Although she was immediately aware of the fact that the other girls had superior manners and were more restrained in their activities, she was not about to let this inhibit her. Just as she had romped through the countryside with her peasant friends and turned her grandmother's house into a meeting place for dozens of rowdy companions, so too she demonstrated the same restless energy in her first year at the convent: run-ning into the courtyard at recess, prying into every nook and cranny, exploring underground passages and dangerous rooftops.

The three years at the convent school from age thirteen to sixteen, covering some two hun-dred pages in *Histoire de ma vie,* provide an excel-lent tableau of female adolescence among the privileged classes in early nineteenth century France. While it is true that Aurore Dupin was an unusual child, that she had superior gifts and a superior education, and that she had above all a greater ability to exercise her will than most of her contemporaries, her adolescence has many features which we think of as typical, not only for girls in nineteenth century France but for most Western female adolescents in modern times.

1) First, there is the initial restlessness and energy, which seems, from the vantage point of adults, to have no direction and to "get out of hand." This energy expresses itself physically in raucous activities characterized by unrestrained movement and a sense of adventure, often in defiance of the social norms. This burst of physical energy was recognized by Rousseau, for one, as the first hallmark of puberty.

In this respect, it is interesting to compare George Sand's description of her adolescent years with the prescriptive medical literature of the same period. In Sand's autobiographical accounts, we see numerous robust teen-agers with an insatiable drive toward movement and activity. The prescriptive medical literature, on the other hand, depicted adolescence as a time of great fragility for females, a life crisis where the budding woman was particularly vulnerable to all sorts of disease and fatal conditions.

Sand remembers herself as an unusually strong and active adolescent, making dangerous excursions underground and on the rooftops, enduring the cold of an attic room and the truly spartan conditions that were *de rigueur* in French convent schools and in English boarding schools even in this century. And despite chilblains and sores on hands and feet, she not only survives with no trace of cough or consumption but she enjoys a healthful constitution—in her case, into her seventies. Adolescence for George Sand was no passage into an adulthood of feminine fragility, but into a vigorous and forceful womanhood. Certainly this was not true of all, or even most female adolescents of her time and place. Many did indeed die of consumption and other ills, but this was probably due more to unhygienic conditions and to poor diet than to a natural vulnerability induced by menarche.

2) Second, there is a spirit of rebellion that characterizes her early adolescence, as indeed her entire adult life. When George Sand entered the convent at the age of thirteen, she immediately allied herself with a group called "les diables." She could have chosen to have joined "les sages," or "les bêtes," but it is, she tells us, in protest against the injustices of Mlle D., headmistress of the children's division. There are several aspects of this alignment with "les diables" which are par-

ticularly fascinating. First, there is the very fact that such clearly defined groups exist. What is this need of early adolescents to lock themselves into tightly bound peer groups whose major mission seems to be the exclusion of others from it? Psychologists like Erik Erikson would emphasize the fact that such group affiliation is very important in the process of developing a sense of identity at a time when one is separating oneself from parents and all the familiar supports of childhood.[12] The group proffers an instant sense of identity. But why should some of the girls have chosen to be "good girls" and some have chosen to be "devils?" And why is there so much antisocial behavior during the adolescent years— juvenile delinquency, as we call it today in its extreme form? Clearly, for Aurore Dupin at least, joining "les diables" offered a clearcut means of rebelling against the social norms which she found repugnant.

The leader in this enterprise was one Mary G. and she was surely the antithesis of the fragile Victorian woman, who was the ideal in France as well as in England. Strength, braveness, boldness—these were not characteristics that the convent had set out to inculcate in their young ladies. Little wonder that strong-willed adolescent females like George Sand and Mary G. and others (Juliette Adam springs to mind) refused to become the passive porcelain figures that society wished to make of them.

In common with our twentieth century memories of adolescence, Sand recalls a "secret society" with its rite of initiation, the written notes passed secretly in class, and the spontaneous outbursts of laughter understandable only to the initiated. Certain characteristics seem particularly French; for example, the French regard for form, as in Aurore's first meeting with Mary G., of which she wrote: "C'était à elle, comme plus ancienne, de me faire les avances."[13] Though the forms were more explicitly hierarchical than our own and the students more embedded in a literary tradition, there is nonetheless a very familiar quality for all who have discovered rebellion in adolescence and enlisted private group support to condone anti-parental or antisocial behavior.

3) Another aspect is, of course, the intense female friendships that are established in this period of life, all the more intense when one is isolated from boys. Sand at the age of fifty remembers in detail a large number of girls whom she loved with great tenderness, not only Mary G., in the lower division, but Valentine de Gouy and

Louise de la Rochejaquelein, later Eliza Austen, the most intelligent girl in the school, and also the nuns who served as mother figures. Sand wrote of her great worshipful love for Madame Alicia, "la perle du couvent,"[14] and of her great attachment to the lay sister, Sister Hélène, who did the dirtiest work in the convent. For a small convent of some one hundred and twenty or one hundred and thirty persons, it offered a wide range of deep attachments to various types of persons.[15]

4) The religious awakening and conversion experienced by Aurore Dupin during her convent years provides another focal point for the study of adolescence, and one that is closely linked to the historical time in which she lived and to her particular culture, although spiritual awakening in adolescence is not uncommon in all times. Sand divides her convent life into three periods: "La première année, je fus plus que jamais l'enfant terrible. La seconde année, je passais presque subitement à une dévotion ardente et agitée. La troisième année, je me maintins dans un état de dévotion calme, ferme et enjouée."[16]

This experience of religious conversion as told by George Sand is not unlike many other experiences undergone by other adolescent girls in France, England and the United States at the same period in history. It may be somewhat ironic to realize that something so infinitely personal as the experience of grace and communion with God can have, in certain historical moments, almost a vogueish quality. In early nineteenth century France, the restoration of the Bourbon monarchy ushered in a vigorous revival of Catholic doctrine in both public and private life. Similarly, in England and America, the Christian revivalist movement promoted the reading of Gospel and the examination of conscience as fundamental nourishment for the soul seeking salvation. Conversion was a socially sanctioned event, a rite of passage from childhood to adulthood. In all three countries, it was expected to occur around the time of adolescence and was interpreted as a sign of divine grace marking a new beginning. According to the prevailing philosophy, this much encouraged religious awakening, accompanying the physical awakening of puberty, would give direction to one's resurgent physical and emotional needs. As Barbara Gelpi has written in her work on Victorian girlhood, "To young children religion may well have been drab, boring or repressive, but for many adolescents it became an emotional outlet and an escape from repres-

sion."[17] Citing the examples of Sainte Thérèse in France and Catherine Beecher in America, Gelpi concludes that "even those who were not susceptible to the fervent spirituality of their peers . . . formed their adult personalities in the dialectic between their feelings and the religious expectations for them of those about them."[18]

Like many other converts, Sand's attention was drawn to the mystical experience by reading from the "Lives of the Saints," and stimulated through the eye and the ear. At mass there was the superb picture of Jesus in the Garden of Olives, the glitter of stained glass windows, the charm of the chapel at night, the silver candlesticks, the beautiful flowers, all of which seem to blend in that moment of insight—that flash of white light which she experienced in the convent chapel.

> L'heure s'avançait, la prière était sonnée, on allait fermer l'église. J'avais tout oublié. Je ne sais ce qui se passait en moi. Je respirais une atmosphère de suavité indicible, et je la respirais par l'âme plus encore que par les sens. Tout à coup je ne sais quel ébranlement se produisit dans tout mon être, un vertige passe devant mes yeux comme une lueur blanche dont je me sens enveloppée. Je crois entendre une voix murmurer à mon oreille: *tolle, lege*. Je me retourne, croyant que c'est Marie-Alicia qui me parle. J'étais seule.
>
> Je ne me fis pas d'orgueilleuse illusion, je ne crus point à un miracle. Je me rendis fort bien compte de l'espèce d'hallucination où j'étais tombée. Je n'en fus ni enivrée ni effrayée. Je ne cherchai ni à l'augmenter ni à m'y soustraire. Seulement je sentis que la foi s'emparait de moi, comme si je l'avais souhaité, par le coeur. J'en fus si reconnaissante, si ravie, qu'un torrent de larmes inonda mon visage. Je sentis encore que j'aimais Dieu, que ma pensée embrassait et acceptait pleinement cet idéal de justice, de tendresse et de sainteté que je n'avais jamais révoqué en doute, mais avec lequel je ne m'étais jamais trouvée en communication directe; je sentis enfin cette communication s'établir soudainement, comme si un obstacle invincible se fût abîmé entre le foyer d'ardeur infinie et le feu assoupi dans mon âme.[19]

Sand's emotionally-charged description of the experience of grace is not unlike those described by others who have been similarly illumined. It is, of course, difficult to know to what extent she embroidered upon her recollection and recreated an experience that was more poetic, more mystical than its historic reality. But we have no reason to doubt the significance of this religious epiphany; during the next sixty years, despite her highly unconventional existence as a novelist, adulteress, cigar-smoking woman in male clothes, political radical, she never completely lost her faith; indeed, she always wrote and spoke reverently of the religious sentiment as an inborn and beneficent force.

Her adolescent religious conversion had immediate social benefits. Just as identification with "les diables" permitted a reprieve from activities for which she felt herself unready, so too the experience of "conversion" provided a rite of passage into a more socially acceptable young womanhood. She wrote that she had exhausted the resources of a disorderly career and was ready for something else, and with Madame Alicia as her role model, the one and only attractive role was that of a believer. Once converted, Aurore set herself a course of piety and goodness that quite astonished her friends. "J'étais devenue sage, obéissante et laborieuse."[20] She entertained for some time the notion of becoming a nun, although with little encouragement from the nuns themselves, who realized that her grandmother had other plans for her grand-daughter—namely, to establish her in a marriage suitable to her station.

This period of intense devotion was critical in Sand's adolescence and in her developing sense of self. It forced her to make choices that entailed identifying with socially acceptable behavior and renouncing behaviors that were considered unacceptable for women. At sixteen when George Sand left the convent, she was, by her own retrospective accounts, a cheerful and pious young woman. She left the convent to live once more with her grandmother, while the latter set about finding her a husband.

From the point of view of Sand's time and culture, adolescence had run its course; a rebellious girl had been suitably tamed and transformed into "une femme." Let us pause to remark that the French word "femme" means both woman and wife. (The French have only one word where we have two). Adolescence was thus implicitly and explicably conceived of as a period of transition from the state of being a child or girl to the state of being a woman and wife. This same supposition underlies the structure of a radically different piece of Sand's writing: **La Petite Fadette.** In that remarkable story of adolescence among the Berrichon peasants, Sand demonstrates the difficulties of growing up female without the support of family and institutions that socialize a girl into her "proper" role. Because **Fadette** is essentially a pastoral romance, the heroine's adolescent apprenticeship ends happily with an ideal

peasant marriage. As we know, Sand's adolescence also culminated in marriage at the age of nineteen, but her story was not to end there.[21]

Notes

1. George Sand, *Histoire de ma vie* in *Oeuvres Autobiographiques* [OA], ed. Georges Lubin, 2 Vols. (Paris: Gallimard, 1970). All translations are my own.

2. Philippe Ariès, *Centuries of Childhood,* trans. Robert Baldick (New York: Vintage Books, 1962), pp. 29-30.

3. Ibid., p. 30.

4. Justin O'Brien, *The Novel of Adolescence in France* (New York: Columbia University Press, 1937).

5. Ibid., pp. 12-13.

6. Much of this work is based upon the collaborative research undertaken by Hellerstein, Hume, Offen, Freedman, Gelpi and Yalom in *Victorian Women* (Stanford, CA: Stanford University Press, 1981).

7. Ariès, p. 30.

8. Hellerstein, et al., pp. 91-93.

9. Ibid., p. 93.

10. Sand, *OA,* I, p. 861.

11. Albertine-Adrienne Necker de Saussure, *The Study of the Life of Woman* (Philadelphia, 1844). Originally published in Paris in 1838.

12. Erik Erikson, *Identity, Youth and Crisis,* (New York: W. W. Norton, 1968).

13. Sand, *OA,* I, p. 881.

14. Ibid., I, p. 921.

15. For a comparative analysis of female friendship in nineteenth century America, see Caroll Smith-Rosenberg, "The Female World of Love and Ritual: Women in the Nineteenth Century America," *Signs,* I, 1 (Autumn 1975), pp. 1-29.

16. Sand, *OA,* I, p. 869.

17. Barbara Gelpi, Introduction to Part I, "The Girl," in Hellerstein, et al., p. 15.

18. Ibid.

19. Sand, *OA,* I, pp. 953-954.

20. Ibid., p. 965.

21. Between the writing of this essay and its publication four years later, some literary scholars have begun to pay attention to female, as well as male, models of adolescence, for example, Patricia Meyer Spacks, *The Adolescent Idea: Myths of Youth and the Adult Imagination* (New York: Basic Books, 1981) and Richard N. Coe, *When the Grass Was Taller: Autobiography and the Experience of Childhood* (New Haven: Yale University Press, 1984).

TITLE COMMENTARY

Indiana

PETER DAYAN (ESSAY DATE APRIL 1998)

SOURCE: Dayan, Peter. "Who Is the Narrator in *Indiana*?" *French Studies* 52, no. 2 (April 1998): 152-61.

In the following essay, Dayan examines the complex point of view in Indiana *in which the male narrator presents a distinctly paternalistic stance.*

George Sand's first novel **Indiana** has been one of the set texts on our second-year literature course for several years now. It is, on the whole, popular with the students. They like it partly because, unlike the work of the uncontroversially canonized (such as Baudelaire or Flaubert), it provides topics for debate on which the students feel they can take sides, for or against. One such topic has been dividing readers and critics since the novel was first published: the question of the literary desirability of the conclusion. At the end of the fourth part of the novel, we are promised the perfect Romantic lovers' suicide: Ralph takes Indiana in his arms, 'et l'emporta pour la précipiter avec lui dans le torrent . . .'. But, in the conclusion which follows, we find they have decided to live happily ever after instead. This has always been felt by some to be a bold rupture with the realist tradition, and by others to be a let-down, an abdication both of verisimilitude and of Romantic nobility for reasons of unworthy sentimentality. The 'points de suspension' at the end of the above quotation, however, do not merely signal the suspension of the realist mode, replaced in the conclusion by the idealist (according to the contrast between realism and idealism so well established by Naomi Schor).[1] The conclusion also differs from the rest of the novel in having an intradiegetic first person narrator, whereas the rest of the novel seems to have an extradiegetic omniscient narrator in the Balzacian mould.

In the conclusion, the point of view is strictly, in accordance with the traditional rules governing such narration, that of the narrator. We can only see what he can see. To him, Ralph and Indiana are enigmas, and he clearly knows virtually nothing about them other than through public rumour until Ralph himself tells him their story. The question of point of view in the rest of the novel is more complex and problematic. It is certainly impossible to believe that the apparently omniscient narrator is simply coterminous with George

Sand.[2] Particularly, even if one could discount the question of gender (he is masculine), he appears to have paternalist ideas concerning the character of women and their proper place in society which are obviously opposed to those of Sand herself. He consistently presents women as intellectually weak and necessarily dependent on men. He never even considers the possibility that a woman could lead the kind of independent life that Sand herself had just embarked on at the time she wrote the book. This possibility emerges in many of the novels Sand wrote in the following decade—*André, Jacques, Lélia, Consuelo,* for example; but I think it would be uncontroversial to say that, in **Indiana**, women are unable to imagine a fulfilling life that does not rely on a man as partner, support, or father-figure, or at the very least as interface with the public sphere. Indeed, the very structure of the narrative depends on the assumption that Indiana needs a man to make her happy. We are told near the beginning that this is the case, and that she is dying for want of a lover. Raymon saves her—then betrays her; and final salvation comes through Ralph. **Indiana** tells the story of a woman who achieves happiness not through independence and self-realization, but by finding the right man. The assumption that she needs a man is never questioned.

In many of Sand's later novels, there is a fascinating contradiction between the point of view of the narrator and the apparent signification of the events that he describes. One can often analyse this as the product of the friction between the paternalist, realist narrative stance that Sand used to structure her novels, and a more complex human and especially feminine reality that disturbs that structure, often without perturbing the narrator himself. It is fairly easy, in such cases, to tease out a distinction between the author (responsible for the subversive features) and the narrator (responsible for the discourse that attempts, happily and necessarily without success, to suppress the meaning of those subversive features). However, in **Indiana** there is no such contradiction. The events correspond to and support the discourse. In other words, **Indiana,** considered on its own, has an ideological coherence that many other Sand novels lack, because there is little internally obvious difference between the narrator and the implied author. If one read the novel without knowing any of Sand's other work (and since it was her first novel, that is how it was originally read), one would have little reason to suspect that its author's opinions were in many ways diametrically opposed to those of its narrator; that opposition becomes plain only when one compares the ideas expressed in the novel to those put forward elsewhere by Sand, especially in her letters, articles, and autobiographical writings. Within *Indiana,* the morals suggested by the events and characters seem, on the whole, to support the views of the narrator (save, as we shall see, in one exceptional passage). One might ask who this narrator is, and why Sand appears to have delegated to him such wideranging control over the world view presented in her work. I would like to propose a simple answer to these questions, which also aims to elucidate the relationship between the extradiegetic narrator of the first four parts and the intradiegetic narrator of the conclusion.

Frequently—for example, in *Mauprat, Le Dernier Amour, Les Maîtres Sonneurs*—Sand begins her novel with a first-person frame narrator who introduces to us one of the novel's main protagonists, and tells us how that protagonist told him his story; then the frame narrator recounts for us that story, which constitutes the body of the novel. (Thus the first-person frame narrator appears intradiegetic in the frame, but extradiegetic in the main story.) Normally, the story is recounted orally to the frame narrator, and he claims to reproduce with the minimum of editorial intervention the words of the teller; so, in the main part of the text, 'je' refers not to the frame narrator, but to the story-telling protagonist who is being quoted more or less verbatim. This is what happens, for example, in *Mauprat,* or in *Le Dernier Amour.* However, it is not unknown for the frame narrator to retell the story in the third person, basing it entirely on the information given to him by the protagonist, but not claiming to reproduce exactly the protagonist's words. This is how *La Mare au diable* is presented. In the second chapter of that novel, the narrator (who refers to himself as 'l'auteur') describes how Germain has told him his story; he then states his intention to write this story down for the benefit of his literate readers. Germain, being an illiterate peasant, 'n'en saura rien et ne s'en inquiétera guère'. But the narrator will enjoy retelling it. In the retelling, he, the frame narrator, remains in the first person; and Germain, who originally told it, is in the third person.

It is possible to read *Indiana* in the same way, as a story told to the narrator by Ralph, although in the retelling, Ralph, like Germain, remains in the third person. In the conclusion, the intradiegetic narrator goes to visit Ralph and Indiana at their remote home on the île Bourbon. He describes his main motivation as a desire to learn about Ralph and his history. Just before he leaves, disappointed at having learnt little, he stings Ralph with a tactless remark concerning the islanders' low opinion of him. Ralph is at first angry, particularly because Indiana, who knows nothing of this low opinion, has overheard the remark; but then he consents to tell all, once Indiana is safely out of the way.

> Quand la nuit fut venue, elle se retira dans sa chambre, et sir Ralph, me faisant asseoir à côté de lui sur un banc dans le jardin, me raconta son histoire jusqu'à l'endroit où nous l'avons laissée dans le précédent chapitre.[3]

The words 'précédent chapitre', here, can only refer to the end of the novel's fourth part. Who, then, is 'nous'? It seems to me only logical to suppose that it includes 'vous' (the addressee, whom one could see as either the reader, or J. Néraud, to whom the conclusion is dedicated, and who is addressed in the second person) and 'je', the narrator; in which case we must assume that 'je' and 'vous' reached the end of the 'précédent chapitre' together. This clearly implies that the narrator of the conclusion is the same person as the narrator of the rest of the novel; and that the story in the novel's first four parts is the one which Ralph told to him on that night in Bourbon. The formal difference between *La Mare au diable* and *Indiana* would then be simply this: in the former, we are told at the beginning that the narrator had the story from Germain; in the latter, it is only at the end, in the conclusion, that we discover the relationship between Ralph and the narrator.

But even this discovery, as Kathryn Crecelius says, 'does not resolve all the ambiguities of the narrative'.[4] For in many ways, the attitudes and the narrative strategies of the authoritative and extradiegetic narrator of the first four parts seem incompatible with those of the hesitant and intradiegetic narrator of the conclusion. It is these incompatibilities which lead Robert Godwin-Jones simply to propose that the narrator of the conclusion should not be seen as the same person as the narrator of the first four parts.[5] In this, he articulates the gut feeling of the average reader: in my experience, everyone, on a first reading, tends to assume that there are indeed two different narrators, and no one sees any need to conflate them. Nonetheless, as I have shown, and as most critics recognize, the text does explicitly invite us to operate just such a conflation. So are there two narrators in *Indiana,* or one? This question ceases to be problematic if one understands the sudden change in the narrative approach which distinguishes the conclusion from the rest of the novel as a consequence of the fact that in the first four parts, the narrator is giving us Ralph's version and interpretation of events, from Ralph's point of view, though in the third person; whereas in the conclusion, he is speaking in his own voice.

My intention, in this essay, then, is to see what happens when one reads the first four parts of *Indiana* resolutely and consistently as the transposed narration of Ralph, as Ralph's story ('son histoire', as the narrator calls it), a story both about Ralph and told by Ralph, rather than about Indiana and told from the point of view of the narrator. I do not think that a rigorous attempt at such a reading has been made before; and it has wide-reaching implications. The first is that Ralph's ideology must be assumed to pervade the narrative. And that ideology is certainly not a neutral or uncontroversial one. Ralph is a man of strong views, deeply idealistic, with a much firmer grasp on principle than on reality. We need not, therefore, look in the novel either for an 'objective' view, or for George Sand's (or Indiana's) view; it is an exercise, sustained with peculiar virtuosity, in reconstructing the world from the point of view of a certain masculine idealism.

Ralph's opinion concerning the difference between the sexes is clear and almost uncontested in the novel. Women, to him, are less rational, less intelligent than men; they are more generally prone to enthusiasm, to fanaticism, and to deceiving and being deceived. This, of course, corresponds to the traditional Romantic equation of femininity with the heart, and masculinity with the head. In the case of Indiana herself, Ralph has done his best to turn it into a self-fulfilling prophecy. It was he who brought her up, who was her teacher, guide and mentor; and he gave her the education he thought appropriate to her sex. He taught her to love nature and beauty, but not to reason. (It is perhaps worth remembering that George Sand was also educated by a male tutor— Deschartres; but he gave her a man's education, very different from Indiana's.)

> Ignorante comme une vraie créole, madame Delmare [. . .] avait été élevée par sir Ralph, qui avait une médiocre opinion de l'intelligence et du raisonnement chez les femmes, et qui s'était borné à lui donner quelques connaissances positives et d'un usage immédiat. Elle savait donc à peine l'histoire abrégée du monde, et toute dissertation sérieuse l'accablait d'ennui.[6]

Except, that is, when it is the man she loves who is talking; then 'la poésie de son langage' ap-

peals to her. It is not reason which convinces a woman; it is love. This unfortunately means that a woman can be convinced to do irrational and indeed dishonourable things in the name of love, as the fanatic does in the name of religion.

> L'amour, c'est la vertu de la femme; c'est pour lui qu'elle se fait une gloire de ses fautes, c'est de lui qu'elle reçoit l'héroïsme de braver ses remords. [. . .] C'est le fanatisme qui met le poignard aux mains du religieux.[7]

Thus it is, the narrator tells us, the imbecility of woman, her inability to understand the full context of her actions and her willingness to dupe and be duped, that explains the apparent heroism and strength of character of Indiana. She does not, as a man would, think through and face up to the often terrifying social and ideological implications of what she does; that would indeed require exceptional force. But a woman is as untroubled by prescience as by notions of categorical imperatives or collective responsibility. She is able to base her whole world view on 'un jour de délire', to see the world not as it is, but as her fantasies would wish it to be; so that in behaving in accordance with those fantasies, she can commit extraordinary acts without extraordinary courage or intellectual merit. (In the following quotation, 'nous' obviously refers to men, as opposed to women, and supposes, therefore, that both the narrator and his primary addressee are men.)

> La femme est imbécile par nature; il semble que, pour contrebalancer l'éminente supériorité que ses délicates perceptions lui donnent sur nous, le ciel ait mis à dessein dans son cœur une vanité aveugle, une idiote crédulité. [. . .] Voilà ce que je vous répondrais si vous me disiez qu'Indiana est un caractère d'exception [. . .]. Je vous demanderais où vous avez trouvé une femme qui ne fût pas aussi facile à tromper que facile à l'être; qui ne sût pas renfermer dix ans au fond de son cœur le secret d'une espérance risquée si légèrement un jour de délire.[8]

These are the terms in which Indiana is always presented by the narrator. From the very beginning, we are told that she has a dream—that one day a saviour, a 'libérateur', a 'messie', will appear and spirit her away from her dull life. '"Un jour viendra . . . un homme viendra . . ."'.[9] When she believes Raymon is that man, she is happy; when she loses faith in him, she lives only for death, until she acquires a new faith in Ralph as true saviour. Only once, I think, does this elementary analysis of Indiana's character fail to account for her words or deeds.

When critics wish to present Indiana as a genuinely progressive feminine character (rather than as the projection of a sexist male imagination or as a simple rebel against oppression), the passage they turn to is the letter which she sends to Raymon from the île Bourbon.[10] In that letter, she describes a quite astonishingly daring and ferociously anti-Catholic and anti-royalist system of beliefs, based on the principle that might must never be confused with right, and that the right to flee is the most fundamental of all. This is revolutionary stuff, and it is doubtless as incompatible with Ralph's republicanism as with Raymon's royalism (it foreshadows, in its assertion of the rights of the individual against the rule of the collectivity, Sand's later anti-Jacobinism). Surely it shows that Indiana is by no means a stranger to philosophical, religious and political speculation. Furthermore, she is also well aware of the gap between her ideals and reality. She has no illusions concerning the likely realization of her dreams, she analyses lucidly the circumstances in which she was able to believe that Raymon would sacrifice all for her, and she is clearly capable of seeing through and refuting his arguments in self-justification. This contrasts strangely with the way she had been presented to us, as a 'faible femme' buffeted by circumstance, and at the mercy of Raymon's flattery.

If one takes it that the narrator's point of view is Ralph's, the exceptional status of this letter becomes explicable. It is used by Sand as a device to give Indiana, just once in the novel, a chance to speak for herself, and to allow us to judge to what extent her future partner does her justice. The narrator's reaction (which, I repeat, I take as synonymous with Ralph's) is indeed revealing. He sees in the letter nothing more than another manifestation of her feeble-mindedness. The words that follow it are: 'L'infortunée se vantait'; and the following paragraph is the one beginning 'La femme est imbécile par nature', which I have quoted and discussed above. In fact, he ignores the content of four-fifths of the letter. He does not comment at all on its ideological or intellectual implications. To him, its sense is this: Indiana is trying to persuade Raymon that she is now in a state of 'douleur profonde et calme', and has ceased to long for him. It is on that interpretation of the letter that he bases his affirmation that she 'se vantait', and is easily deceived; after all, with hindsight, he knows that she will soon succumb to Raymon's wiles again. But is that really what she says in the letter? Surely not. She speaks neither of 'profondeur' nor of 'calme'; she says only: 'ma douleur est digne de l'amour que j'eus pour vous' . . . which, given the violently para-

doxical nature of that love as she has just described it, certainly does not suggest a stable resignation. In fact, I would suggest that she is well aware of the weakness of her position. She knows full well what no man in the novel will admit: that as a woman, she would be able to realize herself fully only if she could escape from them all—for all of them see woman as subject to their law. But she also knows that escape is impossible. She cannot obey the laws of God; she must submit to the law of man. That submission will be a derogation; but she can have no life without it.

> En me soumettant, c'est au pouvoir des hommes que je cède. Si j'écoutais la voix que Dieu a mise au fond de mon cœur, et ce noble instinct d'une nature forte et hardie, qui peut-être est la vraie conscience, je fuirais au désert, je saurais me passer d'aide, de protection et d'amour; j'irais vivre pour moi seule au fond de nos belles montagnes [. . .]. Mais, hélas! l'homme ne peut se passer de son semblable, et Ralph lui-même ne peut pas vivre seul.[11]

The narrator ignores this deep and eternally frustrated longing for independence, and continues to present Indiana as a 'faible femme' in need of a strong man. Certainly, Indiana is unable to do what Sand herself did (and many of her female protagonists, such as Thérèse, in *Elle et Lui*; Geneviève, in *André*, Consuelo and Jeanne, in the novels named after them): she cannot work for a living, and thereby acquire a social status of her own. But the reason for that is surely simple. One cannot work if one has no education and no skills. Indiana has none because of the way she was brought up—by Ralph. Ralph has thus made her dependent; at the end of the novel, he plainly means to keep her dependent; and in the story as he tells it, all evidence that she might not want to be dependent has been erased—except in the letter to Raymon, which, we may assume, is quoted verbatim, and has thus not been filtered through Ralph's eyes. The narrator is clearly aware that the letter's content needs to be belittled; he does not, however, see any need to take account of its real message.

Indiana's character, then, is presented by the narrator as constant, coherent, and fairly simple. Her circumstances change dramatically in the course of the novel, but her personality does not; the portrait of her that we receive in the first part remains valid. One could say the same of Delmare, of Raymon, indeed of all the characters in the book with one exception: Ralph; and this seems to me one of the clearest indications of the special relationship between Ralph and the narrator. Ralph remains an enigma almost until the end of the fourth part. He is an enigma to the reader, in that his behaviour is clearly not fully explained. But he also seems, strangely, to be an enigma to the narrator, challenging the latter's omniscience. Indeed, it is possible to put together quite an impressive catalogue of instances in which Ralph's behaviour seems to be either ignored or flatly contradicted by the narratorial commentary, whereas explanations are always forthcoming where the other characters are concerned. I shall take just two examples. Right at the beginning of the book, in the opening scene, we are given first a long portrait of Delmare, which subsequent events confirm; then an equally prophetic portrait of Indiana, and then a portrait of Ralph of which practically every detail turns out to be a red herring. He appears physically handsome, 'dans toute la force et dans toute la fleur de la jeunesse', elegant, self-satisfied, 'vermeil et blond', 'dormeur et bien mangeant'; but 'fade' and 'monotone', passionless and cold as his English origins would stereotypically suggest. In fact, we learn later that he has led a complex and tormented life, is emotionally old before his time, indeed 'flétri', exists in a permanent state of internal turmoil and self-contradiction, cares nothing for public opinion, and is, without exception, the most obsessively passionate character in the book, as well as the one with the greatest capacity to vary his appearance and social role. One is tempted to say that the portrait is designed to deceive. But the most extreme example of deception occurs halfway through the book, when Indiana is telling Raymon about Ralph's life, and how he approached her husband to ask for permission to come and live with them.

> 'Monsieur, lui dit-il, j'aime votre femme; c'est moi qui l'ai élevée; je la regarde comme ma sœur, et plus encore comme ma fille. C'est la seule parente qui me reste et la seule affection que j'aie. Trouvez bon que je me fixe auprès de vous et que nous passions tous trois notre vie ensemble. [. . .] Quand je vous aurai donné ma parole que je n'eus jamais d'amour pour elle et que je n'en aurai jamais, vous pourrez me voir avec aussi peu d'inquiétude que si j'étais réellement votre beau-frère. N'est-il pas vrai, monsieur?'[12]

This is quite simply a lie, as we discover at the end of the novel. He had always loved her. But the curious fact is not that a character should lie; after all, Raymon lies often enough. It is that, throughout, the narrator presents Ralph as a paragon of probity; and yet this lie is allowed to pass without comment. Obviously, the narrator simply does not want to tell us the truth either about Ralph's emotions, or about his character,

which, given his ability first to tell and then to sustain this lie, must be much more complex than is ever suggested. Why not? There is one obvious answer: to maintain suspense and tension in the book. We slowly discover, one step ahead of Indiana all the way, that Ralph is not what he seems, and that despite appearances he is destined to be her soul-mate, for 'c'était lui qu'il aurait fallu aimer'.[13] But if one accepts my suggestion that the narrator is merely a front for Ralph, another reason, more essential, emerges.

However honest Ralph may be in other ways, he is in most circumstances constitutionally incapable of telling the truth about himself. Particularly, he can never engage in meaningful dialogue. In all the conversations he has, he turns out to have been playing a role which betrays his true nature. That nature can only emerge in narrative monologue. Furthermore, that monologue cannot be internal; Ralph needs a sympathetic and admiring ear. His first such monologue comes at the end of part IV, when he tells his story to Indiana. His second is the tale he tells to the narrator in the conclusion, and which, I have been suggesting, serves as the basis for the whole novel. Why should Ralph thus refuse both dialogue and self-analysis in the abstract? Naturally, it is partly because his circumstances make it impossible for him to tell the truth without causing scandal. But a broader consideration of the refusal of dialogue and of self-analysis in Sand's work suggests a more organic explanation. There is a whole class of characters in her novels who are apparently unable or unwilling to discuss their thoughts and feelings with others. These characters are necessarily, in one sense, not central; they cannot have the main speaking part in the book, for they speak little. However, they exert a certain fascination on those around them. They often inspire passionate attachments, sometimes temporary, sometimes permanent; above all, they have a curious ability to appear somehow more authentic, more real, than those who readily express themselves. They tend thus to become the centre of gravity of the work. I have in mind, for example, Marie in *La Mare au diable*, or la petite Fadette; Edmée, in *Mauprat*; Félicie, in *Le Dernier Amour*; Jeanne, in *Jeanne*; Boisguilbault, in *Le Péche de Monsieur Antoine*. There is a parallel to be drawn, though I have not the space to do it here, between their mutism, and that which Sand so frequently attributes to herself, not least in *Histoire de ma vie*. Mutism, loss of voice, frequently equates with loss or lack of social power, as Isabelle Hoog Naginski shows.[14] But it also signifies hidden depths; and it is an unquestioned tenet of Romantic fiction that a character with hidden depths is more interesting than a character who is clearly explained. Ralph, in *Indiana,* alone has these depths; his is the only character that one cannot appreciate without not only re-reading, but also careful reconstruction. In that sense, reading *Indiana* means discovering Ralph. The other characters appear simple, because that is how Ralph sees them. He does not, however, see himself as simple. Like most people, he is able to pigeon-hole others, but he can only conceive of himself through narrative, through the story of how he became what he is; static portraits always seem betrayals to the sitter. It is, then, because Ralph is the hidden narrator that he appears qualitatively different from the other characters. *Indiana* is indeed Ralph's story—not only the tale he tells, but also the narrative that constitutes him. And that is the reason for what one might call the inversion of the frame in the novel. Why is it only at the end that we discover who told the story? and why is Ralph in the third person, not the first? Because the novel traces his acquisition of a voice. At the beginning, he has none; he is unable even to think thoughts worthy of expression. It is only when he becomes able to live (or die) according to his ideals that he acquires the capacity to establish his personality in language, by speaking himself through narrative. Central to those ideals, as to that narrative, is a certain status relative to woman: Ralph needs a 'femme faible' to love and protect, he needs to save a woman from the world. Indiana gives him the opportunity to do so. It is her submission to him that gives him a history and therefore a voice; before that, he had been divorced from his own first person.

Notes

1. In *George Sand and Idealism* (New York, Columbia University Press, 1993). Kristina Wingård Vareille analyses similarly the 'rupture franche avec le code "réaliste" que constitue la fin'; see her *Socialité, sexualité et les impasses de l'histoire: L'évolution de la thématique sandienne d'"Indiana" à 'Mauprat'* (Uppsala, Acta Universitatis Upsaliensis, 1987), p. 61.

2. As many critics have pointed out; see, for example, Robert Godwin-Jones, *Romantic Vision: The Novels of George Sand* (Birmingham, AL, Summa Publications, 1995), p. 15.

3. George Sand, *Indiana* ed. Béatrice Didier, Folio (Paris, Gallimard, 1984), p. 339. All references will be to this edition.

4. In *Family Romances* (Bloomington, Indiana University Press, 1987), p. 62.

5. See R. Godwin-Jones, op. cit., p. 303, n. 15. I am grateful to Nigel Harkness for bringing the critical debate on this matter to my attention.

6. *Indiana*, p. 174.

7. Ibid., p. 279.

8. Ibid., pp. 251-52.

9. Ibid., p. 89.

10. See, for example, R. Godwin-Jones, op. cit., p. 24; I. Hoog Naginski, *George Sand: Writing for her Life* (New Brunswick, Rutgers University Press, 1991), p. 73; K. Wingård Vareille, op. cit., pp. 54-55; K. Crecelius, op. cit., p. 72.

11. *Indiana*, p. 250.

12. Ibid., p. 159.

13. Ibid., p. 330.

14. Op. cit., pp. 218-20. Although Naginski does not go so far as to see Ralph as the source of the narrative perspective, her analysis of the novel as a narrative of the acquisition of speech does lead her to view Ralph as in many ways its emblematic character, 'la grande figure du livre' (p. 76).

FRANÇOISE MASSARDIER-KENNEY (ESSAY DATE 2000)

SOURCE: Massardier-Kenney, Françoise. "Victimization in *Indiana* and *Jacques.*" In *Gender in the Fiction of George Sand*, pp. 15-52. Amsterdam, Netherlands: Rodopi, 2000.

In the following excerpt, Massardier-Kenney explores Sand's presentation and treatment of female protagonists in her fiction, particularly the novel Indiana.

George Sand's life-long investigation of the meaning of "woman" and her questioning of the hierarchical binary oppositions between men and women is evident in her first novel, the famous *Indiana* (1832) and the lesser known fine epistolary novel *Jacques* (1834). In these two works, Sand began to lay bare the cultural mechanisms responsible for gender inequalities and began a pattern of using ambiguous protagonists in order to bring attention to the incoherence of established gender positions. Sand's first novel (1832) attracted considerable attention when it was first published and is one of the few among her works to be systematically discussed by contemporary critics. In 1832, critics focused on its realism and compared it to the work of Stendhal, while recent critics have perceived it as Sand's attempt to find a literary voice separate from realism (i.e., something called "idealism"). As Sandy Petrey has demonstrated in his analysis of the critical reception of 1832, *Indiana*'s appeal at the time was a "realist" appeal whereby the novel shows that life is formed by forces that vary with time and place, and it is also the reason for its appeal now: gender is one of the "components of human existence that vary with time, place and customs" (134); and gender is interrelated with genre.[1]

However, beyond the continuity of its appeal, *Indiana* continues to give rise to opposite interpretations of what Sand's novel says about gender matters and what character is used to represent Sand's position. In *Working for Her Life*, Isabelle Naginski has argued that the novel registers Sand's new found literary voice, which is embodied by the character of Ralph[2]; whereas Marilyn Lukacher reads *Indiana* as the impossible attempt to choose between two mother figures: Sand's aristocratic grandmother and her plebeian mother and sees a parallel, not between Sand and Ralph, but between Sand and Raymon[3]. Some critics see the end of the novel where Ralph and Indiana escape to the idyllic setting of Bernica, as a flaw in a realist text[4] while others attempt to justify the ending as befitting an idealist and/or a feminist text. For instance, in his justification of the end, Nigel Harkness rereads *Indiana* as proposing an essentialist view and the end as claiming a feminist silence[5], while Petrey demonstrates that the novel is based on a constructivist notion of gender. Last, some, like Leslie Rabine, argue that Sand represents woman as passive and chaste (i.e., as reproducing a conservative nineteenth-century ideology) while others, like Kathryn Crecelius, point out that Sand shows how "religious, social, and political systems combine to oppress women" (73)[6]. Kristina Wingard Vareille also stresses the importance of Sand's critique of marriage and of the condition of women in *Indiana* but also points out that this critique is not limited to women since Sand shows that men almost as much as women are victimized by traditional marriage.[7]

These varied and sometimes contradictory interpretations stem from the novel's own contradictions and from a number of narrative shifts that prevent critical attempts to interpret it as a coherent narrative because precisely the novel's theme is the incoherence of gender positions. In *Indiana* Sand is analyzing and bringing to the surface mechanisms of victimization based on gender, race, and class and is questioning the stability of gender boundaries that buttress power inequalities through a systematic undermining of narrative authority and consistency. Although the final episode of the plot is usually the place where the disruption of the "idealist" is perceived, Sand has undermined the coherence of her own narrative well before the end through the manipulation of the omniscient narrator and through contradictory presentations of characters.

Although interpretations of *Indiana* vary greatly, there seems to be a critical consensus about the fact that the final episode of *Indiana* is

FROM THE AUTHOR

ON THE COMPOSITION OF *INDIANA*

I do not think that I have ever written anything under the influence of a selfish passion; I have never even thought of avoiding it. They who have read me without prejudice understand that I wrote *Indiana* with a feeling, not deliberately reasoned out, to be sure, but a deep and genuine feeling that the laws which still govern woman's existence in wedlock, in the family and in society are unjust and barbarous. I had not to write a treatise on jurisprudence but to fight against public opinion; for it is that which postpones or advances social reforms. The war will be long and bitter; but I am neither the first nor the last nor the only champion of so noble a cause, and I will defend it so long as the breath of life remains in my body.

Sand, George. From the preface to the 1842 edition of *Indiana*. Translated by George Burnham Ives. Philadelphia: George Barie & Son, 1900.

an idealist happy ending. Whether critics approve of it or criticize it for its switch in mode, they consider what happens after the scene where Ralph and Indiana leap to their death a positive outcome: the protagonists don't die and live together happily ever after. However, their lives on a secluded plantation where they employ old or weak former slaves that they have freed may seem an "idealist" or "happy" solution only if readers identify with the patriarchal omniscient narrator. For this final episode obliterates the character of Indiana who becomes passive and silent[8]. The narrative is made by the male narrator for a male friend as recounted by Ralph the male protagonist who thus becomes the hero of the novel.

Indiana's transformation from a rebellious and articulate victim[9] into a sweet and languid character [according to the narrator, her eyes have a "douceur incomparable / unique sweetness" (337) and her manners have "quelque chose de lent et de triste qui est naturel aux créoles / something slow and sad that comes naturally to creole women" (337)] starts with the suicide scene where

Ralph not only takes over discourse and recounts his long hidden passion for her but also directs all their actions ["il prit sa fiancée dans ses bras et l'emporta pour la précipiter avec lui dans le torrent / he took his fiancée in his arms and led her away to hurl her with him in the torrent" (330)]. The following "idyllic" episode repeats this pattern whereby Ralph controls discourse and action. When the narrator alludes to gossip concerning them among the colonists, Ralph silences him, and once Indiana is out of earshot, he accepts to tell his story "je vous dirai mon histoire, mais pas devant Indiana. Il est des blessures qu'il ne faut pas réveiller / I shall tell you my story, but not in front of Indiana. There are wounds that should not be reopened." (338) [note that he refers to it as *his* story, not hers], repeating a pattern of silence and withdrawal of information justified by the mistaken goal of protecting weak women. All of a sudden, Indiana's story has become Ralph's story and the novel ends with a dramatic shift away from the mechanisms of victimization of women to the emergence of the male Romantic hero.

While Ralph's own victimization and opposition to patriarchal structures may explain some critics' acceptance of his Romantic positioning as representing the voice of the author, his participation in those very patriarchal power structures and his final effective silencing of Indiana should warn the readers that identifying the author's position may be more difficult than the surface narrative would lead us to expect.

Ralph's surprising and seductive transformation into a passionate, articulate opponent of the debased values of Restoration society, and his endorsement by the omniscient narrator trap the readers into glossing over Indiana's erasure and, more importantly, into ignoring Sand's careful construction of Ralph as a character who participates in the victimization of women even though he is himself the victim of patriarchal law and even though, as Doris Kadish has noticed, he has been "symbolically emasculated and feminized through analogy with women, slaves, and members of oppressed groups" (27).

Sand's association of Ralph with some feminized traits, however, must be seen as part of her attempt to show that the unequal status of the two "sexes" is not based on any natural division but is a complex set of gender positions occupied by men and women who have different amounts of control over their lives. To see that Ralph is silent and submissive (i.e., positioned as a woman) does not mean that he represents the voice of the author. An examination of Ralph's history and personality reveals both his victimization and the extent of his participation in the structures that disenfranchise most women. Thus Sand's construction of Ralph is paradoxical.

Sand uses the omniscient narrator to present Ralph in a deceiving and ultimately inconsistent way. As Crecelius has noted, the presentation of Ralph gives rise to "certain inconsistencies" (77) because he is presented from the point of view of Indiana rather than in an objective way, as Sand's use of an omniscient narrator would lead the readers to expect. I would argue that the entire presentation of Ralph is suspect. The details describing Ralph given at the beginning of the novel consistently undermine the portrait made later. The Ralph of the beginning of the novel is characterized by the omniscient narrator as a well fed, dull character, an "homme dormeur et bien mangeant" (51). His features are "régulièrement fades / regularly dull" (51), his portrait in Indiana's room is insignificant and "only the original is more insignificant than the portrait" (108); still according to the narrator Indiana's and Ralph's personalities are totally incompatible (51). Moreover, Ralph is presented as a friend of Delmare, Indiana's tyrannical husband. Ralph also despises women as the narrator's description of his innermost thoughts indicate. When Ralph expresses his distrust of rhetoric as opposed to ideas (in the idealist belief, one assumes, that ideas can be evaluated separately from the language in which they are articulated), he blames women especially for paying more attention to form than to content, and for being highly susceptible to flattery. Indiana's reaction to his remarks "vous avez un profond dédain pour les femmes / you have a great disdain for women" (58) correctly interprets his comments as expressing his belief in the inferiority of women.

When Noun, Indiana's servant becomes agitated upon hearing that Delmare is out with a gun and risks wounding her secret lover Raymon de Ramière, and when Indiana also shows concern, the narrator makes us privy to Ralph's thoughts "Ces deux femmes sont folles, pensa Sir Ralph. D'ailleurs ajouta-t-il en lui-même, toutes les femmes le sont / these two women are crazy, thought Sir Ralph. Anyway, he thought on to himself, all women are" (61). He adds later "Quelles misérables terreurs de femmes / what miserable women terrors" (62). This is the same Ralph who at the end of the novel is presented as Indiana's ideal lover and interpreted as Sand's voice.

Furthermore, the theme of women's ignorance and specifically of Indiana's ignorance is linked throughout the novel to Ralph's conception of women as intellectually deficient. When, near the end of the novel, Ralph finally tells Indiana of his passion for her and recounts his role in her life: "Je fis de vous ma soeur, ma fille, ma compagne, mon élève, ma société / I made you my sister, my daughter, my companion, my student, my community" (316), the reader may be seduced by his passionate language (his "rhetoric") and forget that it is Ralph's upbringing that has made Indiana into an ignorant person whose subsequent intellectual weakness confirms his patriarchal belief about women's innate inferiority. As the omniscient narrator had reminded the reader, Indiana had been brought up by Ralph "qui avait une médiocre opinion de l'intelligence et du raisonnement chez les femmes . . . Elle savait donc à peine l'histoire agrégée du monde et toute discussion sérieuse l'accablait d'ennui / who had a poor opinion of women's intelligence and capacity for reasoning . . . Thus she hardly knew any world history and any serious discussion bored her to tears" (174). This reminder by the narrator about Ralph's responsibility in Indiana's lack of intellectual maturity not only contradicts the same narrator's later endorsement of Ralph but is part of the novel's insistence on the role of men's prejudice in propagating women's ignorance and then blaming them for it. Sand ties the question of women's ignorance to the mechanisms of victimization through which knowledge is withheld from disenfranchised groups, be they women, servants or slaves. Because of her class, Indiana has at least learned to read and write as her letters to Raymon indicate. However, such is not the case for her servant and friend Noun; she makes a number of spelling errors in her letter to the same Raymon, who, upon receiving her letter, decides to leave her as such lack of control of French grammar clearly marks Noun's social inferiority and reminds him of the impossibility of continuing his affair with her.

The withholding of knowledge and of information because of the male characters' belief in the inability of women to understand the information is not the sole prerogative of Ralph; it characterizes all the male characters who have some power but it indicates that Ralph participates in the reproduction of patriarchal structures that are inimical to women. Besides his denial of education to Indiana, who is his sole love and anchor, Ralph also withholds from her crucial information about Noun and Raymon. In agreement with Delmare, Ralph keeps silent about the fact that Indiana's friend and maid is having a secret affair with Raymon, and thus further isolates Noun and allows Indiana to fall prey to Raymon's schemes. Similarly, at the end of the novel, he prevents the narrator from repeating what he has heard in order to protect Indiana as if she were a child. Ralph's role in denying women access to knowledge is incompatible with interpreting him as an ideal androgynous character. On the contrary it suggests that weak and silent characters may participate in their own victimization, as we shall see with Indiana' and Noun's attitudes toward their lover.

Even the facts of Ralph's early life as recounted by Indiana suggest Ralph's acquiescence and implication in the victimization of women. Significantly, it is Indiana who tells Ralph's story, in contrast to the end of the novel where Ralph is in control of the narrative. Indiana recounts to Raymon Ralph's first unhappy years during which he is rejected by his parents who prefer his less shy and more demonstrative older brother. Ralph is so depressed by his life that he is on the verge of committing suicide by drowning in the ocean[10] when he sees his young cousin Indiana (then five years old) who runs to him and hugs him. He decides to live for her and to take care of her (158). Ralph is thus saved from despair by the love of a child. As an adolescent he takes care of the orphaned Indiana, but after his own brother's death, he is forced to marry his brother's fiancee for unspecified family reasons (the reader assumes it is a financial arrangement between the two families). Ralph leaves for England with his wife who loved his brother and abhors him; has a son, and returns to the island of Bourbon after the death of his wife and son. Raymon, to whom Indiana is recounting this story, astutely wonders why Ralph didn't marry Indiana and she invokes her lack of wealth as a reason. The narrative of Ralph's life emphasizes the necessity of having a child-like woman for the melancholy hero to survive, but also Ralph's own victimization. The novel represents the patriarchal pattern of victimization which includes women, slaves, and men who don't occupy a position of power. Ralph is the second son, rejected by his parents and forced to marry for social and financial reasons while Indiana is also ignored by her relatives and married off to a much older man. In both cases families have broken down and have lost their protective vocation. Family structure is presented as the occasion to consolidate power positions. The pervasive corruption of the traditional family in which fathers no longer protect and mothers no longer nurture indicate Sand's conviction that the oppression of the weak—children, women, men, slaves—is endemic to the Restoration society she represents and that, by the logic of their own participation in such family structures, her characters can turn oppressors too.

By agreeing to marry his dead brother's betrothed, even though he knows of her love for his brother, Ralph puts himself in the position of a Delmare. Moreover, since Ralph had a son with this woman, whereas the question of Delmare's actually consummating his marriage with Indiana is left ambiguous, the reader must assume that Ralph forced himself on his wife to produce an heir or at least that he consumed his union knowing of her repulsion. Ralph's consent to marry is explained by his unwillingness to be disowned by his father (by which one assumes he will be disinherited since he has already been rejected emotionally by his parents).

Thus his allegiance to patriarchal values and his participation in oppressive practices, and his long lasting contempt for women must not be forgotten even in the context of his being later presented as the prototypical melancholy and isolated Romantic hero of the "idyllic" end of the novel. Ironically, Ralph is the character who had claimed the superiority of actions and ideas over words, but who is absolved because of his final control of the narrative. The complexity of Ralph's role, the mix of victim and victimizer allows Sand to show the difficulty of escaping oppression as long as human beings accept binary systems of opposition whereby one category is posed as inferior to the other (women to men, slaves to masters). By luring the reader into accepting Ralph as the "idealist" solution to Indiana's fate, by carefully constructing him as the Romantic figure who finally comes to speech, Sand problematizes any notion of liberation that is not accompanied by a radical rethinking of gender and social categories. Ralph loves and saves Indiana but his adherence to paternalistic views of women condemns him to play the role of a traditional husband, one surely more palatable than the old, tyrannical Delmare, but still one which spells the end of Indiana's psychological and moral autonomy.[11]

This interiorization of patriarchal values by characters who articulate their opposition to the political or social aspects of these structures is shared by women characters as well, an idea to which Sand will return on several occasions and even more pointedly in later novels and which explains in part her reluctance to accept the category "women" as a rallying point because this very notion of woman often stands, as she demonstrates, for definitions of women articulated by and for the benefit of patriarchal subjects.

Women characters in **Indiana** follow Ralph's pattern of rebellion against the patriarchy while internalizing its norm or simply accepting and reproducing these structures if their position on the power scale allows it. Sand uses a range of women to show their implication in these oppressive practices: from a wealthy aristocrat (Laure de Nagy) to a servant who is possibly a former slave (Noun).

At one end of the power spectrum, Laure de Nagy who marries Raymon because he has the right pedigree and she can control him, occupies the position of "male" power. As Petrey has noticed, "the power granted Laure by historical changes affects nothing less than the obliteration of male hegemony" (141), but it is not so much male hegemony that is obliterated as the demonstration that gender performance has replaced notions of natural biological sexual differences to found inequalities. Laure de Nagy performs as a male. The obliteration of the power of the individual male leaves the structure intact. The character of Laure occupies a "masculine" position and thus further demonstrates the constructedness of notions of masculinity and femininity. Her social and economic position (an orphan from an old noble family who has been adopted by a rich industrialist), gives her the power to assess the desirability of potential male partners and to decide whom she will marry. Even before she becomes a major character, Sand introduces her as one of the spectators and commentators at the ball where Raymon recognizes Indiana and starts flirting with her. While Indiana innocently falls for Raymon's attentions, Laura watches him and invites gossip and information about him in a scene that inverts gender roles by placing her as the subject gazing. Laura's biological sexual identity is compensated by her social position; her gender role is that of male domination in contrast to Indiana's lower position and victimization, and later adoption of female submission. By providing these opposite examples of feminine performance, a tactic she will use as well in the novels discussed in subsequent chapters, Sand suggests that masculinity and femininity are positions that are linked to social and economic power more than to "nature" and that they could be negotiated. Sand shows that these gender inequalities are enforced through external pressures and through internal mechanisms (when individuals internalize imposed definitions and come to consider them natural, i.e., women can't think, women are weak, women are natural mothers, etc).

Whereas Laure de Nagy's mental attitude is one of extreme power, Indiana's and Noun's reflect their inferior status and their ultimate acceptance of their inferiority. The orphan Indiana, daughter of an impoverished noble family was given to a much older man (she is sixteen and he is sixty), ex-soldier turned business man whose money endeared him to her relatives, whereas Noun is a servant who follows Indiana wherever she moves. Although we are given no details (we don't know whether Noun's mother was a slave or free, or even whether Noun is black), her position as a domestic is clear and provides a more pronounced version of Indiana's own situation of servitude.

What is less evident is the importance of servitude in shaping these characters' own attitudes. Indiana may denounce the inequity of the laws that allow her husband's domination but when she leaves Bourbon to join Raymon, she can only speak in terms of abjection and servitude "c'est ton esclave que tu as rappelée de l'exil / here is your slave that you called back from exile" (296), and "Je viens pour te donner du bonheur, pour être ce que tu voudras, ta compagne, ta servante ou ta maîtresse / I come to give you some happiness, to be what you want, your companion, your servant or your mistress" (296), "je suis ton bien, tu es mon maître / I am your thing, you are my master" (297). Indiana's discourse, which is steeped in the vocabulary of slavery and which is a part of a pattern where relationships between men and women are described with a vocabulary of enslavement and subjection, reveals Sand's understanding of the mechanisms of subjection: the long-lasting subjection and state of ignorance in which women have been forced to live have resulted in their acceptance and internalization of the hierarchical structures that created their bondage; as a result, even when these structures of coercion are removed (i.e., when Indiana escapes from her husband), the women characters retain a mental frame that conceptualizes "love" as bondage or as a relation of inequality.

When Noun attempts to regain Raymon's favors after she finds out that she is pregnant, she rejects his offers of financial support and uses the same metaphors that Indiana would later use. She even proposes to Raymon to work as his servant (as she is already his mistress, it is the only position that she can envision). She tells him "Je ne suis pas exigeante; je n'ambitionne point ce qu'une autre à ma place aurait peut-être eu l'art d'obtenir. Mais permettez-moi d'être votre servante / I am not demanding; I don't hope for what another woman in my place would have been artful enough to obtain. But allow me to be your servant." (110). So while Noun feels insulted by Raymon's offer of money (an offer which clearly means the end of their relationship), she is ready to surrender her whole being in order to be next to him. Isabelle Naginski has remarked that Noun is almost without speech (64) but actually it is the force of her eloquence that convinces Raymon not to break up as he intended. The narrator's comment on her appeal "Noun parla longtemps ainsi. Elle ne se servit peut-être pas des mêmes mots, mais elle dit les mêmes choses, bien mieux, cent fois que je ne pourrais les redire / Noun spoke thus for a long time. She perhaps did not use exactly the same words, but she said the same things, much better, a hundred times better than I could repeat them" (102). Noun may use the language of female subjection as Naginski and others have argued, but it is an extremely articulate language that describes accurately that state of mental bondage that characterizes women who don't benefit from a social position that can counterbalance gender positions. Indiana's and Noun's statements both articulate their acceptance that what they are is defined by what the male other wants. Indiana's "Je serai ce que tu voudras / I will be what you want" (296) echoes Noun's "Je me hais puisque je ne vous plais plus / I hate myself since I no longer please you" (102). The grammatical slip of the "what" instead of a "who" indicates the extent of Indiana's vision of herself as an object rather than as a subject, even in a situation which is the result of her will and of remarkable determination and courage.

In *Indiana,* love is thus presented as another locus for women's oppression. Not surprisingly Laure de Nagy, the only powerful woman in the novel, rejects the idea of "love" because she knows that, paradoxically, her wealth will make it impossible for her to disentangle genuine affection from ambition or greed. The ignorant and powerless Indiana and Noun who embrace romantic notions of love are destroyed by their acceptance of love as a relation that disempowers them. Whether this love includes a sexual relation or not, it is a negative experience[12]. The sexual relation just increases the chance that the woman will be victimized more quickly, as happens with Noun or with the other women that Raymon has discredited. Sexuality, like romantic love and marriage, has no positive ideological function in *Indiana.* The new order proposed at the end of the novel is very problematic as the previous analysis of its implication has shown. Although Kristina Wingard argues that Sand discretely suggests that Ralph and Indiana consummate their union[13] and that Indiana can finally accept her sexuality without danger or suffering, the final episode is curiously ambiguous about their status as a couple. This ambiguity reflects Sand's own ambiguity about the limits of the figure of Ralph as a solution. Her heroes are cut off from the external social structures of the world but they have interiorized gender roles. Thus the question of sexuality is erased[14]. Criticism of Sand for representing Indiana as a chaste *bourgeoise* fails to notice that Sand presents all the scenarios possible for a woman: marriage with sex (Laure de Nagy), love and sex (Noun), love without sex (Indiana), and that none of these scenarios can be fulfilling because of the power structure[15].

Sand's commitment to providing her readers with a constructivist conception of gender is such that the novel presents an unusual number of women who either are not mothers (thus whose lives as women contradicts traditional conceptions of "femininity" that rely on maternity as its linchpin or who as mothers or mother figures function as agents of reproduction of the social order. Sand's deconstruction of stable gender categories includes a reexamination of the roles of mothers in the reproduction of patriarchy and femininity.

First of all maternity and the ability to procreate among women of child bearing age is associated with death. Ralph's wife and his young son are dead by the beginning of the novel and, of course, Noun commits suicide while pregnant because her lover Raymon no longer wishes to carry on their affair. The other protagonists who are young women and who survive—Indiana and Laure de Nagy—are both childless and their own mothers are dead, an interesting coincidence if one recalls Sand's discussion of gender differences in which she mentions maternity as the only difference separating the sexes.

The older women who are actual mothers (for instance, Raymon's mother) or who are mother substitutes (Mme de Carvajal, Indiana's aunt) are both aristocrats who are presented as opportunistic survivors of political and social upheavals or as educating their male offsprings to be victimizers. Mme de Carjaval, who has ignored her niece, starts to show her much affection when she realizes that Delmare has become a successful businessman ("Madame de Carvajal aux yeux de qui la fortune était la première recommandation, témoigna beaucoup d'affection à sa nièce et lui promit le reste de son héritage / Madame de Carvajal who considered wealth of foremost importance, showed her niece much affection and promised her the rest of her inheritance" (86). The details of her life provided by the narrator draw the portrait of an opportunist for whom fortune and appearances are foremost: a widowed Spanish aristocrat who was an admirer of Napoleon, she has made a fortune speculating on the stock market and, according to the narrator "A force d'esprit, d'intrigues et de dévotion elle avait obtenu, en outre, les faveurs de la cour / Through her wit, schemes, and devotion she had moreover obtained the favors of the court" (85). Mme de Carjaval uses her pretty niece Indiana to attract young fashionable men to her salon. She sees no objection to her niece's involvement with Raymon but is ready to disown her when gossip about their alleged affair threatens to break out and sully her reputation as a pious older woman. Sand's biting portrait of Mme de Carjaval as a crafty maneuverer who adopts the current ideologies (religiousness and the monarchy) and who gains power and money shows how little room there is to nurture and protect younger women like Indiana. These characters represent such disparate human types (one powerful, savvy, and independent; the other powerless, naive, and ignorant) that the fact that they are both women becomes irrelevant and cannot lead to any allegiance based on their sex.

In fact, Sand's presentation of women protagonists who belong to an older generation suggests that what these older women nurture is the reproduction of the very patriarchal structures that allow younger women without power to be bartered and exploited. An analysis of the presentation of Raymon's mother also shows the care with which Sand constructed her not as the positive character which most critics have seen, but as a very ambiguous, misguided, not to say negative, figure[16]. Sand's portrait of Raymon's mother as a good mother is ironic since that characteristic is always invoked in the context of his mistreatment of women. When the narrator describes Raymon's desertion of the pregnant Noun, he links his action to a class prejudice "Pour lui, une grisette n'était pas une femme / for him a *grisette* was not a woman" (75), which the narrator exonerates by commenting "Tout cela n'était pas la faute de Raymon; on [read his mother since his father has been long dead] l'avait élevé pour le monde / All this was not Raymon's fault; he had been brought up for fashionable society" (75). His mother is held responsible for his considering lower class women sub-human and not warranting the treatment reserved to "women," that is women of one's class who can provide social and financial alliances.

Thus in **Indiana** . . . being a woman has a host of different meanings depending on the class to which an individual woman belongs. The higher the class, the more power she has and the less she shares with other women. The disparity of interests between younger poorer women and older aristocratic women is emphasized by Raymon's reactions to Noun after he attempts to break off with her. The omniscient narrator explains Raymon's eagerness to get rid of Noun by invoking his mother "Il en coûtait à Raymon de tromper une si bonne mère / It was difficult for Raymon to deceive such a good mother" (76).

Raymon's mother is thus directly linked to his treatment of Noun. The narrator follows with an ironically positive portrait of Raymon's mother as a woman with intellectual and moral qualities who has given him "ces excellents principes qui le ramenaient toujours au bien / those excellent principles that always brought him back to good" (78). Since the reader was just told how Raymon avoids responsibility [that would be the "bien" to which he returns] by invoking the need to spare his mother, the principles that his mother has taught him are reduced to simple narcissism[17]. Sand thus uses the omniscient narrator to say one thing but to mean another. The positive portrait of Raymon's mother seems to be used to excuse the behavior of the son but actually serves to implicate his mother in his corruption.

The ambiguity of the role of Raymon's mother is further developed through the narrator's comments alluding to the vicissitudes of her life. She is a woman who went through "des époques si différentes que leur esprit a pris toute la souplesse de leur destinée / such different times that their mind has adopted the suppleness of their destiny" (78). While the narrator presents this information positively, it parallels his other comments about Mme de Carjaval's ability to adapt to different moral codes, an ability, as we have seen, which is a sign of corruption. After Noun's suicide, the narrator explains that Raymon feels remorse and thinks of blowing his brains out but "un sentiment louable l'arrêta. Que deviendrait-sa mère . . . sa mère âgée, débile / a worthy feeling stopped him. What would become of his mother,

so old and weak?" (127). Again his mother is the excuse for his failure to act.

The role of Raymon's mother as the explanation and justification for his narcissistic behavior is linked not only to Noun's fate but also to Indiana's. After Noun's suicide, Indiana refuses to see Raymon, but her husband imposes Raymon's visit on her because he has been charmed by Raymon's mother (122). Raymon in turn uses his mother to come visit Indiana who is seduced by her charm "qu'un esprit supérieur joint à une âme noble et généreuse, sait répandre dans ses moindres relations / that a superior mind linked to a noble and generous soul can infuse in all her relationships" 140. Indiana's "fascination de coeur" with Madame de Ramière is linked to her not having known her own mother (141).

The complexity of Raymon's mother's role is further demonstrated in the episode in which Indiana compromises herself by coming to see him late at night and he attempts to make her leave by asking his mother to help. Mme de Ramière acts very generously toward Indiana but as the narrator's analysis makes clear, she has created Raymon's selfishness and self-indulgence: "Le caractère de ce fils impétueux et froid, raisonneur et passionné était une conséquense de son inépuisable amour et de sa tendresse généreuse pour lui . . . mais elle l'avait habitué à profiter de tous les sacrifices qu'elle consentait à lui faire . . . A force de générosité, elle n'avait réussi qu'à former un coeur égoïste / The character of this impetuous and cold, reasoning and passionate son was a consequence of her unending love and her generous affection . . . but she had accustomed him to profit from all the sacrifices she was willing to make for him . . . By dint of generosity, she had only succeeded in shaping a selfish heart" (223). This analysis presents Raymon's narcissism, not as a natural "male" trait, but as the product of his mother's indulgence, that is as the product of specific cultural practices that reproduce hierarchies. Loving a son means encouraging narcissistic behavior and victimizing women. Ironically, mothers, as Sand presents them in **Indiana,** are the social agents through which gender inequalities are passed on to the next generation. . . .

Notes

1. See Sandy Petrey "George and Georgina: Realist Gender in *Indiana*. Pp. 133-47 in *Textuality and Sexuality: Reading Theories and Practices*. Eds. Judith Still and Michael Worton. Manchester: Manchester University Press, 1993.

2. She states "the story of Ralph recapitulates the writer's progress from initial uncertainty and hesitation to ultimate assurance and eloquence" (56).

3. Lukacher specifically argues that Raymon figures Sand herself "before the impasse of the double feminine identification" (77). Marilyn Lukacher, *Maternal Fictions*. Durham: Duke University Press, 1994.

4. This seems to be the view of the French editors of *Indiana*. See for instance the introduction of Pierre Salomon, ed. *Indiana*. Paris: Garnier, 1962; and Béatrice Didier, ed. *Indiana*. Paris: Gallimard (Folio): 1984.

5. See Nigel Harkness, "Writing under the Sign of Difference: The Conclusion of *Indiana*" *Forum for Modern Language Studies* 33.2 (1997): 115-128.

6. See Kathryn Crecelius, *Family Romances*. Bloomington: Indiana University Press, 1987. Like Harkness, Crecelius also believes that Sand posits a difference between men's and women's language (73).

7. Vareille focuses on the character of Delmare to show that, for Sand, the victims of mariage are men as well as women since they are also frozen in a social role over which they have no control See Kristina Wingard Vareille, *Socialité, sexualité et les impasses de l'histoire: l'évolution de la thématique sandienne d'Indiana (1832) à Mauprat (1837)*, 32-34.

8. I have showed elsewhere that Sand has constructed Indiana as a very strong character both morally and physically. See Françoise Massardier-Kenney, "*Indiana*: Lieux et personnages féminins" *Nineteenth-Century French Studies* (1990): 65-71. Vareille has also showed that while Indiana is presented as a "faible femme" who faints, cries, is emotional, she is also very strong morally: she attends to wounded men, she stands up to her husband, etc. As she will do later in *Jeanne*, Sand redefines traditional notions of physical and moral strength. It should be noted as well that the very characteristics that mark her as a "femme faible" (crying, fainting, etc) are also typical of the male characters: all three male characters cry at one point or another. Raymon faints when the body of Noun is discovered and Ralph almost swoons when he thinks Indiana died from a horse accident.

9. Although Indiana is clearly presented as the victim of patriarchal institutions and although the narrative is controlled by a male voice, it is her voice whether in direct discourse or through letters that is the most present. Even the prolix Raymon is not given more space in letters or actual speech than is Indiana.

10. While a number of critics have noted the link that Sand establishes between water and women, I maintain that they miss a number of occurrences when water is associated with men as well. Noun does commit suicide in the river and, after wandering in Paris, Indiana, almost drowns in the Seine, but there are as many incidents linked to water that are associated by male characters: for instance, Ralph's early suicide thoughts, Raymon's near fall in the very river where Noun drowned, and of course, Ralph's later planned leap in the waterfalls of the Bernica. As I have showed in "*Indiana*: Lieux et personnages féminins," Ophelia is not a figure for women; it is the name of Indiana's dog and it is the dog that dies from drowning, not Indiana. When Indiana escapes her husband to sail back to France, the dog follows the boat and is killed by coarse sailors. It should not surprise us that Sand refrain from associating women with water, since it would be an essentialist gesture.

11. Sand's contradictory portrait of Ralph as a positive Romantic figure who opposes conservative social and political practices but whose own gender ideology is ultimately patriarchal will find a development in *Jacques* (1834), where she will explore the very possibility of the contradictions expressed by the Ralph figure.

12. Vareille Wingard notes the negativeness of sexuality for women: "for women, sexuality can only be a trap, a threat, an aggressive and destructive domination exerted by the male" (43), but she does not extend her remarks to romantic love in general which is also a domination exerted by the male in that it destroys the female's subjectivity.

13. Her evidence is mostly based on the fact that the word "virginal" is no longer used in the utopic episode (footnote 61, p. 63) and that Indiana dresses as a bride in the suicide scene.

14. Of course, Sand's decision to leave the couple childless is a further detail that marks the absence of sexuality from their relation.

15. In any case, chastity is by no means reserved for women: since Ralph's wife died, he has remained single and sexless.

16. For example Maryline Lukacher interprets Raymon's mother as a figure representing Sand's grandmother because her last words to Raymon are the same as those Sand's grandmother actually said to her on her death bed (77). Similarly Vareille Wingard, who is usually a very astute reader, fails to notice Sand's irony in depicting Madame de Ramière.

17. The theme of male narcissism and the role of mothers in fostering such narcissism will be developed and amplified in later novels, most notably in *Lucrezia Floriani* (1846).

Valentine

DEBRA L. TERZIAN (ESSAY DATE SPRING-SUMMER 1997)

SOURCE: Terzian, Debra L. "Feminism and Family Dysfunction in Sand's *Valentine*." *Nineteenth-Century French Studies* 25, nos. 3-4 (spring-summer 1997): 266-79.

In the following essay, Terzian analyzes Sand's particular brand of feminism by exploring the construction of her female characters in Valentine.

C'étaient de beaux et chastes livres, presque tous écrits par des femmes sur des histoires de femmes: Valérie, Eugène de Rothelin, Mademoiselle de Clermont, Delphine. Ces récits touchants et passionnées, ces aperçus d'un monde idéal pour moi élevèrent mon âme, mais ils la dévorèrent. Je devins romanesque, caractère le plus infortuné qu'une femme puisse avoir.

George Sand, Leone Leoni

In the passage cited above, a female character from one of Sand's fictional works cites the works of fiction that have most influenced her and that have marked decisive moments in what can be termed her sentimental education. The novels she lists form a veritable corpus of women's literature. Evoking the notion of a continuum of women writers, Sand's protagonist makes plain the problematic and troublesome feature that these works share—their power to both "elevate" and "devour" the reader. For while Sand's Juliette is moved by the beauty and purity of these texts, she is not unaware of the often disheartening, disquieting ways in which women, as gendered subjects, are represented in these works.

Sand's second novel, *Valentine* (1832), participates in this novelistic tradition of fictionalizing the feminine. *Valentine* takes its place alongside such literary works as Germaine de Staël's *Delphine,* published 30 years earlier, and included above by Juliette in her roster of women's fiction. In *Valentine,* Sand yields to the dominant nineteenth-century textual codes and cultural conventions that govern the social relation of the sexes, and she conforms to the nineteenth century's agenda of subservient femininity in her narration of female *Bildung.* Yet, in the story she tells, and this is true as well for her Staëlian pre-text, Sand couples this conformity to narrative codes with a feminist critique of the ways in which these codes define and circumscribe the feminine. Admittedly, the feminism inherent in Sand's *Valentine* has none of the feminist rhetoric and pathos that we read for example, in Staël's *Delphine.* But, I should like to begin this reading of a Sandian tale of growing up female by taking up the issue of Sand's feminism from the outset.

As Naomi Schor has pointed out, the question of Sand's feminism is an inevitable one for many Sandian critics (71). For some readers of Sand's earliest fictions, *Indiana,* as well as *Valentine,* Sand's narratives do not contest, but capitulate to the nineteenth century's construction of the feminine stereotype. This is the view of Leslie Rabine, who writes that the heroine in *Indiana* "fulfills the desire to epitomize the social ideal of nineteenth-century womanhood" (9). And should any reader need clarification of this point, Rabine defines her terms: "not only is *Indiana* an imitation of the male nineteenth-century wish-fulfillment work, but also the wish or dream the heroine fulfills is to be the perfect dream-object of the male dreamer" (5). Kathryn Crecelius takes a similar position in her reading of *Valentine.* Comparing the two novels, she concludes that "as a feminist work, *Valentine* is surprisingly thin compared to *Indiana*" (92). For both Rabine and

MIROIR DROLATIQUE.

Si de Georges Sand ce portrait
Laisse l'esprit un peu perplexe,
C'est que le génie est abstrait,
Et comme on sait n'a pas de sexe.

George Sand is remembered for bold behavior, including wearing men's clothing, as depicted here circa 1840.

Crecelius then, Sand's early feminocentric fictions represent disappointing works of nineteenth-century feminism.

I foreground their critical perspectives here, for as well argued as they are, I would like to propose a reading of *Valentine* that takes another look at Sand's feminism, and finds no abandonment of feminist principles, no forsaking of a feminist sensibility. In her recent book, *George Sand and Idealism,* Naomi Schor undertakes the rather thorny issue of Sand's feminism, and moves the Sandian critic beyond that most formulaic of questions, namely, is Sand a good feminist or a bad one. And, although the nineties have brought about the displacement of feminist criticism from the more privileged status it held in the seventies and eighties—the interrogation of its very conceptual underpinnings—Sand's writings continue to invite and invoke the reader to consider the question of her feminism.[1] Indeed, Schor locates Sand's feminism in her contradictions—the very contradictions that lead Rabine to indict Sand's *Indiana* as a work that conceals its "conformity to the feminine stereotypes then in force" within its "rhetoric of rebellion" (2). What is important then is that Sand's works put forth these contradictions, not that she fails to resolve them. How Sand does or does not resolve the contradictions in her writings on women's experience is not the issue, for as Schor explains, "Feminism is the debate itself" (76). What follows is an effort to identify the terms of this debate, and to trace how it plays itself out in *Valentine.*

Valentine's story begins in the absence of the father. Unlike Balzac's *Eugénie Grandet,* for example, published just one year after *Valentine,* Sand's novel of female development is not father-driven; female *Bildung* is not subject to the constraining law of the father. But, we could say that Sand's fiction is sister-driven. Indeed, the first significant event in the heroine's story comes in the early part of the novel with the return of Valentine's sister, Louise, after fifteen years spent in exile. Louise was banished from the château de Raimbault by Valentine's mother (Louise's stepmother) for having fallen victim to the seduction of a Monsieur de Neuville, who, it turns out, was Madame de Raimbault's lover as well. The early part of the novel, dealing with Louise's return and reunion with Valentine is an episode of Valentine's narrative that I will refer to as the sisters' story. It is within the pages of the sisters' story that Sand begins the fiction that is *Valentine.* The heroine's developmental trajectory is initially presented and articulated within the narrative framework of the sister's story; the heroine's text, to borrow a term from Nancy Miller, is subsumed within, and grows out of this story.[2] This merging of story marks the novel's opening pages. One example is the following passage in which Valentine's thoughts turn to her sister, whose misfortune and imposed exile have kept them apart:

> Cette dernière pensée amena une larme au bord de sa paupière. C'était là le seul événement de la vie de Valentine; mais il l'avait remplie; il avait influé sur son caractère, il lui avait donné à la fois de la timidité et de la hardiesse; de la timidité pour elle-même, de la hardiesse quand il s'agissait de sa soeur. Elle n'avait, il est vrai, jamais pu lui prouver le dévouement courageux dont elle se sentait animée; jamais le nom de sa soeur n'avait été prononcé par sa mère devant elle; jamais on ne lui avait fourni une seule occasion de la servir et de la défendre. Son désir en était d'autant plus vif, et cette sorte de tendresse passionnée, qu'elle nourrissait pour une personne dont l'image se présentait à elle à travers les vagues souvenirs de l'enfance, était réellement la seule affection romanesque qui eût trouvé place dans son âme.
>
> (42)

Louise's first appearance in the novel is also predicated on her tie to Valentine: "je n'aurai pas de repos que je n'aie vu ses traits, entendu le son de sa voix" (11).

The kind of narrative fusion that Sand enacts as she recounts the story of her heroine in relation to that of the sisters puts me in mind of Nancy Chodorow's psychoanalytic account of female development, which is grounded in a sense of "self-in-relationship" to another woman—the mother.[3] Sand's narrative makes plain the strong mother-daughter bond that underlies the relationship of the sisters, and it gives fresh articulation to Chodorow's contention that there exists "a tendency in women toward boundary confusion" (110). The parallel between Sand's fiction and Chodorow's theory seems to me to be inevitable for the reader who confronts the novel's opening pages, constructed as they are in such a way as to mirror the permeable ego boundaries that define the relationship between Valentine and her sister.[4]

The sisters' story, at once tragic and idyllic, takes its place in the context of a rather curious fictional family romance. The constellation of family members around Valentine—all of whom are female—makes for an unusual cast of characters to play the role of formative influences in a tale of growing up female. Indeed, the story of Valentine's family reads like a nineteenth-century fictional account of a dysfunctional family. There is Louise, a young single woman raising a child out of wedlock, and banished from her family home by her malicious stepmother. Yet, prior to her exile, Louise did nonetheless play a significant role in raising her younger sister. This stepmother, Madame de Raimbault, biological mother to Valentine, depicted throughout as an aging, repressive, and bitter woman, looks upon her daughters as rivals for male attention and approval. Their youth and beauty are a painful reminder of her own aging, fading attractiveness. Bitter, angry, and resentful, Madame de Raimbault is happiest when she can appear in society alone and without Valentine. As for the third member of the family, Valentine's grandmother, she is presented to the reader as a young and scatterbrained woman: "étourdie et jeune" (41).

Valentine's relationships to these women who have raised her are marked by some curious slippages and displacements, and since these family ties are central to the developmental tale that Sand writes for her heroine, I should like to consider them in some detail. The subject of relationships between women in Sandian fiction represents, of course, a meaningful point of inquiry for the feminist reader, and **Valentine** offers an interesting case in point. With this novel, Sand gives her fictional account of the mother-daughter relationship under patriarchy. She casts this story in bleak, impoverished terms; she fictionalizes no instances of female bonding between them, and the text effectively severs any notion of female genealogy or transmission from mother to daughter. Sand is far from reinscribing the mother-daughter story as told by Madame de Lafayette in *La Princesse de Clèves,* or even, to cite a more contemporary example, that told by Balzac in *Eugénie Grandet.* Instead, the novel enacts a schism in the figure of the mother. This schism is at once prefigured and encapsulated in the episode of Louise's dream in the novel's opening pages. Prior to being reunited with her sister, Louise has a dream in which Valentine falls into the river, and Valentine's mother impedes Louise's efforts to save the drowning child. Her dream plays out the conflict of the good versus the bad mother, and the novel makes it clear that Mme de Raimbault is the bad mother, lacking in maternal feeling, completely alienated from her own child. The text leaves no doubt that Louise is the good mother, linking, in a kind of affective continuum, the love and maternal feelings that she had for the young Valentine with the maternal love she has for her son: "Cet amour d'autrefois pour sa sœur s'était réveillé plus intense et plus maternel avec celui qu'elle avait eu pour son fils" (59). Louise tells of her experience of motherhood in the following way:

> Mon fils existe, il ne m'a jamais quittée; c'est moi qui l'ai élevé. Je n'ai point essayé de dissimuler ma faute en l'éloignant de moi ou en lui refusant mon nom. Partout il m'a suivie, partout sa présence a révélé mon malheur et mon repentir. Et le croirastu, Valentine? j'ai fini par mettre ma gloire à me proclamer sa mère. . . .
>
> (92-93)

A mother-daughter bond grounds the relationship between the sisters and affectively displaces Valentine's biological mother from the mother-daughter dyad. When the sisters are reunited, they confirm the tie that binds them, and that consequently invalidates the figure of Madame de Raimbault as mother:

> —Pourquoi ce *vous*? dit Louise; ne sommes-nous pas sœurs?
>
> —Oh! c'est que vous êtes ma mère aussi! répondit Valentine. Allez, je n'ai rien oublié! Vous êtes encore présente à ma mémoire comme si c'était hier . . .

> — . . . C'est moi qui t'ai élevée, Valentine, tu t'en souviens! . . . car ta mère ne s'occupait guère de toi; moi seule, je veillais sur tous tes instants. . . .
>
> (60-61)

As for Madame de Raimbault, the novel reinforces her distance from her daughter in the very way that it names her. Referred to alternately in the text by her maiden name, Mademoiselle de Chignon, or her title by marriage, la Comtesse de Raimbault, she is firmly rooted in social and patriarchal convention. She is the one who holds the title to the Raimbault property. It was her wealth and fortune that enabled the reacquisition of the Château de Raimbault, which had been sold as national property during the Revolution. In fact, this Sandian mother essentially coopts the role of the father: she assures the transmission of property to the daughter and thus provides her daughter's dowry for her marriage to Monsieur de Lansac. Assimilating Madame de Raimbault into the role of the father, the novel dispossesses this patriarchal mother even further of her textual identification with maternity. On the eve of her wedding day, Madame de Raimbault summons her daughter for a most peculiar mother-daughter chat:

> Alors madame de Raimbault entama une grave dissertation d'affaires avec sa fille; elle lui fit remarquer qu'elle lui laissait le château et la terre de Raimbault, dont le nom seul constituait presque tout l'héritage de son père, et dont la valeur réelle, détachée de sa propre fortune, constituait une assez belle dot. . . . Elle entra dans des détails d'argent qui firent de cette exhortation maternelle une véritable consultation notariée, et termina sa harangue en lui disant qu'elle espérait, au moment où la loi allait les rendre *étrangères* l'une à l'autre, trouver Valentine disposée à lui accorder des *égards* et des soins.
>
> (164)

More father-surrogate than nurturing mother, it is Madame de Raimbault who bequeaths the patrimonial legacy to the daughter—"elle lui laissait le château et la terre de Raimbault, dont le nom seul constituait presque tout l'héritage de son père." And, lest the reader need additional evidence of Madame de Raimbault's singular lack of mothering skills—her distaste for the role of motherhood, we need only look to one of the novel's last references to her. After Valentine's marriage to Monsieur de Lansac, Madame de Raimbault takes her leave, relieved to leave her maternal role behind her once and for all: "En se sentant débarrassée des devoirs de la maternité, il lui sembla qu'elle rajeunissait de vingt ans . . ." (221).

After Valentine's marriage, Madame de Raimbault essentially writes off her daughter. We scarcely hear of her again, and when we do, it is disparagingly, for in the final half of the novel, when the dissolute husband carefully selected for her by her mother has sold Valentine's home and property out from under her, Madame de Raimbault is quick to reject her daughter's pleas for help. And so it is that this mother, who has so summarily written off her daughter, finds herself, in turn, written out of the fiction itself. According to Marianne Hirsch, this is a common feature of nineteenth-century fiction authored by women. Studying the way in which women writers have gone about writing the story of the mother, Hirsch finds that the plots of nineteenth-century women writers are based on maternal repression—the mother's absence, silence, and negativity (The Mother/Daughter Plot 47). Hirsch's book points to what she sees as "the thoroughness with which female realist writers eliminate mothers from their fiction" (50). The novel of female development, anchored as it is in plots of romantic love, is predicated on the absence of the mother. Indeed, the sacrifice of the mother becomes the organizing principle of such fiction.[5]

Valentine takes her place alongside other nineteenth-century heroines by virtue of her motherlessness.[6] For, long before Sand writes the mother out of her story, she depicts her heroine as an orphan. This is, of course, one significant feature of Sand's fiction of family dysfunction. As we saw earlier, Valentine credits Louise with having raised her, and she discounts and dismisses her mother's role. Yet, since her female role models are all essentially anti-role models, Valentine endeavors to write a new story for her life. She most clearly rejects the script of female conduct that the women in her life have followed. Sand describes her motherless, orphaned heroine in the following way:

> La jeune Valentine, élevée tour à tour par sa sœur bannie, par sa mère orgueilleuse, par les religieuses de son couvent, par sa grand'mère étourdie et jeune, n'avait été définitivement élevée par personne. Elle s'était faite elle-même ce qu'elle était, et, faute de trouver des sympathies bien réelles dans sa famille, elle avait pris le goût de l'étude et de la rêverie.
>
> (41)

> Elle se promettait d'échapper à ces inclinations ardentes qui faisaient sous ses yeux le malheur des autres: à l'amour du luxe, auquel sa grand'mère sacrifiait toute dignité; à l'ambition, dont les espérances déçues torturaient sa mère; à l'amour, qui avait si cruellement égaré sa sœur.
>
> (42)

This brief excerpt from the narrative of Valentine's family ties speaks volumes about Sand's fiction of female *Bildung*. Curiously enough, in spite of the fact that Valentine has been mothered by three different women of three different generations, the text ultimately casts her as an orphan and thereby invalidates any trace of female transmission between the women: "La jeune Valentine . . . n'avait été définitivement élevée par personne. Elle s'était faite elle-mëme ce qu'elle était. . . ." Valentine will not participate in that which has been the experience and destiny of the women around her. The text disinherits her from any female legacy, and it disidentifies her from her maternal models. She most clearly does not want to be her mother's daughter. Yet, Sand's representation of this failed relationship is not evidence of an anti-feminist stance on the part of the novelist. For what the novel underlines in this story of mother and daughter is the daughter's singularity with respect to the mother. Sand's heroine turns away from the mother. If there is ultimately no female legacy or transmission passed on from mother to daughter, it is due to Valentine who rejects the notion of womanhood and the patriarchal conception of femininity that her mother embodies. To read in Sand's story her inability to fictionalize a nurturing relationship between women without rivalry or jealous rancor seems to me to be a failed reading. For, what it fails to read in this story is the novelist's refusal to make of her heroine a daughter in the economy of patriarchy.

The work of Luce Irigaray can be helpful to a reading of this feature of Sand's fiction, since Irigaray confronts the reality and the consequences of women's existence in Western, male-ordered culture, and, by extension, in its literary productions. She speaks about the rupture in female genealogy as a casualty in the foundation and logic of Western culture. The perpetuation of Western society and culture resides, according to Irigaray, in the silence of, and separation between women: "Pourquoi, en quoi, la société, la socialité trouvent-elles intérêt à leur silence? Pour perpétuer toutes les normes de la société et de la culture existantes qui reposent aussi sur la séparation entre les femmes" (*Ethique* 103). It is the break in female genealogy, reflected in the relationships between the women in Sand's novel, which, if we play out Irigaray's reasoning, inexorably signals and underlies women's relation to women in a patriarchal economy, subject to the laws of male desire. Irigaray writes: "La verticalité est en quelque sorte toujours enlevée au devenir femme. Le lien entre mère et fille, fille et mère, doit être rompu pour que la fille devienne femme. La généalogie féminine doit être supprimée, au bénéfice de la relation fils-Père, de l'idéalisation du père et du mari comme patriarches" (106).[7] Reading Irigaray, it is impossible not to think here of the way in which Sand casts Madame Raimbault's troubled relationship to her daughters. Sandra Gilbert and Susan Gubar's *The Madwoman in the Attic: The Woman Writer and the Nineteenth-Century Literary Imagination,* is another important critical intertext for a reading of Sand. The mother-daughter narrative in **Valentine** calls to mind Gilbert and Gubar's reading of Grimm's "Snow White." This story of (step)mother and daughter also takes place in the absence of the father. Yet, as Gilbert and Gubar read it, the father/king is present to the extent that the mother has internalized and assimilated his "patriarchal voice of judgment that rules the Queen's—and every other woman's—self-evaluation" (38). Reading the mother-daughter narratives of Grimm and Sand alongside one another reveals the parallel that exists between them: "It is true, of course, that in the patriarchal kingdom of the text these women inhabit, the Queen's life can be literally imperiled by her daughter's beauty, and true . . . that, given the female vulnerability such perils imply, female bonding is extraordinarily difficult in patriarchy: women almost inevitably turn against women because the voice of the looking glass sets them against each other" (38). Thus, patriarchal plots and representations of the feminine are mirrored in fiction from fairy tale to novel. Textual constructions of the feminine across fictional genres are grounded in the ideology of patriarchy, and bound up in this ideology are both the causes of, and explanations for women's difficult and problematic relationship to women in fiction.

But, shouldn't things work out differently in female-authored fiction? Doesn't gender make a difference? Of course it does, and **Valentine** provides one example. In **Valentine,** we can read, on the one hand, the novelist's effort to be faithful to dominant literary traditions, and on the other, her attempt to envision alternate ways in which to write the heroine's text. The course of development for nineteenth-century heroines is marked throughout by their inscription as gendered subjects in culture and fiction. The nineteenth-century feminocentric novel moves its heroine towards the heterosexual romance plot; the most characteristic organization of nineteenth-century narrative.[8] And, in this, **Valentine** is no exception. The novel is marked by a writing

posture that both inscribes and attempts to circumscribe dominant literary tradition and its ideological underpinnings. Sand's struggle to resist this tradition can be read in the very structure and organization of her narrative. We have already seen that the novel begins with the story of the sisters. And in these early pages, the novel's presentation of the sisters, bound up in their preoedipal attachment to one another, is at once a powerful and a sensuous one. With the exception perhaps of Sand's **Lélia,** I can think of no other nineteenth-century text that can possibly come close to matching or rivaling the depiction of the sensuality that pervades **Valentine** and Louise's reunion within the pages of the sisters' story:

> Louise, en se redressant sur son chevet, perdit le mouchoir de soie qui retenait ses longs cheveux bruns. Dans ce désordre, pâle, effrayée, éclairée par un rayon de la lune qui perçait furtivement entre les fentes du rideau, elle se pencha vers la voix qui l'appelait. Deux bras l'enlacent; une bouche fraîche et jeune couvre ses joues de saintes caresses; Louise, interdite, se sent inondée de larmes et de baisers; Valentine, près de défaillir, se laisse tomber, épuisée d'émotion, sur le lit de sa sœur. Quand Louise comprit que ce n'était plus un rêve, que Valentine était dans ses bras, qu'elle y était venue, que son cœur était rempli de tendresse et de joie comme le sien, elle ne put exprimer ce qu'elle sentait que par des étreintes et des sanglots.
>
> (60)

Sand clearly stages and valorizes the heroine's "homosexual" ties to her sister and sets forth the importance of the preoedipal in her presentation of the heroine. Yet, the sisters' story then gives way to the heterosexual romance plot, and thus the story of preoedipal love between the sisters yields to the narrative of the heroine's passage through oedipalization. In this way, Sand respects the prevailing narrative pattern of dominant literary tradition, for her novel enacts a passage from a valorization of homosexual ties to the characteristic preoccupation with heterosexual ones.

By grounding the heroine in a preoedipally organized narrative, and thus depicting the instance of affective merging between the heroine and another woman, Sand opens up the possibility of telling a different developmental story—one that is perhaps more complete—at the least, more faithful to the specificity of female development. The preoedipal is a story that goes untold in the tradition of nineteenth-century narrative; it is a story that is suppressed by the romance plot. The preoedipal is the untold story in Freudian theory as well. Freud acknowledged only belatedly and superficially the importance of the preoedipal for women. In his essay, "Femininity," Freud begins to stress its lingering importance for the specificity of female development: "We knew, of course, that there had been a preliminary stage of attachment to the mother, but we did not know that it could be so rich in content and so long-lasting, and could leave behind so many opportunities for fixations and dispositions. . . . In short, we get an impression that we cannot understand women unless we appreciate this phase of their pre-Oedipal attachment to the mother" (118). Sand, however, does not neglect to tell this story. On the contrary, she goes to great lengths to do so. Yet, if indeed Sand's attempt to inscribe her heroine in a different story—a preoedipally organized one—ultimately gives way to that more traditional of stories—romantic love, she does, in fact, return to it in an effort to reinscribe it throughout the novel. In the part of the novel concerned with the developing romance between Valentine and Bénédict, it is true that the sisters' story is no longer primary.[9] Yet, there is an effort on the part of the novelist to bind Louise to this part of Valentine's story. The heterosexual love story in this novel grows out of the sisters' story: Valentine's initial attachment to Bénédict grows out of her love for Louise. It is Bénédict who is responsible for reuniting the sisters, and the love that Valentine comes to feel for Bénédict is initially, as far as the heroine is concerned, a displacement and an extension of her strong feelings for her sister: "elle se levait et courait à la fenêtre; appelant dans son coeur Louise et Bénédict; car Bénédict, ce n'était pour elle, du moins elle le croyait ainsi, qu'une partie de sa soeur détachée vers elle" (78). As the novel moves from recounting the sisters' story to plotting the romance between Valentine and Bénédict, Bénédict plays as important a role in the sisters' story as Louise does in the story of the lovers. Bénédict's role in the sisters' story is clear: he reunites them and serves as intermediary between them, delivering their messages and letters to one another. And, on one occasion, he literally stands in for Louise, when he sings a song to Valentine that she clearly associates with her sister:

> —Cet air, dit Valentine dans un instant où elle fut seule avec Bénédict, est celui que ma soeur me chantait de prédilection lorsque j'étais enfant. . . . Je ne l'ai jamais oublié, et tout à l'heure j'ai failli pleurer quand vous l'avez commencé.
>
> —Je l'ai chanté à dessein, répondit Bénédict; c'était vous parler au nom de Louise.
>
> (83)

In this way, the novel does not simply trade off the preoedipally invested story in favor of the romance. Rather, this subsequent story builds out of and feeds off of the earlier story. The novel binds Louise to the romance plot, making clear that the heroine's love for Bénédict stems from love for her sister. Sand plots Valentine's story in such a way as to continually situate her within a relational triangle with her sister and her lover. In fact, at one point in the romance plot when Valentine clearly understands how deeply she loves Bénédict and how perilous the stakes of romantic love can be, the heroine attempts to draw Louise into the lovers' story, as if Louise's presence could, in some way, legitimize the passion between the lovers: "De son côté, celle-ci s'abandonnait à des dangers dont elle n'était pas trop fâchée de voir sa soeur complice. Elle se laissait emporter par sa destinée, sans vouloir regarder en avant, et puisait dans l'imprévoyance de Louise des excuses pour sa propre faiblesse" (226). Thus, narrative structure in **Valentine**, passing as it does from the preoedipal to the oedipal, does not simply supplant one story for the other in a kind of hegemonic ordering of story. Instead, it merges the two stories. Fusing the sisters' story and the story of the lovers, the novel presents its heroine in a kind of bisexual relational triangle.[10]

In terms of the narrative organization of the novel, the story of the lovers is in turn displaced by the story of the pavilion. There is much to be said of the episode of the pavilion, and this very topic has received important critical attention.[11] The novel's story of the pavilion represents the heroine's attempt to reclaim her own story. It is in the absence of her mother and husband that Valentine's quest for self finds definition and fulfilment in the sphere of activity and relationships that she creates within the walls of the pavilion. The importance of the mother's absence on Valentine's freedom and well-being cannot be stressed enough: "Jamais Valentine ne s'était sentie si heureuse; loin des regards de sa mère, loin de la roideur glaciale qui pesait sur tous ses pas, il lui semblait respirer un air plus libre, et, pour la première fois depuis qu'elle était née, vivre de toute sa vie" (105). The pavilion story makes clear that the mother needs to be removed from the daughter's story in order for the daughter to be able to shape and create her own story. It is here that she summons a family of her own choosing and writes a story for herself that takes place outside of, and in opposition to, society's conventions and prejudices: "Ainsi une réunion de circonstances favorables concourait à protéger le bonheur que Louise, Valentine et Bénédict volaient pour ainsi dire à la loi des convenances et des préjugés" (247). Interestingly enough, where the novel sets up a conflict for the mother between motherhood and selfhood—her role as mother clearly effacing any possibility of self-fulfilment for the countess—it celebrates the heroine's quest for self and achievement of self-fulfilment through her creation of family. Valentine's fictional quest is bound up in this desire for family. The story of the pavilion is all about the harmonious coexistence of Louise and her son, Valentin, Bénédict and his cousin and former fiancée, Athénaïs, and Valentine, a group that the novel indeed refers to as a family (257). The novel goes to great lengths to describe the blissful, idyllic refuge from the reality of the social order that the heroine has succeeded in establishing:

> Le pavilion était donc pour tous, à la fin du jour, un lieu de repos et de délices. . . . C'était l'Elysée, le monde poétique, la vie dorée de Valentine; au château, tous les ennuis, toutes les servitudes, toutes les tristesses; . . . au pavilion, tous les bonheurs, tous les amis, tous les doux rêves, l'oubli des terreurs, et les joies pures d'un amour chaste. C'était comme une île enchantée au milieu de la vie réelle, comme une oasis dans le désert.
>
> (250)

The pavilion is also a space in which social difference is collapsed and where an aristocratic heroine can coexist happily with those from a lower social class (Bénédict and Athénaïs) and those that society has expelled (Louise and Valentin). The pavilion represents Valentine's attempt to create a space for herself and her "family" outside of social difference, as well as outside of desire. The notion of the pavilion as a place for the sublimation of the lovers' desire ultimately proves, as Nancy Miller suggests, to be outside the possibilities of fiction ("Writing (From) the Feminine" 138).

Yet, there is another way in which to read the story of the pavilion. Although the pavilion episode continues to tell the story of the lovers, it shifts and dislocates this story by factoring in the story of Louise, Athénaïs, and Valentin. For the pavilion is not only figured as a site for the sublimation of the lovers' desire, it also opens up a space in which female genealogy, severed throughout the novel, is restored and reaffirmed. Louise is drawn back into the narrative. Her role expands beyond that of being her sister's jealous rival for Bénédict's love[12]; and the legitimate ties to family that had been denied to her are restored in the pavilion story. One of the main activities of this part of the novel becomes the education of Valentin, undertaken and transmitted by both Valentine and Bénédict. Thus, the pavilion story shifts the focus away from the romance plot and figures in other stories. It seems to me that this shift is another example of Sand's effort to rework and revise traditional narrative convention. She marks her dissent from dominant tradition by dislocating the romance plot from the center of the fiction and introducing a story organized around the notion of a group of collective protagonists, a feature of Sandian fiction.

I would like to conclude by returning to Crecelius's indictment of *Valentine*: "as a feminist work, *Valentine* is surprisingly thin compared with *Indiana*." In the conclusion to her chapter on *Valentine,* she further states that *Valentine*'s "literary innovations are also more circumscribed than previously" (92). The reading of the novel that I present here takes issue with these remarks. Granted, the novel does stage women's problematic relation to women in a society in which they compete for male desire and romance. And granted, the novel, although it celebrates the strong, affective ties that can exist between women in its recounting of the sisters' story, it does, as well, debase these ties, in the story of Louise's jealousy. Ties between mother and daughter are severed, and those between sister and sister are compromised in Sand's fiction. Her heroine is the site of this break in female genealogy, and Sand's narrative is an attempt to negotiate a place and a role for her heroine within the terms of such a fiction.

Is *Valentine* a disappointing feminist work? Let's consider the novel's conclusion. Although it is true that the novel's feminism is subsumed within the social consciousness and conception of social equality that pervades the novel's conclusion, this conclusion does point toward the grounding of a more just and egalitarian society, and heralds the birth of a new generation (reflected in the marriage of Valentin and Athénaïs), founded on the notion of social equality. The novel's ending is not an abandonment of feminist principles. Rather, the novel's conclusion gestures towards the possibility of a society, very much like the one created by Valentine in the brief episode of the pavilion, where feminism is just another word for a more balanced, egalitarian, social relation between the sexes, between men and women as gendered subjects.

Notes

1. In Schor's reading, the question to be asked is "if a definition of feminism exists that can account for practices and convictions that are heterogeneous and sometimes irreconcilable" (75). According to Schor, a definition of feminism appropriate to a discussion of

Sand would be one that "makes of it a sum of contradictions, the nodal point where dissatisfactions with contemporary society and the place it assigns women, claims for equality, claims for singular or plural differences, assertions of an essential and transhistorical female nature, and denunciations of a subaltern condition stemming from specifically historical and contingent factors clash and intertwine" (75-76).

2. See Nancy K. Miller, *The Heroine's Text: Readings in the French and English Novel, 1722-1782.*

3. See Nancy Chodorow, *The Reproduction of Mothering: Psychoanalysis and the Sociology of Gender.*

4. Although Chodorow's theories have come under attack from a number of scholars in different disciplines, many feminist critics have acknowledged the usefulness of Chodorow's work for an understanding of female experience in literature. See, for example, Marianne Hirsch, "Mothers and Daughters: A Review Essay" 218.

5. Hirsch traces the mother's evacuation from the daughter's story to her reading of Freud's "Family Romances" with its androcentric bias. Playing out the implications of the Freudian family romance pattern for a female child, Hirsch concludes that the female family romance depends on elimination of the mother from the daughter's fiction and on attachment to the husband/father. Hirsch also draws on Luce Irigaray and her definition of Western culture as inherently matricidal. See Marianne Hirsch, *The Mother/Daughter Plot* 43-58. See also Luce Irigaray who writes: "Dès lors, ce qui apparaît dans les faits les plus quotidiens comme dans l'ensemble de notre société et de notre culture, c'est que celles-ci fonctionnent originairement sur un matricide. Quand Freud décrit et théorise, notamment dans *Totem et Tabou,* le meurtre du père comme fondateur de la horde primitive, il oublie un meurtre plus archaïque, celui de la femme-mère nécessité par l'établissement d'un certain ordre dans la cité" (*Le Corps-à-Corps avec la Mère* 15-16).

6. Adrienne Rich has also written on the motherless heroine. In a compelling essay on *Jane Eyre,* Rich draws on Phyllis Chesler's assertion that "women are motherless children in patriarchal society" (qtd. in Adrienne Rich, *On Lies, Secrets, and Silence* 91).

7. On the subject of the mother-daughter relationship, Irigaray has this to say: "Pour se faire désirer, aimer de l'homme, il faut évincer la mère, se substituer à elle, l'anéantir pour devenir même. Ce qui détruit la possibilité d'un amour entre mère et fille. Elles sont à la fois complices et rivales pour advenir à l'unique position possible dans le désir de l'homme" (*Ethique* 101).

8. See Rachel Blau DuPlessis who points out that the telic romance plot of these fictions is "a trope for the sex-gender system." Heterosexuality, as DuPlessis writes, is "not a natural law," "but a cultural and narrative ideology" (5).

9. Valentine's romance with Bénédict both predates and survives her marriage to Monsieur de Lansac.

10. See Nancy Chodorow, who writes that the feminine oedipal configuration is triangular—the course of female development is not seen as an abandonment of the preoedipal. The developmental narrative that Sand writes for Valentine mirrors, in many ways, the narrative of female development put forth by Chodorow and other object relations theorists. See Chodorow 140.

11. I am thinking here of Nancy Miller's "Writing (From) the Feminine: George Sand and the Novel of Female Pastoral."

12. Madame de Raimbault, Louise, and Athénaïs, suffer from jealousy over male desire, but this emotion is never attributed to Valentine.

Works Cited

Chodorow, Nancy. *The Reproduction of Mothering: Psychoanalysis and the Sociology of Gender.* Berkeley: U of California P, 1978.

Crecelius, Kathryn J. *Family Romances: George Sand's Early Novels.* Bloomington: Indiana UP, 1987.

DuPlessis, Rachel Blau. *Writing Beyond the Ending: Narrative Strategies of Twentieth-Century Women Writers.* Bloomington: Indiana UP, 1985.

Freud, Sigmund. "Femininity." in *The Standard Edition of the Complete Works of Sigmund Freud.* Vol. 22. London: Hogarth Press, 1964.

Gilbert, Sandra M., and Susan Gubar. *The Madwoman in the Attic: The Woman Writer and the Nineteenth-Century Literary Imagination.* New Haven: Yale UP, 1979.

Hirsch, Marianne. *The Mother/Daughter Plot: Narrative, Psychoanalysis, Feminism.* Bloomington: Indiana UP, 1989.

——. "Mothers and Daughters: A Review Essay." *Signs* 7.1 (1981): 200-222.

Irigaray, Luce. *Le Corps-à-Corps Avec la Mère.* Montréal: Editions de la Pleine Lune, 1981.

——. *Ethique de la Différence Sexuelle.* Paris: Minuit, 1984.

Miller, Nancy K. *The Heroine's Text: Readings in the French and English Novel, 1722-1782.* New York: Columbia UP, 1980.

——. "Writing (From) the Feminine: George Sand and the Novel of Female Pastoral." *The Representation of Women in Fiction: Selected Papers from the English Institute, 1981.* Ed. Carolyn J. Heilbrun and Margaret Higonnet. Baltimore: The Johns Hopkins UP, 1983. 124-151.

Rabine, Leslie. "George Sand and the Myth of Femininity." *Women and Literature* 4.2 (1976): 2-9.

Rich, Adrienne. *On Lies, Secrets, and Silence: Selected Prose, 1966-1978.* New York: Norton, 1979.

Sand, George. *Valentine.* Paris: Michel Lévy Frères, 1869.

Schor, Naomi. *George Sand and Idealism.* New York: Columbia UP, 1993.

FURTHER READING

Biographies

Cate, Curtis. *George Sand: A Biography,* Boston: Houghton Mifflin, 1975, 812 p.

Provides an in-depth look at Sand's life and work.

Winegarten, Renée. *The Double Life of George Sand, Woman and Writer.* New York: Basic Books, 1978, 339 p.

Critical biography of Sand, examining in particular her struggle to understand herself as a woman and a human being.

Criticism

Barry, Joseph. *Infamous Woman: The Life of George Sand.* Garden City, N.Y.: Doubleday, 1977, 436 p.

Addresses Sand's achievement in terms of her works and the events of her life, asserting that she was "quintessentially the modern woman."

Brée, Germaine. "George Sand: The Fictions of Autobiography." *Nineteenth-Century French Studies* 4, no. 4 (summer 1976): 438-49.

Argues that Sand's autobiography and fiction constitute attempts to define herself by integrating the opposing tendencies represented by the two mother figures in her life.

Crecelius, Kathryn J. "Writing a Self: From Aurore Dudevant to George Sand." *Tulsa Studies in Women's Literature* 14, no. 1 (spring 1985): 47-59.

Traces Sand's literary development through her early writings, most of which were not published in her lifetime.

———. *Family Romances: George Sand's Early Novels.* Bloomington: Indiana University Press, 1987, 183 p.

Focusing on Sand's use of the father figure, explores a woman's depiction of the Oedipal triangle from the daughter's perspective.

———. "Female Fantastic: The Case of George Sand." *L'Esprit Createur* 28, no. 3 (fall 1988): 49-62.

Considers Sand's fiction in the context of nineteenth-century fantastic literature.

———. "'Fille majeure, etablie, maitresse de ses actions': George Sand's Unusual Heroines." In *Women in French Literature*, edited by Michael Guggenheim, pp. 137-433. Saratoga, Calif.: Anma Libri, 1988.

Investigates the range of Sand's female protagonists.

Danahy, Michael. "*La Petite Fadette*: The Dilemma of Being a Heroine." In *The Feminization of the Novel*, pp. 159-91. Gainesville: University of Florida Press, 1991.

Analyzes Fadette as a heroine without role models or social support.

Datlof, Natalie, Jean Fuchs, and David A. Powell, eds. *The World of George Sand*, New York: Greenwood Press, 1991, 352 p.

Collection of essays on Sand, with articles exploring the author's political affinities, sexual politics, and autobiographical techniques.

Deutelbaum, Wendy and Cynthia Huff. "Class, Gender, and Family System: The Case of George Sand." In *The (M)other Tongue: Essays in Psychoanalytic Interpretation*, edited by Shirley Nelson Garner, Claire Kahane, and Madelon Sprengnether, pp. 260-79. Ithaca, N.Y.: Cornell University Press, 1985.

Argues that class and sexual politics together shaped Sand as an anti-feminist socialist who could envision utopia emerging only through male endeavor.

Dickenson, Donna. *George Sand: A Brave Man—The Most Womanly Woman.* Oxford, England: Berg, 1988, 190 p.

Emphasizes Sand's position as a hardworking professional writer in the nineteenth century.

Ender, Evelyne. *Sexing the Mind: Nineteenth-Century Fictions of Hysteria.* Ithaca, N.Y.: Cornell University Press, 1995, 300 p.

Studies Sand, Henry James, and George Eliot in the context of the construction of gender difference during the nineteenth century, when gender divisions were being clearly demarcated in literary and scientific discourse through the codification of the "hysterical" woman.

Glasgow, Janis, ed. *George Sand: Collected Essays*, Troy, N.Y.: Whitson, 1985, 329 p.

Collection of essays exploring Sand's creative process, her literary influences, her reputation, and her ideas on the woman question and other issues.

Grant, Richard B. "George Sand's *La Mare au Diable*: A Study in Male Passivity." *Nineteenth-Century French Studies* 13, no. 4 (summer 1985): 211-23.

Analysis of La Mare au Diable which explores a man's maturity and his masculinity, analyzing its importance for the position of women.

———. "George Sand's *Lélia* and the Tragedy of Dualism." *Nineteenth-Century French Studies* 19, no. 4 (summer 1991): 499-516.

Studies the characters in Lélia psychologically in order to explore the theme of dualism at the heart of the novel.

Gray, Margaret E. "Silencing the (M)other Tongue in Sand's *François Le Champi*." *Romanic Review* 83, no. 3 (May 1992): 339-56.

Analysis of the theatrical or dialogicized "female" narration of François Le champi.

Jurgrau, Thelma. "Critical Introduction: Gender Positioning in *Story of My Life*." In *Story of My Life: The Autobiography of George Sand*, edited by Thelma Jurgrau, pp. 7-29. Albany: State University of New York Press, 1991.

Focuses on Sand's representation of gender and the gap between the writer's declared intentions and her actual narrative, arguing that Sand's autobiography is a carefully constructed life story that foregrounds the idea of "gender in flux."

Lukacher, Maryline. "Sand: Double Identity." In *Maternal Fictions: Stendhal, Sand, Rachilde, and Bataille*, pp. 61-89. Durham, N.C.: Duke University Press, 1994.

Examines the function of the doubled female figures in Indiana and their connection to Sand's relationship with the two mother figures in her life.

Massardier-Kenney, Françoise. "A Question of Silence: George Sand's *Nanon*." *Nineteenth-Century French Studies* 21, nos. 3-4 (spring-summer 1993): 357-65.

Explores the narrative techniques in Nanon.

———. Introduction to *Gender in the Fiction of George Sand*, pp. 1-14. Amsterdam, Netherlands: Rodolpi, 2000.

Examines the strategies Sand uses in her novels to question the definitions of gender.

Miller, Nancy K. "Writing from the Pavilion: George Sand and the Novel of Female Pastoral." In *Subject to Change: Reading Feminist Writing*, pp. 206-28. New York: Columbia University Press, 1988.

Explores the spatial and sexual economy of Valentine to highlight Sand's attempt to provide an alternative to marriage for women.

Naginski, Isabelle Hoog. *George Sand: Writing for Her Life.* Brunswick, N.J.: Rutgers University Press, 1991, 281 p.

Focuses on Sand's contribution to the development of the modern novel in terms of her conscious distancing from the dominant nineteenth-century French male tradition and her attempts to create a female poetics based upon an androgynous vision.

O'Brien, Dennis. "George Sand and Feminism." In *George Sand Papers: Conference Proceedings, 1976*, pp. 76-79. New York: AMS Press, 1980.

Attempts to place Sand in her own socio-historical context, highlighting her commitment to equality and to the revolt against male domination as evidence of her proto-feminism.

Petrey, Sandy. "George and Georgina Sand: Realist Gender in *Indiana.*" In *Textuality and Sexuality: Reading Theories and Practices,* edited by Judith Still and Michael Worton, pp. 133-47. Manchester, England: Manchester University Press, 1993.

Places Indiana *in the tradition of French realism by reading it as a novel that focuses on the socio-historical forces that determine the construction of gender identities.*

Prasad, Pratima. "Deceiving Disclosure: Androgony and George Sand's *Gabriel.*" *French Forum* 24, no. 3 (September 1999): 331-51.

Discusses the issues of transvestism and androgony and the related theme of masquerade in the novel Gabriel.

Rea, Annabelle. "Maternity and Marriage: Sand's Use of Fairy Tale and Myth." *Studies in the Literary Imagination* 12, no. 2 (fall 1979): 37-47.

Examines Sand's transformation of fairy tales into vehicles for her ideas on social change.

——. "Toward a Definition of Women's Voice in George Sand's Novels: The Siren and the Witch." In *George Sand: Collected Essays,* edited by Janis Glasgow, pp. 227-38. Troy, New York: Whitson, 1985.

Asserts that Sand's portrayal of women emphasizes women's need to speak out and deconstruct stereotypes, which casts vocal women as sirens or witches.

Rogers, Nancy. "Psychosexual Identity and the Erotic Imagination in the Early Novels of George Sand." *Studies in the Literary Imagination* 12, no. 2 (fall 1979): 19-35.

Examines Sand's treatment of female sexuality.

Schor, Naomi. "Female Fetishism: The Case of George Sand." *Poetics Today* 6, nos. 1-2 (1985): 301-310.

Examines Sand's use of fetishism as a deliberate strategy that foregrounds her characters' and her own bisexuality.

——. "The Portrait of a Gentleman: Representing Men in (French) Women's Writing." *Representations* 20 (fall 1987): 113-33.

Analyzes a recurrent scene in works by Sand, Mme. de Staël, and Mme. de Lafayette with a view to opening a broader discussion of the representation of men by women writers.

——. "Idealism in the Novel: Recanonizing Sand." *Yale French Studies* 75 (1988): 56-73.

Examines reasons for Sand's virtual exclusion from the literary canon in the late nineteenth century and most of the twentieth century.

——. *George Sand and Idealism.* New York: Columbia University Press, 1993, 275 p.

Explores the relationship between feminism and idealism in Sand's writing, discussing the effect of this conjunction on Sand's problematic position in the literary canon.

Singer, Armand E., Mary W. Singer, and Janice S. Spleth, eds. *West Virginia George Sand Conference Papers,* Morgantown: Department of Foreign Languages, West Virginia University, 1981, 111 p.

Collection of essays that includes commentary on Sand's ideas about gender, language, and politics.

Sivert, Eileen Boyd. "*Lélia* and Feminism." *Yale French Studies* 62 (1981): 45-66.

Compares Sand's treatment in Lélia *of various problems surrounding the representation and recognition of women with the treatment of similar problems by twentieth-century French feminists Luce Irigaray and Hélène Cixous.*

OTHER SOURCES FROM GALE:

Additional coverage of Sand's life and career is contained in the following sources published by the Gale Group: *Dictionary of Literary Biography*, Vols. 119, 192; *DISCovering Authors; DISCovering Authors: British Edition; DISCovering Authors: Canadian Edition; DISCovering Authors Modules: Most-studied Authors* and *Novelists; DISCovering Authors 3.0; European Writers*, Vol. 6; *Feminist Writers; Guide to French Literature, 1789-Present; Literature Resource Center; Nineteenth-Century Literature Criticism*, Vols. 2, 42, 57; *Reference Guide to World Literature*, Eds. 2, 3; *Twayne's World Authors;* and *World Literature Criticism.*

CATHARINE MARIA SEDGWICK

(1789 - 1867)

American novelist.

A popular as well as critically acclaimed writer in her own time, Sedgwick is best remembered for her novels depicting colonial and early-nineteenth-century New England life. Sedgwick's contemporaries praised her use of distinctly American characters, history, morals, values, and ideals. She was also noted for her realistic descriptions of domestic detail and regional culture. Sedgwick's first novel, *A New-England Tale,* was published in 1822, and she is numbered among a group of nineteenth-century writers who helped found a uniquely American body of literature. Although neglected by scholars and critics for many years, Sedgwick's work was rediscovered in the 1970s, and since then most attention has been focused on *Hope Leslie; or, Early Times in Massachusetts* (1827), a historical novel that treats Puritan attitudes towards religion, women's role in the new American republic, and the relationship between whites and Native Americans. Feminist scholars have analyzed Sedgwick's subversion of the traditional frontier romance genre in *Hope Leslie* to expose the political and ideological contradictions of the early nineteenth century and address the opression of women and Native Americans.

BIOGRAPHICAL INFORMATION

Sedgwick was born December 28, 1789 into a prestigious family in Stockbridge, Massachusetts. Her father, Theodore Sedgwick, was an early and prominent member of the newly formed U.S. Congress, and his political obligations kept him from home for long periods of time. Left to manage the large household by herself, Sedgwick's mother, Pamela, suffered debilitating bouts of mental illness. Consequently, the responsibility for raising Sedgwick and her younger brother often fell upon their older siblings, to whom she remained deeply attached all her life. Offered the best education available to girls at the time, Sedgwick nevertheless always felt disadvantaged because of the poor educational opportunities open to girls. She attended a local grammar school, which offered a limited curriculum, and later went to boarding schools in Albany and Boston. When her mother died in 1807, Sedgwick went to live with relatives in New York, where she became friends with a number of literary figures, including poet William Cullen Bryant and noted theologian and Unitarian minister William Ellery Channing, whose liberal beliefs left a strong impression on her. Sedgwick returned to her family home in Stockbridge following her father's death in 1813. His conversion from Calvinism to Unitarianism shortly before his death, as well as her own admiration for Channing, fueled Sedgwick's already strong interest in religion; in 1821 she also converted to the Unitarian faith. The hostile reaction to her conversion from conservative friends and relatives helped inspire her lifelong quest for religious tolerance and also prompted her to begin writing. In 1822 she composed a tract about religious persecution, which, with her brother's encouragement, she eventually developed into her first novel, *A New-England Tale*. Sedgwick continued to write for most of the rest of her life, composing moral tracts and didactic tales as well as novels. She divided her time between New York City and Massachusetts, where she became renowned for her tea parties. These gatherings brought together some of the leading American writers, including Herman Melville, Nathaniel Hawthorne, Ralph Waldo Emerson, and James Fenimore Cooper. Sedgwick also became involved with social causes, helping to promote improvements in prisons and schools. Sedgwick avoided taking controversial stances. For example, she opposed slavery, but considered the abolitionists too extreme in their views; she remained unmarried, but idealized matrimony; and she supported a woman's right to own property, but not a woman's right to vote. Sedgwick continued to champion social reform until late into her seventies when she became ill and moved to Boston. There, a niece cared for her until her death at the age of seventy-eight.

MAJOR WORKS

Sedgwick wrote both fiction and nonfiction, and there is a didactic tone in her work that stresses the need for religious and racial tolerance, as well as social and political reform. Her first novel, *A New-England Tale,* focuses on the evils of organized religion. Set in the early nineteenth century, the novel concerns a noble young woman who is the victim of corrupt church leaders. Because most novels written in America at this time were modeled on the works of English authors, *A New-England Tale* received special critical attention for its American setting and characters. The focus on moral concerns and domestic themes also met with immediate acclaim, and Sedgwick soon became one of the country's most popular authors. Her novel *Redwood* (1824), featuring a highly principled protagonist, Debbie Lenox, and again focusing on religious concerns, has often been praised for the creation of one of the most realistically drawn woman characters in early American literature. Despite the success of these two novels, it is Sedgwick's fourth novel,

Hope Leslie, that is considered by most critics to be her best work. In this historical romance set in New England, Sedgwick describes the customs of the Native American Pequot tribe, delineates relations between whites and Native Americans, and introduces the theme of miscegenation into American literature. The novel tells the story of Hope Leslie, her sister Faith, and Magawisca, a Pequot Indian. Through the stories of these women and within the boundaries of the romance, Sedgwick confronts authorized versions of history, offering an alternate perspective to the Puritans' largely ethnocentric view of the Pequot War and the displacement of Native Americans during the early years of the American Republic.

CRITICAL RECEPTION

Sedgwick's works were considered innovative during her own time, as she was among the first American writers to use local scenery, customs, and characters. While many of her contemporaries considered her writing style awkward and her works overbearingly didactic, she was universally praised for her well-realized characters and lively plots. Additionally, she was lauded for the realism of her work. Critical interest in her writing, however, began diminishing soon after the publication of her last novel, *Married or Single?*, when other authors began writing novels about American locales, customs, and characters. It was not until the mid-twentieth century that Sedgwick's work once again received critical attention, beginning with the release of a new edition of *Hope Leslie* in the late 1980s. This novel has garnered the most attention from modern critics, who admire Sedgwick's innovative writing style and subjects. Critics have examined the work in the context of other contemporary historical accounts of the Pequot War and praised Sedgwick's revisionist interpretation of Puritan historiography through the eyes of those traditionally marginalized or oppressed by it—women and Native Americans. Other commentators have maintained that the novel explores the possibilities of a more inclusive definition of American identity and culture and refashions the frontier romance tradition to offer an alternative, feminist, and racially diverse vision of American women and American culture. Feminist critics have praised the way in which Sedgwick's fiction subverts racial and gender stereotypes and offers characters that have nontraditional views of society and nature. Several scholars have also examined Sedgwick's short story "Cacoethes Scribendi" (1835) to illuminate the author's impression of the relationship between culture, writing, and women. Contemporary and modern critics alike have acknowledged Sedgwick as one of the first American writers to focus on moral themes that address issues of both social and political significance for nineteenth-century America.

PRINCIPAL WORKS

Mary Hollis: An Original Tale (novel) 1822

A New England Tale; or, Sketches of New England Character and Manners (novel) 1822; revised as *A New England Tale, and Miscellanies* 1852

Redwood: A Tale 2 vols. (novel) 1824

Hope Leslie; or, Early Times in the Massachusetts (novel) 1827

Clarence; or, A Tale of Our Own Times (novel) 1830

Home (novel) 1835

The Linwoods; or, "Sixty Years Since" in America (novel) 1835

Tales and Sketches 2 vols. (short stories) 1835-44

The Poor Rich Man, and the Rich Poor Man (novel) 1836

Live and Let Live; or, Domestic Service Illustrated (novel) 1837

Means and Ends; or, Self-Training (essays) 1839

Letters from Abroad to Kindred at Home (letters) 1841

Married or Single? (novel) 1857

Life and Letters of Catharine M. Sedgwick (unfinished autobiography and letters) 1871; revised as *The Power of Her Sympathy: The Autobiography and Journal of Catharine Maria Sedgwick* [edited by Mary Kelly] 1993

PRIMARY SOURCES

CATHARINE MARIA SEDGWICK (ESSAY DATE 1827)

SOURCE: Sedgwick, Catharine Maria. *Hope Leslie*, pp. 198-201. New York: White, Gallaher, and White, 1827.

In the following excerpt from her novel Hope Leslie, *the Native American character Magawisca demands liberty from her white male captors.*

The governor replied, with a severe gravity, ominous to the knight, "that the circumstances he had alluded to certainly required explanation; if that should not prove satisfactory, they would demand a public investigation. In the mean time, he should suspend the trial of the prisoner, who, though the decision of her case might not wholly depend on the establishment of Sir Philip's testimony, was yet, at present, materially affected by it."

"He expressed a deep regret at the interruption that had occurred, as it must lead," he said, "to the suspension of the justice to be manifested either in the acquittal or condemnation of the prisoner. Some of the magistrates being called away from town on the next morning, he found himself compelled to adjourn the sitting of the court till one month from the present date,"

"Then," said Magawisca, for the first time speaking with a tone of impatience, "then, I pray you, send me to death now. Anything is better than wearing through another moon in my prisonhouse, thinking," she added, and cast down her eyelids, heavy with tears, "thinking of that old man—my father. I pray thee," she continued, bending low her head, "I pray thee now to set my spirit free. Wait not for his testimony"—she pointed to Sir Philip—"as well may ye expect the green herb to spring up in your trodden streets, as the breath of truth to come from his false lips. Do you wait for him to prove that I am your enemy? Take my own word, I am your enemy; the sunbeam and the shadow cannot mingle. The white man cometh—the Indian vanisheth. Can we grasp in friendship the hand raised to strike us? Nay—and it matters not whether we fall by the tempest that lays the forest low, or are cut down alone by the stroke of the axe. I would have thanked you for life and liberty; for Mononotto's sake I would have thanked you; but if ye send me back to that dungeon—the grave of the living, feeling, thinking soul, where the sun never shineth, where the stars never rise nor set, where the free breath of heaven never enters, where all is darkness without and within"—she pressed her hand on her breast—"ye will even now condemn me to death, but death more slow and terrible than your most suffering captive ever endured from Indian fires and knives." She paused—passed unresisted without the little railing that encompassed her, mounted the steps of the platform, and advancing to the feet of the governor, threw back her mantle, and knelt before him. Her mutilated person, unveiled by this action, appealed to the senses of the spectators. Everell involuntarily closed his eyes, and uttered a cry of agony, lost indeed in the murmurs of the crowd. She spoke, and all again were as hushed as death. "Thou didst promise," she said, addressing herself to Governor Winthrop, "to my dying mother, thou didst promise, kindness to her children. In her name, I demand of thee death or liberty."

Everell sprang forward, and clasping his hands exclaimed, "In the name of God, liberty!"

The feeling was contagious, and every voice, save her judges, shouted, "Liberty!—liberty! grant the prisoner liberty!"

The governor rose, waved his hand to command silence, and would have spoken, but his voice failed him; his heart was touched with the general emotion, and he was fain to turn away to hide tears more becoming to the man, than the magistrate.

The same gentleman who, throughout the trial, had been most forward to speak, now rose; a man of metal to resist any fire. "Are ye all fools and mad!" he cried; "ye that are gathered here together, that like the men of old, ye shout, 'Great is Diana of the Ephesians!' For whom would you stop the course of justice? for one who is charged before you, with having visited every tribe on the shores and in the forests, to quicken the savages to diabolical revenge!—for one who flouts the faith once delivered to the saints, to your very faces!—for one who hath entered into an open league and confederacy with Satan against you!—for one who, as ye have testimony within yourselves, in that her looks and words do so prevail over your judgments, is presently aided and abetted by the arch enemy of mankind!—I call upon you, my brethren," he added, turning to his associates, "and most especially on you, Governor Winthrop, to put a sudden end to this confusion by the formal adjournment of our court."

The governor bowed his assent. "Rise, Magawisca," he said, in a voice of gentle authority, "I may not grant thy prayer; but what I can do in remembrance of my solemn promise to thy dying mother, without leaving undone higher duty, I will do."

"And what mortal can do, I will do," said Everell, whispering the words into Magawisca's ear as she rose. The cloud of despondency that had settled over her fine face, for an instant vanished, and she said aloud; "Everell Fletcher, my dungeon will not be, as I said, quite dark, for thither I bear the memory of thy kindness."

TITLE COMMENTARY

Hope Leslie

CHRISTOPHER CASTIGLIA (ESSAY DATE FALL 1989)

SOURCE: Castiglia, Christopher. "In Praise of Extravagant Women: *Hope Leslie* and the Captivity Romance." *Legacy* 6, no. 2 (fall 1989): 3-16.

In the following essay, Castiglia presents an analysis of Hope Leslie *as a frontier romance that subverts racial and gender stereotypes.*

The many exploits of the American Adam are by now well recorded. Adam is the quintessential adventurer, devoting his life to what Thoreau in *Walden* calls "extra-vagance": "I fear chiefly lest my expression may not be *extra-vagant* enough, may not wander far enough beyond the narrow limits of my daily experience, so as to be adequate to the truth of which I have been convinced. . . . I desire to speak somewhere *without* bounds" (240). Life beyond limits, beyond restriction, lived by a wandering hero unencumbered by the mundane details of home and society—this is the nineteenth-century Adam's American dream.[1]

But if extra-vagance was Adam's lot, what was Eve's? Stating that "there is no picaresque tradition among women who are novelists," Mary Morris is not alone in lamenting the less adventurous plots allotted to women.

> From Penelope to the present, women have waited—for a phone call, for a date, for a marriage proposal, for the man to return from sea or war or a business trip. To wait is to be powerless. Like patients and prisoners, women have waited for the freedom to enter the world.
>
> (C2)

A literature of imprisonment implies, however, a potential compensatory mythology of jail-break. Just such a tradition is established in the women-authored captivity romances, beginning with Susanna Rowson's *Reuben and Rachel* in 1798 and reaching an apogee in 1827 with Catharine Maria Sedgwick's **Hope Leslie**.[2] Rejecting the agency of men and overcoming the limitations imposed on women, finding strength in shared female identity and history, it is, ironically, the captivity romance that creates the first expression of female extra-vagance in America. In its fictionalization, the captivity narrative becomes not a tale of imprisonment primarily, but a tale of liberation, uniquely woman-centured.

In creating novels of female extra-vagance in the American wilderness, the authors of the captivity romance simultaneously altered stereotypes about people of color and about the "proper" character and domain of women. Recognizing in *Hope Leslie* a frontier romance with a difference, critics have focused on Sedgwick's subversion of the racial and gender stereotypes endorsed by the wilderness mythology of James Fenimore Cooper and his male contemporaries, which privileges weak, infantilized women, isolated and in need of protection from the attacks of savage barbarians.[3] Edward Foster notes that Cooper's novels "never center primarily on women—or 'females' as he often calls them—and . . . he had a decided preference for passive rather than self-reliant women" (91). Leland Person draws the contrast even more sharply. While Cooper's novels "establish triangular, doubly exploitative relationships among Indian and white males and white women that reinforce male fantasies of chivalrous protection, rescue, and revenge" (671), the woman-authored frontier romance represents "an alternative tradition that was more sympathetic to women and Indians—and to their intermarriage" (677). Featuring strong women who draw fortitude from interracial cooperation and empowering sisterhood, the woman-authored frontier narrative subverts the elements of narratives such as Cooper's, and by so doing challenges what Sandra Zagarell calls "the collusion between established narrative structures and racist, patriarchal definitions of the nation" (233).

While I agree completely with readings of *Hope Leslie* as a subversion of the racist and misogynistic assumptions of the traditional wilderness tale, I question the situating of Sedgwick's subversion solely within the framework of *The Last of the Mohicans*. The frontier mythology was not, after all, the only source of restrictive stereotypes about women, nor was it, therefore, the only narrative needing Sedgwick's revision. Cooper's novels stand synecdochically for a larger cultural inscription of women's proper character found in the enormous outpouring of domestic literature—pamphlets, editorials, manuals, and novels—authored by both men and women. While challenging the assumptions of the frontier romance, *Hope Leslie* also questions a more pervasive system of definitions of "womanhood," stereotypes that inform—but are in no sense limited to—Cooper's characterizations of women. Using a "domestic" perspective to render Cooper's wilderness more humane, Sedgwick also deploys the frontier romance to dismantle many of the assumptions of domestic literature, bringing the wilderness—

and American history—into the home. Questioning her culture's situation of "female virtue" within a specific and potentially narrow site—the home—the captivity romance, as *Hope Leslie* best demonstrates, allows women to take their domesticity on the road.

I am not arguing that the captivity romance represents a complete abandonment of domestic ideals. On the contrary, the captivity romance bears many of the marks of domestic fiction: sentimental depictions of homelife; the centrality of motherhood; faith in Christian mercy. Above all, the captivity romance comes to celebrate a system of "separate spheres" that creates strong female communities. In these novels, the heroine's adoption into an alternative community is the apparently inherent result of and the surest means of escape from her confinement.[4] The dialectic of confinement and community central to the captivity romance embodies the phenomenon, documented by Nancy Cott, of the "group consciousness" that emerged among early nineteenth-century American women due to a separation of spheres. Cott describes how industrialization forced women's consignment to a domestic sphere ideologically and physically divorced from the public sphere of commerce and politics. To justify their exclusion from the public realm, women were credited with a "natural" aptitude for "domestic influence, religious morality, and child nurture"—in short, for domesticity. But the attribution of special characteristics that marked each woman as inherently different from all men yet like all others of her sex, gave women, along with their domestic confinement, a common ground on which to gather, to sympathize, to identify. "Women's sphere" became, then, not only a site of exclusion, but of identity that, shared with others in the same social category, provided the basis of community. The intended cultural invisibility of women led instead to a strong cultural presence, giving rise to the sense of a specifically female identity that made American feminism possible (201).

The phenomenon described by Cott provides a specific example of the dialectic between restriction and knowledge written of by Michel Foucault. A society enacts "punishment, supervision, and constraint" (29), Foucault writes, in order "to repress, to prevent, to exclude, to eliminate" (24) some portion of itself. The social exercise of constraint, for Foucault, manipulates the labor forces of the body (25). Yet the confined body becomes, paradoxically, not invisible or submissive, but the site of a "field of knowledge," which Foucault calls "the soul": "psyche, subjectivity, personality, consciousness, etc." (29-30). Foucault's discussion of power-knowledge also accounts for the emergence of a group identity. When, through regulation and control, society isolates and contains an entire set of people, the act of containment gives the group status *as a group*. The constituted "body of knowledge" is not a single but a collective soul, with definable boundaries and codes, rituals and characteristics. While serving as the machinery of repression, then, confinement also constitutes a recognizable community.[5]

In the fictional topography of the captivity romance, the social transformation of the home from a place of constraint to one of empowerment is literalized into two separate sites: the former represented by the place of the heroine's confinement, the latter by her new-found community. Between lies the wilderness, the liminal space in which the heroine moves from captivity to community; historical change is dramatized as a physical journey—a jail-break—from one space to the other. By making the frontier a precondition for domestic community, the women-authored captivity romances challenge a literary and critical tradition that more typically opposes the wilderness to society.[6] While masculine extra-vagance seeks to leave behind a stifling community in favor of a romanticized solitude, female extra-vagance offers escape from a stifling isolation into an empowering community.

Although *Hope Leslie* and the other captivity romances in some ways resemble the domestic novel, to ignore Sedgwick's challenge to central elements of domestic literature is to underestimate her subversive critique of "religion, motherhood, home, and family" (145)—the four elements Jane Tompkins identifies as the roots of sentimental, or "domestic," fiction. Through the following discussion of *Hope Leslie,* I hope to keep both sides of Sedgwick's critique in view, in order to see how, by conflating and altering two genres, Sedgwick creates a heroine who can dwell in the wilderness without becoming a "rugged" (i.e., racist, misogynistic, antisocial) individualist, but can also enjoy the best of nineteenth-century domesticity without becoming, In Barbara Welter's words, a "hostage in the house" (151).

The captivity romance in general, and *Hope Leslie* in particular, challenge the twin narratives of religion and sentiment that together defined women's character in Victorian America. In contract to the mercantile practicality of the masculine sphere of politics and commerce, Victorian women were characterized, at least ideologically, by their religious devotion and by their sovereignty over matters of the heart. Often, however, the rhetoric of women's mastery of virtue and emotion idealized and therefore masked the reality of women's restriction and disempowerment. While hearing their moral superiority extolled, women were also reminded of their subordination to the needs of their families and to the wills of their husbands. As one minister told his female congregants in 1832, "the world concedes to you the honor of exerting an influence, all but divine; but an influence you lose the power to exert, the moment you depart from the sphere and delicacy of your proper character" (Cott 158). While religion sanctified women for their centrality—and subjugation—within the limited world of their families, the rhetoric of romance, by glorifying marriage, idealized the loss of a woman's financial and social autonomy. Nominally privileging women for their transcendence over the brutish standards of the marketplace, then, religion and sentimentalism also formed the cornerstones of women's domestic prison. The captivity romance's challenge to dominant nineteenth-century assumptions about woman's "natural" character and her "proper sphere" begins, then, with its refusal of religion and of romance, with their attendant "captivities" of marriage and housewifery.

The principal villain in the captivity romance is organized religion. While initially placing great stock in the promise of religion—especially Puritanism—to better the lives of women, the captivity romance eventually shows instead the efforts of religious leaders to control women by prescribing their romantic and domestic identities. The depiction of the domestic hypocrisy of Puritanism and of its disastrous consequences for women is a central concern of Harriet Cheney's *A Peep at the Pilgrims* (1824). Cheney's novel contains a humorous yet pointed debate between Mr. Wilson and Mrs. Winthrop. When the latter points out the hypocrisy of Roger Williams, who fought for freedom of conscience and then punished his wife for disagreeing with him, the former contends that in this, anyway, Williams was correct: men owe their loyalty to God; women owe theirs to husbands. A more serious and haunting presence in the novel is Anne Hutchinson, whose trial demonstrates the unwillingness of Puritan men to grant women the same freedom of conscience for which they themselves, according to Cheney, came to America.

Opposed to the masculine Puritanism—judgmental, hypocritical, and intolerant—Cheney represents a more gentle, forgiving, and open-minded theology: Puritanism as practiced by the novel's women. "Feminized" Puritanism, Cheney implies, is not only the healthiest and most virtuous, but has the power to convert the men of America. When near the end of the novel Edward Atherton (the only character apart from the narrator to praise Hutchinson) converts to Puritanism in order to marry the novel's heroine, he explicitly names Puritanism as the faith of his mother. *A Peep at the Pilgrims* ends with a different vision of Puritanism, then, and of "home rule." In Cheney's novel husbands are brought by their wives to a matriarchal religion: a truly woman-centered faith.

Less sanguine than Cheney, Sedgwick presents a strong indictment of religion in the opening chapters of **Hope Leslie**. Sedgwick's novel begins in England, where the nefarious William Fletcher has maneuvered to have his nephew (also named Will Fletcher), a wayward Puritan-sympathizer, fall in love with his daughter, Alice. By arranging this match, William hopes to force his nephew to forego his Puritan leanings and return to the established church. Will does in fact fall in love with his cousin, but when the elder Fletcher presents him with an ultimatum—disavow Puritanism or lose Alice's hand—Will resolves to flee temptation by taking passage to the New World. Alice, ignoring the wishes of her father, follows her beloved to the pier, determined to join him in his emigration. While Will is on board, arranging for Alice's passage and for a minister to marry them *en route,* Alice's father and a host of guards arrive to restrain Alice and to separate her from the young Puritan. Will stays in England hoping to remedy his situation, but to no avail. Finally he joins his friend John Winthrop aboard the *Arbella,* and Alice is eventually married to a respectable Anglican, Sir Leslie.

Throughout this episode, Puritanism is privileged as a means to break with the wills—and the pun is surely deliberate—of the English Fathers (even if in doing so one is subjected to another Will), and for its promise of a community ruled by values advantageous to women. Sedgwick shows Puritanism breaking the patrimony of traditional English values; in fact, the greedy and

manipulative Uncle William portrays Puritanism in terms of a matrilineage: "'Liberty, what is it! Daughter of disloyalty and mother of all misrule'" (8). Puritanism further carries with it an anti-hierarchical rhetoric of equality, democracy, and community: as Uncle William says, the Puritans in the New World "'might enjoy with the savages that primitive equality, about which they make such a pather'" (8). Finally, by offering women the option of duty and sacrifice to God, Puritanism provides women with an escape from traditional romance plots. As Jane Tompkins writes, "By ceding themselves to the source of all power, [women] bypass worldly (male) authority, and as it were, cancel it out" (*Sensational Designs* 163). Alice Fletcher, a captive in England, becomes a conventional abandoned heroine of sentimental fiction:[7] "impotent," living "in absolute retirement," she "in the imbecility of utter despair, submitted to her father's commands" (13-14).

Once in the New World, Will Fletcher remains, in a sense, true to the original promise of Puritanism. But before long Will, "mortified at seeing power, which had been earned at so dear a rate, and which he had fondly hoped was to be applied to the advancement of man's happiness, sometimes perverted to purposes of oppression and personal aggrandizement" (16), shuns the Puritan community by moving to a village on the edge of the colony, then to the edge of the village, and finally to the edge of Puritan morality itself.

Yet the more obvious victim of the betrayal of Puritan rhetoric—of its perversion into a mode of oppression—is not Will but Martha, the pitiable orphan Will marries in America. Knowing that Will still loves Alice, Martha nevertheless joins him in a wilderness settlement where she raises a son, Everell, and a number of daughters. Without consulting her, Will further burdens Martha with two captive Indian children—Magawisca and Oneco—as well as Hope and Faith, the two orphaned children of Alice Leslie who, widowed, dies during the voyage she is finally able to make to the New World. Will Fletcher goes to Boston to take custody of his wards. Sending Faith on to Springfield, he stays behind in Boston with Hope, the image of her mother—the Oedipal, as well as allegorical, attachment of Will and Hope continues unresolved tension throughout the novel. While Mr. Fletcher remains for no fewer than three seasons in Boston.

his little community at Bethel proceeded more harmoniously than could have been hoped from the discordant materials of which it was composed. This was owing, in great part, to the wise and gentle Mrs. Fletcher, the sun of her little system.

(29-30)

In Sedgwick's depiction of the first generation of settlers, only Mrs. Fletcher's home comes close to realizing the equality and community with which the Puritans were associated in England. It is also a world without authoritative men (there are male servants, whom, due to their low position in the social hierarchy, Sedgwick aligns with the other disempowered members of Mrs. Fletcher's household). This depiction of a peaceful, equitable domestic world devoid of the harsh and hierarchizing law of men sows the narrative seeds of a vision—of a harmonious world composed of women, children, servants, and Indians—that the rest of the novel will struggle to bring to fruition. It also reveals Sedgwick's link with the domestic novel, in which, as Tompkins writes, "The removal of the male from the center to the periphery of the human sphere" is "one of the most radical components" (*Sensational Designs* 145).

While apparently offering a domestic model, however, Mrs. Fletcher's community also questions the ideals of family and religion upon which Victorian domesticity was based. The Fletcher "home" is more like an orphanage than the traditional nuclear family that became the core of domestic morality. All the central characters except Everell are either orphans or have been taken from their natural homes. The disruption of the nuclear family, furthermore, is ironically the product of religion: the death of Alice Fletcher and the subsequent orphaning of her children is the result, Sedgwick implies, of her weakened state, brought about by the religious intolerance of her father. Magawisca and Oneco still have a father—the Pequod chief, Mononotto—but are separated from him by Puritan warfare waged against the Indians, justified by religious rhetoric. Mrs. Fletcher's household stands, then, as a challenge to the linkage of biological kinship and social harmony, and as a critique of religions that dismember the families they claim to revere.

Even "motherhood" is questioned in Sedgwick's depiction of Martha Fletcher's "little community." As her name indicates, Martha is the woman who serves—she serves the myth of English, male superiority.[8] She has unwavering faith in the protection offered by men. Although she has been warned by the old Indian woman, Nelema, that the Fletcher home is in danger of an Indian attack, Martha does not move her family to a nearby fort because she hears that her hus-

band is expected from Boston shortly, and trusts in his protection. Because of this decision Martha and most of her children are slaughtered by Pequods, and Everell and Faith taken hostage. Martha must be murdered—in the way Virginia Woolf writes of needing to murder the Angel in the House[9]—if Magawisca and Hope, her surrogate daughters, are to achieve their potential as women heroes. With the death of Martha Fletcher, her daughters are freed from the living proof of Puritanism's failure to relieve women from the limits of their existence, or to substitute "feminine" values for "masculine" ones.[10]

The model for Martha Fletcher was perhaps Sedgwick's own mother, Pamela Dwight Sedgwick, whose life Sedgwick describes in *The Life and Letters of Catharine M. Sedgwick* (1872). Like Martha, Pamela Sedgwick was her husband's second love. Theodore Sedgwick first married Eliza Mason, who died within a year of their marriage. Throughout Theodore's life, he received annual visits from the spirit of his "girl wife," who "always came to restore to him those days of young romantic love—the passages of after life vanished" (25-26). Like Will Fletcher, Theodore remarried, not for love, but for convenience: "In that time, marriage was essential to a man's life; there were no arrangements independent of it, no substitutions for it" (26). As a Congressman, Theodore Sedgwick was away from home for most of the year, leaving his wife, as Will leaves Martha, "for many months in this cold northern country, with young children, a large household, complicated concerns, and the necessity of economy" (27). Like her Puritan precursor, Pamela Sedgwick, although "oppressed with cares and responsibilities" and frequently "afflicted with the severest anguish, from an apprehension that her life was useless," "never once expressed a feeling of impatience" (37). Her mother was kept silent, Sedgwick implies, by the double-bind of sentiment and piety. She "uttered no complaint" (28) because "she knew she was most tenderly beloved, and held in the very highest respect by my father" (28). Harry Sedgwick adds that his mother "'seemed sweetly to repose on the pillow of Faith, and, when tortured by pain and debilitated by disease, she not only sustained herself, but was the comfort, support, and delight of her family.'" "'Such,'" he notes, "'was the strength of her submissive piety'" (37). Sedgwick concludes that the pressures placed upon her mother caused bouts of insanity and her death at the age of 54. Theodore Sedgwick remarried a year later.

Despite Sedgwick's purported admiration for her mother's patience—and for Martha's—she ultimately valorizes her father's life over her mother's.

> Her sufferings are past, and, I doubt not, prepared her to enjoy more keenly the rest and felicities of heaven. The good done by my father in trying to establish the government, and to swell that amount of political virtue which makes the history of the Federal party the record of the purest patriotism the world has known—*that remains.*
>
> (34)

Theodore's claim that Pamela was "'exemplary in all her sufferings'" (30) notwithstanding, Catharine had other, less patient, less passive roles in mind. Significantly, it is precisely those instruments of her mother's martyrdom—romantic sentiment and piety—that Sedgwick—who left the orthodox church and never married—chose to reject in her own life.[11]

Hope faces a further threat that her creator—choosing "to stamp all the coin of my kindness with a *sister's* affection" (**Life** 98) rather than to marry—managed successfully (although not without effort) to avoid. More dangerous than the restrictive model of womanhood offered by the heroine's mother is the deployment of romance—that mainstay of domestic literature—by her fathers, both biological and surrogate. Jessy Oliver in *Reuben and Rachel* is locked in a secluded castle until she agrees to marry the man her father has chosen for her, while in *A Peep at the Pilgrims* Miriam Grey is pressured by her father to marry the most intolerant and lifeless of the Puritans. John Winthrop himself stoops to matchmaking in **Hope Leslie**, contriving to involve Hope with Sir Philip Gardiner, whom Winthrop, along with the other elders, sees as "the selected medium of a special kindness of Providence to them" (249). The reader knows, however, that Sir Philip is an Anglican and a follower of the heretic, Thomas Morton. Winthrop is blinded to Gardiner's heresies, Sedgwick implies, because he perceives Hope Leslie, with her flouting of "feminine" roles, as more dangerous to the state than the Popish affectations of a male stranger. Winthrop deploys Gardiner as a mode of restriction; as he tells Will Fletcher, by arranging a romance for Hope, he means to put "jesses" on the overly-independent girl. Through the association of Winthrop and Gardiner, Sedgwick makes it clear that, where women are concerned, romance is the foremost tool of official restriction. Sedgwick makes the connection even more obvious in a subtle play on Calvinist theology. Governor Winthrop comments on the wayward Hope, "'I have thought

the child rests too much on *performances*; and you must allow, that she hath not, I speak it tenderly, that passiveness, that, next to godliness, is a woman's best virtue'" (153). Sedgwick shows Winthrop converting the Puritan skepticism towards a covenant of works into a justification for theocratically enforced female passivity.

Despite the restrictions imposed upon her, however, the heroine of the captivity romance inevitably chooses—and achieves—adventure over romance. Jessy Oliver escapes her father's prison and joins her friend Rachel "'in search of adventure.'" She tells Rachel, "'We will live together in humble, but contented independence'" (II:278). And rather than marry a stuffy Puritan, Miriam Grey takes to the wilderness, where she is taken captive by Indians, "adopted" by the sachem's wife, and eventually freed. In **Hope Leslie,** too, despite the efforts of the matchmaking brethren (Sedgwick nicely reverses gender stereotypes by making men the gossips and arrangers), Hope maintains her independence from all romantic entanglements, preferring the life of an extra-vagant adventurer. When Sir Philip tells Hope, "'If I had a charmed shield, I would devote my life to sheltering you from all harm,'" she responds, "'It's useless talking in this rattling storm, your words drop to the ground with the hail-stones'" (193). When Sir Philip then gallantly offers Hope his cloak, she protests, "'the cloak will but encumber me'" (193). Representing chivalric romance, Philip believes that "'ladies must have lovers—idols must have worshippers, or they are no longer idols'" (201). When it comes to fetishized women, Sedgwick momentarily realigns herself with Puritan theology and its iconoclastic aversion to idols.

Sedgwick's association of orthodox religion and romance, and her ultimate rejection of both,[12] is most clear at the conclusion of **Hope Leslie.** Sir Philip is escaping Boston on a pirate ship with a disguised woman the reader believes to be Hope Leslie. Also on board is Rosa, a young girl Sir Philip wooed from a convent, seduced, and then abandoned. Rosa, who spends the entire novel pining and sighing, is a stereotypical sentimental heroine, wasting away under the spell of romantic enthrallment. Ironically, Rosa's one act of disobedience brings both herself and Sir Philip to their deaths. Descending into the hull of the ship, Sir Philip asks Rosa to hand him the lantern she carries, but instead Rosa flings the lantern into a powder-keg, exploding the ship and all its passengers. The woman blown up with the ship is not, of course, Hope Leslie. Arriving at the Winthrop house late at night to abduct Hope, the pirate sent for that purpose instead kidnaps Jennet, the Fletchers' servant. Moralizing and interfering, Jennet represents Puritanism at its most intolerant and restrictive. She is what one might call today "male identified," seeking to out-Puritan the brethren. In one fell swoop, then, Sedgwick kills off—literally and figuratively—the two New World threats to the freedom of her female hero: romantic enthrallment and religious restriction.

Although the novel ends with the marriage of Everell and Hope Leslie, their union does not constitute a traditional euphoric ending, in which heterosexual coupling is rendered as the perfect closure to a heroine's life and of a woman author's narrative. Defying narrative conventions, Sedgwick minimalizes the importance of the marriage: while we are told the ultimate fate of every minor character in the novel in some detail, we learn nothing about the actual wedding: all we learn is that it makes society happy. Sedgwick concludes the novel by commenting of Esther Downing, who has escaped heartbreak by devoting her life to Christian duty.

> She illustrated a truth, which if more generally received by her sex, might save a vast deal of misery: that marriage is not *essential* to the contentment, the dignity, or the happiness of woman.
> (349-50)

In the end the restrictions of the heterosexual romance—exposed as the means by which the fathers proscribe the lives of their daughters—are replaced in *Hope Leslie* by sibling affection and female community. Magawisca hails Everell as a brother more than as a lover. Esther, too, in the note informing Everell and Hope of her departure to England, writes that she "'shall hereafter feel a sister's love [for Everell], who will not withold a brother's kindness'" (347). Even Hope's feelings for Everell are described by Sedgwick in terms that valorize sisterly affection over romantic love: "It has been said that the love of a brother and sister is the only platonic affection. This truth (if it be a truth) is the conviction of an experience far beyond our heroine's" (224). Passion and possession are replaced at the end of the novel with mutuality and friendship. The epigraph to the final chapter is taken from La Rochefoucald, and encapsulates the novel's social vision—and Sedgwick's contribution to the frontier romance tradition. "Quelque rare que soit le veritable amour, il l'est encore moins que la veritable amitie" ("However rare true love is, it is less rare than true friendship") (336).

Sedgwick refuses to depict her heroines as antagonistic rivals for the novel's eligible bachelor, a novelistic device that makes a woman's relationship to a man more important than any she might have with another woman. Rather, traditional romance is subordinated to an ideal of female community that spans racial difference.[13] Magawisca, Hope, and Faith become literal sisters when, in the only happy interracial marriage in nineteenth-century American literature,[14] Faith Leslie marries Magawisca's brother, Oneco. But the novel's women become comrades as well, providing mutual support and sharing a spiritual motherhood (the meeting of Faith, Hope, and Magawisca occurs at the gravesites of their two mothers, who, Magawisca tells Hope, bless the reunion). Even Rosa, the most remote woman in the novel, is mourned at the end as "a fallen, unhappy sister" (348). The sisterhood that evolves in *Hope Leslie* contrasts ironically with the men who, although "brethren," rarely act as brothers. Romance is displaced by the end of the novel by friendship, between Hope and Everell, but more significantly among the various women in the novel—white and Indian—substituting mutuality and support for subservience and hierarchy.

To further subvert religion and romance, Sedgwick's female heroes defy Puritan rule (both the active rule of the Fathers and the passive acquiescence of the Mothers) by turning the Puritan errand into a female quest. The quest is embodied by Sedgwick in a sophisticated narrative pattern of female imprisonment and escape. Although the image of imprisonment by men and release by women is pervasive, the most striking depictions of female extra-vagance come in the middle of volume one, beginning with Magawisca's rescue of Everell Fletcher and ending with Hope's release of Nelema. In these chapters Sedgwick successfully writes, in Rachel Blau DuPlessis's phrase, "beyond the ending"—beyond, that is, the endings of death and marriage that characterized the domestic novel.

The tale of Magawisca's heroism recasts the debate central to *A Peep at the Pilgrims* between masculine and feminine religion. As chapter seven begins, Everell Fletcher and Faith Leslie are the captives of the Pequod chief, Mononotto, who plans to sacrifice Everell to avenge his own son, murdered by attacking English. As Magawisca pleads for Everell's life, she looks at her father with "her mother's eyes and speaketh with her voice" (84), evoking the mother as a principle of mercy in a gesture echoed by Everell, who prays as he is led to execution that "my mother and sisters are permitted to minister to me" (88). Everell's impending execution evokes a tension between the male world of the Old Testament—based on violence, vengeance, and "artificial codes of law" (92)—and the feminine world of the New Testament—based on mercy and love, represented by the evoked spirits of the mothers. Mononotto uses the language of the Old Testament: "'Nay, brothers—the work is mine—he dies by my hand—for my first-born—life for life.'" He further explains that to give up this code would be to become "feminized": "'My people have told me I bore a woman's heart toward the enemy. Ye shall see, I will pour out this English boy's blood to the last drop, and give his flesh and bones to the dogs and wolves'" (92). Afraid that Magawisca will help Everell escape (as she in fact has tried to do during the voyage), Mononotto has her placed under guard in the dwelling of the chief's elderly and ailing sister. The reader is presented, in this episode, with the first of a series of prison-breaks, as Magawisca feels that "if she were to remain pent in that prison-house, her heart would burst" (91). Magawisca tries to spring past her guard, but he "caught her arm in his iron grasp," pushing her back into the hut. It is then that Magawisca devises a plan that enacts one of the prominent themes of the novel: the "art" of the mother-figure allows the younger woman to escape her imprisonment by men. The ailing woman has been brewing a sleeping remedy to ease her pain, some of which Magawisca now slips into the guard's drink, enabling her to escape. While Everell is prepared for execution, Magawisca runs through the forest, scaling rocks and overcoming precipices with all the natural grace of a forest-dweller, and, at the very moment that Mononotto brings his tomahawk down towards Everell's exposed neck, Magawisca leaps from a clearing, interposes her arm, and, as the "lopped, quivering member dropped over the precipice," Everell hugs her "as he would a sister that had redeemed his life with her own" (93) and makes his escape.

The story of Magawisca's rescue of Everell derives from the legend of Pocahontas, who lay her head on John Smith's to protect his life from the wrath of her father. Mary Dearborn discusses the metaphoric implications of Pocahontas's sacrifice, noting that if the act implies, as critics have claimed it does, a "ritual marriage" between the Indian princess and the white man, it does not speak well of the benefits of matrimony for women, who, literally or symbolically, risk their necks for husbands who are free to desert them. Sedgwick further implies that the law of the Old Testament—the law of the Fathers—ultimately punishes, not the sons, but the daughters. For a woman to engage in the masculine plot of heroism—betraying her "femininity" and, therefore, her "inferior" body—the betrayal must be inscribed upon her very body, like Hester's Scarlet "A," in a symbolic act of mutilation. Under the law of an eye for an eye, a mutilation of the boundaries of gender must be repaid with a mutilation of that on which those boundaries are based. When Magawisca attempts to escape the imprisonment of the father, a guard catches her by the arm. Her symbolic act of liberation from that hold is brutally ritualized here by the literal loss of the site of control.

Neither traditional romance nor adventure plots are able to accommodate the degree to which Magawisca is an active agent in her own heroism. For the witnesses, her act follows a tradition of heavenly intervention, as Sedgwick again shows religious rhetoric returning women to divine passivity: "To all it seemed that this deliverance had been achieved by miraculous aid. All—the dullest and coldest—paid involuntary homage to the heroic girl, as if she were a superior being, guided and upheld by supernatural power" (93). Sedgwick further suggests that history, authored for a white male audience, will erase the heroism of women—women of color in particular. A painting commemorating Everell's rescue depicts a man saving the sleeping boy from the attack of wild animals. *This* version—in which female heroism is "masculinized" and the Indians, so often metaphorized as animals, become literal ones—is, we are told, the one that will endure and become the official story, "'a kind of history for Mr. Everell's children'" (96). The objectivity of male-centered "history" is undermined, however, by the inclusion of a description of the painting *and* of Magawisca's actions within a letter Hope writes to Everell, in which Hope's sarcasm undercuts the legitimacy of the painting. Hope refers to her letter as her "Bethel chronicles" (111), replacing a masculine history with a feminine version. By presenting the letter verbatim, furthermore, Sedgwick allows Hope—as she allows Magawisca, Mrs. Fletcher, Esther, and even the frivolous Bertha Grafton at other points in the text—her own voice. Sedgwick's art includes those people—women, Indians—the tales of male heroism exclude.

Sedgwick extends the subversion of male myth/history—for the two are shown to be indistinguishable—through Hope's extra-vagant heroism on the trip to the newly forming settlement at Northampton. This episode mirrors Magawisca's extra-vagance, redeeming Magawisca's suffering and rendering it fruitful. First, while Magawisca loses a limb to the unequal system of male power and female captivity, Hope gains "a right godly and suitable appendage to a pilgrim damsel" (98). That "appendage" is Craddock, the most ineffectual male in the novel. But whereas Magawisca loses an "appendage" because of her extra-vagance, because of Craddock's presence, Hope can travel. When subsequently this appendage is "sacrificed"—Hope moves too quickly for Craddock and soon leaves him behind—it will be not as punishment inflicted on Hope for her heroism, but as a self-willed act to allow freer movement. Furthermore, whereas Magawisca is a victim of the Old Testament, Hope subverts one of its most misogynistic myths—the fall of Adam and Eve. In the descent from Mt. Holyoke, Craddock is bitten by a rattlesnake. Hope offers to suck the venom from the wound, "for I well knew it could not harm me, and I believed it to be life or death to my poor tutor" (102). The serpent no longer has power to harm Eve in this New World paradise; she is now an active hero rather than a passive victim. Rather, it wounds the New World Adam, no longer a powerful name but rather a comic scholar of dead languages and a "poor tutor."

Finally, whereas Magawisca is able to escape her imprisonment because of the art/magic of the disempowered mother, Hope is now able to return the favor, freeing in turn the imprisoned mother. The old Indian woman, Nelema, cures the poisoned tutor with a snake-dance, assuming "the living form of the reptile whose image she bore" as a "sign of honour" (104). But as a consequence Nelema is arrested, condemned as a witch, and imprisoned in Governor Winthrop's basement. It is from this prison that Hope Leslie sets her free. The release of the mother/artist is essential to the formation of female community; if Nelema is killed, Hope Leslie writes Everell, "you will never again hear of Magawisca, I shall never hear more of my sweet sister" (110).

By writing a novel of female extra-vagance, circumventing the narrative options presented to nineteenth-century women authors, Sedgwick frees herself as well as her heroines. Sedgwick's self-empowerment is evident in the "amplification" (119) she offers following Hope's letter, in which she thematizes the generational coming to legibility in the novel. From the mothers, who work in perishables (potions, food, weavings) or write, like Nelema, "hieroglyphics on the invisible air" (104), springs the daughter, Hope, who begins

to create an encoded text, her letter, in a semi-permanent form. Finally the narrator, writing from the nineteenth century, can explicate openly in a published text.

While Sedgwick successfully imagines a narrative of female heroism, she also seems aware that, because of the different risks she faced, extra-vagance could never be for a women what it was for a man, as Hope's most dramatic adventure demonstrates. At the midnight meeting of Hope, Faith, and Magawisca, the women are surprised by the Governor's guards, who seize Faith and Magawisca. Hope, however, is carried away in a canoe by Oneco and Mononotto, but soon the latter is struck by lightning. Oneco lands on shore, and while he frantically tries to revive his father, Hope makes her escape. She runs through the forest, until she stumbles upon a troop of drunken pirates who try to rape her. Hope again escapes and, seeing a dinghy moored nearby, leaps aboard and sets out to sea. No sooner does she push off from shore, however, than she is surprised by another pirate, Antonio, who has been sleeping in the boat. Antonio, convinced that Hope is a sacred apparition, agrees to row the "saint" back to Boston (where John Winthrop rebukes Hope for encouraging the pirate's "popish" beliefs.) Hope, arriving in Boston wet and exhausted, faints into Rosa's arms, and is carried to the Winthrop home.

Sedgwick externalizes in these "adventures" the inherent threats to women of romance: entrapment, sexual violation, and an idealization that puts the fetishized woman at the mercy of the purported adorer. All the forces Hope encounters, furthermore, immobilize her, putting her at the mercy of men, who command the means of movement (the canoe, the ship, the dinghy). Hope is exposed to these dangers through the romantic machinations of Sir Philip, who hopes by recapturing Faith to further his suit with Hope. It is fitting that Hope is returned to safety, finally, by Rosa, who puts a final end to Sir Philip's schemes, and represents the one stage of Hope's conveyance controlled by a woman. Hope's adventures—which highlight the physical danger that men threaten against women—contrast sharply with those of male characters such as Natty Bumppo, who in *The Last of the Mohicans* claims that a "secret love of desperate adventure . . . had increased with his experience, until hazard and danger had become, in some measure, necessary to the enjoyment of his existence" (270).

Despite the potential dangers to women, however, female extra-vagance in ***Hope Leslie*** challenges nineteenth-century definitions of "womanhood" by problematizing the oppositions underlying the increasingly rigid division of masculine and feminine spheres. Above all, the captivity romance deconstructs the "natural" division between "home and the world" (Cott 64) by giving women a plot outside the house, set within the American wilderness. Jane Tompkins argues that the Western arose in the early twentieth century as a reaction to the "feminine culture" of the nineteenth century. Tompkins contends that the Western *"answers* the domestic novel," becoming "the antithesis of the cult of domesticity that dominated American Victorian culture" ("West" 371). The captivity romance, I am arguing, is another response to the "cult of domesticity," and in some ways resembles the Western. Like the Western, the captivity romance challenges orthodox Christianity and privileges the frontier as an alternative to home and civilization. But while the Western rejects women as the natural representatives of religion and the home, the captivity romance rejects religion and the home as tools men use to deprive women of their independence. While the Western sees home and frontier as inherently antagonistic, the captivity romance creates a female hero who embodies the best of both worlds. The captivity romancers refute the notion that domesticity must be entirely repudiated before a heroine can live an adventurous life in the wilderness.

Dissatisfaction with "home"—as an ideological nexus if not as a lived reality—is perhaps best represented in the captivity romance through the trope of imprisonment, which, as my analysis of *Hope Leslie* should demonstrate, was stressed—even overstressed—as women's experience in America. Sandra Gilbert writes that "women writers have frequently responded to sociocultural constraints by creating symbolic narratives that express their common feelings of constriction, exclusion, dispossession" (35). Through the trope of "captivity," these romances create a uniquely American version of the madwoman in the attic. But novels such as *Reuben and Rachel* and *Hope Leslie* create neither madwomen nor dutiful, devout housewives, but adventurous and daring heroines. In offering female characters a story set in the wilderness rather than in the parlor or in the kitchen, and by representing women who are tough and shrewd enough to perform in both spheres, the captivity romances challenge the "natural" division between home and the outside world—between inside and outside, heart and head, public and private, feminine and masculine—upon which nineteenth-century separate sphere ideologies were based. In doing so, they also produce America's most striking literary expression of female extra-vagance, of women granting each other permission to enter the world.

Notes

1. For the most extensive discussions of the American Adam, see Leslie A. Fiedler, *Love and Death in the American Novel* (New York: Dell, 1960); R. W. B. Lewis, *The American Adam: Innocence, Tragedy, and Tradition in the Nineteenth Century* (Chicago: U of Chicago P, 1985); and Richard Poirier, *A World Elsewhere* (New York: Oxford, 1966).

2. By "captivity romance" I mean to indicate historical romances, authored by women between 1793 and 1827, that dramatize the experiences of women taken captive by Indians: Susanna Rowson's *Reuben and Rachel* (1799); Harriet Cheney's *A Peep at the Pilgrims* (1824); and Catharine Maria Sedgwick's *Hope Leslie* (1827). Although they share many strategies and concerns, the fictionalization of the captivity narrative distinguishes these novels from other frontier romances written by women, such as Lydia Maria Child's *Hobomok* (1824) and Eliza Laneford Cushing's *Saratoga* (1824).

3. For analyses of Sedgwick's divergence from—and subversion of—Cooper, see Foster, Person, and Zagarell.

4. Sandra Zagarell describes the subversive potential of women's communities in the context of *Hope Leslie*. Calling Sedgwick's vision of women's cooperation "communitarianism," Zagarell notes, "While historical romance usually concerns itself with individual liberty," the sisterhood of *Hope Leslie* "opposes a communitarian ethic to the rigid legalism that for Sedgwick undergirds all authoritarian male rule" (238).

5. In Foucault's analysis of how a society "supervises, trains and corrects madmen, children at home and at school, the colonized, . . . those who are stuck at a machine and supervised for the rest of their lives" (29), he neglects the exercises of restraint and confinement against women. Given the obvious connection between the control of women's production and of their bodies (through abortion laws, welfare regulation, and salary and benefit disparities, for instance), gender seems a particularly potent example of the "modalities of knowledge" (28) Foucault writes of.

6. Nina Baym writes that male critics of American literature have established that "the essential quality of America comes to reside in the unsettled wilderness and the opportunities that such a wilderness offers to the individual as the medium on which he may inscribe, unhindered, his own destiny and his own nature" (71). Baym concludes that such theories exclude women authors, since mobility, upon which wilderness mythologies are based, is a "male prerogative" (72).

7. For a full discussion of the conventions of the Richardsonian abandonment plot and of its influence on early American literature, see Herbert Ross Brown, *The Sentimental Novel in America, 1789-1860* (Durham: Duke UP, 1940). See also Cathy Davidson, *Revolution and the Word: the Rise of the Novel in America* (New York:

Oxford UP, 1986). Davidson reads the sentimental abandonment plot as a challenge to the limited options offered women in early America. While I am entirely convinced by Davidson's reading, I would argue that Sedgwick attempts to leave behind that relatively enabling plot in favor of a narrative that offers its heroine options other than marriage or seduction.

8. On Martha Fletcher's ethnocentrism, see Mary Kelley's Introduction to *Hope Leslie*, p. xxx. See also Suzanne Gossett and Barbara Ann Bardes for a discussion of Martha Fletcher's "obedient passivity," and the subsequent punishment inflicted upon her by Sedgwick.

9. Woolf writes that the Angel "was intensely sympathetic. She was immensely charming. She was utterly unselfish. She excelled in the difficult arts of family life." In order to avoid becoming such a martyred woman herself, Woolf concludes, "I turned upon her and caught her by the throat. I did my best to kill her . . . I acted in self-defense. Had I not killed her she would have killed me" (59).

10. In killing off Martha Fletcher as a way of circumventing traditional domesticity, Sedgwick follows the lead of previous captivity romances, most of which feature heroines who either have no mothers at all—Jessy Oliver in *Reuben and Rachel* and Miriam Grey of Harriet Cheney's *A Peep at the Pilgrims* are cases in point—or have at best ambivalent feelings towards a mother who soon dies, as in Lydia Maria Child's *Hobomok* and Eliza Cushing's *Saratoga*. By removing mothers from these novels, the authors free their heroines from a limited model of womanhood, for as Cathy Davidson writes, "A motherless daughter is unguided, uneducated, unprotected, but also unencumbered" (120). The only mothers who empower their daughters subvert—rather than embody—traditional definitions of womanhood. When Isabel Arundel is taken captive in Rowson's *Reuben and Rachel*, for example, she prepares her daughter Columbia for escape by telling her:

> "We are women, it is true, and ought never to forget the delicacy of our sex; but real delicacy consists in purity of thought, and chastity of words and actions; not in shuddering at an accidental blast of wind, or increasing the unavoidable evils of life by affected weakness and timidity."
>
> (I: 189)

Ironically, "delicacy" comes to mean hardiness, assurance, bravery—exactly the opposite of its traditional definition. Rowson does not choose to kill off Isabel Arundel.

11. Sedgwick tacitly acknowledges in her autobiography that she, like Hope Leslie, was released from strangling conventions of femininity by her mother's death. Left with "no regular instruction" (43), Sedgwick concludes that her "life in Stockbridge was a most happy one. I enjoyed unrestrained the pleasures of a rural childhood" (44). Her manner, Sedgwick notes, was "not conventional" (75). In place of a mother, Sedgwick "clung . . . with instinctive love and faith" (42) to a family servant, a freed slave named Mumbet, who "though perfect in service, was never servile" (41). Sedgwick's childhood was, in short, much like Hope Leslie's. Freed from the model of an overburdened yet silently suffering mother, Catharine and Hope are both released into the unconventional lives promised by an unsettled landscape and endorsed by a strong,

beloved woman of color. Not surprisingly, Sedgwick later recalls her affection for her home in Stockbridge as "too much like that of the savage" (109)—identifying herself with the Indians in her love of the land and the freedom it allows her to enjoy.

12. Sedgwick's life provided her with ample evidence of the complicit relationship between orthodox religion and domestic subservience. In *The Life and Letters of Catharine M. Sedgwick,* she describes the beliefs that led her to leave the church in 1821. Sedgwick found Calvinism "unscriptural and very unprofitable, and, I think, very demoralizing" (119). "I thought myself bound," she wrote to her sister Frances, "not to lend [my] sanction to what seems to me a gross violation of the religion of the Redeemer, and an insult to a large body of Christians entitled to respect and affection" (119). Particularly "demoralized" by orthodox Calvinism were the women of Sedgwick's family, especially her eldest sister, Eliza, who "suffered from the horrors of Calvinism. She was so true, so practical, that she could not evade its realities; she believed its monstrous doctrines, and they made her gloomy" (68). Worse than the gloom instilled by its doctrines were the "modesty," "self-diffidence," and "humility" of her sisters and mother, "so authorized and enforced by their religion that to them . . . [self-sacrifice] took the potent form of a duty" (33). Her religious beliefs, Sedgwick implies, left Eliza "occupied with household duties, first in her father's house, and then in her own; first nursing her mother, and supplying a mother's place to the children, and in her married life having twelve children of her own to care for" (70). Shortly after her departure from the orthodox church, Sedgwick joined her "enlightened, rational, and liberal" brothers (117) in the more generous Unitarian Church—"that religion which alone can give us grace in this world and life in the next" (98)—and was soon followed in her conversion by Eliza, who "escaped from the thraldom of orthodox despotism" (144). It is not surprising, given the "despotic" character assigned Calvinism in *Hope Leslie,* that Sedgwick, describing her sister's flight from orthodoxy, uses the very language she uses to narrate Hope and Magawisca's release from the lord-brethren's prisons. Sedgwick reported to Mrs. Frank Channing (sister-in-law to William Ellery Channing) that Eliza "rejoices in her freedom. But I beg your pardon, my dear friend; you do not know my sister, and you live beyond the sound of our gloomy polemics, so that you can not even imagine what liberty to such a captive is!" (144).

13. For an excellent discussion of interracial relationships in *Hope Leslie* see Leland Person. To Person's analysis I would add only that for Sedgwick interracial "sisterhood" seems more important than interracial marriage; the relationship between Hope and Magawisca is much more developed than that between Faith and Oneco, although, as Person notes, the latter relationship is characterized as more loving and respectful than any marriage between whites.

14. William Dudley and Oberea in Rowson's *Reuben and Rachel* have a loving marriage, but William is killed because he cannot surrender his English background. In Lydia Child's *Hobomok*, Mary respects her Indian husband, but never truly loves him. Child ends the novel by returning Hobomok to the forest when Mary's true love, an Englishmen who has been reported killed at sea, returns to claim Mary's hand.

Works Cited

Bardes, Barbara Ann, and Suzanne Gossett. "Women and Political Power in the Republic: Two Early American Novels." *LEGACY* 2. 2 (1985): 13-30.

Baym, Nina. "Melodramas of Beset Manhood: How Theories of American Fiction Exclude Women Authors." *The New Feminist Criticism: Essays on Women, Literature and Theory.* Ed. Elaine Showalter. New York: Pantheon, 1985: 63-80.

Cheney, Harriet. *A Peep at the Pilgrims.* Boston: Phillips, Samson, 1824.

Cooper, James Fenimore. *The Last of the Mohicans: A Narrative of 1757.* 1826. New York: Signet, 1962.

Cott, Nancy F. *The Bonds of Womanhood: "Women's Sphere" in New England, 1780-1835.* New Haven: Yale UP, 1977.

Davidson, Cathy N. "Mothers and Daughters in the Fiction of the New Republic." *The Lost Tradition: Mothers and Daughters in Literature.* Eds. Cathy N. Davidson and E. M. Broner. New York: Frederick Ungar, 1980: 115-27.

Dearborn, Mary. *Pocahontas's Daughters: Gender and Ethnicity in American Culture.* New York: Oxford UP, 1986.

DuPlessis, Rachel Blau. *Writing Beyond the Ending: Narrative Strategies of Twentieth Century Women.* Bloomington: Indiana UP, 1985.

Foster, Edward Halsey. *Catharine Maria Sedgwick.* New York: Twayne, 1974.

Foucault, Michel. *Discipline and Punish: The Birth of the Prision.* Trans. Alan Sheridan. New York: Vintage, 1979.

Gilbert, Sandra M. "What Do Feminist Critics Want? A Postcard from the Volcano." *The New Feminist Criticism: Essays on Women, Literature and Theory.* Ed. Elaine Showalter. New York: Pantheon, 1985: 29-45.

———, and Susan Gubar. *The Madwoman in the Attic: The Woman Writer and the Nineteenth-Century Literary Imagination.* New Haven: Yale UP, 1979.

Morris, Mary. "Hers." *New York Times* 30 Apr. 1987: C2.

Person, Leland, Jr. "The American Eve: Miscegenation and a Feminist Frontier Fiction." *American Quarterly* 37 (1985): 668-85.

Rowson, Susanna Haswell. *Reuben and Rachel; or, Tales of Old Times.* 2 vols. London: Minerva, 1799.

Sedgwick, Catharine Maria. *Hope Leslie; or, Early Times in the Massachusetts.* 1827. Ed. and Intro. Mary Kelley. New Brunswick: Rutgers UP, 1987.

———. *The Life and Letters of Catharine M. Sedgwick.* Ed. Mary E. Dewey. New York: Harper & Brothers, 1872.

Thoreau, Henry David. *Walden; or Life in the Woods.* 1854. New York: Harper & Row, 1965.

Tompkins, Jane. *Sensational Designs: The Cultural Work of American Fiction, 1790-1860.* New York: Oxford UP, 1985.

———. "West of Everything." *South Atlantic Quarterly* 86 (1987): 357-77.

Welter, Barbara. "The Cult of True Womanhood: 1820-1860." *American Quarterly* 18 (1966): 151-74.

Woolf, Virginia. "Professions for Women." *Women and Writing.* Ed. and Intro. Michele Barrett. New York: Harcourt Brace Jovanovich, 1979: 57-63.

Zagarell, Sandra. "Expanding 'America': Lydia Sigourney's *Sketch of Connecticut,* Catharine Sedgwick's *Hope Leslie."* *Tulsa Studies in Women's Literature* 6 (1987): 225-45.

KAREN RICHARDSON GEE (ESSAY DATE DECEMBER 1992)

SOURCE: Richardson Gee, Karen. "Women, Wilderness, and Liberty in Sedgwick's *Hope Leslie."* *Studies in the Humanities* 19, no. 2 (December 1992): 161-70.

In the following essay, Richardson Gee asserts that Hope Leslie and Magawisca in Hope Leslie *are free from their societies' conventions and have nontraditional ways of viewing themselves and nature.*

In her greatest novel, **Hope Leslie: Or, Early Times in the Massachusetts,** Catharine Maria Sedgwick implies that the equality of women and Native Americans and the continued wildness of nature are qualities that Americans should value. They are an extension of Puritan defiance of artificial power structures such as the crown and the church. Two characters particularly exemplify and support freedom and wilderness: Magawisca, a Native American woman, and Hope Leslie, a white woman. Both women are free from their societies' conventions if not from their societies' tensions; through freedom of conscience, they have developed a non-traditional way of seeing themselves and their world. They see one another as individuals, not merely as representatives of different races;[1] they see themselves as free people of conscience—not passive, impotent women; and they see nature as the body of God, not something to be molded and used by human beings.

Sedgwick supports liberty and naturalness throughout the novel, as Michael Davitt Bell states in "History and Romance Convention in Catharine Sedgwick's *Hope Leslie."* He writes that "Miss Sedgwick is celebrating the historical movement from artificial to natural or, as romantic historians liked to express it, from 'tyranny' to 'liberty' . . . it is possible for the forces of liberty to defeat the forces of tyranny" (220). Catharine Maria Sedgwick begins her attack on Puritan society by showing the noble beginnings of the Puritan movement. She tells the story of Mr. Fletcher, Hope's guardian, who personally betrays the patriarchal structures of his own British society by becoming a Puritan against the wishes of his uncle—the head of the Fletcher family. Mr. Fletcher continues this betrayal by settling in the new world, and then by leaving the town of Boston, which is controlled by a new hierarchy of Puritan fathers, and he brings up his children to have independent consciences.

Mr. Fletcher flees the town of Boston because it is a Puritan re-creation of the world from which he escaped. He sees abuses of power and notices that the players have changed but that the game remains the same. The first example of an abuse of power occurred in Mr. Fletcher's early life in England. He and his cousin, Alice Fletcher, who would later become Hope Leslie's mother, were in love. However, her father did not approve of Mr. Fletcher's religion, so he refused to allow Alice to marry her cousin. Alice's father says to Mr. Fletcher, "'I forewarn you, no daughter or guinea of mine shall ever go to one who is infected with [Puritanism]'" (1: 8); one cannot doubt that he sees his own child as a commodity—as much as is his money. This pattern continues in the Massachusetts Bay Colony as its leaders arrange matches for the young people, such as Everell Fletcher, Mr. Fletcher's son; Hope Leslie; and Esther Downing, the governor's niece. The Puritan male power structure intends to control the lives of its subjects just as clearly as its Anglican and royalist antecedents did. All the while, the male colonists speak the language of liberty.

Throughout the novel Sedgwick critiques the white male rhetoric of freedom of conscience. She points out that the white settlers of America based their new world on defiance and betrayal of patriarchal structures, such as those of the Catholic and Anglican churches and the British government and way of life. However, Sedgwick claims that freedom-loving Puritan men loved only their own freedom and betrayed the principle of freedom. In "Women and Political Power in the Republic: Two Early American Novels," Suzanne Gossett and Barbara Ann Bardes point out that "Sedgwick demonstrates that though the Puritans came to America seeking freedom to practice their religious beliefs, they established a religious polity which punished those members who claimed to act on individual conscience" (20). The Puritans were unwilling to extend freedom to their pawns—women. Native Americans, and the natural world.[2] Instead, freedom-loving Puritan men see and use people—particularly if they are women or "savages"—and the natural world to re-create the world they fled.

Mr. Fletcher feels so strongly about the abuses of the Puritans that he leaves Boston to settle in the wilderness. After coming to Massachusetts, he makes the complaint against his Puritan brothers that many of us in the 20th century make—that they came to America to obtain freedom of religion for themselves but would not extend it to others. Sedgwick says he

> was mortified at seeing power . . . sometimes perverted to purposes of oppression and personal aggrandizement. . . . [H]is heart sickened when he saw those, who had sacrificed whatever man holds dearest to religious freedom, imposing those shackles on others . . . he determined to retire from the growing community of Boston to [a] frontier settlement.
>
> (2: 16)

Like other romantics, Mr. Fletcher believes that in the wilderness, he can remain outside of civilization, of societal control, and of patriarchal authority. Unfortunately, even Mr. Fletcher is unable to completely extend freedom to those around him; for example, he is content for his own wife to remain passive and submissive to him. Sedgwick tells us of the Fletchers' removal to the wilderness:

> Mrs. Fletcher received his decision as all wives of that age of undisputed masculine supremacy (or most of those of our less passive age) would do, with meek submission . . . passive obedience to the resolve of her husband
>
> (1:16).

Mr. Fletcher praises his wife for her "obedience—; your careful conformity to my wishes; [and] your steady love" (20). Mr. Fletcher is not the only white male character to prize his own personal freedom enough to leave oppressive Boston for the wilderness. Digby, one of Mr. Fletcher's former servants, leaves Boston for an uninhabited island, thereby breaking away from his former status and escaping to the wilderness. On this island, and in wilderness in general, both Hope and Digby find independence from the rules of Boston society. In a discussion of freedom with Hope, Digby concurs with Hope's assertion that "'I like to have my own way,'" and he tells her that "'this having our own way, is what every body likes; it's the privilege we came to this wilderness world for; . . . though the gentles up in town there, with the Governor at their head, hold a pretty tight rein'" (2: 225). For white men and women of independent conscience, in the wilderness they can find freedom from societal constraints. As Michael Davitt Bell points out, this passage shows that "Hope Leslie's 'spirit,' in short, is the spirit of American history. She *is* liberty; she *is* progress" (221).

However, even the positive white male characters in this novel, the foremost of whom is Mr. Fletcher, see nature as a tool with which to create a new world in the likeness of the old world. As white men explore America's forests, groves, and plains, they ask themselves what the land can give them or what they can take from it. For instance, as Mr. Fletcher, Mr. Holioke, Hope, and her tutor explore what will become known as Mount Holyoke, the men comment only briefly on the majestic and profound beauty around them; then they speed from that observation and spend the afternoon planning how to use the land.

In a letter to Everell narrating this episode, Hope reports that "'We lingered for an hour or two on the mountain. Mr. Holioke and your father were noting the sites for future villages, already marked out for them by Indian huts'" (1: 100). Even these good men's study of the wilderness includes removing the indigenous population and turning the American wilderness into something like the tame English countryside. Hope does not condemn Mr. Fletcher's and Mr. Holioke's attitudes explicitly, but she does say, and note the masculine pronoun, that "'He must have a torpid imagination, and a cold heart, I think, who does not fancy these vast forests filled with invisible intelligences'" (1: 100).

Hope's eyes and heart are open to the beauty surrounding her. Sedgwick writes three paragraphs detailing Hope's ecstatic response to the wilderness. Hope identifies with the wildness she sees. After all, she is not a *civilized* heroine. Sedgwick later describes Hope as "rash and lawless . . . [and] open, fearless, and gay" (1: 121-2). In nearby passages, Sedgwick compares Hope to a mountain stream and to a bird flying free on the wind. Catharine Maria Sedgwick privileges Hope's vision of life and wilderness and leads us to condemn white men for seeing nature as a tool to be used—just as they see women.

Hope is as at home in the forest as is Magawisca, a Native American born and reared there. However, this novel does not state that all women have these feelings about their land. Sedgwick never gives examples of conventional women enjoying the wilderness. Like Sarah Kemble Knight, they may have to travel through it to get somewhere, but they have no sympathy with it. They avoid it or fear it, and they hunger to return to civilization, which they really define as England, with the town of Boston as an adequate substitute. The city, with its fashion, laces, millinery, and baubles which Hope disdains, is the conventional woman's only natural environment.

This kind of woman has not developed a free conscience, nor has she developed into a real American. Such a conventional woman is Hope's Anglican aunt, Bertha Grafton, whom Michael Davitt Bell calls "the most 'artificial' and European of the novel's minor characters" (219). Hope tells Everell that Aunt Grafton calls Hope's exploring the wilderness:

> very unladylike, and a thing quite unheard of in England, for a young person, like me, to go out exploring a new country. I urged, that our new country developes faculties that young ladies, in England were unconscious of possessing. She maintained, as usual, that whatever was not practised and known in England, was not worth possessing.
>
> (1: 98)

Similarly, Esther, the pattern maiden of Massachusetts, never goes into the wilderness. If Hope is a mountain rill, Esther is a canal. While Hope's hair is curly and free of regulation, Esther's hair "which was of a sober brown line, [was] parted on her forehead, and confined behind in a braid" (1:135). While Sedgwick never condemns or pokes fun at Esther, as she does at Aunt Grafton, she makes it clear throughout her text that Hope and Magawisca are the true heroines of her novel.[3]

During Hope's visit to Mt. Holyoke, she comes close to a pantheistic, Native American view of the world when she says "'I love to lend my imagination to poets' dreams, and to fancy nature has her myriads of little spirits'" (1: 99). In this passage, Hope considers the possibility that nature is not just a tool to be wielded but a living, intelligent presence to be revered, even deified. For Hope and Magawisca, the wilderness is not something to use and change, nor is it something to fear: it is a place to find God, whichever of God's names they use.

As Hope visits Mount Holyoke, she feels awe, wonder, and adoration for God because of the magnificence of nature, and she concludes that Native Americans, who live with this beauty everyday, are likely to be profoundly religious. She sees a pile of stones and comments that "It has, I believe, been the custom of people, in all ages, who were instructed only by nature, to worship on high places" and she wonders if her Christian God would find that worship acceptable. Mr. Holioke rebukes her ecumenical spirit, and while she does not come to a conclusion about this question, she does not forget this revelation, the moment when

> My senses were enchanted on that high place. I listened to the mighty sound that rose from the forest depths of the abyss, like the roar of the distant ocean, and to the gentler voices of nature, borne on the invisible waves of air—the farewell notes of the few birds that still linger with us—the rustling of the leaves beneath the squirrel's joyous leap.
>
> (1: 101)

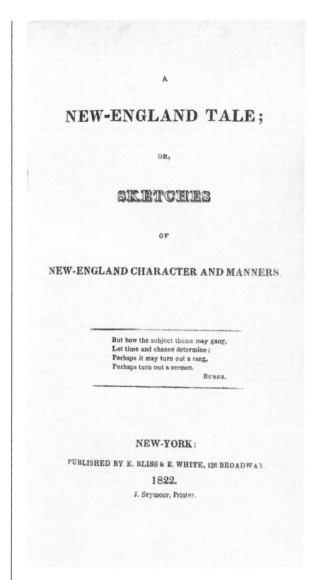

A

NEW-ENGLAND TALE;

OR,

SKETCHES

OF

NEW-ENGLAND CHARACTER AND MANNERS.

But how the subject theme may gang,
Let time and chance determine;
Perhaps it may turn out a sang,
Perhaps turn out a sermon.

BURNS.

NEW-YORK:

PUBLISHED BY E. BLISS & E. WHITE, 128 BROADWAY.
1822.
J. Seymour, Printer.

Title page of *A New England Tale* (1822).

Unlike the Christianity of other Puritans, Hope's faith and creed do not come from the Bible or any other text, but from revelation. Mr. Fletcher says that "what is difficult duty to others, hath ever seemed impulse in [Hope]" (1: 153) and Sedgwick's biographer, Edward Foster, claims that "Hope Leslie is a Christian not because the Puritan doctrines have taught her how a Christian should act; rather, she knows *instinctively* how a Christian should act" (87-8). Her instinctive response to nature is part of her generous Christianity. This religious response to nature helps Hope and Magawisca understand one another.[4]

They have a great deal in common, personally and circumstantially. Both have experienced great losses, particularly with the deaths of their moth-ers; both are close to their fathers (or father-figure in Hope's case). They also occupy similar positions in their societies. As women, both Hope and Magawisca are heir to powerless positions in their patriarchal communities. To achieve freedom, they must rebel, struggling against artificial structures to act in the history of their world and in the exploration of the wilderness. In an article discussing women and power in this novel, Suzanne Gossett and Barbara Ann Bardes state that "Both [Hope and Magawisca] make independent decisions and each at some point directly challenges the rules or laws of her own culture" (22).

Both women also respond similarly to nature. Unlike the conventional women and the men in the novel,[5] Hope and Magawisca see nature through instinctive religion and imagination. Susan K. Harris, in *19th-Century American Women's Novels: Interpretative Strategies,* claims that Sedgwick proposes a similar connection in Sedgwick's *A New England Tale.* Harris states that this novel's Rebecca is also "projected as closely in touch with nature and nature's God. . . . Rebecca's love of nature is a sign that she is one of those virtuous women . . . [her words] exhibit Rebecca's affinity for nature and amplify the narrator's affirmation of her piety" (55).

Sedgwick uses the same kind of association for Hope and Magawisca that she uses for Rebecca. However, the emphasis on nature in this novel is more basic than it is in *A New England Tale.* In passages discussing Hope and nature, Sedgwick uses conventional pronouns for both nature—she—and people—he. By using the feminine pronoun for nature, Sedgwick creates an equation between nature and women, especially because in this novel men attempt to control both. In her most positive description of wilderness, Sedgwick speaks in an authorial voice, portraying feminine wilderness inhabited by Native American men:

> not a trace of man's art was seen save the little bark canoe that glided over [the rivers] or lay idly moored along the shore. The savage was rather the vassal, than the master of nature; obeying her laws, but never usurping her dominion. He only used the land she prepared, and cast in his corn but where she seemed to invite him by mellowing and upheaving the rich mould. He did not presume to hew down her trees, the proud crest of her uplands, and convert them into "russet lawns and fallows grey." The axman's stroke, that music to the *settler's* ear, never then violated the peace of nature, or made discord in her music.
>
> (1: 83).

In this description of wilderness, Native American men become the lovers of the land, not the rapists that the settlers are. While Native American men wait for invitations to inseminate nature, white men "presume" to "violate" its prerogatives. Because this passage was written by a woman, who by definition was a rapable object—just as the land was—the argument about wilderness versus settlement reaches an intensity that is not usually found in discussions of cutting down tress.

When Sedgwick describes the attitudes of particular Native American men, they are less perfect in their understanding of the land and, similarly, in their treatment of women, than the previous idealistic passage suggests. Sedgwick does not condemn white men alone for controlling nature and women. Although she says that Native American men are generally less destructive to nature than are white men, they still see themselves as separate from nature and they still try to control women.

In the scenes Sedgwick sets in Magawisca's village, she shows Native American men controlling and excluding women and at odds with the feminine wilderness. Mononotto, her father and a Pequod chief, has lost his people, wife, and son. After these losses he can no longer find comfort in the feminine wilderness. As he and Magawisca travel through the forest, he points to a "leafless tree . . . a fit emblem of the chieftain of a ruined tribe." Magawisca tells him that he is listening to the wrong voice in the wilderness:

> listen not to the sad strain; it is but the spirit of the tree mourning over its decay; rather turn thine ear to the glad song of the bright stream, image of the good. She nourishes the aged trees, and cherishes the tender flowrets, and her song is ever of happiness, till she reaches the great sea—image of our eternity.
>
> (1: 84)

In Sedgwick's novel, Mononotto represents the Native American man who is traditionally masculine: he will not hear nature's feminine voice, just as he rejects the voices of women.

Mononotto responds to the destruction of his people and his family by taking violent action against the settlers not only out of grief, anger, or what we might call survivor's guilt, but also in order to prove that he has regained his masculinity. As he prepares to sacrifice Everell, he addresses his tribesmen: "Brothers—My people have told me I bore a woman's heart towards the enemy. Ye shall see. I will pour out this English boy's blood to the last drop and give his flesh and bones to the dogs and wolves" (1:92). Throughout the sacrifice scene, Sedgwick underlines the masculin-

ity of the ritual and Magawisca's banishment from any participation in her tribe's government. One of many examples comes when Magawisca asks her father to spare Everell. Mononotto tells her, "No—though thou lookest on me with thy [dead] mother's eye, and speakest with her voice" (1: 84). He will never again submit to his feminine self, nor will he listen to a woman.

Hope and Magawisca face many of the same problems. Neither lives in a society in which women's opinions are valued. Hope, after all, lives in a community in which the full weight of Miltonic misogyny falls on her head. She has been taught that man is the intermediate between woman and God and that God gave the natural world to man to name and use. Hope refuses to accept her society's creed, just as Magawisca continues to challenge her tribe's misogyny. Each woman continues to act with freedom of conscience, and each considers an ecumenical approach to religion. In the middle of the second volume of the novel, Hope and Magawisca meet in Boston near the graves of their mothers; they discuss their different creeds and mutual faith. Magawisca explains that "'to me the Great Spirit is visible in the life-creating sun. I perceive Him in the gentle light of the moon that steals in through the forest boughs. I feel Him here,' she continued, pressing her hand on her breast, while her face glowed with the enthusiasm of devotion. 'I feel Him in these ever-living, ever-wakeful thoughts'" (2: 189).

Neither woman sees nature as an instrument to be used. Each sees it as a temple of God. Magawisca tells Hope and Everell, as she prepares to leave them forever, that "'the Great Spirit, and his ministers, are every where present and visible to the eye of the soul that loves him; nature is but his interpreter; her forms are but bodies for his spirit'" (2: 332). Interestingly enough, Sedgwick reveals her own lack of imagination in these passages on religion and nature. She does not allow Magawisca or Hope to make the leap that many modern feminists make, that God is not male—but female or without gender. Despite Magawisca's reference to "the Great Spirit," both she and Hope continue to present God as the capitalized Him of the King James Bible.

For Sedgwick, as for Hope, Everell, and modern readers, Magawisca's leaving is mournful. Mary Kelley and other critics point out that Sedgwick wrote this novel at a time when the wilderness was disappearing with its Native American inhabitants. In a series of speeches, Magawisca connects the destruction of the wilderness with the extermination and disenfranchisement of her race. For example, at her trial, she tells her judges that "'The white man cometh—the Indian vanisheth . . . it matters not whether we fall by the tempest that lays the forest low, or are cut down alone, by the stroke of the axe'" (2: 292). While good white characters, such as Everell and Hope, cannot see the impossibility of friendship between white settlers and Native Americans, Magawisca and Sedgwick are wiser. They recognize that Native Americans cannot peacefully coexist with whites anymore than the land can remain wild under the axe.

The only hope for racial relations is the tolerant ecumenical spirit Hope struggles to learn—that blind belief in one's own vision of God and lack of respect for other visions of God are wrong. Nature, Sedgwick suggests, can teach this lesson to spirits free enough to listen. To be that free, one must not be a member of an artificial and oppressive patriarchal structure. One must be able to respond to nature with an eager ear, an open eye, and a waiting heart. If we are to learn the lessons nature teaches, we must add another caveat—that wilderness must exist to teach.

Notes

1. Hope fails to do so at one point in the novel, when she is confronted with her sister's marriage to Oneco, Magawisca's brother. In the words of the novel, "'God forbid!' exclaimed Hope, shuddering as if a knife had been plunged in her bosom. 'My sister married to an Indian!'" (2: 188). After getting to know Faith slightly, Hope learns to accept her sister's marriage and her return to her husband.

2. Sedgwick does not address the fact that black slaves were also inhabitants of this new world.

3. I do not agree with Bell's assertion that Magawisca represents untrustworthy wilderness and that Hope symbolizes trustworthy nature. I, and many readers, both modern and nineteenth-century, find Magawisca more heroic and admirable than Hope is—and equally trustworthy. Bell probably does not recognize Magawisca's greatness because he is analyzing this novel in terms of the conventional marriage plot, which places Hope in the role of "heroine." While he is correct that such a plot occurs, I think that he places too much emphasis on it and ignores other important patterns in the novel.

4. Compare Hope's instinctive religion to the artificial Christianity of the Puritans: Sedgwick says that in their view, "[w]hatever gratified the natural desires of the heart was questionable, and almost every thing that was difficult or painful, assumed the form of duty" (I: 156).

5. I should say that we do not see Everell's response to the wilderness. The first episode in which he spends a substantial amount of time in the wilderness occurs when he is on a forced march to Mononotto's camp. His mother and siblings have been killed before his

eyes and he suspects rightly that the same fate awaits him when he reaches his destination. Understandably, he does not notice anything about the wilderness at that time. When he visits the island on which Digby lives, we do not see his response to the wilderness. At that point all of the characters are preoccupied by the marriage plot. However, as Bell rightly points out, Sedgwick suggests that Everell has the right attitude toward nature because he chooses the natural Hope instead of the artificial Esther (219).

Works Cited

Bell, Michael Davitt. "History and Romance Convention in Catharine Sedgwick's *Hope Leslie.*" *American Quarterly* 22 (1970): 213-21.

Foster, Edward Halsey. *Catharine Maria Sedgwick.* Twayne's United States Authors Series TUSAS 233. (NY: Twayne, 1974): 87-88.

Gossett, Suzanne and Barbara Ann Bardes. "Women and Political Power in the Republic: Two Early American Novels." *Legacy* 2.2 (Fall 1985): 13-30.

Harris, Susan K. *19th-Century American Women's Novels: Interpretative Strategies.* Cambridge: Cambridge UP, 1990.

Kelley, Mary. "Introduction." *Hope Leslie: Or, Early Times in the Massachusetts.* By Catharine Maria Sedgwick. Ed. Mary Kelley. American Women Writers Series. New Brunswick: Rutgers UP, 1990.

Sedgwick, Catharine Maria. *Hope Leslie: Or, Early Times in the Massachusetts.* Ed. Mary Kelley. American Women Writers Series. New Brunswick: Rutgers UP, 1990.

CHERI LOUISE ROSS (ESSAY DATE MARCH 1996)

SOURCE: Ross, Cheri Louise. "(Re)writing the Frontier Romance: Catharine Maria Sedgwick's *Hope Leslie.*" *College Language Association Journal* 39, no. 3 (March 1996): 320-340.

In the following essay, Ross contends that Hope Leslie *transforms the frontier romance genre by giving it a feminist, non-racist character.*

During the nineteenth century, four writers were credited as being "the great founders of American literature": Catharine Maria Sedgwick, Washington Irving, James Fenimore Cooper, and William Cullen Bryant.[1] Sedgwick's work was extremely popular with the reading public and critically acclaimed by her contemporaries. Nathaniel Hawthorne called her "our most truthful novelist" and Washington Irving remarked on her "classic pen."[2] Margaret Fuller reported that Sedgwick is "a fine example of the independent and beneficent existence that intellect and character can give to Woman, no less than Man" and believed that her work had "permanent value."[3] As Edward Halsey Foster notes in his study of Sedgwick, "*The North American Review* consistently praised her novels, and . . . this was the most scholarly and learned journal in the country."[4] After the publication of her fourth novel, *The Linwoods* (1835), the members of Boston's Athenaeum ranked her with Irving, Bryant, and Cooper in a survey of American literary achievements.[5] Her work, like that of the male founders of American literature, was "well-received on both sides of the Atlantic."[6]

Sedgwick, the sole woman in the group, is also the only writer among the founders whose name and works had disappeared from the American canon long before the mid-twentieth century. Denigrated by powerful critics such as Van Wyck Brooks, who wrote in 1936, "No one could have supposed that her work would live," Sedgwick's novels lost the place in American letters which had once seemed assured.[7] Michael Davitt Bell continues the pattern of marginalization in his discussion of her third novel, *Hope Leslie* (1827). He finds the plot of this novel "incredibly complicated" and on several occasions refers to "the confusion of the plot."[8] He seems to share that confusion, faulting Sedgwick on these grounds, yet at the same time capably summarizing the plot in four paragraphs. He also flatly states that "it is no master piece" and calls it "an extraordinarily conventional book."[9] In the last decade, however, feminist scholars such as Mary Kelley and Nina Baym have challenged the judgment of critics who have marginalized Sedgwick's work, and so it is once again beginning to receive the critical attention and acclaim it deserves.

Particularly deserving of critical attention is Sedgwick's frontier romance, *Hope Leslie*, in which she transforms the conventions of the genre in order to propound a feminist, nonracist view. Conflating the issues concerning Native Americans, the woman question, and the historical record, Sedgwick challenges the assumptions of the patriarchy of her time: White, androcentric society has dispossessed both Native Americans and women of their inherent rights. Either vilified or ignored by the white male guardians of historical "fact," these groups found a spokesperson in Sedgwick. For once, it seems, the side of the apparently alien Other has been told, and told in such a way that it might be folded into the individual and collective self. Writing less than four decades before the Civil War, Sedgwick also prefigures the later alliance of blacks and women in presenting an alliance of Native Americans and women. The parallels between race and gender are unmistakable; they are also unprecedented in the frontier romance.

ABOUT THE AUTHOR

EXCERPT FROM AN EARLY REVIEW OF *HOPE LESLIE*

Hope Leslie, the white heroine of the work, is a finely drawn character, full of enthusiasm, affection, truth, and yet sparkling with gaiety and wit. Her friend and rival—yes, both friend and rival—Esther Downing, is lovely too, in her way, which, as was to be expected in those times, was rather a precise one, and her loveliness is as distinct from Hope's as possible. Magawisca too is another friend and rival, as we before hinted. Here are three ladies, who seem to love and admire each other as much as they do Everell Fletcher; who, by the way, excellent as he is, hardly deserves such an accumulation of honor. Is this, or is it not, a greater improbability than the character of the Indian heroine? We are afraid to leave the decision of the question to our authoress, who, if the truth must be told, appears to entertain a decided partiality for her own sex. Nor can we blame her for it. We are in no humor, indeed, to find fault with her at all, or for anything. We only hope, that as we have been tardy in noticing the last production of her pen, another will very soon be ready for our inspection. We pray her to go on, in the path in which she must excel, and has excelled, and which she ought consequently to make her peculiar one. We pray her to go on, in the name of her friends, for the public's sake, and for the honor of our youthful literature.

From *The North American Review* 26 (April 1828): 420.

The frontier romance emerged as a genre in the 1790s and declined in the 1850s.[10] It is a particularly American genre, melding the characteristics of the captivity narrative and the major features of the English historical romance, especially as presented by Sir Walter Scott in his Waverley novels. Louise Barnett has identified the main conventions of the frontier romance as follows: (1) a racist-nationalistic philosophy of white-Indian relations; (2) captivity as the central plot episode; and (3) stereotyped Native American characters ("good" and "bad" Indians); (4) a passive, imperiled white heroine who is the object of white and Indian attempts to possess her; and (5) a white hero who rescues the heroine from captivity. Other conventions include a white hero and heroine of aristocratic lineage, who are married at the end of the novel, and a grounding in historical data and use of historical personages. By 1824 these conventions were well established.[11]

In the present canon of American literature James Fenimore Cooper's preeminence is firmly established among the exemplars of this genre. Any of the five *Leatherstocking Tales* could be discussed as a representative frontier romance, but for the purposes of this study, I will follow the lead of scholars such as Barnett, who link *The Last of the Mohicans* (1826) to *Hope Leslie* and both of these to the captivity narrative.[12] In this novel, Cooper utilizes every convention described above. Several captivity episodes occur; at one time or another, all the major white characters are captured by Indians. Stereotyped characters include the lone woodsman, Hawk-eye; the good Indians, Chingachgook and his son Uncas; the bad Indian, Magua; the white hero, Duncan Heyward; the passive, imperiled, sentimental heroine, Alice, and her less passive sister, Cora, but whose mixed blood disqualifies her from consideration as heroine. The racist-nationalistic philosophy is demonstrated by the attitude of the whites who see the extermination of the Indians as inevitable and necessary to the white Westward expansion movement. The pious, noble, and often tearful Alice and Duncan are married at the end; the more self-assertive Cora, along with the bad Indian Magua and the good Indian Uncas, dies before the narrative ends; none leaves heirs.[13] The story is set in Northern New York state at the time of the French and Indian Wars in the mid-eighteenth century and includes historical personages such as General Montcalm.

Hope Leslie, set during the so-called King Philip's War (1675-76) in the environs of Boston, uses historical personages, including the Winthrops, John Eliot, Mononotto, and Sir Christopher Gardiner (here named Sir Philip Gardiner), and it ends with the marriage of the white hero and heroine. These lesser conventions of the frontier romance, however, are the only ones that Sedgwick leaves unchanged. In this essay, I will focus on three areas which subsume the major conventions. First, I will analyze Sedgwick's attitude toward Native American issues; then I will discuss her portrayal of male characters; finally, I will examine her portrayal of women characters.

Part I: Native American Issues

In *Hope Leslie,* Sedgwick presents an alternative history of white-Native American relations during and shortly after King Philip's War.[14] She dislikes the racist-nationalistic philosophy of whites toward Native Americans which she found while researching the histories written by Puritan forefathers.[15] These male-authored chronicles valorize the behavior of the white expansionist settlers while exhibiting intolerance and bigotry toward Native Americans. In contrast, Sedgwick recognizes the problem inherent in any history: ostensibly objective, histories are, in fact, written from the point of view of those who hold the power and who assume that their exercise of power is correct. Sedgwick presents her opposing view at the outset. In her "Preface" she declares:

> The Indians of North America are, perhaps, the only race . . . of whom it may be said, that though conquered, they were never enslaved. They could not submit, and live. When made captives, they courted death, and exulted in torture. These traits of character will be viewed by an impartial observer, in a light very different from that in which they were regarded by our ancestors. In our histories, it was perhaps natural that they should be presented as "surly dogs," who preferred to die rather than to live, from no other motive than a stupid or malignant obstinacy. Their own historians or poets, if they had such, would as naturally, and with more justice, have extolled their high-souled courage and patriotism.[16]

Detailed descriptions of white atrocities mark Sedgwick's alternative history. By allowing Magawisca to narrate the new version of history only after she is firmly established as intelligent, virtuous, and credible, Sedgwick underscores the violence inherent in the displacement and conquest of Native Americans. As Mary Kelley notes:

> Written during a decade in which nineteenth-century Americans were demanding still more land from the Cherokees, the Chicksaws, and the Choctaws, Sedgwick's portrayal of earlier conflicts between Puritans and the indigenous population stood in opposition to tenets that sanctioned American expansion and Indian dispossession in both centuries. *Hope Leslie* resounded with an unmistakable challenge to the morality of a nation.
>
> (xxviii)

The start of a new version of history is prompted by the warning token which Nelema, an old Native American woman, leaves behind when she visits Magawisca, who has been forced to work as a servant at Bethel, the Fletchers' homestead. Mrs. Fletcher asks Magawisca to interpret it, but torn between her loyalty to her father and her love for the Fletchers, she says only that it denotes impending danger. The trusting Fletchers do not take the warning seriously because Magawisca gives no specific details. When Everell, the Fletchers' teenage son, questions her later, she paints a graphic and moving picture of the night that the English attacked her village.

Men were away at a council when the English attacked the sleeping women and children, she explains. The invaders showed no mercy, eventually setting the Native Americans' huts on fire with the brand "taken from our hearthstone, where the English had been so often warmed and cherished" (50). Only Mononotto's family was spared. Of course, the other men suspected him of collusion because

> [h]e had been the friend of the English; *he* had counselled peace and alliance with them; *he* had protected their traders; delivered the captives taken from them, and restored them to their people; now *his* wife and children alone were living and they called him traitor. From that moment my father was a changed man.
>
> (50)

She also tells of the fate of her sixteen-year-old brother who was first captured, then brutally murdered by the English when he refused to guide them to the Indians' stronghold, and asks Everell,

> You English tell us . . . that the book of your law is better than that written in our hearts, for ye say it teaches mercy, compassion, forgiveness—if ye had such a law and believed it, would ye thus have treated a captive boy?
>
> (51)

Magawisca convinces him that "this new version of an old story . . . was putting the chisel into the hands of truth, and giving it to whom it belonged" (53). Everell, of course, has heard the events recounted many times by the whites, but "from Magawisca's lips they took on a new form and hue; she seemed to . . . embody nature's best gifts, and her feelings to be the inspiration of heaven" (53). Through Magawisca, Everell finally learns of the white provocation which led to Indian attacks. Mononotto has seen his tribe decimated by the ferocious assaults of the Puritan militias defending the expanded settlements and expropriation of land. Mononotto's wife and children have been taken captive and his eldest son decapitated. Originally a friend to the settlers, Mononotto learns to hate them because of these tribal and personal disasters. In consequence, the attack on Bethel is inevitable. Shortly after Magawisca tells her story to Everell, Mononotto and his men do attack Bethel, and although Ma-

gawisca begs her father to stop the massacre, she cannot stem the tide of death.

Sedgwick depicts this massacre in as much horrific detail as that of the English massacre of the Indians, thus giving equal treatment to the atrocities perpetrated by both sides. Sandra Zagarell remarks that

> [by] situating Indian brutality within Puritan expansionism, *Hope Leslie* strongly challenges the ways in which several popular narrative modes repressed the fundamental connections between white settlement and conflicts with the Indians. The downplaying of historical connection was conspicuous in the Puritan histories that Sedgwick researched to write *Hope Leslie* and in the frontier romances popular in the earlier nineteenth century. In both genres, Indians tend to be inherently malevolent, their violence against whites unprovoked.
>
> (233-34)

Clearly, Sedgwick provides a more balanced view of the issue than was commonly found in other works in the frontier romance. Even though "good" and "bad" Indians are portrayed, few are of the Noble Savage or Devilish Heathen stereotype. Even "bad" Indians are provided with psychological motivations which partially mitigate the cruelty of their actions.

Captivity episodes, although central to the plot of *Hope Leslie,* are not always typical of this genre because not only do Indians hold whites captive, but Puritan authorities hold Indians captive, and a Puritan impersonator attempts to abduct the title character. (Significantly, the exemplars of feminine passivity, Mrs. Winthrop and Esther Downing, are never captured.) In the major captivity episode of the novel, after William Fletcher's family is attacked by Indians and most are killed, two captives are taken: his son, Everell, the nominal hero, and Fletcher's ward, Faith Leslie. Everell escapes death not through his own cunning or bravery but through the intervention of the chief's daughter, Magawisca. In an effort to redirect "history," she pleads with her father to spare Everell's life. Mononotto, however, denies her plea; he plans to kill him to avenge the death of his son Samoset. Magawisca feigns submission, but at the same time, she unsuccessfully tries to help Everell escape. Her father separates the two when they reach an Indian village, and Magawisca correctly interprets this action as one preparatory to the captive's death. Guarded by a Mohawk, she cleverly adds an opiate to his cup, thus enabling her to escape while he is drugged. She reaches the sacrificial rock just in time to interpose her body between the victim and the knife, thus saving Everell's life but losing her right arm in the process.

As for the fate of Faith Leslie, Sedgwick undermines the code against miscegenation that Cooper so thoroughly promoted. Enamoured of Oneco since childhood and married to him during her captivity, Faith Leslie has no desire to return to live among the Puritans. As Annette Kolodny has noted, "Sedgwick offered a white heroine whose romantic attachment to an Indian included a happy accommodation to life in the woods."[17] Although Hope desperately wants to be reunited with her sister, Magawisca wisely warns her, "Those arms . . . could no more retain thy sister, than a spider's web" (188). Magawisca's words prove true when Hope and Faith finally meet. Hope pleads eloquently with her, and when that fails, uses every possible bribe to lure her away from her Indian life, but Faith determinedly refuses. From Faith's perspective, white society offers nothing. As Richard Slotkin has noted,

> Sedgwick violates Puritan psychology and aligns herself with the more radical environmentalists in asserting that Mary's [Faith's] proper place is now with her Indian husband and in seeing this acculturation in a positive light, rather than as a sort of degeneracy.[18]

Sedgwick finds nothing degenerate in Native American culture; instead, she presents it as nourishing to white culture. This presentation represents a radical departure: from the time of Mary Rowlandson on, white settlers considered Native Americans to be subhuman; in consequence, their lifestyle was also denigrated.

"Rescued" at the same time that Magawisca is taken prisoner, Faith is miserable: "All day, and all night . . . she goes from window to window, like an imprisoned bird fluttering against the bars of its cage; and so wistfully she looks abroad, as if her heart sent forth with the glance of her eye" (265-66). Oneco, too, is heartbroken, thinking of nothing but how to reclaim his "white bird" (326). Disguising himself as a sailor, he gains admittance to the Winthrop household and signals to his wife. Faith may not be as inventive as Hope (more on this later), but she is clever enough to conceal her emotions until the time is propitious for her to approach Oneco and thus vouchsafe their escape. Sedgwick characterizes Faith and Oneco as well-adjusted, loyal spouses who genuinely love each other. Authorial approval of their union permeates the novel. According to Louise Barnett, they make up "the only interracial couple in the frontier romance to achieve a happy ending."[19] Thus, taking an unprecedented stand against a long line of authors repelled by the thought of miscegenation, Sedgwick presents a strong and subversive critique of this taboo.[20]

Through her rewriting of the Puritan histories, Sedgwick succeeds in presenting a more balanced account of the white-Native American conflicts in the seventeenth century and, by extension, argues against further Native American displacement in the nineteenth century. She also promotes racial tolerance through her approbation of Native American culture and the marriage of Faith and Oneco.

Part II: Portrayal of Male Characters

Everell, the central male character, possesses heroic attitudes, but he is never allowed to become a heroic figure. In each of three major episodes, he proves to be ineffectual. During his Indian captivity, he is unable to escape even with the covert guidance of Magawisca. He resigns himself to death, and only Magawisca's last-second intervention saves him. When she is incarcerated, he attempts to remove the bars from her prison window to allow her to escape, but he is frightened away by the sound of approaching voices before he can accomplish the task. When Hope is captured—first by Oneco and Mononotto and then when Chaddock's men attempt to capture her—Everell plays no part in her escape, therefore disqualifying himself from the role of conventional hero.

Even in his personal relationships, Everell cannot seem to take charge of his life. He becomes engaged to marry Esther through a concatenation of events over which he seems unable to exert any control. In love with Hope but bound to Esther against his will, he resigns himself to his fate. Only because Esther finally breaks their engagement upon realizing that he does not love her, is he free to marry the woman of his, not his elders', choice. She does not, however, absolve him from responsibility. In a letter addressed to Everell and Hope, she asks, "Would it not have been better, as well as kinder, to have said, 'Esther, I do not love thee,' than to have permitted me to follow my silly imaginings, and thereby have sacrificed my happiness for this world—and thine—and Hope Leslie's?" (346).

Although the novel does end with marriage for the white hero and heroine, it is significant that Everell chooses the independent Hope Leslie over the passive Esther. The question remains, however, why Hope accepts Everell. Several possible reasons may explain her choice. First, she and Everell spent their formative years together in the Fletcher household, and childhood affection may lay the foundation for stronger feelings. Second, perhaps Everell's sojourn in England has made him more tolerant than other less flexible young men of her acquaintance and has, consequently, added to his original appeal. Neither Hope nor Everell holds typical Puritan views; but the two of them share many attitudes. Everell simply cannot translate his ideas into viable plans as Hope does. He recognizes Hope's true abilities, however, and treats her as his equal—and better. Hope recognizes Everell's good qualities; with her independent personality, she does not need a strong-willed man who will attempt to dominate her.

Interestingly for a frontier romance, *Hope Leslie* portrays the Puritan impersonator, Sir Philip Gardiner, rather than a Native American, as villain. Clearly, Gardiner is treated as a reprehensible character. Having no morals and no scruples, he calculates his every action to further his own nefarious plans. First he tries to win Hope's favor, but when she fails to succumb to his charms, he plans to take her captive and then coerce her into becoming his mistress. As Leland Person has stated,

> Hope Leslie has far more to fear from the white, civilized male than her sister has to fear from her Indian abductor. . . . The novel suggests very clearly that the threat of assault or forced marriage inheres in cultural attitudes of possession and authority—in a view of women as objects. . . . Sedgwick seems to have realized that the most serious threat to frontier women did not necessarily proceed from Indians.[21]

Gardiner, the epitome of the "white, civilized male," instigates the only threats to Hope's chastity. It is his machinations which cause Hope to be at risk among Chaddock's men.

Gardiner also possesses a history of using and abusing women; Hope is not his first victim. Prior to his arrival in Boston, he had seduced Rosa, his present mistress, whom he forces to impersonate a male page. He has ruined her life, for although he cares nothing about her, she has fallen in love with him. Aware of her feelings, Gardiner abuses and ignores her. Tired of her and finding her an ever-increasing threat to his real anti-Puritan identity, he wants only to dispose of her. With Rosa in mind, he visits Magawisca in jail and offers her freedom on the condition that she take Rosa with her into the wilderness. He suggests that Magawisca give her to Oneco to take the place of his captive wife. If Oneco does not agree to this plan, perhaps she can be guided to a French Canadian convent. Appalled, Magawisca refuses such a condition for her freedom although she desperately wants to be free: "And dost thou think . . . that I would make my heart as black as thine, to save my life?" (257). Here is Sedgwick's strongest reminder that white males can be much more dangerous to women than Native Americans are.

Part III: Portrayal of Women

The alternative history which Sedgwick writes also presents a critique of Puritan attitudes toward women. Unless, like Anne Hutchinson, they had committed transgressions, women's voices were silenced in these male-authored chronicles. In *Hope Leslie* women's voices are heard, and it is clear which voices Sedgwick favors. For instance, Governor Winthrop's wife is characterized contemptuously as "a horse easy on the bit" and as a woman whose submission to her husband's will is total (145). With the creation of the title character and her Native American counterpart, Sedgwick valorizes a different heroine. Even some of the male critics of the day found her strong women characters appealing. A writer for the *North American Review* asserted that Hope Leslie is "a finely drawn character, full of enthusiasm, affection, truth, and yet sparkling with gaiety and wit" and called Magawisca "a glorious creature."[22] A writer for the *Western Monthly Review,* however, faulted Sedgwick for her portrayal of Magawisca, stating, "We should have looked in any place for such a character rather than in an Indian wigwam."[23] It is such an attitude, among others, that Sedgwick's novel addresses. Hope and Magawisca share many traits. They are, in effect, spiritual sisters who bridge the supposed color barrier. Sedgwick presents them as brave, intelligent, strong-willed, independent women who follow the dictates of their consciences. Both Hope and Magawisca attempt to redress the wrongs of their separate but equally male-dominated societies. Both defy patriarchal authority and risk their lives to rescue captives of the other race.

Hope's first real demonstration of these characteristics comes when her tutor, the good-hearted but bumbling Master Cradock, suffers a rattlesnake bite while accompanying Hope on an outing. She wants to suck the venom from the wound, but Digby, her supervisor within the patriarchal society, deems the proposed action too dangerous and prevents her. Hope ignores his status and *acts,* turning to nonwhite healing arts. She convinces Mr. Fletcher to let Nelema, who can provide an antidote, treat Cradock. Nelema's ministrations succeed.

Sedgwick, however, does not ignore possible negative repercussions; she honestly depicts the impact of the patriarchy exercising its power. Nelema is accused of practicing witchcraft and is held as a prisoner in Judge Pynchon's cellar. Hope courageously testifies on her behalf, but the town patriarchs find her presumptuous and dismiss her attempt to gain mercy for Nelema: "Thou art forward, maiden . . . in giving thy opinion; but thou must know, that we regard it but as the whistle of a bird; withdraw, and leave judgment to thy elders" (109). Refusing to "leave judgment" to those whom she believes to be wrong, Hope steals the key to the cellar when Nelema is condemned to death, frees her, and with the connivance of Digby (significantly now her ally), effects Nelema's escape from the town. The narrator commends Hope's action:

> This was a bold, dangerous, and unlawful interposition, but Hope Leslie took counsel only from her own heart, and that told her that the rights of innocence were paramount to all other rights, and as to danger to herself, she did not weigh it, she did not think of it.
>
> (120)[24]

Hope's intervention is indeed unlawful and precipitates a direct power struggle. The male authorities do not publicly censure her, but Judge Pynchon suspects her of aiding and abetting in the "disappearance" of Nelema. Consequently, the Puritan fathers decree that Hope must reside with Governor Winthrop's family in Boston to learn proper maidenly behavior. Furious, the seventeen-year-old Hope refuses to leave her home with the Fletcher family, yet she has no choice but to go. Judge Pynchon "felt the necessity of taking instant and efficient measures to subdue to becoming deference and obedience, the rash and lawless girl, who had dared to interpose between justice and its victim" (121).

The other Puritan leaders agree that Hope is too independent and strong-willed. Governor Winthrop remarks that "she hath not . . . that passiveness, that next to godliness, . . . a woman's best virtue" (153). His wife agrees that Hope is hardly a role model for Puritan maidenhood:

> Our heroine's independent temper, and careless gaiety of heart, had more than once offended against the strict notions of Madam Winthrop, who was of the opinion that the deferential manners of youth, which were the fashion of the age, had their foundation in immutable principles.
>
> (206)

Mrs. Winthrop has bought the whole bill of goods; conditioned to accepting male authority, she confuses moral principle with societal expectations.

Hope's friend Esther Downing, the Winthrops' niece, also chastises her for unseemly behavior:

> Hope Leslie . . . you do allow yourself too much liberty of thought and word: you certainly know that we owe implicit deference to our elders and superiors;—we ought to be guided by their advice, and governed by their authority.
>
> (180)

Hope, however, is adamant, rejoining, "I do not entirely agree with you about advice and authority. . . . I would not be a machine to be moved at the pleasure of anybody a little older than myself" (180).

Ironically, Hope's removal to Boston does not change her personality; predictably, it only affords more opportunities for her to come into conflict with the patriarchal authorities. Soon after her arrival in Boston, she goes off alone late at night to meet with Magawisca in order to hear tidings of her sister Faith, who had been captured by the Pequods seven years ago.

Hope defies the conventions of her society not only by attending this clandestine meeting but also by refusing to explain her absence to Governor Winthrop and the rest of his household upon her return. Because of her pledge of secrecy, she cannot tell the truth; because of her honest and forthright nature, she cannot manufacture a lie. The narrator refers to Hope's refusal to explain as an action denoting "moral courage," but "Governor Winthrop was not accustomed to have his inquisitorial rights resisted by those of his own household, and he was more struck than pleased" by Hope's silence (175).

A series of captivities soon ensues, including those of Faith and Magawisca by the Puritan militia and that of Hope by Mononotto and Oneco—from whom she escapes. This, Hope's first captivity, underscores Sedgwick's inversion of the usual convention; instead of passively waiting to be rescued by the hero, Hope takes the initiative and rescues herself.

Her relief, however, is only temporary because she soon happens upon the notorious pirate Chaddock and his men, who are in the midst of a drunken revel on the island. Momentarily lacking self-confidence, Hope naively asks for help and promises a monetary reward if they will take her to Boston. One of the men replies, "There's no reward could pay for you, honey" (240). Horrified, Hope runs away, but Chaddock's men pursue her until she discovers a boat, unties it, and pushes off. Once again, she saves herself.

Hope displays her quick wit under pressure when she discovers that one of Chaddock's men, Antonio Bastista, already occupies the boat. The Catholic Antonio mistakes her appearance for a visitation by the Virgin Mary. Because she has faithfully studied under Cradock, she understands the Italian language and informs Antonio that she is not what he believes her to be. Still under the impression that she is a celestial visitant, Antonio desperately begins guessing which saint she is. Thinking quickly, Hope allows him to believe that she is his patron saint, Petronilla, and asks him to take her to Boston. In this manner, she turns the situation to her advantage and safely arrives home without help from the hero and others who seek to rescue her.

Hope not only effects her own escape from captivity but also makes sure that others escape. When Magawisca is imprisoned and faces trial and a possible death sentence, Hope takes charge. She first courageously speaks to Governor Winthrop, asking for Magawisca's release. Of course, he denies her request; he also warns her against further intercession. Feeling strongly that Magawisca will not receive an unbiased trial and thus must be freed, Hope originates a plan and enlists the help of Everell, Digby, and Cradock. This daring plan succeeds, ending with Hope escorting Magawisca (disguised as Cradock) from prison under the watchful eye of the jailer.

Hope manifests intelligence, courage, and independence during every crisis. She absolutely will not abide by manmade laws—or even some Biblical laws as interpreted by men—if they oppose the dictates of her conscience. Unable to countenance injustice, she cannot help but intervene.

Like Hope, Magawisca evinces the traits which Sedgwick privileges. Magawisca, at fifteen, "was slender, flexible, and graceful; and there was a freedom and loftiness in her movement, which though tempered with modesty, expressed a consciousness of high birth" (23). She wore "an expression of dignity [and] thoughtfulness" (23). Mrs. Fletcher comments in a letter shortly before her death, "I have, sometimes, marvelled at the providence of God, in bestowing on this child of the forest, such rare gifts of mind, and other outward beauties" (32).

Throughout the novel, Magawisca evinces courage, along with pride in her heritage. When she comes to the Winthrop house to arrange for the meeting between the sisters, her ethnic pride surfaces as Hope reacts negatively to Faith and Oneco's marriage. Shocked, Hope cries, "My sister married to an Indian!" (188). Magawisca is equally scornful:

"An Indian!" exclaimed Magawisca, recoiling with a look of proud contempt, that showed she reciprocated, with full measure, the scorn expressed for her race. "Yes—an Indian, in whose veins runs the blood of the strongest, the fleetest children of the forest, who never turned their backs on friends or enemies, and whose souls have returned to the Great Spirit, stainless as they came from him. Think ye that your blood will be corrupted by mingling with this stream?"

(188)

She also displays her pride when she appears before the magistrates at her trial: "There was certainly nothing of the culprit, or suitor in the aspect of Magawisca; neither guilt, nor fearfulness, nor submission" (282). Accused of conspiracy, Magawisca looks at her judges and speaks: "I am your prisoner, and ye may slay me, but I deny your right to judge me. My people have never passed under your yoke—not one of my race has ever acknowledged your authority" (286). When the trial must be recessed for a month, Magawisca, hating to return to her dungeon, commands Governor Winthrop to give her "death or liberty" (293).

In direct contrast to Hope and Magawisca, Esther embodies the domestic virtues of piety, submissiveness, and obedience, and she is extremely inflexible in her beliefs. In the course of the novel, she repeatedly disappoints both Hope and Everell when either asks her to help in a good (but subversive) cause. Esther, clearly, would like very much to please them, but she cannot bring herself to do so. Her stern Puritan conscience and concomitant obedience to authority prevent her from thinking for herself. For instance, after Hope explains the ruse which she used to persuade Antonio to row her to shore, Esther is asked to comment on Hope's behavior: "I would rather, Hope, thou hadst trusted thyself wholly to that Providence that had so wonderfully wrought for thee thus far" (272). Esther, like the model Puritan maiden that she is, sees the hand of Providence behind Hope's deliverance. Sedgwick, however, clearly demonstrates that Hope alone, through her initiative, intelligence and quick wit, should have the credit for her escape.

Another instance which is emblematic of Esther's personality occurs when Magawisca is incarcerated. Everell begs her to help him in a scheme to free Magawisca; Esther adamantly denies him. The narrator comments on her refusal: "No earthly consideration could have tempted her to waver from the strictest letter of her religious duty. . . . [S]he thought they had not Scripture warrant for interfering between the prisoner and the magistrates" (277-78). Instead, she visits Magawisca daily in order to convert her to Puritanism, for the authorities have intimated that such a conversion may lighten her sentence. Thus, Esther and Magawisa become involved in a power play. Esther's attempt is doomed from the start—Magawisca wants no such instruction. So while Esther plays by the rules and fails, Hope enlists the help of Everell, Cradock, and Digby, and thereby secures Magawisca's escape. Undoubtedly, Esther would lay down her life for her friends, but she lacks the ability to bend the rules for them. Esther Downing, like her Aunt Winthrop, epitomizes the "passiveness, that, next to Godliness, is woman's best virtue" which was so esteemed by the patriarchy (153). Sedgwick's impatience with this attitude is obvious when she refers to the two women as "the straight-laced Mrs. Winthrop and her perpendicular niece" (114).

Catharine Maria Sedgwick valorized personality characteristics in Hope and Magawisca that are directly opposed to those promoted by patriarchal society. These two strong, active female characters evince traits which most other writers of frontier romances assigned to male characters. The combined force of Hope and Magawisca provide a devastating critique of women as inherently passive and weak. Through her portrayals of Hope and Magawisca, Sedgwick manipulated the conventions of the frontier romance to offer a covert feminist message critical of both Puritan and nineteenth-century society's treatment of women. This covert feminist message combines with a nonracist history of the events of King Philip's War to critique the androcentric Puritan histories which she used as sources. Sedgwick's subtext draws parallels between the disenfranchised Native Americans and white women, prefiguring the alliance between women and blacks later in the nineteenth century. Throughout the novel, she de-authorizes the presumed authority of white, male androcentric society; in this respect, **Hope Leslie** is even more radical than it appeared to be to its nineteenth-century readers.

Notes

1. Edward Halsey Foster, *Catharine Maria Sedgwick* (New York: Twayne, 1974) 20.

2. Foster 169 and 58, respectively.

3. Margaret Fuller, as quoted in Bell Gale Chevigny, ed., in *The Woman and the Myth: Margaret Fuller's Life and Writings* (Old Westbury, NY: Feminist Press, 1976) 190. Catharine Maria Sedgwick was the only American woman writer whom Fuller ever cited by name.

4. Foster 22.

5. Mary Kelley, introd., *Hope Leslie: or Early Times in the Massachusetts* (New Brunswick: Rutgers UP, 1987) xi. Hereafter cited parenthetically in the text.

6. Foster 23.

7. Van Wyck Brooks, *The Flowering of New England* (New York: Dutton, 1936) 188.

8. Michael Davitt Bell, "History and Romance Convention in Catharine Sedgwick's *Hope Leslie*," *American Quarterly* 22 (1970): 215.

9. Bell 214-15.

10. Early examples of the genre include Ann Eliza Bleecker's *History of Maria Kittle* (1793) and Susannah Rowson's *Reuben and Rachel* (1798). These early novels display "an uncertain welding of plot elements." *Maria Kittle* is little more than a fictionalized captivity narrative, while *Reuben* does connect the captivity narrative to the romances as later frontier romances do. See Louise K. Barnett, *The Ignoble Savage: American Literary Racism, 1790-1890* (Westport, CT: Greenwood, 1975).

11. Lydia Maria Child's *Hobomok* (1824) varies from the established conventions of the genre in that the heroine Mary Conant marries the Indian Hobomok while in a deranged state of mind after learning of the apparent death of her white lover, Charles. After several years of marriage and the birth of a child, Charles reappears. Hobomok relinquishes his wife and fades into the forest; the child later goes to Harvard, and all traces of his Indian heritage are erased. See Lydia Maria Child, *Hobomok* (1824; rpt. New Brunswick: Rutgers UP, 1986). As Carolyn Karcher has maintained, however, Child does not "contest the Puritan chroniclers' version of the wars that decimated the Indians . . . nor had she come to view the Indians . . . as the true heroes of the American epic" as she would a few years later. In *The First Settlers of New-England* (1828) Child does, however, argue against patriarchal authority and links the issues of male dominance and white supremacy. The message of *Hobomok* is that the alternative to war between Native Americans and whites is assimilation of Native Americans into white society. This, however, will involve eradication of Indian heritage and culture. See Karcher's "Introduction" to *Hobomok and Other Writings on Indians* (New Brunswick: Rutgers UP, 1986), ix-xxxviii.

12. Edward Halsey Foster states, "*Hope Leslie* was published a year after *The Last of the Mohicans*, and it is entirely possible that Miss Sedgwick's novel is in part an answer to Cooper's" (Foster 91).

13. Sandra Zagarell notes that "Uncas was not 'the last of the Mohicans,' and one of his sons was named Oneco," the name Sedgwick chooses to give Faith Le-

slie's husband. See Zagarell's essay, "Expanding America: Lydia Sigourney's *Sketch of Connecticut* and Catharine Sedgwick's *Hope Leslie*," *Tulsa Studies in Women's Literature* 6 (Fall 1987): 239; hereafter cited parenthetically in one text.

14. Richard Slotkin points out that during King Philip's War (1675-78), "the New England colonies were driven nearly to the brink of destruction by a loose federation of formerly friendly tribes. . . . [It] was extraordinary from an historical standpoint: it was the last of the wars fought by New England without the aid or intervention of outside powers." See Slotkin, *Regeneration Through Violence: The Mythology of the American Frontier, 1600-1800* (Middletown, Conn: Wesleyan UP, 1973), 79.

15. Sedgwick relied on the histories penned by Hubbard, Winthrop, and Trumbell, according to Foster.

16. Catharine Maria Sedgwick, *Hope Leslie* (1827; rpt. New Brunswick: Rutgers UP, 1987) 6. Subsequent references are to this edition and will be cited parenthetically by page reference only.

17. Annette Kolodny, *The Land Before Her: Fantasy and Experience of the American Frontiers, 1630-1860* (Chapel Hill: U of North Carolina P, 1984) 81.

18. Slotkin 453.

19. Barnett 119.

20. Zagarell, Foster, and Gossett and Bardes assert that the marriage of Faith and Oneco alludes to Cooper's abhorrence of miscegenation and consequent separation of Cora and Uncas. See Suzanne Gossett and Barbara Bardes, *Declarations of Independence: Women and Political Power in Nineteenth-Century American Fiction* (New Brunswick: Rutgers UP, 1990). See, also, Gossett's "Women and Political Power in the Republic: Two Early American Novels," *Legacy* 2 (Fall 1985): 13-30.

21. Leland Person, "The American Eve: Miscegenation and a Feminist Frontier Fiction," *American Quarterly* 37 (Winter 1985): 680-81.

22. *North American Review* 26 (1828): 411.

23. *Western Monthly Review* 1 (1828): 294.

24. Erica R. Bauermeister notes that "Hope almost never fails in her endeavors; her one blunder is to attempt to make a match between Esther and Everell, mistakenly believing that submission against her nature would be a virtue. . . ." See Bauermeister, "*The Lamplighter, The Wide, Wide World, and Hope Leslie*: Reconsidering the Recipes for Nineteenth-Century American Women's Novels," *Legacy* 8 (Spring 1991), 22.

FURTHER READING

Biographies

Foster, Edward Halsey. *Catherine Maria Sedgwick.* New York: Twayne Publishers, Inc., 1974, 171 p.

Offers a full-length biography of Sedgwick.

Kelley, Mary. "Catherine Maria Sedgwick, 1789-1867." *Legacy* 6, no. 2 (fall 1989): 43-50.

Provides a biographical and critical overview.

———. "A Woman Alone: Catherine Maria Sedgwick's Spinsterhood in Nineteenth-Century America." *New England Quarterly* 51, no. 2 (June 1978): 209-25.

Compares the feminine ideal that Sedgwick professed in her fiction with the realities of her personal life.

Saulsbury, Rebecca R. "Catharine Maria Sedgwick (1789-1867)." In *Nineteenth-Century American Women Writers: A Bio-Bibliographical Critical Sourcebook,* edited by Denise D. Knight, pp. 351-60. Westport, Conn.: Greenwood Press, 1997.

Offers an overview of Sedgwick's life, her major works and themes, and the critical reception of her writing.

Criticism

Bauermeister, Erica R. "*The Lamplighter, The Wide, Wide, World* and *Hope Leslie*: Reconsidering Recipes for Nineteenth-Century American Women's Novels." *Legacy* 8, no. 1 (spring 1991): 17-28.

Provides a comparative study of three novels written by prominent nineteenth-century women writers, commenting on the novels standing as autonomous works of literature.

Fetterley, Judith. "'My Sister! My Sister!': The Rhetoric of Catherine Sedgwick's *Hope Leslie*." *American Literature* 70, no. 3 (September 1998): 491-516.

Contends that Hope Leslie *is a novel that examines and reflects the political and ideological contradictions of its times.*

Ford, Douglas. "Inscribing the 'Impartial Observer' in Sedgwick's *Hope Leslie*." *Legacy* 14, no. 2 (1997): 81-92.

Discusses the manner in which Hope Leslie *addresses the repressive treatment of women and Native Americans.*

Garvey, T. Gregory. "Risking Reprisal: Catharine Sedgwick's *Hope Leslie* and the Legitimation of Public Action by Women." *American Transcendental Quarterly* 10, no. 1 (March 1996): 41-58.

Asserts that Hope Leslie *dramatizes the challenge of female authorship in nineteenth-century America while also displaying the advantages of expanding women's responsibility for moral values of the public arena.*

Gossett, Suzanne and Barbara Ann Bardes. "Women and Political Power in the Republic: Two Early American Novels." *Legacy* 2, no. 2 (fall 1985): 13-30.

Analysis and comparison of Hope Leslie *and Sarah Josepha Hale's* Northwood *as fictive expressions of the contemporary political culture.*

Gould, Philip. "Catherine Sedgwick's 'Recital' of the Pequot War." *American Literature* 66, no. 4 (December 1994): 641-62.

Examines Sedgwick's revisionary history of the Pequot War in Hope Leslie *and discusses the significance of its anti-patriarchalism.*

Higonnet, Margaret R. "Comparative Reading: Catherine M. Sedgwick's *Hope Leslie*." *Legacy* 15, no. 1 (1998): 17-22.

Examines Sedgwick's novel by noting parallels and differences with works by other nineteenth-century women writers, including George Sand and Germaine de Staël.

Holly, Carol. "Nineteenth-Century Autobiographies of Affiliation: The Case of Catherine Sedgwick and Lucy

Larcom." In *American Autobiography: Retrospect and Prospect,* edited by Paul John Eakin, pp. 216-34. Madison, Wis.: University of Wisconsin Press, 1991.

Discusses nineteenth-century women's autobiographies as texts of affiliation that present the autobiographical act as an intimate, interactive, and female event.

Karafilis, Maria. "Catherine Maria Sedgwick's *Hope Leslie*: Fostering Radical Democratic Individualism in the New Nation." *American Transcendental Quarterly* 12, no. 4 (December 1998): 327-44.

Proposes that a conflict exists in Hope Leslie *between Sedgwick's desire for an alternative model of government and her desire to foster a domestic national literature.*

————. Introduction to *Hope Leslie; Or, Early Times in the Massachusetts,* by Catherine Maria Sedgwick, edited by Mary Kelley, pp. ix-xxxvii. New Brunswick, N.J.: Rutgers University Press, 1987.

Examines Sedgwick's most famous novel and its reception against its historical and social background.

Kelley, Mary. "Negotiating a Self: The Autobiography and Journals of Catherine Maria Sedgwick." *New England Quarterly* 66, no. 3 (September 1993): 366-98.

Appraises Sedgwick's autobiography and journals in the context of the larger contemporary political and ideological landscape in which they were written.

LaMonaca, Maria. "'She Could Make a Cake as Well as Books'." *Women's Writing: The Elizabethan to Victorian Period* 2, no. 3 (1995): 221-34.

Examines and compares the impact of Sedgwick's and Anna Jameson's "domestic advice manuals" and "conduct books" on nineteenth-century women.

Mitchell, Domhnall. "Acts of Intercourse: 'Miscegenation' in Three 19th Century American Novels." *American Studies in Scandinavia* 27, no. 2 (1995): 126-41.

Discusses three nineteenth-century novels—Lydia Maria Child's Hobomok, *James Fenimore Cooper's* The Wept of Wish-ton-Wish, *and Sedgwick's* Hope Leslie—*that imagine the possibility of union between Native Americans and whites.*

Nelson, Dana. "Sympathy as Strategy in Sedgwick's *Hope Leslie*." In *The Culture of Sentiment: Race, Gender, and Sentimentality in Nineteenth-Century America,* edited by Shirley Samuels, pp. 191-202. Oxford, England: Oxford University Press, 1992.

Contends that the sympathetic frame of reference employed by Sedgwick and other women authors in their frontier romances fostered a more positive cultural vision by attempting to promote similarities between races and cultures.

Singley, Carol J. "Catherine Maria Sedgwick's *Hope Leslie*: Radical Frontier Romance." In *Desert, Garden, Margin, Range: Literature on the American Frontier,* edited by Eric Heyne, pp. 110-22. New York: Twayne Publishers, 1992.

Examines Hope Leslie *as a frontier romance that offers an alternative vision of American women and culture.*

Stadler, Gustavus. "Magawisca's Body of Knowledge: Nation-Building in *Hope Leslie*." *The Yale Journal of Criticism* 12, no. 1 (spring 1999): 41-56.

Claims that by investing narrative authority in the figure of Magawisca, Sedgwick uses an individual to dramatize the public issues of conflict between the colonists and Native Americans in her novel.

Welsh, Sister Mary Michael. "An Analysis of Miss Sedgwick's Novels." In *Catharine Maria Sedgwick: Her Position in the Literature and Thought of Her Time Up to 1860,* pp. 21-34. Washington, D.C.: Catholic University Press, 1937.

Overview of Sedgwick's best-known novels, including A New-England Tale, Hope Leslie, *and* The Linwoods.

OTHER SOURCES FROM GALE:

Additional coverage of Sedgwick's life and career is contained in the following sources published by the Gale Group: *Dictionary of Literary Biography,* Vols. 1, 74, 183, 239, 343, 254; *Literature Resource Center; Nineteenth-Century Literature Criticism,* Vols. 19, 98; and *Reference Guide to American Literature,* Ed. 4.

MARY WOLLSTONECRAFT SHELLEY

(1797 - 1851)

English novelist, short story writer, and travel writer.

The daughter of noted authors Mary Woll-stonecraft and William Godwin, Shelley became widely known as a literary talent of her own right with the 1818 publication of *Frankenstein; or, the Modern Prometheus*. The story of a scientist who attempts to bring life to a dead body, *Frankenstein* has become one of the most iconic and recognizable novels of the past two centuries. Though Shelley produced a variety of works throughout her career—including novels, short stories, and essays—the bulk of critical scholarship has focused on *Frankenstein*. Feminist critics have argued that the novel explores a range of themes, including the repression of women, childbirth and parental responsibility, and gender roles at the beginning of the nineteenth century. Such scholars claim that *Frankenstein* acts as a manifestation of Shelley's own feelings about motherhood and her role as a wife as well as an early attempt to articulate a feminist position. The most famous assessment of Shelley comes from the poet Leigh Hunt, who called Shelley "four-fam'd," referring to her parents, her husband—poet Percy Bysshe Shelley—and the monstrous creature she created.

BIOGRAPHICAL INFORMATION

Shelley was born August 30, 1797, to two of the foremost intellectuals of the eighteenth century. Wollstonecraft, an outspoken advocate for women's rights, died shortly after Shelley's birth, leaving Shelley in the care of her father. Godwin, a novelist and political philosopher, was by all accounts an undemonstrative and self-absorbed intellectual, but Shelley's attachment to him was powerful. This later became a major theme in her work, particularly in *Mathilda* (1959; believed to have been written c. 1819). In 1801 Godwin married a widow named Mary Jane Clairmont. Shelley's relationship with her stepmother was strained from the beginning for several reasons, such as Shelley's intense feelings for her father, her idolization of her dead mother, and Clairmont's preference for her own children over Shelley and her half sister. Shelley did not receive any formal education, but instead learned to read at home, having access to her father's extensive library. In 1812 tensions between Shelley and her stepmother prompted Godwin to send his daughter to stay with William Baxter and his family. On her return to London later that year, she met Percy Bysshe Shelley, who had become a disciple and financial supporter of her father. In 1814 the couple declared their love for each other and eloped to France. Although the couple married—following the suicide of Percy's first wife, Harriet—

their initial relationship caused a long-term estrangement between Shelley and her father. The Shelleys had four children together, though only one survived to adulthood. Shelley lapsed into a deep depression after the deaths of her children, and her relationship with her husband became strained.

Despite their personal losses as well as considerable financial hardships, the Shelleys devoted a great deal of time and energy to the study of literature, language, music, and art, associating with some of the most noted writers of their day, including Lord Byron and Leigh Hunt. During an evening with her husband, Byron, and Byron's companion John Polidori at Lake Leman, Switzerland, Shelley first conceived the idea for *Frankenstein*. After reading a selection of Gothic stories, the four challenged each other to create their own horrific tales. Shelley became inspired by a discussion between Byron and her husband regarding the notion of creating life with electricity and that night awoke mesmerized by a vision of a creature animated by such means. She began to write the monster's narrative, which Percy Shelley urged her to expand into a novel. In 1822 Percy drowned while the couple was living in Lenci, Italy. A year later, Shelley returned to England with her son. Her life after her husband's death was marked by melancholy and hardship as she tried to support herself and her child. Her husband's father offered her a meager stipend, but ordered that she keep the Shelley name out of print—thus, all her works were published anonymously. She earned money by contributing biographical and critical sketches to *Chamber's Cyclopedia* and writing short stories for literary annuals. Her financial situation improved when her father-in-law increased her allowance after her son came of age, and the pair traveled to Europe, where Shelley wrote a number of travel essays. Too ill in her last years to complete her most cherished project, a biography of her husband, Shelley died on February 1, 1851, at the age of fifty-four.

MAJOR WORKS

A story steeped with mythic allusions—as suggested by the subtitle *The Modern Prometheus*—*Frankenstein* has been characterized variously as either a Gothic, Romantic, horror, or science fiction novel. However, acting in sharp contrast to the rationality of Enlightenment literature, the Gothic atmosphere of *Frankenstein* rejects the scientific objectivity of modern science fiction in its sense of the strange and the irrational. An epistolary novel told in increasingly tightening circles, or frames, and interspersed with poetry, *Frankenstein* concerns a driven medical student, Victor Frankenstein, who desires to use science to bypass God and create human life in his laboratory. Piecing together a cadaver from discarded corpses, Victor reanimates the body using electricity, bringing "life" to his horrific creation. After the creature awakens, Victor becomes disgusted and abandons his new offspring, leaving the monster to wander the forests alone. The creature eventually learns language and finds Victor's journal, recounting the details of his creation. Tracking Victor to his family home, the creature demands that Victor take responsibility for his existence and suggests that Victor should build him a mate. When Victor refuses, the creature murders Victor's wife on their wedding night. Victor pursues the creature, who leads him north into the Arctic Circle. Here, Victor meets the captain of a doomed polar expedition, Robert Walton, to whom he narrates his tale—the novel is structured as a letter from Walton to his sister. Victor eventually dies from illness, and the creature appears, explaining to Walton his reasons for seeking vengeance and his remorse at his creator's death. The creature leaves Walton's ship, vowing to destroy himself, so no one else will ever know of his existence.

Although *Frankenstein* has consistently dominated critical discussions of her oeuvre, Shelley was a prolific author. After *Frankenstein*, her most recognized work is *The Last Man* (1826), which describes a post-apocalyptic future. Set in the twenty-first century, the novel depicts a plague that devastates Europe and the efforts of the "last man"—Lionel Verney—to reach Rome in a search for other survivors. The work is noted for its inventive descriptions of the future and is considered an early prototype of contemporary science fiction. *Valperga; or, The Life and Adventures of Castruccio, Prince of Lucca* (1823) and *The Fortunes of Perkin Warbeck* (1830) are historical novels that have received scant attention from critics, while *Lodore* (1835) and *Falkner* (1837), thought by many to be autobiographical, have frequently been examined by literary historians for their insight into the lives of the Shelleys and their circle of peers. Shelley's posthumously-published novel *Mathilda* concerns the incestuous attraction between a father and daughter which results in the father's eventual suicide. The daughter, Mathilda, reveals the story to a poet whom she meets while mourning her father in Scotland. Scholars have come to a general consensus regarding *Mathilda,* suggesting that the characters are largely based on Shelley, her father, and Percy Shelley.

CRITICAL RECEPTION

Since Shelley's death, critics have devoted little attention to her range of works, focusing almost entirely on *Frankenstein.* Early commentators relegated the novel to the Gothic genre, practiced by such popular authors of the era as Ann Radcliffe and Matthew Gregory "Monk" Lewis. While most early Victorian reviewers reviled what they considered the sensationalist and gruesome elements in *Frankenstein,* many praised the anonymous author's imagination and powers of description. Since the latter part of the nineteenth century, critics have reassessed *Frankenstein,* analyzing the novel's mythic-philosophic theme of Prometheanism, and its expression of Romantic ideals and attitudes. Scholars have also focused on the influence of Percy Shelley's poetry, Godwin's humanitarian social views, and Wollstonecraft's feminism on the text. Critics have noted the influence of John Milton's *Paradise Lost,* Goethe's *Faust,* and Samuel Taylor Coleridge's "The Rime of the Ancient Mariner" on Shelley's narrative. Criticism on *Frankenstein* has proliferated since the 1950s, encompassing a wide variety of themes and approaches. Feminist scholars have often viewed Frankenstein's creature as a representation of the repression of women, arguing that the novel expresses Shelley's own feelings regarding her self-identity and her feelings of anxiety as a female writer. Such critics have also noted that *Frankenstein,* along with Shelley's other works, offers commentary on the social construction of gender, the marginalization of women, and the ways in which women figure into the public world. In recent years, feminist scholars have additionally begun to examine Shelley's other, more neglected writings. In particular, they have explored the themes of incest, familial relationships, and psychological trauma in *Mathilda,* offering psychobiological interpretations of the work and viewing it as a revelatory text regarding her relationship with her father. Feminist academics have called for a critical reassessment of Shelley's oeuvre, arguing that her prose reveals a writer with a wide range of stylistic abilities and thematic interests. Overall, critics have maintained that Shelley's writing echoes her mother's early feminist views and addresses complex questions of multiple sexualities, gender roles, and the pressures facing female writers in the nineteenth century.

PRINCIPAL WORKS

History of a Six Weeks' Tour through a Part of France, Switzerland, Germany, and Holland, with Letters Descriptive of a Sail round the lake of Geneva, and the Glaciers of Chamouni [with Percy Bysshe Shelley] (travel essays) 1817

Frankenstein; or, the Modern Prometheus (novel) 1818

Valperga; or, The Life and Adventures of Castruccio, Prince of Lucca (novel) 1823

The Last Man (novel) 1826

The Fortunes of Perkin Warbeck, A Romance (novel) 1830

Lodore (novel) 1835

Falkner: A Novel (novel) 1837

Rambles in Germany and Italy in 1840, 1842, and 1843 (travel essays) 1844

Tales and Stories (short stories) 1891

*Mathilda (novel) 1959

Collected Tales and Stories (short stories) 1976

The Journals of Mary Shelley. 2 vols. (journals) 1987

The Letters of Mary Wollstonecraft Shelley. 3 vols. (letters) 1988

---

*   Originally titled *The Fields of Fancy, Mathilda* is believed to have been written c. 1819.

PRIMARY SOURCES

MARY WOLLSTONECRAFT SHELLEY (ESSAY DATE 1818)

SOURCE: Shelley, Mary Wollstonecraft. Preface to *Frankenstein; or, The Modern Prometheus,* pp. 1-2. London: Henry Colburn and Richard Bentley, 1831.

In the following preface to her 1818 edition of Frankenstein; or, The Modern Prometheus, *Shelley introduces her work, touching on its purpose and how it was conceived.*

The event on which this fiction is founded has been supposed, by Dr. Darwin and some of the physiological writers of Germany, as not of impossible occurrence. I shall not be supposed as according the remotest degree of serious faith to such an imagination; yet, in assuming it as the basis of a work of fancy, I have not considered myself as merely weaving a series of supernatural terrors. The event on which the interest of the story depends is exempt from the disadvantages of a mere tale of spectres or enchantment. It was recommended by the novelty of the situations which it develops, and however impossible as a physical fact, affords a point of view to the imagination for the delineating of human passions more comprehensive and commanding than any which thee ordinary relations of existing events can yield.

I have thus endeavoured to preserve the truth of the elementary principles of human nature, while I have not scrupled to innovate upon their combinations. The Iliad, the tragic poetry of Greece, Shakespeare in the Tempest and Midsummer Night's Dream, and most especially Milton in Paradise Lost conform to this rule; and the most humble novelist, who seeks to confer or receive amusement from his labours, may, without presumption, apply to prose fiction a license, or rather a rule, from the adoption of which so many exquisite combinations of human feeling have resulted in the highest specimens of poetry.

The circumstance on which my story rests was suggested in casual conversation. It was commenced partly as a source of amusement, and partly as an expedient for exercising any untried resources of mind. Other motives were mingled with these as the work proceeded. I am by no means indifferent to the manner in which whatever moral tendencies exist in the sentiments or characters it contains shall affect the reader; yet my chief concern in this respect has been limited to the avoiding the enervating effects of the novels of the present day, and to the exhibition of the amiableness of domestic affection, and the excellence of universal virtue. The opinions which naturally spring from the character and situation of the hero are by no means to be conceived as existing always in my own conviction; nor is any inference justly to be drawn from the following pages as prejudicing any philosophical doctrine of whatever kind.

It is a subject also of additional interest to the author that this story was begun in the majestic region where the scene is principally laid and in society which cannot cease to be regretted. I passed the summer of 1816 in the environs of Geneva. The season was cold and rainy, and in the evenings we crowded around a bluing wood fire and occasionally amused ourselves with some German stories of ghosts which happened to fall into our hands. These tales excited in us a playful desire of imitation. Two other friends (a tale from the pen of one of whom would be far more acceptable to the public than anything I can ever hope to produce) and myself agreed to write each a story founded on some supernatural occurrence.

The weather, however, suddenly became serene; and my two friends left me on a journey among the Alps and lost, in the magnificent scenes which they present, all memory of their ghostly visions. The following tale is the only one which has been completed.

GENERAL COMMENTARY

A. A. MARKLEY (ESSAY DATE 1997)

SOURCE: Markley, A. A. "'Laughing That I May Not Weep': Mary Shelley's Short Fiction and Her Novels." *Keats-Shelley Journal* 66 (1997): 97-124.

In the following excerpt, Markley attempts to reassess Shelley's reputation by examining her stories and novels, arguing that a fresh look at her neglected stories, which explore themes such as the loyalty of women and arranged marriage, shows the breadth of her interests and stylistic abilities.

I

Still fixed in the general cultural memory as a grieving widow who was unable to reproduce the success of her first novel, Mary Wollstonecraft Shelley has not been known as a writer skilled in a range of generic conventions. Until very recently her reputation has been based almost solely upon *Frankenstein* (1818), and occasionally *The Last Man* (1826), both of which are serious works of science fiction within which Mary Shelley also refashioned the genre of her father's popular confessional narratives, such as *Things As They Are, or the Adventures of Caleb Williams* (1794), *St. Leon, A Tale of the Sixteenth Century* (1799), *Fleetwood* (1805), and *Mandeville* (1817). Nevertheless, Mary Shelley also wrote the historical novels *Valperga* (1823) and *The Fortunes of Perkin Warbeck* (1830), the Victorian domestic novels *Lodore* (1835) and *Falkner* (1837), and two travel books, *History of a Six Weeks' Tour* (1817) and *Rambles in Germany and Italy* (1844), all of which demonstrate significant differences in style and tone from her better-known Godwinian confessional narratives. It has only been within the last few years that significant numbers of scholars have begun to move beyond *Frankenstein* in assessing her work, and 1996 marked the first publication of all of her novels together in a complete edition, indeed the first publication of several of the novels in this century.[1]

If we are to give Mary Shelley her due as an artist, it is important to establish a framework for analyzing her work that does not derive solely from *Frankenstein,* a framework that takes into account her versatility and range from multiple stylistic and generic perspectives. An analysis of many of her shorter pieces, for example, reveals that not only did she experiment with more than one literary genre, but she very often reworked her serious themes and conventions, employed so effectively in such novels as *Frankenstein* and *The Last Man,* in a lighter, more artistically playful vein. Mostly short stories that Mary Shelley wrote for gift-book annuals—as financial necessity dictated in the mid to late 1820s and 1830s— many of these works display her wit and ability as a humorist, an aspect of her literary personality which has not been sufficiently acknowledged.[2] Moreover, an analysis of these stories offers a rare view of Mary Shelley the writer at work, in this case using and reusing material that inspired her in the composition of her more serious, longer novels.

Mary Shelley produced the majority of her short stories for publication in *The Keepsake,* a popular annual published every November in time for holiday gift-giving. In working in the rapidly growing gift-book genre, she faced a number of restrictions quite different from those of the three-decker novel. In his Introduction to the *Collected Tales and Stories,* Charles E. Robinson explains that annuals such as *The Keepsake* often contracted with writers to compose stories of a certain rigidly-set length to accompany plates they had already chosen to publish (p. xvi). In *The Keepsake* for 1831 (publ. 1830), for example, Mary Shelley's stories **"Transformation: A Tale,"** and **"The Swiss Peasant"** were published to accompany plates depicting young women entitled "Juliet" and "The Swiss Peasant."[3] The plates were a particular point of pride for *The Keepsake*'s editor, Mary Shelley's friend Frederic Mansel Reynolds, who in the Preface to this number heartily thanks a contributor for permission to publish a frontispiece engraving of a painting of "Haidée," which has no apparent connection to the contents of the annual. Although Mary Shelley's stories are often linked to their respective plates of necessity, the relationship between the illustration and the story is in most cases artificial and rather tenuous.[4] A study of her work for the annuals reveals Mary Shelley's remarkably consistent production of high quality work true to her own literary designs, which simultaneously satisfy the necessity of illustrating predetermined engravings.[5]

Indeed, in many of these short pieces, Mary Shelley manages to complement the plate which she was obligated to "illustrate" in a creative, sometimes even humorous manner. This may suggest something of her attitude toward the restricting genre of the annuals. After all, her feelings must have been mixed about frequently having to put aside work on her novels during the 1820s to compose short stories in order to support herself and her son. And most of her work for the annuals involves treating themes of love and romance, meeting the editors' requirements for stories involving beautiful young women aimed at a largely female readership. The various twists that Mary Shelley is able to put on the themes of these stories provides an array of evidence for her professional poise and artistic skills within a set genre.

No doubt the limited attention paid to Mary Shelley's short stories, along with the majority of her other works, is partly the result of the critical assumption, beginning as early as her own lifetime, that her post-*Frankenstein* work is aesthetically inferior. Perhaps the most unfortunate fact of her publishing career is that the genius behind *Frankenstein* often has been attributed in varying degrees to her husband, Percy Bysshe Shelley.[6] Even Richard Garnett, one of the most important nineteenth-century figures responsible for the preservation of Mary Shelley's reputation and the first editor of her short stories, contributed to the abiding perception of Mary Shelley's work after *Frankenstein* as inferior. In his Introduction to Mary Shelley's *Tales and Stories* of 1891, Garnett attempted to defend Mary Shelley against those who attributed her success in *Frankenstein* solely to her relationship with her husband. Nevertheless, he undercuts his defense by dismissing her later novels, with the exception of *The Last Man:*

> None of Mary Shelley's subsequent romances approached *Frankenstein* in power and popularity. The reason may be summed up in a word— Languor. After the death of her infant in 1819, she could never again command the energy which had carried her so vigorously through *Frankenstein.* Except in one instance, her work did not really interest her. Her heart was not in it.[7]

Garnett did, however, see many of the virtues of Mary Shelley's short stories, although he credited their general success to the restrictions of the short story format of the period. He wrote that "the necessary limitations of space afforded less scope for that creeping languor which relaxed the

FROM THE AUTHOR

SHELLEY ON THE AUTHORSHIP OF
FRANKENSTEIN
To [Sir Walter Scott]

Bagni di Lucca 14 June-1818

Sir

Having received from the publisher of Frankenstein the notice taken of that work in Blackwood's magasine, and intelligence at the same time that it was to your kindness that I owed this favourable notice I hasten to return my acknowledgements and thanks, and at the same time to express the pleasure I receive from approbation of so high a value as yours.

Mr Shelley soon after its publication took the liberty of sending you a copy but as both he and I thought in a manner which would prevent you from supposing that he was the author we were surprised therefore to see him mentioned in the notice as the probable author,—I am anxious to prevent your continuing in the mistake of supposing Mr Shelley guilty of a juvenile attempt of mine; to which—from its being written at an early age, I abstained from putting my name—and from respect to those persons from whom I bear it. I have therefore kept it concealed except from a few friends.

I beg you will pardon the intrusion of this explanation—

Your obliged & c & c Mary Wollst^ft Shelley.

Shelley, Mary Wollstonecraft. "A Letter to Sir Walter Scott." In *The Mary Shelley Reader*, edited by Betty T. Bennett and Charles E. Robinson, pp. 391-92. New York: Oxford University Press, 1990.

nerve of her more ambitious productions" (Introduction, p. xi). In addition, he claims that the annual's tendency to affect "an exalted order of sentiment" was "perfectly suited" to Mary Shelley as a writer of passion and emotion (p. x). Although Garnett credited her for her ability to create "poetical atmosphere" and for the deeply interwoven biographical elements in her work, he did not acknowledge the range of her work. He did not comment on the humorous and parodic elements of such works as **"Transformation"** and **"The Mortal Immortal,"** for example, nor did he credit either of these stories for their subtle reworkings of the Godwinian confessional narrator; **"The Mortal Immortal"** he saw merely as "a variation on the theme of *St. Leon*" (p. xiii).

In reassessing Mary Shelley's reputation as a writer, it must be acknowledged that her short stories vary widely in both tone and generic form, and that the "grieving widow" was in fact capable of great originality, wit, and humor. Her supposed "languor" after the deaths of her children and husband neither stifled Mary Shelley's ability to produce great literature, nor prevented her from exercising a marked ingenuity, even a kind of ironic playfulness, in some works. She frequently achieves these effects by imaginatively playing off the engravings provided her, putting a creative twist on the typical literary fare published in the annuals at that time.

I begin by looking at three stories in which Mary Shelley treats the theme of the loyalty of women, in each case reworking what constitutes a frequently recurring theme in her longer fiction, namely *Valperga*, *The Last Man*, and *Perkin Warbeck*, novels written during the mid to late 1820s. In **"The Bride of Modern Italy,"** Mary Shelley provides a wryly ironic critique of the Italian custom of arranged marriages, which she witnessed while living in Italy from 1818-1823, as well as a humorous response to her husband's infatuation with the young Emilia Viviani. **"The False Rhyme"** is a comic treatment of the extent of one woman's loyalty; and **"The Dream"** a humorous deflation of many of the conventions of gothic literature that Mary Shelley often drew on in her own novels. The protagonist of **"The Dream"** is in many ways a comic recasting of such figures as Ellen in **"The Mourner,"** written two years earlier, or even the heroine of *Mathilda*—both characters whose obsessive grief cripple them emotionally.

Next I will look at three stories in which Mary Shelley reworks conventions of science fiction and the fantastic—like those found in her well-known novels *Frankenstein* and *The Last Man*. In **"Roger Dodsworth: The Reanimated Englishman,"** for example, Mary Shelley gently satirizes contemporary British culture through the device of a European "Rip Van Winkle," whose reanimation in a later century allows her to associate nineteenth-century England with the revolutionary England of the Interregnum. In this story she provides a lighter treatment of the same situation that she had taken up in the unfinished "**Valerius: The Reanimated Roman**" and *The Last Man.* In "**The Mortal Immortal**" and "**Transformation,**" Mary Shelley reaches the height of her gift for humor. In these stories she develops the themes of human immortality and of body-swapping, and while doing so she also recasts the Godwinian confessional narrator, a character-type that strongly influenced her conception of both Victor Frankenstein and Lionel Verney. In addition, she draws on the popular figure of the Byronic hero, traces of whom are also evident in such figures as *Valperga*'s Castruccio, and *The Last Man*'s Lord Raymond. And, in her humorous treatment of fantastic plot elements, she reworks elements of science fiction and the supernatural that characterize her own more serious fiction, *Frankenstein* in particular.

Mary Shelley was driven to the necessity of having to produce short works quickly in order to support herself and her son Percy Florence in the years following Percy Bysshe Shelley's death, so it is not surprising to find that she occasionally found it worthwhile to rework some of the serious themes to which she devoted herself in her novels. That she reworked the themes with such wit, and sometimes in parodic or humorous ways, however, may be surprising to readers who know her only for her more serious longer fiction. Perhaps Mary Shelley found in these lighter short stories a welcome release from the serious themes that she was continually drawn to in her novels; one may think of Byron's lines from *Don Juan*: "And if I laugh at any mortal thing / 'T is that I may not weep" (IV.iv.1-2).

II

"**The Bride of Modern Italy**" is an excellent example among Mary Shelley's shorter fiction of her artful, playful mode. First published in 1824 in the *London Magazine,* in it Mary Shelley took the opportunity to respond to her husband's obsession with the young Italian Emilia Viviani in 1820-1821, who was the inspiration for Percy Bysshe Shelley's "Italian Platonics," and his poem *Epipsychidion.* Although "**The Bride of Modern Italy**" is a rather gentle treatment of this situation, a passage in a letter that Mary Shelley wrote to Maria Gisborne on 7 March 1822 clarifies her feelings. In reporting to Mrs. Gisborne Emilia's marriage, Mary Shelley writes, "The conclusion of

our friendship *a la Italiana* puts me in mind of a nursery rhyme which runs thus—

> As I was going down Cranbourne lane,
> Cranbourne lane was dirty,
> And there I met a pretty maid,
> Who dropt to me a curt'sey;
> I gave her cakes, I gave her wine,
> I gave her sugar candy,
> But oh! the little naughty girl!
> She asked me for some brandy

Now turn Cranbourne lane into Pisan acquaintances, which I am sure are dirty enough, & brandy into that wherewithall to buy brandy (& that no small sum *pero*) & you have [the] whole story of Shelley['s] Italian platonics."[8]

During the time in which she composed "**The Bride of Modern Italy**," or soon thereafter, Mary Shelley was at work on another fiction, in which she idealizes Percy Bysshe Shelley in the character of Adrian, Earl of Windsor, a major figure in *The Last Man.* Adrian embodies the virtues of genius, gentleness, and altruism that Mary Shelley most admired in her husband. Emily Sustein notes that Mary Shelley had to put aside her work on the novel from time to time in order to write short stories for more ready money; her work on "**The Bride of Modern Italy**" therefore offered her an alternative site for working through the anguished feelings regarding the difficult issues in her marriage in the years immediately preceding Shelley's death.[9]

The Shelleys became acquainted with Emilia Viviani while living in Pisa in 1820, and both Mary and Shelley were drawn to her out of sympathy for her plight. The daughter of the governor of Pisa, Emilia was confined to a convent until her family arranged her marriage—a process which excluded Emilia's wishes altogether. Mary Shelley's initial response was horror at Italian conventions concerning arranged marriages. In a letter to Leigh Hunt, she described the pitiful, lamenting Emilia: "Her only hope is to marry but her very existence is almost a secret—what an exceptional wedding! I will tell you, my friend, how they marry in this country."[10] Her diatribe against the conventions of arranged marriages continues in a long description of a sample marriage contract, in which a groom's physical and financial attributes are described in detail; his name is to be withheld until the contract was agreed upon by both families. But it is not merely the contemporary Italian mode of arranging marriages that Mary Shelley satirizes in "**The Bride of Modern Italy**"; she also draws a gently critical portrait of her husband in the story—perhaps in part to balance the idealization of Shelley in **The Last Man**'s Adrian. Shelley had become infatuated with Emilia Viviani soon after the Shelleys made her acquaintance, and his feelings for the young girl and the emotional relationship he carried on with Emilia drove a wedge between him and his wife at a time when the marriage was strained by the deaths of Harriet Shelley, their children Clara and William, and problems between Claire Clairmont and Byron concerning Claire's daughter Allegra. As Shelley grew more enamoured of Emilia Viviani, Mary may well have grown gradually more suspicious of the girl's duplicity despite her innocuous demeanor.

In the story, Mary Shelley represents Emilia as "Clorinda Saviani," a woman whose very name, "Clorinda," playfully recalls the military Clorinda of Tasso's *Gerusalemme Liberata* in order to exploit the comic potential of the woman-warrior. Clorinda's last name, "Saviani," ironically comes from the Italian *savio* or "wise," a detail that suggests that the girl is not the innocent that she appears to be. Like Emilia, Clorinda is shut up in a convent until her marriage is arranged, and Mary Shelley's long, de-romanticized description of Clorinda's convent itself parodies a convention of gothic literature. "If my reader has never seen a convent," Mary Shelley writes, "let him dismiss from his mind all he may have heard or imagined of such abodes, or he can never transport himself into the garden of St. S———" (p. 32). The narrator describes the weather-stained building and the kitchen garden (overgrown, untended, and strewn with "broken earthen-ware, ashes, cabbage-stalks, orange-peel, bones, and all that marks the vicinity of a much frequented, but disorderly mansion" [p. 32]), creating an exceptionally prosaic setting, something far more earthy than readers might expect. In effect Mary Shelley deflates the conventional gothic setting of the convent, destroying any likelihood that it will invoke the darkness and mystery of gothic fiction. From the beginning of the story Mary Shelley stresses Clorinda's fickleness. The dejected Clorinda pines for her lover Giacomo and explains to her friend Teresa that she changes her patron saint to match her lovers' changing names, a comment that recalls Claire Clairmont's journal entry of 23 July 1821 regarding Emilia Viviani: "Emilia says that she prays always to a Saint, and every time she changes her lover, she changes her Saint, adopting the one of her lover."[11] Even for the real Emilia, religious devotion is subjected to amorous whims. Mary Shelley undermines Clorinda's sworn "eternal devotion" to Giacomo by plotting a tale in which

that devotion is shaken as soon as the young artist Marcott Alleyn enters the scene. Alleyn, described as "a man of infinitely pleasing manners" and possessing "a soft tone of voice and eyes full of expression," is clearly based in part on Percy Bysshe Shelley. At this point Mary Shelley adds a comic twist to Dante's famous story of the pathethic figures of Paolo and Francesca in the *Inferno*. Dante's Paolo, having been sent as his brother's representative in obtaining Francesca's hand, falls in love with Francesca himself. Like Paolo, Alleyn comes to Clorinda as a messenger for his friend Giacomo, commenting that "if I do not lose my heart, I shall at least gain some excellent hints for my picture of the Profession of Eloisa." Since the narrator has already described the real state of the convent, the reader can imagine the irony of the disappointment awaiting Alleyn, much like Mary Shelley's disappointment on her first visit to Emilia's dirty convent, which smelled of garlic (Sunstein, p. 193). The depiction of Marcott Alleyn and his artist's hope that he will, at the very least, gain material for a new painting, along with his infatuation—Alleyn's compassion is "excited in various ways"—is obviously satirical. Alleyn's initial infatuation with Clorinda begins to fade as soon as Clorinda begins to return it, the narrator explaining that young men that age "look on women as living Edens which they dare not imagine they can ever enjoy; they love, and dream not of being loved; they seek, and their wildest fancies do not picture themselves as sought" (p. 38). Thematically, the male figure in this scenario turns out to be as fickle as the inconstant Clorinda.

"The Bride of Modern Italy" obviously builds on Mary Shelley's reaction to her husband's interest in Emilia Viviani, but it also offers an excellent example of her sense of humor and her facility for subtle satire. In *Valperga,* published just a year before (1823), she devoted herself to depicting unflagging feminine devotion in the characters of Euthanasia and Beatrice as opposed to the ambitious and single-minded Castruccio. Here, she allows herself the freedom to satirize masculine devotion. Because Mary Shelley more often tended to idealize her husband in her fiction, and because she went to great lengths throughout her life to establish his reputation as a poet by providing the public with annotated editions of his works, readers may be surprised by the tone of **"The Bride of Modern Italy."** But the story is perhaps most valuable as proof that Mary Shelley's reputation after her husband's death as a languorous and remorseful widow is based on a substantial underestimation of her mind, her art, and her understanding of the complexities of human relationships.

In the case of "**The False Rhyme**," Mary Shelley turns again in a comic vein to the theme of feminine loyalty, here making the most of the given engraving and the forced necessity to compose a romantic love story. Written in 1829 for *The Keepsake* for 1830, this story is built around the premise of a king's mourning a failed love affair, thus imaginatively complementing the plate. The engraving depicts King Francis languishing on a couch with two dogs at his feet, with his sister Margaret, Queen of Navarre, standing beside him and drawing the curtain back from a window to expose an epigram that has been etched into the windowpane.[12] In Mary Shelley's extrapolation from the plate, Margaret teases the king for his exaggerated pronouncements on the unfaithfulness of all women, and for his having etched into the window the couplet, "Souvent femme varie / Bien fou qui s'y fie!" (Often a woman is inconstant / A great fool is he who has faith in her!). Margaret jokes that the epigram may just as well read "Souvent homme varie, / Bien folle qui s'y fie," in which she reverses the genders in the couplet and suggests that it is greatly amended thus. The siblings' discussion concludes with a bet that Margaret cannot produce for the king one instance of a woman's faithfulness. Margaret's success in doing so ultimately proves to the king that his couplet is a "false rhyme," the title itself thus working as a pun on this poetic term.

A remarkably concise story, Mary Shelley's light tone and comic treatment of Francis' and Margaret's wager is strengthened by the story's debt to Shakespeare.[13] Mary Shelley's characterization of the brooding Francis, who has impetuously imprisoned his knight, Enguerrard de Lagny, on a false charge, is drawn in the tradition of Shakespeare's jealous Othello or Leontes of *The Winter's Tale*. Moreover, the plot hinges on a traditional case of hidden identity—the king learns that de Lagny's wife Emilie has donned men's clothing in order to take her husband's place in prison so that he can continue to fight for the king. The mistaken-identity and cross-dressing in "**The False Rhyme**" *is* traditionally Shakespearean, but in this case it may also be something of a disguised disclosure of a real-life situation for Mary Shelley. In 1991 Betty T. Bennett uncovered proof that Mary Shelley was involved in the long-term success of her friend Mary Diana Dods' dressing and passing as a man, "Walter Sholto Douglas," the "husband" of Isabel Robinson, in Paris social circles in the late 1820s.[14] In light of this discovery

it is no surprise that the theme of cross-dressing recurs in Mary Shelley's fiction of the mid to late 1820s; other instances include "A Tale of the Passions," "Ferdinando Eboli," *The Last Man* and *Perkin Warbeck.*

Much of the humor of "**The False Rhyme**" derives from its exaggeration of the theme of feminine devotion. Rather than merely provide an example of a woman who is faithful to her husband in the sexual sense, Queen Margaret finds an extreme example in the case of Emilie de Lagny, who is not only the ideal of a woman's loyalty to her husband, but also the ideal of loyalty to the king, since the couple's switch of identity had been orchestrated entirely for the purpose of serving Francis. Having lost his bet, Francis dutifully breaks the window upon which he had etched his "false rhyme," as he had agreed he would do. The story exaggerates the ideal of loyalty to comic proportions, but the issue of loyalty is one that plays a major role in Mary Shelley's serious fiction of this period, including *Valperga,* which depicts extreme feminine loyalty in both Euthanasia and Beatrice, and *The Last Man* (1826), in the characters of Perdita and Evadne. In July 1827 Mary Shelley discovered that she had been betrayed for years by her close friend Jane Williams, who had been spreading rumors regarding the problems in Mary's marriage to P. B. Shelley.[15] Then, in *Perkin Warbeck* (1830), she explored the theme of loyalty in the story of Richard Plantagenet, the Yorkist heir to the throne during the reign of Henry VII, with particular focus on the faithfulness and devotion of his wife Katherine. One passage is clearly relevant to Mary Shelley's situation with Jane Williams; when Richard learns of the betrayal of his friend Robin Clifford, he says, "The whole wide world of misery contains no pang so great, as the discovery of treachery where we pictured truth; death is less in the comparison, for both destroy the future, and one, with Gorgon countenance, transforms the past."[16]

Mary Shelley again explores the theme of female devotion in "**The Dream**," written for *The Keepsake* for 1832, and here she chooses to exaggerate elements of Keatsian gothic as represented by such works as "Isabella; or the Pot of Basil" (1818) and "The Eve of St. Agnes" (1819). "**The Dream**" was composed to accompany an illustration of a woman sitting in the woods, entitled "Constance," and it would be difficult to conceive of a more imaginative story line than Mary Shelley's drawn from such an illustration. Mary Shelley's Constance is an exaggeration of that virtue—a woman who lives her life to mourn the deaths of her father and brother, and who vows to deny her love for Gaspar, whom she deems responsible for their deaths. Constance is an exaggerated figure of the grieving woman, a rather comic counterpart to a figure such as Ellen in Mary Shelley's melodramatic story, **"The Mourner"** (1830), who inadvertently causes her father's drowning at sea, or to the mournful Mathilda in the novel of that name (written 1819-1820 and unpublished until the twentieth century), in which the heroine inadvertently drives her father to suicide as a result of their incestuous attraction to each other. In the particular scene written to accommodate the illustration, Mary Shelley's heroine hears a rustling in the leaves in the woods around her and despairs that such a sound will never again indicate the approach of her former lover, Gaspar. Just then Gaspar leaps from the bushes to confront her. The situation of the lamenting Constance and her interview with the lover she had been sure she would never see again recalls the appearance of the dead Lorenzo to Keats's crazed "Isabella." The story's similarity to "Isabella" was even clearer in the original manuscript version, in which Constance's interview with Gaspar was set in the dark, gloomy bedroom that she had converted into "black hung rooms" to suit her state of mourning. Charles Robinson notes that Mary Shelley was forced to alter her story to fit the illustration of "Constance" outside in the woods, thus diminishing what seems to have been originally an even stronger evocation of Keats.[17]

The story's similarity to Keats's "The Eve of St. Agnes" is even stronger than its resemblance to "Isabella," however, for Constance's inability to decide between her devotion to the dead and her love for Gaspar leads her to consult her patron saint, Catherine.[18] Like the legend of St. Agnes on which Keats structures his poem, Mary Shelley describes a local legend that a young woman who spends a night asleep on "Saint Catherine's bed" will be guided by the saint in a dream. Here Mary Shelley takes the gothic setting to the extreme, for Saint Catherine's bed turns out to be a precarious ledge jutting out over the river, and the reader is told that those who formerly attempted to sleep there either fled in fear or met their death in the turbulent waters below. True to her name, however, Constance cannot be dissuaded from her decision to seek St. Catherine's guidance, and the description of her perilous night spent on the "bed" extends Keats's use of folktale. In the exag-

gerated gravity and devotion of "Constance," Mary Shelley recasts Keats's Madeline with her maidenly purity and devotion. In addition, she humorously reworks Keats's theme of appearance and reality: Constance nearly falls from the ledge crying out in a dream that she will save Gaspar, only to be caught and rescued by the real Gaspar, who is standing over her, watching her sleep. Mary Shelley rounds out the humorous ending of **"The Dream"** by having Constance's maid Manon, who has slept the night in the chapel near St. Catherine's bed, awaken to find Constance's wedding ceremony underway. In addition, Gaspar himself makes light of the events of the story when Constance finally confides to him that it was a vision of his suffering in prison "in soiled and tattered garments, with unkempt locks and wild matted beard," in form "a mere skeleton" that caused her to cry out in her dream and which nearly cost her her life (p. 164). Gaspar answers, "And was it my appearance in that attractive state and winning costume that softened the hard heart of Constance?" (p. 164), thus laughing himself at the ordeal that Constance went through before being able to abandon her grief and excess of devotion, and to accept the opportunity of love.

"The Dream" provides further evidence for Mary Shelley's abilities as a humorist. She exaggerates gothic conventions, in this case as they were employed by Keats, poking fun at some examples of popular fiction, including the "constant" woman whose blind devotion to the dead and to religious folk belief inhibits her present life and happiness until she is saved from the restrictions she has created for herself. The biographical context is unavoidable. Mary Shelley may well be "laughing that [she] may not weep" in this case, given her strong devotion to her husband's memory and her guilt over the dead, as well as the treatments of the theme of the constant woman in her more serious works. Both **"The False Rhyme"** and **"The Dream"** are comic treatments of what was obviously a serious issue for Mary Shelley, and as such these stories demonstrate a flexibility and resilience in handling themes that inform her major writings at the time, including *Mathilda*, *Valperga*, *The Last Man*, *Perkin Warbeck*, and **"The Mourner."** In these stories Mary Shelley again managed to produce original and creative works within the restrictions of market demands. These stories must have far superseded any expectations the reader of the annuals must have derived from the accompanying engravings. . . .

Having produced both *Frankenstein* and *The Last Man* in the direct lineage of her father's popular confessional narratives, Mary Shelley in "The Mortal Immortal" and "Transformation" may have sought (and found) an outlet for recasting those serious confessionals in a lighter manner. Certainly one of the most valuable legacies of her short stories for the modern reader is the view they provide us of Mary Shelley as an author, playfully reworking the exaggerated and oftentimes morose conventions of gothic fiction, portraying the self-absorbed figures of both Godwin's and Byron's works with wit and humor, and even finding new ways to rework serious themes, such as feminine devotion, that repeatedly inspired her own longer, more serious fiction. In many of her short stories, Mary Shelley not only greatly superseded one of the few publishing venues available to her as a woman writing in the early nineteenth century, and a fairly rigidly confining one at that, but she also produced works of subtle humor—even brilliant imagination—which, as a group, contribute to a reappraisal of her genius and her reputation.

Notes

1. *The Novels and Selected Works of Mary Wollstonecraft Shelley,* Nora Crook, ed., with Pamela Clemit. Consulting ed. Betty T. Bennett, 8 vols. (London: William Pickering, 1996).

2. In his edition *Mary Shelley: Collected Tales and Stories with Original Engravings* (Baltimore: Johns Hopkins University Press, 1976), Charles E. Robinson acknowledges the humorous elements in the short fiction; in this paper I hope to focus on the range and the contexts of Mary Shelley's use of humor in her stories as she reworks major themes from her novels. References to Mary Shelley's short stories are in Robinson's edition.

3. Mary Shelley also contributed the poems "A Dirge," and "A Night Scene," and "Absence" to the 1831 *Keepsake.* The stories and poems are attributed in the Table of Contents and under the title of each work in the text as "The Author of *Frankenstein,*" with the exception of "A Night Scene" ("I see thee not, my gentlest Isabel;"), which is attributed to "Mary S."

4. See Robinson, Introduction, p. xvi.

5. For a treatment of the challenges Mary Shelley faced in writing for the annuals, and especially for an astute assessment of her success within the limitations of the genre, see Sonia Hofkosh, "Disfiguring Economies: Mary Shelley's Short Stories," in *The Other Mary Shelley,* Audrey Fisch, Anne Mellor, and Esther Schor, eds. (Oxford: Oxford University Press, 1993), pp. 204-19.

6. Charles E. Robinson's publication of *The Frankenstein Notebooks,* 2 vols. (New York: Garland, 1996) at last puts this controversy to rest by providing physical proof of the relatively small degree to which P. B. Shelley made editorial additions or changes to the novel.

7. Richard Garnett, ed. *Tales and Stories by Mary Wollstonecraft Shelley* (London: William Paterson, 1891), p. vii. The exception that Garnett allows in this assessment of Mary Shelley's work is *The Last Man,* although he again undercuts his praise by contributing to the reductive stereotype of Mary Shelley as grieving widow: "*The Last Man* demands great attention, for it is not only a work of far higher merit than commonly admitted, but of all her works the most characteristic of the authoress, the most representative of Mary Shelley in the character of pining widowhood which it was her destiny to support for the remainder of her life" (pp. vii-viii).

8. Betty T. Bennett ed., *The Letters of Mary Wollstonecraft Shelley,* 3 vols. (Baltimore: Johns Hopkins University Press, 1980), I, 223. Bennett explains that Mary Shelley's comment on "that wherewithall to buy brandy" refers to Emilia's attempt to borrow a large sum of money from Shelley (225, n14).

9. Emily Sunstein, *Mary Shelley: Romance and Reality* (New York: Little, Brown & Co., 1989), p. 254. Mary Shelley's journals attest to the anguish that she suffered in coming to terms with Shelley's death. See Paula R. Feldman and Diana Scott-Kilvert, *The Journals of Mary Wollstonecraft Shelley,* 2 vols. (Oxford: Oxford University Press, 1987).

10. Mary W. Shelley to Leigh Hunt, 3 December 1820, *The Letters of Mary Wollstonecraft Shelley,* ed. Betty T. Bennett, 3 vols. (Baltimore: Johns Hopkins University Press, 1980), I, 162-66.

11. *The Journals of Claire Clairmont,* ed. Marion Kingston Stocking (Cambridge: Harvard University Press, 1968), p. 243; cited by Robinson, p. 376.

12. See Robinson, *Tales,* p. xiv. Mary Shelley would have been familiar with Francis I's history from William Godwin's novel *St. Leon,* in which the narrator witnesses and describes Francis' ceremonial meeting with Henry VIII at the Field of the Cloth of Gold, and participates in certain military engagements in Francis' ranks, including the defeat of the French at Pavia.

13. Mary Shelley's journal records that she and Shelley read at least 26 of Shakespeare's plays between 1814-1821, and she would have been familiar with all of the plays to some degree from Charles and Mary Lamb's *Tales from Shakespear,* published by M. J. Godwin and Co. in 1807.

14. Betty T. Bennett, *Mary Diana Dods: A Gentleman and a Scholar* (Baltimore: Johns Hopkins University Press, 1991). Mary Shelley's interest in the theme of cross-dressing is no doubt likewise due to influences such as Tasso and Byron's *Don Juan,* during much of the composition of which she served Byron as a copyist.

15. For Mary Shelley's relationship with Jane Williams, see Emily Sunstein's biography, and Paula R. Feldman and Diana Scott-Kilvert, eds., *The Journals of Mary Shelley* (Oxford University Press, 1987).

16. *The Fortunes of Perkin Warbeck, a romance,* by the author of "*Frankenstein,*" 3 vols. (London: Henry Colburn and Richard Bentley, 1830), II, p. 68.

17. See Robinson, *Tales,* p. 383.

18. Robinson, *Tales,* p. 383.

TITLE COMMENTARY

Frankenstein

ANNE K. MELLOR (ESSAY DATE 1988)

SOURCE: Mellor, Anne K. "Possessing Nature: The Female in *Frankenstein.*" In *Romanticism and Feminism*, edited by Anne K. Mellor, pp. 220-32. Bloomington: Indiana University Press, 1988.

In the following essay, Mellor argues that Frankenstein *is a feminist novel which depicts the consequences of a social construction of gender that places greater value on the male.*

When Victor Frankenstein identifies Nature as female—"I pursued nature to *her* hiding places"[1]— he participates in a gendered construction of the universe whose ramifications are everywhere apparent in *Frankenstein.* His scientific penetration and technological exploitation of female nature, which I have discussed elsewhere,[2] is only one dimension of a more general cultural encoding of the female as passive and possessable, the willing receptacle of male desire. The destruction of the female implicit in Frankenstein's usurpation of the natural mode of human reproduction symbolically erupts in his nightmare following the animation of his creature, in which his bride-to-be is transformed in his arms into the corpse of his dead mother—"a shroud enveloped her form, and I saw the grave-worms crawling in the folds of the flannel" (p. 53). By stealing the female's control over reproduction, Frankenstein has eliminated the female's primary biological function and source of cultural power. Indeed, for the simple purpose of human survival, Frankenstein has eliminated the necessity to have females at all. One of the deepest horrors of this novel is Frankenstein's implicit goal of creating a society for men only: his creature is male; he refuses to create a female; there is no reason that the race of immortal beings he hoped to propagate should not be exclusively male.[3]

On the cultural level, Frankenstein's scientific project—to become the sole creator of a human being—supports a patriarchal denial of the value of women and of female sexuality. Mary Shelley, doubtless inspired by her mother's *A Vindication of the Rights of Woman*, specifically portrays the consequences of a social construction of gender that values the male above the female. Victor Frankenstein's nineteenth-century Genevan society is founded on a rigid division of sex roles: the male inhabits the public sphere, the female is relegated to the private or domestic sphere.[4] The

men in Frankenstein's world all work outside the home, as public servants (Alphonse Frankenstein), as scientists (Victor), as merchants (Clerval and his father), or as explorers (Walton). The women are confined to the home; Elizabeth, for instance, is not permitted to travel with Victor and "regretted that she had not the same opportunities of enlarging her experience and cultivating her understanding" (151). Inside the home, women are either kept as a kind of pet (Victor "loved to tend" on Elizabeth "as I should on a favorite animal" [p. 30]); or they work as house wives, childcare providers, and nurses (Caroline Beaufort Frankenstein, Elizabeth Lavenza, Margaret Saville) or as servants (Justine Moritz).

As a consequence of this sexual division of labor, masculine work is kept outside of the domestic realm; hence intellectual activity is segregated from emotional activity. Victor Frankenstein cannot do scientific research and think lovingly of Elizabeth and his family at the same time. His obsession with his experiment has caused him "to forget those friends who were so many miles absent, and whom I had not seen for so long a time" (p. 50). This separation of masculine work from the domestic affections leads directly to Frankenstein's downfall. Because Frankenstein cannot work and love at the same time, he fails to feel empathy for the creature he is constructing and callously makes him eight feet tall simply because "the minuteness of the parts formed a great hindrance to my speed" (p. 49). He then fails to love or feel any parental responsibility for the freak he has created. And he remains so fixated on himself that he cannot imagine his monster might threaten someone else when he swears to be with Victor "on his wedding-night."

This separation of the sphere of public (masculine) power from the sphere of private (feminine) affection also causes the destruction of many of the women in the novel. Caroline Beaufort dies unnecessarily because she feels obligated to nurse her favorite Elizabeth during a smallpox epidemic; she thus incarnates a patriarchal ideal of female self-sacrifice (this suggestion is strengthened in the 1831 revisions where she eagerly risks her life to save Elizabeth). She is a woman who is devoted to her father in wealth and in poverty, who nurses him until his death, and then marries her father's best friend to whom she is equally devoted.

The division of public man from private woman also means that women cannot function effectively in the public realm. Despite her innocence of the crime for which she is accused,

Justine Moritz is executed for the murder of William Frankenstein (and is even half-persuaded by her male confessor that she is responsible for William's death). And Elizabeth, fully convinced of Justine's innocence, is unable to save her: the impassioned defense she gives of Justine arouses public approbation of Elizabeth's generosity but does nothing to help Justine, "on whom the public indignation was turned with renewed violence, charging her with the blackest ingratitude" (p. 80). Nor can Elizabeth save herself on her wedding night. Both these deaths are of course directly attributable to Victor Frankenstein's self-devoted concern for his own suffering (the creature will attack only him) and his own reputation (people would think him mad if he told them his own monster had killed his brother).

Mary Shelley underlines the mutual deprivation inherent in a family and social structure based on rigid and hierarchical gender divisions by portraying an alternative social organization in the novel: the De Lacey family. The political situation of the De Lacey family, exiled from their native France by the manipulations of an ungrateful Turkish merchant and a draconian legal system, points up the injustice that prevails in a nation where masculine values of competition and chauvinism reign. Mary Shelley's political critique of a society founded on the unequal distribution of power and possessions is conveyed not only through the manifest injustice of Justine's execution and of France's treatment first of the alien Turkish merchant and then of the De Lacey family, but also through the readings in political history that she assigns to the creature. From Plutarch's *Parallel Lives of the Greeks and Romans* and from Volney's *Ruins, or Meditations on the Revolutions of Empires,* the creature learns both of masculine virtue and of masculine cruelty and injustice. "I heard of the division of property, of immense wealth and squalid poverty; . . . I learned that the possessions most esteemed . . . were high and unsullied descent united with riches" (p. 115). "Was man, indeed, at once so powerful, so virtuous, and magnificent, yet so vicious and base?" the creature asks incredulously. Implicit in Mary Shelley's attack on the social injustice of established political systems is the suggestion that the separation from the public realm of feminine affections and compassion has caused much of this social evil. Had Elizabeth Lavenza's plea for mercy for Justine, based on her intuitively correct knowledge of Justine's character, been heeded, Justine would not have been wrongly murdered by the courts. As Elizabeth exclaims,

how I hate [the] shews and mockeries [of this world]! when one creature is murdered, another is immediately deprived of life in a slow torturing manner; then the executioners, their hands yet reeking with the blood of innocence, believe that they have done a great deed. They call this *retribution.* Hateful name! when the word is pronounced, I know greater and more horrid punishments are going to be inflicted than the gloomiest tyrant has ever invented to satiate his utmost revenge.

(p. 83)

In contrast to this pattern of political inequality and injustice, the De Lacey family represents an alternative ideology: a vision of a social group based on justice, equality, and mutual affection. Felix willingly sacrificed his own welfare to ensure that justice was done to the Turkish merchant. More important, the structure of the De Lacey family constitutes Mary Shelley's ideal, an ideal derived from her mother's *A Vindication of the Rights of Woman.* In the impoverished De Lacey household, all work is shared equally in an atmosphere of rational companionship, mutual concern, and love. As their symbolic names suggest, Felix embodies happiness, Agatha goodness. They are then joined by Safie (*sophia* or wisdom). Safie, the daughter of the Turkish merchant, is appalled both by her father's betrayal of Felix and by the Islamic oppression of women he endorses; she has therefore fled from Turkey to Switzerland, seeking Felix. Having reached the De Lacey household, she promptly becomes Felix's beloved companion and is taught to read and write French. Safie, whose Christian mother instructed her "to aspire to higher powers of intellect, and an independence of spirit, forbidden to the female followers of Mahomet" (p. 119), is the incarnation of Mary Wollstonecraft in the novel. Wollstonecraft too traveled alone through Europe and Scandinavia; more important, she advocated in *A Vindication* that women be educated to be the "companions" of men and be permitted to participate in the public realm by voting, working outside the home, and holding political office.

But this alternative female role-model of an independent, well-educated, self-supporting, and loving companion, and this alternative nuclear family structure based on sexual equality and mutual affection, is lost in the novel, perhaps because the De Lacey family lacks the mother who might have been able to welcome the pleading, pitiable creature. When Safie flees with the De Lacey family, we as readers are deprived of the novel's only alternative to a rigidly patriarchal construction of gender and sex roles, just as Mary Shelley herself was deprived of a feminist role-model when her mother died and was subsequently denounced in the popular British press as a harlot, atheist, and anarchist. Safie's disappearance from the novel reflects Mary Shelley's own predicament. Like Frankenstein's creature, she has no positive prototype she can imitate, no place in history. That unique phenomenon envisioned by Mary Wollstonecraft, the wife as the lifelong intellectual equal and companion of her husband, does not exist in the world of nineteenth-century Europe experienced by Mary Shelley.

The doctrine of the separate spheres that Victor Frankenstein endorses encodes a particular attitude to female sexuality that Mary Shelley subtly exposes in her novel. This attitude is manifested most vividly in Victor's response to the creature's request for a female companion, an Eve to comfort and embrace him. After hearing his creature's autobiographical account of his sufferings and aspirations, Frankenstein is moved by an awakened conscience to do justice toward his Adam and promises to create a female creature, on condition that both leave forever the neighborhood of mankind. After numerous delays, Frankenstein finally gathers the necessary instruments and materials together into an isolated cottage on one of the Orkney Islands off Scotland and proceeds to create a female being. Once again he becomes ill: "my heart often sickened at the work of my hands . . . my spirits became unequal; I grew restless and nervous" (p. 162).

Disgusted by his enterprise, Frankenstein finally determines to stop his work, rationalizing his decision to deprive his creature of a female companion in terms that repay careful examination. Here is Frankenstein's meditation:

> I was now about to form another being, of whose dispositions I was alike ignorant; she might become ten thousand times more malignant than her mate, and delight, for its own sake, in murder and wretchedness. He had sworn to quit the neighborhood of man, and hide himself in deserts; but she had not; and she, who in all probability was to become a thinking and reasoning animal, might refuse to comply with a compact made before her creation. They might even hate each other; the creature who already lived loathed his own deformity, and might he not conceive a greater abhorrence for it when it came before his eyes in the female form? She also might turn with disgust from him to the superior beauty of man; she might quit him, and he be again alone, exasperated by the fresh provocation of being deserted by one of his own species.
>
> Even if they were to leave Europe, and inhabit the deserts of the new world, yet one of the first results of those sympathies for which the daemon thirsted would be children, and a race of devils would be propagated upon the earth, who might make the very existence of the species of man a condition precarious and full of terror. Had I a right, for my own benefit, to inflict this curse upon everlasting generations? . . . I shuddered to think that future ages might curse me as their pest, whose selfishness had not hesitated to buy its own peace at the price perhaps of the existence of the whole human race.
>
> (p. 163)

What does Victor Frankenstein truly fear, which causes him to end his creation of a female? First, he is afraid of an independent female will, afraid that his female creature will have desires and opinions that cannot be controlled by his male creature. Like Rousseau's natural man, she might refuse to comply with a social contract made before her birth by another person; she might assert her own integrity and the revolutionary right to determine her own existence. Moreover, those uninhibited female desires might be sadistic: Frankenstein imagines a female "ten thousand times" more evil than her mate, who would "delight" in murder for its own sake. Third, he fears that his female creature will be more ugly than his male creature, so much so that even the male will turn from her in disgust. Fourth, he fears that she will prefer to mate with ordinary males; implicit here is Frankenstein's horror that, given the gigantic strength of this female, she would have the power to seize and even rape the male she might choose. And finally, he is afraid of her reproductive powers, her capacity to generate an entire race of similar creatures. What Victor Frankenstein truly fears is female sexuality as such. A woman who is sexually liberated, free to choose her own life, her own sexual partner (by force, if necessary). And to propagate at will can appear only monstrously ugly to Victor Frankenstein, for she defies that sexist aesthetic that insists that women be small, delicate, modest, passive, and sexually pleasing—but available only to their lawful husbands.

Horrified by this image of uninhibited female sexuality, Victor Frankenstein violently reasserts a male control over the female body, penetrating and mutilating the female creature at his feet in an image that suggests a violent rape: "trembling with passion, [I] tore to pieces the thing on which I was engaged" (p. 164). The morning after, when he returns to the scene, "The remains of the half-finished creature, whom I had destroyed, lay scattered on the floor, and I almost felt as if I had mangled the living flesh of a human being" (p. 167). However he has rationalized his decision to

Boris Karloff as the monster in the 1935 film adaptation of *Frankenstein*.

murder the female creature, Frankenstein's "passion" is here revealed as a fusion of fear, lust, and hostility, a desire to control and even destroy female sexuality.

Frankenstein's fear of female sexuality is endemic to a patriarchal construction of gender. Uninhibited female sexual experience threatens the very foundation of patriarchal power: the establishment of patrilineal kinship networks together with the transmission of both status and property by inheritance entailed upon a male line. Significantly, in the patriarchal world of Geneva in the novel, female sexuality is strikingly repressed. All the women are presented as sexless: Caroline Beaufort is a devoted daughter and chaste wife while Elizabeth Lavenza's relationship with Victor is that of a sister.

In this context, the murder of Elizabeth Lavenza on her wedding night becomes doubly significant. The scene of her death is based on a painting Mary Shelley knew well, Henry Fuseli's famous "The Nightmare." The corpse of Elizabeth lies in the very attitude in which Fuseli placed his succubus-ridden woman: "She was there, lifeless and inanimate, thrown across the bed, her head hanging down, and her pale and distorted features half covered by her hair" (p. 193). Fuseli's woman is an image of female erotic desire, both lusting for and frightened of the incubus (or male demon) that rides upon her, brought to her bed-chamber by the stallion that leers at her from the foot of her bed; both the presence of this incubus and the woman's posture of open sexual acceptance leave Fuseli's intentions in no doubt.[5] Evoking this image, Mary Shelley alerted us to what Victor fears most: his bride's sexuality.[6] Significantly, Elizabeth would not have been killed had Victor not sent her into their wedding bedroom *alone*. Returning to the body of the murdered Elizabeth, Victor "embraced her with ardour; but the deathly languor and coldness of the limbs told me, that what I now held in my arms had ceased to be the Elizabeth whom I had loved and cherished" (p. 193). Victor most ardently desires his bride when he knows she is dead; the conflation with his earlier dream, when he thought to embrace the living Elizabeth but instead held in his arms the corpse of his mother, signals Victor's most profound erotic desire, a necrophiliac and incestuous desire to possess the dead female, the lost mother.

To put this point another way, we might observe that Victor Frankenstein's most passionate relationships are with men rather than with women. He sees Clerval as "the image of my former self" (p. 155), as his "friend and dearest companion" (p. 181), as his true soul mate. His description of Clerval's haunting eyes—"languishing in death, the dark orbs covered by the lids, and the long black lashes that fringed them" (p. 179)—verges on the erotic. Similarly, Walton responds to Frankenstein with an ardor that borders on the homoerotic. Having desired "the company of a man who could sympathize with me; whose eyes would reply to mine" (p. 13), Walton eagerly embraces Frankenstein as "a celestial spirit" (p. 23) whose death leaves him inarticulate with grief: "what can I say," Walton writes to his sister, "that will enable you to understand the depth of my sorrow?" (p. 216) Finally, Frankenstein dedicates himself to his scientific experiment with a passion that can be described only as erotic: as Mary Shelley originally described Frankenstein's obsession, "I wished, as it were, to procrastinate my feelings of affection, until the great object of my affection was compleated." Frankenstein's homoerotic fixation upon his creature, whose features he had selected as "beautiful" (p. 52) in a parody of Pygmalion and Galatea, was underlined by Mary Shelley in a revision she made in the Thomas copy of *Frankenstein.* Describing his anxious enslavement to his task, Frankenstein confesses: "my voice became broken, my trembling hands almost refused to accomplish their task; I became as timid as a lovesick girl, and alternate tremor and passionate ardour took the place of wholesome sensation and regulated ambition" (51:31-35). In place of a normal heterosexual attachment to Elizabeth, Victor Frankenstein has substituted a homosexual obsession with his creature,[7] an obsession that in his case is energized by a profound desire to reunite with his dead mother, by becoming himself a mother.

To sum up, at every level Victor Frankenstein is engaged upon a rape of nature, a violent penetration and usurpation of the female's "hiding places," of the womb. Terrified of female sexuality and the power of human reproduction it enables, both he and the patriarchal society he represents use the technologies of science and the laws of the polis to manipulate, control, and repress women. Thinking back on Elizabeth Lavenza strangled on her bridal bier and on Fuseli's image of female erotic desire that she replicates, we can now see that at this level Victor's creature, his monster, realizes his own most potent lust. The monster, like Fuseli's incubus, leers over Elizabeth, enacting Victor's own repressed desire to rape, possess, and destroy the female. Victor's creature here becomes just that, his "creature," the instrument of his most potent desire: to destroy female reproductive power so that only men may rule.

However, in Mary Shelley's feminist novel, Victor Frankenstein's desire is portrayed not only as horrible and finally unattainable but also as self-destructive. For Nature is not the passive, inert, or "dead" matter that Frankenstein imagines.[8] Frankenstein assumes that he can violate Nature and pursue her to her hiding places with impunity. But Nature both resists and revenges herself upon his attempts. During his research, Nature denies to Victor Frankenstein both mental and physical health: "my enthusiasm was checked by my anxiety, and I appeared rather like one doomed by slavery to toil in the mines, or any other unwholesome trade, than an artist occupied by his favourite employment. Every night I was oppressed by a slow fever, and I became nervous to a most painful degree" (p. 51). When his experiment is completed, Victor has a fit that renders him "lifeless" for "a long, long time" and that marks the onset of a "nervous fever" that confines him for many months (p. 57). Victor continues to be tormented by anxiety attacks, bouts of delirium, periods of distraction and madness. As soon as he determines to blaspheme against Nature a second time, by creating a female human being, Nature punishes him: "the eternal twinkling of the stars weighed upon me, and . . . I listened to every blast of wind, as if it were a dull ugly siroc on its way to consume me" (p. 145). His mental illness returns: "Every thought that was devoted to it was an extreme anguish, and every word that I spoke in allusion to it caused my lips to quiver and my heart to palpitate" (p. 156); "my spirits became unequal; I grew restless and nervous" (p. 162). Finally, Frankenstein's obsession with destroying his creature exposes him to such mental and physical fatigue that he dies at the age of twenty-five.

Appropriately, Nature prevents Frankenstein from constructing a normal human being: an unnatural method of reproduction produces an unnatural being, in this case a freak of gigantic stature, watery eyes, a shriveled complexion, and straight black lips. This physiognomy causes Frankenstein's instinctive withdrawal from his child, and sets in motion the series of events that produces the monster who destroys Frankenstein's family, friends, and self.

Moreover, Nature pursues Victor Frankenstein with the very electricity he has stolen: lightning, thunder, and rain rage around him. The November night on which he steals the "spark of being" from Nature is dreary, dismal, and wet: "the rain . . . poured from a black and comfortless sky" (p. 54). He next glimpses his creature during a flash of lightning as a violent storm plays over his head at Plainpalais (p. 71); significantly, the almighty Alps, and in particular Mont Blanc, are represented in this novel as female, as an image of omnipotent fertility"—on his wedding day, Victor admires "the beautiful Mont Blanc, and the assemblage of snowy mountains that in vain endeavour to emulate *her*" (p. 190; my italics). Before Frankenstein's first encounter with his creature among the Alps, "the rain poured down in torrents, and thick mists hid the summits of the mountains" (p. 91). Setting sail from the Orkney island where he has destroyed his female creature, planning to throw her mangled remains into the sea, Frankenstein wakes to find his skiff threatened by a fierce wind and high waves that portend his own death: "I might be driven into the wide Atlantic, and feel all the tortures of starvation, or be swallowed up in the immeasurable waters that roared and buffetted around me. I . . . felt the torment of a burning thirst; . . . I looked upon the sea, it was to be my grave" (p. 169). Frankenstein ends his life and his pursuit of the monster he has made in the arctic regions, surrounded by the aurora borealis, the electromagnetic field of the North Pole. The atmospheric effects of the novel, which most readers have dismissed as little more than the traditional trappings of Gothic fiction, in fact manifest the power of Nature to punish those who transgress her boundaries. The elemental forces that Victor has released pursue him to his hiding places, raging round him like avenging Furies.

Finally, Nature punishes Victor Frankenstein the life-stealer most justly by denying him the capacity for natural procreation. His bride is killed on their wedding night, cutting off his chance to engender his own children. His creature—that "great object, which swallowed up every habit of my nature" (50)—turns against him, destroying not only his brother William, his soul mate Clerval, his loyal servant Justine, his grief-stricken father, and his wife, but finally pursuing Victor himself to his death, leaving Frankenstein entirely without progeny. Nature's revenge is absolute: he who violates her sacred hiding places is destroyed.

Mary Shelley's novel thus portrays the penalties of raping Nature. But it also celebrates an all-creating Nature loved and revered by human beings. Those characters capable of deeply feeling the beauties of Nature are rewarded with physical and mental health. Even Frankenstein in his moments of tranquillity or youthful innocence can respond powerfully to the glory of Nature. As Walton notes, "the starry sky, the sea, and every sight afforded by these wonderful regions, seems still to have the power of elevating his soul from earth" (p. 23). In Clerval's company Victor becomes again

> the same happy creature who, a few years ago, loving and beloved by all, had no sorrow or care. When happy, inanimate nature had the power of bestowing on me the most delightful sensations. A serene sky and verdant fields filled me with ecstasy.
>
> (p. 65)

Clerval's relationship to Nature represents one moral touchstone of the novel: since he "loved with ardour . . . the scenery of external nature" (p. 154), Nature endows him with a generous sympathy, a vivid imagination, a sensitive intelligence and an unbounded capacity for devoted friendship. His death annihilates the possibility that Victor Frankenstein might regain a positive relationship with Nature.

Mary Shelley envisions Nature as a sacred life-force in which human beings ought to participate in conscious harmony. Elizabeth Lavenza gives voice to this ideal in her choice of profession for Ernest Frankenstein:

> I proposed that he should be a farmer. . . . A farmer's is a very healthy happy life; and the least hurtful, or rather the most beneficial profession of any. My uncle [wanted him] educated as an advocate . . . but . . . it is certainly more creditable to cultivate the earth for the sustenance of man, than to be the confidant, and sometimes the accomplice, of his vices.
>
> (p. 59)

Nature nurtures those who cultivate her; perhaps this is why, of all the members of Frankenstein's family, only Ernest survives. Mary Shelley shares Wordsworth's concept of a beneficial bond between the natural and the human world, which is broken only at man's peril. Had Victor Frankenstein's eyes not become "insensible to the charms of nature" (p. 50) and the affections of family and friends, he would not have defied Mary Shelley's moral credo:

> A human being in perfection ought always to preserve a calm and peaceful mind, and never to allow passion or a transitory desire to disturb his

tranquillity. I do not think that the pursuit of knowledge is an exception to this rule. If the study to which you apply yourself has a tendency to weaken your affections, and to destroy your taste for those simple pleasures in which no alloy can possibly mix [e.g., the "beautiful season"], then that study is certainly unlawful, that is to say, not befitting the human mind.

(p. 51)

As an ecological system of interdependent organisms, Nature requires the submission of the individual ego to the welfare of the family and the larger community. Like George Eliot after her, Mary Shelley is profoundly committed to an ethic of cooperation, mutual dependence, and self-sacrifice. The Russian sea-master willingly sacrifices his own desires that his beloved and her lover may marry; Clerval immediately gives up his desire to attend university in order to nurse his dear friend Victor back to health; Elizabeth offers to release her beloved Victor from his engagement should he now love another. Mary Shelley's moral vision thus falls into that category of ethical thinking which Carol Gilligan has recently identified as more typically female than male. Where men have tended to identify moral laws as abstract principles that clearly differentiate right from wrong, women have tended to see moral choice as imbedded in an ongoing shared life. As Gilligan contrasts them, a male "ethic of justice proceeds from the premise of equality—that everyone should be treated the same" while a female "ethic of care rests on the premise of nonviolence—that no one should be hurt."[10] This traditional female morality can probably be traced to what Nancy Chodorow and Dorothy Dinnerstein have shown to be the daughter's greater identification with the mother.[11] Whereas the son has learned to assert his separateness from the mother (and the process of mothering), the daughter has learned to represent that gendered role and thus has felt more tightly (and ambivalently) bound to the mother. Less certain of her ego boundaries, the daughter has been more likely to engage in moral thinking which gives priority to the good of the family and the community rather than to the rights of the individual.

Insofar as the family is the basic social unit, it has historically represented the system of morality practiced by the culture at large. The hierarchical structure of the Frankenstein family embodies a masculine ethic of justice in which the rights of the individual are privileged: Frankenstein pursues his own interests in alchemy and chemistry, cheerfully ignoring his family obligations as he engages

"heart and soul" in his research, and is moreover encouraged to leave his family and fiancée for two years ("for a more indulgent and less dictatorial parent did not exist upon earth" [p. 130]). In contrast, the egalitarian and interdependent structure of the De Lacey family ideologically encodes a female ethic of care in which the bonding of the family unit is primary. Felix blames himself most because his self-sacrificing action on behalf of the Turkish merchant involved his family in his suffering. Agatha and Felix perform toward their father "every little office of affection and duty with gentleness; and he rewarded them by his benevolent smiles"; they willingly starve themselves that their father may eat (106). Safie's arrival particularly delighted Felix but also "diffused gladness through the cottage, dispelling their sorrow as the sun dissipates the morning mists" (112). In portraying the De Laceys as an archetype of the egalitarian, benevolent, and mutually loving nuclear family, Mary Shelley clearly displayed her own moral purpose, which Percy Shelley rightly if somewhat vaguely described in his Preface as "the exhibition of the amiableness of domestic affection, and the excellence of universal virtue" (7).

Mary Shelley's grounding of moral virtue in the preservation of familial bonds (against which Frankenstein, in his failure to parent his own child, entirely transgresses) entails an aesthetic credo as well. While such romantic descendants as Walter Pater and Oscar Wilde would later argue that aesthetics and morality, art and life, are distinct, Mary Shelley endorsed a traditional mimetic aesthetic that exhorted literature to imitate ideal Nature and defined the role of the writer as a moral educator. Her novel purposefully identifies moral virtue, based on self-sacrifice, moderation, and domestic affection, with aesthetic beauty. Even in poverty, the image of the blind old man listening to the sweetly singing Agatha is "a lovely sight, even to me, poor wretch! who had never beheld aught beautiful before" (103). In contrast, Frankenstein's and Walton's dream of breaking boundaries is explicitly identified as both evil and ugly. As Walton acknowledges, "my day dreams are . . . extended and magnificent; but they want (as the painters call it) *keeping*" (p. 14). "Keeping," in painting, means "the maintenance of the proper relation between the representations of nearer and more distant objects in a picture"; hence, in a more general sense, "the proper subserviency of tone and colour in every part of a picture, so that the general effect is harmonious to the eye" (*OED*). Walton thus introduces Mary Shelley's ethical norm as an aesthetic norm; both in life and in art, her ideal is a balance or golden mean between conflicting demands, specifically here between large and small objects. In ethical terms, this means that Walton must balance his dreams of geographical discovery and fame against the reality of an already existing set of obligations (to his family, his crew, and the sacredness of Nature). Similarly, Frankenstein should have better balanced the obligations of great and small, of parent and child, of creator and creature. Frankenstein's failure to maintain *keeping,* to preserve "a calm and peaceful mind" (p. 51), is thus in Mary Shelley's eyes both a moral and an aesthetic failure, resulting directly in the creation of a hideous monster.

Notes

1. Mary W. Shelley, *Frankenstein, or The Modern Prometheus* (London: Lackington, Hughes, Harding, Mavor and Jones, 1818); all further references to *Frankenstein* will be to the only modern reprint of this first edition, edited by James Rieger (New York: Bobbs-Merrill, 1974; reprinted, Chicago: University of Chicago Press, 1982), and will be cited by page number only in the text. This phrase occurs on page 49.

2. Anne K. Mellor, "*Frankenstein*: A Feminist Critique of Science," in *One Culture: Essays on Literature and Science,* ed. George Levine (Madison: University of Wisconsin Press, 1988), pp. 287-312.

3. Mary Shelley thus heralds a tradition of literary utopias and dystopias that depict single-sex societies, a tradition most recently appropriated by feminist writers to celebrate exclusively female societies. For an analysis of the strengths and weaknesses of such feminist utopian writing, in which female societies are reproduced by parthenogenesis, see my "On Feminist Utopias," *Women's Studies* (1982): 241-62. Leading examples of this genre include Charlotte Perkins Gilman's *Herland,* Sally Miller Gearhart's *The Wanderground,* Joanna Russ's *The Female Man,* James Tiptree, Jr.'s "Houston, Houston Do You Read?" and Suzy McKee Charnas's trilogy *The Vampire Tapestry.*

4. On the gender division of nineteenth-century European culture, see Jean Elshtain, *Public Man, Private Woman: Women in Social and Political Thought* (Oxford: Robertson, 1981); and *Victorian Women: A Documentary Account of Women's Lives in Nineteenth-Century England, France, and the United States,* ed. E. Hellerstein, L. Hume, and K. Offen (Stanford: Stanford University Press, 1981). For a study of sex roles in *Frankenstein,* see Kate Ellis, "Monsters in the Family: Mary Shelley and the Bourgeois Family," in *The Endurance of Frankenstein,* ed. George Levine and U. C. Knoepflmacher (Berkeley, Los Angeles, London: University of California Press, 1979), pp. 123-42; and Anca Vlasopolos, "*Frankenstein*'s Hidden Skeleton: The Psycho-Politics of Oppression," *Science-Fiction Studies* 10 (1983): 125-36.

William Veeder, in his insightful but occasionally reductive psychological study of Mary and Percy Shelley and *Frankenstein, Mary Shelley and Frankenstein: The Fate of Androgyny* (1986), wishes to define masculinity and femininity as the complementary halves of an ideally balanced androgynous or agapic personality that is destroyed or bifurcated by erotic self-love; his book traces the reasons why Mary Shelley's fictional characters realize or fail to achieve her androgynous ideal. While he is right to argue that Mary Shelley believed in balancing "masculine" and "feminine" characteristics, he consistently defines as innate psychological characteristics those patterns of learned behavior (masculinity, femininity) that I prefer to see as socially constructed gender roles. His readings thus unintentionally reinforce an oppressive biological determinism and sex-stereotyping, even as they call attention to the dangers of extreme masculine and feminine behaviors.

5. Henry Fuseli, *The Nightmare,* first version, 1781; The Detroit Institute of Art. This famous painting was widely reproduced throughout the early nineteenth century and was of particular interest to Mary Shelley, who knew of her mother's early passionate love for Fuseli. H. W. Janson has suggested that Fuseli's representation of the nightmare is a projection of his unfulfilled passion for Anna Landolt, whose portrait is drawn on the reverse side (H. W. Janson, "Fuseli's *Nightmare,*" *Arts and Sciences* 2 [1963]: 23-28). When Fuseli learned that Anna Landolt had married, he wrote to her uncle and his good friend Johann Lavater from London on 16 June 1779 that he had dreamed of lying in her bed and fusing "her body and soul" together with his own. Fuseli's painting is thus a deliberate allusion to traditional images of Cupid and Psyche meeting in her bedroom at night; here the welcomed god of love has been transformed into a demonic incubus of erotic lust (see also Peter Tomory, *The Life and Art of Henry Fuseli,* London: 1972, pp. 92ff.; and the Catalogue Raisonnée by Gert Schiff, *Johann Heinrich Fussli,* Zurich: 1973, pp. 757-59).

Gerhard Joseph first noted the allusion to Fuseli's painting, "Frankenstein's Dream: The Child Is Father of the Monster," *Hartford Studies in Literature* 7 (1975): 97-115, 109. William Veeder denies the association (*Mary Shelley and Frankenstein,* 192-93) on the grounds that Elizabeth's hair half-covers her face; in this regard, it may be significant that Fuseli's woman's face is half-covered in shadow.

6. Paul A. Cantor has discussed Frankenstein's rejections both of normal sexuality and of the bourgeois lifestyle, in *Creature and Creator: Myth-making and English Romanticism* (New York: Cambridge University Press, 1984), pp. 109-15.

7. William Veeder has emphasized the homosexual bond between Frankenstein and his monster (*Mary Shelley and Frankenstein,* pp. 89-92). Eve Kosofsky Sedgwick arrives at this conclusion from a different direction. In her *Between Men: English Literature and Male Homosocial Desire* (New York: Columbia University Press, 1985), she observes in passing that *Frankenstein,* like William Godwin's *Caleb Williams,* is "about one or more males who not only is persecuted by, but considers himself transparent to and often under the compulsion of, another male. If we follow Freud [in the case of Dr. Schreber] in hypothesizing that such a sense of persecution represents the fearful, phantasmic rejection by recasting of an original homosexual (or even merely homosocial) desire, then it would make sense to think of this group of novels as embodying strongly homophobic mechanisms" (pp. 91-92).

8. While I largely agree with Mary Poovey's intelligent and sensitive analysis of Frankenstein's egotistic desire (in *The Proper Lady and the Woman Writer*, pp. 123-33), I do not share her view that the nature we see in the novel is "fatal to human beings and human relationships." Poovey fails to distinguish between Frankenstein's view of nature and the author's and between the first and second editions of the novel in this regard.

9. On Mary Shelley's subversive representation of the traditionally masculinized Alps as female, see Fred V. Randel, "*Frankenstein*, Feminism, and the Intertextuality of Mountains," *Studies in Romanticism* 23 (Winter, 1984): 515-33.

10. Carol Gilligan, *In a Different Voice: Psychological Theory and Women's Development* (Cambridge, Mass: Harvard University Press, 1982), p. 174.

11. See Nancy Chodorow, *The Reproduction of Mothering: Psychoanalysis and the Sociology of Gender* (Berkeley and Los Angeles: University of California Press, 1978); Dorothy Dinnerstein, *The Mermaid and the Minotaur: Sexual Arrangements and Human Malaise* (New York: Harper and Row, 1976); cf. Nancy Friday, *My Mother/My Self: The Daughter's Search for Identity* (New York: Dell, 1977).

JOHANNA M. SMITH (ESSAY DATE 1992)

SOURCE: Smith, Johanna M. "'Cooped Up': Feminine Domesticity in *Frankenstein*." In *Mary Shelley*: Frankenstein, edited by Johanna M. Smith, pp. 270-85. New York: Bedford Books of St. Martin's Press, 1992.

In the following essay, Smith analyzes the influence of the nineteenth-century doctrine of "separate spheres" for men and women on Shelley's Frankenstein.

It is important to note that *Frankenstein* was published anonymously, that its woman author kept her identity hidden. Similarly, no women in the novel speak directly: everything we hear from and about them is filtered through the three masculine narrators. In addition, these women seldom venture far from home, while the narrators and most of the other men engage in quests and various public occupations. These facts exemplify the nineteenth century's emerging doctrine of "separate spheres," the ideology that split off the (woman's) domestic sphere from the (man's) public world and strictly defined the "feminine" and "masculine" traits appropriate to each sphere. My essay will analyze the operations of this ideology in the writing of *Frankenstein* and in the novel itself.

From the novel's women we may infer that Mary Shelley approved the separate-spheres doctrine; Elizabeth, for example, fully embodies the ideologically correct feminine qualities Victor—and the author—attribute to her. Yet it is equally clear that Elizabeth and the domestic sphere she represents fail signally in their raison d'être, which is to prepare young men like Victor to resist the temptations of the public sphere. *Frankenstein* shows that the private virtues inculcated through domestic affection cannot arm men against the public world unless men emulate these feminine and domestic qualities. Although Victor waxes eloquent on the domestic "lesson of patience, of charity, and of self-control" taught him as a child (40),[1] his quest for scientific glory shows that none of this lesson took; and while he often reiterates his "warmest admiration" (129) for Elizabeth's qualities, he perceives them not as a model but as a "reward" and "consolation" for his trials (131). Through these contradictions the novel may be suggesting that domestic affection can achieve its educational aim only if it is "hardy enough to survive in the world outside the home" (Ellis, "Monsters" 140); but *Frankenstein* also dramatizes how all but impossible is that aim.

The problem is that the domestic ideology is bifurcated: the home is to provide not only a moral education for involvement in the public world but also a shelter against this world. Instead of a nursery of virtue, then, the home could become, as one of domesticity's stoutest ideologues put it, a "relief from the severer duties of life" (Ellis, *Women* 12); a man could thus "pursue the necessary avocation of the day" but also "keep as it were a separate soul for his family, his social duty, and his God" (Ellis, *Women* 20). Although written some twenty years after *Frankenstein*, this picture of a man with two separate souls perfectly represents a contradictory domestic ideology and its product, a Victor divided between his masculine "necessary avocation" of scientific glory and his admiration of Elizabeth's feminine domesticity.

Feminist criticism of *Frankenstein* has addressed the similar conflict between public and private that troubled Victor's creator. Mary Shelley's 1831 introduction states her desire for the public fame both her parents had achieved by writing, but she adds that her private, domestic role—"the cares of a family"—kept her from pursuing this goal (20). Even when she went public with *Frankenstein* in 1818, she remained to some extent private by publishing it anonymously. Several possible explanations of this desire for privacy suggest themselves. While Mary claimed that she withheld her name out of respect for those "from whom I bear it" (*Letters* 1.71), she may also have feared a repetition of the public contumely directed at both of her parents as well as their writings. The experience of her husband

Percy and their friend Byron, two published poets whose work and unconventional lives had been vilified by critics, must have intensified these fears. And, although by 1818 she was legally married, her experience of publicity after eloping—she knew the rumors that her father had sold her to Percy (*Letters* 1.4)—may have made her especially wary of inviting public attention. Finally, Mary's caution could well have been gender-specific: she may have wanted to prevent critics from dismissing her as a woman writer.

Several elements of this last possibility—the terms of such a critical judgment, Mary Shelley's own view of women's writing, the difficulty of writing her way out of the woman's private into the man's public sphere—are well illustrated by the peregrinations of a letter she wrote to Percy. On September 30, 1817, the letter's date, *Frankenstein* was at the publisher, halfway between a private and a public state; Percy Shelley, not Mary, was in London editing the proofs. In her letter Mary animadverted at some length on the politics of a pamphlet by the radical William Cobbett. Percy apparently showed these private comments on public affairs to their mutual friend Leigh Hunt, editor of the *Examiner*. Without informing Mary, Hunt published her comments in the October 15 *Examiner*; he did not name her but did note her gender, describing her as "a lady of what is called a masculine understanding, that is to say, of great natural abilities not obstructed by a *bad* education" (*Letters* 1.54, fn. 2). Mary's letter reads somewhat breathlessly—like much of the manuscript *Frankenstein,* for instance, it is punctuated only by dashes—and she felt it "cut a very foolish figure" in print (*Letters* 1.53). Had she known Hunt planned to make her comments public, she told Percy, she would have written with "more print-worthy dignity"; instead, the letter was "so femeninely [sic] expressed that all men of letters will on reading it acquit me of having a *masculine* understanding."

The incident of the letter and its author's response illuminate several of her difficulties as a woman writer. To begin with, she would come up against one element of the separation of spheres, namely a strict ideological distinction of "masculine" from "feminine" qualities. In Hunt's editorial note, for instance, "great natural abilities" are gendered; that is, they are equated with "a masculine understanding." If "obstructed" by the "bad" education most women could expect to receive, these abilities would be feminized—that is, obscured and weakened. For Mary Shelley to name herself as *Frankenstein's* author, then, would be

to endanger her status as honorary man, to risk having her "masculine understanding" impugned as "femininely expressed."

Writing a novel of "print-worthy dignity" had already presented its author with similar problems. As I have noted, her domestic duties interfered with the time available for writing, and as editor her husband may have been a further impediment. Mary Poovey has cogently argued that Mary Shelley's own editing of the 1831 *Frankenstein* was meant to bring her younger, unorthodox self into line with the conventional image of a proper lady, and it seems to me that a similar image-making motivated Percy's revisions of his wife's manuscript. In some ways, of course, his idea of a proper lady diverged wildly from contemporary ideology; after he and Mary eloped, for instance, he suggested to his wife Harriet that she join them. Nonetheless, Percy Shelley shared his culture's desire to mold women according to a masculine idea of femininity, a narcissistic complement to masculine traits. Such narcissism colored his view of his relationship with Mary: they were so "united," he wrote, that in describing her "excellencies" he seemed to himself "an egoist expatiating upon his own perfections" (qtd. in Spark 21). His editing displays the same self-satisfied desire to "unite" Mary's work to his, to see his perfections mirrored in her manuscript.

While some of Percy Shelley's changes are clarifications and others are grammatical, even these minimal alterations show his desire to control the text and shape it in his own image. As he consistently changes Mary's dashes to colons and semicolons, for instance, or her coordinating "that" to the subordinating "which," he is imposing his order on her ideas. More striking are his revisions of her language. Anne K. Mellor has exhaustively documented the extent to which Percy altered Mary's straightforward and colloquial diction into a more ponderous and latinate prose,[2] and my own examination of the rough-draft and fair-copy manuscripts confirms that he is largely responsible for what George Levine calls the novel's "inflexibly public and oratorical" style (3). This "public" style is masculine—the product of a public-school and university education, available only to men, which taught writing by using Latin prose as a model—and so it confers "print-worthy dignity" on what might otherwise seem "femininely expressed."

Where Percy Shelley's changes extended beyond clarification, grammar, and diction, Mellor charges that they "actually distorted the meaning of the text" (62). I will return to this questionable notion that any text has a single meaning, but certainly Percy's heavy editorial hand marks the novel throughout. He rewrote some sections extensively; his fair copy of the conclusion (from Victor's death on) significantly revises the rough draft; and his wife gave him "carte blanche to make what alterations you please" while he was editing certain sections of the proofs (*Letters* 1.42).

Accustomed as we are to regarding authorship as independent creation we may wonder why Mary Shelley allowed her husband to rewrite her novel in these fairly substantial ways. Every writer knows how dispiriting it is to have one's deathless prose altered, no matter how kindly—especially when, as in Mary's case, the alterations come from a more experienced and thus (presumably) authoritative writer. Yet most writers have also felt the benefits of what might be called a collaborative editing, one that does not "distort" a text's single meaning but rather teases out its several inchoate or chaotic possibilities. It is at least arguable, then, that Mary acceded to her husband's changes not simply out of "deference to his superior mind" (Mellor 69) but also because she viewed him as a collaborator. Moreover, if Percy's revisions were in some ways protective coloration, they were also empowering: his attentions must have encouraged her to believe that she "possessed the promise of better things hereafter" (Introduction 20) and to produce a substantial body of "better things" after his death.

But the issue of a man's influence on a woman writer remains complicated. Mary Shelley felt unable "to put [her]self forward unless led, cherished & supported," and she perceived this need for support as feminine, "the woman's love of looking up and being guided" (*Journals* 555). It might be, then, that this ideology of dependent femininity rendered her unable to write her own text without her husband's help. Moreover, collaboration forced by a more dominant writer on a less powerful and perhaps unwilling "partner" is a kind of rape; if *Frankenstein* is the product of such a union, then it evinces a debilitating femininity. But to perceive writing as noncollaborative, as a necessarily independent act, betokens a concept of masculinity that raises another set of problems. One has only to think of Victor as self-sufficient "author"[3]—of the monster (91), "unalterable evils" (84), and "[his] own speedy ruin" (92)—to see such authorship as a monstrous, masculine version of creativity. If Mary Shelley rejected this view of creation as autochthonous, of a work as wholly self-engendered, *Frankenstein* becomes

"an incipient critique of the individualistic notion of originary creativity" (Carson 436). By welcoming help, then, she challenged a destructive version of "masculine understanding." But even if her collaboration was willing, it could be seen as self-suppression, an acceptance of "feminine" weakness: as the journal entry cited above shows, a woman of her time was *conditioned* to think she needed a man's help. From this perspective, her willingness to accept her husband's revisions is analogous to the novel's oppressively feminine women: all are efforts to straddle the line between public and private, to ensure that a masculine understanding is expressed without feminine obstructions but with feminine propriety.

This "but"-laden formulation leaves the question of Percy Shelley's influence open, and I have done so deliberately—partly because editing this book showed me the difficulty of distinguishing between encouragement and coercion, partly because we cannot ascertain Mary Shelley's motives with any certainty, but mainly because the problem of influence shows that the relations between prescribed femininity and women's actual experience are so convoluted as to resist single-answer formulations.

If we now turn from the author to her novel, we can see how domestic relationships in *Frankenstein* embody this complex and uneasy negotiation between ideology and experience.

The Frankenstein home seems a model of ideologically correct relationships. Not only are Alphonse and Caroline happily married, as parents they are "possessed by the very spirit of kindness and indulgence" (43). Together, we are told, they guide Victor with "a silken cord" (40); they are joint "agents and creators" of his childhood joys (43); and he derives as much pleasure from his father's "smile of benevolent pleasure" (40) as from his mother's "tender caresses." This shared parenting shows that men as well as women have an important domestic role; indeed, insofar as Alphonse is a Good Father, he is feminine. His nurturant qualities were commonly associated with femininity, and it is significant that he has "relinquished all his public functions," withdrawn from the man's sphere of government into the woman's domestic sphere. Yet he also fulfills the traditional masculine role of protector toward his wife, by rescuing her from want and "shelter[ing] her, as a fair exotic is sheltered by the gardener, from every rougher wind." In these ways Alphonse becomes a sort of feminine patriarch, and his gentle rule by "silken cord" is the reverse of paternal tyranny.

Also ideologically sound is the harmony produced among the household's children by their opposite yet complementary traits. Where the original manuscript focused on diversity, the final version was revised to focus on harmony. In the rough draft, for instance, an electrical storm produced "a very different effect" on each child: Victor wanted "to analyze its causes," Henry "said that the fairies and giants were at war," and Elizabeth "attempted a picture of it" (Abinger Dep.c.477/1, p. 45). Although the 1831 *Frankenstein* retains such differences between Elizabeth and Victor, the focus shifts to how "diversity and contrast . . . drew us nearer together" (42). Elizabeth accepts "with a serious and satisfied spirit the appearance of things" while Victor "delight[s] in investigating their causes," but no "disunion or dispute" mars this gender difference between feminine passivity and masculine activity. Here as throughout the novel, gender opposites are represented as complements. The young Victor Frankenstein and his friend Henry Clerval actively prepare for public futures while Elizabeth simply exists as a domestic icon, but what might seem an *opposition* between separate spheres is rewritten as complementary *difference*. In other words, while Elizabeth is little more than "the living spirit of love" (43), as such she has feminine functions. Her "sympathy," smile, etc. are "ever there to bless and animate" Henry and Victor; she teaches Henry "the real loveliness of beneficence" (43), and she keeps Victor from becoming "sullen" and "rough" by "subdu[ing him] to a semblance of her own gentleness" (43).

In Henry, moreover, Victor has a paradigm for the successful complementarity of masculine and feminine traits within himself. While Henry wants to be one of "the gallant and adventurous benefactors of our species" (43), he is also a domestic benefactor: as Victor's "kind and attentive nurse" (61) at Ingolstadt, he fulfills the role Elizabeth wished for herself (63). In addition, he tempers his masculine "passion for adventurous exploit" (43) with Elizabeth's feminine desire that he make "doing good the end and aim of his soaring ambition." Unlike Victor's "mad enthusiasm" (154), Henry's "wild and enthusiastic imagination was chastened by the sensibility of his heart" (133). Clearly, Victor's "eager desire" to learn "the *physical* secrets of the world" should have been balanced by Henry's preoccupation with "the *moral* relations of things" (43; emphasis added).

Why, then, does this domestic enclave of virtue not protect Victor? Why does he not remain within the boundaries marked off by the "silken cord" of domestic affection? Why does he not profit from the "lesson of patience, of charity, of self-control" taught by his parents and embodied in his friends, Elizabeth and Henry? The answers lie in Victor's complicated relations to nature, feminized domesticity, and masculine science.

For Victor, nature is "maternal" (87), and its life-giving and "kindly influence" has a domestic equivalent in Elizabeth's feminine fosterage. Just as Elizabeth "subdued Victor to a semblance of her own gentleness," so a "cloudless blue sky" can bestow "a tranquillity to which [he] had long been a stranger" (132); just as Elizabeth can "inspire [him] with human feelings" (159), so a "divine spring" can "revive" in him "sentiments of joy and affection" (62). In these moods of openness to nature, Victor is feminized into passive tranquillity and domestic affection. In other moods, however, he thrills to a more masculine nature; when he experiences a storm in the Alps, for instance, "This noble war in the sky elevated my spirits" (72). It is this idea of war, of attempted conquest or dominion, that most frequently informs Victor's masculine attitude toward nature. It is no accident, then, that he chooses the masculine realm of science as a means of discovering and thereby mastering the secrets of feminine nature. From childhood Victor had regarded the world as "a secret which I desired to divine"; repeatedly he tells us of his obsessive curiosity about "the hidden laws of nature" (42), his "eager desire" to learn "the secrets of heaven and earth" (43), his "fervent longing to penetrate the secrets of nature" (44). Because "her immortal lineaments were still a wonder and a mystery" to him (45), this unknown nature offers a field for the masculine mastery promised by scientific knowledge.[4] At Ingolstadt M. Waldman assures him that modern scientists can "penetrate into the recesses of nature and show how she works in her hiding-places" (51), and so Victor determines to "pursue nature to her hiding-places" (56).

Now, this language describing masculine penetration of feminine nature may be scientific, but it also sounds insistently sexual; to post-Freudian ears, it may suggest a woman writer's uneasiness with masculine sexuality.[5] But another explanation may lie in Mary Shelley's conflicted desire both to achieve public fame by writing and to escape the consequent publicity by remaining in the private sphere. If Percy Shelley's "incitement" (23) reinforced her "persistent association of writing with an aggressive quest for public notice" (Poovey 121), then writing *Frankenstein* must have seemed to *invite* the consequent invasions by publicity. The novel's language of penetration, that is, may have less to do with sexuality per se than with a woman writer's fear that walled-off domesticity cannot guarantee the privacy it promises. More troubling would be the possibility that, if writing masculinizes, then it might make a woman Victor-like, aggressive, a scientific violator of domesticity's secrets.

But if domesticity can be penetrated, especially from within, does this not suggest that it was never inviolable, that its apparent strengths were in fact its weaknesses or even its immanent destruction? This question moves back toward the problem of feminized domesticity, and here we need to look again at Alphonse's role as feminine patriarch. While Victor says that Waldman's promises of scientific prowess were "enounced to destroy me" (51), he blames not Waldman but his father. Instead of offhandedly dismissing Cornelius Agrippa as "sad trash" (44), Victor complains, Alphonse should have explained that modern science "possessed much greater powers" than Agrippa's outmoded alchemical methods; Victor would then have bowed to the authority of paternal knowledge and "possibl[y]" escaped "the fatal impulse that led to my ruin" (44). Well, maybe. But if the revelation of modern science's "new and almost unlimited powers" (51) is an "evil influence" when it comes from M. Waldman (49), it would be no less evil coming from the elder Frankenstein. Significant here are the author's revisions rendering Alphonse "not scientific" (45). She omitted from the rough draft both his scientific experiments and his wish that Victor attend lectures in natural philosophy, and she altered the decision to send Victor to university, originally made by "my father," to the wish of "my parents" (Abinger Dep.c.477/1, pp. 6, 47). All these changes suggest that the author intended to reduce Alphonse's culpability for Victor's skewed science.

Yet Alphonse *does* contribute to Victor's ruin, not because he is a bad scientist but because he is a good father. What I am suggesting is a destructive domesticity enforced by the feminized patriarch. Despite Victor's insistence on his perfect childhood, his relation to his "remarkably secluded and domestic" upbringing (48) is in fact conflicted. On the one hand, he is "reluctant" to leave home for Ingolstadt, where he must become "[his] own protector"; on the other, he has "longed to enter the world," to no longer be "cooped up" by domesticity and its protections. In a novel ostensibly written to exhibit "the amiableness of domestic affection" (Preface 25),[6] Victor's admis-

sion jars: can it be that his home is too domestic, his feminized father too protective?

Although Victor insists on his "gratitude" for his parents' care (43), we may speculate that this very gratitude has made him feel "cooped up." Gratitude, no matter how heartfelt, implies obligation, which in turn implies the power of the person to whom one is grateful or obligated. The insistence on gratitude and obligation induces a bookkeeping mentality that permeates all the relations in this novel. Victor acknowledges Henry Clerval's nursing by asking "How shall I ever repay you?" (62); Felix De Lacey views Safie as "a treasure which would fully reward his toil and hazard" in rescuing her father (108); when shot by the peasant, the monster fumes that "the reward of [his] benevolence" is "ingratitude" (122). This emotional quid pro quo is most evident, however, in the novel's domestic relations. In these terms the Frankenstein family is "a paradigm of the social contract based on economic terms" (Dussinger 52), for kinship and domestic affection are "secondary to the indebtedness incurred by promises exchanged for gifts." That is, in this family what seems freely given in fact requires something in exchange, so that the relation between parents and children is one of "unpayable debt."

Rather than Victor's picture of a gentle patriarch guiding by "silken cord," what then emerges is a cord or bond of constricting domestic relations. Among the Frankensteins, a gift requires gratitude and so produces a sense of obligation that can be discharged only by endless repetition of this pattern. Victor's parents had "a deep consciousness of what they *owed* towards the being to which they had *given* life" (40). To them the child was

> the innocent and helpless creature *bestowed* on them by Heaven, . . . whose future lot it was in their hands to direct to happiness or misery, according as they fulfilled their duties towards me.
> (40; emphases added)

Caroline and Alphonse pay off their debt of gratitude to "heaven" by fulfilling the duties they owe their child. Victor in turn owes gratitude for the life "given" him and for his parents' care, but their power and his consequent obligations form the cord that, no matter how silken, confines and encloses him within the family. Hence he repeats this domestic pattern when he contemplates creating a new species, and his view of the parent-child relation revealingly focuses on himself as patriarch. The members of his new species "would *owe* their being to me," he gloats, and so "[n]o father could *claim* the *gratitude* of his child so completely as I should deserve theirs" (55; emphases added). Alphonse may have seemed a gentle patriarch, but Victor's words suggest there was an iron hand in this velvet glove: a father can *claim* gratitude from the child who owes existence to him.

Judged simply from this paternal point of view, there is a certain logic in Victor's abandonment of the "child" he created: if the sheer bestowal of existence is a sufficient claim to gratitude, why be an Alphonse-like Good Father? Of course, in abandoning the monster Victor forgets the distinction he had earlier made between merely claiming gratitude and really deserving it. To deserve gratitude, parents must "fulfill their duties" toward their child; because Victor does not do so, he is a Bad Father and his child is not embodied filial gratitude but "my own vampire, my own spirit . . . forced to destroy all that was dear to me" (73). But if a bad father produces a bad child, and Victor like the monster is a bad child, does this not suggest that Alphonse too was a bad father, that he somehow failed to fulfill his duties toward his child? Or was it *fulfilling* those duties that made him a bad father? In other words, can the ideologically correct Good Father be so nurturant that he becomes a Bad Father? If so, then Alphonse's paternal protection is as damaging to his child as Victor's paternal indifference is to his. In other words, while the monster becomes monstrous in part because he has been denied parental care, Victor becomes monstrous in part because he has been *given* this care and made subject to the attendant obligations. In this reading, the "spirit" that Victor releases through the monster is the masculinity so "cooped up" by Alphonse's feminized domesticity that it breaks out as "the male principle in its extreme, monstrous form" (Veeder 190). Hence Victor can enter the masculine sphere of science only by destroying the feminine sphere, and that includes his feminized father. Victor's kinship to the monster reveals the dark side of the Frankenstein family's oppressive domesticity and too-nurturant patriarch.

But Victor is not the only victim of this pattern of domestic indebtedness: it is the novel's women who are literally destroyed by it. In the relations of Caroline, Elizabeth, and Justine to the Frankenstein family, we can again see something excessive, something too enveloping in Frankensteinian domesticity. Certainly the image of Caroline as Alphonse's "fair exotic" (39) suggests a hothouse atmosphere, and when she transplants the "garden rose" Elizabeth (41) to the Frankenstein home as Victor's "more than sister" (42), "the

amiableness of domestic affection" comes precariously close to incest. Of course Elizabeth is not literally Victor's sister, and he later assures his father that he loves her not as a brother but as a husband (129). But pursuing the hint of incest will clarify how blood kinship among the Frankensteins is secondary to familial indebtedness; we can then see how the resulting insistent domesticity kills off the novel's women.

Class selection determines which women are worthy to enter the upper class Frankenstein family; as Anca Vlasopolos suggests, this criterion is "a form of aristocratic protectionism that encourages, in fact engineers, incest" (126) by closing the family off from otherness or difference. Although plunged into straw-plaiting poverty by her father's business failure, Caroline's lineage and beauty mark her as still deserving the "rank and magnificence" he once enjoyed (38); by marrying her, then, Alphonse is restoring the status quo, rescuing Caroline from the otherness of a working-class milieu and returning her to her proper place. This pattern is even more overt in the adoption of Elizabeth. Because Elizabeth is "of a different stock" from her rude guardians (40), Caroline rescues this nobleman's daughter from the lower orders and then uses the "powerful protection" (41) of the Frankenstein family to restore Elizabeth to her proper status. Difference is further excluded as Elizabeth takes on all the family's feminine roles; Victor's "more than sister" and destined to be his wife, she also becomes Caroline by "supply-[ing her] place" as mother after her death (47). Although Justine is brought less fully into the family, she is perhaps the most Frankensteinized: when Caroline rescues her from a Bad Mother, Justine so "imitate[s] her phraseology and manners" (64) as to become her clone. The Frankenstein family's incestuous pattern of reproducing itself by excluding difference could hardly be clearer. And although none of these women is a born Frankenstein, they all—unlike Victor—fully internalize the family pattern of gratitude that enforces obligation.

This insistent replication of the grateful icon of domesticity shows how completely the pattern of indebtedness permeates the Frankenstein definition of femininity. Caroline is an especially rich example of this definition. We first see her as a daughter; even though her father's culpably "proud and unbending disposition" (38) forces her into his (masculine) role of breadwinner, the daughterly "tenderness" that discharges obligations to even a bad father (39) ensures her elevation to Frankenstein status. After Alphonse becomes her "protecting spirit," Caroline almost literally owes all she has to this marriage, and his oppressive benevolence constitutes another silken cord of enjoined gratitude. When she tries to discharge her obligations by "act[ing] in her turn the guardian angel to the afflicted" (40)—that is, by becoming a Frankenstein—her benevolence takes the usual form of enforced gratitude and obligation. When she gives Justine an education, for instance, "this benefit was fully repaid" (64) when Justine becomes "the most grateful little creature in the world." And when Caroline tries to discharge her debt to Alphonse by rescuing Elizabeth as she herself was rescued, she eventually pays with her life when she catches scarlet fever while nursing her protegée; unlike Victor, she has learned her own lesson "of patience, of charity" only too well.

A similar sacrifice is Elizabeth. Indebted to Caroline for rescue from peasant life, she must discharge this debt by taking Caroline's place as the Frankenstein ideal of femininity. As "a shrine-dedicated lamp in our peaceful home" (43) and "the tie of our domestic comfort and the stay of [Alphonse's] declining years," she is embodied domesticity. She is also Victor's "possession" (41), as he puts it: "my pride and my delight," "mine to protect, love, and cherish." But just as Alphonse's "protecting spirit" is ultimately responsible for Caroline's death, so Victor fails signally to "protect and cherish" his wife. His dream, that his kiss kills Elizabeth and turns her into his dead mother, is proleptic of the price she must pay for being Caroline's "pretty present" to him (41): in the form of the monster, Victor's aggressive masculinity murders the domestic femininity that had tried to "subdue [him] to a semblance of her own gentleness."

Justine is perhaps the most pathetic victim of this pattern of replicated femininity. Exhausted by her Caroline-like maternal care in searching for William, she falls asleep and so becomes the monster's prey. Her likeness to Caroline reminds him that he is "forever robbed" of any woman's "joy-imparting smiles" (123), so he determines that "she shall atone" for all women's indifference. While Justine suffers here from being Caroline's stand-in, more generally her crime is being seductive; according to this masculine logic, women are "to blame for having been desired" (Jacobus 133). To the townspeople, however, the crime for which Justine must "atone" is "blackest ingratitude" toward her benefactors (79). Once again the portrait of Caroline seals Justine's fate:

planted on her by the monster, it becomes circumstantial evidence of this ingratitude. Elizabeth's statement of her own and Caroline's kindness to their servant backfires; Justine, like Caroline and Elizabeth, must pay her obligations to the Frankensteins with her life, and furthermore dies all but convinced "that I was the monster" of ingratitude she is accused of being (80). These dramatic ironies, one victimized woman convicting another and that second victim convicting herself, in fact convict the Frankenstein family of omnivorous benevolence. Victor is right to call himself Justine's murderer (149), for it is the masculinity he represents that destroys its own creation of perfect femininity.

Victor's creation and destruction of the female monster is a kind of parody of these three women's fates. From watching the De Laceys and Safie, the monster learns to value the delights of domesticity they represent but also learns that he is "shut out" from such intercourse (106); hence he asks Victor for a mate with whom to "interchange [the] sympathies necessary for my being" (124). Given the failure of his exchange of sympathies with the De Laceys, it is more than a little ironic that the monster should make this request. And his desire for a female complement, a woman "as hideous as myself" (125), parodies not only Victor's insistence on Elizabeth's complementary relationship to himself, but also Victor's bride-to-be as both the creation and the gift of his parents. This traffic in women via Frankensteinian quid pro quo is at its most overt in the murders of the monsterette and Elizabeth: deprived of a bride by Victor, the monster retaliates by killing Victor's bride. Victor, of course, assumes that he and not Elizabeth will be the monster's target, and in one sense he is correct: like the monsterette's, Elizabeth's creation and murder show that women function not in their own right but rather as signals of and conduits for men's relations with other men.

Against this dreary record of dead women we may place Safe. Her mother was rescued from slavery just as Caroline was rescued from poverty (Ellis, "Monsters" 141), but there the resemblance ends. From her mother Safie learns "to aspire to higher powers of intellect and an independence of spirit" (108); hence she flouts her father's "tyrannical mandate" (110) against marrying Felix and travels across Europe to rejoin him. Both her maternal inspiration and her active adventurousness contrast with Caroline's influence on her passive "daughters" Elizabeth and Justine. Unlike their iconic femininity, Safie is "subtly androgynous" (Rubinstein 189); we might see her as a female Henry, combining the standard feminine "angelic beauty" (103) with a masculine energy and enterprise lacking in the novel's other women. But the challenge she might represent to conventional ideas of femininity is in effect "absorbed" by various cultural norms (Vlasopolos 132). In the first place, her desire to marry Felix has a class bias, for she is "enchant[ed]" (109) by the prospect of "tak[ing] a place in society." In addition, unlike Henry or Walton she seeks adventure not for its own sake or to benefit humankind but to get a man. This is not to say that Walton's quest is unambiguously benevolent: like Victor's desire to "pioneer a new way" (51) and thus achieve "more, far more" than his predecessors, Walton's urge to "confer on all mankind" (26) an "inestimable benefit" is motivated at least as much by a self-absorbed itch for glory as by humanitarianism. It is nonetheless true that Safie, albeit much less drastically than the Frankenstein women, represents the view that women are "relative creatures" whose value derives from "promoting the happiness of others" (Ellis, *Women* 48, 16). It is thus apt that she joins the De Lacey family, for while their interactive domestic style stands in stark contrast to the rigid gift / debt structure of the Frankensteins, still it is a conventionally separate-spheres arrangement: Felix is "constantly employed out of doors" (98), for instance, while his sister Agatha's work consists of "arranging the cottage" (97). Moreover, just as Victor's family attempts to make a select few women into Frankensteins, so the De Lacey family circle opens only to admit the beautiful Safie. That Felix, like Victor, excludes the ugly monster indicates again how strictly men control where "the amiableness of domestic affection" is allowed to operate.

By using several feminist methodologies—studying one woman writer's experience of domestic and public roles, analyzing the cultural formation and literary representation of these gender roles—I have been reading **Frankenstein** as a woman's text concerned with women's issues. While Victor's story shows that the constraints of domesticity bear down hard on men, it is clear that the novel's women—who must not only create the familial sanctuary and sacrifice themselves to maintain it but also be punished for its failures—take the heavier share of the burden. If **Frankenstein** is about Victor, it is also about what his monstrous masculinity does to women, and even though none of these women speaks directly, Mary Shelley's novel speaks to us for them.

Notes

1. Note that page numbers refer to *Frankenstein,* by Mary Shelley. Edited by Johanna M. Smith. New York: Bedford Books, 1992.

2. See Mellor 58-69. Murray 62-68 prints a useful side-by-side listing of the rough draft, fair copy, and 1831 revisions.

3. Mellor 65 argues that Percy Shelley introduced all uses of the word "author." Granted I am not a handwriting expert, the manuscript evidence for this assertion does not seem to me conclusive; moreover, even if it were he who introduced the word, surely Mary Shelley would have had her own ideas of what it connoted.

4. Mellor's Chapter 5 fully documents the masculinist language of domination used by the scientists Mary consulted while writing *Frankenstein;* on more recent uses of such language, see Kranzler.

5. There is some biographical evidence for this view. In 1815 Percy was apparently urging Mary toward an affair with his friend T. J. Hogg, who was nothing loath; this combined sexual pressure may have been at least unsettling for Mary, at worst the same kind of masculine domination that Victor wants to impose on nature. See *Letters* 1.6-14; the most even-handed treatment of this episode is Spark 40-46.

6. In her 1831 introduction Mary Shelley claims that Percy Shelley wrote this Preface, but an 1817 journal entry suggests otherwise. On May 14 she writes "S. [i.e., Percy] reads History of Fr[ench] Rev[olution] and corrects F[rankenstein]. write Preface.—Finis" (*Journal* 169). The verb "write" indicates that the omitted subject of this sentence is not Percy but "I"; this may be a slip of the pen, but if not it is interesting to speculate why Mary remembered Percy and not herself as the author of the Preface.

Works Cited

Carson, James B. "Bringing the Author Forward: *Frankenstein* through Mary Shelley's Letters." *Criticism* 30.4 (Fall 1988): 431-53.

Dussinger, John A. "Kinship and Guilt in Mary Shelley's *Frankenstein.*" *Studies in the Novel* 8 (1976): 38-55.

Ellis, Kate. "Monsters in the Garden: Mary Shelley and the Bourgeois Family." Levine and Knoepflmacher 123-42.

Ellis, Sarah Stickney. *The Women of England: Their Social Duties and Domestic Habits.* 1838. In *The Select Works of Mrs. Ellis.* New York: Langley, 1854.

Jacobus, Mary. "Is There a Woman in This Text?" *New Literary History* 14.1 (Autumn 1982): 117-41.

Kranzler, Laura. "Frankenstein and the Technological Future." *Foundation* 44 (Winter 1988-89): 42-49.

Levine, George. "The Ambiguous Heritage of *Frankenstein.*" Levine and Knoepflmacher 3-30.

Levine, George, and U. C. Knoepflmacher, eds. *The Endurance of Frankenstein: Essays on Mary Shelley's Novel.* Berkeley: U of California P, 1979.

Mellor, Anne K. *Mary Shelley: Her Life, Her Fiction, Her Monsters.* New York: Routledge, 1988.

Murray, E. B. "Shelley's Contribution to Mary's *Frankenstein.*" *Keats-Shelley Memorial Bulletin* 29 (1978): 50-68.

Poovey, Mary. *The Proper Lady and the Woman Writer: Ideology as Style in the Works of Mary Wollstonecraft, Mary Shelley, and Jane Austen.* Women in Culture and Society series. Chicago: U of Chicago P, 1984. 114-42.

Rubinstein, Marc A. "'My Accursed Origin': The Search for the Mother in *Frankenstein.*" *Studies in Romanticism* 15 (Spring 1976): 165-94.

Shelley, Mary. *The Journals of Mary Wollstonecraft Shelley.* Ed. Paula R. Feldman and Diana Kilvert-Scott. Oxford: Clarendon, 1987.

———. *The Letters of Mary Wollstonecraft Shelley.* Ed. Betty T. Bennett. 3 vols. Baltimore: Johns Hopkins UP, 1980-1988.

Spark, Muriel. *Mary Shelley.* Rev. ed. London: Sphere-Penguin, 1987.

Veeder, William. *Mary Shelley and "Frankenstein": The Fate of Androgyny.* Chicago: U of Chicago P, 1986.

Vlasopolos, Anca. "*Frankenstein's* Hidden Skeleton: The Psycho-Politics of Oppression." *Science-Fiction Studies* 10.2 (July 1983): 125-36.

STEPHEN BEHRENDT (ESSAY DATE 1995)

SOURCE: Behrendt, Stephen. "Mary Shelley, *Frankenstein,* and the Woman Writer's Fate." In *Romantic Women Writers: Voices and Countervoices,* edited by Paula R. Feldman and Theresa M. Kelley, pp. 69-87. Hanover, N.H.: University Press of New England, 1995.

In the following essay, Behrendt argues that Frankenstein *embodies the dilemma of the nineteenth-century female writer and that it comments on women's marginalization and place in the public world.*

Frankenstein is a woman author's tale of almost exclusively male activity, a tale whose various parts are all told by men. Women are conspicuously absent from the main action; they are significantly displaced (Agatha de Lacey, Safie) or entirely eliminated (Justine, Elizabeth, and the Creature's partially constructed mate). The only woman truly *present* in the tale is paradoxically not "there" at all: the unseen, silent auditor/reader Margaret Walton Saville (MWS), who exists only in Walton's letters. Walton's letters make clear that Margaret figures into his part of the tale as both confidante and confessor, much as Walton himself serves Victor Frankenstein. Indeed, Walton's explanations to Margaret of his own behavior suggest that he casts her in a role as *sanctifier,* whose province it is to hear, understand, sympathize, and approve (see Letter 2, for instance), rather in the manner of the roles in which Dostoyevsky later casts Liza in *Notes from Underground* and Sonia Marmeladov in *Crime and Punishment.* Walton manipulates his sister much as William Wordsworth encircles and silences his sister Dorothy in "Tintern Abbey": the brother's own future viability (which the text explicitly demands) is to be engineered precisely by the resonance of his own words in his sister's consciousness (ll. 134-59).

As "silent bearers of ideology" in Western literature and art, women have traditionally been made "the necessary sacrifice to male secularity," which finds its expression in materialistic public activity in a world that cannot—indeed will not—accommodate the woman of action.[1] Ellen Moers sees in Ann Radcliffe an alternative to both the intellectual, philosophical woman typified by Mary Wollstonecraft and the super-domesticated image of the submissive wife and mother extolled by earlier eighteenth-century culture. Moers claims that Radcliffe's vision of female selfhood involved neither the wholly intellectual nor the traditionally "loving" nurturant role but rather that of the traveling woman: "the woman who moves, who acts, who copes with vicissitude and adventure."[2] This very public role of the woman of action fits authors like Mary Darby Robinson and Helen Maria Williams, as well as the many Gothic heroines who, like Emily St. Aubert in *The Mysteries of Udolpho,* cope exceedingly well with continual reversals of fortune and circumstance. It is not, however, the model of experience embraced by Mary Shelley, who, despite her considerable travels and public activity, wrote in pointedly gender-specific terms in 1828 that "my sex has precluded all idea of my fulfilling public employments."[3] For modern readers her comment hints painfully both at the encultured tendency of many women of the time—and today—to perpetuate women's oppression by discouraging public roles for women and at a narrowed and more biologically based rationalization of reserve on women's part.

In her important 1982 article, Barbara Johnson examines the troubled relationship among mothering, female authorship, and autobiography in *Frankenstein,* revealing some of the ways Mary Shelley associated authorship with monstrousness, and the products of authorship with the violent and unpredictable Creature. Anne Mellor has subsequently extended and refined the discussion in terms of Shelley's life and other writings.[4] My own reading is informed by their critical insights. I argue further that the initially well-intentioned and humane Creature resembles the idealistic author seeking to benefit her or his society, and so, tragically, does Victor Frankenstein. Both see their desires frustrated, however, as their intentions are first misunderstood and then misrepresented by others. Their interlaced histories thus pose a strong warning to authors—whether of literary texts or of cultural texts, such as revolutions—about the dangers of creating that which can destroy even its own author. The author must acknowledge the fact that her or his text's potential for mischief is at least as great as its potential for good. Because *Frankenstein*'s embedded lessons about the hazards of authorship bear particular relevance to the Romantic woman author, I shall here treat the novel as a touchstone as I examine some broader issues.

Although *Frankenstein* is a novel about *acts* and *actions,* it comes to us not in actions but in *reports* of actions, almost in the manner of classical theater, where much of the offstage action is represented only in verbal reports. The more contemporary parallel lies in Gothic fiction, in which the violence is often kept offstage and thereby rendered powerfully imminent, a menace whose physical manifestations are only barely held in abeyance by a combination of virtue, fortitude, coincidence, and plain good luck. In *Frankenstein* the reports are in fact frequently multilayered: they are reports of reports. The most heavily layered is Walton's report of Victor's report of the Creature's report of his self-education and experiences. Mary Shelley adds to this layering by beginning her novel in epistolary fashion, with a series of embedded reports that draw our attention to the writing acts of Walton and, by extension, to Shelley herself, both as original anonymous author and as the subsequently public, ex post facto authorial presence in the 1831 Introduction who reports on the novel's genesis. Moreover, in adopting the epistolary form of discourse, Walton adopts a genre long associated with *women's* writing. Just as he appropriates woman's procreative activity in creating his own "Creature," so does he appropriate the ostensibly uninhibited literary form (the letter form has been called "spontaneity formalized") that women—otherwise denied voice and hence access to male literary culture—"could practice without unsexing" themselves.[5]

To what extent does the nature of *Frankenstein* as a construct of words, rather than a direct representation of actions, embody the dilemma of the woman writer at the beginning of the nineteenth century? In what ways does the marginalization of women, their activities, and their perceived cultural worth figure in *Frankenstein*'s elimination or destruction of them? And what relation do these questions bear to the circumstances and the literary productions of other women writers of the Romantic period? Inherent in *Frankenstein* are some telling reflections of the ways in which women figured in the public world. In Mary Shelley's novel, women are occasionally the *objects* of discourse—most notably Margaret Saville, who cannot respond (or is at least represented as not responding), but also Justine and Elizabeth, whose responses to discourse aimed at them are in each case truncated by their deaths at the hands (in Elizabeth's case, quite literally) of the violent system of male authority within which the narrative is inscribed. When they are the *subjects* of discourse, on the other hand, they fare little better, for every woman of any importance who is spoken of in the main narrative is likewise destroyed: Victor's mother, Elizabeth, Justine, and the Creature's mate (who dies before even being "born"). In the public literary world of the time, the story is much the same. As objects of discourse, women were continually reminded of their "proper" and "natural" place in private familial and public extrafamilial interaction. The woman writer (who becomes herself an originator of discourse by publishing) is "represented" within public culture as an object of discourse when her work is reviewed by the (generally male) critic. But she is also translated into the *subject* of discourse when her literary efforts are indiscriminately interchanged with, or substituted for, her self—her individual person—within the public discourse of criticism.

Mary Shelley's first novel demonstrates that men's actions are typically either overtly destructive and therefore disruptive of social bonding or simply so thoroughly counterproductive that they result in paralysis, much as Walton's ship becomes immobilized in the ice. This message is repeated in one form or another in her subsequent novels and tales, and it appears in perhaps its starkest terms in *Mathilda,* where the psychological and sexual oppressions are so powerful that they resist language's capacity to record them at all. The writings of Shelley and others reveal the consequences of the cultural pressures exerted upon the woman author, pressures whose cumulative weight often served either to drive women to misrepresent themselves by adopting the masculinist culture's literary conventions or to silence them altogether.[6] In the case of Mary Shelley—daughter of politically radical philosophers, wife of a particularly notorious radical artist, and member of a glittering literary circle—the residue of this enculturated sense of inferiority is startling. The terrible cost of her search for personal fulfillment in a permanent, secure relationship based equally upon affection and intellectual equality have been documented by her biographers. Sufficiently telling are two comments from her letters to two women, the first of whom (Frances Wright [Darusmont]) was herself an active political and social reformer transplanted in 1818 to America:

> [W]omen are . . . per[pet]ually the victims of their generosity—& their purer, & more sensitive feelings render them so much less than men capable of battling the selfishness, hardness & ingratitude [which] is so often the return made, for the noblest efforts to benefit others.
>
> In short my belief is—whether there be sex in souls or not—that the sex of our material mechanism makes us quite different creatures—better though weaker but wanting in the higher grades of intellect.[7]

The second remark, in which "weaker" clearly refers to physical strength and stature, comes from a letter that is unusual even for Mary Shelley in the violence of its self-deprecation. But Dorothy Wordsworth expressed her fear of disappointing Coleridge in much the same terms: "I have not those powers which Coleridge thinks I have—I know it. My only merits are my devotedness to those I love and I hope a charity towards all mankind."[8] John Stuart Mill expressed the nature of the dilemma when he wrote in 1861 that "all the moralities tell [women] that it is the duty of women, and all the current sentimentalities that it is their nature, to live for others, to make complete abnegations of themselves, and to have no life but in their affections."[9] Comments like Shelley's and Wordsworth's provide compelling evidence of the validity of Mary Jacobus's much more recent observation that women's attempts to gain access to a male-dominated culture tend often to produce feelings of alienation, repression, and division: "a silencing of the 'feminine,' a loss of woman's inheritance" (27).

Indeed, expressions of self-disgust and self-hatred recur in the personal, private statements of Mary Shelley and other women who indulged their ambition (or, like Mary Robinson, Charlotte Smith, Felicia Hemans, and Shelley herself, their plain financial *need*) to enter the public arena of authorship. Entering explicitly into competition with the dominant caste of male authors, the woman writer seemed to violate not just social decorum but also the nature and constitution of her own sex. Not surprisingly, her efforts generated both anxiety and hostility among the male literary establishment, particularly when the woman dared to venture outside genres such as Gothic fiction that were more or less reserved for the heightened emotionalism expected of women writers.[10] It is instructive to remember that when Percy Bysshe Shelley composed a review of *Frankenstein* in 1818 his language implied that the author was male (perhaps, as was believed, Shelley himself).[11] Although this may have been yet another instance of Shelley's exaggerated, chivalric protectiveness toward his wife, the result was nevertheless to strip her of her authorship, even as she had been stripped of her early literary efforts in 1814 when the trunk containing her papers was left behind in Paris and subsequently vanished.[12]

I do not mean to minimize the growing impact women had on the Romantic literary market, either as authors or as readers.[13] But for nearly two centuries their place has been defined largely in terms of their relation to sentimentalism, which has had the effect of stereotyping the majority and effectively silencing the rest. By the later Romantic period it was becoming apparent that men no longer held quite the stranglehold on the literary scene that we have generally assumed. While publishing and criticism remained male-dominated fields, publishers especially were shrewd enough to understand their markets and to cater to the apparent tastes of a growing female readership, in part by employing women authors who addressed that readership. Nevertheless, the literary woman's activity remained circumscribed. Although women were free to write the literature of sentiment and were, in fact, encouraged to do so, the invitation did not customarily extend to the literature of science or, for the most part, of philosophy, political science, or economics. Indeed, the criticism of the would-be intellectual woman typically turned on assumptions about both the proper "nature" of women and the attributes that make them desirable to men, who are still the ultimate "consumers." This comment is typical: "[T]his woman had utterly thrown off her sex; when nature recalled it to her, she felt only distaste and tedium; sentimental love and its sweet emotions came nowhere near the heart of a woman with pretensions to learning, wit, free thought, politics, who has a passion for philosophy and longs for public acclaim. Kind and decent men do not like women of this sort."[14] The woman is Charlotte Corday, the famous man-killer; the account, from a Jacobin newspaper of the time. Such terminology recurs repeatedly in the English press and in the culture it both reflects and molds, and it suggests the extent to which the male establishment feared the "monstrous" advances being made by women. Like other novels (Smith's *Desmond* or Wollstonecraft's *Maria*, for example) whose rhetorical and thematic threads include the political, *Frankenstein* at once trespasses on "forbidden" territory and at the same time comments on the nature and consequences of that incursion.

The Romantic reading public's voracious appetite could consume authors as easily as their works, but their lack of access to the male-dominated, symbiotic twin industries of publishing and criticism made women writers particularly vulnerable. When Joseph Johnson hired Mary Wollstonecraft in 1787, he was taking an unconventional step, even though his decision was undoubtedly rooted more in pragmatic economic reasons than in progressive, gender-sensitive political ones; just back from France, she offered him both a contact (as well as a translator and editor familiar with the Continental literary milieu) and an intelligent author in her own right. Mary Darby Robinson's work for the *Morning Post* (which placed her squarely in the company of—and partly in competition with—Coleridge and Southey) offers another exception to the all-but-universal rule of male dominance. This overall dominance inevitably lent publishers and critics an inordinate power to silence the woman writer by denying her access to an audience or by so characterizing her efforts as to render them wholly unattractive to the inquisitive reader and thus to the prospective publisher of any subsequent efforts. Both of these forces stood poised to strike as soon as the woman writer overstepped the boundaries of propriety; they stood ready to step in "the moment she appeared to them as too palpably a manifestation of that monstrously capricious readership that has given birth to her" (Ross, *Contours*, 232).

This is not to say, however, that women poets (and women writers in general) were not acknowledged. Indeed, women poets seem to have been anthologized more frequently in the nineteenth century than they have been until recently in the twentieth, whereas women novelists like Ann Radcliffe, Charlotte Turner Smith, Amelia Opie, Jane Austen, and Mary Shelley, who *began* on the margins, achieved a more immediate and lasting enfranchisement. But the *manner* of that acknowledgment of women poets and of that anthologization tells its own tale. Let us take one example: Frederic Rowton's 1853 edition of *The Female Poets of Great Britain: Chronologically Arranged with Copious Selections and Critical Remarks*.[15] An enterprising editor and publisher, Rowton was active in such liberal causes as the Society for the Abolition of Capital Punishment. His anthology achieved a wide readership, both in England and in America, and there is no question that the volume called

attention to women's contributions to England's poetic heritage. Nevertheless, Rowton's "critical remarks" typify the narrow post-Romantic characterization of women's writing in terms analogous to those in which women's "domestic" work was being characterized at the outset of the Romantic period. Rowton's comments on Felicia Hemans, for example, are illustrative:

> She seems to me to represent and unite as purely and completely as any other writer in our literature the peculiar and specific qualities of the female mind. Her works are to my mind a perfect embodiment of woman's soul:—I would say that they are *intensely* feminine. The delicacy, the softness, the pureness, the quick observant vision, the ready sensibility, the devotedness, the faith of woman's nature find in Mrs. Hemans their ultra representative. . . . In nothing can one trace her feminine spirit more strikingly than in her domestic *home*-loving ideas. . . . No where, indeed, can we find a more pure and refined idea of home than that which pervades Mrs. Hemans's writings on the subject.
>
> (Pp. 386-87)

The delicacy that Rowton so admires in Hemans is in fact a recessive, deferential attitude that is more a critical overlaying, an interpretive imposition, than an essential quality of Hemans's verse. Just as female subordinates are kept in their "place" at the office by being called by first name (frequently in a diminutive form, at that) by supervisors whom they are expected to call by formal surname, so too is Hemans (and many others) "placed" by Rowton's condescending but nevertheless firmly authoritarian language, shored up by his "selection" of verse, which guarantees that the reader will see in Hemans precisely what Rowton intends. Interestingly, when H. T. Tuckerman wrote an introduction for the American edition of Hemans's *Poems* that appeared in 1853 (the same year as Rowton's anthology), he employed many of the same critical tactics, engaging in a form of "psychic defense" under the guise of critical appraisal. Such tactics, as Marlon Ross has demonstrated, "enable the critic to perform the crucial cultural endeavor of putting women in their natural and social place while ostensibly simply going about the mundane task of literary criticism" (*Contours*, 237).

The deferential, self-deprecating introduction or preface was a familiar literary fixture, whether it was employed by a Wordsworth or a Shelley in offering the world works that were proposed to be somehow "experimental" or adopted by a Mary Tighe (as in *Psyche,* 1805). But while readers seem to have "seen through" the affected posture when men employed it, they were more likely to regard that disclaimer, when women adopted it, not as a mere convention but rather as a statement of fact. And if the woman author failed to make the expected apologies, others stood ready to do it for her. Thus, the editorial introduction addressed "To the Reader" in later editions of Tighe's *Psyche, with Other Poems* assigns gender-driven terms to Tighe—and Tighe to them: "To possess strong feelings and amiable affections, and to express them with a nice discrimination, has been the attribute of many female writers . . . [but Tighe is] a writer intimately acquainted with classical literature, and guided by a taste for real excellence, [who] has delivered in polished language such sentiments as can tend only to encourage and improve the best sensations of the human breast."[16] Notice that the praiseworthy features—nicety, amiability, polish, sentiment—are intimately associated with such archetypal attributes of the Western female as cleanliness, orderliness, softness, and pliability. Even the exceptional (i. e., unfeminine) attributes—strong feelings, classical learning—are tempered by their being assigned to the support of essentially "feminine" concerns, the nurturing of the best *sensations* of the human heart chief among them. This sort of bracketing commentary is the norm for the period, both for the woman authors themselves and for the (male) interlocutors who felt compelled to speak for them in order to "introduce" them to their audiences.

Ironically, the notions of "home-loving" domesticity that Tighe's publisher, Rowton, and others sought to impose on women's writing have been succinctly summed up a century and a half later in—of all places—an anthropological study of dining etiquette:

> If "a woman's place is in the home," her place implies all the "female" characteristics: interiority, quietness, a longing to nurture, unwillingness to stand forth, and renunciation of the "male" claims to authority, publicity, loudness, brightness, sharpness. These qualities have a multitude of practical applications; for example, they either make a woman altogether unfit and unwilling to attend feasts, or they influence the way she behaves while participating in them.[17]

Substitute "publish" for "attend feasts," and the fit is nearly perfect. Indeed, according to traditional Western (especially Anglo-American) etiquette, what could be less womanly, less feminine, than *public*-ation, which injects the woman into a visible world held to be as thoroughly and exclusively masculine an arena as that to which gentlemen adjourned after dining for cigars and port?

In exercises like Rowton's, ideology is represented as "natural" fact, and begging the question is then passed off as exposition. Elsewhere, Rowton observes of Hemans that "to *passion* she is well nigh a stranger." Unlike Byron (who is "indeed, of all others *the* poet of passion"), "affection is with her a serene, radiating principle, mild and ethereal in its nature, gentle in its attributes, pervading and lasting in its effects" (p. 388). And Letitia Landon (Maclean), whom Rowton explicitly compares (favorably) with Byron ("the Byron of our poetesses" [p. 424]) is nevertheless censured for treating materials and attitudes for which Byron was even in 1853 routinely praised—however cautiously. Rowton remarks of Landon's skill at portraying sorrow:

> Persons who knew her intimately say that she was *not* naturally sad: that she was all gaiety and cheerfulness: but there is a mournfulness of soul which is never to be seen on the cheek or in the eye: and this I believe to have dwelt in Mrs. Maclean's breast more than in most people's. How else are we to understand her poetry? We cannot believe her sadness to have been put on like a player's garb: to have been an affectation, an unreality: it is too earnest for that. We must suppose that she *felt* what she wrote: and if so, her written sadness was real sadness.
>
> (Pp. 426-27)

Rowton's conclusions reveal a built-in ideological inability to credit the female poet with the imaginative capacity to *create* powerful moods or attitudes, a capacity attributed to a Wordsworth or a Byron without question. The male poet can create, invent; the female poet can only replicate and transcribe. Worse, Rowton extrapolates from his own faulty causal logic a narrowly moralistic (and predictably negative) literary-critical judgment: "This strong tendency towards melancholy frequently led Mrs. Maclean into most erroneous views and sentiments; which, though we may make what excuses we will for them out of consideration for the author, should be heartily and honestly condemned for the sake of moral truth" (p. 429).

We are dealing here with codes of behavior, with manners, considered within the sphere of literary production. Behaviors that are *tolerated* among male authors—even when they are disapproved—are intolerable in female authors. Morally reactionary critical responses to productions like *Don Juan, Prometheus Unbound,* or *Endymion* stemmed at least in part from a recognition that their authors were writers of substance and power, whose productions stood to shake up the conservative establishment on whose stability (and capital) the critical industry of the time had already come to depend. Women were writing powerful, socially volatile poetry, too; but rather than launch a comparable frontal attack on women writers like Mary Darby Robinson, Joanna Baillie, Charlotte Turner Smith, Letitia Landon, or even Hannah More, gender-driven criticism adopted the psychologically subtle device of *undermining* by misrepresentation, of assessing works in terms of their adherence to or deviation from presumed standards of "femininity." The male-dominated publishing industry and its accompanying critical establishment had, of course, a great store in preserving, codifying, *and enforcing* this construct of "the feminine" in writing, perhaps especially so in the field of poetry, which was, in the Romantic period, still the preeminent vehicle for "high" art. If the membership of the club could not be preserved indefinitely for males only, it could at least be stratified: separate, lesser rooms in the clubhouse could be apportioned to women to keep them out of the way.

Johnson and Mellor have helped us to see that Frankenstein's Creature shares the situation of Romantic women, marginalized and spurned by a society to whose patriarchal schemata they fail to conform. Moreover, the values and sensibilities typically assigned to women during the Romantic period are not unlike those that Shelley assigns the Creature, including instinctive responsiveness to Nature, the impulse toward emotional human bonding (especially apparent in the deLacey episode), and an experiential rather than an abstract empirical way of "knowing"—all of which are the heritage of eighteenth-century sentimentalism. In the pursuit of all of these impulses the Creature is thwarted, both by his irresponsible creator and by the members of the society that has produced Victor and countless others like him. That the Creature is not "beautiful"—another attribute stereotypically associated with women—indicates the seemingly deforming nature of nonconformity as measured by the standards and sensibilities of the dominant majority. Ironically, as the representative of the masculinist culture that places such a premium on physical beauty among women (note especially his descriptions of Elizabeth), Victor Frankenstein creates a being whose hideousness contravenes any proper instinctive and loving parental response on his part to the Creature as "child." He has created that which he abhors, a situation entirely analogous to what the masculinist social and political establishment wrought upon women, writers or otherwise, and with the same consequences: the victim is led to self-deprecation and ultimately self-destructive behavior. Likewise, the author who thinks highly enough of her work to publish it nevertheless compromises herself in publishing with it self-effacing, apologetic, or temporizing prefaces that devalue or even destroy the work that follows. This is a necessary compromise, it would seem, for those who would be heard at all. But the cost in honesty and self-esteem to the author is considerable.

Victor renounces the product of his activities when the creative seeks to usurp the procreative. Hence, physically destroying the Creature's mate is only an emblem of the real act of devastation implicit in Victor's actions: the demolition of those who will not retreat to passive, silent existence on the margins of human experience. Silent neglect, however, is an equally powerful response. This fact lends particular significance to a literary project Mary Shelley proposed in 1830 to John Murray III and to which he apparently turned a (predictably) deaf ear. Suggesting topics on which she might write for publication, she says, "I have thought also of the Lives of Celebrated women—or a history of Woman—her position in society & her influence upon it—historically considered. [sic] and a History of Chivalry."[18]

Did Murray simply assume that the market-driven "buying public" (despite the very large number of women *readers* in it) would be uninterested in a volume of prose about women, perhaps especially one about "Woman"? The topic itself was certainly not prohibitively unpopular: Hemans's *Records of Woman* had appeared in 1828, with a second edition the same year and a third in 1830, as Shelley must have known (although there is no mention of it, nor of Hemans, in her letters or journals of this period). The balance (or *im*balance) in Mary Shelley's query between the worthy and promising topic of the position *and influence* of women in society and the much "safer" "History of Chivalry" (in which women might be expected to figure as ornament rather than as agent) is unintentionally revealing of the cultural bind from which neither Mary Shelley nor any other woman writer of her generation could entirely escape. Certainly, when one considers the sentimental concessions to traditional expectations about gender and genre that mar *Records of Woman*, one cannot help acknowledging the truth of what Jennifer Breen says about women writers' dilemma of creating in their works a woman's point of view: they were forced by social pressure "to conceal the split between what was expected of them and what they actually felt."[19] Hence, most of the women in *Records of*

Woman are, in fact, reflections of male social and cultural expectations only slightly displaced from their customary passive, recessive, nurturant roles to relatively more aggressive ones whose activity is typically generated by default, by the disappearance, death, or incapacitation of the male figure who would otherwise play the active role in the scenario (e.g., "Arabella Stuart," "The Switzer's Wife," or "Gertrude," whose subtitle, "Fidelity till Death," says it all).

One of **Frankenstein**'s lessons is that all creative activity (whether physically procreative or aesthetically/scientifically creative) drives individuals into seclusion and isolation and *away from* the salutary human interaction that is the proper objective of all human *action*. Shelley's introduction to the 1831 edition details the countersocializing aspect of her own experience as creative writer. That she chose to include that information and therefore to publicly detail her physical and psychological anxiety and her attempt to compete with the literary men who surrounded her is instructive, for her experience as a woman of words[20] ties her to contemporaries like Anna Letitia Barbauld, Jane Taylor, Mary Robinson, Ann Radcliffe, and Charlotte Smith, as well as to Dorothy Wordsworth, whose words were repeatedly appropriated by her brother in poems that for two centuries have blithely been regarded as "his." That still others, like Felicia Browne Hemans, unhesitatingly identified themselves by their married names (e.g., Mrs. Hemans, Mrs. Opie, or Mrs. Montolieu) indicates the extent to which they elected (whether freely or under cultural coercion) to reduce their actions and their identities to mere *words* (denoting marital status and recessive identity). What Stuart Curran says specifically of Felicia Hemans and Letitia Landon might be said of many of the women who were their contemporaries: In addition to the comfortable domesticity and sentimentality that may be glimpsed in their work, we can see also "darker strains," which include "a focus on exile and failure, a celebration of female genius frustrated, a haunting omnipresence of death."[21] This aspect of women's writing is as troubling today as it was two centuries ago, and it should not surprise us that intrusive contemporary commentators, editors, and anthologizers (like Frederic Rowton) attempted to deny the validity or even the meaningful presence of that aspect, either explicitly by branding it as subject matter inappropriate for women, in roundabout fashion by refusing to credit female authors with adequate imagination or intellect, or in slightly more covert fashion by calling their efforts on this front derivative from male models such as Byron.

Writing literature may be a form of communication, but it is decidedly not dialogue. Like Margaret Saville, the reader (or audience) is kept at a distance; functional interactive discourse with the author is precluded by the nature of the literary work of art. The one-sidedness of this arrangement is quite unlike the dialogic nature of the familiar letter (and I stress the adjective), a genre Mary Shelley seems to have much enjoyed.[22] The act of *literary* communication—the writing act and the production of a public, published text—distances both the writer and the reader from the subjective substance that the text mediates by means of language. In her preface to *Psyche* (1805), Mary Tighe presents a view of her work opposite to the one reflected in Shelley's 1831 reference to her "hideous progeny": "The author, who dismisses to the public the darling object of his solitary cares, must be prepared to consider, with some degree of indifference, the various receptions it may then meet."[23] Whether "hideous progeny" or "darling object," the fate of the published work is out of its author's hands, as is the author's private self, which soon becomes the property of critics and others who appropriate it by reading it both into and in the literary work, as is evident from this remark about Mary Darby Robinson's poetry:

> Of Mrs. Robinson's general character, it can only be added that she possessed a sensibility of heart and tenderness of mind which very frequently led her to form hasty decisions, while more mature deliberation would have tended to promote her interest and worldly comfort; she was liberal even to a fault; and many of the leading traits of her life will most fully evince, that she was the most disinterested of human beings. As to her literary character, the following pages, it may be presumed, will form a sufficient testimony.[24]

Here again are the terms we have seen applied to Hemans and Tighe; they include the standard catalog of "feminine" virtues of softness, tenderness, and pliability, as well as the converse (and therefore culpable) traits of independence, immaturity, hastiness, and lack of foresight. The concluding sentence of the "Preface" makes perfectly clear the writer's rhetorical strategy: having detailed for the reader a literary life characterized by failures to behave "properly," both in life and in print, the writer injects the works themselves ("the following pages") into this pejorative context. Co-opted into disapproving of the author's life and life-style, the reader is invited to carry along that sense of disapprobation while reading the poetry. It is a classic tactic of reader manipulation and an unusually effective one, as history affords us ample opportunities to observe.

To create literary art is ultimately to falsify both the person and the *act*—whether external and immediate or internal and imaginative—that motivates the verbal text. It is not just a matter of producing fading coals, as Percy Bysshe Shelley suggests in *A Defence of Poetry,* but rather of burning up the raw material entirely. In the process the individual self gets burned up as well, consumed and extinguished. For the woman writer, no less than for the man, who and what one *is* gets superseded in the process of publication by the *words* that may represent—but more likely *mis*represent—that individual private entity. Fame devours personhood, as Tennyson's Ulysses reminds us later when he ironically announces that "I am become a name." In a "man's world," which is very much what the Romantic era was in England despite the presence of literary women in it, men are better able to overcome this dissolution of the self because they are the principal *actors* (act-ors) on the public stage, as well as the controllers of language and other cultural determinants. But because of their social, political, and cultural marginalization, women have few resources for countering the extinguishing of the personal self. When they did write, as Susan J. Wolfson observes of Dorothy Wordsworth, their experiences frequently generated in their texts "countertexts and spectres of defeat."[25]

Wolfson reminds us that in professing to "detest the idea of setting myself up as author" (p. 140) Dorothy Wordsworth effectively accepted the marginalized and *un*authoritative female role assigned her by the masculinist society epitomized in her brother and valorized by his public audiences. As journal keeper and documenter of domestic affairs both personal and public, rather than self-promoting, publishing author, she played out the culturally conditioned expectations of woman as domestic engineer, historical and social housekeeper, and minder of minor details of order and appearance. Nevertheless, Dorothy Wordsworth did write, both in prose and in poetry, and even her characteristic self-deprecating tone cannot entirely hide the clear strain in her writings of ambition and of longing for a more authoritative and self-expressive voice.[26] Much the same might be said about Mary Shelley, whose letters are filled with protestations against public visibility: "There is nothing I shrink from more fearfully than publicity—. . . far from wishing to stand forward to assert myself in any way, now that I am alone in the world, [I] have but the desire to wrap night and the obscurity of insignificance around me."[27] Despite her very considerable oeuvre, she often deprecated both her literary talent and her intellectual acuity by referring to her writing, as she once did to John Murray, as "my stupid pen & ink labors."[28]

Part of the Romantic woman writer's predicament involves what Sandra Gilbert and Susan Gubar have called the "anxiety of authorship"— the woman's radical fear "that she cannot create, that because she can never become a 'precursor' the act of writing will isolate or destroy her."[29] This is a potentially and often an actually crippling anxiety. And yet this fear need not be gender-specific to women. Sonia Hofkosh has demonstrated that no less "male" a male writer than Byron exemplifies the author who "dreads, as he desires, being read by others—a reading that rewrites him and thus compromises his powers of self-creation."[30] The problem is particularly acute for the woman writer, however, who in the Romantic period was working with only the bare thread of a literary heritage. Battling the powerful forces that everywhere reminded her of her cultural and intellectual marginality and the impropriety of her artistic aspirations—forces that fed (and rewarded) timidity and submissiveness—the woman writer was very like Mary Shelley's Creature. This gender-driven cultural stifling both of experience and of expression lies behind what Mary Jacobus, among others, sees as the themes of "dumbness and utterance" and of the powerful quest to fulfill an impossible desire (*Reading Woman,* 28).

We do well to catch in the Creature's history a glimpse of the history of the woman artist during the Romantic period—and indeed during much of the history of Western culture. What is at issue, finally, is the ongoing radical marginalization of the unconventional, a phenomenon as much political as social and cultural. The dominant social milieu severs communication with the Creature because neither its appearance nor its acts conform to the expectations of that majority culture. The society in which Frankenstein and Walton alike opt for the isolation of individual pursuits over the socializing impulses of human interaction proves to be the real agent in redefining the parameters of creative activity. Acts are replaced by words, activity by passivity, responsibility by the irresponsibly ambivalent, and individuality by abstraction. The person is dissolved.

Mary Shelley's first major literary project after Percy's death was ***The Last Man,*** which presents itself as a set of fragmentary papers—Sibylline leaves—that trace the vanishing of an entire civilization in a prolonged universal cataclysm. Since the indifferent universe of time and history effectively ends in the skeptical intellectual framework of that novel, all that remains to lend meaning to mortal existence are human interaction and human language systems, both of which, being temporal, are themselves inevitably doomed to end. The alternative to this desolate picture lies in Shelley's frequently iterated commitment to "an ethic of cooperation, mutual dependence, and self-sacrifice" as the means for salvaging individual and collective dignity and meaning from the wreckage of temporal human existence. She argued in work after work that civilization can achieve its full promise only when "individuals willingly give up their egotistical desires and ambitions in order to serve the greater good of the community."[31] But this situation leaves the writer in a particularly precarious position, with her or his printed words dependent for value on a community of readers to whom the author is nevertheless a stranger, whose language and *identity* is subject to gross misconstruing over time. Mary Shelley's life of Alfieri offers insight into her view of authorship, which itself seems to echo both Wordsworth's and Percy Bysshe Shelley's views: "The author has something to say. . . . An Author . . . is a human being whose thoughts do not satisfy his mind . . . he requires sympathy, a world to listen, and the echoes of assent. [The author desires] to build up an enduring monument . . . [and] court the notoriety which usually attends those who let the public into the secret of their individual passions or peculiarities."[32] But this is risky business, surely, for even if the assenting voice is loud and unified, the author still exposes her or his own autonomous personhood ("individual passions or peculiarities") for public view and public reading—or misreading. As the daughter of Wollstonecraft and Godwin and wife of Percy Bysshe Shelley, she would have appreciated more than most that the "sympathy" of which she writes here could be a rare commodity indeed among the early-nineteenth-century English reading public.

At the same time, though, to write is not just to yield authority but also to *take* it, to exercise it. In the preface composed for the anonymous first edition of *Frankenstein,* Percy Bysshe Shelley claims that the author has gone beyond what Erasmus Darwin and other speculative physiologists have postulated about the nature of life and "the elementary principles of human nature." Indeed,

the author is presented as having surpassed not only these *scientists* but also other culturally ensconced male *literary* luminaries, including Homer, the Greek dramatists, Shakespeare, and Milton, as well as the two "friends" to whose conversations the story is said to owe. In her own 1831 introduction to *Frankenstein,* Shelley pointedly reminds us that her story originated with a set of conversations between Percy Bysshe Shelley and Byron to which she was essentially a silent auditor. Yet *hers* is the story that was completed *and* published *and* that became sufficiently popular to demand republication. Making her claim of authorship explicit, Mary Shelley in the process claims possession not only of the novel's language but also of the material—the apparently unremittingly *male* material—of its subject matter. Moreover, the new introduction constitutes a gesture of authority by which her own authorial voice supersedes the ventriloquistic voice of her dead husband in the preface. By 1831 she had, after all, survived both Shelley and Byron, and the popularity of her novel had far exceeded that of her husband's works and had rivaled and in some quarters even surpassed that of Byron's.

The Last Man extends some of the issues I have already raised in terms of *Frankenstein.* Is the author's role (whether the author be female or male) merely to record the real or invented acts of others? That is, after all, what Mary Shelley turned to in her later years when she wrote the lives of eminent *men.* The *historian* characteristically steps *out* of the history she or he writes, functioning as nameless, invisible recorder, although even in the best of cases an element of fiction enters—or is inserted—into the writing of history. This ostensibly detached role appears to have become increasingly attractive to Mary Shelley, who in 1834, while working on her contributions to the *Lives of the Most Eminent Literary and Scientific Men of Italy, Spain, and Portugal,* wrote at length about her imagination's fleeting visitations and suggested that, as Wordsworth wrote in the "Intimations" ode, the years that bring the philosophic mind provide recompense (though not necessarily so "abundant" as the poet regards it in "Tintern Abbey") for the imagination's fading: "I hope nothing & my imagination is dormant—She awakes by fits & starts; but often I am left *alone* (fatal word) even by her. My occupation at present somewhat supplies her place—& my life & reason have been saved by these "Lives"—Yes—let the lonely be occupied—it is the only cure."[33]

And yet is not this consuming indulgence in words both the goal and the supermarginalizing consequence of authorship generally—to be reduced to *words,* to be captured, "pictured," and read not as person but as textual construct, as a sort of shadow existence, a phantasm of the reader's own distorting imagination?

The author constantly runs the risk of being made into a fiction by the reader who formulates or extrapolates the author from the text. The woman author is "read" within a system of culturally encoded patriarchal authority over which she has virtually no control but within which she is expected to express herself. She is thus deprived at once of subjectivity, creativity, and autonomy. The assessment not just of Romantic women's writing but also of the cultural and intellectual position of the woman writer in general underscores the urgency of Annette Kolodny's observation that what unites and invigorates feminist criticism is neither dogma nor method but rather "an acute and impassioned *attentiveness* to the ways in which primarily male structures of power are inscribed (or encoded) within our literary inheritance."[34] Worst danger of all, one runs the risk of becoming an accomplice to the substitutional fictionalization of the "real" (the actual, autonomous, personal, and historical individual) self by the very act of writing. For the text that results from that act contains the self that the reader may reformulate and reconstruct in a living lie that reflects not the author but the *reader,* who has, in the act of reading her, appropriated her and torn her to pieces, much as Victor Frankenstein first assembles and then tears to pieces the Creature's mate.

Virginia Woolf suggested that George Eliot's decision to combine womanhood and writing was very costly indeed; as Mary Jacobus observes, it was a mortally significant decision that entailed "the sacrifice not only of happiness, but of life itself" (*Reading Woman,* 29). Women writers are particularly sensitive to the conflict between the "domesticity" that society expects of them and their own authorial aspirations for public fame, Marlon Ross writes, precisely because "the conflict is so palpable in their private lives and in their poetic careers" (*Contours,* 289). Mary Shelley understood the personal cost of authorship, writing of it to Trelawny that "I know too well that that excitement is the parent of pain rather than pleasure."[35] Writing, especially for publication, is an act of society, of civilization: a surrender of the autonomous self and identity to, and ostensibly on behalf of, the collective public. But as Rousseau had foreseen, the impulse toward formal civilization brings with it a radical reduction of one's options and, for the writer, "an enclosure within the prisonhouse of language" (Mellor, *Mary Shelley,* 50). One becomes what one writes, to paraphrase Blake, even as one writes what one is. In this endlessly revolving cycle one becomes imprisoned in temporality and topicality; one is reduced, finally, to a cipher, to a sheaf of papers, to reports of actions—or to reports of *ideas* that purport to be actions.

Like her contemporaries, Mary Shelley wrestled with the assault upon the personal ego inherent in the public response to one's formal writing. She wrote—after 1822 primarily because she *had* to, to support herself and her son—and only occasionally did she allow herself to stare back at the potential uselessness of it all: "What folly is it in me to write trash nobody will read— . . . I am—But all my many pages—future waste paper—surely I am a fool—."[36] At more optimistic and self-assured moments she could at least find consolation in the *activity* of writing, even if it was merely a matter of filling the hours.

That Walton finally redirects his ship toward the south (and symbolically toward warmth and society) at the conclusion of *Frankenstein* might indicate that he has learned from his experience, were it not that Walton does not choose freely in the matter but rather accedes in the face of a mutiny. I suggest that the practical struggle to be true to oneself and to one's ideals and aspirations—for the woman writer as for the man Arctic explorer—inevitably involves compromise and with it the reduction and subjection of one's essential self to a report embedded in words. Literature traditionally introduces us not to authors but to their words, the words by which they represent impressions of their ideas and of the "selves" in which they live their days. Living with the diminished self whose record is the journal of papers that makes up the novel will haunt Walton, even as the Creature haunts the obsessive-compulsive Victor Frankenstein (who is no victor at all but the ultimate cosmic loser). But so too must the writer—woman or man—inevitably be haunted by the specter of herself or himself reduced to a cipher, to a construct of words, the work itself becoming a "hideous progeny" that dissolves the author as self, as living, acting entity. Whatever the inherent formal value of the literary product, it nevertheless both mutilates and misrepresents its author. In this sense, among others, it seems to me entirely valid to read in *Frankenstein,* as in much of Romantic women's writing, the enigmatic warning that creativity may be hazardous to one's health—indeed to one's entire existence.

Notes

1. See Mary Jacobus, *Reading Woman: Essays in Feminist Criticism* (New York: Columbia University Press, 1986), 28.

2. Ellen Moers, *Literary Women: The Great Writers* (1963; reprint, New York: Oxford University Press, 1985), 126.

3. 5 January 1828, *The Letters of Mary Wollstonecraft Shelley*, ed. Betty T. Bennett, 3 vols. (Baltimore and London: Johns Hopkins University Press, 1983), 2:22.

4. Barbara Johnson, "My Monster/My Self," *Diacritics* 12 (1982): 2-10; Anne K. Mellor, *Mary Shelley: Her Life, Her Fiction, Her Monsters* (New York and London: Methuen, 1988).

5. Moers, *Literary Women*, 163; Virginia Woolf, "Dorothy Osborne's 'Letters,'" in *The Second Common Reader*, ed. Andrew McNeillie (San Diego, Calif.: Harcourt Brace Jovanovich, 1986), 59-70.

6. Deborah Cameron, *Feminism and Linguistic Theory* (New York: St. Martin's, 1985), 161. Mellor writes that "that unique phenomenon envisioned by Mary Wollstonecraft, the wife as the lifelong intellectual equal and companion of her husband, does not exist in the world of nineteenth-century Europe experienced by Mary Shelley" ("Possessing Nature: The Female in *Frankenstein*," in *Romanticism and Feminism*, ed. Anne K. Mellor [Bloomington: Indiana University Press, 1988], 223).

7. Shelley to Frances Wright [Darusmont], 12 September 1827, and to Maria Gisborne, 11 June 1835, *Letters* 2:4, 246.

8. *The Letters of William and Dorothy Wordsworth*, ed. Ernest de Selincourt et al., 2nd ed., 6 vols. (Oxford: Clarendon Press, 1967-93), vol. 1, no. 239.

9. John Stuart Mill, *The Subjection of Women*, ed. Sue Mansfield (Arlington Heights, Ill.: AHM Publishing, 1980), 15. Mill's essay was written in 1861 and published in 1869.

10. See Mary Poovey, *The Proper Lady and the Woman Writer: Ideology as Style in the Works of Mary Wollstonecraft, Mary Shelley, and Jane Austen* (Chicago: University of Chicago Press, 1984); and Mellor, *Mary Shelley*, 56.

11. Percy Bysshe Shelley's review may have been intended for Leigh Hunt's *Examiner*. It did not appear until Thomas Medwin published it in *The Atheneum* in 1832.

12. See Mellor, *Mary Shelley*, 22-23, and Emily W. Sunstein, *Mary Shelley: Romance and Reality* (Boston, Toronto and London: Little, Brown, 1989), 85-86.

13. Stuart Curran, Gaye Tuchman, and Marlon Ross have most notably reminded us of women's significant presence in the literary milieu. See Stuart Curran, *Poetic Form and British Romanticism* (New York: Oxford University Press, 1986); Gaye Tuchman, with Nina E. Fortin, *Edging Women Out: Victorian Novelists, Publishers, and Social Change* (New Haven, Conn.: Yale University Press, 1989); Marlon Ross, *The Contours of Masculine Desire: Romanticism and the Rise of Women's Poetry* (New York: Oxford University Press, 1989). See too Cheryl Turner, *Living by the Pen: Women Writers in the Eighteenth Century* (London: Routledge, 1992).

14. Quoted in Rupert Christiansen, *Romantic Affinities: Portraits from an Age, 1780-1830* (London: Cardinal, 1988), 102.

15. This volume, which is readily available in a facsimile edited by Marilyn Williamson (Detroit: Wayne State University Press, 1981), typifies the woman writer's treatment by the (male) Victorian anthologizer. Parenthetical page citations in this portion of my discussion refer to this facsimile.

16. Mrs. Henry [Mary] Tighe, *Psyche, with Other Poems*, 5th ed. (London: Longman, 1816), iii-iv.

17. Margaret Visser, *The Rituals of Dinner: The Origins, Evolution, Eccentricities, and Meaning of Table Manners* (New York: Grove Weidenfeld, 1991), 273.

18. Shelley to John Murray III, 8 September 1830, *Letters*, 2:115.

19. *Women Romantic Poets, 1785-1832: An Anthology*, ed. Jennifer Breen (London: J. M. Dent, 1992), xix.

20. This is, in fact, the picture often painted of Mary Shelley: "Mary was never a woman of action. Her pursuits were intellectual, her pleasure domestic" (Jane Dunn, *Moon in Eclipse: A Life of Mary Shelley* [London: Weidenfeld and Nicolson, 1978], 278).

21. Stuart Curran, "Romantic Poetry: The 'I' Altered," in *Romanticism and Feminism*, ed. Anne K. Mellor (Bloomington: Indiana University Press, 1988), 189.

22. As Betty T. Bennett's three volumes of Shelley's letters amply demonstrate, she was an avid letter writer, and the style of those letters is richly interactive, inviting a variety of kinds of response from her correspondents. Even in letters from the years immediately following Percy Bysshe Shelley's death, letters in which postured self-pity mingles with spontaneous expressions of genuine misery, the correspondent is never shut off from *communication* or from what Shelley clearly structures as an ongoing dialogue.

23. [Mary Tighe], *Psyche, or the Legend of Love* (London, privately printed, 1805), ii.

24. "Preface," in *The Poetical Works of the Late Mrs. Mary Robinson*, 3 vols. (London: Jones and Company, 1824), 1:4.

25. Susan J. Wolfson, "Individual in Community: Dorothy Wordsworth in Conversation with William," in Mellor, *Romanticism and Feminism*, 162.

26. The painful ambivalences about ambition, ability, and gender-related expectations that surface so frequently in what Dorothy Wordsworth's writings tell us about herself, her situation, and the life she led have at last been addressed in a number of sympathetic revisionist studies. See esp. Wolfson, "Individual in Community," Margaret Homans, *Women Writers and Poetic Identity: Dorothy Wordsworth, Emily Bronte, and Emily Dickinson* (Princeton, N.J.: Princeton University Press, 1980); and Susan M. Levin, *Dorothy Wordsworth and Romanticism* (New Brunswick, N.J.: Rutgers University Press, 1987).

27. Shelley to Edward J. Trelawny, 1 April 1829, *Letters*, 2:72.

28. Shelley to John Murray III, 10 February 1835, *Letters*, 2:223.

29. Sandra M. Gilbert and Susan Gubar, *The Madwoman in the Attic: The Woman Writer and the Nineteenth-Century Literary Imagination* (New Haven, Conn., and London: Yale University Press, 1979), 49-50.

30. Sonia Hofkosh, "The Writer's Ravishment: Women and the Romantic Author—the Example of Byron," in Mellor, *Romanticism and Feminism* 94.

31. Mellor, "Possessing Nature," 129, and *Mary Shelley,* 169, 215.

32. Mary Shelley [with James Montgomery], *Lives of the Most Eminent Literary and Scientific Men of Italy, Spain, and Portugal,* 3 vols. (London: Longman, 1835), 2:351.

33. Shelley, December 1834, *The Journals of Mary Shelley: 1814-1844,* ed. Paula R. Feldman and Diana Scott-Kilvert, 2 vols. (Oxford: Clarendon Press, 1987), 2:543.

34. Annette Kolodny, "Dancing through the Minefield: Some Observations on the Theory, Practice, and Politics of a Feminist Literary Criticism," in *The New Feminist Criticism: Essays on Women, Literature, and Theory,* ed. Elaine Showalter (New York: Pantheon Books, 1985), 162.

35. Shelley to E. J. Trelawny, 27 July 1829, *Letters,* 2:82.

36. Shelley, 30 January 1825, *Journals,* 2:489.

FURTHER READING

Bibliography

Lyles, W. H. *Mary Shelley: An Annotated Bibliography.* New York: Garland Publishing, Inc., 1975.

Lists sources by and about Shelley through 1975.

Biographies

Mellor, Anne K. *Mary Shelley: Her Life, Her Fiction, Her Monsters.* New York: Routledge, 1989, 350 p.

Draws on unpublished material and Shelley's fiction to present an analysis of Shelley's life.

Seymour, Miranda. *Mary Shelley.* New York: Grove Press, 2000, 672 p.

Utilizes feminist scholarship to present a balanced picture of Shelley's life.

Williams, John. *Mary Shelley: A Literary Life.* London: Palgrave, 2000, 222 p.

Provides an overview of Shelley's life.

Criticism

Batchelor, Rhonda. "The Rise and Fall of the Eighteenth Century's Authentic Feminine Voice." *Eighteenth-Century Fiction* 6, no. 4 (July 1994): 347-68.

Suggests that Frankenstein *offers formal and thematic echoes of earlier, revolutionary feminist thought.*

Bunnell, Charlene E. "*Mathilda*: Mary Shelley's Romantic Tragedy." *Keats-Shelley Journal* 66 (1997): 75-96.

Analyzes the theatrical aspects of Mathilda.

Conger, Syndy McMillen. "Mary Shelley's Women in Prison." In *Iconoclastic Departures: Mary Shelley After Frankenstein; Essays in Honor of the Bicentenary of Mary Shelley's Birth,* edited by Syndy M. Conger, Frederick S. Frank, and Gregory O'Dea, pp. 81-97. Madison, N.J.: Farleigh Dickinson University Press, 1997.

Explores Shelley's treatment of the metaphoric imprisonment of women, a topic taken up by her mother in her writings, and claims that Shelley thus endorses her mother's profeminist views.

Davis, William. "*Mathilda* and the Ruin of Masculinity." *European Romantic Review* 13, no. 2 (2002): 175-81.

Argues that Mathilda *presents a vision of male subjectivity that Shelley both adored and detested.*

Favret, Mary A. "A Woman Writes the Fiction of Science: The Body in *Frankenstein.*" *Genders* 14 (fall 1992): 50-65.

Discusses Shelley's role in the reproduction of scientific and cultural ideas about human nature.

Gilbert, Sandra M., and Susan Gubar. "Horror's Twin: Mary Shelley's Monstrous Eye." In *The Madwoman in the Attic: The Woman Writer and the Nineteenth-Century Literary Imagination,* pp. 213-47. New Haven: Yale University Press, 1979.

Stresses the literary and sexual themes of Frankenstein, *claiming it is a version of the misogynist story found in Milton's* Paradise Lost.

Harpold, Terrence. "'Did You Get *Mathilda* from Papa?': Seduction Fantasy and the Circulation of Mary Shelley's *Mathilda.*" *Studies in Romanticism* 28 (spring 1989): 49-67.

Offers a psychobiographical interpretation of the novel Mathilda.

Hatlen, Burton. "Milton, Mary Shelley, and Patriarchy." In *Rhetoric, Literature, and Interpretation,* edited by Harry R. Garvin, pp. 19-47. Lewisburg, Pa.: Bucknell University Press, 1986.

Contends that Shelley wrote from a radical political position, imbuing her writings with egalitarian and libertarian motifs.

Hoeveler, Diane Long. "Mary Shelley's and Gothic Feminism: The Case of 'The Mortal Immortal.'" In *Iconoclastic Departures: Mary Shelley After Frankenstein; Essays in Honor of the Bicentenary of Mary Shelley's Birth,* edited by Syndy M. Conger, Frederick S. Frank, and Gregory O'Dea, pp. 150-63. Madison, N.J.: Farleigh Dickinson University Press, 1997.

Argues that the short story "The Mortal Immortal" suggests that just as there may be a way to make mortals immortal, there may be a way to equalize men and women.

Joseph, Gerhard. "Virginal Sex, Vaginal Text: The 'Folds' of *Frankenstein.*" In *Virginal Sexuality and Textuality in Victorian Literature,* edited by Lloyd Davis, pp. 25-32. Albany: State University of New York Press, 1993.

Focuses on dreams and sexuality to understand Frankenstein.

Liggins, Emma. "The Medical Gaze and the Female Corpse: Looking at Bodies in Mary Shelley's *Frankenstein.*" *Studies in the Novel* 32, no. 2 (summer 2002): 129-46.

Argues that Frankenstein *draws on contemporary debates about surgery and medical practice, comments on the medical control and violation of women, and explores ideas about sexual desire.*

Lokke, Kari. "'Children of Liberty': Idealist Historiography in Staël, Shelley, and Sand." *PMLA* 118, no. 3 (May 2003): 502-20.

Examines how Shelley responded to and refashioned ideas presented by male idealist philosophers.

London, Bette. "Mary Shelley, *Frankenstein,* and the Spectacle of Masculinity." *PMLA* 108, no. 3 (March 1993): 253-67.

Examines the presence of the male body in Frankenstein, contending that it serves as the site of an ineradicable masculinity.

Moers, Ellen. "Female Gothic: The Monster's Mother." *New York Review of Books* 21 (March 1974): 24-8.

Notes that Shelley's most famous novel became the model for the "female" Gothic, a dominant strain in Gothic fiction.

Poovey, Mary. "My Hideous Progeny: Mary Shelley and the Feminization of Romanticism." *PMLA* 95, no. 3 (May 1980): 332-47.

Explores the pressures faced by Shelley who was expected to be both an original writer and a conventional feminine model of propriety.

———. "'My Hideous Progeny': The Lady and the Monster." In *The Proper Lady and the Woman Writer: Ideology as Style in the Works of Mary Wollstonecraft, Mary Shelley, and Jane Austen*, pp. 114-42. Chicago: University of Chicago Press, 1984.

Depicts Shelley as torn between the desire for self-expression and the desire to conform.

Purinton, Marjean D. "Polysexualities and Romantic Generations in Mary Shelley's Mythological Dramas *Midas* and *Prosperine*." *Women's Writing* 6, no. 3 (1999): 385-411.

Examines how Shelley's dramas undermine conventional constructions of male and female genders and how her reconstructions of the mother/daughter relationship open up possibilities of multiple sexualities.

Randel, Fred V. "*Frankenstein*, Feminism, and the Intertextuality of Mountains." *Studies in Romanticism* 23, no. 4 (winter 1984): 515-32.

Discusses Frankenstein's feminism, romanticism, and greatness as a work of art.

Rubenstein, Marc A. "'My Accursed Origin': The Search for the Mother in *Frankenstein*." *Studies in Romanticism* 15, no. 2 (spring 1976): 165-94.

Analyzes Frankenstein as a struggle focusing on the role of motherhood.

Sussman, Charlotte. "'Islanded in the World': Cultural Memory and Human Mobility in *The Last Man*." *PMLA* 118, no. 2 (March 2003): 286-301.

Discusses The Last Man in the context of contemporary sociopolitical debates, especially those about emigration.

OTHER SOURCES FROM GALE:

Additional coverage of Shelley's life and career is contained in the following sources published by the Gale Group: *Authors and Artists for Young Adults*, Vol. 20; *Beacham's Encyclopedia of Popular Fiction: Biography and Resources*, Vol. 3; *Beacham's Guide to Literature for Young Adults*, Vol. 5; *British Writers*, Vol. 3; *British Writers: The Classics*, Vol. 2; *British Writers Supplement*, Vol. 3; *Concise Dictionary of British Literary Biography, 1789-1832*; *Dictionary of Literary Biography*; Vols. 110, 116, 159, 178; *DISCovering Authors*; *DISCovering Authors: British Edition* and *Canadian Edition*; *DISCovering Authors Modules: Most-studied* and *Novelists*; *DISCovering Authors 3.0*; *Exploring Novels*; *Literary Movements for Students*, Vols. 1, 2; *Literature and Its Times*, Vol. 1; *Literature Resource Center*; *Nineteenth-Century Literature Criticism*, Vols. 14, 59, 103; *Novels for Students*, Vol. 1; *Reference Guide to English Literature*, Ed. 2; *Science Fiction Writers*; *Something About the Author*, Vol. 29; *St. James Guide to Horror, Ghost, & Gothic Writers*; *St. James Guide to Science Fiction Writers*, Ed. 4; *Twayne's English Authors*; *World Literature and Its Times*, Ed. 3; and *World Literature Criticism*.

GERMAINE DE STAËL

(1766 - 1817)

(Born Anne Louis Germaine Necker; later Baronne de Staël-Holstein; also known as Madame de Staël) French critic, novelist, historian, and playwright.

Although for many years her reputation rested largely on her critical works, de Staël has, since the 1970s, been viewed by feminist scholars as an important novelist. As a critic, de Staël is credited with inculcating the theories of Romanticism into French literary and political thought. Her belief that critical judgment is relative and based on a sense of history sharply altered the French literary attitudes of her time. In her *De la littérature considérée dans ses rapports avec les institutions sociales* (1800; *A Treatise on Ancient and Modern Literature*), she delineated the distinction between the classical literature of southern Europe and northern Europe's Romantic literature. Feminist scholars have focused on de Staël's depiction of the oppressive effects of patriarchal hegemony. De Staël's novels *Corinne; ou, L'Italie* (1807; *Corinne; or, Italy*) and *Delphine* (1802) in particular have been praised by feminist scholars as perceptive explorations of female subjugation.

BIOGRAPHICAL INFORMATION

De Staël, born Anne Louise Germaine Necker in Paris on April 22, 1766, was the daughter of the French politician Jacques Necker, Louis XVI's minister of finance. Her literary interests were encouraged by her parents, and as a girl she was exposed to the intellectual salon that her mother hosted in her house, which included such notables as Edward Gibbon, Denis Diderot, and Friedrich Grimm. In 1786 de Staël married Baron de Staël-Holstein, the Swedish ambassador to Paris. Although initially sympathetic to the cause of the French Revolution, she turned away from its ideals. During the Revolution, her husband's political immunity enabled de Staël to remain in France and arrange the escape of numerous refugees. Ultimately, however, she was forced to flee to Switzerland in 1792. When she returned to France in 1797, she established her own salon as a center of progressive political and intellectual discussions. She separated amicably from her husband and became intimately associated with the French painter and author Benjamin Constant, and for the rest of her life she enjoyed a series of unconventional romantic attachments. In 1803 the publication of de Staël's *Delphine* angered Napoleon Bonaparte and resulted in her exile from Paris. She retired to her estate at Coppet on the Lake of Geneva, where she once again attracted a circle of well-known intellectuals. She fled France again in 1810 after Napoleon took issue with her historical-critical work *De l'Allemagne* (*Germany*; 1810) and criticized it as "un-French." She returned to Paris in 1813 and attempted to establish another literary salon, but she died within a few years.

MAJOR WORKS

De Staël became known as a theorist with the publication of *Letters sur les ouvrages et le caractère de J. J. Rousseau* (1788; *Letters on the Works and Character of J. J. Rousseau*). Published just before the outbreak of the French Revolution, the book advocated liberal thinking and the ideas of the Enlightenment as antidotes to the then current political crisis. Upon her return to Paris, de Staël began what many critics consider to be the most brilliant segment of her career. She published several important political and literary essays, notably *De l'influence des passions* (1796; *A Treatise on the Influence of the Passions upon the Happiness of Individuals and Nations*), a document of European Romanticism. By 1800, her political and literary concepts had become more defined, as evidenced in *A Treatise on Ancient and Modern Literature*. The book holds that a literary work must reflect the moral and historical reality, or *Zeitgeist,* of the country in which it is created. De Staël's other famous work of historical criticism, *Germany,* a study of the Sturm und Drang movement (a movement that dealt with the individual's revolt against society), introduced German Romanticism in France and inspired new modes of thought and expression. De Staël idealized Germany and saw its culture as a model for French intellectual development, a position that Napoleon found subversive and intolerable, and he ordered the work's proof sheets to be destroyed before exiling the author.

The novels *Delphine* and *Corinne* have been viewed by some critics as limited illustrations of de Staël's literary concepts. *Corinne* centers on a love affair between the Englishman Oswald, Lord Nelvil, and a beautiful Italian poetess, a woman of genius. It is also an homage to the landscape, literature and art of Italy. In the epistolary novel *Delphine,* a woman fights the social codes of France—in particular, codes regarding divorce and social disdain for older, unmarried women—in an attempt to gain individual freedom.

CRITICAL RECEPTION

Contemporary critics of de Staël praised her as a powerful literary figure and a champion of liberal ideas. Her unconventional life and views about women garnered negative attention from conservative critics, but many acknowledged the importance of her literary theories and her role in awakening her native France to an interest in foreign literature. For more than a century de Staël's reputation rested solely on her critical and historical work, but feminist critics have revisited her novels as important works for their portrayal of female characters and their use of a distinctly female narrative voice. Scholars note in her novels depictions of the fallen woman, and an overarching view of the challenges that talented, intellectual women faced. Her anonymously published 1793 essay on the trial of Marie Antoinette, *Réflexions sur le procés de la Reine, par une Femme* (*Reflections on the Trial of a Queen, by a Woman*), has also been of interest to feminist scholars because of its political attitudes and representation of the female self.

PRINCIPAL WORKS

Lettres sur les ouvrages et le caractère de J. J. Rousseau [*Letters on the Works and Character of J. J. Rousseau*] (essays) 1788

Jane Grey, tragédie en cinq actes et en vers (verse drama) 1790

Réflexions sur le procés de la Reine, par une Femme [*Reflections on the Trial of a Queen, by a Woman*] (essay) 1793

De l'influence des passions [*A Treatise on the Influence of the Passions upon the Happiness of Individuals and Nations*] (essays) 1796

De la littérature considérée dans ses rapports avec les institutions sociales [*A Treatise on Ancient and Modern Literature*] (criticism) 1800; also published as *The Influence of Literature upon Society* 1813

Delphine (novel) 1802

Corinne; ou, L'Italie [*Corinne; or, Italy*] (novel) 1807

De l'Allemagne 3 vols. [*Germany*] (history and criticism) 1810

Considérations sur les principaux événemens de la Révolution française, [*Considerations on the Principal Events of the French Revolution*] (criticism) 1818

Dix Années d'Exil [*Ten Years' Exile*] (memoirs) 1818

GERMAINE DE STAËL (ESSAY DATE 1810)

SOURCE: de Staël, Germaine. "Of the Women." In *Germany*, pp. 43-45. New York: Houghton Mifflin and Company, 1859.

In the following excerpt from her nonfiction work Germany, originally published in 1810, de Staël offers an analysis of the character of the German woman, who she says is distinguished by her perfect loyalty.

Nature and society give to women a habit of endurance; and I think it can hardly be denied that, in our days, they are generally worthier of moral esteem than the men. At an epoch when selfishness is the prevailing evil, the men, to whom all positive interests are related, must necessarily have less generosity, less sensibility, than the women. These last are attached to life only by the ties of the heart; and even when they lose themselves, it is by sentiment that they are led away: their selfishness is extended to a double object, while that of man has himself only for its end. Homage is rendered to them according to the affections which they inspire; but those which they bestow are almost always sacrifices. The most beautiful of virtues, self-devotion, is their enjoyment and their destiny; no happiness can exist for them but by the reflection of another's glory and prosperity; in short, to live independently of self, whether by ideas or by sentiments, or, above all, by virtues, gives to the soul an habitual feeling of elevation.

In those countries where men are called upon by political institutions to the exercise of all the military and civil virtues which are inspired by patriotism, they recover the superiority which belongs to them; they reassume with dignity their rights, as masters of the world; but when they are condemned, in whatever measure, to idleness or to slavery, they fall so much the lower as they ought to rise more high. The destiny of women always remains the same; it is their soul alone which creates it; political circumstances have no influence upon it. When men are ignorant or unable to employ their lives worthily and nobly, Nature revenges herself upon them for the very gifts which they have received from her; the activity of the body contributes only to the sloth of the mind; the strength of soul degenerates into coarseness; the day is consumed in vulgar sports and exercises, horses, the chase, or entertainments which might be suitable enough in the way of relaxation, but brutalize as occupations. Women, the while, cultivate their understanding; and

sentiment and reflection preserve in their souls the image of all that is noble and beautiful.

The German women have a charm exclusively their own—a touching voice, fair hair, a dazzling complexion; they are modest, but less timid than Englishwomen; one sees that they have been less accustomed to meet with their superiors among men, and that they have besides less to apprehend from the severe censures of the public. They endeavor to please by their sensibility, to interest by their imagination; the language of poetry and the fine arts are familiar to them; they coquet with enthusiasm, as they do in France with wit and pleasantry. That perfect loyalty, which distinguishes the German character, renders love less dangerous for the happiness of women; and, perhaps, they admit the advances of this sentiment with the more confidence, because it is invested with romantic colors, and disdain and infidelity are less to be dreaded there than elsewhere.

Love is a religion in Germany, but a poetical religion, which tolerates too easily all that sensibility can excuse. It cannot be denied, that the facility of divorce in the Protestant States is prejudicial to the sacredness of marriage. They change husbands with as little difficulty as if they were arranging the incidents of a drama; the good-nature common both to men and women is the reason that so little bitterness of spirit ever accompanies these easy ruptures; and, as the Germans are endowed with more imagination than real passion, the most extravagant events take place with singular tranquillity; nevertheless, it is thus that manners and character lose every thing like consistency; the spirit of paradox shakes the most sacred institutions, and there are no fixed rules upon any subject.

One may fairly laugh at the ridiculous airs of some German women, who are continually exalting themselves even to a pitch of affectation, and who sacrifice to their pretty softnesses of expression, all that is marked and striking in mind and character; they are not open, even though they are not false; they only see and judge of nothing correctly, and real events pass like a phantasmagoria before their eyes. Even when they take it into their heads to be light and capricious, they still retain a tincture of that *sentimentality* which is held in so high honor in their country. A German woman said one day, with a melancholy expression, "I know not wherefore, but those who are absent pass away from my soul." A French woman would have rendered this idea with more gayety, but it would have been fundamentally the same.

Notwithstanding these affectations, which form only the exception, there are among the women of Germany numbers whose sentiments are true and manners simple. Their careful education, and the purity of soul which is natural to them, render the dominion which they exercise gentle and abiding; they inspire you from day to day with a stronger interest for all that is great and generous, with more of confidence in all noble hopes, and they know how to repel that desolating irony which breathes a death-chill over all the enjoyments of the heart. Nevertheless, we seldom find among them that quickness of apprehension, which animates conversation, and sets every idea in motion; this sort of pleasure is scarcely to be met with anywhere out of the most lively and the most witty societies of Paris. The chosen company of a French metropolis can alone confer this rare delight; elsewhere, we generally find only eloquence in public, or tranquil pleasure in familiar life. Conversation, as a talent, exists in France alone; in all other countries it answers the purposes of politeness, of argument, or of friendly intercourse. In France, it is an art to which the imagination and the soul are no doubt very necessary, but which possesses, besides these, certain secrets, where, by the absence of both may be supplied.

GENERAL COMMENTARY

ELLEN MOERS (ESSAY DATE SPRING 1975)

SOURCE: Moers, Ellen. "Mme de Staël and the Woman of Genius." *The American Scholar* 44, no. 2 (spring 1975): 225-41.

In the following essay, Moers maintains that Corinne *is as much a guidebook to Italy as it is a guide to the woman of genius.*

I am not used to Hope—
It might intrude upon—
Its sweet parade—blaspheme the place—
Ordained to Suffering—

It might be easier
To fail—with Land in Sight—
Than gain—My Blue Peninsula—
To perish—of Delight—

—EMILY DICKINSON

Of all the books that have had a special meaning for gifted women, Mme de Staël's *Corinne ou l'Italie* is the most important. There is ample testimony from George Eliot, Margaret Fuller, Elizabeth Barrett Browning, Harriet Beecher Stowe, George Sand, Kate Chopin, and many others to the place Mme de Staël's myth of the woman of genius held in their own adolescent unfolding. I cannot imagine a revival of the myth of Corinne in modern times, any more than I can imagine a revival of Manfred or Childe Harold. But that Mme de Staël did for women what Byron did for men—dramatized the romantic ego in all its extravagance, pain, and glory—was quite clear to her nineteenth-century readers, including Byron. Thanks to Lady Blessington, we have a hilarious record of the debate between Mme de Staël and Byron over which of them had done more harm to their generation with their heroic creations.

Published in 1807, *Corinne* of course preceded the Byronic myth and in at least one way affected it. The farewell to Rome that Mme de Staël's heroine pays in reckless and dramatic fashion by visiting the Colosseum by moonlight became a *locus romanticus* for Byron, then for Lamartine, then for Italian tourists in general. Appropriately enough, the most famous literary reworking of the scene dramatizes the independence of the American girl on tour in Italy. "Well, I *have* seen the Coliseum by moonlight!" cries Daisy Miller. "That's one good thing."

Corinne is not, properly speaking, a feminist work. Like most people of genius, Mme de Staël was concerned more with demonstrating the pride and penalty of the elite, the special case, than with widening the options or diminishing the inhibitions that affect the average woman. Her Corinne is superspecial: the super-heroine of genius who writes poetry, improvises, sings, paints, lectures, dances, acts, has a wider range of talents and a wider audience for their display than any woman before or after her. The public component of her genius, what Mme de Staël called *la gloire*, is the nub of the myth of Corinne; for the achievement of wide public fame, which in a man's story (at least in fiction) is normally rewarded by private happiness in the form of a woman's adoration, in a woman's story makes equivalent happiness difficult or impossible. *Corinne* is a very old-fashioned, in some ways a very silly novel; but from what I see around me, and from what I read, modern times have still not resolved the woman's dilemma of reconciling enormous public success with private romance.

Corinne first appears to the reader at her moment of greatest public triumph. Through the ringing of bells and the cannonades, through processions and ceremonies, through the odes of poets and the shouts of the populace, she is carried in a chariot drawn by four white horses to the Capitoline Hill, there to be crowned with the laurel wreath of genius. This fantasy of a woman's glory, which no writer has ever surpassed in extravagance, is filtered to the reader through the eyes of a British tourist, Oswald Lord Nelvil, who is surprised, shocked, fascinated, then transfixed by love for the woman of genius. He proves to be a serious, earnest, and adoring lover; but finally, out of the highest motives, and to no one's surprise, he leaves her for another.

All the critical discussion I have seen about Corinne's love story centers on its sources in the life of Mme de Staël (a biographical approach particularly common when the writer is a woman). Certainly Mme de Staël did tour Italy—she was then a widow with two children—shortly before she wrote **Corinne,** and she did, while traveling, suffer the joys and sorrows of an *affaire du cœur*—but which affair? Various biographers, for a hundred years or more, have been certain that Oswald is a portrait of a Portuguese nobleman, or a Swiss diplomat, or an Irish soldier of fortune. I myself can find no compelling biographical reason not to identify Mme de Staël's Lord Nelvil—who is little more than a pattern of an English nobleman constructed to make an ideal husband (for someone other than Corinne)—with the great original pattern of such a figure, Samuel Richardson's Sir Charles Grandison, who was much in Mme de Staël's mind. I rather suspect that she intended to retell Richardson's story: that of an Englishman who loves an Italian woman, but finally exchanges her—out of the noblest motives—for an English bride. But Mme de Staël retold the story from the Italian woman's point of view—and made the woman a Corinne.

One of the oddest things about **Corinne** is that it is as much a guidebook to Italy as it is a guide to the woman of genius. Mme de Staël called the novel **Corinne; or, Italy** to signify its double usefulness, and there is a puzzle about her priorities. Did she plot the movement of her love story across the map of Italy in such a way as to cover the principal monuments—the catacombs, St. Peter's, Pompeii, Vesuvius, the Bay of Naples, the canals of Venice? Or did her idea of Italian culture evoke the spirit, and shape the destiny, of her mythic heroine?

And why Italy? Mme de Staël was Geneva-born and utterly French. She had written extensively about England and France in **De la Littérature** (1800), the work for which she was known around the world. She had traveled to Germany in 1803, and was already at work on **De l'Allemagne.** She interrupted her ambitious, epoch-making study of German culture to tour Italy in the winter of 1804-1805 with the definite intention of finding the materials for a novel. Why Italy? may seem a foolish question, for what northern European needs an excuse to go south in search of sun—to know the land of *Mignonslied* where lemons grow? But this question, like so many others, poses itself differently for a literary woman (like Mme de Staël) than for a literary man (like J. W. von Goethe). If **Corinne** did at least as much as *Wilhelm Meister* to arouse the passion for Italy among the English Romantics, and if **Corinne** played as large a role in the making of Victorian Italophilia as would appear from the writings of Elizabeth Barrett Browning and Margaret Fuller, who were deeply affected by Mme de Staël's ideas about Italy as *the* place for the woman of genius, then Richardson's share in the making of those ideas would indeed be remarkable.

Richardson never set foot in Italy. The "data" on which he drew for the sizable Italian sections of *Sir Charles Grandison* consisted of the fact that it was a Catholic country, that Ariosto's marvels took place there, and that people there were somehow different from the norm. He divided his huge cast of characters into "Men—Women—and Italians." Grandison's Clementina, met on his Grand Tour, is a romance heroine of the highest social and moral class; she seems Italian only in that she grows a bit more hysterical, has a few more mad scenes, and altogether suffers more dramatically from the griefs of love than would her English equivalent. Clementina is no Corinne, except in her passionate attachment to her Italian homeland and her Catholic faith, which are the grounds for her rejection of Grandison's proposal of marriage. Neither, though, is a barrier to Grandison, who proposes that she spend half her years in Italy, half in England, and that their male issue be raised as Protestant Englishmen, while their girls may be Catholics. Nothing could be fairer—and it appears that Richardson was animated primarily by a spirit of toleration (a religious toleration unusual for his age) when he introduced the Italian matter into the novel. Richardson keeps *Sir Charles Grandison* going through thousands of pages of epistolary sensibility by fanning Grandison's scruples, and by sending him on journeys to Italy to try to change Clementina's mind and allay any suspicion among his English friends that he has merely trifled with a lady of foreign fascination encountered on his travels.

That such suspicions were both natural and commonplace Corinne herself points out. "Listen to me," she says to Lord Nelvil on the eve of his departure from Italy:

> When you get to London they will tell you, the men about town, that promises of love do not engage a man's honor; that all the Englishmen who have ever lived have fallen in love with Italian women met on their travels and forgotten upon their return; that a few months of happiness tie down neither the woman who bestows, nor the man who enjoys it; and that, at your age, the whole future course of your life cannot be determined by whatever delight you have found, for a brief period, in the society of a foreign woman. And they will appear to be right, right as the world sees it; but you, you who have known this heart, known how it loves you, will you find the sophisms to excuse, . . .

Oswald protests his troth in all sincerity, for he is not a mere man of the world—an *homme léger*—but a Grandison; that is why Corinne loves him in preference to all the brilliant Italian and witty French noblemen who surround and court her. It is, however, Oswald's British morality that parts him from Corinne, with a cultural irrevocability that makes their final separation an affair of state.

The story of Oswald's past—which he divulges to Corinne halfway up the slope of Mount Vesuvius, where "all that has life disappears, you enter the empire of death, and only ashes shift beneath uncertain feet"—centers on his worship of his dead father, repository of the wisdom of his native land and faith. Detained in revolutionary France during his father's last illness by an entanglement with a scheming Frenchwoman, Oswald had hastened his father's death through grief over his son's unwise love and apparent disloyalty to his native land—France and England then being enemies. Now a guilty and melancholy man, Oswald is resolved to fulfill every wish of the dead man, especially in regard to his own marriage; and he knows that his father wished him to marry Lucile Edgermond, the young daughter of an old family friend, and did not want him to marry Corinne. The reasons for this preference are far more interesting to Mme de Staël (and to us) than are the tricks of plot whereby Corinne is enmeshed in Nelvil-Edgermond family affairs, without ever having met Oswald until the day she is crowned on the Capitoline as the most celebrated of Italian women. It seems that Corinne is only half-Italian; that her father was the same Lord Edgermond, by his first (Italian) wife; that she is a half-sister of Lucile and a rejected first choice by Oswald's father for his son's bride.

"Will you forgive me, my friend," the senior Lord Nelvil had written to Lord Edgermond (in a letter that Oswald travels home from Italy to read)

> if I propose a change in our plan for a union between our two families? My son is eighteen months younger than your older daughter; it would be better to make his destined bride Lucile, your second daughter, who is twelve years younger than her sister. But since I knew the age of Miss Edgermond when I asked her hand for Oswald, I owe to our friendship a frank statement of my reasons for wishing that their marriage not take place. . . .

> Your daughter is charming, but I seem to perceive in her one of those beautiful Greek women who enchanted and subjugated the world. Don't be offended—of course your daughter has been brought up to possess only the purest of feelings and principles; but she needs to please, to captivate, to impress.

> She has more talent than she has self-love; but talents of so rare a kind necessarily inspire the desire to develop them; and I do not know what stage can contain that activity of mind, that impetuous imagination, that ardent character which one senses in every word she speaks. She would of course take my son away from England, for such a woman cannot be happy here. Only Italy would suit her.

Why Italy? Because Italy is a country (I am now following the cultural analysis Mme de Staël spreads through the novel) where one lives openly, in the open air and the sun, and where the populace is always at hand to cheer artistic genius. The Italian past was glorious, the Italian future may be so as well, but "in the present condition of the Italians, artistic glory is the only kind they are permitted"—one of numerous offhand social commentaries to infuriate Napoleon, whose empire had included most of Italy since 1804. Life in Italy is free in a way unknown to more advanced, more politically liberated nations, and therefore most suited to women of artistic talent. For in Italy there is no hypocrisy about morals, as in England, no malicious gossip as in France, no false modesty or artifice, no obsession with rank or convention, but only spontaneity in love and art. If a woman can give delight with her dancing or reciting, she does so at once, without being begged, without simpering; if a woman loves a man, she can tell him she does so—"a terrible fault in England, but so pardonable in Italy." For married happiness and domestic virtues, England is undoubtedly the place, but for love outside marriage, go to Italy.

There is simply no way to "compromise" a woman's reputation in Italian society, as Corinne tells a nervous Oswald: women are expected always to be in love in Italy, always to speak of love and their lovers. "Thus, in this country, where no one thinks of anything but love, there isn't a single novel, because love is so rapid here, so public, that it doesn't lend itself to any kind of development; to give a true account of love Italian style, you would have to begin and end on the first page."

The result of these special conditions of Italian society, as far as Corinne is concerned, is not the possibility of attaining perfect happiness in love (no heroine ever felt herself more doomed to suffering through her heart) but that of leading an independent life as a woman of genius, and developing all her talents to the full with the open encouragement, rather than the shocked disapproval, of society. And in fact, beneath all her ranting and posing, her lyre strumming and drapery shaking, Corinne does illustrate a way of life for women of such novel fascination (perhaps even today?) that it turned the heads of young women from Paris to Yorkshire to New England, and gave them "a wild desire for an existence of lonely independence," as Fanny Kemble put it, along with "a passionate desire to go to Italy."

Corinne lives alone on her own money; she maintains her own establishment, is waited on by her own servants. She uses her own name, an invented one, and never refers to her family or even her true nationality. She goes into society without protector or escort; she has friends and lovers of her own free choosing. She does her own work—publishes, exhibits, performs—and is famous in her own right. She travels everywhere, alone or with a man as she chooses; she guides her own life.

So does George Sand's Lélia, and so, more remarkably, does Aurora Leigh. The scenes in Mrs. Browning's novel-poem which present Aurora's life in a London flat, writing and publishing her own poems and enjoying her own social existence in the best circles, are among the most delightful, the most modern, and apparently the most realistic (though how far they were from real experience, anyone who knows Elizabeth Barrett's life with father up to the age of forty will quickly recognize). Swinburne, whose passion for Aurora Leigh almost equaled Virginia Woolf's, assumed that its heroine was "in all essentials a conscious and intentional portrait of the author by herself," and protested against this fantasy material. "The career of Aurora in London," he wrote (in 1898!), "is rather too eccentric a vision to impose itself upon the most juvenile credulity: a young lady of family who lodges by herself in Grub Street,

preserves her reputation, lives on her pen, and dines out in Mayfair, is hardly a figure for serious fiction."

"Genius cannot do everything," Swinburne apologized for Mrs. Browning in conclusion; but female genius very much wanted to act out that fantasy of the independent woman's life called *Corinne* which Mme de Staël first located in an Italy of dreamland, the feminine Somewhere-else, where people were Men, Women, and Italians. For Emily Dickinson that land was simply "My Blue Peninsula" of hope and dreamed delight, one of several images which (as Rebecca Patterson has convincingly demonstrated) she derived from Mrs. Browning's Italy in *Aurora Leigh*.

As far as Mme de Staël was concerned, neither Geneva nor Paris, the places of her young womanhood, was any sort of Italy. In spite of the drama and independence of her mature life (greater than any woman had achieved before), she knew perfectly well what it was like to be Germaine Necker: that is, to be raised as a proper young lady in a strict Protestant family, to be laughed at and criticized in society for her mannerisms, and to be married off, at the age of nineteen, to a man chosen by her family for his title (from the very restricted field of available Protestant aristocrats). She carried her heroine's story back to childhood, and I believe this was another important originality of her novel; for when, before *Corinne*, had the sufferings of the gifted girl been told in fiction? The young Corinne more distinctly foreshadows the young Maggie Tulliver than does Fanny Burney's Evelina.

Corinne postpones the revelation of her early life to Oswald until she can give him the full tour of Naples and its environs, and pose with lyre in hand on Cape Misena (see the Vigée-Lebrun portrait of Mme de Staël). There, inspired by the nearby tomb of Vergil, Corinne makes one of her famous improvisations. The poets, the heroes, the women of Greece and Italy come to her mind, those whose genius flowered and whose suffering climaxed on these storied shores. O Fate! she cries, why has it always pursued the exalted spirits, the poets whose imagination derives from their power to love and to suffer? Cruel Destiny, of which the ancients spoke with such terror, means nothing to ordinary people ("*les êtres vulgaires*") who simply follow the course of the seasons in the habitual round of their peaceful lives. But the elite (*le petit nombre des élus*) are of another sphere, removed from the influence of the Universal Good; some unknown force drives genius toward misery. Protect us, O Sublime Creator: we hear a music of the spheres not caught by ordinary mortals, we feel stronger passions, think higher thoughts, are doomed to greater suffering, et cetera, et cetera. This is the extravagant prelude to Corinne's story, a tale of childhood wholly recognizable to middle-class Victorian women.

She was born in Italy, her mother a Roman, her father an Englishman, Lord Edgermond of Northumberland—a province as close to the edge-of-the-world as Mme de Staël could imagine and to which he was deeply attached. There he returned when his wife died, leaving Corinne behind in Florence with memories of a mother who "spoke of nothing from my infancy but the misfortune of not living in Italy." Until the age of fifteen, Corinne was raised by an Italian aunt who kept warning her that she would be damned if she lived in a Protestant country, and reminding her that "it was the fear of leaving her native land that had made her mother die of grief." Nevertheless, Corinne did have to leave Italy, and, *"avec un sentiment de tristesse inexprimable,"* she went to England to live for the next six years—explanation of the mystery that most puzzles Oswald in the first half of the novel—Corinne's faultless English accent.

Corinne was right to grieve. Her father had married again, and the second Lady Edgermond, a dignified, cold woman, cared for nothing but English provincial life and domestic virtue, and hated nothing so much as the Italian spirit, and language, and style of womanhood represented by Corinne. In spite of the single gleam of happiness provided by her darling little three-year-old stepsister Lucile, Corinne suffered terribly in rainy and gloomy England, full of teacups and boring neighbors. These last much resemble, when due allowance is made for Jane Austen's genius, the good ladies of Highbury in *Emma*.

Corinne's conversation is censored and silenced; her Italian expansiveness and spontaneity are simply squelched. One night at a gloomy formal dinner she attempts to enliven the atmosphere by quoting a few lines of Italian poetry which refer, in all delicacy, to the subject of love. So shocked is her stepmother that she enforces much earlier than usual that dreadful English custom, the after-dinner separation of women from men. (Mme de Staël's contemporaries saw in this material only a reflection of her discomfort when in exile in England in 1793; but Victorian women clearly perceived, what today we know to

be the fact, that Lady Edgermond is a version of Mme de Staël's own extremely strict mother.)

All of Corinne's nascent talents—for music, recitation, literature—are repressed and despised, not through active malice or cruelty but because her stepmother adheres to a cultural standard different from her own. When Corinne spends more and more time by herself, in her own room, studying and developing her native gifts, Lady Edgermond protests:

> "What is the good of all that?" she asked: "will it make you happy?"—and the question plunged me into despair. For what is happiness, I asked myself, if not the development of our faculties? Is not mental suicide as bad as physical? And if I must repress my mind and my spirit, what's the use of preserving the miserable rest of my life, which begins to drive me wild?

> But there was no use saying these things to my step-mother. I once tried to, and she had answered that a woman was created to take care of her husband's household and her children's health; all other ambitions led only to trouble, and I should conceal any that I had. And these words, in all their commonness, left me absolutely speechless; for emulation and enthusiasm, those motive forces of genius, require encouragement, or they fade like withered flowers beneath a cold grey sky. . . .

> . . . Narrow spirits and mediocre people attempt in the name of Duty to impose silence on talent, to get rid of enthusiasm, of genius, in short, of all their enemies. . . . But is it true that Duty prescribes the same rules for all? . . . Every woman, just like every man, must forge her own path according to her character and her talents.

Little wonder that Harriet Beecher "felt an intense sympathy" for Corinne. "But in America," she wrote, "feelings vehement and absorbing like hers become still more deep, morbid, and impassioned by the constant forms of self-government which the rigid forms of our society demand. They are repressed, and they burn inward till they burn the very soul."

And little wonder that Elizabeth Barrett invented for Aurora Leigh a Florentine mother, an English father, and an Italian homeland to mourn throughout her years of oppressive upbringing in England by her spinster aunt.

> I broke the copious curls upon my head
> In braids, because she liked smooth-ordered hair.
> I left off saying my sweet Tuscan words. . . .

For the Corinne that we first encounter riding to the Capitol behind four white horses was not to triumph born, but to the sufferings of the gifted girl in a strict home and a conventional society. Italy was in her soul—a quality of spirit more than an actual heritage; to Italy she dreamed of going, there to live the independent life of the woman of genius. And Corinne in fact runs away—from home, stepmother, neighbors, England. What happens between her flight to Italy and her crowning on the Capitoline, Mme de Staël does not tell us, except that in some marvelous way it all works out in Italy—the training, developing, publishing, applauding of the woman of genius. For "Italy," as Mrs. Browning wrote in *Aurora Leigh,* "Italy / Is one thing, England one."

It will be noticed that Harriet Beecher's reaction to **Corinne** led her to comment on "the rigid forms of our society," not on the strict New England stepmother who, in actual fact, had soured her own childhood. (And Miss Ophelia in *Uncle Tom's Cabin,* the New England spinster whose efforts to tame, without love, the wild black spirit of Topsy, provides a subtle criticism of New England values, and a comedy, rather than a running sore of remembered childhood pain.) In the same way, Miss Leigh, the spinster aunt in Mrs. Browning's novel-poem, is drawn with witty malice but no bitterness to represent English cultural attitudes toward the raising of women:

> she owned
> She liked a woman to be womanly,
> And English women, she thanked God and
>   sighed
> (Some people always sigh in thanking God),
> Were models to the universe.

Among Mme de Staël's legacies to literary women was the ability to generalize social value and cultural law from domestic fact.

The curious split in form, part novel and part guidebook, that puzzles readers of **Corinne** suggests on a small scale the problem that all students of Mme de Staël must face when attempting to fix her place in the history of thought. Her principal contribution was the extension of the central point of Montesquieu's *Esprit des Lois*—that political systems grow out of, and are inseparable from, social custom and national tradition—to other fields than politics, and most of all to literature. In the history of literature and its study, Mme de Staël's influence has in fact been enormous. Her analysis of European literature as made up of two separate but equal cultural traditions, the northern Anglo-Germanic and the southern Franco-classical, made way for Romanticism, a term she was the first to use. She introduced German

Romanticism not only to France but to England, for it was the reading of **De l'Allemagne** that led Carlyle to study German and to pay a most uncharacteristic tribute to intellectual womanhood: Mme de Staël, he said, had "the loftiest soul of any female of her time."

Irving Babbitt later saluted her as founder of the study of comparative literature, and in our own time no less a critic of the novel than Ian Watt has honored her as a precursor. But "Madame de Staël was not really a belle-lettrist or a literary critic, nor even a literary historian," as Morroe Berger observes; "today . . . we should call her a social scientist, since she sought to find in social institutions the influences that shaped the ideas and forms of literary expression."

Mme de Staël does not argue as a feminist; **Corinne** is hardly propaganda for an adjustment of marriage to female requirements. Instead, Mme de Staël's point is to demonstrate that regional or national, or what we call cultural, values determine the female's destiny even more rigidly, even more inescapably than the male's. For as women are the makers and transmitters of those minute local and domestic customs upon which rest all the great public affairs of civilization (that perception, as Susan Tenenbaum makes clear, had been in Montesquieu), so women suffer more than men in their daily and developing lives from the influences of nationality, geography, climate, language, political attitudes, and social forms.

Oswald's father is quite right. Corinne really is not a proper wife for a Lord Nelvil, or for anyone else. She belongs on the open, sunlit stage of Italy, and he in the retired domestic privacy of rainy England. Corinne is a wild spirit, and England, as Mrs. Browning puts it, is a tame place:

> All the fields
> Are tied up fast with hedges, nosegay like;
> The hills are crumpled plains, the plains
>   parterres,
> The trees, round, woolly, ready to be clipped,
> And if you seek for any wilderness,
> You find, at best, a park. A nature tamed
> And grown domestic like a barn-door fowl

—and like the clucking, strutting, pecking, barnyard women who are as much a part of the English landscape as are Aunt Pullet and Aunt Glegg in *The Mill on the Floss.*

George Eliot, in her scrupulous attention to the domestic habits of rural England; Charlotte Brontë in *Villette,* a novel which in its title, as in its every scene and event, is concerned with the power of place; Harriet Beecher Stowe, in the wide geographical and socioeconomic sweep of her novel on slavery; George Sand, in her thousand brilliant pages on the clashing values transmitted by the women of her own family; Willa Cather in "Old Mrs. Harris," the most delicate cultural study that we have in fiction of the ages of women—all are worthy descendants of the tradition of *Corinne.*

I hesitate to name in this connection the distinguished women anthropologists, for fear of suggesting, as I definitely am not, that anthropology is a woman's field. The reason for Ruth Benedict's and Margaret Mead's success in the new profession, which clearly emerges from their memoirs, was economic opportunity: there were jobs for women in anthropology in the 1920s because half the field work, that half concerned with investigation of female customs in remote societies, simply had to be done by women. (If such assignments had not come their way, both Mead and Benedict might have gone on writing the poetry and fiction that they wrote in college.)

Nor will I affirm the cliché that the delicate sensibility of women to the little ways of home makes them preservers and, in their literature, celebrants of conservative and local values. In some writings by some women, of course, just as in some writings by some men, there can indeed be found conservative views and regional affections, but these are hardly the hallmark of the tradition of *Corinne.* For what Mme de Staël passed on to her disciples was a heady sense of cutting loose from custom, an intoxicating awareness of the possibility of otherness in the human condition, resting on a thoroughly unsentimental perception of its various forms in varying societies. As in anthropological writing at its cautious best, *Corinne* provides no easy choices, no simple prescriptions for ideal happiness under the blue sky of Italian culture.

Indeed one of the most remarkable things about the novel, and the one that most justly infuriated Napoleon, is Mme de Staël's enthusiasm for England, the enemy nation of women as well as of France. For the kind of literary treason that in our barbarous times means imprisonment or death, Napoleon punished her by forbidding her residence in Paris. "'I leave you the universe to exploit'," the Emperor remembered telling Mme de Staël. "'I abandon the rest of the earth to you and reserve only Paris for myself'—but Paris was

all she wanted." Paris, its salons and its enlightenment, was her center and the source of all her own values: her personal culture as well as the historical and geographical cultures that were being undermined, as Mme de Staël well knew, by the north European and romantic values that sift through the pages of *Corinne.*

In the person of Oswald, Corinne herself worships the English ideal of *home,* a word Mme de Staël used without translating (there is no French equivalent for what is more a value than a place). And for such an ideal of life and of manhood, the ideal woman is in fact not Corinne but her blond rival—ideal of English womanhood, English culture, and English Romanticism. Lucile is young, pale, innocent, and silent. She has no personality, no education, no talent, no society but her mother, no thought but for Oswald; but her very nullity as a person is the source of her charm—a mysterious and subtle charm that Corinne, with all her demonstrative brilliance, does not provide. Lucile is Oswald's *princesse lointaine à la tour abolie,* his "still unravish'd bride of quietness," as Mme de Staël had neither the poetry nor the romantic sensibility to say. But she did turn her remarkable analytic powers on Oswald's reflections:

> Lucile was on her knees beside her mother, and it was Lucile who was reading first a chapter of the Bible and then a prayer adapted to domestic and rural life. . . . Tears fell from her eyes . . . she covered her face . . . but Oswald saw them. . . . He studied that air of youth which is so close to infancy, that glance which seems to preserve a recent memory of heaven. . . . Lord Nelvil reflected upon her austere and retired life, without pleasures, without the homage of the world. . . . Corinne delighted the imagination in a thousand ways, but there was nevertheless a species of thought [*un genre d'idées*] and, if one can use the expression, a musical sound which went only with Lucile. Images of domestic happiness were more easily combined with her Northumberland retreat than with Corinne's triumphal chariot. . . .

> He fell asleep thinking of Italy; yet during his sleep he thought he saw Lucile passing gently before him in the form of an angel. . . .

Patterns of contrast fill the conclusion of the novel. Lucile is pale and blond, with white plumes in her hat; Corinne is dark, and covers herself with the black Venetian domino. Lucile is the quintessential virgin; Corinne, in spite of Mme de Staël's sporadic efforts to clean up her past and order her present, is clearly a woman who has lived. Lucile in her extreme youth "presents the innocent image of the springtime of life"; and Corinne, while not precisely the spirit of autumn—for Mme de Staël was only a woman—is very ripe.

Lucile has no existence apart from her family, and Corinne has no family. Lucile is a Protestant who prays at home, and Corinne honors all the public rituals and ceremonies of the Catholic church. Corinne is open, spontaneous, talkative, bold, talented, famous; Lucile is silent and shy—a girl for a man to dream of, for a man to worship, for a man to marry. Corinne is the city and civilization, is art and joy; Lucile is melancholy, country retirement, and boredom. For as the epilogue points out—Mme de Staël was only human—Oswald is dreadfully bored by his marriage to Lucile, which, the reader feels, is just what he deserves. As for Corinne, much as she grieves for Oswald, much as she yearns for domestic happiness, all she gets is what she deserves—Italy.

I rather like the way Mme de Staël ties up the novel without attempting to resolve any of the cultural dilemmas that face the woman of genius. On the arm of a frivolous French count, who turns out to be a good sort of chap to have around in time of trouble, Corinne staggers back from Scotland to Italy, after managing to release Oswald from his troth to herself and free him for marriage to Lucile. In Italy she finds that love has destroyed her talents as well as her happiness, and she retreats from the public eye. Years later, Oswald and Lucile, now man and wife, make a trip to Florence and search out Corinne. She stages a final public triumph in the Academy, and then expires (finding time, however, to coach their little daughter to be a Corinne of the future and a terrible handful, one assumes, for her strict mama).

All this takes place in northern Italy, the one region of the country not already covered, guidebook style, by the novel. Perhaps Mme de Staël felt that Florence was the only possible locale for the finale of the woman of genius. What she actually drew upon in the last chapters, as we know from her letters, were memories of the start of her own Italian tour. The surprise and disappointment that she then felt, travelers from the north, both before her time and after, have shared. For northern Italy is cold, cold as the rest of Europe, "and winter displeases more there than anywhere else, because the imagination is not prepared for it." The skies are leaden and grey; the snow falls, the fog thickens, the rivers flood; even the architecture (at least of the Cathedral of Milan) is Gothic. One might as well have stayed at home.

"Où donc est votre belle Italie?" Lucile asks her husband. "'So where is your beautiful Italy?' 'I don't know,' Lord Nelvil sadly answered, 'when I shall ever find it again'."

TITLE COMMENTARY

Reflections of the Trial of a Queen, by a Woman

LORI J. MARSO (ESSAY DATE SPRING 2002)

SOURCE: Marso, Lori J. "Defending the Queen: Wollstonecraft and Staël on the Politics of Sensibility and Feminine Difference." *The Eighteenth Century* 43, no. 1 (spring 2002): 43-60.

In the following excerpt, Marso analyzes de Staël's Reflections on the Trial of a Queen, by a Woman *discussing how she negotiates the politics of sense and sensibility and uses a masculine model to offer a notion of the female self.*

I shall therefore only speak of that verdict, analyzing the political, in telling what I have seen, what I know of the queen, and in depicting the hideous circumstances which have led to her condemnation.[1]

GERMAINE DE STAËL, *Reflections on the Trial of the Queen, by a Woman.* August 1793

Staël's essay in defense of Marie Antoinette at the time of her trial was initially published anonymously as authored only "by a woman." Staël's identification of herself as a woman is significant. The Revolutionary Criminal Tribunal, consisting of a male jury and nine male judges, ultimately decided Marie Antoinette's fate, yet the lower-class women of Paris were among her most notorious and vicious enemies. Indeed, the first time that women organized politically was to march to Versailles in October 1789 to demand that the royal couple guarantee bread to the people and approve the Declaration of the Rights of Man and of the Citizen. The direct confrontation between the Queen of France and the mostly lower-class Parisian women who marched to Versailles to capture the queen serves as a political moment peculiarly open to a variety of readings. In this essay, I am particularly interested in analyzing the readings of the two female political theorists who write about this event, Mary Wollstonecraft and Germaine de Staël.

As a feminist working in the field of political theory. I am drawn to specific historical moments and literary metaphors that function within theoretical texts as sites where ideas of femininity (as well as masculinity) are (re)produced and mediated. I have isolated the October 1789 Women's March to Versailles and the August 1793 trial of Marie Antoinette to be studied here because the status of femininity and women's role in politics are at the center of each event. The Women's March was the first moment in the Revolution that women came together *as a group of women* in order to act politically and make demands of their sovereigns.[2] One of these sovereigns is a woman who herself will be slandered and executed for stepping outside the role of proper femininity. In the bill of indictment against Marie Antoinette at her trial, she is accused of squandering public monies, siphoning money to Austria, and most outrageously, of engaging in incest with her son. A host of contemporary feminist scholars have studied the ways in which Marie Antoinette's status as queen symbolized, for revolutionaries, the feminization and corruption of the Old Regime. Propaganda at the time painted Marie Antoinette as woman, foreigner, prostitute, adulteress, and coquette.[3] And indeed, her trial and execution in August 1793 marks the moment after which all possibilities for women's formal participation in politics were closed off.

Thus, we see the interpretive and political perils of these historical events for writers who sought to advance women's potential role in the New Republic. Marie Antoinette, the female victim said to symbolize the feminine excess of the aristocracy, is attacked by lower-class market women testing and enacting their newly found political power. How was the woman writer to understand the potential role of women in politics and notions of the feminine when faced with such contradictory behavior of women and diverse meaning attached to the feminine? To attempt to analyze the role of "women" in these events, one becomes increasingly drawn into an eighteenth-century discursive dynamic that Gunther-Canada has called the "politics of sense and sensibility."[4] Simply put, sensibility was identified with female virtues of sympathetic feeling, empathetic behavior, and romanticism; sense was associated with masculine rational discourse as exemplified in Enlightenment philosophy. Negotiating the gendered politics of sense and sensibility proved to be significant challenge for women who wished to see gender inequality alleviated. To continue to view women and define the feminine self through the lens of sensibility was to run the risk of

identifying women with the very qualities that had been said to justify their exclusion from politics in the first place. To turn the tables and claim that women could indeed be associated with sense, just as well as men, was to risk reifying a masculine model of political discourse rendering sexual difference incompatible with democratic politics.

Mary Wollstonecraft and Germaine de Staël boldly entered into this debate. Wollstonecraft, a woman writer of the middle classes who wrote to earn her keep, firmly forged her allegiance with the common people in analyzing the conditions of the majority, claiming that women faced the most wretched circumstances of all. Wollstonecraft is most famous for two early political essays. Her *Vindication of the Rights of Men* (1790)[5] was written in defense of the principles of the French Revolution in response to Edmund Burke's attack on the Revolution; the *Vindication of the Rights of Woman* (1792)[6] was written to persuade Talleyrand, French Minister of Education at the time, that a national education program should include girls alongside boys. While these two essays were written from England, *An Historical and Moral Overview of the French Revolution* (1794)[7] was authored by Wollstonecraft after she came to Paris to experience the Revolution for herself. She arrived in time to see Louis XVI being taken off to prison and to witness the beginning of the Terror. Yet, despite the increasing radicalization of the Revolution, until her death in 1797, Wollstonecraft remained committed to the view of the "French Revolution [as] part of the human destiny for improvement" and sought to secure the rights of her sex through democratic politics.[8]

In contrast, Germaine de Staël, daughter of Jacques Necker, Finance Minister on the eve of the Revolution, and Suzanne Necker, Parisian salonnière, [Staël] was an aristocrat by birth and initially sought to prepare herself to preside over a salon and "exert an influence in the manner appropriate to women of the aristocracy."[9] Initially loyal to the idea of an enlightened constitutional monarchy, Staël became a committed republican. Geneviève Fraisse calls Staël "the most visible woman of her generation" (Fraisse 1994, 103). Swept up into the center of revolutionary events by her father's position, Staël remained fascinated by politics, and especially the role of women, throughout her life and put these concerns at the forefront of her work. Though the lives of women were central to almost everything Staël wrote, she was most interested in the lives of exceptional women and never explicitly made the case for politically empowering every woman. After the fall of the monarchy, Staël took refuge in Switzerland, returned to France in 1795, eventually became a forceful opponent of Napoleon and was exiled in 1803. Her three-volume treatise, *Considerations on the Principal Events of the French Revolution,*[10] was left unfinished in 1817 upon her death and published one year later. . . .

While Wollstonecraft was authoring her *Vindication of the Rights of Men* and the *Rights of Woman,* both of which sought to "confound the rhetorical distinctions of sex in political writing" (Gunther-Canada 1996, 62), Germaine de Staël was busy *appealing to her sex,* to a distinctly feminine sensibility. Though employing very different political strategies, both women theorists were attempting to reverse the direction in which the Revolution was increasingly headed, towards defining "woman" and "citizen" as exclusive categories. Wollstonecraft sought to "deny men the authority of defining womanhood as difference" (Gunther-Canada 1996, 63) while Staël embraced that difference as a way to critique the violence, excess, and irrationality of revolutionary politics as peculiarly "male."

Staël's rhetorical stance, whereby she valorized many of the attributes of a stereotyped femininity in order to call for women's inclusion in revolutionary politics, was rooted in her burgeoning awareness that to be a woman was increasingly becoming a *political fact,* an attribute to which revolutionaries attached an overwhelming significance. For Staël, this becomes most clear when looking at the significance that Marie Antoinette took on as a public and visible woman, and in the way women's revolutionary activity and their desire to participate in revolutionary politics were viewed. In order to contrast Staël's analysis of gender in the Revolution with Wollstonecraft's, and use the two as a starting point for a broader discussion of the risks involved in defining "woman," I look to Staël's *Reflections on the Trial of the Queen, by a Woman* (1793), buttressed by her continuing analysis in the three-volume *Considerations on the Principal Events of the French Revolution* (1817). It is important to note that, though her three volume *Considerations* was written long after revolutionary events when Staël had the benefit of hindsight, in fact her *Reflections on the Trial of the Queen,* written in the midst of these political events, expresses similar sentiments and promotes the same primary focus, that of an emphasis on positive feminine traits and how we might understand these in terms of the potential role of women in politics. Though it

was written much later, I consult the *Considerations* primarily because here she applies her analysis derived in *Reflections on the Trial of a Queen* as applied to the Women's March on Versailles.

In her account of the March, as in all her work, Staël emphasizes the many ways that emotion affects reason and credits women for the ability to bring that special quality into political situations that require good judgment. She appeals to the *hearts of women* in all situations that demand political and moral deliberation. Staël praises the group of "women and children, armed with pikes and scythes" (*Considerations* I, 340), whose "political rage became appeased" upon "seeing the queen, as a mother" (*Considerations* I, 343). Staël claims that "the populace, in a state of insurrection, are, in general, inaccessible to reasoning, and are to be acted on only by sensations rapid as electricity, and communicated in a similar manner" (*Considerations* I, 343). When the crowd saw the queen, "her hair disheveled, her countenance pale, but dignified" (*Considerations* I, 343) standing alongside her two children, "those, who that very night had perhaps wished to assassinate her, extolled her name to the skies" (*Considerations* I, 343).

When the Revolution takes its turn towards the Terror, Staël blames the zeal for violence and excess partially on the exclusion of women from the revolutionary process. In constructing a hypermasculinist conception of politics, the Revolution totally disregarded "truth" which is, according to Staël, made up of "every fact and every individual being."[11] It is women who are able to discern this source of truth and keep it in sight as a goal. In contrast, revolutionary men (regardless of their political perspective) ran roughshod over individual lives and individual dreams. Staël argues that during the Terror, men lost their hearts, their ability to feel; political dogmas reigned, not men: "Robespierre had acquired the reputation of high democratical virtue, and was believed incapable of personal views" (*Considerations* II, 142). And much later, of her first meeting with Napoleon Bonaparte, Staël writes: "I had a vague feeling that no emotion of the heart could act upon him. . . . [H]e regards a human being as an action or a thing, not as a fellow creature. . . . [H]e does not hate nor does he love" (*Considerations* II, 197-198). During Napoleon's reign, "friendship and love . . . were frozen in every heart. . . . [M]en no longer cared for one another" (*Considerations* II, 306). Staël emphasizes what she sees as women's special political talent of persuading men to act within a more compassionate model of reason, according to rules of engagement, generosity, and compassion:

> It is the duty of us women at all times to aid individuals accused of political opinions of any kind whatsoever; for what are opinions in times of faction? Can we be certain that such and such events, such and such a situation, would not have changed our own views? and, if we except a few invariable sentiments, who knows how difference of situation might have acted on us
> (*Considerations* II, 193, my emphasis).

This philosophy is the source of Staël's defense of Marie Antoinette, both at the time of the October Days and at the moment of Marie Antoinette's impending trial and execution. Staël had the remarkable foresight to realize what Wollstonecraft had not: Marie Antoinette was not simply a fallen queen. Her image was manipulated to represent a too-powerful and too-political woman. Staël worried that if women failed to defend the queen, the most prominent and visible woman in France, women's future in the Revolution might be forever compromised. As Lynn Hunt reminds us, Marie Antoinette was accused of crimes mostly on account of her sex. She writes, "Promiscuity, incest, poisoning of the heir to the throne, plots to replace the heir with a pliable substitute—all of these charges reflect a fundamental anxiety about queenship as the most extreme form of women invading the public sphere" (Hunt 1991, 123). Staël recognizes this anxiety and uses it to appeal, as she puts it, to "women of all nations, of all classes of society" to see that "the destiny of Marie Antoinette encompasses all which can possibly touch [women's] hearts" (*Queen*, 366). Staël attempts to erase divisions amongst women (particularly class divisions which initially drove the market women to descend on Versailles) in order to get women to see in Marie Antoinette what Staël believes all women have in common. See how Marie Antoinette is just like you—your destiny could be hers, she argues: "if you are sensitive, if you are mothers, she has loved with all of the same power of soul as you" (*Queen*, 366). Staël argues that as a woman, Marie Antoinette always put her family first; the crime of keeping her contacts with her family in Austria should be something we should praise her for: "her entire life has been proof of her respect for the ties of nature—but this virtue, far from frightening us, should set our minds at ease about all of the others" (*Queen*, 373). Moreover, according to Staël, in any acts she has done she has only been motivated by a love for her family:

You, who saw her look at her children, you who know that no danger could reconcile her to being separated from her spouse, even when so many times he left paths open for her to return to her country—can you believe that her heart was barbarous or tyrannical? Ah! no one who knows what it is to love would make others suffer; perhaps no one who has been punished through those whom one cherishes could doubt celestial vengeance.

(*Queen*, 377)

The only time, according to Staël, that the queen lost her composure or acted out of anything even approaching self-interest was when one of her family members was in danger. "If you want to weaken a grand character," Staël writes, "arrest her children" (*Queen*, 379). According to Staël's account, when Marie Antoinette was separated from her son, he refused to "take the slightest nourishment" (*Queen*, 390). Despite the boy's young age, he was kept separate from his mother, yet Marie Antoinette continued to live; "she remains alive because she loves, because she is a mother: ah, but for this sacred bond, she would excuse herself from the company of those who want to prolong her life" (*Queen*, 391)!

Unfortunately, there were few that wanted to prolong, and many that desired to end, Marie Antoinette's life. Anne Mini insightfully notes that the essence of Staël's defense of the queen hinges on an account of how Marie Antoinette's roles as "woman" suddenly "crashed into one another—roles over which the young queen had even less control than most women."[12] Mini elaborates that on Staël's criteria, condemned as a woman, Marie Antoinette was simply seen as "asking for it."

> She was famous—and since, society's logic runs, no virtuous woman attracts public attention, she must necessarily have been lacking in virtue. She was wealthy—and since no woman can deserve wealth on her own behalf, she must have stolen it from the French people, using her feminine wiles to distract attention from her avarice. . . . She was the King's wife—and therefore must have used her feminine wiles to blandish him into bad policies, since as a woman, she could not possess the reason to favor good ones. . . . She was the daughter of Maria-Theresa—and thus must have been a traitoress to France.
> (Mini 1995, 243)

Thus, Marie Antoinette's worst crime: to be a highly visible woman. Anne Mini reminds us of something that Wollstonecraft had pointed out quite forcefully: Marie Antoinette did not step out of the prescribed social roles for women. Yet, her adherence to those social roles, especially when they "crashed into one another" was no guarantee that she would not be slandered. To many women who supported the Revolution, hatred of Marie Antoinette came to symbolize their loyalty to the Revolution. Though the queen adhered to a feminine role, in the context of revolutionary politics, many women came to hate the queen for having escaped the traditional female vices: ignorance, poverty, sexual bondage, slavery to her reproductive life, unfreedom to act (Gutwirth 1992, 242-3). In Lynn Hunt's analysis "the queen, then, was the emblem (and sacrificial victim) of the feared disintegration of gender boundaries that accompanied the Revolution" (Hunt 1991, 123).

Defining the Feminine

Taken together, these accounts by Wollstonecraft and Staël propose different lenses through which to view historical notions of the female self and how they were invoked by these two female political theorists to argue for the potential role of women in politics. Wollstonecraft sees a broad and participatory role for women but holds women to what she calls a "masculine" model of educated citizenship and reasonable reflection (Revolution, 6). She maintains that structural inequality is at the root of gendered accounts of virtue, and that individuals should pursue enlightened virtue regardless of gender. In line with this reasoning, Marie Antoinette and the women who participated in the march equally fail to live up to Wollstonecraft's idea of virtue: Marie Antoinette was a coquette, and the women who marched were part of a "mob" mimicking male behavior. While Wollstonecraft certainly felt that women had a special social role to play in being mothers and would uplift politics through this unique sensibility, she thought women were, first and foremost, human beings with reason who should exercise their reason in playing their political role, Mary Lyndon Shanley writes that Wollstonecraft believed "exaggerated notions of female sensibility corrupted both women and men, and worked against the extension of fundamental rights of citizenship to women."[13]

Staël puts women's feminine identity at the center of her analysis to lay the groundwork for a protofeminist politics based exclusively in feminine identity. She invokes traditional, even stereotyped, notions of women's virtue, claiming that these are the ideals that are needed in public life. Staël glorifies an appeal to emotions and to the sensuous imagination as a way to understand the situations of persons such as Marie Antoinette.[14] . . . [S]he seems to imply that our feelings might be more deeply rational than our intellect. After all, revolutionary men from the Terror to Napoleon claimed to rule in accordance with reason; women were traditionally excluded. The question arises, however, as to whether women's exclusion necessarily fosters the kinds of emotions Staël depicts. Her appeal to the "hearts of women" fails to account for women's anger, women's violence, and women's deviation from a model of motherhood and compassionate understanding. Staël's move could convincingly be read as simply another essentializing strategy. How much, after all, do the women marchers really have in common with Marie Antoinette, who represents the Old Regime and is consequently a class rival of the marchers? Because of the model of femininity that Staël employs in this particular instance, she is unable to consider the many motivations behind the women's march and the various ways this political action represents possibilities for women's revolutionary activity and their potential relationship to the state. Staël's reading of women's "common" interests in family, emotion, attachment to particular others, and disdain for the "excesses" of politics may indeed misunderstand what the marchers themselves understood about their own political subjectivity and their desire and ability to act on that very subjectivity. In this vein, one would need to inquire whether the marchers' actions were at odds with their own conceptions of womanhood.

From our perspective as contemporary scholars, we stand fully aware of the problems of ever attempting to securely define "woman" and hold women to a standard based in any notion of the eternal feminine. Joan Scott has stressed the indeterminacy of gender categories, noting that "man" and "woman" are at once empty and overflowing categories. They are empty in that they have no ultimate, transcendent meaning; overflowing because even when they appear to be fixed, they still contain within them alternative, denied, or suppressed definitions.[15] Denise Riley writes about the peculiar temporality of "women" and distinguishes the levels of indeterminacy that characterize the category. These include "the individual indeterminacy (when am I a woman?), the historical indeterminacy (what do "women" mean, and when?), and the political indeterminacy (what can "women" do?)."[16] Madelyn Gutwirth applies these in her own account of the October Days:

> The huge existential gap between the ideology of gender and the in-the-home and on-the-street realities of women's actual behavior is nowhere more evident than in the story of the October Days. Just as we still jockey mentally in daily life

DE

L'INFLUENCE DES PASSIONS

SUR

LE BONHEUR DES INDIVIDUS

ET

DES NATIONS.

PAR

MAD. LA BARONNE STAEL DE HOLSTEIN.

Quæsivit cœlo lucem ingemuitque repertà.

A LAUSANNE *en Suisse,*

Chez {JEAN MOURER, Libraire.
HIGNOU ET COMPᵉ. Imp. Lib.

1 7 9 6.

Title page of *A Treatise on the Influence of the Passions upon the Happiness of Individuals and Nations* (1796).

with insistent ideas of female "goodness," "purity," and "beauty" we encounter, so did the eruption of a mob of women armed with pikes and muskets strain the ability of the Revolution's contemporaries to sort out the solecism of the Frenchwomen's playing so unforeseen a militant role as they did in their march on Versailles.

(Gutwirth 1992, 239)

Dominique Godineau documents that women's revolutionary action does not follow any preconceived patterns of "feminine" behavior, no matter how defined. When women acted politically, they acted from a number of different axes and with a variety of demands and expectations; women do not necessarily act solely (though of course they do sometimes act primarily) as women.

Yet, though we are reminded that it is ill advised to seek firmly fixed notions of woman and the female self, women activists and theorists during the Revolution were faced with a peculiarly difficult situation. In *Only Paradoxes to Offer: French Feminists and the Rights of Man,* Joan Scott has argued that we should understand the dilemma of

needing to invoke qualities of group identity even while denying their negative characteristics in terms of a "politics of undecidability."[17] Due to the political situation whereby the Rights of Man were presumed to be universal, yet posited as against and exclusive of women's rights, women were forced to accept definitions of gender in order to argue on behalf of their sex, while maintaining that gender should not matter if rights are indeed "universal."

This paradoxical political situation sheds light on Staël's strategy of invoking a stereotyped notion of the female self. Recall that Staël's political strategy is born in a crucial moment. Staël felt quite certain that manipulation of the image of the queen as the most visible political woman would have dire political consequences for women as a whole in terms of revolutionary politics. Her appeal in the face of this danger, and at the moment of Marie Antoinette's trial, seeks to forge a female community across class and political boundaries upon emotional grounds suggesting the "hearts" of all women would recognize the queen's plight. Though the women marchers and the queen were class enemies, they were acting in a political moment when the category of "woman" was being manipulated within revolutionary rhetoric. The salient question becomes, in both historical and contemporary terms, when it is possible, and politically strategic, to invoke categories of identity that have heretofore served as disciplinary and/or exclusionary. While marks of identity are oppressive, they are also constitutive of a person's very existence. At the moment of the Women's March, the class oppression of the Old Regime, the queen's status as foreigner and as woman, and French women's revolutionary role were simultaneously in flux.

Across her oeuvre, Staël is well aware of the risks of the attempt to "fix" a notion of feminine subjectivity in any appeal to nature or even social behavior. In light of living through a historical moment in which women were denied access to citizenship based on claims of nature, Staël fractures the category of "woman" throughout her works in talking explicitly about women intellectuals and their various representations and women's "indeterminate" nature. As her work on Marie Antoinette and the representation of women in the Revolution indicates, Staël is quite clearly aware that it is precisely because of the inability to posit a strict feminine subjectivity that the category of woman is open to both overt and covert forms of political manipulation. In championing the emotive and the performative as against the rational and the transparent. Staël willingly engages in the political acts by which women must claim political space and action despite the risks inherent in any such political strategy. She seems to imply that engaging in a political performance might be less risky than forever glorifying a masculine model of reason that makes sexual difference incompatible with rational political discourse.

Moreover, despite (or maybe because of) our inability to read transparently the intentions of the marchers themselves and to understand their own conceptions of womanhood and feminine subjectivity, it is imperative to theorize how best women can act in the name of women without attributing a regulatory and disciplinary categorical status to the concept of woman. Contrary to the instinct to read an appeal to the "hearts" of women as reactionary or stereotyped, I would like to suggest the possibility of claiming this move as an appeal to a utopian moment that, when invoked, points simultaneously towards the possibility of community and laments the current lack of community. Might an affirmation of identity be liberating within the context of a larger struggle to transform wider material and institutional forms of oppression?

Writing almost two hundred years after Germaine de Staël, in her introduction to *The Second Sex*, Simone de Beauvoir writes that because women are scattered across all social groups, "the bond that unites her to her oppressors is not comparable to any other."[18] Consequently, women tend to feel solidarity with men in their own social class (or we might add, racial category) rather than with women in general. "Women do not say 'We.' . . . they do not authentically posit themselves as Subject" (Beauvoir 1984, 19). Depending then on women's particular social class, race, and other circumstances, feminine subjectivity is a strange mix of freedom and alienation. This mix, for Beauvoir, is a highly specific kind of oppression necessarily difficult to break out of due to the problem of the lack of a feminist subjectivity. When we think about Staël's political strategy of asserting a politics of sexual difference in light of Beauvoir's comments, we might better understand the necessity of speaking *of* and *to* women as a politicization of the category on the way to its ultimate depoliticization. Despite the fact that Staël herself is well aware of class and political divisions amongst women (witness her analysis of the relationships between women in her famous novel **Delphine,** for example) she does not give

up the hope that women will realize that in order to be free, they must assert themselves *as women.*

This hope may seem a highly naïve and utopian political strategy. It also may seem a dangerous and debilitating one in light of concerns raised by some feminist scholars who charge that the women's movement posited an identity of women across class and race lines by advancing the middle-class white woman as model.[19] While I would insist that feminists constantly be aware of our own exclusionary and disciplinary kinds of moves in attempts to posit woman as a category, in light of this reading of the Women's March, I would also claim that we abandon utopian and collective narratives only at the peril of losing sight of feminist goals for the improvement of the lives of all kinds of women. Staël was eerily aware that in a highly charged political moment, one woman could come to stand in for all women. Staël sought to invoke the utopian dream of women coming together to forge an alternative path to these dangerous options. Because neither history nor philosophy has offered feminists a way beyond the dilemma of feminine subjectivity, I suggest that an alternative path lies in political strategy. If the ultimate goal of feminism is to abolish the need for its own existence, we can learn from Staël's historical moment that the seemingly utopian strategy of speaking collectively as women, carefully and cautiously, may be usefully called upon along the way.

Notes

1. *Réflexions sur le procès de la Reine par une Femme* (Bibliotèque Nationale Librarie 3272: August, 1793). Unless otherwise indicated, all references to this piece will be to the English translation by Anne A. A. Mini cited in Appendix B. 365-92 in *An Expressive Revolution: the political theory of Germaine de Staël*, Ph.D. dissertation. University of Washington, 1995, and cited within the text as (*Queen*, page number).

2. Dominique Godineau remarks that in this crowd there were "six to seven thousand women and some men [who] forced their way into the Hotel-de-Ville and then began to march toward Versailles." See Dominique Godineau, *The Women of Paris and Their French Revolution*, trans. Katherine Streip (Berkeley, 1998), 98.

3. On the ways Marie Antoinette was used to undermine the position of all women as possible political actors or citizens see. Madelyn Gutwirth, "Marie-Antoinette, Scourge of the French People." *The Twilight of the Goddesses: Women and Representation in the French Revolutionary Era* (New Brunswick, NJ, 1992), 228-45; Elizabeth Colwill, "Just Another Citoyenne? Marie-Antoinette on Trial, 1790-1793," *History Workshop* 28 (Autumn 1989), 63-87; and Lynn Hunt, "The Many Bodies of Marie-Antoinette: Political Pornography and the Problem of the Feminine in the French Revolution," as well as "The Diamond Necklace Affair Revisited (1785-1786): The Case of the Missing

DE STAËL

Queen," in *Eroticism and the Body Politic,* Ed. Lynn Hunt (Baltimore, 1991), 108-30 and 63-89.

4. Wendy Gunther-Canada, "The politics of sense and sensibility: Mary Wollstonecraft and Catharine Macaulay Graham on Burke's *Reflection on the Revolution in France*" in Hilda L. Smith, ed., *Women Writers and the Early Modern British Political Tradition* (Cambridge, 1998), 127-47.

5. Mary Wollstonecraft, *A Vindication of the Rights of Men,* in Janet Todd and Marilyn Butler, eds., *The Works of Mary Wollstonecraft,* Volume 5 (New York, 1989). Reference to this work will be cited within the text as (*Men,* page number).

6. Mary Wollstonecraft, *A Vindication of the Rights of Woman,* Ed. Carol Poston (New York, 1988). Reference to this work will be cited within the text as (*Woman,* page number).

7. Mary Wollstonecraft, *An Historical and Moral Overview of the French Revolution,* in Janet Todd and Marilyn Butler, eds., *The Works of Mary Wollstonecraft,* Volume 6 (New York, 1989). Reference to this work will be cited within the text as (*Revolution,* page number).

8. See Virginia Sapiro, "Wollstonecraft, Feminism, and Democracy: 'Being Bastilled'" In Maria J. Falco, ed., *Feminist interpretation of Mary Wollstonecraft* (University Park, PA, 1996), 33-45 at 39 as well as Sapiro's *A Vindication of Political Virtue: The Political Theory of Mary Wollstonecraft* (Chicago, 1992).

9. Geneviève Fraisse, *Reason's Muse: Sexual Difference and the Birth of Democracy,* trans. Jane Marie Todd (Chicago and London, 1994), 104.

10. Germaine de Staël, *Considerations on the Principal Events of the French Revolution.* Three Volumes (London, 1818). References to this work will be cited within the text as (*Considerations,* Volume Number, page number).

11. See Germaine de Staël, *On Literature in Relation to Social Institutions,* in Morroe Berger, ed., *Madame de Staël on Politics, Literature, and National Character* (Garden City, NY, 1964), 247.

12. See Anne Mini, *An Expressive Revolution,* cited above, 234.

13. Mary Lyndon Shanley, "Mary Wollstonecraft on sensibility, women's rights, and patriarchal power," in Hilda L. Smith, ed., *Women Writers and the early Modern British Political Tradition* (Cambridge, 1998), 148-67 at 150.

14. For an analysis of Staël as a political thinker able to include particular identities and loyalties within the call to universal principles, see my *(Un)Manly Citizens: J. J. Rousseau's and Germaine de Staël's Subversive Women* (Baltimore, 1999).

15. See Joan Scott's *Gender and the Politics of History* (New York, 1988), 49.

16. Denise Riley, "A Short History of Some Preoccupations," in Judith Butler and Joan W. Scott, eds., *Feminists Theorize the Political* (New York, 1992), 121-9 at 121.

17. See Joan Scott, *Only Paradoxes to Offer: French Feminists and the Rights of Man* (Cambridge, 1996), xi.

18. See Simone de Beauvoir, *The Second Sex,* trans. H. Parshley (New York, 1984), 19.

19. For one (of many) argument concerning the dangers and problems inherent in claiming solidarity for women across class and race lines, see Elizabeth Spelman, *Inessential Woman* (Boston, 1988).

Corinne

ARMINE KOTIN MORTIMER (ESSAY DATE 1992)

SOURCE: Kotin Mortimer, Armine. "Male and Female Plots in Staël's *Corinne*." In *Studies in Literature, History, and the Arts in Nineteenth-Century France: Selected Proceedings of the Sixteenth Colloquium in Nineteenth-Century French Studies,* edited by Keith Busby, pp. 149-56. Amsterdam: CIP-Gegevens Koninklijke, 1992.

In the following excerpt, Kotin Mortimer explores the male subjugation of the fallen woman in Corinne.

Through the fictive transcription of her artistic personality in the character of Corinne, Germaine de Staël addressed a vindictive reproach to any man who failed to give due consideration to her genius.[1] She plotted to kill her heroine, and to blame her death on Lord Oswald Nelvil, an amalgam of several real men in Staël's circle who, in Madelyn Gutwirth's phrase, held the "analogous role of unreliable lover in Mme de Staël's life."[2]

From the outset Staël projected Oswald's situation between two women, one superior, the other ordinary; Oswald was to marry the ordinary woman, and have a daughter; Corinne was to die. Writes Simone Balayé of the early outline: "Le héros tue l'héroïne ou l'abandonne . . . le choix n'est pas fait. Mais on sait d'ores et déjà que Corinne se trouvera dans cette situation, l'abandon, la mort et peut-être le pardon, pendant qu'Oswald sera livré au remords."[3]

Yet though the accusation is palpable throughout, Staël's final judgment of Oswald remains ambiguous. The last paragraph of the novel is a coda in which a series of questions lays doubt on the future destiny of Nelvil:

Que devint Oswald? . . . se pardonna-t-il sa conduite passée? le monde, qui l'approuva, le consola-t-il? se contenta-t-il d'un sort commun, après ce qu'il avait perdu? Je l'ignore; je ne veux, à cet égard, ni le blâmer ni l'absoudre.[4]

The veiled accusations against Oswald, and his troubled or common fate, could well have carried against all the men in Staël's coterie who, like Benjamin Constant, failed to recognize that they had been chosen for a unique destiny, as if singled out by a divine power, which it was their error to reject. The novel's closure is marked by this vengeful "I told you so." But the dominant image at

Corinne's death in the final pages is that of a cloud that darkens the sky, and symbolically obnubilates any clear finalities. Most romantic closures display this double characteristic: against the brutal certainty of death there stands in counterpoise the ambiguity affecting the final moral judgment on Oswald Nelvil and the uncertainty that Corinne's death will have changed Oswald for the better. Any apotheosis of the female as artist, which is, to be sure, a function of the ending, is counter-balanced by the failure of the novel to close on the decisive punishment of Nelvil. In this Staël sacrificed not to any man but to a tenacious romantic commonplace according to which the moral of a work of art must remain "dans le vague."

There are several masculine standards and morals, or "male plots," that a feminist reading of the novel would expose. Such a reading would show Oswald Nelvil to be rather a stereotypical male chauvinist even in his love of Corinne. It would dwell on Oswald's masculine vanity, as when he is proud to be seen in public with a woman of such fame as Corinne, which later takes an ironic turn when he is thrilled at being with Lucile while her beauty is admired by the crowds in the London theater or in Hyde Park. Staël also treats with some irony a common male plot, according to which women need male protection, a pervasive ethic propounded here by Corinne's friend Castel-Forte: "ces fragiles idoles adorées aujourd'hui peuvent être brisées demain, sans que personne prenne leur défense, et c'est pour cela même que je les respecte davantage" (p. 565). In her decline Corinne herself falls prey to another male plot, a kind of mythological playing out of the older-woman syndrome, who sees her glory eclipsed by the younger, blonder, and fresher Lucile (pp. 488-90). The *Phèdre* intertext, alluded to in a painting, might be pertinent here (p. 236). Apocalypse, not apotheosis, threatens. Finally, a double paternal authority stands in direct antagonism to female desires (p. 504).

Staël had the courage to develop these male plots while at the same time finding support for her feminist theses in them. Oswald's tendency to judge Corinne too superior and too uncommon is the female author's assessment of the ordinary man's failing; it is a reproach to the men in Staël's circle. The central theme opposing "English" and "Italian" values raises the heated question of a woman's virtue: can a woman of talents and imagination be pure? (It was a heated question at the time, and we can guess Staël's answer.) Corinne's stepmother Lady Edgermond, the *nec plus ultra* of the straitlaced English, sees only that a woman who has ideas beyond the common ones cannot be pure, according to a socially defined virtue (p. 370). To this Staël opposed the idea of dedication ("dévouement"), and the natural virtues of generosity, goodness, tenderness, and frankness; or as Nelvil warmly defends Corinne to Lady Edgermond:

> "Vous confondez dans les règles vulgaires une personne douée comme aucune femme ne l'a jamais été; un ange d'esprit et de bonté; un génie admirable, et néanmoins un caractère sensible et timide; une imagination sublime, une générosité sans bornes, une personne qui peut avoir eu des torts, parce qu'une supériorité si étonnante ne s'accorde pas toujours avec la vie commune."
>
> (p. 459)

As in *Paul et Virginie,* where Virginie's French education violently disrupts the idyll, the scorn for natural virtues leads to death. But when we reflect on Germaine de Staël's life of talent and character, and on her many lovers, we can readily see that the link "opinion" might have established between "esprit" or "génie" and a lack of virtue might have been of some concern to her. The portrait of herself in **Corinne,** idealized in so many other ways, is above all idealistically "clean" and "moral"—in the "English" way, ironically. For such an idealism does Corinne die at Germaine de Staël's hands. And it is a troubling deconstructive undercurrent.

The deconstruction lies in a reading which attempts to reconcile the *exaggerated idealism* of the (feminist) interpretation with the referential reality from which the character is drawn. In this reading we must take into account an occulted subtext. I speak of the "fallen-woman" subtext. Corinne is most emphatically not a fallen woman. Yet in the highly charged chapters of Book 17, "Corinne en Écosse," in which she compares herself to the angelically pure Lucile, such a repressed plot suggests itself, if only by antithesis, to the reader's mind, in direct contradiction to the idealized portrait. Contemplating Lucile's innocent and pious face, Corinne reflects that the younger woman has before her "un avenir qui n'était troublé par aucun souvenir, par aucune vie passée dont il fallût répondre ni devant les autres, ni devant sa propre conscience" (p. 503). Such a reflection would not be in disagreement with the plot of the fallen but repentant woman. Corinne is definitely a Woman with a Past, even though we are told that she is virtuous, and has given only her heart. But the consequences for her are *as if* she had given all, so that the plot requires and depends on such a subtext. The "faute de la

FROM THE AUTHOR

DE STAËL ON JEAN JACQUES ROUSSEAU'S VIEW ON WOMEN'S LITERARY-TALENTS

I do reproach Rousseau on women's behalf with one wrong, however: of claiming in a note to the *Letter on Spectacles* [*Lettre a d'Alembert sur les spectacles* (*Letter to d'Alembert on the Theater*)] that women are incapable of painting passion with warmth and truth. Let him deny women, if he likes, the vain literary talents that make them struggle with men instead of being loved by them; let him refuse women the intellectual power, the profound capacity for attention with which great geniuses are endowed; women's feeble organs are opposed to this, and their hearts too often preoccupied, monopolizing their minds, so that they cannot concentrate on other meditations; but let Rousseau not accuse women of just being able to write coldly, and of being unable to portray even love. The soul alone is what distinguishes women: the soul gives women's minds some movement; the soul alone makes them find any charm in a destiny whose only events are feelings, whose only interests are affections; the soul makes them identify with the fate of their beloved, and arranges a happiness for them whose only source is the happiness of the things they love; finally, the soul takes the place of both education and experience for them, making them worthy of feeling what they are unable to judge. According to Rousseau, Sappho was the only woman capable of making love speak. Ah! women might blush to use the burning language that is the sign of insane delirium rather than deep passion, and still express what they feel: the sublime abandon, the melancholy sorrow, the overpowering feelings that make them live and die, would touch their readers' hearts more deeply than all the raptures born of the exalted imagination of poets.

De Staël, Germaine. Excerpt from "On the *Letter on Spectacles*." Reprinted in *An Extraordinary Women: Selected Writings of Germaine de Staël*. Translated with an introduction by Vivian Folkenflik New York: Columbia University Press, 1987.

femme" is an implied necessary precondition for this story, or at least a preexisting plot line on which the plot we do have establishes itself by occulting it. In this occulting of the source of the plot lies the romantic genius of the novel, the attraction of its ambiguous ending, and the mystery of its murderous intent.

Thus the heat with which Oswald defends Corinne to Lady Edgermond has an unnamed source, and indeed he speaks of her faults: "une personne qui peut avoir eu des torts, parcequ'une supériorité si étonnante ne s'accorde pas toujours avec la vie commune, mais qui possède une ame si belle, qu'elle est au-dessus de ses fautes, et qu'une seule de ses actions ou de ses paroles les efface toutes" (p. 459). Other "lovers" before Oswald—"un grand seigneur allemand" and "un prince italien" (p. 387)—are put neatly into place in Corinne's written recital of her past; they too arise from the subtext, though they appear to exist in the actual plot to *deny* any dishonor. But before Oswald knows her story, he does have moments of doubt, at least one of which is caused by Corinne's own allusions to "une vie sans tache." A line from an elegy by Properce (Cornélie says: "aucune tache n'a souillé ma vie depuis l'hymen jusqu'au bûcher") inspires in Corinne so passionate an envy that Oswald is overcome with a "soupçon pénible": "Corinne, s'écria-t-il, Corinne, votre ame délicate n'a-t-elle rien à se reprocher?" (pp. 131-32). Corinne's response is anything but unambiguous: "Et n'y a-t-il pas dans le coeur de l'homme une pitié divine pour les erreurs que le sentiment, ou du moins l'illusion du sentiment, aurait fait commettre!" (p. 132). And in her deathbed confession she will recognize that "mes fautes ont été celles des passions" (p. 585). The subtext suggests itself too in Corinne's lessons to Lucile, lessons that otherwise lend themselves readily to quite a smile of mockery, as Corinne unabashedly teaches Lucile to resemble the person Oswald had loved the most, Corinne herself! Here she likens the woman of charm to the woman who needs to "réparer des torts": "On a vu, dit Corinne à Lucile, des femmes aimées non seulement malgré leurs erreurs, mais à cause de ces erreurs mêmes" (p. 578).

But it is Corinne's trip to Naples with Oswald, and what happens there, that is the most revealing, and the most symbolically attentive to the subtext. Already highly charged with the implication of a public confession of a love affair, and a sacrifice Corinne risks of her honor, the descent to Naples is a kind of perilous journey to the id.

There the intense heat and Corinne's brilliance contribute to the first expressions of Oswald's sexual desire:

> Plusieurs fois il serra Corinne contre son coeur, plusieurs fois il s'éloigna, puis revint, puis s'éloigna de nouveau, pour respecter celle qui devait être la compagne de sa vie. Corinne ne pensait point aux dangers qui auraient pu l'alarmer, car telle était son estime pour Oswald, que, s'il lui avait demandé le don entier de son être, elle n'eût pas douté que cette prière ne fût le serment solennel de l'épouser; mais elle était bien aise qu'il triomphât de lui-même et l'honorât par ce sacrifice . . . Oswald était bien loin de ce calme: il se sentait embrasé par les charmes de Corinne. Une fois il embrassa ses genoux avec violence, et semblait avoir perdu tout empire sur sa passion . . .
>
> (pp. 288-89)

The metonymic sexual embrace takes place in this *elsewhere* that Naples represents, where Oswald gives his ring to Corinne, both indulge in self-exposure by telling the much-awaited stories of their pasts, presentiments of death occur, masked as obnubilated sexual desire (a cloud passes over the moon, and Corinne says "ce soir il condamnait notre amour"), and the whole emotional scenario is crowned by the powerful eruption of Vesuvius, producing more clouds in the sky and rivers of fire in the night.

The Naples episode explicitly rejects the sexual interpretation of the couple's passion, which it displaces to the symbolic level with the eruption of Vesuvius. The novel is in contradiction with itself, virtue and passion being made to coexist both in extreme degrees. It is a sort of *Lys dans la vallée* without Lady Dudley to deflect or absorb the sexual current—in this *Corinne* is a far more daring work than Balzac's novel. After Naples, and the ruins of Pompeii, the relation between Oswald and Corinne changes, and Corinne begins a long decline. The arrival in Venice is marked by bells ringing for a woman's entry into a convent, her death to the world, which proposes to Corinne's imagination a possible solution that she will nevertheless reject (pp. 421-22).

For clearly Corinne dies of "douleur," and her suffering is imposed on her by Nelvil. To Castel-Forte she says about Oswald: "C'est un homme qui m'a fait trop de mal. L'ennemi qui m'aurait jetée dans une prison, qui m'aurait bannie et proscrite, n'eût pas déchiré mon coeur à ce point" (565). Just as Oswald "killed" his father—"la douleur qui venait de moi avait déchiré son coeur" (p. 332)—so he kills his mistress: "elle désira que l'ingrat qui l'avait abandonnée sentît encore une fois que c'était à la femme de son temps qui savait le mieux aimer et penser qu'il avait donné

la mort" (p. 580). Nothing could be clearer: Corinne thinks Oswald has killed her. And a final letter from Corinne, the last words she addresses directly to Oswald, condemns him no less sternly and finally than Ellénore's last letter to Adolphe:

> qu'avez-vous fait de tant d'amour? qu'avez-vous fait de cette affection unique en ce monde? un malheur unique comme elle. Ne prétendez donc plus au bonheur; ne m'offensez pas en croyant l'obtenir encore.
>
> (p. 572)

Germaine de Staël plots to kill Corinne in order to propose her a martyr to feminine genius. No man may rise to the level of her pretensions. Oswald, or the amalgam of his various real models, was finally as great a disappointment as the "grand seigneur allemand" and the "prince italien"—promising, but lacking a just appreciation of female genius. In a chapter rejected from *De l'Allemagne*, Staël wrote:

> Je voulois faire ressortir les malheurs qu'entraînent de certaines qualités dans une femme et quel malheur pourroit-il y avoir pour une femme si elle étoit parfaitement aimée d'un homme digne d'elle?[5]

It is partly the function of the ending "dans le vague" to remind the reader that the moral of a work of imagination is in the impression left after the reading. In the end, the *moral* reason Germaine de Staël sacrifices Corinne might well depend on the fallen-woman subtext the narrative suggests by rejecting it. Had Corinne found a man worthy of her, she might not have died; but might the novel have left a moral impression if Corinne had not died? The narrative model of the plot with the death of the woman is parallel to an ideological tradition according to which the woman alone pays the price of disobeying social imperatives, and one may well claim that Corinne is sacrificed to this tradition. But much more important is the ideal truth for Germaine de Staël, or what I call the truth of the drive.

The "fallen-woman" subtext might also be named "seduced and abandoned." Germaine de Staël used her plot as a message to particular readers, to show what would happen to her if she were to become the abandoned woman: suffering, then death. She had already, as it were, fulfilled the first half of that plot; the second was a potential outcome. In this the plot serves more as a lightning rod than as a wish-fulfillment, like those dreams Freud analyzed whose function was to ward off dreaded events by dreaming their very realization. This subtext is one of the determinants of the fiction, never realized, but molding the plot:

Corinne is *not* seduced by Oswald, as the authorial voice has taken great pains to assure us, but she is abandoned. It is as if the plot has taken over the fiction, making Oswald so guilty that the seduction might just as well have happened. It is the plot that makes Corinne an idealized portrait of the seduced and seductive Germaine, and it is the plot that puts Oswald in the murderer's shoes, loading the guilt on his shoulders, then leaving his punishment in the interrogatory mode. According to this very weighty literary model, the heroine must either finish her days in a convent (a solution preferred by the eighteenth century) or finish her days right away (the modern preference). It is thus the fiction that kills the heroine, as the text speaks for itself and performs a plot that has its own end in death. Here the truth of the drive irresistibly takes over and rewrites plain truth, casting the reference to reality adrift in the space of what Doubrovsky calls autofiction, which is neither true nor false.[6]

The occulted plot of the fallen woman, the subtext, contributed to the end to which the plot of the novel came. Corinne is the victim of a murder at the hands of her creator because the author could not die of her suffering, as she so often claimed she would. Her text borrowed the plot of the subtext to make Oswald guilty of causing Corinne's death. This divergence from real life shows that the plot has a life of its own. The text executes for the author the plot the author does not execute in life; it turns this realism into an operable real, in spite of Barthes's assertion that *"le réel romanesque n'est pas opérable."*[7]

Notes

1. A different version of this text has appeared as part of a chapter on *Corinne* and *Adolphe* in my book *Plotting to Kill* (New York: Peter Lang, 1992).

2. Madelyn Gutwirth, *Madame de Staël, Novelist: The Emergence of the Artist as Woman* (Urbana, IL.: Univ. of Illinois Press, 1978), p. 232.

3. Simone Balayé, *Les carnets de voyage de Madame de Staël. Contribution à la genèse de ses œuvres* (Genève: Droz, 1971), p. 246.

4. Germaine de Staël, *Corinne ou l'Italie* (Paris: Gallimard, 1985), pp. 586-87. All further quotations are from this recent edition.

5. Quoted in Simone Balayé, "*Corinne* et les amis de Madame de Staël," *Revue d'Histoire Littéraire de la France*, 66 (1966), p. 148.

6. Serge Doubrovsky, "Autobiographie/Vérité/Psychanalyse," *L'Esprit Créateur*, 20, 3 (1980), p. 90.

7. Roland Barthes, *S/Z* (Paris: Seuil, 1970), p. 87.

FURTHER READING

Biographies

Andrews, Wayne. *Germaine: A Portrait of Madame de Staël.* New York: Atheneum, 1963, 237 p.

Conveys a modern view of the life of de Staël.

Besser, Gretchen Rous. *Germaine de Staël Revisited.* New York: Twayne Publishers, 1994, 180 p.

Offers an analysis of the life, works, and contributions of de Staël in light of new data and a changing feminist perspective.

Blennerhassett, Lady Charlotte. *Madame de Staël: Her Friends and Her Influence in Politics and Literature*, 3 vols., translated by J. E. Cumming. London: Chapman and Hall, 1889.

Provides a definitive biography of de Staël.

Criticism

Birkett, Jennifer. "Speech in Action: Language, Society, and Subject in Germaine de Staël's *Corinne.*" *Eighteenth-Century Fiction* 7, no. 4 (July 1995): 393-408.

Discusses the dynamics of subjective and collective narrative voice within the feminist text of Corinne.

Borowitz, Helen O. "The Unconfessed *Précieuse*: Madame de Staël's Debt to Mademoiselle Scudéry." *Nineteenth-Century French Studies* 11, nos. 1&2 (fall-winter 1982-83): 32-59.

Explores de Staël's use of de Scudery's literary self-portrait as a model for her fictional heroine Corinne.

Coleman, Patrick. "Exile and Narrative Voice in *Corinne.*" *Studies in Eighteenth-Century Culture* 24 (1995): 91-105.

Contends that the influential narrative voice of Corinne *is traceable to de Staël's own experience with exile and other political expressions.*

DeJean, Joan. "Staël's *Corinne*: The Novel's Other Dilemma." *Stanford French Review* (spring 1987): 77-88.

Examines de Staël's adoption of the patriarchal third-person perspective and rejection of the first person, conversational form in Corinne.

Deneys-Tunney, Anne. "*Corinne* by Madame de Staël: The Utopia of Feminine Voice as Music within the Novel." *Dalhousie French Studies* 28 (fall 1994): 55-63.

Discusses the crisis of the feminine voice portrayed in Corinne.

Goldsmith, Margaret. *Madame De Staël: Portrait of a Liberal in the Revolutionary Age.* London: Longmans, Green, 1938, 276 p.

Analyzes de Staël's political concepts.

Gutwirth, Madelyn. *Madame De Staël, Novelist: The Emergence of the Artist As Woman.* Urbana, Ill.: University of Illinois Press, 1978, 324 p.

Detailed critical study of de Staël, beginning with a presentation of woman's place in the eighteenth century and which includes in-depth biographical information and analyses of the author's best-known novels.

——. "Forging a Vocation: Germaine de Staël on Fiction, Power, and Passion." *Bulletin of Research in the Humanities* 86, no. 3 (1983-1985): 242-54.

Analyzes de Staël's views on love, passion, and ambition as expressed in De l'influence des passions.

Heller, Deborah. "Tragedy, Sisterhood, and Revenge in *Corinne*." *Papers on Language & Literature* 26, no. 2 (spring 1990): 212-32.

Evaluates the impact of de Staël's feminist narrative in Corinne *on twentieth-century readers.*

Hogsett, Charlotte. "History and Story." In *The Literary Existence of Germaine de Staël*, pp. 71-93. Carbondale, Ill.: Southern Illinois University Press, 1987.

Examines de Staël's attempts to insert feminine ways of narration into a masculine-oriented history and literature in A Treatise on Ancient and Modern Literature *and* Delphine.

Isbell, John. "The Painful Birth of the Romantic Heroine: Staël as Political Animal, 1786-1818." *Romanic Review* 87, no. 1 (January 1996): 59-66.

Argues that de Staël chose to produce literary art in response to her exclusion from politics as a woman.

Massardier-Kenney, Francoise. "Staël, Translation, and Race." In *Translating Slavery: Gender and Race in French Women's Writing*, edited by Doris Y. Kadish and Francoise Massardier-Kenney, pp. 135-45. Kent, Ohio: Kent State University Press, 1994.

Investigates de Staël's critique of cultural values in her work, particularly the antislavery sentiment of Mirza.

Moi, Toril. "A Woman's Desire to Be Known: Expressivity and Silence in *Corinne*." *Bucknell Review* 45, no. 2 (2002): 143-75.

Explores the obsessive concern with Corinne's expressivity and the protagonist's silence in book 17 of the novel, noting the author's concern with the aesthetics of theatricality and absorption.

Peel, Ellen. "Contradictions of Form and Feminism in *Corinne ou L'Italie*." *Essays in Literature* 14, no. 2 (fall 1987): 281-98.

Analyzes patterns and oppositions in the feminism of Corinne.

Schor, Naomi. "*Corinne*: The Third Woman." *L'Esprit Createur* 34, no. 3 (fall 1994): 99-106.

Examines the relationship between death and femininity in Corinne.

Swallow, Noreen J. "Portraits: A Feminist Appraisal of Mme de Staël's *Delphine*." *Atlantis* 7, no. 1 (fall 1981): 65-76.

Assesses Delphine *as it depicts the oppressive effects of patriarchal hegemony.*

Vallois, Marie-Claire. "Voice as Fossil, Madame de Staël's *Corinne or Italy*: An Archaeology of Feminist Discourse." *Tulsa Studies in Women's Literature* 6, no. 1 (spring 1987): 47-60.

Interprets de Staël's use of passive and impersonal modes of narration in Corinne.

Winegarten, Renee. "An Early Dissident: Madame de Staël." *The New Criterion* 16, no. 9 (May 1998): 17-22.

Probes the results of de Staël's exile from France during the Napoleonic regime.

OTHER SOURCES FROM GALE:

Additional coverage of Staël's life and career is contained in the following sources published by the Gale Group: *Dictionary of Literary Biography*, Vols. 119, 192; *Feminist Writers*; *Guide to French Literature 1789 to the Present*; *Literature Resource Center*; *Nineteenth-Century Literature Criticism*, Vols. 3, 91; and *Twayne's World Authors*.

ELIZABETH CADY STANTON

(1815 - 1902)

(Born Elizabeth Cady) American nonfiction writer and editor.

Stanton was one of the leaders of the women's suffrage movement in the United States during the nineteenth century. More radical in her views than her close friend Susan B. Anthony, Stanton advocated a wide range of feminist reforms in law, society, and religion. Stanton promoted her ideas in both writing and by touring as a public speaker. Many of her speeches and other works were produced in collaboration with Anthony and other suffragists. Her most famous speech, "Solitude of Self" (1892), which details the necessity of women's rights, is regarded as a work of exceptional rhetorical and ideological power. Since the late twentieth century, feminist critics have been especially interested in Stanton's autobiography, *Eighty Years and More* (1898), because of the insights it provides into the author's views on the female self and body as well her political beliefs.

BIOGRAPHICAL INFORMATION

Born November 12, 1815 in Johnston, New York, the daughter of a politician and jurist Daniel Cady, Stanton developed an early interest in liberal causes, such as abolishing slavery and promoting women's civil rights. She allegedly pledged her life to study in 1826 when, after her brother's untimely death, her father remarked "Oh, my daughter, would that you were a boy!" Stanton received a privileged education, attending Johnstown Academy, where she studied Latin, Greek, and mathematics. During this time, she also frequented her father's law office, which adjoined the house, and gained first-hand knowledge of women who were affected by unfair laws. In 1830, Stanton enrolled in Troy's Female Seminary, where she furthered her study in physiology, geography, higher mathematics, Greek, Latin, French, music, and elocution. In 1840 she married antislavery activist Henry Brewster Stanton; she combined her duties as a housewife and mother of seven with increasing involvement as a writer, public speaker, and political organizer on behalf of women's suffrage. Stanton co-organized the First Woman's Rights Convention held in 1848. The convention took place in Seneca Falls and resulted in several resolutions concerning rights to property and children. In 1851 she met Susan B. Anthony, who became her lifelong partner in working toward voting rights for women. From 1868 to 1870 Stanton edited the *Revolution,* an influential pro-suffrage newspaper she cofounded with Anthony. She also contributed letters and articles to many other periodicals and went on cross-country lecturing tours to promote her feminist ideas. During the early 1880s Stanton, Anthony, and Matilda Joslyn Gage edited the first three volumes of *History of Woman Suffrage* (1881-86), which compiled the documents and letters of the suffrage movement for the years 1848-1885. After her husband's death in 1887 Stanton moved to New York City, where she served as president of the American Woman Suffrage Association for two years and later published two controversial books, *The Woman's Bible* (1895-98) and *Eighty Years and More (1815-1897): Reminiscences of Elizabeth Cady Stanton*. Stanton died October 26, 1902.

MAJOR WORKS

Stanton often collaborated with others, usually Anthony, when producing her books, articles, and speeches. When working together, Anthony reportedly contributed facts and ideas, while Stanton, who had stronger rhetorical skills, did most of the actual writing. Indeed, commentators often credit Stanton as the author of the speeches she delivered, noting that her ideas about feminist reform tended to be more wide-ranging and controversial than those of Anthony and her other associates. Her best-known speech, "Solitude of Self," reflects a highly personal philosophical vision, arguing for women's freedom on the grounds that all human beings live and die alone, and so must be responsible for themselves. Although she invited others to contribute to her *Woman's Bible,* a highly controversial assemblage of feminist revisionist commentaries on biblical passages dealing with women, she edited the work and composed most of it herself. Critics note that Stanton was adept at shaping her own public image as well as expressing her political views. Her autobiography, *Eighty Years and More,* offers an upbeat portrayal of her career, emphasizing her well-rounded life as both a family woman and political activist.

CRITICAL RECEPTION

Stanton's success as a writer and orator was necessarily tied to the political nature of her work. Although she was one of the most famous and influential leaders of the American suffrage movement, her revolutionary ideas often set her at odds with fellow activists as well as more conservative opponents. For instance, the National American Woman Suffrage Association, which she founded, turned against her by passing a resolution disassociating itself from *The Woman's Bible.* As her immediate influence waned and she retired from public life, emphasis was placed more on her importance as a historical figure than on the merits of her writings. The resurgence of feminist criticism in the late twentieth century stimulated new scholarly interest in both Stanton's political ideas and her literary works. Critics have paid particular attention to the representation of her as an "ordinary" woman and reformer in her autobiography, her notions of selfhood, her religious ideas, her sometimes troubled relationship with other feminists and abolitionists, the rhetorical strategies she uses in her speeches, and her ideas about the female body.

PRINCIPAL WORKS

History of Woman Suffrage 3 vols. [editor and contributor, with Susan B. Anthony and Matilda Joslyn Gage] (prose) 1881-86

The Woman's Bible 2 vols. [editor, contributor] (prose) 1895-98

Eighty Years and More (1815-1897): Reminiscences of Elizabeth Cady Stanton 2 vols. (autobiography) 1898

Elizabeth Cady Stanton as Revealed in Her Letters, Diary and Reminiscences 2 vols. (prose) 1922

Elizabeth Cady Stanton/Susan B. Anthony: Correspondence, Writings, Speeches (prose) 1981

PRIMARY SOURCES

ELIZABETH CADY STANTON (SPEECH DATE 19 JANUARY 1848)

SOURCE: Stanton, Elizabeth Cady. "Address: First Women's Rights Convention." In *Elizabeth Cady Stanton Unpublished Manuscript Collection.* Washington, D.C.: Library of Congress, 1848.

In the following essay, originally delivered as a speech before the first women's rights convention in Seneca Falls on July 19, 1848, Stanton demands freedom and political representation of women. Stanton calls women to the task of fighting for equality and to protest unjust laws.

We have met here today to discuss our rights and wrongs, civil and political, and not, as some have supposed, to go into the detail of social life alone. We do not propose to petition the legislature to make our husbands just, generous, and courteous, to seat every man at the head of a cradle, and to clothe every woman in male attire. None of these points, however important they may be considered by leading men, will be touched in this convention. As to their costume, the gentlemen need feel no fear of our imitating that, for we think it in violation of every principle of taste, beauty, and dignity; notwithstanding all the contempt cast upon our loose, flowing garments, we still admire the graceful folds, and consider our costume far more artistic than theirs. Many of the nobler sex seem to agree with us in this opinion, for the bishops, priests, judges, barristers, and lord mayors of the first nation on the globe, and the Pope of Rome, with his cardinals, too, all wear the loose flowing robes, thus tacitly acknowledging that the male attire is neither dignified nor imposing. No, we shall not molest you in your philosophical experiments with stocks, pants, high-heeled boots, and Russian belts. Yours be the glory to discover, by personal experience, how long the kneepan can resist the terrible strapping down which you impose, in how short time the well-developed muscles of the throat can be reduced to mere threads by the constant pressure of the stock, how high the heel of a boot must be to make a short man tall, and how tight the Russian belt may be drawn and yet have wind enough left to sustain life.

But we are assembled to protest against a form of government existing without the consent of the governed—to declare our right to be free as man is free, to be represented in the government which we are taxed to support, to have such disgraceful laws as give man the power to chastise and imprison his wife, to take the wages which she earns, the property which she inherits, and, in case of separation, the children of her love; laws which make her the mere dependent on his bounty. It is to protest against such unjust laws as these that we are assembled today, and to have them, if possible, forever erased from our statute books, deeming them a shame and a disgrace to a Christian republic in the nineteenth century. We have met to uplift woman's fallen divinity upon an even pedestal with man's.

And, strange as it may seem to many, we now demand our right to vote according to the declaration of the government under which we live. This right no one pretends to deny. We need not prove ourselves equal to Daniel Webster to enjoy this privilege, for the ignorant Irishman in the ditch has all the civil rights he has. We need not prove our muscular power equal to this same Irishman to enjoy this privilege, for the most tiny, weak, ill-shaped stripling of twenty-one has all the civil rights of the Irishman. We have no objection to discuss the question of equality, for we feel that the weight of argument lies wholly with us, but we wish the question of equality kept distinct from the question of rights, for the proof of the one does not determine the truth of the other. All white men in this country have the same rights, however they may differ in mind, body, or estate.

The right is ours. The question now is: how shall we get possession of what rightfully belongs to us? We should not feel so sorely grieved if no man who had not attained the full stature of a Webster, Clay, Van Buren, or Gerrit Smith could claim the right of the elective franchise. But to have drunkards, idiots, horse-racing, rum-selling rowdies, ignorant foreigners, and silly boys fully recognized, while we ourselves are thrust out from all the rights that belong to citizens, it is too grossly insulting to the dignity of woman to be longer quietly submitted to. The right is ours. Have it, we must. Use it, we will. The pens, the tongues, the fortunes, the indomitable wills of many women are already pledged to secure this right. The great truth that no just government can be formed without the consent of the governed we shall echo and re-echo in the ears of the unjust judge, until by continual coming we shall weary him

There seems now to be a kind of moral stagnation in our midst. Philanthropists have done their utmost to rouse the nation to a sense of its sins. War, slavery, drunkenness, licentiousness, gluttony, have been dragged naked before the people, and all their abominations and deformities fully brought to light, yet with idiotic laugh we hug those monsters to our breasts and rush on to destruction. Our churches are multiplying on all sides, our missionary societies, Sunday schools, and prayer meetings and innumerable charitable and reform organizations are all in operation, but still the tide of vice is swelling, and threatens the destruction of everything, and the battlements of righteousness are weak against the raging elements of sin and death. Verily, the world waits the coming of some new element, some purifying power, some spirit of mercy and love. The voice of woman has been silenced in the state, the church, and the home, but man cannot fulfill his destiny alone, he cannot redeem his race unaided. There are deep and tender chords of sympathy and love in the hearts of the downfallen and oppressed that woman can touch more skillfully than man.

The world has never yet seen a truly great and virtuous nation, because in the degradation of woman the very fountains of life are poisoned at their source. It is vain to look for silver and gold from mines of copper and lead. It is the wise mother that has the wise son. So long as your women are slaves you may throw your colleges and churches to the winds. You can't have scholars and saints so long as your mothers are ground to powder between the upper and nether millstone of tyranny and lust. How seldom, now, is a father's pride gratified, his fond hopes realized, in the budding genius of his son! The wife is degraded, made the mere creature of caprice, and the foolish son is heaviness to his heart. Truly are the sins of the fathers visited upon the children to the third and fourth generation. God, in His wisdom, has so linked the whole human family together that any violence done at one end of the chain is felt throughout its length, and here, too, is the law of restoration, as in woman all have fallen, so in her elevation shall the race be recreated.

"Voices" were the visitors and advisers of Joan of Arc. Do not "voices" come to us daily from the haunts of poverty, sorrow, degradation, and despair, already too long unheeded. Now is the time for the women of this country, if they would save our free institutions, to defend the right, to buckle on the armor that can best resist the keenest weapons of the enemy—contempt and ridicule. The same religious enthusiasm that nerved Joan of Arc to her work nerves us to ours. In every generation God calls some men and women for the utterance of truth, a heroic action, and our work today is the fulfilling of what has long since been foretold by the Prophet—Joel 2:28: "And it shall come to pass afterward, that I will pour out my spirit upon all flesh; and your sons and your daughters shall prophesy." We do not expect our path will be strewn with the flowers of popular applause, but over the thorns of bigotry and prejudice will be our way, and on our banners will beat the dark storm clouds of opposition from those who have entrenched themselves behind the stormy bulwarks of custom and authority, and who have fortified their position by every means, holy and unholy. But we will steadfastly abide the result. Unmoved we will bear it aloft. Undauntedly we will unfurl it to the gale, for we know that the storm cannot rend from it a shred, that the electric flash will but more clearly show to us the glorious words inscribed upon it, "Equality of Rights."

ELIZABETH CADY STANTON (SPEECH DATE LATE 1870S)

SOURCE: Stanton, Elizabeth Cady. "Dare to Question." In *Elizabeth Cady Stanton Unpublished Manuscript Collection.* Washington, D.C.: Library of Congress, n.d.

In the following essay, originally delivered as a speech before the Liberal League, Stanton challenges those who would prevent others from questioning popular theology. The speech was transcribed from the author's handwritten notes.

Though we have passed beyond the Inquisition, the stake, the rack and the thumb screw, yet those who dare publicly question the popular theology, are as effectually persecuted to day, as ever. Though in different ways, from the coarse, brutal modes of the past, we have more refined methods of torturing the spirit rather than the flesh. Go into any community, and if there is a person or family who does not belong to some one of the leading sects, who expresses doubts as to the truth of any of the dogmas, traditions, and superstitions of the popular theology and you will invariably find such a person or family, ignored, ostracized, slandered, unless by great wealth, and genius they conquer by power, the positions denied them by right.

Hence Liberal Leagues are needed to make all forms of religion, all shades of thought equally respectable. We occasionally hear, even in our country at this late day, of physical inflictions for opinion's sake, as the recent case in Texas proves. It was stated in the leading Journals that a respectable physician who was supposed to entertain liberal theological opinions, was taken from his home, severely beaten, tarred and feathered:—the assailants declaring that all infidels in that state should be similarly dressed and treated.

When Col. Robert Ingersoll lectured in the chief cities of New York last winter, the press, the pulpit at once put him in the pillory of abuse and denunciation. Bishop Doane of Albany wrote a protest against him as a dangerous man unfit to be heard! and tried to secure the signatures of all the leading clergy. None declined. The people crowded to hear him, were enchained with his eloquence and in spite of Bishop Doane's protest [Ingersoll] was invited there a second time. The clergy throughout the state attacked him fiercely, and treated him with as much arrogance as if the constitution of the United States had not said in its first amendment, "Congress shall make no law respecting an establishment of religion; or prohibiting the free exercise thereof, or abridging the freedom of speech." The question naturally arises, shall the clergy in this land be permitted to do by clamor, what Congress is forbidden to do by law? It may be a small matter to denounce one man in every pulpit from Maine to Texas, but if the principle of free speech and free thought be questioned and religious persecution tolerated, we have rung the death knell of American liberties. We cannot watch with too jealous an eye the slightest aggression on individual rights by the church, remembering that the moral wrongs, oppressions and persecutions inflicted on humanity through the centuries have all been in the name of religion. . . .

The preference is invariably given to those who sustain the popular faith. With all his resources in himself, he [the freethinker] is often made to feel painfully conscious of his isolation from human sympathy. One of the most touching chapters in the Autobiography of Theodore Parker is that in which he describes his sense of loneliness. While conscious of his own unflinching integrity to principle, his lofty aspirations for all that is good, true in a noble mankind, his devotion to the best interests of humanity, he was traduced and shunned; almost to the end of his life, beyond human sympathy. Many who read his great thoughts now, would not have dared to listen to the living voice that first uttered them.

I recently met a young woman just ordained in the Universalist Church and installed over a congregation. She is as grand a type of womankind as I ever met. Well developed in body and mind, beautiful to look upon, a charming companion, and effective preacher, a woman whose influence in any community must be most desirable. In expressing for her the enthusiasm I felt to the wife of a clergyman, a very inferior type of womanhood, narrow, bigoted, morose, ah! she replied, "Miss K. is a very dangerous woman. She does not believe in the personality of the Devil, in hell and eternal punishment. She is a Universalist, and my one regret is that she is so ladylike, so charming, so unexceptional in thought, word and deed; for that only makes her the more dangerous." And thus everywhere we find character, influence, development, all made secondary to belief in unimportant dogmas. A mere speculative faith of what lies beyond our earthly horizon of which no mortal can possibly know anything, is made primal to all the great facts of existence which we do know, and for the right use of which we are responsible. When we sum up all that the generations have lost in development, and suffered through fear of the power of the Devil, and the torments of Hell, we feel that the Canons of Westminster have been far too slow in rolling back the huge iron gates of the bottomless pit, and letting the oppressed go free. Seeing that with all their learning they have been so lamentably tardy in lifting humanity out of such gloomy depths, it would be well for us now one and all to begin to do our own thinking, and not to blindly henceforward trust to the leadership of those no wiser than ourselves.

A new thought in morals and religion is as important as in art, science, discovery and invention, and instead of persecuting those who utter it, we should encourage the expression of individual opinion, resting in the faith that truth is more powerful than error and must conquer at last. In estimating the character of the noble men and women identified with the Liberal movement compared with their assailants, I am forcibly reminded of the morality and religion of the Fejee Islands. The United States Exploring Expedition in their reports of uncivilized nations compare the Samoans and Fejians. While the Samoans have no religion, no Gods, no rites, they are kind, good humored, desirous of pleasing and very hospitable. Both sexes show great regard and love for their children, and age is much respected. The men cannot bear to be called stingy, and disobliging. The women are remarkably domestic, and virtuous. Infanticide after birth is unknown.

Their cannibal neighbors the Fejians are indifferent to human life; they live in constant dread of each other: shedding blood is no crime but a glory, they kill the decrepit, maimed and sick, and treachery is an accomplishment. Infanticide covers one half the births and the first lesson taught the child is to strike its mother. A chief's wives, courtiers, and aides-de-camp are strangled at his death. Cannibalism is rampant. They sometimes roast their victims alive. When Gods have like characters, they live on the souls of those devoured by men and yet these Fejians look with horror at the Samoans, because they have no Gods, no rites, no religion. What better are we who measure men by their creeds rather than character? . . .

I am often asked what do those Liberals mean by a complete secularization of the government? Surely we have no established church in this country. We have not in theory:—but we have practically, so long as all church property is exempt from taxation, so long as the Protestant Bible is read in our schools, and the state enforces by law the observance of the Holy days of any one religion in preference to all others. If the Seventh-day Baptists and the Jews prefer to observe Saturday as holy time they should not be forbidden to work on Sunday and the masses compelled to toil six days should be protected in all rational amusements on the seventh. Yet in more of our towns and cities there is no provision whatever for the amusement and instruction of the masses.

We must guard with vigilance all approaches at union of church and state . . . Though we see its [theocracy's] crippling power in France, and

Italy, the enemy of science, and liberal ideas in both politics and religion, yet we imagine we have no danger to apprehend from that quarter, forgetting that even in our republic the clergy are a privileged order, and all church property exempt from taxation.

. . . But mothers give their sons no lessons on these great questions because they are not yet awake to their importance themselves. And yet the position of woman is the great factor in civilization to day. During the discussion on Catholicism a few years ago in England Gladstone said in one of his pamphlets that most ready converts to this religion as might be expected are women, through them the men are made victims of priestcraft and superstition. A recent writer on Turkish civilization says the great block to all progress in that nation is the condition of the women, and their improvement is hopeless, because they are taught by their religion that their position is ordained of heaven. Thus has the religious nature of woman been played upon in all ages and under all forms of religion for her own complete subjugation, and our religion in the republic of America is no exception. See how many Liberal clergymen we have seen in the last two years brought before Synods and General Assemblies, tried and condemned for preaching the doctrine of woman's equality and admitting women to their pulpits. Our scriptures, and our religion as taught by the majority of our ordained leaders, assign woman the same subject position as under all other forms, and it is through the perversion of her religious element that she is held in that condition.

As the son always reaps the disadvantages suffered by the mother, we need not wonder that the man who dares to think, reason, investigate, and protest against the traditions, and superstitions of our popular religion is considered the marvel of this day and generation. How many men have we who dare to stand up in Congress, or the state legislature, and talk on the real interests of the people, to tell what he knows to be the absolute truth in any subject? We shall never have brave men until we first have free women. . . .

Let the rising generation of young men learn that justice, freedom and equality are principles of which it is safe to build alike the state, the church, and the home, and that it is impossible for them to ever realize a full, complete, noble mankind, until their mothers, wives and sisters are recognized as equal factors in the progress of civilization.

GENERAL COMMENTARY

SIDONIE SMITH (ESSAY DATE 1992)

SOURCE: Smith, Sidonie. "Resisting the Gaze of Embodiment: Women's Autobiography in the Nineteenth Century." In *American Women's Autobiography: Fea(s)ts of Memory,* edited by Margo Culley, pp. 75-110. Madison: University of Wisconsin Press, 1992.

In the following excerpt, Smith explores Stanton's expression of her selfhood in her autobiography.

Elizabeth Cady Stanton announces in the preface to *Eighty Years and More, 1815-1897* that the story of her life is actually split, doubly inscribed: "The story of my private life as the wife of an earnest reformer, as an enthusiastic housekeeper, proud of my skill in every department of domestic economy, and as the mother of seven children, may amuse and benefit the reader. The incidents of my public career as a leader in the most momentous reform yet launched upon the world—the emancipation of woman—will be found in *The History of Woman Suffrage*" (v). Textually splitting both story and "selfhood" into the dual spheres of private ("feminine") and public ("masculine") activity, Stanton gestures to the "commonplaces"[1] of female identity in the nineteenth century. She apparently positions the public achievements of "metaphysical selfhood" in an elsewhere distant from her autobiographical project, thereby banishing to the margins of her "woman's" text the story of agency and autonomy. In that textual elsewhere she claims her place as a "leader" in "the most momentous reform yet launched upon the world," no small claim to notoriety. Yet even there, in that elsewhere, public achievement is displaced into "self"-less history as her centrifugal role disperses into a "communal" rather than "personal" story of the suffrage movement. Refusing to make "unwomanly" or monstrous claims to publicity, Stanton signals at the gateway to her narrative her resistance to self-promotion. Even her purposes in writing are conventionally "feminine" ones: she writes self-sacrificially for the amusement and the edification of her reader.

Stanton at first appears to embrace the cultural figuration of "woman" by positioning herself squarely inside the enclosure of domestic space, the territory of "embodied selfhood." As she traces her childhood, youth, courtship, and marriage through the opening chapters of the text, she attends to the teleological pattern of "embodied selfhood," those defining moments of the female life cycle. Moreover, she wraps the commonplaces of "woman's" story of courtship in the language and figures of sentimental fiction: "When walking slowly through a beautiful grove, he laid his hand on the horn of the saddle and, to my surprise, made one of those charming revelations of human feeling which brave knights have always found eloquent words to utter, and to which fair ladies have always listened with mingled emotions of pleasure and astonishment" (60). Representing herself as the desirable and decorous heroine of "romance," Stanton invokes the idealized script of young "womanhood." Once past this point in the text she appears to fulfill her opening promise to focus on her life as wife, mother, and housekeeper, invoking the idealized script of nurturant self-sacrifice. Sometimes she invests commentary about motherhood in similarly sentimental garb. Talking of young women whose singing is much remarked she announces: "One has since married, and is now pouring out her richest melodies in the opera of lullaby in her own nursery" (414). More often in talking about motherhood she assumes the posture of the experienced grandmother, practical, authoritative, aggressive in her concern for the welfare of children. In the discourse of housewifery, the older woman offers advice on such domestic concerns as healthy ventilation, stoves, childrearing practices.

However, the representation of Stanton the wife and mother is disturbed and destabilized throughout the text in a variety of ways.[2] The narrative of "embodied selfhood" ends fairly early when the roles have been fulfilled, when the courtship and romance culminate in marriage and childbearing. Henry Stanton appears in the early pages and then disappears almost entirely once he has married her and fathered her first children. Stanton erases him so effectively that the reader is not really clear whether he has died when she concludes her narrative. Nor do her children assume much prominence in the text. They are noted when she talks about the early trials of marriage and housekeeping, but then they too disappear until the end when they reappear, woven in and out of the text, given as much narrative space as the hundreds of other friends she visits.

Nonetheless the shadow existence of both husband and children in the text serves the function of legitimizing Stanton's "excessive" narrative. Since her cultural authority and readability depend upon her fulfillment of that generic contract whereby she presents herself as a "woman," husband and children establish her identity and credibility as a narrating woman. No virgin spinster (like Susan B. Anthony) Stanton assures her reader that female "embodiment" has

FROM THE AUTHOR

STANTON ON THE RESPONSIBILITY FOR THE SELF

I remember once, in crossing the Atlantic, to have gone upon the deck of the ship at midnight, when a dense black cloud enveloped the sky, and the great deep was roaring madly under the lashes of demoniac winds. My feelings was not of danger or fear (which is a base surrender of the immortal soul), but of utter desolation and loneliness; a little speck of life shut in by a tremendous darkness. Again I remember to have climbed the slopes of the Swiss Alps, up beyond the point where vegetation ceases, and the stunted conifers no longer struggle against the unfeeling blasts. Around me lay a huge confusion of rocks, out of which the gigantic ice peaks shot into the measureless blue of the heavens, and again my only feeling was the awful solitude.

And yet, there is a solitude, which each and every one of us has always carried with him, more inaccessible than the ice-cold mountains, more profound than the midnight sea; the solitude of self. Our inner being, which we call ourself, no eye nor touch of man or angel has ever pierced. It is more hidden than the caves of the gnome; the sacred adytum of the oracle; the hidden chamber of eleusinian mystery, for to it only omniscience is permitted to enter.

Such is individual life. Who, I ask you, can take, dare take, on himself the rights, the duties, the responsibilities of another human soul?

Stanton, Elizabeth Cady. An excerpt from "Solitude of Self." Delivered before the Committee of the Judicary of the United States Congress, January 18, 1892.

operated in culturally respectable and expected ways. All parts having assumed their proper places, her body has fulfilled its destiny. Having positioned herself toward the body in this way, Stanton achieves at least two effects. She diffuses the lurking threat of the monstrous female body, which always threatens to return from the margins of "woman's" text to disrupt the processes and practices of patriarchal culture. Second, she provides herself with a strategic counter: she can use brief, fleeting references to husband and children to reinforce her legitimacy again and again in a text that quickly begins to contest the institution of marriage itself.

For the preface and sentimental posturings notwithstanding, the thrust of Stanton's narrative contests the sanctity of marriage and even the motherhood Stanton would promote. To the roles of wife and mother and their attendant responsibilities she traces her profound dissatisfaction with the fate of "woman" and the constraints of female embodiment. Her domestic life in Seneca Falls she presents as drudgery, isolating, hard, dulling. Parenting she constantly assesses as constricting, brutalizing. Describing her experience as a young mother she writes:

> I now fully understood the practical difficulties most women had to contend with in the isolated household, and the impossibility of woman's best development if in contact, the chief part of her life, with servants and children. . . . The general discontent I felt with woman's portion as wife, mother, housekeeper, physician, and spiritual guide, the chaotic conditions into which everything fell without her constant supervision, and the wearied, anxious look of the majority of women impressed me with a strong feeling that some active measures should be taken to remedy the wrongs of society in general, and of women in particular.
>
> (147-48)

Throughout her text she interjects commentary on the pettiness, tyranny, and brutality of men and their victimization of women, emotional, physical, political, economic.

Moreover, Stanton locates mutual understanding and comradeship in her relationship with Susan B. Anthony (and with women generally) rather than in her relationship to men, whether husband or father. Pointedly she does not dedicate her narrative to either husband or children but to Anthony, "my steadfast friend for half a century." Textually, Anthony takes the place of the marriage partner, displacing Henry Stanton as source of inspiration. In offering a brief biography of Anthony, Stanton draws upon a rhetoric that celebrates the complementarity traditionally identified with the marriage partner:

> So entirely one are we that, in all our associations, ever side by side on the same platform, not one feeling of envy or jealousy has ever shadowed our lives. . . . To the world we always seem to agree

and uniformly reflect each other. Like husband and wife, each has the feeling that we must have no differences in public. . . . So closely interwoven have been our lives, our purposes, and experiences that, separated, we have a feeling of incompleteness—united, such strength of self-assertion that no ordinary obstacles, difficulties, or dangers ever appear to us insurmountable.

> (166, 184)

Stanton spends considerable narrative time weaving Anthony's presence into the text, testifying to the priority of female friendship over wifehood and motherhood.

And whatever lip service she might give to the centrality of the "home" for women, the text constantly displays a kind of homelessness, albeit a wealthy homelessness, not one of poverty but one of constant travel. Stanton describes her travels across the West, back and forth to Europe, from one home to another, one friend to another, one public speaking engagement to another. In her mobile existence even the home to which she returns constantly shifts from place to place.

For a narrative which purports to be about the stable roles of wife, mother, housekeeper, this one incessantly frays, breaks apart, goes off in pursuit of another kind of "selfhood" as Stanton seeks to escape the confinement of "embodied selfhood," to escape enclosure in "woman's place," to escape encoding in "woman's" life script, that narrative marginal to the contractual expectations of autobiography. Thus, Stanton pursues another story, albeit one that is sketchy, not prominently linear but suggestively so. Through the barest shell of an alternative teleology, she locates the originary moments of her developmental "selfhood." First she recalls her experience at the death of her brother when her father refuses to acknowledge her as the substitute son she would be. Then she describes her experience in her father's law office listening to the wives, mothers, and widows who find themselves powerless economically. From there she proceeds to track her involvement in first the abolitionist and then the suffrage movements with their various and complex stages of development.

Charting the course of her education and public involvement, Stanton reifies the liberal humanism and individualism that served as cornerstones of the ideology of "metaphysical selfhood" in the nineteenth century. Effectively, she figures herself as a kind of "unembodied" and "self-made man," fiercely rational, intellectually keen, independent, agentive, mobile, outspoken, tenacious, combative. Again and again she describes her engagements with men, in the process claiming her place alongside them, even claiming a superiority of position. For instance, she confidently denounces the advice of the doctors attending her after her first delivery and describes how ineffective they were, how she assumed their place, determining her own solution to the problem of the baby's health. Recalling how she sparred with various clergy, she dismisses them as reactionary conservatives, arguing her own position on the Bible and on biblical interpretation. Toward the conclusion of the text she discusses her very rewriting of the Bible itself as *The Woman's Bible.*

Textually, Stanton enacts her pledge to her father—"I will try to be all my brother was" (21)—by assuming the position of "son," figuring herself as pseudo-lawyer, reformer, politician, interpreter. In what she claims to be a personal and domestic narrative, Stanton stakes her claim to an empowered "metaphysical selfhood" for herself and for women generally. Resisting the position of "woman" which allows her only a vague "influence," she emphasizes in the text her exercise of "direct power": "A direct power over one's own person and property, an individual opinion to be counted, on all questions of public interest, are better than indirect influence, be that ever so far reaching" (376). Stanton travels from the territory of the margins, travels from the shadow of influence, to the territory of direct action, analysis, and speech. Thus, she appropriates for herself the fiction of "man," reproducing the culturally valued story of "metaphysical selfhood" with its powers of self-reflectiveness and self-fabrication and its preoccupation with quest. In this way Stanton "unsexes" herself, uncouples her "selfhood" from embodiment. In this way she legitimates her desire (and the desire of women in the suffrage movement) to achieve equal political rights with men, to achieve the status of "voter" alongside men.

But lest, in her ventriloquization of "man," she become a *lusus naturae*, a truly powerful but truly monstrous "woman," Stanton heeds the cultural injunction against unremitting self-assertion in "woman." Rhetorically she tries to maintain a posture of "feminine" self-effacement. For instance, she mutes the agency inherent in her decision to engage in political activism in response to her experience of motherhood by the claim of external determinacy: "My experience at the World's Anti-slavery Convention, all I had read of the legal status of women, and the oppression I saw everywhere, together swept across my soul, intensified now by many personal experi-ences. It seemed as if *all the elements had conspired to impel me* to some onward step" (148; emphasis mine). Manifesting resistance to the appearance of aggressive self-assertion, she invests the story of her purposeful life quest with the conventions of the "romance of the calling." In doing so she displays what Carolyn G. Heilbrun, in discussing the autobiographies of public women of the late nineteenth century in America, suggests is the etiology of bourgeois woman's activity: "The only script for women's life insisted that work discover and pursue them, like the conventional romantic lover" (17).[3] She also emphasizes, throughout the descriptions of her various journeys to promote the suffrage cause, the physical discomforts and tribulations of her self-sacrificing activities. Moreover, as Jelinek suggests, even as she represents herself as the exceptional "woman," as the "son," she insists on her identification with a broad range of women, even the lonely, isolated, impoverished plainswoman (87-90). Effectively, Stanton uses her position as wife and mother to screen her self-asserting presentation of herself as "individual," as "man," as "metaphysical self." This double-positioning underwrites the tensions, points of opposition, and contradictions of and in the text. . . .

Notes

1. The phrase is borrowed from Felicity A. Nussbaum's provocative study "Eighteenth-Century Women's Autobiographical Commonplaces."

2. Estelle Jelinek also notes this resistance in "The Paradox and Success of Elizabeth Cady Stanton" (72).

3. Heilbrun is reviewing at this point in her essay a study by Jill Conway, "Paper on Autobiographies of Women of the Progressive Era," delivered at Workshop on New Approaches to Women's Biography and Autobiography, Smith College Project on Women and Social Change, June 12-17, 1983.

Works Cited

Heilbrun, Carolyn G. "Women's Autobiographical Writings: New Forms." *Prose Studies,* 8 (September 1985), 14-28.

Jelinek, Estelle. "The Paradox and Success of Elizabeth Cady Stanton." In *Women's Autobiography: Essays in Criticism,* ed. Estelle Jelinek, 71-92. Bloomington: Indiana University Press, 1980.

Nussbaum, Felicity A. "Eighteenth-Century Women's Autobiographical Commonplaces." In *The Private Self: Theory and Practice of Women's Autobiographical Writings,* ed. Shari Benstock, 147-71. Chapel Hill: University of North Carolina Press, 1988.

Stanton, Elizabeth Cady. *Eighty Years and More (1815-1897): Reminiscences of Elizabeth Cady Stanton.* New York: European Publishing, 1898.

TITLE COMMENTARY

The Woman's Bible

ELLEN DUBOIS (ESSAY DATE 1984)

SOURCE: DuBois, Ellen. "The Limitations of Sister-hood: Elizabeth Cady Stanton and the Division of the American Suffrage Movement, 1875-1902." In *Women and the Structure of Society: Selected Research from the Fifth Berkshire Conference on the History of Women*, edited by Barbara J. Harris and JoAnn K. McNamara, pp. 160-69. Durham, N. C.: Duke University Press, 1984.

Explores the conflicts in the early feminist movement, focusing on Stanton's ideas on religion, and how the publication of the Woman's Bible *influenced perceptions of her within the movement.*

In the 1850s and 1860s, divisive political conflict characterized most efforts of American feminists, but by the mid-1870s and on through the end of the century, these conflicts had less-ened. During the Gilded Age, politically active women made a strong commitment to consolida-tion. Ideologically, women emphasized their similarities rather than their differences; organiza-tionally, they emphasized unity over division. Women of the period tended to create multi-issue, all-inclusive, and nonideological organizations that, at least theoretically, embraced all women and united them in a sisterhood dedicated to the elevation of their sex. The consolidation of wom-en's reform efforts might be said to have begun with Frances Willard's assumption of the presi-dency of the Women's Christian Temperance Union (WCTU) in 1879 and to have reached maturity with the formation of the National Council of Women and the General Federation of Women's Clubs, both in the late 1880s.[1] By this time, suffragists participated enthusiastically in the move to unite women politically, consolidate them organizationally, and harmonize them ideologically. In 1890 the suffrage movement, which had divided in 1869, reunified into a single organization that foreswore all political distinc-tions among proponents of woman suffrage and welcomed all women, whatever their differences, to work for "the Cause."[2] Even Susan B. Anthony, who had always gloried in a good factional fight, embraced this strategy. She displayed an excessive reverence for harmony in fighting for the suffrage and avoided any issue that would split the unity she was intent on building around the demand for the vote.[3]

How real in fact was the harmony and consen-sus that seemed to predominate in late nineteenth-century feminism? Under the calm surface feminists presented to the world, there is evidence of a considerable amount of conflict, which their belief in the overriding importance of unity and dedication to the principle of sisterhood led them to obscure in the historical record. Here I wish to examine the ideas and experiences of the leading feminist dissident of the late nine-teenth century, Elizabeth Cady Stanton. The qual-ity of Stanton's thought is so extraordinary, so original and thought-provoking, that it is always profitable to examine her ideas closely. Moreover, in a situation in which she had to fight against a stifling ideological consensus to get a hearing, her insights and criticism were considerably sharp-ened. The issues that divided the late nineteenth-century women's movement—religion, sex, and family, and the role of the state in women's libera-tion—are critical for an understanding of the development of feminism. We can gain a perspec-tive on our own situation by considering how feminists differed over these matters and how the relation of these issues to women's liberation has changed over the last eighty years.

Central to the conflict between Stanton and other leaders of the late nineteenth-century feminist movement were differences over the role of religion, especially Christianity, in the oppres-sion of women.[4] Stanton had been a militant an-ticleric since she was a teenager, when exposure to secular and rationalist ideas helped her to recover her emotional balance after an evangelical re-vival.[5] Politically, she was much more influenced by secular than by evangelical radicalism. Encour-aged by Lucretia Mott, she read Frances Wright, Mary Wollstonecraft, and Tom Paine.[6] In the 1840s she knew of and was influenced by the two leading secular feminists in the United States, Robert Dale Owen and Ernestine Rose.[7] In the early phases of her career, she advocated reforms for women that these two had championed and that were generally associated with secular radical-ism—the liberalization of divorce law and property rights for married women.[8] Even Stanton's role in developing the demand for the vote, and the emphasis she placed on politics, is most compre-hensible when we recognize the militantly secular and anti-evangelical character of her approach to change, and her preference, throughout her career as a leader of American feminism, for political as opposed to moral reform.

In the 1860s and early 1870s, Stanton's inter-est in religion temporarily abated—perhaps be-cause she concerned herself more with other reforms, perhaps because the clergy were less uniform in their opposition to women's rights, perhaps because women of orthodox religious belief were drawing closer to feminism. In 1878 Stanton's friend and political comrade, Isabella Beecher Hooker, held a prayer meeting in connection with the National Woman Suffrage Association convention and introduced pro-Christian resolutions at its proceedings. "I did not attend," Stanton wrote to Anthony, ". . . as Jehovah has never taken a very active part in the suffrage movement, I thought I would stay at home and get ready to implore the [Congressional] committee, having more faith in their power to render us the desired aid."[9]

In the early 1880s, however, she became convinced once again that religion held the key to women's oppression. What led to this reawakening of her interest in religion, and how did it differ from her pre-Civil War anticlericalism? Social developments in the United States, particularly the revival of crusading Protestantism, helped to alert her to the continuing hold religion had on women's consciousness. Postwar Christianity spoke less of hellfire than of divine love and, in part because of the growth of the women's rights movement itself, women were especially active in its spread. Indeed, one of the major avenues for the growth both of revivalism and feminism in the late nineteenth century was the Women's Christian Temperance Union.

Stanton was also affected by political developments in England, where she went in 1882 to be with her daughter and lived, on and off, for the next decade. In England Stanton was involved with and influenced by many political movements—Fabian socialism, the movement to repeal the Contagious Diseases Act, the suffrage movement, and above all, British secularism. The continued existence in England of an established church meant that the secularist demand for separation of church and state remained a powerful political issue. Non-Christians still could not sit in Parliament, and blasphemy, which included antigovernment remarks, remained a civil crime.[10] Stanton's diary in this period is filled with remarks about religion. Soon after she arrived in London, she gave a speech on the religious dimension of women's subordination to the progressive congregation of her old friend, Moncure Conway. "I never enjoyed speaking more than on that occasion," she wrote in her autobiography, "for I had been so long oppressed with the degradation of woman under canon law and church discipline, that I had a sense of relief in pouring out my indignation."[11]

Stanton was especially impressed with Annie Besant, one of the foremost leaders of British secularism. Besant was a feminist and a sexual radical as well as a militant secularist. In 1878 she was arrested, along with Charles Bradlaugh, for distribution of a pamphlet advocating birth control. While the more moderate wing of the secularist movement held to ideas about gender and sexuality that were too genteel for Stanton's taste, Besant combined militant secularism with sexual radicalism and the kind of uncompromising individualism that had always been so important to Stanton's feminism.[12] Stanton wrote of Besant, "I consider her the greatest woman in England."[13] As a result of Stanton's experiences in England, as well as the impact on her of the American Protestant revival, her approach to religion in the 1880s was closely linked to her ideas about sexuality and to new questions she began to form about social coercion and state interference with individual development and personal freedom.

Stanton contributed to late nineteenth-century secularism by examining the impact religion had on women. She believed that all organized religions degraded women and that women's religious sentiments had been used to keep them in bondage. However, she concentrated her fire on Christianity, and on refuting the assertion, made in its defense, that Christianity had elevated woman's status by purifying marriage, spreading social justice, and insisting on the spiritual equality of men and women.[14] On the basis of considerable historical scholarship, she demonstrated that the status of women in pre-Christian societies had been high, and conversely, that the impact of Christianity had been to debase and degrade the position of women. She also argued that historically the church had tolerated prostitution, polygamy, and other practices associated with the slavery of women. Christianity, she charged, excluded women from the priesthood and identified the deity solely with the male element. Finally, she argued that, with the Reformation, Christianity had abandoned what little respect it had retained for women, in particular the cult of the Virgin Mary and the existence of the religious sisterhoods. Given the confidence with which late nineteenth-century Protestants believed their faith represented the absolute height of human civilization, we can imagine that they found Stanton's assertion that Catholicism treated women with more respect than Protestantism especially infuriating.

Stanton's criticisms of Christianity's spiritual claims were closely related to her challenge to its sexual morality. She suspected that part of the explanation for Christianity's hold over women was the fact that it denied the power of female sexuality, while at the same time drawing on it in the form of religious passion. To her daughter she suggested that "the love of Jesus, among women in general, all grows out of sexual attraction."[15] Stanton was particularly critical of the doctrine of original sin, which identified sex with evil and both with the carnal nature of women.[16] This fear of female sexuality permeated Pauline doctrine, which treated marriage primarily as an institution to permit men to satisfy their sexual cravings without having to resort to sin.[17] Stanton dissented from the idea, at the center of late nineteenth-century Christian morality, that the "civilized" approach to human sexuality was the establishment of a single, absolute standard of sexual behavior, a morality to which all individuals should be held. Stanton had always been suspicious of official standards of sexual conduct, but the debates of the 1880s and 1890s clarified her position and made her profoundly skeptical of the idea that a universal standard of sexual morality could be ascertained. Of one thing she was sure: sexual purity did not prevail under nineteenth-century Christianity. "There never has been any true standard of social morality and none exists today," she insisted. "The true relation of the sexes is still an unsolved problem that has differed in all latitudes and in all periods from the savage to the civilized man. What constitutes chastity changes with time and latitude; its definition would be as varied as is public opinion on other subjects."[18]

On the basis of her interest in Christianity and its role in the oppression of women, Stanton began as early as 1886 to plan an ambitious feminist analysis of the Bible. She wanted to avoid treating the book as a "fetish," but to assess what it had to say about women's position "as one would any book of human origin."[19] General developments in Biblical criticism, the publication in 1881 of a new revised version of the Bible, and the growing tendency of Biblical scholars to treat the Bible historically rather than metaphysically no doubt inspired her. Stanton's own opinion was that the Bible taught "the subjection and degradation of women."[20] She realized, however, that other feminists interpreted its teachings more positively, and she genuinely sought to stir debate on the nature of the Bible's ethical teachings about women.[21] Years before she had read Voltaire's *Commentary* on the Bible, which was organized in the form of selected Biblical passages at the head of the page, followed by Voltaire's own "arch skeptical" analyses.[22] Stanton adopted this form, but proposed that the commentaries be written by several women of different opinions. The editors would then "add a few sentences, making some criticisms of our inconsistencies." "Our differences would make our readers think," Stanton wrote enthusiastically, "and teach them to respect the right of individual opinion."[23]

Stanton was genuinely surprised when most of the feminists to whom she wrote refused to join the **Woman's Bible** project. She had invited women with a wide range of opinions, including those "belonging to orthodox churches," and at first some of them showed interest in the idea.[24] Ultimately, almost all refused to participate. The reasons they gave varied. Harriot Hanson Robinson and her daughter Harriet Shattuck, close political allies of Stanton for several years, claimed that they did not see why the project was important and doubted their ability to make any contribution of significance.[25] Frances Willard and her friend Lady Henry Somerset withdrew their support because the project did not include enough "women of conservative opinion" and therefore could not "find acceptance with the women for whom we work."[26] Even Anthony refused to cooperate on the grounds that a battle over religion would divert attention from the fight for suffrage. "I don't want my name on that Bible Committee," she wrote Stanton. "I get my share of criticism. . . . Read and burn this letter."[27] Mary Livermore, who shared Stanton's goal of bringing the masses of women to more liberal religious ideas, also feared that any effort to which "the mad dog cry of atheist, infidel, and reviler of holy things" could be attached would do more harm than good.[28] In part, what was at work here were different ideas about how to build and develop a social movement. Livermore thought that leaders should move their followers' ideas gradually, carefully, by persuasion and reassurance, always seeking to preserve ideological consensus. Stanton believed in the value of debate and conflict, in sharpening differences rather than muting them.

This leaves us with the question of why religion should be the source of such deep differences among late nineteenth-century feminists. What did Christianity signify, especially for those who revered the Bible and found Stanton's ideas objectionable? In the context of late nineteenth-century capitalism, surrounded by intensely competitive individualism, many reformers were drawn to Christian values as an alternative to the ideology of laissez-faire. Christianity represented to them a set of beliefs about loving and selfless conduct toward others that, if universally followed, would eliminate tyranny and injustice. "Wherever we find an institution for the care and comfort of the dependent and defective classes," Frances Willard explained, "there the spirit of Christianity is at work."[29] Even to feminists, women were among the dependent classes, placed there by their maternity and the economic relation it put them in with respect to men. "That woman is handicapped by peculiarities of physical structure seems evident," wrote Ednah Dow Cheney, another feminist who objected to the *Woman's Bible*; "but it is only by making her limitations her powers"—her motherhood her glory—"that the balance can be restored."[30] Thus, the most important Christian institution for the care of dependent classes was the family, and women were at its center—dedicated to the care of dependent children, while themselves relying on the protection and goodwill of men. Women's inescapable dependence is what made Christian morality so important to feminists: a common belief in Christian ethics was the only thing that would insure that men treated women with respect and that the family functioned to protect women and children rather than permit their abuse. "The gospel of Christ has mellowed the hearts of men until they become willing to do women justice," wrote Frances Willard, the most impassioned preacher of feminist Christianity. "To me the Bible is the dear and sacred home book which makes a hallowed motherhood possible because it raises woman up."[31]

While Stanton agreed with some of the elements of this argument—for instance, the practice of appealing to women's position as mother of the race—at the most basic level she disagreed with this approach to women's emancipation. She believed that the task of the women's movement was not to assume women's vulnerability and to protect them from its consequences, but to so transform women and the condition in which they lived that they would no longer need protection, but would be fully independent. Even while recognizing that the structures of inequality were very strong, she held to the classical feminist goal of equality and continued to emphasize the necessity of achieving it with respect to the sexes. Her most powerful assertion of these ideas can be found in "The Solitude of Self," her 1892 meditation on the relative importance to women's liberation of protection versus freedom, differences between the sexes versus similarities, and community morality and Christian ethics versus individual autonomy and self-determination.

Christianity's message was "to bear ye one another's burdens," and Stanton granted that humanity would be better off if we did, but the point of her speech was "how few the burdens that one soul can bear for another." "No matter how much women prefer to lean, to be protected and supported, nor how much men desire them to do so," she explained, "they must make the voyage of life alone, and for safety's sake . . . should know something of the laws of navigation." Stanton believed that the idea of safe dependence was an illusion for women for several reasons: because no matter how secure one's home life, how kindly the husband, emergencies arose and women had to be prepared to care for themselves; because each life was different, each woman had her "individual necessities" with which no one else could grapple but herself; above all, because the philosophical truth of human existence was the same for women as for men, "that in the tragedies and triumphs of human experience, each mortal stands alone." "The talk of sheltering woman from the fierce storms of life is the sheerest mockery," Stanton argued, "for they beat on her just as they do on man, and with more fatal results, for he has been trained to protect himself." Faced with these truths, the only security for women, as for men, was in full self-development. As a positive vision of women's liberation, Stanton stressed women's emancipation into the "infinite diversity in human character," the human condition that simultaneously distinguishes each of us from the other, and is common to all of us, men and women alike.[32]

These philosophical differences became political differences, and debates over religion became debates over government, as Christian reformers worked to introduce religious values into law and religious feminists sought to marshal the power of the government behind their idea of the family. By the end of the century, the idea that government should enforce Christian morality was becoming popular with reformers, as were proposals for Bible education in the public schools, legal enforcement of Sunday closings, a wide variety of sexual morals legislation, and—most hauntingly—a Constitutional amendment recognizing the Christian basis of the American political system.[33] The 1888 platform of the Prohibition party, for instance, called for Sunday closing laws and restrictive divorce legislation, as well as for antimonopoly and prolabor measures. Feminists played an important role in this Christian political movement. Their special concern was sexual morality legislation: social purity laws to raise the age of consent, strengthen the bonds of marriage, limit the number of divorces, censor obscene literature, and eliminate prostitution. Feminists involved in social purity politics included Mary Livermore, Julia Ward Howe, Anna Garlin Spencer, Frances Harper, and all of the Blackwells.[34] The WCTU was especially active in social purity politics. Under the leadership of Frances Willard, it allied with Anthony Comstock, formed its own department for repressing impure literature, endorsed a Constitutional amendment recognizing Christianity, and formed a department of "Christian citizenship."[35]

Although Christian morality and social purity ideology dominated the late nineteenth-century feminist movement, these ideas did not go unchallenged. A minority of feminists—Matilda Gage, Josephine Henry, Clara Colby, and Olympia Brown, to name a few—tried to halt the interpenetration of feminism and Christian reform in the 1890s.[36] Stanton provided secular feminists with leadership. Despite Anthony's urgings to keep conflict out of the women's movement, Stanton insisted on raising the level of debate and bringing feminists' differences into the open. At the 1890 suffrage unity convention, where pressure to present a united face to the world was great, Stanton's keynote speech challenged feminists' efforts to introduce Christian morality into civil law. "As women are taking an active part in pressing on the consideration of Congress many narrow sectarian measures," she declared, ". . . I hope this convention will declare that the Woman Suffrage Association is opposed to all Union of Church and State and pledges itself . . . to maintain the secular nature of our government."[37] She was particularly incensed over efforts to suppress all nonreligious activities on Sunday, especially the upcoming Chicago World's Fair.[38] She also opposed Christian reformers' attempts to make divorce laws more conservative and divorces harder to get.[39] She criticized both measures on the grounds that they were destructive of individual liberty, especially for women. She particularly objected to the suppression of individual choice when it came to divorce, because women as yet enjoyed so little self-determination in matters of marriage and sexuality. In contrast to her social purity opponents, she argued that liberal divorce laws were in women's interests, that more and more women were initiating divorce, and that the obligation of the women's movement was to encourage this development, not to repress it. "The rapidly increasing number of divorces, far from showing a lower state of morals, proves

exactly the reverse," she contended. "Woman is in a transition period from slavery to freedom, and she will not accept the conditions in married life that she has heretofore meekly endured."[40]

Underlying Stanton's objections to the coercive character of social purity legislation was a growing concern over the uses of state power in general. Most late nineteenth-century reformers, including most feminists, relied on a unified community faith, backed by the power of the government, for the creation of a just social order. One has only to think of Edward Bellamy's *Looking Backward,* with its vision of a state-run utopia, where national government organized all aspects of social life and met—one might say anticipated—all one's personal needs.[41] While many reformers embraced this vision, there were those who saw problems with it. "The spring of the [Bellamy nationalist] movement is the very best cooperation in the place of the deadly competition of our so-called Christian civilization," William F. Channing wrote Stanton, "But the spring is made to drive the wheels of a state socialism more arbitrary than the government of the czar or the Emperor William."[42] Stanton was of the same opinion. "All this special legislation about faith, Sabbath, drinking, etc. is the entering wedge of a general government interference," she wrote in 1888, "which would eventually subject us to espionage, which would become tyrannical in the extreme."[43] Stanton's concerns about the impact of Christian ideology on American reform politics are worth considering. The explicitly religious dimension of this approach to reform soon faded, but its coercive and paternalistic aspects remained and formed the basis of the most disturbing, undemocratic elements of twentieth-century progressivism.[44]

Stanton's ideas about religion and sex were not very popular in the late nineteenth-century women's movement. In 1890 she was narrowly elected president of the National American Woman Suffrage Association (NAWSA), and two years later she resigned, frustrated at the opposition she consistently encountered.[45] In 1895 she finally published the **Woman's Bible,** which only heightened the opposition to her leadership. At the 1896 suffrage convention, Rachel Foster Avery, corresponding secretary of NAWSA and one of Anthony's protégées, criticized the **Woman's Bible** as "a volume with a pretentious title . . . without either scholarship or literary merit, set forth in a spirit which is neither that of reverence or inquiry."[46] Avery recommended that the suffrage association "take some action to show that it was not responsible for the individual actions of its officers"—Stanton was no longer an officer—and moved that NAWSA disavow any connection with the **Woman's Bible.** There was considerable debate: Charlotte Perkins Gilman, at her first suffrage convention, defended Stanton eloquently, but the resolution of censure passed, 53 to 41. The censorship left Stanton bitter. "Much as I desire the suffrage," she wrote in 1896, "I would rather never vote than to see the policy of our government at the mercy of the religious bigotry of such women. My heart's desire is to lift women out of all these dangerous and degrading superstitions and to this end will I labor my remaining days on earth."[47] The low regard in which suffrage leaders held Stanton at the end of her life was carried after her death in 1902 into the historical record of the movement, through organizational histories and autobiographies, so that her historical contribution and her conception of the emancipation of women continued to be undervalued in the feminist tradition. There was not even a full-length biography of Stanton until 1940, in contrast to several written about Anthony within years of her death.

As a modern feminist, I find myself a good deal closer to Stanton's ideas about women's liberation, her focus on independence and egalitarianism, her emphasis on freedom rather than protection, than I feel to her social purity opponents. When I read "Solitude of Self" and ask myself what I think of it, I truly believe that Stanton's description of the dangerous, unpredictable, necessarily "solitary" nature of life describes what it means for women to leave the sheltered world of home and sexually stereotyped social role, each individual to find a way of life and a sense of self appropriate to her. It is interesting that the arguments of Stanton's feminist opponents—that religious values, a strengthened family, and a more uniform social morality offer women the best protection—are no longer put forward primarily by feminists. Although we can hear echoes of such ideals in some aspects of cultural feminism, Christian reform arguments are now primarily the province of the antifeminist movement—the moral majority, the right-to-lifers, Phyllis Schlafly, and STOP-ERA. What are we to make of this curious development? On the one hand, the similarities between feminist arguments of the past and antifeminist arguments of the present should give feminists pause and make us think more carefully about just how precisely feminists represent all women's aspirations. Pro-family politicians, for all their conservatism, are addressing aspects of

ON THE SUBJECT OF...

STANTON'S FRIENDSHIP WITH SUSAN B. ANTHONY

If there is one part of my life that gives more satisfaction than another, it is my friendship of forty years' standing with Susan B. Anthony . . . I do believe that I have developed into much more of a woman under Susan's jurisdiction, fed on statute laws and constitutional amendments, than if left to myself reading novels in an easy-chair, lost in sweet reveries of the golden age to come, without any effort of my own

Stanton, Elizabeth Cady. From "The Friendship of a Woman." *Woman's Tribune,* (22 February 1890).

If I have ever had any inspiration she has given it to me. I want you to understand that I never could have done the work I have if I had not had this woman at my right hand.

Anthony, Susan B. *Woman's Tribune,* (22 February 1890).

women's discontent and offering visions of family and social reform that are attractive, at least to some women.[48] There is no one solution to women's oppression; there may not even be one "women's oppression," and the history of women's efforts to reform their social position, to give voice to their discontent, is as complex a phenomenon as American reform in general, and as contradictory in its development.

At the same time the appropriation of protectionist arguments by modern antifeminists is also a reason for optimism, a development on which feminists can pin historical faith. Nineteenth-century Christian feminists focused on women's weaknesses and vulnerability, and on the creation of safe environments and external power to protect them from exploitation and abuse. Given the position of the masses of women in the nineteenth century—economically dependent, unable to support themselves or their children, absolutely deprived of personal freedom, either sexual or reproductive—even the feminist movement could aspire to little more than this defensive and protectionist program on women's behalf. This no longer need be the case. Women's lives are no longer so completely circumscribed, at least no longer circumscribed in precisely the same ways. Modern feminist programs are much less protectionist as a result, women's goals much more libertarian and egalitarian. Once we understand that as the conditions of women's lives change, so do their visions of freedom, our approach to the history of feminism changes. We must study feminism's byways as well as its mainstreams, its dissidents as well as its representative voices; we must understand that our heritage is complex, so that we uncover the whole range of precedents on which we can draw.

Notes

1. Karen J. Blair, *Clubwoman as Feminist: True Womanhood Redefined, 1868-1914* (New York: Holmes and Meier, 1980); Barbara Leslie Epstein, *Politics of Domesticity: Women, Evangelism, and Temperance in Nineteenth-Century America* (Middletown, Conn.: Wesleyan University Press, 1981).

2. Ellen C. DuBois, ed., *Elizabeth Cady Stanton, Susan B. Anthony: Correspondence, Writings, Speeches* (New York: Schocken, 1981), 179-81, 222-27.

3. "Our intention . . . is simply to make every one . . . believe in the great principles of equality of rights and chances for woman. . . . Neither you nor I have the right to complicate the question." Anthony to Stanton, 1884, in *The Life and Work of Susan B. Anthony,* ed. Ida H. Harper (Indianapolis: Bowen and Merrill, 1899), 2: 586. The issue that Anthony feared would complicate the suffrage movement was racism.

4. My emphasis on feminists' conflicts over religion contrasts with that of William R. Leach, in *True Love and Perfect Union: Feminist Reform of Sex and Society* (New York: Basic Books, 1981); Leach stresses the common commitment to religious liberalism, which he believes was shared by virtually all nineteenth-century feminists.

5. Elizabeth Cady Stanton, *Eighty Years and More: Reminiscences, 1815-1897* (New York: T. Fischer Unwin, 1898), 43-44.

6. Lucretia Mott to Richard Webb, 5 Sept. 1855, in *James and Lucretia Mott, Life and Letters,* ed. Anna D. Hallowell (Boston: Houghton Mifflin and Co., 1884), 357; Stanton to Elizabeth Smith Miller, 20 Sept. 1855, in *Elizabeth Cady Stanton as Revealed in Her Letters, Diary, and Reminiscences,* ed. Theodore Stanton and Harriot Stanton (New York: Harper & Bros., 1922), 60-61.

7. Stanton, *Eighty Years and More,* 150.

8. Owen advocated divorce reform and property rights for married women in Indiana in the 1830s; the two issues were also linked in Massachusetts by Mary Upton Ferin. Rose and Judge Hertell, also a freethinker, led the drive for women's property rights in New York in the 1840s. Stanton helped to circulate petitions for property rights in 1845. She first advocated liberal divorce laws in 1852, in connection with the New York women's temperance movement.

9. Elizabeth Stanton to Susan B. Anthony, 14 Jan. 1878, Stanton Papers, Manuscripts Division, Library of Congress (hereafter cited as Stanton Papers, LC).

10. Susan Budd, *Varieties of Unbelief: Atheists and Agnostics in English Society, 1850-1960* (London: Heinemann, 1977).

11. Stanton, *Eighty Years and More,* 356.

12. "Spent the afternoon with some Positivists whom I was invited to meet at Mr. William Hertz's. Though clear on religious questions, I found many of them narrow in their ideas as to the sphere of woman." Diary, 26 Nov. 1882, *Stanton as Revealed in Her Letters,* 198. For Stanton's first meeting with Besant, see ibid., 25 Nov. 1882, 198. In her first months in England, Stanton also met with Victoria Woodhull and Ernestine Rose, both important figures in the individual rights tradition of feminism at an earlier period.

13. Diary, 18 July 1891, in *Stanton as Revealed in Her Letters,* 274-75.

14. Stanton presented a series of resolutions to the 1885 National Woman Suffrage Association convention indicting "Christian theology" for the oppression of women. The convention altered the resolutions to focus on "religious creeds derived from Judaism." See Stanton, *Eighty Years and More,* 381-82. Stanton developed her ideas on religion fully in "Has Christianity Benefitted Woman?" *North American Review* 342 (May 1885): 389-99.

15. Elizabeth Stanton to Harriot Stanton, 17 Apr. 1880, Stanton Papers, LC.

16. Stanton, "Has Christianity Benefitted Woman?" 395.

17. Ibid.

18. Stanton, "Patriotism and Chastity," *Westminster Review* 135 (Jan. 1891): 1-5.

19. Elizabeth Stanton to Elizabeth Boynton Harbert, 15 Sept. no yr., Harbert Papers, Huntington Library, San Marino, California.

20. Stanton, *Eighty Years and More,* 396.

21. Stanton to May Wright Sewall, 10 Oct. 1886, Harbert Collection, Huntington Library, San Marino, California.

22. Diary, 13 Aug. 1882, in *Stanton as Revealed in Her Letters,* 193.

23. Stanton to Harbert, 15 Sept. no yr., in ibid.

24. Stanton, *Eighty Years and More,* 452.

25. Stanton to Harriot Hanson Robinson, 30 Sept. 1886, Robinson Papers, Schlesinger Library, Cambridge, Massachusetts.

26. Lady Henry Somerset to Stanton, 5 June 1895, Stanton Papers, LC.

27. Anthony to Stanton, 24 July 1895, Harbert Collection, Huntington Library.

28. Mary Livermore to Stanton, 1 Sept. 1886, Stanton Papers, LC.

29. Frances Willard to Elizabeth Stanton, n.d., in *The Woman's Bible,* Part II (New York: European Publishing Co., 1898), 200.

30. Ednah Dow Cheney to Stanton, n.d., in ibid., 190.

31. Willard to Stanton, n.d., in ibid., 200-201.

32. Stanton, "The Solitude of Self," in DuBois, *Elizabeth Cady Stanton, Susan B. Anthony*, 246-54.

33. David Pivar, *Purity Crusade: Sexual Morality and Social Control, 1868-1900* (Westport, Conn.: Greenwood Press, 1973). Also see Judith R. Walkowitz, *Prostitution and Victorian Society* (Cambridge: Cambridge University Press, 1980), for similar developments in England.

34. Pivar, *Purity Crusade*, 250; "Purity Conference," *Woman's Journal*, 7 Dec. 1895: 388.

35. Parker Pillsbury to Lillie Devereux Blake, 11 Apr. 1890, Blake Papers, Missouri Historical Society, St. Louis, Missouri. See also Epstein, *Politics of Domesticity*.

36. *Women's National Liberal Union: A Report of the Convention for Organization* (Syracuse: Masters and Stone Printers, 1890); also see Margaret Marsh, *Anarchist Women* (Philadelphia: Temple University Press, 1980).

37. Elizabeth Cady Stanton, "Address to the Founding Convention of the National American Woman Suffrage Association," in DuBois, *Elizabeth Cady Stanton, Susan B. Anthony*, 222-27.

38. Elizabeth Cady Stanton, "Sunday at the World's Fair," *North American Review* 154 (1892): 254-56.

39. Stanton, "Address to the Founding Convention of the National American Woman Suffrage Association," DuBois, *Elizabeth Cady Stanton, Susan B. Anthony*, 225; Elizabeth Cady Stanton, "Divorce Versus Domestic Warfare," *Arena* 1 (1890): 560-69.

40. Stanton, "Divorce Versus Domestic Warfare," 568.

41. Dolores Hayden, *The Grand Domestic Revolution: History of Feminist Designs for American Homes, Neighborhoods, and Cities* (Cambridge, Mass.: MIT Press, 1981), chap. 7; William R. Leach, "Looking Forward Together: Feminists and Edward Bellamy," *Democracy* (Winter 1982).

42. Channing to Stanton, 7 May 1890, Stanton Papers, LC.

43. Diary, 8 Feb. 1888, in *Stanton as Revealed in Her Letters*, 247.

44. Robert M. Crunden, *Ministers of Reform: The Progressive Achievement in American Civilization, 1889-1920* (New York: Basic Books, 1982), stresses the religious aspects of Progressivism.

45. *Life and Work of Susan B. Anthony*, 2:631-32.

46. *Washington Post*, 27 Jan. 1896 and 29 Jan. 1869, clippings in the Anthony Papers, Manuscript Division, Library of Congress; also, "The Washington Convention," *Woman's Journal*, 1 Feb. 1896: 1.

47. Stanton to Elizabeth Boynton Harbert, 7 June 1900, Harbert Papers, Huntington Library, San Marino, California.

48. Susan Harding, "Family Reform Movements: Recent Feminism and its Opposition," *Feminist Studies* 7, no. 1 (Spring 1981): 57-75; Barbara Ehreinreich, "The Women's Movements: Feminist and Antifeminist," *Radical America* 1, no. 1 (Spring 1981): 93-104.

Eighty Years and More

ESTELLE C. JELINEK (ESSAY DATE 1980)

SOURCE: Jelinek, Estelle C. "The Paradox and Success of Elizabeth Cady Stanton." In *Women's Autobiography: Essays in Criticism*, edited by Estelle C. Jelinek, pp. 71-92. Bloomington: Indiana University Press, 1980.

In the following essay, Jelinek discusses the paradoxical self-image of an ordinary woman and an extraordinary public figure that Stanton presents in Eighty Years and More, *noting that Stanton was a success in both roles in her life.*

In 1895, when Elizabeth Cady Stanton began her autobiography at the age of eighty, she was still a vigorous and active person, writing and publishing even during the last year of her life. *Eighty Years and More: Reminiscences, 1815-1897* (1898) followed close on the heels of two other of her major publications, *History of Woman Suffrage* (I-II, 1881-86) and *The Woman's Bible* (I, 1895; II, 1898), and she had been a prolific writer of articles and speeches during a period of fifty years of service to the cause that occupied most of her life—and shaped her autobiography—the women's suffrage movement.

Stanton was not a literary person, making her representative of most women who produced autobiographies in America and in England at the turn of the century—they were women who devoted their lives to careers in the reform movements of the nineteenth and early twentieth centuries. She was the major intellectual figure of her time, and her autobiography reflects both the excitement and the reserve of her era. It also bears the particular stamp of her personality and reflects her specific intent in writing her life story.

Stanton's intention as stated in her preface—to write about her "private life" as opposed to her "public career"—does not exactly give us the whole picture.

> The story of my private life as wife of an earnest reformer, as an enthusiastic housekeeper, proud of my skill in every department of domestic economy, and as the mother of seven children, may amuse and benefit the reader.

> The incidents of my public career as a leader in the most momentous reform yet launched upon the world—the emancipation of woman—will be found in **"The History of Woman Suffrage."**

The account of her private life as wife-housekeeper-mother is not given enough coverage in *Eighty Years* for us to believe Stanton's assertion. Though her marriage to Henry Stanton lasted for forty-seven years until his death in 1887, her role as his wife is hardly mentioned. Except for a brief sketch of their meeting and marriage journey, Henry himself is hardly present in the book; from 1848, when Stanton's political work started in earnest, until 1885—a period of thirty-seven years—he is never mentioned, and thereafter only three times, very briefly and insignificantly. Though Stanton offers many helpful suggestions on the subject of housekeeping, like the value of efficient stoves, of circulating heat throughout a house, of adequate ventilation, and of the joys of creative cooking, the anecdotes on these matters are scattered through the book and hardly constitute the major theme. Her own motherhood is barely covered and then only, after the birth of her first child, as a kind of handbook for other new mothers; she urges them to trust their own judgment rather than the dictates of rigid and ignorant doctors. Though Stanton bore seven children from 1842 to 1858 and did not undertake her out-of-state lecturing until 1869 when the youngest was eleven, we rarely hear anything about these children until the 1880s when they are all grown and married and pleasant people to visit in her less active years.

Stanton's actual intention is twofold. She wants to present herself as an *ordinary* human being, but *not* as a wife-housekeeper-mother. She is ordinary because she mixes easily with ordinary people, has a cheerful disposition, is self-reliant and healthy, and has varied domestic interests in addition to her political ones. This ordinary person plays an important role in the anecdotes she relates to relieve the narrative of its more weighty and actual though unstated goal: to educate her readers about the women's suffrage movement in order to convert them to her cause. Everything she includes or excludes in this autobiography, even the way she portrays her own self-image, is determined by this overriding educational aim. Her "public career" is indeed the major objective of the autobiography, but she tries to present it as painlessly as she can by means of her humorous, human interest anecdotes in order to persuade her readers to accept her and her reformist ideas.

When Stanton wrote *Eighty Years and More*, she was well known, actually a celebrity among reformists and a name that had figured prominently in the news for fifty years. By casting her views within the framework of an ordinary life, she was attempting to counter the unidimensional public image of herself as a brilliant, argumentative, sharp-witted, unrelenting reformer from a prestigious upper-class family. How was she to integrate this overdetermined image of herself as a superior human being—certainly one worthy of full citizenship as an equal with men—with a multidimensional image of an ordinary human being so that her readers would be receptive to the "most momentous reform yet launched upon the world"?

The dilemma that this paradoxical self-image presented for the writing of her autobiography derived from the two roles she played out in her life, one as wife-housekeeper-mother, the other as public, professional person. It was the struggle of her entire life as a feminist, and it still remains a dilemma for today's feminists. In every way, for Stanton, and for us, there is this dialectic between this ordinary woman, product of the conditions that produce women in this society, *and* at the same time, this *not* ordinary but exceptional woman who is not trapped in those conditions but can see her way out of them.

It is evident from reading her autobiography that Stanton was a success at both roles in her life. But in the autobiography itself, she needed to submerge the superior person in order to win over her readers. Yet in presenting herself as an ordinary person who could accomplish so much, she produces a narrative that is rife with paradox, contradiction, and, at the very least, ambivalence. While she writes an apparently linear and chronological narrative that emphasizes the stability of her personality and her faith in the order and progress of the world as well as in the successful outcome of her life's mission, the narrative is constantly interrupted by a variety of discontinuous forms—anecdotes, for the most part, but also letters and excerpts from speeches and published articles by herself and others. Though she is writing about weighty and controversial issues, she resorts to light and humorous anecdotes to make her points. While she wants to convince us that her childhood was a happy and normal one, she also must show the unusual emotional and intellectual sources of her dedication to the cause of women's rights. Though she treats her father with the greatest respect, it is apparent even at the age of eighty-two that she still thinks of him with fear and a great deal of unrecognized anger. While she regales us with her exploits aboard trains, bathing crying babies or airing stuffy parlor cars, she turns out speeches, lectures, petitions, and pamphlets undauntedly, traveling day and night under superhuman conditions. While in her travels on the lyceum lecture circuit, she feels comfortable and sisterly with ordinary women whose hospitality she accepts despite often unhealthful food and unsanitary sleeping accommodations, she has easy access to the homes of famous people in and out of the reform movement in her own country and abroad because of her family's social position. While she is completely reticent about her sex life, she is outspoken on such controversial issues as hypocrisy in the Bible, incompatibility as grounds for divorce, and the enfranchisement of former slaves only on condition of enfranchisement for women also—positions that brought the profoundest attacks upon her not only from the mass public but even from within her own movement.

The final paradox is that at the time Stanton wrote her autobiography, she had not achieved the goal to which she had dedicated her entire life—the enfranchisement of women. Yet campaigns, attacks on bills, struggles for propositions and amendments, petitions, speeches, etc., all the various efforts she describes here appear as victories. We complete this autobiography with the very positive impression that Stanton's public career was a success.

The primary means by which she conveys this image of her work, despite its immediate failure, are to omit anything that might cast a negative light on her achievements and always to emphasize the positive. She excludes anything about her personal or public life that is irrelevant to the movement or that might give detractors ammunition to undermine the cause. Stanton's unflinching self-confidence and her positive vision of her work—qualities that produce leaders and heroes—made a success of her effort to educate her readers and to convince them of her cause and resulted in their acceptance of her two-pronged self-image. The resolution of her self-image—the dialectic between her being one with all women and at the same time above them—has contemporary overtones, especially in Kate Millett's efforts in her autobiography *Flying* to reconcile her individual needs with the collective goals of her cause.

Let us look at how Stanton develops her two unstated intentions—presenting herself as an ordinary human being and furthering the cause of women's suffrage. In the first third of the book, she deals with the influences that shaped her personality and character during her childhood, girlhood, marriage, and early motherhood, to the age of thirty-three in 1848. Here we see the most ambivalent or paradoxical treatment of her life study, for she is dealing with her personality more than the movement. In the second and longest section, the emphasis shifts to her efforts for the cause, from 1848 to 1881; here we see less ambiva-

lence and more direct omitting of information to further her intention. In the final section, which continues the theme of her work for women's suffrage, she spends more time describing her travels and visits with her grown children; here, there is both omission and paradox, but to a lesser degree than in either of the two earlier sections.

First, let us look at the ambivalence evident in Stanton's description of her early years. She pictures herself, on the one hand, as a healthy, romping girl full of enthusiasm and energy, enjoying her school work, her games with her two younger sisters, and all kinds of outdoor activities at her central New York state home of Johnstown. Her upper-class family supported a number of servants, nurses, and tutors, and the three girls played joyfully in the attic or the cellar, where the many barrels of produce from her father's tenants served as playthings. She presents no terrifying experiences or a sense of deprivation either emotional or physical in these descriptions.

So intent is she on demonstrating that she had a happy childhood that whenever she does introduce a "sorrow" from her childhood, it is immediately followed by one of joy. Some complaints are common to children, like the starched collars that tore at her neck but about which she was rebuked for even complaining. Or the all-red outfits that she and her younger sisters wore throughout their childhood, leaving with Stanton a permanent hatred of that color.

Her more sorrowful memories are of the worms that dangled from the poplar trees of the town, the sight of which made her tremble, and the many bells that tolled on every conceivable occasion and seemed to her like "so many warnings of an eternal future."[1] Years later, in her sixties, she experienced the same frightened reaction that she had as a child to the mournful sound of church bells. Of the many festivities that early nineteenth-century Americans celebrated with such enthusiasm like the Fourth of July, it is the terrifying sounds of the cannon she most remembers.

Stanton evidences ambivalence not only toward the "joys and sorrows" of her childhood but also toward authority. On the one hand, she is incapable of defying her nurses until her younger sister convinces her that they will be punished anyhow, so they might as well have some fun. "Having less imagination than I, she took a common-sense view of life and suffered nothing from anticipation of troubles, while my sorrows were intensified fourfold by innumerable apprehensions of possible exigencies" (p. 11). On the other hand, she rails against the nurses who "were the only shadows on the gayety of these winter evenings. . . . I have no doubt we were in constant rebellion against their petty tyranny" (p. 6).

Her upbringing must have been strict and rigid though she gives us little clue to the rules which suffocated her enthusiasm and energy.

> I have a confused memory of being often under punishment for what, in those days, were called "tantrums." I suppose they were really justifiable acts of rebellion against the tyranny of those in authority. I have often listened since, with real satisfaction, to what some of our friends had to say of the high-handed manner in which sister Margaret and I defied all the transient orders and strict rules laid down for our guidance. If we had observed them we might as well have been embalmed as mummies, for all the pleasure and freedom we should have had in our childhood. As very little was then done for the amusement of children, happy were those who *conscientiously* took the liberty of amusing themselves.
>
> (p. 12)

But perhaps the source of her fear of authority came as much from a severe religious code of behavior as from the nurses in her home. At the time Stanton was writing this autobiography, she was also writing **The Woman's Bible**, an exegesis and attack on the Bible and the clergy who preached women's inferiority. Writing the **Bible** must have reawakened her anger against the tyranny of the church, one source of authority in her childhood about which she evidences no ambivalence. "I can truly say, after an experience of seventy years, that all the cares and anxieties, the trials and disappointment of my whole life, are light, when balanced with my suffering in childhood and youth from the theological dogmas which I sincerely believed . . ." (p. 24).

When in her teens she attended Emma Willard's Troy Seminary for girls, she was so overcome by the hellfire sermons of the Reverend Charles G. Finney, that "terrifier of human souls," that because of "my gloomy Calvinistic training in the old Scotch Presbyterian church, and my vivid imagination," she became one of the first of his "victims" (p. 41). She roused her father so often at night to pray for her soul that he, her sister, and her brother-in-law took her on a six-week summer trip where the subject of religion was tabooed and they talked about nothing but "rational ideas and scientific facts." She then concludes this unpleasant subject with a rather rapid recovery, lest her

readers be too saddened by her account. After this trip, "my mind was restored to its normal condition" (p. 44).

Stanton's mention of waking her father at night to help her and of his taking her on a trip to cure her would seem to indicate a warm relationship. However, about her father she exhibits much ambivalence. He was, she writes, "a man of firm character and unimpeachable integrity," "sensitive and modest to a painful degree," and though "gentle and tender, he had such a dignified repose and reserve of manner that, as children, we regarded him with fear rather than affection" (p. 3). With her father, Stanton had probably the most traumatic experience of her childhood. When she was eleven, her only brother, who had recently graduated from Union College, died. "He was the pride of my father's heart. We early felt that this son filled a larger place in our father's affections and future plans than the five daughters together" (p. 20). Stanton yearns so much for her father's affection that she accompanies him on his almost daily visits to the boy's gravesite. When she tries to comfort him, he says:

> "Oh, my daughter, I wish you were a boy!" Throwing my arms about his neck, I replied: "I will try to be all my brother was."
>
> Then and there I resolved that I would not give so much time as heretofore to play, but would study and strive to be at the head of all my classes and thus delight my father's heart. All that day and far into the night I pondered the problem of boyhood. I thought that the chief thing to be done in order to equal boys was to be learned and courageous. So I decided to study Greek and learn to manage a horse. . . . They were resolutions never to be forgotten—destined to mold my character anew.
>
> (pp. 20-21)

Her efforts are futile, however, though she accomplishes her two goals.

> I surprised even my teacher, who thought me capable of doing anything. I learned to drive, and to leap a fence and ditch on horseback. I taxed every power hoping some day to hear my father say: "Well, a girl is as good as a boy, after all." But he never said it.
>
> (p. 22)

In 1854 when Stanton was thirty-nine, her father asked to hear her first speech on the issue of divorce that she was to deliver before the New York legislature.

> On no occasion, before or since, was I ever more embarrassed—an audience of one, and that the one of all others whose approbation I most desired, whose disapproval I most feared. I knew he

condemned the whole movement, and was deeply grieved at the active part I had taken.

(p. 188)

When she finished her rehearsal, Judge Cady offered no opinion for or against her political work then or ever after but "gladly gave me any help I needed, from time to time, in looking up the laws, and was very desirous that whatever I gave to the public should be carefully prepared" (p. 189). But more important to this study is the fact that Stanton evidences no bitterness toward her father's disapproval of her as a female. She treats him as one more influence on her life. At the above meeting, Judge Cady's response on hearing her speech is primarily surprise at her emotional complaints.

"Surely you have had a happy, comfortable life, with all your wants and needs supplied; and yet that speech fills me with self-reproach; for one might naturally ask, how can a young woman, tenderly brought up, who has had no bitter personal experience, feel so keenly the wrongs of her sex? Where did you learn this lesson?"

(pp. 188-89)

And Stanton's response is, "'I learned it here, in your office, when a child, listening to the complaints women made to you'" (p. 189). Stanton does not want to remind her readers of her emotional crisis at eleven lest her readers attribute her devotion to her cause to merely a neurotic source.

Even her father's objection to her marriage to Henry Brewster Stanton did not seem to change her affection for him. Her cousin Gerrit Smith, the abolitionist, at whose Peterboro, New York, home she met Henry, also objected to the marriage and for similar reasons, that an abolitionist reformer and orator, as Henry was, would not be a good provider. After their wedding trip to Europe, however, Judge Cady took Henry into his law office to train him for the bar, and for three years the couple and their growing family lived in the Cady household. Apparently Daniel Cady was both a stern father and a reasonable man. Though Stanton does not include it in her autobiography, it is known that at one time he disinherited his suffragist daughter but changed his mind before his death in 1859.[2]

Of her mother, Mary Livingston, from the prestigious colonial family, Stanton writes hardly anything at all. We know that her mother "took the deepest interest in her father's political campaign for Congress, at which he succeeded during the year of her birth; this prenatal influence, Stanton suggests, may account for her own interest in

politics. To her mother's side of the family, she attributes her self-reliance, derived no doubt from General Livingston, whose Revolutionary War fame came from using his own judgment and firing upon a British man-of-war. This action earned him not only General Washington's commendation because it saved many of his troops, but also a warning that under normal circumstances the action would have earned him a court-martial. Stanton describes her mother as a "tall, queenly looking woman, . . . courageous, self-reliant, and at her ease under all circumstances and in all places" (p. 3). One wonders how she evidenced her courage and what control was mustered to be at "ease under all circumstances and in all places." It is clear that Stanton, who was short and progressively stouter as she grew older, must have envied her mother's queenliness because she attributes this characteristic to women she most admires. Stanton never mentions her mother after the first early pages, a curious omission, for which she gives no clue.[3]

Stanton's relationship with her husband seems to have been a satisfactory one though she gives us very little to go on in this autobiography. When she met him, he was considered

the most eloquent and impassioned orator on the anti-slavery platform. . . . Mr. Stanton was then in his prime, a fine-looking, affable young man, with remarkable conversational talent, and was ten years my senior, with the advantage that that number of years necessarily gives.

(p. 58)

On their first outing together on horseback, they seem to have fallen immediately in love, though they had talked in groups on other occasions.

When walking slowly through a beautiful grove, he laid his hand on the horn of the saddle and, to my surprise, made one of those charming revelations of human feeling which brave knights have always found eloquent words to utter, and to which fair ladies have always listened with mingled emotions of pleasure and astonishment.

One outcome of those glorious days of October, 1839, was a marriage, in Johnstown . . . and a voyage to the Old World.

(pp. 59-60)

That is the extent of Stanton's description of her courtship and marriage to Henry Stanton. We can only guess whether or not he objected to her taking out the word "obey" from their marriage ceremony, but she does tell us, quite objectively, that at the World's Anti-Slavery Convention in London in 1840, which they attended as part of their honeymoon trip, when the issue of women's participation in the proceedings came up for a vote, Henry cast his in the negative. She expresses no feelings on this early event of her marriage, but she does recount enthusiastically the position of abolitionist William Lloyd Garrison, who sat in the observation gallery with the women and refused to take part in the segregated proceedings.

She briefly mentions Henry when, because of his frequent travels to courts and abolitionist meetings, he delegates to her the complete management of their homes, first in Boston and Chelsea, later in Seneca Falls. After 1848, when Stanton's political work began, Henry is not mentioned until thirty-seven years later at his eightieth birthday celebration in 1885.

There must have been a policy of live-and-let-live during their forty-seven years together until Henry's death in 1887, which also is not mentioned. We know from sources other than this autobiography that he, like her father, though reformist in every other political cause, always objected to her work for women's rights. We know that he threatened to leave town if the first women's rights convention was held in their town of Seneca Falls, and he did.[4] We also know that Stanton's father frequently helped the couple financially and that she undertook the lyceum tours in part to earn money for their children's education. But Elizabeth Stanton does not include this information in her life study; it might discredit her husband, herself, and the movement. Writing in 1897, in *Eighty Years,* of their minister's superstitious objection to their marriage on a Friday, she sums up her view of her relationship with her husband:

> as we lived together, without more than the usual matrimonial friction, for nearly a half a century, had seven children, all but one of whom are still living, and have been well sheltered, clothed, and fed, enjoying sound minds in sound bodies, no one need be afraid of going through the marriage ceremony on Friday for fear of bad luck.
>
> (pp. 71-72)

Though Stanton also leaves out any personal references to sexuality, her awareness of it is evident. For one thing, she frequently notices the good looks or fine physiques of the men she meets in her travels, but even earlier, she writes of her experiences as a child when she studied with boys at the Johnstown Academy, then moved on to Emma Willard's Troy Seminary for girls only. She was flabbergasted by the intrigue stirred up by the

girls there without boys present and argues strongly for coeducation, which most adults of her time opposed.

Stanton describes the period between her graduation from Willard's seminary to her marriage as "the most pleasant years of my girlhood" primarily because she "rejoiced in the dawn of a new day of freedom in thought and action" (p. 45). Her description of this time of her life is filled with echoes of sexual awakening:

> Then comes that dream of bliss that for weeks and months throws a halo of glory round the most ordinary characters in everyday life, holding the strongest and most common-sense young men and women in a thraldom from which few mortals escape. The period when love, in soft silver tones, whispers his first words of adoration, painting our graces and virtues day by day in living colors in poetry and prose, stealthily punctuated ever and anon with a kiss or fond embrace. What dignity it adds to a young girl's estimate of herself when some strong man makes her feel that in her hands rest his future peace and happiness! Though these seasons of intoxication may come once to all, yet they are seldom repeated. How often in after life we long for one more such rapturous dream of bliss, one more season of supreme human love and passion!
>
> (pp. 44-45)

Closely following this passage is Stanton's effusive description of her brother-in-law Edward Bayard, "ten years my senior . . . an inestimable blessing to me at this time" (p. 45). We know that Stanton was infatuated with Bayard, but she judiciously rejected his advances beyond a platonic attachment[5] and soon after fell in love with Henry Stanton, like Bayard ten years her senior. She excluded any hint of an attachment to a member of her own family, which might have been construed as an unrequited love affair "explaining" her "discontent" with the male way of running the world.

Of the intellectual influences on her life, we have already learned how, as a youngster, Stanton frequented her father's law office and heard the complaints of abandoned wives and mothers with no recourse to the law. Nonetheless, from these experiences and her frequent visits to the county jail, she writes, "I gleaned some idea of the danger of violating the law" (p. 14). Her respect for the law explains why Stanton was conservative when it came to tactics and deferred in that department to her complement Susan B. Anthony; it also explains why she was such a logical and thorough debater. But her respect never seems to have intimidated her or deterred her from fighting laws she felt were unjust or discriminated against women.

Stanton's political and reform spirit was nurtured in the home of Gerrit Smith, where as a late teenager she met her first runaway slave. But Stanton never felt the force of the tyranny of slavery as much as she did that tyranny of her own childhood and womanhood. When push came to shove, she opposed enfranchisement for male blacks when it was denied women after the Civil War, though she had given up her suffrage efforts for five years to help the cause of the North.

It is not surprising that the tyranny Stanton felt was exercised over her as a child was the foundation for her later rebellion against the tyranny over her and all her sex as female. And it is not surprising that she should use the very same phrase to describe those two areas of tyranny over her life: "the constant cribbing and crippling of a child's life" (p. 11) and "the most cribbed and crippled of Eve's unhappy daughters" (p. 204).

The crucial experience that ignited her already informed sympathies for the lot of women came at that antislavery convention in London on her honeymoon trip. It wasn't until eight years later, when longing for more intellectual challenges than those evoked by the management of a large house, servants, and many children, that she and Lucretia Mott placed a brief notice in the local newspaper. Four days later, fifty women met at the Methodist church in Seneca Falls, New York, and started the first feminist movement in North America.

At this point in her life story, female readers probably have no trouble in identifying with Stanton's frustrations after eight years of dedicating herself exclusively to domestic duties. She has convincingly proven herself an ordinary human being and justified her gradual involvement in a "public career." Perhaps now her audience will be receptive to her as a person and treat her ideas seriously.

We now turn to the bulk of *Eighty Years and More,* where Stanton concentrates on her public career, the stated nonintention of her book. While the first part was informed by ambivalence and paradox because of the need to convey the self-image of both an ordinary and superior person, with some omission to protect the women's movement, this second section is informed more by omission than paradox because her political work is the central focus. Her aim is to educate her audience about women's rights, and she does

so by creating a positive image of the cause by leaving out anything that might devalue it in any way. There is still some paradoxical treatment or ambivalence in her presentation of herself, but it is less evident here than in the first section. Here everything is positively shaped for the cause.

All the chapters in this middle section have titles that refer to issues or events in the women's rights movement. Nonetheless, the subjects of these chapters are usually minimally treated. As in the first section, Stanton continues to use amusing and pleasant anecdotes, now to educate her audience painlessly about serious issues. The transition chapter "The First Woman's Rights Convention" deals less with that event than with Stanton's preconvention boredom as her duties become tedious, with her postconvention relief in talking to women about their rights, and with her door-to-door efforts for signatures to petition the state legislature for more liberal property and divorce laws. Her female readers, no doubt, could identify more with her concrete domestic experiences than with the convention itself, though she manages to convey its significance in bringing together for the first time an organized protest against women's inferior legal treatment. True to her determination to be positive, Stanton tells us nothing about her husband's negative reaction to the meeting.

The next two chapters, which constitute a portrait of Susan B. Anthony, break the chronology, for it extends from 1851 when the two women met, three years after the Seneca Falls convention, to the 1890s. By including this portrait of Anthony (a revision of one she wrote for *Eminent Women of the Age,* 1868), Stanton reveals how far from her stated intention this autobiography is. For Anthony was the lifelong friend of her public career, and her portrait emphasizes how closely the two worked together.

> In thought and sympathy we were one, and in the division of labor we exactly complemented each other. In writing we did better work than either could alone. While she is slow and analytical in composition, I am rapid and synthetic. I am the better writer, she the better critic. She supplied the facts and statistics, I the philosophy and rhetoric, and, together, we have made arguments that have stood unshaken through the storms of long years; arguments that no one has answered. Our speeches may be considered the united product of our two brains.
>
> (p. 166)

Stanton omits any tension or problems with her friend. Their partnership was, indeed, predominantly a harmonious one, but they did disagree at times. Though Stanton was more revolutionary in respect to the movement's ideas, Anthony was more militant when it came to tactics. Nonetheless, Stanton exposes none of the disagreements or tensions in the upper echelons of the movement, nothing that might give cause for dissention in the ranks or for gossip among their detractors.

In this chapter Stanton also reminds her readers that she is not neglecting her children while she and Anthony work. She describes the mischievous games her children play around them that often require quick rescues and adult participation. She also directly faces the issue of Anthony's single life, which she knows her readers are curious about. She uses the portrait as an occasion to praise all single women who dedicate their lives to important causes: "All honor to the noble women who have devoted earnest lives to the intellectual and moral needs of mankind!" (p. 157). She quotes Anthony's stand on the question of marriage, thus educating her audience in the process:

> She could not consent that the man she loved, described in the Constitution as a white male, native born, American citizen, possessed of the right of self-government, eligible to the office of President of the Great Republic, should unite his destinies in marriage with a political slave and pariah. "No, no; when I am crowned with all the rights, privileges, and immunities of a citizen, I may give some consideration to this social institution; but until then I must concentrate all my energies on the enfranchisement of my own sex."
>
> (p. 172)

It is unstated, but one may infer that Stanton is aware that *she* had accomplished what few women before, during, or since her lifetime had accomplished, and that is the total dedication to a political cause *and* the achievement of a career as wife and mother.

It is in the next chapter, "My First Speech Before a Legislature" (in 1854 on behalf of the civil rights of married women), that Stanton gives her father her intellectual explanation for her sense of "keenly felt wrongs" against women—hearing the complaints of women in his law office—not the "negative" explanation of her traumatic emotional experience at eleven. Certainly, it was a common experience in her day for female children to be treated as inferiors to boys, but Stanton's explanation reflects her preferred emphasis on the law as the basis for her struggle.

In chapter after chapter, Stanton treats her material with this positive emphasis. In "Views on Marriage and Divorce" she manages to convey the

impression of success in 1860 as she traveled around New York state trying to get a liberal divorce bill passed. We hear amusing anecdotes about generous people and her pleasant experiences while traveling from one city to another, but nothing of the results of the bill. In "Westward Ho!" she describes her trip in the early 1870s to lecture throughout the state of Nebraska for a proposition to strike the word "male" from the state constitution. She gives a favorable description of the results of her efforts, but we really do not know if the proposition passed or not.

For the 1876 centennial celebration, she attempted to get enough tickets so that every state was represented by a woman, but received only six tickets in response to her polite but firm letters, which she quotes in their entirety. She concentrates, however, on Anthony's daring rush to the platform to shove the Woman's Declaration of Rights into the presiding officer's hand, thus succeeding in making it a part of the day's proceedings. Of the Woman's Pavilion at the centennial, though she praises the woman engineer who ran its turbine to the surprise of the male organizers, she was obviously not satisfied with its contents. Rather than criticize what was in it, however, she lists all the things that *should* have hung on its walls: "the yearly protest of Harriet K. Hunt against taxation without representation," "all the laws bearing unjustly upon women," "the legal papers in the case of Susan B. Anthony, who was tried and fined for claiming her right to vote under the Fourteenth Amendment," and "decisions in favor of State rights which imperil the liberties not only of all women, but of every white man in the nation" (pp. 316-17).

It is only in the case of the proposition to extend suffrage to women in Kansas in 1867 that Stanton evidences any anger at the failure of their efforts. She blames the failure on those in the East who "feared the discussion of the woman question would jeopardize the enfranchisement of the black man" (p. 247). But women also learned another

> important lesson—namely, that it is impossible for the best of men to understand women's feelings or the humiliation of their position. When they asked us to be silent on our question during the War, and labor for the emancipation of the slave, we did so, and gave five years to his emancipation and enfranchisement. . . . I am now . . . sure that it was a blunder. . . .
>
> (p. 254)

The issue of black enfranchisement without women's suffrage split the women's movement into two factions, those who were willing to wait and take a back seat to black (male) suffrage and those who were not willing to support one without the other. Stanton led the latter camp, but nothing is mentioned in **Eighty Years and More** of this split in the movement nor of the establishment of two rival women's organizations in 1869. The union of the two groups eleven years later, in 1890, is easily missed in a quoted letter in which she mentions her election to the presidency of the new national organization.

Though Stanton expresses some anger about the Kansas failure early in the chapter "Pioneer Life in Kansas," the dispute over black and women's suffrage is pretty much buried thereafter as she concentrates on her harrowing experiences among settlers in the backwoods, sleeping in soiled and flea-ridden beds and eating starchy and sometimes inedible foods, but always admiring the frontier women whose sacrifices in settling the west go unrecognized. Many of the anecdotes in these chapters where Stanton is touting her seemingly successful efforts focus on her encounters with people, usually women, whom she praises with obvious pride in their accomplishments.

Many of the anecdotes, however, have to do with her own experiences traveling around states as a lyceum lecturer from 1869 to 1881, from the age of fifty-four to sixty-six, from October through June, enduring an extremely physically demanding regime with crowded schedules, often twelve-to-eighteen-hour train rides with no time to rest or eat before appearances, even frequent blizzards that snowbound the hardiest. But not Stanton: "As I learned that all the roads in Northern Iowa were blocked, I made the entire circuit, from point to point in a sleigh, traveling forty and fifty miles a day" (pp. 261-62).

Stanton never complains about the many difficulties she encounters in her travels but describes her experiences with enthusiasm and cheerful good humor. For example, in Dubuque, she arrives by train at a desolate station in the early hours of the morning but manages to attract attention by shouting, "John! James! Patrick!" When her feminist friends rib her for not hollering for "Jane, Ann, and Bridget," she retorts, "as my sex had not yet been exalted to the dignity of presiding in dépots and baggage rooms, there would have been no propriety in calling Jane and Ann" (p. 281). In Kansas, where her experiences seem to have been the most trying physically, she writes, "In spite of the discomforts we suffered in the Kansas campaign, I was glad of the experience. It

ON THE SUBJECT OF...

THE *REVOLUTION*, A NEWSPAPER DEVOTED TO WOMEN'S RIGHTS OF WHICH STANTON WAS A CONTRIBUTOR

[It] made a contribution to the women's cause out of all proportion to either its size, brief lifespan, or modest circulation . . . Here was news not to be found elsewhere—of the organization of women typesetters, tailoresses, and laundry workers, of the first women's clubs, of pioneers of the professions, of women abroad.

But the *Revolution* did more than just carry news, or set a new standard of professionalism for papers edited by and for women. It gave their movement a forum, a focus, and direction. It pointed, it led, and it fought, with vigor and vehemence. . . .

Flexner, Eleanor. "The Emergence of a Suffrage Movement." In *Century of Struggle: The Woman's Rights Movement in the United States*, p. 154. Cambridge: Harvard University Press, 1975.

gave me added self-respect to know that I could endure such hardships and fatigue with a great degree of cheerfulness" (p. 252).

The amazon image that Stanton conveys throughout this second section of her autobiography sits side by side with her image as an ordinary person. She sleeps on a lounge in the woman's salon of a ship during a two-week voyage because she can open a window there and avoid the stuffy staterooms. While all others are suffering with seasickness below, she enjoys the ocean breezes while strolling or reading on deck. She precariously descends a mountain in Yosemite National Park, grabbing for roots and branches to steady herself, an undignified but impressive picture for a heavy woman in her sixties. Stanton never mentions a single illness in her life study; she rarely, and then discreetly, refers to her weight which grew considerably each year; and only parenthetically does she refer to her lameness from a "severe fall" in her seventies.

Not only do we get this paradoxical self-image of Stanton as both an ordinary person and one of almost superhuman physical stamina, but in her descriptions of the people she meets and stays with, we also get a double message. On one hand, she stays with poor pioneer women in cabins in the midwest and west; on the other, she is hosted by famous people in the United States and abroad. Her egalitarian attitude came from her genuine political commitment, whereas her pleasure in meeting the famous came from her upper-class family background, which opened doors to her not open to the usual suffragist. It is also clear from the many names listed, most of which are unknown to readers today, that she is using this autobiography to thank these people for their generous support of the women's movement in hosting her and financing her efforts. There is no question, finally, that her name-dropping is meant to indicate her superior status not just in intelligence but also in social position, which should certainly entitle her in any just society to full citizenship with the right to vote and hold office.

In her travels Stanton emphasizes the women she meets rather than their usually more famous husbands. And on only one occasion does she deviate from her usual tolerance for women who are unable to support the movement:

> The history of the world shows that the vast majority, in every generation, passively accept the conditions into which they are born, while those who demanded larger liberties are ever a small, ostracized minority, whose claims are ridiculed and ignored. . . . That only a few, under any circumstances, protest against the injustice of long-established laws and customs, does not disprove the fact of the oppression, while the satisfaction of the many, if real, only proves their apathy and deeper degradation. That a majority of the women of the United States accept, without protest, the disabilities which grow out of their disfranchisement is simply an evidence of their ignorance and cowardice, while the minority who demand a higher political status clearly prove their superior intelligence and wisdom.
>
> (pp. 317-18)

Such an outburst, which might antagonize those she most wants to win to her cause, is the exception rather than the rule in *Eighty Years*. Generally, the presentation and tone of the autobiography are mild and low-keyed. Stanton explains how she and the other women, often writing as a group, would argue, discuss, and plan their strategy in order to prepare speeches with acceptable arguments and ones that would not reap the abuse so often leveled at them:

> so long as woman labors to second man's endeavors and exalt his sex above her own, her virtues pass unquestioned; but when she dares to demand rights and privileges for herself, her motives, man-

ners, dress, personal appearance, and character are subjects for ridicule and detraction.

> (p. 241)

Anyone reading Stanton's *History of Woman Suffrage* or *The Woman's Bible* will be startled by the comparison with *Eighty Years*. The effort not to antagonize readers of her autobiography made her soften the presentation of her ideas here with anecdote. Her other writings are complex and brilliantly argued expositions; this life study appears simple and straightforward, almost childlike, by comparison. Where her public writings express the full force of her anger and rage at the injustice of the laws against women, here there is no anger, no rage, and no bitterness.

While some men have felt uncomfortable reading the autobiography, it is not because she ever affronts them personally but because of the force of her very logical attacks on the laws which discriminate against women. She is no man-hater and often expresses her appreciation for men who supported the movement and her understanding for those who could not. Though she wore the bloomer outfit for two years, she desisted when it was apparent that it caused her male companions too much embarrassment. When she reflects on how much abuse and ridicule men have suffered in supporting the women's movement, she understands, even in her eighties, why so few have been its supporters.

The third section of Stanton's autobiography, after 1881 when she was sixty-six and had retired from her lyceum lecturing chores, relies on the diary she began keeping at the suggestion of friends. The result is a more precisely documented narrative with notations of day, month, and year scrupulously recorded. The narrative thus becomes choppy and less integrated, with fewer extended anecdotes and much less humor. Though she continues to write, deliver speeches, and attend the annual meetings of the National American Woman Suffrage Association, the emphasis in this last section is once again on her private life. In the ten years between 1881 and 1891, she made six trips to Europe, primarily to visit her two children most active in women's work, Harriot Stanton Blatch and Theodore Stanton, who together edited her letters and other writings in 1922.

The emphasis here returns to the two-faceted image of ordinary woman and exceptional person. Though in 1881 her youngest child was twenty-two, she describes the joys of spending time with her "seven boys and girls dancing round the fireside, buoyant with all life's joys opening before them . . ." (p. 322). Invited to give an address at the sixtieth anniversary of her graduation from the Troy Seminary, she regales her audience with the memory of the time when she and a friend woke the entire school by ringing bells in the middle of the night without being caught. Her observations on differences in domestic accommodations between England and France continue her image of a woman concerned with ordinary matters. But she clearly wants to keep alive her exceptional image as well. Even in her seventies, she boasts of hiding her fatigue after a long trip when she arrives at a friend's house. And wherever she goes all over the world, she is treated as a celebrity with receptions in her honor and invitations to give keynote addresses at women's convocations.

Stanton ends her autobiography with a chapter on her eightieth birthday celebration in 1895, when she was honored for her fifty years of service to womankind with a gala reception at the Metropolitan Opera House. She leaves her readers here with the final paradox of the autobiography, the impression that her efforts were a huge success. She achieves this effect here by quoting several pages of an effusive article that reviewed the occasion, and then by quoting her own address where she summed up her life's work. Now it no longer required courage "to demand the right of suffrage, temperance legislation, liberal divorce laws, or for women to fill church offices—these battles have been fought and won and the principle governing these demands conceded" (p. 467).

As to the most important effort of her life, women's suffrage, rather than conclude with what still needed to be accomplished, she summarizes the victories: "municipal suffrage has been granted to women in England and some of her colonies; school suffrage has been granted to women in half of our States, municipal suffrage in Kansas, and full suffrage in four States of the Union" (p. 465). Though it wasn't until 1920, seventy years after her first call for suffrage in 1848 and eighteen years after her death in 1902, that the Nineteenth Amendment was finally passed, yet the reader closes this autobiography with the distinct impression that Stanton's life was a success.

For after all, it was, and ***Eighty Years and More***, indeed, *is* a success story. Without Elizabeth Cady Stanton, ordinary *and* exceptional woman that she was, the present women's liberation movement would now be in the dark ages. She provided the foundation and the tradition for contemporary feminists, who are closer—because

of her—to an amalgam of the sexual with the political, the private with the public.

Notes

1. *Eighty Years and More: Reminiscences, 1815-1897* (New York: Schocken Books, 1971), p. 8. Subsequent page references, given in the text, are from this edition.

2. *Notable American Women, 1607-1950*, ed. Edward T. James et al. (Cambridge: Harvard University Press, 1971).

3. Ellen DuBois (*Feminism and Suffrage*, Cornell University Press, 1978), an authority on Stanton, notes that nothing among Stanton's papers indicates her feelings about her mother.

4. Catharine Stimpson, "'Thy Neighbor's Wife, Thy Neighbor's Servants': Women's Liberation and Black Civil Rights," in *Woman in Sexist Society*, ed. Vivian Gornick and Barbara K. Moran (New York: Basic Books, 1971), p. 625.

5. *Notable American Women.*

FURTHER READING

Biographies

Adams, Elmer C., and Warren Durham Foster. "Elizabeth Cady Stanton." In *Heroines of Progress*, pp. 58-88. New York: Sturgis and Walton, 1913.

Comprises a short biography.

Burns, Kenneth, and Geoffrey C. Ward. *Not For Ourselves Alone: The Story of Susan B. Anthony and Elizabeth Cady Stanton.* New York: Knopf, 1999, 256p.

Offers insight into Anthony and Stanton's friendship and advocacy for women's rights.

Morris, Charles. "Elizabeth Cady Stanton, the Women's Rights Pioneer." In *Heroes of Progress in America,* pp. 226-31. Philadelphia, Pa.: J. B. Lippincott, 1906.

Biographical sketch.

Criticism

Campbell, Karlyn Kohrs. "Stanton's 'The Solitude of Self': A Rationale for Feminism." *The Quarterly Journal of Speech* 66, no. 3 (October 1980): 304-12.

Explores the rhetorical and ideological aspects of the 1892 address to the National American Woman Suffrage Association.

Goodman, James E. "The Origins of the 'Civil War' in the Reform Community: Elizabeth Cady Stanton on Women's Rights and Reconstruction." *Critical Matrix* 1, no. 2 (1985): 1-29.

Examines the rift between Stanton and leading abolitionists before and after the Civil War.

Gordon, Ann D. "The Political is the Personal: Two Autobiographies of Woman Suffragists." In *American Women's Autobiography: Fea(s)ts of Memory,* edited by Margo Culley, pp. 111-27. Madison: University of Wisconsin Press, 1992.

Analyzes how Stanton and Abigail Scott Duniway portray themselves in their autobiographies.

Kern, Kathi L. "Rereading Eve: Elizabeth Cady Stanton and *The Woman's Bible.*" *Women's Studies* 19, nos. 3-4 (1991): 371-83.

Discusses the controversy in the women's suffrage movement surrounding The Woman's Bible.

Loeffelholz, Mary. "Posing the Woman Citizen: The Contradictions of Stanton's Feminism." *Genders* 7 (March 1990): 87-98.

Discusses Stanton's 1860 speech after the campaign for the married women's property act, focusing on her ideas about the female body.

Masel-Waters, Lynne. "Their Rights and Nothing More: A History of *The Revolution, 1868-70.*" *Journalism Quarterly* 53, no. 2 (summer 1976): 242-51.

Discusses Stanton's role in developing the suffragist weekly newspaper.

Masur, Louis P. "Notes and Documents: Elizabeth Cady Stanton on Capital Punishment." *The Huntington Library Quarterly* 53, no. 3 (summer 1990): 237-42.

Comments on a letter by Stanton expressing her views on capital punishment.

Nies, Judith. "Elizabeth Cady Stanton." In *Seven Women: Portraits from the American Radical Tradition*, pp. 63-93. New York: Viking Press, 1977.

Discusses Stanton's work as a reformer beginning with the 1848 Seneca Falls convention.

Pellauer, Mary D. *Toward a Tradition of Feminist Theology: The Religious Social Thought of Elizabeth Cady Stanton, Susan B. Anthony, and Anna Howard Shaw.* New York: Carlson Publishing, 1991, 427 p.

Examines religious aspects of Stanton's writings.

Riegel, Robert E. "Elizabeth Cady Stanton." In *American Feminists*, pp. 41-64. Lawrence: University Press of Kansas, 1963.

Provides an overview of Stanton's life and work and an assessment of her contributions, describing her as the force that kept the early women's movement together.

Smith, Sidonie. "Elizabeth Cady Stanton, Harriet Jacobs, and Resistances to 'True Womanhood'." In *Subjectivity, Identity, and the Body: Women's Autobiographical Practices in the Twentieth Century*, pp. 24-52. Bloomington: Indiana University Press, 1993.

Analyzes Stanton's portrayal of herself in Eighty Years and More.

Stevenson-Moessner, Jeanne. "Elizabeth Cady Stanton, Reformer to Revolutionary: A Theological Trajectory." *Journal of the American Academy of Religion* 62, no. 3 (fall 1994): 673-97.

Traces the evolution of Stanton's views on women in Christianity.

Waggenspack, Beth M. *The Search for Self-Sovereignty: The Oratory of Elizabeth Cady Stanton.* New York: Greenwood Press, 1989, 204 p.

Critical survey of Stanton's speeches.

Wolff, Cynthia Griffin. "Emily Dickinson, Elizabeth Cady Stanton, and the Task of Discovering a Usable Past." *The Massachusetts Review* 30, no. 4 (winter 1989): 629-44.

Compares feminist ideas in writings by Stanton and Emily Dickinson.

OTHER SOURCES FROM GALE:

Additional coverage of Stanton's life and career is contained in the following sources published by the Gale Group: *Contemporary Authors*, Vol. 171; *Dictionary of Literary Biography*, Vol. 79; *Literature Resource Center*; *Feminist Writers*; and *Twentieth-Century Literary Criticism*, Vol. 73.

HARRIET BEECHER STOWE

(1811 - 1896)

(Also wrote under the pseudonym Christopher Crowfield) American novelist, short story writer and essayist.

Stowe stirred the conscience of the nation and the world with her famous antislavery novel, *Uncle Tom's Cabin; or, Life Among the Lowly* (1852). Its overtly didactic advocacy of abolitionism and humanitarianism made the work popular, controversial, and influential. Despite her prolific output of novels, short stories, and nonfiction works, Stowe is chiefly remembered for *Uncle Tom's Cabin* because of its compelling historical significance. Critics have generally agreed that Stowe's works address the great issues and events which shaped her century: slavery, the rise of industrialism, the decline of Calvinism, and the role of women in society. Feminist commentators have argued that, despite their sentimental tone, Stowe's novels contain a sustained and ardent critique of patriarchal social conventions.

BIOGRAPHICAL INFORMATION

Stowe was born in Litchfield, Connecticut, on June 14, 1811, the seventh of eight surviving children in a deeply religious family. Her father, Lyman Beecher, was a Presbyterian minister, and her mother, Roxanna Foote, was a well-educated Episcopalian from a prosperous family. When Stowe was five years old, her mother died of consumption, and her older sister Catherine took over as a mother figure to Harriet and her younger brother Henry Ward. Stowe's disposition as a child has been described as sad, even depressed. Hoping to ease this depression, Catherine took her younger sister, at the age of thirteen, to Hartford to live in the women's seminary she had established. There Stowe learned languages, natural and mechanical science, composition, ethics, logic, and mathematics. In 1832 Stowe's father was appointed as president of Lane Theological Seminary, and the family, including Stowe, relocated with him to Cincinnati, Ohio. Once the Beecher family had settled in their new home, Harriet and Catherine founded a new seminary called the Western Female Institute.

In Cincinnati Stowe met her husband, Calvin Stowe, who taught biblical studies at Lane. They married in 1836 and had seven children by 1850. The early years of their marriage were marked by poverty, and Stowe wrote stories and essays for magazines in part to supplement her husband's meager income. While living in Cincinnati, Stowe first came into contact with fugitive slaves from the South; further, she visited a plantation in neighboring Kentucky and witnessed first-hand the poor treatment of slaves. In 1850 Stowe's husband accepted a teaching position at Bowdoin College in Brunswick, Maine, and the family moved from Ohio back to New England. That same year, Congress passed the controversial Fugitive Slave Law, which made it illegal to help an escaped slave. A staunch supporter of abolitionism, Stowe responded to this legislative action by writing *Uncle Tom's Cabin.* The work was first serialized in the antislavery newspaper *The National Era* before being published in book form. *Uncle Tom's Cabin* evoked swift and strident reactions from readers on both sides of the slavery issue; indeed, some ardent abolitionists considered the novel too lenient on the institution of slavery, while most Southern slave-owners reviled it as slanderous and inaccurate. Based on the notoriety that she had gained from *Uncle Tom's Cabin,* Stowe received invitations to publish her writings in many of the most influential literary magazines of the day, including the *Atlantic Monthly.* She also became an international celebrity, traveling to Europe several times between 1853 and 1859. During her travels, Stowe became acquainted with such literary figures and famous admirers as George Eliot, Elizabeth Barrett Browning, Lady Byron, and Queen Victoria.

During the Civil War, Stowe resided in Hartford, Connecticut, where she wrote periodical articles on such topics as the social integration of freed slaves and developing a policy of political and economic compassion towards the Confederacy once it had been reincorporated into the Union after the war. After the conflict, Stowe invested in several ventures in the deep South to employ freed slaves and to assist in the reconstruction of the Confederacy's devastated economy. Stowe spent her later years in poor health and seclusion under the care of her twin daughters who never married. She died at the age of eighty-five in 1896.

MAJOR WORKS

Stowe's early stories, published in local and religious journals and collected in *The Mayflower* (1843), are morally didactic sketches describing American life and people. While many critics have maintained that the stories are not particularly well crafted, they have also contended that the pieces offer valuable insights into Stowe's formative years of religious and moral instruction. *Uncle Tom's Cabin,* her second published work, was written at the suggestion of her sister-in-law, who urged Stowe to use her literary skills to aid the abolitionist cause. Though Stowe claimed that her Christian passion compelled her to write the novel, she also conducted extensive research

before composing her novel, writing to Frederick Douglass and others for help in creating a realistic picture of slavery in the Deep South. The novel, inspired by the real life of the slave Josiah Henson, traces the fortunes of a slave, Uncle Tom, who is sold by his owner in Kentucky to pay off debts to Augustine St. Clair in New Orleans. Eva, the young daughter of St. Clair, becomes fond of Tom and life is relatively happy. However, following the deaths of St. Clair and his daughter, Tom is sold to a cruel cotton plantation owner, Simon Legree. The novel also tells a parallel tale of another slave, Eliza, who is sold by the same slave trader as Tom, and who tries to escape after learning that her son is to be taken away from her and sold to another slaveholder. While the principal aim of *Uncle Tom's Cabin* is to expose the horrors of the institution of slavery, the novel also addresses questions about the position of women in nineteenth-century America. In particular, the work elucidates the role of the mother as the agent of moral regeneration in a corrupt and godless society. The novel also depicts women as equal to men in intelligence, bravery, and spiritual strength, and female characters direct the book's morality, serving as vital advisors who counsel their husbands to defy convention and popular opinion.

Upon its publication, *Uncle Tom's Cabin* came under virulent attack from Southerners, who flatly denied the work's veracity. This passionate debate led Stowe to publish *A Key to Uncle Tom's Cabin* (1853), which includes the primary sources upon which Stowe based the main characters; various religious and legal arguments on the subject of slavery and prejudice; and excerpts of newspaper articles which influenced the development of the novel's narrative. In 1856 Stowe published a second antislavery novel entitled *Dred: A Tale of the Great Dismal Swamp,* which details the circumstances surrounding an attempted slave rebellion. Three years later, Stowe published *The Minister's Wooing* (1859), a historical novel and domestic comedy that critiques the rigid theological doctrine of Calvinism. The novel recounts the story of Mary Scudder, who marries a Calvinist minister who advocates the abolition of slavery and who aids and abets fugitive slaves. Critics have noted that *The Minister's Wooing* provides important insights into slavery, history, and gender, with many of its characters based on historical figures, including the early black feminist Sojourner Truth. Another of Stowe's historical novels, *Agnes of Sorrento* (1862), is based on the fall of Girolamo Savonarola, the fifteenth-century monk who attempted to bring social and religious reform to Florence. Stowe's later novels, *The Pearl of Orr's Island* (1862), *Oldtown Folks* (1869), and *Poganuc People* (1878), are based partly on her husband's childhood reminiscences and are among the first examples of local color writing in New England. Stowe's notable nonfiction works include an 1863 essay about Sojourner Truth published in *The Atlantic Monthly; Woman in Sacred History* (1873), a compilation of sketches, poems, essays, and artwork about Biblical women; and a preface to *Tell It All* (1875)—a critique of Mormonism—in which Stowe calls for an end to polygamy, a practice that she considered to be another form of slavery.

CRITICAL RECEPTION

Many literary historians have averred that *Uncle Tom's Cabin* is one of the most important works of American literature, culture, and history. Indeed, most critics agree that Stowe's reputation as a writer and social activist is due to the unparalleled success of that novel. *Uncle Tom's Cabin* had a modest inception, appearing in serial form in the antislavery weekly *The National Era* from 1851 to 1852. Despite initially reaching a relatively small circulation of abolitionist readers, word of mouth about the story spread; soon copies of it were passed from family to family until it achieved unprecedented status as a national sensation. The installments attracted the attention of Boston publisher J. P. Jewett, who published *Uncle Tom's Cabin* as a novel in March of 1852. The novel quickly surpassed all previous sales records for a book, selling 300,000 copies in the first year alone. With the success of the novel, Stowe became an international celebrity and was invited to write and speak about antislavery issues across the United States and in Europe. Public fascination with the Uncle Tom story also led to the production of numerous unauthorized dramatic adaptations of the work performed across the United States throughout the remainder of the nineteenth century. Stowe's subsequent works were also financially successful, although none achieved the popularity of *Uncle Tom's Cabin*. By the early twentieth century, despite the fact that the novel had achieved iconic status as an historical artifact, the term "Uncle Tom" had come to be associated with any black person demonstrating a passive submission to the white social establishment. This burgeoning negative sentiment culminated in James Baldwin's 1949 critical assault on *Uncle Tom's Cabin* as racist because it faulted the system of slavery rather than its administrators. Ultimately, Baldwin concluded that the novel's moral position was fundamentally flawed because it did not encourage personal accountability for performing evil acts. Baldwin's views influenced much of the Stowe scholarship in succeeding decades until feminist critics began to reexamine the characters and themes in *Uncle Tom's Cabin* in the 1970s. These commentators advocated admiration for Stowe's underlying theme of feminine moral fortitude and approvingly compared Uncle Tom's passivity to Mahatma Gandhi's strategy of peaceful resistance in his struggle to free colonial India from Great Britain in the twentieth century. Stowe's other works also began to attract scholarly attention in the late twentieth century. Feminist critics reviewing her works have argued that a consistent theme in Stowe's writings is the fundamental necessity to infuse the rigid patriarchal order with nurturing femininity and humanitarianism. As a result, she is regarded by some as an important early Christian feminist who utilized Calvinist ideology to assert that the Madonna should serve as the paradigmatic mother for society; who used Christianity to criticize contemporary male-dominated institutions; and who appropriated the popular language of sentimentality and domesticity to bring national attention to issues of race, gender, and oppression.

PRINCIPAL WORKS

The Mayflower; or, Sketches of Scenes and Characters among the Descendants of the Pilgrims [reprinted as *The Mayflower; or, Scenes and Sketches among the Descendants of the Pilgrim Fathers.*] (short stories) 1843

Uncle Tom's Cabin; or, Life among the Lowly (novel) 1852

A Key to Uncle Tom's Cabin; Presenting the Original Facts and Documents upon which the Story is Founded. Together with Corroborative Statements Verifying the Truth of the Work (nonfiction) 1853

Sunny Memories of Foreign Lands. 2 vols. (memoir) 1854

The Christian Slave: A Drama Founded on a Portion of Uncle Tom's Cabin (play) 1855

Dred: A Tale of the Great Dismal Swamp. 2 vols. (novel) 1856

The Minister's Wooing (novel) 1859

Agnes of Sorrento (novel) 1862

The Pearl of Orr's Island: A Story of the Coast of Maine (novel) 1862

Oldtown Folks (novel) 1869

†*Lady Byron Vindicated: A History of the Byron Controversy, from Its Beginning in 1816 to the Present Time* (essay) 1870

My Wife and I: or, Harry Henderson's History (novel) 1871

Pink and White Tyranny: A Society Novel (novel) 1871

Woman in Sacred History (essays) 1873

We and Our Neighbors: or, the Records of an Unfash-ionable Street (novel) 1875

Footsteps of the Master (religious prose) 1877

Poganuc People: Their Loves and Lives (novel) 1878

---

*   *Uncle Tom's Cabin* was initially published serially in *The National Era.*

†   *Lady Byron Vindicated* was written in response to negative public response to Stowe's 1869 article in *The Atlantic* called "The True Story of Lady Byron."

PRIMARY SOURCES

HARRIET BEECHER STOWE (ESSAY DATE 1856)

SOURCE: Stowe, Harriet Beecher. "Preface." In *Dred: A Tale of the Great Dismal Swamp,* pp. iii–vi. London: Sampson Low, Son & Co., 1856.

In the following preface to her antislavery novel Dred, *Stowe declares that she aims to show the general effect of the institution of slavery on society as well as its corruptive influence on Christianity.*

The publishing of **Uncle Tom's Cabin** disclosed the sorrows of the American slave.

When the existence of such sorrows was disputed, the **Key to Uncle Tom's Cabin** was published, and to this no answer has ever been returned; a most profound silence has always reigned with regard to that book in quarters whence there was the most clamor with regard to the tale.

The author has never seen or heard of one attempt to disprove or refute a single statement of the Key.

Meanwhile, during the five years that have passed since the publication of the story, the great Evil has marched on to its results with a terrible and undeviating tread. The foolish virgins, who all slumbered and slept, the respectable and tender-hearted, who, in ignorant sincerity, cried peace when there was no peace, have one by one been awakened in wild surprise; and the foolish have said unto the wise, Give us of your oil, for our lamps have gone out.

The few who then fought the battle of liberty almost single-handed, those Cassandras who for many years saw the coming evil and prophesied to unheeding ears, now find themselves at the head of a mighty army, and in a crisis that must speedily determine what shall be the working out of this great evil, whether it shall issue peaceably or in blood.

When **Uncle Tom** was published, sentimental humanity was shocked that its author could represent a Legree beating defenceless Uncle Tom on the head with a cow-hide; but sentimental humanity has lately seen, with her own eyes, the accomplished scholar and gentleman, the senator of a sovereign state, struck down unarmed and unsuspecting, by a cowardly blow, and, while thus prostrate, *still* beaten by the dastard arm which had learned its skill on a South Carolina plantation.

Sentimental humanity then loudly declared her belief that the chivalry of South Carolina would repudiate the act. The chivalry of South Carolina presented the ruffian with a cane, bearing the inscription, "Hit him again;" and presents of silver plate and congratulatory letters from public meetings flowed in, mixed with tenderer testimonials from the gentler sex; and the cowardly bully, forced by public sentiment to resign his seat, has been, in insulting defiance of that sentiment triumphantly returned by the citizens of South Carolina: and his act was openly vindicated by Southern members in their places in both houses of Congress.

After this who will doubt what the treatment of slaves has been, or is likely to be, in the hands of men educated under such influences?—"If these things are done in the green tree, what shall be done in the dry?"

The Author's object in this book is to show the general effect of slavery on society—the various social disadvantages which it brings even on its most favoured advocates—the thriftlessness and misery and backward tendency of all the economical arrangements of slave states—the retrograding of good families into poverty—the deterioration of land—the worse demoralization of all classes from the aristocratic tyrannical planter to the oppressed and poor white—which is the result of the introduction of slave labour.

It is also an object to display the corruption of Christianity which arises from the same source; a corruption which has gradually lowered the standard of the Church, North and South, and been productive of more infidelity than the works of all the Encyclopædists put together.

As an illustration of the corrupted state of Christianity, the author need only adduce the following fact, related to her by one of her family connexions—a minister of the Gospel, resident in Missouri at the time when orginizations were being formed to go into Kansas and forcibly take away the rights of the ballot-box from the citizens of that territory.

This gentleman had gone to Missouri, with the fond hope that he would be allowed to preach the Gospel, if he would say nothing about slavery. He informed the writer that all the church members and elders, and even ministers in his vicinity, openly justified and spoke in favour of this movement, and in many cases even joined the party who went to effect it; and for daring to lift his voice in very gentle remonstrance, his situation was made so uncomfortable that he was obliged to leave the state.

The regiment of Colonel Buford, which has distinguished itself by indiscriminate pillage and murder, left Alabama amid an enthusiastic popular concourse, with addresses and prayers from clergymen cheering them on.

This winter has witnessed the most shocking cold-blooded murders of men in Kansas, for the simple crime of avowing opposition to slavery. The city of Lawrence has been sacked, with atrocities which it was hoped had been discarded in modern warfare; and yet neither the new nor the old school assembly of the Presbyterian church, assembled in their public capacity, have uttered one word indicative of disapprobation of these proceedings, and the defences of slavery in both these bodies have never been so open and unblushing. The same is true with regard to the Methodist general conference, although not quite to the same extent.

These facts speak for themselves. They show more strongly than anything else the force of the demoralizing power that is at work.

The author desires to anticipate one criticism, which may be made on the dramatic representations of this volume:—

It was represented to her, after the publication of **Uncle Tom's Cabin,** that the profanity attributed to some of the characters was a painful shock to the religious feelings of the community.

The author has given this subject a serious consideration, and it is a deliberate opinion formed as the result, that in a dramatic exhibition made for moral purposes, it is necessary sometimes even to pain the moral sense in order to give the full force of the lesson.

If a certain style of society induces profaneness and contempt of all reverential considerations, an author cannot make this realized without in some cases shocking the reverential feelings of the readers. How is it possible to represent the conversation of men, whose every breath is an oath, without the admission of some touches of the pencil, shocking to the minds of the pious? We are apt to think in such cases that what pains us must necessarily injure, when, in fact, that pain is an indication of a healthy state of the moral organization. The Scriptures, whose representations of evil and of good are always dramatic, give, without reserve, the boastings of the profane, who defy the Lord, as well as the adorations of those who worship Him. The haughty Pharaoh says, "Who is the Lord that I should obey him?" The sensitive and irritable Jonah expostulates in language quite unlike the reverence of a common prayer, and the words and deeds of the wicked are told with a homely plainness which makes the fastidious shudder.

In considering, therefore, how far a moral artist may go on this subject—the moral purpose and result is to be taken into account.

If profanity and vice are rendered interesting in the person of a gay and accomplished hero, the good would indeed have reason to complain; but while it is held up in the characters of those confessedly formed under the influences of an evil system, it may be a necessary part of the exhibition.

Let it not be said that the people of England do not need the enlightening power of such exhibitions—that they have nothing to do with the evil. They have *much* to do with it; it is vital to them as well as to us. When they read in these pages how good men to secure good purposes are led first to endure, then to pity, then to embrace the monster which has been the cause of all this evil—when they see how the standard of Christianity in a whole nation has been insensibly lowered—let them not be high-minded, but fear. England is connected with America by the same ties of interest, trade, relationship, and religious fraternity, that have bound together the North and the South.

Every year the power of steam is drawing these ties closer, and it is for her Christianity to decide whether, for the sake of good or gain of any description, it will begin that course of endurance which has always ended at last in an embrace. Are there not some signs of the times in England? When defences not only of slavery, but of the slave-trade, *begin* to appear in respectable quarters, is it not time to ask whereto these things will grow?

The party in America, who in the coming election are to make a stand against this tremendous evil, may possibly meet a temporary defeat; it is always best to look the worst issue steadily in the face. The Christianity of England have to ponder the question, whether if slavery becomes triumphant, they for the sake of trade and gain will join the acclamation and follow the victorious car? Will the British Lion be led in cotton bands by such hands as smote down Charles Sumner?

One word more is due to the Free States in America: much as they have erred, it is but justice to them to say that the error has not been entirely one either of cowardice or of interest; something is certainly due to a generous credulity unwilling to believe the worst of brethren, and that slowness to wrath which is characteristic of those who have been taught to rule their own spirit.

That they have not yet avenged the insult to their senator, the violation of their free ballot-box, the burning of their towns, and the murders of their brethren and sons, is no sign that they have not *felt* them; it simply shows the grandeur of that law-abiding education which is given by true freedom, which seeks its redress not by immediate violence, but by those surer methods provided by national law. Should all these fail, we have only to say, "Wo to the aggressor when *they who are slow to anger* are at last aroused."

But though we have alluded to the worst possibilities, we rejoice in saying that everything now promises in our next election a triumphant vindication of Liberty and Right in America.

GENERAL COMMENTARY

JOHN GATTA (ESSAY DATE 1995-96)

SOURCE: Gatta, John. "Calvinism Feminized: Divine Matriarchy in Harriet Beecher Stowe." *Connotations* 5, nos. 2-3 (1995-96): 147-66.

In the following essay, Gatta explores Stowe's use of the image of the Madonna as the paradigmatic Mother, representing the Catholic symbol in Calvinist terms.

I

Confronting her New England religious heritage with more personal credulity than Hawthorne ever did his, the seventh child of Lyman and Roxana Beecher found herself engaged in a lifelong struggle to assimilate—and to remake—her ancestral Calvinism. The fruit of this engagement is evident in the subject matter of later novels such as *The Minister's Wooing, Oldtown Folks,* and *Pogunuc People,* as well as in the apocalyptic urgency and evangelical fervor of *Uncle Tom's Cabin.* Deficient in several crafts of the belletristic novelist, Stowe yet knew how to infuse her writing with the powerful rhetoric of conversion preaching. In fact, her best fiction often shows a temper closer to symbolic romance than to novelistic realism, with the author drawing on mythic and personal energies to sustain her heightened rhetoric. Thus, episodes in *Uncle Tom's Cabin* such as Eliza's perilous crossing of the Ohio River or the deaths of Eva and Tom amount to rituals of passage laden with mythological import.

Inspired with regenerative confidence that the last will be first in God's Kingdom, Stowe exalted society's powerless people—children, blacks, and women—in her tales of the lowly. And as critics like Elizabeth Ammons and Dorothy Berkson have demonstrated for *Uncle Tom's Cabin,*[1] her recognition of women and endorsement of feminine piety centered especially on the saving force of maternity. Stowe's agnostic involvement with Jonathan Edwards and the original faith of New England's fathers issued at length in a reconceived Christianity of American mothers.

At one level, of course, this paean to motherly love betrays the influence of a post-revivalist and sentimental Christianity, of emerging bourgeois values, and of feeling loosed from all strictures of logic. As Berkson suggests, it also shows Stowe's theological impulse to displace the monarchical God of Edwardsean Calvinism with a divine principle of maternal compassion. At the same time, one can see the author's matrifocal spirituality flowing directly from evangelical tradition insofar as her motherhood theme grounds more incarnationally that classic Reformation-Pauline metaphor of conversion as a "new birth."

For Stowe the resulting focus on divine womanhood, which is central to her vision of this life and the next, drew particular inspiration from the biblical Mary. That Stowe reflected deeply on the Marian Madonna is a little-known fact one might not have predicted in a woman of her era, place, and religious background. She shared this interest with her brothers Charles and Henry Ward Beecher.[2] One indication of it can be seen in her zeal for visual art, particularly as stimulated by her three visits to Europe. In her Hartford residence on Forest Street, tour guides today may point to a copy of Raphael's *Madonna of the Goldfinch* hanging conspicuously in the front parlor to illustrate her pioneering display of Madonna artifacts among the households of local Protestant gentility. What is more, Stowe owned copies of at least three other sacred Madonnas—including the *Holy Family del Divino Amore* and Raphael's *Madonna del Gran Duca*—in addition to secular renderings of the Mother and Child motif. After her first European tour in 1853, she reported in a letter to her sister-in-law that she had just installed a copy of Raphael's Sistine Madonna, the original of which she had viewed at Dresden, in her home at Andover, Massachusetts. She remarked elsewhere that this picture "formed a deeper part of my consciousness than any I have yet seen."[3]

So her iconographic fascination with the theme is plain. And in conjunction with her fiction, Stowe's written discourses on Mary in her verse and nonfictional prose—especially as delineated in *Woman in Sacred History*—offer us valuable understanding of the personal, cultural, and theological significance of her interest. Her Marian attitudes help to clarify, in turn, the distinctive sort of domestic, matrifocal feminism that informs her fictions. It is scarcely accidental that several of Stowe's redemptive heroines—Mary Scudder in *The Minister's Wooing*, Mara in *The Pearl of Orr's Island,* and Mary Higgins in *Pogunuc People*—even bear Marian names. In the limited purview of this essay, however, my first aim is simply to describe the character of Stowe's attraction to the mythical image of divine womanhood—or, in Christian terms, the Madonna—as indicated in nonfictional prose and poetic writings. What is the import of this Protestant writer's interest in the ostensibly Catholic image of the Madonna?[4] I then want to consider how this interest might bear particularly on *Uncle Tom's Cabin* and on one less familiar novel, *The Minister's Wooing.*

II

Stowe's revalorization of the Madonna presented Mary not as Virgin so much as paradigmatic Mother, focusing especially on her conjunctive relation to a maternal Jesus. Thus accommodating Marian piety to Protestant orthodoxy, Stowe sought to refashion her inherited Calvinism into what she conceived to be a more encompassing Christianity. In biographical terms, Stowe's interest in the Marian Madonna may have been stirred not only by her European travel experiences but also by highly sanctified memories of her own deceased mother, Roxana Beecher, who died when Harriet was only five years old. Brother Henry Ward Beecher even testified that "My mother is to me what the Virgin Mary is to a devout Catholic."[5]

Two revealing expressions of Stowe's responses to the biblical Mary can be located in her devotional account of "The Blessed Woman"—included in her *Footsteps of the Master* (1877)—and in her volume of character portraits celebrating **Woman in Sacred History.**[6] Devoting separate chapters of **Woman in Sacred History** to "Mary the Mythical Madonna" and "Mary the Mother of Jesus," Stowe seems at first to reject the mythical Mary altogether on the usual Protestant grounds of scant biblical evidence. To allow unscriptural legends, iconography, and pagan associations to image a Mary who overshadows Jesus is, she charges, a grave mistake.

Yet the resistance here to deifying Jesus' mother may derive less from biblical hermeneutics than from Mrs. Stowe's urge to identify with Mary's palpable experience of womanhood. For Stowe, the woman highly favored is no timeless goddess but a figure of history. Though "the crowned queen of women," Mary manifests her blessedness for Stowe not through supernal powers but in her exemplary bearing among those "that have lived woman's life."[7] And not surprisingly, Stowe identifies this womanhood chiefly with maternity.

Indeed, Stowe's domestic sense of Mary as Mother is so strong that it all but effaces the title of Virgin from her nonfictional commentary. Rejecting in usual Protestant fashion the theory of Mary's perpetual virginity, Stowe reflects instead with knowing sympathy on the trials Mary faced by virtue of "the unbelief of her other children."[8] Moreover, Mary's maternity extends beyond the momentous act of birthing Christ to include her teaching of Jesus and domestic familiarity with him.

This sense of an integral association between Mary and Jesus is central to Stowe's theology. It helps to explain not only her Protestant reluctance to view Mary as an autonomous goddess, but also her arresting insistence on the feminine character of Jesus. For if Jesus lacked a biological father, "all that was human in him" derived from Mary's nature. Accordingly, "there was in Jesus more of the pure feminine element than in any other man. It was the feminine element exalted and taken in union with divinity." So intimate is this association that to express it, Stowe combines imagery of marriage and parthenogenesis: "He was bone of her bone and flesh of her flesh—his life grew out of her immortal nature."[9]

Yet Mary herself retains for Stowe a crucial role as exemplar. It is evident that Stowe identified personally not only with Mary's motherhood, but also with Mary's ironic attainment of public significance through values and activities centered in the private, domestic sphere.[10] Stowe does praise Mary's self-abnegating acceptance of the divine will, to the point of echoing the blessed woman's "Behold the handmaid of the Lord" in the course of describing the newfound faith and vocation beyond perplexity she found in her own religious experience.[11] But Stowe also attributes to Mary the divine fire of poet and prophet, as reflected presumably in her one great effusion, the Magnificat.[12]

Plainly Stowe identifies, too, with Mary's perseverance in facing keen personal loss. She dedicates her 1867 verses on **"The Sorrows of Mary"** quite explicitly "to mothers who have lost sons in the late war,"[13] and surely the "anguish of disappointed hopes"[14] that pierced the *stabat mater* was comprehensible to a mother who in 1849 lost one son to plague and in 1857 another, nineteen years old, to death by drowning in the Connecticut River. In fact, Stowe's ability to draw mythic power from her own maternal mourning over baby Charley became crucial to her conception of *Uncle Tom's Cabin,* just as her affliction over Henry's state of soul at the time of his drowning helped to precipitate *The Minister's Wooing.*[15]

In the final analysis, Stowe's nonfictional writings testify that she could not fully resist the imaginative attraction of "Mary the Mythical Madonna." Even as she laments displacement of "the real Mary" by poeticized imagery, she writes appreciatively of iconographic representations by Raphael, Titian, and Fra Angelico as well as of legends passed down through apocryphal writings. She confesses she is attracted, for example, by the mythic tradition of the Greek Church that "Mary alone of all her sex was allowed to enter the Holy of Holies, and pray before the ark of the covenant."

By envisioning Mary as a "second Eve" and quintessential mother worthy of "love and veneration," Stowe comes close to recognizing her—if not invoking her—as the mother of us all. But she

is careful to distance herself from Catholic allegiances, observing that the Mariological excesses of the Roman Church "have tended to deprive the rest of the world of a great source of comfort and edification by reason of the opposite extreme to which Protestant reaction has naturally gone."[16]

III

Against the backdrop of such concerns, the prophetic purpose of *Uncle Tom's Cabin* can be seen all the more clearly. Just as the Marian Magnificat looks toward that era when God shall put down the mighty but exalt the humble and meek, so also Stowe's bestseller represents a womanly triumph of evangelical rhetoric on behalf of "the lowly." And despite the book's technical deficiencies as novel, it is indeed a masterwork of rhetoric. Addressed above all to the maternal soul and conscience of the nation, *Uncle Tom's Cabin* is also a book full of motherly characters—to the point where even its black hero, Tom, has been aptly described as figuring a feminized and maternal Christ.[17]

Already in the book's second chapter, entitled "The Mother," Stowe invokes an heroic image of motherhood in the flight of Eliza Harris. Warned as Mary had been that on account of her male child "a sword will pierce through your soul,"[18] Eliza nonetheless enjoys almost miraculous protection as she flees from bondage across the Ohio River, her figurative Jordan and Red Sea, on dancing icefloes. What drives this thrilling Exodus, Stowe suggests, is Eliza's powerful assent to faith and hope combined with "maternal love, wrought into a paroxysm of frenzy by the near approach of a fearful danger" (105). And just as Stowe perceived something stronger in Mary's assent to Gabriel's annunciation than shrinking submissiveness, so also she highlights the fierceness of Eliza's parental commitment.

Another case of compelling maternity is presented by Senator Bird's wife, named Mary, who intercedes successfully with her husband on behalf of the fugitives. In view of the familiar charge that Stowe's sentimental portrayal of womanhood reduces all argument to mere feeling, it is worth observing that Mary applies a fairly rigorous logic of consistency and biblical authority in making her case against the fugitive slave law. By contrast Senator Bird, who lacks Mary's concrete, integral sense of moral reality, succumbs initially to a fallacy of uprooted abstraction in which "his idea of a fugitive was only an idea of the letters that spell the word" (155). Yet ironically, he patronizes his wife as having more heart than head, just as Haley dismisses Mrs. Shelby's concern for her slaves as irrational because women "ha'nt no sort of calculation" (46).

Even more than Mrs. Shelby or Mary Bird, Rachel Halliday, whose comfort Eliza enjoys in the Quaker settlement, presents an image of archetypal maternity. It is surely no accident that in the epigraph appearing one chapter before Halliday's introduction, Stowe cites Jeremiah's prophetic account of Rachel weeping for her children. (192) For Rachel Halliday supplies potential nurture to the whole of afflicted humankind since "hers was just the face and form that made 'mother' seem the most natural word in the world" (216). As Jane Tompkins observes, Halliday personifies for Stowe something of divine presence because as she is "seated in her kitchen at the head of her table, passing out coffee and cake for breakfast, Rachel Halliday, the millennarian counterpart of little Eva, enacts the redeemed form of the last supper."[19]

Yet Stowe portrays only one virgin mother within her gallery of memorable women. Or at least one could argue that the childsaint Eva, who is evidently a holy virgin, qualifies metaphorically as a mother by virtue of her role in mediating the new birth to characters such as Topsy, Miss Ophelia, and her father Augustine. Hers is thus a true, spiritual motherhood in opposition to the false, fleshly motherhood of Marie St. Clare. Consistent with the book's ironic reversals in which the last become first, Stowe develops here a curious sort of reverse typology in which Eva replaces Mary (or second Eve), and in which the child emerges as more effectively maternal than her own mother.

Beyond the ironic nomenclature by which Eva supplants Marie, Stowe exploits other dimensions of Eva's name. As Evangeline, she serves of course as the book's strongest evangelical instrument of conversion. For the author of *Uncle Tom's Cabin*, conversion to the cause of immediate emancipation, with its conviction of slavery as sin, must be founded at base on the heart's conversion to Christ. But Stowe portrays Eva as stimulating this twofold conversion not through her speech, so much as through a quality of presence that bears the Word into the world. As an antitype of Eve, Eva epitomizes—within the sentimental terms of Stowe's narrative—the saving power of natural womanhood. Recreating her namesake's title as "the mother of all living" (Gen. 3:20), Eva also epitomizes a more universal maternity than that presented by Marie.

At the same time, Eva reveals herself to be a new Eve in that she bears the Word into a world enslaved by sin and offers herself as agent of the New Birth. She also absorbs the pain of others; for like the *mater dolorosa* of Luke 2:51, she knows what it is for such sorrow to "sink into" her heart (326). Through her devotional exercises, this "fair star" (383) consents to act as feminine intercessor before God for her sinful father. When St. Clare sees her off to church where he will not follow, he nonetheless bids her "pray for me" (278). This intercessory role parallels and supports that of St. Clare's own mother.

However embarrassing by present-day standards of critical taste, Eva's deathscene plainly occupies a pivotal place in the book—and in this character's brief career as mother of conversions. Of course, Stowe does not hesitate to milk the episode for all the Victorian sentiment that a pious maiden's early demise could supply. Precisely the sort of nineteenth-century conventions regarding death that Dickinson mocks so brilliantly in "I heard a fly buzz when I died" come in for solemn treatment here: the circle of chastened mourners, the sacramentalized curls of hair Eva confers as "a last mark of her love," an edifying farewell discourse reminiscent of that given by Jesus in St. John's gospel, and the mourners' urge to glimpse something of the saint's dying vision of joy, peace and love.

Yet beyond its individual demonstration of holy dying, Eva's translation is intended to signal the larger birthpangs of a new order opening from the womb of eternity. As such, the scene incorporates birthing similitudes in its mention of Eva's spasmodic agony leading toward exhaustion, its passage through the tension of midnight vigil when eternity's veil "grows thin" (426) to that blessed change which Tom describes as an opening wide of heaven's door. Still presented as beautiful despite her crimson coloring, Eva dies nobly of consumption, as had the author's mother. In Stowe's idealized fable she is indeed consumed—immediately and integrally, without apparent corruption of body or conflict of spirit—into the dawn of God's Kingdom. No wonder a favorite hymn of Stowe's was the comforting song of death beginning "O mother dear, Jerusalem."[20] This untraumatic form of Eva's rebirth parallels the translation of Mary, otherwise termed her assumption or (in Eastern Orthodox usage) dormition, as set forth in apocryphal and iconographic traditions later described by Stowe in detail. Such traditions regard Mary's assumption as an instance of realized eschatology in which Jesus returns to escort Mary not merely in his role as Son but also as Bridegroom of his beloved.[21] So also Tom counsels watchfulness for the bridegroom's rendezvous with Eva at midnight.

In tandem with this scene, Stowe later depicts a more traumatic version of passage toward the new birth in Tom's martyrdom at the hand of Simon Legree. Already a reconceived *alter Christus*, Tom is delivered to the Kingdom's larger life as "He began to draw his breath with long, deep inspirations; and his broad chest rose and fell, heavily" (591). Moreover, Stowe associates his death mystically with the birthpangs of the apocalyptic endtime. And plainly the archetype of Tom's triumphant passion is found in Jesus' life-giving labor on the cross: "In his patient, generous bosom he bears the anguish of a world. Bear thou, like him, in patience, and labor in love; for sure as he is God, 'the year of his redeemed shall come.'"[22] In the closing pages of her book, the author underscores the natal trauma of this coming age of cataclysm or millennialistic renewal, "an age of the world when nations are trembling and convulsed," when "a mighty influence is abroad, surging and heaving the world." (629) As George Harris interprets the signs of these times, "the throes that now convulse the nations are . . . but the birth-pangs of an hour of universal peace and brotherhood" (611).

Predictably, readers unsympathetic to Stowe's religious values have scorned Tom's nonviolent resistance, his self-sacrificing resignation, as a form of passive docility demeaning to African Americans. No matter that in his defiant love Tom refuses to flog a fellow slave, that he will die rather than betray Cassy and Emmeline, that his response makes possible both their escape and the liberation of slaves on the Shelby estate in Kentucky. In dramatizing her belief in the spiritual force of kenotic or self-emptying love, Stowe does indeed draw on conventional pieties surrounding motherhood and childhood; at the same time she subverts normative values, insofar as she argues not simply for a redistribution but for a redefinition of power. That the "powerfully made" (68) and indubitably masculine Tom nonetheless functions as a kind of heroine, incorporating values traditionally branded as feminine or maternal, is a notable finding of recent feminist criticism. And when Tom assures Legree that he (Tom) "can die," the affirmation carries for Stowe an active import understandable only within the visionary terms of his role—shared with Eva—as divine mother of the nascent Kingdom of God.

Because Tom carries maternal compassion so fully in the body of his own person, his biological mother need not play a role in this narrative. Yet two other mothers in **Uncle Tom's Cabin**, both deceased, continue to influence their sons despite or through their absence. These are the absent mothers of Simon Legree and of Augustine St. Clare. Even Simon Legree, it seems, might have claimed salvation had he not rejected definitively the humanizing and divinizing influence of his mother. From beyond the grave she haunts this would-be reprobate with the spectre of an unresolved identity and almost irresistable grace. Linked to Eva by association with a golden hairthread, Legree's mother signifies not only the shadow of potential regeneracy, but also the suppressed anima of this "grotesquely masculine tyrant."[23] Despite her son's perdition, her intercessory power bears fruit—even at a heavenly distance—by making possible the escape of Emmeline and Cassy.

As a choice version of what Puritans would recognize as the "natural man," an unconverted but sympathetic man of the world, the ironically named Augustine St. Clare does achieve full conviction of his personal depravity. He might therefore be considered ripe for regeneration. Yet before his deathbed change, he is incapable of passing beyond this stage toward the assurance of grace and forgiveness needed for "effectual calling." He also abandons hope when he fails in his romantic ideal of love. Briefly, this Augustine believes more deeply in his capacity for sin than in his ability to embrace the saving goodness of God. He can appreciate, intellectually, the evil of slavery though he is helpless to affirm, existentially, the imperative of emancipation. Accordingly, his predicament reflects Stowe's moral critique of Calvinism. Without the intervention of heaven-sent intermediaries, "Saint Clare" can be neither saintly nor clear of vision.

Yet he is peculiarly susceptible to the influence of feminine grace by virtue of his "marked sensitiveness of character, more akin to the softness of woman than the ordinary hardness of his own sex" (239). And we know that his bible-loving mother had been, literally, another Evangeline. In St. Clare's estimation she "was divine," or at least immaculately conceived in the sense that she betrayed "no trace of any human weakness or error about her" (333). We are told that St. Clare's father once over-ruled her, despite his supreme reverence for her, as brazenly as he would have "the virgin Mary herself" (336). Yet as a woman of Protestant (French Huguenot) stock who plays Catholic organ music, she transcends sectarian categories. That St. Clare's maternal piety leads toward a virtual identification of motherhood with divinity seems apparent when, on his deathbed, he declares he is returning "HOME, at last" and invokes "Mother!" as his final word. Thus St. Clare's absent mother ultimately regains Presence.

In her closing exhortation to the congregation of all America, Stowe warns of wrath from above unless the nation reverses its course toward a dis-union effected by slavery and sin. If "this Union" is "to be saved," to regain health and wholeness, her readers must seize the "day of grace" and assist the birth of God's Kingdom in a convulsive era. (629) But by the close of *Uncle Tom's Cabin,* Stowe establishes that within her hopeful vision of the mother-savior lies the mother-healer who could restore integrity to dismembered families, souls, and sections of the United States.

IV

Seven years after releasing *Uncle Tom's Cabin* in book form, Stowe confronted more directly her own religious and familial heritage in a New England novel featuring an overtly Marian protagonist. Despite its title, *The Minister's Wooing* (1859) focuses less on the historically based character of Samuel Hopkins than it does on the saintly figure of Mary Scudder. If Hopkins fictionally encompasses Lyman Beecher so as to epitomize for Stowe New England's Calvinist patriarchy,[24] it is telling that Mary ends up displacing Hopkins as the novel's theological center. Similarly, Stowe had already advanced her own claim, within a family of noted clergymen, to exercising a ministry of the Word through her authorship of works like *Uncle Tom's Cabin.*

It is telling that the opening still life of Mary Scudder in *The Minister's Wooing* shows her enshrined as the New England maiden, an image superimposed on her iconographic portrayal as the original Virgin Mary. The picture of this girl who at first means never to marry comes complete with a descending dove, forming an overall impression of "simplicity and purity" reminiscent "of some old pictures of the girlhood of the Virgin."[25] Indeed the Roman Catholic Virginie de Frontignac later confides to Mary that "I always think of you when I think of our dear Lady." (394). In her grief, Stowe's American heroine is also likened to the Sistine Madonna and associated with one of da Vinci's Madonnas. Linked repeatedly to the ocean beside Newport, she is

even decked out playfully for her nuptials by Madame de Frontignac to resemble a "sea-born Venus." (423)

This image of Mary's divine womanhood—reinforced by further comparisons to Catherine of Siena, to Dante's Beatrice, and to the saintly wife of Jonathan Edwards—is qualified only slightly by recognition that the dove painted into the *mise en scène* actually belongs to her heathenish cousin James. For Stowe quickly establishes that at another level Mary is herself the dove, one in whom the Holy Spirit ultimately bears vitalizing power as "priestess, wife, and mother" (567).

Like Eva, Mary Scudder fulfills a crucial vocation as the mother of new birth for others. She is a regenerative agent not only for James Marvyn—her cousin, future husband, lusty sailor, and natural man—but also, if with less certain results, for the notorious Aaron Burr, grandson of Jonathan Edwards. She even succeeds in "wooing" the learned Doctor some distance from his overcerebral, self-tormenting Calvinism toward a Christianity allowing greater scope for beauty and divine compassion.

While preserving Mary's image of unspotted virtue, Stowe attributes to her the same initiated understanding of affliction that James remembers seeing pictorialized in "the youthful Mother of Sorrows" (36). Even before she finally achieves biological motherhood at the story's conclusion, then, and particularly after gaining precocious wisdom in her grief over James's supposed death at sea, Mary appears less the virginal innocent than her friend, the nearly ruined "Virginie." Stowe's New England maiden qualifies as a mother-nurturer to others because of her initiation "as a sanctified priestess of the great worship of sorrow" (380).

Yet the way in which Mary Scudder quickens conversion differs in at least one crucial respect from that displayed by Eva St. Clare. For Mary, unlike Eva, draws on sexual energies directed initially toward herself on the way to stirring male desires for the love of God.

Thus, in *The Minister's Wooing* Stowe ventures to affirm that *agape* need not efface *eros* in the divine economy of grace. To be sure, disordered *eros* gives rise to the rapaciousness of Burr, or the psychic bondage of Virginie. Rightly directed, however, natural impulses might elevate the soul toward higher loves, as in the instance of Dante's love for Beatrice. Stowe demonstrates this theological hypothesis by indicating how much of the regenerative inspiration Mary supplies to

ABOUT THE AUTHOR

STOWE AND SOJOURNER TRUTH

Sojourner Truth and Harriet Beecher Stowe met only once, in 1853, when Sojourner made a special trip to Andover to visit the author of *Uncle Tom's Cabin.* Fascinated with the towering Negro woman, Mrs. Stowe called in the members of her eminent family. To Henry Ward Beecher, the influential clergyman, Sojourner exclaimed, "You dear Lamb! The Lord bless you. I love preachers. I'm kind of a preacher myself." In discussing the Woman Movement, Sojourner expressed approval for women's rights but declared laughingly that she would not wear bloomers. Following this meeting, Mrs. Stowe wrote the introduction to a new edition of Sojourner's life story. She also described Sojourner to the sculptor William Wetmore Story when she spoke with him in Rome. As a result, Story transformed his impressions of Sojourner Truth into a marble statue called the Libyan Sibyl, an important prize-winner at the 1862 World's Exhibition in London.

It seems clear, and inevitable, that Sojourner Truth, the itinerant and illiterate orator in the antislavery and feminist movements, won the admiration of Harriet Beecher Stowe. In *The Minister's Wooing,* one of the most important novels in the genre of New England regionalism, Mrs. Stowe presents a character who strongly resembles the black feminist. Candace, the Negro servant, is a large, vigorous, outspoken woman. When a deacon reminds her that she is "the weaker vessel," Candace glances at Cato, her shy and fumbling husband, and replies, "I de weaker vessel? Umph!" The narrator adds: "A whole woman's rights convention could not have expressed more in a day than was given in that single look and word."

Lebeden, Jean. Excerpt from "Harriet Beecher Stowe's interest in Sojourner Truth, Black Feminist." *American Literature* 46 (November 1974): 362.

James Marvyn, Hopkins, and Burr is fueled by eroticism. So *this* Mary is clearly lover as well as spiritual mother—and, without conscious design, she fulfills much of her latter role through the former. The figurative ambiguity corresponds to some traditional symbolizations of the Madonna as both mother and spouse of God.

In *The Minister's Wooing,* then, Stowe underscores her conviction that a progressive scale of affections connects the theological orders of nature and grace, that natural love is indeed sacramental. In contrast to the all-or-nothing ideality of austere Calvinism, she insists that "There is a ladder to heaven, whose base God has placed in human affections, tender instincts, symbolic feelings, sacraments of love, through which the soul rises . . . into the image of the divine." (87).

Within this sacramental scheme, Mary Scudder clearly qualifies as high priestess. Thus James testifies that Mary's image, standing "between me and low, gross vice" (70), elevated his character. In her office as mediator and intercessor, Mary Scudder typifies for Stowe that charism of spiritual maternity shared by many women and some men.

In contrast to this sacramental theology, the hyper-Calvinistic theology of the rungless ladder demands an heroic, unmediated leap of virtue to the point of accepting one's own damnation for the greater glory of God. Stowe suggests that Hopkins' sublime theory of benevolence betrays a masculinized privileging of heroic achievement and individual force of will. For at its worst, the damned theology of Hopkins ends up exalting the nobility of man's self-abnegating exertions over the gracious benevolence of a God who presumably wills to save all repentant sinners. Ironically, this New Divinity comes close to supplanting Calvinism's favored Covenant of Grace with a new Covenant of Works centered in human volition, to replacing the charitable bonds of communitarian Christianity with a virtue borne of heroic individualism.

Depicted novelistically as a sound-hearted eccentric, Doctor Hopkins embodies true virtue both in his personal charity toward African slaves and in his willingness to free Mary from her promise to marry him. But the novel portrays him as a good man largely despite, rather than because of, the theological system he espouses. For Stowe, the rationalistic, disjunctive logic supporting his theology is far less sound than the pneumenal wisdom that sustains the faith of characters like Mary and Candace, the Scudder family's black housekeeper and nurse. In underscoring this point, the author elaborates a gender division in which the epistemology and semiotic expression of male clerics are superseded by those of holy women.

The male-sponsored, rationalistic approach emphasizes verbal knowledge and expression as epitomized by the Doctor's monumental treatise. It is essentially analytic, cerebral, abstracted. By contrast, Stowe's pneumenal way accents iconic or wordless communication, intuitive and poetic knowledge, and matrifocal values.

It is fair to question the gender-specific validity of this opposition, or what appears to be the anti-intellectual tenor of Stowe's sentimental focus on a religion of feeling. Yet the pneumenal epistemology favored in **The Minister's Wooing** does respect a logic of its own.

Thus, the Puritan logic of "evidences" for election is shown to be ultimately illogical insofar as it purports to find rationalistic criteria for judging pneumenal motions of the Spirit. During James's fearful absence at sea, there is no external, empirical evidence to prove that this natural man ever found personal evidence of his conversion and salvation. Hence Hopkins offers no hope for him. Yet Candace, eschewing the "white folks' way of tinkin" and following another "mode of testing evidence," rightly affirms that "Mass'r James is one o' de 'lect' and I'm clar dar's considerable more o' de 'lect than people tink." (447-88, 349)

By contrast with Hopkins, Candace and Mary demonstrate other, more womanly ways of knowing. As Stowe's African re-embodiment of the archaic earth mother, Candace not only displays special powers of intuitive prophecy but also exercises the universal motherhood typified by the Christian Madonna. Thus, Candace rocks the grieving Mrs. Marvyn "as if she had been a babe" (347), reminding her of how tenderly Jesus of Nazareth "looked on His mother" and assuring her that such a Savior "knows all about mothers' hearts" and "won't break yours" (348).

This black mother's pneumenal and aboriginal power as intercessor likewise emboldens her to invoke the authority of the Spirit when she assures Ellen Marvyn, contrary to one version of Calvinist evidence, that James has been "called an' took" (349) among God's elect. Candace bustles about the house, half comically, as a latter-day goddess of abundance and the hearth, an "African Genius of Plenty" (445) resembling one of those rotund fertility figurines from the Neolithic era. But she also performs Christian interces-sion as a Black Madonna who spreads her "ample skirts" over the transgressions of her white and black children and who has "secret bowels of mercy" (112) for James when he is convicted of youthful misbehavior. Hers is indeed a queenly motherhood, as underscored by Doctor Hopkins' joking reference to her name as that of an ancient Ethiopian queen (138); and for nineteenth-century scholars like J. J. Bachofen, "Candace" became a generic term associated with a phase of material and spiritual matriarchy.[26]

In her office as evangelizing intercessor, Mary Scudder likewise mediates the Spirit—as when she quickens Hopkins' soul, passions, and instinct for beauty through "the silent breathing of her creative presence" (93). And though James finds her "a living gospel" who shelters the Word, she achieves this end not mainly through verbalized discourse but through an iconic force issuing from silence. Particularly in her pain, she is framed descriptively as an image of reflective and attentive meditation, like her namesake who ponders words in her heart. Stowe underscores the inspirative power mediated through her face, gestures, and listening presence. As Kristeva says of the Virginal Maternal, Mary Scudder's semiotic import extends "to the extralinguistic regions of the unnamable."[27] Because the language of the Virginal Maternal issues from the Spirit's silence, it is fitting that James progresses toward his shipboard conversion not through any direct verbal initiative but through possession of Mary's Bible, that physical relic whose extra-linguistic power extends the presence of her physical body.

Yet the author's feminized theology reflects more of an adaptation and transformation than a wholesale rejection of masculine precedents in her Christian tradition. It is scarcely surprising that within the sacred bower of Mary Scudder's bedchamber, the library that feeds her imagination includes not only the Bible and a few secular writings but also the works of Jonathan Edwards. For holy New England women could find much to sustain them in the contemplative Edwards—the Edwards who recognized the beauty of divine virtue and the virtue of beauty, or who appreciated the emotive power of affections in drawing souls toward conversion.

Only the ultraCalvinist Edwards, the rigorist who highlighted divine sovereignty and human depravity, needed to be shelved. For Stowe this less congenial exponent of the rungless ladder and a monarchical God had, like his follower Hopkins, lost contact with that homelier life sanctified by Mother and Child:

These hard old New England divines were the poets of metaphysical philosophy, who built systems in an artistic fervor, and felt self exale from beneath them as they rose into the higher regions of thought. But where theorists and philosophers tread with sublime assurance, woman often follows with bleeding footsteps;— women are always turning from the abstract to the individual, and feeling where the philosopher only thinks.

(25)

In a subsequent letter, Virginie de Frontignac enlarges the meaning of these "bleeding footsteps" when she exclaims with reference to Mrs. Marvyn's loss that "the bleeding heart of the Mother of God can alone understand such sorrows" (382) as the book's grieving women—and, presumably, its author—have known. No wonder Mrs. Marvyn, after James's return, sits "looking into her son's eyes, like a picture of the Virgin Mary" (566). Stowe's narrative returns often to this notion that the *heart of the mater dolorosa* lies close to the mystery of a suffering God and that "Sorrow is divine" (360). For "the All-Father treats us as the mother does her 'infant crying in the dark;' he does not reason with our fears, or demonstrate their fallacy, but draws us silently to His bosom, and we are at peace" (425-26).

V

As I hope to establish in a forthcoming full-length study of six literary figures, Stowe was not unique among Protestant writers in expressing fascination with the idea of a Christian Magna Mater at odds with the pragmatic, rationalistic, and competitive impulses of American culture. Especially for writers like Hawthorne and Stowe, figures of Divine Maternity also challenged the predominantly masculine symbol-system inherited from Puritan forebears. But a distinctive mark of Stowe's treatment of Divine Womanhood is the way her fiction draws from Catholic antecedents but re-presents them in Calvinist instances—in characters like Eva St. Clare, Mary Higgins, or Mary Scudder, who are infused in turn with reminiscence of real-life New Englanders such as Sarah Pierrepont. For Stowe this feminized amalgam of Calvinist rectitude and Catholic mythography attached itself, in addition, to Romantic notions of salvific womanhood and to Victorian glorifications of Motherhood. Praising Goethe's great Romantic poem, Stowe observes that Faust is raised from sin not simply through the abstract force of "the eternal womanly" but through the particular intervention of Margaret, "who, like a tender mother, leads the new-born soul to look

upon the glories of heaven." And of course many works published in nineteenth-century America, including Lydia Sigourney's *Letters to Mothers* (1838) or Charles Goodrich's *The Influence of Mothers* (1835), witness to popular faith in the sacred power of a mother's influence in home and community.[28]

Yet for Stowe, post-Calvinist Christian piety supplied an essential continuity beneath all these elements. Thus, her reading of Faust credits Goethe not for articulating a Romantic vision but for displaying appreciation of Christian forgiveness and redemption. It is, after all, not through works but through the womanly mediation of grace that Faust is ultimately saved. And a conspicuous companion of Margaret in the "shining band" of purified women encircling him at his death is "Mary the mother of Jesus."[29] For Stowe, then, the archetype of Divine Maternity found its historic center in the conjoined Mother and Son of Nazareth—the unified epitome of compassionate mother-love.

In personal terms, though, the experience of motherhood seems to have yielded considerable bitterness as well as satisfaction for Stowe.[30] Accordingly, her theologizing imagination drew her persistently toward images of God as suffering servant rather than as superintending monarch, and toward a Jesus who learned something of that servanthood in the household of the *mater dolorosa*. Stowe could envision only such a woman, recalled in her several variants as Eva, Mary Scudder, or Mara with roots in the "salt, bitter waters of our mortal life," interceding on behalf of struggling humankind.

Notes

1. Elizabeth Ammons, "Heroines in *Uncle Tom's Cabin*," *American Literature* 49 (1977): 161-79; Ammons, "Stowe's Dream of the Mother-Savior," *New Essays on Uncle Tom's Cabin*, ed. Eric Sundquist (New York: CUP, 1986) 155-95; Dorothy Berkson, "Millennial Politics and the Feminine Fiction of Harriet Beecher Stowe," *Critical Essays on Harriet Beecher Stowe*, ed. Elizabeth Ammons (Boston: G. K. Hall, 1980) 244-58.

2. For a summary of views on Mary expressed in writings by Charles and Henry Ward Beecher, see Peter Gardella's *Innocent Ecstasy: How Christianity Gave America an Ethic of Sexual Pleasure* (New York: OUP, 1985) 108, 128. In Charles Beecher's *The Incarnation; or, Pictures of the Virgin and her Son* (New York: Harper & Bros., 1849), the author supposes that Mary's beauty of soul was matched by an "exquisite symmetry of physical development" (53).

3. Letter to Sarah Beecher, November 11, 1853 at Stowe-Day Library; Harriet Beecher Stowe, *Sunny Memories of Foreign Lands* (Boston: Phillips, Sampson, 1854) 2:343.

For information concerning the inventory of Stowe's art works, I am indebted to Kristen Froehlich at the Stowe-Day Library and to Renee T. Williams of the New Britain Museum of American Art for her detailed notes on file at Stowe-Day.

4. I say "ostensibly" because Marian devotion also figures notably in Eastern Orthodox spirituality and to some lesser degree in the Anglican and Lutheran traditions, as Frau Inge Leimberg reminded us at the recent *Connotations* conference in Cologne. Yet Marian piety found scant encouragement indeed within the more Calvinist scheme of faith and practice to which Stowe was first exposed.

5. Charles Foster, *The Rungless Ladder: Harriet Beecher Stowe and New England Puritanism* (Durham: Duke UP, 1954) 115.

6. The footsteps material is also available in the collection, *Religious Studies: Sketches and Poems,* vol. 15 of the Riverside Edition (Boston: Houghton Mifflin, 1896). Although Stowe produced many of these religious writings (which typically appeared first as articles in the *Christian Union*) considerably later than her best-known novels, the views they offer of theology generally and of Marian themes in particular show a consistent development from earlier brief statements such as her 1849 Introduction to Charles Beecher's book on *The Incarnation; or Pictures of the Virgin and her Son. The Incarnation* volume also includes an early printing of Stowe's poem "Mary at the Cross," which demonstrates the role Mariology already played in her thinking by 1849. "The Sorrows of Mary," another relevant poem collected (with minor revisions) in *Religious Studies,* first appeared in the Supplement to the *Hartford Courant* for February 16, 1867.

7. *Religious Studies* 31.

8. *Woman in Sacred History* (1873; rpt. New York: Portland House, 1990) 193.

9. *Religious Studies* 36.

10. *Woman in Sacred History* 183, 185-86, 198; *Religious Studies* 36.

11. "For many years my religious experience perplexed me—I could see no reason for it—why God led me thus and so, I have seen lately, and I believe that He has a purpose for which He has kept me hitherto. I am willing to be just such and so much and be used for what He wills—'Behold the handmaid of the Lord.'" Letter to Charles Beecher, likely date fall 1852, at Stowe-Day Library and printed in *Stowe Day Foundation Bulletin* 1:2 (September 1960).

12. *Woman in Sacred History* 198, 183; *Religious Studies* 70.

13. Reprinted in *Religious Studies* 190, 70; *Woman in Sacred History* 183, 70, 190.

14. *Woman in Sacred History* 190.

15. Joan D. Hedrick, *Harriet Beecher Stowe: A Life* (New York: OUP, 1994) 190-91, 214, 254, 274-83. Written after Stowe had lost both Charley and Henry, "The Sorrows of Mary" exposes the poignance of her identification with the *stabat mater:* "Had ye ever a son like Jesus / To give to a death of pain?" (*Religious Studies* 353). But her earlier verses on the same theme, published in 1849 as "Mary at the Cross," were composed before Charley's death. In Charles Beecher's *Plymouth Collection of Hymns and Tunes* (New York: A. S. Barnes and Burr, 1863), a Protestant work with which Stowe was closely associated, Hymn #26 extends involvement of the *stabat mater* figure to any instance of oppression, grief, or terror.

16. *Woman in Sacred History* 172; *Religious Studies* 31.

17. In addition to Berkson and Ammons, critics Alice Crozier (*The Novels of Harriet Beecher Stowe* [New York: OUP, 1969]) and Jane Tompkins (*Sentimental Designs*) have stressed the central role of mothers in Stowe's novel.

18. *Uncle Tom's Cabin, Or Life Among the Lowly,* ed. and intro. Ann Douglas (New York: Viking, 1981) 63. Subsequent references, identified parenthetically, are to this edition.

19. Jane Tompkins, *Sensational Designs* 142.

20. Joan A. Hedrick, *Harriet Beecher Stowe* 8.

21. *Woman in Sacred History* 174-75.

22. In her *Revelations of Divine Love,* which Stowe could not have read, the fourteenth-century English mystic Julian of Norwich envisions a similar connection between birthpangs and the Passion of Jesus.

23. Elizabeth Ammons ("Heroines" 175) aptly describes Legree as "a caricature, and a very serious one, of supermasculinity, which Stowe associates with the devil."

24. See Lawrence Buell, "Calvinism Romanticized: Harriet Beecher Stowe, Samuel Hopkins, and The Minister's Wooing," *ESQ: A Journal of the American Renaissance* 24 (1978): 121.

25. *The Minister's Wooing* (Hartford: Stowe-Day, 1859, 1988) 19. Subsequent references, indicated parenthetically, are to this edition.

26. I am grateful to my graduate student Kurt Heidinger for pointing out this significance of Candace's name. I have also benefitted from discussion of this issue in an unpublished essay by Monica Hatzberger.

27. Julia Kristeva, "Stabat Mater," in *Tales of Love,* trans. Leon S. Roudiez (New York: Columbia UP, 1987) 250.

28. *Religious Studies* 93-94. In her *Letters to Mothers* (New York: Harper and Bros., 1840), Sigourney extols maternal love as changeless and "next in patience to that of a Redeemer" such that it fulfills a "sacred mission." The nearly complete "dominion" of mothers over their children allowed Christian mothers to perform an angelic ministry within the household (49, 53, 16, 10). Elizabeth Ammons ("Stowe's Dream of the Mother-Savior," 158-59), drawing in turn on historian Ruth H. Block, points out that a distinctly idealized concept of "feminized parenthood" or "'motherhood'" did not take hold in America until after the Industrial Revolution.

29. *Religious Studies* 93.

30. In *Harriet Beecher Stowe* (esp. 127, 140-41), Joan A. Hedrick points out that Stowe suffered not only bereavement but also persistent failure in attempting to raise her children and govern her household in a manner consistent with her professed ideology.

TITLE COMMENTARY

Uncle Tom's Cabin

LORA ROMERO (ESSAY DATE WINTER 1989)

SOURCE: Romero, Lora. "Bio-Political Resistance in Domestic Ideology and *Uncle Tom's Cabin*." *American Literary History* 1, no. 4 (winter 1989): 715-34.

In the following essay, Romero offers a biological-political reading of Uncle Tom's Cabin, *arguing that the novel was influenced by Stowe's own sense of her victimization as a woman by a patriarchal system.*

Throughout the decade before she wrote *Uncle Tom's Cabin* (1852), Harriet Beecher Stowe suffered from hysterical episodes that left her bedridden for weeks at a time. These attacks were so severe that from May 1846 to March 1847 she left her husband and their three young children in Cincinnati for Dr. Wesselhoeft's Hydropathic Institute, a fashionable water-cure establishment in Brattleboro, Vermont, recommended to her by her sister Catharine Beecher.[1]

The illness from which Stowe suffered in the 1840s may have, in part, dictated her choice of the subject matter for *Uncle Tom's Cabin* (1852). When read together, *Uncle Tom's Cabin* and Stowe's letters on her illness suggest that the novelist identified the white hysterical housewife with the black Southern slave, seeing both as victims of a patriarchal power that violates the integrity of the self.[2] Because the discourse on hysteria addresses the issue of subjectivity at the same time that it expresses concern for the health of the body, Stowe's figuration of the hysteric as the archetypal victim of patriarchal government in *Uncle Tom's Cabin* encodes, as we shall see, a feminist-abolitionist critique within hygienist norms. Not only does Stowe's medicalizing of feminist critique derive from her sister Catharine Beecher's hygienist concept of bodily economy in her writings on housekeeping, but Beecher's domestic ideology also provides a medical feminism to which Stowe added an abolitionist component when writing *Uncle Tom's Cabin*.[3]

The biographical factors informing Stowe's political consciousness take shape within, and themselves evince, a larger restructuring of political power in relation to medical knowledge in antebellum America. Foucault suggests that "bio-power" or "bio-politics"—the integration of the medical and political—increasingly characterizes the exercise of governmental power in Western countries beginning in the eighteenth century.[4]

Since that time "political technologies that [invest] the body, health, modes of subsistence and lodging" have proliferated—technologies directed toward "*policing*" but of a sort not to be "understood in the limiting, repressive sense we give the term today, but according to a much broader meaning that encompasse[s] all the methods for developing the quality of the population and the strength" of nations (Donzelot 6). Reading the relation between Stowe's hysteria and political critique in *Uncle Tom's Cabin* articulates the history of the bio-political both as discourse and as "the materiality of power operating on the very bodies of individuals" ("Body/Power" 5), in this case the body of the hysterical Stowe.

Feminist scholarship has long recognized the status of both domestic ideology and *Uncle Tom's Cabin* as political critique, but my claim that feminist-abolitionist resistance itself forms an important part of the history of the exercise of governmental power might, at first, seem to imperil such a reading of Stowe's and Beecher's work. Jane Tompkins, for example, asserts that the domesticity of Stowe's novel delineates a feminist "*alternative* . . . world, one which calls into question the whole structure of American society" (144). In Tompkins's remark feminist-abolitionist critique stands in a relationship of alterity to political power and social institutions. Political resistance originates *outside* of established political relations, in the home. In the critical tradition represented by Tompkins, only from such a privileged point can cultural critique transcend "the whole structure of . . . society."[5]

Although my reading of abolitionism and feminism as integral to the rise of bio-power in the United States undermines an oppositional analysis of the two movements, it does *not* illustrate the recuperation of resistance by that which it opposes. Bio-power renders irrelevant the power/resistance binarism upon which Tompkins's analysis depends. In *The History of Sexuality* Foucault displaces the binary with the multiple, asserting that society is "not a structure," but a network of "nonegalitarian and mobile" power relations (93). All of these relations have their limits. While he allows for "hegemonic effect" when some superstructural force "traverses the local oppositions" within otherwise competing power relations and "links them together" (94), Foucault de-essentializes hegemony. A "whole" society to whose monolithic sameness resistance could oppose an equally monolithic difference does not exist; for Foucault, resistance to power *cannot* be grounded in radical alterity. Without a "binary and all-encompassing opposition between rulers and ruled at the root of power relations," there can be "no single locus of great Refusal, no soul of revolt, source of rebellions, or pure law of the revolutionary" (95-96). "Bio-political resistance" is *not* oxymoronic. Thus resistance may be retheorized as historical rather than radical alterity. My reading of the bio-politics of antebellum feminist and abolitionist critique analyzes political resistance as *defined* rather than *contained* by its entanglement in power relations.

1. Feminist Hygiene and Stowe's Hysteria

A conflict between two perceptual modes, absorption and abstraction, structures Stowe's private letters on housekeeping from the late 1830s and the 1840s, a conflict which expresses the impact of the hygienist component of domestic ideology upon Stowe's interpretation of her own hysteria. These letters suggest that Stowe believed that she had a tendency to become absorbed in the physical details of domestic work and that, in order to recover from her illness, she needed to develop a household system, a domestic economy, to abstract herself from "minutiae."

In an 1845 letter to her husband, Stowe describes the drudgery of housework as a perilous visual activity. She describes herself not just (like all other nineteenth-century housewives) "working hard," but also "looking into closets, and seeing a great deal of that dark side of domestic life which a housekeeper may who will investigate too curiously into minutiae . . ." (qtd. in Charles Stowe 111). If this letter presents the dark side of domestic labor as the somatic activity of focusing on particular household details, the specific symptomatology of Stowe's hysteria represents a retreat from such absorptive domestic vision. The author found herself paying for periods of intense domestic labor with ensuing episodes of hysterical blindness and a related "neuralgic complaint that settled in [her] eyes," which, as she put it, rendered her unable "to fix them with attention on anything" (101). Stowe was not so much blinded by her hysteria as incapable of discerning discrete objects. Confined to a darkened room during these attacks, she symbolically eluded absorptive vision at the same time that she actually eluded domestic labor.

Stowe's letters suggest that the author imagined that her failure to impose a larger intellectual system or economy upon household specifics had resulted in her absorption in domestic details and her consequent illness. Stowe opposes absorption

Poster advertising *Uncle Tom's Cabin* (c. 1850).

in domestic minutiae to what she calls "systematic" housekeeping. She writes to a friend in 1838 that "all [her] days [are] made up" of domestic "details" (92), and in a later letter to her husband admits that she is "constitutionally careless and too impetuous and impulsive easily to maintain that consistency and order which is necessary in a family . . ." (qtd. in Wagenknecht 54). The topic of "system and order in a family" inspires Stowe to effuse in one letter she wrote while at Brattleboro, "I know that nothing can be done without it; it is the keystone, the *sine qua non* . . ." (qtd. in Charles Stowe 115). Systematic household organization, symbolizing the housewife's control over otherwise unorganized physical details, represents Stowe's attempt to imagine household labor as something more than manual labor. Expressing a rejection of absorptive domestic vision, Stowe's hysterical blindness answers her fear of being reduced to "a mere drudge with few ideas" (92).

Like Stowe, Beecher understood hysteria to result from absorption in details. In *Letters to the People on Health and Happiness* (1855), Beecher translates external multiplicity, the myriad of household details, into internal fragmentation, hysteria. She rapturously hails systematization as remedying the increasing "nervousness" of American women (111). Systematization, the domestic skill that allowed women to displace the patriarch from the home, conjoins faculties dissevered by patriarchal government and in doing so repairs the self-division that, for Beecher, defines hysteria.

The competing terms (discrete details versus overarching systems) shaping Stowe's interpretation of the origin of her illness also structure Beecher's domestic ideology. A single hygienist dictum informs virtually all of Beecher's writing on housekeeping: no faculty should be developed at the expense of any other. Disproportion must be avoided at all costs. Hysteria is the mark of patriarchal oppression. Beecher uses the concept of bodily economy to articulate a feminist critique of patriarchal government of the home.[6] Beecher, like others committed to educational reform in the late eighteenth and early nineteenth centuries, believed that patriarchal interests had dictated the content of traditional, middle-class female education.[7] In instructing girls exclusively in the ornamental graces requisite for obtaining an advantageous familial alliance through the marriage contract, that education had privileged the development of certain pleasing and marketable skills in women, such as dancing and piano playing. Educational reformers lamented the rarefied and partial product of such an upbringing. They responded with an educational method that they believed would cultivate the whole woman instead of only a few marketable accomplishments—hence Beecher's obsessive dismissal of partiality from female experience.

Beecher banishes disproportion by banishing precisely those absorbing household details that her sister found so problematic. "There is no one thing, more necessary to a housekeeper, in performing her varied duties," proclaims Beecher, who dedicates an entire chapter of her *Treatise on Domestic Economy* (1841) to the subject, "than *a habit of system and order,*" for "the affairs of a housekeeper [are] made up . . . of ten thousand desultory and minute items" (18). In regard to the organization of the troublesome "minutiae of domestic arrangements" (149), Beecher recommends that the housewife devote specific days to specific tasks. In a systematic household Monday might be devoted to mending, Tuesday to washing, Wednesday to ironing, and so forth. For Beecher, the real issue is hygienic rather than merely practical, for a "wise economy is nowhere more conspicuous, than in the right *apportionment of time* to the different pursuits" (144-45). Systematization "modif[ies] any mistaken proportions" in a woman's development (147). It allows her to cultivate various faculties instead of only a few.

Beecher links disproportion to the opening of a gap between mind and body. She designs her postpatriarchal pedagogy to close this gap through the harmonious development of all the faculties (an economy of the body). Referring in her *Letters* to the use of domestic help in wealthy families, Beecher laments that even in America, where there is no genuine aristocracy, one "portion of the women have all the exercise of the *nerves of motion,* and another have all the *brain-work.*" She explains the great virtue of properly systematic housework: "it would exercise every muscle in the body, and at the same time interest and exercise the mind" (111). Disproportional development leads to self-division, hence the alarming incidence of "nervousness" and hysteria among Americans, for, when "equalization of the nervous fluid" is "withheld, the sensibility of the other portions of the brain is liable to become excessive, unnatural, and less under the control of the will" (103). Beecher thinks of labor in the systematic household as active rather than reactive, its stimulus being internal not external, determined by the housekeeper rather than by factors out of her control. Systematic housekeepers, writes Beecher, "control circumstances" rather than allowing "circumstances [to] control them" (*Treatise* 148). For Beecher, domestic economy maintains bodily economy by encouraging women to exercise their will over physical details. In narrowing the gap between mind and body, domestic economy enhances subjectivity and thus combats hysteria.

Stowe's representation of absorptive labor in an essay she wrote on nervousness helps explain the logic of Beecher's belief that the housewife's enslavement to circumstances creates hysterical women. In "Irritability" the novelist speaks of overwork as an "overdraft on the nervous energy, which helps us to use up in one hour the strength of whole days" (76) and compares it to alcohol, tobacco, and coffee, indulgences Beecher repeatedly denounces. According to Stowe, such stimulants permit one to shine "for a few hours of extra brightness," but with an artificial glow. Artificial brightness, produced under the stimulus of excessive labor or narcotic indulgence, destabilizes subjectivity. To be artificially stimulated is to surrender self-determination and willpower and to make the body work independently of the mind. Beecher believes that systematization enhances female subjectivity by coordinating handwork and brainwork, relocating the stimulus for activity within the housewife by creating an economy of the self in which all the faculties surrender control to the will.

Beecher's call for the educational conjunction of physical and intellectual culture partakes in a larger grounding of female subjectivity in resistance to patriarchal control over the home. Other domestic ideologues (both British and American) called for the creation of an integrated female self. These educators also wanted to institute the home, rather than the marriage market, as the focus of female education. If women were to spend the greater part of their adult lives in the home, then their education should prepare them for that life, not prepare them for a lifetime in the ballroom, the theater, or the drawing room. Hannah More, the British author who influenced Beecher, asks, "Do not we educate [our daughters] for a crowd, forgetting they are to live at home? for the world, and not for themselves? for show, and not for use?" (40). According to More, patriarchal education engenders a craving for excitement that domestic life could never gratify and hence produces fragmented female selves, torn between desire and domestic duty. Domestic education of the sort envisaged first by More and later Beecher represents the attempt to imagine a form of household government that would enhance, not undermine, subjectivity.

Because the sphere of female activity defined by Beecher and other female educators is circumscribed by the boundaries of the home, one could argue that domestic ideology extends rather than subverts patriarchal power. Carroll Smith-Rosenberg presents the hysterical woman as a rebel against the coercive ethos of "will, control, and hard work" personified in the ideal domestic woman, whom Smith-Rosenberg sees as the discursive product of patriarchal power. As Jacques Donzelot points out, however, analyses such as these essentialize patriarchal hegemony. "For feminists," writes Donzelot, the rise of the domestic woman "seems of slight importance when weighed against a patriarchal domination seen as essentially unchanged across the centuries." The power/resistance binarism supporting Smith-Rosenberg's argument may "nurture . . . combat," but it also "conceals" historical changes in the family (xxii). Women's colleges, the growth of teaching and nursing as careers for women, the entrance of women into public life through their alliance with social professions, were "the springboard" women "needed for the recognition of [their] political rights" (xxiii). Even if such developments enforced behavioral norms and values that, to use Smith-Rosenberg's words, prepare women "to undertake the arduous and necessary duties of wife and mother" (205), they also legitimated certain versions of female financial and social autonomy, without which female political enfranchisement was unthinkable. Although antebellum domestic feminism may at points intersect and even collaborate with patriarchal power, that does not make the former reducible to the latter.

2. Social and Bodily Economy

Nancy Armstrong has argued that British domestic ideology signals a "cultural change from an earlier form of power based on sumptuary display to a modern form that works through the production of subjectivity" (80). Armstrong's comment applies also to American domesticity, which produces a female subject in the act of resisting patriarchal power.

Beecher's domestic ideology also bears resemblance to a late eighteenth-century European educational analysis of the body's relationship to the state that, according to Donzelot, expressed itself through a political discourse on the health and welfare of the working classes and through a domestic discourse on the preservation of women and children. French educators, physicians, and politicians expressed a concern for the waste of labor resources through state oppression of the working classes at the same time that they exposed the "wasteful" and "artificial" education of the children of the wealthy. Valuable human resources were being squandered both at the bottom and the top of the social scale. The "impoverishment of the nation and the etiolation of its elite" would result, warned these authorities (9). Donzelot describes the bio-politics as a two-part agenda, one, a call for bodily economy to preserve the bodies of upper-class women and children, and the other, a call for social economy to preserve the bodies of the working classes (12-13). Biopolitical resistance unites the working classes with upper-class women and children against the patriarch. It demands that these two groups wrest control over their bodies away from him, stabilize their unstable subjectivities, and practice self-government.

Donzelot's account of bio-politics helps explain Stowe's apparent translation of the terms by which she understood her hysteria into a fictional representation of Southern slavery. In **Uncle Tom's Cabin** bodily economy and social economy merge in a feminist-abolitionist critique of patriarchal power. The very same hygienist logic behind Stowe's understanding of her hysteria governs her analysis of slavery, a coincidence suggested by the parallels her novel articulates between "nervous" white women and overworked black slaves.

In *Uncle Tom's Cabin* the lack of an economy of the body among white women raised in unsystematic aristocratic households recapitulates in its structure the dissociation of mind and body produced by a society in which "a lower class" is "given up to physical toil and confined to an animal nature" so that "a higher one thereby acquires leisure and wealth for a more expanded intelligence and improvement and becomes the directing soul of the lower" (II: 21). This system, as pro-slavery apologist Henry Hughes put it, makes blacks "manualizers" and whites "mentalizers" (86).

The Southern white woman's lack of *wholeness* reflects and is predicated upon the division of labor into mentalizers and manualizers. Significantly, the hysterical and sickly Marie St. Clare is not, as Stowe puts it, a "whole woman." Rather, as Stowe twice repeats, she is "a fine figure, a pair of bright dark eyes, and a hundred thousand dollars" (I: 222, 224). The partial product of patriarchal education, the daughter raised for what Armstrong calls "sumptuary display," becomes an "unsystematic" housekeeper (I: 295). As in Beecher's narrative of the etiology of nervous disease, ill-health in *Uncle Tom's Cabin* originates in the division between mind and body, a gap to whose presence Marie St. Clare's "enervated" nervous system (II: 144), her lapses into "hysterical spasms" (II: 118), and her failure to be a "whole woman" attest.

Even more vividly than Marie's hysterical outbursts, however, Little Eva's fatal illness suggests the bio-political dimension of Stowe's feminism. In representing Eva's slow decline, Stowe wages a bio-political critique of patriarchal power. The novelist describes how the child's body is being used up too quickly. In her illness Eva, who is about eight years old, seems suddenly to undergo puberty. The consumptive flush, as has often been remarked of nineteenth-century representations of the disease, resembles the flush of awakening sexuality—a similarity that suggests that Stowe thinks of Eva, as much as the slave, as a victim of preindustrial southern discipline. Eva's father Augustine St. Clare notes something unnatural and precocious about his daughter. He is struck by "the daily increasing maturity of the child's mind and

feelings," and all notice a new "womanly thoughtfulness" gracing Eva's behavior as her disease progresses (II: 67).

Contemporaneous discussions of consumption further illuminate how Eva's illness symbolizes the dissociation of mind and body produced by patriarchal government. Dr. William Alcott advises that the "common custom of pushing forward the intellect at the expense of the body" lies behind many cases of consumption (273). Alcott sees in consumption a failure to maintain an economy of the body, a dangerous and disproportionate development of one faculty (the imagination) at the expense of development of another faculty (the body).

Moreover, in the dissociation of mind and body depicted in Eva's illness, the novelist creates a version of her own hysteria. At one point St. Clare wonders if Eva isn't growing "nervous"—a suggestion that Eva dismisses, while Stowe notes "a nervous twitching about the corners of her mouth" (II: 28). As Dr. James Clark, a mid-century authority on consumption, writes, there "is more nervous sensibility than is natural to the [consumptive] patient" (31), and Alcott concurs (269). According to Stowe, the nervous are "soon used up" ("Irritability" 71), consumed. Little Eva's precociousness, the rapid consumption of her flesh, her apparent nervous susceptibility, all express Stowe's feminist critique of a patriarchal power that discourages proportional development in women and deprives them of self-government.[8]

In *Uncle Tom's Cabin*, the South uses up black slaves even more conspicuously than it consumes white women. Stowe deems slave labor in the southernmost states as less hygienic than those of more northern regions, for the "general prevalence of agricultural pursuits of a quiet and gradual nature, not requiring those periodic seasons of hurry and pressure that are called for in the business of more southern districts, makes the task of the negro [in states like Kentucky] a more healthful and reasonable one" (I: 23). Because preindustrial Southern labor is task- rather than time-oriented, Stowe can transform the intense physical activity of slaves engaged in absorptive labor into a kind of consumptive fever. As Simon Legree summarizes his treatment of slaves, "Use up, and buy more, 's my way . . ." (II: 173). During the "heat and hurry of the [cotton-picking] season" (II: 183), the overseer's whip temporarily "stimulate[s]" slaves "to an unnatural strength" (II: 191), and hence, in the logic of mid-century hygiene, the bodies of blacks are used up all the more quickly. The term "used up" adumbrates the hygienist maxim upon which Stowe dilates "Irritability": it is better "to labor for years steadily, diligently . . . avoiding those cheating stimulants that overtax Nature" than it is "to pass life in exaltations and depressions, resulting from over-strained labors, supported by unnatural stimulus" (82). The patriarchal stimulus to labor is unnatural in that it comes from outside rather than from within and thus leaves the slave exhausted.

There is nothing remarkable about the fact that Stowe's representation of slavery should refer to the horrific intensity of labor in the fields or that part of Stowe's appeal comes from depicting the toll that slavery takes upon the body. Obviously, attention to the physical effects of slavery on the body furthers both Stowe's realism and her polemic intent; that Stowe embeds her critique of coercive power in the specific logic of bodily economy *does* warrant remark.

Hygienist notions of absorptive labor, and their implicit political critique, even determine Stowe's representation of slave labor of a less intensive variety than field work. The St. Clare's cook Dinah reproduces the southern disciplinary system in her method of managing the St. Clare kitchen. Stowe notes that, even though the kitchen is generally characterized by the most extreme disorder, Dinah "had, at irregular periods, paroxysms of reformation and arrangement, which she called 'clarin' up times'" (I: 302). Labor manifests itself like a spasm or a fever in these "irregular periods." Stowe's language suggests an analogy between Dinah's "clarin' up times" and those "periodic seasons of heat and hurry" characteristic of field work when she refers to the cook's occasional attempts to put the kitchen in order as "periodic seasons" of household reform (I: 303).

Dinah's spasmodic relation to labor symbolizes her spasmodic relation to discipline, the gap that patriarchal government generates between power and subject, the same gap that Stowe also suggests in her representation of Marie St. Clare's lack of "wholeness" and of Little Eva's illness. Stowe's hygienist critique of patriarchal government stresses the inadequacy of power that disrupts the economy of the self. My point is not that Stowe's abolitionist-feminism addresses issues of the body but rather that a nineteenth-century concept of physical health structures the entire logic of Stowe's critique of patriarchal power. Stowe's critique, in other words, is bio-political.

3. The Subject of Resistance

Although Beecher's feminism can be aligned with Stowe's feminist-abolitionism on the basis of the bio-politics they share, bio-politics does not stipulate a conservative or progressive political position. While Stowe translated her belief in the need for an economy of the body into an abolitionist best-seller, Beecher's hygienist fear of the partial and of the detail led her to oppose abolitionism. In her *Essay on Slavery and Abolitionism* (1837), Beecher represents the antislavery movement as a variety of mania by which "the minds of men are thrown into a ferment" (94). Abolitionist leaders, writes Beecher, are probably otherwise moral and reasonable individuals, but because of political measures that require disproportionate fixation on a single idea, a significant portion of the movement's leadership is composed of "men accustomed to a contracted field of observation, and more qualified to judge of immediate results than of general tendencies" (21). Bio-power determines the discursive materials through which various political positions articulate themselves but does not completely determine individual interpretations of those materials into specific political affiliations.

Because the materials of bio-power are subject to multiple, although not infinite, interpretations and uses, Foucault asks that we reconceive power as "power relations" and resistance as "resistances" (*HS* 96); however, in the particular versions of bio-politics represented in Beecher's and Stowe's work, the integration of the political and medical discourages us from thinking of the relationship between power and resistance as anything other than a "binary and all-encompassing opposition." Perhaps we should think of bio-politics not as a particular political interest or stance so much as a way of conceiving the political. Beecher's hygienist analysis of abolitionism is really less concerned with that particular movement than it is a critique of politics in general. Any engagement in politics, for Beecher, threatens the self (throws "the mind of men . . . into a ferment"), because all political beliefs are partial and involve devotion to details at the expense of larger systems. Any relation to power, whether as its victim (in the case of the hysterical housewife) or as its agent (in the case of the hysterical abolitionist), leads to self-division.

To imagine power as something that creates self-division is to imagine power as simultaneously absolute and negative. In discussing the "separation in the subject between *psyche* and *soma*" figured in hysteria, D. A. Miller suggests that, paradoxically, the hysteric, whom I have been representing as like the slave, may be the figure of the liberal subject par excellence. Hysteria, Miller writes, allows us to imagine the radical autonomy

FROM THE AUTHOR

STOWE ON RACIAL PREJUDICE

It is very easy to see that, although slavery has been abolished in the New England States, it has left behind it the most baneful feature of the system—that which makes American worse than Roman slavery—the prejudice of caste and colour. In the New England States the negro has been treated as belonging to an inferior race of beings; forced to sit apart by himself in the place of worship; his children excluded from the schools; himself excluded from the railroad-car and the omnibus, and the peculiarities of his race made the subject of bitter contempt and ridicule.

This course of conduct has been justified by saying that they are a degraded race. But how came they degraded? Take any class of men, and shut them from the means of education, deprive them of hope and self-respect, close to them all avenues of honourable ambition, and you will make just such a race of them as the negroes have been among us.

Stowe, Harriet Beecher. Excerpt from *The Key to Uncle Tom's Cabin*, pp. 52-3. London: Clarke, Beeton, and Co., 1853.

of the individual from the society around her, for "what the body suffers, the mind needn't think" (148). The body of the hysteric, like the body of the slave, is coerced by power, but the mind of both hysteric and slave remains absent and aloof. In Stowe's and Beecher's bio-political imaginations, the nervous woman and the slave are archetypal *objects of power,* but the hygienist body/mind binarism built into the representation of hysteric and slave does not permit them to become the *subjects of power.* Subjectivity, selfhood, individualism are invested in one half of the binarism whereas political relations, power, and society pertain only to the other half. This negative inscription of power enables the oppositionalist understanding of resistance. The hysteric and the slave, as discursive entities, serve simultaneously as figures of utter disempowerment and transcen-

dental resistance, of a resistance whose purity is guaranteed by its radical alterity from what Tompkins calls "the whole structure of society."

That the mind and body could become utterly dissevered, no matter how oppressive the circumstances, is, at best, a dubious proposition. If people could be made into just bodies, slavery would seem less appalling than it is, but Henry Hughes's division of society into manualizers and mentalizers rests on a proposition not just offensive but absurd, that some people are things. Stowe's original subtitle for her novel—*The Man That Was a Thing*—conveys the absurdity of the legal fiction that makes subjects into objects. It expresses the pathos of the situation of human beings treated as though they were simply bodies, and yet, paradoxically, Stowe's concept of resistance to enslavement requires that sometimes people be things.

Even when Stowe represents the resistance to patriarchal government that her novel would appear to legitimate, the hygienist mind/body binarism allows her to imagine the self in a relation of complete exteriority to the political power exercised in the act of rebellion. When George Harris can no longer tolerate his master's abuse and determines to escape slavery or die trying, Stowe represents this as George's loss of control over his body. He "had [formerly] been able to repress every disrespectful word; but the flashing eye, the gloomy and troubled brow, were part of a natural language that could not be repressed—indubitable signs, which showed too plainly that the man could not become a thing" (I: 29). Curiously, in the very moment that George becomes determined to be more than a body, more than a thing, Stowe reduces him to his body.

When George's wife Eliza learns her master has sold their son to a slave trader, she too loses the capacity for self-government. Although she believes she is "wicked" to run away, she explains to her friends that she "can't help it" (I: 63, 64). They express approbation of her actions by asserting that she did "what no kind o' mother could help a doin'!" (I: 139). Eliza's loss of control over her body manifests itself in "[p]ale, shivering . . . rigid features and compressed lips" that make her look like "an entirely altered being from the soft and timid creature she had been hitherto" (I: 60). Not until she has reached Indiana with her son does the "supernatural tension of [her] nervous system [lessen]" and the apparently hysterical Eliza falls into a sort of nervous exhaustion (I: 82).

Stowe's insistence on the mind/body binarism in her representation of first George's and later Eliza's acts of resistance allows the body to suffer "what the mind needn't feel." These two episodes record Stowe's inability to conceive of the subject in any relation to the political. Rebellion in *Uncle Tom's Cabin* is not a political act but rather the radical separation of the individual from all political activity. In Stowe's mind, power and resistance are so polarized that she cannot imagine resistance as the assertion of a legitimate political position against an illegitimate one. Instead, the novelist represents resistance as what Foucault calls the "great soul of revolt," a radically independent self, rebelling against political power in general, rather than some particular and malignant manifestation of power.

Stowe's inability to think of the subject in relation to the political is perhaps even clearer in her characterization of the abolitionist Ophelia's demeanor. St. Clare's cousin from Vermont is as "inevitable as a clock, and as inexorable as a railroad engine." The mechanical metaphors express her disdain for "all modes of procedure which [have] not a direct and inevitable relation to accomplishment of some purpose they definitely had in mind" (I: 229). Stowe represents Ophelia (in what has to be a significant metaphor in an abolitionist novel) as the "absolute bond-slave" of her personal moral code (I: 230), including her abolitionism. Despite Ophelia's obedience to a personal political code rather than external coercion, Stowe suggests Ophelia's mechanical deportment is a self-division comparable to that of the slave laboring under the whip. Although St. Clare's cousin comes from an abolitionist family and expresses strong political views on the issue of slavery, Stowe undermines the legitimating grounds of the abolitionism as a political position when she shows Ophelia recoiling in horror at the sight of whites touching black slaves. Ophelia's automatism suggests that the gap between the subject and the political cannot be bridged.

Even though Simon Legree represents a political position antithetically opposed to Ophelia's, Stowe also understands his pro-slavery ideology too as fundamentally exterior to the self. The novel's final chapters, which show Legree descending into alcoholism and insanity, suggest that Stowe's villain had all along been maddeningly ambivalent about the morality of slavery and that only a Herculean act of self-government, analogous to Ophelia's enslavement to her politics, has enabled him to hold slaves in the first place. His "bullet head" and aggressively mechanical behav-

ior testify to the effort of repressing a pre-political consciousness of the moral sin involved in slave-holding.

Significantly, when Legree's self-government begins to unravel, Stowe symbolizes it with an image of the body uncannily coming to life. On her deathbed Eva gives a lock of her hair to Tom, who later comes into Legree's possession. This lock of hair "like a living thing, twine[s] itself round Legree's fingers" and his memories when he confiscates it from his new possession (II: 216). Eva's memento animates Legree's long-dead memory of the lock of hair that his own saintly mother sent him on her deathbed, hair which also "twined about his fingers" (II: 218). Legree wonders "if hair could rise from the dead!" (II: 220). The uncanniness of this scene consists in the body's (the hair's) refusal to act like a *thing*. Stowe identifies Legree's repressed feelings about slavery with Mrs. Legree's lock of hair, and she configures Legree's eroding ability to repress those emotions as the body uncannily taking on a life of its own.

Integrating the medical and political permits Stowe to imagine in the split between body and mind a transcendent liberal subject radically independent of political power and society in general. One episode especially conveys how absorptive vision returns as the novel's abolitionist desideratum. Augustine St. Clare compares the danger of looking too minutely into the details of the slave system to the danger of looking too minutely into his cook Dinah's slovenly habits of kitchen management. "If we are to be prying and spying into all the dismals of life," he informs his northern cousin Miss Ophelia, who asks him how he can live with his knowledge of the abuse suffered by slaves, "we should have no heart to anything. 'T is like looking too close into the details of Dinah's kitchen . . ." (II: 8). St. Clare later quotes the axiom by which his father conveniently disposed of the matter of the maltreatment of slaves: "General rules will bear hard on particular cases" (II: 17).

In her letters on hysteria Stowe represents herself as a "housekeeper" who "investigate[s] too curiously into minutiae." Stowe was committed to eliciting on behalf of her political cause the absorptive vision and commitment to the particular that St. Clare disavows. According to *A Key to Uncle Tom's Cabin* (1853), general rules, like those promoted by Bird and St. Clare, have impeded emancipation: "The atrocious and sacrilegious *system*," Stowe claims, referring to the institution of slavery, "fails to produce the impression on the mind that it ought to produce because it is lost in generalities." She concludes that she herself "cannot give any idea of the horribly cruel and demoralizing effect of [slavery], except by presenting *facts in detail*" (349; my emphasis). Facts in detail, investigation into minutiae, absorptive vision—these can topple political belief and abstract theories. Whereas Stowe's earlier letters on hysteria express a Beecherian feminist critique of the detail in favor of the system, in ***Uncle Tom's Cabin*** the hysterical violation of economy and wholeness entailed by privileging the detail functions simultaneously as the product of patriarchal power and the grounds of resistance to it.

4. The Cultural Subject

The difficulty of divesting our political imaginations of the prophylactic binarism, the difficulty of imagining a *subject* of power, is suggested by the tendency of even Foucauldian literary criticism to depend upon a body/mind dyad in describing how power works. Foucauldian critics speak of power in the nineteenth century as "internalized . . . institutional control" (Miller 122) and the "inward" relocation of "external discipline's traditional corrective tools" (Brodhead 78). To understand bio-power as internalized physical discipline, as the introjection of the prison cell or the slave master's whip, is to apply the mind/body binarism to consciousness itself. In these tropes power stands in a belated relation to subjectivity. Foucault interrogates this strictly negative concept of power when he questions the "repressive hypothesis" in *The History of Sexuality.* In figuring power as introjected social control these critics fail to challenge "a human subject on the lines of the model provided by classical philosophy, endowed with a consciousness which power is then thought to seize on" ("Body/Power" 58). In *Discipline and Punish* Foucault insists that we "must cease once and for all to describe the effects of power in negative terms." Power "produces," he writes, and precisely what it produces is a subject (194).

Foucauldian criticism on nineteenth-century literature has relied on the oppositional concept of resistance as radical alterity, no doubt because of the difficulty of imagining a productive relationship between the self and power. Inspired by *The History of Sexuality*'s assertion that where "there is power, there is resistance, and yet, or rather consequently, this resistance is never in a position of exteriority in relation to power," followers of Foucault have deconstructed the central binarism of oppositional criticism by demonstrating how political critique fails to occupy such a

position of exteriority and hence is recuperated by power.[9] Only within the logic of the oppositionalist binarism, however, are the failure to stand outside of power and the fact of containment synonymous. Resistance may not transcend power relations altogether, but that does not mean that it merely reproduces the same power relations or that all power relations must reproduce the status quo.

Similarly, thinking of bio-power as having a productive relation to the self does not render it the mere pawn of social control. Foucault writes that "the subject constitutes himself in an active fashion, by the practices of self, these practices are nevertheless not something that the individual invents by himself. They are patterns that he finds in his culture and which are proposed, suggested and imposed on him by his culture, his society and his social group" ("Care of the Self" 11).

In a somewhat different context, the feminist philosopher Judith Butler suggests an alternative model of subjectivity in relation to power which does not depend upon the existence of the liberal subject radically free of "the whole structure of society." Butler describes a "cultural self" created as a "process of interpretation within a network of deeply entrenched cultural norms" (128). This "cultural self" is grounded but not contained, and power invests it in both positive and nondeterminist ways. Butler's concept of the cultural subject suggests a way of thinking ourselves out of the power/resistance binarism informing ***Uncle Tom's Cabin*** and domestic ideology and still operating in feminist oppositional criticism and, far more subtly, in Foucauldian criticism itself.

Notes

1. Forrest Wilson provides the most detailed account available of Stowe's illness. On Dr. Wesselhoeft's Hydropathic Institute, see Kemble and Weiss, 209-18, and on Beecher's relationship to the water cure, see Sklar, 204-09.

2. A discussion of the political problematics of Stowe's identification of white women and slaves is beyond the scope of this study. They are very ably detailed by Sanchez-Eppler.

3. Ammons in "Stowe's Dream of a Mother-Savior," Brown, Tompkins, Brodhead, Fisher, Matthews, and Crumpacker all discuss Stowe's relation to her sister's domestic ideology.

4. Foucault writes that bio-power takes on issues such as "the problems of birthrate, longevity, public health, housing, and migration" and that "its aim is to strengthen the social forces—to increase production, to develop the economy, spread education, raise the level of public morality; to increase and multiply" (*History of Sexuality* 140; *Discipline and Punish* 208).

5. For other examples of feminist oppositional readings of Stowe and domesticity, see Ammons's "Heroines in *Uncle Tom's Cabin*" 153 and Baym 189.

6. Cf. Barker-Benfield's discussion of what he sees as the inherently misogynist concept of bodily economy, and Leach's statement that the concept of bodily economy served the interests of "an emerging hierarchical corporate capitalist system dominated by men" (350-51).

7. On the reform of female education in this period, see Cott 115-16; Kerber 203-21; Sklar 75-76; Donzelot 39; and Armstrong 59-95.

8. I realize that my interpretation of Little Eva's illness and death goes against critical consensus, which has represented Eva's consumption in positive terms, as part and parcel of the larger transcendence of "the physical" necessitated by evangelical belief that "it is the spirit alone that is finally real" (see Tompkins 133). But Stowe's Christianity was of a more muscular variety than critics have generally assumed. In an article appearing in her "The Chimney-Corner" series, Stowe actually attacked revivals of religion because they so "often end in periods of bodily ill-health." Stowe states in this article that the body *need not* be transcended by the true believer. In fact, "[t]he body, if allowed the slightest degree of fair play, so far from being a contumacious infidel and opposer, becomes a very fair Christian helper, and, instead of throttling the soul, gives it wings to rise to celestial regions" ("Bodily Religion" 90).

9. A particularly relevant example of the tendency of Foucauldian criticism to reproduce a pre-Foucauldian conception of power is Brodhead's "Sparing the Rod." There Brodhead asserts that Stowe wants to abolish slavery—but only to replace it with a disciplinary maternal love that is not at all liberating but rather a "new [order] of coercive power" (87). When he suggests that because bourgeois antebellum child-rearing practices enforced behavioral norms they were a form of "coercive power" analogous to slavery, Brodhead effectively collapses the difference Foucault posits between punishment and discipline. While Brodhead is right that neither black slave nor white child is "free" in an absolute sense, Foucault's point is precisely that there exists a whole spectrum of power relations occupying the space between enslavement and absolute freedom.

Works Cited

Alcott, William A. *Lectures on Life and Health.* Boston: Phillips, Sampson, 1853.

Ammons, Elizabeth. "Heroines in *Uncle Tom's Cabin*." *Critical Essays on Harriet Beecher Stowe.* Ed. Elizabeth Ammons. Boston: Hall, 1980. 152-65.

———. "Stowe's Dream of the Mother-Savior: *Uncle Tom's Cabin* and American Women Writers Before the 1920s." *New Essays on* Uncle Tom's Cabin. Ed. Eric J. Sundquist. New York: Cambridge UP, 1986. 155-95.

Armstrong, Nancy. *Desire and Domestic Fiction: A Political History of the Novel.* New York: Oxford UP, 1987.

Barker-Benfield, G. J. *The Horrors of the Half-Known Life: Male Attitudes Toward Women and Sexuality in Nineteenth-Century America.* New York: Harper, 1976.

Baym, Nina. *Novels, Readers, and Reviewers: Responses to Fiction in Antebellum America.* Ithaca: Cornell UP, 1984.

Beecher, Catharine E. *An Essay on Slavery and Abolitionism.* 1837. Freeport, New York: Books For Libraries, 1970.

———. *Letters to the People on Health and Happiness.* New York: Harper, 1855.

———. *Treatise on Domestic Economy.* 1841. New York: Schocken, 1977.

Brodhead, Richard H. "Sparing the Rod: Discipline and Fiction in Antebellum America." *Representations* 21 (Winter 1988): 67-96.

Brown, Gillian. "Getting in the Kitchen with Dinah: Domestic Politics in *Uncle Tom's Cabin*." *American Quarterly* 36 (Fall 1984): 503-23.

Butler, Judith. "Variations on Sex and Gender: Beauvoir, Wittig and Foucault." *Feminism as Critique: On the Politics of Gender.* Ed. Seyla Benhabib and Drucilla Cornell. Minneapolis: U of Minnesota P, 1987. 128-42.

Clark, James. *The Sanative Influence of Climate.* Philadelphia: A. Waldie, 1841.

Cott, Nancy F. *The Bonds of Womanhood: "Woman's Sphere" in New England, 1780-1835.* New Haven: Yale UP, 1977.

Crumpacker, Laurie. "Four Novels of Harriet Beecher Stowe: A Study in Nineteenth-Century Androgyny." *American Novelists Revisited: Essays in Feminist Criticism.* Ed. Fritz Fleischmann. Boston: Hall, 1982. 78-106.

Donzelot, Jacques. *The Policing of Families.* Trans. Robert Hurley. New York: Pantheon, 1979.

Fisher, Philip. *Hard Facts: Setting and Form in the American Novel.* New York: Oxford UP, 1985.

Foucault, Michel. "Body/Power." Trans. Colin Gordon, et al. *Power/Knowledge: Selected Interviews and Other Writings, 1972-1977.* Ed. Colin Gordon. New York: Pantheon, 1980. 55-62.

———. *Discipline and Punish: The Birth of the Prison.* Trans. Alan Sheridan. New York: Vintage, 1979.

———. "The Ethic of Care for the Self as a Practice of Freedom: An Interview." Trans. J. D. Gauthier. *The Final Foucault.* Ed. James Bernauer and David Rasmussen. Cambridge: MIT P, 1988. 1-20.

———. *The History of Sexuality: An Introduction.* Trans. Robert Hurley. New York: Vintage, 1980.

Hughes, Henry. *Treatise on Sociology.* Philadelphia: Lippincott, 1854.

Kemble, Howard R., and Harry B. Weiss. *The Great American Water-cure Craze: A History of Hydropathy in the United States.* Trenton: Past Times, 1967.

Kerber, Linda K. *Women of the Republic: Intellect and Ideology in Revolutionary America.* Chapel Hill: U of North Carolina P, 1980.

Leach, William. *True Love and Perfect Union: The Feminist Reform of Sex and Society.* New York: Basic, 1980.

Matthews, Glenna. *"Just a Housewife": The Rise and Fall of Domesticity in America.* New York: Oxford UP, 1987.

Miller, D. A. "*Cage aux folles*: Sensation and Gender in Wilkie Collins's *The Woman in White*." *The Novel and the Police.* Berkeley: U of California P, 1988. 146-191.

More, Hannah. *Strictures on the Modern System of Female Education.* 3rd American ed. Boston: J. Bumstead, 1802.

Rugoff, Milton. *The Beechers: An American Family in the Nineteenth Century.* New York: Harper, 1981.

Sanchez-Eppler, Karen. "Bodily Bonds: The Intersecting Rhetorics of Feminism and Abolitionism." *Representations* 24 (Fall 1988): 28-59.

Sklar, Kathryn Kish. *Catharine Beecher: A Study in American Domesticity.* New York: Norton, 1976.

Smith-Rosenberg, Carroll. "The Hysterical Woman: Sex Roles and Role Conflict in Nineteenth-Century America." *Disorderly Conduct: Visions of Gender in Victorian America.* New York: Knopf, 1985. 197-216.

Stowe, Charles. *Life and Letters of Harriet Beecher Stowe.* Boston: Houghton, 1889.

Stowe, Harriet Beecher. "Bodily Religion: A Sermon on Good Health." *Atlantic Monthly* Jan. 1866: 85-93. 93.

——. *A Key to Uncle Tom's Cabin.* New York: AMS, 1967. Vol. 2 of *The Writings of Harriet Beecher Stowe.* 16 vols. London: Thomas Bosworth, 1853.

——. "Irritability." *Little Foxes.* Boston: Ticknor and Fields, 1868. 53-90.

——. *Uncle Tom's Cabin; or, Life Among the Lowly.* 2 vols. Boston: J. P. Jewett, 1852.

Sweetser, William. *A Treatise on Consumption.* Boston: T. H. Carter, 1836.

Tompkins, Jane. *Sensational Designs: The Cultural Work of American Fiction, 1790-1860.* New York: Oxford UP, 1985.

Wagenknecht, Edward. *Harriet Beecher Stowe: The Known and the Unknown.* New York: Oxford UP, 1965.

Wilson, Forrest. *Crusader in Crinoline: The Life of Harriet Beecher Stowe.* Philadelphia: Lippincott, 1941.

The Minister's Wooing

ANNE WEST RAMIREZ (ESSAY DATE SPRING 2002)

SOURCE: Ramirez, Anne West. "Harriet Beecher Stowe's Christian Feminism in *The Minister's Wooing*: A Precedent for Emily Dickinson." *Christianity and Literature* 51, no. 3 (spring 2002): 407-24.

In the following essay, Ramirez argues that A Minister's Wooing, with its use of Christian teaching to challenge the dominant patriarchal institutions of its day, illuminates the shared cultural heritage of Stowe and Emily Dickinson.

Fear not, little flock; for it is your Father's good pleasure to give you the kingdom.

—Luke 12:32

God will not let us have heaven here below, but only such glimpses and faint showings as parents sometimes give to children, when they show them beforehand the jewelry and pictures and stores of rare and curious treasures which they hold for the possession of their riper years.

—Harriet Beecher Stowe, *The Minister's Wooing*

The Love a Life can show Below
Is but a filament, I know,

Of that diviner thing
That faints upon the face of Noon—
And smites the Tinder in the Sun—
And hinders Gabriel's Wing—

—Emily Dickinson, Fr285/J673

As Thomas Wentworth Higginson maintains in his 1867 essay "A Plea for Culture," the great minds who are best remembered by posterity are "rarely isolated mountain-peaks" but rather "the summits of ranges" (18). The same argument has been brilliantly expanded by critic David S. Reynolds, who concludes that the great writers of the nineteenth century "memorably reconstructed the popular subversive imagination" and that Emily Dickinson was the "highest product of a rebellious American sisterhood" (567, 413). Many of these rebellious sisters were revisionists rather than radicals. Amid the social constraints and political inequalities they endured, they sought and found liberating principles within their cultural traditions. By privately and sometimes publicly appropriating for themselves the ideals of equality and individualism professed within Christianity, Romanticism, and American democracy, many nineteenth-century women contrived to maintain their sanity and inspire their contemporaries and descendants. From reading Scripture and other literature, they were increasingly empowered to challenge the very institutions that had taught them how and what to read. A striking expression of that challenge is *The Minister's Wooing* (1859) by Harriet Beecher Stowe.

In this novel Stowe balances her themes celebrating romance and domesticity with a good admixture of comedy and satire, all expressed in a remarkably descriptive and leisurely style. Certainly *The Minister's Wooing* is no action-packed adventure story, but it is a shrewd psychological study, a feast for the visual imagination, and a compassionate critique of the New England Puritan tradition. Christianity, Romanticism, and feminism are blended in the portraits of Mary Scudder and several other admirable female characters. Mary is courageous, unselfish, and unconventional, expanding traditional definitions of female virtue. She upholds yet transforms the rigorous Puritan belief system, establishing through her example the possibility of a new community founded upon love rather than fear.

It seems likely that Dickinson may have read and enjoyed *The Minister's Wooing,* inasmuch as it was originally serialized in early issues of the *Atlantic Monthly,* shortly before the peak of Dickinson's creative productivity. As Beth Maclay Doriani has pointed out, Stowe would have provided Dickinson with at least one literary model of an assertive female voice "speaking prophetically while not seeming to transgress cultural boundaries" (149-50). Doriani's *Emily Dickinson, Daughter of Prophecy* provides a wide-ranging examination of Dickinson's prophetic vocation in the context of her religious and intellectual milieu. The present discussion complements this invaluable study by focusing on a single literary contemporary of the poet in detail, partially to establish Stowe as a precedent and potential resource not only for Dickinson but also for other readers (past and present) familiar with the same theological and cultural heritage.[1]

Both Stowe and Dickinson merit the attention of anyone interested in interdisciplinary women's studies, perhaps especially those who continue to grow up, as did these writers, in an evangelical tradition that impresses upon them the concept of the divine presence as unquestionably *there*, no matter how alarming or indifferent that presence might seem. Like Stowe and Dickinson, they cannot escape into comfortable unbelief and thus have no alternative but to seek a more bearable interpretation of their faith. For example, one of the most influential spokeswomen of the evangelical feminist movement in recent decades has been Reta Halteman Finger, for many years editor of the Christian feminist periodical *Daughters of Sarah*. In an analysis of three theories of Christ's atonement, Finger outlines the inadequacies of the commonly promoted substitutionary and moral-influence models of salvation and calls attention to the "Christus Victor" paradigm that predominated in the Church for the first thousand years after Christ. In this model humanity is delivered not from God the Father's wrath but from domination by evil powers, whether invisible or visible, societal or internal. The incarnation, death, and resurrection of Christ are seen as "one continuing conflict with the powers of evil" ("How Can Jesus Save Women?" 16; see also "Your Daughters Shall Prophesy," "The Bible and Christian Feminism"). As we will see, *The Minister's Wooing* likewise modifies the image of a wrathful Father-God, partly by creating a female protagonist as the character most fully reflecting divine grace, and partly by presenting the Puritan minister himself as a more loving and admirable character than might be inferred from his stern theology. Such revisionist perspectives are justifiable in the tradition shared by Stowe, Dickinson, and Finger on the grounds that one's belief system is assumed to be based upon the interpretation of certain primary texts and that all individuals should be educated enough to analyze these texts. Conflicts of interpretation are thus to be resolved by justifying one's theory of literary criticism, so to speak, rather than by deferring to institutional authority. In the long run, as in Stowe's novel, these assumptions have undermined unjust social structures as women and disadvantaged men have drawn support for their liberationist thought and action from biblical texts and finally from one another's texts.

Both Stowe's novel and Dickinson's poems illustrate the psychological suffering shared by many other sensitive spirits growing up in the Calvinist tradition. On the other hand, both writers celebrate love and nature and other joys of earthly existence as precious foretastes of the Kingdom of Heaven rather than distractions from it. Both affirm women's right to develop their own spiritual vision rather than blindly following institutional dictates, even though both reveal some interest in more liturgical Christian traditions. Both contrive to transform the image of virtuous womanhood even while affirming various traditional domestic activities and values, and both reflect concern for the difficulties of other women. Both eloquently describe the suffering of thwarted love and imply that settling for "second best" is an undesirable alternative. Both suggest that learning to live with pain is an inescapable reality of life rather than a source of masochistic pleasure, and both portray the dream of reunion with loved ones in an afterlife. These many similarities are significant regardless of whether it can ever be demonstrated that Dickinson wrote any given poem in direct response to a particular passage by Stowe. Although such specific influence is quite possible, it is in no way essential to the point that *The Minister's Wooing*'s vivid illumination of their shared cultural heritage discourages the image of Dickinson as a masochistic neurotic and supports the impression of her as a relatively well integrated individual who sensitively articulated thoughts and experiences familiar to her contemporaries. The similarities of these two writers are also significant because they anticipate evangelical feminist thinkers of later generations, providing precedents for reinterpreting Christian teachings in ways conducive to theological and social reforms. *The Minister's Wooing* deserves greater attention for these reasons as well as for its own artistic merits.

Set in the late 1700s, Stowe's novel centers on Mary Scudder's love for the young sailor James Marvyn and her strength of character during his absence and after his reported death. Her widowed mother sympathizes with Mary's grief but has never wanted her to marry James because of his religious skepticism. Mother and daughter keep house for the minister, Dr. Samuel Hopkins (an actual figure of colonial history), whose rigorous neo-Edwardsian doctrines distress several members of his congregation. However, the good-hearted Doctor does credit to his faith by denouncing the slave trade, thereby losing his richest parishioner. Mrs. Scudder is delighted as the minister slowly falls in love with her daughter, who resigns herself to her lover's death and agrees to marry Hopkins.

In the meantime Mary has made friends with a young French Catholic woman, who is already married to a pleasant older man but who now has lost her heart to the unscrupulous Aaron Burr (another historical figure and, ironically, the grandson of Jonathan Edwards). As Virginie de Frontignac brings out Mary's best characteristics, the heroine's personality seems increasingly credible as the novel progresses. Upon realizing that Burr sees her as a mere plaything for his leisure hours, Virginie comes to stay with the Scudders while she tries to calm her emotional turmoil and remain a faithful wife. In a remarkably feminist scene Mary firmly impresses upon Aaron Burr that he must cease all contact with Madame de Frontignac. In turn, when James unexpectedly proves to have survived shipwreck, Virginie advises Mary to follow her heart and explain her feelings to the Doctor, rather than place herself in Virginie's predicament of loving one man while being married to another. Predictably, the unselfish Mary believes that she must not break her promise to the minister. However, the village dressmaker (a superbly comic character) takes it on herself to tell Dr. Hopkins that Mary has always loved James, leaving the issue in his hands. After a painful night the Doctor releases his bride-to-be to the young sailor. This generous sacrifice deeply impresses James, who has already become a more serious Christian during his long absence from Mary.

The novel's sentimental tendencies are counterbalanced by Stowe's humorous account of James Marvyn's mischievous childhood (see 64-65), the hilarious figure of Miss Prissy the dressmaker, the relationship of the servants Candace and Cato, and the informal diction of many of the characters. Moreover, although a superficial reader might classify Mary Scudder as a familiar stereotype of sentimental Victorian piety, Mary's inner conflicts over her love for James, her duty to her mother, and her genuine affection for Dr. Hopkins are realistically described. Furthermore,

Stowe carefully contrasts Mary's spiritual influence on others with the ministry of Dr. Hopkins so as to demonstrate that a woman can manifest the image of God as thoroughly as any institutional male authority—a point perennially disputed by those opposed to the official ordination of women. Mary's character testifies to certain strengths in her religious tradition yet undercuts it in that her holiness does not derive from the kind of formal theological study to which the Doctor devotes his life. Stowe even cites Jonathan Edwards' deservedly famous description of his future wife, Sarah Pierrepoint, as an historical example supporting the credibility of her heroine (155-56).

Another model for Mary Scudder appears to have been the author's mother, Roxana Foote Beecher. Dying when Harriet was scarcely five, Roxana was remembered in the large family as a saint. However, Stowe's biographer, Joan D. Hedrick, implies that Roxana's life was in some respects at least as tragic as her early death. When as a child Harriet visited her mother's relatives at Nutplains, she found a very different world from Lyman Beecher's strict regime, even though Beecher had discarded some of the harsher Puritan teachings such as infant depravity. Grandmother Foote and Aunt Harriet were Episcopalians and sent the Beecher children presents at Christmas, a day not celebrated in their household. In her youth the cultured and well read Roxana had heard of distant lands and customs from her seafaring brother Samuel, and even learned French from a West Indian emigrant, but in her busy years as a minister's wife and mother of nine children she had very little time to read and reflect. Completely worn out, she died of tuberculosis at the age of forty-one (Hedrick 7).

In *The Minister's Wooing* Roxana's daughter has Virginie de Frontignac warning Mary what will happen if she sends James away and marries the minister: "[M]ust you struggle always, and grow whiter and whiter, and fall away into heaven, like the moon this morning, and nobody know what is the matter? People will say you have the liver-complaint, or the consumption, or something. Nobody ever knows what we women die of" (304). Here it seems likely that Stowe indirectly recalls the difficulties of her mother's life, worn down by the needs and demands of those who made her into the household saint. Although the author gives Dr. Hopkins truly admirable qualities, from the beginning she enlists the reader's sympathies on the side of James Marvyn, the cheerful and adventurous sailor reminiscent of her Uncle Samuel Foote (who, incidentally, prevailed upon Lyman Beecher to allow novel-reading in his home). Hedrick perceptively concludes: "Combining the prophetic intensity of her father with the literary and cultural heritage of her mother, Harriet Beecher Stowe fused the best of her paternal and maternal heritage. She transformed the role of the angel in the house from a purely self-denying (and ultimately fatal) script into one in which she was a facilitator of and minister to the spirits of others" (9).

The commendable tolerance of Mary and Virginie for one another's religious beliefs reflects this ability to synthesize different perspectives. Harriet Beecher grew up hearing not only her father's exhortations to seek the Calvinist high road to salvation, but also her maternal relatives' concern for the soul of Lyman Beecher himself. The names of Mary and Virginie both recall the mother of Jesus, as if to suggest that they represent parts of one whole.

Like Stowe, Dickinson seems to deplore the self-sacrificial existence often expected of women in their society, as in Fr857/J732:

> She rose to His Requirement—dropt
> The Playthings of Her Life
> To take the honorable Work
> Of Woman, and of Wife—

If the character feels any regret, "It lay unmentioned" as if buried in the sea. Of course, the marvelous irony of this poem lies in its third-person perspective; the speaker is in fact able to perceive what the dutiful wife bravely tries to conceal from the world. Here Dickinson implicitly criticizes the same fate that Virginie de Frontenac fears for Mary if she marries the Doctor, despite his merits.

As Ann Douglas notes, Mary's spiritual sensitivity is combined with the "faculty" of making the lightest biscuits and creamiest butter in the village; she is her mother's daughter as well as her father's. Thus Stowe gently criticizes the absent-mindedness of Dr. Hopkins, who devotes himself to thought and study while the two women provide for all his material needs (Douglas 75). Mary also does her own spinning and weaving, as did Stowe's pre-industrial Nutplains relatives. She is thus much more economically productive than the stereotypical Victorian domestic angel. As Mary spins in her little garret overlooking an apple tree, one is tempted to see her as yet another "madwoman in the attic," embodying the famous metaphor applied by Sandra M. Gilbert and Susan Gubar to Dickinson and several other women writers.[2] Of course, this is not to say that Mary is forc-

ibly isolated by anyone, as is Bertha Antoinetta Mason in Charlotte Brontë's *Jane Eyre*. Rather, she apparently draws inner strength from voluntary times of solitude (as Dickinson seems to have done), enabling her mysterious transformation of the religious conventions she seems to follow so carefully into a spirituality so uniquely her own that Dr. Hopkins himself is humbled by her unswerving confidence in God's love. As for James, the seeds of his conversion are sown by his shamed realization that his love for Mary seems pathetically self-serving compared to her passionate willingness to give up her own salvation if only it could somehow ensure his entry into heaven.

Stowe is emphatically Romantic and painfully honest in portraying the struggles of Mary and Virginie to forget the men to whom they have lost their hearts. Neither James's supposed death nor Aaron Burr's self-centeredness makes it any easier for either woman to control her deep love. Stowe's plot recalls a cluster of traditional ballads in which a maiden hears that her beloved is lost at sea, marries another man, and subsequently is persuaded to desert him by the returning lover—or the devil who takes his shape—only to meet her death by shipwreck. A similar scenario is poignantly rendered in the literary ballad "Auld Robin Gray" by Lady Ann Lindsay (1750-1825). In this case the speaker marries to help her poverty-stricken parents. When her supposedly dead lover unexpectedly returns, she feels it is her duty to remain loyal to her husband (exactly as Mary Scudder would have done had James come home a week later):

> I gang like a ghaist, and I carena to spin;
> I daurna think on Jamie, for that wad be a sin,
> But I'll do my best a gude wife ay to be,
> For auld Robin Gray he is kind unto me.
>
> (153)

Stowe might easily have known Lindsay's ballad, just as she knew the songs of Robert Burns. It may not be coincidence that her sailor lover is named James and that her title, like "Auld Robin Gray" and the "House Carpenter" ballad, oddly refers to the woman's second lover rather than to the woman herself who would seem to be the protagonist.

Still another obvious literary analogy, directly alluded to in the novel (178), is the story of Penelope staving off her suitors as she waits for Odysseus to come home, although in that case the couple are already married before Odysseus goes away. The common theme among all these narratives is the virtue of fidelity: under no circumstances should the young woman marry anyone other than her lost beloved, for this decision leads to disaster if she leaves the marriage or to misery if she stays. Every character in Stowe's novel appears to agree with this conventional wisdom except for Mary herself and her protective mother.

Similarly, we may never be certain whether Dickinson suffered a single great bereavement that outweighed all other sorrows, but if she did she evidently chose to remain faithful to that relationship's memory. As she affirms in Fr884/J781: "To wait Eternity—is short— / If Love reward the end." Many of her more somber poems that describe the aftermath of tragic loss reflect this same principle of fidelity even when hope of earthly reunion is gone. In Fr683/J618 the persona describes the terrible "Width of Life . . . / Without a thing to do" spreading before her and begs for simple tasks such as the "humblest Patchwork— Children do— / To still it's noisy Hands—[Help it's Vacant Hands—]." After her bereavement Mary Scudder's "care about the details of life seemed more than ever minute; she was always anticipating her mother in every direction, and striving by a thousand gentle preveniences to save her from fatigue and care" (218). When Madame de Frontignac takes refuge with the Scudders, she too devotes herself to helping with the domestic tasks and continues to adorn her appearance as she tries to subdue her feelings for Aaron Burr. Much the same attitude is expressed in a haunting Dickinson poem, Fr522/J443, in which the speaker disciplines herself to meet her responsibilities and achieve external calm despite great suffering:

> I tie my Hat—I crease my Shawl—
> Life's little duties do—precisely—
> As the very least
> Were infinite—to me—

Like Stowe's heroines, Dickinson's speaker feels that she is facing "Miles on Miles of Nought," yet she commits herself to "life's labor— / Though life's Reward—be done."

The imperceptible easing of pain, experienced by both Mary and Virginie, is paralleled by Dickinson's "It ceased to hurt me, though so slow / I could not feel the trouble [Anguish] go" (Fr421/J584), in which the speaker, "looking back," begins to sense that "whereas 'twas Wilderness— / It's better—almost Peace—." At first Virginie is startled that Mary has agreed to marry the Doctor, as she clearly sees it is "not the light of any earthly love" in her friend's face "but only the calmness of a soul that knows itself no more" (248). However, she sadly concludes that Mary will "have peace" by this means (249).

The subplot is essential to Stowe's achievement in *The Minister's Wooing,* for Mary's character is perhaps most successfully dramatized by her passionate interview with Aaron Burr on behalf of her friend. The author's analysis of Burr resembles her father's view of Lord Byron as a tragic figure who went astray and wasted his great gifts (Crozier 207). Burr is utterly astonished to hear the gentle Puritan maiden pronounce that he has "done a very great injury" to Madame de Frontignac and "taken the very life out of her." Dismissing his cultivated protests, Mary continues:

> You men can have everything—ambition, wealth, power; a thousand ways are open to you: women have nothing but their heart; and when that is gone, all is gone. . . . You have stolen all the love she had to give . . . and you can never give her anything in return, without endangering her purity and her soul. . . . [A]nd if you die, as I fear you have lived, unreconciled to the God of your fathers, it will be in her heart to offer up her very soul for you, and to pray that God will impute all your sins to her, and give you heaven.
>
> (275-76)

Similarly, in Dickinson's "I cannot live with you" (Fr706/J640) the speaker affirms that "were You lost, I would be— / Though my name / Rang loudest / On the Heavenly fame."

Mary's indignation reveals a deeply feminist awareness that women's suffering is multiplied because society allows them to define themselves only in terms of their relationships, whereas men have many other ways to define themselves and seek fulfillment. The fact that no painless alternatives exist for either young woman at this point seems to reflect stark realism rather than the sentimental masochism described at length by Marianne Noble. Even though Virginie experiences one form of suffering by avoiding Burr, the alternative of becoming illicitly involved with him would also result in suffering. Similarly, Mary will continue to grieve for James no matter whether she does or does not marry the Doctor. Neither Mary nor Virginie welcomes pain, and Stowe specifically undercuts Mary's mood of extreme self-abnegation after James's shipwreck as "a state not purely healthy" (217), in which her spirit is "utterly divided from the world" (218). Although Dickinson is noted for her eloquent expression of suffering, she too can be seen as resisting rather than collaborating with the patriarchal culture so often responsible for women's pain. Doriani argues that "Dickinson transformed renunciation. . . . Certainly such a transformation was necessary for the woman prophet in America, who had to alter a conventional social role of renunciation into renunciation as prophetic stance" (162-63). Neither Stowe nor Dickinson implies that coping with pain as constructively as possible is necessarily equivalent to passively accepting, or desiring, suffering on society's terms.

Paradoxically, it is only in the arena of religious faith—despite the elements in Calvinism that Stowe deplores—that society allows a woman such as Mary to be the equal or superior of any man, no matter what his learning or institutional office. At the same time, Stowe suggests that the impossibly high standards for salvation and full church membership, as promoted by Hopkins and other followers of Edwards, are much to blame for inadvertently alienating the James Marvyns and Aaron Burrs of the world from Christianity. The damage sometimes wrought by such disturbing doctrines as predestination is painfully evident in the scene at the Marvyn home when word comes that James is lost at sea. Mrs. Marvyn is a deeply sensitive and well read woman who cannot help fearing that she fails to meet the strict criteria for salvation set forth by her religious community. Worse yet, she fears for the souls of those she loves and thus is thrown into agonies lest James has been condemned for all eternity. (Mrs. Marvyn is commonly thought to be modeled on the author's sister, Catherine, who suffered similar distress upon her fiancé's death). Neither Mr. Marvyn nor Mary can halt the tide of the mother's near-insane despair: "The number of the elect is so small we can scarce count them for anything! Think what noble minds, what warm generous hearts, what splendid natures are wrecked and thrown away by thousands and tens of thousands!" she cries out in honest rage (199). "It is *not* right! . . . I never can think it right,—never!" (200). It is Candace, the maternal African freedwoman, who brings Mrs. Marvyn some measure of comfort as she challenges the teachings of their church with her description of a compassionate Christ whose love cannot possibly be less than that of fallen human creatures.

Dickinson parallels the reactions of Stowe's characters in such poems as Fr1675/J1601:

Of God we ask one favor,
That we may be forgiven—
For what, he is presumed to know—
The Crime, from us, is hidden—

Similarly, in Fr1752/1719 she describes a "jealous" Deity who "cannot bear to see / That we had rather not with Him / But with each other play." Dickinson's poems repeatedly express torments lest the world to come be less precious than the beauty and relationships enjoyed on earth. Never-

theless, in other poems she finds her way to an image of Christ much like that of Stowe's Candace, as Dorothy Huff Oberhaus has explained.

On the whole, *The Minister's Wooing* is not so much a forum for conventional piety as it is an effort to take seriously the emotional and philosophical problems arising within Puritan culture and to dramatize them through the interaction of characters as lively as many in the novels of Charles Dickens. Even if some readers cannot find Mary credible, Stowe lavishes vivid description and considerable wit upon her portraits of Mrs. Katy Scudder, Miss Prissy, Cerinthy Ann, Madame de Frontignac, and several minor characters from the community. The resulting heteroglossia is delightfully illustrated by Miss Prissy's description of Madame de Frontignac's decoration of the best room for Mary's wedding:

> . . . she spent nobody knows what time in going round and getting evergreens and making wreaths, and putting up green boughs over the pictures, so that the room looked just like the Episcopal Church at Christmas. In fact, Mrs. Scudder said, if it had been Christmas, she shouldn't have felt it right, but, as it was, she didn't think anybody would think it any harm.
>
> (322)

For a wedding the Puritan conscience accepted the colorful decoration and ritual that would be avoided at Christmas to emphasize the community's separation from Anglo-Catholic tradition. Ironically, the only rituals to thrive in Puritan New England were those of nature (as Stowe reminds us through repeated mention of morning birdsong, lilacs, apple blossoms, and apples), as well as the dressmaking and decorating rituals maintained by women in honor of great events in the natural life cycle.

Similarly, among the descendants of Calvinist tradition, a fondness for decorative domestic arts, natural foods, organic gardening, and the like still continues to coexist with a preference for relatively unadorned church buildings and ritual-free worship services. Lawrence Buell speaks of the "obsolescence of Stowe's literary renditions of Puritanism as opposed to Hawthorne's" as being due to his greater ability to transform "Puritan categories into techniques that could be transported across regional and temporal lines" (280). It could be argued, however, that the Puritans of *The Minister's Wooing* resemble many Americans of today much more than do the stern characters in *The Scarlet Letter*, even though Stowe may not be Nathaniel Hawthorne's rival as an artist in some other respects.

Dickinson is entirely at one with Stowe in her imaginative appreciation of the New England countryside and in her resistance to the separation of life into secular and sacred compartments. She too seems to have measured time by the smallest details of the changing seasons. The robin is a favorite image with both writers; more than thirty Dickinson poems mention robins. A memorable example is "The Robin's my Criterion for Tune—" (Fr256/J285), in which the images move through the signs by which the speaker anticipates each season. Both Stowe and Dickinson "see— New Englandly" and recreate their vision for the delight of their readers. Although the Puritans rejected the colorful celebrations of the Anglo-Catholic liturgical year, Dickinson virtually reinvented a similar symbolic system for herself, as Barton Levi St. Armand has demonstrated through a detailed chart of her imagery (317), and Stowe enjoyed attending Episcopal services in her later years—sometimes in Grace Church, Amherst, where her daughter Georgianna's husband served as rector.

Critic Gayle Kimball assumes that Stowe concurred with the supposedly common Victorian belief that women had no sexual passions and were above the carnal temptations afflicting males (100-02). Mary Scudder's saintliness, however, is combined throughout the novel with her ineradicable Romantic yearning for the body and soul of her tall, black-haired lover whom she never expects to meet again in this life. Just before he reappears, she is meditating upon her approaching marriage, still unable in the privacy of her imagination to see anyone but James as bridegroom: "She fell into one of those reveries which she thought she had forever forbidden to herself, and there rose before her mind the picture of a marriage-ceremony,—but the eyes of the bridegroom were dark, and his curls were clustering in raven ringlets, and her hand throbbed in his as it had never throbbed in any other" (291).

In every respect Stowe predisposes the reader to agree with Virginie's argument against keeping Mary's secret love from the Doctor: "My dear child, do you think, if he should ever find it out after your marriage, he would think you used him right?" (304). James similarly points out, "Is it a kindness to a good and noble man to give yourself to him only seemingly, when the best and noblest part of your affections is gone wholly beyond your control?" (306-07). At the same time, we are meant to admire Mary's self-sacrificing concern for the Doctor's feelings and her deep joy over James's conversion. The latter circumstance literally transforms Mary's appearance during the last Sunday service before she is to marry the Doctor, in a scene almost certainly intended to recall the Transfiguration of Christ: "Everybody noticed, as she came into church that morning, how beautiful Mary Scudder looked. It was no longer the beauty of the carved statue, the pale alabaster shrine, the sainted virgin, but a warm, bright, living light" (309). The author blends earthly and heavenly longings into one as Mary's exalted vision of eternity is founded on her now-certain hope of reunion with James, even though in this scene she still fully intends to marry Dr. Hopkins: "And as Mary sang, she felt . . . that life is but a moment and love is immortal, and seemed, in a shadowy trance, to feel herself and him, far over on the shores of that other life, . . . all tears wiped away, and with full permission to love and be loved forever" (310). Dickinson imagines a similar celestial "Bridal" in Fr691/J625:

> 'Twas a long Parting—but the time
> For Interview—had Come—
> Before the Judgment Seat of God—
> The last—and second time
>
> These Fleshless Lovers met—
> A Heaven in a Gaze—
> A Heaven of Heavens—the Privilege
> Of one another's Eyes—

With gentle irony Stowe proceeds to bring about the happy ending, not through the heroine's much-extolled virtues but through Miss Prissy's kind-hearted revelation to the Doctor, encouraged by Madame de Frontignac and old Candace. Instead of dying like Little Eva of **Uncle Tom's Cabin** and other sentimental heroines of popular culture, Mary survives to enjoy the fulfillment of her love on earth. Perhaps the marriage of Mary and James symbolizes the union of the more positive elements of the Puritan heritage with the good things of earthly life—precisely the resolution evidently sought by Dickinson, as well as by many others within their tradition. However, Dickinson's integration of earth and heaven did not include marriage and motherhood, a choice that Stowe indirectly helps to clarify.

According to Kimball, Stowe must be recognized as an influential voice who "did much to shackle women to domesticity and the avoidance of competition with men," hindering the "achievement of equal rights for women" (168). It is true that in essays such as "Woman's Sphere" Stowe expressed the common belief that the majority of women would continue to seek and find their greatest happiness in marriage and motherhood, and she does exalt the good mother as the ultimate source of all efforts to transform the evils of society (*Household Papers* 249-73). Kimball's conclusion nevertheless must be questioned in light of *The Minister's Wooing,* for here Stowe, whether consciously or not, subverts the cult of motherhood to a startling extent. Both Mary and James are explicitly described as having independent personalities that continually surprise their mothers. Neither Mrs. Scudder nor Mrs. Marvyn could be labeled a bad mother, but neither is presented as primarily responsible for molding her child into the kind of young adult each has become. The same might reasonably be said of Dickinson's mother as well. Each mother does the best she can according to her lights, but Mrs. Scudder and Mrs. Marvyn are far more human and realistic than the stereotypical ideal that Stowe might elsewhere seem to endorse. If anything, the affection between Mary and her mother seems rather like the relationship between Emily and Lavinia Dickinson, one marked by mutual respect for their different temperaments.

In her helpful introduction to the new Penguin edition of *The Minister's Wooing,* Susan K. Harris rightly notes that it can be read as a feminist text, "especially in its focus on the transition from textual to experiential piety" (xx). However, Stowe and other nineteenth-century Americans lived in a period of increasing tension between the improvement of educational opportunities for women and the economic pressures of industrialization to keep hearth and home separate from the world of commerce. This separation of spheres was much less evident in the late eighteenth-century culture in which Stowe places Mary Scudder. Although division of labor certainly existed, couples such as the Marvyns interacted with one another in the course of a day considerably more than would their counterparts in later decades. As Hedrick puts it, "When women's informal ministry was enshrined in Victorian parlors swathed in tapestries and filled with worldly goods, its radical challenge to male structures of power was sharply curtailed" (287). If there was a feminization of Christianity during the course of the nineteenth century, its potential to reform society was partially negated by the secularization of power; a woman-centered religion is not necessarily a feminist one. A consequence of these cultural conditions was the compromising view that women—perhaps exceptional women—could indeed do most of the same things as men but that they could not raise a family at the same time.

In theory this view is sorely outdated; in practice the dilemma it recognizes is far from being solved. In the meantime many talented women besides Dickinson have felt obliged to make choices not faced by men. Kimball notes that 60-70% of the first generation of graduates from women's colleges did not marry (161). One begins to wonder who actually lived according to the stereotype of the cultured Victorian mother who devoted herself primarily to husband and children. Stowe was fortunate enough to have household help in order to obtain some time to write, but as she explains in *The Minister's Wooing* (282) and in a perceptive essay titled "**The Lady Who Does Her Own Work**" (*Household Papers* 85-101), a great many refined and educated American women, outside of the South, had to spend considerable time doing household tasks that would have been done by servants in comparable English homes. Children were commonly expected to help, rather than receive undivided attention from their mothers. In this context Dickinson's lifestyle seems quite explicable and rational.

It is true that the Dickinsons had an Irish maid and gardeners for many years, but they fit Stowe's description of American hired help who assisted the family members with the work as opposed to doing all of it for them. It must be recalled that the poet contributed long hours of active labor to the maintenance of a leading citizen's large home. Aife Murray argues that the ebb and flow of Dickinson's writing corresponds with the absence and presence of a maid (although there probably were other factors as well). After the creativity of the early 1860s, the poet wrote less from 1865 until 1869, when Maggie Maher was hired (286). Although Dickinson appears to have composed—or at least copied out—her poems more plentifully again in the early 1870s, she also worked side by side with Maggie and her sister as long as her health permitted (287-88). As it was, Dickinson had enough to distract her from perfecting her art. It is not surprising that she, like many other intellectual women of the era, did not undertake the additional responsibilities of marriage and motherhood.

Dickinson's "Don't put up my Thread and Needle" (Fr681/J617) poignantly hints at the poet's efforts to integrate different facets of her life. The speaker, apparently too ill to rise from her pillow, is regretting her "zigzag stitches" and promising to do better:

These were bent—my sight got crooked—
When my mind—is plain

I'll do seams—a Queen's endeavor
Would not blush to own—

Read metaphorically, the poem might be interpreted as an expression of anxiety about her vision and of eagerness to resume her writing as soon as her health permitted. However, the persona of the frustrated seamstress who longs to perfect her fine embroidery suggests the poet's respect for the gifts of other women, and perhaps her identification with their distress when temporarily unable to fulfill their domestic responsibilities. At the same time, the seamstress persona may reflect Dickinson's ironic awareness that many people would sympathize with a woman apologizing for the interruption of domestic activities, but not with a woman concerned about neglecting her calling as prophetic artist. Even more ironically, the poem might be read as a half-sincere, half-mocking apology for falling behind in the household arts *because* of taxing her sight and energies by writing.

The Minister's Wooing enables readers to understand better the heritage underlying Dickinson's art and life. If she ever experienced a romantic crisis in which she suffered a separation from her beloved, as many have speculated, Stowe's novel makes it the more credible that she refused to settle for second best (the bereaved Catherine Beecher also remained single). If, as others infer, the poet personally suffered the religious doubts and fears expressed in her poetry, *The Minister's Wooing* lays bare the theological system that evoked such reactions and, once again, makes the poet's responses seem more natural than neurotic. As Alfred Habegger points out in his recent biography, "not one document from her many literate and outspoken contemporaries speaks of her as crazy" (411)—extraordinary and enigmatic, admittedly, but far from dysfunctional. If the contradictory perspectives on love, religion, and death within Dickinson's poems seem baffling, it is plausible to hypothesize that she sometimes imaginatively articulates the thoughts and emotions of characters encountered in her reading (or of friends and acquaintances). Perhaps it is within reason to see some affinities between the impact of Mary Scudder on other characters and the impressions of Dickinson recorded by those who knew her.

In an eloquent obituary in the *Springfield Republican,* Susan Gilbert Dickinson felt moved to eulogize her sister-in-law with unqualified respect:

So intimate and passionate was her love of Nature,
she seemed herself a part of the high March sky,
the summer day and bird-call. Keen and eclectic

in her literary tastes, she sifted libraries to Shakespeare and Browning; quick as the electric spark in her intuitions and analyses, she seized the kernel instantly, almost impatient of the fewest words, by which she must make her revelation. To her life was rich, and all aglow with God and immortality. With no creed, no formulated faith, hardly knowing the names of dogmas, she walked this life with the gentleness and reverence of old saints, with the firm step of martyrs who sing while they suffer.

(qtd. in Leyda 2:473)

Similarly, Susan's daughter, Martha Dickinson Bianchi, would later recall her aunt's "accomplished cheerfulness," surmising that her "unfailing demeanor in her daily life" may have been influenced by her perusal of the *Imitation of Christ,* the fifteenth-century classic. "In certain moods she would likely have tossed up the crown for the immediate earthly gift withheld her," Bianchi acknowledges, yet, echoing one of Dickinson's frequent metaphors, she concludes, "That her soul had a guest has never been doubted" (303). Like Stowe's Mary Scudder, however, the poet seems to have been rather less ascetic than Thomas a Kempis, considering her passionate appreciation for the most commonplace joys of earthly life.

In addition to these tributes, an article by Dickinson's first cousin Clara Newman Turner recalls the poet as angelic, sensitive, extraordinarily moved by the beauties of nature, and sympathetically available to the orphaned Clara and her sister Anna, who were placed in Austin's family to help care for Ned and Mattie (see Sewall 1:264-75). In all these accounts we catch glimpses of a courageously independent spirit living in accordance with her own conscience rather than by the rules of institutional authority, just as Mary Scudder's inward grace seems to transcend the spiritual processes set forth in Calvinist doctrine. If the character of Mary was not among the resources contributing to the poet's "accomplished cheerfulness," it would seem fair to observe that Dickinson's personality, as described by those closest to her in life, independently supports the realism of Mary's characterization.

An 1854 editorial by one Paula Wright Davis argues that women's rights are advanced not only by public oratory and political activity but also "by any independent working woman, by any woman novelist, by any woman editor," and by any woman who is a creative artist, "the holiest reformer of them all" (qtd. in Reynolds 397). Karen Dandurand has established that a considerable audience had begun to appreciate Dickinson's gifts during her lifetime through the sharing of poems enclosed in letters and the reprinting of a few poems that were published in the newspapers—as well as Colonel Higginson's reading of her manuscripts to the New England Women's Club in 1875 (255-68). Although this semi-public dissemination was often anonymous, allowing Dickinson to maintain the seclusion her temperament and goals required, in "I Sing to use the Waiting" (Fr955/J850) she anticipates the "journey to the Day" amid companions who will freely "tell each other how We sang / To keep the Dark away." Cheryl Walker's landmark study *The Nightingale's Burden: Women Poets and American Culture before 1900* maintains that the poet's "sensibility was consistent in many important respects with the sensibility of other women writers of her time" (109). This conclusion should be construed as a compliment to Dickinson as well as to her contemporaries.

Among them Stowe, outwardly so different from Dickinson, deserves increased recognition for her detailed illumination of their common cultural heritage and for the very real literary merits of **The Minister's Wooing**. Few nineteenth-century novels maintain such a delicate balance between honest disillusionment with conventional religion and the imaginative invocation of that very religion's ideals as the foundation for a more egalitarian and holistic spiritual vision. History tells us what has been; literature tells us what might be.

Notes

1. Also complementing Doriani's work is my essay "The Art to Save: Emily Dickinson's Vocation as Female Prophet," in which thematic clusters of prophetic poems are classified and examined. An influential earlier source providing some relevant analysis of the poet's relationship to religious faith is Eberwein's *Dickinson: Strategies of Limitation*.

2. See Gilbert and Gubar's analysis in "A Woman—White: Emily Dickinson's Yarn of Pearl" (581-650), which includes some discussion of the poet's strategy of adopting personae.

Works Cited

Bianchi, Martha Dickinson. "The Books of Revelation." Appendix A. St. Armand 299-305.

Buell, Lawrence. *New England Literary Culture: From Revolution through Renaissance.* New York: Cambridge UP, 1986.

Crozier, Alice C. *The Novels of Harriet Beecher Stowe.* New York: Oxford UP, 1969.

Dandurand, Karen. "Dickinson and the Public." *Dickinson and Audience.* Ed. Martin Orzeck and Robert Weisbuch. Ann Arbor: U of Michigan P, 1996. 255-77.

Dickinson, Emily. *The Poems of Emily Dickinson.* Ed. Thomas H. Johnson. 3 vols. Cambridge: Belknap-Harvard UP, 1955.

———. *The Poems of Emily Dickinson.* Variorum edition. Ed. Ralph W. Franklin. 3 vols. Cambridge: Belknap-Harvard UP, 1998.

Doriani, Beth Maclay. *Emily Dickinson, Daughter of Prophecy.* Amherst: U of Massachusetts P, 1996.

Douglas, Ann. *The Feminization of American Culture.* New York: Avon, 1977.

Eberwein, Jane Donahue. *Dickinson: Strategies of Limitation.* Amherst: U of Massachusetts P, 1985.

Finger, Reta Halteman. "The Bible and Christian Feminism." *Daughters of Sarah* May/June 1987: 5-12.

———. "How Can Jesus Save Women? Three Theories on Christ's Atonement." *Daughters of Sarah* Nov./Dec. 1988: 14-18.

———. "Your Daughters Shall Prophesy: A Christian Feminist Critiques Feminist Theology." *The Other Side* Oct. 1988: 28-41.

Gilbert, Sandra M., and Susan Gubar. *The Madwoman in the Attic: The Woman Writer and the Nineteenth-Century Literary Imagination.* New Haven: Yale UP, 1979.

Habegger, Alfred. *My Wars Are Laid Away in Books: The Life of Emily Dickinson.* New York: Random, 2001.

Harris, Susan K. Introduction. *The Minister's Wooing,* by Harriet Beecher Stowe. New York: Penguin, 1999. vii-xxiii.

Hedrick, Joan D. *Harriet Beecher Stowe: A Life.* New York: Oxford UP, 1984.

Higginson, Thomas Wentworth. "A Plea for Culture." 1867. *Atlantic Essays.* Boston: Osgood, 1871. 3-22.

Kimball, Gayle. *The Religious Ideas of Harriet Beecher Stowe: Her Gospel of Womanhood.* Studies in Women and Religion 8. New York: Mellen, 1982.

Leyda, Jay. *The Years and Hours of Emily Dickinson.* 2 vols. New Haven: Yale UP, 1960.

Lindsay, Lady Ann. "Auld Robin Gray." *The Golden Treasury.* Ed. Francis Turner Palgrave. 1861. New York: Oxford UP, 1986. 152-53.

Murray, Aife. "Kitchen Table Poetics: Maid Margaret Maher and Her Poet Emily Dickinson." *Emily Dickinson Journal* 5 (1996): 285-96.

Noble, Marianne. *The Masochistic Pleasures of Sentimental Literature.* Princeton: Princeton UP, 1999.

Oberhaus, Dorothy Huff. "'Tender Pioneer': Emily Dickinson's Poems on the Life of Christ." *American Literature* 59 (1987): 341-58.

Ramirez, Anne West. "The Art to Save: Emily Dickinson's Vocation as Female Prophet." *Christianity and Literature* 47 (1998): 387-401.

Reynolds, David S. *Beneath the American Renaissance: The Subversive Imagination in the Age of Emerson and Melville.* Cambridge: Harvard UP, 1988.

St. Armand, Barton Levi. *Emily Dickinson and Her Culture.* Cambridge: Cambridge UP, 1984.

Sewall, Richard B. *The Life of Emily Dickinson.* 2 vols. 1974. New York: Farrar, 1980.

Stowe, Harriet Beecher. *Household Papers and Stories*. Vol. 8 of *The Writings of Harriet Beecher Stowe*. 16 vols. New York: AMS-Houghton, 1967.

———. *The Minister's Wooing*. 1859. New York: Penguin, 1999.

Walker, Cheryl. *The Nightingale's Burden: Women Poets and American Culture before 1900*. Bloomington: Indiana UP, 1982.

FURTHER READING

Bibliography

Stowe-Day Memorial Library and Margaret Granville Mair. *The Papers of Harriet Beecher Stowe*. Hartford, Conn.: Stowe-Day Foundation, 1977, 74 p.

Contains an alphabetized list of recipients, chronology, and correspondence.

Biographies

Adams, John R. *Harriet Beecher Stowe*. Boston: Twayne Publishers, 1989, 131 p.

Offers a succinct biography of Stowe.

Boydston, Jeanne, Mary Kelley and Anne Throne Margolis. *The Limits of Sisterhood: The Beecher Sisters on Women's Rights and Woman's Sphere*. Chapel Hill: University of North Carolina Press, 1988, 393 p.

Provides documents and correspondence from the Beecher sisters and offers insight into their roles and relationships.

Hedrick, Joan D. *Harriet Beecher Stowe: A Life*. New York: Oxford University Press, 1994, 544 p.

Provides a contextual overview of Stowe's life.

Knight, Denise D. "Harriet Beecher Stowe (1811-1896)." In *Nineteenth-Century American Women Writers: A Bio-Bibliographical Critical Sourcebook*, edited by Denise D. Knight, pp. 406-13. Westport, Conn.: Greenwood Press, 1997.

Overview of Stowe's life, her major works and themes, and the critical response to her writing.

Criticism

Ammons, Elizabeth. *Critical Essays on Harriet Beecher Stowe*, edited by Elizabeth Ammons. Boston: G. K. Hall, 1980, 307 p.

Offers a variety of critical perspectives on Stowe's work.

Berkson, Dorothy. "'So We All Became Mothers': Harriet Beecher Stowe, Charlotte Perkins Gilman, and the New World of Women's Culture." In *Feminism, Utopia, and Narrative*, edited by Libby Falk Jones and Sarah Webster Goodwin, pp. 100-15. Knoxville: University of Tennessee Press, 1990.

Argues that Stowe, Charlotte Perkins Gilman, and other early feminist writers believed that the only way to correct the patriarchal system was to put the values of motherhood at the center of the culture.

Boyd, Richard. "Models of Power in Harriet Beecher Stowe's *Dred*." *Studies in American Fiction* 19, no. 1 (spring 1991): 15-30.

Considers how Dred *offers hope for an alternative to the system that generated and sustained slavery, suggesting that a proposed model is based on a benevolent matriarchal structure.*

Crane, Gregg D. "Dangerous Sentiments: Sympathy, Rights, and Revolution in Stowe's Antislavery Novels." *Nineteenth-Century Literature* 51, no. 2 (September 1996): 176-204.

Explores Stowe's ideas about natural rights in Dred *and* Uncle Tom's Cabin.

Crozier, Alice C. *The Novels of Harriet Beecher Stowe*. New York: Oxford University Press, 1969, 235 p.

The first major reassessment of Stowe's novels in the twentieth century.

Crumpacker, Laurie. "Four Novels of Harriet Beecher Stowe: A Study in Nineteenth-Century Androgyny." In *American Novelists Revisited: Essays in Feminist Criticism*, edited by Fritz Fleischmann, pp. 78-106. Boston: G. K. Hall & Co., 1982.

Examines the evolution of Stowe's thinking in her four major novels, focusing on the author's changing ideas about the role of women.

Donovan, Josephine. "Harriet Beecher Stowe's Feminism." *American Transcendental Quarterly* 47-48 (summer-fall 1980): 141-57.

Discusses the feminist aspects of Stowe's writing.

Fetterley, Judith. "Only a Story, Not a Romance: Harriet Beecher Stowe's *The Pearl of Orr's Island*." In *The (Other) American Traditions: Nineteenth-Century Women Writers*, edited by Joyce W. Warren, pp. 108-25. New Brunswick, N. J.: Rutgers University Press, 1993.

Discusses the composition of The Pearl of Orr's Island *and the author's ambivalent attitude toward the work.*

Formichella, Annamaria. "Domesticity and Nationalism in Harriet Beecher Stowe's *Agnes of Sorrento*." *Legacy: A Journal of American Women Writers* 15, no. 2 (1998): 188-203.

Claims that Agnes Sorrento, which is set in Italy, is a cultural critique of Stowe's own country and patriarchal institutions.

Hedrick, Joan D. "Harriet Beecher Stowe." In *Prospects for the Study of American Literature: A Guide for Scholars and Students*, edited by Richard Kopley, pp. 112-32. New York: New York University Press, 1997.

Presents a broad overview of Stowe's writings and their critical reception in an attempt to assess the research required in Stowe scholarship.

Hovet, Theodore. "Rummaging Through the Past: The Cultural Work of Nostalgia in Harriet Beecher Stowe's *My Wife and I*." *Colby Quarterly* 32, no. 2 (June 1996): 113-24.

Explores issues of cultural and religious nostalgia and mass culture in My Wife and I.

———. "The Power of the Popular: The Subversion of Realism in Harriet Beecher Stowe's *My Wife and I*." *American Literary Realism, 1870-1910* 29, no. 2 (winter 1997): 1-13.

Discusses the tension between realism and popular culture—specifically between modern urban life and sentimental romance—in My Wife and I.

Kirkham, E. Bruce. "The Writing of Harriet Beecher Stowe's *The Pearl of Orr's Island*." *Colby Library Quarterly* 16, no. 3 (September 1980): 158-65.

Discusses the composition of The Pearl of Orr's Island *and what it reveals about Stowe's writing habits and her relationship with publishers.*

Lowance, Jr., Mason I., Ellen E. Westbrook, and R. C. De Prospo, eds. *The Stowe Debate: Rhetorical Strategies in* Uncle Tom's Cabin. Amherst: University of Massachusetts Press, 1994, 315 p.

Collection of twelve essays that explores issues of language, rhetoric, narrative, domesticity, sentimentality, race, and slavery in Uncle Tom's Cabin.

Newman, Judie. "Stowe's Sunny Memories of Highland Slavery." In *Special Relationships: Anglo-American Affinities and Antagonisms 1854-1936,* edited by Janet Beer and Bridget Bennett, pp. 28-41. Manchester: Manchester University Press, 2002.

Discusses a travel letter by Stowe in which the author is misinformed about the conditions of European laborers.

Noble, Marianne. "The Ecstasies of Sentimental Wounding in *Uncle Tom's Cabin.*" *The Yale Journal of Criticism* 10, no. 2 (fall 1997): 295-320.

Examines the problems involved with Stowe's use of intersubjectivity at the level of the body for her feminist and abolitionist project.

Robbins, Sarah. "Gendering Gilded Age Periodical Professionalism: Reading Harriet Beecher Stowe's *Hearth and Home* Prescriptions for Women's Writing." In *"The Only Efficient Instrument": American Women Writers and the Periodical, 1837-1916,* edited by Aleta Feinsod Cane and Susan Alves, pp. 45-65. Iowa City: University of Iowa Press, 2001.

Discusses the articles written for the domestic women's magazine Hearth and Home *and Stowe's advice to aspiring authors.*

Ryan, Susan M. "Charity Begins at Home: Stowe's Antislavery Novels and the Forms of Benevolent Citizenship." *American Literature* 72, no. 4 (December 2000): 751-82.

Argues that Stowe's moral and racial politics should be understood in their historical context.

Sajé, Natasha. "Open Coffins and Sealed Books: The Death of the Coquette in Harriet Beecher Stowe's *Dred.*" *Legacy: A Journal of American Women Writers* 15, no. 2 (1998): 158-70.

Explores the role of the coquette and the question of "true womanhood" in Dred.

Smith, Gail K. "Reading with the Other: Hermeneutics and the Politics of Difference in Stowe's *Dred.*" *American Literature* 69, no. 2 (June 1997): 289-313.

Details Stowe's awareness of the hermeneutic debates of her day and her interest in reading, interpretation, and textual ambiguities.

Sundquist, Eric J. *New Essays on* Uncle Tom's Cabin, edited by Eric J. Sundquist. Cambridge: Cambridge University Press, 1986, 208 p.

Includes critical and historical essays on the novel and discussions of Stowe's influence on fellow women writers.

Tompkins, Jane P. "'Sentimental Power': *Uncle Tom's Cabin* and the Politics of Literary History." In *The New Feminist Criticism: Essays on Women, Literature, and Theory,* edited by Elaine Showalter, pp. 81-104. New York: Pantheon Books, 1985.

Offers a discussion of the elements and uses of the sentimental in the novel.

Warhol, Robyn R. "Poetics and Persuasion: *Uncle Tom's Cabin* as a Realist Novel." *Essays in Literature* 13, no. 2 (fall 1986): 283-97.

Discusses past assessments of Uncle Tom's Cabin, *arguing that the work should be seen as a realist novel, focusing in particular on its so-called "sentimental" narrative strategies.*

OTHER SOURCES FROM GALE:

Additional coverage of Stowe's life and career is contained in the following sources published by the Gale Group: *American Writers Supplement,* Vol. 1; *Authors and Artists for Young Adults,* Vol. 53; *Concise Dictionary of American Literary Biography,* 1865-1917; *Dictionary of Literary Biography,* Vols. 1, 12, 42, 74, 189, 239, 243; *DISCovering Authors; DISCovering Authors: British Edition; DISCovering Authors: Canadian Edition; DISCovering Authors Modules: Most-studied Authors and Novelists; DISCovering Authors 3.0; Exploring Novels; Junior DISCovering Authors; Literature and Its Times,* Vol. 2; *Literature Resource Center; Major Authors and Illustrators for Children and Young Adults,* Eds. 1 and 2; *Nineteenth-Century Literature Criticism,* Vols. 3, 50, 133; *Novels for Students,* Vol. 6; *Reference Guide to American Literature,* Ed. 4; *Twayne's United States Authors; World Literature Criticism; Yesterday's Authors of Books for Children.*

INDEXES

The main reference

Austen, Jane 1775-1817 **1**: 122, 125, 220; **2**: 104, 196, **333-384**

lists the featured author's entry in volumes 1, 2, 3, 5, or 6 of Feminism in Literature; *it also lists commentary on the featured author in other volumes of the set, which include topics associated with* Feminism in Literature. *Page references to substantial discussions of the author appear in boldface.*

The cross-references

See also AAYA 19; BRW 4; BRWC 1; BRWR 2; BYA 3; CD-BLB 1789-1832; DA; DA3; DAB; DAC; DAM MST, NOV; DLB 116; EXPN; LAIT 2; LATS 1; LMFS 1; NCLC 1, 13, 19, 33, 51, 81, 95, 119; NFS 1, 14, 18; TEA; WLC; WLIT 3; WYAS 1

list entries on the author in the following Gale biographical and literary sources:

AAL: Asian American Literature

AAYA: Authors & Artists for Young Adults

AFAW: African American Writers

AFW: African Writers

AITN: Authors in the News

AMW: American Writers

AMWR: American Writers Retrospective Supplement

AMWS: American Writers Supplement

ANW: American Nature Writers

AW: Ancient Writers

BEST: Bestsellers (quarterly, citations appear as Year: Issue number)

BG: The Beat Generation: A Gale Critical Companion

BLC: Black Literature Criticism

BLCS: Black Literature Criticism Supplement

BPFB: Beacham's Encyclopedia of Popular Fiction: Biography and Resources

BRW: British Writers

BRWS: British Writers Supplement

BW: Black Writers

BYA: Beacham's Guide to Literature for Young Adults

CA: Contemporary Authors

CAAS: Contemporary Authors Autobiography Series

CABS: Contemporary Authors Bibliographical Series

CAD: Contemporary American Dramatists

CANR: Contemporary Authors New Revision Series

CAP: Contemporary Authors Permanent Series

CBD: Contemporary British Dramatists

CCA: Contemporary Canadian Authors

CD: Contemporary Dramatists

CDALB: Concise Dictionary of American Literary Biography

CDALBS: Concise Dictionary of American Literary Biography Supplement

CDBLB: Concise Dictionary of British Literary Biography

CLC: Contemporary Literary Criticism

CLR: Children's Literature Review

CMLC: Classical and Medieval Literature Criticism

CMW: St. James Guide to Crime & Mystery Writers

CN: Contemporary Novelists

CP: Contemporary Poets

CPW: Contemporary Popular Writers

CSW: Contemporary Southern Writers

CWD: Contemporary Women Dramatists

CWP: Contemporary Women Poets

CWRI: St. James Guide to Children's Writers

CWW: Contemporary World Writers

DA: DISCovering Authors

DA3: DISCovering Authors 3.0

DAB: DISCovering Authors: British Edition

DAC: DISCovering Authors: Canadian Edition

DAM: DISCovering Authors: Modules

    DRAM: Dramatists Module; *MST:* Most-Studied Authors Module;

    MULT: Multicultural Authors Module; *NOV:* Novelists Module;

    POET: Poets Module; *POP:* Popular Fiction and Genre Authors Module

DC: Drama Criticism

DFS: Drama for Students

DLB: Dictionary of Literary Biography

DLBD: Dictionary of Literary Biography Documentary Series

DLBY: Dictionary of Literary Biography Yearbook

DNFS: Literature of Developing Nations for Students

EFS: Epics for Students

EXPN: Exploring Novels

EXPP: Exploring Poetry

EXPS: Exploring Short Stories

EW: European Writers

FANT: St. James Guide to Fantasy Writers

FW: Feminist Writers

GFL: Guide to French Literature, Beginnings to 1789, 1798 to the Present

GLL: Gay and Lesbian Literature

HGG: St. James Guide to Horror, Ghost & Gothic Writers

HLC: Hispanic Literature Criticism

HLCS: Hispanic Literature Criticism Supplement

HR: Harlem Renaissance: A Gale Critical Companion

HW: Hispanic Writers

IDFW: International Dictionary of Films and Filmmakers: Writers and Production Artists

IDTP: International Dictionary of Theatre: Playwrights

LAIT: Literature and Its Times

LAW: Latin American Writers

JRDA: Junior DISCovering Authors

LC: Literature Criticism from 1400 to 1800

MAICYA: Major Authors and Illustrators for Children and Young Adults

MAICYA: Major Authors and Illustrators for Children and Young Adults Supplement

MAWW: Modern American Women Writers

MJW: Modern Japanese Writers

MTCW: Major 20th-Century Writers

NCFS: Nonfiction Classics for Students

NCLC: Nineteenth-Century Literature Criticism

NFS: Novels for Students

NNAL: Native North American Literature

PAB: Poets: American and British

PC: Poetry Criticism

PFS: Poetry for Students

RGAL: Reference Guide to American Literature

RGEL: Reference Guide to English Literature

RGSF: Reference Guide to Short Fiction

RGWL: Reference Guide to World Literature

RHW: Twentieth-Century Romance and Historical Writers

SAAS: Something about the Author Autobiography Series

SATA: Something about the Author

SFW: St. James Guide to Science Fiction Writers

SSC: Short Story Criticism

SSFS: Short Stories for Students

TCLC: Twentieth-Century Literary Criticism

TCWW: Twentieth-Century Western Writers

WCH: Writers for Children

WLC: World Literature Criticism, 1500 to the Present

WLCS: World Literature Criticism Supplement

WLIT: World Literature and Its Times

WP: World Poets

YABC: Yesterday's Authors of Books for Children

YAW: St. James Guide to Young Adult Writers

The Author Index lists all of the authors featured in the Feminism in Literature *set. It includes references to the main author entries in volumes 1, 2, 3, 5, and 6; it also lists commentary on the featured author in other author entries and in other volumes of the set, which include topics associated with* Feminism in Literature. *Page references to author entries appear in boldface. The Author Index also includes birth and death dates, cross references between pseudonyms or name variants and actual names, and cross references to other Gale series in which the authors have appeared. A complete list of these sources is found facing the first page of the Author Index.*

A

Akhmatova, Anna 1888-1966 **5: 1–38**
  See also CA 19-20; 25-28R; CANR 35; CAP 1; CLC 11, 25, 64, 126; DA3; DAM POET; DLB 295; EW 10; EWL 3; MTCW 1, 2; PC 2, 55; RGWL 2, 3

Alcott, Louisa May 1832-1888 **2: 78, 147, 297–332**
  See also AAYA 20; AMWS 1; BPFB 1; BYA 2; CDALB 1865-1917; CLR 1, 38; DA; DA3; DAB; DAC; DAM MST, NOV; DLB 1, 42, 79, 223, 239, 242; DLBD 14; FW; JRDA; LAIT 2; MAICYA 1, 2; NCLC 6, 58, 83; NFS 12; RGAL 4; SATA 100; SSC 27; TUS; WCH; WLCWYA; YABC 1; YAW

Allende, Isabel 1942- **5: 39–64**
  See also AAYA 18; CA 125; 130; CANR 51, 74, 129; CDWLB 3; CLC 39, 57, 97, 170; CWW 2; DA3; DAM MULT, NOV; DLB 145; DNFS 1; EWL 3; FW; HLC 1; HW 1, 2; INT CA-130; LAIT 5; LAWS 1; LMFS 2; MTCW 1, 2; NCFS 1; NFS 6, 18; RGSF 2; RGWL 3; SSC 65; SSFS 11, 16; WLCS; WLIT 1

Angelou, Maya 1928- **5: 65–92**
  See also AAYA 7, 20; AMWS 4; BLC 1; BPFB 1; BW 2, 3; BYA 2; CA 65-68; CANR 19, 42, 65, 111; CDALBS; CLC 12, 35, 64, 77, 155; CLR 53; CP 7; CPW; CSW; CWP; DA; DA3; DAB; DAC; DAM MST, MULT, POET, POP; DLB 38; EWL 3; EXPN; EXPP; LAIT 4; MAICYA 2; MAICYAS 1; MAWW; MTCW 1, 2; NCFS 2; NFS 2; PC 32; PFS 2, 3; RGAL 4; SATA 49, 136; WLCS; WYA; YAW

Atwood, Margaret (Eleanor) 1939- **5: 93–124**
  See also AAYA 12, 47; AMWS 13; BEST 89:2; BPFB 1; CA 49-52; CANR 3, 24, 33, 59, 95; CLC 2, 3, 4, 8, 13, 15, 25, 44, 84, 135; CN 7; CP 7; CPW; CWP; DA; DA3; DAB; DAC; DAM MST, NOV, POET; DLB 53, 251; EWL 3; EXPN; FW; INT CANR-24; LAIT 5; MTCW 1, 2; NFS 4, 12, 13, 14; PC 8; PFS 7; RGSF 2; SATA 50; SSC 2, 46; SSFS 3, 13; TWA; WLC; WWE 1; YAW

Austen, Jane 1775-1817 **1: 122, 125, 220; 2: 104, 196, 333–384**
  See also AAYA 19; BRW 4; BRWC 1; BRWR 2; BYA 3; CD-BLB 1789-1832; DA; DA3; DAB; DAC; DAM MST, NOV; DLB 116; EXPN; LAIT 2; LATS 1; LMFS 1; NCLC 1, 13, 19, 33, 51, 81, 95, 119; NFS 1, 14, 18; TEA; WLC; WLIT 3; WYAS 1

B

Beauvoir, Simone (Lucie Ernestine Marie Bertrand) de 1908-1986 **5: 125–174**
  See also BPFB 1; CA 9-12R; 118; CANR 28, 61; CLC 1, 2, 4, 8,

F

French, Marilyn 1929- **5**: 469–484
    See also BPFB 1; CA 69-72;
    CANR 3, 31; CLC 10, 18, 60,
    177; CN 7; CPW; DAM DRAM,
    NOV, POP; FW; INT CANR-31;
    MTCW 1, 2

Fuller, Margaret 1810-1850 **3**:
167–198
    See also AMWS 2; CDALB 1640-
    1865; DLB 1, 59, 73, 183, 223,
    239; FW; LMFS 1; NCLC 5, 50;
    SATA 25

G

Gilman, Charlotte (Anna) Perkins
(Stetson) 1860-1935 **1**: 3–5, 314,
325, 462–463; **5**: 485–528
    See also AMWS 11; BYA 11; CA
    106; 150; DLB 221; EXPS; FW;
    HGG; LAIT 2; MAWW; MTCW
    1; RGAL 4; RGSF 2; SFW 4;
    SSC 13, 62; SSFS 1, 18; TCLC
    9, 37, 117

H

Hansberry, Lorraine (Vivian)
1930-1965 **6**: 1–30
    See also AAYA 25; AFAW 1, 2;
    AMWS 4; BLC 2; BW 1, 3; CA
    109; 25-28R; CABS 3; CAD;
    CANR 58; CDALB 1941-1968;
    CLC 17, 62; CWD; DA; DA3;
    DAB; DAC; DAM DRAM, MST,
    MULT; DC 2; DFS 2; DLB 7,
    38; EWL 3; FW; LAIT 4;
    MTCW 1, 2; RGAL 4; TUS

Head, Bessie 1937-1986 **6**: 31–62
    See also AFW; BLC 2; BW 2, 3;
    CA 29-32R; 119; CANR 25, 82;
    CDWLB 3; CLC 25, 67; DA3;
    DAM MULT; DLB 117, 225;
    EWL 3; EXPS; FW; MTCW 1,
    2; RGSF 2; SSC 52; SSFS 5, 13;
    WLIT 2; WWE 1

Hellman, Lillian (Florence)
1906-1984 **6**: 63–88
    See also AAYA 47; AITN 1, 2;
    AMWS 1; CA 13-16R; 112;
    CAD; CANR 33; CLC 2, 4, 8,
    14, 18, 34, 44, 52; CWD; DA3;
    DAM DRAM; DC 1; DFS 1, 3,
    14; DLB 7, 228; DLBY 1984;
    EWL 3; FW; LAIT 3; MAWW;
    MTCW 1, 2; RGAL 4; TCLC
    119; TUS

Holley, Marietta 1836(?)-1926 **3**:
199–220
    See also CA 118; DLB 11; TCLC
    99

Hurston, Zora Neale 1891-1960 **4**:
31–32, 249–251, 485–492; **6**:
89–126
    See also AAYA 15; AFAW 1, 2;
    AMWS 6; BLC 2; BW 1, 3; BYA
    12; CA 85-88; CANR 61;
    CDALBS; CLC 7, 30, 61; DA;
    DA3; DAC; DAM MST, MULT,
    NOV; DC 12; DFS 6; DLB 51,
    86; EWL 3; EXPN; EXPS; FW;
    HR 2; LAIT 3; LATS 1; LMFS 2;
    MAWW; MTCW 1, 2; NFS 3;
    RGAL 4; RGSF 2; SSC 4; SSFS
    1, 6, 11, 19; TCLC 121, 131;
    TUS; WLCS; YAW

J

Jacobs, Harriet A(nn) 1813(?)-1897
3: 221–242
    See also AFAW 1, 2; DLB 239;
    FW; LAIT 2; NCLC 67; RGAL 4

Jewett, (Theodora) Sarah Orne
1849-1909 **3**: 243–274
    See also AMW; AMWC 2;
    AMWR 2; CA 108; 127; CANR
    71; DLB 12, 74, 221; EXPS;
    FW; MAWW; NFS 15; RGAL 4;
    RGSF 2; SATA 15; SSC 6, 44;
    SSFS 4; TCLC 1, 22

Juana Inés de la Cruz, Sor
1651(?)-1695 **1**: 321–358
    See also FW; HLCS 1; LAW; LC
    5; PC 24; RGWL 2, 3; WLIT 1

K

Kempe, Margery 1373(?)-1440(?) **1**:
87, 193, 222, **359–392**
    See also DLB 146; LC 6, 56;
    RGEL 2

Kingston, Maxine (Ting Ting)
Hong 1940- **4**: 493–496; **6**:
127–150
    See also AAL; AAYA 8, 55;
    AMWS 5; BPFB 2; CA 69-72;
    CANR 13, 38, 74, 87, 128;
    CDALBS; CLC 12, 19, 58, 121;
    CN 7; DA3; DAM MULT, NOV;
    DLB 173, 212; DLBY 1980;
    EWL 3; FW; INT CANR-13;
    LAIT 5; MAWW; MTCW 1, 2;
    NFS 6; RGAL 4; SATA 53; SSFS
    3; WLCS

L

Lessing, Doris (May) 1919- **4**: 272,
291, 294, 299; **6**: 151–178
    See also AFW; BRWS 1; CA
    9-12R; CAAS 14; CANR 33, 54,
    76, 122; CD 5; CDBLB 1960 to
    Present; CLC 1, 2, 3, 6, 10, 15,
    22, 40, 94, 170; CN 7; DA;
    DA3; DAB; DAC; DAM MST,
    NOV; DLB 15, 139; DLBY
    1985; EWL 3; EXPS; FW; LAIT
    4; MTCW 1, 2; RGEL 2; RGSF
    2; SFW 4; SSC 6, 61; SSFS 1,
    12; TEA; WLCS; WLIT 2, 4

M

Millay, Edna St. Vincent 1892-1950
4: 245, 259; **6**: 179–200
    See also AMW; CA 104; 130;
    CDALB 1917-1929; DA; DA3;
    DAB; DAC; DAM MST, POET;
    DLB 45, 249; EWL 3; EXPP;
    MAWW; MTCW 1, 2; PAB; PC
    6; PFS 3, 17; RGAL 4; TCLC 4,
    49; TUS; WLCS; WP

Montagu, Mary (Pierrepont)
Wortley 1689-1762 **1**: 116,
118–119, 122, 193, 219–220,
225–226, 393–422; **2**: 504, 506
    See also DLB 95, 101; LC 9, 57;
    PC 16; RGEL 2

Moore, Marianne (Craig)
1887-1972 **4**: 244; **6**: 201–232
    See also AMW; CA 1-4R; 33-36R;
    CANR 3, 61; CDALB 1929-
    1941; CLC 1, 2, 4, 8, 10, 13,
    19, 47; DA; DA3; DAB; DAC;
    DAM MST, POET; DLB 45;
    DLBD 7; EWL 3; EXPP;
    MAWW; MTCW 1, 2; PAB; PC
    4, 49; PFS 14, 17; RGAL 4;
    SATA 20; TUS; WLCS; WP

Morrison, Toni 1931- **4**: 349–353;
6: 233–266
    See also AAYA 1, 22; AFAW 1, 2;
    AMWC 1; AMWS 3; BLC 3;
    BPFB 2; BW 2, 3; CA 29-32R;
    CANR 27, 42, 67, 113, 124;
    CDALB 1968-1988; CLC 4, 10,
    22, 55, 81, 87, 173; CN 7;
    CPW; DA; DA3; DAB; DAC;
    DAM MST, MULT, NOV, POP;
    DLB 6, 33, 143; DLBY 1981;
    EWL 3; EXPN; FW; LAIT 2, 4;
    LATS 1; LMFS 2; MAWW;
    MTCW 1, 2; NFS 1, 6, 8, 14;
    RGAL 4; RHW; SATA 57, 144;
    SSFS 5; TUS; YAW

Z

SUBJECT INDEX

Provincetown Players **4:** 306, 324

Pulitzer Prize **4:** 311, 316, 330, 469

suffrage in **4:** 312–330

Theatre of the Absurd **6:** 9–10

transformational **4:** 472–473, 475

Women's Project **4:** 469

See also names of playwrights and plays

"Drawing-Room Naturalism in Edith Wharton's Short Stories" (Emmert) **6:** 511–518

"The Dream" (Cruz). *See* "El sueno"

"The Dream" (Shelley) **3:** 368, 371–372

"Dream Land" (Rossetti) **3:** 277

The Dream of a Common Language: Poems 1974-1977 (Rich) **4:** 512–514; **6:** 330, 338–342

"The Dream of a Common Language: Vietnam Poetry as Reformation of Language and Feeling in the Poems of Adrienne Rich" (Greenwald) (sidebar) **6:** 342

Dreaming Emmett (Morrison) **6:** 234, 243–244

"Dreams" (anonymous) (sidebar) **3:** 132

Dred: A Tale of the Great Dismal Swamp (Stowe) **3:** 456, 458–460

Drexler, Rosalyn **4:** 468–469, 476

The Drinking Gourd (Hansberry) **6:** 2, 8–9, 11

Driver, Dorothy **6:** 47–61

Du Bois, W. E. B. **4:** 331–332; **6:** 15–16

Dubek, Laura **5:** 237–244

Dubois, Ellen Carol
   on Blatch, Harriet Stanton **4:** 198–214
   on conflicts of early feminist movement **3:** 436–442
   on internationalism of suffrage movement **4:** 147–160
   on Seneca Falls convention **2:** 236–248
   on suffragism as social movement **2:** 229–232

Ducrest, Stéphanie-Félicité **2:** 91–93

Dumas, Alexandre **1:** 478–479

Duncan, Carol **4:** 85

Duncan, Isadora **3:** 23–24

Duncan, Robert **5:** 329

Duniway, Abigail Scott **2:** 276–277, 279

Dupin, Aurore. *See* Sand, George

Durand, Lionel **5:** 324–325

Duras, Marguerite **5:** *359,* **359–403**
   adultery and **5:** 379

Andréa, Yann and **5:** 384–385

Antelme, Robert and **5:** 378–379, 380–381

autobiographies **5:** 380

Breton, André and **5:** 380–381

Cixous, Héléne on **5:** 387

connection between life and writing **5:** 380

drama of **5:** 389–396

feminine aesthetic **5:** 386–387

Gauthier, Xavière and **5:** 381

inferred meaning in writings **5:** 368–375

Mascolo, Dionys and **5:** 378–379, 381

on misogyny **5:** 362

Nouveau Roman movement and **5:** 379–380

political activism of **5:** 377–379

principal works **5:** 360–361

Prix Goncourt **5:** 360, 379

psychoanalysis and **5:** 374

rejection of archetypal female protagonists **5:** 368–375

remembrance in works of **5:** 389–390

sexism and **5:** 379

Surrealistic poetics of **5:** 381–388

writing process of **5:** 385–388

Dürer, Alfred **1:** 61

Dust Tracks on a Road (Hurston) **6:** 90, 95, 96–97; (sidebar) **6:** 103; **6:** 105, 106

The Duties of Women (Cobbe) **2:** 187–193

Dworkin, Andrea **1:** 565–566; **5:** *405,* **405–432**
   on female colonized mind (sidebar) **5:** 411
   on gender relations **5:** 415–416
   Jong, Erica on **5:** 409–415
   lesbianism of **5:** 412–413
   on patriarchy **5:** 413
   on pornography **5:** 406–410, 413
   principal works **5:** 407
   on rape **5:** 413
   on sexual intercourse **5:** 406
   on sexual violence **5:** 408–410

"Dworkin Critiques Relations between the Sexes" (Glasgow) **5:** 415–416

Dyer, Mary **1:** 147

"The Dying Fugitive" (Harper) **2:** 143

Dykes **4:** 521–533

E

E. E. S. **2:** 9–10

Each His Own Wilderness (Lessing) **6:** 164, 168–172

Eagleton, Terry **1:** 495–497; **2:** 399–406

The Early Diary of Frances Burney, 1768-1778 (Burney, F.) **2:** 509

"Early Factory Labor in New England" (Robinson) **2:** 10–12

"Early Losses: A Requiem" (Walker) **6:** 473

Eastman, Crystal **4:** 9–11, 18–19, 30

Eastman, Max (sidebar) **6:** 194

Eaton, Edith Maude **4:** 339–340

"Eavesdropper" (Plath) **6:** 300–302, 303

"The Echoing Spell of H. D.'s *Trilogy*" (Gubar) **5:** 342

Echols, Alice **4:** 380–395

Economics **4:** 365–368
   Great Depression **4:** 33–36
   of male-dependent women **5:** 493–494
   New Deal and **4:** 40–41
   poverty **4:** 367–368
   restrictions on women **5:** 487–488

Edgar, George **4:** 5–7

"Edge" (Plath) **6:** 294, 314–315

Edgeworth, Maria **3:** *93,* **93–127**
   on education for women **3:** 93–99
   principal works **3:** 94–95

Edgeworth, Richard Lovell **3:** 103–104

"Edgeworth's Ireland: History, Popular Culture, and Secret Codes" (Butler) **3:** 98–114

The Edible Woman (Atwood) **5:** 93, 94, 102–105, 107, 108; (sidebar) **5:** 114

Edison Company **4:** 95, 97–102

Edith Wharton Society **6:** 503

"The Editor's Preface" (Bianchi) (sidebar) **3:** 54

Education
   benefits of equality **2:** 96–97
   of Brontë, Charlotte **2:** 413–414
   college in 1920s **4:** 23
   Cruz, Sor Juana Inés de la on **1:** 323–326
   Defoe, Daniel on **1:** 109–111
   Edgeworth, Maria on **3:** 95–98
   Eliot, George and **2:** 135–137
   Fuller, Margaret on **3:** 172
   Makin, Bathsua on **1:** 223
   Pan Chao on **1:** 75–76
   reform **2:** 4–6
   sexual discrimination in **4:** 413–414
   of Spartan girls **1:** 13–14
   in Victorian era **2:** 134–137

Lunardini, Christine **4:** 187–197
Lupton, Mary Jane **5:** 67–77
Luther, Martha **5:** 489–490
Lyell, Charles **2:** 414
Lynching **4:** 169, 335
Lynd, Helen and Robert **4:** 26–27
"A Lyrical Opera Made By Two" (Stein) **6:** 430

M

Mabille, Zaza **5:** 163–165
Macaulay Graham, Catharine **1:** 535–536
Macbeth (Shakespeare) **1:** *216*
MacCarthy, Desmond **6:** 538–539
MacDonald, Ruth K. **2:** 322
Macfarlane, Alan **1:** 181–182
MacKinnon, Catharine A. **5:** 406, 413
Madame Bovary (Flaubert) (sidebar) **3:** 6; **3:** 14–15, 21–22
Madame Dodin (Duras) **5:** 367
Madariaga, Isabel de **1:** 172–177
Madness
  Gilman, Charlotte Perkins **4:** 462; **5:** 491–493, 511–512, 520–521
  in literary heroines **4:** 462–463
Madsen, Deborah L. **5:** 256–267
Magazines. *See* Periodicals
Magical realism **5:** 53–54
Maher v. Doe (1977) **4:** 419
Mailer, Norman **4:** 289–290, 464
Les Maîtres Sonneurs (Sand) **3:** 310
Major, Elizabeth **1:** 231, 249–251
Make Bright the Arrows (Millay) **6:** 180
Make, Vusumzi **5:** 91
Makin, Bathsua **1:** 223–224
The Making of Americans (Stein) **6:** 390–391, 403–404, 411–412, 427, 429
"The Making of *The Awful Rowing Toward God*" (Middlebrook) (sidebar) **6:** 371
La maladie de la mort (Duras) **5:** 360, 384, 390–391, 395
The Malady of Death (Duras) **5:** 360
"Male and Female Plots in Staël's *Corinne*" (Mortimer) **3:** 420–424
Male criminals, Equal Rights Amendment and **4:** 420–421
"'A Male Magdalene,' from *Samantha vs. Josiah*" (Holley) **3:** 200–204
"A Man in My Bed Like Cracker Crumbs" (Cisneros) **5:** 261
"The Man in the Brooks Brothers Shirt" (McCarthy) **4:** 464

"The Management of Grief" (Mukherjee) **4:** 456–458
Les mandarins (Beauvoir) **5:** 139–140, 144, 153, 167
"Mango Says Goodbye Sometimes" (Cisneros) **5:** 270
The Man-Made World; or, Our Androcentric Culture (Gilman) **5:** 486
Mann, Emily **4:** 479–480
A Man's World (Crothers) **4:** 318–320
Mansfield, Katherine **4:** 69–70
Mansfield Park (Austen) **2:** 334, *372*
"*Mansfield Park:* Slavery, Colonialism, and Gender" (Ferguson) **2:** 371–382
  colonialism in **2:** 371–380
  compared to *Emma* **2:** 354–355
  feminism in **2:** 352
  influence of Kotzebue, August von on **2:** 352–353
  stylistic conventions in **2:** 341–342
Marchand, Mary V. **6:** 518–531
Marcus, Jane **6:** 561; (sidebar) **6:** 569
Marcus, Leah **1:** 187–190
Marcus v. Marcus (1975) **4:** 420
Marder, Herbert **6:** 539–551, 560
La mare au diable (Sand) **3:** 300, 310, 313
"Margaret Atwood's *Cat's Eye:* Re-Viewing Women in a Postmodern World" (Ingersoll) **5:** 108–112
"Margaret Fuller, Rebel" (Parrington) (sidebar) **3:** 174
"Margaret Fuller, the Eternal Feminine, and the 'Liberties of the Republic'" (Fleischmann) **3:** 173–181
"Margery Kempe's visit to Julian of Norwich" (Kempe) **1:** 364
"Marguerite Duras" (Duras and Jardine) **5:** 361–365
Maria; or, The Wrongs of Woman (Wollstonecraft) **1:** 525, 556, 562
Mariam, the fair Queen of Jewry (Cary) **1:** 203–205
"Marianne Moore" (Auden) (sidebar) **6:** 208
A Marianne Moore Reader (Moore) **6:** 229
"Marianne Moore's 'Marriage'" (Wasserman) (sidebar) **6:** 226
Marie of Champagne **1:** 38
Marilley, Suzanne M. **2:** 253–262
Le marin de Gibraltar (Duras) **5:** 360
Marini, Marcelle **5:** 368
Markley, A. A. **3:** 366–373
"The Marlboro Man" (Cisneros) **5:** 258

The Marne (Wharton) **6:** 496
Marriage
  in *Aurora Leigh* **2:** 486
  Austen, Jane on **2:** 335–337
  in *The Awakening* **3:** 31–34
  balance between career and **4:** 23
  Browning, Elizabeth Barrett on **2:** 484–487
  of Cavendish, Margaret **1:** 207–208
  Coleridge, Mary Elizabeth on **2:** 98–99
  emphasis in 1920s **4:** 28–30
  Gilman, Charlotte Perkins and **5:** 490–491
  Halifax, George Savile, Marquis of on **1:** 108–109
  illness and **2:** 69–71
  law in 19th-century England **2:** 35, 98, 486–487
  licensing **4:** 420
  in Middle Ages **1:** 40–43
  Moore, Marianne on **6:** 206
  in *Night and Day* **6:** 546–547
  Pan Chao on **1:** 76–77
  patriarchal practices in "Hymn to Demeter" **3:** 83–89
  same-sex **4:** 419
  in "Tom's Husband" **3:** 245–251
  in Victorian era **2:** 19–22
  in *The Voyage Out* **6:** 546
  Wollstonecraft, Mary on **1:** 546–547
  women's last names **4:** 420
"Marriage" (Moore) **6:** 202, 208, 212, 217, 225–231
Marriage and Love in England 1300-1840 (Macfarlane) **1:** 181–182
Marriage as a Trade (Hamilton, Cecily) **4:** 140
Marriage of Heaven and Hell (Blake) **6:** 383
Marriages and Infidelities (Oates) **6:** 268
Married or Single? (Sedgwick) **3:** 334
Marsden, Dora **4:** 143–145
Marshall, Paule **4:** 295–296
Marsh-Lockett, Carol P. **6:** 118–124
Marso, Lori J. **3:** 413–420
"Martha" (Lorde) **4:** 520
Martha Quest (Lessing) **6:** 152
Martin, Susannah **1:** 147–148
Martineau, Harriet **2:** *135*
  career of **2:** 201
  excerpt from an obituary for Charlotte Brontë (sidebar) **2:** 432
  on feminism **2:** 137

"Voracities and Verities Sometimes Are Interacting" (Moore) **6:** 212
Votes for Women (Robins) **4:** 138–139
Voting rights. *See* Suffrage
Vowell, Faye **1:** 239–244
The Voyage Out (Woolf, V.) **6:** 535–536, 546

W

WAC (Women's Action Coalition) **4:** 376–377
Wade, Roe v. (1973) **4:** 353–356, *356*, 359, 361, 411–412, 418–419
Waelti-Walters, Jennifer **2:** 50–53
Wages and salaries **4:** 5–7
　in 19th century France **2:** 35–36
　increase with New Deal **4:** 42
　minimum wage legislation **4:** 18, 135–136
　in post-WW II society **4:** 50
　See also Equal pay
Wagner-Martin, Linda **6:** 272–279, 309–316, 503–511
"The Waiting Head" (Sexton) **6:** 382
Walker, Alice **6:** *465*, **465–494**
　on African American women's voice (sidebar) **6:** 469; **6:** 484
　black manhood **6:** 470
　civil rights and **6:** 475–481
　compared to Whitman, Walt **6:** 469–470
　compared to Woolf, Virginia **6:** 483
　female protagonists of **6:** 485–487
　gender relations and **6:** 471–472, 474–481
　on Hurston, Zora Neale **6:** 485
　irony in poetry of **6:** 472
　principal works **6:** 467
　Pulitzer Prize **6:** 465
　quilting metaphor and **6:** 482–488
　race issue and **6:** 474–481
　on Woolf, Virginia **6:** 574
The Walls Do Not Fall (H. D.) **5:** 314, 317, 342–347
The Wanderer; or, Female Difficulties (Burney, F.) **2:** 504, 511, 514–515, 518
"The Wandering Text: Situating the Narratives of Isabel Allende" (Frenk) **5:** 47–55
"Wanting to Die" (Sexton) **6:** 352
The War (Duras). *See La Douleur*

The War Against Women (French) **5:** 470
Ward, Mary A. **2:** 441–448
Ward, Maryanne C. **2:** 420–427
Ward, Mrs. Humphry **2:** 202–203; **4:** 141–142, 143
Warner, Sylvia Townsend **4:** 287
Warren, Mercy Otis (sidebar) **1:** 239
Warrior Marks (Walker) **6:** 466
Wars I Have Seen (Stein) **6:** 390, 409–410
Washington (State) **4:** 424
Washington, George (sidebar) **1:** 492
Wasserman, Roseanne (sidebar) **6:** 226
Wasserstein, Wendy **4:** 469
Watanabe, Kazuko **2:** 325–330
Watch on the Rhine (Hellman) **6:** 64, 79
The Waterfall (Drabble) **4:** 466
Watts, Linda S. **6:** 422–431
The Waves (Woolf, V.) **6:** 536, 551, 560, 562–565
WCTU. *See* Woman's Christian Temperance Union
"We Cover Thee—Sweet Face—" (Dickinson) **3:** 68–69
"'We Must Grant a Romance Writer a Few Impossibilities': 'Unnatural Incident' and Narrative Motherhood in Maria Edgeworth's *Emilie de Coulanges*" (Myers) (sidebar) **3:** 99
"We pray—to Heaven—" (Dickinson) **3:** 73
"We Real Cool" (Brooks) **5:** 176
WEAL (Women's Equity Action League) **4:** 413–414
Weatherford, Doris **2:** 272–286
The Weaver's Uprising (Kollwitz) **4:** 88
Webster v. Reproductive Health Services (1989) **3:** 359–360; **4:** 411–412
"Wedded" (Dickinson) **3:** 50, 62–64
Weeton, Nellie **2:** 3–4
"A Welcome Song for Laini Nzinga" (Brooks) **5:** 197
Welles, Orson **2:** *406*
Wells, Emmeline B. **2:** 280
Wells, H. G. **4:** 72–73; **6:** 541
Wells-Barnett, Ida B. (sidebar) **4:** 169
West, Nathanael **4:** 82–83
West, Rebecca **4:** 5–7, 69, 144
Weston, Ruth D. **6:** 469–474
WHAM (Women's Health Action Mobilization) **4:** 377
Wharton, Edith **6:** *495*, **495–533**, 564
　criticism of **6:** 503–509, 519
　cultural criticism **6:** 520–522

Edith Wharton Society **6:** 503
fiction compared to regionalism **6:** 522–528
Jewett, Sarah Orne and **6:** 522–527
letters **6:** 505
narrative voice and **6:** 514
naturalism **6:** 512–518
Pierpont, Claudia Roth on (sidebar) **6:** 513
principal works **6:** 497–498
Pulitzer Prize **6:** 496, 504
repression of **6:** 511–512
short stories of **6:** 512–518
Wolff, Cynthia Griffin on (sidebar) **6:** 527
What Are Years (Moore) **6:** 202
"What Ever Happened to Jochebed? Motherhood as Marginality in Zora Neale Hurston's *Seraph on the Suwanee*" (Marsh-Lockett) **6:** 118–124
What Happened (Stein) **6:** 390
What Happened to Mary (Edison Company) **4:** 95, 96, 101–102, 108–112
"What I Love" (anonymous) **1:** 245
What Is Found There: Notebooks on Poetry and Politics (Rich) **6:** 330
"What Made Seneca Falls Possible?" (Dubois) **2:** 236–239
"What shall I give my children? who are poor" (Brooks) **5:** 200–201
"What 'Speaks in Us': Margaret Fuller, Woman's Rights, and Human Nature" (Davis) **3:** 181–188
"What the Black Woman Thinks about Women's Lib" (Morrison) **4:** 349–353; **6:** 244
"What the South Can Do" (Blackwell, H.) **2:** 255–256
What Use Are Flowers? (Hansberry) **6:** 2, 9–10, 12
"What White Publishers Won't Print" (Hurston) **6:** 109
What's O'Clock (Lowell) **4:** 255
Wheathill, Anne **1:** 104–108
Wheatley, Phillis **1:** 149, *471*, **471–522**
　American Revolution and **1:** 487–492
　compared to Horton, George Moses **1:** 480
　compared to Pope, Alexander **1:** 476
　criticism of **1:** 474–481, 493–498
　cultural awareness as author **1:** 511–519
　Jefferson, Thomas on **1:** 475–476, 496–497
　Middle Passage **1:** 501–507